Encyclopedia of Sociology

Second Edition

Encyclopedia of Sociology

Second Edition

VOLUME 1

Edgar F. Borgatta
Editor-in-Chief
University of Washington, Seattle

Rhonda J. V. Montgomery
Managing Editor
University of Kansas, Lawrence

Macmillan Reference USA
an imprint of the Gale Group
New York • Detroit • San Francisco • London • Boston • Woodbridge, CT

Encyclopedia of Sociology
Second Edition

Macmillan Reference USA
an imprint of The Gale Group
1633 Broadway
New York, NY 10019

Library of Congress Catalog in Publication Data
Encyclopedia of Sociology / Edgar F. Borgatta, editor-in-chief, Rhonda Montgomery, managing editor.—2nd ed.
    p. cm.
    Includes bibliographical references and index.
    ISBN 0-02-864853-6 (set: alk paper)—ISBN 0-02-864849-8 (v. 1: alk. paper)—0-02-864850-1 (v. 2)—0-02-864851-X (v. 3)—0-02-864852-8 (v. 4)—0-02-865581-8 (v. 5)
    1. Sociology—Encyclopedias. I. Borgatta, Edgar F., 1924- II. Montgomery, Rhonda J. V.

HM425 .E5 2000
301'.03—dc21
                                         00-028402
                                           CIP

Printed in the United States of America by the Gale Group
Gale Group and Design is a trademark used herein under license.

Staff

Publisher
Elly Dickason

Project Editors
Timothy Prairie
Pamela Proffitt

Editorial Assistants
Shawn Beall
Wayne Yang

Assistant Manager, Composition
Evi Seoud

Buyer
Rhonda Williams

Senior Art Director
Michelle DiMercurio

Contents

Preface

The idea for this *Encyclopedia of Sociology* was in gestation for a long time. Probably the notion arose when, as Sociology Advisory Editor for Rand McNally and Company, I arranged for a series of handbooks that were published in the 1960s and 1970s. This influential group of volumes covered most of sociology, especially with the *Handbook of Modern Sociology* (Robert E. L. Faris, 1964) as a key volume. Other titles in the list included: *Handbook of Marriage and the Family* (Harold T. Christensen, 1964); *Handbook of Organizations* (James G. March, 1965); *Handbook of Socialization Theory and Research* (David A. Goslin, 1968); *Handbook of Personality Theory and Research* (Edgar F. Borgatta & William W. Lambert, 1968); *Handbook on the Study of Social Problems* (Erwin O. Smigel, 1971); and *Handbook of Criminology* (Daniel Glaser, 1974). Effectively, the series functioned as an encyclopedia, especially since there was additional related coverage already provided by the *Handbook of Social Psychology* (Gardner Lindzey and Elliot Aronson, 1968). At that time Macmillan's *International Encyclopedia of the Social Sciences* (David L. Sills, ed., 1968) was also available, and a separate encyclopedia for sociology seemed superfluous.

With time, however, as social-science research and professional involvement grew, along with the proliferation of subfields, each of the social and behavioral sciences and, indeed, other specialties, such as statistics, area studies, and applied areas, developed useful encyclopedias. In the late 1970s I talked about an encyclopedia of sociology with F. E. (Ted) Peacock (F. E. Peacock Publishers, Inc.), who encouraged the development of the project.

However, since it takes time for these things, it was not until the early 1980s that I actually started reflecting actively on what would need to be done, and I sought advice on what actually would be involved in such a project. Fortunately, Raymond J. Corsini, a good friend with whom I had worked on other matters, invited me to be an Associate Editor for the *Encyclopedia of Psychology* (Corsini, 1984). I got a close look at what was involved in undertaking a project of this magnitude and I was persuaded that the task would be a feasible one for sociology.

The field of sociology had been growing and evolving rapidly in the post-World War II period. Possibly the decades of the 1960s and 1970s will be seen in retrospect as one of the periods of great change for the discipline. Of course, different people will judge past developments differently, but some of the changes that have to be recognized as important include the following:

First. Sociology, which August Comte had blessed with the title of the "Queen of the Social Sciences," seemed to be losing much of the empire. In particular, applied fields dealing with social behavior blossomed, but as they did so, sociology seemed indifferent, uninvolved. The field of social work developed its advanced degree programs and established research interests that sociology relinquished as uninteresting because they were "applied." The field of industrial sociology virtually disappeared as the interest in research flourished in several specialties in psychology and in schools of business and management. Interest in the key institution, the family, was largely lost to the special applied organizations in that area. And so it went in a number of other fields. The "Queen" appeared indifferent, possibly with the exception of the field of medical sociology, in which there was considerable development.

Second. Technical training in sociology became increasingly more demanding. When I taught the first graduate course in statistics for sociology at the New York University Graduate School in 1954, it included regression analysis and factor analysis. The reception and reputation was a bit like that greeting the arrival of extraterrestrials. The title (or epithet) "Factor Analyst" was definitely not meant to be complimentary. Nevertheless, in the 1950s, the Social Science Research Council (SSRC) and others supported the idea that the formal theory and technical bases of the social sciences required attention, and programs were initiated to foster a greater appreciation of mathematics and statistics. Particularly with the support of the National Institutes of Mental Health (NIMH) graduate training grants, the University of Wisconsin, the University of Michigan, and other centers concentrated on "research methods" during and following the 1960s. The discipline reflected this focus in its journals. Sociology also became known as the leader in research training in the social sciences, with the new generation of scholars becoming conversant with statisticians, econometricians, and psychometricians, and providing service to history, political science, and anthropology. The "Queen" again had some empire.

Third. The 1960s experienced the civil-rights movement, the student movement, the feminist movement, and, implicitly or explicitly, sociologists reacted to and sometimes participated actively in these social movements. Challenges arose to the "traditional" values of objective and "value free" science in sociology. These challenges ranged from positions asserting knowledge by intuition to the posing of more serious epistemological questions. Attention was drawn to the fact that sociology apparently had little utility in solving social problems, aside from assisting in exposing them, but, further, sociologists were often accused of not studying complex problems because they were limited and hampered by their methodologies. A resurgence of interest in "qualitative" approaches developed, which also provided a stimulus for a reexamination of existing research approaches.

Fourth. At the same time, the scope of what sociologists could accomplish more generally expanded with technical development. Two of the more prohibitive cost factors in research and scholarship have progressively been reduced, since the development of computing packages made possible the elimination of computing clerks at the same time that it made possible complex numerical and statistical analyses. Additionally, this development eliminated time losses as the labor intensive aspects were eliminated. Also, the availability of word processing packages made it possible for even the most helpless scholar to by-pass the secretary or typing pool and get materials into a readable and revisable format. As these earlier "barriers" to productivity were removed, presumably the social sciences responded accordingly. In any event, there has been a proliferation of journals, and increasing collateral publication continues in various media.

Fifth. The continued development of the field of sociology can be marked by the increase of special subfields. Aside from the increases in publication, the number of specialization sections in the American Sociological Association (ASA) continues to grow, as do the Research Committees in the International Sociological Association (ISA). A reflection of this may be seen by glancing at the topical coverage of *Contemporary Sociology*, the ASA journal of book reviews.

This broadening of the field of sociology affected the way topics were chosen for the *Encyclopedia of Sociology*. In the early stages, a broad set of topics was used to accumulate the important concepts and subfields included in sociology. Initially, the objective was to be as inclusive as possible and to avoid errors of omission. A constant problem in the process was that topics did not fit neatly into only one broad category. Often they could fit as easily into two, three, or four. In fact, the number of broad categories became increasingly elastic, but eventually these were reduced to seventeen, corresponding to no known system of organization other than expedience. The broad categories did not have any obvious theoretical basis of division, which was disconcerting, but represented the pragmatic result of many revisions. Our Advisory and Associate Editors participated in reviews of the total set of categories or of selected subsets for a few of the broad categories. It is fair to report that while we often saw consensus in the process, sometimes we felt that there was no effective way to manage the procedure for selection of topics or to satisfy every piece of advice, sound as it might seem. At one point we had more than 1,700 potential entry titles. These eventually were consolidated into about 400 titles with notations of how overlapping concepts were handled, how related concepts were to be combined, and so forth. In making the arrangements with authors, further consolidation brought the final number of entries to the 370 in this 4-volume set.

The process of defining topics, thus, while driven by theoretical interests and strategic representations of the field, ultimately resulted in a pragmatic and eclectic product. Thus some topics became very comprehensive while others have more specific content. In areas where there is intensive attention by sociologists, such as social stratification, race and ethnic studies, gender, medical sociology, and aging, coverage by authors may overlap in a way that provides emphasis.

Other factors that guided the formulation of entry topics included defining the audience for whom the encyclopedia was intended. It was expected that sociologists would read about areas with which they were not familiar, but we wanted the materials to be useful to other scholars and professionals who need information about topics in sociology. Further, encyclopedias are gold mines for students, and so a central concern was that articles could be read and understood by younger and uninitiated persons looking for a first introduction to a sociological topic. This latter message was communicated to authors, and in large part it has been possible to provide presentations that will reach a broad range of literate audiences. There are some obvious exceptions. In some technical areas the presentations, while self-contained and elegantly presented, do require a preexisting knowledge base in order to be fully understood by the readers.

OCTOBER 1991
EDGAR F. BORGATTA, *EDITOR-IN-CHIEF*

REFERENCES

Borgatta, Edgar F., and William W. Lambert 1968 (eds.) *Handbook of Personality Theory and Research.* Chicago: Rand McNally and Company.

Christensen, Harold T. 1964 (ed.) *Handbook of Marriage and the Family.* Chicago: Rand McNally and Company.

Corsini, Raymond J. 1984 (ed.) *Encyclopedia of Psychology.* New York: John Wiley & Company.

Faris, Robert E. L. 1964 (ed.) *Handbook of Modern Sociology.* Chicago: Rand McNally and Company.

Glaser, Daniel 1974 (ed.) *Handbook of Criminology.* Chicago: Rand McNally and Company.

Goslin, David A. 1968 (ed.) *Handbook of Socialization Theory and Research.* Chicago: Rand McNally and Company.

Lindzey, Gardner, and Elliot Aronson 1968 (eds.) *Handbook of Social Psychology*, 2nd ed. Boston: Addison-Wesley Publishing Company.

March, James G. 1965 (ed.) *Handbook of Organizations.* Chicago: Rand McNally and Company.

Sills, David L. 1968 (ed.) *International Encyclopedia of the Social Sciences.* New York: Macmillan Company and Free Press.

Smigel, Erwin O. 1971 (ed.) *Handbook on the Study of Social Problems.* Chicago: Rand McNally and Company.

Preface for Second Edition

After the *Encyclopedia of Sociology* had been in print only three years, we began to receive inquiries about when there would be a revised edition. This was surprising given that the *Encyclopedia* was so well received, that its distribution had been much broader than even optimistic supporters of the project had anticipated, and that the articles were largely broad reviews and summaries of areas of knowledge in sociology. However, some areas in sociology changed quickly during the last decade as we approached the Millennium so that interest in a recapitulation and updating did not seem inappropriate. In addition, the social sciences appear to have softened their borders, and thus we realized that a substantial and thoughtful addition of titles would add breadth and depth to the *Encyclopedia*.

August Comte's description of sociology as the "queen" of the social sciences seems to have been awakened in a new generation, and the relevance of sociology to the social and behavioral sciences has been renewed. We took seriously our obligation to improve the representation of the areas of sociology in this edition of the *Encyclopedia*. The *Encyclopedia* was greatly improved through the input of Advisory Editors and authors who identified new content areas and titles that should be included and indicated which titles could be eliminated or consolidated. Some provided comprehensive reviews of the *Encyclopedia's* scope and coverage, as well as reviews of the content of many individual articles. Suggestions for additional titles for the revised *Encyclopedia* accumulated to a list of over 80 concepts and themes, resulting in the addition of 66 new titles, but in addition some of the revised articles also included substantially new and expanded topics.

With the help of the Advisory Editors and quite a few authors, we reviewed articles and sectors of coverage to determine what changes would be important in a new edition. We distilled the major points of emphasis provided by reviews and user comments, and incorporated them into the guidelines for revision provide to authors.

Reflecting the kind of question that comes up so often in sociology doctoral exams, reviewers repeatedly asked us why a particular article was included in an encyclopedia of sociology. Authors who are expert in a particular subject area assume too frequently that readers will know their topic's relevance for sociology. To guard against this we asked authors to note the sociological relevance of the topic and to show how it fit into not only the scheme of sociological knowledge but also social and behavioral knowledge in general. As a consequence, most articles have been expanded.

Authors, experts in their fields, often concentrate on the knowledge and the issues within their field but do not give sufficient attention to the *practical value* of that knowledge, particularly how it is important for policy formation and in applications to everyday life. Of course, this is a comment often made about academic scholars in general, namely, that they sometimes forget that an important reason for research and the accumulation of knowledge is to provide bases for useful and informed applications.

Reviewers raised another theme. Articles often did a wonderful job of summarizing knowledge but did not indicate what to expect from future endeavors in the field. In other words, what areas need more attention in scholarship and research to expand the knowledge in a given field? While this kind of presentation is speculative, we reminded authors of the need to give direction for future work.

An additional theme for the revised edition is one that is temporally controlled. There is no way that references can provide more information than what already has been published. Updating content is important, but equally important is providing information about easily accessible general resources for those who want to go beyond the relatively brief discussions in the *Encyclopedia.* We reminded authors that the purpose of the reference section is to provide users with an opportunity to explore the area further. Academic scholars can too easily become exhaustive bibliographers. Thus, we asked authors to give special attention to providing direction rather than overwhelming the reader, and we are impressed that most authors have been extremely successful in this task. In addition to the work of the authors, the professional sociological staff of the *Encyclopedia* prepared for some article a short list of additional references to broaden the scope of coverage and provide additional transitions to related concepts. We updated and provided new references for 20 articles from the earlier edition of the *Encyclopedia.*

Finally, reviewers commented that some of the presentations in the first edition were too brief, and some topics were too narrowly drawn. Thus, some topics have been combined, some topics have been eliminated and the content incorporated into related broader articles, and many articles have been expanded to cover neglected aspects of a topic and to provide greater detail for a more well-rounded presentation. Thirty-nine titles were eliminated and incorporated into more substantial articles, but some additional titles were changed when the original topic was expanded. In summary, there were 370 articles in the original edition, 39 were eliminated and 66 new articles were added, resulting in 397 in this revised edition.

In short, we have greatly improved the breadth and depth of coverage in the *Encyclopedia,* and we have paid particular attention to those articles that relate to other social and behavioral sciences. We have substantially increased the content of the Encyclopedia in this edition, and we have made every effort to ensure that the content is current, accurate, and representative of the field.

EDGAR F. BORGATTA, *EDITOR-IN-CHIEF*

Acknowledgments

The revision of the *Encyclopedia of Sociology* began with the optimistic hope that following reasonably on the original edition it would turn out to be easier to do. It did not turn out that way, but for good reasons. With the support and encouragement of Elly Dickason, Macmillan Reference USA's Publisher, the research and development for the project was more extensive than anticipated. On this score, our debt to the Advisory Editors in providing broad reviews and suggestions can hardly be emphasized enough. Further, as we proceeded in inviting old and new authors it became apparent that the Encyclopedia was getting a great deal of use and authors provided guidance from their experience on directions for development. Our authors are, of course, truly responsible for the Encyclopedia, but in addition through much interaction they provided support that was both welcome and of enormous value.

Marie L. Borgatta was the managing editor for the original publication, and for this edition she requested a less demanding role as a consulting editor. It was a nice idea, but she inevitably became involved and delivered support in quantities and quality that can only be described as exploitation.

Many ideas and innovations are due to her participation in the project. As Managing Editor for the revision, Rhonda J. V. Montgomery provided a work and intellectual partnership for the project that contributed enormously to the breadth and quality of the Revised Edition. Her initiatives kept the progress of the project smooth and on a reasonable schedule in spite of often unanticipated demands.

During the preparation of this Revised Edition, the Gale Group acquired Macmillan Reference USA, and production moved from New York to Michigan. This was done with only minimal loss of time and effort because of the planning and management of Elly Dickason, the Publisher, but also because in the New York office Timothy Prairie generated a very effective program for copyediting manuscripts and managing the records of progress. Of course, the shift to Michigan was obviously not effortless, but Linda Hubbard guided the project into the capable hands of Pamela Proffitt, who took on the mammoth task of making the Revised Edition of the *Encyclopedia of Sociology* a reality. The devoted efforts of the publisher's staff are greatly appreciated.

List of Articles

List of Authors

Alan C. Acock
Department of Human
Development and Family
Sciences
Oregon State University
STATISTICAL INFERENCE

Patricia A. Adler
University of Colorado,
Boulder
COUNTERCULTURES

Patrick Akard
Department of Sociology,
Anthropology, and
Social Work
Kansas State University
SOCIAL AND POLITICAL
ELITES

Ronald L. Akers
Criminology and Law
University of Florida,
Gainesville
ALCOHOL

Richard D. Alba
Department of Sociology
State University of New
York, Albany
ETHNICITY

A. George Alder
Department of Psychology
University College of
the Cariboo
HIERARCHICAL LINEAR
MODELS

Howard E. Aldrich
Department of Sociology
University of North Carolina
COMPLEX ORGANIZATIONS

Walter R. Allen
Department of Sociology
University of California, Los
Angeles
AFRICAN STUDIES

Paul D. Allison
Sociology Department
University of Pennsylvania
EVENT HISTORY ANALYSIS

Gunnar Almgren
School of Social Work
University of Washington
COMMUNITY

Rodolfo Alvarez
Department of Sociology
University of California, Los
Angeles
ORGANIZATIONAL
STRUCTURE

Duane F. Alwin
Department of Sociology
University of Michigan
FACTOR ANALYSIS
SOCIAL JUSTICE

Elke Koch-Weser Ammassari
University of Rome "La
Sapienza"
TIME USE RESEARCH

Craig A. Anderson
Department of Psychology
Iowa State University
AGGRESSION

Ronald E. Anderson
University of Minnesota
COMPUTER APPLICATIONS
IN SOCIOLOGY

Robert J. Antonio
Department of Sociology
University of Kansas
MATERIALISM

Sharon K. Araji
Department of Sociology
University of Alaska
SEXUAL VIOLENCE AND
EXPLOITATION

J. Michael Armer
Department of Sociology
Florida State University
MODERNIZATION THEORY

David J. Armor
George Mason University
MILITARY SOCIOLOGY

Carol D. Austin
Department of Social Work
The University of Calgary
SOCIAL WORK

Roya Ayman
Illinois Institute of
Technology
LEADERSHIP

Kenneth D. Bailey
Department of Sociology
University of California, Los
Angeles
TYPOLOGIES

Paul Morgan Baker
Department of Sociology
University of Victoria
DIVISION OF LABOR

Robert D. Benford
Department of Sociology
University of Nebraska
SOCIAL MOVEMENTS

Neil G. Bennett
Branch School of Public
Affairs and Columbia
University
DEMOGRAPHIC METHODS

Felix M. Berardo
Department of Sociology
University of Florida
LOVE
WIDOWHOOD

Ivar Berg
University of Pennsylvania
INDUSTRIAL SOCIOLOGY

Richard Berk
Departments of Statistics
and Sociology
University of California, Los
Angeles
TIME SERIES ANALYSIS

Lakshmi Bharadwaj
University of Wisconsin
HUMAN ECOLOGY AND
ENVIRONMENTAL
ANALYSIS

Bruce J. Biddle
Center for Research in
Social Behavior
University of Missouri
ROLE THEORY

Monica Biernat
Department of Psychology
University of Kansas
SEX DIFFERENCES

Dwight B. Billings
Department of Sociology
University of Kentucky
CRITICAL THEORY

Albert W. Black
Department of Sociology
University of Washington
SEGREGATION AND
DESEGREGATION

Hubert M. Blalock
CAUSAL INFERENCE
MODELS

Fred Block
Department of Sociology
University of California,
Davis
ECONOMIC INSTITUTIONS

Robert Boguslaw
SYSTEMS THEORY
UTOPIAN ANALYSIS AND
DESIGN
LIBERALISM/
CONSERVATISM

George W. Bohrnstedt
American Institutes for
Research
VALIDITY

Edna Bonacich
Department of Sociology
University of California,
Riverside
CLASS AND RACE

Edgar F. Borgatta
Department of Sociology
University of Washington
HUMAN RIGHTS/
CHILDREN'S RIGHTS
MEASUREMENT

Lynn Borgatta
Department of Obstetrics
and Gynecology
Boston University School of
Medicine
PREGNANCY AND
PREGNANCY
TERMINATION

Augustine Brannigan
Department of Sociology
The University of Calgary
LEGISLATION OF MORALITY
POSTMODERNISM

George S. Bridges
Department of Sociology
University of Washington
DEVIANCE THEORIES

Julie Brines
Department of Sociology
University of Washington
FAMILY AND POPULATION
POLICY IN LESS
DEVELOPED COUNTRIES

Steven G. Brint
Department of Sociology
University of California,
Riverside
HIGHER EDUCATION

David W. Britt
Department of Sociology
Wayne State University
APPLIED SOCIOLOGY

Kendal Broad
Department of Sociology
University of Florida
SEXUAL BEHAVIOR
PATTERNS

Kris Bulcroft
Department of Sociology
Western Washington
University
MATE SELECTION
THEORIES

Richard A. Bulcroft
Department of Sociology
Western Washington
University
ANALYSIS OF VARIANCE
AND COVARIANCE

Peter J. Burke
Department of Sociology
Washington State University
FEMININITY/MASCULINITY

Craig Calhoun
Social Science Research
Council
SOCIAL CHANGE

Richard T. Campbell
LONGITUDINAL RESEARCH

Francesca Cancian
Department of Sociology
University of California,
Irvine
PARTICIPATORY RESEARCH

Theodore Caplow
Department of Sociology
University of Virginia
COALITIONS

Bernardo Cattarinussi
Dipartimento di Economia
Societa e Territorio
University of Udine, Italy
SENTIMENTS

Heather Cecil
Department of Maternal and
Child Health
University of Alabama,
Birmingham
CHILDHOOD SEXUAL
ABUSE

Costantino Cipolla
Universita di Parma
EPISTEMOLOGY

Lee Clarke
Rutgers University
SOCIETY AND
TECHNOLOGICAL RISKS

Bernard P. Cohen
Department of Sociology
Stanford University
PARADIGMS AND MODELS

Randall Collins
CONFLICT THEORY

Karen S. Cook
Department of Sociology
Stanford University
SOCIAL EXCHANGE
THEORY

Peter Cordella
Department of Sociology
Saint Anselm College
CRIMINAL SANCTIONS

William A. Corsaro
Department of Sociology
Indiana University
CROSS CULTURAL
ANALYSIS

Sarah M. Corse
Department of Sociology
University of Virginia
LITERATURE AND SOCIETY

Raymond J. Corsini
Honolulu, Hawaii
MAJOR PERSONALITY
THEORIES

Herbert L. Costner
Department of Sociology
University of Washington
CORRELATION AND
REGRESSION ANALYSIS
MEASURES OF
ASSOCIATION

Richard M. Coughlin
University of New Mexico
CONVERGENCE THEORIES

Andrew L. Creighton
University of California,
Berkeley
DEMOCRACY

Eileen M. Crimmins
Andrus Gerontology Center
University of Southern
California, Los Angeles
LIFE EXPECTANCY

Robert Crutchfield
Department of Sociology
University of Washington
ANOMIE
CRIMINOLOGY

Vaneeta D'Andrea
Roehampton Educational
Development Centre
Roehampton Institute,
London
BRITISH SOCIOLOGY

William V. D'Antonio
Catholic University
VOLUNTARY ASSOCIATIONS

Glynis Daniels
Department of Sociology
Pennsylvania State
University
ENVIRONMENTAL EQUITY

Jacqueline Darroch
The Alan Guttmacher
Institute
FAMILY PLANNING

Guillermo de la Pena
CIESAS del Occidente
MEXICAN STUDIES

John D. DeLamater
Center for Demography and
Ecology
University of Wisconsin,
Madison
ATTITUDES

Giovanni Delli Zotti
Department of Human
Sciences
University of Trieste, Italy
TOURISM

N. J. Demerath
Department of Sociology
University of Massachusetts
SECULARIZATION

Linda Derksen
    Department of Sociology
    University of Alberta
        SCIENTIFIC EXPLANATION

William DiFazio
    Department of Sociology
    St. John's University
        ECONOMIC DETERMINISM

Don A. Dillman
    Washington State University
        INFORMATION SOCIETY

Thomas A. DiPrete
    Department of Sociology
    Duke University
        SOCIAL MOBILITY

Mattei Dogan
    National Center of Scientific
    Research, Paris
        SOCIOLOGY AMONG THE
        SOCIAL SCIENCES
        STATUS INCONGRUENCE

Kevin Dougherty
    Manhattan College
        EDUCATIONAL
        ORGANIZATION

Frank Dumont
    Educational and Counseling
    Psychology Department
    McGill University
        PERSONALITY THEORY

Riley E. Dunlap
    Department of Sociology
    Washington State University
        ENVIRONMENTAL
        SOCIOLOGY

Nancy E. Durbin
    University of Washington
        COMPARABLE WORTH

Alex Durig
    Sociology Program
    California State University,
    San Marcos
        QUALITATIVE MODELS

Glen H. Elder
    Carolina Population Center
    University of North
    Carolina, Chapel Hill
        LIFE COURSE, THE

Laura L. Ellingson
    Department of Sociology
    University of South Florida
        QUALITATIVE METHODS

Janice M. Engsberg
    Department of Journalism
    and Communication
    Xiamen University, People's
    Republic of China
        MASS MEDIA RESEARCH

Carroll L. Estes
    Institute for Health and
    Aging
    University of California, San
    Francisco
        HEALTH POLICY ANALYSIS
        MEDICAL-INDUSTRIAL
        COMPLEX

Amitai Etzioni
    George Washington
    University
        COMMUNITARIANISM

William M. Evan
    Department of Sociology
    University of Pennsylvania
        LAW AND SOCIETY

Bernard Farber
    Department of Sociology
    Arizona State University
        KINSHIP SYSTEMS AND
        FAMILY TYPES

J Forbes Farmer
    Division of Behavioral
    Sciences
    Franklin Pierce College
        PENOLOGY

Joe R. Feagin
    Department of Sociology
    University of Florida
        AFRICAN-AMERICAN
        STUDIES

Richard B. Felson
    Department of Sociology
    Pennsylvania State
    University
        SELF-CONCEPT

Robert A. Fiala
    Department of Sociology
    University of New Mexico
        POSTINDUSTRIAL SOCIETY

Thomas J. Figurski
    Department of Psychology
    Eastern Michigan University
        MORAL DEVELOPMENT

Anne Foner
    Rutgers University
        STRUCTURAL LAG (AND
        CULTURAL LAG)

William Form
    Department of Sociology
    Ohio State University
        LABOR MOVEMENTS AND
        UNIONS

Martha Foschi
    Department of
    Anthropology and
    Sociology
    University of British
    Columbia
        EXPECTATION STATES
        THEORY

John Fox
    Department of Sociology
    McMaster University
        STATISTICAL GRAPHICS

Jan Fritz
    University of Cincinnati
        CLINICAL SOCIOLOGY

Frank F. Furstenberg
    Department of Sociology
    University of Pennsylvania
        ILLEGITIMACY

David Gartrell
    Department of Sociology
    University of Victoria
        AGRICULTURAL
        INNOVATION

Alberto Gasparini
Dipartimento di Scienze
dell 'Uomo
Universita degli Studi di
Trieste, Italy
PREDICTION AND FUTURES
STUDIES
ITALIAN SOCIOLOGY

Viktor Gecas
Department of Sociology
Washington State University
SOCIALIZATION

Linda K. George
Center for the Study of
Aging and Human
Development
Duke University
AGING AND THE LIFE
COURSE

Don C. Gibbons
Portland State University
CRIME, THEORIES OF

Mary Gilmore
School of Social Work
University of Washington
SEXUALLY TRANSMITTED
DISEASES

Samuel L. Gilmore
Department of Sociology
University of California,
Irvine
CULTURE

Nathan Glazer
Harvard University
AFFIRMATIVE ACTION

Paul C. Glick
Arizona State University
MARRIAGE AND DIVORCE
RATES

Jack A. Goldstone
Department of Sociology
University of California,
Davis
STATE, THE

Leonard Gordon
Office for Academic
Programs
Arizona State University
STUDENT MOVEMENTS
PROTEST MOVEMENTS

Linda S. Gottfredson
Department of Educational
Studies
University of Delaware
INTELLIGENCE

Howard P. Greenwald
Sacramento Center, School
of Public Administration
University of Southern
California
ETHICS IN SOCIAL
RESEARCH
RESEARCH FUNDING IN
SOCIOLOGY
CIVIL LIBERTIES

Larry Griffin
Vanderbilt University
COMPARATIVE-HISTORICAL
SOCIOLOGY

Allen D. Grimshaw
Indiana University
SOCIOLINGUISTICS

Edward Gross
Department of Sociology
University of Washington
COURT SYSTEMS AND LAW

David B. Grusky
Department of Sociology
Cornell University
SOCIAL STRATIFICATION

Oscar Grusky
Department of Sociology
University of California, Los
Angeles
INTERGROUP AND
INTERORGANIZATIONAL
RELATIONS

Renzo Gubert
Dipartimento di Sociologia e
Ricerca Sociale
Universita di Trento, Italy
TERRITORIAL BELONGING

Avery M. Guest
University of Washington
DEMOGRAPHIC
TRANSITION

Christopher W. Gunn
University of Kansas
INTERNET

Regan A. R. Gurung
Department of Psychology
University of Wisconsin
DEPRESSION

Jeffrey K. Hadden
Department of Sociology
University of Virginia
RELIGIOUS MOVEMENTS

John Hagan
Faculty of Law
Northwestern University and
American Bar Foundation,
Chicago
JUVENILE DELINQUENCY,
THEORIES OF

Lee J. Haggerty
Department of Sociology
Portland State University
URBAN SOCIOLOGY

Warren Hagstrom
Department of Sociology
University of Wisconsin,
Madison
SCIENCE

Archibald O. Haller
Sociology and Rural
Sociology
University of Wisconsin,
Madison
SOCIETAL STRATIFICATION
SOCIAL PSYCHOLOGY OF
STATUS ALLOCATION

Richard F. Hamilton
The Mershon Center
The Ohio State University
MASS SOCIETY

Janet Hankin
Wayne State University
LIFESTYLES AND HEALTH
POSITIVE MENTAL HEALTH

Russell Hardin
Department of Political
Science
Stanford University
RATIONAL CHOICE THEORY

Melissa A. Hardy
Department of Sociology
Florida State University
RETIREMENT

Lowell L. Hargens
Ohio State University
SAMPLING PROCEDURES
REPLICATION

Charlene Harrington
Social and Behavioral
Sciences
University of California, San
Francisco
HEALTH CARE UTILIZATION
AND EXPENDITURES

Riaz Hassan
Department of Sociology
University of California, Los
Angeles and Flinders
University of South
Australia
SOCIOLOGY OF ISLAM

Laurie Russell Hatch
Department of Sociology
University of Kentucky
AMERICAN FAMILIES

Lawrence E. Hazelrigg
Department of Sociology
Florida State University
INDIVIDUALISM

Todd F. Heatherton
Department of Psychology
Dartmouth College
SELF-ESTEEM

R. Alan Hedley
Department of Sociology
University of Victoria
INDUSTRIALIZATION IN
LESS DEVELOPED
COUNTRIES
TRANSNATIONAL
CORPORATIONS

David M. Heer
University of Southern
California
INTERNATIONAL
MIGRATION

Karen A. Hegvedt
Department of Sociology
Emory University
SOCIAL COMPARISON
PROCESSES

David R. Heise
Indiana University
AFFECT CONTROL THEORY
AND IMPRESSION
FORMATION

Jon Hendricks
Department of Sociology
Oregon State University
DEPENDENCY THEORY

John Heritage
Department of Sociology
University of California, Los
Angeles
ETHNOMETHODOLOGY

Beth B. Hess
County College of Morris
INCOME DISTRIBUTION IN
THE UNITED STATES

Christine L. Himes
Center for Policy Research
and Department of
Sociology
Syracuse University
STANDARDIZATION

Charles Hirschman
Russell Sage Foundation
University of Washington
SOUTHEAST ASIA STUDIES

Dennis Hogan
Department of Sociology
Brown University
LIFE CYCLE

Charles E. Holzer III
Department of Psychiatry
and Behavioral Science
University of Texas
Medical Branch
EPIDEMIOLOGY

John Houghton
St. Edwards University
ADULT EDUCATION

Judith Howard
Department of Sociology
University of Washington
ATTRIBUTION THEORY
ALTRUISM

Carla B. Howery
American Sociological
Association, Washington,
D.C.
AMERICAN SOCIOLOGICAL
ASSOCIATION AND OTHER
SOCIOLOGICAL
ASSOCIATIONS

Marilyn Ihinger-Tallman
Department of Sociology
Washington State University
MARRIAGE

James M. Inverarity
Department of Sociology
Western Washington
University
SOCIOLOGY OF LAW

Rita Jalali
Bethesda, Maryland
CASTE AND INHERITED
STATUS

David R. James
Department of Sociology
Indiana University
SLAVERY AND
INVOLUNTARY SERVITUDE

Carl Gunnar Janson
Department of Sociology
Stockholm University
SCANDINAVIAN SOCIOLOGY

J. Craig Jenkins
Department of Sociology
Ohio State University
POLITICAL SOCIOLOGY

Brian Michael Jenkins
Kroll Associates, Los
Angeles
TERRORISM

Leif Jensen
Agricultural Economics and
Rural Sociology
Pennsylvania State
University
MARGINAL EMPLOYMENT

Timothy D. Jewell
Allen Library
University of Washington
LIBRARY RESOURCES AND
SERVICES FOR SOCIOLOGY

Blair T. Johnson
University of Connecticut
META-ANALYSIS

Anupama Joshi
Department of Child and
Family Studies
California State University,
Los Angeles
INTERPERSONAL CONFLICT
RESOLUTION

Eva Kahana
Department of Sociology
Case Western Reserve
University
LONG TERM CARE
FACILITIES

Yoshinori Kamo
Department of Sociology
Louisiana State University
MARITAL ADJUSTMENT

Howard B. Kaplan
Department of Sociology
Texas A & M University
SOCIAL PSYCHOLOGY

Tracy Karner
Gerontology Center
University of Kansas
SOCIAL CAPITAL

David R. Karp
Department of Sociology
Skidmore College
VALUE THEORY AND
RESEARCH

John D. Kasarda
University of North
Carolina, Chapel Hill
URBAN UNDERCLASS

John M. Katsillis
Department of Education
University of Patras, Greece
EDUCATION AND MOBILITY

John R. Kelly
Department of Sociology
University of Illinois
LEISURE

Theodore D. Kemper
Department of Sociology
St. John's University
EMOTIONS

Stephen A. Kent
Department of Sociology
University of Alberta
HISTORICAL SOCIOLOGY

Kyle Kercher
Department of Sociology
Case Western Reserve
University
QUASI-EXPERIMENTAL
RESEARCH DESIGNS
MULTIPLE INDICATOR
MODELS

Richard B. Kettner-Polley
Business Administration
Jones International
University
OBSERVATION SYSTEMS
FIELD THEORY

Jae-On Kim
The Center for Asian and
Pacific Studies
University of Iowa
TABULAR ANALYSIS

Paul W. Kingston
Department of Sociology
University of Virginia
SOCIOLOGY OF EDUCATION

Edgar Kiser
Department of Sociology
University of Washington
WAR

Carl B. Klockars
Department of Sociology
University of Delaware
POLICE

David Knoke
Department of Sociology
University of Minnesota
POLITICAL
ORGANIZATIONS

Igor S. Kon
Institute of Ethnography,
Moscow
SOVIET AND POST-SOVIET
SOCIOLOGY

Karl Kosloski
Department of Gerontology
University of Nebraska
EVALUATION RESEARCH

Louis Kriesberg
Maxwell School of
Citizenship and Public
Affairs
Syracuse University
PEACE

Manfred Kuechler
Department of Sociology
Hunter College, CUNY
VOTING BEHAVIOR

Daphne Kuo
Department of Sociology
University of Washington
DESCRIPTIVE STATISTICS

Mary Riege Laner
  Department of Sociology
  Arizona State University
  COURTSHIP

Gladys Engel Lang
  University of Washington
  ART AND SOCIETY

Kurt Lang
  University of Washington
  PUBLIC OPINION

Barrett A. Lee
  Department of Sociology
  Pennsylvania State
  University
  HOMELESSNESS

Gary R. Lee
  Department of Sociology
  Bowling Green State
  University
  FAMILY AND HOUSEHOLD
    STRUCTURE

Janet Lever
  Department of Behavioral
  Sciences
  California State University,
  Los Angeles
  SPORT

Nan Lin
  Department of Sociology
  Duke University
  STRESS
  SOCIAL RESOURCES
    THEORY

Robert C. Liebman
  Department of Sociology
  Portland State University
  REVOLUTIONS

Seymour Martin Lipset
  INTELLECTUALS

Allen E. Liska
  SOCIAL CONTROL

William T. Liu
  National University of
  Singapore and University
  of Illinois, Chicago
  ASIAN AMERICAN STUDIES

Clarence Y. H. Lo
  Department of Sociology
  University of Missouri
  ALIENATION

John R. Logan
  Department of Sociology
  State University of New
  York
  SUBURBANIZATION

J. Scott Long
  Department of Sociology
  Indiana University
  STATISTICAL METHODS

Charles F. Longino, Jr.
  Wake Forest University
  INTERNAL MIGRATION

Joseph Lopreato
  University of Texas
  SOCIOBIOLOGY, HUMAN

Judith Lorber
  City University of New York
  and Brooklyn College
  GENDER

David R. Maines
  Department of Sociology
  Oakland University
  PRAGMATISM
  LIFE HISTORIES AND
    NARRATIVE

Margaret Mooney Marini
  Department of Sociology
  University of Minnesota
  OCCUPATIONAL AND
    CAREER MOBILITY
  SOCIAL VALUES AND
    NORMS

Ronald W. Maris
  Center for the Study of
  Suicide
  University of South Carolina
  SUICIDE

Kyriakos S. Markides
  Division of Sociomedical
  Sciences
  University of Texas Medical
  Branch, Galveston
  QUALITY OF LIFE

Barry Markovsky
  Program Director for
  Sociology
  University of Iowa
  SOCIAL PERCEPTION

Cora B. Marrett
  CORPORATE
    ORGANIZATIONS

Peter V. Marsden
  Department of Sociology
  Harvard University
  SOCIAL NETWORKS

Kerry Marsh
  Department of Psychology
  University of Connecticut
  PERSONAL AUTONOMY

Guido Martinotti
  Departimento di Sociologia
  Universita degli Studi di
  Milano
  DATA BANKS AND
    DEPOSITORIES

Gerald Marwell
  Department of Sociology
  University of Wisconsin
  EXPERIMENTS

Alexandra Maryanski
  Department of Sociolgy
  University of California,
  Riverside
  FUNCTIONALISM AND
    STRUCTURALISM

Eleonora Barbieri Masini
  Faculty of Social Sciences
  Gregorian University, Rome
  FUTURES STUDIES AS
    HUMAN AND SOCIAL
    ACTIVITY

Douglas S. Massey
Department of Sociology
University of Pennsylvania
SEGREGATION INDICES

Armand L. Mauss
Department of Sociology
Washington State University
SOCIAL PROBLEMS

E. Doyle McCarthy
Department of Sociology
Fordham University
SOCIOLOGY OF
KNOWLEDGE

Lisa J. McIntyre
Department of Sociology
Washington State University
FAMILY LAW

James M. McPartland
Johns Hopkins University
EQUALITY OF
OPPORTUNITY

Susan McWilliams
Department of Sociology
University of Southern
Maine
PERSUASION

David Mechanic
Institute for Health, Health
Care Policy, and Aging
Research
Rutgers University
HEALTH AND ILLNESS
BEHAVIOR

Barbara F. Meeker
Department of Sociology
University of Maryland,
College Park
MATHEMATICAL
SOCIOLOGY

H. Andrew Michener
Department of Sociology
University of Wisconsin,
Madison
GAME THEORY AND
STRATEGIC INTERACTION

Mario Mikulincer
Department of Psychology
Bar-Ilan University, Israel
PERSONAL DEPENDENCY

Gale E. Miller
Department of Social and
Cultural Sciences
Marquette University
CASE STUDIES

Rhonda J. V. Montgomery
Gerontology Center
University of Kansas
FILIAL RESPONSIBILITY

Patrick H. Mooney
CAPITALISM

Raymond A. Morrow
Department of Sociology
University of Alberta
MARXIST SOCIOLOGY

Jeylan T. Mortimer
Life Course Center
University of Minnesota
ADULTHOOD

Charles W. Mueller
Obermann Center for
Advanced Studies
University of Iowa
WORK ORIENTATION

Chandra Mukerji
Department of
Communications
University of California,
San Diego
POPULAR CULTURE

Joane Nagel
Department of Sociology
University of Kansas
INDIGENOUS PEOPLES

Saad Nagi
The Ohio State University
NATIONALISM

Keiko Nakao
Department of Sociology
Tokyo Metropolitan
University
OCCUPATIONAL PRESTIGE

Todd D. Nelson
Psychology Department
California State
University, Turlock
COGNITIVE CONSISTENCY
THEORIES

David G. Nickinovich
NRC, Inc.
BUREAUCRACY

Steven L. Nock
Department of Sociology
University of Virginia
DIVORCE

Robert M. O'Brien
Department of Sociology
University of Oregon
LEVELS OF ANALYSIS
CRIME RATES

Mary Ellen O'Connell
INTERNATIONAL LAW

Angela M. O'Rand
Department of Sociology
Duke University
SOCIAL INEQUALITY

Richard Ofshe
Department of Sociology
University of California,
Berkeley
EXTREME INFLUENCE:
THOUGHT REFORM, HIGH
CONTROL GROUPS,
INTERROGATION, AND
RECOVERED MEMORY
PSYCHOTHERAPY

Valerie K. Oppenheimer
Department of Sociology
University of California, Los
Angeles
LABOR FORCE

Myron Orleans
Department of Sociology
California State University,
Fullerton
PHENOMENOLOGY

Suzanne T. Ortega
Department of Sociology
University of Nebraska,
Lincoln
MENTAL ILLNESS AND
MENTAL DISORDERS

Fred C. Pampel
Department of Sociology
University of Colorado
SOCIAL SECURITY SYSTEMS

Jeffrey G. Pankhurst
Department of Sociology
Wittenberg University
FAMILY AND RELIGION

Toby L. Parcel
Social and Behavioral
Sciences
Ohio State University
SECONDARY DATA
ANALYSIS AND DATA
ARCHIVES

Ronald W. Perry
Arizona State University
DIFFUSION THEORIES

Richard A. Peterson
Department of Sociology
and Social Policy
University of Leeds
MUSIC

Thomas F. Pettigrew
Stevenson College
University of California,
Santa Cruz
DISCRIMINATION

David R. Phillips
Asia-Pacific Institute of
Ageing Studies, Faculty of
Social Sciences
Lingnan University,
Hong Kong
LONG-TERM CARE

W. David Pierce
Department of Sociology
University of Alberta
BEHAVIORISM

Karl Pillemer
Department of Human
Development
Cornell University
INTERGENERATIONAL
RELATIONS

Susan R. Pitchford
University of Washington
RACE

Gabriele Pollini
Dipartimento di Sociologia e
Ricerca Sociale
Universita degli Studi di
Trento, Italy
SOCIAL BELONGING

Lin Poyer
Department of
Anthropology
University of Wyoming
SOCIOCULTURAL
ANTHROPOLOGY

Evan Pritchard
Department of Psychology
University of Winnipeg
DECISION-MAKING THEORY
AND RESEARCH

Thomas W. Pullum
Department of Sociology
University of Texas
POPULATION

E. L. Quarantelli
Disaster Research Center
University of Delaware
DISASTER RESEARCH

Barbara F. Reskin
Department of Sociology
Harvard University
WORK AND OCCUPATIONS

Sean Ó Riain
University of California,
Davis
GLOBALIZATION AND
GLOBAL SYSTEMS
ANALYSIS

Maurice N. Richter, Jr.
Sociology Department
State University of New
York at Albany
EVOLUTION: BIOLOGICAL,
SOCIAL, CULTURAL

Cecilia L. Ridgeway
Department of Sociology
Stanford University
COMPLIANCE AND
CONFORMITY

Matilda White Riley
National Institutes of Health
COHORT PERSPECTIVES

John W. Riley, Jr.
Chevy Chase, Maryland
DEATH AND DYING

Georgina Rojas-Garcia
Population Research Center
University of Texas
INFANT AND CHILD
MORTALITY

Patricia A. Roos
Rutgers University
PROFESSIONS

Steve Rytina
Department of Sociology
McGill University
SOCIAL STRUCTURE

George Sabagh
Department of Sociology
University of California
MIDDLE EASTERN STUDIES

Joseph Sanders
University of Houston
LAW AND LEGAL SYSTEMS

Masamichi Sasaki
Hyogo Kyoiku University,
Japan
JAPANESE SOCIOLOGY

Gerard Saucier
Department of Psychology
University of Oregon
PERSONALITY
MEASUREMENT

Erwin K. Scheuch
GERMAN SOCIOLOGY

David R. Schmitt
Department of Sociology
University of Washington
GROUP SIZE

Ronald J. Schoenberg
Department of Sociology
University of Washington
PROBABILITY THEORY

Howard Schuman
Institute for Social Research
University of Michigan
SURVEY RESEARCH

Joseph Scimecca
Department of Sociology
George Mason University
HUMANISM

David Sciulli
Department of Sociology
Texas A & M University
INTERNATIONAL
ASSOCIATIONS IN
SOCIOLOGY

Karen Seccombe
Department of Sociology
Portland State University
ALTERNATIVE LIFESTYLES

Vimal P. Shah
Gujarat University, India
INDIAN SOCIOLOGY

Michael J. Shanahan
Center for Advanced Study
in the Behavioral Sciences
Pennsylvania State
University
ADOLESCENCE

Constance L. Shehan
Department of Sociology
University of Florida
PARENTAL ROLES

Larry D. Shinn
Berea College
WORLD RELIGIONS

James F. Short
Department of Sociology
Washington State University
CRIMINAL AND
DELINQUENT
SUBCULTURES

Robert W. Shotola
Department of Sociology
Portland State University
SMALL GROUPS

William Simon
Department of Sociology
University of Houston
SEXUAL ORIENTATION

John H. Simpson
Department of Sociology
University of Toronto
RELIGION, POLITICS, AND
WAR

Richard Mcgrath Skinner
University of Virginia
POLITICAL AND
GOVERNMENTAL
CORRUPTION

David Smith
University of Kansas
GENOCIDE

C. Matthew Snipp
Department of Sociology
Stanford University
AMERICAN INDIAN STUDIES

David Snow
Department of Sociology
University of Arizona
CROWDS AND RIOTS

Subhash Sonnad
Department of Sociology
Western Michigan University
NONPARAMETRIC
STATISTICS

Kenneth I. Spenner
Department of Sociology
Duke University
PERSONALITY AND SOCIAL
STRUCTURE

Rodney Stark
Department of Sociology
University of Washington
SOCIOLOGY OF RELIGION

Lauri Steel
American Institutes for
Research
FAMILY SIZE

Sonia Stefanizzi
Department of Sociology
and Social Research
University of Milan-Bicocca
DATABANKS AND
DEPOSITORIES

Ardyth Stimson
Kean University
INTERPERSONAL
ATTRACTION

John Stimson
Sociology Department
William Paterson University
SOCIAL FORECASTING

Philip J. Stone
Department of Sociology
Harvard University
CONTENT ANALYSIS

David Strang
Center for Advanced Study
in the Behavioral Sciences
Cornell University
IMPERIALISM,
COLONIALISM, AND
DECOLONIZATION

Jeffrey J. Strange
Public Insight
CENSORSHIP AND THE
REGULATION OF
EXPRESSION

Raimondo Strassoldo
Dipartimento EST
University of Udine, Italy
NATIONAL BORDER
RELATIONS,
MANAGEMENT OF

Murray A. Straus
University of New
Hampshire
FAMILY VIOLENCE

Robin Stryker
Department of Sociology
University of Iowa
GOVERNMENT
REGULATION

Sheldon Stryker
Department of Sociology
Indiana University
IDENTITY THEORY
SYMBOLIC INTERACTION
THEORY

Donald E. Stull
Department of Sociology
University of Akron
HEALTH AND THE LIFE
COURSE
INTERGENERATIONAL
RESOURCE TRANSFERS

J. Jill Suitor
Department of Sociology
Louisiana State University
INTERGENERATIONAL
RELATIONS
REMARRIAGE

Teresa A. Sullivan
Univesity of Texas at Austin
BANKRUPTCY AND CREDIT

Deborah A. Sullivan
Department of Sociology
Arizona State University
BIRTH AND DEATH RATES

Gene F. Summers
Department of Rural
Sociology
University of Wisconsin,
Madison
RURAL SOCIOLOGY

Marvin B. Sussman
INHERITANCE

Richard Swedberg
Department of Sociology
Stockholm University
ECONOMIC SOCIOLOGY

Szonja Szelenyi
Department of Sociology
Cornell University
SOCIALISM AND
COMMUNISM

Jacek Szmatka
Jagiellonian University,
Poland
POLISH AND EASTERN
EUROPEAN SOCIOLOGY

Karl E. Taeuber
Department of Sociology
University of Wisconsin
CENSUS

Irving Tallman
Department of Sociology
Washington State University
FAMILY POLICY IN
WESTERN SOCIETIES

Marylee C. Taylor
Department of Sociology
Pennsylvania State
University
PREJUDICE

James E. Teele
Department of Sociology
Boston University
JUVENILE DELINQUENCY
(AND JUVENILE CRIME)
WHITE COLLAR CRIME

Bruno Tellia
Dipartimento Economia,
Società, Territorio
Universita di Udine, Italy
NEGOTIATION OF POWER

Ann R. Tickamyer
Department of Sociology
The Ohio University
MACROSOCIOLOGY
INFORMAL ECONOMY, THE

Marta Tienda
Office of Population
Research
Princeton University
HISPANIC AMERICANS

Jackson Toby
Sociology Department
The State University of New
Jersey, Rutgers
CRIMINALIZATION OF
DEVIANCE

Donald J. Treiman
Department of Sociology
University of California at
Los Angeles
STATUS ATTAINMENT

Gaye Tuchman
Department of Sociology
University of Connecticut
FEMINIST THEORY

Nancy Brandon Tuma
Department of Sociology
Stanford University
SOCIAL DYNAMICS

Austin T. Turk
Department of Sociology
University of California,
Riverside
POLITICAL CRIME

Herman Turk
SOCIAL ORGANIZATION

Jonathan H. Turner
Department of Sociology
University of California,
Riverside
POSITIVISM

Ralph H. Turner
University of California, Los Angeles
COLLECTIVE BEHAVIOR

Bernard Valade
The Sorbonne
FRENCH SCHOOL OF SOCIOLOGY, THE

Maurice D. Van Arsdol, Jr.
Institute of International Studies
University of Southern California and Monterey
CITIES

Pierre L. van den Berghe
Department of Sociology
University of Washington
POLITICAL CORRECTNESS

Brenda J. Vander Mey
Department of Sociology
Clemson University
INCEST

Wayne J. Villemez
Department of Sociology
University of Connecticut
POVERTY

Carlos H. Waisman
Department of Sociology
University of California, San Diego
LATIN AMERICAN STUDIES

Walter L. Wallace
Department of Sociology
Princeton University
METATHEORY

Marilyn E. Walsh
ORGANIZED CRIME

Carol A. B. Warren
Department of Sociology
University of Kansas
ETHNOGRAPHY

Susan Cotts Watkins
Department of Sociology
University of Pennsylvania
FERTILITY DETERMINANTS

Frederick D. Weil
Department of Sociology
Louisiana State University
POLITICAL PARTY SYSTEMS

Joseph G. Weis
Department of Sociology
University of Washington
PROBATION AND PAROLE

Jack Whalen
Xerox Palo Alto Research Center
CONVERSATION ANALYSIS

Martin K. Whyte
Department of Sociology
George Washington University
CHINA STUDIES

Marion C. Willetts
Department of Sociology and Anthropology
Illinois State University
SEXUAL BEHAVIOR IN MARRIAGE AND CLOSE RELATIONSHIPS

Robin M. Williams, Jr.
University of California, Irvine and Cornell University
AMERICAN SOCIETY

Charles Winick
The Graduate School and University Center
City University of New York
PORNOGRAPHY
DRUG ABUSE

Halliman H. Winsborough
DEMOGRAPHY

Christopher Winship
Department of Sociology
Harvard University
SAMPLE SELECTION BIAS

Lynne Woehrle
Wilson College
GROUP CONFLICT RESOLUTION

Alan Wolfe
Boston College
SOCIAL PHILOSOPHY
HUMAN NATURE

James R. Wood
Department of Sociology
Indiana University
RELIGIOUS ORGANIZATIONS

James D. Wright
Department of Sociology
Tulane University
PUBLIC POLICY ANALYSIS

Robert Wuthnow
Department of Sociology
Princeton University
RELIGIOUS ORIENTATIONS

Grace J. Yoo
Asian-American Studies Department
San Francisco State University
INTERMARRIAGE

John H. Yost
Department of Psychology
John Carroll University
ROLE THEORY: FOUNDATIONS, EXTENSIONS, AND APPLICATIONS

Rosalie F. Young
Department of Community Medicine
Wayne State University
HEALTH PROMOTION AND HEALTH STATUS

Yih-Jin Young
Nassau Community College
EDUCATION AND DEVELOPMENT

Morris Zelditch, Jr.
Department of Sociology
Stanford University
INTERPERSONAL POWER

Viviana Zelizer
  Department of Sociology
  Princeton University
    MONEY

Richard A. Zeller
  Department of Sociology
  Bowling Green State
    University
    RELIABILITY

Mary Zimmerman
  Health Policy and
    Management
  University of Kansas
    MEDICAL SOCIOLOGY
    COMPARATIVE HEALTH-
    CARE SYSTEMS

Editorial Board

ABORTION

See Family Planning; Pregnancy and Pregnancy Termination.

ACCULTURATION

See Ethnicity.

ADDICTION

See Alcohol; Drug Abuse.

ADOLESCENCE

Recognition of the life stage between childhood and adulthood as a subject of modern scientific inquiry began in the early twentieth century with the publication of Antonio Marro's *La Puberta* (1898) and G. Stanley Hall's highly influential compendium *Adolescence* (1904). Although Hall's book represented an initial effort to describe adolescence, it nevertheless resonated with themes already familiar among scholars and the public. In Europe, romantic conceptions of a sexually charged, troubled youth (e.g., in Rousseau's *Émile*) circulated among the socially concerned. In America, an established tradition of cautionary literature emphasized the impressionable nature of young people and their vulnerability to sin (e.g., in the essays and sermons of Cotton Mather). Hall incorporated many of these ideas into a Darwinian framework to conjure an "adolescence" recognizable to

his readers (Ross 1972). Although the work is viewed as a curious and difficult amalgam today, it nevertheless emphasized themes that continue to shape the study of youth.

Hall viewed adolescence through the lens of Ernst Haeckel's biogenetic principle, which holds that the human life span recapitulates the phases of human biological and social evolution (Gould 1977). Hall maintained that late childhood corresponds to a period of peaceful savagery in the distant past, whereas adolescence represents a "neo-atavistic" period of migration into a challenging environment, which prompted physical, social, and psychological conflict and growth. This characterization of the adolescent, as troubled by all-encompassing turmoil, was contested early in the twentieth century by prominent behavioral scientists such as Edwin Thorndike (1917) and has been repeatedly challenged since then, perhaps most famously by Margaret Mead's *Coming of Age in Samoa* (1928) (but see Freeman 1983; Côté 1994). Likewise, sociologists such as Robert and Helen Lynd (1929) and August Hollingshead (1949) found little evidence of pervasive trouble among the youth of Middletown or Elmtown. Contemporary behavioral scientists take a more moderate view than Hall's, depicting adolescence as a time of both change and continuity (e.g., Douvan and Adelson 1966). Nevertheless, the study of adolescence has been indelibly marked by the "storm and stress" motif.

Hall also maintained that adolescents are highly responsive to adult guidance. Drawing on work by

Edward Cope, a leading American proponent of the biogenetic principle, he believed that the influence of the environment in producing acquired characteristics that were then transmissible by heredity was greatest during adolescence. The implication of this Lamarckian view was momentous: The future development of the human race depended on improvements in the adolescent (Hall 1904, v. 1, p. 50). Indeed, as a leader of the Child Study Movement, Hall forcefully argued for collaborative efforts between pedagogy and the emerging discipline of psychology, creating schools that push adolescents to their physical and mental limits, and effect the "moral rejuvenation" of youth, society, and indeed the human race. A view of adolescence as a source of manifold revitalization was especially appealing to Hall's readership, a Gilded Age middle class weary from concern over urbanization and the perceived cultural and eugenic threats posed by large-scale immigration into the United States (Kett 1977; Ross 1972). The view that adults can constructively regulate the socialization of youth is reflected in continuing scientific and public interest in the settings of youth (e.g., the workplace) and their implications for development.

Hall's *Adolescence* was an interdisciplinary work, and drew from a wide range of sources, including writings by early sociologists such as Auguste Comte, Herbert Spencer, Gustave Le Bon, and Adolphe Quételet. The interdisciplinary study of youth remains an important theme, with many fields recognizing adolescence as a significant area of inquiry, including psychology (Petersen 1988), history (Modell and Goodman 1990), and anthropology (Schlegel and Barry 1991). Yet each discipline has its unique presuppositions and focal points. Psychologists tend to focus on adolescents' cognitive, motivational, and emotional capacities; their maturation (often along universalistic lines, as one finds in the work of Piaget and Erikson), their interrelationships, and how they are shaped by experiences in proximal settings, including the family, peer group, school, and workplace. Anthropologists and historians focus on the range of experiences that adolescence encompasses across cultures and through historical time: the existence

of the adolescent life phase, its distinctive social and cultural traditions, and interrelationships among youth, other age groups, and social institutions.

Sociological studies of adolescence often overlap with these concerns, reflecting interests in the social settings of youth and their implications for the self, as well as variability in this stage of life across societies and through historical time. Yet sociologists have also maintained a unique view by drawing on the life course paradigm as an analytic framework. The life course focuses on age-graded roles, opportunities, and constraints; how these differ through historical time, and how they shape the biography. The analytic focus is on the structural complexity and diversity of social settings through time and place, as well as the plasticity of humans in these settings (Dannefer 1984).

The remainder of this entry will focus on three distinctive features of adolescence as viewed from a life-course perspective (see Table 1). The first feature concerns adolescence as a life phase in historical perspective: Has adolescence been a recognized part of the life course through historical time? And how have the factors that mark the transition both into and out of adolescence changed? Implicit in the concept of markers that distinguish adolescence from childhood and adulthood is the rate of movement from one phase to the next. Accordingly, the second feature concerns how quickly young people move through the adolescent role set and the social circumstances that promote an accelerated life course.

The third feature focuses on the central role of institutionalized pathways through adolescence. In this context, pathways refer to routes from childlike dependence on the family of origin to the autonomies of adulthood. At the same time, individuals actively construct their lives. Within the structured pathways from childhood to adulthood, how do adolescents actively shape their biographies? Throughout this essay, social historical accounts are presented to underscore the highly variable nature of adolescence in the last two centuries; in turn, these accounts are juxtaposed with current sociological efforts to understand the social worlds of youth. The entry concludes by considering the dual role of sociologists in the study of adolescence: To contribute to substantive debates about the place of youth in society, but

Adolescence As a Phase of the Life Course

Features of Adolescence	Core Idea
1. Adolescence in social historical perspective	Variability in the adolescent experience can be studied through the social history of youth.
A. Historical permanence of adolescence	Adolescence is a semi-autonomous phase of life that is not of modern origin. Adolescence is always changing in response to social forces.
B. The boundaries of adolescence	Adolescence is differentiated from childhood and adulthood by transition markers and roles.
(1) From childhood to adolescence	The pubertal transition was not always a critical marker between childhood and adolescence.
(2) From adolescence to adulthood	The transition markers have been compressed and their sequence has become more complex.
2. Pace of movement through adolescent roles	Social stressors may promote rapid movement into, through, and out of adolescent roles.
3. Pathways through adolescence	Pathways direct youth through social positions in organizations.
A. Pathways in the school	This pathway is defined by the transition to 8th grade, tracks, and transitions out of high school.
B. Pathways in the workplace	This pathway is defined by the adolescent work career: extent of work involvement, quality of work, and fit with other roles and life goals.
C. Agency in pathways	Adolescent planfulness is a critical resource with which to actively negotiate the life course.

Table 1

also to identify how the contours of these debates are themselves the products of social forces.

Two additional features of adolescence are not covered in this entry. One involves the social relationships of youth, a subject that has been examined from several vantage points. Considerable attention has been devoted to the "sociometric" properties of peer relationships, mapping out affiliations among young people in high schools (see Hallinan and Smith, 1989 for a contribution to this tradition). Relatedly, sociologists have also examined the typical personalities, behavioral patterns, and group identities of youth as they reflect responses to the social organization of the high school and this phase of life (e.g., Matza 1964). Sociologists have also focused on youth and their intergenerational relationships: How youth are integrated into adult society (for example, see Coleman 1994), how they and their parents interrelate (for a useful review, see Dornbusch 1989), and how youth serve as agents of social change (for

a classic statement, see Mannheim 1928/1952). The second feature is juvenile delinquency (see *JUVENILE DELINQUENCY*).

ADOLESCENCE AS A LIFE PHASE

Each phase of life reflects social norms and institutional constraints and serves as a principal source of identity for the individual by specifying appropriate behaviors and roles (Elder 1980). The study of adolescence as a life phase requires that it be situated in the life course, that its distinctive features be identified in comparison to both childhood and adulthood. Indeed, adolescence is frequently depicted as a transitional period of semiautonomy, reflecting movement from the complete dependence of children on their parents to the establishment of one's own livelihood and family in adulthood (e.g., Kett 1974; Katz 1979; Gillis 1974). Yet the study of adolescence as a life phase also requires that it be situated in history, that the changing norms and institutions that shape adolescence be identified, and correspondingly, that the changing nature of adolescent semiautonomy be recognized. Within this frame of life-stage analysis, social scientists have studied the historical permanence of adolescence and the factors that have circumscribed this phase of life, marking its beginning and end.

"Adolescence" in historical time. Initial efforts to interpret the social history of youth concluded that adolescence did not exist before the modernization of societies (modernization refers to a constellation of societal changes thought to mark a break with previous forms of social organization: rapid technological changes, the emergence of market economies, urbanization, industrialization, the decline of agricultural life, secularization, broad-based political participation, the use of currency, and the spread of science [Kleiman 1998]). Norbert Elias (1994) suggested that children and adults became increasingly distinct in their behaviors as etiquette became more widespread and refined, particularly with the collapse of feudal societies. Indeed, Elias implied that the life span recapitulates the history of manners, an instance of Haeckel's biogenetic law.

More focused on youth was Philippe Ariés's path-setting *Centuries of Childhood* (1962). Drawing on a diverse array of evidence—including art history, linguistics, and literature—Ariés argued that in medieval times children merged directly into adult roles starting at around seven years of age. Medieval society distinguished between adults and nonadults, but, in the latter category, distinctions were not maintained between children and adolescents. Most medieval and premodern children did not attend school, but were incorporated into adult life as quickly as possible by way of daily interactions with their elders in tightly knit communities. The few youth who did attend school remained integrated in adult society by way of a vocational curriculum designed largely to train lawyers and the clergy. According to Ariés, beginning as early as the sixteenth century, a wide range of factors—from Cartesianism to technological advancements—led to the prolongation of childhood and the emergence of adolescence as a life phase. Youth were to be educated in age-segregated settings according to curricula that were less concerned with vocational training. With this prolongation of education and segregation from the adult world, adolescence emerged as a distinct age-graded identity.

Like Hall's *Adolescence*, Ariés's work was read by a receptive audience (Ben-Amos 1995). The prominent functionalist Kingsley Davis (1944) had already argued that the transmission of adult norms and values took less time in "simpler" societies. Similarly, in his highly influential *The Lonely Crowd*, David Riesman (1950) argued that children could assume adult roles in tradition-directed societies (see also Eisenstadt 1956). But Ariés was unique in his use of the historical record, and his work was a point of departure for the social history of children and adolescence that subsequently emerged in the 1970s (e.g., Demos 1970; Gillis 1974). Accordingly, some commentators maintained that adolescence was "discovered" or "invented" in the eighteenth century, as shown in part by more precise distinctions among words like "child," "adolescent," and "youth" (e.g., Musgrove 1964). Yet a linguistic analysis says little about the historical permanence of adolescence as a set of transitional experiences marked by semiautonomy between childhood and adulthood. Indeed, many of Ariés's arguments have been seriously contested, including his description of education in medieval and Renaissance Europe and his lack of appreciation for the semiautonomous roles youth often played in these societies as servants or apprentices (e.g., Davis 1975).

The guiding principle of most contemporary social historical research is that adolescence reflects ever-changing values and societal structures, encompassing demographic, political, economic, and social realities. For example, Kett (1977) views American adolescence as a set of behaviors imposed on youth beginning in the late nineteenth century. This imposition was justified by "psychological laws" (e.g., the necessity of religious decision during adolescence) freighted with middle-class concerns over the dangers of cities, immigrants, bureaucracies, and the pace of social change. Not surprisingly, social historians have detected "different adolescences" in diverse settings defined by historical time and place.

Reflecting a continuing engagement with Ariés, a focal point of social historical research has been the experience of adolescence before, during, and after the emergence of industrialism. An overview of research on England highlights the contingent nature of adolescence as a social category. Two realities were prominent in defining adolescence in premodern England (Gillis 1974). First, children of all social classes were often sent out of their household of origin to become servants for another family at about age seven. "Binding out" coincided with the adoption of adult dress and codes of behavior, although the young person was viewed as neither fully adult nor child. Rather, this practice marked a form of semiautonomy: they participated in the labor market and resided outside their parents' home, but they did not marry and they were not financially independent.

Second, marriage was often linked with the establishment of an independent household. The timing of this transition, which marked full adulthood, was in turn determined by when the father conveyed dowries for daughters and annuities or land to sons. Although the specifics of inheritance were often far more complex than the rule of primogeniture would suggest (Stone 1979), the net result was that marriage was typically postponed among the poor and lower-middle classes (that is, most of society) until young people were in their late twenties, with males marrying about two years later than females. For the proportion of the population that never married (about one in five), the commencement of adulthood hinged on occupational achievements and financial independence, which probably took place in the late twenties as well.

The coming of industrialism changed the adolescent experience dramatically. Reactions to industrialism differed greatly by class and were complicated by a wide array of factors. For many strata of society, however, economic livelihood was often enhanced by encouraging several wage laborers within the family (Gillis 1974). In turn, wage labor was a strong force in creating new and popular pathways into marriage. Concerns over inheritance were less common than in the earlier period, and kin ties were defined along more pragmatic lines that allowed youth greater freedom to marry and to establish a household. The absence of strong patriarchal control and new-found pocket money led many youth to courting and consumption patterns that shocked their elders. A new adolescence had emerged.

This broad-brush view varied in important ways from place to place, among social classes, and by gender (for related accounts of the English experience, see Anderson 1971; Musgrove 1964; Smelser 1959; for the Continental experience, see Mittauer and Sieder 1982; for the American experience see Demos 1970; Handlin and Handlin 1971; Hareven 1982; Kett 1977; Prude 1983). Yet it is instructive for two reasons. First, most scholars now agree that as a transitional stage of semiautonomy, adolescence existed before the emergence of modern societies, although it had distinctive "premodern" characteristics. For example, premodern adolescence was typically not a period of identity formation, as Erik Erikson's (1963) putatively universal model of psychosocial development maintains (Mitterauer 1992). Young people knew their occupational and educational futures, their parents arranged both their marriages and home-leaving, and the realities of inheritance, fecundity, and infant mortality dictated their reproductive behaviors. Furthermore, for most youth, few real political or religious options presented themselves. Although there are recorded instances of youth riots in urban areas and many adolescents and young adults were active in the Protestant Reformation, political and religious beliefs generally reflected the traditions and customs of the locale.

Second, although adolescence existed in preindustrial times, historians such as Ariés maintain too sharp a distinction between premodern and modern phases of the life course (Ben-Amos 1995). The adolescences of both the preindustrial and contemporary West are not entirely dissimilar, suggesting that there are distinctly "modern" features of preindustrial adolescence and "traditional" features of contemporary adolescence. For example, many adolescents of both periods lack a parent. In seventeenth-century England, life expectancy was approximately thirty-two years, so that many youth, born when the mother was in her early to mid-twenties, lacked at least one parent. In contemporary society, parental separation is not uncommon through the early life course. For example, among cohorts born between 1967 and 1973, about 20 percent of white males and 60 percent of black males have lived in a mother-only family between birth and age 15 (Hill et al. 1999). Parental separation and absence today is a substitute for the parental mortality of the premodern period.

Similarly, the adolescence of both historical eras was a drawn-out process. Because of early home-leaving and late marriage, preindustrial adolescence in England spanned two decades. In contemporary times, it is commonly asserted that the span between puberty and the transition to adulthood is excessive because of delays in school completion, marriage, and home-leaving. Indeed, some sociologists have suggested adding a "postadolescence" stage to the life course (e.g., Hurrelmann 1989). Although the duration of adolescence today appears extended against the backdrop of the early to mid-twentieth century, it is nevertheless brief when compared to preindustrial adolescence (about twelve versus twenty years).

In short, adolescence traces back to at least the High Middle Ages in the West, but its form and content have been remarkably responsive to social setting (Mitterauer 1992). Furthermore, one often observes both similarities and differences among the "adolescences" defined by historical time and place.

The transition from childhood to adolescence. Sociologists have not studied the transition to adolescence extensively, perhaps because it is typically equated with the onset of puberty, which strongly reflects individual differences in genetics, nutrition, and physical exertion (Tanner 1978). This lack of interest is unfortunate, as the effects of these factors on pubertal timing have always been conditioned by social circumstances (e.g., improvements in nutrition diffused through many societies on the basis of class and urban-rural distinctions; see Mitterauer 1992).

In any event, historical analyses suggest that puberty was not always the primary marker of the transition to adolescence. By today's standards, physical changes associated with puberty occurred notably later in the premodern and early modern periods. For example, the average age of menarche was about fifteen for girls in early eighteenth-century America and final height was not attained among men until around age twenty-five (Kett 1977). Sources from mid-sixteenth century Europe suggest even later dates and a much more gradual progression of physical changes than is observed today (for a review of earlier sources and their critical evaluation, see Tanner 1981).

In the premodern period, young people were probably viewed as semi-autonomous when they were sent to other households as servants or apprentices (often between ages seven and ten). Other local customs (such as religious confirmation and conversion, and membership in a wide array of village groups) also marked the end of childhood, and these frequently occurred before the pubertal transition. Thus historical evidence suggests that physical changes associated with puberty were not prominent factors that distinguished children from adolescents, and this generalization may be valid into the mid-nineteenth century, when improvements in nutrition began to take hold for large segments of society. Indeed, the pubertal transition often represented an important step into adult roles. Before the mid-nineteenth century, puberty in America was associated with a sense of rising power and energy and the ability to assume adult work responsibilities. It was largely after the Civil War that puberty came to represent a vulnerable and awkward stage closely associated with the adolescence of today (Kett 1977).

The transition from adolescence to young adulthood. A range of "transition markers" are typically used to indicate movement out of adolescence and into adulthood. These include leaving school, starting a full-time job, leaving the home of origin, getting married, and becoming a parent. These markers can not be used uncritically, however, because their relevance in defining stages of the life course changes through historical periods (Mitterauer 1992). Furthermore, although young people in the contemporary West rely on these markers to distinguish between adolescence and adulthood, they also draw on other criteria, including cognitive self-sufficiency, emotional self-reliance, and behavioral self-control (Arnett and Taber 1994). Nevertheless, most sociological research has focused on these transition markers and has generated valuable insights about the changing life course. Paradoxically, many commentators argue that markers of the transition from adolescence to adulthood have become both more standardized and variable.

Standardization: The compression of transition markers. Standardization reflects the increasing importance of age-grading and is seen in the increasing "compactness" of transition markers, particularly the ages of school completion, first job, and marriage. Theorists argue that the organization of public services, transfer payments, and employment opportunities according to age renders the life course more orderly and calculable (Beck 1992; Kohli 1986). Also, as the state increased the number of rights that an individual could claim on a universalistic, standardized basis, it also restricted the individual's right to organize many aspects of life (e.g., with respect to education and entry into, and exit from, the labor market) (Buchmann 1989).

Evidence from historical demography suggests that the transition to adulthood has indeed become more standardized. Examining the prevalence of different female life-course patterns (e.g., spinster, dying mother, widowed mother) among cohorts of women born between 1830 and 1920, Uhlenberg (1969) observes a convergence on the "typical" pattern, involving marriage, having children, and surviving with husband until age 55. Among women born in 1830, about 21 percent experienced this "typical" pattern in contrast to about 57 percent of women born in 1920. In addition, the age range in which women typically married and had children narrowed. The primary factor promoting standardization of the life course was improvement in mortality due to the management of contagious and infectious diseases such as smallpox, typhoid and scarlet fever, diphtheria, and measles. Similarly, the time it took 80 percent of both men and women to leave the household of origin, marry, and establish their own households decreased markedly between 1880 and 1970 among those who experienced these transitions (Modell et al. 1976). A considerable body of evidence suggests that the transition to adulthood was standardized between about 1830 and 1960, as measured by a constriction of the time in which most people pass through a range of transition markers (for further discussion, see Shanahan forthcoming).

Theoreticians have emphasized the critical role of "modernity" in explaining this long-term pattern, but this formulation, with its connotation of a monotonic pace and continuous process, has not been supported by empirical study. Instead, age standardization has been affected by historically specific conditions, including improvements in health (Uhlenberg 1969) and age-grading in the school system (Hogan 1981). And as historians have noted, legal reforms, public debates about the rights and responsibilities of age groups, and cultural innovations have come into play at different times and with varying degrees of import (Kett 1977; Modell 1989; Zelizer 1994). Evidence thus points to a long-term trend of compression of the transition markers, but that trend reflects manifold factors proceeding at an uneven pace.

Variability: The complex sequencing of transition markers. Variability is found in the increasing complexity of role overlap and sequencing during the transition to adulthood. Theorists of modernity maintain that as individuals were freed from the traditional constraints of family and locale, they were able to exercise more agency in the construction of their biographies (e.g., Beck 1992; Giddens 1991). Consistent with these arguments, Modell, Furstenberg, and Hershberg (1976) observe that as transition markers occurred in briefer periods of time, they exhibited greater diversity in their sequencing. Between 1880 and 1970, the familial and nonfamilial transition markers increasingly overlapped, creating variability in the transition to adulthood in the form of more sequence patterns of school completion, leaving home, starting a family and career, and becoming a parent.

Hogan (1981) provides important empirical evidence for variability in the sequencing of markers among cohorts born between 1907 and 1946. The percentage of men experiencing an "intermediate nonnormative" order of transition markers (beginning work before completing school or marriage before beginning work but after school completion) increased from about 20 percent in the cohorts born between 1907 and 1912 to about 30 percent for men born in 1951. The prevalence of "extreme nonnormative" ordering (marriage before school completion) increased from less than 10 percent among cohorts born between 1907 and 1911 to over 20 percent for cohorts born between 1924 and 1947. "Modernity" has a large negative effect on the prevalence of the normative pattern, but a large positive effect on the prevalence of the extreme nonnormative pattern. That is, in historical times marked by greater educational attainment, lower infant mortality, greater longevity, and fewer youth in the adult labor market, men are more likely to make extremely nonnormative transitions to adulthood. Evidence thus suggests a trend toward individualization of the life course as found in the increased variability in the sequencing and overlap of transitions (for further discussion, see Shanahan forthcoming).

THE ACCELERATED LIFE COURSE AND ADOLESCENCE

A conception of adolescence as bounded by markers implies a normative rate of movement through roles that indicate childhood, adolescence, and adulthood. Accordingly, influential accounts of youth view adolescence as a transitory period, marking normatively paced movement from childlike to adult roles (e.g., Linton 1942). The individual is construed as more or less adultlike depending on the acquisition of symbols, the provision of opportunities, and demands for responsibility that indicate adulthood. With respect to the second decade of life, behavioral scientists recognize three forms of an accelerated life course, reflecting the nonnormatively rapid (1) transition into adolescence, (2) movement through adolescence, and (3) transition into adulthood. These manifestations of the accelerated life course are frequently linked to stressors operating on the parents and the young person.

Precocious youth represent an early form of accelerated life course in American history. Since at least the mid-eighteenth century, some young people have been portrayed as astonishingly adultlike in their intellectual, moral, physical, and social capacities. Early American history is replete with admiration for youth who grew up in log cabins only to rise to high levels of prominence while still young, a rise often linked to exceptional talents exhibited in childhood. Yet precocity was also viewed as an inconvenience. Thus, the father of an eleven-year-old graduate from Yale at the end of the eighteenth century lamented that his son was "in no way equipped to do much of anything" (Graff 1995, p. 47). Instances such as these became rare as the social institutions of youth became age-graded, beginning in the mid-nineteenth century.

In contemporary times, an accelerated life course may reflect an early transition to adolescence. For example, Belsky and his colleagues (1991) have proposed a sociobiological model of early menarche and sexual activity. According to this model, high levels of stress during childhood—reflecting marital discord, inconsistent and harsh parenting, and inadequate financial resources—lead to aggression and depression in late childhood, which in turn foster early puberty and sexual activity. In contrast, children whose families enjoy spousal harmony, adequate financial resources, and sensitive, supportive parenting tend to experience a later onset of puberty and sexual activity. That is, depending on environmental cues about the availability and predictability of resources (broadly defined), development follows one of two distinct reproductive strategies.

Empirical studies provide partial support for this model. Menarche occurs earlier among girls who live in mother-only households or with stepfathers. Conflict in parent-child relationships or low levels of warmth are also associated with earlier menarche (Ellis and Graber forthcoming; Graber, Brooks-Gunn, and Warren 1995; Surbey 1990). Drawing on longitudinal data, Moffitt and her colleagues (1992) report that family conflict and the absence of a father in childhood lead to earlier menarche, although this relationship is not mediated by any psychological factors examined in their study. Research findings to date, however, are open to genetic interpretation. It may be that early-maturing mothers transmit a genetic predisposition toward early puberty and the same genes produce traits in the mother that affect parenting (Rowe forthcoming) finds some support for both models. Maccoby (1991) suggests an additional class of explanations, namely that these findings reflect social psychological processes (e.g., the adolescent's imitation of the mother's permissiveness).

The accelerated life course may also involve the rapid assumption of autonomy not typically associated with adolescent roles. This form may appear in the adoption of the parent role by adolescents in their family of origin, what Minuchin (1974) refers to as the "parental child." Children and adolescents may respond to the family's emotional and practical needs through activities such as serving as a confidant to a parent, mediating family disputes, and the extensive parenting of younger siblings. Young people may assume responsibilities such as these in single, working-parent homes, which can have positive consequences for adolescents but detrimental effects for younger children (Weiss 1979). The contextual and interpersonal factors that promote "parentification," however, are potentially numerous and complex, perhaps encompassing family structure, sibship size, marital dysfunction, and the employment status of the parents (Jurkovic 1997).

Likewise some critics of youth employment suggest that extensive involvement in the workplace during the high school years can promote "pseudomaturity," the appearance of adult status that nevertheless lacks the full set of rights and responsibilities that accompany adulthood. (Psychologists have also expressed concern about "pseudomaturity" among contemporary youth, although they define it as a disjunction between the apparent ability to play adult roles and a lack of "commensurate psychological differentiation" [e.g., Erikson 1959].) For example, although youth may earn considerable amounts of money during high school, they spend a relatively high percentage of their income on entertainment because they lack the financial responsibilities of true adults (e.g., insurance, housing). In turn, this "premature affluence" may interfere with the development of realistic financial values (Bachman 1983; Bachman and Schulenberg 1993). However, studies show that youth spend their earnings on a wide range of things, not all of which are concerned with leisure, including savings for future education, car insurance, and even loans and contributions to parents (Shanahan et al. 1996). Moreover, studies of families during the Great Depression suggest that economic hardship can lead to the assumption of more adultlike work responsibilities among children and adolescents, which can benefit the latter group (Elder 1974).

Finally, the accelerated life course may reflect a rapid transition to adulthood. For example, because young black men have markedly shorter life expectancies than white men, they often accelerate their transition behaviors (Burton et al. 1996). There may also be an important element of intentionality in the "search for role exit" from adolescence (Hagan and Wheaton 1993). Although the desire to leave home, marry, and have children may be normative, the intent to exit the adolescent role set too early is nonnormative and often associated with deviant acts. Indeed, the search for adolescent role exits significantly predicts frequency of dating and the timing of first marriage and parenthood. That is, some adolescents may seek rapid transition to adulthood because they are substantially dissatisfied with their experience of adolescence as a life phase. In any event, sociologists have offered numerous explanations for adolescent parenthood including, for example, the lack of role models and opportunities that would otherwise encourage postponing intercourse and pregnancy (Brewster 1994).

PATHWAYS AND AGENCY THROUGH ADOLESCENCE

The preceding discussion highlights the variable meanings of adolescence in the life course; a related issue is the structured pathways that constitute likely sequences of social positions through which the adolescent moves. Pathways reflect institutional arrangements that both provide and restrict opportunities, channeling youth from one social position to another. Pathways are a prominent feature in the school and workplace—and between these institutions (see ADULTHOOD)—where social forces match individuals to social opportunities and limitations. Pathways are also evident in the family, as a sequence of roles that the child assumes and that offer progressively greater autonomy.

Before the mid-nineteenth century in America, the immediate environments of youth were casual and unstructured; mortality and frequent moves from the home placed limits on the direct and sustained application of parental discipline, and schools were decidedly unstructured settings marked by violence and informality (Kett 1977). Between 1840 and 1880, a different viewpoint emerged in both Britain and the United States, a viewpoint that emphasized character formation in planned, "engineered" environments. For example, Horace Bushnell's influential *Christian Nurture* (1848) argued for carefully controlled settings that would promote in youth qualities necessary to succeed in a world threatened by urbanization and non-Protestant immigrants. By the end of the nineteenth century, efforts to standardize the settings of youth—particularly schools—led to the emergence of recognized tracks of educational and occupational experiences for young men entering the medical and legal professions. Educational and occupational pathways from adolescence to adulthood were becoming standardized.

Although pathways sort individuals and assign them to various positions in social systems, people are also active agents who attempt to shape their biographies. In life-course perspective, agency at the level of the person can be defined as the ability to formulate and pursue life plans. Young people are constrained and enabled by opportunity structures of school and work, but they also construct their life course through their active efforts. This section provides a set of examples that highlight structured pathways that describe likely sequences of social positions in terms of education and work. It also discusses sociological efforts to understand the active efforts of adolescents to shape their biographies in these structured settings.

Educational pathways through adolescence. At the turn of the nineteenth century, youth fortunate enough to attend school typically started their educations late and attended class sporadically. Academies of education, not uncommonly a single room in a private residence, were eager to accommodate the seasonal demands of agriculture. Consequently student bodies encompassed a wide range of pupils, whose ages often said little about their academic accomplishments. This situation was more pronounced in district schools, where attendance was said to fluctuate from hour to hour. Furthermore, teaching was not yet an occupation that required credentials, and teachers frequently resorted to violence to impart lessons or to maintain order, as did the students in response to frequent humiliation.

At the college level, the violence was pronounced. There were riots at Harvard, Yale, and Princeton, nightly stoning of the president's house at Brown through the 1820s, and frequent beating of blacks, servants, fellow students, and professors (Kett 1977). During the early years of the republic, little in the educational system was standardized. Beginning in the mid-nineteenth century, the educational system changed as Horace Mann, Henry Barnard, and Calvin Stowe led the common school revival, aimed at creating regulated, controlled school settings. In addition to the efforts of early reformers, many social, economic, political, and cultural forces contributed to the standardization of schools, particularly in the late nineteenth century (Tyack 1974; Tyack, James, and Benavot 1987).

Today, the educational system is highly standardized and adolescent pathways through school are readily identifiable: Adolescent pathways through the educational system can be described in terms of the transition to the seventh grade and tracking through the high school years. A considerable

body of sociological research also examines the many structured connections among secondary education, tertiary institutions such as colleges and vocational schools, and the workplace.

At the transition to seventh grade, children may remain in the same school (a "K–8" system) or change to a junior high school. The latter structure is thought to be more stressful by sociologists, as it typically brings with it a disruption in social networks and the student's first exposure to a bureaucratic setting with a high degree of specialization. Students in K–8 systems continue to have one teacher and one set of classmates for all subjects, while students attending junior high school often have a different teacher and classmates for each subject. In fact, students in K–8 systems are more influenced by peers, date more, and prefer to be with close friends more than students making the transition to junior high school. The latter report higher levels of anonymity. Further, girls who make the transition to junior high school appear especially vulnerable to low levels of self-esteem when compared with girls in a K–8 system and boys in either system (Blyth et al. 1978; Simmons and Blyth 1987; Simmons et al. 1979).

It may be that the negative effects of the transition to junior high school are amplified as the number of transitions experienced by a young person increases. A "focal theory of change" maintains that young people are better able to cope with significant life events serially rather than simultaneously (Coleman 1974). Some evidence supports this view: As the number of transitions—including school change, pubertal change, early dating, geographic mobility, and major family disruptions such as death—that students must cope with concurrently increase, their grades, extracurricular involvements, and self-esteem decrease (Simmons et al. 1987). These associations are particularly deleterious for girls. How the transition to seventh grade is organized can thus have pervasive implications for the well-being of youth.

Within secondary schools students are frequently assigned to "tracks," different curricula for students of differing talents and interests. Sociologists have identified several noteworthy features of tracks, including selectivity (the extent of homogeneity within tracks), electivity (the extent to which students choose their tracks), inclusiveness (the extent to which tracks leave open options for future education), and scope (the extent to which students are assigned to the same track across subjects and through time). Scope—particularly the extent to which students are in the same track across grade levels—predicts math and verbal achievement, when earlier scores of achievement are controlled.(Gamoran 1992).

In turn, these differences in educational achievement largely reflect socialization and allocation processes (for a useful review, see Gamoran 1996). Socialization refers to systematically different educational experiences across tracks. Allocation refers to the decisions made by teachers to assign students to tracks, assignments that provide information to students about their abilities and that elicit differential responses from others. That is, students of differing ability are assigned to different educational opportunities, which in turn creates inequalities in outcomes, even if initial differences in ability are taken into account. Unfortunately, tracking systems are often unfair in the sense that students of similar ability are assigned to different tracks, and assignments may be based on factors other than intellectual talents and interests (see Entwisle and Alexander 1993). Furthermore, status allocations from primary through tertiary school and to the labor force are remarkably consistent (Kerckhoff 1993). The advantages or disadvantages of one's position in the educational and occupational systems cumulate as individuals increasingly diverge in their educational and labor market attainments. Thus, educational tracks can exert substantial influence on socioeconomic achievements throughout the life course.

Pathways in the workplace. Work responsibilities have always indicated one's status in the life course. Through the early nineteenth century in America, young people began performing chores as early as possible in childhood and often assumed considerable work responsibilities by age seven, either on the farm or as a servant in another household. Many youth were fully incorporated into the workforce with the onset of physical maturity, in the mid- to late teens (Kett 1977). During this same period, however, agricultural opportunities waned in the Northeast while expansions in commerce, manufacturing, and construction provided new employment for youth in and around cities. Many families adopted economic strategies whereby parents and children were involved in complex combinations of farming, work in factories, and other sources of wage labor (Prude 1983) or whereby entire families were recruited into factory work (Hareven 1982; for the case of England, see Anderson 1971; Smelser 1959).

The second Industrial Revolution, commencing after the Civil War and extending to World War I, led in part to less reliance on children as factory workers (Osterman 1979). Technological innovations in the workplace—the use of internal combustion engines, electric power, and continuous-processing techniques—created an economic context conducive to the consolidation of primary schools in the life course as many youth jobs were eliminated by mechanization (Troen 1985) and manufacturers required more highly skilled employees (Minge-Kalman 1978). These economic factors operated in concert with progressive political movements, as well as cultural, demographic, social, and legal changes (Hogan 1981; Zelizer 1985), all of which fueled debates about the appropriate role of youth in the workplace. These debates continue to the present, particularly focusing on the work involvements of high school students (for useful overviews, see Institute of Medicine/National Research Council 1998; Mortimer and Finch 1996). Today, almost all adolescents work in paid jobs and time commitments to the workplace can be substantial (Bachman and Schulenberg 1993; Manning 1990). Whereas youth work at the beginning of the twentieth century often centered around agriculture and involved family, kin, and neighbors, today's adolescent is more frequently employed in "entry-level" jobs among unrelated adults in the retail and restaurant sectors. These changes have prompted arguments that contemporary adolescent work interferes significantly with the basic developmental tasks of youth.

Yet the transition to paid work represents a large step toward autonomy and can promote a sense of contribution, of egalitarianism, and of being "grown up" among youth. Although very little research has examined the adolescent work career, several generalizations are currently plausible. First, adolescents have work careers in that they typically progress from informal work (e.g., babysitting and yard work for neighbors) to a surprisingly diverse set of occupations as seniors in high school, a trend that is accompanied by an increase in earnings. That is, work tends to become more complex and to produce more earnings through the high school years (Mortimer et al. 1994).

Second, adolescent work can have positive or negative consequences, depending on the extent and the quality of the experience, as well as its meaning. For example, work of high intensity (that is, exceeding twenty hours of work on average across all weeks employed) curtails postsecondary education among boys and increases alcohol use and smoking among high school girls (Mortimer and Johnson 1998). But adolescents engaged in low-intensity work during high school have favorable outcomes with respect to schooling (for boys) and part-time work (for both boys and girls).

Third, the quality of work matters. For example, several studies show that jobs that draw on or confer skills deemed useful in the workplace are associated with feelings of efficacy during the high school years as well as success in the job market three years after high school (Finch et al. 1991; Stern and Nakata 1989). Similarly, adolescent work experiences can have positive implications for development depending on how they fit into the adolescent's life. Thus, when earnings are saved for college, working actually has a positive effect on grades (Marsh 1991), and nonleisure spending (e.g., spending devoted to education or savings) may enhance relationships with parents (Shanahan et al. 1996). In short, the adolescent work career can pose positive or negative implications for subsequent attainment and adjustment.

Life course agency in adolescence. Whereas the concept of pathways reflects an interest in how organizations and institutions allocate youth to social positions and their attendant opportunities and limitations, young people are also active agents attempting to realize goals and ambitions. It is unlikely that most youth were agents in this sense before or during the founding of the republic. In a detailed study of autobiographical life histories between 1740 and 1920, Graff (1995) observes that lives marked by conscious choice and self-direction, a search for opportunities including social mobility, the instrumental use of further education, and risk-taking in the commercial marketplace, were atypical before the nineteenth century. In some accounts this emerging orientation

was expressed in explicit emulation of the widely circulated autobiography of Benjamin Franklin, who emphasized planning, thrift, decision making, and independence. Before this period, the major features of the life course—including education, occupation, and family life—were largely determined by family circumstances. (The notable exception to a lack of decision making about one's life was religious "rebirth." Departing from Catholic and Lutheran doctrine, religious sects such as the Anabaptists emphasized the adolescent's conscious decision to be baptized and then lead an appropriately Christian life [Mitterauer 1992].)

This active orientation toward the life course gained currency as "conduct-of-life" books in the first decades of the nineteenth century departed from Puritan hostility to assertiveness in order to emphasize the building of a decisive character marked by "a strenuous will" (e.g., as found in John Foster's popular essay "Decision of Character" of 1805). The message was especially appealing to the large number of young men leaving rural areas for the city in search of jobs. Since that time, themes such as self-reliance, decisiveness, willpower, and ambition have recurred in popular advice books and social commentaries directed to adolescents and their parents (Kett 1977). Indeed, a view of "youth as shapers of youth" has become prominent among social historians of the twentieth century (for a superb example, see Modell 1989).

In contemporary times, a conception of life as shaped through decision-making, planning, and persistent effort is common. A particularly useful concept to study this phenomenon is *planful competence*, the thoughtful, assertive, and self-controlled processes that underlie selection into social institutions and interpersonal relationships (Clausen 1991a). Although these traits can be found in approaches to personality (e.g., conscientiousness), planful competence is uniquely concerned with the ability to select social settings that best match a person's goals, values, and strengths. That is, planful competence describes the self's ability to negotiate the life course as it represents a socially structured set of age-graded opportunities and limitations. Clausen (1991b, 1993) maintains that a planful orientation in mid-adolescence (about ages 14 and 15) is especially relevant to the life course because it promotes realistic decision-making about the roles and relationships of adulthood. That is, one's self-reflexivity, confidence, and self-regulation at mid-adolescence lead to better choices during the transition to adulthood, choices that in turn have implications for later life. Clausen reasons that children are not capable of planful competence, but most adults possess at least some; therefore interindividual differences at mid-adolescence are most likely to differentiate people during the transition to adulthood and through later life. Adolescents who are planfully competent "better prepare themselves for adult roles and will select, and be selected for, opportunities that give them a head start" (1993, p. 21).

Drawing on extensive longitudinal archives from the Berkeley and Oakland samples at the Institute of Child Welfare, Clausen (1991b, 1993) demonstrated that planful competence in high school (age 15 to 18 years) had pervasive effects on functioning in later life. Planfulness significantly predicted marital stability, educational attainment for both males and females, occupational attainment and career stability for males, and life satisfaction in later adulthood. Satisfaction with marriage was often associated with adolescent planfulness among men and women, especially among men who were capable of interpersonal warmth. Men who were more planful earlier in life reported greater satisfaction with their careers, more job security, and better relationships with their coworkers.

Some research suggests that the effects of planfulness are conditioned by historical experience, an insight that joins the concepts of pathways and agency. Drawing on the Terman Sample of Gifted Children, Shanahan and his colleagues (1997) examined the lifetime educational achievement of two cohorts of men who grew up during the Great Depression. The older cohort, those born between 1900 and 1910, often were in college or had just begun their careers when the Great Depression hit. The younger cohort, those born between 1910 and 1920, typically attended college after the Depression and began their careers in the post-World War II economic boom. For the older cohort, it was hypothesized that adolescent planful competence would not predict adult educational attainment. Rather, very high levels of unemployment during the Depression would support a prolonged education for this cohort—through continuity in or return to school—regardless of their planfulness. In contrast, planful competence in adolescence was expected to predict adult educational attainment in the younger cohort, which was presented with practical choices involving employment opportunities and further education.

As expected, planfulness at age fourteen positively predicted educational attainment, but only for the men born between 1910 and 1920, who often finished school during the postwar economic boom. Planful competence did not predict educational attainment for men from the older cohort, who typically remained in school or returned to school after their nascent careers floundered. Thus, for the older cohort, the lack of economic opportunity precluded entry into the workplace and under these circumstances, personal agency did not predict level of schooling. In short, the Terman men's lives reflect "bounded agency," the active efforts of individuals within structured settings of opportunity.

ADOLESCENCE IN RETROSPECT AND PROSPECT

A historically sensitive inquiry into the sociology of adolescence reveals several prominent features of this life phase. First, although adolescence as a state of semiautonomy between childhood and adulthood has long been part of the Western life course, it has nevertheless been highly responsive to social, political, economic, and cultural forces. Indeed, adolescence acts like a "canary in the coal mine:" As successive generations of youth encounter adult society for the first time, their reactions tell us much about the desirability of social arrangements. These reactions have ranged from enthusiastic acceptance to large-scale revolt and have often led to the emergence of new social orders.

Second, the many "adolescences" revealed through historical time and place are both different and similar in significant ways. Many supposedly universalistic accounts of social and psychological development would not describe adolescent experiences and interpretive frames in the past (Mitterauer 1992). On the other hand, few, if any, aspects of the adolescent experience are without precedent. Statistics on adolescent sexual behavior are met with great alarm today, and yet alarm was already sounded in pre-Colonial times: Leaving England for America in the 1630s, the Puritans hoped to establish an "age-relations utopia" between young people and their elders, which had not been possible in the Old World because of the "licentiousness of youth" (Moran 1991; for the related problem of adolescent pregnancy, see Smith and Hindus 1975; Vinovskis 1988). Likewise, contemporary debates about whether adolescents should be allowed to engage in paid work echo exchanges over child labor laws a century ago (Zelizer 1985). Analogous observations could be made about drug abuse, violence in schools, gangs, and troubled urban youth with diminished prospects.

Yet each generation of adults insists that its adolescence is uniquely vulnerable to social change and the problems that come with it. Indeed, this orientation has spawned a large and often alarmist and contradictory literature about the American adolescent (see Graff 1995, especially Chap. 6). Although many strands of scientific evidence show that adolescence as a state of semiautonomy has lengthened over the past several decades, a torrent of books nonetheless warn of "the end of adolescence." And although many studies show that adolescence is not a period of sudden and pervasive distress, scientific journals devoted to adolescence are filled with contributions examining psychological disorder, substance use, antisocial behavior, sexually transmitted disease, delinquency, troubled relationships with parents, and poor academic performance. Denials of "storm and stress" frequently accompany implicit statements of "doom and gloom."

Unfortunately, these negative images run the risk of defining adolescence (Graff 1995). Studies and social commentaries that highlight the troubled nature of youth may alert the public to social problems in need of redress, but they may also create dominant cultural images that ultimately define what it means to be an adolescent in negative terms, breeding intergenerational mistrust and, among youth, alienation (Adelson 1986).

In this context of research and representation, sociology has much to contribute to an understanding of adolescence. What is needed are balanced accounts of their lived experiences and how these vary by social class, race, gender, and other indicators of inequality. These descriptions need to be situated in both place and time. Place refers to the many contexts of youth, encompassing families and neighborhoods, urban and rural distinctions, ideologies, modes of production, and national and international trends. Time refers to the history of youth, with its many continuities and discontinuities, but it also refers to the life course, how adolescence fits into the patterned sequence of life's phases. Through such efforts, sociologists can contribute to public discourse about youth and comprehend this discourse as being itself a product of social forces.

(SEE ALSO: Adulthood; Juvenile Delinquency and Juvenile Crime; Juvenile Delinquency, Theories of; The Life Course)

REFERENCES

Adelson, Joseph 1986 *Inventing Adolescence: The Political Psychology of Everyday Schooling*. New Brunswick, N. J.: Transaction Books.

Anderson, Michael 1971 *Family Structure in Nineteenth Century Lancashire*. Cambridge, Eng.: Cambridge University Press.

Ariés, Philippe 1962 *Centuries of Childhood: A Social History of Family Life*. Translated by Robert Baldick. New York: Vintage Books.

Arnett, Jeffrey J., and Susan Taber 1994 "Adolescence Terminable and Interminable: When Does Adolescence End?" *Youth and Society* 29:3–23.

Bachman, Jerald G. 1983 "Premature Affluence: Do High School Students Earn Too Much?" *Economic Outlook* 10:64–67.

———, and John Schulenberg 1993 "How Part-time Work Intensity Relates to Drug Use, Problem Behavior, Time Use, and Satisfaction Among High School Seniors: Are These Consequences or Merely Correlates?" *Developmental Psychology* 29:220–235.

Beck, Ulrich 1992 *Risk Society: Towards a New Modernity*. Translated by Mark Ritter. London: Sage.

Belsky, Jay, Laurence Steinberg, and Patricia Draper 1991 "Childhood Experiences, Interpersonal Development, and Reproductive Strategy: An Evolutionary Theory of Socialization." *Child Development* 62:647–670.

Ben-Amos, Ilana Krausman 1995 "Adolescence as a Cultural Invention: Philippe Ariés and the Sociology of Youth." *History of the Human Sciences* 8:69–89.

Blyth, Dale A., Roberta G. Simmons, and Diane Mitbush 1978 "The Transition into Early Adolescence: A Longitudinal Comparison of Youth in Two Educational Contexts." *Sociology of Education* 51:149–162.

Brewster, Karen 1994 "Race Differences in Sexual Activity Among Adolescent Women: The Role of Neighborhood Characteristics." *American Sociological Review* 59:408–424.

Buchmann, Marlis 1989 *The Script of Life in Modern Society: Entry into Adulthood in a Changing World.* Chicago: University of Chicago Press.

Burton, Linda M., Dawn A. Obeidallah, and K. Allison 1996 "Ethnographic Insights on Social Context and Adolescent Development Among Inner-city African-American Teens." In Richard Jessor, Anne Colby, and Richard Shweder, eds., *Ethnography and Human Development.* Chicago: University of Chicago Press.

Bushnell, Horace 1848 *Views of Christian Nurture, and of Subjects Adjacent Thereto.* Hartford, Conn.: E. Hunt.

Clausen, John 1993 *American Lives: Looking Back at the Children of the Great Depression.* Berkeley: University of California Press.

—— 1991a "Adolescent Competence and the Shaping of the Life Course." *American Journal of Sociology* 96:805–842.

—— 1991b "Adolescent Competence and the Life Course, Or Why One Social Psychologist Needed a Concept of Personality." *Social Psychology Quarterly* 54:4–14.

Coleman, James S. 1994 "Social Capital, Human Capital, and Investment in Youth." In Anne C. Petersen and Jeylan T. Mortimer, eds., *Youth Unemployment and Society.* New York: Cambridge University Press.

Coleman, J. C. 1974 *Relationships in Adolescence.* Boston: Routledge and Kegan Paul.

Côté, James E. 1994 *Adolescent Storm and Stress: An Evaluation of the Mead-Freeman Controversy.* Hillsdale, N.J.: Lawrence Erlbaum Associates.

Dannefer, Dale 1984 "Adult Development and Social Theory: A Paradigmatic Reappraisal." *American Sociological Review* 49:100–116.

Davis, Kingsley 1944 "Adolescence and the Social Structure." *The Annals of the American Academy of Political and Social Science* 236:8–16.

Davis, Natalie Z. 1975 *Society and Culture in Early Modern France.* Stanford, Calif.: Stanford University Press.

Demos, John 1970 *A Little Commonwealth: Family Life in Plymouth Colony.* New York: Oxford University Press.

Dornbusch, Sanford 1989 "The Sociology of Adolescence." *Annual Review of Sociology* 15:233–259.

Douvan, Elizabeth, and Joseph Adelson 1966 *The Adolescent Experience.* New York: Wiley.

Eisenstadt, Shmuel N. 1956 *From Generation to Generation: Age Groups and Social Structure.* Glencoe, Ill.: Free Press.

Elder, Glen H., Jr. 1980 "Adolescence in Historical Perspective." In Joseph Adelson, ed., *Handbook of Adolescent Psychology.* New York: Wiley.

—— 1974 *Children of the Great Depression: Social Change in Life Experience.* Chicago: University of Chicago Press.

Elias, Norbert 1994 *The Civilizing Process.* Translated by Edmund Jephcott. Oxford: Blackwell.

Ellis, Bruce J., and Judy Graber forthcoming. "Psychosocial Antecedents of Variation in Girls' Pubertal Timing: Maternal Depression, Stepfather Presence, and Marital and Family Stress." *Child Development.*

Entwisle, Doris R., and Karl L. Alexander 1993 "Entry into Schools: The Beginning School Transition and Educational Stratification in the United States." In *Annual Review of Sociology*, vol. 19. Palo Alto, Calif.: Annual Reviews, Inc.

Erikson, Eric H. 1963 *Childhood and Society.* New York: Norton.

—— 1959 *Identity and the Life-Cycle.* New York: International Universities Press.

Finch, Michael D., Michael J. Shanahan, Jeylan T. Mortimer, and Seongryeol Ryu 1991 "Work Experience and Control Orientation in Adolescence." *American Sociological Review* 56:597–611.

Freeman, Derek 1983 *Margaret Mead and Samoa: The Making and Unmaking of an Anthropological Myth.* Cambridge, Mass.: Harvard University Press.

Gamoran, Adam 1996 "Educational Stratification and Individual Careers." In Alan C. Kerckhoff, ed., *Generating Social Stratification: Toward a New Research Agenda.* Boulder, Colo.: Westview Press.

—— 1992 "The Variable Effects of High School Tracking." *American Sociological Review* 57:812–828.

Giddens, Anthony 1991 *Modernity and Self-identity: Self and Society in the Late Modern Age.* Stanford, Calif.: Stanford University Press.

Gillis, John R. 1974 *Youth and History: Tradition and Change in European Age Relations 1770–Present.* New York: Academic Press.

Gould, Stephen Jay 1977 *Ontogeny and Phylogeny.* Cambridge, Mass.: Belknap Press of Harvard University.

Graber, Judy, Jeanne Brooks-Gunn, and M. P. Warren 1995 "The Antecedents of Menarcheal Age: Heredity, Family Environment, and Stressful Life Events." *Child Development* 66:346–359.

Graff, Harvey J. 1995 *Conflicting Paths: Growing Up in America.* Cambridge, Mass.: Harvard University Press.

Hagan, John, and Blair Wheaton 1993 "The Search for Adolescent Role Exits and the Transition to Adulthood." *Social Forces* 71:955–980.

Hall, G. Stanley 1904 *Adolescence: Its Psychology and its Relations to Physiology, Anthropology, Sociology, Sex, Crime, Religion, and Education.* New York: D. Appleton and Co.

Hallinan, Maureen, and Steven S. Smith 1989 "Classroom Characteristics and Student Friendship Cliques." *Social Forces* 67:898–919.

Handlin, Oscar, and Mary F. Handlin 1971 *Facing Life: Youth and the Family in American History*. Boston: Little, Brown.

Hareven, Tamara 1982 *Family Time and Industrial Time: The Relationship Between the Family and Work in a New England Industrial Community*. New York: Cambridge University Press.

Hill, Martha S., W. Yueng, and Greg J. Duncan 1999 "How Has the Changing Structure of Opportunities Affected Transitions to Adulthood?" In Alan Booth, Nan Crouter, and Michael Shanahan, eds., *Transitions to Adulthood in a Changing Economy*. Greenwood, Conn.: Greenwood Publishing.

Hogan, Dennis P. 1981 *Transitions and Social Change: The Early Lives of American Men*. New York: Academic Press.

Hollingshead, August 1949 *Elmstown's Youth, The Impact of Social Classes on Adolescents*. New York: Wiley.

Hurrelmann, Klaus 1989 "The Social World of Adolescents: A Sociological Perspective." In Klaus Hurrelmann and Uwe Engel, eds., *The Social World of Adolescents: International Perspectives*. Berlin: Walter de Gruyter.

Institute of Medicine/National Research Council 1998 *Protecting Youth at Work: Health, Safety, and Development of Working Children and Adolescents in the United States*. Washington, D.C.: National Academy Press.

Jurkovic, Gregory J. 1997 *Lost Childhoods: The Plight of the Parentified Child*. New York: Brunner Mazel.

Katz, Michael B. 1975 *The People of Hamilton, Canada West: Family and Class in a Mid-Nineteenth Century City*. Cambridge, Mass.: Harvard University Press.

Kerckhoff, Alan C. 1993 *Diverging Pathways: Social Structure and Career Deflections*. Cambridge, Eng.: Cambridge University Press.

Kett, Joseph F. 1977 *Rites of Passage: Adolescence in America, 1790 to the Present*. New York: Basic Books.

Kleiman, Jordan 1998 "Modernization." In Richard W. Fox and James T. Kloppenberg, eds., *Companion to American Thought*. Malden, Mass.: Blackwell.

Kohli, Martin 1986 "The World We Forgot: A Historical Review of the Life Course." In Victor Marshall, ed., *Later Life*. Beverly Hills, Calif.: Sage.

Linton, Ralph 1942 "Age and Sex Categories." *American Sociological Review* 7:589–603.

Lynd, Robert S., and Helen M. Lynd 1929 *Middletown: A Study of American Culture*. New York: Harcourt, Brace and Co.

Maccoby, Eleanor E. 1991 "Differential Reproductive Strategies in Males and Females." *Child Development* 62:676–681.

Mannheim, Karl (1928) 1952 "The Problem of Generations." In Paul Keckskemeti, ed., *Essays on the Sociology of Knowledge*. New York: Oxford University Press.

Manning, Wendy 1990 "Parenting Employed Teenagers." *Youth & Society* 22:184–200.

Marro, Antonio 1898 *La Puberta*. Torino: Fratelli Bocca Editori.

Marsh, Herbert W. 1991 "Employment During High School: Character Building or a Subversion of Academic Goals?" *Sociology of Education* 64:172–189.

Matza, David 1964 "Position and Behavior Patterns of Youth." In Robert E. L. Faris, ed., *Handbook of Modern Sociology*. Chicago: Rand McNally & Company.

Mead, Margaret 1928 *Coming of Age in Samoa: A Psychological Study of Primitive Youth for Western Civilization*. New York: Blue Ribbon Books.

Minge-Kalman, Wanda 1978 "The Industrial Revolution and the European Family: The Institutionalization of 'Childhood' as a Market for Family Labor." *Comparative Studies in Society and History* 20:454–468.

Minuchin, Salvador 1974 *Families and Family Therapy*. Cambridge, Mass.: Harvard University Press.

Mitterauer, Michael 1992 *A History of Youth*. Translated by Graeme Dunphy. Oxford: Basil Blackwell.

——, and Reinhard Sieder 1982 *The European Family: Patriarchy to Partnership from the Middle Ages to the Present*. Oxford, Eng: Basil Blackwell.

Modell, John 1989 *Into One's Own*. Berkeley: University of California.

——, Frank F. Furstenberg Jr., and Theodore T. Hershberg 1976 "Social Change and Transitions to Adulthood in Historical Perspective." *Journal of Family History* 1:7–32.

——, and Madeline Goodman 1990 "Historical Perspectives." In S. Shirley Feldman and Glen R. Elliott, eds., *At the Threshold: The Developing Adolescent*. Cambridge: Harvard University Press.

Moffitt, Terrie E., Avshalom Caspi, Jay Belsky, and Phil A. Silva 1992 "Childhood Experience and Onset of Menarche: A Test of a Sociobiological Model." *Child Development* 63:47–58.

Moran, Gerald F. 1991 "Adolescence in Colonial America." In Richard M. Lerner, Anne C. Petersen, and Jeanne Brooks-Gunn, eds., *Encyclopedia of Adolescence*. New York: Garland Publishers.

Mortimer, Jeylan T., and Michael D. Finch 1996 "Work, Family, and Adolescent Development." In Jeylan T.

Mortimer and Michael D. Finch, eds., *Adolescents, Work, and Family: An Intergenerational Developmental Analysis*. Thousand Oaks, Calif.: Sage Publications.

——, Katherine Dennehey, Chaimun Lee, and Timothy Beebe 1994 "Work Experience in Adolescence." *Journal of Vocational Behavior* 19:39–70.

Mortimer, Jeylan T., and Monika K. Johnson 1998 "New Perspectives on Adolescent Work and the Transition to Adulthood." In Richard Jessor, ed., *New Perspectives on Adolescent Risk Behaviors*. New York: Cambridge University Press.

Musgrove, Frank 1964 *Youth and the Social Order*. Bloomington: Indiana University Press.

Osterman, Paul 1979 "Education and Labor Markets at the Turn of the Century." *Politics and Society* 9:103–122.

Petersen, Anne C. 1988 "Adolescent Development." *Annual Review of Psychology* 39:583–607.

Prude, Jonathan 1983 *The Coming of the Industrial Order: Town and Factory Life in Rural Massachusetts, 1810–1860*. Cambridge, Eng.: Cambridge University Press.

Riesman, David, in collaboration with Reuel Denney, and Nathan Glazer 1950 *The Lonely Crowd: A Study of the Changing American Character*. New Haven, Conn.: Yale University Press.

Ross, Dorothy 1972 *G. Stanley Hall: The Psychologist as Prophet*. Chicago, Ill.: University of Chicago Press.

Rowe, David C. forthcoming "Environmental and Genetic Influences on Pubertal Development: Evolutionary Life History Traits?" In J. Rogers and David Rowe, eds., *Genetic Influences on Fertility and Sexuality*. Boston: Kluwer.

Schlegel, Alice, and Herbert Barry III 1991 *Adolescence: An Anthropological Inquiry*. New York: Free Press.

Shanahan, Michael J. forthcoming "Pathways to Adulthood in Changing Societies: Variability and Mechanisms in Life Course Perspective." *Annual Review of Sociology*.

——, Glen H. Elder Jr., Margaret Burchinal, and Rand D. Conger 1996 "Adolescent Paid Labor and Relationships with Parents: Early Work-Family Linkages." *Child Development* 67:2183–2200.

——, Glen H. Elder Jr., and Richard A. Miech 1997 "History and Agency in Men's Lives: Pathways to Achievement in Cohort Perspective." *Sociology of Education* 70:54–67.

Simmons, Roberta G., and Dale A. Blyth 1987 *Moving Into Adolescence: The Impact of Pubertal Change and School Context*. New York: Aldine de Gruyter.

——, Edward F. Van Cleave, and Diane Mitsch Bush 1979 "Entry into Early Adolescence: The Impact of School Structure, Puberty, and Early Dating on Self-Esteem." *American Sociological Review* 44:948–967.

Simmons, Roberta G., Richard Burgeson, Steven Carlton-Ford, and Dale A Blyth 1987 "The Impact of Cumulative Change in Early Adolescence." *Child Development* 58:1220–1234.

Smelser, Neil J. 1959 *Social Change in the Industrial Revolution: An Application of Theory to the British Cotton Industry*. Chicago: University of Chicago Press.

Smith, Daniel S., and Michael S. Hindus 1975 "Premarital Pregnancy in America, 1640–1971: An Overview and Interpretation." *Journal of Interdisciplinary History* 4:537–570.

Stern, D., and Y. F. Nakata 1989 "Characteristics of High School Students, Paid Jobs, and Employment Experience After Graduation." In D. Stern and Dorothy Eichorn, eds., *Adolescence and Work: Influences of Social Structures, Labor Markets, and Culture*. Hillsdale, N.J.: Lawrence Erlbaum Associates.

Stone, Lawrence 1977 *The Family, Sex and Marriage in England, 1500–1800*. New York: Harper & Row, Co.

Surbey, M. 1990 "Family Composition, Stress, and Human Menarche." In F. Bercovitch and T. Zeigler, eds., *Socioendocrinology of Primate Reproduction*. New York: Liss.

Tanner, James M. 1981 *A History of the Study of Growth*. Cambridge, Eng.: Cambridge University Press.

—— 1978 *Foetus into Man: Physical Growth from Conception to Maturity*. Cambridge, Mass.: Harvard University Press.

Thorndike, Edwin 1917 "Magnitude and Rate of Alleged Changes at Adolescence." *Educational Review* 54:140–147.

Troen, Selwyn 1985 "Technological Development and Adolescence: The Early 20th Century." *Journal of Early Adolescence* 5:429–439.

Tyack, David 1974 *The One Best System: A History of American Urban Education*. Cambridge, Mass.: Harvard University Press.

Tyack, David, Thomas James, and Aaron Benavot 1987 *Law and the Shaping of Public Education, 1785–1954*. Madison: University of Wisconsin Press.

Uhlenberg, Peter 1969 "A Study of Cohort Life Cycles: Cohorts of Native Born Massachusetts Women, 1830–1920." *Population Studies* 23:407–420.

Vinovskis, Maris A. 1988 *An "Epidemic" of Adolescent Pregnancy: Some Historical and Policy Perspectives*. New York: Oxford.

Weiss, R. S. 1979 "Growing Up a Little Faster: The Experience of Growing Up in a Single-parent Household." *Journal of Social Issues* 35:97–111.

Zelizer, Viviana 1985 *Pricing the Priceless Child*. New York: Basic Books.

MICHAEL J. SHANAHAN

ADULT EDUCATION

Most basically defined, adult education is the intentional, systematic process of teaching and learning by which persons who occupy adult roles acquire new values, attitudes, knowledge, skills, and disciplines. As a concept, "adult education" demarcates a subfield of education that is distinct from the latter's historical and still general identification with the formal schooling of youth in primary and secondary schools, colleges, and universities. Once lacking the central social significance long recognized for this formal schooling, adult education expanded rapidly after 1950. Changing social, economic, and demographic forces occasioned new educational forms and organizations and new levels of adult participation in existing forms. Adult education is now so widespread and important a feature of societies worldwide that it increasingly occupies the attention of social scientists, policy makers, businesses, and the public.

TYPES OF ADULT EDUCATION

Adult education now permeates modern societies. It does not do so, however, with the kind of public funding, legislative sanction, organizational cohesion, and standardization of practice that have made universal schooling a highly visible and central institution. Precise substantive definition and classification of adult education is frustrated by the great and changing variety that characterizes the field (Courtney 1989). The complex circumstances of adult life and development lead to the informal, nonformal, and formal pursuit of education for many different purposes. In response to an intricate array of social, economic, and political conditions, formal and nonformal organizations—from multi-state international agencies to corporations to local recreational clubs—support and develop adult education programs. In consequence, an eclectic set of professions, occupations, disciplines, and practices forms the division of adult education labor.

Adults seek a wide variety of educational goals. These include basic literacy and work readiness skills; knowledge and technical competencies required for entering and improving performance of occupational, avocational, and recreational roles; credentials for status attainment; information for the improvement of family life, health, and psychological well-being; knowledge, values, and disciplines for spiritual growth and intellectual enrichment; and tools for addressing community problems and advancing political and social-action agendas. An equally diverse set of organizations and groups provides such education. Publishers and producers of print and electronic educational media serve a growing market for informal adult education with products that range from golf tutorials to taped lectures on the history of philosophy. A large and rapidly expanding nonformal sector (i.e., educational organizations that are not a part of the formal school and college system), now mobilizes very considerable resources to educate adults. Businesses, government agencies, and nonprofit organizations train employees to enhance productivity, organizational effectiveness, and client satisfaction, to spur innovation in products and services, and as an employment benefit to attract workers. Proprietary schools and training companies seek profits by providing similar training to both businesses and individuals. National, regional, and local governments fund adult education programs to reduce welfare dependency and promote economic development. Political parties and special-interest groups deliver adult education designed to foster either dominant or insurgent civic values, knowledge, and action. Professional associations sponsor and certify continuing education to maintain and enhance member competence, ensure the value of their credentials, and maintain market advantages for their members.

Other major providers of nonformal education programs that expressly target adults include unions; churches; libraries, and museums; the armed forces; prison systems; charitable, fraternal, service, and cultural associations; and the health care industry. The formal educational system itself no longer serves only the young. Community school adjuncts to primary and secondary schools teach basic literacy, prepare adults for high school equivalency exams, and offer classes in subjects ranging from the latest computer software to traditional arts and crafts. Colleges and universities now educate almost as many adults as youth; in the United States almost half of all college students are adults above twenty-five years of age. With increasing frequency, these students study in divisions of colleges and universities specifically dedicated to adults.

The functional and organizational diversity of adult education is mirrored in its professions and occupations. Those working in the field include the administrators, researchers, and professors in university graduate programs that train adult educators and maintain adult education as an academic discipline. Teachers and student-service personnel in university, governmental, and proprietary organizations deliver graduate, undergraduate, and continuing education to adults. Managers, trainers, and associated marketing and support personnel staff the employee, technical, and professional training industry. Adult literacy and basic education practitioners form a specialization of their own. Professional activists, organizers, and volunteers consciously include adult education in the portfolio of skills that they apply to pursuits ranging across the full spectrum of ideologies and interests. Policy analysts, planners, researchers, and administrators staff the adult education divisions of international organizations, national and regional governments, and independent foundations and development agencies.

While those who occupy these professional statuses and roles are clearly doing adult education, not all identify themselves as adult educators or, even when sharing this identity, see themselves as engaged in similar practice. The field is conceptually, theoretically, and pedagogically heterogeneous both within and among its many sectors. Role identity and performance differences based in organizational setting and population served are compounded by differences in fundamental aims and methods. One of the sharpest divides is between many in the "training and development" industry and those in academia and elsewhere who identify with "adult education" as a discipline, as a profession and, sometimes, as a social movement.

Training and development specialists tend to define their task as cultivating human resources and capital that can be used productively for the purposes of businesses, armed forces, government agencies, and other formal organizations. For training line employees, and all employees in technical areas, they tend to emphasize teaching and learning methodologies that maximize the efficiency and effectiveness of individual acquisition of skill sets that can be easily and usefully applied to well-established performance objectives. For executive and managerial development, they tend to emphasize leadership, team, problem-solving, strategy, and change management competencies in the context of developing general organizational learning, effectiveness, and continuous quality improvement (Craig 1996).

Those who identify themselves as adult educators, on the other hand, tend to emphasize theories and methods designed to "facilitate" individual transformation and development. Variants of the facilitation model advocated by the adult education profession include the following: one perspective focuses on the special characteristics of learning in adulthood, and on "andragogy" as a new type of specifically adult teaching and learning distinct from pedagogy, as critical to successful adult education (Knowles 1980); another emphasizes adult life circumstances and experiences as key variables (Knox 1986); a third sees facilitating new critical and alternative thinking as the key to successful adult transformation (Brookfield 1987); and yet another sees adult education as active, consciousness-transforming engagement with social conditions to produce individual liberation and progressive social change (Coben, Kincheloe, and Cohen 1998). Common to all of the facilitation approaches is the ideal of adult education as a democratic, participatory process wherein adult educators facilitate active learning and critical reflection for which adult learners themselves assume a large measure of responsibility and direction.

Theoretical and ideological differences among adult education practitioners draw sharper lines than does their actual practice. Active learning techniques through which concepts, information, and skills are acquired in the course of real or simulated practical problem solving, strongly advocated by professional adult educators, have been embraced by the corporate training and development industry. Educational technology tools such as interactive, computer-based learning modules and Web-based tutorials, tools most robustly developed by the training industry, enable precisely the kind of independent, self-directed learning celebrated by the adult education profession. In most of its settings and branches, adult educators of all types deploy the entire array of pedagogies from rote memorization to classic lecture-recitation to the creation of self-sustaining "learning communities." Few central methodological tendencies demarcate distinct factions within the field, or the field itself from other types of education. Visible variants, such as the training and facilitation models, serve only partially to distinguish different segments of the field; and even these differences stem more from the particular histories, conditions, aims, and clients of those segments than from distinct disciplines, theories, or methods. Other methodological tendencies, such as widespread reliance on adult experience and self-direction as foundational for instructional design and delivery, reflect differences between adult and childhood learning more than a distinctly adult pedagogy (Merriam and Cafferella 1991).

Adult learning has several well-established characteristics that distinguish it from learning earlier in the life cycle: greater importance of clear practical relevance for learning, even of higher-order reasoning skills; the relatively rich stock of experience and knowledge to which adults relate new learning; "learner" or "student" as a role secondary to and embedded in adult familial, occupational and social roles; and the application of adult levels of responsibility and self-direction to the learning process. Indeed, at the level of practice, the learning characteristics of those being educated (i.e., adults) serve to distinguish adult education as a distinct field much more clearly than do distinctively adult educators, organizations, or methods.

DEVELOPMENT OF ADULT EDUCATION

The remarkable variety of contemporary adult education directly reflects complexity in the social environment and the necessities and rewards associated with mastering that complexity. Like schooling, adult education emerged and developed in response to the social, economic, political, cultural, and demographic forces that produced increasing structural and functional differentiation as one of the few clear trends in human social evolution. As social roles and practices proliferated, conveying the skills, knowledge, and disciplines that they embodied required the intentional and organized teaching and learning that is education. As productivity, wealth, power, and status became more dependent on the mastery and application of knowledge, education to acquire it increasingly occupied the interest and resources of individuals and groups.

The long and discontinuous trajectory of increasing social complexity within and among human societies yielded very little formal and nonformal adult education before the advent of industrialism. Prior to the Neolithic revolution, education of any type was rare; informal socialization without conscious, systematic intent to train or study sufficed for most cultural transmission and role acquisition. Agrarian, state-organized societies, especially the early and late classical civilizations of the Middle East, Asia, and Europe, developed the first formal and nonformal schooling in response to the increasing complexity of knowledge, administration, social control, and production. This schooling was delivered by professional tutors and early versions of primary and secondary schools to educate the children of political, military, and religious aristocracies for their rulership roles; in schools and colleges to train bureaucratic and religious functionaries, professionals in law and medicine, and the elite in the liberal arts; and by nonformal systems of apprenticeship, such as the medieval guilds, for specialized crafts and trades. Although there are many examples of adults seeking informal education from adepts in the arts, religion, and natural philosophy, the educational systems of agrarian societies were devoted mostly to preparation for adult roles.

The widespread and diverse adult education of the present era emerged in response to the development of modern, urban, scientifically and technologically complex societies. Education became an important and dynamic institutional sector, one that gradually extended its territory from basic schooling for the literacy, numeracy, and general knowledge necessary to market relationships, industrial production, and democratic politics to adult continuing education for advanced professional workers in the theoretical and applied sciences. With some exceptions, the pattern of extension was from earlier to later stages of the life cycle (finally yielding education for learning that is "lifelong") from the upper to the lower reaches of class and status hierarchies (yielding "universal education") and from informal education occurring in avocational and domestic contexts, to nonformal education conducted by voluntary organizations to increasingly institutionalized formal systems.

Prior to industrialization, informal and nonformal adult education was relatively widespread in Europe, especially in England and North America, and especially among the growing urban middle class of artisans and merchants. As this new middle class sought to acquire its share of the growing stock of culture, and as literacy spread and became intrinsic to social and economic participation, adults increasingly engaged in self-directed study (aided by a publishing explosion that included a growing number of "how-to" handbooks) participated in informal study groups, and established cultural institutes and lyceums that delivered public lectures and evening courses of study.

Systematic efforts to spread adult education to the working class and the general population emerged during the process of industrialization. Until the last decades of the nineteenth century, these were almost entirely voluntary efforts devoted to democratization, social amelioration, and social movement goals. In both Britain and the United States, mechanics' institutes, some with libraries, museums, and laboratories, delivered education in applied science, taught mechanical skills, and conducted public lectures on contemporary issues. In Scandinavia, "folk high schools" performed similar functions. Religious groups conducted literacy campaigns among the new urban masses and established adult educational forums in organizations such as the Young Men's Christian Association (YMCA). Women's suffrage groups, labor unions, abolitionists, socialists, and many others developed educational programs both to develop their members and as an organizing tool. After 1860 and until World War I, efforts to popularize education among adults continued in various ways: in an extensive network of lyceums, rural and urban Chautauquas and settlement homes; in educational efforts to aid and acculturate immigrants to the burgeoning industrial cities; and in post-slavery self-improvement efforts of African Americans. These middle- and working-class adult education activities received considerable support and extension from the spread of public libraries.

In most societies, state support for and sponsorship of adult education has always been scant in comparison to that for schooling children and adolescents. Late nineteenth- and twentieth-century imperialism included modest adult educational efforts designed to selectively spread literacy and educate indigenous peoples as functionaries for colonial administrations. Some higher-level adult education of the type delivered by the mechanics' and folk institutes received public funding, especially in Nordic societies where leisure time and adult continuing education were well provisioned by the state. With the Hatch Act of 1887 and enabling legislation in 1914, American land-grant universities were charged with developing "extension" services to deliver a wide range of educational and technical assistance to farmers and rural populations. The agricultural extension model later expanded to include technical training and assistance for industry, and night schools and continuing education for adults. Public funding for these developments was minimal; extension services beyond the land-grant mandate, to the present, have usually been expected to operate as fiscally self-supporting units.

Robust state support for adult education occurred only in the socialist societies that emerged after the Russian Revolution of 1917. Beginning with the mass literacy campaign initiated by the Bolsheviks, adult education was an important priority of the Soviet regime (Lee 1998). It established a large and wide-ranging formal adult continuing education system, with branches in virtually all institutional sectors of Soviet life. It was intended to foster ideological allegiance to the Soviet system, develop the Soviet workforce, spread socialist culture, and foster progress in sports and the arts. A nonformal, decentralized system of "people's universities" paralleled and reinforced the formal system. After World War II, Soviet-style adult education was transplanted to most of its Eastern European satellites and, usually in severely truncated form, to the developing societies of Asia, Africa, and Latin America that followed the Soviet model. After the communist victory in 1949, China began its own mass literacy campaign for adults. Later it developed a near-universal system of "spare-time" and other adult schools that trained students for very specific political, economic, and cultural roles in the new society, and for political and ideological conformity to the tenets and goals of the revolution. In the decade following 1966, China conducted one of the largest and most disastrous adult education programs in history. The Cultural Revolution spawned a severe and mandatory form of experiential learning that replaced much of higher education by sending professionals and officials with suspect class pedigrees, intellectuals, professors, and students into agricultural villages and factories to be reeducated by proletarian labor and incessant exposure to Mao-sanctioned communist propaganda.

In spite of the social control service to the dominant regime that it was designed to deliver, socialist adult education played a very significant role in the rapid industrialization and modernization of agrarian Russia and China. In the market societies of the West, the unplanned and longer-term realization of such development did not entail centralized efforts to transform adults for new roles. The systems of political and social control did not generally require the systematic and continuous indoctrination of adults. Thus, until the second half of the twentieth century, adult education in the West remained largely a function of individual and small group informal education, voluntary and philanthropic organizations, relatively small government efforts, specialty units of the system of formal schooling, and small training programs in proprietary schools and businesses.

CONTEMPORARY STRUCTURES AND PARTICIPATION

After 1950, adult education grew in scale and organization. The pattern of this growth involved a shift from adult education delivered by community-based organizations to that provided by formal educational institutions and the training industry. Demand for education among adults grew because of increasing rates of technological innovation, professional specialization, organizational complexity, knowledge intensiveness in goods-and-services production, and rising credential requirements for employment. Adults returned to secondary and postsecondary education in steadily increasing numbers. In the United States, the GI Bill sent the first large wave of these new students into colleges and universities after World War II (Olson 1974). In the 1960s and 1970s new or expanded units of formal education were organized to accommodate and recruit adult students in

both Europe and the United States: college adult degree programs, open universities, evening colleges, programs for accrediting experientially based adult learning, and government and school-district sponsored adult high school completion programs.

Higher education attendance among adults continued to accelerate in the 1980s and 1990s as a result of several factors: multiple stop-in, stop-out college career paths; rapid obsolescence of knowledge and associated multiple career changes throughout a lengthening cycle of life and work; increased requirements and rewards for specialized graduate, certificate, and technical education; and, most significantly, the large returning student population among Baby Boom adults. In turn, the growing market of adult students spawned new forms of higher education. In the 1990s, the for-profit, fully accredited University of Phoenix became the largest private university in the United States, with over 65,000 adult graduate and undergraduate students (Winston 1999). Phoenix provides a library that is entirely electronic, uses both branch campuses in strip malls and office buildings and Internet-delivered courses to provide education nationwide, and employs only forty-five full-time faculty and more than 4,500 adjuncts. Internationally, "mega-universities," such as Britain's Open University and China's TV University—100,000 and 500,000 students respectively—deliver education to adults through diffuse networks of distance education technologies and part-time local mentors. Collectively, the new virtual (i.e. based entirely on the Internet), distance, for-profit, and mega-universities, all oriented primarily to adults, are beginning to significantly alter the structure and practice of higher education worldwide.

Training and development programs witnessed similar growth after World War II under the impact of a combination of forces. New technologies, especially those associated with information technology production and use, and increased rates of innovation, required education for entirely new skill sets and for continuous upgrading of existing knowledge. Increased job mobility required more new worker training. More intense, global economic competition and new understandings of the contribution of training to productivity and profitability led to greater training investments by firms, agencies, and individuals.

The growing volume of adult training is delivered in many forms and sectors of society and has important consequences. In the advanced industrial societies of Europe and Asia, training and development systems, usually involving employers, unions, and governments, provide training in a substantial majority of firms and to most workers (Lynch 1994). Yearly participation rates by both firms and individuals are highest in the European and Japanese systems and may be an important factor in their high rates of productivity growth. Even in the more diffuse U.S. system with lower participation, over 60 percent of adults between twenty-eight and fifty years of age had participated in some variety of part-time adult education or training by the early 1990s (Hight 1998). Workplace training alone became a $60-billion a year industry with 53,000 providers (Martin 1998). Some firms supply most of their own training through another new institutional form of adult education, the "corporate university." With curricula ranging from basic employee orientation to the most advanced technical and business subjects, several of these universities are now fully accredited to grant baccalaureate and graduate degrees. As the U.S. military's reliance on technologically complex strategies, tactics, logistics and equipment grew, it became the largest single provider of training in the United States. Even with post-Cold War downsizing, the military's adult training activities remain significant contributors to labor-force development, especially in computer, electronics, and mechanical specialties (Barley 1998). Higher education institutions are also major training providers. Collectively, college and university adult continuing and professional education now rivals or surpasses the volume of military training (Gose 1999). Harvard serves over 60,000 adults each year in continuing education classes. New York University's School of Continuing and Professional Studies offers more than one hundred certificate programs and has revenues of over $90-million a year. The involvement of universities in the expansion of training presents something of a paradox. In many instances, the new training complex is endowing its adult students with professional and industry certifications that are beginning to rival standard degrees as the credentials of both individual and employer choice. This training may also be working significant changes in the social structure. Considerable evidence suggests that a large measure of the growing income inequality characteristic of advanced industrial societies is a function of technological change and associated wage premiums paid for workers with the kind of technical credentials and competencies that much of the new training is designed to deliver (Bassie 1999).

Contemporary developing societies of Africa, Asia, and Latin America contain all of the forms of adult education found in the West, as well as forms of popular adult education now only minimally present there. While virtually all of the less developed societies have succeeded in establishing systems of primary, secondary, and higher education for youth, participation rates vary widely among and within them. Some Latin American countries, for example, have higher college attendance rates than their European counterparts while many poor children never enter or complete primary school (Arnove et al. 1996). In such contexts, adult education is often bifurcated (Torres 1990). The poor are served by literacy programs, popular education efforts developed by local nongovernmental organizations, and the health and technical education programs of international agencies. Middle and upper classes participate in corporate training, government-sponsored adult higher education, and professional continuing education programs that are little different from and, in the case of training delivered distance education technologies and global firms, exactly the same as those found in the most advanced societies. However, under the impact of globalization, the distinctions among higher education, human resource training, and popular education are softening. There is a growing recognition among education professionals and policy makers that widespread and inclusive lifelong learning is a critical common good (Walters 1997).

Lifelong learning and adult education that is on a par with schooling are increasingly articulated goals of social policy. The United Nations concluded its fifth Conference on Adult Education in 1997 with a call for worldwide lifelong learning to promote social and economic development, empower women, support cultural diversity, and incorporate new information technologies. Adult education and training is now a central focus of the United Nations Education Scientific and Cultural Organization's (UNESCO) development policy, planning, and programs. The European Union designated 1996 the "European Year of Lifelong Learning" and established the European Lifelong Learning Initiative to research, coordinate, and develop lifelong learning policies and programs throughout Europe. In 1997, the Commission for a Nation of Lifelong Learners, representing U.S. business, labor, government, and education interests, called for policies that would ensure equity of access to lifelong learning, optimize the use of new technologies, reorganize the education and training system into one providing comprehensive lifelong learning, and commit private and public resources sufficient to these ends. The federal administration established a yearly summit on lifelong learning to pursue implementation of these goals. Similar policy formation and advocacy is now widespread at the local level, and cities recognize the importance of lifelong learning to workforce development and urban economic viability in the new "knowledge economy." It remains to be seen whether the new focus on adult education policy will result in the kind of resource deployment or accessible, comprehensive system for lifelong learning recommended by most analysis.

SOCIOLOGY OF ADULT EDUCATION

The sociology of education has traditionally focused on the processes, structures, and effects of schooling, with very little attention to adult education. Thus, there is no scholarly or applied field, no distinct body of theory or research that can be properly labeled "the sociology of adult education." Expositions of a sociology of adult education that do exist tend to be general characterizations of the field in terms drawn from general sociological and schooling literature (e.g., Rubenson 1989; Jarvis 1985). Certainly much of this is applicable. Adult education presents many opportunities for sociological interpretation in terms of the functionalist, conflict, reproductive, or postmodernist educational models applied to schooling; in terms of adult education's impact on social mobility, status attainment, and distributional equity; or in terms of its contribution to organizational effectiveness, social welfare, or economic development. The small body of sociological research in the area takes just such an approach, focusing on issues such as: the patterns and causes of adult enrollment in higher education (e.g., Jacobs and Stoner-Eby 1998); the consequences of women's return to

higher education (e.g., Felmlee 1988); and the patterns of access to and provision of employer-provided training (e.g., Jacobs, Lukens, and Useem 1996). However, neither the extent nor the depth of sociological study in the area matches its potential importance.

Adult education is clearly no longer a social activity marginal to schooling. The information-technology revolution, the knowledge society, the learning organization, and the increasingly critical concern of individuals and organizations with the development and control of human and knowledge capital are representative of trends that are bringing adult education into the mainstream of social interest, analysis, and policy. Responses to these trends for which adult education is central include new and powerful forms of higher education, new determinants of the structure and process of social inequality, new bases for economic and social development, and new conceptions of the relationship of education to the human life cycle. Many opportunities for the application of sociological theory, research, and practice to adult education await realization.

REFERENCES

Arnove, Robert F., Alberto Torres, Stephen Franz, and Kimberly Morse 1996 "A Political Sociology of Education and Development in Latin America." *International Journal of Comparative Sociology* 37:140–158.

Barley, Stephen R. 1998 "Military Downsizing and the Career Prospects of Youths." *The Annals* 559:41–157.

Bassi, Laurie J. 1999 "Are Employers' Recruitment Strategies Changing?" In N. G. Stacey, project manager, *Competence Without Credentials*. Jessup, M.: U.S. Department of Education.

Brookfield, Stephen D. 1987 *Developing Critical Thinkers: Challenging Adults to Explore Alternative Ways of Thinking and Acting*. San Francisco: Jossey-Bass.

Coben, Diana, Joe L. Kincheloe, and Diana Cohen 1998 *Radical Heroes: Gramsci, Freire and the Politics of Adult Education*. New York: Garland Publishing.

Courtney, Sean 1989 "Defining Adult and Continuing Education." In S. B. Merriam and P.M. Cunningham, eds., *Handbook of Continuing and Adult Education*. San Francisco: Jossey-Bass.

Craig, Robert L. (ed.) 1996 *The ASTD Training and Development Handbook: A Guide to Human Resource Development*, 4th ed. New York: McGraw Hill Text.

Felmlee, Diane 1988 "Returning to School and Women's Occupational Attainment." *Sociology of Education* 61:29–41.

Gose, Ben 1999 "Surge in Continuing Education Brings Profits for Universities." *The Chronicle of Higher Education* 45(February 9):A, 24.

Hight, Joseph E. 1998 "Young Worker Participation in Post-School Education and Training." *Monthly Labor Review* 121:14–21.

Jacobs, Jerry A., Marie Lukens, and Michael Useem 1996 "Organizational, Job, and Individual Determinants of Workplace Training: Evidence from the National Organizations Survey." *Social Science Quarterly* 77:159–177.

Jacobs, Jerry A., and Scott Stoner-Eby 1998 "Adult Enrollment and Educational Attainment." *The Annals* 559:91–108.

Jarvis, Peter 1985 *The Sociology of Adult and Continuing Education*. London: Croom-Helm.

Knowles, Malcolm S. 1980 *The Modern Practice of Adult Education: From Pedagogy to Andragogy*, 2nd ed. Chicago: Association/Follett.

Knox, Alan B. 1986 *Helping Adults Learn*. San Francisco: Jossey-Bass.

Lee, David Currie 1998 *The People's Universities of the USSR*. Westport, Conn.: Greenwood.

Lynch, Lisa M. 1994 "Payoffs to Alternative Training Strategies at Work." In Richard B. Freeman, ed., *Working Under Different Rules*. New York: Russell Sage.

Martin, Justin 1998 "Lifelong Learning Spells Earnings." *Fortune* 138(July 6):197–200.

Merriam, Sharan B., and Rosemary S. Cafferella 1991 *Learning in Adulthood*. San Francisco: Jossey-Bass.

Olson, Keith W. 1974 *The GI Bill, the Veterans, and the Colleges*. Lexington, Ky.: The University Press of Kentucky.

Rubenson, Kjell 1989 "The Sociology of Adult Education." In S. B. Merriam and P. M. Cunnigham, eds., *Handbook of Adult and Continuing Education*. San Francisco: Jossey-Bass.

Torres, Carlos Alberto 1990 *The Politics of Nonformal Education in Latin America*. New York: Preager.

Walters, Shirley (ed.) 1997 *Globalization, Adult Education and Training: Impacts and Issues*. Cape Town: Zed.

Winston, Gordon C. 1999 "For Profit Higher Education." *Change* 31(January/February):13–19.

JOHN HOUGHTON

ADULTHOOD

Becoming an adult is a life-cycle transition signified by multiple markers (Hogan and Astone 1986). These include the completion of education, the establishment of an independent residence, the attainment of economic self-sufficiency, marriage, parenthood, permission to vote and serve in the military, and the entry into full-time work. These multifaceted, objective markers of adult status, variability in the ages at which they occur, and differences in both preadult and adult roles, make the character of this transition variable across societies, historically relative, and subject to diverse interpretations and subjective meanings. Each new generation's experience of transition to adulthood is somewhat unique, dependent on the particular economic, political and social currents of the time (Mannheim 1952). Institutional contexts (cultural, social, educational, economic) determine the pathways through which the transition to adulthood occurs, as well as the competencies that enable successful adaptation to adult roles.

In addition to the formal markers of transition, there are clearly recognized prerogatives of adult status (e.g., smoking, alcohol use, and sexuality) that are widely frowned upon or legally prohibited when engaged in by minors. Youth's engagement in these "problem behaviors" can be attempts to affirm maturity, gain acceptance by peers, or to negotiate adult status (Jessor and Jessor 1977, p. 206; Maggs 1997). Finally, there are even more subtle, subjective indicators of adulthood—for example, the development of "adult-like" psychological orientations or the acquisition of an adult identity. Considering oneself as an adult may or may not coincide with the formal markers of transition.

There has been a trend in the United States and Western Europe toward earlier assumption of full adult civil rights (e.g., the age at which it is legal to vote or to marry without parental consent) from the age of twenty-one to eighteen (Coleman and Husen 1985). Youth must be age eighteen to vote in France, Germany, Great Britain, and the United States, but must be twenty to vote in Japan (The World Factbook 1998).

Within countries, legal restrictions on the age at which certain events can occur, signifying adulthood to a greater or lesser degree, vary depending on the marker in question. For example, in the United States, a person has the right to vote and serve in the military at the age of eighteen, but must be twenty-one to purchase alcoholic beverages. At age sixteen, a young person can leave school and work in paid jobs without federal restriction on hours of work. (However, restrictions on work hours of sixteen and seventeen year olds exist in many states; see Committee on the Health and Safety Implications of Child Labor 1998). The legal age of marriage varies widely across U.S. states, from none to twenty-one (The World Factbook 1998), but the age of consent is sixteen to eighteen in most states (www.ageofconsent.com).

However, many eighteen, and even twenty-one year olds in the United States and other modern countries would not be socially recognized as "adults," since they have not yet accomplished other key markers of transition. The law only sets minimum standards, and may have little relation to the age at which young people actually make the various transitions in question. Despite prohibitions on the use and purchase of alcohol until the age of twenty-one, "it is more normative to drink during adolescence than it is not to drink" (Maggs 1997, p. 349). The majority of young people in the United States stay in school beyond the age of sixteen; they graduate from high school and receive at least some postsecondary education. With the extension of formal education, contemporary youth in modern countries delay the acquisition of full-time employment, and remain economically dependent for longer periods of time. Moreover, the legal age of marriage hardly reflects the average age of first marriage. Since the 1950s, it has been increasing (from 20.3 for women and 22.8 for men in 1950 to 24.4 for women and 26.5 for men in 1992; Spain and Bianchi 1996).

HISTORICAL AND SOCIETAL VARIATION IN THE TRANSITION TO ADULTHOOD

Neither the timing nor the process of becoming adult are universalistic or biologically determined. Throughout Western history, there has been increasing differentiation of early life stages, postponement of entry to adulthood, and change in the status positions from which adulthood is launched (Klein 1990). Some scholars argue that in medieval times persons moved directly from a

period of infancy, when small size and limited strength precluded productive work, to adulthood, at which time younger persons began to work alongside their elders (Ariés 1962).

A new stage of childhood, between infancy and adulthood, arose with the emergence of schools. As economic production shifted from agriculture to trade and industry, persons increasingly entered adulthood after a stage of apprenticeship or "child labor." By the beginning of the twentieth century, with schooling extended and child labor curtailed, adolescence gained recognition as the life stage preceding adulthood (Hall 1904). The adolescent, though at the peak of most biological and physiological capacities, remained free of adult responsibilities.

With more than 60 percent of contemporary young people obtaining some postsecondary education (Halperin 1998), a new phase of "youth" or "postadolescence" has emerged, allowing youth in their mid-to-late twenties, and even older youth, to extend the preadult "moratorium" of continued exploration. This youth phase is characterized by limited autonomy but continued economic dependence and concern about the establishment of adult identity (Keniston 1970; Coleman and Husen 1985; Buchmann 1989).

Various forms of independent residence are now common in the United States before marriage (Goldscheider and Goldscheider 1993). Youth's residence in dormitories (or, less commonly, military barracks) allows independence from familial monitoring, while a formal institution assumes some control (Klein 1990). Even greater freedom from supervision occurs when young people, still economically dependent on parents, live in their own apartments. For contemporary young people in the United States who enter the labor force after high school, a continuing period of "moratorium" (Osterman 1989) lasts several years. During this time, youth hold jobs in the secondary sector of the economy to satisfy immediate consumption needs. They experience high unemployment and job instability (Borman 1991). At the same time, employers express preference for low-wage workers who do not require fringe benefits and are not likely to unionize. When filling adultlike "primary" jobs, such employers seek evidence of stability or "settling down."

But youth "irresponsibility" and employer reluctance to offer desirable jobs to youthful recruits are not universal in modern societies. Instead, they derive from particular institutional arrangements. In the United States, the absence of clear channels of mobility from education to the occupational sector, and youths' lack of occupation-specific educational credentials, fosters a prolonged period of trial and instability in the early career (Kerckhoff 1996). In contrast, the highly developed institution of apprenticeship in Germany implies the full acceptance of young workers as adults, and encourages employers to invest in their human capital (Hamilton 1990, 1999; Mortimer and Kruger forthcoming).

The onset of adulthood has thus been delayed through historical time by the emergence of successive preadult life stages. This historical progression of preadult phases refers to the normative, legitimate pathways to adulthood. A highly problematic, but increasingly prevalent way station in the transition is supervision by the criminal justice system; indeed, it is estimated that a full ten percent of U.S. males, aged twenty to twenty-nine, is in jail, in prison, on parole, or on probation on any one day (Halperin 1998).

Obstacles to "growing up" are sometimes presented when assuming adultlike statuses threatens adult interests and values. The extension of required schooling was motivated, at least in part, by a desire to curb competition for jobs with older workers (Osterman 1980). "Warehousing" the young in secondary and tertiary education has reduced adolescent unemployment during times of economic contraction; earlier movement out of school into the workforce is promoted by economic expansion (Shanahan et al. 1998).

Societal wealth may also encourage postponement of adulthood and the extension of "youthful" values and life styles to older ages. Japanese young people, traditionally oriented to the extended family, obedience, educational achievement, and hard work, seem to be becoming more rebellious and interested in immediate enjoyment as delayed gratification becomes more difficult to sustain in a more affluent society (Connor and De Vos 1989; White 1993).

Although age-related increases from birth through the second decade of life—in strength, cognitive capacity, and autonomy (Shanahan, this volume)—are probably recognized in some form in all human societies, the social construction of the early life course clearly reflects societal diversity and institutional change. Processes of modernization, encompassing changes in education, the labor force, and the emergence of the welfare state, produce age standardization of the early life course (Shanahan forthcoming). For example, the social differentiation of children and adolescents was less pronounced in the educational system in nineteenth- and early twentieth-century America than in the contemporary period (Graff 1995). Secondary school students have become increasingly homogeneous in age; this more pronounced age grading promotes "adolescent" life styles and orientations. Similarly, the extension of postsecondary schooling promotes the perpetuation of "youth." However, during the past century in the United States the changes marking the transition have taken place first in quicker, and then in more lengthy, succession (Shanahan forthcoming; Modell et al. 1976).

As a result of technological and economic change and increasing educational requirements (Hogan and Mochizuki 1988; Arnett and Taber 1994; Côté and Allahar 1994), as well as family instability (Buchmann 1989), the entry to adulthood has been characterized as increasingly extended, diversified, individualized (Buchmann 1989; Shanahan forthcoming), "disorderly" (Rindfuss et al. 1987), variable (Shanahan forthcoming), and less well defined (Buchmann 1989). For example, while the acquisition of full-time work is widely considered to mark the transition to adulthood, distinctions between "youth work" and "adult work" blur as young people increasingly combine, and alternate, student and occupational roles, in various forms and levels of intensity through a lengthy period of adolescence and youth (Mortimer and Johnson 1998, 1999; Mortimer et al. 1999; Morris and Bernhardt 1998; Arum and Hout 1998). Markers of family formation likewise become less clear as young people move in and out of cohabiting and marital unions (Spain and Bianchi 1996).

Orderly sequences of transition events have become less common (Shanahan forthcoming). For example, many youth return to their parental homes after leaving for college or other destinations (Cooney 1994). Divergence from normative timing or sequencing sometimes generates public alarm, becomes defined as a social problem, and leads to difficulties for the young people whose lives exhibit such patterns. Whereas parenting is becoming more common outside of marriage (approximately one-third of births in the United States occur to unmarried women; Spain and Bianchi 1996), it is widely thought that nonmarital birth in the teenage years marks a too-early transition to adulthood. Adolescent parenting is linked to school dropout, difficulties in the job market, restricted income and marital instability (Furstenberg, et al. 1987). (However, Furstenberg and colleagues' 1987 study of a panel of black adolescent mothers sixteen to seventeen years after their children were born actually showed considerable diversity in maternal socioeconomic outcomes.)

Still, assertions that the transition to adulthood is especially indeterminate, or becoming more difficult, in contemporary Western societies remain controversial. Graff (1995) documents the extended and equivocal nature of this transition in eighteenth- to twentieth-century America. Foner and Kertzer (1978) noted ambiguity even in premodern contexts, where elders and the rising adult generation often struggled over the timing of age-set transitions and corresponding transfers of power, wealth, and privilege. It is certain, however, that the transition to adulthood assumes a quite different character historically and across national contexts, and may be more clear in some than in others.

THE SUBJECTIVE TRANSITION TO ADULTHOOD

A series of psychological, or subjective, changes are expected to occur as young people move into adulthood. The adolescent is said to be oriented to fun, sports, popular music, and peers; receptive to change; and ready to experiment with alternative identities and sometimes, mood-altering substances (Hall 1904). Youth are encouraged to enjoy themselves as they continue to explore their interests and potentials. Osterman (1989) describes out-of-school employed youth as lacking career orientation; instead, they emphasize peer relationships, travel, adventure, and short-term jobs.

Young adults, in contrast, are expected to relinquish such dependent, playful, experimental,

carefree, and even reckless stances of adolescence and youth, so that they can address the "serious business" of life. Those who become financially and emotionally independent, productive, hardworking, and responsible are considered "adult" (Klein 1990). Moreover, they themselves are expected to "feel like" adults (Aronson 1998).

The concept of "maturity" is integrally tied to adulthood. Most generally, it refers to the psychological competencies deemed necessary to adapt to the roles and responsibilities of adulthood (Galambos and Ehrenberg 1997). For Greenberger and Sorenson (1974), the term signifies autonomy, the capacity to make decisions on the basis of life goals and to function independently in work and other spheres; skills in communicating and relating to others; and social responsibility, the motivation and ability to contribute to the wider society. Greenberger and Steinberg (1986) worry that teenagers who have paid jobs become "pseudomature," as they take on adult identities and behavioral prerogatives without being psychologically equipped for them. Such pseudomaturity can precipitate disengagement from more beneficial, albeit dependent and childlike, roles (especially the role of student). Bachman and Schulenberg (1993) similarly note syndromes of adultlike roles, activities, and identities that promote premature entry to adult family and occupational roles.

But like the objective markers of transition, beliefs about the specific attributes that define maturity, and how these competencies may be fostered and recognized, vary across time and social space (Burton et al. 1996). The extent to which youth feel that they possess such capacities, and the likelihood that adults will attribute these qualities to them, may be highly variable across social situations. Furthermore, in postmaterialist societies and especially in the more highly educated and affluent social niches within them, orientations promoting success in the economic sphere may recede in importance as criteria of maturity, in favor of continued "youthful" emphases on freedom and self-actualization throughout adulthood (Vinken and Ester 1992; Inglehart 1990).

Meanings and interpretations of the various transitions signifying acquisition of adult status, such as those linked to family formation (Modell

1989), also exhibit historical and cross-societal variability. In contemporary modern societies, structural differences in the link between school and work (Shavit and Muller 1998) are reflected in the phenomenal experience of the transition into the labor force. Variation in the institutional connection between school and work in the United States and Germany influences the ages at which young people begin to actively prepare for the highly consequential decisions (especially regarding postsecondary schooling and career) that lie ahead of them, and the degree of stress and uncertainty they encounter in doing so (Mortimer and Kruger forthcoming).

It is widely believed that age norms, specifying the timing and order of key life events, influence the subjective passage, as well as the objective trajectory, through the life course (Neugarten et al. 1965; Neugarten and Datan 1973). "On-time" transitions are "culturally prepared" by socialization and institutional arrangements (Model 1989, p. 13), and are thereby rendered psychologically salutary. Those who are "off-time," too early or too late, are thought to be the target of negative social sanctions and to experience psychological strain (Rossi 1980). National polls on the ideal age to marry and become a parent yield age distributions that cluster around the modal ages at which these changes generally occur. But consistency in expectations, "ideal ages," or even in the actual timing of transitions, may have more to do with institutionally determined pathways and other structural constraints than personal norms.

The notion that norms control timing behavior is contradicted by evidence that age preferences ("ideal" ages for marker events) lag behind behavioral change (Modell 1980; McLaughlin et al. 1988, ch. 9). Marini (1984) notes that there is little direct evidence regarding the existence or content of social norms governing the timing of life events. She asserts that if norms (and associated sanctions) do exist, they probably vary by population subgroup (e.g., by socioeconomic status, gender, and ethnicity), and encompass such a wide range of acceptable ages that they lack causal import. In one study, college students' expectations about the ages at which they would most likely traverse various markers of transition were found to be more variable than those of high school students (Greene 1990).

Older ages of marriage and finishing school, coupled with the increasing reversibility of status changes (serial marriages and cohabiting unions, adult education, etc.) could erode age norms, to the extent that they do exist, since such passages are "no longer viewed in a linear way as transitions passed at a given point and left behind permanently" (Arnett 1997, p. 20). Historically, as objective markers of adulthood have become increasingly variable in their timing and sequencing, age norms may have lost whatever force they once had. But in fact, we do not know whether the failure to make particular transitions at an age when one's contemporaries have mostly done so engenders a subjective sense of being "too early" or "too late" and creates stress, either for earlier cohorts or for contemporary young people.

Arnett (1997) found that youth themselves were more likely to choose psychological traits indicative of individualism and responsibility as necessary for a person to be considered an adult; as criteria for adult status, youth reject role transitions or "objective markers" of adulthood, such as finishing school, marriage, or parenthood. Rituals, such as marriage and graduation, have traditionally allowed public recognition of successful passage to adulthood. If such objective markers of transition have less psychological salience than in the past, they may be less important in signifying and reinforcing adult status.

However, in Arnett's study, two such transitions were endorsed by the majority: living outside the parental household and becoming financially independent of parents. These linked changes, signifying autonomy from parents, may have important symbolic meaning for young people as they contemplate becoming adults. So too, three-fourths of the participants endorsed "decide on personal beliefs and values independently of parents or other influences" (p. 11) as criteria of adulthood.

Consistent with Arnett's research, there is apparently no clear correspondence between particular objective markers (e.g. graduating from college, beginning a full-time job) and young people's subjective identification of themselves as "adults." Aronson (1999b) found that some contemporary young women in their mid-twenties do not "feel like" adults, even when occupying roles widely considered to be indicative of adulthood. Interviews revealed a great deal of ambiguity about adult identity, as well as career uncertainty, despite having already graduated from college and begun full-time work linked to postsecondary areas of study.

Asynchronies in the age-grading systems of different societal institutions generate status inconsistencies (Buchmann 1989) with important psychological implications. If adultlike identities are confirmed in some contexts, such as the workplace, but not in others, such as the family, this discrepancy could produce strain. Moreover, the "loosening" of age-grading and structured sequencing in transitional activities decreases the ability to predict the future from current circumstances (Buchmann 1989), and may thereby engender both stressful situations and depressive reactions (Seligman 1988).

It is widely believed that adolescence and youth are stressful life stages, and that problems diminish with successful acquisition of adult roles (Modell et al. 1976). Consistent with this supposition, youth have been found to exhibit less depressed mood from late adolescence to early adulthood, as they move from high school into postsecondary education and, especially, into full-time work roles (Gore et al. 1997). Moreover, there is evidence that men's self-perceptions of personal well-being and competence decline during college, but rise during the following decade (Mortimer et al. 1982).

However, women's morale may follow a less sanguine trajectory from adolescence through midlife (Cohler et al. 1995). Contemporary women are more likely than those in the historical past to take on multiple and conflicting roles. Difficulties in balancing work and family may be particularly acute and stressful during the transition to adulthood (Aronson 1999a), as increasing numbers of young women attempt to balance the conflicting demands of single motherhood, work, and postsecondary education.

Though the literature tends to focus on problematic outcomes of historical change and the loosening of age-graded social roles, greater diversity in the sequencing and combination of roles (schooling and work, parenting and employment) have promoted more diversified, and autonomous,

courses of action. Indeed, the allowance of more diverse sequences of transitions enables some youth to escape from dissatisfying circumstances in adolescence, for example, by leaving home (Cooney and Mortimer 1999).

The greater individualization and lengthening of the adult transition and early life course in recent times may increase the potential for freedom, and the effective exercise of choice, as well as stress. The extension of formal education allows more time for the exploration of vocational and other life-style alternatives (Maggs 1997). Although change in occupational choice in the years after high school (Rindfuss et al. 1990) may be seen as indicative of a kind of "floundering" and instability, it also may reflect youth's increasing capacity to assess alternatives before making a firm vocational commitment. Modell's (1989) social history of the transition to adulthood in twentieth-century America finds youth increasingly taking charge of their heterosexual relationships and the formation of new families, becoming ever freer of adult surveillance and control. Aronson (1998) found that contemporary young women appreciate their life-course flexibility (Aronson 1998).

THE TRANSITION TO ADULTHOOD AS A CRITICAL PERIOD OF HUMAN DEVELOPMENT

The transition to adulthood is a highly formative period for the crystallization of psychological orientations relating to work, leisure (Inglehart 1990), and politics (Glenn 1980). Alwin and colleagues' (1991) study of a panel of Bennington college women from the 1930s to the 1980s reports extraordinary persistence of political attitudes formed while in college over an approximately fifty-year period (a stability coefficient of .781). Work orientations also become more stable following early adulthood (Lorence and Mortimer 1985; Mortimer et al. 1988). Three explanations have been put forward to account for this pattern: The first implicates the environment; the second, features of the person; the third combines both elements. According to the first line of reasoning, the relatively dense spacing of major life events during the transition to adulthood generates external pressures to form new attitudes or to change previous views (Glenn 1980). While similar events can occur later in life (e.g., a job or career change, remarriage, or entry into an adult education program), they are usually spaced more widely and are like those experienced previously, rather than wholly new circumstances requiring adaptation. Similarly, experiences at work generally assume greater constancy after an initial period of job instability (Osterman 1980). Primary relationships that provide support for attitudes are often in flux during the transition to adulthood; thereafter, stable primary groups may provide continuing support for previously crystallized attitudinal positions (Sears 1981; Backman 1981; Alwin et al. 1991). According to this perspective, there may be continuing capacity to change throughout life (Baltes et al. 1980), but if environments become more stable after the adult transition, there will be less impetus for such change (Moss and Susman 1980).

A second explanation links the "aging stability" pattern to intrapersonal processes that increasingly support the maintenance of existing personality traits, and resistance to change. Mannheim's (1952) classic concept of generation implies that the young are especially receptive to influences generated by the key historical changes of their time (economic upheaval, war, or political revolution). Analysis of data from the European Values Survey shows that younger cohorts are less religiously traditional, are more sexually and morally permissive, and value personal development more highly than older cohorts (Vinken and Ester 1992).

Alwin and colleagues (1991) find evidence for a "generational/persistence model," which similarly combines notions of vulnerability in youth and persistence thereafter. Before role and character identities are formed, the person may be quite malleable. However, preserving a consistent, stable sense of self is a major motivational goal (Rosenberg 1979); and once self-identities are linked to key attitudes and values, the person's self may become inextricably tied to those views (Sears 1981). Moreover, feelings of dissonance (Festinger 1957) arise when attitudes and beliefs that provide a sense of understanding are threatened (Glenn 1980). Consistent with the notion that young adults may be more ready to change, occupational experiences (i.e., related to autonomy) have stronger influences on the work orientations of younger

workers (ages sixteen to twenty-nine) than of those who are older (Lorence and Mortimer 1985; Mortimer et al. 1988).

According to a third point of view, an interaction between the young person and the environment fosters a process of "accentuation" of preexisting traits. While early experiences provide initial impetus for personal development, attitudes and values formed in childhood or adolescence are later strengthened through the individual's selection, production, and/or maintenance of environmental circumstances that support earlier dispositions. According to this view, youth making the transition to adulthood select and/or mold their environments (Lerner and Busch-Rossnagel 1981) often so as to maintain (or to reinforce) initial psychological states. This process typically results in an "increase in emphasis of already prominent characteristics during social transitions in the life course" (Elder and Caspi 1990, p. 218; see also Elder and O'Rand 1995).

Such processes of accentuation take many forms. For example, students choosing particular college majors become increasingly similar in interests and values over time (Feldman and Weiler 1976). Mortimer and colleagues' (1986) study of a panel of young men showed that competence measured in the senior year of college predicted work autonomy ten years later, which in turn, fostered an increasing sense of competence. Similarly, intrinsic, extrinsic and people-oriented values prior to adult entry to the workforce led to the selection of occupational experiences that served to strengthen these value preferences. A similar pattern was found among high school students seeking part-time jobs; intrinsic values predicted opportunities to acquire skills and to help others at work, and further opportunities for skill development strengthened intrinsic values (Mortimer et al. 1996). Alwin and colleagues' (1991) follow-up study of women who attended Bennington College in the 1930s indicated that the choice of associates and the formation of supportive reference groups—e.g., spouses, friends, and children—played a substantial part in maintaining the women's political values.

Elder's longitudinal study of young people growing up during the Great Depression amassed considerable evidence that successful encounters with problems in adolescence can build confidence and resources that promote effective coping with events later in life, fostering personality continuity (Elder 1974; Elder et al. 1984). Thus, early achievements and difficulties can give rise to "spiralling" success and failure. For members of the Oakland cohort, early economic deprivation provided opportunity to help the family in a time of crisis; the consequent increase in self-efficacy, motivation, and capacity to mobilize effort fostered adult work and family security. Elder and Caspi (1990) similarly find that adolescents with more resilient personalities reacted more positively as young adults to combat in World War II. Such reciprocities are also evident among women in the National Longitudinal Survey of Youth; early self-esteem predicted educational attainment and more substantively complex employment, which, in turn, further enhanced their sense of worth (Menahgan 1997).

In contrast, negative early events may set in motion processes that accentuate problems. Early failures can produce psychological reactions and cognitive attributes that perpetuate poor outcomes. There is evidence from several studies that early unemployment fosters distress, self-blame, and negative orientations toward work in general, engendering continued failure in the labor market (Mortimer 1994). Traumatic war experiences in early adulthood can threaten marriage and thereby reinforce a cycle of irritability (Elder and Caspi 1990, p. 235).

Whereas sociologists emphasize the social determination of early adult outcomes, and social psychologists have noted enduring personality traits that influence the process of transition to adulthood, changes in both socioeconomic and personal trajectories do occur, frequently at times of life-course transition. Change can occur as a result of "fortuitous events" that intervene in the developmental process rather than reinforcing patterns of preadult behavior (Elder and Caspi 1988, p. 102). For example, marriage to a nondeviant spouse, the quality of a first marriage, or of economic self-sufficiency from a full-time job may lead to change in direction of a previously "disorderly" or otherwise problematic early life course (Rutter and Quinton 1984; Sampson and Laub 1993; Gore et al. 1997). "Identity transformations" (Wells and

Stryker 1988) can also result when "turning points" (Strauss 1959) in personal history intersect with a rapidly changing historical context to alter a previously held worldview (Aronson forthcoming).

FACTORS INFLUENCING SUCCESSFUL ACQUISITION AND ADAPTATION TO ADULT ROLES

Social scientists are giving increasing attention to processes of individual agency, including goal setting, choice among alternative lines of action, and the mobilization of effort, which influence trajectories of attainment throughout the life course. Early orientations toward, and expectancies about, competent action are critical for later adult success (Mainquist and Eichorn 1989). Jordaan and Super (1974) report that adolescents' planfulness, responsibility, and future orientation predicted their level of occupational attainment at the age of twenty-five. The more explorative adolescents, who were actively engaging of the environment, had more positive early adult outcomes. "Planful competence," denoting ambition, productivity, and dependability in adolescence, has also been linked to men's adult occupational status and marital stability (Clausen 1991, 1993). These attributes imply planfulness, delayed gratification, an intellectual orientation, and a sense of control over goal attainment. Planfully competent adolescents actively explore future options and opportunities, and select those that match their developing proclivities and potentialities. This process gives rise to a better fit between the person and the environment, fostering satisfaction and stability in adult social roles (see Shanahan and Elder 1999).

However, the institutional structure, and the individual's place within hierarchies establishing unequal resources and opportunities, may either facilitate or limit the effective exercise of agency. Shanahan (forthcoming) speaks of "limited strategic action," resulting from "the dynamic tension between selection and assignment." Because the relation between courses of study and higher educational outcomes is often obscure, students may have limited ability to alter negative educational trajectories (Dornbusch 1994). The consequences of planfulness may also be historically variable, depending on the degree of opportunity available to a cohort at critical phases of its life course (Shanahan and Elder 1999).

As the process of acquiring adultlike markers of transition becomes more complex and ambiguous, a wide variety of psychological orientations—including aspirations, values, goals, life plans, self-concepts, and identities—may become increasingly determinative of subsequent outcomes (Mortimer 1996). In fact, both general (Bandura 1996) and facet-specific (Grabowski et al. 1998) dimensions of efficacy are predictive of goal-directed behavior and achievement. Fact-specific orientations include expectations relevant to particular spheres, such as school and work.

The social structural conditions and circumstances that enable some young people to continue to pursue their goals despite obstacles, and others to relinquish them, deserve further study. However, in some circumstances, more favorable outcomes will accrue to those who are more flexible. Kerckhoff and Bell (1988) find that the achievement of postsecondary educational credentials in the form of some vocational certificates yield higher earnings than attaining only some college. The relative merit of tenacious goal pursuit (e.g. a baccalaureate degree) versus the substitution of new, more realistic, alternative objectives ("assimilation" and "accommodation" in Brandtstadter's [1998] terminology) may be determined by structurally constrained resources as well as opportunities.

The character and outcomes of the transition to adulthood are clearly dependent on diverse resources that are differentially distributed among young people (Shanahan forthcoming). There are social class differences in the age at which adult roles are acquired, in the character of marking events, and even in the availability of opportunities to assume adult-status positions (Meijers 1992). The socioeconomic background of the family of origin sets the level of available resources, fostering intergenerational continuity in attainment (Blau and Duncan 1967; Sewell and Hauser 1976; Kerckhoff 1995). Relative advantage or disadvantage can derive from placement in familial and other networks that provide information (Granovetter 1974; Osterman 1989), for example, about higher educational opportunities, jobs (Lin 1992), or even prospective marital partners. A lack of resources, as well as instability (McLanahan and Sandefur 1994),

in the family of origin is associated with disadvantaged transitions to adulthood. Moreover, structural sources of cumulative advantage, such as advantageous placement in ability groups, high school tracks or secondary schools, increase the likelihood of higher education (Kerckhoff 1993; Garmoran 1996).

Personal resources facilitating the educational and occupational attainment process have been linked to social class background. Adolescents' educational and occupational aspirations, and their educational attainments, are important mediators of the effects of occupational origins on destinations (Featherman 1980; Featherman and Spenner 1988). The transmission of self-directed values may also constitute a mechanism through which socioeconomic status is perpetuated across generations (Kohn and Schooler 1983; Kohn et al. 1986). Close father–son relationships in late adolescence engender continuity in paternal occupations and values, and sons' work values and early adult-occupational destinations (Mortimer and Kumka 1982; Ryu and Mortimer 1996). Parents of higher socioeconomic level typically engage in more supportive child-rearing behavior (Gecas 1979), which fosters the development of personality traits such as competence, work involvement, and positive work values, that facilitate early adult socioeconomic attainments (Mortimer et al. 1986).

Gender differences in future orientations can foster differences in achievement. For example, if young women view their futures as contingent on the needs of future spouses, children, and others, this will diminish their propensity to make firm plans (Hagestad 1992), thereby diminishing their attainment. Despite dramatic changes in adult women's employment (McLaughlin et al. 1988; Moen 1992), and in contrast to young men's occupational aspirations, many young women are "talking career but thinking job" (Machung 1989, pp. 52–53).

Geissler and Kruger (1992) have identified different patterns of contemporary "biographical continuity" among young German women, each having important implications for career achievement. Traditionally-oriented women expect to have limited labor force participation and to be economically dependent on a husband. Career-oriented young women emphasize the acquisition of professional qualifications and delay marriage. Still others are actively concerned with both work and family spheres. Such divergence in future orientations and planning influences the intensity of striving for achievement and attainment during the transition to adulthood.

Moreover, to the extent that young women are aware of the difficulties adult women face, resulting from employer discrimination and the unequal division of family work, this would likely depress expectations for labor market success. Ambivalence about work could exacerbate the detrimental consequences of other psychological differences (relative to males) for socioeconomic attainment, such as lower self-efficacy, lower self-esteem, and higher levels of depressive affect (Simmons and Blyth 1987; Gecas 1989; Finch et al. 1991; Shanahan et al. 1991; Mortimer 1994). It is therefore not surprising that although women have narrowed the historical gap in educational attainment (McLaughlin et al. 1988), they often get "diverted" from their initial plans, emphasizing romance over academics (Holland and Eisenhart 1990). For today's women, taking on adult work and family roles is more likely than for men to result in the termination of schooling (Pallas 1993).

If the family is an important institutional context for the acquisition of economic and other resources for the adult transition, family poverty or disintegration may be expected to have negative consequences. Experiences in youth may thus set in motion a train of events that have a profound impact on the early life course. Disruption and single parenthood in the family of origin, and the economic loss and emotional turmoil that frequently ensue, may jeopardize parental investment in children and youth. However, Coleman (1994) argues that declining investments in the next generation may occur even in more favorable and affluent circumstances. As the functions of the family are transferred to other agencies in welfare states (e.g., as the government takes over education, welfare, support of the aged, and other functions), there is a declining economic dependence of family members on one another. As the multigenerational organization and functions of the family weaken, parental motivation to invest attention, time, and effort in the younger generation may also decrease throughout the population.

However, Shanahan (forthcoming) speaks of "knifing off" experiences during the transition to adulthood, which can enable some youth to escape from poverty, familial conflict, stigmatization, and other debilitating circumstances of their childhood and teen years. For example, service in the military enabled many men from disadvantaged backgrounds to extricate themselves from the stressful circumstances of their families, mature psychologically, and therefore be in a better position to take advantage of educational benefits for veterans after World War II (Elder and Caspi 1990).

The availability of opportunities for anticipatory socialization or practice of adult roles may also affect adaptation to them. Contemporary youth spend much of their time in schools, cut off from meaningful contact with adult workers (excepting their teachers). Some have expressed concern that this isolation from adult work settings reduces opportunities for career exploration and encourages identification with the youth subculture (Panel on Youth 1974). Many parents encourage adolescent children to work, believing that this experience will help them to become responsible and independent, to learn to handle money, and to effectively manage their time (Phillips and Sandstrom 1990). However, "youth jobs" are quite different from adult work, involving relatively simple tasks and little expectation of continuity.

The impacts of part-time employment during adolescence for the transition to adulthood is the subject of much controversy (Committee on the Health and Safety Implications of Child Labor 1998, ch. 4). While the full impact of employment in adolescence is not known, there is evidence that increasing investment in paid work (as indicated by the number of hours spent working per week) is associated with reduced educational attainment (Marsh 1991; Chaplin and Hannaway 1996; Carr et al. 1996). However, several studies have shown that employment during high school also predicts more stable work histories and higher earnings in the years immediately following (Mortimer and Finch 1986; Marsh 1991; Ruhm 1995, 1997; Mortimer and Johnson 1998). Stern and Nakata (1989), using data from noncollege youth in the National Longitudinal Survey of Youth, report that more complex work activity in adolescence is associated with lower incidence of unemployment and higher earnings three years after high school.

The meaning of adolescent work also influences subsequent educational and occupational outcomes. For example, employment has been found to have a positive effect on high school students' grades when the workers are saving their earnings to go to college (Marsh 1991; Ruscoe et al. 1996). Consistently, youth who effectively balance their part-time jobs with school, working near continuously during high school but restricting the intensity of their employment to twenty hours a week or fewer, were found to have high early-achievement orientations and obtained more months of post-secondary education (Mortimer and Johnson 1998).

There is further evidence that the quality of adolescent work experience matters for psychological outcomes that are likely to influence adult attainment (Mortimer and Finch 1996). For example, adolescent boys who felt that they were obtaining useful skills and who perceived opportunities for advancement in their jobs exhibited increased mastery (internal control) over time; girls who thought that they were being paid well for their work manifested increasing levels of self-efficacy (Finch et al. 1991). Exposure to job stressors, in contrast, heightened depressive affect (Shanahan et al. 1991).

For the most disadvantaged segments of society there is concern that poor educational opportunities and a rapidly deteriorating economic base in the inner cities preclude access to youth jobs as well as to viable adult work roles (Wilson 1987), irrespective of personal efficacy, ambition, or other traits. The shift from an industrial- to a service-based economy has lessened the availability of entry-level employment in manufacturing. Economic and technological change has created a class of "hard-core unemployed"; those whose limited education and skills place them at a severe disadvantage in the labor market (Lichter 1988; Halperin 1998). Black males' lack of stable employment in U.S. inner cities limits their ability to assume the adult family role (as male provider) and fosters the increasing prevalence and legitimacy of female-headed families.

Research on African-American adolescents suggests that the transition to adulthood may differ significantly from that of non-minority teens. Ogbu (1989) implicates beliefs about success as critical to understanding the paradox of high aspirations among black adolescents and low subsequent achievement. The "folk culture of success," fostered by a history of discrimination and reinforced by everyday experience (e.g., the observation of black career ceilings, inflated job qualifications, housing discrimination, and poor occupational achievement despite success in school), convinces some young blacks that desired occupational outcomes will not be assured by educational attainment. Given the belief that external forces controlled by whites determine success, alternative strategies for achievement may be endorsed— hustling, collective action, or dependency on a more powerful white person. These, in turn, may diminish the effort in school that is necessary to obtain good grades and educational credentials.

In the context of urban poverty and violence, youth expectations for a truncated life expectancy (an "accelerated life course"), may lessen the salience of adolescence as a distinct life stage (Burton et al. 1996). With few employment and educational opportunities available, these youth often focus on alternative positive markers of adulthood, such as becoming a parent, obtaining material goods, or becoming involved in religious activities. Under such conditions, even a menial job can engender and reinforce "mainstream" identities and "possible selves" as economically productive working adults (Newman 1996). However, structural opportunities pervasively influence achievement orientations and outcomes throughout the social class hierarchy; such processes are clearly not limited to any particular societal stratum (Kerckhoff 1995).

Supportive families and other social bonds are predictive of successful adjustment in the face of poverty and other disadvantages (Ensminger and Juon 1998). Families who are successful in these circumstances place great emphasis on connecting their adolescent children with persons and agencies outside the immediate household, in their neighborhoods and beyond, thereby enhancing their social networks and social capital, invaluable resources in the transition to adulthood (Furstenberg et al. 1999; Sullivan 1989).

In summary, becoming an adult involves changes in objective status positions and in subjective orientations. The transition to adulthood has changed through historical time as a result of economic, political, and social trends. Contemporary young people face increasingly extended and individualized paths in the timing and sequencing of their movement into adult roles. The transition to adulthood is found to be a critical period for the crystallization of key orientations and values. Adult status placement and adjustment are influenced by socioeconomic background and poverty, gender, early employment experiences, and psychological resources.

The multiplicity of transition markers, the variety of macrostructural and personal influences, and the little-studied subjective component give rise to important challenges and complexities in the study of this phase of life.

REFERENCES

Alwin, Duane F., Ronald L. Cohen, and Theodore M. Newcomb 1991 *Political Attitudes over the Life Span: The Bennington Women after Fifty Years*. Madison: University of Wisconsin Press.

Ari@eacute;s, Philippe 1962 *Centuries of Childhood: A Social History of Family Life*. New York: Vintage.

Arnett, Jeffrey Jensen 1997 "Young People's Conceptions of the Transition to Adulthood." *Youth and Society* 29:3–23.

——, and Susan Taber 1994 "Adolescence Terminable and Interminable: When Does Adolescence End?" *Journal of Youth and Adolescence* 23:5, 517–537.

Aronson, Pamela 1999a "The Balancing Act: Young Women's Expectations and Experiences of Work and Family." In Toby Parcel, ed., *Research in the Sociology of Work*. Greenwich, Conn.: JAI Press.

—— 1999b Blurring life course stages: Young women's transition from adolescence to adulthood in the contemporary era. Paper under review.

—— 1998 "Coming of age in the 1990s: Women's identities, life paths, and attitudes towards feminism." Ph.D. diss., Minneapolis: University of Minnesota.

—— Forthcoming "The Development and Transformation of Feminist Identities under Changing Historical Conditions." In Timonthy J. Owens, ed., *Advances in Life Course Research: Identity across the Life Course in Cross-Cultural Perspective*. Greenwich, Conn.: JAI Press.

Arum, Richard, and Michael Hout 1998 "The Early Returns: The Transition from School to Work in the United States." In Yossi Shavit and Walter Muller, eds., *From School to Work: A Comparative Study of Educational Qualifications and Occupational Destinations*. Oxford: Clarendon Press.

Bachman, Jerald G., and John Schulenberg 1993 "How Part-time Work Intensity Relates to Drug Use, Problem Behavior, Time Use, and Satisfaction among High School Seniors: Are These Consequences or Merely Correlates?" *Developmental Psychology* 29:220–235.

Backman, Carl W. 1981 "Attraction in Interpersonal Relationships." In M. Rosenberg and R. H. Turner, eds., *Social Psychology: Sociological Perspectives*. New York: Basic Books.

Baltes, Paul B., Hayne W. Reese, and Lewis P. Lipsitt 1980 "Life-Span Developmental Psychology." *Annual Review of Psychology* 31:65–110.

Bandura, Albert 1996 *Self-Efficacy: The Exercise of Control*. New York: W. H. Freeman.

Blau, Peter M., and Otis Dudley Duncan 1967 *The American Occupational Structure*. New York: Wiley.

Borman, Kathryn M. 1991 *The First 'Real' Job: A Study of Young Workers*. Albany: State University of New York Press.

Brandtstadter, Jochen 1998 "Action Perspectives on Human Development." In Richard M. Lerner, ed., *Handbook of Child Psychology*. Vol. 1, *Theoretical Models of Human Development*. New York: John Wiley & Sons, Inc.

Buchmann, Marlis 1989 *The Script of Life in Modern Society: Entry into Adulthood in a Changing World*. Chicago: University of Chicago Press.

Burton, Linda M., Dawn A. Obeidallah, and Kevin Allison 1996 "Ethnographic Insights on Social Context and Adolescent Development among Inner-City African-American Teens." In R. Jessor, A. Colby, and R. Shweder, eds., *Ethnography and Human Development: Context and Meaning in Social Inquiry*. Chicago: University of Chicago Press.

Carr, R. V., J. D. Wright, and C. J. Brody 1996 "Effects of High School Work Experience a Decade Later: Evidence from the National Longitudinal Survey." *Sociology of Education* 69 (January):66–81.

Chaplin, D., and J. Hannaway 1996 High school enrollment: meaningful connections for at-risk youth. Paper presented at the Annual Meeting of the American Educational Research Association, New York. Washington, D.C.: Urban Institute.

Clausen, John A. 1993 *American Lives: Looking Back at the Children of the Great Depression*. New York: Free Press.

—— 1991 "Adolescent Competence and the Shaping of the Life Course." *American Journal of Sociology* 96:805–842.

Cohler, Bertram J., Frances M. Stott, and Judith S. Musick 1995 "Adversity, Vulnerability, and Resilience: Cultural and Developmental Perspectives." In

Dante Cicchetti and Donald J. Cohen, eds., *Developmental Psychopathology*. Vol. 2, *Risk, Disorder, and Adaptation*. New York: John Wiley & Sons, Inc.

Coleman, James S. 1994 "Social Capital, Human Capital, and Investment in Youth." In Anne C. Petersen and Jeylan T. Mortimer, eds., *Youth Unemployment and Society*. Cambridge, Eng.: Cambridge University Press.

——, and Torsten Husen 1985 *Becoming Adult in a Changing Society*. Paris: Organization for Economic Co-operation and Development.

Committee on the Health and Safety Implications of Child Labor, National Research Council 1998 *Protecting Youth at Work: Health, Safety, and Development of Working Children and Adolescents in the United States*. Washington, D.C.: National Academy Press.

Connor, John W., and George A. De Vos 1989 "Cultural Influences on Achievement Motivation and Orientation toward Work in Japanese and American Youth." In D. Stern and D. Eichorn, eds., *Adolescence and Work: Influences of Social Structure, Labor Markers, and Culture*. Hillsdale, N.J.: Lawrence Erlbaum.

Cooney, Teresa M. 1994 "Leaving Home and Coming Back: The Influence of Parental Divorce and Family Dynamics on Young Adults' Residential Transitions." *Sociological Studies of Children* 6:159–179.

——, and Jeylan T. Mortimer Forthcoming "Family Structure Differences in the Timing of Leaving Home: Exploring Mediating Factors." *Journal of Research on Adolescence*.

Côté, James E., and Anton L. Allahar 1994 *Generation on Hold: Coming of Age in the Late Twentieth Century*. New York: New York University Press.

Dornbusch, Sanford M. 1994 Off the track. Presidential address at the meeting of the Society for Research on Adolescence, 10–13 February, at San Diego, Calif.

Elder, Glen H., Jr. 1974 *Children of the Great Depression*. Chicago: University of Chicago Press.

——, and Avshalom Caspi 1990 "Studying Lives in a Changing Society: Sociological and Personological Explorations." In A. I. Rabin, R. A. Zucker, and S. Frank, eds., *Studying Persons and Lives*. New York: Springer-Verlag.

—— 1988 "Human Development and Social Change: An Emerging Perspective on the Life Course." In N. Bolger, A. Caspi, G. Downey, and M. Moorehouse, eds., *Persons in Context: Developmental Processes*. New York: Cambridge University Press.

Elder, Glen H., Jr., J. K. Liker, and C. E. Cross 1984 "Parent-Child Behavior in the Great Depression:

Life Course and Intergenerational Influences." In P. B. Baltes, ed., *Life-Span Development and Behavior*. New York: Academic Press.

Elder, Glen H., Jr., and Angela M. O'Rand 1995 "Adult Lives in a Changing Society." In K. S. Cook, G. A. Fine and J. S. House, eds., *Sociological Perspectives on Social Psychology*. New York: Allyn and Bacon.

Ensminger, Margaret E., and Hee Soon Juon 1998 "Transition to Adulthood among High-Risk Youth." In Richard Jessor, ed., *New Perspectives on Adolescent Risk Behavior*. New York: Cambridge University Press.

Featherman, David L. 1980 "Schooling and Occupational Careers: Constancy and Change in Worldly Success." In O. G. Brim, Jr. and J. Kagan, eds., *Constancy and Change in Human Development*. Cambridge, Mass.: Harvard University Press.

——, and Kenneth I. Spenner 1988 "Class and the Socialization of Children: Constancy, Change, or Irrelevance?" In E. Mavis Hetherington, R. M. Lerner, and M. Perlmutter, eds., *Child Development in Perspective*. Hillsdale, N.J.: Lawrence Erlbaum.

Feldman, Kenneth A., and John Weiler 1976 "Changes in Initial Differences among Major-Field Groups: An Exploration of the 'Accentuation Effect.'" In W. H. Sewell, R. M. Hauser, and D. L. Featherman, eds., *Schooling and Achievement in American Society*. New York: Academic Press.

Festinger, Leon 1957 *A Theory of Cognitive Dissonance*. Stanford, Calif.: Stanford University Press.

Finch, Michael D., Michael J. Shanahan, Jeylan T. Mortimer, and Seongryeol Ryu 1991 "Work Experience and Control Orientation in Adolescence." *American Sociological Review* 56 (October):597–611.

Foner, Anne, and David Kertzer 1978 "Transitions over the Life Course: Lessons from Age-Set Societies." *American Journal of Sociology* 83:1081–1104.

Furstenberg, Frank F., Jr., J. Brooks-Gunn, and S. Philip Morgan 1987 *Adolescent Mothers in Later Life*. Cambridge, Eng.: Cambridge University Press.

Furstenberg, Frank F., Jr., and Thomas D. Cook, Jacquelynne Eccles, Glen H. Elder, Jr., and Arnold Sameroff 1999 *Managing to Make It: Urban Families and Adolescent Success*. Chicago: University of Chicago Press.

Galambos, Nancy L., and Marion F. Ehrenberg 1997 "The Family as Health Risk and Opportunity: A Focus on Divorce and Working Families." In John Schulenberg, Jennifer L. Maggs, and Klaus Hurrelmann, eds., *Health Risks and Developmental Transitions during Adolescence*. Cambridge, Eng.: Cambridge University Press.

Gamoran, Adam 1996 "Educational Stratification and Individual Careers." In Alan C. Kerckhoff, ed., *Generating Social Stratification: Toward a New Research Agenda*. Boulder, Colo.: Westview Press.

Gecas, Viktor 1989 "The Social Psychology of Self-Efficacy." *Annual Review of Sociology* 15:291–316.

—— 1979 "The Influence of Social Class on Socialization." In W. R. Burr, R. Hill, F. I. Nye, and I. L. Reiss, eds., *Contemporary Theories about the Family*. Vol. 1, *Research-Based Theories*. New York: Free Press.

Geissler, B., and Helga Kruger 1992 "Balancing the Life Course in Response to Institutional Arrangements." In Walter Heinz, ed., *Institutions and Gatekeeping in the Life Course*. Weinheim, Germany: Deutscher Studien Verlag.

Glenn, Norval D. 1980 "Values, Attitudes, and Beliefs." In O. G. Brim, Jr. and J. Kagan, eds., *Constancy and Change in Human Development*. Cambridge, Mass.: Harvard University Press.

Goldscheider, Frances K., and Calvin Goldscheider 1993 *Leaving Home Before Marriage: Ethnicity, Familism, and Generational Relationships*. Madison: University of Wisconsin Press.

Gore, Susan, Robert Aseltine, Jr., Mary Ellen Colten, and Bin Lin 1997 "Life after High School: Development, Stress, and Well-Being." In Ian H. Gotlib and Blair Wheaton, eds., *Stress and Adversity over the Life Course: Trajectories and Turning Points*. Cambridge, Eng.: Cambridge University Press.

Grabowski, Lorie Schabo, Kathleen T. Call. and Jeylan T. Mortimer 1998 Global and economic self-efficacy in the attainment process. Paper presented at the annual meeting of the American Sociological Association, August, San Francisco, Calif.

Graff, Harvey 1995 *Conflicting Paths: Growing Up in America*. Cambridge, Mass.: Harvard University Press.

Granovetter, Mark S. 1974 *Getting a Job*. Cambridge, Mass.: Harvard University Press.

Greenberger, Ellen, and A. B. Sorenson 1974 "Toward a Concept of Psychosocial Maturity." *Journal of Youth and Adolescence* 3:329–358.

Greenberger, Ellen, and Laurence Steinberg 1986 *When Teenagers Work*. New York: Basic Books.

Greene, A. L. 1990 "Great Expectations: Constructions of the Life Course During Adolescence." *Journal of Youth and Adolescence* 19:289–306.

Hagestad, Gunhild 1992 "Assigning Rights and Duties: Age, Duration, and Gender in Social Institutions." In Walter Heinz, ed., *Institutions and Gatekeeping in the Life Course*. Weinheim, Germany: Deutscher Studien Verlag.

Hall, G. S. 1904 *Adolescence: Its Psychology and its Relations to Physiology, Anthropology, Sociology, Sex, Crime, Religion, and Education*. New York: Appleton.

Halperin, Samuel (ed.) 1998 *The Forgotten Half Revisited: American Youth and Young Families, 1988–2008*. Washington, D.C.: American Youth Policy Forum, Inc.

Hamilton, Stephen F. 1990 *Apprenticeship for Adulthood. Preparing Youth for the Future*. New York: Free Press.

Hogan, Dennis P., and Nan Marie Astone 1986 "The Transition to Adulthood." *Annual Review of Sociology* 12:109–130.

Hogan, Dennis P., and Takashi Mochizuki 1988 "Demographic Transitions and the Life Course: Lessons from Japanese and American Comparisons." *Journal of Family History* 13:291–305.

Holland, Dorothy, and Margaret Eisenhart 1990 *Educated in Romance: Women, Achievement, and College Culture*. Chicago: University of Chicago Press.

Inglehart, R. 1990 *Culture Shift in Advanced Industrial Society*. Princeton, N.J.: Princeton University Press.

Jessor, Richard, and Shirley L. Jessor 1977 *Problem Behavior and Psychosocial Development. A Longitudinal Study of Youth*. New York: Academic Press.

Jordaan, Jean Pierre, and Donald E. Super 1974 "The Prediction of Early Adult Vocational Behavior." In D. F. Ricks, A. Thomas, and M. Roff, eds., *Life History Research in Psychopathology*. Minneapolis: University of Minnesota Press.

Keniston, Kenneth 1970 "Youth as a Stage of Life." *American Scholar* 39:631–654.

Kerckhoff, Alan C. 1996 "Building Conceptual and Empirical Bridges between Studies of Educational and Labor Force Careers." In A. C. Kerckhoff, ed., *Generating Social Stratification: Toward a New Research Agenda*. Boulder, Colo.: Westview Press.

—— 1995 "Social Stratification and Mobility Processes: Interaction between Individuals and Social Structures." In Karen S. Cook, Gary Alan Fine, and James S. House, eds., *Sociological Perspectives on Social Psychology*. Boston: Allyn and Bacon.

—— 1993 *Diverging Pathways. Social Structure and Career Deflections*. New York: Cambridge University Press.

—— and Lorraine Bell 1998 "Hidden Capital: Vocational Credentials and Attainment in the United States." *Sociology of Education* 71:152–174.

Klein, Hugh 1990 "Adolescence, Youth and Young Adulthood: Rethinking Current Conceptualizations of Life Stage." *Youth and Society* 21:446–471.

Kohn, Melvin L., and Carmi Schooler 1983 *Work and Personality: An Inquiry into the Impact of Social Stratification*. Norwood, N.J.: Ablex Publishing.

Kohn, Melvin L., Kazimierz M. Slomczynski, and Carrie Schoenbach 1986 "Social Stratification and the Transmission of Values in the Family: A Cross-National Assessment." *Sociological Forum* 1:73–102.

Lerner, Richard M., and N. A. Busch-Rossnagel (eds.) 1981 *Individuals as Producers of Their Development: A Life-Span Perspective*. New York: Academic Press.

Lichter, Daniel T. 1988 "Racial Differences in Underemployment in American Cities" *American Journal of Sociology* 93:771–792.

Lin, Nan 1992 "Social Resources Theory." In Edgar F. Borgatta and Marie L. Borgatta, eds., *Encyclopedia of Sociology*. New York: Macmillan.

Lorence, Jon, and Jeylan T. Mortimer 1985 "Job Involvement through the Life Course: A Panel Study of Three Age Groups." *American Sociological Review* 50:618–638.

McLanahan, Sara, and Gary Sandefur 1994 *Growing up with a Single Parent*. Cambridge, Mass.: Harvard University Press.

McLaughlin, Steven D., Barbara D. Melber, John O. G. Billy, Denise M. Zimmerle, Linda D. Winges, and Terry R. Johnson 1988 *The Changing Lives of American Women*. Chapel Hill: University of North Carolina Press.

Machung, Anne 1989 "Talking Career, Thinking Job: Gender Differences in Career and Family Expectations of Berkeley Seniors." *Feminist Studies* 15:35–39.

Maggs, Jennifer L. 1997 "Alcohol Use and Binge Drinking as Goal-Directed Action during the Transition to Postsecondary Education." In John Schulenberg, Jennifer L. Maggs, and Klaus Hurrelmann, eds., *Health Risks and Developmental Transitions during Adolescence*. Cambridge, Eng.: Cambridge University Press.

Mainquist, Sheri, and Dorothy Eichorn 1989 "Competence in Work Settings." In D. Stern and D. Eichorn, eds., *Adolescence and Work: Influences of Social Structure, Labor Markets, and Culture*. Hillsdale, N.J.: Lawrence Erlbaum.

Mannheim, Karl 1952 "The Problem of Generations." In P. Kecskemeti, ed., *Essays in the Sociology of Knowledge*. London: Routledge and Kegan Paul.

Marini, Margaret Mooney 1984 "Age and Sequencing Norms in the Transition to Adulthood." *Social Forces* 63:229–244.

Marsh, H. W. 1991 "Employment during High School: Character Building or Subversion of Academic Goals?" *Sociology of Education* 64:172–189.

Meijers, Frans 1992 "'Being Young' in the Life Perceptions of Dutch, Moroccan, Turkish and Surinam Youngsters." In Wim Meeus, Martijn de Goede, Willem Kox, and Klaus Hurrelmann, eds., *Adolescence, Careers, and Cultures*. Berlin: Walter de Gruyter.

Menaghan, Elizabeth G. 1997 "Intergenerational Consequences of Social Stressors: Effects of Occupational and Family Conditions on Young Mothers and Their Children." In Ian Gotlib and Blair Wheaton, eds., *Stress and Adversity over the Life Course: Trajectories and Turning Points*. Cambridge, Eng.: Cambridge University Press.

Modell, John 1989 *Into One's Own. From Youth to Adulthood in the United States, 1920–1975*. Berkeley: University of California Press.

—— 1980 "Normative Aspects of American Marriage Timing since World War II." *Journal of Family History* 5:210–234.

——, Frank Furstenberg, and Theodore Hershberg 1976 "Social Change and Transitions to Adulthood in Historical Perspective." *Journal of Family History* 1:7–32.

Moen, Phyllis 1992 *Women's Two Roles: A Contemporary Dilemma*. Westport, Conn.: Auburn House.

Morris, Martina, and Annette Bernhardt 1998 The transition to work in the post-industrial labor market. Paper presented at the annual meeting of the American Sociological Association, August, San Francisco, Calif.

Mortimer, Jeylan T. 1996 "Social Psychological Aspects of Achievement." In Alan C. Kerckhoff, ed., *Generational Social Stratification: Toward a New Generation of Research*. Boulder, Colo.: Westview.

—— 1994 "Individual Differences as Precursors of Youth Unemployment." In Anne C. Petersen and Jeylan T. Mortimer, eds., *Youth Unemployment and Society*. New York: Cambridge University Press.

——, Carolyn Harley, and Pamela J. Aronson 1999 "How do Prior Experiences in the Workplace Set the Stage for Transitions to Adulthood?" In Alan Booth and Nan Crouter, eds., *Transitions to Adulthood in a Changing Economy: No Work, No Family, No Future?* New York: Greenwood Press.

Mortimer, Jeylan T., and Michael D. Finch 1986 "The Effects of Part-time Work on Self-Concept and Achievement." In K. Borman and J. Reisman, eds., *Becoming a Worker*. Norwood, N.J.: Ablex Publishing.

—— 1996 "Work, Family, and Adolescent Development." In J. T. Mortimer and M. D. Finch, eds., *Adolescents, Work and Family: An Intergenerational Developmental Analysis*. Thousand Oaks, Calif.: Sage Publications.

———, and Donald S. Kumka 1982 "Persistence and Change in Development: The Multidimensional Self-Concept." In P. D. Baltes and O. G. Brim, Jr., eds., *Life-Span Development and Behavior*. New York: Academic Press.

Mortimer, Jeylan T., Michael D. Finch, and Geoffrey Maruyama 1988 "Work Experience and Job Satisfaction: Variation by Age and Gender." In J. T. Mortimer and K. M. Borman, eds., *Work Experience and Psychological Development through the Life Span*. Boulder, Colo.: Westview Press.

Mortimer, Jeylan T. and Monica K. Johnson 1999. "Adolescent Part-Time Work and Post-Secondary Transition Pathways in the United States." Walter Heinz, ed., *From Education to Work: Cross National Perspectives*. New York: Cambridge University Press.

——— 1998 "New Perspectives on Adolescent Work and the Transition to Adulthood." In Richard Jessor, ed., *New Perspectives on Adolescent Risk Behavior*. New York: Cambridge University Press.

Mortimer, Jeylan T., and Helga Kruger (Forthcoming) "Transition from School to Work in the United States and Germany: Formal Pathways Matter." In M. Hallinan, ed., *Handbook of the Sociology of Education*. New York: Plenum Publishing Company.

Mortimer, Jeylan T., and Donald S. Kumka 1982 "A Further Examination of the 'Occupational Linkage Hypothesis.'" *Sociological Quarterly* 23:3–16.

Mortimer, Jeylan T., Jon Lorence, and Donald S. Kumka 1986 *Work, Family, and Personality: Transition to Adulthood*. Norwood, N.J.: Ablex Publishing.

Mortimer, Jeylan T., Ellen Efron Pimentel, Seongryeol Ryu, Katherine Nash, and Chaimun Lee 1996 "Part-Time Work and Occupational Value Formation in Adolescence." *Social Forces* 74:1405–1418.

Moss, Howard A., and Elizabeth J. Susman 1980 "Longitudinal Study of Personality Development." In O. G. Brim, Jr., and J. Kagan, eds., *Constancy and Change in Human Development*. Cambridge, Mass.: Harvard University Press.

Neugarten, Bernice L., and Nancy Datan 1973 "Sociological Perspectives on the Life Cycle." In P. B. Baltes and K. Warner Schaie, eds., *Life Span Developmental Psychology: Personality and Socialization*. New York: Academic Press.

Neugarten, Bernice L., Joan W. Moore, and John C. Lowe 1965 "Age Norms, Age Constraints, and Adult Socialization." *American Journal of Sociology* 70:710–717.

Newman, Katherine 1996 "Working Poor: Low Wage Employment in the Lives of Harlem Youth." In J.

Graber, J. Brooks-Gunn, and A. Petersen, eds., *Transitions through Adolescence: Interpersonal Domains and Context*. Hillsdale, N.J.: Erlbaum Associates.

Ogbu, John U. 1989 "Cultural Boundaries and Minority Youth Orientation toward Work Preparation." In D. Stern and D. Eichorn, eds., *Adolescence and Work: Influences of Social Structure, Labor Markets, and Culture*. Hillsdale, N.J.: Lawrence Erlbaum.

Osterman, Paul 1989 "The Job Market for Adolescents." In D. Stern and D. Eichorn, eds., *Adolescence and Work: Influences of Social Structure, Labor Markets, and Culture*. Hillsdale, N.J.: Lawrence Erlbaum.

——— 1980 *Getting Started: The Youth Labor Market*. Cambridge, Mass.: MIT Press.

Pallas, Aaron 1993 "Schooling in the Course of Human Lives: Social Context of Education and Transition to Adulthood in Industrial Society." *Review of Educational Research* 63, 4, Winter: 409–447.

Panel on Youth of the President's Science Advisory Committee 1974 *Youth: Transition to Adulthood*. Chicago: University of Chicago Press.

Phillips, Sarah, and Kent Sandstrom 1990 "Parental Attitudes toward 'Youthwork'" *Youth and Society* 22:160–183.

Rindfuss, Ronald R., Elizabeth C. Cooksey, and R. L. Sutterlin 1990 Young adult occupational achievement: early expectations versus behavioral reality. Paper presented at the World Congress of Sociology, July, Madrid.

Rindfuss, Ronald R., C. Gray Swicegood, and Rachel Rosenfeld 1987 "Disorder in the Life Course: How Common and Does it Matter?" *American Sociological Review* 52:785–801.

Rosenberg, Morris 1979 *Conceiving the Self*. New York: Basic Books.

Rossi, Alice S. 1980 "Life-Span Theories and Women's Lives." *Signs: Journal of Women in Culture and Society* 6:4–32.

Ruhm, C. J. 1997 "Is High School Employment Consumption or Investment?" *Journal of Labor Economics* 15:735–776.

——— 1995 "The Extent and Consequences of High School Employment." *Journal of Labor Research* 16:293–303.

Ruscoe, G., J. C. Morgan, and C. Peebles 1996 "Students Who Work." *Adolescence* 31:625–632.

Rutter, Michael, and David Quinton 1984 "Long-Term Follow-Up of Women Institutionalized in Childhood: Factors Promoting Good Functioning in Adult Life." *British Journal of Developmental Psychology* 2:191–204.

Ryu, Seongryeol, and Jeylan T. Mortimer 1996 "The 'Occupational Linkage Hypothesis' applied to Occupational Value Formation in Adolescence." In Jeylan T. Mortimer and Michael D. Finch, eds., *Adolescents, Work, and Family: An Intergenerational Developmental Analysis.* Thousand Oaks, Calif.: Sage.

Sampson, Robert J., and John H. Laub 1993 *Crime in the Making: Pathways and Turning Points through Life.* Cambridge: Harvard University Press.

Sears, David O. 1981 "Life-Stage Effects on Attitude Change, Especially among the Elderly." In B. Kiesler, J. N. Morgan, and V. Kincade Oppenheimer, eds., *Aging: Social Change.* New York: Academic Press.

Seligman, Martin 1988 "Boomer Blues." *Psychology Today* (October): 50–55.

Sewell, William H., and Robert M. Hauser 1976 "Causes and Consequences of Higher Education: Models of the Status Attainment Process." In W. H. Swell, R. M. Hauser, and D. L. Featherman, eds., *Schooling and Achievement in American Society.* New York: Academic Press.

Shanahan, Michael J. (Forthcoming) "Pathways to Adulthood in Changing Societies: Variability and Mechanisms in Life Course Perspective." *Annual Review of Sociology.*

—— This volume "Adolescence." In Edgar F. Borgatta and Marie L. Borgatta, eds., *Encyclopedia of Sociology.* New York: Macmillan.

——, and Glen H. Elder, Jr. 1999 History, agency and the life course. Paper presented at the Lincoln, Nebraska Symposium on Motivation.

Shanahan, Michael J., Richard A. Miech, and Glen H. Elder, Jr. 1998 "Changing Pathways to Attainment in Men's Lives: Historical Patterns of School, Work, and Social Class." *Social Forces* 77:231–256.

Shanahan, Michael J., Michael D. Finch, Jeylan T. Mortimer, and Seongryeol Ryu 1991 "Adolescent Work Experience and Depressive Affect." *Social Psychology Quarterly* 54:299–317.

Shavit, Yossi, and Walter Muller 1998 *From School to Work: A Comparative Study of Educational Qualifications and Occupational Destinations.* Oxford: Clarendon Press.

Simmons, Roberta, and Dale Blyth 1987 *Moving into Adolescence: The Impact of Pubertal Change and School Context.* New York: Aldine.

Spain, Daphne, and Suzanne M. Bianchi 1996 *Balancing Act: Motherhood, Marriage, and Employment among American Women.* New York: Russell Sage Foundation.

Stern, David, and Yoshi-Fumi Nakata 1989 "Characteristics of High School Students' Paid Jobs, and Employment Experience after Graduation." In D. Stern and D. Eichorn, eds., *Adolescence and Work. Influences of Social Structure, Labor Markets, and Culture.* Hillsdale, N.J.: Lawrence Erlbaum.

Strauss, Anselm 1959 *Mirrors and Masks: The Search for Identity.* Glencoe, Ill.: The Free Press.

Sullivan, Mercer L. 1989 *Getting Paid: Youth Crime and Work in the Inner City.* Ithaca, NY: Cornell University Press.

Vinken, Henk, and Peter Ester 1992 "Modernization and Value Shifts: A Cross-Cultural and Longitudinal Analysis of Adolescents' Basic Values." In Wim Meeus, Martijn de Goede, Willem Kox, and Klaus Hurrelmann, eds., *Adolescence, Careers, and Cultures.* Berlin: Walter de Gruyter.

Wells, L. Edward, and Sheldon Stryker 1988 "Stability and Change in Self over the Life Course." In Paul Baltes, David Featherman, and Richard Lerner, eds., *Life Span Development and Behavior.* Hillsdale, N.J.: Lawrence Erlbaum.

White, Merry 1993 *The Material Child: Coming of Age in Japan and America.* New York: Free Press.

Wilson, William Julius 1987 *The Truly Disadvantaged. The Inner City, the Underclass, and Public Policy.* Chicago: University of Chicago Press.

World Factbook, The 1998 Compiled by the Central Intelligence Agency. Washington, D.C.: U.S. Government Printing Office.

JEYLAN T. MORTIMER
PAMELA ARONSON

AFFECT CONTROL THEORY AND IMPRESSION FORMATION

Sociologist Erving Goffman (1969) argued that people conduct themselves so as to generate impressions that maintain the identities, or "faces," that they have in social situations. Human action—aside from accomplishing tasks—functions expressively in reflecting actors' social positions and in preserving social order. Affect control theory (Heise 1979; Smith-Lovin and Heise 1988; MacKinnon 1994) continues Goffman's thesis, providing a mathematized and empirically grounded model for explaining and predicting expressive aspects of action.

AFFECTIVE MEANING

Cross-cultural research among people speaking diverse languages in more than twenty-five nations around the world (Osgood, May, and Miron 1975) revealed that any person, behavior, object, setting, or property of persons evokes an affective response consisting of three components. One component consists of approval or disapproval of the entity—an evaluation based on morality (good versus bad), aesthetics (beautiful versus ugly), functionality (useful versus useless), hedonism (pleasant versus unpleasant), or some other criterion. Whatever the primary basis of evaluation, it tends to generalize to other bases, so, for example, something that is useful tends also to seem good, beautiful, and pleasant.

Another component of affective responses is a potency assessment made in terms of physical proportions (large versus small, deep versus shallow), strength (strong versus weak), influence (powerful versus powerless), or other criteria. Again, judgments on the basis of one criterion tend to generalize to other criteria, so, for example, a powerful person seems large, deep (in a metaphorical sense), and strong.

The third component of affective responses—an appraisal of activity—may depend on speed (fast versus slow), perceptual stimulation (noisy versus quiet, bright versus dim), age (young versus old), keenness (sharp versus dull), or other criteria. These criteria also generalize to some degree so, for example, a young person often seems metaphorically fast, noisy, bright, and sharp.

The evaluation, potency, and activity (EPA) structure in subjective responses is one of the best-documented facts in social science, and an elaborate technology has developed for measuring EPA responses on "semantic differential scales" (Heise 1969). The scales consist of adjectives separated by a number of check positions. For example, a standard scale has Good–Nice at one end and Bad–Awful at the other end, and intervening positions on the scale allow respondents to record the direction and intensity of their evaluations of a stimulus. The middle rating position on such scales represents neutrality and is coded 0.0. Positions moving outward are labeled "slightly," "quite," "extremely," and "infinitely," and they are coded 1.0, 2.0, 3.0, and 4.3 respectively—positive on the good, potent, and active sides of the scales; and

negative on the bad, impotent, and inactive sides (Heise 1978).

EPA responses tend to be socially shared within a population (Heise 1966, 1999), so a group's average EPA response to an entity indexes the group sentiment about the entity. Group sentiments can be computed from as few as thirty ratings since each rater's transient response originates from a single shared sentiment rather than a separately held position (Romney, Weller, and Batchelder 1986). Sentiments vary across cultures. For example, potent authorities such as an employer are evaluated positively in U.S. and Canadian college populations, but German students evaluate authorities negatively; small children are evaluated positively in Western nations but neutrally in Japan.

IMPRESSION FORMATION

Combinations of cognitive elements bring affective meanings together and create outcome impressions through psychological processes that are complex, subtle, and yet highly predictable (Gollob 1974; Heise 1979; Anderson 1996).

One kind of impression formation amalgamates a personal attribute with a social identity resulting in a sense of how a person is different from similar others (Averett and Heise 1987). For example, among U.S. college students (the population of raters for examples henceforth), someone who is rich is evaluatively neutral, very powerful, and a little on the quiet side. Meanwhile, a professor is fairly good, fairly powerful, and a bit quiet. The notion of a "rich professor" combines these sentiments and yields a different outcome. A rich professor is evaluated somewhat negatively, mainly because the personalized power of wealth generates an uneasiness that is not overcome by esteem for academic status. A rich professor seems very powerful because the average potency of wealth and of professors is high, and the mind adds an extra increment of potency because of the personalized power deriving from wealth. A rich professor seems even quieter than the component statuses because activity connotations do not merely average, they summate to some degree.

The processes that are involved in combining a social identity with a status characteristic like "rich" also are involved in combining a social identity with personal traits. Thus, an authoritarian professor evokes an impression roughly similar to a rich professor since the affective association for authoritarian is similar to that for rich.

Another example involving emotion illustrates additional processes involved in combining personal characteristics with social identities (Heise and Thomas 1989). Being outraged implies that one is feeling quite bad, somewhat potent, and somewhat lively. A child is felt to be quite good, quite impotent, and very active. The combination "outraged child," seems fairly bad, partly because the child is flaunting personalized power deriving from an emotion and partly because the mind discounts customary esteem for a person if there is a personal basis for evaluating the person negatively: The child's negative emotion undercuts the regard one usually has for a child. The child's impotency is reduced because of a bad and potent emotional state. And the child's activity is greater than usual because the activity of the emotion and the activity of the identity combine additively.

The combining of attributions and identities involves somewhat different processes in different domains. For example, North American males and females process attributions in the same way, though both make attributions about females that are more governed by morality considerations than attributions about males (Heise 1999). Meanwhile, Japanese males are socialized to be more concerned than Japanese females with evaluative consistency in attributions and with matching goodness and weakness, so Japanese males process attributions about everything with more concern for morality than do Japanese females (Smith, Matsuno, and Ike 1999).

Events are another basis for impression formation. A social event—an actor behaving on an object or person within some setting—amalgamates EPA impressions of the elements comprising the event and generates a new impression of each element. For example, when an athlete strangles a coach, the athlete seems bad, and the coach seems cowardly because the coach loses both goodness and potency as a result of the event. The complex equations for predicting outcome impressions from input impressions have been found to be similar in different cultures (Heise 1979; Smith-Lovin 1987a; Smith-Lovin 1987b; Smith, Matsuno, and Umino 1994).

To a degree, the character of a behavior diffuses to the actor who performs the behavior. For example, an admired person who engages in a violent act seems less good, more potent, and more active than usual. Impressions of the actor also are influenced by complex interplays between the nature of the behavior and the nature of the object. For example, violence toward an enemy does not stigmatize an actor nearly so much as violence toward a child. That is because bad, forceful behaviors toward bad, potent objects seem justified while such behaviors toward good, weak objects seem ruthless. Moreover, the degree of justification or of ruthlessness depends on how good the actor was in the first place; for example, a person who acts violently toward a child loses more respect if initially esteemed than if already stigmatized.

Similarly, diffusions of feeling from one event element to another and complex interplays between event elements generate impressions of behaviors, objects, and settings. The general principle is that initial affective meanings of event elements combine and thereby produce new impressions that reflect the meaning of the event. Those impressions are transient because they, in turn, are the meanings that are transformed by later events.

IMPRESSION MANAGEMENT

Normal events produce transient impressions that match sentiments, whereas events that generate impressions deviating widely from sentiments seem abnormal (Heise and MacKinnon 1987). For example, "a parent assisting a child" creates impressions of parent, child, and assisting that are close to sentiments provided by our culture, and the event seems normal. On the other hand, "a parent harming a child" seems abnormal because the event produces negative impressions of parent and child that are far different than the culturally-given notions that parents and children are good.

According to affect control theory, people manage events so as to match transient impressions with sentiments and thereby maintain normality in their experience. Expressive shaping of events occurs within orderly rational action, and ordinarily the expressive and the rational components of action complement each other because cultural sentiments incite the very events that are required by the logic of social institutions like the family, law, religion, etc.

Having adopted an appropriate identity at a scene and having cast others in complementary identities, a person intuits behaviors that will create normal impressions. For example, if a person in the role of judge is to act on someone who is a proven crook, then she must do something that confirms a judge's power and that confirms the badness of a crook, and behaviors like "convict" and "sentence" produce the right impressions. Fitting behaviors may change in the wake of prior events. For example, a father who is fulfilling his role in a mediocre manner because his child has disobeyed him strives to regain goodness and power by controlling the child or by dramatizing forgiveness. Other people's identities may serve as resources for restoring a compromised identity (Wiggins and Heise 1987); for example, a father shaken by a child's disobedience might recover his poise by supporting and defending mother.

Behaviors that confirm sentiments are the intrinsically motivated behaviors in a situation. Actors sometimes comply to the demands of others and thereby forego intrinsically motivated behaviors. Yet compliance also reflects the basic principle since compliant behavior is normal in one relationship even though it may be abnormal in another relationship. For example, a child acts normally when calling on a playmate though also abnormally if his mother has ordered him not to do so and he disobeys her. The actor maintains the relationship that is most salient.

Sometimes other people produce events that do not confirm sentiments evoked by one's own definition of a situation. Affect control theory suggests several routes for restoring consistency between impressions and sentiments in such cases. First, people may try to reinterpret other's actions so as to optimize expressive coherence. For example, an actor's movement away from another person can be viewed as departing, leaving, escaping, fleeing, deserting—and one chooses the interpretation that seems most normal, given participants' identities and prior events (Heise 1979). Of course, interpretations of a behavior are bound by determinable facts about the behavior and its consequences, so some behaviors cannot be interpreted in a way that completely normalizes an event.

Another response to disturbing events is construction of new events that transform abnormal impressions back to normality. Restorative events with the self as actor might be feasible and enacted, as in the example of a father controlling a disobedient child. Restorative events that require others to act might be elicited by suggesting what the other should do. For example, after a child has disobeyed his mother, a father might tell the child to apologize.

Intractable disturbances in interaction that cannot be handled by reinterpreting others' actions or by instigating new events lead to changes in how people are viewed, such as attributing character traits to people in order to form complex identities that account for participation in certain kinds of anomalous events. For example, a father who has ignored his child might be viewed as an inconsiderate person.

Changing base identities also can produce the kind of person who would participate in certain events. For example, an employee cheating an employer would be expressively coherent were the employee known to be a lawbreaker, and a cheating incident may instigate legal actions that apply a lawbreaker label and that withdraw the employee identity. The criminal justice system changes actors in deviant events into the kinds of people who routinely engage in deviant actions, thereby allowing the rest of us to feel that we understand why bad things happen.

Trait attributions and labels that normalize particular incidents are added to conceptions of people, and thereafter the special identities may be invoked in order to set expectations for a person's behavior in other scenes or to understand other incidents. Everyone who interacts with a person builds up knowledge about the person's capacities in this way, and a person builds up knowledge about the self in this way as well.

EMOTION

Affect control theory is a central framework in the sociology of emotions (Thoits 1989; Smith-Lovin 1994), and its predictions about emotions in various situations match well with the predictions of real people who imagine themselves in those situations (Heise and Weir 1999). According to affect control theory, spontaneous emotion reflects the state a person has reached as a result of events and also how that state compares to the ideal experience of a person with a particular social identity. For example, if events make a person seem neutral on goodness, potency, and activity, then the tendency is to feel emotionally neutral, but someone in the sweetheart role ends up feeling blue because he or she is experiencing so much less than one expects in a romantic relationship.

Because emotions reflect the impressions that events have generated, they are a way of directly sensing the consequences of social interaction. Because emotions simultaneously reflect what kinds of identities people are taking, emotions also are a way of sensing the operative social structure in a situation. Moreover, because displays of emotion broadcast a person's subjective appraisals to others, emotions contribute to intersubjective sharing of views about social matters.

People sometimes mask their emotions or display emotions other than those that they feel spontaneously in order to hide their appraisal of events from others or to conceal personal definitions of a situation. For example, an actor caught in misconduct might display guilt and remorse beyond what is felt in order to convince others that he believes his behavior is wrong and that he is not the type who engages in such activity. Such a display of negative emotion after a deviant act makes the actor less vulnerable to a deviant label—an hypothesis derived from the mathematics of affect control theory (Heise 1989).

APPLICATIONS

Affect control theory provides a comprehensive social-psychological framework relating to roles, impression formation, behavior, emotion, attribution, labeling, and other issues (Stryker and Statham 1985). Consequently it is applicable to a variety of social-psychological problems. For example:

- Smith-Lovin and Douglass (1992) showed that sentiments about relevant identities and behaviors are positive in a deviant subculture, and therefore subcultural interactions are happier than outsiders believe.

- MacKinnon and Langford (1994) found that moral evaluations determine the prestige of occupations with low and middle but not high levels of education and income; and they found that income affects occupational prestige partly by adjusting feelings about the potency of the occupation.

- Robinson and Smith-Lovin (1992) found that people with low self-esteem prefer to associate with their critics rather than their flatterers. Robinson (1996) showed that networks can emerge from self-identities, with cliques reflecting differing levels of self-esteem, and dominance structures reflecting differing levels of self-potency.

- Francis (1997a, 1997b) showed that therapists often promote emotional healing by embedding clients in a social structure where key identities have particular EPA profiles; the identities are associated with different functions in different therapeutic ideologies.

- Studies of courtroom scenarios (Robinson, Smith-Lovin, and Tsoudis 1994; Tsoudis and Smith-Lovin 1998) showed that people (such as jurors) deal more leniently with convicted criminals who show remorse and guilt over their crimes, as predicted by affect control theory. In a related study, Scher and Heise (1993) suggested that perceptions of injustice follow justice-related emotions of anger or guilt, so social interactional structures that keep people happy can prevent mobilization regarding unjust reward structures.

- Heise (1998) suggested that solidarity comes easier when a group identity is good, potent, and lively so that group members engage in helpful actions with each other and experience emotions in parallel. Britt and Heise (forthcoming) showed that successful social movements instigate a sequence of member emotions, culminating in pride, which reflect a good, potent, and lively group identity.

Affect control theory's mathematical model is implemented in a computer program that simulates social interactions and predicts the emotions and interpretations of interactants during expected or unexpected interpersonal events. Simulations can be conducted with EPA measurements obtained in a variety of nations—Northern Ireland, Canada, Germany, Japan, and the United States. The computer program, the datasets, and other materials are available at the affect control theory web site at: www.indiana.edu/~socpsy/ACT.

CONCLUSION

Goffman (1967, p. 9) called attention to the expressive order in social relations:

By entering a situation in which he is given a face to maintain, a person takes on the responsibility of standing guard over the flow of events as they pass before him. He must ensure that a particular expressive order is sustained—an order that regulates the flow of events, large or small, so that anything that appears to be expressed by them will be consistent with his face.

Affect control theory's empirically based mathematical model offers a rich and productive foundation for studying the expressive order.

REFERENCES

Anderson, Norman H. 1996 *A Functional Theory of Cognition*. New York: Lawrence Erlbaum.

Averett, C. P., and D. R. Heise 1987 "Modified Social Identities: Amalgamations, Attributions, and Emotions." *Journal of Mathematical Sociology* 13:103–132.

Britt, Lory, and D. Heise (Forthcoming) "From Shame to Pride in Identity Politics." Forthcoming. In Sheldon Stryker, Tim Owens, and Robert White, eds., *Self Identity, and Social Movements.*

Francis, Linda 1997a "Ideology and interpersonal Emotion Management: Redefining identity in Two Support Groups." *Social Psychology Quarterly* 60:153–171.

——1997b "Emotion, Coping, and Therapeutic Ideologies." *Social Perspectives on Emotion* 4:71–101.

Goffman, Erving 1967 *Interaction Ritual: Essays on Face-to-Face Behavior*. Garden City, N.Y.: Anchor Books.

Gollob, Harry F. 1974 "A Subject-Verb-Object approach to social cognition." *Psychological Review* 81:286–321.

Heise, David R. 1966 "Social Status, Attitudes, and Word Connotations." *Sociological Inquiry* 36:227–239.

——1969 "Some Methodological Issues in Semantic Differential Research." *Psychological Bulletin* 72:406–422.

——1979 *Understanding Events: Affect and the Construction of Social Action*. New York: Cambridge University Press.

——1989 "Effects of Emotion Displays on Social Identification." *Social Psychology Quarterly* 52:10–21.

——1998 "Conditions for Empathic Solidarity." In Patrick Doreian and Thomas Fararo, eds., *The Problem of Solidarity: Theories and Models*, 197–211 Amsterdam: Gordon and Breach.

——1999 "Controlling Affective Experience Interpersonally." *Social Psychology Quarterly*. Forthcoming.

——, and Neil MacKinnon 1987 "Affective Bases of Likelihood Judgments." *Journal of Mathematical Sociology* 13:133–151.

——, and Lisa Thomas 1989 "Predicting Impressions Created by Combinations of Emotion and Social Identity." *Social Psychology Quarterly* 52:141–148.

——, and Brian Weir 1999 "A Test of Symbolic Interactionist Predictions About Emotions in Imagined Situations." *Symbolic Interaction*. Forthcoming.

MacKinnon, Neil J. 1994 *Symbolic Interactionism as Affect Control*. Albany, N.Y.: SUNY Press.

——, and Tom Langford 1994 "The Meaning of Occupational Prestige Scores: A Social Psychological Analysis and Interpretation." *Sociological Quarterly* 35:215–245.

Osgood, C. H., W. H. May, and M. S. Miron 1975 *Cross-Cultural Universals of Affective Meaning*. Urbana: University of Illinois Press.

Robinson, Dawn T. 1996 "Identity and friendship: Affective Dynamics and Network Formation." *Advances in Group Process* 13:91–111.

——, and Lynn Smith-Lovin 1992 "Selective Interaction as a Strategy for Identity Maintenance: An Affect Control Model." *Social Psychology Quarterly* 55:12–28.

——, Lynn Smith-Lovin, and Olga Tsoudis 1994 "Heinous Crime or Unfortunate Accident? The Effects of Remorse on Responses to Mock Criminal Confessions." *Social Forces* 73:175–190.

Romney, A. Kimball, Susan C. Weller, and William H. Batchelder 1986 "Culture as Consensus: A Theory of Culture and Informant Accuracy." *American Anthropologist* 88:313–338.

Scher, Steven J., and D. R. Heise 1993 "Affect and the Perception of Injustice." *Advances in Group Process* 10:223–252.

Smith, Herman W., Takanori Matsuno, and Michio Umino 1994 "How Similar are Impression-Formation Processes among Japanese and Americans?" *Social Psychology Quarterly* 57:124–139.

Smith, Herman W., Takanori Matsuno, and Shuuichirou Ike 1999 "The Social Construction of Japanese and American Attributional Expectations." St. Louis University of Missouri Press.

Smith-Lovin, Lynn 1987a "Impressions from Events." *Journal of Mathematical Sociology* 13:35–70.

——1987b "The Affective Control of Events within Settings." *Journal of Mathematical Sociology* 13:71–101.

——1994 "The Sociology of Affect and Emotion." In K. Cook, G. Fine, and J. House, eds., *Sociological Perspectives on Social Psychology*. New York: Allyn and Bacon.

——, and D. R. Heise 1988 *Analyzing Social Interaction: Advances in Affect Control Theory*. New York: Gordon and Breach.

——, and William Douglass 1992 "An Affect-Control Analysis of Two Religious Groups." In V. Gecas and D. Franks, eds., *Social Perspectives on Emotion*, vol. 1. Greenwich, Conn.: JAI Press.

Stryker, S., and A. Statham 1985 "Symbolic Interaction and Role Theory." In G. Lindzey and E. Aronson, eds., *Handbook of Social Psychology*, vol.1, 3rd ed. New York: Random House.

Thoits, P. A. 1989 "The Sociology of Emotions." *Annual Review of Sociology* 15:317–342.

Tsoudis, Olga, and Lynn Smith-Lovin 1998 "How Bad Was It? The Effects of Victim and Perpetrator Emotion on Responses to Criminal Court Vignettes." *Social Forces* 77:695–722.

Wiggins, Beverly, and D. R. Heise 1987 "Expectations, Intentions, and Behavior: Some tests of Affect Control Theory." *Journal of Mathematical Sociology* 13:153–169.

DAVID R. HEISE

AFFIRMATIVE ACTION

The term *affirmative action* has been used in the United States since the late 1960s to refer to policies that go beyond the simple prohibition of discrimination on grounds of race, national origin, and sex in employment practices and educational programs. These policies require some further action, "affirmative action," to make jobs and promotions and admissions to educational programs available to individuals from groups that have historically suffered from discrimination in gaining these opportunities or are, whether discriminated against or not by formal policies and informal practices, infrequently found in certain occupations or educational institutions and programs.

Affirmative action policies may be policies of governments or governmental units, affecting their own procedures in employment or in granting contracts; or they may be policies of governments, affecting the employment procedures of companies or nonprofit agencies and organizations over whom the governments have power or with whom they deal; or they may be the policies of profit and nonprofit employers, adopted voluntarily or under varying degrees of public or private pressure. Affirmative action policies may include the policies of philanthropic foundations, when they affect the employment policies of their grantees, or educational accrediting agencies, when they affect the employment or admissions policies of the institutions they accredit.

The range of policies that can be called affirmative action is wide, but the term also has a specific legal meaning. It was first used in a legal context in the United States in an executive order of President John F. Kennedy. Subsequent presidential executive orders and other administrative requirements have expanded its scope and meaning, and since 1971 affirmative action so defined has set employment practice standards for contractors of the United States, that is, companies, colleges, universities, hospitals, or other institutions that have business with the U.S. government. These standards are enforced by an office of the Department of Labor, the Office of Federal Contract Compliance Programs. Because of the wide sweep of the executive order and its reach into the employment practices of almost every large employer, affirmative action policies have become extremely controversial.

Affirmative action, under other names, is also to be found in other countries to help groups, whether majority or minority, that have not fared as well as others in gaining employment in higher status occupations or admissions to advanced educational programs.

Affirmative action has been controversial because it appears to contradict a central objective of traditional liberalism and the U.S. civil rights movement, that is, the treatment of individuals on the basis of their individual talents and not on the basis of their color, race, national origin, or sex. Affirmative action, as it has developed, requires surveys by employers of the race, national origin, and sex of their employees to uncover patterns of "underutilization" and to develop programs to overcome this underutilization and thus to take account of the race, national origin, and sex of applicants for employment and of candidates for promotion. To many advocates of expanded civil rights, this is seen as only the next and a most necessary step in achieving equality for groups that have in the past faced discrimination. To others, who may also deem themselves advocates of civil rights and of the interests of minority groups, affirmative action, in the form in which it has developed, is seen as a violation of the first requirement for a society that promises equal opportunity, that is, to treat individuals as individuals independent of race, national origin, or sex.

This apparent contradiction between civil rights and affirmative action may be glimpsed in the very language of the Civil Rights Act of 1964, the central piece of legislation that banned discrimination in government programs, public facilities, and employment. In the debate over that act, fears were expressed that the prohibition of discrimination in employment, as codified in Title VII, would be implemented by requiring certain numbers of employees to be of a given race. This fear was dealt with by placing language in the act that was understood at the time specifically to forbid the practices that are required under affirmative action since the late 1960s and early 1970s. Title 703 (j) reads:

> *Nothing contained in this title shall be interpreted to require any employer . . . to grant preferential treatment to any individual or to any group because of the race, color, religion, sex, or national origin of such individual or group on account of an imbalance which may exist with respect to the total number or percentage of persons of any race, color, religion, sex, or national origin employed by any employer.*

However, federal executive orders governing how the federal government does its business may set their own standards, independent of statutory law. The first executive order using the term *affirmative action* was issued by President John F. Kennedy in 1961. It created a President's Committee on Equal Employment Opportunity to monitor the obligations contractors undertook to extend affirmative action. At this time, the general understanding of affirmative action was that it

required such things as giving public notice that the employer did not discriminate, making the availability of positions and promotions widely known, advertising in minority media, and the like. With the Civil Rights Act of 1964—which not only prohibited discrimination on grounds of race, color, and national origin but also on grounds of sex—a new executive order, no. 11,246, was formulated by President Lyndon B. Johnson and came into effect. It replaced the President's Committee on Equal Employment Opportunity with an Office of Federal Contract Compliance Programs (which still operates). Subsequent federal regulations of the late 1960s and early 1970s specified what was meant by affirmative action in the executive order, and the meaning of affirmative action was considerably expanded into the full-fledged program that has existed since 1971. Revised order no. 4 of that year, which is part of the *Code of Federal Regulations* and is still in effect, reads in part:

> *An affirmative action program is a set of specific and result-oriented procedures to which a contractor commits itself to apply every good effort. The objective of those procedures plus such efforts is equal employment opportunity. Procedures without efforts to make them work are meaningless; and effort, undirected by specific and meaningful procedures, is inadequate. An effective affirmative action program must include an analysis of areas within which the contractor is deficient in the utilization of minority groups and women, and further, goals and timetables to which the contractor's good faith efforts must be directed to correct the deficiencies and, [sic] thus to achieve prompt and full utilization of minorities and women, at all levels and in all segments of its work force where deficiencies exist.* (Code of Federal Regulations 1990, pp. 121–122)

Much of the controversy over affirmative action is over the term *goals and timetables*: Are these "quotas"? Supporters of affirmative action say not—only good faith efforts are required, and if they fail the contractor is not penalized. Further controversy exists over the term *utilization*: What is the basis on which a group is found "underutilized," and to what extent is this evidence of discrimination? Similarly, there is considerable dispute over how to label these programs. "Affirmative action" has a positive air, and in public opinion polls will receive considerable support. Label the same programs "racial preference"—which indeed is specifically what they are—and public support drops radically. In the 1990s, as campaigns were launched to ban affirmative action programs by popular referendum, just what language could or should be used in these referenda became hotly disputed.

Controversy also arises over the categories of employees that contractors must report on and over whose utilization they must be concerned. The executive order lists four categories: blacks, Spanish-surnamed Americans, American Indians, and Orientals. (These are the terms in the order as of 1971 and are still used in the *Code of Federal Regulations*.) The preferred names of these groups have changed since then to Afro- or African Americans, Hispanics or Latinos, Native Americans, and Asians. While the original executive order and the Civil Rights Act was a response to the political action of black civil rights groups, and it was the plight of blacks that motivated both the executive order and the Civil Rights Act, it was apparently deemed unwise in the mid-1960s to limit affirmative action requirements to blacks alone. The Civil Rights Act bans discrimination against any person on grounds of race, national origin, and sex and specifies no group in particular for protection; but the Equal Employment Opportunity Commission, set up by the Civil Rights Act to monitor discrimination in employment, from the beginning required reports on the four groups listed above, despite the fact that even in the 1960s it could be argued that discrimination against Asians was far less acute and much less of a problem than discrimination against blacks, that discrimination against American Indians also differed in severity and character from discrimination against blacks, and that discrimination against Spanish-surnamed Americans ranged from the nonexistent or hardly existent (Spaniards from Spain? Cubans? Sephardic Jews?) to the possibly significant. Nevertheless, these four categories set up in the mid-1960s are still the groups that governmental programs of affirmative action target for special attention (Glazer 1987).

Since affirmative action is a governmental program operated by government agencies that grant contracts and is overseen by the Office of Federal Contract Compliance Programs, one major issue of controversy has been over the degree to which these programs are really enforced. It is generally believed that enforcement is more severe under Democratic administrations than under Republican administrations, even though the program was first fully developed under the Republican administration of President Richard Nixon. President Ronald Reagan was an avowed opponent of affirmative action, but despite his eight-year administration no modification of the program took place. Changes were proposed by some parts of the Republican administration but opposed by others. Business, in particular big business, had learned to live with affirmative action and was not eager to upset the apple cart (Belz 1990).

One of the most controversial areas in which affirmative action is applied is in the employment and promotion of police, firefighting and sanitation personnel, and teachers and other local government employees. Here strict racial quotas often do apply. They are strongly resented by many employees when new employees are hired by race and even more when promotions are given out by race and layoffs are determined by race. The basis of these quotas is not the presidential executive order but rather consent decrees entered into by local government on the basis of charges of discrimination brought by the federal government. These charges are brought on the basis of the Civil Rights Act; under this act, if discrimination is found, quotas can be required by courts as a remedy. Since local government employment is generally on the basis of tests, one very controversial aspect of such cases is the role of civil service examinations. Blacks and Hispanics characteristically do worse than white applicants. Are these poorer results to be taken as evidence of discrimination? A complex body of law has been built up on the basis of various cases determining when a test should be considered discriminatory. In the Civil Rights Act of 1964, one provision read "it shall not be an unlawful employment practice . . . for an employer to give and act upon the results of any professionally developed ability test provided that such test . . . is not designed, intended, or used to discriminate." But the courts decide whether the test is "designed, intended, or used to discriminate." Because of the frequency with which courts have found tests for the police, fire, or sanitation force discriminatory, and because state and local governments believe they will lose such cases, many have entered into "consent decrees" in which they agree to hire and promote on the basis of racial and sex criteria.

Affirmative action is also used in the granting of government contracts on the basis of either statutes (federal, state, or local) or administrative procedures. It is in this area that the edifice of affirmative action was first effectively attacked in the 1980s and 1990s, in the wake of the failure of Republican administrations to take any action limiting affirmative action. The first major crack came in the U.S. Supreme Court's decision in *City of Richmond v. Croson*, in which the Court ruled against a Richmond, Virginia, city program to set aside 30 percent of city contracts for minority-owned businesses. The Court ruled that such programs could only stand, under the judicial "strict scrutiny" standard triggered by apparent government discrimination, if it could be demonstrated there had been discrimination against these groups by the city in the past. The response of cities to this judicial limitation on their minority "set-aside" programs was often to commission studies to demonstrate they had indeed discriminated, in order to save the set-aside programs (LaNoue 1993). In a later decision, *Adarand v. Pena* (1995), the Court ruled against a federal statute requiring that 10 percent of public works contracts be set aside for minorities. While these programs still continue in many jurisdictions, including the federal government, they are all legally threatened.

One issue in minority contract set-asides has been that of possible fraud, as various contractors find it to their advantage to take on black partners so as to present themselves as minority contractors and thus to get whatever advantages in bidding that status provides. In this area, as in other areas where advantage might follow from minority status, there have been debates over what groups may be included as minorities. It was unclear, for example, whether Asian Indians—immigrants and American citizens of Indian origin—were to be considered Asian. Asian Indian Americans were divided among themselves on this question, but during the Reagan administration they were reclassified as Asian, presumably in part for the modest political advantage this gave the Republican administration.

Affirmative action also governs the employment practices of colleges and universities, whether public or private, because they all make use of federal grants and loans for their students, and many have government research contracts. Colleges and universities therefore must also survey their faculties and other staffs for underutilization, and they develop elaborate affirmative action programs. Affirmative action applies to women as well as to racial and ethnic minority groups. There has been, perhaps in part because of affirmative action programs, a substantial increase in female faculty. But there has been little increase in black faculty during the 1980s. The numbers of blacks taking doctorates in arts and sciences has been small and has not increased. The higher rewards of law, business, and medicine have attracted into those fields black students who could prepare themselves for an academic career. Many campuses have been shaken by controversies over the small number of black faculty, with administrators arguing that few were available and protestors, often black students, arguing that greater effort would change the situation.

In the 1990s, the most controversial area of affirmative action became admissions to selective colleges and universities and professional schools. Affirmative action in admissions is not required by government regulations, as in the case of employment, except in the special case of southern public higher education institutions. There parallel and separate black and white institutions existed, and while all of these institutions have been open to both white and black students since at least the early 1970s, an extended lawsuit has charged that they still preserve their identity as traditionally black and traditionally white institutions. As a result of this litigation, many of these institutions must recruit a certain number of black students. But the major pressure on many other institutions to increase the number of black students has come from goals voluntarily accepted by administrators or as a result of black student demands. (In one case, that of the University of California, the state legislature has called on the institution to mirror in its racial-ethnic composition the graduating classes of California high schools.) Voluntary affirmative action programs for admission of students, targeted on black, Hispanic, and Native American students, became widespread in the late

1960s and early 1970s, particularly after the assassination of Martin Luther King.

The first affirmative action cases to reach the Supreme Court challenged such programs of preference for black and other minority students. A rejected Jewish applicant for admission to the University of Washington Law School, which had set a quota to increase the number of its minority students, sued for admission, and his case reached the Supreme Court. It did not rule on it. The Court did rule on a subsequent case, in 1978, that of Allan Bakke, a rejected applicant to the University of California, Davis, Medical School, which also had set a quota. The Court, splitting into a number of factions, rejected fixed numerical quotas but asserted race was a factor that could be taken into account in admissions decisions for purposes of promoting academic diversity. Under the protection offered by this complex decision, most colleges and universities and professional schools do grant preferences to black and Hispanic students. Asian Americans, also considered a minority, did not receive preference, but this was hardly necessary since their academic achievement is high. Indeed, by the 1980s, Asian American students were protesting that it was more difficult for them than whites to gain admission to selective institutions (Bunzel and Au 1987).

Matters turned around in the mid-1990s. In 1995, the regents of the University of California banned any consideration of race or ethnicity in admission to the university. In 1996 the voters of California approved the California Civil Rights Initiative, which banned the use of race or ethnic criteria in state government action, in employment and contracts as well as college admissions. This initiative, launched by one academic and one former academic, became the basis of a movement to extend the ban on affirmative action. In 1998 the State of Washington became the second state to pass such an initiative. In Texas, the assault on affirmative action in admissions led to a wide-ranging decision by the Fifth Circuit Court of Appeals in 1996 banning the use of race and ethnicity in admissions to the University of Texas Law School. This decision affects all institutions of higher education in the states covered by the fifth Circuit. Massive changes have followed in the admissions procedures of the University of California, the peak institution in the system of public

higher education in California, and the University of Texas, which holds a similar position in Texas.

Initially, there were substantial drops in enrollment of black and Hispanic students, but energetic action by the university administrations has stemmed this fall-off, and the decline statistically is not as drastic as originally projected or feared. The commitment by university administrators to maintain a substantial representation of black and Hispanic students is so strong that they have devised new admissions practices and procedures designed to keep the number up, and have had some success in doing so. Further, the Texas legislature has voted that the top 10 percent of every high school graduating class be eligible for admission to the University of Texas, and the Board of Regents of the University of California has similarly voted that the top 4 percent of California high school graduating classes should be eligible for enrollment in the University of California. The effect of such actions, in view of the high concentration of black and Hispanic students in low-achieving high schools, which ordinarily send few students to the selective state institutions, is to keep up the number of black and Hispanic students.

Affirmative action in admissions has become perhaps the best-researched area of affirmative action as a result of these controversies. An important study by William Bowen and Derek Bok of admissions procedures in selective institutions has argued effectively that "race-sensitive" admissions have been good for the students, good for the institutions, and good for the country. Their conclusions, however, have been sharply disputed by critics of affirmative action. (Bowen and Bok 1998; Trow 1999). At this writing (Fall, 1999) the Supreme Court has not yet ruled on the issue of the degree to which public colleges and universities may take race into account. In view of the fact that neither Congress nor state legislatures will take decisive action on race preference owing to the political sensitivity of the issue, it is clear the key decisions in this area will have to be taken by the Supreme Court. It is possible that the age of affirmative action in American race relations and race policy is coming to an end.

Affirmative action has been a divisive issue in American political life and has sometimes been raised effectively in political campaigns. It has divided former allies on civil rights issues, in particular American Jews, normally liberal, from blacks. Jews oppose quotas in admissions to medical and law schools because they were in the past victims of very low quotas imposed by American universities.

Affirmative action under various names and legal arrangements is found in many countries: in India, to provide opportunities to scheduled castes, scheduled tribes, and other backward classes, where different requirements operate at the national level and within the states and where some degree of preference has existed in some areas and for some purposes as far back as the 1920s (Galanter 1984); in Malaysia, to protect the native Malay population; in Sri Lanka, to benefit the majority Sri Lankan population (Sowell 1990); and in Australia and Canada, where milder forms of affirmative action than those found in the United States operate. It is now being raised in the countries of Western Europe, which have received since World War II large numbers of immigrants who now form distinctive communities who lag behind the native populations in education and occupational status. The policies called affirmative action in the United States are called "reservations" in India, and "positive discrimination" in some other countries.

There is considerable debate as to the effects of affirmative action policies and how weighty these can be as against other factors affecting employment, promotion, and educational achievement (Leonard 1984a; 1984b). A summary judgment is difficult to make. Black leaders generally consider affirmative action an essential foundation for black progress, but some black intellectuals and publicists have been skeptical. Black leaders often denounce opponents of affirmative action as racists, hidden or otherwise, yet it is clear that many opponents simply find the use, required or otherwise, of racial and sexual characteristics to determine job and promotion opportunities and admission to selective college programs in contradiction with the basic liberal principles of treating individuals without regard to race, national origin, color, and sex. Affirmative action has undoubtedly increased the number of blacks who hold good jobs and gain admission to selective programs. But it has also had other costs in the form of increased racial tensions. It has coincided with a period in which a pattern of black advancement occupationally and educationally since World War II has been surprisingly slowed. The defenders of affirmative action argue that this is because it has not yet been applied vigorously enough. The opponents argue that the concentration on affirmative action encourages the neglect of the key factors that promote educational and occupational progress, which are basically the acquisition of qualifications for better jobs and superior educational programs.(SEE ALSO: Discrimination; Equality of Opportunity)

REFERENCES

Belz, Herman 1990 *Equality Transformed: A Quarter-Century of Affirmative Action*. New Brunswick, N.J.: Transaction Books.

Bowen, William G., and Derek Bok 1990 *The Shape of the River: Long-term Consequences of Considering Race in College and University Admissions*. Princeton, N.J.: Princeton University Press.

Bunzel, John H., and Jeffrey K. D. Au 1987 "Diversity or Discrimination? Asian Americans in College." *The Public Interest* 87:49–62.

Code of Federal Regulations 1990 Title 41, section 60-2.10, pp. 121–122.

Galanter, Marc 1984 *Competing Equalities: Law and the Backward Classes in India*. Berkeley: University of California Press.

Glazer, Nathan 1987 *Affirmative Discrimination: Ethnic Inequality and Public Policy*. Cambridge, Mass.: Harvard University Press. (Originally published 1975 and 1978, New York: Basic Books.)

LaNoue, George R. 1993 "Social Science and Minority Set-Asides."*The Public Interest* 110:49–62.

Leonard, Jonathan 1984a "The Impact of Affirmative Action on Employment." Working Paper No. 1,310. Cambridge, Mass.: National Bureau of Economic Research.

——1984b "What Promises Are Worth: The Impact of Affirmative Action Goals." Working Paper no.1,346. Cambridge, Mass.: National Bureau of Economic Research. (Also published in *Journal of Human Resources* (1985) 20:3–20.)

McWhirter, Darien A. 1996 *The End of Affirmative Action: Where Do We Go From Here?* New York: Birch Lane Press.

Orfield, Gary, and Edward Miller (eds.) 1998 *Chilling Admissions: The Affirmative Action Crisis and the Search for Alternatives*. Cambridge, Mass.: Harvard Education Publishing Group.

Skrentny, John David 1996 *The Ironies of Affirmative Action*. Chicago: University of Chicago Press.

Sowell, Thomas 1990 *Preferential Policies: An International Perspective.* New York: William Morrow.

Trow, Martin 1999 "California After Racial Preferences." *The Public Interest* 135:64–85.

NATHAN GLAZER

AFRICAN-AMERICAN STUDIES

Research on African Americans covers many important areas, only a few of which will be discussed here: theories of white-black relations; the enslavement of African Americans; the development of an antiblack ideology; the creation of white wealth with black labor; the idea of whiteness; racial discrimination today; and possibilities for social change.

THEORIES OF WHITE-BLACK RELATIONS

Explanatory theories of U.S. racial relations can be roughly classified into *order-deficit theories* and *power-conflict theories.* Order-deficit theories accent the gradual inclusion and assimilation of an outgroup such as African Americans into the dominant society and emphasize the barriers to progress that lie within the outgroup. Power-conflict theories, in contrast, emphasize past and present structural barriers preventing the full integration of African Americans into the society's institutions, such as the huge power and resource imbalance between white and black Americans. They also raise larger questions about the society's historically racist foundations.

Milton Gordon (1964) is an order-deficit scholar who distinguishes several types of initial encounters between racial and ethnic groups and an array of subsequent assimilation outcomes ranging from acculturation to intermarriage. In his view the trend of immigrant adaptation in the United States has been in the direction of substantial conformity—of immigrants giving up much of their heritage for the Anglo-Protestant core culture. Gordon and other scholars apply this scheme to African Americans, whom they see as substantially assimilated at the cultural level (for example, in regard to language), with some cultural differences remaining because of "lower class subculture" among black Americans. This order-deficit model and the accent on defects in culture have been popular among many contemporary analysts who often seek to downplay discrimination and accent instead problems internal to black Americans or their communities. For example, Jim Sleeper (1990) has argued that there is no institutionalized racism of consequence left in United States. Instead, he adopts cultural explanations—for example, blacks need to work harder—for present-day difficulties in black communities.

In contrast, power-conflict analysts reject the assimilationist view of black inclusion and eventual assimilation and the inclination to focus on deficits within African-American individuals or communities as the major barriers to racial integration. From this perspective, the current condition of African Americans is more oppressive than that of any other U.S. racial or ethnic group because of its roots in centuries-long enslavement and in the subsequent semislavery of legal segregation, with the consequent low-wage jobs and poor living conditions. Once a system of extreme racial subordination is established historically, those in the superior position in the hierarchy continue to inherit and monopolize disproportionate socioeconomic resources over many generations. One important power-conflict analyst was Oliver C. Cox. His review of history indicated that from the 1500s onward white-on-black oppression in North America arose out of the European imperialistic system with its profit-oriented capitalism. The African slave trade was the European colonists' Away of recruiting labor for the purpose of exploiting the great natural resources of America" (Cox 1948, p. 342). African Americans provided much hard labor to build the new society—first as slaves, then as sharecroppers and tenant farmers, and later as low-wage laborers and service workers in cities.

In the late 1960s civil rights activist Stokely Carmichael (later renamed Kwame Ture) and historian Charles Hamilton (1967) documented contemporary patterns of racial discrimination and contrasted their power-conflict perspective, which accented institutional racism, with an older approach focusing only on individual whites. They were among the first to use the terms "internal colonialism" and "institutional racism" to describe discrimination by whites as a group against African Americans as a group. Adopting a similar power-conflict perspective, sociologist Bob Blauner (1972) argued that there are major differences between black Americans and the white immigrant groups at the center of assimilationist analysis. Africans brought across the ocean became part of an internally subordinated colony; white slaveowners incorporated them against their will. Black labor built up white wealth. European immigrants, in contrast, came more or less voluntarily.

More recently, sociologist Molefi Kete Asante (1988) has broken new ground in the development of a new power-conflict perspective, termed *afrocentricity*, that analyzes the Eurocentric bias in U.S. culture and rejects the use of the concepts such as "ethnicity," "minority," and "ghetto" as antithetical to developing a clear understanding of racism and to building antiracist movements. Similarly, anthropologist Marimba Ani (1994) has shown how from the beginning European colonialism was supported by a well-developed theory of white supremacy, a worldview that attempted to destroy the cultures of other non-European peoples. Yet other analysts (Feagin 2000) have argued for a power-conflict framework that understands white oppression of black Americans—with its racist ideology—as the foundation of U.S. society from the beginning. From this perspective much in the unfolding drama of U.S. history is viewed as a continuing reflection of that foundation of systemic racism.

THE ENSLAVEMENT OF AFRICAN AMERICANS

Research on slavery emphasizes the importance of the power-conflict perspective for understanding the history and conditions of African Americans. Manning Marable (1985, p. 5) demonstrates that before the African slave trade began, Europeans were predisposed to accept slavery. Western intellectuals from Aristotle to Sir Thomas More defended slavery.

Research by sociologists, historians, and legal scholars emphasizes the point that slavery is the foundation of African-American subordination. Legal scholar Patricia Williams has documented the dramatic difference between the conditions faced by enslaved Africans and by European immigrants: "The black slave experience was that of lost languages, cultures, tribal ties, kinship bonds, and even of the power to procreate in the image of oneself and not that of an alien master" (Williams 1987, p. 415). Williams, an African American, discusses Austin Miller, her great-great grandfather, a white lawyer who bought and enslaved her great-great-grandmother, Sophie, and Sophie's parents. Miller forced the thirteen-year-old Sophie to become the mother of Williams's great grandmother Mary. Williams's white great-great grandfather was thus a rapist and child molester. African Americans constitute the only U.S. racial group whose heritage involves the forced mixing of its African ancestors with members of the dominant white group.

Eugene Genovese (1974) has demonstrated that the enslavement of African Americans could produce both servile accommodation and open resistance. Even in the extremely oppressive slave plantations of the United States, many peoples from Africa—Yorubas, Akans, Ibos, and others—came together to create one African-American people. They created a culture of survival and resistance by drawing on African religion and values (Stuckey 1987, pp. 42–46). This oppositional culture provided the foundation for many revolts and conspiracies to revolt among those enslaved, as well as for later protests against oppression.

In all regions many whites were implicated in the slavery system. Northern whites built colonies in part on slave labor or the slave trade. In 1641, Massachusetts was the first colony to make slavery legal; and the state's merchants and shippers played important roles in the slave trade. Not until the 1780s did public opinion and court cases force an end to New England slavery. In 1786 slaves made up 7 percent of the New York population; not until the 1850s were all slaves freed there. Moreover, an intense political and economic subordination of free African Americans followed abolition (Higginbotham 1978, pp. 63–65, 144–149). As Benjamin Ringer (1983, p. 533) puts it, "despite the early emancipation of slaves in the North it remained there, not merely as fossilized remains but as a deeply engrained coding for the future." This explains the extensive system of antiblack discrimination and "Jim Crow" segregation in northern states before the Civil War. Later, freed slaves and their descendants who migrated there from the South came into a socioeconomic system already coded to subordinate African Americans.

THE DEVELOPMENT OF AN ANTIBLACK IDEOLOGY

Truly racist ideologies—with "race" conceptualized in biologically inferiority terms—appear only in modern times. St. Clair Drake (1987) has shown that in the Greek and Roman periods most Europeans attached greater significance to Africans' culture and nationality than to their physical and biological characteristics. Beginning with Portuguese and Spanish imperialism in the fifteenth century, a racist ideology was gradually developed to rationalize the brutal conquest of the lands and labor undertaken in the period of European imperialism (Snowden 1983).

The system of antiblack racism that developed in the Americas is rooted deeply in European and Euro-American consciousness, religion, and culture. Europeans have long viewed themselves, their world, and the exploited "others" within a parochial perspective, one that assumes European culture is superior to all other cultures, which are ripe for exploitation (Ani 1994). For the colonizing Europeans it was not enough to bleed Africa of its labor. A well-developed anti-African, antiblack ideology rationalized this oppression and thus reduced its moral cost for whites. As it developed, this ideology accented not only the alleged physical ugliness and mental inferiority of Africans and African Americans, but also their supposed immorality, family pathologies, and criminality. Notions that African Americans were, as the colonial settlers put it, "dangerous savages" and "degenerate beasts," were apparently an attempt by those who saw themselves as civilized Christians to avoid blame for the carnage they had created. As historian George Frederickson put it, "otherwise many whites would have had to accept an intolerable burden of guilt for perpetrating or tolerating the most horrendous cruelties and injustices" (Frederickson 1971, p. 282).

CREATING WHITE WEALTH WITH BLACK LABOR

In his masterpiece *The Souls of Black* (1903), the pioneering sociologist W. E. B. Du Bois anticipated current research on the significance of African Americans for U.S. prosperity and development:

"Your country. How came it yours? Before the Pilgrims landed we were here. Here we have brought our three gifts and mingled them with yours: a gift of story and song—soft, stirring melody in an ill-harmonized and unmelodious land; the gift of sweat and brawn to beat back the wilderness, conquer the soil, and lay the foundations of this vast economic empire two hundred years earlier than your weak hands could have done it; the third, a gift of the spirit" (Du Bois 1989 [1903], pp. 186–187). The past and present prosperity of the nation is substantially the result of the enforced labor of millions of African Americans under slavery and segregation.

Under common law, an innocent individual who benefits unknowingly from wealth gained illegally or by unjust actions in the past generally cannot, if the ill-gotten gains are discovered, claim a right to keep them (Cross 1984, p. 510; Williams 1991, p. 101). A coerced taking of one's possessions by an individual criminal is similar to the coerced taking of one's labor by a white slaveholder or discriminator. Over centuries great wealth was unjustly created for white families from the labor of those enslaved, as well as from the legal segregation and contemporary racist system that came after slavery.

Some researchers (see America 1990) have examined the wealth that whites have unjustly gained from four hundred years of the exploitation of black labor. Drawing on James Marketti (1990, p. 118), one can estimate the dollar value of the labor taken from enslaved African Americans from 1620 to 1861—together with lost interest from then to the present—as between two and five *trillion* dollars (in current dollars). Adding to this figure the losses to blacks of the labor market discrimination in place from 1929 to 1969 (plus lost interest) would bring the total figure to the four to nine trillion dollar range (see Swinton 1990, p. 156). Moreover, since the end of legal segregation African Americans have suffered more economic losses from continuing discrimination. For more than two decades now the median family income of African-American families has been about 55 to 61 percent of the median family income of white families. Compensating African Americans for the value of the labor stolen would clearly require a very large portion of the nation's current and future wealth. And such calculations do not take into account the many other personal and community costs of slavery, segregation, and modern racism.

Research has shown that for centuries whites have benefited from large-scale government assistance denied to African Americans. These programs included large-scale land grants from the 1600s to the late 1800s, a period when most blacks were ineligible. In the first decades of the twentieth century many government-controlled resources were given away, or made available on reasonable terms, to white Americans. These included airline routes, leases on federal lands, and access to radio and television frequencies. During the 1930s most federal New Deal programs heavily favored white Americans. Perhaps the most important subsidy program benefiting whites was the Federal Housing Administration (FHA) loan insurance that enabled millions of white families to secure homes and accumulate equity later used for education of their children (Sitkoff 1978). During the long segregation period from the 1890s to the late 1960s, black families received much less assistance from government programs and were unable to build up wealth comparable to that of white families.

WHITENESS DEVELOPS IN RELATION TO BLACKNESS

From the beginning of the nation, the ideas of "whiteness" and "blackness" were created by whites as an integral part of the increasingly dominant racist ideology. The first serious research on whiteness was perhaps that of Du Bois (1992 [1935]), who showed how white workers have historically accepted lower monetary wages in return for the *public and psychological wage* of white privilege. In return for not unionizing or organizing with black workers, and thus accepting lower monetary wages, white workers were allowed by employers to participate in a racist hierarchy where whites enforced deference from black Americans. Several social scientists (Roediger 1991; Allen 1994; Brodkin 1998) have shown how nineteenth-century and twentieth-century immigrants from Europe—who did not initially define themselves as "white" but rather as Jewish, Irish, Italian, or other European

identity—were pressured by established elites to view themselves and their own groups as white. Racial privileges were provided for new European immigrants as they aligned themselves with the native-born dominant Anglo-American whites and actively participated in antiblack discrimination.

Today, whites still use numerous myths and stereotypes to defend white privilege (Frankenberg 1993; Feagin and Vera 1995). Such fictions often describe whites as "not racist" or as "good people" even as the same whites take part in discriminatory actions (for example, in housing or employment) or express racist ideas. In most cases, the positive white identity is constructed against a negative view of black Americans.

RACIAL DISCRIMINATION TODAY

Racial discrimination involves the practices of dominant group members that target those in subordinate groups for harm. Discrimination maintains white wealth and privilege. A National Research Council report noted that by the mid-1970s many white Americans believed "the Civil Rights Act of 1964 had led to broad-scale elimination of discrimination against African Americans in public accommodations" (Jaynes and Williams 1989, p. 84). However, social science research still finds much racial discrimination in housing, employment, education, and public accommodations.

Many scholars accent current black economic progress. In the 1980s and 1990s the number of black professional, technical, managerial, and administrative workers has increased significantly. Yet African Americans in these categories have been disproportionately concentrated in those jobs with lower status. Within the professional-technical category, African Americans today are most commonly found in such fields as social and recreational work, public school teaching, vocational counseling, personnel, dietetics, and health-care work; they are least often found among lawyers and judges, dentists, writers and artists, engineers, and university teachers. Within the managerial-administrative category African Americans are most commonly found among restaurant and bar managers, health administrators, and government officials; they are least commonly found among top corporate executives, bank and financial managers, and wholesale sales managers. Such patterns of job channeling indicate the effects of intentional and indirect racial discrimination over several centuries.

Studies have shown that housing segregation remains very high in U.S. metropolitan areas, North and South. This is true for both low-income and middle-income African Americans. Change in residential balkanization has come very slowly. Census data indicate that from 1980 to 1990 there were only small decreases in the level of residential segregation in thirty major U.S. metropolitan areas; fewer changes than for the previous decade. Two-thirds of the black residents of the southern metropolitan areas and more than three-quarters in northern metropolitan areas would have to move from their present residential areas if one wished to create proportional desegregation in housing arrangements in these cities (Massey and Denton 1993, pp. 221–223). U.S. cities remain highly segregated along racial lines.

At all class levels, African Americans still face much discrimination. After conducting pioneering interviews with forty black women in the Netherlands and the United States, social psychologist Philomena Essed (1990) concluded that racial discrimination remains an omnipresent problem in both nations. She showed that black accounts of racism are much more than discrete individual accounts, for they also represent systems of knowledge that people collectively accumulate to make sense of the racist society. Research by U.S. social scientists has confirmed and extended these findings. Lois Benjamin (1991), Kesho Y. Scott (1991), and Joe Feagin and Melvin Sikes (1994) conducted in-depth interviews to move beyond the common litany of black underclass pathologies to document the racial discrimination that still provides major barriers to black mobility in U.S. society. These field studies have revealed the everyday character of the racial barriers and the consequent pain faced by blacks at the hands of whites in employment, housing, education, and public accommodations.

Researchers Nancy Krieger and Stephen Sidney (1996) gave about 2,000 black respondents a list of seven settings where there might be discrimination. Seventy percent of the female respondents and 84 percent of the male respondents reported facing discrimination in at least one area.

The majority reported discrimination from whites in at least three settings. Several national surveys as well have found substantial racial discrimination. For example, a 1997 Gallup survey (1997, pp. 29–30, 108–110) inquired of black respondents if they had faced discrimination in five areas (work, dining out, shopping, with police, in public transportation) during the last month. Forty-five percent reported discrimination in one or more of these areas in that short period.

Discrimination for most black Americans entails much more than an occasional discriminatory act, but rather a lifetime of thousands of blatant, covert, and subtle acts of differential treatment by whites—actions that cumulate to have significant monetary, psychological, family, and community effects. African Americans contend against this discrimination in a variety of ways, ranging from repressed rage to open resistance and retaliation (Cobbs 1988). This cumulative and persisting discrimination is a major reason for the periodic resurgence of civil rights organizations and protest movements among African Americans (see Morris 1984).

ANTIBLACK RACISM AND OTHER AMERICANS OF COLOR

During the 1990s numerous researchers from Latino, Asian, and Native-American groups accented their own group's perspective on racial and ethnic relations and their experience with discrimination in the United States. They have often criticized a binary black-white paradigm they feel is dominant in contemporary research and writing about U.S. racial-ethnic relations (see Perea 1997). From this perspective, the binary black-white paradigm should be abandoned because each non-European group has its distinctive experiences of oppression.

However, a few scholars (Feagin 2000; Ani 1994) have shown the need to adopt a broader view of the long history and current realities of U.S. racism. The racist foundation of the nation was laid in the 1600s by European entrepreneurs and settlers as they enslaved Africans and killed or drove off Native Americans. By the middle of the seventeenth century African Americans were treated by whites, and by the legal system, as chattel property—a position held by *no other group* in the four centuries of American history. This bloody article-of-property system created great wealth for whites and was soon rationalized in the aforementioned racist ideology. Ever since, whites have remained in firm control of all major U.S. institutions; they have perpetuated a racist system that is still imbedded in all these institutions.

White-on-black oppression is a comprehensive system originally designed for the exploitation of African Americans, one that for centuries has shaped the lives of every American, regardless of background, national origin, or time of entry. This long-standing white-racist framework has been extended and tailored for each new non-European group brought into the nation. Immigrants from places other than Europe, such as Chinese and Japanese immigrants from the mid-1800s to the 1950s and Mexican immigrants after 1900, were often oppressed for white gain and constructed as racialized inferiors without citizenship rights (Takaki 1990). Other types of white racism have been important in U.S. history, but white-on-black racism is the most central case. While it has changed in some ways as time has passed, this systemic racism has stayed roughly constant in its fundamentals. U.S. society is not a multiplicity of disconnected racisms, but has a central white-racist core that was initially developed by whites as they drove Native Americans off their lands and intensely exploited enslaved African Americans. Scholarship (Takaki 1990; Feagin 2000) has shown how this framework was gradually extended and adapted for the oppression of all other non-European groups.

POSSIBILITIES FOR CHANGE

Some African-American scholars have expressed great pessimism about the possibility of significant racial change in the United States. The constitutional scholar Derrick Bell (1992) argues that racism is so fundamental that white Americans will never entertain giving up privileges and thus that black Americans will never gain equality.

There is a long history of African Americans and other people of color resisting racism. The development of resistance movements in the 1950s and 1960s was rooted in activism in local organizations, including churches, going back for centuries

(Morris 1984). Given these deep and persisting roots, many other analysts, black and nonblack, remain optimistic about the possibility of civil rights action for social change. Thus, legal scholar Lani Guinier (1994) has spelled out new ideas for significantly increasing the electoral and political power of black Americans. While the Voting Rights Act (1965) increased the number of black voters and elected officials, it did not give most of these officials an adequate or substantial influence on political decisions in their communities. Guinier suggests new strategies to increase black influence, including requiring supermajorities (a required number of votes from black officials who are in the minority) on key political bodies when there are attempts to pass major legislation.

Some scholars and activists are now pressing for a two-pronged strategy that accents both a continuing civil rights struggle outside black communities and an internal effort to build up self-help projects within those communities. A leading scholar of civil rights, Roy Brooks (1996), has documented the failures and successes of the traditional desegregation strategy. Though still supportive of integration efforts, Brooks has argued that blacks must consider separatist, internally generated, community development strategies for their long-term economic, physical, and psychological success. Working in the tradition of W. E. B. Du Bois and Malcolm X, numerous African-American scholars and community leaders have reiterated the import of traditional African and African-American values for the liberation of their communities from continuing discrimination and oppression by white Americans.

REFERENCES

Allen, Theodore W. 1994 *The Invention of the White Race: Racial Oppression and Social Control.* London: Verso.

America, Richard F. (ed.) 1990 *The Wealth of Races: The Present Value of Benefits from Past Injustices.* New York: Greenwood Press.

Ani, Marimba 1994 *Yurugu: An African-Centered Critique of European Cultural Thought and Behavior.* Trenton, N.J.: Africa World Press.

Asante, Molefi Kete 1988 *Afrocentricity.* Trenton, N.J.: Africa World Press.

Bell, Derrick 1992 *Faces at the Bottom of the Well: The Permanence of Racism.* New York: Basic Books.

Benjamin, Lois 1991 *The Black Elite: Facing the Color Line in the Twilight of the Twentieth Century*. Chicago: Nelson-Hall.

Blauner, Bob 1972 *Racial Oppression in America*. New York: Harper and Row.

Brodkin, Karen 1998 *How The Jews Became White Folks: And What That Says About Race in America*. New Brunswick, N.J.: Rutgers University Press.

Brooks, Roy L. 1996 *Integration or Separation? A Strategy for Racial Equality*. Cambridge, Mass.: Harvard University Press.

Carmichael, Stokely, and Charles Hamilton 1967 *Black Power*. New York: Random House/Vintage Books.

Cross, Theodore 1984 *Black Power Imperative: Racial Inequality and the Politics of Nonviolence*. New York: Faulkner.

Drake, St. Clair 1987 *Black Folk Here and There*. Los Angeles: UCLA Center for Afro-American Studies.

Du Bois, William E. B. (1935) 1992 *Black Reconstruction in America: An Essay Toward a History of the Part which Black Folk Played in the Attempt to Reconstruct Democracy in America, 1860–1880*. New York: Atheneum.

—— (1903) 1989 *The Souls of Black Folk*. New York: Bantam Books.

Essed, Philomena 1990 *Everyday Racism: Reports from Women of Two Cultures*. Claremont, Calif.: Hunter House.

Feagin, Joe R. 2000 *Racist America*. New York: Routledge.

——, and Melvin P. Sikes 1994 *Living with Racism: The Black Middle Class Experience*. Boston: Beacon.

Feagin, Joe R., and Hernan Vera 1995 *White Racism: The Basics*. New York: Routledge.

Frankenberg, Ruth 1993 *White Women, Race Matters: The Social Construction of Whiteness*. Minneapolis: University of Minnesota.

Fredrickson, George M. 1971 *The Black Image in the White Mind: The Debate on Afro-American Character and Destiny, 1817–1914*. Hanover, N.H.: Wesleyan University Press.

Gallup Organization 1997 *Black/White Relations in the United States*. Princeton, N.J.: Gallup Organization.

Gordon, Milton 1964 *Assimilation in American Life*. New York: Oxford University Press.

Guinier, Lani 1994 *The Tyranny of the Majority: Fundamental Fairness in Representative Democracy*. New York: Free Press.

Higginbotham, A. Leon 1978 *In the Matter of Color*. New York: Oxford University Press.

Jaynes, Gerald D., and Robin Williams, Jr. (eds.) 1989 *A Common Destiny: Blacks and American Society*. Washington, D.C.: National Academy Press.

Krieger, Nancy, and Stephen Sidney 1996 "Racial Discrimination and Blood Pressure." *American Journal of Public Health* 86:1370–1378.

Marketti, James 1990 "Estimated Present Value of Income Diverted during Slavery." In Richard F. America, ed., *The Wealth of Races: The Present Value of Benefits from Past Injustices*. New York: Greenwood Press.

Massey, Douglas S., and Nancy A. Denton 1993 *American Apartheid: Segregation and the Making of the Underclass*. Cambridge, Mass.: Harvard University Press.

Morris, Aldon D. 1984. *The Origins of the Civil Rights Movement*. New York: Free Press.

Perea, Juan F. 1997 "The Black/White Binary Paradigm of Race: The 'Normal Science' of American Racial Thought." *California Law Review* 85:1219–1221.

Ringer, Benjamin B. 1983 *"We the People" and Others*. New York: Tavistock.

Roediger, David R. 1991 *The Wages of Whiteness*. London and New York: Verso.

Scott, Kesho Y. 1991 *The Habit of Surviving: Black Women's Strategies for Life*. New Brunswick, N.J.: Rutgers University Press.

Sitkoff, Harvard 1978 *A New Deal for Blacks*. New York: Oxford.

Sleeper, Jim 1990 *The Closest of Strangers: Liberalism and the Politics of Race in New York*. New York: Norton.

Snowden, Frank 1983 *Color Prejudice*. Cambridge, Mass.: Harvard University Press.

Stuckey, Sterling 1987 *Slave Culture*. New York: Oxford University Press.

Swinton, David H. 1990 "Racial Inequality and Reparations." In Richard F. America, ed., *The Wealth of Races: The Present Value of Benefits from Past Injustices*. New York: Greenwood Press.

Takaki, Ronald 1990 *Iron Cages: Race and Culture in 19th Century America*. New York: Oxford University Press.

Williams, Patricia 1991 *The Alchemy of Race and Rights*. Cambridge, Mass.: Harvard University Press.

—— 1987 "Alchemical Notes: Reconstructing Ideals from Deconstructed Rights." *Harvard Civil Rights and Civil Liberties Review* 22:401–434.

JOE R. FEAGIN

AFRICAN STUDIES

African studies simply defined is the systematic, scientific study of African peoples, and their institutions, culture, and history. But such a simple definition fails to encompass adequately the complexity of this important but often neglected arena for sociological theory and research.

THE GEOGRAPHY OF AFRICA

In sociology, the definition of one's unit of study is prerequisite to undertaking any research project. However, facts of history make the task of defining what encompasses African studies elusive. Geographic or spatial definitions are generally clearcut, so if one asks, "Where is Africa?" a concise answer is expected. The continent of Africa is easily identifiable on any atlas or globe. By association African studies could be defined as all research falling within the identified physical boundaries of this continental landmass. This is a simple and neat solution—or so it would seem. In reality, however, even the task of defining the physical boundaries of Africa can be daunting. As a vast continent of rich cultural, linguistic, political, and historical diversity, Africa is subject to considerable geographical disaggregation. Thus, what is one continent is approached and conceived of as several subcontinents or subregions. For example, many people—both lay and professional alike—are not accustomed to thinking of Egypt and the northern Islamic states (e.g., Algeria, Libya, Algeria, Morocco) as part of the African continent. These African states are routinely separated in scholarly discourse from Africa and African studies, and are generally treated as parts of the Middle East or Mediterranean.

The tendency toward geographic disaggregation in the conceptualization and study of Africa is also apparent at levels beyond the "North African" versus "sub-Saharan African" distinction. African studies in the so-called "sub-Saharan" context is usually divided into presumably distinct regions of this vast continent: East Africa (e.g., Kenya, Somalia, Tanzania, Uganda); West Africa (e.g., Nigeria, Ghana, Senegal); Central Africa (e.g., Zaire, Congo, Central African Republic); and Southern Africa (e.g., South Africa, Zimbabwe, Lesotho).

An additional complication in approaching the geography of Africa is represented by the partitioning of the continent into arbitrarily designated and imposed nation-states. Climaxing during the critical decades between 1870 and 1914, Western European imperialists divided Africa among themselves in order to share in the exploitation of the continent's rich natural and human resources. The Berlin Conference, a meeting among various European powers, was held from November 15, 1884 to February 26, 1885 in response to envy and mistrust spurred by competing attempts to claim and colonize Africa. The gathering produced negotiated guidelines for the division and governance of Africa by Europeans. As one striking example, the Congo River basin, envied and hotly contested by several European powers (e.g., Portugal, Britain, France, Germany, Belgium), was by consensus ceded to King Leopold II and Belgium. As another example, while some contested claims were settled, West Africa continued to be divided unequally among the colonizing countries that were fighting amongst themselves for the land and the people: Portugal claimed 14,000 square miles; Germany took possession of 33,000 square miles; Britain declared ownership of 450,000 square miles; and France laid claim to 1.8 million square miles of African soil. In claiming the land, these European powers also declared dominion over the people who occupied these lands.

By 1898 Europeans had colonized most of Africa. Since the lines of demarcation were drawn with European rather than African interests in mind, these artificially imposed geographic boundaries often dissected cultural and national groups or tribes that had been unified entities for centuries before the arrival of Europeans. The political or national boundaries arbitrarily established by European conquest had profound, far-reaching consequences. These boundaries are largely responsible for contemporary borders and nation-states in Africa. Moreover, these artificial divisions or mergers, or both, damaged historic patterns and relationships and, by so doing, contributed in some degree to ongoing ethnic conflicts in Africa. As with icebergs formed over centuries where we only can see the tip, these historic machinations provided the impetus for many "modern" conflicts in Africa. In these cases, colonial influence persists long after independence was proclaimed.

As a strategy, colonizers chose and groomed new African leadership to reinforce the ideals of newly formed, imposed nation-states, thereby creating a native elite and fostering division and mistrust among the colonized. The strategic approach to implementation varied for different colonial powers. France and Britain were the most successful Western European colonizing powers. Interestingly, their approaches to subduing and exploiting the African colonies differed vastly. The French saw traditional African heads-of-state as occupying the least important position within their new administrative system. Existing African governments were viewed as obstacles to the ultimate integration of Africans with French culture and society. Thus, achieving the French goal necessitated the utter destruction of established governmental systems as well as the absolute eradication of traditional cultures. Similar to American laws during the era of slavery, practicing ancestral religions, speaking traditional languages, and participating in customs such as dancing were deemed unlawful and were punishable by whipping, torture, and even death. The British, on the other hand, were more indirect. They sought to mold traditional governmental structures to accomplish their goals at the district level, while closely regulating the colonial administration nationally. The intention was for their African colonies to follow the examples of Canada and Australia, eventually emerging as self-governing extensions of the British Empire.

The institutionalized practice of misrepresenting the scale of Africa in relation to other continents is another point of contention. A European-inspired and -dominated cartography has successfully institutionalized blatantly misrepresentative views of African topography. The traditional world map portrays Europe's landmass as much larger than its true physical reality. Since the 1700s, the Mercator map scale, the most widely used cartographic scale in the world, has distorted the sizes of continents to favor the Northern Hemisphere. While traditional mapmaking and representations have instilled a picture of North America as equal in size to Africa, the Sahara Desert alone is in fact roughly the same size as the United States. The African continent has nearly four times the landmass of North America and comprises approximately twenty percent of the world's landmass.

More subtly, the world's geographic view of Africa has evolved to attribute a unidimensional image of Africa as consisting wholly of lush, impenetrable, tropical forests. This view of African geography fails to do justice to the rich, variegated landscape of this vast continent. Tropical rainforests represent only the smallest fraction of Africa's myriad landscape, which ranges from snow-capped mountains to deserts to high plains to hardwood forests, from rippling fields of grain to placid lakes. In fact the world's largest desert, the world's longest river, and natural wonders from the spectacular Victoria Falls to snow-capped Mount Kilamanjaro, all characterize the diversified topography of this continent.

THE PEOPLE OF AFRICA

"Where is Africa?" We see that the answer to this, the most essential or rudimentary of originating questions for sociological research, can be quite elusive. Facts of history and perception combine to make what should be a simple interrogatory quite complicated. Equally elusive, if not more so, is the task of defining "Who is African?" The answer to this seemingly straightforward question seems obvious. More often than not, answers to this question conform to the widespread view of Africans as a race of black people characterized by dark skin, curly hair, broad noses and numerous other physical features. In fact, the biological diversity of Africans matches and, at points, surpasses Africa's vast geographic diversity. Few other continents in the world approach or match the breadth of human biology and physiology historically found in Africa. Africans run the gamut of the human color spectrum, encompassing the range of human prototypes—the Negroid, the Mongoloid, the Caucasoid. For centuries the continent of Africa has been home not only to people of traditional biophysical description, but also to people descended from Europeans, Asians, Arabs, and Hispanics. Moreover, centuries of biological intermingling have produced a continent of hybrid people. Africa is truly a continent where the human reality defies attempts to neatly categorize race and racial identity.

Traditional images of race fail to embrace or represent the African reality adequately. Modern conceptions of race are derived from a hierarchical European worldview that assigns the lowest status to Africans, who are equated with blackness—the opposite of whiteness or European ancestry. When carefully examined in either an African or European context, racial identity loses much of its force as a concept. "White" and "black" are more political designations than physical ones. Thus, although there are indigenous Africans who have lighter complexions than some indigenous Europeans, widespread views of Europe as white and Africa as black persist. By the same token, race is often reified and incorrectly attributed characteristics that are in point of fact intellectual, social, cultural, or economic rather than biological. Generally speaking, race is incorrectly presumed to incorporate characteristics that extend far beyond human physical traits.

Apartheid in South Africa provides an excellent example of the politically motivated, exclusionary nature of racial classification systems (as does the historical case of "Jim Crow" segregation in the U.S. South). The assignment of people to categories of White, Coloured, and African (Black) in South Africa, coupled with the subdivision of each racial category into smaller racial groups (e.g., Whites = Afrikaner and English-speaking; Asians = East Indian and Malaysian; Coloureds = European/African and Asian/African; and Blacks = Zulu, Xhosa, Sotho), was largely determined by white efforts, as a demographic minority of the population, to maintain their historic political, economic, and social dominance. Apartheid relied on an elaborate system of "racial markers," such as hair texture, skin color, and parentage, to classify people into distinct racial groups. Associated with each racial group were certain privileges and restrictions. Restrictions were heaviest and privileges least for black Africans, the group at the bottom of the South African color hierarchy. Thus race, as a socially constructed, politically manipulated reality in South Africa, exerted overwhelming force in limiting black and coloured Africans' access and opportunities. The myth of the color hierarchy became—to some degree—a self-fulfilling, self-perpetuating prophecy in that many people, irrespective of race, internalized this value system. The result was often self-imposed ranking, with people of color creating additional levels within the established hierarchy, thereby constructing

intricate designations for race that extended far beyond traditional definition.

Discussions of African racial identity are additionally complicated by the vast global population of people of African ancestry. People of African descent are present in sizeable numbers in the Americas, Western Europe, and in parts of Asia and the South Pacific. In most instances, the dispersion of African people around the world—notably in Brazil, the United States, the Caribbean, and Britain—is directly traceable to the European conquest, domination, and distribution of African people. Europe created, installed, and operated a system of racial slave trade that fueled the economic, agricultural, and industrial development of the Americas and of Europe. The slave trade displaced millions of Africans and struck a crippling blow to social, economic, political, and cultural life on the African continent. The traffic in slaves was a demographic disaster for the African continent, taking away people in the prime of their reproductive and productive lives. The African slave trade left in its wake destroyed villages, ruined crops, disrupted cultures, and crumbling social institutions. So traumatic was the devastation of this trade in human lives, and the subsequent colonial exploitation of Africa for natural resources, that four centuries later Africa has not yet fully recovered.

Dramatic and extensive dispersion of Africans confounded questions of race and racial identity because of the extensive intermingling of Africans with other so-called racial groups. This was particularly true in the Americas, where systematic and legalized rape was characteristic of the era of enslavement. The manipulation of race and racial identity was a central feature in this drama. White men used sexual subjugation as another means of reinforcing their domination, resulting in the established pattern of African hybrid identity. Yet under the legal guidelines of American enslavement, the children who resulted from this institutionalized rape were considered black, and thereby referred to by Chief Justice Taney (*Dred Scott v. Sandford*, U.S. Supreme Court, 1857) as a people with "no rights which the white man was bound to respect." African ancestry combined with Native American, Asian, and European bloodlines to further diversify the already rich biological heritage of Africans. The extension of the African diaspora to the Americas produced a people represented by black Chinese in Mississippi, Jamaica, and Trinidad; black Amerindians in Florida (Seminoles), Oklahoma (Cherokee), and Surinam (Arawaks); black Irish in Virginia, black English in Barbados, black Portuguese in Brazil; and black East Indians in Guyana, black French Canadians in Montreal; and black Mexicans in Vera Cruz. A veritable human rainbow resulted from the transplantation of Africans to the "New World" and points beyond. Yet throughout the diaspora, Social Darwinism assigned Africans the lowest position on the evolutionary hierarchy and laid the foundation for elaborate ideology and pseudoscience that offered justifications for the continued subjugation of Africans. Ideologies founded upon the rationalization that lent credence to this travesty persist today, further plaguing Africans throughout the diaspora.

THE CULTURAL AND SOCIAL INSTITUTIONS OF AFRICA

We have seen the complexity that underlies the seemingly simple questions of "Where is Africa" and "Who is African." The task of defining for sociological study a people who are both geographically and genetically dispersed is extremely challenging. Additional complication results when we ask the next question, "What is African?" Here we simply raise the logical question of which institutions, customs, values, institutions, cultural features, and social forms can be characterized or labeled as distinctively African.

The survival (albeit in evolved form) of indigenous African customs, values, and institutions is remarkable, especially considering the abundance of historical barriers and complications. First among these is the reality of African conquest and domination by other cultures, most notably European, but also including cultures from the Islamic world. The experience of conquest and domination by external powers, often designed to annihilate African civilization, makes the myriad existing retentions all the more amazing. One of the best examples of these retentions is what Africa and people of African ancestry have done with the abundance of nonindigenous languages that were imposed upon them during colonization.

Language plays a vital role in the process of cultural and personal affirmation. Therefore, it is not surprising to note that the conquest experience of Africa and Africans in the diaspora was commonly associated with systematic attempts to suppress or eliminate indigenous languages. The African continent can be divided into European language communities that parallel the geographic regions associated with European domination and partition of Africa (e.g., Anglophone, Francophone). In a similar fashion, members of the African diaspora have adopted the dominant languages of the cultures and regions where they found themselves, speaking Arabic, Portuguese, Spanish, English, French, or Dutch. However, before European languages were introduced, there were well over 800 languages spoken by various African ethnic groups, most of which can be classified between three of the principal language families—Niger-Kordofian, Nilo-Saharan, and Khoisian. Numerically, these African-selected language groups incorporate approximately 300 million people.

Many if not most Africans are minimally bilingual, routinely speaking several languages in addition to their own. However, colonial tongues are generally recognized as the country's "official" language. Part of the devastation of colonization is the demise of original languages as the primary means of communication. These languages are forgotten, ignored, and sometimes even mocked by those who would assimilate into Westernized ideals. Strikingly, many independent African nations have embarked on programs aimed at the regeneration of indigenous languages, often creating written forms for languages that were previously solely oral. Other African nations have substituted indigenous languages for European languages (derived from the country's colonial experience) as the country's "official" language. South Africa is an example of a country where multiple national languages were officially established in a process that validated the myriad of mother tongues as well as the colonizers' language.

Attempting to strip Africans of their languages was an essential feature of the move to supplement military, economic, and political domination with cultural domination. However, understanding the essential connection between language, worldview, personal identity, and cultural survival, many Africans fought to retain their indigenous languages. They believed their survival as a unique people hinged on successful retention of their original languages, and the culture, values, self-affirmation, and history embodied within those native tongues. Interesting variations in the retention of African language forms are observable throughout Africa and the African diaspora. The patois (patwa) spoken in Jamaica contains many words that need no translation from Twi, the language spoken by the Ghanaian Ashanti who constituted the majority of the slaves brought in to work on Jamaican plantations. French has been transformed in both Louisiana and Haiti with varieties of Kreyol. In North America we can observe the Gullah people, primarily found in South Carolina and Georgia, who infuse their English-based Creole with the language of their enslaved African ancestors. Standard black American English (sometimes referred to as Ebonics) also retains evidence of similar African-derived language structures. A related case is provided by places like Bahia in Brazil where Yoruba, an indigenous African language, was successfully transplanted and maintained outside the continent. There are nations on the African continent where indigenous languages were practiced throughout the colonial experience and reinstituted after independence. However, as we have observed, the most common case across the diaspora is the synthesis of African syntax with the dominant European language syntax to create a new language.

The pattern of adaptive acculturation or synthesis that occurs with language also characterizes other sociocultural institutions in Africa and across the diaspora. Art and music provide distinctive examples. African people traditionally use visual art as a means of communication. Cloth making, for example, is not simply an aesthetic undertaking. Often, messages are inscribed or embedded within the very combinations of patterns and colors chosen to create the fabric. Among the Ashanti in Ghana, funeral cloth is often adorned with what are known as Adinkra symbols. The symbols impressed upon the cloth convey different meanings, thereby transmitting messages to those who are knowledgeable. The Touaregs, a people concentrated in Niger, are also known to transcribe messages on cloth in the distinctive alphabet that characterizes their language. Within Rastafarian culture in Jamaica, sculpture is used as another method of communicating and reinforcing the beliefs of the practitioners. Moreover, African-American artists often draw from the diaspora in their creation of visual art. Lois Mailou Jones traversed the French-speaking African world, and her work was influenced by the various cultures she studied.

Artistic products of African people, especially those living outside of the continent, reflect the mixture of cultural influences—part indigenous, part nonindigenous—that characterize the African experience. The synthesis contains elements that are obviously African-derived alongside elements that are obviously European or Islamic. Yet the final tune or drawing is often truly syncretic, possessing emergent qualities greater than the sum of the influences. It is in the realm of cultural production, music and art, where the African influence on world society has been most readily apparent. During the period of colonization, ruling cultures often defined the oppressed as "others" in an effort to justify their subhuman treatment. Historic views of African-American culture provide powerful examples of objectification and stereotypes such as "Sambo," the happy darkie, or "Jezebel," the promiscuous black female. These false perceptions permeated the fabric of American society, allowing whites to embrace the racial stereotypes and notions that blacks were content in their status as second-class citizens. In order to perpetuate these false images, blacks were allowed to prosper in media and occupations that coincided with and reinforced views of their subservient status. To do otherwise was to risk retribution from whites. Thus, the entertainment industry (and its related variant, professional sports) has historically provided socially acceptable, non-threatening roles for blacks.

Many blacks recognized the power inherent in these media and used them for empowerment and to accomplish larger goals. For example, we can note the themes of resistance embodied in traditional spirituals sung during slavery. It is also interesting to observe the tremendous impact of music during the civil rights movement. In many instances, a syncretic merger has been achieved that fuses indigenous African "authenticity" with nonindigenous traits to create new forms of music (e.g., rap). People of African descent have facilitated the growth of myriad musical genres, such as reggae, zouk, jazz, blues, soca, zaico, calypso, gogo, Hip Hop, and gospel. In yet other instances, Africans have chosen to embrace, master, and operate within the unmodified European form (e.g., opera, classical music).

Religion is another excellent example of a sociocultural institution that challenges us to define what is distinctively African. Forms of indigenous African religion are as diverse as the continent and people themselves. Christianity, Islam, and Judaism all have long histories on the continent. The same is true for traditional, animistic African religions that imbue all features of the environment with spiritual qualities. It is perhaps the long tradition of polytheism—or, more correctly, the belief in, and acceptance of a Supreme God who is in turn represented in the world by several intermediary spirits—that made Africa and African people such fertile ground for the spread of diverse religions.

In addition, colonial powers felt a need to control all forms of thought and expression in order to ensure their continued dominion over the indigenous people. Religion was recognized as an especially powerful medium with immense capacity to control the daily behavior of people. Thus, religion was a central component in the colonial arsenal and pattern of domination. In spite of this, many traditional African religions have survived the test of time. Both the original forms and syncretic amalgamations of Western and traditional religion are found throughout the diaspora. On the island of Jamaica, one can observe how the Ashanti religion Kumina has flourished and grown over time into the distinctly Jamaican Pukumina (Pocomania). Linkages such as the one between the Gabonese sect known as Bwiti and Haitian vodun continue, in which the words for traditional healer are almost the same. Continuities are also seen in Shango/Santeria (Brazil) and Rastafarianism (Jamaica and internationally). Religious forms throughout the African diaspora range from the classical European through the traditional African into the Islamic, with a large variety of syncretic forms interspersed throughout.

The organization of social and community life in Africa and across the African diaspora also runs the spectrum from indigenous to nonindigenous. In a now familiar pattern, there exist places in Africa or in the African diaspora where traditional African forms of family life, dating back centuries, persist. Similarly, there are places where family forms are closer to the European or the Islamic model. The same observations can be offered about education and the organization of schools among Africans in a given society.

Predictably, given Africa's history of subjugation, it is in realms of international power and influence, economics, government, and the military, that African development has been most restricted. Historical deprivation has resulted in the ranking of Africa and people of African ancestry at the bottom of all indicators of economic development. While other formerly colonized countries have managed to advance economically (e.g., Brazil, Singapore, and Korea), much of Africa and the African diaspora continue to be economically dependent. Coupled with this economic dependence are persistently high rates of unemployment, disease, educational disadvantage, and population growth. Africans continue to be without significant representation at the centers of international power, judged by economic clout, political influence, and military might. In each of these aspects, Africa remains the suppressed giant, unable to exert world influence commensurate to her nearly billion people, strategic geopolitical location, and rich mineral and human resources. The emergence of Africa onto the world stage, like Japan's in 1960 and China's in 1980, will have to wait.

UNIFYING THEMES IN AFRICAN STUDIES

Due to historical context, we have seen there are no simple answers to the basic questions for orienting any scientific, sociological study of Africa and her people. The African diaspora has been uniquely shaped by experiences of conquest and domination, resistance and survival. The experiences of slavery, colonization, and external domination have left in their wake considerable devastation. Yet one also sees the amazing strength of a people able to adapt and diversify, and to love and live, and ultimately continue to be.

Studies of African people and institutions commonly reveal the creative retention of authentic or indigenous traits. Such creative responses have been, in their own way, acts of resistance enabling cultural perpetuation. These adaptive responses have assured the ultimate survival of many aspects of African culture and institutions. It must also be noted that with time comes transition. Many things traditionally African have been altered, progressing from their original, indigenous form to completely new and different forms. It is perhaps in this tension, the reconciliation of the old with the new, the indigenous with the nonindigenous, that African studies will find its most exciting terrain for future inquiry. The challenge will be to discover the cultures and the people who have been historically distorted by the twin activities of concealment from within, and degradation and misperception from without.

AMERICAN SCHOLARSHIP AND AFRICAN STUDIES

The dismissal of the importance of African studies preceded its acceptance as a scholarly discipline. While clearly diminished today, the white male Eurocentric focus has historically dominated university curricula. Both grassroots and academic movements pointed to the need for recognition of the African contribution to world and American culture. The early to mid-1900s saw the emergence of black intellectuals in Africa (e.g., Léopold Sédar Senghor, Patrice Lumumba, Cheikh Anta Diop), the Caribbean (Frantz Fanon, Aimé Césaire, Claude McKay), and America (W.E.B. Du Bois, Langston Hughes, Anna Julia Cooper), who spoke of parallel movements based on the assumption that black people in all parts of the world were a community with shared interests and identity (e.g., Negritude, Pan-Africanism). The goals of these scholars emphasized the uplift of people of African ancestry worldwide through education, research, politics, and cultural activities. These international movements among black intellectuals were in direct response to theories of black inferiority and the systematic oppression of Africans (both on the continent and abroad). Herbert Spencer, among others, launched the ideology of Social Darwinism, which developed into a popular, pseudoscientific justification for racial hierarchies. Social Darwinism assigned Africans, and thereby African Americans, to the lowest rung in the evolutionary ladder.

A nineteenth-century phenomenon, Social Darwinism and its associated beliefs persisted well into the twentieth century. Its philosophy is still heard in the remnants of eugenics, in the present-day interest in sociobiology, and in recurring assertions of black innate intellectual inferiority.

Before the incorporation of African studies into predominantly white colleges, black educators and leaders had stressed the value of black America's ties to Africa for decades. Notable activists from William Monroe Trotter to Booker T. Washington and Marcus Garvey called for "Back to Africa" movements. Zora Neale Hurston was an anthropologist whose studies of African Americans emphasized retentions and links with original African cultures. The distinguished sociologist W.E.B. Du Bois founded the Pan-African Congress in 1921, supported by notables such as the author Jessie Redmon Fauset, in order to explicitly link the problems and fortunes of African Americans to those of blacks in Africa and elsewhere. Moreover, much of his work over a long and illustrious career focused on Africa. Ultimately Du Bois renounced his American citizenship and accepted Kwame Nkrumah's invitation to settle in Ghana.

Within white-dominated institutions, the value of African studies had strange origins. Egyptologists and anthropologists gathered information from Africa during colonial rule. In such instances, sociology was both friend and foe. Early sociologists promoted cross-cultural studies as well as research into the social conditions under which blacks lived. However, many of these sociologists embraced Social Darwinism and its belief in the inherent inferiority of blacks. Rarely did these early academics speak out or take active stances against the oppression of Africa and African people by Europeans.

Some American colleges remained racially segregated until the 1960s. The inclusion of African-American students, and later African-American studies classes, came in response to student activism, which occurred against the backdrop of the push for civil rights and amidst significant racial unrest. The black power movement of this time strongly influenced many African Americans to reclaim their heritage in everyday life and to demand that black history and culture be included in school and university curricula. There was—and continues to be—significant struggle around these questions, since what is at risk here was (is) the control and validation of knowledge in the society. The black studies movement paved the way for further interest in African studies. The publication of Alex Haley's *Roots*, a volume which traced his family lineage back to Gambia, West Africa, followed by a popular television miniseries, was a signal moment in the development of black Americans' interest in Africa. In addition, many African Americans celebrate Kwaanza, a holiday founded upon principles of the African harvest, as another conscious link with their cultural roots. Ironically, the growing interest of black Americans in their cultural roots in Africa helped to fuel a resurgence of ethnic pride and the search for roots among other racial groups in this country. Interestingly, in contemporary universities, the field of African-American studies tends to be dominated by African Americans, while African-studies programs tend to be dominated by European Americans.

CONCLUSION

African studies is a woefully underdeveloped area of institutionalized research in the field of sociology. Researchers need to mount aggressive programs determined to "ask new questions and to question old answers." For this research to be successful, it must be located in broader context, recognizing the unique historical, economic, social, cultural, political, and academic relationships that determine reality for Africans on the continent and throughout the diaspora. In each of these areas, relationships are generally structured hierarchically, with African worldviews, values, institutional forms, methodologies, and concerns being considered subordinate to those of Europeans or whites. Such distorted structural relations lead inevitably to distortions in research and conclusions. The irony is that clear understanding of African people and institutions will help pave the way to better understanding Whites and European heritage, institutions, and experiences.

REFERENCES

Appiah, Anthony 1992 *In My Father's House: Africa in the Philosophy of Culture*. New York: Oxford University Press.

Asante, Molefi 1987 *The Afrocentric Idea*. Philadelphia: Temple University Press.

Bates, Robert H., V. Y. Mudimbe, and Jean O'Barr, (eds.) 1993 *Africa and the Disciplines: The Contributions of Research in Africa to the Social Sciences and Humanities*. Chicago, Ill.: University of Chicago Press.

Césaire, Aimé 1972 *Discourse on Colonialism* New York: Macmillan Reference USA.

Chinweizu 1975 *The West and the Rest of Us*. New York: Vintage.

Diawara, Manthia 1998 *In Search of Africa*. Cambridge, Mass.: Harvard University Press.

Diop, Cheikh Anta 1989 *The Cultural Unity of Black Africa: The Domains of Patriarchy and of Matriarchy in Classical Antiquity*. London: Karnak House.

Fanon, Frantz 1986 *The Wretched of the Earth*. New York: Grove Press.

Franklin, John Hope, and Alfred A. Moss, Jr. 1994 *From Slavery to Freedom: A History of African Americans*, 7th ed. New York: McGraw-Hill.

Fyfe, Christopher (ed.) 1976 *African Studies Since 1945: A Tribute to Basil Davidson*. London: Longman.

Gilroy, Paul 1993 *The Black Atlantic: Modernity and Double Consciousness*. Cambridge, Mass.: Harvard University Press.

Gromyko, Anatoly, and C. S. Whitaker (eds.) 1990 *Agenda for Action: African-Soviet-U.S. Cooperation*. Boulder, Colo.: L. Rienner.

Haley, Alex 1976 *Roots*. Garden City, N.Y.: Doubleday.

Hochschild, Adam 1998 *King Leopold's Ghost: A Story of Greed, Terror and Heroism in Colonial Africa*. Boston, Mass.: Houghton-Mifflin.

Jackson, Henry 1984 *From the Congo to Soweto: U.S. Foreign Policy Toward Africa Since 1960*. New York: Quill.

James, C. L. R. 1969 *A History of Pan-African Revolt*, 2nd ed. Washington, D.C.: Drum and Spear Press.

Mazrui, Ali 1986 *The Africans: A Triple Heritage*. London: BBC Publications.

Mbiti, J. S. 1969 *African Religions and Philosophy*. London: Heinemann.

Mudimbe, V. Y. 1988 *The Invention of Africa: Gnosis, Philosophy, and the Order of Knowledge*. Bloomington, Ind.: Indiana University Press.

Nkrumah, Kwame 1965 *Neo-Colonialism: The Last Stage of Imperialism*. New York: International.

Rodney, Walter 1974 *How Europe Underdeveloped Africa*. Washington, D.C.: Howard University Press.

Soyinka, Wole 1976 *Myth, Literature and the African World*. New York: Cambridge University Press.

Sunshine, Catherine 1988 *The Caribbean: Survival, Struggle and Sovereignty*. Boston: South End Press.

Thompson, Robert Farris 1984 *Flash of the Spirit: African and Afro-American Art and Philosophy.* New York: Random House.

Thompson, Vincent 1969 *Africa and Unity: The Evolution of Pan-Africanism.* London: Longman.

Winston, James 1998 *Holding Aloft the Banner of Ethiopia: Carribean Radicalism in Early Twentieth-Century America.* London: Verso.

WALTER R. ALLEN
SHANI O'NEAL

AGGRESSION

In its most extreme forms, aggression is human tragedy unsurpassed. Hopes that the horrors of World War II and the Holocaust would produce a worldwide revulsion against the taking of another human's life, resulting in the end of genocidal practices and a reduction in homicide rates, have been dashed by the realities of increasing homicide and genocide in the last half of the twentieth century. The litany of genocidal events is both long and depressing, including major massacres in Uganda, Cambodia, Rwanda, Burundi, Zaire, Bosnia, Serbia, Croatia, and Herzegovina, among others. Homicide rates have risen in a number of industrialized countries since World War II, most notably in the United States.

We have seen slight declines in the homicide rate in the United States during the 1990s. But despite six consecutive years of decreases, the 1997 homicide rate was still 133 percent of the 1965 rate, and 166 percent of the 1955 rate. For these and related reasons, interest in understanding the causes of aggression remains high, and there have been major advances in the social psychology of aggression.

WHAT IS AGGRESSION?

Definitions have varied widely over time and across research domains. However, a consensus has emerged among most social psychologists studying human aggression about what constitutes "aggression" in general and what constitutes the major forms or "ideal types" of aggression. (See the following books for current definitions and perspectives on aggression: Baron and Richardson 1994; Berkowitz 1993; Geen 1990; Geen and Donnerstein 1998; Tedeschi and Felson 1994).

Basic Definitions. *Aggression vs. Assertiveness vs. Violence.* Human aggression is behavior performed by one person (the aggressor) with the intent of harming another person (the victim) who is believed by the aggressor to be motivated to avoid that harm. "Harm" includes physical harm (e.g., a punch to the face), psychological harm (e.g., verbal insults), and indirect harm (e.g., destroying the victim's property).

Accidental harm is not "aggressive" because it is not intended. Harm that is an incidental by-product of actions taken to achieve some superordinate goal is also excluded from "aggression" because the harm-doer's primary intent in such cases is to help the person achieve the superordinate goal and because the harm-recipient doesn't actively attempt to avoid the harm-doer's action. For example, pain delivered during a dental procedure is not "aggression" by the dentist against the patient.

In their scientific usages "aggressiveness" is very different from "assertiveness" even though the general public frequently uses these words interchangeably. When people say that someone is an "aggressive" salesperson they typically mean that he or she is assertive—pushy or confident or emphatic or persistent—but they do not truly mean "aggressive" unless, of course, they believe that the salesperson intentionally tries to harm customers. Similarly, coaches exhorting players to "be more aggressive" seldom mean that players should try to harm their opponents; rather, coaches want players to be more assertive—active and confident.

Violence, on the other hand, is a subtype of aggression. The term "violence" is generally used to denote extreme forms of aggression such as murder, rape, and assault. All violence is aggression, but many instances of aggression are not violent. For example, one child pushing another off a tricycle is considered aggressive but not violent. For example, one child pushing another off a tricycle is considered aggressive but not violent.

Affective vs. Instrumental Types of Aggression. "Affective" aggression has the primary motive of harming the target, and is thought to be based on anger. It is sometimes labeled hostile, impulsive, or reactive aggression, though these labels often carry additional meaning. When aggression is merely a tool to achieve another goal of the aggressor, it is labeled "instrumental" aggression. Most robberies are primarily instrumental, whereas most murders and assaults are affective. Similarly, Jack may hit Jim merely to obtain a desirable toy, a case of instrumental aggression. Jim may get angry and respond by hitting Jack in order to hurt him, a case of affective aggression.

Proactive vs. Reactive Types of Aggression. "Proactive" aggression occurs in the absence of provocation. It is usually instrumental, as when Jack hit Jim to get the toy. "Reactive" aggression is a response to a prior provocation, such when Jim retaliated. There is an asymmetrical relation between proactive and reactive aggression. Children who are high on proactive aggression usually are high on reactive aggression as well, but many children who are high on reactive aggression engage in little proactive aggression.

Thoughtful vs. Thoughtless Aggression. A more recent distinction among types of aggression concerns whether the aggressive act resulted from thoughtful or thoughtless (impulsive) psychological processes. In past work, instrumental aggression has usually been seen as thoughtful, involving the careful weighing of potential costs and benefits. But more recent work reveals that frequent use of aggression to obtain valued goals can become so automatized that it also becomes thoughtless. Affective aggression has usually been seen as thoughtless, but people sometimes consider various possible courses of action and decide that an angry outburst is the best way to achieve those goals. This distinction between thoughtful and thoughtless aggression has important implications for the development of and intervention in aggression.

Distinguishing among types of aggression is difficult because underlying motives and psychological processes must be inferred. Is Jim's angry attack on Jack purely anger-based, solely intended to harm Jack, or is there also some instrumental component? There is a growing realization that these ideal types of aggression rarely exist in pure form in the real world of human interaction. Indeed, a few scholars have argued that all aggression is instrumental, serving goals such as social control, public-image management, private-image

management (i.e., self-esteem), and social justice. Nonetheless, most aggression scholars still find these distinctions helpful for theoretical, rhetorical, and application-oriented reasons.

WHAT CAUSES AGGRESSION?

The causes of aggression can be analyzed at two different levels: the proximal causes (in the immediate situation) and the more distal causes that set the stage for the emergence and operation of proximate causes.

Distal Causes: Biological Factors. Distal causes of aggression are those that make people ready and capable of aggression. Some are structural, built into the human species. Others are developmental, based on the particular environmental history of the individual, and result in individual differences in preparedness to aggress.

Genetics. In the broadest sense aggression is a species characteristic. That is, the human species has physical, cognitive, and emotional systems capable of intentionally inflicting harm on other humans. The genetic basis of aggression is easier to identify in nonhuman species, in which fighting behaviors can be produced by stimulating certain regions of the limbic system. Similar physiological systems exist in humans, but human behavior is much more complexly determined.

In the more usual sense genetic influences refer to individual differences in aggressiveness that are linked to genetic differences within the species. Human twin studies have yielded mixed results in estimates of the genetic contribution to human aggression. Miles and Carey (1997) did a meta-analysis (i.e., statistical review) on twenty-four "genetically informative" studies. Two important conclusions were: (1) up to 50 percent of variation in self- or parent-reported aggression was attributable to genetic effects; and (2) when aggressiveness was measured by careful observation of laboratory behaviors, the genetic effect disappeared and a strong family-environment effect emerged. These contradictory findings highlight the complexity of human aggression as well as the need for additional studies.

Mechanisms. Several biological mechanisms appear plausible as potential causes of individual differences in aggressiveness. Hormones (e.g., testosterone), neurochemicals (e.g., serotonin), attention deficit hyperactivity disorder, and general levels of arousal have all been linked to aggression. For example, Eysenck and Gudjonsson (1989) proposed that individuals whose nervous system is relatively insensitive to low levels of environmental stimulation seek out high-risk activities, including criminal ones, to increase their arousal.

But many biological effects on aggression are neither as strong nor as consistent as the general public believes. For example, testosterone is frequently cited as the explanation for male/female differences in violence rates, but the human literature on testosterone effects is far from clear. Testosterone levels in humans seems more closely linked to social dominance, which in turn may well influence aggression under some limited circumstances (Campbell, Muncer, and Odber 1997; Geary 1998).

Other psychological variables with links to aggression also appear to have some genetic basis. Empathy, behavioral inhibition, negative affectivity, extraversion, neuroticism, and psychoticism all have yielded evidence of some genetic heritability, and have obvious links to aggression. General intelligence may also link biological variation to aggressiveness; low intelligence increases the occurrence of frustrating failures and aversive conditions, which might increase the likelihood of a person developing an aggressive personality.

Distal Causes: Environmental and Psychological Factors. Numerous social, environmental, and psychological factors contribute to the development of habitual aggressiveness. Learning stands out as the most important factor of all.

Learning. Bandura's social-learning theory of aggression (1973) has been most influential. One key idea in this and all modern learning approaches is that much of human development is based on learning by observing how other people behave. Patterson, DeBaryshe, and Ramsey (1989) presented a detailed look at the maladaptive social-learning processes found in families of aggressive children. Among the key problems are parental use of poor disciplinary measures and inadequate monitoring of their children's activities. Similarly, Olweus (1995) has identified a number of child-rearing factors that are conducive to creating bullies: caretakers with indifferent attitudes toward the child; permissiveness for aggressive behavior

by the child; and the use of physical punishment and other power-assertive disciplinary techniques.

Cognitive psychology has also been crucial in the present understanding of the aggressive personality, as can be seen in books by Berkowitz (1993) and Geen (1990), and in Huesmann's (1998) information-processing theory of aggressive personality development. In brief, humans begin learning from infancy how to perceive, interpret, judge, and respond to events in the physical and social environment. We learn perceptual schemata that help us decide what to look for and what we "see." We learn rules for how the social world works. We learn behavioral scripts and use them to interpret events and actions of others and to guide our own behavioral responses to those events. These various *knowledge structures* develop over time. They are based on the day-to-day observations of and interactions with other people: real (as in the family) and imagined (as in the mass media). For example, the long-term exposure to media violence can increase later aggressive behavior by influencing a variety of aggression-related knowledge structures. Such long-term media violence effects have been shown to be substantial in size and long lasting in duration (Huesmann and Miller 1994).

As knowledge structures develop, they become more complex, interconnected, and difficult to change. Developing knowledge structures are like slowly hardening clay. Environmental experiences shape the clay. Changes are relatively easy to make at first, when the clay is soft, but later on changes become increasingly difficult. Longitudinal studies suggest that aggression-related knowledge structures begin to harden around age eight or nine, and become more perseverant with increasing age.

People learn specific aggressive behaviors, the likely outcome of such behaviors, and how and when to apply these behaviors. They learn hostile perception, attribution, and expectation biases, callous attitudes, and how to disengage or ignore normal empathic reactions that might serve as aggression inhibitors.

The pervasiveness, interconnectedness, and accessibility of any learned knowledge structure is largely determined by the frequency with which it is encountered, imagined, and used. With great frequency even complex perception-judgment-behavior knowledge structures can become *automatized*—so overlearned that they are applied automatically with little effort or awareness. Frequent exposure to aggressive models is particularly effective in creating habitually aggressive people, whether those models are in the home, neighborhood, or mass media. Once the use of any particular knowledge structure has become automatized, it becomes very difficult for the person to avoid using it because the perceptions and behavioral impulses it produces seem to be based on "how the world really is."

Social Processes. Several common social processes contribute to disproportionate exposure to and learning of aggression-related knowledge structures. Low intellect (social or academic) creates excessive failures and frustration in a variety of developmental contexts. Low social intelligence, for example, leads to problems in interpersonal interactions, whereas low academic intelligence creates problems in school settings. Problems in either context typically lead to higher-than-normal levels of aggression, which lead to further frustrating encounters with parents, teachers, and peers. The resulting social ostracism often forces children to spend more time with other social misfits who also have highly aggressive behavior patterns. This "gang" can impede further intellectual development and reward additional antisocial tendencies.

Environments. Many social environments foster the development of an aggressive personality. Such factors include poverty; living in violent neighborhoods; deviant peers; lack of safe, supervised child recreational areas; exposure to media violence; bad parenting; and lack of social support. Growing up in a culture of fear and hate, as in many ethnic-minority communities around the world, may well be the most extreme version of an aggressive-personality–fostering environment, and may well account for the generation after generation of ethnic and religious hatreds and genocidal tendencies that occasionally erupt into genocidal wars (Keltner and Robinson 1996; Staub 1989, 1998). The perceptual knowledge structures modeled and explicitly taught in these contexts guarantee continued mistrust, misunderstanding, and hatred of key outgroups.

Even in its simplest form, poverty is associated with more frustrations, bad role models, and lack of good role models. Bad parenting includes several particularly common and damaging factors such as lack of parental attention, inconsistent discipline, harsh and abusive discipline, and inattention to nonaggressive efforts at problem solving by the child. Privation, victimization, and violence in a social milieu of long-standing ethnic/religious conflicts provide a powerful learning environment that is mightily resistant to change.

Short-term impoverishment, such as that brought on by a general decline in economic activity (e.g., a recession or depression), has been proposed as a causal factor in aggression directed against ethnic minorities. The dominant model is that the frustration engendered by such economic downturns leads to increased aggression against relatively powerless target groups. However, research casts considerable doubt on this hypothesis. For example, Green, Glaser, and Rich (1998) reanalyzed data on lynchings and data on "gay-bashing," and showed no evidence of short-term fluctuations in economic conditions and violence directed at minorities.

Child abuse and neglect. Child abuse and neglect itself are self-perpetuating problems. Abused or neglected children are particularly likely to become abusing and neglecting parents and violent criminal offenders. Children learn maladaptive beliefs, attitudes, and values from their abusive or neglectful parents (Azar and Rohrbeck 1986; Peterson, Gable, Doyle, and Ewugman 1997).

Proximate Causes: Individual Differences. The distal causes described in earlier sections set the stage for human aggression of various types. Proximate causes are those that are present in the current situation. One type of proximate cause consists of individual differences between people that have been created by their biological and social pasts. People differ widely in readiness for aggressing. These differences show considerable consistency across time and situations (Huesmann and Moise 1998).

Hostility Biases. Hostility biases have been identified in aggressive adults and children, some as young as six years. The *hostile perception bias* is the tendency of aggression-prone people to perceive social behaviors as more aggressive than do normal people, whereas the *hostile expectation bias* is the tendency of aggression-prone people to expect and predict others to behave relatively more aggressively (Dill, Anderson, Anderson, and Deuser 1997). The more widely studied *hostile attribution bias* is the tendency of aggression-prone people to attribute hostile intent to others' accidentally harmful behaviors. For example, Dodge (1980) had aggressive and nonaggressive children listen to a story about a boy who hurt another boy by hitting him with a ball. When asked, aggressive children attributed more hostile intent to the boy who threw the ball than did nonaggressive children.

Attitudes and Beliefs. Aggression-prone people hold favorable attitudes toward aggression, believing that aggressive solutions to problems are effective and appropriate. Aggressive thoughts and aggressive solutions come to mind quickly and easily. However, creating nonaggressive alternatives is particularly difficult for the aggressive person.

For example, Malamuth, Linz, Heavey, Barnes, and Acker (1995) found that sexually aggressive males hold relatively positive attitudes toward the use of aggression against women, believe in numerous rape myths, engage in more impersonal sex, and are likely to aggress against women in nonsexual contexts as well. Research (Anderson and Anderson 1999) reveals that sexually aggressive men are specifically aggressive only against women, in both sexual and nonsexual contexts, but are not unusually aggressive against other men.

Narcissism and Self-Esteem. The predominant view of the link between self-esteem and violence has been that low self-esteem contributes to high violence. However, research from several perspectives has demonstrated a very different pattern. Certain individuals with high self-esteem are most prone to anger and are most aggressive when their high self-image is threatened. Specifically, it is high self-esteem people who react most violently to threats to their self-esteem—if their high self-esteem is inflated (undeserved), unstable, or tentative. In other words, narcissists are the dangerous people, not those with low self-esteem or those who are confident in their high self-image (Baumeister, Smart, and Boden 1996; Bushman and Baumeister 1998; Kernis, Grannemann, and Barclay 1989).

Sex. Males and females differ in aggressive tendencies, especially in the most violent behaviors of homicide and aggravated assault. The ratio of male to female murderers in the United States is almost 10:1. Laboratory studies show the same type of sex effect, but provocation has a greater effect on aggression than does sex. Bettencourt and Miller (1996) used meta-analytic procedures and found that sex differences in aggression practically disappear under high provocation.

Men and women also appear to differ in what provokes them. Bettencourt and Miller showed that males are particularly sensitive to negative intelligence provocations whereas females are particularly sensitive to insults by a peer and to physical attacks. Geary, Rumsey, Bow-Thomas, and Hoard (1995) showed that males are more upset by sexual infidelity of their mates than by emotional infidelity, whereas the opposite pattern occurs for females. Buss and Shackelford (1997) showed similar sex differences in the effects of infidelity on mate-retention tactics, including use of violence.

Biology. Other biological differences that people bring with them to the current situation may also contribute to aggression, but as noted earlier many biological effects on aggression are neither as strong nor as consistent as the general public believes. For example, testosterone is frequently cited as the explanation for male/female differences in violence rates, but the human literature on testosterone effects is mixed.

Proximate Causes: Situational Factors. The second type of proximate causes of aggression consists of the situational factors currently present. Some of these factors are so powerful that even normally nonaggressive individuals can be made to behave aggressively.

Provocation. Most aggressive incidents can be directly linked to some type of perceived provocation. Some are direct and obvious, such as verbal insults and physical assaults. Some are less direct, as when an expected pay raise fails to materialize. Most murders and assaults in normal (i.e., nonwar) contexts are the result of provocations of one kind or another, usually in a series of escalatory provocations, threats, and counterthreats. Federal Bureau of Investigation data reveal that most murders in the United States occur during arguments among family, friends, or acquaintances. The tendency for stranger-based homicides to be relatively rare is even more pronounced in other industrialized cultures than in the United States. Frequently, the provocations involve sexual or emotional infidelity, or perceived insults to one's honor.

Frustration. Frustration is both an event and an emotional reaction. It occurs when something blocks the attainment or threatens the continued possession of a valued goal objective. For example, a supervisor's bad report may prevent a promotion, a spouse's infidelity may threaten the continued existence of a marriage, or a flood may destroy one's home. If the frustrating agent is another person, then the frustrating event is also a provocation.

The original form of the frustration-aggression hypothesis by Dollard, Doob, Miller, Mowrer, and Sears (1939) stated that: (1) all acts of aggression are the result of previous frustration; (2) all frustration leads to aggression. But some frustrations do not yield aggression, and some aggression is not the result of a prior frustration. Indeed, many contemporary scholars believe that if a frustrating event is fully justified, the frustrated person would show no residual inclination to aggress. However, Berkowitz (1989) claimed that even fully justified frustration can produce aggressive tendencies. This prediction was recently confirmed by Dill and Anderson (1995).

In a similar vein, Miller and Marcus-Newhall (1997) have shown that provocations can lead to increased aggressive tendencies against individuals who were not part of the frustrating event at all, a phenomenon typically labeled *displaced aggression.* Miller and Marcus-Newhall also suggest that such displaced aggression is increased if the displacement target provides a minor "triggering" provocation, and if the displacement target is a member of a disliked outgroup.

Incentives. Incentives are the rewards or benefits a person expects for having performed a particular action. Many situations in politics, the business world, and sports encourage aggression by their incentives. People often expect their chances of winning an election, getting a contract, or defeating an opponent to be enhanced by harming their competitor. Research on television violence has shown that seeing a character rewarded (or not punished) for aggressing increases subsequent aggression by the viewer more so than does unrewarded (or punished) television violence, presumedly by increasing the perceived incentive value of aggressive behavior.

The prototypical incentive-based example of individual aggression is the contract killer, who murders purely for money. The Iraqi assault and takeover of Kuwait, as well as NATO's subsequent attack on Iraq are clear examples of incentive-based institutional aggression (though other factors also clearly played a role). Contract murders account for only a small percentage of homicide totals, but they nicely illustrate the concept of relatively anger-free instrumental aggression.

Aversive Stimulation and Stress. Almost any form of aversive stimulation can increase the likelihood of aggression—noise, pain, crowding, cigarette smoke, heat, daily hassles, and interpersonal problems illustrate a few such aversive factors. When the cause of an aversive stimulus is an identifiable person, such as a smoker, these factors are also provocations. As such, they can increase aggression directed at the person identified as the provocateur, as well as against other "displaced" targets.

In cases where there is no identifiable human agent causing the aversive stimulation the effects on aggression are often less noticeable, but much research demonstrates their reality. The most studied of these effects, with relevant data gathered for over one hundred years, is the heat effect. Anderson and Anderson (1998) showed that a wide array of studies across time, culture, and method converge on the conclusion that hot temperatures increase aggressive tendencies. People who live in hotter cities have higher violent crime rates than those in cooler cities. This effect persists even when controlling for poverty, education, and culture. Violent crime rates are higher during hotter years, seasons, months, and days. When people are hot, they think more aggressive thoughts, feel more hostile, and behave more aggressively.

Alcohol and Drugs. Bushman (1993) reviewed studies on alcohol and drug effects on aggression, and found that central nervous system depressants increase aggression. Neither actual alcohol consumption nor the mere belief that one has consumed alcohol were individually sufficient to produce reliable increases in aggression, but when research participants believed they had consumed alcohol and had actually consumed alcohol, aggression increased. The exact mechanisms underlying these drug effects are not yet fully understood. Steele and Josephs (1990) proposed an "alcohol myopia" explanation, in which alcohol impairs key perceptual processes necessary to normal inhibitions against extreme and risky behavior. Bushman's review (1997) confirmed this view.

Aggression Cues. Objects or events associated with aggression in semantic memory can cue or "prime" aggression-related thoughts, affects, and behavior programs also stored in memory. For instance, seeing a gun can prime aggressive thoughts (Anderson, Benjamin, and Bartholow 1998) and increase aggressive behavior. This phenomenon, labeled the "weapons effect" by Berkowitz and LePage (1967), has been found in field and laboratory studies, in several different countries, with pictures of weapons and with real weapons.

As mentioned earlier, one prevalent source of aggressive cues in modern society is the mass media. Television shows, movies, and video games are filled with violence. Over 1,000 empirical comparisons, compiled by Paik and Comstock (1994) have conclusively demonstrated that even short-term exposure to media violence increases aggression. The immediate impact of viewing violent media is more pronounced for people with strong aggressive tendencies (Bushman 1995). Unfortunately, aggressive people also are the most likely to seek out violent media.

Many people in modern society believe that viewing aggression (e.g., on television) or behaving in a mildly aggressive way within protected environments (e.g., playing football) will reduce later aggressive behavior. This catharsis hypothesis, though, has been thoroughly debunked (Bushman, Baumeister, and Stack in press; Geen and Quanty 1977).

Opportunity. Some situations restrict opportunities to aggress; others provide "good" opportunities. Church service situations have many impediments to aggression—there are witnesses, strong social norms against aggression, and specific nonaggressive behavioral roles for everyone in attendance. Country and Western bars on Saturday nights present better opportunities for aggression, because many aggression facilitators are present: alcohol, aggression cues, aggression-prone individuals, males competing for the attention of females, and relative anonymity.

Removal of Self-Regulatory Inhibitions. One often-neglected facet of human aggression has

garnered increased attention; the aggression inhibitions that normally operate in most people. Several different research groups have independently identified and discussed how these inhibitions are sometimes overridden (Bandura, Barbaranelli, Caprara, and Pastorelli 1996; Keltner and Robinson 1996; Staub 1989, 1998). Most people do not commit extreme acts of violence even if they could do so with little chance of discovery or punishment. Such self-regulation is due, in large part, to the fact that people cannot easily escape the consequences that they apply to themselves. Self-image, self-standards, and sense of self-worth—in other words moral standards—are used in normal self-regulation of behavior.

However, people with apparently normal moral standards sometimes behave reprehensibly toward others, including committing such actions as murder, torture, even genocide. Two particularly important mechanisms that allow people to disengage their normal moral standards involve moral justification and dehumanizing the victim. Common justifications for extreme and mass violence include "it is for the person's own good," or the good of the society, or that personal honor demands the violent action. These justifications can be applied at multiple levels, from a parent's abuse of a child to genocidal war. Dehumanizing the victim operates by making sure that one's moral standards are simply not applicable. War propaganda obviously fits this mechanism, but people also use this mechanism at an individual level. Potential victims are placed in the ultimate outgroup—one that has no human qualities.

The Escalation Cycle. Many proximate causal factors seem too trivial or weak to contribute to serious aggression. How can seeing a weapon, being uncomfortably hot, or watching a violent movie increase murder rates? The answer lies in the escalation cycle. As noted earlier, assaults and homicides do not typically result from one brief encounter or provocation. The parties involved usually know each other and have had a series of unpleasant exchanges. The final encounter may well begin as a relatively minor dispute, but one person escalates the level of aggression. The other person responds in kind and subsequently increases the aggressiveness of the next response. A shouting match can quickly become a shoving match, which can lead to fists, guns, and death. Seemingly trivial factors increase the likelihood of violence by increasing the accessibility of aggressive thoughts, affect, and behavioral acts at each turn of the escalation cycle.

INTERVENTION: PREVENTION AND TREATMENT

The knowledge structure approach explains the difficulty of rehabilitating adults who repeatedly commit violent crimes, or of changing the genocidal climate of groups that have long histories of hate and violence. At the individual level, a lifetime of developing aggressive behavior scripts and automatized hostile perception, expectation, and attribution biases cannot be unlearned easily. However, this approach also reveals that preventing the development of an aggressive or genocidal personality is a more reasonable goal if appropriate steps are taken prior to full maturation.

Preventing and Treating Aggressive Personality. There are three main loci for preventing a child from developing into an aggressive adult. First, one can reduce exposure to events that teach aggressive behaviors or scripts. This would include direct modeling (e.g., by abusive or violent parents) as well as indirect modeling (e.g., exposure to media violence). Second, one can reduce exposure to events that teach that aggression is rewarding. For example, most media violence is highly rewarding for the perpetrator, especially when it is the protagonist who is committing the violence. Similarly, adult violence against children (e.g., by parents or school officials) appears highly rewarding to the child because the adult "wins" the encounter and there are no obvious costs to the adult for harming the child. Third, one can reduce exposure to events that teach hostile perception, expectation, and attribution biases. Once again, the entertainment media is one source of violence exposure that increases the perception that the world is a dangerous place. A heavy dose of media violence (e.g., television, movies, video games, music) can increase all three hostility biases. Witnessing high levels of violence in one's neighborhood also increases these biases.

At all three loci, reducing exposure to aggression-enhancing factors would seem much easier to do in the context of a normal and relatively nonviolent culture than in the context of a genocidal culture. Though the following statements focus on dealing with the aggressive personality, the general principles apply to dealing with the genocidal personality.

Furthermore, treating people who have already developed a strong and stable aggressive personality is much more difficult than preventing the development of such a personality. People with aggressive personalities must learn new nonhostile knowledge structures ranging from perceptual schemata through attributional ones to behavioral scripts. The knowledge structure approach outlined earlier explains why it is easiest to intervene successfully in younger children whose personalities are still malleable, harder to succeed with violent juvenile offenders and young abusive parents, and hardest of all to succeed with habitually violent adult criminals.

Child Abuse: Treatment and Prevention. Early intervention attempts relied primarily on intensive dynamic psychotherapy with the abuser, but this approach has repeatedly failed. Cognitive behavioral interventions have had much greater success, largely because they deal directly with the knowledge structure issues that are so important in this domain (Wolf 1994). This approach succeeds by teaching abusive caregivers to use nonaggressive child compliance techniques, personal anger control, and developmentally appropriate beliefs about childhood abilities.

Reducing Exposure to Aggressive Social Models. Reducing children's exposure to aggressive social models would reduce the percentage who grow up believing in and using aggressive tactics. One way of doing this is to reduce exposure to violent media, especially television and video games. The research literature on television violence has conclusively demonstrated that early and repeated exposure to violent television causes children to develop into aggressive adults. For example, kids who watch a lot of violent television at age eight are more likely to have criminal records at age thirty, even after statistically controlling for a variety of other relevant social variables. Research has suggested that exposure to violent video games has a similar effect.

Reducing other types of exposure to violent social models would also help. Reducing parental violence towards children, reducing the frequency and visibility of violence in children's neighborhoods, reducing violence in schools—including violence by school authorities in attempts to control children—would all have a positive impact on the overall level of aggressiveness in society.

Treating Violent Juvenile Offenders. Many treatments have been tried with violent juvenile offenders, including such things as "boot camps," individual therapy, "scared straight" programs, and group therapy; there is little evidence of sustained success for any of these approaches. One problem is that these standard approaches do not address the wide range of factors that contribute to the development and maintenance of violent behavior. However, there is evidence that treatment can have a significant beneficial impact on violent juvenile offenders (e.g., Simon 1998). Tate, Reppucci, and Mulvey (1995) drew attention to one approach with impressive results—the Multisystemic Therapy developed by Henggeler and Borduin (e.g., Henggeler, Schoenwald, Borduin, Rowland, and Cunningham 1998). Multisystemic Therapy is a family-based approach that first identifies the major factors contributing to the delinquent and violent behaviors of the particular individual undergoing treatment. Biological, school, work, peers, family, and neighborhood factors are examined. Intervention is then tailored to fit the individual constellation of contributing factors. Opportunities to observe and commit further violent and criminal offenses are severely restricted, whereas prosocial behavior opportunities (including studying school subjects, developing hobbies) are greatly enhanced, and are rewarded. Both the long-term success rate and the cost/benefit ratio of this approach have greatly exceeded other attempts at treating this population.

Adults. Attempts at treatment or "rehabilitation" of violent adults, usually done in the context of prison programs, have led to a general consensus of failure. However, several studies have yielded some evidence of a positive effect of treatment on the behavior of violent adults (e.g., Simon 1998). Rice (1997) reported that an intensive program for violent offenders cut recidivism rates in half for nonpsychopathic offenders. Unfortunately, the recidivism rate for psychopathic offenders was significantly increased by this particular treatment program.

MAKING MODERN SOCIETIES LESS VIOLENT

Several controversial suggestions for social change emerge from the past forty years of research on human aggression. These suggestions, designed to decrease aggression and violence levels generally rather than to treat already-violent individuals, are controversial for political rather than scientific reasons. Research results clearly support each of them.

1. Reduce exposure to media violence and other aggressive role models, especially for children and adolescents.

2. Replace the use of corporal punishment with more positive child-control techniques.

3. Reduce social rewards for aggressive activities, including those previously thought to be cathartic.

4. Increase social rewards and social support for nonaggressive prosocial activities (e.g., learning in school) while making success at such activities possible (e.g., reducing class sizes).

5. Increase the quality of prenatal and postnatal care, to decrease the proportion of the population suffering from developmental difficulties that interfere with normal learning and socialization processes (Anderson in press).

6. Increase the quality of parenting, by providing instruction, social support, and economic support.

REFERENCES

Anderson, C. A. (in press) "Aggression and Violence." *The Encyclopedia of Psychology*. Washington, D.C.: American Psychological Association.

——, A. J. Benjamin, and B. D. Bartholow 1998 "Does the Gun Pull the Trigger? Automatic Priming Effects of Weapon Pictures and Weapon Names." *Psychological Science* 9:308–314.

Anderson, C. A., and K. B. Anderson 1998 "Temperature and Aggression: Paradox, Controversy, and a (Fairly) Clear Picture." In R. Geen and E. Donnerstein, eds., *Human Aggression: Theories, Research and Implications for Social Policy*. New York: Academic Press.

Anderson, K. B., and C. A. Anderson 1999 *Men who Target Women: Specificity of Target, Generality of Aggressive Behavior*. Unpublished manuscript.

Azar, S. T., and C. A. Rohrbeck 1986 "Child Abuse and Unrealistic Expectations: Further Validation of the Parent Opinion Questionnaire." *Journal of Consulting and Clinical Psychology* 54:867–868.

Bandura, A. 1973 *Aggression: A Social Learning Analysis*. Englewood Cliffs, N.J.: Prentice-Hall.

——, C. Barbaranelli, G. V. Caprara, and C. Pastorelli 1996 "Mechanisms of Moral Disengagement in the Exercise of Moral Agency." *Journal of Personality and Social Psychology* 71:364–374.

Baron, R. A., and D. R. Richardson 1994 *Human Aggression*, 2nd ed. New York: Plenum Press.

Baumeister, R. F., L. Smart, and J. M. Boden 1996 "Relation of Threatened Egotism to Violence and Aggression: The Dark Side of High Self-Esteem." *Psychological Review* 103:5–33.

Berkowitz, L. 1989 "Frustration-Aggression Hypothesis: Examination and Reformulation." *Psychological Bulletin* 106:59–73.

—— 1993 *Aggression: Its Causes, Consequences, and Control*. New York: McGraw-Hill.

——, and A. LePage 1967 "Weapons as Aggression-Eliciting Stimuli." *Journal of Personality and Social Psychology* 7:202–207.

Bettencourt, B. A., and N. Miller 1996 "Gender Differences in Aggression as a Function of Provocation: A Meta-Analysis." *Psychological Bulletin* 119:422–447.

Bushman, B. J. 1993 "Human Aggression While Under the Influence of Alcohol and Other Drugs: An Integrative Research Review." *Current Directions in Psychological Science* 2:148–152.

—— 1995 "Moderating Role of Trait Aggressiveness in the Effects of Violent Media on Aggression." *Journal of Personality and Social Psychology* 9:950–960.

—— 1997 "Effects of Alcohol on Human Aggression: Validity of Proposed Explanations." In M. Galanter, et al., eds., *Recent Developments in Alcoholism: Alcohol and Violence*, vol. XIII. New York: Plenum Press.

——, and R. F. Baumeister 1998 "Threatened Egotism, Narcissism, Self-Esteem, and Direct and Displaced Aggression: Does Self-Love or Self-Hate Lead to Violence?" *Journal of Personality and Social Psychology* 75:219–229.

——, and A. D. Stack 1999 "Catharsis, Aggression, and Persuasive Influence: Self-Fulfilling or Self-Defeating Prophecies?" *Journal of Personality and Social Psychology* 76:367–376.

Buss, D. M., and T. K. Shackelford 1997 "From Vigilance to Violence: Mate Retention Tactics in Married Couples." *Journal of Personality and Social Psychology* 72:346–361.

Campbell, A., S. Muncer, and J. Odber 1997 "Aggression and Testosterone: Testing a Bio-Social Model." *Aggressive Behavior* 23:229–238.

Dill, K. E., C. A. Anderson, K. B. Anderson, and W. E. Deuser 1997 "Effects of Aggressive Personality on Social Expectations and Social Perceptions." *Journal of Research in Personality* 31:272–292.

Dodge, K. A. 1980 "Social Cognition and Children's Aggressive Behavior." *Child Development* 51:162–170.

Dollard, J., L. Doob, N. Miller, O. H. Mowrer, and R. R. Sears 1939 *Frustration and Aggression*. New Haven, Conn.: Yale University Press.

Eysenck, H. J., and G. Gudjonsson 1989 *The Causes and Cures of Criminality*. New York: Plenum Press.

Geary, D. C. 1998 *Male, Female: The Evolution of Human Sex Differences*. Washington, D.C.: American Psychological Association.

——, M. Rumsey, C. C. Bow-Thomas, and M. K. Hoard 1995 "Sexual Jealousy as a Facultative Trait: Evidence from the Pattern of Sex Differences in Adults from China and the United States." *Ethology and Sociobiology* 16:355–383.

Geen, R. G. 1990 *Human Aggression*. Pacific Grove, Calif.: Brooks/Cole.

——, and E. Donnerstein (eds.) 1998 *Human Aggression: Theories, Research and Implications for Social Policy*. New York: Academic Press.

Geen, R. G., and M. B. Quanty 1977 "The Catharsis of Aggression: An Evaluation of a Hypothesis." In L. Berkowitz, ed., *Advances in Experimental Social Psychology*, vol. 10. New York: Academic Press.

Green, D. P., J. Glaser, and A. Rich 1998 "From Lynching to Gay Bashing: The Elusive Connection between Economic Conditions and Hate Crime." *Journal of Personality and Social Psychology* 75:82–92.

Goldstein, A. P. 1994 *The Ecology of Aggression*. New York: Plenum.

Henggeler, S. W, S. K. Schoenwald, C. M. Borduin, M. D. Rowland, and P. B. Cunningham 1998 *Multisystemic Treatment of Antisocial Behavior in Children and Adolescents*. New York: The Guilford Press.

Huesmann, L. R. 1998 "The Role of Social Information Processing and Cognitive Schema in the Acquisition and Maintenance of Habitual Aggressive Behavior." In R. Geen and E. Donnerstein, eds., *Human Aggression: Theories, Research and Implications for Social Policy*. New York: Academic Press.

—— (ed.) 1994 *Aggressive Behavior: Current Perspectives*. New York: Plenum.

——, and L. S. Miller 1994 "Long-Term Effects of Repeated Exposure to Media Violence in Childhood." In L. R. Huesmann, ed., *Aggressive Behavior: Current Perspectives*. New York: Plenum Press.

Huesmann, L. R., and J. F. Moise 1998 "The Stability and Continuity of Aggression from Early Childhood to Young Adulthood." In D. J. Flannery and C. F. Huff, eds., *Youth Violence: Prevention, Intervention, and Social Policy*. Washington, D.C.: American Psychiatric Press.

Keltner, D., and R. J. Robinson 1996. "Extremism, Power, and the Imagined Basis of Social Conflict." *Current Directions in Psychological Science* 5:101–105.

Kernis, M. H., B. D. Grannemann, and L. C. Barclay 1989 "Stability and Level of Self-Esteem as Predictors of Anger Arousal and Hostility." *Journal of Personality and Social Psychology* 56:1013–1022.

Malamuth, N. M., D. Linz, C. L. Heavey, G. Barnes, and M. Acker 1995 "Using the Confluence Model of Sexual Aggression to Predict Men's Conflict with Women: A 10-Year Follow-Up Study." *Journal of Personality and Social Psychology* 69:353–369.

Miles, D. R., and G. Carey 1997 "Genetic and Environmental Architecture of Human Aggression." *Journal of Personality and Social Psychology* 72:207–217.

Miller, N., and A. Marcus-Newhall 1997 "A Conceptual Analysis of Displaced Aggression." In R. Ben-Ari and Y. Rich, eds., *Enhancing Education in Heterogeneous Schools: Theory and Application*. Ramat-Gan: Bar-Ilan University Press.

Olweus, D. 1995 "Bullying or Peer Abuse at School: Facts and Intervention." *Current Directions in Psychological Science* 4:196–200.

Paik, H., and G. Comstock 1994 "The Effects of Television Violence on Antisocial Behavior: A Meta-Analysis." *Communication Research* 21:516–546.

Patterson, G. R., B. D. DeBaryshe, and E. Ramsey 1989 "A Developmental Perspective on Antisocial Behavior." *American Psychologist* 44:329–335.

Peterson, L., S. Gable, C. Doyle, and B. Ewugman 1997 "Beyond Parenting Skills: Battling Barriers and Building Bonds to Prevent Child Abuse and Neglect." *Cognitive and Behavioral Practice* 4:53–74.

Rice, M. E. 1997 "Violent Offender Research and Implications for the Criminal Justice System." *American Psychologist* 52:414–423.

Rubin, J. Z., D. G. Pruitt, and S. H. Kim 1994 *Social Conflict: Escalation, Stalemate, and Settlement*, 2nd ed. New York: McGraw-Hill.

Simon, L. M. J. 1998 "Does Criminal Offender Treatment Work?" *Applied & Preventive Psychology* 7:137–159.

Staub, E. 1989 *The Roots of Evil: The Origins of Genocide and Other Group Violence*. New York: Cambridge University Press.

—— 1998 "Breaking the Cycle of Genocidal Violence: Healing and Reconciliation." In J. Harvey, ed., *Perspectives on Loss: A Sourcebook*. Philadelphia: Taylor and Francis.

Steele, C. M., and R. A. Josephs 1990 "Alcohol Myopia: Its Prized and Dangerous Effects." *American Psychologist* 45:921–933.

Strasburger, V. C. 1995 *Adolescents and the Media: Medical and Psychological Impact*. Thousand Oaks, Calif.: Sage.

Straus, M. A., and R. J. Gelles 1990 *Physical Violence in American Families: Risk Factors and Adaptations to Violence in 8,145 Families*. New Brunswick, N.J.: Transaction.

Tate, D. C., N. D. Reppucci, and E. P. Mulvey 1995 "Violent Juvenile Delinquents: Treatment Effectiveness and Implications for Future Action." *American Psychologist* 50:777–781.

Tedeschi, J. T., and R. B. Felson 1994 *Violence, Aggression, & Coercive Actions*. Washington, D.C.: American Psychological Association.

Wolfe, D. A. 1994 "The Role of Intervention and Treatment Services in the Prevention of Child Abuse and Neglect." In G. B. Melton and F. D. Barry, eds., *Protecting Children from Abuse and Neglect: Foundations for a New National Strategy*. New York: Guilford Press.

CRAIG A. ANDERSON

AGING

See Aging and the Life Course; Cohort Perspectives; Filial Responsibility; Intergenerational Relations; Intergenerational Resource Transfer; Long Term Care, Long Term Care Facilities; Retirement; Widowhood.

AGING AND THE LIFE COURSE

Social gerontology, or the sociology of aging, has two primary foci: (a) social factors during late life, and (b) social antecedents and consequences of aging. Thus, social gerontology includes examination of both the status of being old and the process of becoming old. Increasingly, theories and methods of the life course are replacing the earlier emphasis on late life as a separate topic of inquiry. This is a vast arena, and the sociology of aging is appropriately informed by the theories and methods of many sociological subspecialities ranging from macrohistorical and demographic perspectives to the microorientations of social psychology and interpretive sociology.

HISTORY OF THE FIELD

Historically, social gerontology emerged from a social-problems orientation and focused on the deprivations and losses that were expected to characterize late life (e.g., Burgess 1960; Cain 1959). Early research in the field focused on issues such as poverty during late life; old age as a marginal status, reflecting problems of social integration; the negative effects of institutionalization and poor quality of long-term care; and ageism and age discrimination. Early on, however, some investigators saw the dangers of allowing a crisis orientation to dominate the study of aging and focused attention on patterns of "normal" and "successful" aging (Havighurst 1963; Palmore 1970). A significant proportion of research also focuses on the problems of late life. Investigators remain concerned about social integration and adaptation to loss. The majority of funding for aging research is provided by the National Institute on Aging, which is mandated to support health-related research. Consequently, much aging research focuses on illness and the health care delivery system. The dramatic aging of the population (U.S. Bureau of the Census 1987)—a trend that will peak with the aging of the Baby Boom cohorts—leads to questions about the capacities of social institutions and public policies to meet the needs of an unprecedented number and proportion of older adults. Scholars using political economy theories focus on the ways in which societies respond to the dependency needs of older adults and the social implications of those responses.

Although much research remains focused on the problems of late life, sociologists now recognize the broader importance and implications of old age and aging. Two primary factors appear to have been the driving forces that account for this broader and more complex view. First, despite the social-problems orientation of most early research,

empirical data failed to confirm a uniformly bleak picture of old age. For example, in spite of higher rates of illness and disability, the vast majority of older adults are competent and able to live independent lives (Kunkel and Applebaum 1992). Similarly, rather than representing involuntary loss of a treasured role, retirement is actively sought by the majority of older workers and seldom poses adaptive problems (e.g., Hardy and Quadagno 1995). In addition, some of the problems observed in early studies of older adults have been remedied by the increased resources that recent cohorts have brought to late life, as well as to effective public policies. Thus, although health care costs remain a burden for many older adults, Medicare and Medicaid substantially reduced barriers to health care among older people. Similarly, as a result of improvements in Social Security benefits and increased participation in private pensions, older Americans now are no more likely to live in poverty than younger adults and, indeed, are less likely to live in poverty than children (U.S. Bureau of the Census 1997). Such findings pushed social gerontology toward more complex and empirically defensible perspectives on old age and aging.

Second, sociologists came to recognize that age plays a fundamental role in social structure and social organization. As a parameter of social organization, age affects the allocation of social resources and social roles. Along with sex and race, age is an ascribed status. But age is unique among ascribed statuses in that it changes over time, and movement across age categories results in changing expectations for behavior, changing access to social resources, and changing personal and social responsibilities. The structural quality of age is best articulated in *age stratification theory* (Riley 1987). Age stratification refers to the division of society into meaningful age groups that differ in social value and the allocation of social resources. The concept of age stratification has proven to be useful in a variety of ways. At the broadest level, it reminds us that age is a fundamental parameter of social organization. Age stratification has been particularly useful in highlighting age-related roles and norms. It has a social-psychological facet as well: age consciousness or awareness and identification with members of one's age group (Day 1990). Moreover, the structural and individual facets of age stratification operate in both directions. On the one hand, the structural component of age stratification allocates roles and resources and assigns differential social value to age strata. Thus, ageism is largely an effect of age stratification. On the other hand, by promoting age consciousness, age stratification sets the stage for age-based public policies and collective efforts by older adults to protect or increase their share of societal resources (e.g., voting and lobbying efforts based on the self-interests of the elderly).

In the 1990s, the sociology of aging focused on change and stability across the life course. Life-course perspectives have enriched aging research in several ways (e.g., Elder 1995; George 1993). First, a life-course approach is attractive because it recognizes that the past is prologue to the future. That is, status and personal well-being in late life depend in large part on events and achievements experienced earlier in the life course. Second, life-course perspectives emphasize relationships across life domains, recognizing that, for example, family events affect and are affected by work and health. Traditionally, sociological research has focused on specific life domains (e.g., the sociology of work, the sociology of the family); life-course perspectives, in contrast, are person-centered rather than domain-centered. Third, life-course perspectives focus on the intersection of history and personal biography. Although the macro-micro schism remains difficult to bridge, life-course research has documented some of the complex ways that historical conditions affect personal lives both contemporaneously and over subsequent decades.

THE AGE-PERIOD-COHORT PROBLEM

Isolating the effects of age and characterizing the aging process are difficult tasks. Because many factors affect social structure and individual behavior, it is always difficult to isolate the effects of a specific factor. But this task is especially difficult with regard to age, because it is inherently confounded with the effects of two other factors: cohort and period. *Age*, of course, refers to time since birth, and *age effects* refers to patterns resulting from the passage of time or sheer length of life. *Cohort* refers to the group of persons born at approximately the same time (e.g., the 1920 cohort, the 1940–1944 cohort). There are two primary kinds of *cohort effects*. One type results from historical factors. For example, cohorts who lived through the Great Depression or World War II

had different life experiences than cohorts who were not exposed to those historical events. And, as a further complication, the effects of historical events vary depending on the ages of those who experience them. The second type of cohort effect reflects compositional characteristics. For example, large cohorts (such as the Baby Boomers) may face greater competition for social resources than smaller cohorts (e.g., those born during the Great Depression, when fertility rates were low). Both types of cohort effects can have persistent effects on the life course, and, hence, late life. *Period effects* (also called *time of measurement effects*) result from events or situations that happen at a specific time, and tend to affect individuals regardless of age or cohort. For example, faith in government decreased in all Americans (regardless of age or cohort) at the time of the Watergate scandal.

Age, cohort, and period effects are intertwined. If one knows when an individual was born and also knows the time of measurement, simple subtraction provides accurate information about the individual's age. Similarly, if one knows an individual's age and time of measurement, one can easily calculate date of birth or birth cohort. Statistically, there are no easy methods for disentangling age, period, and cohort. In general, however, the most compelling research results are those that are based on examination of multiple cohorts at multiple times of measurement. If the same age patterns are observed across different cohorts measured at different times, those patterns are likely to reflect age effects. If patterns are not similar across cohorts and times of measurement, however, they are likely to reflect cohort or period effects.

The issue of age-period-cohort effects has lost some of its appeal; critics point out that simply knowing, for example, that there is a cohort effect leaves unanswered what it is about those cohorts that generated the observed differences. This is an appropriate criticism; nonetheless, it is immensely helpful in searching for causal explanations to know whether the underlying mechanism is consistent across time and place (an aging effect), had strong contemporaneous effects on persons of all ages (a period effect), or affected only specific cohorts (a cohort effect). Age, cohort, and period effects are all important in aging research. Age effects provide information about human development as it unfolds in social context. Cohort effects permit us to observe the social implications of shared history and cohort composition. Period effects provide information about the effects of contemporaneous events and situations on social structure and individual behavior. Distinguishing among age, period, and cohort effects also has important implications for the generalization of research results. Age effects are the same or highly similar across time and place; thus, they are generalizable. In contrast, cohort and period effects are, by definition, variable across time. Consequently, generalization is limited.

Examination of age-period-cohort effects requires large data bases in which multiple cohorts are observed on multiple occasions over long periods of time. Because of these stringent requirements, few aging studies focus specifically on disentangling these confounded factors. But recognition of these sources of confounding appropriately temper investigators' generalizations. In addition, this issue has sensitized researchers to the need to examine change over time, with the result that longitudinal studies have become the dominant research design in efforts to characterize the aging process.

No single theme nor easily summarized list of topics does justice to the scope and diversity of research on aging and the life course. However, three major research domains can provide a general sense of the current major avenues of aging and life-course research: aged heterogeneity, life-course dynamics, and life-course trajectories.

AGED HETEROGENEITY

The majority of research on older adults focuses on heterogeneity in that population. In many ways, this is the legacy of the problem orientation upon which initial aging research in the social sciences rested. Even now, most aging research focuses on differences among older adults and the complex configurations of social factors that can account for individual differences during late life. And, although there are many exceptions, a majority of research in this domain focuses on the social factors that explain individual behavior and personal well-being.

The specific topics that are examined in research on aged heterogeneity are extensive. Health and disability are major concerns in this research tradition, including physical illness; mental illness,

especially depression; cognitive status and dementing illness; functional status and disability; and health behaviors. Health service utilization is a corollary emphasis; there are numerous studies on both utilization in general (e.g., doctors visits, hospitalizations) and specialized health care settings and providers (e.g., long-term care facilities, emergency room visits, screening programs and other preventative services, mental health professionals, dentists). There also has been extensive research on the use of social and community services and living arrangements—both of which are strongly driven by health during late life.

Along with health, socioeconomic status has been a high-volume, long-standing focus in research on aged heterogeneity. Economic status, in the form of income and, to a lesser extent, assets has been the primary emphasis of this research, with studies of the antecedents and consequences of retirement ranking as a close second. Pensions have been shown to have strong effects upon the adequacy of postretirement income, which has spurred substantial investigation of the determinants of pension acquisition and value.

From a more social-psychological perspective, there are strong research traditions examining multiple psychosocial states that can be subsumed under the umbrella of "quality of life." Life satisfaction and morale have received paramount attention in this regard. But several dimensions of the self (e.g., self-esteem, locus of control, sense of mastery) also have rich research traditions.

Two common elements of the wide range of research conducted on the topic of aged heterogeneity merit note. First, a common thread in this research is the desire to understand the processes that render some older adults advantaged and others disadvantaged. This is often described as the "applied" character of aging research. However, it also is a focus on stratification in the broadest sense, which is one of the most persistent and cherished issues in mainstream sociology. Research on aging and the life course has contributed much to our understanding of how broadly life chances and life quality are linked to social factors, as well as to the multiple powerful social bases of stratification.

Second, examination of heterogeneity among the elderly has proven to be a strategic site for testing and refining multiple middle-range theories and concepts that are central to sociological research. A few examples will illustrate this point. Research on health and disability during late life has been enriched by attention to issues of social stress and social support; conversely, the older population has proven to be ideal for testing theoretical propositions about the effects of stress and social support. Similarly, the issue of social integration, which has an honored tradition in sociology, has been reactivated in studies of older adults, who vary widely in number and quality of links to social structure. And issues such as the "feminization of poverty" and the "double/triple jeopardy hypothesis" (i.e., the potential interacting deprivations associated with being female, nonwhite, and old) have highlighted the extent to which socioeconomic stratification rests on ascribed rather than achieved statuses.

LIFE-COURSE DYNAMICS

While the issue of heterogeneity focuses attention on differences across individuals, life-course dynamics focus on the persisting effects of social factors over time and stages of life; that is, on intraindividual change. At least three types of life-course studies have received substantial attention in aging research.

The Intersection of History and Personal Biography. There now is substantial evidence that historical events can permanently alter personal lives. Most research to date has focused on two historical events: the Great Depression and World War II; both historical events have been linked to life circumstances during late life. Elder (1974, 1999) has compellingly documented, for example, that entering the labor market during the Depression had a permanent negative effect on occupation and income, which in turn affected socioeconomic status during late life. In contrast, younger men, who entered the labor force immediately after World War II experienced historically unparalled occupational opportunities (and, if they were veterans, government-subsidized college educations).

Other studies by Elder and colleagues focused on the life-course consequences of combat experience during World War II (Elder, Shanahan, and Clipp 1994, 1997). Exposure to combat was strongly related to subsequent health problems, not only immediately after the war, but also during late life. Social factors loom large in these dynamics. First, social factors were strongly predictive of which soldiers were exposed to combat. Second, social resources and deprivations were strong predictors of the onset or avoidance of health problems.

The effects of historical events on the life course appear on two levels. When an historical event is pervasive, one method of observing its effects is via cohort differences. That is, an event with wide-ranging effects will render those who experience it discernibly different from cohorts that come before and after it. At the same time, historical events do not have the same immediate or long-term consequences for all members of a cohort. For example, families were differentially affected by the economic dislocations of the Depression, with some suffering extensive economic deprivation and others experiencing little or no change in their economic fortunes. Thus, not everyone who "lives through" a major historical event will experience serious life-course consequences. One of the tasks of the life-course scholar is to identify the social factors that determine whether or not an historical event alters personal biography.

The Persisting Effects of Early Traumas and Deprivations. A second research focus that illustrates the power of life-course perspectives is investigation of the consequences of early traumas and deprivations on well-being in middle and late life. A growing body of research documents the far-reaching effects of severe childhood experiences—including parental divorce and, to a lesser extent, parental death; childhood poverty; and childhood physical and sexual abuse—on the course of adulthood. Most research to date has focused on the implications of these traumas and deprivations on physical and mental health (e.g., Krause 1998; Landerman, George, and Blazer 1991). The robust relationships between events experienced during childhood and health fifty to sixty years later, controlling on contemporaneous risk factors for morbidity, is strong evidence of the power of fateful events to alter the life course.

Again, social factors are strongly implicated in the processes that account for the relationships between childhood traumas and health and well-being during late life. First, the availability of social resources *at the time* of the trauma can dampen its negative effects in both the short and the long term. For example, financial security and adequate supervision ameliorate most of the negative effects of parental divorce on subsequent socioeconomic achievements and physical and mental health (e.g., Kessler and Magee 1994). Second, two of the primary mechanisms by which childhood traumas generate poor health in later life are socioeconomic achievement and high-quality social relationships (e.g., McLeod 1991). That is, childhood traumas are often associated with lower socioeconomic status and poor-quality relationships during adulthood—both of which are risk factors for physical and mental illness. If, however, individuals who experienced childhood traumas manage to achieve adequate financial resources and supportive social ties during adulthood, their excess risk of illness in middle and late life is reduced substantially.

The Persisting Effects of Early Life Decisions. There now is substantial evidence that the decisions that individuals make during early adulthood have important consequences for their life circumstances in late life. Studies of retirement income provide perhaps the best illustration of this research domain. The strongest predictor of retirement income is occupational history. Throughout adulthood, individuals "sort themselves" into jobs that differ not only in income, but also in benefits (i.e., total compensation packages). Of these, the availability and quality of pensions is most important for retirement income. There is strong evidence that the provision of pensions differs not only by occupation, but also by industrial sector (Quadagno 1988). Thus, when individuals make occupational choices—including job changes throughout adulthood—they are inevitably determining, in part, their retirement incomes.

Research on women's retirement income has broadened our understanding of the life-course consequences of early decisions. Women and men tend to be concentrated in different occupations and different industrial sectors—and those in which women dominate have, on average, lower earnings and lower likelihood of pension coverage (O'Rand 1988). Moreover, family formation decisions strongly affect women's job histories. Compared to men, women are less likely to work full-time and work fewer total years, largely as a result of parental responsibilities. All of these factors combine to produce substantially lower retirement incomes for women than for men (O'Rand and Landerman 1984).

LIFE-COURSE TRAJECTORIES AND PERSON-CENTERED RESEARCH

The two research domains described above focus on *interindividual differences* in late life and *intraindividual change* over the life course. A third domain, less developed than the others but exciting in its scope, attempts to examine interindividual differences and intraindividual change simultaneously. At this point, two emerging research traditions illustrate the nature and potential of this approach.

Life-Course Trajectories. Trajectories refer to long-term patterns of stability and change. They can be examined at both the aggregate (e.g., the "typical" career, the modal pathway to nursing home placement) and individual levels. Thus, trajectories capture patterns of intraindividual change. Examination of heterogeneity can be pursued in two ways. In the first, the trajectory that best describes the sample or population is constructed. Subsequently, using techniques such as hierarchical linear modeling or growth-curve analysis, investigators can examine the extent to which factors of interest alter the shape of the trajectory. For example, a trajectory of earnings across adulthood can be constructed for a given sample. Investigators can then examine the degree to which factors such as sex, education, and race affect the shape of the earnings trajectory. In the second approach, multiple common trajectories are identified and investigators then determine the characteristics associated with those trajectories. Using this approach, for example, several common trajectories of earnings during adulthood could be identified (e.g., consistently increasing earnings, earnings peaking during mid-life and then decreasing, consistently decreasing earnings, a relatively flat earnings history). Factors such as sex, education, and race could then be examined to determine their association with these distinctive earnings trajectories.

Trajectory-based research, with its focus on both interindividual differences and intraindividual change, is very attractive. The major limitation to the use of this approach is the availability of data, because longitudinal data covering long periods of time are required if one wishes to understand life-course patterns. It should be noted, however, that trajectory-based research can also be useful for studying shorter processes (e.g., patterns of illness outcome, with relatively short-term trajectories of death, chronicity, recovery, and relapse).

Trajectory-based research relevant to our understanding of middle and late life is gradually accumulating. This is especially true for long-term patterns of health and functioning, providing evidence about both the dynamics of disability during late life (e.g., Maddox and Clark 1992; Verbrugge, Reoma, and Gruber-Baldini 1994) and long-term patterns of stability, improvement, and decline in health over the course of adulthood (e.g., Clipp, Pavalko, and Elder 1992). Important trajectory-based research on pathways to retirement (Elder and Pavalko 1993) and place of death (Merrill and Mor 1993) is also available.

The concept of trajectories has been valuable in theoretical development, as well as empirical inquiry. The theory of *cumulative advantage/disadvantage* has intersected well with studies of life-course trajectories. This theory posits that heterogeneity is greater in late life than earlier in the life course as a result of the accumulation of assets (advantage) or liabilities (disadvantage) over time. The theory of cumulative advantage/disadvantage has been especially useful in understanding socioeconomic heterogeneity in late life, especially differences in total net worth (e.g., Crystal and Shea 1990; O'Rand 1996). However, it can be applied to other sources of heterogeneity in late life as well (e.g., health). Investigators who prefer examination of the multiple distinctive trajectories within a sample would offer a caution to cumulative advantage/disadvantage theory, however. They would note that although trajectories of increasing and decreasing advantage are undoubtedly common, there are likely to be other important trajectories as well—e.g., a trajectory of cumulating advantage that is reversed as a result of a personal (e.g., serious illness) or societal (e.g., severe economic downturn) catastrophic event.

Person-centered research. A more recent contribution to the sociological armamentarium for understanding aging and the life course is *person-centered research*. As the label implies, the focus of this emerging research strategy is to analyze "people" rather than "variables." In practice, this means that members of a sample are first grouped into subsets on the dependent variable of interest. Subsequently, those categories are further disaggregated into groups based on distinctive pathways or life histories associated with the outcome of interest.

Work by Singer, Ryff, and Magee (1998) provides the richest example of person-centered aging research to date. The dependent variable of interest was mental health. In the first stage of their research, groups of middle-aged women were divided into groups that differed on levels of mental health. Subsequently, the large archive on longitudinal data obtained from these women over the previous three decades was examined to identify distinctive pathways associated with mid-life mental health. For example, the group of women who exhibited high levels of mental health and well-being were further subdivided into two groups that Singer et al. (1999) labeled the healthy and the resilient. Healthy women were those who had life histories that were relatively free of major stressors or traumas, enjoyed adequate or higher levels of social and economic resources, and exhibited stable patterns of robust mental health. Resilient women were those who had achieved robust mental health at mid-life despite earlier evidence of poor mental health and/or histories of stress and/or inadequate social and economic resources. Clearly the life histories of women who were mentally healthy at mid-life varied in important ways. Moreover, the healthy women illustrate the benefits of leading relatively "charmed" lives, while the resilient women help us to understand the circumstances under which "risky" life histories can be turned around to produce health and personal growth.

There are clear similarities between person-centered research and trajectory-based research. Both are based on long-term patterns of change and stability and both are designed to understand both life-course dynamics and heterogeneity in those dynamics. But there also are important differences between the two approaches. In trajectory-based research, the trajectory or pathway itself is the "dependent variable" of interest and the "independent variables" are factors that have the potential to alter the shape(s) of those pathways. In person-centered research, the "dependent variable" is an outcome of interest (e.g., mental health), and trajectories of the "independent variables" are constructed to explain that outcome. Both are currently at the cutting edge of research that attempts to simultaneously examine life-course dynamics and life-course heterogeneity.

Aging and the life course is an important sociological specialty. It provides us with information about aging and being "old," and about the antecedents and consequences of stability and change during late life. The increasing life-course focus of aging research is especially important in that it concentrates sociologists' attention on the dynamics of intraindividual change and on the intersections of social structure, social change, and personal biography. At its best, aging and life-course research effectively link processes and dynamics at the macrohistorical and societal levels with individual attitudes and behaviors. In addition, the life course in general, and late life in particular, provide excellent contexts for testing and, indeed, challenging some commonly held assumptions and hypotheses about the dynamics of social influence. In this way, it offers valuable contributions to the larger sociological enterprise.

REFERENCES

Burgess, Ernest W. 1960 "Aging in Western Culture." In E. W. Burgess, ed., *Aging in Western Societies.* Chicago: The University of Chicago Press.

Cain, Leonard D., Jr. 1959 "The Sociology of Aging: A Trend Report and Bibliography." *Current Sociology* 8:57–133.

Clipp, Elizabeth C., Eliza K. Pavalko, and Glen H. Elder, Jr. 1992 "Trajectories of Health: In Concept and Empirical Pattern." *Behavior, Health, and Aging* 2:159–177.

Crystal, Stephen, and Dennis Shea 1990 "Cumulative Advantage, Cumulative Disadvantage, and Inequality among Elderly People." *The Gerontologist* 30:437–443.

Day, Christine L. 1990 *What Older People Think.* Princeton, N.J.: Princeton University Press.

Elder, Glen H., Jr. 1999 *Children of the Great Depression* (twenty-fifth anniversary ed.). Boulder, Colo.: Westview Press.

—— 1995 "The Life Course Paradigm: Historical, Comparative, and Developmental Perspectives." In P. Moen, G. H. Elder, and K. Luscher, eds., *Examining Lives in Context: Perspectives on the Ecology of Human Development.* Washington, D.C.: American Psychological Association Press.

—— 1974 *Children of the Great Depression.* Chicago: University of Chicago Press.

——, and Eliza K. Pavalko 1993 "Work Careers in Men's Later Years: Transitions, Trajectories, and Historical Change." *Journal of Gerontology: Social Sciences* 48:S180–S191.

Elder, Glen H., Jr., Michael J. Shanahan, and Elizabeth C. Clipp 1997 "Linking Combat and Physical Health: The Legacy of World War II in Men's Lives." *American Journal of Psychiatry* 154:330–336.

—— 1994 "When War Comes to Men's Lives: Life-Course Patterns in Family, Work, and Health." *Psychology and Aging* 9:5–16.

George, Linda K. 1993 "Sociological Perspectives on Life Transitions." *Annual Review of Sociology* 19:353–373.

Hardy, Melissa A., and Jill Quadagno 1995 "Satisfaction with Early Retirement: Making Choices in the Auto Industry." *Journal of Gerontology: Social Sciences* 50:S217–S228.

Havighurst, Robert A. 1963 "Successful Aging." In R. Williams, C. Tibbets, and W. Donahue, eds., *Processes of Aging.* New York: Atherton.

Kessler, Ronald C., and William J. Magee 1994 "Childhood Family Violence and Adult Recurrent Depression." *Journal of Health and Social Behavior* 35:13–27.

Krause, Neal 1998 "Early Parental Loss, Recent Life Events, and Changes in Health." *Journal of Aging and Health* 10:395–421.

Kunkel, Susan R., and Robert A. Applebaum 1992 "Estimating the Prevalence of Long-Term Disability for an Aging Society." *Journal of Gerontology: Social Sciences* 47:S253–S260.

Landerman, Richard, Linda K. George, and Dan G. Blazer 1991 "Adult Vulnerability for Psychiatric Disorders: Interactive Effects of Negative Childhood Experiences and Recent Stress." *Journal of Nervous and Mental Disease* 179:656–663.

Maddox, George L., and Daniel O. Clark 1992 "Trajectories of Functional Impairment in Later Life." *Journal of Health and Social Behavior* 33:114–125.

McLeod, Jane D. 1991 "Childhood Parental Loss and Adult Depression." *Journal of Health and Social Behavior* 32:205–220.

Merrill, Deborah M., and Vincent Mor 1993 "Pathways to Hospital Death Among the Oldest Old." *Journal of Aging and Health* 5:516–535.

O'Rand, Angela M. 1996 "The Precious and the Precocious: Understanding Cumulative Disadvantage and Cumulative Advantage Over the Life Course." *The Gerontologist* 36:230–238.

—— 1988 "Convergence, Institutionalization, and Bifurcation: Gender and the Pension Acquisition Process." *Annual Review of Gerontology and Geriatrics* 8:132–155.

——, and L. Richard Landerman 1984 "Women's and Men's Retirement Income: Early Family Role Effects." *Research on Aging* 6:25–44.

Palmore, Erdman B. 1970 *Normal Aging: Reports from the Duke Longitudinal Studies, 1955–1969*. Durham, N.C.: Duke University Press.

Quadagno, Jill 1988 "Women's Access to Pensions and the Structure of Eligibility Rules: Systems of Production and Reproduction." *Sociological Quarterly* 29:541–558.

Riley, Matilda White 1987 "On the Significance of Age in Sociology." *American Sociological Review* 52:1–14.

Singer, Burton, Carol D. Ryff, Deborah Carr, and William J. Magee 1998 "Life Histories and Mental Health: A Person-Centered Strategy." In A. Rafferty, ed., *Sociological Methodology, 1988*. Washington, D.C.: American Sociological Association.

U. S. Bureau of the Census 1997 *Statistical Abstracts of the United States, 1997*. Washington, D. C.: U. S. Government Printing Office.

U. S. Bureau of the Census 1987 *An Aging World*. Washington, D. C.: U. S. Government Printing Office.

Verbrugge, Lois M., Joseto M. Reoma, and Ann L. Gruber-Baldini 1994 "Short-Term Dynamics of Disability and Well-Being." *Journal of Health and Social Behavior* 35:97–117.

LINDA K. GEORGE

AGRICULTURAL INNOVATION

Getting a new idea adopted can be very difficult. This is all the more frustrating when it seems to the proponents of the new idea that it has very obvious advantages. It can be a challenge to try to introduce new ideas in rural areas, particularly in less-developed societies, where people are somewhat set in their ways—ways that have evolved slowly, through trial and error. It's all the more difficult when those introducing new ideas don't understand why people follow traditional practices. Rural sociologists and agricultural extension researchers who have studied the diffusion of agricultural innovations have traditionally been oriented toward speeding up the diffusion process (Rogers 1983). Pro-innovation bias has sometimes led sociologists to forget that "changing people's customs is an even more delicate responsibility than surgery" (Spicer 1952).

Although innovation relies on invention, and although considerable creativity often accompanies the discovery of how to use an invention, innovation and invention are not the same thing. Innovation does, however, involve more than a change from one well-established way of doing things to another well-established practice. As with all innovations, those in agriculture involve a change that requires significant imagination, break with established ways of doing things, and create new production capacity. Of course, these criteria are not exact, and it is often difficult to tell where one innovation stops and another starts. The easiest way out of this is to rely on potential adopters of an innovation to define ideas that they perceive to be new.

Innovations are not all alike. New ways of doing things may be more or less compatible with prevalent norms and values. Some innovations may be perceived as relatively difficult to use and understand (i.e., complex), while others are a good deal simpler. Some can be experimented with in limited trials that reduce the risks of adoption (i.e., divisible). Innovations also vary in the costs and advantages they offer in both economic and social terms (e.g., prestige, convenience, satisfaction). In the economists' terms, innovation introduces a new production function that changes the set of possibilities which define what can be produced (Schumpeter 1950). Rural sociologists have studied the adoption of such agricultural innovations as specially bred crops (e.g., hybrid corn and high-yield wheat and rice); many kinds of machines (e.g., tractors, harvesters, pumps); chemical and biological fertilizers, pesticides, and insecticides; cropping practices (e.g., soil and water conservation); and techniques related to animal husbandry (e.g., new feeds, disease control, breeding). Often they have relied upon government agencies such as the U.S. Department of Agriculture to tell them what the recommended new practices are.

The diffusion of agricultural innovations is a process whereby new ways of doing things are spread within and between agrarian communities. Newness implies a degree of uncertainty both because there are a variable number of alternatives and because there is usually some range of relative probability of outcomes associated with the actions involved. Rogers (1983) stresses that the diffusion of innovations includes the communication of information, by various means, about these sets of alternative actions and their possible outcomes. Information about innovations may come via impersonal channels, such as the mass media, or it may pass through social networks. From an individual's point of view, the process of innovation is usually conceived to start with initial awareness of the innovation and how it functions. It ends with adoption or nonadoption. In between these end points is an interactive, iterative process of attitude formation, decision making, and action. The cumulative frequency of adopters over time describes an S-shaped (logistic) curve. The frequency distribution over time is often bellshaped and approximately normal.

Individual innovativeness has been characterized in five ideal-type adopter categories (Rogers 1983). The first 2 to 3 percent to adopt an innovation, the "innovators," are characterized as venturesome. The next 10 to 15 percent, the "early adopters," are characterized as responsible, solid, local opinion leaders. The next 30 to 35 percent are the "early majority," who are seen as being deliberate. They are followed by the "late majority" (30 to 35 percent), who are cautious and skeptical, and innovate under social and economic pressures. Finally, there are the "laggards," who comprise the bottom 15 percent. They are characterized as "traditional," although they are often simply in a precarious economic position. Earlier adopters are likely to have higher social status and better education, and to be upwardly mobile. They tend to have larger farms, more favorable attitudes toward modern business practices (e.g., credit), and more specialized operations. Earlier adopters are also argued to have greater empathy, rationality, and ability to deal with abstractions. They are less fatalistic and dogmatic, and have both positive attitudes toward change and science, and higher achievement motivation and aspirations. Early adopters report more social participation and network connections, particularly to change agents, and greater exposure to both mass media and interpersonal communication networks.

Although Rogers (1983) provides dozens of such generalizations about the characteristics of early and late adopters, he admits that the evidence on many of these propositions is somewhat mixed (Downs and Mohr 1976). Even the frequently researched proposition that those with higher social status and greater resources are likely to innovate earlier and more often has garnered far less than unanimous support (Cancian 1967, 1979; Gartrell 1977). Cancian argues that this is a result of "upper middle-class conservatism," but

subsequent meta-analysis has clearly demonstrated that the relationship between status and innovation is indeed linear (Gartrell and Gartrell 1985; Lewis et al. 1989). If anything, those with very high status or resources show a marked tendency to turn their awareness of innovations into trial at a very high rate (Gartrell and Gartrell 1979).

Ryan and Gross (1942) provide a classic example of diffusion research. Hybrid corn seed, developed by Iowa State and other land-grant university researchers, increased yields 20 percent over those of open-pollinated varieties. Hybrid corn also was more drought-resistant and was better suited to mechanical harvesting. Agricultural extension agents and seed company salesmen promoted it heavily. Its drawback was that it lost its hybrid vigor after only one generation, so farmers could not save the seed from the best-looking plants. (Of course, this was not at all a drawback to the seed companies!)

Based on a retrospective survey of 259 farmers in two small communities, Ryan and Gross found that 10 percent had adopted hybrid corn after five years (by 1933). Between 1933 and 1936 an additional 30 percent adopted, and by the time of the study (1941) only two farmers did not use the hybrid. Early adopters were more cosmopolitan, and had higher social and economic status. The average respondent took nine years to go from first knowledge to adoption, and interpersonal networks and modeling were judged to be critical to adoption. In other cases diffusion time has been much shorter. Beginning in 1944, the average diffusion time for a weed spray (also in Iowa) was between 1.7 years for innovators and 3.1 years for laggards (Rogers 1983, p. 204). Having adopted many innovations, farmers are likely to adopt others more quickly.

Adoption-diffusion research in rural sociology has dominated all research traditions studying innovation. Rural sociology produced 791 (26 percent) of 3,085 studies up to 1981 (Rogers 1983, p. 52). Most of this research relied upon correlational analysis of survey data based on farmers' recall of past behaviors. This kind of study reached its peak in the mid 1960s. By the mid 1970s the farm crisis in the United States and the global depression spurred rural sociologists to begin to reevaluate this tradition. By the 1980s global export markets had shrunk, farm commodity prices had fallen, net farm incomes had declined, and high interest rates had resulted in poor debt-to-asset ratios. What followed was a massive (50 percent) decapitalization of agriculture, particularly in the Midwest and Great Plains.

Criticisms of adoption-diffusion research include (1) pro-innovation bias; (2) a lack of consideration of all the consequences of innovation; (3) an individual bias; (4) methods problems; (5) American ethnocentric biases; (6) the passing of the dominant modernization-development paradigm. The pro-innovation bias of researchers has led them to ignore the negative consequences of innovation (van Es 1983). Indeed, innovativeness itself is positively valued (Downs and Mohr 1976). The agencies that fund research and the commercial organizations (e.g., seed companies) that support it have strong interests in promoting diffusion. Furthermore, successful innovations leave visible traces and can be more easily studied using retrospective social surveys, so researchers are more likely to focus on successful innovations.

Since most researchers are well aware of this problem, it can be addressed by deliberately focusing on unsuccessful innovations, and by studying discontinuance and reinvention. It can also be avoided by the use of prospective research designs, including qualitative comparative case studies, that track potential innovation and innovators' perceptions and experiences. This should facilitate the investigation of noncommercial innovations and should result in a better understanding of the reasons why people and organizations decide to use new ideas. Moreover, these methods will likely lead to a better understanding of the system context in which innovations diffuse.

One of the most strident critiques of the pro-innovation bias of the "land-grant college complex" was voiced by Hightower (1972). Agricultural scientists at Davis, California, worked on the development and diffusion of hard tomatoes and mechanized pickers (Friedland and Barton 1975). They ignored the effects of these innovations on small farms and farm labor, except in the sense that they designed both innovations to solve labor problems expected when the U.S. Congress ended the bracero program through which Mexican workers were brought in to harvest the crops. In the six years after that program ended (1964 to 1970) the mechanical harvester took over the industry. About

thirty-two thousand former hand pickers were out of work. They were replaced by eighteen thousand workers who rode machines and sorted tomatoes. Of the four thousand farmers who produced tomatoes in California in 1962, only six hundred were still in business in 1971. The tomato industry honored the inventor for saving the tomato for California, and consumers got cheaper, harder tomatoes—even if they preferred softer ones.

Several other classic examples of agricultural innovation illustrate problems that result from not fully considering the consequences of innovation (Fliegel and van Es 1983). Until the late 1970s rural sociologists, among others, studiously ignored Walter Goldschmidt's 1940s study (republished in 1978) of the effects of irrigation on two communities in California's San Joaquin Valley. Dinuba had large family farms, and it also had more local business, greater retail sales, and a greater diversity of social, educational, recreational, and cultural organizations. Arrin was surrounded by large industrial corporate farms supported by irrigation. These farms had absentee owners and Mexican labor. This produced a much lower quality of life that was confirmed three decades later (Buttel et al. 1990, p. 147).

The enforced ban on earlier chemical innovations in agriculture by the U.S. Food and Drug Administration provides another interesting example. Chemical innovations such as DDT insecticide, 2,4-D weed spray, and DES cattle feed revolutionized farm production in the 1950s and 1960s. In 1972, DDT was banned because it constituted a health threat (Dunlap 1981), and 2,4-D, DES, and similar products were banned soon afterward. Finally, in 1980 the U.S. Department of Agriculture reversed its policy and began to advise farmers and gardeners to consider alternative, organic methods that used fewer chemicals.

The impact of technical changes in U.S. agriculture, particularly the rapid mechanization begun in the Great Depression, put farmers on the "treadmill of technology" (Cochran 1979; LeVeen 1978). Larger farmers who are less risk-aversive adopt early, reap an "innovation rent," reduce their per-unit costs, and increase profits. After the innovation spreads to the early majority, aggregate output increases dramatically. Prices then fall disproportionately, since agricultural products have low elasticity of demand. Lower, declining prices force the late majority to adopt, but they gain little. They have to adopt to stay in business, and some late adopters may be forced out because they cannot compete. This treadmill increases concentration of agricultural production and benefits large farmers, the suppliers of innovations, and consumers. Indeed, it helps to create and to subsidize cheap urban labor. When it comes to environmental practices, however, large farms are not early innovators (Pampel and van Es 1977; Buttel et al. 1990).

The individual bias of adoption-diffusion research is evident in its almost exclusive focus upon individual farmers rather than upon industrial farms or other agribusiness. There is also a tendency to blame the victim if anything goes wrong (Rogers 1983). Change agents are too rarely criticized for providing incomplete or inaccurate information, and governments and corporations are too infrequently criticized for promoting inappropriate or harmful innovations. Empirical surveys of individual farmers also lead to a number of methodological problems. As noted above, if surveys are retrospective, recall relies on fallible memory and renders unsuccessful innovations difficult to study. These surveys are commonly combined with correlational analysis that makes it difficult to address issues of causality. After all, the farmer's attitudes and personality are measured at the time of the interview, and the innovation probably occurred some time before. As we have pointed out, these issues can be addressed by prospective designs that incorporate other methods, such as qualitative case studies and available records data, and focus on the social context of innovation.

Taking into account the social context of innovation involves shifting levels of analysis from individual farmers to the social, economic, and political structures in which they are embedded. Contextual analysis of social structures has evolved in two directions, both of which have been inspired by the adoption-diffusion paradigm. The first considers social structure as a set of social relations among farmers, that is, a social network. Typically, social network structure has been studied from the point of view of individual farmers. For instance, farmers are more likely to innovate if they are connected to others with whom they can discuss new farming ideas (Rogers and Kincaid 1981; Rogers 1983; Warriner and Moul 1992). In

this type of analysis, "connectedness" becomes a variable property of individual farmers that is correlated with their innovativeness. It is much less common to find studies that consider how agricultural innovation is influenced by structural properties of entire networks, such as the presence of subgroups or cliques, although other types of innovation have been studied within complete networks (see, e.g., Rogers and Kincaid 1981 on the diffusion of family planning in Korean villages). Field studies of subcultural differences in orientations to innovation report what amount to network effects, though networks are rarely measured directly. For instance, studies of Amish farmers have revealed that members of this sect restrict certain kinds of social contacts with outsiders in order to preserve their beliefs, which include environmental orientations based on religious beliefs (for a review, see Sommers and Napier 1993). Given the growing importance of social network analysis in contemporary sociology (Wasserman and Faust 1995), and the demonstrated importance of networks of communication and influence in innovation research (Rogers and Kincaid 1981), future studies of agricultural innovation could profitably incorporate network models and data in their research designs.

A second type of social structural analysis has considered how agricultural innovation is influenced by distributions of resources within farming communities. Much of this research has focused on the so-called "Green Revolution." This term refers to the increases in cereal-grain production in the Third World, particularly India, Pakistan, and the Philippines, in the late 1960s, through the use of hybrid seeds and chemical fertilizer. In Indian villages where knowledge of new farming technology and agricultural capital were highly concentrated, the rate at which individual farmers translated their knowledge into trial was higher (Gartrell and Gartrell 1979). Yet overall levels of innovation tended to be lower in such high-inequality villages. Had the primary goal of India's development programs been to maximize the rate at which knowledge of new farming practices is turned into innovation, then these results could have been seen as a vindication of a development strategy that concentrated on well-to-do cultivators and high-inequality villages. Yet, this and other assessments of the Green Revolution in the

1970s suggested that development would likely exacerbate rural inequality; that most of the benefits of innovation would accrue to farmers who were wealthy enough to afford the new inputs (Frankel 1971; Poleman and Freebairn 1973); and that the rural poor would be further marginalized and forced to seek employment in the increasingly capital-intensive industries developing in cities. The Green Revolution, so the thinking went, contained the seeds of civil unrest in the cities—an urban Red Revolution (Sharma and Poleman 1993).

Recent research in agricultural economics paints a more optimistic portrait of the long-run distributional effects of the Green Revolution. Once small farmers were given the necessary infrastructural support, their productivity and incomes increased. Growing rural incomes and the resulting growth in consumption demand stimulates the development of a wide variety of off-farm and noncrop employment opportunities. Through participation in these "second generation" effects of the Green Revolution, the incomes of landless and near-landless households have increased dramatically (Sharma and Poleman 1993). These indirect consequences of agricultural innovation are not limited to the Green Revolution. Innovation in agriculture and the expansion of rural, nonagricultural manufacturing were strongly associated in the development of Western Europe and East Asia as far back as the eighteenth century (Grabowski 1995). We tend to think of the Industrial Revolution as an urban phenomenon in which agricultural surplus labor was transferred from occupations of low productivity in agriculture to those of high productivity in urban manufacturing. Yet in this early phase of industrialization, the flow of people and economic activity went the other way—from town to country. Then, as now, agricultural innovation influenced and was influenced by the growth of rural manufacturing. Expanding commercialization of rural areas fosters innovation by providing many of the inputs needed by agriculture, as well as sources of credit for farm operations and alternative sources of income to buffer the risks associated with innovations. These reciprocal effects have been observed in the experience of China in the 1990s (Islam and Hehui 1994).

Economists have argued that agricultural innovation is induced by changes in the availability and cost of major factors of production, particularly land and labor (Binswanger and Ruttan 1978). Historical, cross-national studies show that countries differently endowed with land and labor have followed distinct paths of technological change in agriculture. Population pressures on land resources have impelled technological change and development (Boserup 1965, 1981; Binswanger 1986). Rather than focusing on individual farmers' adoption decisions, research in this tradition has examined variation in innovation by region according to demographic and other conditions.

The social context of innovation also has an important political dimension. Political structures powerfully influence the path of innovation. When family farms were turned over to collective management by the Democratic Republic of Vietnam, local farmers in both the lowland and upland areas were unable to use their own knowledge of farm management (Jamieson et al. 1998). Traditional knowledge passed down over many generations became lost to new generations of farmers. Yet local knowledge systems are often crucial to the successful implementation of modern farming technologies brought in from the outside. Such problems are compounded when the power to make decisions about the course of development is centralized in national agencies, as is the case in Vietnam.

Innovation can also call forth new political structures. India's Green Revolution became politicized as the terms and prices at which agricultural inputs could be obtained and the price at which agricultural products could be sold were determined by government and its local agencies. Peasant movements arose as a response to concern about access to the new farming technology. The incidence of improved agricultural practices has been associated with the rise of political parties such as the Lok Dal of Uttar Pradesh, which most clearly articulated rural interests (Duncan 1997). By asserting new identities and interests created in the changed circumstances brought about by the Green Revolution, the Lok Dal was able to mobilize across traditional lines of caste and locality.

The social, economic, and political structures of the social context of innovation do not exist in isolation from one another. In any development setting, a contextually informed understanding of agricultural innovation must consider the relationships among these different types of structures (Jamieson et al. 1998). While it may no longer be as fashionable as it once was, the adoption-diffusion model still has much to offer in such efforts. The model refers implicitly to structural effects of socioeconomic status and communication behavior, though these are conceptualized at an individual level (Black and Reeve 1992). Structural analysis has recently moved more firmly into this interdisciplinary realm, particularly in economics (see "Economic Sociology"). With the appropriate structural tools, rural sociologists could make notable contributions to our understanding of how the social structures of markets influence innovation.

Technological change in agriculture is still vitally important throughout the world and, correctly applied, diffusion research can assist in its investigation. It is important to consider the consequences of technological change as well as the determinants of adoption of innovation. It is critical to apply the model to environmental practices and other "noncommercial" innovations in agriculture. In-depth case studies over time are needed to further our understanding of how and why individuals and agricultural social collectives adopt technological change. Above all, the social, economic, and political contexts of innovation must be studied with the models and methods of modern structural analysis. All this provides a basis for continuing to build on a wealth of research materials.

(SEE ALSO: *Diffusion Theories; Rural Sociology*)

REFERENCES

Binswanger, Hans P. 1986 "Evaluating Research System Performance and Targeting Research in Land-abundant Areas of Sub-Saharan Africa." *World Development* 14:469–475.

——, and Vernon W. Ruttan 1978 *Induced Innovation: Technology, Institutions, and Development*. Baltimore: Johns Hopkins University Press.

Black, Alan W., and Ian Reeve 1993 "Participation in Landcare Groups: the Relative Importance of Attitudinal and Situational Factors." *Journal of Environmental Management* 39:51–71.

Boserup, Ester 1965 *The Conditions of Agricultural Growth*. Chicago: Aldine.

—— 1981 *Population and Technological Change: A Study of Long-term Trends*. Chicago: University of Chicago Press.

Buttel, Frederick, Olav Larson, and Gilbert Gillespie, Jr. 1990 *The Sociology of Agriculture*. New York: Greenwood Press.

Cancian, Frank 1967 "Stratification and Risk Taking: A Theory Tested on Agricultural Innovations." *American Sociological Review* 32:912–927.

—— 1979 *The Innovator's Situation: Upper-Middle Class Conservatism in Agricultural Communities*. Stanford, Calif.: Stanford University Press.

Cochran, Willard 1979 *The Development of American Agriculture*. Minneapolis: University of Minnesota Press.

Downs, George, and Lawrence Mohr 1976 "Conceptual Issues in the Study of Innovations." *Administrative Science Quarterly* 21:700–714.

Duncan, Ian 1997 "Agricultural Innovation and Political Change in North India: The Lok Dal in Uttar Pradesh." *The Journal of Peasant Studies* 24:246–248.

Dunlap, Thomas 1981 *DDT: Scientists, Citizens and Public Policy*. Princeton, NJ.: Princeton University Press.

Fliegel, Frederick, and John van Es 1983 "The Diffusion-Adoption Process in Agriculture: Changes in Technology and Changing Paradigms." In Gene Summers, ed., *Technology and Social Change in Rural Areas*. Boulder, Colo.: Westview Press.

Frankel, Francine R. 1971 *India's Green Revolution: Economic Gains and Political Costs*. Princeton: Princeton University Press.

Friedland, William, and Amy Barton 1975 *Destalking the Wily Tomato: A Case Study in Social Consequences in California Agricultural Research*. Research Monograph no. 15. Davis: Department of Applied Behavioral Sciences, University of California Press.

Gartrell, David, and John Gartrell 1985 "Social Status and Agricultural Innovation: A Meta-analysis." *Rural Sociology* 50(1):38–50.

Gartrell, John 1977 "Status, Inequality and Innovation: The Green Revolution in Andhra Pradesh, India." *American Sociological Review* 42:318–337.

——, and David Gartrell 1979 "Status, Knowledge and Innovation." *Rural Sociology* 44:73–94.

Goldschmidt, Walter 1978 *As You Sow*. New York: Harcourt, Brace.

Grabowski, Richard 1995 "Commercialization, Nonagricultural Production, Agricultural Innovation, and

Economic Development." *The Journal of Developing Areas* 30:41–62.

Hightower, James 1972 *Hard Tomatoes, Hard Times: The Failure of America's Land-Grant College Complex*. Cambridge, Mass.: Schenkman.

Islam, Rizwanul, and Jin Hehui 1994 "Rural Industrialization: An Engine of Prosperity in Postreform Rural China." *World Development* 22:1643–1659.

Jamieson, Neil L., Le Trong Cuc, and A. Terry Rambo 1998 *The Development Crisis in Vietnam's Mountains*. Honolulu: East-West Center Special Reports No. 6.

LeVeen, Phillip 1978 "The Prospects for Small-Scale Farming in an Industrial Society: A Critical Appraisal of Small Is Beautiful." In Richard Dorf and Yvonne Hunter, eds., *Appropriate Visions*. San Francisco: Boyd and Fraser.

Lewis, Scott, David Gartrell, and John Gartrell 1989 "Upper-Middle-Class Conservatism in Agricultural Communities: A Meta-analysis." *Rural Sociology* 54 (3):409–419.

Pampel, Fred, and J. C. van Es 1977 "Environmental Quality and Issues of Adoption Research." *Rural Sociology* 42:57–71.

Poleman, Thomas T., and D. K. Freebairn 1973 *Food, Population and Employment: The Impact of the Green Revolution*. New York: Praeger.

Rogers, Everett 1983 *The Diffusion of Innovations*, 3rd ed. New York: Free Press.

——, and D. Lawrence Kincaid 1981 *Communication Networks: Toward a New Paradigm for Research*. New York: Free Press.

Ryan, Bryce, and Neal Gross 1942 "The Diffusion of Hybrid Corn Seed in Two Iowa Communities." *Rural Sociology* 8:15–24.

Schumpeter, Joseph 1950 *Capitalism, Socialism, and Democracy*. New York: Harper and Row.

Sharma, Rita, and Thomas T. Poleman 1993 *The New Economics of India's Green Revolution*. Ithaca, N.Y.: Cornell University Press.

Sommers, David G., and Ted L. Napier 1993 "Comparison of Amish and Non-Amish Farmers: A Diffusion/Farm-Structure Perspective." *Rural Sociology* 58:130–145.

Spicer, Edward 1952 *Human Problems in Technological Change*. New York: Russell Sage Foundation.

van Es, J. C. 1983 "The Adoption/Diffusion Tradition Applied to Resource Conservation: Inappropriate Use of Existing Knowledge." *The Rural Sociologist* 3:76–82.

Warriner, G. Keith, and Trudy M. Moul 1992 "Kinship and Personal Communication Network Influences on the Adoption of Agriculture Conservation Technology." *Journal of Rural Studies* 8:279–291.

Wasserman, Stanley, and Katherine Faust 1994 *Social Network Analysis*. Cambridge, Eng.: Cambridge University Press.

JOHN GARTRELL
DAVID GARTRELL

ALCOHOL

INTRODUCTION

The sociological study of alcohol in society is concerned with two broad areas. (1) The first area is the study of alcohol behavior, which includes: (a) social and other factors in alcohol behavior, (b) the prevalence of drinking in society, and (c) the group and individual variations in drinking and alcoholism. (2) The second major area of study has to do with social control of alcohol, which includes: (a) the social and legal acceptance or disapproval of alcohol (social norms), (b) the social and legal regulations and control of alcohol in society, and (c) efforts to change or limit deviant drinking behavior (informal sanctions, law enforcement, treatment, and prevention). Only issues related to the first area of study, sociology of alcohol behavior, will be reviewed here.

PHYSICAL EFFECTS OF ALCOHOL

There are three major forms of beverages containing alcohol (ethanol) that are regularly consumed. Wine is made from fermentation of fruits and usually contains up to 14 percent of ethanol by volume. Beer is brewed from grains and hops and contains 3 to 6 percent ethanol. Liquor (whisky, gin, vodka, and other distilled spirits) is usually 40 percent (80 proof) to 50 percent (100 proof) ethanol. A bottle of beer (12 ounces), a glass of wine (4 ounces), and a cocktail or mixed drink with a shot of whiskey in it, therefore, each have about the same absolute alcohol content, one-half to three-fourths of an ounce of ethanol.

Alcohol is a central nervous system depressant, and its physiological effects are a direct function of the percentage of alcohol concentrated in the body's total blood volume (which is determined mainly by the person's body weight). This concentration is usually referred to as the BAC (blood alcohol content) or BAL (blood alcohol level). A 150-pound man can consume one alcoholic drink (about three-fourths of an ounce) every hour essentially without physiological effect. The BAC increases with each additional drink during that same time, and the intoxicating effects of alcohol will become noticeable. If he has four drinks in an hour, he will have an alcohol blood content of .10 percent, enough for recognizable motor-skills impairment. In almost all states, operating a motor vehicle with a BAC between .08 percent and .10 percent (determined by breathalyzer or blood test) is a crime and is subject to arrest on a charge of DWI (driving while intoxicated). At .25 percent BAC (about ten drinks in an hour) the person is extremely drunk, and at .40 percent BAC the person loses consciousness. Excessive drinking of alcohol over time is associated with numerous health problems. Cirrhosis of the liver, hepatitis, heart disease, high blood pressure, brain dysfunction, neurological disorders, sexual and reproductive dysfunction, low blood sugar, and cancer, are among the illnesses attributed to alcohol abuse (National Institute on Alcohol Abuse and Alcoholism 1981, 1987; Royce 1990; Ray and Ksir 1999).

SOCIAL FACTORS IN ALCOHOL BEHAVIOR

Alcohol has direct effects on the brain, affecting motor skills, perception, and eventually consciousness. The way people actually behave while drinking, however, is only partly a function of the direct physical effects of ethanol. Overt behavior while under the influence of alcohol depends also on how they have learned to behave while drinking in the setting and with whom they are drinking with at the time. Variations in individual experience, group drinking customs, and the social setting produce variations in observable behavior while drinking. Actions reflecting impairment of coordination and perception are direct physical effects of alcohol on the body. These physical factors, however, do not account for "drunken comportment"— the behavior of those who are "drunk" with alcohol before reaching the stage of impaired muscular coordination (MacAndrew and Edgerton 1969). Social, cultural, and psychological factors are more important in overt drinking behavior. Cross-cultural studies (MacAndrew and Edgerton 1969), surveys in the United States (Kantor and Straus 1987), and social psychological experiments (Marlatt and Rohsenow 1981), have shown that both conforming and deviant behavior while "under the influence" are more a function of sociocultural and individual expectations and attitudes than the physiological and behavioral effects of alcohol. (For an overview of sociocultural perspectives on alcohol use, see Pittman and White 1991)

Sociological explanations of alcohol behavior emphasize these social, cultural, and social psychological variables not only in understanding the way people act when they are under, or think they are under, the influence of alcohol but also in understanding differences in drinking patterns at both the group and individual level. Sociologists see all drinking behavior as socially patterned, from abstinence, to moderate drinking, to alcoholism. Within a society persons are subject to different group and cultural influences, depending on the communities in which they reside, their group memberships, and their location in the social structure as defined by their age, sex, class, religion, ethnic, and other statuses in society. Whatever other biological or personality factors and mechanisms may be involved, both conforming and deviant alcohol behavior are explained sociologically as products of the general culture and the more immediate groups and social situations with which individuals are confronted. Differences in rates of drinking and alcoholism across groups in the same society and cross-nationally reflect the varied cultural traditions regarding the functions alcohol serves and the extent to which it is integrated into eating, ceremonial, leisure, and other social contexts. The more immediate groups within this sociocultural milieu provide social learning environments and social control systems in which the positive and negative sanctions applied to behavior sustain or discourage certain drinking according to group norms. The most significant groups through which the general cultural, religious, and community orientations toward drinking have an impact on the individual are family, peer, and friendship groups, but secondary groups and the media also have an impact. (For a social learning theory of drinking and alcoholism that specifically incorporates these factors in the social and cultural context see Akers 1985, 1998; Akers and La

Greca 1991. For a review of sociological, psychological, and biological theories of alcohol and drug behavior see Goode 1993.)

SOCIAL CHARACTERISTICS AND TRENDS IN DRINKING BEHAVIOR

Age. Table 1 shows that by time of high school graduation, the percentages of current teenage drinkers (still under the legal age) is quite high, rivaling that of adults. The peak years for drinking are the young adult years (eighteen to thirty-four), but these are nearly equaled by students who are in the last year of high school (seventeen to eighteen years of age). For both men and women, the probability that one will drink at all stays relatively high from that time up to age thirty-five; about eight out of ten are drinkers, two-thirds are current drinkers, and one in twenty are daily drinkers. The many young men and women who are in college are even more likely to drink (Berkowitz and Perkins 1986; Wechsler et al. 1994). Heavy and frequent drinking peaks out in later years, somewhat sooner for men than women. After that the probability for both drinking and heavy drinking declines noticeably, particularly among the elderly. After the age of sixty, both the proportion of drinkers and of frequent or heavy drinkers decrease. Studies in the general population have consistently found that the elderly are less likely than younger persons to be drinkers, heavy drinkers, and problem drinkers (Cahalan and Cisin 1968; Fitzgerald and Mulford 1981; Meyers et al. 1981-1982; Borgatta et al. 1982; Holzer et al. 1984; Akers 1992).

Sex. The difference is not as great as it once was, but more men than women drink and have higher rates of problem drinking in all age, religious, racial, social class, and ethnic groups and in all regions and communities. Teenage boys are more likely to drink and to drink more frequently than girls, but the difference between male and female percentages of current drinkers at this age is less than it is in any older age group. Among adults, men are three to four times more likely than women (among the elderly as much as ten times more likely) to be heavy drinkers and two to three times more likely to report negative personal and social consequences of drinking (National Institute on Alcohol Abuse and Alcoholism 1987).

Percentages Reporting Drinking by Age Group (1997)

Age Group	Lifetime	Past Year	Past Month
12-17	39.7	34	20.5
High School Seniors	81.7	74.8	52.7
18-25	83.5	75.1	58.4
26-34	88.9	74.6	60.2
35+	87	64.1	52.8

Table 1

SOURCE: Substance Abuse and Mental Health Services Administration 1998; University of Michigan (for high school seniors) 1998.

Social Class. The proportion of men and women who drink is higher in the middle class and upper class than in the lower class. The more highly educated and the fully employed are more likely to be current drinkers than the less educated and unemployed. Drinking by elderly adults increases as education increases, but there are either mixed or inconsistent findings regarding the variations in drinking by occupational status, employment status, and income (Holzer 1984; Borgatta 1982; Akers and La Greca 1991).

Community and Location. Rates of drinking are higher in urban and suburban areas than in small towns and rural areas. As the whole country has become more urbanized the regional differences have leveled out so that, while the South continues to have the lowest proportion of drinkers, there is no difference among the other regions for both teenagers and adults. Although there are fewer of them in the South, those who do drink tend to drink more per person than drinkers in other regions (National Institute on Alcohol Abuse and Alcoholism 1998a).

Race, Ethnicity, and Religion. The percent of drinking is higher among both white males and females than among African-American men and women. Drinking among non-Hispanic whites is also higher than among Hispanic whites. The proportion of problem or heavy drinkers is about the same for African Americans and white Americans (Fishburne et al. 1980; National Institute on Drug Abuse, 1988; National Institute on Alcohol Abuse and Alcoholism 1998a). There may be a tendency for blacks to fall into the two extreme categories, heavy drinkers or abstainers (Brown and Tooley

1989), and black males suffer the highest rate of mortality from cirrhosis of the liver (National Institute on Alcohol Abuse and Alcoholism 1998b). American Indians and Alaskan Natives have rates of alcohol abuse and problems several times the rates in the general population (National Institute on Alcohol Abuse and Alcoholism 1987).

Catholics, Lutherans, and Episcopalians have relatively high rates of drinking. Relatively few fundamentalist Protestants, Baptists, and Mormons drink. Jews have low rates of problem drinking, and Catholics have relatively high rates of alcoholism. Irish Americans have high rates of both drinking and alcoholism. Italian Americans drink frequently and heavily but apparently do not have high rates of alcoholism (see Cahalan et al. 1967; Mulford 1964). Strong religious beliefs and commitment, regardless of denominational affiliation, inhibit both drinking and heavy drinking among teenagers and college students (Cochran and Akers 1989; Berkowitz and Perkins 1986).

Trends in Prevalence of Drinking. There has been a century-long decline in the amount of absolute alcohol consumed by the average drinker in the United States. There was a period in the 1970s when the per capita consumption increased, and the proportion of drinkers in the population was generally higher by the end of the 1970s than at the beginning of the decade, although there were yearly fluctuations up and down. The level of drinking among men was already high, and the increases came mainly among youth and women. But in the 1980s the general downward trend resumed (Keller 1958; National Institute on Alcohol Abuse and Alcoholism 1981, 1987, 1998). Until the 1980s, this per capita trend was caused mainly by the increased use of lower-content beer and wine and the declining popularity of distilled spirits rather than a decreasing proportion of the population who are drinkers.

Alcohol-use rates were quite high in the United States throughout the 1970s and into the 1980s (see table 2). Since then, there have been substantial declines in use rates in all demographic categories and age groups. In 1979 more than two-thirds of American adolescents (twelve to seventeen years of age) had some experience with alcohol and nearly four out of ten were current drinkers (drank within the past month). In 1988, these proportions

had dropped to one-half and one-fourth respectively. In 1997, adolescent rates had dropped even lower to four out of ten having ever used alcohol and only two out of ten reporting use in the past month. Current use in the general U.S. population (aged twelve and older) declined from 60 percent in 1985 to 51 percent in 1997. Among the adult population eighteen years of age and older, current use declined from 71 percent in 1985 to 55 percent in 1997. Lifetime use rates have also declined from 88.5 percent in 1979 to 81.9 percent in 1997 (aged twelve and older). Generally, there have been declines in both annual (past year) prevalence of drinking (decreases of 3 to 5 percent) and current (past month) prevalence of drinking (decreases of 7 to 10 percent) among high school seniors, young adults, and older adults. Although lifetime prevalence is not a sensitive measure of short-term change in the adult population (since the lifetime prevalence is already fixed for the cohort of adults already sampled in previous surveys), it does reflect an overall decline in alcohol use. It should be remembered, however, that most of this is light to moderate consumption; the modal pattern of drinking for all age groups in the United States has long been and continues to be nondeviant, light to moderate social drinking.

The relative size of the reductions in drinking prevalence over the last two decades have been rather substantial; however, the proportions of drinkers remains high. By the time of high school graduation, one-half of adolescents are current drinkers and the proportion of drinkers in the population remains at this level throughout the young adult years. Three-fourths of high school seniors and young adults and two-thirds of adults over the age of thirty-five have consumed alcohol in the past year (see table 1).

Although lifetime use and current use rates appear to be continuing a slight decline in all categories, there have been some slight increases in rates of frequent (daily) drinking among high school seniors and young adults. While these increases do not approach the rates observed in the 1980s they may indicate that the overall rates are stabilizing and hint of possible increases in alcohol use rates in the future.

Estimates of Prevalence of Alcoholism. In spite of these trends in lower levels of drinking,

Percentages Reporting Lifetime, Past Year, and Past Month Use of Alcohol in the U.S. Population Aged 12 and Older (1979–1997)

	1979	1985	1991	1993	1997
Lifetime	88.5	84.9	83.6	82.6	81.9
Past Year	72.9	72.9	68.1	66.5	64.1
Past Month	63.2	60.2	52.2	50.8	51.4

Table 2

SOURCE: Substance Abuse and Mental Health Services Administration 1998.

alcoholism remains one of the most serious problems in American society. Alcohol abuse and all of the problems related to it cause enormous personal, social, health, and financial costs in American society. Cahalan et al. (1969) in a 1965 national survey characterized 6 percent of the general adult population and 9 percent of the drinkers as "heavy-escape" drinkers, the same figures reported for a 1967 survey (Cahalan 1970). These do not seem to have changed very much in the years since. They are similar to findings in national surveys from 1979 to 1988 (National Institute on Alcohol Abuse and Alcoholism 1981, 1987, 1988, 1989; Clark and Midanik 1982), which support an estimate that 6 percent of the general population are problem drinkers and that about 9 percent of those who are drinkers will abuse or fail to control their intake of alcohol. Royce (1989) and Vaillant (1983) both estimate that 4 percent of the general population in the United States are "true" alcoholics. This estimate would mean that there are perhaps 10.5 million alcoholics in American society (see also Liska 1997). How many alcoholics or how much alcohol abuse there is in our society is not easily determined because the very concept of alcoholism (and therefore what gets counted in the surveys and estimates) has long been and remains controversial.

THE CONCEPT OF ALCOHOLISM

The idea of alcoholism as a sickness traces back at least 200 years (Conrad and Schneider 1980). There is no single, unified, disease concept, but the prevailing concepts of alcoholism today revolve around the one developed by E. M. Jellinek (1960) from 1940 to 1960. Jellinek defined alcoholism as a disease entity that is diagnosed by the "loss of control" over one's drinking and that progresses through a series of clear-cut "phases."

The final phase of alcoholism means that the person is rendered powerless by the disease to drink in a controlled, moderate, nonproblematic way.

The disease of alcoholism is viewed as a disorder or illness for which the individual is not personally responsible for having contracted. It is viewed as incurable in the sense that alcoholics can never truly control their drinking. That is, sobriety can be achieved by total abstention, but if even one drink is taken, the alcoholic cannot control how much more he or she will consume. It is a "primary" self-contained disease that produces the problems, abuse, and "loss of control" over drinking by those suffering from this disease. It can be controlled through proper treatment to the point where the alcoholic can be helped to stop drinking so that he or she is in "remission" or "recovering." "Once an alcoholic, always an alcoholic" is a central tenet of the disease concept. Thus, one can be a sober alcoholic, still suffering from the disease even though one is consuming no alcohol at all. Although the person is not responsible for becoming sick, he or she is viewed as responsible for aiding in the cure by cooperating with the treatment regimen or participation in groups such as Alcoholics Anonymous.

The disease concept is the predominant one in public opinion and discourse on alcohol (according to a 1987 Gallup Poll, 87 percent of the public believe that alcoholism is a disease). It is the principal concept used by the vast majority of the treatment professionals and personnel offering programs for alcohol problems. It receives widespread support among alcohol experts and continues to be vigorously defended by many alcohol researchers (Keller 1976; Vaillant 1983; Royce 1989). Alcoholics Anonymous, the largest single program for alcoholics in the world, defines alcoholism as a disease (Rudy 1986). The concept of alcoholism as a disease is the officially stated position of the federal agency most responsible for alcohol research and treatment, the National Institute of Alcoholism and Alcohol Abuse (National Institute on Alcohol Abuse and Alcoholism 1987).

Nonetheless, many sociologists and behavioral scientists remain highly skeptical and critical of the disease concept of alcoholism (Trice 1966; Cahalan and Room 1974; Conrad and Schneider 1980; Rudy 1986; Fingarette 1988, 1991; Peele 1989). The concept may do more harm than good by discouraging many heavy drinkers who are having problems with alcohol, but who do not identify themselves as alcoholics or do not want others to view them as sick alcoholics, from seeking help. The disease concept is a tautological (and therefore untestable) explanation for the behavior of people diagnosed as alcoholic. That is, the diagnosis of the disease is made on the basis of excessive, problematic alcohol behavior that seems to be out of control, and then this diagnosed disease entity is, in turn, used to explain the excessive, problematic, out-of-control behavior.

In so far as claims about alcoholism as a disease can be tested, "Almost everything that the American public believes to be the scientific truth about alcoholism is false" (Fingarette 1988, p.1; see also Peele 1989; Conrad and Schneider 1980; Fingarette 1991; Akers 1992). The concept preferred by these authors and by other sociologists is one that refers only to observable behavior and drinking problems. The term *alcoholism* then is nothing more than a label attached to a pattern of drinking that is characterized by personal and social dsyfunctions (Mulford and Miller 1960; Conrad and Schneider 1980; Rudy 1986: Goode 1993). That is, the drinking is so frequent, heavy, and abusive that it produces or exacerbates problems for the drinker and those around him or her including financial, family, occupational, physical, and interpersonal problems. The heavy drinking behavior and its attendant problems are themselves the focus of explanation and treatment. They are not seen as merely symptoms of some underlying disease pathology. When drinking stops or moderate drinking is resumed and drinking does not cause social and personal problems, one is no longer alcoholic. Behavior we label as alcoholic is problem drinking that lies at one extreme end of a continuum of drinking behavior with abstinence at the other end and various other drinking patterns in between (Cahalan et al. 1969). From this point of view, alcoholism is a disease only because it has been socially defined as a disease (Conrad and Schneider 1980; Goode 1993).

Genetic Factors in Alcoholism. Contrary to what is regularly asserted, evidence that there may be genetic, biological factors in alcohol abuse is evidence neither in favor of nor against the disease concept, any more than evidence that there may be genetic variables in criminal behavior demonstrates that crime is a disease. Few serious researchers claim to have found evidence that a specific disease entity is inherited or that there is a genetically programmed and unalterable craving or desire for alcohol. It is genetic susceptibility to alcoholism that interacts with the social environment and the person's drinking experiences, rather than genetic determinism, that is the predominant perspective.

The major evidence for the existence of hereditary factors in alcoholism comes from studies that have found greater "concordance" between the alcoholism of identical twins than between siblings and from studies of adoptees in which offspring of alcoholic fathers were found to have an increased risk of alcoholism even though raised by nonalcoholic adoptive parents (Goodwin 1976; National Institute on Alcohol Abuse and Alcoholism 1982; U.S. Department of Health and Human Services 1987; for a review and critique of physiological and genetic theories of alcoholism see Rivers 1994). Some have pointed to serious methodological problems in these studies that limit their support for inherited alcoholism (Lester 1987). Even the studies finding evidence for an inherited alcoholism report that only a small minority of those judged to have the inherited traits become alcoholic and an even smaller portion of all alcoholics have indications of hereditary tendencies. Whatever genetic variables there are in alcoholism apparently come into play in a small portion of cases. Depending upon the definition of alcoholism used, the research shows that biological inheritance either makes no difference at all or makes a difference for only about one out of ten alcoholics. Social and social psychological factors are the principal variables in alcohol behavior, including that which is socially labeled and diagnosed as alcoholism (Fingarette 1988; Peele 1989).

REFERENCES

Akers, Ronald L. 1998 *Social Learning and Social Structure: A General Theory of Crime and Deviance.* Boston: Northeastern University Press.

—— 1992 *Drugs, Alcohol, and Society.* Belmont, Calif.: Wadsworth.

—— 1985 *Deviant Behavior: A Social Learning Approach.* Belmont, Calif.: Wadsworth.

——, and Anthony J. La Greca 1991 "Alcohol Use among the Elderly: Social Learning, Community Context, and Life Events." In David J. Pittman and Helene White, eds., *Society, Culture and Drinking Patterns Re-examined.* New Brunswick, N.J.: Rutgers University Press.

Berkowitz, Alan D., and H. Wesley Perkins 1986 "Problem Drinking among College Students: A Review of Recent Research." *Journal of American College Health* 35:21–28.

Borgatta, Edgar F., Rhonda J. V. Montgomery, and Marie L. Borgatta 1982 "Alcohol Use and Abuse, Life Crisis Events, and the Elderly. *Research on Aging* 4:378–408.

Brown, Frieda, and Joan Tooley 1989 "Alcoholism in the Black Community." In Gary W. Lawson and Ann W. Lawson, eds. *Alcohol and Substance Abuse in Special Populations,* 115–130. Rockville, Md.: Aspen Publishers.

Cahalan, Don 1970 *Problem Drinkers: A National Survey.* San Francisco: Jossey-Bass.

——, Ira H. Cisin, and Helen M. Crossley 1967 *American Drinking Practices.* Washington, D.C.: George Washington University Press.

Cahalan, Don, and Robin Room 1974 *Problem Drinking Among American Men.* New Brunswick, N.J.: College and University Press.

Clark, Walter B., and Lorraine Midanik 1982 "Alcohol Use and Alcohol Problems among U.S. Adults: Results of the 1979 Survey." *Alcohol Consumption and Related Problems.* Department of Health and Human Services, No. 82–1190. Washington, D.C.: U.S. Government Printing Office.

Cochran, John K., and Ronald L. Akers 1989 "Beyond Hellfire: An Exploration of the Variable Effects of Religiosity on Adolescent Marijuana and Alcohol Use." *Journal of Research on Crime and Delinquency* 26:198–225.

Conrad, Peter, and Joseph W. Schneider 1980 *Deviance and Medicalization.* St. Louis: C.V. Mosby.

Fingarette, Herbert 1991 "Alcoholism: The Mythical Disease." In David J. Pittman and Helene White, eds., *Society, Culture and Drinking Patterns Re-examined.* New Brunswick, N.J.: Rutgers University Press.

—— 1988 *Heavy Drinking: The Myth of Alcoholism as a Disease.* Berkeley: University of California Press.

Fishburne, Patricia, Herbert I. Abelson, and Ira Cisin 1980 *National Survey on Drug Abuse: Main Findings.* Washington, D.C.: U.S. Government Printing Office.

Fitzgerald, J. L., and Harold A. Mulford 1981 "The Prevalence and Extent of Drinking in Iowa, 1979." *Journal of Studies on Alcohol* 42:38–47.

Goode, Erich 1993 *Drugs in American Society,* 4th ed. New York: McGraw-Hill.

Goodwin, Donald 1976 *Is Alcoholism Hereditary?* New York: Oxford University Press.

Holzer, C., Lee Robins, Jerome Meyers, M. Weissman, G. Tischler, P. Leaf, J. Anthony, and P. Bednarski 1984 "Antecedents and Correlates of Alcohol Abuse and Dependence in the Elderly." In George Maddox, Lee Robins, and Nathan Rosenberg, eds., *Nature and Extent of Alcohol Abuse Among the Elderly.* Department of Health and Human Services No. 84–1321. Washington, D.C.: U.S. Government Printing Office.

Jellinek, E. M. 1960 *The Disease Concept of Alcoholism.* New Haven, Conn.: Hillhouse Press.

Johnston, Lloyd D., Patrick M. O'Malley, and Jerald G. Bachman 1989 *Drug Use, Drinking, and Smoking: National Survey Results from High School, College, and Young Adult Populations, 1975–1988.* Washington, D.C.: U.S. Government Printing Office.

Kantor, Glenda K., and Murray A. Straus 1987 "The 'Drunken Bum' Theory of Wife Beating." *Social Problems* 34:213–230.

Keller, Mark 1976 "The Disease Concept of Alcoholism Revisited." *Journal of Studies on Alcohol* 37:1694–1717.

—— 1958 "Alcoholism: Nature and Extent of the Problem." *Annals* 315:1–11.

Lester, David 1987 "Genetic Theory: An Assessment of the Heritability of Alcoholism." New Brunswick, N.J.: Center of Alcohol Studies, Rutgers University.

Liska, Ken 1997 *Drugs and the Human Body,* 5th ed. Upper Saddle River, N.J.: Prentice Hall.

MacAndrew, Craig, and Robert B. Edgerton 1969 *Drunken Comportment: A Social Explanation.* Chicago: Aldine.

Marlatt, G. Alan, and Damaris J. Rohsenow 1981 "The Think-Drink Effect." *Psychology Today* (Dec):60–69, 93.

Meyers, A. R., E. Goldman, R. Hingson, N. Scotch, and T. Mangione 1981 "Evidence of Cohort and Generational Differences in Drinking Behavior of Older Adults." *International Journal of Aging and Human Development* 14:31–44.

Mulford, Harold A. 1964 "Drinking and Deviant Drinking, USA, 1963." *Quarterly Journal of Studies on Alcohol* 25:634–650.

——, Donald Miller 1960 "Drinking in Iowa IV: Preoccupation with Alcohol and Definitions of Alcoholism, Heavy Drinking, and Trouble Due to Drinking." *Quarterly Journal of Studies on Alcohol* 21:279–296.

National Institute on Alcohol Abuse and Alcoholism 1998a *Apparent Per Capita Alcohol Consumption: National, State, and Regional Trends, 1977–1996.* (Gerald D. Williams, Frederick S. Stinson, Lorna L. Sanchez, and Mary C. Dufour) Rockville, Md.: National Institute on Alcohol Abuse and Alcoholism.

—— 1998b *Surveillance Report No. 48: "Liver Cirrhosis Mortality in the United States, 1970–1995.* (Forough Saadatmand, Frederick S. Stinson, Bridget F. Grant, and Mary C. Dufour) Rockville, Md.: National Institute on Alcohol Abuse and Alcoholism.

—— 1987 *Alcohol and Health: Sixth Special Report to the U. S. Congress from the Secretary of Health and Human Services.* Rockville, Md.: National Institute on Alcohol Abuse and Alcoholism.

—— 1982 *"Researchers Investigating Inherited Alcohol Problems, NIAAA Information and Feature Service* No. 99, August 30. Rockville, Md.: National Clearinghouse for Alcohol Information, National Institute on Alcohol Abuse and Alcoholism.

—— 1981 *Fourth Special Report to the U.S. Congress on Alcohol and Health.* Washington, D.C.: U.S. Government Printing Office.

National Institute on Drug Abuse 1989 "Highlights of the 1988 Household Survey on Drug Abuse." *NIDA Capsules*, August. Rockville, Md.: National Institute on Drug Abuse.

—— 1989 *Results from High School, College, and Young Adult Populations, 1975–1988.* Washington, D.C.: U.S. Government Printing Office.

——1985 *National Household Survey on Drug Abuse: Main Findings.* Rockville, Md.: National Institute on Drug Abuse.

Peele, Stanton 1989 *Diseasing of America: Addiction Treatment Out of Control.* Lexington, Mass.: Lexington Books.

Pittman, David J., and Helene White (eds.) 1991 *Society, Culture, and Drinking Patterns Re-examined.* New Brunswick, N.J.: Rutgers University Press.

Ray, Oakley, and Charles Ksir 1999 *Drugs, Society, and Human Behavior.* 8th ed. Boston: WCB/McGraw-Hill.

Rivers, P. Clayton 1994 *Alcohol and Human Behavior: Theory, Research, and Practice.* Englewood Cliffs, N.J.: Prentice Hall.

Royce, James E. 1989 *Alcohol Problems and Alcoholism,* rev. ed. New York: Free Press.

Rudy, David 1986 *Becoming Alcoholic: Alcoholics Anonymous and the Reality of Alcoholism.* Carbondale, Ill.: Southern Illinois University Press.

Substance Abuse and Mental Health Services Administration 1998 *Preliminary Results from the 1997 National Household Survey on Drug Abuse.* Rockville, Md.: (SAMHSA). http://www.samhsa.gov.

Trice, Harrison 1966 *Alcoholism in America.* New York: McGraw-Hill.

University of Michigan 1998 *Monitoring the Future Survey.* http://www.isr.umich.edu/src/mtf/.

U. S. Department of Health and Human Services 1987 *Sixth Special Report to the U. S. Congress on Alcohol and Health from the Secretary of Health and Human Services.* Rockville, Md.: National Institute on Alcohol Abuse and Alcoholism.

Vaillant, George 1983 *The Natural History of Alcoholism.* Cambridge, Mass.: Harvard University Press.

Wechsler, H., A. Davenport, G. W. Dowdall, B. Moeykens, and S. Castillo 1994 "Health and Behavioral Consequences of Binge Drinking in College: A National Survey of Students at 140 Campuses." *Journal of the American Medical Association* 272:1672–1677.

RONALD L. AKERS
THOMAS R. HEFFINGTON

ALIENATION

Since 1964, many commentators have been speaking of a crisis of confidence in the United States, a malaise marked by widespread public belief that major institutions—businesses, labor unions, and especially the government, political parties, and political leaders—are unresponsive, remote, ineffective, and not to be trusted (Lipset and Schneider 1983). *Alienation* became the catchword for these sentiments, detected among discontented workers, angry youth, and militant minority groups. American leaders concerned about the increase in alienation found new relevance in ongoing discussions among sociologists and other social scientists, who have defined alienation, used survey research to measure the level of alienation in society, and have debated the causes, significance, and consequences of alienation and particularly, political alienation.

DIMENSIONS OF ALIENATION AND POLITICAL ALIENATION

Theorists and sociological researchers have developed different definitions of alienation (Seeman 1975). Scholars influenced by the philosophical writings of Karl Marx have used the word *alienation* to mean self-estrangement and the lack of self-realization at work (Blauner 1964; Hodson 1996). Marx argued that although humans by their very nature are capable of creative and intrinsically rewarding work, the Industrial Revolution alienated workers from their creative selves and reduced workers to the unskilled tenders of machines (Braverman 1974). The worker produced machinery and other commodities that formed the capitalist system of workplace hierarchies and global markets, which the worker could not control. Rather, the system dominated workers as an alienated, "reified" force, apart from the will and interests of workers (Meszaros 1970). Whereas this oldest definition links alienation to the development of capitalism in modern society, some scholars see alienation as a characteristic reaction to the postmodern condition of fragmented multiple images and loss of individual identities and any shared meanings (Geyer 1996).

Alienation can also refer to the isolation of individuals from a community—a detachment from the activities, identifications, and ties that a community can provide. In addition, the concept of alienation has included the notion of cultural radicalism or estrangement from the established values of a society. Ingelhart (1981) has argued that the highly educated generation that came of age in the counterculture of the 1960s rejected their elders' traditional values of materialism, order, and discipline. Easterlin (1980, pp. 108–111) suggests that it is the relatively large cohort size of the Baby Boom generation that led them to suffer competition for jobs, psychological stress, discontent, and hence, generalized political alienation. On the contrary, Inglehart (1997) argues that baby boomers and succeeding generations will only express alienation against specific authoritative institutions, such as the police, the military, and churches. With succeeding generations increasingly espousing "postmaterialist" values such as the quality of life, self-realization, and participatory democracy, Inglehart finds a worldwide increase in some activities that reduce alienation such as petition-signing and political conversation.

Much of the literature on alienation in the 1990s focused on alienation from political institutions, and some writers have examined how alienation has changed in former authoritarian nations such as Argentina and South Africa and in Eastern Europe (Geyer 1996; Geyer and Heinz 1992). Sociologists interested in the political well-being of the United States have measured the extent to which individuals feel powerless over government (i.e., unable to influence government) and perceive politics as meaningless (i.e., incomprehensible; Seeman 1975). Such attitudes may be connected to a situation of normlessness, or *anomie*, which occurs when individuals are no longer guided by the political rules of the game (Lipset and Raab 1978). Social scientists have been concerned that alienation might reduce political participation through institutional channels such as voting, and might lead to nonconventional activity like protest movements and collective violence.

MEASUREMENT AND CONSEQUENCES OF POLITICAL ALIENATION

Political alienation consists of attitudes whereby citizens develop (or fail to develop) meanings and evaluations about government and about their own power (or powerlessness) in politics. Specifically, political alienation is composed of the attitudes of distrust and inefficacy. Distrust (also called cynicism) is a generalized negative attitude about governmental outputs: the policies, operations, and conditions produced by government. Compared to the simple dislike of a particular policy or official, distrust is broader in scope. Whereas distrust is an evaluation of governmental outputs, inefficacy is an expectation about inputs, that is, the processes of influence over government. People have a sense of inefficacy when they judge themselves as powerless to influence government policies or deliberations (Gamson 1971).

Researchers have sought to find opinion poll questions that yield responses consistently correlated to only one underlying attitude, of distrust for example. Mason, House, and Martin (1985) argue that the most "internally valid" measures of distrust are two questions: "How much of the time do you think you can trust the government in Washington to do what is right—just about all of the time, most of the time, or only some of the time?" and "Would you say that the government is pretty much run by a few big interests looking out for themselves or that it is run for the benefit of all people?" Similarly, a person's sense of inefficacy can be measured by asking the person to agree or disagree with the following statements, which contain the words "like me": "People like me don't have any say about what the government does" and "I don't think public officials care much what people like me think."

During election years since the 1950s, the Center for Political Studies at the University of Michigan at Ann Arbor has posed these and other questions to national samples of citizens. Those replying that you can trust the government only some of the time or none of the time comprised 22 percent in 1964 but 73 percent in 1980. This percentage fell during President Ronald Reagan's first term but then increased through 1994 (reaching 78 percent) before falling to 67 percent in 1996. Those disagreeing with the statement that public officials care rose from 25 percent in 1960, to 52 percent in 1980 and 66 percent in 1994 (Orren 1997; Poole and Mueller 1998).

In addition, polls indicate that in the same time period, increasing numbers of citizens felt that government was less responsive to the people (Lipset and Schneider 1983, pp. 13–29). This attitude, which can be termed *system unresponsiveness*, was measured by asking questions that did not use the words "like me." Responses to the questions thus focused not on the respondents' evaluations of their own personal power, but rather on their judgments of the external political system. (Craig 1979 conceptualizes system unresponsiveness as "output inefficacy").

What are the consequences of the increase in political alienation among Americans? Social scientists have investigated whether individuals with highly alienated attitudes are more likely to withdraw from politics, engage in violence, or favor protest movements or extremist leaders. Research findings have been complicated by the fact that the same specific alienated attitudes have been linked to different kinds of behaviors (Schwartz 1973, pp. 162–177).

The alienated showed little tendency to support extremist candidates for office. (The only exception was that high-status alienated citizens supported Goldwater's presidential campaign in 1964. See Wright 1976, pp. 227, 251; Herring

1989, p. 98.) Social scientists have generally agreed that politically alienated individuals are less likely to participate in conventional political processes. During four presidential elections from 1956 to 1968, citizens with a low sense of efficacy and a low level of trust were less likely to vote, attend political meetings, work for candidates, contribute money, or even pay attention to the mass media coverage of politics. Although some studies fail to confirm that those with low *trust* are likely to be apathetic (Citrin 1974, p. 982), those with a low sense of political *efficacy* are indeed likely to be nonvoters, mainly because they are also less educated (Lipset and Schneider 1983, p. 341). In the United States, the percentage of eligible voters who actually cast ballots declined between 1960 and 1980, while the percentage who expressed political inefficacy rose in the same period; Abramson and Aldrich (1982) estimate that about 27 percent of the former trend is caused by the latter. (See Shaffer 1981 for confirmation but Cassel and Hill 1981 and Miller 1980 for contrary evidence).

Piven and Cloward (1988) vigorously dispute the notion that the alienated attitudes of individuals are the main cause for the large numbers of nonvoters in the United States. Piven and Cloward construct a historical explanation—that in the early twentieth century, political reformers weakened local party organizations in cities, increased the qualifications for suffrage, and made voting registration procedures more difficult. Legal and institutional changes caused a sharp decrease in voting, which only then led to widespread political alienation. Voting participation, especially among the minority poor in large cities, continues to be low because of legal requirements to register in advance of election day and after a change in residence, and because of limited locations to register.

Some researchers have found that the politically alienated are more likely to utilize nonconventional tactics such as political demonstrations or violence. College students who participated in a march on Washington against the Vietnam War, compared to a matched sample of students from the same classes at the same schools, expressed more alienated attitudes, stemming from an underlying sense of inefficacy and system unresponsiveness (Schwartz 1973 pp, 138–142). Paige's (1971) widely influential study drew on Gamson's distinctions between trust and efficacy and showed that Blacks who participated in the 1967 riot in Newark, New Jersey, had low levels of political trust but high levels of political efficacy (i.e., high capabilities and skills to affect politics, measured indirectly in this instance by the respondents' level of political knowledge). However, Sigelman and Feldman's (1983) attempt to replicate Paige's findings in a seven-nation study discovered that the participants and supporters of unconventional political activity were only slightly more likely to feel both efficacious and distrusting. Rather than being generally distrusting, participants and supporters in some nations were more likely to be dissatisfied about specific policies. (See also Citrin 1974, p. 982 and Craig and Maggiotto 1981 for the importance of specific dissatisfactions).

Even though politically alienated individuals may sometimes be found in social movements, the alienation of individuals is not necessarily the cause of social movements. McCarthy and Zald (1977) have argued that alienation and indeed policy dissatisfactions and other grievances are quite common in societies. Whether or not a social movement arises depends on the availability of resources and the opportunities for success. The civil rights movement, according to McAdam (1982), succeeded not when blacks believed that the political system was unresponsive, but rather when blacks felt that some national leaders showed signs of favoring their cause.

DISTRIBUTION AND SIGNIFICANCE OF POLITICAL ALIENATION

Social scientists have argued that political alienation is concentrated in different types of groups—among those who dislike politicians of the opposing political party, in certain economic and racial groups, and among those dissatisfied with government policy. Each of these findings supports a different assessment of the causes and the importance of political alienation.

Partisan Bickering? First of all, high levels of political distrust can be found among those who have a negative view of the performance of the presidential administration then in office. Citrin (1974) concludes that widespread expressions of political distrust (cynicism) merely indicate Democratic versus Republican Party rivalries as usual.

Cynicism, rather than being an expression of deep discontent, is nothing more than rhetoric and ritual and is not a threat to the system. Even partisans who intensely distrust a president from an opposing party are proud of the governmental system in the United States and want to keep it. However, King (1997) argues that distrust stems from a more serious problem, that congressional leaders and activists in political parties have become more ideological and polarized (see Lo and Schwartz 1998 on conservative leaders). The public has remained in the center but is becoming alienated from politicians whose ideologies are seen as far removed from popular concerns.

The alienation of social classes and minorities. Second, other researchers interested in finding concentrations of the politically alienated have searched not among people with varying partisan identifications, but rather in demographic groups defined by such variables as age, gender, education, and socioeconomic class. Many public opinion surveys using national samples have found alienation only weakly concentrated among such groups (Orren 1997). In the 1960s, the sense of inefficacy increased uniformly throughout the entire U.S. population, rather than increasing in specific demographic groups such as blacks or youth (House and Mason 1975). Using a 1970 survey, Wright (1976) noted that feelings of inefficacy and distrust were somewhat concentrated among the elderly, the poorly educated, and the working class. Still, Wright's conclusion was that the alienated were a diverse group that consisted of both rich and poor, black and white, and old and young, making it very unlikely that the alienated could ever become a unified political force.

Research on the gender gap, that is, the differing political attitudes between women and men (Mueller 1988), indicates that women are not more politically alienated than men (Poole and Muller 1998). In fact, a higher percentage of women compared to men support more government spending on social programs and a more powerful government with expanded responsibilities (Clark and Clark 1996) and thus are less distrustful of the broad scope of government. Some studies have shown that the politically alienated are indeed concentrated among persons with less education and lower income and occupational status (Wright

1976, p. 136; Lipset and Schneider 1983, pp. 311–315; Finifter 1970; Form and Huber 1971). Research that directly focuses on obtaining the opinions of minority and poor respondents has uncovered high degrees of political alienation among these groups. A survey of roughly equal numbers of blacks and whites in metropolitan Detroit in 1992 showed that blacks, compared to whites, evaluated schools and the police more negatively, distrusted local government more, and thought that participation in local politics was less efficacious (Bledsoe et al. 1996). Bobo and Hutchings (1966) oversampled minority residents of Los Angeles County and found that higher percentages of blacks compared to whites expressed "racial alienation," that is, the opinion that blacks faced inferior life chances, fewer opportunities, and unfair treatment. Blacks living in Detroit neighborhoods where over 20 percent of the residents are poor, were more likely than other blacks to say that they had little influence in community decisions and that community problems were complex and unsolvable (Cohen and Dawson 1993).

Wright argues that even though sizable numbers of persons express alienated attitudes, these people pose little threat to the stability of regimes, because they rarely take political action and even lack the resources and skills to be able to do so. Lipset (1963) has argued that apathy is a virtue because it allows elites in democratic societies to better exert leadership. (For a critique see Wolfe 1977, p. 301.) For many social scientists in the 1950s, widespread apathy was a welcome alternative to the alleged mass activism that had produced the fascist regimes in Germany and Italy. However, Wright (1976, pp. 257–301) counters that since the alienated masses actually pose no threat to the contemporary political system, an increase in mass democratic participation, perhaps the mobilization of workers on the issues of class division, could very well be beneficial.

But the class mobilization that Wright envisions might turn out to be a middle-class affair (Teixeira 1996) rather than a working-class revolt. Whereas Lipset and Wright have been concerned about the concentration of political alienation in the lower socioeconomic strata, Warren (1976) emphasizes the alienation among "Middle American Radicals," who believe that they are disfavored by a government that gives benefits to the poor and to the wealthy. Feelings of inefficacy and

distrust have increased the most among the middle strata—private-sector managers, middle-income workers, and a "new layer" of public-sector professionals (Herring 1989).

Unlike the poor, the middle strata have the resources to protest and to organize social movements and electoral campaigns, exemplified by protests against the property tax that culminated with the passage of Proposition 13 in California and Proposition 2 1/2 in Massachusetts. Property tax protesters were middle-class homeowners who expressed their political alienation when they condemned "taxation without representation." Citizens who felt cut off from political decision making were the most likely to support the tax revolt (Lowery and Sigelman 1981). Protests centered around unresponsive government officials who continued to increase assessments and tax rates, without heeding the periodic angry protests of homeowners. Movement activists interpreted their own powerlessness and power in community and metropolitan politics, thereby shaping the emerging tactics and goals of a grass-roots citizens' movement (Lo 1995).

A Crisis for Democracy? Finally, other social scientists have found intense alienation among those with irreconcilable dissatisfactions about government policy, thus threatening to make effective government impossible. Miller (1974) argued that between 1964 and 1970, political distrust (cynicism) increased simultaneously among those favoring withdrawal and those favoring military escalation in the Vietnam War. Similarly, distrust increased both among blacks who thought that the civil rights movement was making too little progress, and among white segregationists who held the opposite view. The 1960s produced two groups—cynics of the left and cynics of the right, each favoring polarized policy alternatives (see also Lipset and Schneider 1983, p. 332). Cynics of the right, for example, rejected both the Democratic and Republican parties as too liberal. (Herring 1989 has developed a similar "welfare split" thesis, that more social spending has different effects on the distrust level of various groups but, overall, raises political distrust.) Miller concludes that increased cynicism, along with a public bifurcated into extreme stances on issues, makes it difficult for political leaders to compromise and build support for centrist policies. While agreeing with Wright that the alienated are divided amongst themselves,

Miller argues that this fragmentation does indeed constitute a crisis of legitimacy for American politics.

For some social theorists, widespread political alienation is a sign of even deeper political contradictions. Throughout American history, as citizens have fought to extend their democratic freedoms and personal rights, businesses have used the notion of property rights to protect their own interests and stifle reform (Bowles and Gintis 1987). Wolfe (1977) sees political alienation as a symptom of how the democratic aspirations of the citizenry have been frustrated by the state, which has attempted to foster the growth of capitalism while at the same time maintaining popular support.

OVERCOMING ALIENATION

One diagnosis for overcoming alienation has been proposed by Sandel, Etzioni (1996), and others from the communitarian perspective, which promotes the values of civic commitment. Sandel (1996) argues that citizens today feel powerless over their fate and disconnected from politics because of an excessively individualist culture in the United States. America's leaders must encourage devotion to the common good, attachments to communities, volunteerism, and moral judgments and dialogues. Political alienation can be overcome through the associations and networks of civil society.

Others also trace political alienation back to its roots in society, but focus on work and economic hardships, which Marx long ago characterized as alienating and that now prevent the emergence of the caring and democratic public life envisioned by the communitarians (Bennett 1998). According to Lerner (1991), people experience a deep and debilitating sense of inefficacy (what he terms "surplus powerlessness") in their personal and family lives. Surplus powerlessness can be overcome through such measures as communities of compassion, occupational stress groups, and family support groups, which will build the attachments and religious values sought by the communitarians, while at the same time compassionate unions will seek to change power relations at work and in the society at large.

Alienation, originally a Marxist concept depicting the economic deprivations of industrial workers, is now a political concept portraying the plight of citizens increasingly subjected to the authority and the bureaucracy of the state in advanced capitalist societies. Perhaps returning to the original theorizing about alienation in the economic sphere can deepen our analysis of contemporary political alienation.

REFERENCES

Abramson, Paul, and John Aldrich 1982 "Decline of Electoral Participation in America." *American Political Science Review* 76:502–521.

Bennett, W. Lance 1998 "The Uncivic Culture: Communication, Identity, and the Rise of Lifestyle Politics." *PS: Political Science and Politics* 31:740.

Blauner, Robert 1964 *Alienation and Freedom: The Factory Worker and His Industry*. Chicago: University of Chicago Press.

Bledsoe, Timothy, Lee Sigelman, Susan Welch, and Michael W. Combs 1996 "The Social Contract in Black and White: Racial Differences in Evaluations of Government." In Stephen C. Craig, ed., *Broken Contract? Changing Relationships between Americans and their Government*. Boulder, Colo.: Westview Press.

Bobo, Lawrence, and Vincent L. Hutchings 1996 "Perceptions of Racial Group Competition: Extending Blumer's Theory of Group Position to a Multiracial Social Context." *American Sociological Review* 61:951–972.

Bowles, Samuel, and Herbert Gintis 1987 *Democracy and Capitalism: Property, Community, and the Contradictions of Modern Social Thought*. New York: Basic Books.

Braverman, Harry 1974 *Labor and Monopoly Capital*. New York: Monthly Review Press.

Cassel, Carol A., and David B. Hill 1981 "Explanations of Turnout Decline: A Multivariate Test." *American Politics Quarterly* 9:181–195.

Citrin, Jack 1974 "Comment: The Political Relevance of Trust in Government." *American Political Science Review* 68:973–988.

Clark, Janet, and Cal Clark 1996 "The Gender Gap: A Manifestation of Women's Dissatisfaction with the American Polity?" In Stephen C. Craig, ed., *Broken Contract? Changing Relationships between Americans and their Government*. Boulder, Colo.: Westview Press.

Cohen, Cathy J., and Michael C. Dawson 1993 "Neighborhood Poverty and African American Politics." *American Political Science Review* 87: 286–303.

Craig, Stephen C. 1979 "Efficacy, Trust, and Political Behavior: An Attempt to Resolve a Lingering Conceptual Dilemma." *American Politics Quarterly* 7:225–239.

——, and Michael Maggiotto 1981 "Political Discontent and Political Action." *Journal of Politics* 43:514–522.

Easterlin, Richard A. 1980 *Birth and Fortune: The Impact of Numbers on Personal Welfare.* New York: Basic Books.

Etzioni, Amitai 1996 *The New Golden Rule: Community and Morality in a Democratic Society.* New York: Basic Books.

Finifter, Ada W. 1970 "Dimensions of Political Alienation." *American Political Science Review* 64:389–410.

Form, William H., and Joan Huber Rytina 1971 "Income, Race, and the Ideology of Political Efficacy." *Journal of Politics* 33:659–688.

Gamson, William 1971 "Political Trust and its Ramifications." In Gilbert Abcarian and John W. Soule, eds., *Social Psychology and Political Behavior: Problems and Prospects.* Columbus, Oh.: Charles E. Merrill.

Geyer, Felix (ed.) 1996 *Alienation, Ethnicity, and Postmodernism.* Westport, Conn.: Greenwood Press.

——, and Walter R. Heinz (eds.) 1992 *Alienation, Society, and the Individual: Continuity and Change in Theory and Research.* New Brunswick, N.J.: Transaction Publishers.

Herring, Cedric 1989 *Splitting the Middle: Political Alienation, Acquiescence, and Activism Among America's Middle Layers.* New York: Praeger.

Hodson, Randy 1996 "Dignity in the Workplace under Participative Management: Alienation and Freedom Revisited." *American Sociological Review,* 61:719–738.

House, James, and William Mason 1975 "Political Alienation in America, 1952–1968." *American Sociological Review* 40:123–147.

Inglehart, Ronald 1997 "Postmaterialist Values and the Erosion of Institutional Authority." In Joseph P. Nye, Jr., Philip D. Zelikow, and David C. King, eds., *Why People Don't Trust Government.* Cambridge, Mass.: Harvard University Press.

—— 1981 "Post-Materialism in an Environment of Insecurity." *American Political Science Review* 75:880–900.

King, David C. 1997 "The Polarization of American Parties and Mistrust of Government." In Joseph P. Nye, Jr., Philip D. Zelikow, and David C. King, eds., *Why People Don't Trust Government.* Cambridge, Mass.: Harvard University Press.

Lerner, Michael 1991 *Surplus Powerlessness: The Psychodynamics of Everyday Life and the Psychology of Individual and Social Transformation.* Atlantic Highlands, N.J.: Humanities Press International.

Lipset, Seymour Martin 1963 *Political Man.* Garden City, N.Y.: Anchor.

——, and Earl Raab 1978 *The Politics of Unreason: Right-Wing Extremism in America, 1790–1977.* Chicago: University of Chicago Press.

——, and William Schneider 1983 *The Confidence Gap: Business, Labor, and Government in the Public Mind.* New York: Free Press.

Lo, Clarence Y.H. 1995 *Small Property versus Big Government: Social Origins of the Property Tax Revolt.* Berkeley and Los Angeles: University of California Press.

——, and Michael Schwartz 1998 *Social Policy and the Conservative Agenda.* Oxford, Eng. and Cambridge, Mass.: Blackwell Publishers.

Lowrey, David, and Lee Sigelman 1981 "Understanding the Tax Revolt: Eight Explanations." *American Political Science Review* 75: 963–974.

McAdam, Doug 1982 *Political Process and the Development of Black Insurgency.* Chicago: University of Chicago Press.

McCarthy, John D., and Mayer N. Zald 1977 "Resource Mobilization and Social Movements: A Partial Theory." *American Journal of Sociology* 82: 1112–1141.

Mason, William W., James S. House, and Steven S. Martin 1985 "On the Dimensions of Political Alienation in America." In Nancy Brandon Tuma, ed., *Sociological Methodology.* San Francisco: Jossey-Bass.

Meszaros, I. 1970 *Marx's Theory of Alienation.* London: Merlin.

Miller, Arthur 1974 "Political Issues and Trust in Government: 1964–1970." *American Political Science Review* 68:951–972.

Miller, Warren E. 1980 "Disinterest, Disaffection, and Participation in Presidential Politics." *Political Behavior* 2:7–32.

Mueller, Carol M. (ed.) 1988 *The Politics of the Gender Gap: The Social Construction of Political Influence.* Beverly Hills, Calif.: Sage.

Orren, Gary 1997 "Fall from Grace: The Public's Loss of Faith in Government." In Joseph P. Nye, Jr., Philip D. Zelikow, and David C. King, eds., *Why People Don't Trust Government.* Cambridge, Mass.: Harvard University Press.

Paige, Jeffery 1971 "Political Orientation and Riot Participation." *American Sociological Review* 36:801–820.

Piven, Frances Fox, and Richard A. Cloward 1988 *Why Americans Don't Vote.* New York: Pantheon.

Poole, Barbara L., and Melinda A. Mueller 1998 "Alienation and the 'Soccer Mom:' A Media Creation or a New Trend in Voting Behavior?" In Thomas J. Johnson, Carol E. Hays, and Scott P. Hays, eds.,

Engaging the Public: How Government and the Media and Reinvigorate American Democracy. Lanham, Md.: Rowman and Littlefield.

Sandel, Michael 1996 *Democracy's Discontent: America in Search of a Public Philosophy.* Cambridge, Mass.: Harvard University Press.

Schwartz, David C. 1973 *Political Alienation and Political Behavior.* Chicago: Aldine.

Seeman, Melvin 1975 "Alienation Studies." In Alex Inkeles, James Coleman, and Neil Smelser, eds. *Annual Review of Sociology,* vol. 8. Palo Alto, Calif.: Annual Reviews.

Shaffer, Stephen D. 1981 "A Multivariate Explanation of Decreasing Turnout in Presidential Elections, 1960–1976." *American Journal of Political Science* 25:68–95.

Sigelman, Lee, and Stanley Feldman 1983 "Efficacy, Mistrust, and Political Mobilization: A Cross-National Analysis." *Comparative Political Studies* 16:118–143.

Teixeira, Ruy A. 1996 *Economic Changes and the Middle-Class Revolt Against the Democratic Party.* In Stephen C. Craig, ed., *Broken Contract? Changing Relationships between Americans and their Government.* Boulder, Colo.: Westview Press.

Warren, Donald I. 1976 *The Radical Center: Middle Americans and the Politics of Alienation.* Notre Dame, Ind.: University of Notre Dame Press.

Wolfe, Alan 1977 *The Limits of Legitimacy: Political Contradictions of Contemporary Capitalism.* New York: Free Press.

Wright, James D. 1976 *The Dissent of the Governed: Alienation and Democracy in America.* New York: Academic Press.

CLARENCE Y.H. LO

ALTERNATIVE LIFESTYLES

Lifestyles that were considered "alternative" in the past are becoming less unusual and increasingly normative. Many people, for example, experience cohabitation, divorce, and remarriage. Other lifestyles, such as singlehood, gay and lesbian relationships, or remaining childfree may not be rising drastically in frequency, but they are less stigmatized and more visible than they were in recent decades.

It was during the 1960s and 1970s that the utility and the structure of many social institutions were seriously questioned. This included the institution of the family. What was the purpose of the family? Was it a useful social institution? Why or why not? How can it be improved? The given cultural milieu of the period, such as resurgence of the women's movement, concerns about human rights more generally, and improvements in our reproductive and contraceptive technology, exacerbated these questions. In increasing numbers individuals began to experiment with new and alternative ways in which to develop meaningful relationships, sometimes outside the confines of marriage. Literature soon abounded among both the academic community and the popular press describing and deliberating on these new lifestyles. In 1972, a special issue of *The Family Coordinator* was devoted to the subject of alternative lifestyles, with a follow-up issue published in 1975. The subject was firmly entrenched within the field of family sociology by 1980 when the *Journal of Marriage and Family* devoted a chapter to alternative family lifestyles in their decade review of research and theory.

Despite the increased visibility and tolerance for a variety of lifestyles during the 1990s, concern is voiced from some people over the "demise" of the family. The high divorce rate, increased rates of premarital sexuality, cohabitation, and extramarital sex are pointed to as both the culprits and the consequences of the deterioration of family values. Popenoe and Whitehead write about cohabitation, for example: "Despite its widespread acceptance by the young, the remarkable growth of unmarried cohabitation in recent years does not appear to be in children's or the society's best interest. The evidence suggests that it has weakened marriage and the intact, two-parent family and thereby damaged our social well-being, especially that of women and children" (1999, p. 16). What do the authors mean by "society's best interest"? And what type of family relationship would be in our "best interest"? What invariably comes to mind is the married, middle-class, traditional two-parent family in which the father works outside the home and the mother stays at home to take care of the children, at least while they are young. This monolithic model, however, excludes the majority of the population; indeed, a growing number of persons do not desire such a model even if it were attainable. It is based on the false notion of a single and uniform intimate experience that many argue has racist, sexist, and classist connotations.

This distress about the demise of the family is not particularly new. For at least a century American observers and social critics have warned against the negative consequences of changes in the family. Yes, the family has indeed changed, but the vast majority of the population, both then and now, still prefers to marry, have children, and live in a committed, monogamous relationship. The most profound changes to date have not occurred in alternatives *to* marriage but rather in alternatives *prior* to marriage, and alternative ways in *structuring* marriage itself, while keeping the basic institution and its purposes intact. For example, nonmarital sex, delayed marriage and childbearing, and cohabitation are practiced with increasing frequency and are tolerated by a larger percentage of the population than ever before. And within marriage itself, new behaviors and ideologies are becoming increasingly popular, such as greater equality between men and women (although gender equality is more an ideal than a reality in most marriages).

NEVER-MARRIED SINGLES

A small but growing percentage of adult men and women remain single throughout their lives. In the United States, approximately 5 percent never marry (U.S. Bureau of the Census 1998). These individuals experience life without the support and obligations of a spouse and usually children. While often stereotyped as either "swingers" or "lonely losers," Stein reports that both categorizations are largely incorrect (1981). Instead, singles cannot be easily categorized and do not constitute a single social type. Some have chosen singlehood as a preferred option, perhaps due to career decisions, sexual preference, or other family responsibilities. Others have lived in locations in which demographic imbalances have affected the pool of eligibles for mate selection. And others have been lifelong isolates, have poor social skills, or have significant health impairments that have limited social contacts.

Attitudes toward singlehood have been quite negative historically, especially in the United States, although change has been noted. Studies report that during the 1950s, remaining single was viewed as pathology, but by the mid-1970s singlehood was not only tolerated but also viewed by many as an avenue for enhancing one's happiness. In the early 1990s, when asked about the importance of being married, approximately 15 percent of unmarried white males and 17 percent of unmarried white females between the ages of 19 and 35 did not agree with the statement that they "would like to marry someday." The percentage of blacks that did not necessarily desire marriage was even higher, at 24 percent and 22 percent of black males and females, respectively. Interestingly, the gap in attitudes between males and females was the largest among Latinos, with only 9 percent of Latino males, but 25 percent of Latina females claiming that they did not necessarily want to marry (South 1993).

Despite this gender gap, single males are viewed more favorably than are single females. Males are stereotyped as carefree "bachelors," while single women may still be characterized as unattractive and unfortunate "spinsters." In the popular card game "Old Maid," the game's loser is the one who is stuck with the card featuring an old and unattractive unmarried woman. Oudijk (1983) found that the Dutch population generally affords greater lifestyle options to women, and only one-quarter of his sample of married and unmarried persons reported that married persons are necessarily happier than are singles.

Shostak (1987) has developed a typology in which to illustrate the divergence among the never-married single population. It is based on two major criteria: the voluntary verses involuntary nature of their singlehood, and whether their singlehood is viewed as temporary or stable. *Ambivalents* are those who may not at this point be seeking mates but who are open to the idea of marriage at some time in the future. They may be deferring marriage for reasons related to schooling or career, or they may simply enjoy experimenting with a variety of relationships. *Wishfuls* are actively seeking a mate but have been unsuccessful in finding one. They are, generally, dissatisfied with their single state and would prefer to be married. The *resolved* consciously prefer singlehood. They are committed to this lifestyle for a variety of reasons; career, sexual orientation, or other personal considerations. A study of 482 single Canadians reported that nearly half considered themselves to fall within this category (Austrom and

Hanel 1985). They have made a conscious decision to forgo marriage for the sake of a single lifestyle. Small but important components of this group are priests; nuns; and others who, for religious reasons, choose not to marry. Finally, *regretfuls* are those who would rather marry but who have given up their search for a mate and are resigned to singlehood. They are involuntarily stable singles.

While the diversity and heterogeneity among the never-married population is becoming increasingly apparent, one variable is suspected to be of extreme importance in explaining at least some variation: gender. Based on data gathered in numerous treatises, the emerging profiles of male and female singles are in contrast. As Bernard (1973) bluntly puts it, the never-married men represent the "bottom of the barrel," while the never-married women are the "cream of the crop." Single women are generally thought to be more intelligent, are better educated, and are more successful in their occupations than are single men. Additionally, research finds that single women report to be happier, less lonely, and have a greater sense of psychological well-being than do their single male counterparts.

One reason why single women are more likely to be the "cream of the crop" as compared to men is that many well-educated and successful women have difficulty finding suitable mates who are their peers, and therefore have remained unmarried. Mate-selection norms in the United States encourage women to "marry up" and men to "marry down" in terms of income, education, and occupational prestige. Thus, successful women have fewer available possible partners, because their male counterparts may be choosing from a pool of women with less education and income. A second reason for the gender difference is that some highly educated and successful women do not *want* what they interpret as the "burdens" of a husband and children. Career-oriented women are not rewarded, as are career-oriented men, for having a family. Someone who is described as a "family man" is thought to be a stable and reliable employee; there is no semantic equivalent for women. Thus, well-educated, career-oriented women may see singlehood as an avenue for their success, whereas well-educated, career-oriented men may see marriage as providing greater benefits than singlehood.

Demographers predict that the proportion of singles in our population is likely to increase slightly in the future. As singlehood continues to become a viable and respectable alternative to marriage, more adults may choose to remain single throughout their lives. Others may remain single not out of choice but due to demographic and social trends. More people are postponing marriage, and it is likely that some of these will find themselves never marrying. For example, the number of women between the ages of forty and forty-four today who have never married is double the number in 1980, at approximately 9 percent (U.S. Bureau of the Census 1998). Some of these women may marry eventually, but many will likely remain unmarried. Moreover, the increasing educational level and occupational aspirations of women, coupled with our continued norms of marital homogamy, help to ensure that the number of never-married single persons—women in particular—is likely to increase somewhat into the twenty-first century.

COHABITATION

Cohabitation, or the sharing of a household by unmarried intimate partners, is quickly becoming commonplace in the United States. Some people suggest that it is now a normative extension of dating. According to the U.S. Bureau of the Census, the number of cohabiting couples topped 4 million in 1997, up from less than one-half million in 1960. Approximately one-half of unmarried women between the ages of twenty-five and thirty-nine have lived with a partner or are currently doing so, and over half of all first marriages are now preceded by cohabitation. Approximately one-third of these unions contain children (U.S. Bureau of the Census 1998). Cohabitation is now seen as an institutionalized component to the larger progression involving dating, courtship, engagement, and marriage.

Given the attitudes of even younger persons, we expect trends in cohabitation to continue to increase in the United States. Nearly 60 percent of a representative sample of high school seniors "agreed," or "mostly agreed" with the statement "it is usually a good idea for a couple to live together before getting married in order to find out whether they really get along" (Survey Research Center, University of Michigan 1995).

Cohabitation is not a recent phenomenon, nor one unique to the United States. In Sweden and other Scandinavian countries, for example, cohabitation has become so common that it is considered a social institution in and of itself. It is a variant of marriage rather than of courtship; approximately 30 percent of all couples in Sweden who live together are unmarried (Tomasson 1998). People who cohabit have the same rights and obligations as do married couples with respect to taxation, inheritance, childcare, and social welfare benefits. Many of these unions have children born within them, and there is little stigma attached to being born "out of wedlock." Another study of eighty-seven Canadian couples, located through newspaper wedding announcements, reported that 64 percent of the couples had cohabited for some period, 43 percent of these for over three months. In contrast, cohabitation is relatively rare in more traditional and Roman Catholic nations such as Italy.

Cohabitors tend to differ from noncohabitors in a variety of sociodemographic characteristics. For example, cohabitors tend to see themselves as being more androgynous and more politically liberal, are less apt to be religious, are more experienced sexually, and are younger than married persons. Although cohabitors may argue that living together prior to marriage will enhance the latter relationship by increasing their knowledge of their compatibility with day-to-day living prior to legalizing the union, such optimism is generally not supported. While some studies indicate no differences in the quality of marriages among those who first cohabited and those that did not, others find that those people who cohabit have higher rates of divorce. This may, however, have nothing to do with cohabitation per se but rather may be due to other differences in the personalities and expectations of marriage between the two groups.

A wide variety of personal relationships exist among cohabiting couples. Several typologies have been created to try to capture the diversity found within these relationships. One particularly useful one, articulated by Macklin (1983), is designed to exemplify the diversity in the stability of such relationships. She discusses four types of cohabiting relationships. These include: (1) *temporary or casual* relationships, in which the couple cohabits for convenience or for pragmatic reasons; (2) *going together*, in which the couple is affectionately involved but has no plans for marriage in the future; (3) *transitional*, which serves as a preparation for marriage; and (4) *alternative to marriage*, wherein the couple opposes marriage on ideological or other grounds.

Although attitudes toward cohabitation have become increasingly positive, especially among younger persons, Popenoe and Whitehead (1999) remind us that cohabitation was illegal throughout the United States before 1970 and remains illegal in a number of states based on a legal code outlawing "crimes against chastity" (Buunk and Van Driel 1989). These laws, however, are rarely if ever enforced. In the Netherlands, or in other countries where cohabitation is institutionalized, the majority of the population sees few distinctions between cohabitation and marriage. Both are viewed as appropriate avenues for intimacy, and the two lifestyles resemble one another much more so than in the United States in terms of commitment and stability.

The future of cohabitation, and the subsequent changes in the attitudes toward it, is of considerable interest to sociologists. Many predict that cohabitation will become institutionalized in the United States to a greater degree in the near future, shifting from a pattern of courtship to an alternative to marriage. Whether it will ever achieve the status found in other countries, particularly in Scandinavia, remains to be seen.

CHILDFREE ADULTS

There is reason to believe that fundamental changes are occurring in the values associated with having children. As economic opportunities for women increase; as birth control, including abortion, becomes more available and reliable; and as tolerance increases for an array of lifestyles, having children is likely to become increasingly viewed as an option rather than a mandate. Evidence is accumulating to suggest that both men and women are reevaluating the costs and benefits of parenthood. Approximately 9 percent of white and African-American women and 6 percent of Latina women indicate that they would like to have no children (U.S Bureau of the Census 1998).

This trend is occurring not only in the United States but in many industrialized countries in Europe as well. The decline in childbearing there has been referred to as the "second demographic transition" (Van de Kaa 1987). Davis (1987) posits that features of industrial societies weaken the individual's desire for children. He lists several interrelated traits of industrialization, including the postponement of marriage, cohabitation, and high rates of divorce, claiming that these trends decrease the need for both marriage and childbearing.

Remaining childfree is not a new phenomenon, however. In 1940, for example, 17 percent of married white women between the ages of thirty-five and thirty-nine were childfree. Some of these women were simply delaying parenthood until their forties; however, many remained childfree. This percentage began to drop considerably after World War II, and by the late 1970s only 7 percent of women in the thirty-five to thirty-nine age group did not have children. Today the figure has risen to over 13 percent among this age group (U.S. Bureau of the Census 1998). This increase is due to a multitude of factors: delayed childbearing, infertility, and voluntary childlessness.

An important distinction to make in the discussion of childlessness is whether the decision was voluntary or involuntary. *Involuntary* childlessness involves those who are infecund or subfecund. For them, being childfree is not a choice. Unless they adopt or create some other social arrangement, they are inevitably committed to this lifestyle. *Voluntary* childlessness, the focus of this discussion, involves those who choose to remain childfree. Large differences exist within members of this group; *early articulators* have made their decision early in their lives and are committed to their choice. *Postponers*, on the other hand, begin first by delaying their childbearing, but wind up being childfree due to their continual postponement. Early articulators generally exhibit less stereotypical gender roles, are more likely to cohabit, and enjoy the company of children less than do postponers. Seccombe (1991) found that among married persons under age forty who have no children, wives are more likely than their husbands to report a preference for remaining childfree (19 percent and 13 percent, respectively).

Despite increasing rates of voluntary childlessness, most research conducted within the United States documents the pervasiveness of pronatalist sentiment. Those who voluntarily opt to remain childfree are viewed as selfish, immature, lonely, unfulfilled, insensitive, and more likely to have mental problems than are those who choose parenthood. In the past, females, persons with less education, those with large families of their own, Catholics, and residents of rural areas were most apt to judge the childfree harshly. However, more recently, data from a nationally representative sample suggest that women are more likely to want to remain childfree than are men (Seccombe 1991).

Most studies report that those persons who opt to remain childfree are well aware of the sanctions surrounding their decision yet are rarely upset by them (see Houseknecht 1987 for a review). In her review of twelve studies, Houseknecht found only three that reported that childfree individuals had trouble dealing with the reaction from others. Sanctions apparently are not strong enough to detract certain persons from what they perceive as the attractiveness of a childfree lifestyle. Houseknecht (1987), in a content analysis of twenty-nine studies reporting the rationales for remaining childfree, identified nine primary motivations. These are, in order of the frequency in which they were found: (1) freedom from child-care responsibilities: greater opportunity for self-fulfillment and spontaneous mobility; (2) more satisfactory marital relationship; (3) female career considerations; (4) monetary advantages; (5) concern about population growth; (6) general dislike of children; (7) negative early socialization experience and doubts about the ability to parent; (8) concern about physical aspects of childbirth and recovery; and (9) concern for children given world conditions. Gender differences were evidenced in a number of areas. Overall, females were more likely to offer altruistic rationales (e.g., concern about population growth, doubts about the ability to parent, concern for children given world conditions). The male samples, conversely, were more apt to offer personal motives (e.g., general dislike of children, monetary advantages).

The consequences of large numbers of persons in industrialized societies forgoing parenthood are profound. For example, the demographic structure in many countries is in the process of radical change; populations are becoming increasingly aged. More persons are reaching old age than ever before, those persons are living longer, and birth rates are low. The cohort age eighty-five or older, in fact, is the fastest-growing cohort in the United States. The question remains: Who will care for the elderly? Some Western European countries provide a variety of services to assist elderly persons in maintaining their independence within the community as long as possible. But social policies in other countries, including the United States, rely heavily on adult children to provide needed care to elderly parents. Formal support services, when available, tend to be uncoordinated and expensive. The question of who will provide that needed care to the large numbers of adults who are predicted to have no children has yet to be answered.

GAY AND LESBIAN RELATIONSHIPS

Not long ago homosexuality was viewed by many professionals as an illness or a perversion. It was only as recently as 1973, for example, that the American Psychiatric Association removed homosexuality from its list of psychiatric disorders. Today, due in large part to the efforts of researchers such as Kinsey and associates (1948, 1953), Masters and Johnson (1979), and to organizations such as the Gay Liberation Front during the late 1960s, homosexuality is slowly but increasingly being viewed as a lifestyle rather than an illness. The work of Kinsey and associates illustrated that a sizable minority of the population, particularly males, had experimented with same-sex sexual relationships, although few considered themselves exclusively homosexual. Thirty-seven percent of males, they reported, had experienced at least one homosexual contact to the point of orgasm, although only 4 percent were exclusively homosexual. Among females, 13 percent had a same-sex sexual contact to the point of orgasm, while only 2 percent were exclusively homosexual in their orientation.

Obviously not all people who have had a homosexual experience consider themselves to be gay or lesbian. Most do not. One national probability sample of adult males interviewed by telephone found that 3.7 percent reported to have either a homosexual or bisexual identity (Harry 1990). Others suggest that the percentages are higher, that perhaps 3 to 5 percent of adult women and 5 to 10 percent of adult men are exclusively lesbian or gay (Diamond 1993).

Cross-cultural evidence suggests that the majority of cultures recognize the existence of homosexual behavior, particularly in certain age categories such as adolescence, and most are tolerant of homosexual behavior. Culturally speaking, it is rare to find an actual *preference* for same-sex relations; a preference tends to occur primarily in societies that define homosexuality and heterosexuality as mutually exclusive, as in many industrial countries.

There still remains a tremendous degree of hostility to homosexual relationships by large segments of society. Many regions in the United States, particularly in the South and in the West, still have laws barring homosexual activity among consenting adults. The results of national polls indicate that the majority of adults believe that homosexuals should still be restricted from certain occupations, such as elementary-school teacher, and should not be allowed to marry. Gays and lesbians report that their sexual orientation has caused a variety of problems in securing housing and in the job market. They often report that negative comments or acts of violence have been levied on them in public.

This contrasts sharply with the view toward homosexuality in the Scandinavian countries. In 1989 Denmark lifted the ban on homosexual marriages, the first country to do so. Norway and Sweden followed suit in the 1990s. These changes extend to gays and lesbians the advantages that heterosexual married couples experience with respect to inheritance, taxation, health insurance, and joint property ownership.

There is a growing amount of research illuminating various aspects of homosexual relationships, such as gender roles; degree of commitment; quality of relationships; and the couples' interface with other relationships, such as children, ex-spouses, or parents. However, because of unique historical reactions to gays and lesbians, and the different socialization of men and women in our society, it is important to explore the nature of lesbian and gay male relationships separately. Gender differences emerge in homosexual relations within a variety of contexts; for example, lesbians are more apt to have monogamous, stable relationships than are gay men, although the popular stereotype of gays as sexually "promiscuous" has been exaggerated. The majority of gay men, just like lesbians, are interested in monogamous, long-term relationships. The lack of institutional support for gay and lesbian relationships and the wide variety of obstacles not encountered among heterosexuals, such as prejudice and discriminatory behavior, take their toll on these relationships, however.

The AIDS epidemic has had an enormous impact on the gay subculture. While the impact on lesbians is significantly less, they have not been untouched by the social impact of the devastating medical issue, despite the slow response of the world's governments.

DIVORCE AND REMARRIAGE

Throughout most of history in America, the primary reason that marriages ended was because of death. In 1970, the trends were reversed, and for the first time in our nation's history, more marriages ended by divorce than by death (Cherlin 1992). The United States now has the highest rate of divorce in the world, at approximately 20 divorces per 1,000 married women aged fifteen and over in the population (U.S. Bureau of the Census 1998). This is twice as high as the divorce rate found in Canada, four times that of Japan, and ten times as high as Italy. But, it's important to note that the divorce rate has actually leveled off, or even declined somewhat in the United States after peaking in the early 1980s.

Who divorces? Research has shown that those at greatest risk for divorcing are people who marry young, especially after only a brief dating period; those who have lower incomes, although very high-earning women are also more likely to divorce; African Americans, who are about 25 percent more likely to divorce than whites; people who have been divorced before or whose parents divorced; and those who are not religious or claim no religious affiliation. The likelihood of divorce is particularly high among couples who marry in their teens because of an unplanned pregnancy. Women are almost twice as likely as men to petition for divorces, reflecting the fact that women are more often dissatisfied with their marriages than are men.

There are a variety of reasons why the rate of divorce has increased so dramatically in many

Western nations during the twentieth century: (1) there is increasing emphasis on individualism and individual happiness over the happiness of the group—or a spouse and children; (2) divorce is more socially acceptable and less stigmatized than in the past; (3) divorce is easier to obtain, as "fault" is generally no longer required; (4) women are less financially dependent on men, on average, and therefore can end an unhappy marriage more easily; (5) there is an increase in the number of adult children who grew up in divorced households, who are more likely to see divorce as a mechanism to end an unhappy marriage; and (6) today's marriages experience increased stress, with outside work consuming the time and energy people used to devote to their marriages and families.

One of the consequences of divorce is that many children will live at least a portion of their lives in single-parent households. Single-parent households are becoming increasingly normative, with approximately half of all children under age eighteen spending some portion of their lives living with only one parent, usually their mother. Single-parent households are more likely to be poor and often lack the social capital available in two-parent households, and consequently place the child at greater risk for a variety of negative social and health outcomes. Commonly the absentee parent does not pay the child support that is due, and fails to see the children with regularity.

Although divorce has become common in many industrialized nations, it would be incorrect to assume that this represents a rejection of marriage. Four out of five people who divorce remarry, most often within five years. Men are more likely to remarry than are women. This difference is due to the greater likelihood that children will be living with their mothers full-time, rather than their fathers; the cultural pattern of men marrying younger women; and the fact that there are fewer men than women in the population in general.

Remarriage often creates "blended families" composed of stepparents and possibly stepsiblings. It is estimated that approximately one-third of all children will live with a stepparent for at least one year prior to reaching age eighteen. Despite the increasing commonality of this type of family, it has been referred to as an "incomplete institution" because the social expectations are less clear than in other family structures. There are no well-established rules for how stepparents and children are supposed to relate, or the type of feelings they should have for one another. Without a clear-cut set of norms, blended families may be seen as "alternative lifestyles," but yet they are becoming increasingly common in modern industrialized societies where divorce is common.

CONCLUDING COMMENTS

There is considerable accumulating evidence to suggest that family lifestyles are becoming more varied and that the public is becoming increasingly tolerant of this diversity. The data indicate that traditional marriage itself *per se* may be less important in sanctioning intimacy. The review by Buunk and Hupka (1986) of seven countries reveals that individualism, as expressed by following one's own personal interests in intimate relationships, was more prevalent in affluent democratic countries such as the United States and in most of Western Europe than in poorer and nondemocratic nations.

This does not mean, however, that people are discarding the institution of marriage. In the United States, as elsewhere, the vast majority of the population continues to endorse marriage and parenthood in general, and for themselves personally. Most still plan to marry and have children, and optimism remains high that theirs will be a lasting union despite high national frequencies of divorce.

Alternative lifestyles are not replacing marriage. Instead, they are gaining acceptance because they involve, for some, modifications of the family structure as an adaptation to changing conditions in society. The lifestyles discussed here, as well as others, reflect the broader social changes in values, relationships, and even technology that are found within society as a whole. As Macklin notes, the family is not disappearing, but "continuing its age-old process of gradual evolution, maintaining many of its traditional functions and structures while adapting to changing economic circumstances and cultural ideologies" (1987, p. 317). This process has merely accelerated during the past several decades, and these changes have caught the attention of the general public. College classes and their corresponding textbooks within this discipline of sociology are still often titled *Marriage and the Family*, as if there were only one model of intimacy. Yet perhaps a more appropriate title would be Marriages, Families, and Intimate Relationships. This would reflect not only the diversity illustrated here but would also acknowledge the tremendous ethnic and class variations that make for rich and meaningful personal relationships.

(SEE ALSO: *American Families*; *Courtship*; *Divorce and Remarriage*; *Marriage*; *Mate Selection Theories*; *Sexual Orientation*)

REFERENCES

Austrom, Douglas, and Kim Hanel 1985 "Psychological Issues of Single Life in Canada: An Exploratory Study." *International Journal of Women's Studies* 8:12–23.

Bernard, Jessie 1973 *The Future of Marriage*. New York: Bantam Books.

Buunk, Bram P., and R. B. Hupka 1986 "Autonomy in Close Relationships: A Cross-Cultural Study." *Family Perspective* 20:209–221.

——, and Barry Van Driel 1989 *Variant Lifestyles and Relationships*. Newbury Park, Calif.: Sage Publications.

Cherlin, Andrew 1992 *Marriage, Divorce, Remarriage*, rev. ed. Cambridge Mass.: Harvard University Press.

Davis, Kingsley 1987 "Low Fertility in Evolutionary Perspective." In K. Davis, M. S. Bernstam, and R. Ricardo-Campbell, eds., *Below Replacement Fertility in Industrial Societies*. Cambridge, Eng.: Cambridge University Press.

Diamond, M. 1993 "Homosexuality and Bisexuality in Different Populations." *Archives Of Sexual Behavior*, 22:291–310.

Harry, Joseph 1990 "A Probability Sample of Gay Men." *Journal of Homosexuality* 19:89–104.

Houseknecht, Sharon K. 1987 "Voluntary Childlessness." In M. B. Sussman and S. K. Steinmetz, eds., *Handbook of Marriage and the Family*. New York: Plenum Press.

Kinsey, Alfred, W. Pomeroy, P. H. Gebhard, and C. E. Martin 1953 *Sexual Behavior in the Human Female*. Philadelphia: W. B. Saunders.

Kinsey, Alfred, W. Pomeroy, and C. E. Martin 1948 *Sexual Behavior in the Human Male*. Philadelphia: W. B. Saunders.

Macklin, Eleanor D. 1987 "Nontraditional Family Forms." In M. B. Sussman and S. K. Steinmetz, eds., *Handbook of Marriage and the Family*. New York: Plenum Press.

—— 1983 "Nonmarital Heterosexual Cohabitation: An Overview." In E. D. Macklin and R. H. Rubin, eds., *Contemporary Families and Alternative Lifestyles: Handbook on Research and Theory*. Beverly Hills, Calif.: Sage Publications.

Masters, William H., and Virginia E. Johnson 1979 *Homosexuality in Perspective*. Boston: Little, Brown.

Oudijk, C. 1983 *Social Atlas of Women* (in Dutch). The Hague: Staatsuitgeverij.

Popenoe, David, and Barbara Dafoe Whitehead 1999 *Should We Live Together? What Young Adults Need to Know About Cohabitation Before Marriage*. New Brunswick, N.J.: The National Marriage Project.

Seccombe, Karen 1991 "Assessing the Costs and Benefits of Children: Gender Comparisons among Child-free Husbands and Wives." *Journal of Marriage and the Family* 53:191–202.

Shostak, Arthur B. 1987 "Singlehood." In M. B. Sussman and S. K. Steinmetz, eds., *Handbook of Marriage and the Family*. New York: Plenum Press.

South, Scott 1993 "Racial and Ethnic Differences in the Desire to Marry." *Journal Of Marriage and the Family* 55:357–370.

Stein, Peter J. 1981 *Single Life: Unmarried Adults in Social Context*. New York: St. Martin's Press.

Survey Research Center, University of Michigan 1995 *Monitoring the Future Survey*. Ann Arbor, Mich.: Survey Research Center.

Tomasson, Richard F. 1998 "Modern Sweden: The Declining Importance of Marriage." *Scandinavian Review* August, 1998:83–89.

United States Bureau of the Census 1998 *Statistical Abstract of the United States, 1998* 118th ed. Washington, D.C.: U.S. Bureau of the Census.

Van de Kaa, Dick J. 1987 "Europe's Second Demographic Transition." *Population Bulletin* 42:1–57.

KAREN SECCOMBE

ALTRUISM

Three terms are commonly used in the broad research area that investigates positive interpersonal action: prosocial behavior, helping behavior, and altruism. "Prosocial behavior" is the broadest of the three; it refers to any behavior that can be construed as consistent with the norms of a given society. Thus, murder, when enacted on behalf of one's country on a battlefield, is as prosocial a behavior as intervening to prevent a crime. "Helping behavior" refers simply to any behavior that provides some benefit to its recipient. "Altruism" is the narrowest of the three concepts. Altruism is behavior that not only provides benefits to its recipient but also provides no benefits to the actor and even incurs some costs. If one conceives of psychological rewards as benefits to the actor, this definition of altruism is so narrow that it excludes virtually all human behavior. Hence, many social psychologists maintain simply that altruistic behavior need exclude only the receipt of material benefits by the actor. Some theorists require as part of the definition that the act be motivated "with an ultimate goal of benefiting someone else" (Batson 1991, p. 2), but do not rule out the incidental receipt of benefits by the actor.

Related terms include philanthropy, charity, volunteering, sharing, and cooperating. Philanthropy and charity have largely come to mean donation of money or material goods. Volunteering, similarly, generally refers to giving time for the ultimate purpose of benefiting others, under the aegis of some nonprofit organization. Sharing and cooperating refer to coordinated actions among members of a group or collectivity in the service of better outcomes for the group as a whole. All of these terms may be subsumed under the generic term "prosocial behavior," and often under "helping behavior," although they would seldom meet the stringent criteria for altruism.

HISTORY

The origins of the contemporary study of altruism have been traced back to August Comte, who explored the development of altruism and "sympathetic instincts." The existence of an altruistic instinct was emphasized in McDougall's *Introduction to Social Psychology* (1908) but argued against by the naturalistic observational research of Lois Murphy (1937). Early symbolic interactionists attributed altruistic behavior to the capacity to "take the role of the other"—to imagine oneself in another person's situation (Mead 1934). The developmental study of altruism has built on the theoretical work of Piaget (1932), who explored stages in the development of sharing behavior, as well as on the work of Kohlberg (1969) on the development of moral judgment. Hartshorne and May conducted one of the earliest series of empirical studies (1928–30), focusing on honesty and altruism in children. Sorokin (1950, 1970[1950]) wrote extensively on love and altruism, and carried out the first empirical work on informal helping and volunteering by studying individuals nominated by others as "good neighbors." It is only since the mid-1960s, however, that altruism has been extensively examined through systematic research.

Most social psychology textbooks attribute this upsurge of interest in altruism and helping behavior to the murder of Kitty Genovese in 1964 and the failure of the thirty-nine witnesses to intervene. The subject of widespread media coverage, this incident motivated Latané and Darley's experimental investigations of bystander inaction, published in *The Unresponsive Bystander: Why Doesn't He Help?* (1970). During the 1970s, helping behavior became one of the most popular topics in social psychological research, although this emphasis declined considerably through the 1980s and 1990s (see Batson 1998 for figures on the number of published studies by decade). Because of this beginning, the vast majority of the studies deal with intervention in the momentary problems of strangers. Only since the 1990s has there been much attention to informal and formal volunteering, charitable donation, and blood donation. Virtually all textbooks now have a chapter on altruism and helping behavior, and a number of books on the topic have been published in the past three decades.

THEORIES OF ALTRUISM AND HELPING BEHAVIOR

Helping behavior has been explained within a variety of theoretical frameworks, among them evolutionary psychology, social learning, and cognitive development. One sociobiological approach maintains that helping behavior and altruism have developed through the selective accumulation of behavioral tendencies transmitted genetically. Three mechanisms have been suggested: kin selection, reciprocal altruism, and group selection (see Sober and Wilson 1998). These mechanisms explain the evolution of altruistic behavior as a function of, in turn: the greater likelihood that altruists would save kin, through perpetuating an altruistic gene shared among them; a tendency to help others who have engaged in helpful acts, presumably based on a reciprocity gene; and the greater

likelihood of survival of entire groups that include a higher proportion of altruists. A second sociobiological theory maintains that helping behavior has developed through sociocultural evolution, the selective accumulation of behavior retained through purely social modes of transmission. (See Krebs and Miller [1985] for an excellent review of this literature.) The cognitive-developmental approach to the development of helping behavior in children emphasizes the transformation of cognitive structures and experiential role-taking opportunities as determinants. Social learning theory explains altruism and helping behavior as learned through interaction with the social environment, mainly through imitation and modeling, but also through reinforcement. Reflecting the same behaviorist principles, exchange theory suggests that individuals perform helping acts while guided by the principles of maximizing rewards and minimizing costs. Helping behavior is instrumental in acquiring rewards that may be material, social, or even self-administered. A more explicitly sociological framework suggests that individuals help out of conformity to social norms that prescribe helping. Three norms have received special attention: the norm of giving, which prescribes giving for its own sake; the norm of social responsibility, which prescribes helping others who are dependent; and the norm of reciprocity, which prescribes that individuals should help those who have helped them.

Reflecting the contemporary social psychological emphasis on cognition, several decision-making models of helping behavior have guided much of the research into adult helping behavior (Latané and Darley 1970; Piliavin et al. 1981; Schwartz and Howard 1981). These models specify sequential decisions that begin with noticing a potential helping situation and end with a decision to help (or not). Research has focused on identifying those personality and situational variables that influence this decision-making process and specifying how they do so. There also has begun to be more attention to the social and sociological aspects of helping—to the context in which helping occurs, to the relationship between helper and helped, and to structural factors that may affect these interactions (Gergen and Gergen 1983; Callero 1986). A very active focus of work, mainly identified with Batson (see, e.g., Batson 1991) and Cialdini and colleagues, has been the attempt to demonstrate (or refute) the existence of "true" altruistic motivations for helping.

RESEARCH ON ALTRUISM AND HELPING BEHAVIOR

Person Variables. There has been an extensive and confused debate, due both to definitional and measurement problems, about the existence of an altruistic personality (see Schroeder et al. 1995). There is now good evidence of a pattern of prosocial personality traits that characterize individuals whose behavior involves long-term, sustained forms of helping behavior (e.g., community mental health workers, see Krebs and Miller 1985; volunteers who work with AIDS patients, see Penner et al. 1995; Penner and Finkelstein 1998). The traits that make up the prosocial personality include empathy, a sense of responsibility, concern for the welfare of others, and a sense of self-efficacy. With regard to helping in emergencies, the evidence is stronger for person by situation effects; that is, interactions of characteristics of both individuals and situations that influence helping in emergencies. For example, self-confidence and independence can predict differentially how individuals will behave in emergency situations when there are others present or when the person is alone (Wilson 1976). And Batson and his colleagues have found that prosocial personality characteristics correlate with helping, but only when helping is egoistically motivated, not when true altruism is involved. The general proposal that individual difference factors are most effective when situational pressures are weak seems generally applicable in the helping area.

Internalized values as expressed in personal norms have also been shown to influence helping. Personal norms generate the motivation to help through their implications for self-based costs and benefits; behavior consistent with personal norms creates rewards such as increased self-esteem, whereas behavior that contradicts personal norms generates self-based costs such as shame. This influence has been demonstrated in high-cost helping such as bone marrow donation (Schwartz 1977). Other personality correlates of helping are less directly related to the costs and benefits of the helping act itself. For example, information-processing styles such as cognitive complexity influence helping.

Clary and Snyder (1991) have pursued a functional approach to understanding motivations for helping. They have developed a questionnaire measure that distinguishes six potential motives for long-term volunteering (e.g. value expression, social motivation, career orientation) and have demonstrated both predictive and discriminant validity for the instrument (Clary, Snyder et al. 1998). In one study, they showed that it was not the more purely altruistic motivations that predicted long-term commitment. Temporary emotional states or moods may also affect helping. A series of studies by Isen (1970) and her colleagues demonstrate that the "glow of good will" induces people to perform at least low-cost helping acts such as helping someone pick up a pile of dropped papers, and research by Cialdini and colleagues has shown that helping can be motivated by the need to dispel a bad mood.

Situation Variables. Characteristics of the situation also influence the decision to help. The salience and clarity of a victim's need influence both the initial tendency to notice need and the definition of the perceived need as serious. Salience and clarity of need increase as the physical distance between an observer and a victim decreases; thus, victims of an emergency are more likely to be helped by those physically near by. Situational cues regarding the seriousness of another's need influence whether need is defined as serious enough to warrant action. Bystanders are more likely to offer aid when a victim appears to collapse from a heart attack than from a hurt knee, for example, presumably because of perceived seriousness. The presence of blood, on the other hand, can deter helping, perhaps because it suggests a problem serious enough to require medical attention.

One of the most strongly supported findings in the area of helping is that the number of others present in a potential helping situation influences an individual's decision to help. Darley and Latané (1968) demonstrated experimentally that the higher the number of others present, the lower the chance of any one individual helping. One process underlying this effect involves the diffusion of responsibility: the higher the number of potential helpers, the less any given individual perceives a personal responsibility to intervene. The presence of an individual who may be perceived as having special competence to help also reduces the felt responsibility of others to help. Thus, when some-one in medical clothing is present at a medical emergency, others are less likely to help. A second process underlying the effect, when bystanders can see each other, involves definition of the situation. If no one moves to intervene, the group may collectively provide a social definition for each other that the event is not one that requires intervention.

Social Variables. Research has also demon-strated the influence of other social variables on helping. Darley and Latané (1968) showed experi-mentally that people were more likely to provide help in an emergency in the presence of a friend rather than in the presence of strangers. They reasoned that in emergency situations in which a friend does not respond, one is not likely to attrib-ute this to lack of concern, but rather will seek other explanations. In addition, bystanders who are acquainted are more likely to talk about the situation. Thus, preexisting social relationships among bystanders affect helping. Individuals are also more likely to help others who are similar to them, whether in dress style or in political ideolo-gy. The perceived legitimacy of need, a variable defined by social norms, also affects rates of help-ing. In one field study of emergency intervention, bystanders were more likely to help a stranger who collapsed in a subway car if the distress was attrib-uted to illness rather than to drunkenness (Piliavin, Rodin, and Piliavin 1969).

Other demographic variables, such as sex, age, socioeconomic status, and race have also been investigated. Race appears to affect helping main-ly when the costs for helping are relatively high, or when failure to help can be attributed to factors other than prejudice (Dovidio 1984). In the study cited above (Piliavin et al. 1969) the rate of helping by white and black bystanders was unrelated to the race of the victim who appeared to be ill, but help offered to the drunk was almost always by people of his own race. Females are usually helped more than males, but who helps more depends heavily on the nature of the help required. Males tend to help females more than they help males, whereas females are equally helpful to females and males (see Piliavin and Unger 1985). This pattern may reflect stereotypic gender roles: Females are stereo-typed as dependent and weaker than males. Other studies of the effect of social statuses on helping

indicate, consistent with social categorization theo-ry, that members of one's own group tend to be helped more than outgroup members. Studies of reactions following natural disasters show that people tend to give aid first to family members, then to friends and neighbors, and last to strangers.

THE SOCIOLOGICAL CONTEXT OF HELPING

Gergen and Gergen (1983) call for increased at-tention to the social structural context of helping and to the interactive history and process of the helping relationship (see also Piliavin and Charng 1990). Social structure is clearly important as a context for helping. Social structure specifies the pool of social roles and meaning systems associat-ed with any interaction (Callero, Howard, and Piliavin 1987). Social structure also influences the distribution of resources that may be necessary for certain helping relationships. One needs money to be able to donate to a charity and medical expert-ise to be able to help earthquake victims. Wilson and Musick (1997) have presented data in support of a model using both social and cultural capital as predictors of involvement in both formal and informal volunteering. Social structure also deter-mines the probability of both social and physical interaction among individuals and thus influences the possibility of helping.

Interaction history is also crucial to under-standing helping behavior. If a relationship has been positive and mutually supportive, this con-text suggests that beneficial actions should be defined as helping. If a relationship has been characterized by competition and conflict, this context does not support defining beneficial ac-tion as helping. In this case, alternative, more self-serving motivations may underlie helping. Thus the provision of U.S. foreign aid to countries with which the United States has had conflict is often viewed as a strategic tool, whereas when such aid has been provided to countries with which the United States has had positive relationships, it is viewed generally as genuine helping. Such pat-terns illustrate this influence of interaction history on the interpretation of helping behavior.

Another sociological approach emphasizes helping as role behavior and is guided by Mead's

(1934) conception of roles as patterns of social acts framed by a community and recognized as distinct objects of the social environment. Roles define individual selves and thus also guide individual perception and action. Helping behavior has been shown to express social roles. A series of studies of blood donors (Callero, Howard, and Piliavin 1987; Piliavin and Callero 1991) demonstrate that role-person merger (when a social role becomes an essential aspect of self) predicts blood donation, independent of the effects of both personal and social norms, and is more strongly associated with a history of blood donation than are social or personal norms. This study demonstrates the importance of helping for self-validation and reproduction of the social structure as expressed in roles. More recent research has shown similar effects for identities tied to volunteering time and giving money (Grube and Piliavin in press; Lee, Piliavin, and Call in press). This attention to concepts such as roles, interaction history, and social structure is evidence of the sociological significance of altruism and helping behavior.

CROSS-CULTURAL RESEARCH IN ALTRUISM

Until the last few decades, little work had been done systematically comparing altruism and helping behavior across cultures. Beginning in the 1970s, researchers have compared helping in rural and urban areas, rather consistently finding that helping of strangers, although not of kin, is more likely in less densely populated areas all around the world. In a real sense, urban and rural areas have different "cultures"; small towns are more communal or collective, while cities are more individualistic. A review of other cross-cultural comparisons (Ting and Piliavin forthcoming) examines similarities and differences not only in the helping of strangers but also in the development of moral reasoning, socialization of prosocial behavior, and participation in "civil society." The collectivism-individualism distinction across societies provides a good organizing principle for understanding many of the differences that are found. Not only do societies differ in the level of helping, but in the pattern. For example, in communal societies, the difference between the amount of help offered to ingroup and outgroup members is exaggerated in comparison with the more individualistic societies.

ALTRUISM RESEARCH IN OTHER FIELDS

Scholars from many fields other than social psychology have also addressed the question of altruism. The long debate in evolutionary biology regarding the possibility that altruism could have survival value appears to have been answered in the affirmative (Sober and Wilson 1998). Some authors (e.g. Johnson 1986; Rushton 1998) in fact view patriotism or ethnic conflict, or both, as rooted in altruism fostered by kin selection. Game theorists have discovered that in repeated prisoner's dilemma games and public goods problems, some individuals consistently behave in more cooperative or altruistic ways than do others (Liebrand 1986). Even economists and political scientists, who have long held to the belief that all motivation is essentially selfish, have begun to come to grips with evidence (such as voting behavior and the public goods issue) that indicates that this is not true (see Mansbridge 1990; Clark 1998).

Recommended reading. The interested reader is referred Schroeder et al., *The Psychology of Helping and Altruism* (1995) for a relatively nontechnical overview of the field, or Batson, "Altruism and Prosocial Behavior" (1998) for a briefer, more technical approach emphasizing work demonstrating that "true altruism" can be a motivation for helping. For an excellent examination of approaches to the topic of altruism by economists and political scientists, read Mansbridge, *Beyond Self-Interest* (1990). For an engaging read on the topic of both evolutionary and psychological altruism, try Sober and Wilson's *Unto Others* (1998). Finally, for a view toward the practical application of ideas from altruism research, read Oliner et al., *Embracing the Other* (1992). (Full citations for these works are in the references that follow.)

(SEE ALSO: *Social Psychology*)

REFERENCES

Batson, C. Daniel 1998 "Altruism and Prosocial Behavior." In Daniel T. Gilbert, Susan T. Fiske, and Gardner Lindzey, eds., *The Handbook of Social Psychology*, vol. 2, 4th ed., Boston, Mass.: McGraw-Hill.

—— 1991 *The Altruism Question: Toward a Social-Psychological Answer*. Hillsdale, N.J.: Erlbaum.

Callero, Peter L. 1986 "Putting the Social in Prosocial Behavior: An Interactionist Approach to Altruism." *Humboldt Journal of Social Relations* 13:15–32.

——, Judith A. Howard, and Jane A. Piliavin 1987 "Helping Behavior as Role Behavior: Disclosing Social Structure and History in the Analysis of Prosocial Action." *Social Psychology Quarterly* 50:247–256.

Cialdini, Robert B., Donald J. Baumann, and Douglas T. Kenrick 1981 "Insights from Sadness: A Three-Step Model of the Development of Altruism as Hedonism." *Developmental Review* 1:207–223.

Clark, Jeremy 1998 "Fairness in Public Good Provision: an Investigation of Preferences for Equality and Proportionality." *Canadian Journal of Economics* 31:708–729.

Clary, E. Gil, and Mark Snyder 1991 "Functional Analysis of Altruism and Prosocial Behavior: the Case of Volunteerism." In M.S. Clark, ed., *Prosocial Behavior* Newbury Park, Calif.: Sage.

——, Robert D. Ridge, John Copeland, Arthur A. Stukas, Julie Haugen, and Peter Miene 1998 "Understanding and Assessing the Motivations of Volunteers: A Functional Approach." *Journal of Personality and Social Psychology* 74:1516–1530.

Darley, John M., and Bibb Latané 1968 "Bystander Intervention in Emergencies: Diffusion of Responsibility." *Journal of Personality and Social Psychology* 8:377–383.

Dovidio, John F. 1984 "Helping Behavior and Altruism: An Empirical and Conceptual Overview." In L. Berkowitz, ed., *Advances in Experimental Social Psychology*, vol. 17. New York: Academic.

Gergen, Kenneth J., and Mary M. Gergen 1983 "Social Construction of Helping Relationships." In J. F. Fisher, A. Nadler, and B. M. DePaulo, eds., *New Directions in Helping*, vol. I. New York: Academic.

Grube, Jean, and Jane A. Piliavin forthcoming "Role Identity and Volunteer Performance." *Personality and Social Psychology Bulletin.*

Hartshorne, H., and M. A. May 1928–30 *Studies in the Nature of Character*, vols. 1–3. New York: Macmillan.

Isen, Alice M. 1970 "Success, Failure, Attention and Reaction to Others: The Warm Glow of Success." *Journal of Personality and Social Psychology* 15:294–301.

Johnson, G. R. 1986 "Kin Selection, Socialization, and Patriotism: An Integrating Theory." *Politics and the Life Sciences* 4:127–154.

Kohlberg, Lawrence 1969 "Stage and Sequence: The Cognitive-Developmental Approach to Socialization." In D. Goslin, ed., *Handbook of Socialization Theory and Research*. Chicago: Rand McNally.

Krebs, Dennis L., and Dale T. Miller 1985 "Altruism and Aggression." In G. Lindzey and E. Aronson, eds., *The Handbook of Social Psychology*, 3rd ed., vol. 2. Hillsdale, N.J.: Erlbaum.

Latané, Bibb, and John M. Darley 1970 *The Unresponsive Bystander: Why Doesn't He Help?* New York: Appleton-Crofts.

Lee, Lichang, Jane A. Piliavin, and Vaughn Call forthcoming "Giving Time, Money, and Blood: Similarities and Differences." *Social Psychology Quarterly.*

Liebrand, Wim B.G. "The Ubiquity of Social Values in Social Dilemmas." In Henk A.M. Wilke, David M. Messick, and Christel G. Rutte, eds., *Experimental Social Dilemmas*, 113–133. Frankfurt am Main: Verlag Peter Lang.

Mansbridge, Jane J. (ed.) 1990 *Beyond Self-Interest*. Chicago: University of Chicago Press.

McDougall, William 1908 *Introduction to Social Psychology*. London: Methuen.

Mead, George Herbert 1934 *Mind, Self and Society from the Standpoint of a Social Behaviorist*, edited by C. W. Morris. Chicago: University of Chicago Press.

Murphy, Lois B. 1937 *Social Behavior and Child Personality: An Exploratory Study of Some Roots of Sympathy*. New York: Columbia University Press.

Oliner, Pearl M., Samuel P. Oliner, Lawrence Baron, Lawrence A. Blum, Dennis L. Krebs, and M. Zuzanna Smolenska 1992 *Embracing the Other: Philosophical, Psychological, and Historical Perspectives on Altruism*. New York: New York University Press.

Oliner, Samuel P., and Pearl M. Oliner 1988 *The Altruistic Personality: Rescuers of Jews in Nazi Europe*. New York: Free Press.

Penner, Louis A., and Marcia A. Finkelstein 1998 "Dispositional and Structural Determinants of Volunteerism." *Journal of Personality and Social Psychology* 74:525–537.

——, Barbara A Fritzsche, J. Philip Craiger, and Tamara S. Freifeld 1995 "Measuring the Prosocial Personality." In James N. Butcher, Charles D. Spielberger, et al., eds., *Advances in Personality Assessment*, vol. 10. Hillsdale, N.J.: Erlbaum.

Piaget, Jean 1932 *The Moral Judgment of the Child*. London: Routledge and Kegan Paul.

Piliavin, Irving M., Judith Rodin, and Jane A. Piliavin 1969 "Good Samaritanism: An Underground Phenomenon?" *Journal of Personality and Social Psychology* 13:289–299.

Piliavin, Jane A., and Peter L. Callero 1991 *Giving Blood: The Development of an Altruistic Identity*. Baltimore: Johns Hopkins University Press.

Piliavin, Jane A., and Hong-wen Charng 1990 "Altruism: A Review of Recent Theory and Research." *Annual Review of Sociology* 16:25–65.

Piliavin, Jane A., John F. Dovidio, Samuel Gaertner, and Russell D. Clark 1981 *Emergency Intervention*. New York: Academic.

Piliavin, Jane A., and Rhoda Kesler Unger 1985 "The Helpful but Helpless Female: Myth or Reality?" In Virginia E. O'Leary, Rhoda K. Unger, and Barbara S. Wallston, eds., *Women, Gender, and Social Psychology*. Hillsdale, N.J.: Erlbaum.

Rushton, J. Philippe 1998 "Genetic Similarity Theory and the Roots of Ethnic Conflict." *The Journal of Social, Political, and Economic Studies* 23:477–486.

Schroeder, David A., Louis A. Penner, John F. Dovidio, and Jane Allyn Piliavin 1995 *The Psychology of Helping and Altruism: Problems and Puzzles*. New York: Mc-Graw-Hill.

Schwartz, Shalom H. 1977 "Normative Influences on Altruism." In L. Berkowitz, ed., *Advances in Experimental Social Psychology*, vol. 10. New York: Academic Press.

——, and Judith A. Howard 1981 "A Normative Decision-Making Model of Altruism." In J. P. Rushton and R. M. Sorrentino, eds., *Altruism and Helping Behavior: Social, Personality, and Developmental Perspectives*. Hillsdale, N.J.: Erlbaum.

Sober, Elliott, and David S. Wilson 1998 *Unto Others: The Evolution and Psychology of Unselfish Behavior*. Cambridge, Mass.: Harvard University Press.

Sorokin, Pitirim A. 1950 *Altruistic Love: A Study of American 'Good Neighbors' and Christian Saints*. Boston: The Beacon Press.

—— (ed.) 1970 [1950] *Explorations in Altruistic Love and Behavior: A Symposium*. New York: Kraus Reprint Co. [Boston: The Beacon Press]

Ting, Jen-Chieh, and Jane A. Piliavin forthcoming "Altruism in Comparative International Perspective." In James Phillips, ed., *Charities: Between State and Market*. Montreal: McGill-Queen's University Press.

Wilson, John P. 1976 "Motivation, Modeling, and Altruism: A Person X Situation Analysis." *Journal of Personality and Social Psychology* 34:1078–1086.

Wilson, John, and Marc A. Musick 1997 "Who Cares? Toward and Integrated Theory of Volunteer Work." *American Sociological Review* 62:694–713.

Judith A. Howard
Jane Allyn Piliavin

AMERICAN FAMILIES

Many long-standing assumptions about American families have been challenged by family scholars.

Among these assumptions is the belief that in colonial times the American family was extended in its structure, with three generations living together under one roof. It has been commonly believed that the nuclear family came about as a result of industrialization, with smaller families better able to meet the demands of an industrialized economy. However, historical data show that the extended family was not typical in the colonial era and that the earliest families arriving from Great Britain and other western European countries were already nuclear in structure (Demos 1970; Laslett and Wall 1972).

Some commonly held views about contemporary families also have been debunked in the research literature. For example, it has been commonly thought that American families neglect their elder members and are quick to place them in nursing homes. However, research shows that most older Americans have frequent contact with one or more members of their family, and that families typically provide extensive, long-term care to older persons when such care is needed. In most cases, families turn to placement in a nursing home as a last resort rather than a first option when elder members grow ill or frail.

More generally, family scholars have successfully challenged the notion of "the American family." As Howe (1972, p. 11) puts it, "the first thing to remember about the American family is that it doesn't exist. Families exist. All kinds of families in all kinds of economic and marital situations." This review will show the great diversity of family patterns that characterize the United States of the past, the present, and the foreseeable future.

HISTORICAL OVERVIEW

It is unfortunate that textbooks intended for courses on the family rarely include a discussion of Native Americans, for a historical examination of these groups shows a striking range of variation in family patterns. In fact, virtually all the variations in marriage customs, residence patterns, and family structures found the world over could be found in North America alone (Driver 1969). Though some of these traditional family patterns have survived to the present day, others have been disrupted over the course of U.S. history. It is important to note however, that research has not confirmed the commonly held assumption that Native-American societies were placid and unchanging prior to European contact and subsequent subjugation. Important changes were taking place in Native-American societies long before the arrival of Europeans (Lurie 1985).

As has been noted, European immigrants to the American colonies came in nuclear rather than extended families (and also came as single persons—for example, as indentured servants). It was long believed that colonial families were very large, with some early writers claiming an average of ten to twelve children per family, and that most people lived in extended rather than nuclear families. Family scholars, however, have cited evidence showing somewhat lower numbers of children, with an average of eight children born to colonial women (Zinn and Eitzen 1987). Scholars also have distinguished between number of children born per woman and family size at a given point in time. Average family size was somewhat smaller than the average number of children born, due to high infant mortality and because the oldest children often left home prior to the birth of the last child. Evidence suggests an average family size of five to six members during colonial times (Nock 1987). Thus, although the average size of colonial families was somewhat larger than today's families, they were not as large as has been commonly assumed. Furthermore, most people in colonial America lived in nuclear rather than extended family settings.

To understand the size and composition of colonial households, consideration must be given to nonrelated persons living in the home. Servants often lived with prosperous colonial families, and other families took in boarders and lodgers when economic conditions required such an arrangement (Zinn and Eitzen 1987). Households might also include apprentices and other employees. The presence of nonfamily members has important implications for family life. Laslett (1973) has argued that the presence of nonkin meant that households offered less privacy to families and hence provided the opportunity for greater scrutiny by "outsiders." Colonial homes also had fewer rooms than most American homes today, which also contributed to the relatively public nature of these households.

Colonial communities placed great importance on marriage, particularly in New England, where sanctions were imposed on those who did not marry (for example, taxes were imposed on single men in some New England colonies). However, historical records indicate that colonists did not marry at especially young ages. The average age at marriage was twenty-four to twenty-five for men and twenty-two to twenty-three for women (Leslie and Korman 1989). Older ages at marriage during this era reflect parental control of sons' labor on the farm (with many sons delaying marriage until their fathers ceded land to them) and also reflect the lower relative numbers of women (Nock 1987). Parents also typically exerted strong influence over the process of mate selection but did not control the decision. Divorce was rare during this period. The low divorce rate cannot be equated with intact marriages, however. Spousal desertion and early widowhood were far more common experiences than they are today.

The population for the American colonies came primarily from Great Britain, other western European countries, and from western Africa. Initially brought to the colonies in 1619 as indentured servants, hundreds of thousands of Africans were enslaved and transported to America during the colonial period (by 1790, the date of the first U.S. census, African Americans composed almost 20 percent of the population; Zinn and Eitzen 1987). It has been commonly assumed that slavery destroyed the cultural traditions and family life of African Americans. The reasoning behind this assumption was that slave families often were separated for sale to other masters, males were unable to provide for or protect their families, and slave marriages were not legal. The stereotype of "matriarchal" black families, in which women are the family heads and authorities, usually assumes that slavery produced this family form. Empirical research challenges these assumptions. Though slave families lived in constant fear of separation (Genovese 1986), many slave marriages were strong and longlasting (Gutman 1976). Marriages were legitimized within the slave community (symbolized, for example, by the ritual of "jumping over a broomstick"; Boris and Bardaglio 1987), and two-parent families were common among slaves as well as among free blacks in the North and the South (Gutman 1976). A variety of family structures, including female-headed households, were found in the slave community and attested to the importance placed on kin ties. Rather than the "absent family" assumed to characterize slave life, slaves were connected to one another through extensive kinship networks (Genovese 1986). Extended kin ties continue to be an important aspect of African-American families today.

For decades, the heritage of slavery and its presumed effects on family life have been invoked to explain social problems in poor black communities (e.g., Moynihan 1965). The historical evidence described above does not lend support to this explanation. Most writers today argue that social problems experienced in poor black communities can more accurately be attributed to the effects of discrimination and the disorganizing effects of mass migration to the urbanized North rather than to the heritage of slavery (e.g., Staples 1986).

Societal changes associated with the Industrial Revolution profoundly affected all types of American families, though the specific nature and extent of these effects varied by social class, race, ethnic origins, and geographic region. Prior to the Industrial Revolution, family members worked together as an economic unit. Their workplace was the home or family farm, with families producing much of what they consumed. Family life and economic life were one and the same, and the boundaries between "private life" in the family and "public life" in the community were blurred. With the development of a commercial economy, the workplace was located away from the family unit. Separation of work and family life created a sharp distinction between the "public" realm of work and the "private" realm of family. Particularly for women's roles, changes initiated by the Industrial Revolution have been long-lasting and far-reaching. Increasingly, women's roles were defined by activities assumed to be noneconomic, in the form of nurturing and caring for family members. This was especially true for middle-class women, and married women were excluded from many jobs. Poor and working-class women often participated in wage labor, but this work was generally seen as secondary to their family roles. Men were viewed as having primary responsibility for the economic welfare of their families. No longer an economically interdependent unit, families were transformed such that women and children became economically dependent on the primary wage earner.

Thus, children's roles and family relationships also changed with industrialization. In contrast to earlier times, in which children were viewed as miniature adults and engaged in many of the same tasks they would also perform as adults, childhood came to be seen as a special stage of life characterized by dependence in the home. And although children in working-class homes were more likely to work for pay, the evidence suggests that these families also viewed childhood as a stage of life distinct from adulthood (Zinn and Eitzen 1987). Overall, the family became increasingly defined as a private place specializing in the nurturance of children and the satisfaction of emotional needs, a "haven in a heartless world" (Lasch 1977).

Family structures also changed during the 1800s. Family size declined to an average of four to five members. (Of course, average numbers obscure variation in family sizes across social classes and other important dimensions such as race and ethnicity.) Though the average size of nineteenth-century American families was close to that of today's families, women bore more children during their lifetimes than do American women today. Infant and child mortality was higher and births were spaced further apart, thus decreasing the average size of families at a given point in time. Household size also declined, with fewer households including nonrelated persons such as boarders or apprentices. The average ages at which women and men married were similar to those of colonial times, with an average of twenty-two for women and twenty-six for men. However, greater life expectancy meant that marriages typically lasted longer than they did during the colonial period (Nock 1987).

From 1830 to 1930 the United States experienced two large waves of immigration. The first wave, from 1830 to 1882, witnessed the arrival of more than ten million immigrants from England, Ireland, Germany, and the Scandinavian countries. During the second wave, from 1882 to 1930, over twenty-two million people immigrated to the United States. Peoples from northern and western Europe continued to come to the United States during this second wave, but a large proportion of immigrants came from southern and eastern Europe as well (Zinn and Eitzen 1987). Immigrants' family lives were shaped by their ethnic origins as well as by the diverse social and economic structures of the cities and communities in which they settled.

Ethnic traditions also helped Mexican-American families adapt to changing circumstances. Annexation of territory from Mexico in 1848 and subsequent immigration from Mexico produced sizable Mexican-American communities in the Southwest. Immigrants from Mexico often reconstructed their original family units within the United States, typically including extended as well as nuclear family members. Extended family households are more common today among Mexican Americans than among non-Hispanic whites, reflecting Mexican Americans' strong family orientation (or "familism") as well as their less advantaged economic circumstances (Zinn and Eitzen 1987).

Imbalanced sex ratios among Chinese and Japanese immigrants greatly influenced the family experiences of these groups. First coming to the United States in the early 1900s, Chinese immigrants were predominantly male. The Chinese Exclusion Act of 1882 barred further immigration, and only wealthy Chinese men were able to bring brides to the United States (Boris and Bardaglio 1987). As of 1910, there were 1,413 Chinese men in the United States to every 100 Chinese women. This sex ratio was still skewed in 1940, when there were 258 men to every 100 women. In contrast to the extended family networks typical of traditional Chinese culture, many Chinese-American households consisted of single men living alone (Marden and Meyer 1973).

Substantial immigration from Japan took place between 1885 and 1924. Like traditional Chinese families, Japanese families were based on strong extended kin networks. As was true for Chinese immigration, most Japanese immigrants were male. In addition to immigration restrictions, Japanese-American families (especially those on the West Coast) were disrupted by property confiscation and the mass relocations that took place during World War II (Marden and Meyer 1973).

In addition to the "old" immigration of the mid-nineteenth century and the "new" immigration of the late nineteenth and early twentieth centuries, a third wave of large-scale immigration to the United States began in the mid-1960s. In contrast to the earlier waves, when most immigrants came from European countries, most immigration in this third wave has been from Latin America and Asia. However, as has been true of earlier periods of immigration, public controversies surround the economic and social absorption of these new groups (Marger 1991). In addition to occupational and economic challenges facing immigrant families, social challenges include the continuing debate over whether schools should provide bilingual education to non-English-speaking children.

MARRIAGE AND FAMILY TRENDS IN THE UNITED STATES

The separation of paid work and family life, associated with the transition to an industrialized society, gave rise to profound changes in family life. Over the course of the twentieth century, women's roles were defined primarily by family responsibilities within the "private sphere" of the home, but except for a brief period following World War II, women's labor-force participation rose steadily. As of 1997, nearly half (46 percent) of all employed workers were women. Increases in labor-force participation were especially great among married women. In 1900, less than 4 percent of married women were in the labor force. By 1997, that figure had risen to 62 percent (U.S. Bureau of the Census 1998). In contrast to earlier eras of American history, when African-American women were more likely to work for pay than white women, rates of labor force participation are now nearly the same for women in these racial groups, for both married and unmarried women. Married Hispanic women are slightly less likely to be employed than married African-American and non-Hispanic white women (U.S. Bureau of Labor Statistics 1991). As discussed below, women's labor-force participation has important implications for many dimensions of family life.

Though American families have changed in important ways over the past 100 years, examination of historical trends also reveals continuation of some family patterns begun long ago. Notably, the period of the 1950s is commonly thought to mark the end of a golden age of family life. However, historical data show that for a number of family patterns, the 1950s was an unusual period. Lower rates of divorce, lower ages at marriage, and higher rates of childbearing observed during the 1950s have been attributed mainly to greater economic prosperity following the Great Depression and World War II (Cherlin 1992).

Age at First Marriage. According to U.S. census data, the average (median) age at first marriage in the United States was twenty-five years for women and 26.7 years for men in 1998 (U.S. Bureau of the Census 1998). These average ages are higher than for most U.S. population censuses of the past century, but the current median age for men is comparable to that documented for (white) men near the turn of the twentieth century. In 1890, the median age at first marriage was twenty-two for women and 26.1 for men. The average age at marriage declined until 1956, when the median age at first marriage was 20.1 for women and 22.5 for men. The average age at marriage subsequently began to rise (Saluter 1996). Comparison of non-Hispanic whites, blacks, and Hispanic whites shows that age at first marriage climbed more rapidly for blacks than for non-Hispanic whites, with blacks marrying later than non-Hispanic whites. In contrast, Hispanics marry at younger ages than do other groups. It is difficult to assess whether Hispanics' lower age at marriage reflects long-term trends within the United States due to the large numbers of Mexican Americans who immigrated in the 1980s and 1990s (Sweet and Bumpass 1987).

Factors promoting later age at marriage include greater societal acceptance of singlehood and cohabitation as well as greater emphasis on educational attainment. The relationship between age at marriage and level of education is nearly linear for non-Hispanic white men and women, with more education associated with later age at marriage. This relationship is more complex for minority groups, and especially for black and Hispanic men. For these men, later age at marriage is associated both with lower and higher educational levels, producing a U-shaped relationship between education and age at marriage. Minority men with low education are likely to have especially poor job prospects, which in turn affect prospects for marriage. Overall, less racial and ethnic diversity in age

at marriage is shown for those with higher educational attainment (Sweet and Bumpass 1987).

Interracial Marriage. Most American marriages are homogamous with regard to race. In 1997, there were 1.3 million interracial marriages, representing only 2.3 percent of all marriages. Many Americans equate interracial marriage with black-white marriage, but only one-quarter of American interracial marriages are between blacks and whites. Currently, 4 percent of black men and 2 percent of black women are married to a white partner. Marriage between African Americans and Asian Americans is even less common than black-white marriages (U.S. Bureau of the Census 1998). Asian Americans are more likely than African Americans to marry a partner of another race. A 1990 study found that 23 percent of Asian Americans intermarry, and that over 40 percent of Japanese-American women are married to a man of a different race (Lee and Yamanaka 1990).

Although the total number of interracial marriages is quite small, the rate of growth in these marriages has been increasing. The number of interracial marriages in the United States increased fourfold between 1970 and 1998. During this period, the total number of marriages grew by only 24 percent (U.S. Bureau of the Census 1998).

Singles. Throughout U.S. history a proportion of individuals have remained unmarried. High levels of singlehood were recorded in the late 1800s, when 15 percent of women and 27 percent of men had not married by the age of thirty-four. In 1940, 15 percent of women and 21 percent of men had not married by this age, but by 1970, these proportions had dropped dramatically. By 1970, just 6 percent of women and 9 percent of women had not married by the age of thirty-four (Kain 1990). The size of the unmarried population has been increasing since the 1970s. In 1994, 20 percent of women and 30 percent of men had not married by age thirty-four (Saluter 1996). Women's changing roles have been linked with the rise in singleness: Women with higher education and higher personal income are less likely to marry or have children. Also, in contrast to earlier eras, there is greater societal tolerance of singlehood, providing greater freedom for both women and men to choose a single lifestyle.

Since few individuals marry for the first time at the age of sixty-five or older, a more accurate picture of the never-married population is provided when attention is restricted to the older population. At present, 3.8 percent of men and 4.7 percent of women age sixty-five and older have never married (Lugaila 1998). Due to the continuing stigmatization of homosexuality, it is difficult to ascertain the numbers of single persons who are gay or lesbian. Researchers have estimated that 4 percent of men and 2 percent of women are exclusively homosexual (Collins 1988). Though homosexual marriages are not legally recognized, many gay and lesbian couples form lasting unions.

Childbearing. Childbearing patterns have varied somewhat over the past century. Women born in 1891 had an average of three children. Women born in 1908, who bore children during the Great Depression, had an average of two children. This figure increased to three children per mother during the 1950s and has since declined to two children per mother on average today (Sweet and Bumpass 1987; U.S. Bureau of the Census 1998). In addition to fewer numbers of children born, current trends in childbearing include higher age at first childbirth and longer intervals of time between births. These trends are interrelated. Waiting longer to have a first child and spacing births further apart decrease the average number of children born per mother. The timing of childbearing also has important effects on other life experiences, including educational and occupational attainment. Lower rates of childbearing are associated with higher educational levels and higher incomes.

Fewer married couples are having their first child in the period immediately following marriage, but there are some important differences by race. In 1960, 54 percent of non-Hispanic white couples had children within twelve to seventeen months of marriage. In 1980 this figure dropped to 36 percent. Little change was shown over this period for black couples, who had children within twelve to seventeen months of marriage. Compared to the total population, black couples are likely to have more children on average and to have a child present at the time of marriage. For whites (Hispanics and non-Hispanics) as well as blacks, nine-tenths of all couples have children within seven to eight years of marriage (Sweet and Bumpass 1987).

Childbearing among single women has increased greatly over the past several decades. While just 5 percent of all births were to single women in 1960, approximately one-third (32.2 percent) of all births were to single women in 1995 (Saluter 1996; U.S. Bureau of the Census 1998). As is true for many family patterns, there are substantial variations across racial-ethnic groups. Asian Americans and Pacific Islanders show a relatively low rate of nonmarital births, at 16.3 percent of all births in this group. In contrast, 25.3 percent of all births among whites are to unmarried women, and the rate for Hispanics (who may be of any race) is 40.8 percent. Nearly 70 percent of African-American children are born to single women (U.S. Bureau of the Census 1998). Although socioeconomic factors do not account completely for births to single women, nonmarital childbearing in the United States tends to be higher among those who are poor. Socioeconomic factors can help to explain why African Americans, who are disproportionately likely to be poor, have had higher rates of nonmarital childbearing.

Divorce. A rising divorce rate has been a feature of U.S. society since the Civil War. At that time, the divorce rate per 1,000 existing marriages was just 1.2 (Jacobson 1959). By the early 1990s, the rate had increased to more than 20 divorces per 1,000 existing marriages (Cherlin 1996). This long-term trend does not show a smooth and progressive rise, however. Divorce rates have risen more sharply after every major war during this century. Divorce also increased following the Great Depression, apparently reflecting stresses associated with unemployment and economic deprivation. Economic prosperity as well as a greater emphasis on family life have been linked to the lower divorce rate observed from 1950 to 1962. Following 1962, dramatic increases in the divorce rate occurred, with a 100 percent increase between 1963 and 1975 (Cherlin 1992). By the early 1970s, the chance of eventual divorce reached almost 50 percent. The divorce rate has more or less stabilized since that time, such that approximately 50 percent of all first marriages are projected to terminate eventually in divorce. The chances of divorce are higher for second marriages, of which 60 percent are projected to end in divorce (Olson and DeFrain 1994).

Population trends have been linked with the increased rate of divorce. Among these trends is greater longevity, with an average life expectancy at birth of approximately eighty years for women and seventy-three years for men who were born in 1991. When they reach the age of sixty-five, women who were born in 1991 can expect to live an additional nineteen years, while men of that birth cohort can expect to live fifteen more years (U.S. Bureau of the Census 1996). (These figures are for the total population. Life expectancies are lower for members of racial and ethnic minorities.) In contrast, the life expectancy at birth for those born in 1900 was forty-eight years for women and forty-six years for men (Grambs 1989). Unsatisfactory marriages that formerly may have been terminated by the death of one partner are now more likely to be dissolved by divorce (Uhlenberg 1986). Scholars have also noted the apparent connection between women's increasing levels of labor-force participation and the increased rate of divorce in the United States. Divorce is more likely to occur in couples where the wife is able to support herself financially.

The risk of divorce also varies with age at marriage, duration of the marriage, education, race, and ethnicity. Age at marriage is one of the most important factors, with the likelihood of divorce twice as great among couples where the wife was seventeen or younger than among couples where the wife was in her early twenties. Further, most divorces take place within the first few years of marriage. The longer a couple has been together, the less likely they will be to get divorced. This pattern also holds among couples in which one or both partners have remarried. Education also seems to be an important factor, with a higher divorce rate observed among high school dropouts than among college graduates. However, the effect of education is due in large part to the fact that college graduates tend to marry at later ages. Looking across racial and ethnic groups, the risk of divorce is greater among African Americans than among whites, and especially high divorce rates are observed for Hispanics (Puerto Ricans in particular), Native Americans, and Hawaiians. Divorce is less common among Asian Americans (Sweet and Bumpass 1987).

Widowhood. Rising life expectancies have increased the average age of widowhood. Among women, the median age at widowhood was fifty-one in 1900, compared to sixty-eight in 1979. The median age at widowhood for men was forty-five in 1900 and seventy-one in 1979 (Grambs 1989). Lower average ages of bereavement for men compared to women in 1900 are linked with women's risks for death in childbirth in that era. Women today can expect to live longer in a widowed status compared to widowed men. This gender gap is explained primarily by higher female life expectancy and lower rates of remarriage among women, and also because women tend to marry men several years older than themselves. Nearly one-half (45 percent) of all American women who are age sixty-five or older are widowed, while 15 percent of men in this age group are widowed. Among the oldest-old—those who are eighty-five years of age and older—these figures rise to 77 percent for women and 42 percent for men (Lugaila 1998).

Remarriage. Due in large part to the fact that widowhood tends to occur later in life, fewer men and women remarry following the death of a spouse, compared to those who remarry following a divorce. Most people who divorce eventually remarry, but the likelihood of remarriage varies greatly according to gender, age, and race. Approximately five out of six men eventually remarry following a divorce, compared to two out of three women who do so (Cherlin 1992). As noted above, men are also more likely than women to remarry following the death of a spouse. The probability of remarriage declines with age, especially among women. Only one in four women who divorce at age forty or older eventually remarry (Levitan, Sar, and Gallo 1988). Race differences also are observed for remarriage. The proportion of women who remarry following divorce is approximately 50 percent for African Americans and 75 percent for whites (Bumpass, Sweet, and Castro Martin 1990).

Increased rates of divorce and remarriage are transforming American families. "Blended" families or stepfamilies are becoming increasingly common, whereby one or both spouses bring children into a remarriage. One in four children will spend some time in a blended family (Furstenberg and Cherlin 1991). Nearly all of these children live with their biological mothers.

Household Structure. As defined by the U.S. Bureau of the Census, "family households" contain persons who are related to the household head (the person in whose name the home is owned or rented) by blood ties, marriage, or adoption. "Nonfamily households" consist of individuals who live alone or with one or more unrelated persons. Historically, most American households have been family households, and most of these have included married couples. In 1910, 80 percent of all households included married couples. By 1998 this percentage had declined to 53 percent (Casper and Bryson 1998). In contrast, the proportion of single-person households has risen dramatically over the century. In 1890, only 4 percent of all households were of this type (Sweet and Bumpass 1987). As of 1998, single-person households accounted for one-quarter of all U.S. households. Nearly 12 percent of all households consist of men living alone, 15 percent consist of women living alone (Lugaila 1998).

Breakdowns of family structure by race and ethnicity have shown that Americans of Korean, Filipino, Vietnamese, and Mexican heritage are most likely to live in family households (for each group, about 84 percent reported living in family households). African Americans and non-Hispanic whites are somewhat less likely to live in family households. Also, compared to other racial and ethnic groups, Puerto Ricans are most likely to live in a household consisting of a mother and one or more children (with 23 percent living in this type of household), followed by African Americans, Native Americans, and Hawaiians (Sweet and Bumpass 1987).

Type of household is tied closely with economic status. While the "typical" dual-earner couple with children earned an average annual income of $46,629 in 1991, the average income for mother-only households was only $13,012 (McLanahan and Casper 1998). Of all household types, those headed by a woman with no husband present have the highest poverty rate. In 1997, nearly 32 percent of these households had incomes that fell below the poverty line (Dalaker and Naifeh 1998).

Due largely to women's risks for poverty and the rise in female-headed households, children are more likely to be poor today than they were several decades ago. The proportion of American children living in poor families declined during the 1960s—from 26.5 percent in 1960 to 15 percent in 1970—but has since increased. Nearly one-quarter of all American children live in poor families. For children who live in a female-headed household,

the chances of living in poverty rise to 46 percent for white-Hispanic and non-Hispanic children, and to 82 percent for African-American children (Ollenburger and Moore 1998).

IMPACT OF FAMILY TRENDS ON CHILDREN AND OLDER PERSONS

The majority of the family patterns described here represent long-term trends in the United States and are unlikely to represent the demise of American families, as has been decried by some social observers. Indeed, marriage remains as "popular" as ever. Although Americans are marrying somewhat later on average than they did in the 1950s and 1960s, the majority of women and men continue to marry and have children. Those who divorce tend to remarry. Although these trends did not originate in the late twentieth century, it is nonetheless true that divorce, single-parent households, employed mothers, and nonmaternal childcare are more typical features of American life today than they were in the past. The impact of these family patterns on children's development and well-being has been a matter of great concern to researchers and policymakers. The impact of women's employment and changes in family composition also have given rise to concerns regarding the provision of informal care to elderly parents.

Divorce. Parents' divorce has been linked with a range of negative outcomes for children in the areas of psychological adjustment, life satisfaction, academic achievement, and social relationships. These effects are strongest in the first year or two following the divorce, but some long-term consequences also have been found. The experience of parents' divorce can continue to have negative effects on a child's well-being as she or he grows into young adulthood (Cherlin, Chase-Lansdale, and McRae 1998).

Although divorce typically is a stressful experience, studies have found a great deal of variation in how children adapt to parents' divorce. Among the factors identified as important to consider are the family's socioeconomic status, race-ethnicity, the child's gender and his or her age at the time of the parents' divorce or separation. For example, the effects of divorce apparently are more acute for children of school age than for preschool children. Marital disruption also brings greater risks to children when the parent-child relationship suffers as a result of the divorce and when one or both parents experience multiple divorces (Amato and Booth 1991).

The level and type of conflict present in the family prior to a divorce also is important in understanding the effects of divorce on children. Children whose families were highly conflictual may show increased well-being following a divorce. Conversely, problems of adjustment have been found among children whose parents did not divorce, but whose family lives were characterized by high levels of conflict (Furstenberg and Cherlin 1991).

Individuals who experienced "low-stress" parental divorces do not appear to differ significantly from those who grew up in happy, intact families (Amato and Booth 1991). In general, negative consequences of divorce are not found for children when parents maintain a positive relationship with the child and with one another, and when the child is provided with adequate social and economic resources. As discussed below, economic difficulties pose a central challenge for single-parent (usually single-mother) households.

Single-parent households. Just as the impact of divorce on children depends upon multiple factors, no one pattern characterizes how children's well-being is influenced by living in a single-parent household. The circumstances of single parenthood are diverse—single parents can be divorced, widowed, or never-married—and they have access to varying levels and types of social and economic resources. Households may include only the single parent and one or more children, or may include extended family or other household members. Noncustodial parents may or may not be part of the child's life.

It has been noted that single-parent households are more likely than dual-parent households to be poor, and that mother-headed households are especially likely to be poor. Following a divorce, women's subsequent income declines 27 percent on average, while men's average income increases by 10 percent (Peterson 1996). Some of this income gap is due to the fact that children are more likely to live with their mothers than their fathers following a divorce. Currently one child in four lives in a single-parent family, and women head 83 percent of these families (U.S. Bureau of the Census 1998).

Many of the problems associated with single-parent households are associated with problems of poverty. The economic difficulties faced by single parents are compounded when child support payments from the noncustodial parent are not provided regularly. About one-half of custodial mothers were awarded child support payments in 1992. Of the women who had been awarded child support, 76 percent received full or partial payment. A significant amount of awarded child support is not received by the custodial parent: one-third of all awarded child support was not paid in 1991. Among custodial parents, mothers have higher child support award rates and payment rates than fathers, but they are also much more likely to be poor. Single custodial mothers are two and one-half times more likely to be poor than single custodial fathers (U.S. Bureau of the Census 1995).

In addition to economic strains, single parents report problems arising from role and task overload, in coordinating a social life and parenting responsibilities, and difficulties with former spouses. Strains experienced by the parent can in turn impact the well-being of children (Richards and Schmiege 1993). Some evidence also suggests that single parents provide less supervision of children compared to two-parent families (married or cohabiting) (e.g., Astone and McLanahan 1991).

Although research has focused primarily on problems of single-parent households, some potential benefits of these households have been identified for children's development and well-being. For example, children in single-parent households have been found to take greater responsibility for household tasks than children in two-parent households. Along with increased responsibilities within the home, children in one-parent households also apparently develop higher levels of personal autonomy and independence (see Richards and Schmiege 1993).

Nonmaternal Childcare. With more American women working for pay than ever before, more preschool-age children are receiving care from their fathers, other family members, or from nonrelatives during their mothers' hours of employment. As of 1991, 9.9 million children age five or younger required care during the hours their mothers were employed. Of these children, the majority were cared for in a home environment:

36 percent were cared for in their own homes (usually by the father or another relative); 31 percent were cared for in another home (usually by a nonrelative in the care provider's home). A further 9 percent were cared for by their mothers while they worked—this was generally in a home environment as well, as most of these mothers had home-based paid work. Approximately one-quarter of the children who required care while their mothers worked were enrolled in an organized day care facility (U.S. Bureau of the Census 1995).

With the increasing use of childcare provided by individuals other than the mother, concerns have been raised regarding the impact of nonmaternal care on children's physical, cognitive, and psychological development. The majority of studies on this topic have concluded that nonmaternal childcare, and nonparental childcare more generally, is not in itself harmful to children. In fact, day care settings apparently aid the development of children's social skills. However, the quality of the care—whether in a family or nonfamily setting—is extremely important for children's development and well-being. A comprehensive report published by the National Research Council found that children whose families were undergoing psychological stress or economic deprivation were more likely to receive care in lower quality settings. Hence, these children are vulnerable not only to poverty and psychological stress within the home, but they are also likely to suffer from the effects of poor-quality care outside the home (Hayes, Palmer, and Zaslow 1990).

Eldercare. Most older Americans live independently in the community and are in relatively good health. Most also provide economic and other support to their adult children, such as providing babysitting or other services. It is only when the elder's health or economic status is severely compromised that the balance of exchange tips in the direction of receiving a greater amount of support than elders provide to their children.

The bulk of care provided to older Americans who are frail or ill is provided by family members, usually women, who are typically spouses or children of the elder (Stone, Cafferata, and Sangl 1987; Wolf, Freedman, and Soldo 1997). If a spouse or child is not available, other relatives or a friend may provide care (though assistance from these latter sources is typically less intensive and for briefer periods of time). Much research attests to the extensive and prolonged care provided by family members to elders within a home environment (see Dwyer and Coward 1992). In many if not most cases, it is only after families have exhausted their physical, economic, and emotional resources that a decision is made to place an elder in a long-term care facility. Indeed, only 5 percent of all Americans age sixty-five and older reside in a nursing home or other long-term care facility at a given point in time. The chances of nursing home placement rise with age: Nearly 25 percent of those age eighty-five or older live in a nursing home. However, even among this "oldest-old" age group, the majority of individuals reside in the community rather than a nursing home (Morgan and Kunkel 1998).

Recognizing that women typically are the primary care providers to older family members, researchers and policymakers have raised concerns that such care will be curtailed in the future due to trends in women's employment and an increasing older population. The prevalence of elder care among the employed population is difficult to estimate due to variations in sampling across studies and how caregiving is defined. However, an averaged estimate from studies on this topic is that about one in five employees has some elder care responsibilities (Gorey, Rice, and Brice 1992).

Research has shown that caregiving can be emotionally gratifying for individuals who are providing care to a loved one (Lechner 1992). However, intensive, long-term caregiving can produce serious physical, economic, and emotional strains, especially when caregiving interferes with the provider's work or household responsibilities (Gerstel and Gallagher 1993). A number of studies have found that employment status does not alter the type or amount of care provided to the elderly by their families, but some family members reduce or terminate their employment in order to provide elder care. A national survey found that 9 percent of employees in the study had quit their jobs and a further 20 percent had altered their work schedules to accommodate their caregiving responsibilities. Women were more likely than men to rearrange their work schedules or to reduce or terminate their employment in order to provide family care (Stone, Cafferata, and Sangl 1987).

The strains of intensive caregiving can compromise the provider's ability to continue in the caregiving role. A number of researchers have concluded that greater assistance from the government as well as from the workplace is needed to assist family members and others who provide care to older adults in the community (e.g. Lechner 1992). Such assistance not only benefits the health and well-being of care providers and recipients, but also allows elders to continue living in the community setting for a longer period of time, as is preferred by most elders and their families.

CROSS-NATIONAL COMPARISONS

The family trends described here are not unique to the United States. Other western societies also have witnessed a rise in the age at first marriage, an increased divorce rate, increased numbers of children born to unmarried women, and an increase in the numbers of women who participate in paid labor. Although the trajectories of these trends are similar for most western societies, differing proportions of individuals and families are represented in these trends across societies. For example, although the average age at marriage has been rising in the United States and most other western societies, the average age at first marriage is lower in the United States than in most of the European countries. And although a rising divorce rate has been a feature of the majority of western societies, the rate of divorce is highest in the United States. Out-of-wedlock births also have increased in western societies over the course of the century. However, in contrast to Scandinavian countries including Sweden and Denmark, more children in the United States live in a single-parent household than with cohabiting parents.

A striking gap between the United States and a number of other countries is found in its relatively high rate of infant mortality. Infant mortality is linked with poverty and the lack of adequate nutrition and health care. The wealth enjoyed by the United States as a nation belies the economic deprivation experienced by subgroups within the society. In 1988, the U.S. infant mortality rate was 10 babies per 1,000 live births. This rate was higher not only as compared with other western societies, but also compared with many nonwestern countries. In a ranking of infant mortality rates worldwide, which were ordered from the lowest to the highest rates, the United States ranked eighteenth from the bottom. This rate was higher than that found in countries including Singapore, Spain, and Ireland, which are poorer relative to the United States, but which have lower levels of economic inequality within the society (Aulette 1994). A statement from the Children's Defense Fund illustrates the high risks for infant mortality faced by racial-ethnic minority groups within the United States: "A black child born in the inner-city of Boston has less chance of surviving the first year of life than a child born in Panama, North or South Korea or Uruguay" (Children's Defense Fund 1990, p. 6, cited in Aulette 1994, p. 405). (The famine experienced within North Korea during the 1990s likely would remove that country from this listing.)

The United States is unique among western societies in its lack of a national health care program, which helps to explain its higher infant mortality rate. In 1997, 43.4 million Americans, or slightly over 16 percent of the U.S. population, had no health insurance coverage for the entirety of that calendar year. The lack of health insurance is especially acute among the poor. Although the Medicaid program is intended to provide health coverage to the poor, 11.2 million poor Americans, or one-third of all poor people in the United States, had no health coverage in 1997 (Bennefield 1998).

In the absence of concerted social policy measures, infant mortality and other risks faced by poor Americans are unlikely to diminish in the near future. Using the Gini index (a measure of income concentration), the U.S. Bureau of the Census reported that income inequalities within the country increased by 16 percent between 1968 and 1992. Even greater inequalities have developed since 1992: Between 1968 and 1994 the rate of increase in U.S. income inequality was over 22 percent (Weinberg 1996). At the same time, the percentage of Americans with incomes below the poverty line also increased—from 11.7 percent in 1979 to 13.3 percent in 1997 (Dalaker and Naifeh 1997).

AMERICAN FAMILIES AND THE FUTURE

Traditional distinctions between "family" and "nonfamily" are increasingly challenged. Though still a relatively small proportion of all households (about 4 percent; U.S. Bureau of the Census 1998), the number of cohabiting heterosexual couples has increased greatly in the past several decades. Marriage between homosexuals is not legally recognized, but some have elected to adopt each other legally, and a growing number are raising children. In addition to the "traditional" nuclear family form of two parents with children, other family types can be expected to continue in the future. These include single parents, blended families resulting from remarriage, and households in which other relatives such as grandparents reside.

Increased longevity has brought about some of the most important changes in American family life over the past century. Children are more likely than ever before to interact with their grandparents. Further, many persons are becoming grandparents while their own parents are still alive (Uhlenberg 1986). Research has documented the prevalence and importance of social interaction, emotional support, financial help, and other assistance between the generations. For all types of American families, indications are that high levels of interaction and assistance between the generations will continue in the future. It remains to be seen how U.S. social policy will respond to the needs of family care-providers, and to the needs of poor Americans and their families, in the years to come.

REFERENCES

Amato, Paul R., and Alan Booth 1991 "Consequences of Parental Divorce and Marital Unhappiness for Adult Well-Being." *Social Forces* 69:895–914.

Astone, Nan Marie, and Sara S. McLanahan 1991 "Family Structure, Parental Practices and High School Completion." *American Sociological Review* 56:309–320.

Aulette, Judy Root 1994 *Changing Families*. Belmont, Calif.: Wadsworth.

Bennefield, Robert L. 1998 *Health Insurance Coverage: 1997*. U.S. Bureau of the Census, Current Population Reports, Series P60–202. Washington, D.C.: U.S. Government Printing Office.

Boris, Eileen, and Peter Bardaglio 1987 "Gender, Race, and Class: The Impact of the State on the Family and the Economy, 1790–1945." In Naomi Gerstel and Harried Engel Gross, eds., *Families and Work*. Philadelphia: Temple University Press.

Bumpass, Larry, James A. Sweet, and Teresa Castro-Martin 1990 "Changing Patterns of Remarriage." *Journal of Marriage and the Family* 52:747–756.

Casper, Lynn M., and Ken Bryson 1998 *Household and Family Characteristics: March 1998 (Update)*. U.S. Bureau of the Census, Current Population Reports, Series P20–515. Washington, D.C.: U.S. Government Printing Office.

Cherlin, Andrew J. 1996 *Public and Private Families*. New York: McGraw-Hill.

—— 1992 *Marriage, Divorce, Remarriage*, rev. ed. Cambridge, Mass.: Harvard University Press.

——, Frank F. Furstenberg, Jr., P. Lindsay Chase-Lansdale, Kathleen E. Kiernan, Philip K. Robins, Donna Ruane Morrison, and Julien O. Teitler 1991 "Longitudinal Studies of Effects of Divorce on Children in Great Britain and the United States." *Science* 252:1386–1389.

Collins, Randall 1988 *Sociology of Marriage and the Family: Gender, Love, and Property*, 2d ed. Chicago: Nelson-Hall.

Dalaker, Joseph, and Mary Naifeh 1998 *Poverty in the United States: 1997*. U.S. Bureau of the Census, Current Population Reports, Series P60–201. Washington, D.C.: U.S. Government Printing Office.

Demos, John 1970 *A Little Commonwealth*. New York: Oxford University Press.

Driver, Harold E. 1969 *Indians of North America*, 2d ed. Chicago: University of Chicago Press.

Dwyer, Jeffrey W., and Raymond T. Coward 1992 "Gender, Family, and Long-Term Care of the Elderly." In Jeffrey W. Dwyer and Raymond T. Coward, eds., *Gender, Families, and Elder Care*. Newbury Park, Calif.: Sage.

Furstenberg, Frank F., Jr., and Andrew J. Cherlin 1991 *Divided Families: What Happens to Children When Parents Part?* Cambridge, Mass.: Harvard University Press.

Genovese, Eugene D. 1986 "The Myth of the Absent Family." In Robert Staples, ed., *The Black Family: Essays and Studies*, 3d ed. Belmont, Calif.: Wadsworth.

Gerstel, Naomi, and Sally K. Gallagher 1993 "Kinkeeping and Distress: Gender, Recipients of Care, and Work-Family Conflict." *Journal of Marriage and the Family* 55:598–607.

Gorey, Kevin M., Robert W. Rice, and Gary C. Brice 1992 "The Prevalence of Elder Care Responsibilities Among the Work Force Population." *Research on Aging* 14(3):399–418.

Grambs, Jean Dresden 1989 *Women over Forty: Visions and Realities*. New York: Springer.

Gutman, Herbert 1976 *The Black Family in Slavery and Freedom, 1750–1925*. New York: Pantheon.

Hayes, Cheryl D., John L. Palmer, and Martha J. Zaslow (eds.) 1990 *Who Cares for America's Children? Child Care Policy for the 1990s*. Washington, D.C.: National Academy Press.

Howe, Louise Knapp 1972 *The Future of the Family*. New York: Simon and Schuster.

Jacobson, Paul H. 1959 *American Marriage and Divorce*. New York: Rinehart.

Kain, Edward 1990 *The Myth of Family Decline: Understanding Families in a World of Rapid Social Change*. Lexington, Mass.: Heath.

Lasch, Christopher 1977 *Haven in a Heartless World: The Family Besieged*. New York: Basic Books.

Laslett, Barbara 1973 "The Family as a Public and Private Institution: An Historical Perspective." *Journal of Marriage and the Family* 35:480–494.

Laslett, Peter, and Richard A. Wall (eds.) 1972 *Household and Family in Past Time*. New York: Cambridge University Press.

Lechner, Viola M. 1992 "Predicting Future Commitment to Care for Frail Parents Among Employed Caregivers." *Journal of Gerontological Social Work* 18:69–84.

Lee, Sharon M., and Keiko Yamanaka 1990 "Patterns of Asian American Intermarriage and Marital Assimilation." *Journal of Comparative Family Studies* 21:287–305.

Leslie, Gerald R., and Sheila K. Korman 1989 *The Family in Social Context*, 7th ed. New York: Oxford University Press.

Levitan, Sar A., Richard S. Belous, and Frank Gallo 1988 *What's Happening to the American Family? Tensions, Hopes, Realities*. Baltimore, Md.: Johns Hopkins University Press.

Lugaila, Terry A. 1998 *Marital Status and Living Arrangements: March 1998 (Update)*. U.S. Bureau of the Census, Current Population Reports, Series P20–514. Washington, D.C.: U.S. Government Printing Office.

Lurie, Nancy Oestreich 1985 "The American Indian: Historical Background." In N.R. Yetman, ed., *Majority and Minority*, 4th ed. Boston: Allyn and Bacon.

Marden, Charles F., and Gladys Meyer 1973 *Minorities in American Society*, 4th ed. New York: D. Van Nostrand.

Marger, Martin N. 1991 *Race and Ethnic Relations: American and Global Perspectives*. Belmont, Calif.: Wadsworth.

McLanahan, Sara, and Lynne Casper 1998 "Growing Diversity and Inequality in the American Family." In Andrew J. Cherlin, ed., *Public and Private Families*. Boston: McGraw-Hill.

Morgan, Leslie, and Suzanne Kunkel 1998 *Aging: The Social Context*. Thousand Oaks, Calif.: Pine Forge Press.

Moynihan, Daniel P. 1965 *The Negro Family: The Case for National Action*. Washington, D.C.: Office of Policy Planning and Research, U.S. Department of Labor.

Nock, Steven L. 1987 *Sociology of the Family*. Englewood Cliffs, N.J.: Prentice Hall.

Ollenburger, Jane C., and Helen A. Moore 1998 *A Sociology of Women: the Intersection of Patriarchy, Capitalism, and Colonization*, 2d ed. Upper Saddle River, N.J.: Prentice Hall.

Olson, David H., and John DeFrain 1994 *Marriage and the Family: Diversity and Strengths*. Mountain View, Calif.: Mayfield.

Peterson, Richard R. 1996 "A Re-Evaluation of the Economic Consequences of Divorce." *American Sociological Review* 61:528–536.

Richards, Leslie N., and Cynthia J. Schmiege 1993 "Problems and Strengths of Single-Parent Families." *Family Relations* 42:277–285.

Saluter, Arlene F. 1996 *Marital Status and Living Arrangements: March 1994*. Current Population Reports, Series P20–484. Washington, D.C.: U.S. Government Printing Office.

Staples, Robert (ed.) 1986 *The Black Family: Essays and Studies*, 3d ed. Belmont, Calif.: Wadsworth.

Stone, Robyn, Gail Lee Cafferata, and Judith Sangl 1987 "Caregivers of the Frail Elderly: A National Profile." *The Gerontologist* 27:616–626.

Sweet, James A., and Larry L. Bumpass 1987 *American Families and Households*. New York: Russell Sage.

Uhlenberg, Andrew 1986 "Death and the Family." In A.S. Skolnick and J.H. Skolnick, eds., *Family in Transition*. Boston: Little, Brown.

U.S. Bureau of the Census 1999 *Interracial Married Couples: 1960 to Present*. http:www.census.gov/population/socdemo/ms-la/tabms-3.txt

U.S. Bureau of the Census 1998 *Statistical Abstract of the United States, 1998*. Washington, D.C.: U.S. Government Printing Office.

U.S. Bureau of the Census 1996 *65+ in the United States*. Current Population Reports, Special Studies, Series P–23, No. 190. Washington, D.C.: U.S. Government Printing Office.

U.S. Bureau of the Census 1995 *Population Profile of the United States: 1995*. Current Population Reports, Series P23–189. Washington, D.C.: U.S. Government Printing Office.

U.S. Bureau of Labor Statistics 1991 *Employment and Earnings*. Washington, D.C.: U.S. Government Printing Office.

Weinberg, Daniel H. 1996 *A Brief Look at U.S. Income Inequality.* U.S. Bureau of the Census, Current Population Reports, Series P60–191. Washington, D.C.: U.S. Government Printing Office.

Wolf, Douglas A., Vicki Freedman, and Beth J. Soldo 1997 "The Division of Family Labor: Care for Elderly Parents." *Journals of Gerontology* 52B:102–109.

Zinn, Maxine Baca, and D. Stanley Eitzen 1987 *Diversity in American Families.* New York: Harper and Row.

LAURIE RUSSELL HATCH

AMERICAN INDIAN STUDIES

American Indian Studies blends many fields in the social sciences and humanities; history and anthropology have been especially prominent, along with education, sociology, psychology, economics, and political science. For convenience, this literature can be grouped into several subject areas: demographic behavior, socioeconomic conditions, political and legal institutions, and culture and religion. Of course, there is a great deal of overlap. To date, this literature deals mostly with aboriginal North Americans and their descendants. As the field has evolved, little attention has been devoted to the natives of South America or the Pacific Islanders. However, there is a growing interest in common experiences of indigenous peoples around the world (e.g. Fleras and Elliot 1992).

DEMOGRAPHY

Historical Demography. Historical demography is important for understanding the complexity of indigenous North American societies and for assessing the results of their contacts with Europeans. For example, complex societies require large populations to generate economic surpluses for trade, and large populations often entail highly developed systems of religion, culture, and governance. Because American Indians almost disappeared in the late nineteenth century, large numbers of pre-Columbian Indians would indicate that devastating mortality rates and profound changes in native social organization followed the arrival of Europeans.

No one knows with certainty when populations of *Homo sapiens* first appeared in the Western Hemisphere. The first immigrants to North America probably followed game from what is now Siberia across the Beringia land bridge, now submerged in the Bering Sea. This land bridge has surfaced during several ice ages, leading to speculation that the first populations arrived as early as 40,000 years ago or as recently as 15,000 years ago—25,000 years ago is a credible estimate (Thornton 1987, p. 9).

In 1918 a Smithsonian anthropologist, James Mooney, published the first systematic estimates of the American Indian population. He reckoned that 1.15 million American Indians were living around 1600. Alfred Kroeber (1934) subsequently reviewed Mooney's early estimates and deemed them correct, though he adjusted the estimate downward to 900,000 (Deneven 1976). The Mooney-Kroeber estimates of approximately one million American Indians in 1600 have been the benchmark for scholars throughout most of this century. These estimates were flawed, however, because they failed to take epidemic disease into account; European pathogens devastated native populations.

Noting the shortcomings of the Mooney-Kroeber figures, Henry Dobyns (1966) revised the estimate for the 1492 precontact population, suggesting that it was as large as twelve million. His article ignited an intense debate that is still not fully resolved. Conservative estimates now number the indigenous 1492 population at approximately three to five million (Snipp 1989). Dobyns (1983) later raised his estimate to eighteen million.

Population estimates substantially larger than the Mooney-Kroeber figures are consistent with the archaeological record, which indicates that relatively complex societies occupied the Southwest, the Pacific Northwest, and the Mississippi River valley before the Europeans arrived (Thornton 1987). The effects of European contact were certainly greater than once believed. European diseases, slavery, genocidal practices, and the intensification of conflicts nearly exterminated the native people. Huge population losses undoubtedly caused large-scale amalgamation and reorganization of groups struggling to survive and wrought profound changes in their cultures and social structures.

Despite long and heated debates about the likely number of pre-Columbian North Americans, there is relatively little consensus about this figure. It seems likely that it will never be known with certainty. As scholars realize the elusiveness of this number, there is less interest in trying to establish the definitive estimate and more in attempting to understand the complex demographic behavior related to depopulation (Thornton et al. 1991; Verano and Ubelaker 1992).

Contemporary Demography. During the twentieth century, the American Indian population grew very quickly, from about 228,000 in 1890 to about 1.96 million in 1990 (Shoemaker 1999). American Indian fertility is exceedingly high (Snipp 1996). Indians often have better access to health care (from the Indian Health Service) than other equally impoverished groups, and they are experiencing diminishing infant mortality and increasing longevity (Young 1994; Snipp 1996).

A peculiar characteristic of American Indian population growth, at least since 1970, is that a large share of the increase has resulted from persons switching the racial identification they report to the census from another category (such as black or white) to American Indian (Passell and Berman 1986; Harris 1994). The U.S. census, virtually the only comprehensive source of data for American Indians, depends on voluntary racial self-identification. Declining racial discrimination, growing ethnic pride, and resurgence in tribal organization have been cited as reasons that persons of mixed heritage may choose to report themselves as American Indian (Passell and Berman 1986). Evidence indicates that persons who change their identity so they may claim their Native-American heritage tend to be relatively well-educated (Eschbach et al. 1998).

The fluidity of the American Indian population underscores a particularly problematic concern for demographers: namely, defining population boundaries. Definitions abound, and there is no single agreed-upon standard. Some federal agencies and a number of tribes use an arbitrary measure of descent, such as one-fourth blood quantum; standards for tribal membership vary greatly from one-half to one-sixty-fourth Indian blood.

For many other applications, genealogical verification of blood quantum standards is too complex. Agencies such as the U.S. Bureau of the Census thus simply rely on self-identification. By default, most studies of American Indians also rely

on self-identification, especially if they use secondary data from federal government sources. To complicate the matter, the Canadian government uses a somewhat different set of standards to define the boundaries of its native Indian population (Boldt 1993).

Beyond the complexities of counting, studies show that American Indians, more than other minorities, are concentrated in rural areas; slightly less than one-half reside in cities. Most live west of the Mississippi River, primarily because nineteenth-century removal programs were directed at eastern American Indians. A large number of studies document that American Indians are one of the least educated, most often unemployed, poorest, and least healthy groups in American society (see Sandefur et al.1996). Nonetheless, American Indians are more likely than other groups, especially blacks, to live in a large husband-wife household, and about one-third of them speak an Indian language—provisional evidence of the continuing influence of traditional culture in family organization and language use (Sandefur and Liebler 1996).

STUDIES OF SOCIAL AND ECONOMIC STATUS

Studies of the early social and economic status of American Indians focus on the historical development of so-called dependency relations between them and Euro-Americans (White 1983, 1991; Chase-Dunn and Mann 1998). Dependency theory, a variant of neo-Marxist World Systems Theory, has been widely criticized for its shortcomings, but it has gained some acceptance among scholars of white-Indian relations (Wolf 1982; White 1983; Hall 1989). In this view, economic dependency arose from trade relations in which Euro-Americans enjoyed disproportionate economic advantage stemming from a near monopoly over items such as manufactured goods and rum (Wolf 1982; White 1983). European business practices, such as the use of credit, also fostered dependency.

Dependency relations promoted highly exploitative conditions that were a frequent source of conflict and periodically erupted into serious violence. Unscrupulous traders and a growing commerce in Indian captives, for example, spawned the Yamassee War, which ended Indian slavery in the Southeast (Merrell 1989). Early colonial officials frequently complained about the conflicts created by the unethical practices of frontier traders and sought to curb their abuses, though with little success (White 1991).

Nevertheless, European traders introduced innovations that altered cultures and lifestyles forever. In the Southwest, for example, guns and horses revolutionized relations between nomadic and sedentary groups and allowed the Spanish to exploit traditional antagonisms (Hall 1989).

The emergence of industrial capitalism, large-scale manufacturing, growing urbanization, and an influx of immigrants from Europe and slaves from Africa changed dramatically the relations between Euro-Americans and indigenous peoples. Trading with Indians subsided in favor of policies and measures designed to remove them from lands desired for development (Jacobsen 1984). Throughout the nineteenth century, American Indians were more or less forcibly induced to cede their lands for the development of agriculture, timber, and water. In the late nineteenth century, U.S. corporations began to develop petroleum, coal, and other minerals on tribal lands (Miner 1976).

Exploitation of Indian lands has continued, prompting some scholars to argue that American Indian tribes have a quasi-colonial status within the U.S. economy (Snipp 1986). Natural resources such as timber, water, and minerals are extracted from reservations and exported to distant urban centers where they are processed. In exchange, manufactured goods are imported for consumption. The value of the imported goods typically exceeds the value of the exported resources. The deficit between imports and exports contributes to the persistent poverty and low levels of economic development on many reservations.

The Meriam Report, published in 1928, furnished the first systematic empirical assessment of the economic status of American Indians. Since its publication, numerous studies have documented the disadvantaged status of American Indians (Levitan and Miller 1993). Although many reports have described economic conditions in detail, fewer have attempted to isolate the causes of poverty and unemployment. Clearly, a number of factors can be blamed. American Indians have very little formal education, limiting their access to jobs.

Whether racial discrimination limits opportunities is unclear. Some research suggests that discrimination is not a significant disadvantage for American Indians (Sandefur and Scott 1983), but other studies disagree with this conclusion (Gwartney and Long 1978).

Conditions on reservations, where about one-third of American Indians live, are particularly harsh. Unemployment rates above 50 percent are not unusual. Studies of reservation economies usually blame the isolated locales for many of their woes. The collision of traditional native values and the ethics of capitalism (Cornell and Kalt 1992) frequently complicates economic development in Indian country. In the 1990s, some reservations have enjoyed limited (and in a few instances, spectacular) success in spurring economic development, especially in tourism, gambling, and light manufacturing (Snipp 1995).

Urban American Indians enjoy a higher standard of living than their counterparts in reservation areas (Snipp 1989). Even so, there is disagreement about the benefits of rural-urban migration for American Indians; earlier studies have identified tangible benefits for urban immigrants (Clinton, Chadwick, and Bahr 1975; Sorkin 1978), but later research found contrary evidence (Gundlach and Roberts 1978; Snipp and Sandefur 1988). Federal programs that encouraged urban immigration for American Indians in the 1950s and 1960s were abandoned amid controversies over their effectiveness and overall results (Fixico 1986).

The economic hardships facing rural and urban American Indians alike have been a major source of other serious distress. Alcoholism, suicide, and homicide are leading causes of death for American Indians (Snipp 1996).

POLITICAL ORGANIZATION AND LEGAL INSTITUTIONS

The political and legal status of American Indians is an extremely complicated subject, tangled in conflicting treaties, formal laws, bureaucratic regulations, and court decisions. Unlike any other racial or ethnic group in U.S. society, American Indians have a distinctive niche in the legal system. As a result of this legal history, a separate agency within the federal government (the Bureau of Indian Affairs [BIA]), a volume of the Code of Federal

Regulations, and a multiplicity of other rules exist for dealing with American Indians.

The political status of American Indian tribes is difficult to characterize. In 1831, Chief Justice John Marshall described tribes as "domestic, dependent nations," setting forth the principle that tribes are autonomous political entities that enjoy a quasi-sovereignty yet are subject to the authority of the federal government (Pommersheim 1995; Boldt 1993). The limits on tribal political autonomy have fluctuated as a result of court decisions and federal legislation curtailing or extending tribal powers. Since the early 1900s, tribal governments have greatly increased their autonomy (Pommersheim 1995).

One of the most significant political developments in this century for American Indians was the passage of the Wheeler-Howard Indian Reorganization Act (IRA) of 1934. This legislation made it possible for tribes legally to reconstitute themselves for the purpose of limited self-government (Prucha 1984, ch. 37). Subject to the democratic precepts imposed by the federal government, tribes were allowed to have representative governments with judicial, executive, and legislative branches. Other forms of tribal governance—based on the inheritance of authority, for example—were not permitted by the IRA legislation. Today, virtually every reservation has a form of representative government (O'Brien 1989).

Tribal sovereignty is a complex legal doctrine affecting the political autonomy of tribal governments. It is distinct from a closely aligned political principle known as self-determination. The principle of self-determination, unlike tribal sovereignty, is relatively recent in origin and was first posed as a claim for administrative control of reservation affairs. As a political ideology, self-determination developed in response to the unilateral actions of the federal government in implementing policies such as the Termination legislation of the 1950s. In the 1960s, it was a rallying theme for promoting greater tribal involvement in federal policies affecting American Indians. The principle was formally enacted into public law with the passage of the Indian Self-Determination and Educational Assistance Act of 1975, P.L 97–638. Since its passage, federal agencies have gradually divested control over programs and services such as those once administered by the BIA. For example, many tribal governments have contracts to provide social services similar to the arrangements made with state and local governments.

In recent years, ideas about self-determination have developed to the point where self-determination is nearly indistinguishable from tribal sovereignty (O'Brien 1989). The most influential statement merging the two is a report presented to the U.S. Senate by the American Indian Policy Review Commission (AIPRC) in 1976. The AIPRC report was a comprehensive, though highly controversial evaluation of federal Indian policy. Every presidential administration since Richard Nixon's has endorsed the principle of tribal sovereignty. Shortly after taking office, the Clinton Administration endorsed this principle and there is no indication of a reversal in the foreseeable future.

The political revitalization of American Indians accelerated with the civil rights movement. Some observers have suggested that Indian political activism in the 1960s was a response to postwar termination policies (Cornell 1988), which tried to dissolve the federal reservation system and liquidate the special status of the tribes. Relocation programs in the 1950s accelerated the urbanization of American Indians and, at the very least, may have contributed to the political mobilization of urban Indians, as well as their reservation counterparts (Fixico 1986). Though often complementary, the political agendas of urban and reservation Indians are not always in strict accord.

The diverse tribal composition of urban Indian populations has meant that it is virtually impossible to organize them around issues affecting only one or a few tribes. In the face of this constraint, the ideology of "pan-Indianism" is particularly appealing to urban Indian groups (Hertzberg 1971; Nagel 1996). Pan-Indianism is a supratribal ideology committed to broad issues such as economic opportunity and social justice and to cultural events such as intertribal pow-wows.

The roots of modern pan-Indian organizations can be traced first to the Ottawa leader Pontiac and later to the Shawnee leader Tecumseh and Joseph Brant, a Mohawk. These men led pan-Indian movements opposing Euro-American frontier settlement in the late eighteenth and early nineteenth centuries (e.g., Pontiac's Revolt 1763). In the late nineteenth century, pan-Indian messianic movements known as Ghost Dances swept across the West (Thornton 1986).

Pan-Indian organizations have been active throughout the twentieth century, but urbanization hastened their development in the 1950s and 1960s (Cornell 1988; Nagel 1996). Some, such as the National Congress of American Indians (founded in 1944), have moderate political agendas focused on lobbying; others, such as the American Indian Movement, are highly militant. The latter was involved in the sacking of the Washington, D.C., BIA office in 1972 and in the armed occupation of Wounded Knee, South Dakota, in 1973 (Smith and Warrior 1996). Today, most cities with large Indian populations have pan-Indian organizations involved in political organization, cultural events, and social service delivery (Johnson et al. 1997).

CULTURE AND RELIGION

The cultures of American Indians are extremely diverse, and the same can be said, in particular, about their religious beliefs. Not much is known about the spiritual life of American Indians before the fifteenth century. Only from archaeological evidence is such knowledge available, and this seldom captures the rich complexity of religious symbol systems. Most of what is known about American Indian religions is based on the later reports of explorers, missionaries, traders, and anthropologists (Brown 1982).

Contemporary spiritual practices reflect several different types of religious observances: Christian, neotraditional, and traditional. Participation in one type does not necessarily preclude participation in another. Furthermore, there is a great deal of tribal variation.

American Indians who are practicing Christians represent the legacy of European missionaries. The Christian affiliation of many, perhaps most, American Indians reflects their tribal membership and the denomination of the missionaries responsible for their tribe's conversion. Numerical estimates are not available, but there are many Catholic Indians in the Southwest, and American Indians in the Midwest are often Lutheran, to mention only two examples.

American Indians who participate in neotraditional religions often belong to a branch of the Native American Church (NAC). NAC is a pan-Indian religion practiced throughout the United States and Canada. It combines elements of Christianity with traditional religious beliefs and practices.

Traditional religions are often practiced in informally organized groups such as sweatlodge or feasting societies. Some of these groups are remnants of older religious movements such as the Ghost Dance. Not much is written about them because they are ordinarily not open to outsiders; the Sun Dance is an exception. It is perhaps best known for the ritual scarification and trances of its participants (Jorgenson 1972).

The secrecy in which many traditional religions are practiced may be due to the intense repression once directed at their observances by the federal government. In 1883, the BIA established Courts of Indian Offenses that prosecuted people for practicing native religions. Among other things, the courts forbade traditional medicines, shaman healers, and all traditional ceremonial observances. Despite their dubious legal foundation, the Courts of Indian Offenses were active until their mandate was rewritten in 1935 (Prucha 1984).

In 1935, the federal government ended its official repression of tribal culture and religion. But the conflicts between government authorities and American Indians trying to practice non-Christian religions did not end. Many Indians regard freedom of religion as an elusive promise. Most controversies involve NAC ceremonies, the preservation of sacred areas, and the repatriation of religious artifacts and skeletal remains in museum collections (Loftin 1989; Echohawk 1993). NAC ceremonies are controversial because they sometimes involve the use of peyote (a hallucinogen) as a sacrament. Although peyote was once outlawed, the NAC won the right to use it within narrowly defined limits prescribed by the courts. The U.S. Supreme Court upheld a case in which Oregon banned the use of peyote, however, raising concerns about how the conservative court will interpret freedom of religion cases in the future (Echohawk 1993).

Preservation of sacred areas places Indian groups at odds with land developers, property owners, local governments, and others who would use sites deemed sacred by spiritual leaders. In one case, the Navajo and Hopi in 1983 went to court to petition against the development of a ski resort that intruded on sacred grounds. In this case and several similar ones, the courts ruled against the Indians (Loftin 1989). Similar conflicts have arisen over the repatriation of religious artifacts and skeletal remains in museums. These issues pit academics such as scientists and museum curators against Indian groups. In some instances, remains and artifacts have been returned to tribes; Stanford University returned burial remains to the Ohlone tribe in California, for example. Other institutions have opposed repatriation or are studying the matter. The Smithsonian has developed a complex policy for repatriation, and the University of California appointed a committee to develop a policy. For the foreseeable future, the controversy is likely to linger in the courts, Congress, and academic institutions.

Compared to repatriation, cultural studies are a less controversial though no less important domain of American Indian Studies. Indian religion represents one of the central forms of native culture, but cultural studies also emphasize other elements of Indian lifestyles, values, and symbol systems. Some of these studies focus on the content of tribal culture; other research deals with the consequences of tribal culture.

For decades, ethnologists recording for posterity details about Indian culture, especially material culture, or documenting the ways that European contact influenced the content of tribal culture dominated studies of American Indians. The popularity of this type of research has declined significantly, partly because there are few "pristine" cultures left anywhere in the world, much less in North America. Another reason, perhaps more damaging, is the growing realization that studies purporting to document precontact Indian culture were based on secondhand accounts of groups that were not truly pristine. The influence of European diseases and trade goods often arrived far in advance of Europeans (Ramenofsky 1987).

Many studies of American Indian culture now resemble literary or artistic criticism. Others focus on how European innovations have been incorporated into tribal culture in unique ways; silversmithing and rug weaving are two well-known examples. A related set of studies deals with the resurgence of traditional culture, such as the increase in the use of American Indian languages (Leap 1988).

The behavioral consequences of culture are perhaps most prominent in a large literature on American Indian mental health, education, and rehabilitation (Bennett and Ames 1985; Foster 1988). Many studies show that education and rehabilitation efforts can be made more effective if they are sensitive to cultural nuances (LaFromboise 1995). In fact, many specialists take this idea as a point of departure and focus their research instead on the ways in which Euro-American educational and therapeutic practices can be adapted to the cultural predisposition of American Indian clients (Lafromboise 1995).

Like the American Indian population, American Indian Studies is a highly diverse and growing field of inquiry. It is interdisciplinary and eclectic in the perspectives it uses. Once primarily the domain of historians and anthropologists, American Indian Studies has rapidly expanded beyond the bounds of these disciplines with contributions from scholars in a wide variety of fields.

REFERENCES

Bennett, Linda A., and Genevieve M. Ames (eds.) 1985 *The American Experience with Alcohol: Contrasting Cultural Perspectives*. New York: Plenum.

Boldt, Menno 1993 *Surviving as Indians: The Challenge of Self-Government*. Toronto: University of Toronto Press.

Brown, Joseph Epes 1982 *The Spiritual Legacy of the American Indian*. New York: Crossroad.

Chase-Dunn, Christopher, and Kelley M. Mann 1998 *The Wintu and Their Neighbors: A Very Small World-System in Northern California*. Tucson: University of Arizona Press.

Clinton, Lawrence, Bruce A. Chadwick, and Howard M. Bahr 1975 "Urban Relocation Reconsidered: Antecedents of Employment among Indian Males." *Rural Sociology* 40:117–133.

Cornell, Stephen 1988 *The Return of the Native. American Indian Political Resurgence*. New York: Oxford University Press.

———, and Joseph P. Kalt (eds.) 1992 *What Can Tribes Do? Strategies and Institutions in American Indian Economic Development*. Los Angeles: American Indian Studies Center, University of California, Los Angeles.

Deneven, William M. (ed.) 1976 *The Native Population of the Americas in 1492*. Madison: University of Wisconsin Press.

Dobyns, Henry F. 1983 *Their Number Become Thinned: Native American Population Dynamics in Eastern North America*. Knoxville: University of Tennessee Press.

—— 1966 "Estimating Aboriginal American Population: An Appraisal of Techniques with a New Hemispheric Estimate." *Current Anthropology* 7:395–416.

Echohawk, Walter R. 1993 "Native American Religious Liberty: Five Hundred Years After Columbus." *American Indian Culture and Research Journal* 17:33–52.

Eschbach, Karl, Khalil Supple, and C. Matthew Snipp 1998 "Changes in Racial Identification and the Educational Attainment of American Indians, 1970–1990." *Demography* 35:35–43.

Fixico, Donald L. 1986 *Termination and Relocation, 1945–1960*. Albuquerque: University of New Mexico Press.

Fleras, Augie, and Jean Leonard Elliott 1992 *The Nations Within: Aboriginal-State Relations in Canada, the United States, and Australia*. New York: Oxford University Press.

Foster, Daniel V. 1988 "Consideration of Treatment Issues with American Indians in the Federal Bureau of Prisons." *Psychiatric Annals* 18:698–701.

Gundlach, James H., and Alden E. Roberts 1978 "Native American Indian Migration and Relocation: Success or Failure." *Pacific Sociological Review* 21:117–128.

Gwartney, James D., and James E. Long 1978 "The Relative Earnings of Blacks and Other Minorities." *Industrial and Labor Relations Review* 31:336–346.

Hall, Thomas D. 1989 *Social Change in the Southwest, 1350–1880*. Lawrence: University Press of Kansas.

Harris, David 1994 "The 1990 Census Count of American Indians: What do the Numbers Really Mean?" *Social Science Quarterly* 75:580–593.

Hertzberg, Hazel W. 1971 *The Search for an American Indian Identity*. Syracuse, N.Y.: Syracuse University Press.

Jacobsen, Cardell K. 1984 "Internal Colonialism and Native Americans: Indian Labor in the United States from 1871 to World War II." *Social Science Quarterly* 65:158–171.

Johnson, Troy, Joane Nagel, and Duane Champagne (eds.) 1997 *American Indian Activism: Alcatraz to the Longest Walk*. Urbana: University of Illinois Press.

Jorgensen, Joseph G. 1972 *The Sun Dance Religion: Power for the Powerless*. Chicago: University of Chicago Press.

Kroeber, Alfred L. 1934 "Native American Population." *American Anthropologist* 36:1–25.

LaFromboise, Teresa D. 1995 *American Indian Life Skills Development*. Madison: University of Wisconsin Press.

Leap, William L. 1988 "Indian Language Renewal." *Human Organization* 47:283–291.

Levitan, Sar A., and Elizabeth I. Miller 1993 The Equivocal Prospects for Indian Reservations. Occasional Paper 1993–2 (May). Washington, D.C.: Center for Social Policy Studies, The George Washington University.

Loftin, John D. 1989 "Anglo-American Jurisprudence and the Native American Tribal Quest for Religious Freedom." *American Indian Culture and Research Journal* 13:1–52.

Merrell, James H. 1989 *The Indian's New World: Catawbas and Their Neighbors from European Contact Through the Era of Removal*. Chapel Hill: University of North Carolina Press.

Miner, H. Craig 1976 *The Corporation and the Indian: Tribal Sovereignty and Industrial Civilization in Indian Territory, 1865–1907*. Columbia: University of Missouri Press.

Nagel, Joane 1996 *American Indian Ethnic Renewal: Red Power and the Resurgence of Identity and Culture*. New York: Oxford University Press.

O'Brien, Sharon 1989 *American Indian Tribal Governments*. Norman: University of Oklahoma Press.

Passel, Jeffrey S., and Patricia A. Berman 1986 "Quality of 1980 Census Data for American Indians." *Social Biology* 33:163–182.

Pommersheim, Frank 1995 *Braid of Feathers: American Indian Law and Contemporary Tribal Life*. Berkeley: University of California Press.

Prucha, Francis Paul 1984 *The Great Father: The United States Government and the American Indians*. Lincoln: University of Nebraska Press.

Ramenoffsky, Ann F. 1987 *Vectors of Death: The Archaeology of European Contact*. Albuquerque: University of New Mexico Press.

Sandefur, Gary D., and Carolyn Liebler 1996 "The Demography of American Indian Families." In Gary D. Sandefur, Ronald R. Rindfuss, and Barney Cohen, eds., *Changing Numbers, Changing Needs: American Indian Demography and Public Health*. Washington, D.C.: National Academy Press.

Sandefur, Gary D., Ronald R. Rindfuss, and Barney Cohen (eds.) 1996 *Changing Numbers, Changing Needs: American Indian Demography and Public Health*. Washington, D.C.: National Academy Press.

Sandefur, Gary D., and Wilbur Scott 1983 "Minority Group Status and the Wages of Indian and Black Males." *Social Science Research* 12:44–68.

Shoemaker, Nancy 1999 *American Indian Population Recovery in the Twentieth Century*. Albuquerque: University of New Mexico Press.

Smith, Paul Chaat, and Robert Allen Warrior 1996 *Like a Hurricane: The Indian Movement from Alcatraz to Wounded Knee*. New York: The New Press.

Snipp, C. Matthew 1996 "The Size and Distribution of the American Indian Population: Fertility, Mortality, Migration, and Residence." In Gary D. Sandefur, Ronald R. Rindfuss, and Barney Cohen, eds., *Changing Numbers, Changing Needs: American Indian Demography and Public Health*. Washington, D.C.: National Academy Press.

—— 1995 "American Indian Economic Development." In Emery N. Castle, ed., *The Changing American Countryside*. Lawrence: University Press of Kansas.

—— 1989 *American Indians: The First of This Land*. New York: Russell Sage Foundation.

—— 1986 "The Changing Political and Economic Status of American Indians: From Captive Nations to Internal Colonies." *American Journal of Economics and Sociology* 45:145–157.

——, and Gary D. Sandefur 1988 "Earnings of American Indians and Alaska Natives: The Effects of Residence and Migration." *Social Forces* 66:994–1008.

Sorkin, Alan L. 1978 *The Urban American* Indian. Lexington, Mass.: D. C. Heath.

Thornton, Russell 1987 *American Indian Holocaust and Survival: A Population History Since 1492*. Norman: University of Oklahoma Press.

—— 1986 *We Shall Live Again: The 1870 and 1890 Ghost Dance Movements as Demographic Revitalization*. New York: Cambridge University Press.

——, Jonathon Warren, and Tim Miller 1992 "Depopulation in the Southeast after 1492." In John W. Verano and Douglas H. Ubelaker, eds., *Disease and Demography in the Americas*. Washington, D.C.: Smithsonian Institution.

Verano, John W., and Douglas H. Ubelaker (eds.) 1992 *Disease and Demography in the Americas*. Washington, D.C.: Smithsonian Institution.

White, Richard 1991 *The Middle Ground: Indians, Empires, and Republics in the Great Lakes Region, 1650–1815*. New York: Cambridge University Press.

—— 1983 *The Roots of Dependency: Subsistence, Environment, and Social Change among the Choctaws, Pawnees, and Navajos*. Lincoln: University of Nebraska Press.

Wolf, Eric R. 1982 *Europe and the People Without History*. Berkeley: University of California Press.

Young, T. Kue 1994 *The Health of Native Americans: Towards a Biocultural Epidemiology*. New York: Oxford University Press.

C. MATTHEW SNIPP

AMERICAN SOCIETY

The term *American society* is used here to refer to the society of the United States of America. This conventional usage is brief and convenient and implies no lack of recognition for other societies of North, Central, and South America.

Boundaries of modern national societies are permeable and often socially and culturally fuzzy and changeable. Lines on maps do not take into account the cross-boundary flows and linkages of trade, tourists, information, workers, diseases, military arms and personnel, ethnic or linguistic affiliations, and the like. As a large, heterogeneous country, the United States well illustrates such interdependence and cultural diversity.

During the second half of the twentieth century it became increasingly plain that an understanding of American society required analysis of its place in a global system. National societies have become highly interdependent through extensive flows of capital, technology, goods and services, ideas and beliefs, cultural artifacts, and symbols. A world system of politico-military relationships (blocs and hierarchies) interacts with a global system of trade, finance, and population transfers, and both systems are influenced by cultural interpenetration (including organizational forms and procedures).

While these developments were under way, the American people became healthier, life expectancy increased, educational levels rose, income and wealth increased, major new technologies developed (e.g., the so-called Information Revolution), and ethnic and racial minorities gained in income, occupational status, and political participation (Farley 1996). On the other hand, economic inequality increased sharply, the prison population grew rapidly (and became disproportionately made up of African Americans), divorce rates remained at high levels, single-parent households increased, and infant mortality remained high, as did violent crime (Farley 1996).

Containing less than 5 percent of the world's population, the United States is a polyglot nation of nations that now accepts a greater and more diverse inflow of legal immigrants than any other country—an average of about one million a year from 1990 to 1995. It is often called a young nation, but elements of its culture are continuous with the ancient cultures of Europe, Asia, and Africa, and its political system is one of the most long-enduring constitutional democracies. Many writers have alleged that its culture is standardized, but it continues to show great diversity of regions, ethnic groupings, religious orientations, rural-urban contrasts, age groupings, political views, and general lifestyles. It is a society in which many people seem convinced that it is undergoing rapid social change, while they hold firmly to many values and social structures inherited from the past. Like all other large-scale societies, in short, it is filled with ambiguities, paradoxes, and contradictions.

This society emerged as a product of the great period of European expansion. From 1790 to 1990, the U.S. land area expanded from fewer than 900,000 square miles to well over three million; its populations from fewer than four million to about 265 million. The United States has never been a static social system in fixed equilibrium with its environment. Peopled primarily by history's greatest voluntary intercontinental migration, it has always been a country on the move. The vast growth of metropolitan areas is the most obvious sign of the transformation of a rural-agricultural society into an urban-industrial society. In 1880, the nation had four million farms; in 1992 it had 1.9 million. From 1949 to 1979 the index of output per hour of labor went from about twenty to about 200. The most massive change in the occupational structure, correspondingly, has been the sharply decreasing proportion of workers in agriculture—now less than 1 percent of the labor force.

The technological transformations that have accompanied these trends are familiar. The total horsepower of all prime movers in 1940 was 2.8 billion; in 1963 it was 13.4 billion; by 1978 it was over 25 billion. Productive capacities and transportation and communication facilities show similar long-term increases. For example, from 1947 to 1995, the annual per capita energy consumption in the United States went from 230 to 345 million

BTUs—an increase of about 50 percent. The American people are dependent to an unprecedented degree on the automobile and the airplane. (As of the late 1980s, the average number of persons per passenger car was 1.8; by 1995, there were 201 million motor vehicles in a population of some 263 million—1.6 persons per vehicle.) Mass transit is only weakly developed. During the single decade of the 1960s there was a 50 percent increase in the number of motor vehicles, and in many cities such vehicles account for 75 percent of the outdoor noise and 80 percent of the air pollution. With about 200 million motor vehicles in 1998, it is even possible to imagine an ultimate traffic jam—total immobilization from coast to coast.

All indicators of what we may call "heat and light" variables have increased greatly: energy consumption, pieces of mail handled by the U.S. Postal Service (from 106 billion in 1980 to 183 billion in 1996), televisions (2.3 sets per household in 1995), telephones (93.9 percent of households had one in 1995), radios, electronic mail (29 million persons using the Internet), cellular phones, and fax. A vast flood of messages, images, and information criss-crosses the continent.

In American households, the average number of hours that the television was on increased from 5.6 in 1963 to 6.8 in 1976, and continues to slowly increase. The effects of television viewing are complex, although there is general agreement among researchers that mass exposure is selective, does focus attention on some matters rather than others (raising public awareness), influence attitudes on specific issues—especially those on which information is scanty—and probably has cumulative effects on a variety of beliefs and preferences (cf. Lang and Lang 1992).

In short, this is a society of high technology and extremely intensive energy use. It is also a country that has developed a tightly organized and elaborately interdependent economy and social system, accompanied by vast increases in total economic productivity. Thus the real gross national product doubled in just two decades (1959–1979), increasing at an average rate of 4.1 percent per year (Brimmer 1980, p. 98). But beginning with the sharp increases in oil prices after 1973, the society entered a period of economic stagnation and low productivity that was marked in the 1980s by large trade deficits, greatly increased federal budget deficits, and increased problems of international competitiveness. Coming after a long period of sustained growth, the changes of the 1980s resulted in an economy of low savings, high consumption, and low investment—a situation of "living beyond one's means." In the 1990s, a sustained period of low inflation and rising stock markets marked a somewhat uneasy sense of prosperity, seen as insecure as the decade ended.

MAJOR INSTITUTIONS

"Institution" here means a definite set of interrelated norms, beliefs, and values centered on important and recurrent social needs and activities (cf. Williams 1970, chap. 3). Examples are family and kinship, social stratification, economic system, the polity, education, and religion.

Kinship and Family. American kinship patterns are essentially adaptations of earlier European forms of monogamous marriage, bilateral descent, neolocal residence, and diffuse extended kinship ties. All these characteristics encourage emphasis on the marriage bond and the nuclear family. In an urbanized society of great geographical and social mobility and of extensive commercialization and occupational instability, kinship units tend to become small and themselves unstable. Since the 1950s, the American family system has continued its long-term changes in the direction of greater instability, smaller family units, lessened kinship ties, greater sexual (gender) equality, lower birth rates, and higher rates of female-headed households. The percentage of married women in the labor force rose from 32 in 1960 to 61 in the 1990s. The so-called "traditional" family of husband, wife, and children under eighteen that comprised 40 percent of families in 1970 had declined to 25 percent in 1995. Over one-fifth of households are persons living alone. Marriage rates have decreased, age at marriage has increased, and rates of divorce and separation continue to be high. The percentage of children under eighteen years of age living in mother-only families increased in the years between 1960 and 1985, from 6 to 16 among white, and from 20 to 51 among black Americans (Jaynes and Williams 1989, p. 522). As individuals, Americans typically retain commitment to family life, but external social and cultural forces are producing severe family stresses.

Social Stratification. Stratification refers to structural inequalities in the distribution of such scarce values as income, wealth, power, authority, and prestige. To the extent that such inequalities result in the clustering of similarly situated individuals and families, "strata" emerge, marked by social boundaries and shared styles of life. When succeeding generations inherit positions similar to previous generations, social classes can result.

The American system is basically one of open classes, with relatively high mobility, both within individual lifetimes and across generations. A conspicuous exception has been a caste-like system of racial distinctions, although this has eroded substantially since the civil rights movement of the 1960s (Jaynes and Williams 1989). The 1980s and 1990s were marked by growing income inequality, as the rich became richer and the poor did not. Large increases in earnings inequality accrued during the 1980s; meanwhile labor unions had large membership losses and labor markets were deregulated (unions lost over 3 million members between 1980 and 1989—see Western 1998, pp. 230–232). Union membership declined from 20.1 percent of workers in 1983 to 14.5 percent in 1996 (*Statistical Abstract of the United States, 1997*, p. 441).

In the early 1990s, the United States had the highest income inequality of any of twenty-one industrialized countries (the income of individuals of the highest decile was over six times the income of the lowest decile). The United States differs from other industrialized countries in the especially great disadvantage of its poorest people. This result arises from very low wages at the bottom of the distribution and low levels of income support from public programs (Smeeding and Gottschalk 1998, pp. 15–19).

The end-of-the-century levels of inequality are less than in the early decades of the 1900s, but represent large increases since the lower levels at the end of the 1960s (Plotnick, Smolensky, Evenhouse, and Reilly 1998, p. 8). By 1996, the richest 20 percent of Americans received about 47 percent of total income, while the poorest got 4.2 percent.

The dominant ideology remains individualistic, with an emphasis on equality of opportunity and on individual achievement and success. Although extremes of income, power, and privilege produce strong social tensions, the system has shown remarkable stability.

The history of stratification has included conquest of Native Americans, slavery of African peoples, and extensive discrimination against Asians, Hispanics, and various immigrants of European origin. Assimilation and other processes of societal inclusion have moved the whole society increasingly toward a pluralistic system, but deep cleavages and inequalities continue. A fundamental tension persists between principles of equality of opportunity and individual merit, on the one hand, and practices of ascribed status and group discrimination, on the other (cf. Myrdal, Sterner, and Rose 1944).

As a consequence of increased openness since the Immigration Act of 1965, the population contains increased proportions of persons whose backgrounds are in Asia and Latin America; this development complicates ethnic/racial boundaries and alignments, including political formations (Edmonston and Pasell 1994). The increased receptivity to immigrants was enhanced by the Refugee Act of 1980, the Immigration and Control Act of 1986, and the Immigration Act of 1990. The result is that the number of immigrants admitted per year has soared to an average of about a million during the period 1990–1995 (*Statistical Abstract of the United States, 1997*, p. 10). Although vigorous political controversy surrounds immigration, the country remains committed to a general policy of acceptance and to citizenship by residence rather than by ethnic origin.

Although much reduced in its most obvious forms, discrimination against African Americans continues to be widespread, in housing (Yinger 1995), credit, and employment (Wilson 1996; Jaynes and Williams 1989). Residential segregation continues at high levels, although the 1980s brought a small movement toward more residential mixing, primarily in smaller Southern and Western cities (Farley and Frey 1994).

The Economy. The American economic system is a complex form of "high capitalism" characterized by large corporations, worldwide interdependence, high levels of private consumption, and close linkages with the state.

Increased specialization leads both to increased complexity and to increased interdependence, two

sides of the same coin. In the United States, as in all industrialized countries, the movement from the primary extractive and agricultural industries to manufacturing was followed by growth of the tertiary exchange-facilitating activities, and then to expansion of occupations having to do with control and coordination and those ministering directly to the health, education, recreation, and comfort of the population. As early as 1970, nearly two-thirds of the labor force was in pursuits other than those in "direct production" (primary and secondary industries).

Since the late 1970s, there has been rapid growth in involuntary part-time jobs and in other insecure and low-paying employment as the economy has shifted toward trade and services and corporations have sought to lower labor costs (Tilly 1996).

As the economy has thus shifted its focus, the dominance of large corporations has become more and more salient. In manufacturing, the total value added that is accounted for by the 200 largest companies went from 37 percent in 1954 to 43 percent in 1970. Of all employees in manufacturing, the percent working in multi-unit firms increased from 56 percent in 1947 to 75 percent by 1972 (Meyer 1979, pp. 27–28). The top 500 industrial companies account for three-fourths of industrial employment (Wardwell 1978, p. 97).

Meanwhile, organized labor has not grown correspondingly; for decades, overall unionization has remained static, increasing only in the service, technical, and quasi-professional occupations. The importance of the great corporations as the primary focus of production and finance continues to increase. Widespread dispersion of income rights in the form of stocks and bonds has made the giant corporation possible, and this same dispersion contributes directly to the concentration of control rights in the hands of salaried management and minority blocs of stockholders. With widened markets for mass production of standardized products, strong incentives were created for effective systems of central control. Although such tendencies often overreached themselves and led to a measure of later decentralization, the modern corporation, not surprisingly, shows many of the characteristics of the most highly developed forms of bureaucracy.

The interpenetration of what were previously regarded as separate political and economic affairs is a central fact. The interplay takes many different forms. For a long time government has set rules for maintaining or lessening business competition; it has regulated the plane or mode of competition, the conditions of employment, and the place and functioning of labor unions. Pressure groups, based on economic interests, ceaselessly attempt to influence law-making bodies and executive agencies. Governmental fiscal and monetary policies constitute a major factor influencing economic activity. As the economic role of the state has expanded, economic forces increasingly affect government itself and so-called private corporations increasingly have come to be "public bodies" in many ways, rivaling some sovereign states in size and influence. The post-1980s political movements for a smaller role for the central government resulted in a partial dismantling of the "welfare state" but did not remove the important linkages of state and economy.

Political Institutions. In ideology and law the American polity is a parliamentary republic, federal in form, marked by a strong central executive but with a tripartite separation of powers. From the highly limited state of the eighteenth century, the actual government has grown in size and scope and has become more complex, centralized, and bureaucratized. Partly because of pervasive involvement in international affairs, since World War II a large permanent military establishment has grown greatly in size and importance. In 1996, the Department of Defense included 3.2 million persons, and total defense and veterans outlays amounted to $303 billion. The executive agencies, especially the presidency, became for decades increasingly important relative to the Congress, although the 1990s brought a resurgence of congressional power. Among other changes, the following appear to be especially consequential:

1. Continuing struggles over the character of the "welfare state," dedicated to maintaining certain minimal safeguards for health and economic welfare;

2. High development of organized interest groups, which propose and "veto" nearly all important legislation. The unorganized general public retains only an episodic and delayed power to ratify or reject whole programs of government action. A rapid increase in the number of Political Action Committees—from 2551 in 1980 to 4016 in 1995—is only one indication of the importance of organized interests;

3. Decreased cohesion and effectiveness of political parties in aggregating interests, compromising parties in conflict, and reaching clear public decisions;

4. Increasingly volatile voting and diminished party regularity and party commitment (split-ticket voting, low rates of voting, large proportion of the electorate with no firm party reference).

American political parties are coalitions of diverse actors and interests, with accompanying weak internal discipline, but they remain relatively stable under a system of single-member districts and plurality voting—"first past the post." Although the polity is subject to the hazards of instability associated with a presidential rather than parliamentary system, the national federal system, the separation of powers, and the centrality of the Constitution and the judiciary combine to support the traditional two-party electoral arrangement, although support for a third party appears to be growing (Lipset 1995, p. 6).

Historically, political parties in the United States have been accommodationist: They have served to articulate and aggregate interests through processes of negotiation and compromise. The resulting "packages" of bargains have converted diverse and diffuse claims into particular electoral decisions. To work well, such parties must be able to plan nominations, arrange for representativeness, and sustain effective competition. In the late twentieth century, competitiveness was weakened by volatile elections—for example, landslides and deadlocks with rapidly shifting votes—and by party incoherence. In the nominating process the mass media and direct primaries partly replaced party leaders and patronage. Representativeness was reduced by polarization of activists, single-issue voting, and low turnouts in primaries. And the inability of parties to protect legislators seemed to increase the influence of single-issue organizations and to enlarge the scope of "symbolic" actions. Hard choices, therefore, tended to be deferred (cf. Fiorina 1980, p. 39).

The existence of an "interest-group" polity was clearly indicated. The political system readily expressed particular interests but found difficulties in articulating and integrating partly incompatible demands into long-term national programs.

As the century drew to a close, many commentators expressed concerns about the increasing expense of political campaigns, the increasing importance of very large contributions through Political Action Committees, the potential influence upon voters of "vivid soundbites" on television, and the increasing centralization of control of the mass media. At the same time, the conspicuous behavior of so-called independent counsels (special prosecutors) raised the fears that a "Fourth Branch" of government had arisen that would be relatively free of the checks and balances, traditional in the tripartite system of governance. Public opinion polls showed increased disaffection with political institutions and processes, and lower voting turnouts indicated much apathy in the electorate. As investigations, prosecutions, and litigation have escalated and have been rendered omnipresent by the media, erosion of trust in government has likewise increased greatly (Lipset 1995).

Yet detailed analysis of data from national public opinion surveys in the last decade of the century failed to find the alleged extreme polarization that had been suggested by acrimonious partisanship between the political parties and in the Congress. Thus, a major study (DiMaggio, Evans, and Bryson 1996) found little evidence of extreme cleavages in social opinions between 1974 and 1994, with two exceptions: attitudes toward abortion diverged sharply, and the attitudes of those who identify with the Democratic and Republican parties have become more polarized. Instead of moderating dissension, the party system between 1970 and the 1990s appears to have sharpened cleavages. There is a possibility that some political leaders have been pulled away from centrist positions by militant factions within their own party. The total picture seemed to be that of extreme contentiousness within the central government while the wider society showed much greater tolerance, consensus, and stability.

Education. In addition to diffuse processes of socialization found in family and community, specialized educational institutions now directly involve one-fifth of the American people as teachers, students, and other participants. In the twentieth century, an unparalleled expansion of mass education occurred. Nearly 80 percent of the appropriate age group graduate from secondary school and 62 percent of these attend college; in 1993, 21.3 percent had completed four years of college or more.

Historically, the educational system was radically decentralized, with thousands of school districts and separate educational authorities for each state (Williams 1970, chap. 8). In contrast to countries with strong central control of education and elitist systems of secondary and higher education, the United States for most of its history has had a weak central state and a mass education system. Education was driven by demands for it rather than by state control of standards, facilities, tests, curricula, and so on (cf. Garnier, Hage, and Fuller 1989).

These characteristics partly derive from widespread faith in education as a means of social advancement as well as from commitments to equality of opportunity and to civic unity. Inequalities of access were long enforced by involuntary racial segregation, now somewhat reduced since 1954, when the Supreme Court declared such segregation unconstitutional. Inequalities of access due to social class and related factors, of course, continue (Jencks et al. 1979). Formal educational attainments have come to be so strongly emphasized as a requirement for employment and advancement that some observers speak of the development of a "credential society" (Collins 1979). Meanwhile the slow but steady decline in students' test scores has aroused much concern but little agreement as to remedial measures.

Religious Institutions. Major characteristics of institutionalized religion include: formal separation of church and state, freedom of religious expression and practice, diversity of faiths and organizations, voluntary support, evangelism, high rates of membership and participation, widespread approval of religion and acceptance of religious beliefs, complex patterns of partial secularization, frequent emergence of new religious groupings, and important linkages between religious affiliations and social class and ethnicity (cf. Williams 1970, chap. 9; Wilson 1978).

Many of these characteristics are causally interrelated. For example, earlier sectarian diversity encouraged separation of church and state and religious toleration, which, in turn, favored further diversity, voluntarism, evangelism, and religious innovations. Self-reported religious affiliations in social surveys shows these percentages: Protestant, 60; Catholic, 25; Jewish, 2; other, 4; none, 9. These broad categories cover hundreds of diverse groupings (General Social Surveys 1994).

Changes include growth in membership of evangelical Protestant denominations (now one-fifth of the population, Hunter 1997), closer ties between religious groupings and political activities, and the rise of many cults and sects. Separation of church and state was increasingly challenged in the 1990s, and religious militancy in politics increased. Nevertheless, national surveys (1991) showed that the religiously orthodox and theological progressives were not polarized into opposing ideological camps across a broad range of issues—although there were sharp divisions on some particular issues (Davis and Robinson 1996).

Among industrialized Western countries, the United States manifests extraordinary high levels of membership and participation. Thus, although there has been extensive secularization, both of public life and of the practices of religious groups themselves, religious influence remains pervasive and important (Stark and Bainbridge 1985).

SOCIAL ORGANIZATION

The long-term increase in the importance of large-scale complex formal organizations, salient in the economy and polity, is evident also in religion, education, and voluntary special-interest associations. Other trends include the reduced autonomy and cohesion of small locality groupings and the increased importance of special-interest formal organizations and of mass publics and mass communication. The long-term effects of the saturation of the entire society with advertising, propaganda, assorted information, and diverse and highly selective world views remain to be ascertained. Local communities and kinship groupings have been penetrated more and more by formal, centralized agencies of control and communication. (Decreasing localism shows itself in many forms. A well-known and striking example is the continuous decrease in the number of public school districts.)

These changes have moved the society as a whole in the direction of greater interdependence, centralization, formality, and impersonality.

VALUES AND BELIEFS

Beliefs are conceptions of realities, of how things are. Values are conceptions of desirability, of how things should be (Williams 1970, chap. 11). Through shared experience and social interaction, communities, classes, ethnic groupings, or whole societies can come to be characterized by similarities of values and beliefs.

The weight of the evidence for the United States is that the most enduring and widespread value orientations include an emphasis on personal achievement (especially in occupational activity), success, activity and work, stress on moral principles, humanitarianism, efficiency and practicality, science, technology and rationality, progress, material comfort, equality, freedom, democracy, worth of individual personality, conformity, nationalism and patriotism; and, in tension with most other values, values of group superiority and racism. Mixed evidence since the 1970s seems to indicate complex shifts in emphasis among these orientations—primarily in the direction of success and comfort, with lessened commitment to more austere values. Some erosion in the emphasis placed on work and some lessening in civic trust and commitment may have occurred.

In contrast to many images projected by the mass media, national surveys show that most Americans still endorse long-standing beliefs and values: self-reliance, independence, freedom, personal responsibility, pride in the country and its political system, voluntary civic action, anti-authoritarianism, and equality within limits (Inkeles 1979; Williams 1970, chap. 11). And for all their real disaffections and apprehensions, most Americans see no other society they prefer: As late as 1971, surveys in eight countries found that Americans were less likely than persons in any other country to wish to live elsewhere (Campbell, Converse, and Rodgers 1976, pp. 281–285). Americans in national public opinion surveys (1998) ranked second among twenty-three countries in pride in the country and in its specific achievements. Thus, popular attitudes continue to reflect a perennial satisfaction and positive nationalism (Smith and Jarkko 1998).

REFERENCES

Brimmer, Andrew F. 1980 "The Labor Market and the Distribution of Income." In Norman Cousins, ed., *Reflections of America*. Washington D.C.: U.S. Government Printing Office.

Campbell, Angus, Phillip E. Converse, and Willard L. Rodgers 1976 *The Quality of American Life*. New York: Russell Sage Foundation.

Cherlin, Andrew J. 1992 *Marriage, Divorce, Remarriage*. Cambridge, Mass.: Harvard University Press.

Collins, Randall 1979 *The Credential Society: An Historical Sociology of Education and Stratification*. New York: Academic Press.

Davis, Nancy S., and Robert V. Robinson 1996 "Are the Rumors Exaggerated? Religious Orthodoxy and Moral Progressivism in America." *American Journal of Sociology* 102(3):756–787.

DiMaggio, Paul, John Evans, and Bethany Bryson 1996 "Have Americans' Social Attitudes Become more Polarized?" *American Journal of Sociology* 102(3):690–755.

Edmonston, Barry, and Jeffrey S. Pasell 1994 *Immigrational Ethnicity: The Integration of America's Newest Arrivals*. Washington D.C.: The Urban Institute Press.

Farley, Reynolds 1996 *The New American Reality: How We Got There, Where We AreGoing*. New York: Russell Sage Foundation.

——, and William H. Frey 1994 "Changes in the Segregation of Whites from Blacks During the 1980s: Small Steps Toward a More Integrated Society." *American Sociological Review* 59(1):23–45.

Fiorina, Morris P. 1980 "The Decline of Collective Responsibility in American Politics." *Daedalus*, Summer: 25–45.

Frank, Robert H., and Phillip J. Cook 1995 *The Winner-Take-All Society*. New York: Free Press.

Garnier, Maurice, Jerald Hage, and Bruce Fuller 1989 "The Strong State, Social Class, and Controlled Expansion in France, 1881–1975." *American Journal of Sociology* 95:279–306.

Hunter, James Davidson 1987 *Evangelism: The Coming Generation*. Chicago: University of Chicago Press.

Inkeles, Alex 1979 "Continuity and Change in the American National Character." In Seymour Martin Lipset, ed., *The Third Century: America as a Post-Industrial Society*. Stanford, Calif.: Hoover Institution Press.

Jaynes, Gerald David, and Robin M. Williams, Jr. (eds.) 1989 *A Common Destiny: Blacks and American Society*. Washington, D.C.: National Academy Press.

Jencks, Christopher, Susan Bartlett, Mary Corcoran, James Crouse, David Eaglesfield, Gregory Jackson, Kent McClelland, Peter Mueser, Michael Olneck, Joseph Schwartz, Sherry Ward, and Jill Williams 1979 *Who Gets Ahead: The Determinants of Economic Success in America*. New York: Basic Books.

Lang, Gladys Engel, and Kurt Lang 1992 "Mass Media Research." In Edgar F.Borgatta and Marie L. Borgatta, eds., *Encyclopedia of Sociology*, vol. 3. New York: Macmillan Publishing Company.

Lipset, Seymour Martin 1995 "Malaise and Resiliency in America." *Democracy* 6(3):4–18.

Meyer, Marshall W 1979 "Debureaucratization?" *Social Science Quarterly* 60:25–34.

Myrdal, Gunnar, Richard Sterner, and Arnold Rose 1944 *An American Dilemma*. New York: Harper and Row.

Plotnick, Robert D., Eugene Smolensky, Eirik Evenhouse, and Siobhan Reilly 1998 "Inequality and Poverty in the United States: The Twentieth-Century Record." *Focus* 19(3):7–14.

Smeeding, Timothy M., and Peter Gottshalk 1998 "Cross-National Income Inequality: How Great Is It and What Can We Learn From It?" *Focus* 19(3):15–19.

Smith, Tom W., and Lars Jarkko 1998 "National Pride: A Cross-National Analysis." *GSS Cross-National Report No. 19*. Chicago: National Opinion Research Center.

Stark, Rodney, and William Sims Bainbridge 1985 *The Future of Religion: Secularization, Revival, and Cult Formation*. Berkeley: University of California Press.

Tilly, Cris 1996 *Half a Job: Bad and Good Part-time Jobs in a Changing Labor Market*. Philadelphia: Temple University Press.

U.S. Bureau of the Census 1998 *Statistical Abstract of the United States, 1997* (117th ed.). Washington, D.C.:

Wardwell, Nancy Needham 1978 "The Corporation." *Daedalus*, Winter: 97–110.

Western, Bruce 1998 "Institutions and the Labor Market." In Mary C. Brinton and Victor Nee, eds., *The New Institutionalism in Sociology*. New York: Russell Sage Foundation.

Williams, Robin M., Jr. 1979 "Change and Stability in Value Systems: A Sociological Perspective." In Milton Rokeach, ed., *Understanding Human Values*. New York: Free Press.

——1970 *American Society: A Sociological Interpretation*. New York: Alfred A. Knopf.

Wilson, John N. 1978 *Religion in American Society: The Effective Presence*. Englewood Cliffs, N.J.: Prentice-Hall.

Wilson, William Julius 1996 *When Work Disappears: The World of the New Urban Poor*. New York: Alfred A. Knopf.

Yinger, John 1995 *Closed Doors, Opportunities Lost: The Continuing Costs of Housing Discriminations*. New York: Russell Sage Foundation.

ROBIN M. WILLIAMS, JR.

AMERICAN SOCIOLOGICAL ASSOCIATION AND OTHER SOCIOLOGICAL ASSOCIATIONS

The American Sociological Association (ASA) will celebrate its centennial year in 2005; since its inception, it has grown in size, diversity, programs, and purpose. Current ASA goals are as follows:

- Serving sociologists in their work,

- Advancing sociology as a science and as a profession,

- Promoting the contributions and use of sociology to society.

While the first goal remains the raison d'etre for the membership organization, over the ASA's 100 years, there have been ebbs and flows, support and controversy, about the latter two goals and how the association embodies them.

ASA MEMBERSHIP TRENDS

An interesting perspective on the ASA's history is revealed through an examination of membership trends. Table 1 shows fairly slow but stable growth up until 1931. During the years of the Great Depression, there were substantial declines. Despite these declines, however, sociologists were becoming very visible in government agencies such as the U.S. Department of Agriculture and the U.S. Bureau of the Census. Between 1935 and 1953, for example, there were an estimated 140 professional social scientists, the great majority of them sociologists, employed in the Division of Farm Population and Rural Life. This activity reached its peak between 1939 and 1942, when there were approximately sixty professionals working in Washington, D.C. and in regional offices. Sociologists are well placed in many federal agencies and non-profit organizations in Washington; however, they are "undercover," working under a variety of job titles.

The years following World War II saw a rapid increase in ASA membership—the number nearly quadrupled between 1944 (1,242) and 1956 (4,682). Between 1957 and 1967, membership more than doubled, from 5,223 to 11,445, and continued upward to 15,000 during the heights of the social protest and anti-Vietnam War movements. However, during the latter half of the 1970s, membership gradually drifted downward and reached a seventeen-year low of 11,223 in 1984. In the next fifteen years, the membership increased by 2,000 and has remained stable at over 13,000 in the 1990s.

The growth and decline in the ASA can be accounted for in part by a combination of ideological and demographic factors as well as the gradually changing nature of work in American society, particularly since the end of World War II. For example, the GI bill made it possible for an ordinary veteran to get a college education. The college population jumped from one-half million in 1945 to several million within three years. Gradually, while urban and metropolitan populations grew, the number and percentage of people in the manufacturing sector of the labor force declined, and the farm population declined even more dramatically, while the service sector grew. Within the service sector, information storage, retrieval, and exchange grew in importance with the coming of the computer age. These societal changes helped to stimulate a growth in urban problems involving areas such as family, work, and drugs, and these changes led to a growth of these specialty areas in sociology.

Membership in the ASA rapidly increased in the 1960s and early 1970s, an era of many social protest movements. Sociology was seen as offering a way of understanding the dynamic events that were taking place in this country. Substantive areas within the ASA and sociology were also affected by these social changes. As Randall Collins (1989) points out, the social protest movements of the 1960s and 1970s coincided with the growth within the ASA of such sections as the Marxist, environmental, population, world systems, collective behavior and social movements, and racial and ethnic minorities sections. In addition, the growing public concerns in the late 1970s and early 1980s about aging and equality for women were reflected within the ASA by new sections on sex and gender and aging. Similarly, the "me" generation, in the aftermath of the protest movements and the

ASA Official Membership Counts
1906–1999

1906	115	1931	1,567	1954	4,350	1977	13,755
1909	187	1932	1,340	1955	4,450	1978	13,561
1910	256	1933	1,149	1956	4,682	1979	13,208
1911	357	1934	1,202	1957	5,233	1980	12,868
1912	403	1935	1,141	1958	5,675	1981	12,599
1913	621	1936	1,002	1959	6,323	1982	12,439
1914	597	1937	1,006	1960	6,875	1983	11,600
1915	751	1938	1,025	1961	7,306	1984	11,223
1916	808	1939	999	1962	7,368	1985	11,485
1917	817	1940	1,034	1963	7,542	1986	11,965
1918	810	1941	1,030	1964	7,789	1987	12,370
1919	870	1942	1,055	1965	8,892	1988	12,382
1920	1,021	1943	1,082	1966	10,069	1989	12,666
1921	923	1944	1,242	1967	11,445	1990	12,841
1922	1,031	1945	1,242	1968	12,567	1991	13,021
1923	1,141	1946	1,651	1969	13,485	1992	13,072
1924	1,193	1947	2,057	1970	14,156	1993	13,057
1925	1,086	1948	2,450	1971	14,827	1994	13,048
1926	1,107	1949	2,673	1972	14,934	1995	13,254
1927	1,140	1950	3,582	1973	14,398	1996	13,134
1928	1,352	1951	3,875	1974	14,654	1997	13,082
1929	1,530	1952	3,960	1975	13,798	1998	13,273
1930	1,558	1953	4,027	1976	13,958	1999	13,056

Table 1

disillusionment that set in after the Vietnam War, may have contributed both to a decline in student enrollments in sociology courses and in ASA membership. The growth of the college student population and some disillusionment with purely vocational majors, as well as sociology's intrinsic interest to students, led to a gradual rise in membership in the 1990s.

ASA membership trends can also be examined in the context of the availability of research money. Postwar federal support for sociology grew with the development of sponsored research and the growth of research labs and centers on university campuses. Coincident with an increase in ASA membership, research funding from federal agencies during the 1960s and 1970s grew steadily. In the early 1980s, however (particularly in 1981 and 1982), cutbacks in research funding for the social sciences were especially noticeable. In the 1990s, major efforts to educate Congress on the importance of social science research won support for sociology and the other social sciences. The result has been a reversal of the negative trend and a slow but steady improvement in funding, not only for basic research but also in greater amounts for research with an applied or policy orientation.

ASA SECTIONS, PUBLICATIONS, AND PROGRAMS

The increase in the number of sections in the ASA and of membership in them is another sign of growth within the ssociation in the 1990s. Despite a decline in overall ASA membership in the early 1980s, the number of sections increased from nineteen in 1980 to twenty-six in 1989 and to thirty-nine a decade later. The new sections represent some new fields of study (or at least a formal nomenclature for these specialties) such as sociology of emotions, sociology of culture, rational choice, and sociology of sexualities. Furthermore, this overall increase in sections was not achieved by simply redistributing members already in sections but resulted from an actual growth in section members from 8,000 to 11,000 to 19,000 in the three time periods. More than half the ASA members belong to at least one section; the modal membership is in two sections. The ASA has learned from other associations, such as psychology and anthropology, about the possible pitfalls of subgroups within "the whole." The ASA continues to require members to belong to ASA as a condition for joining a section, so that everyone has a connection to the discipline at large as well as to their specialty groups. This approach has prevented the ASA from becoming a federation of sections and probably has minimized "split off" groups. The annual meeting grew by a thousand participants in the decade of the 1990s, now topping 5,000 people who find professional development in the broad program as well as in section involvement.

The growth of the ASA is also reflected in the growth of the number of journal publications. Since 1936, when the first issue of the *American Sociological Review* was published, ASA publications have expanded to include seven additional journals: *Contemporary Sociology*; *Journal of Health and Social Behavior*; *Social Psychology Quarterly*; *Sociological Methodology*; *Sociological Theory*; *Sociology of Education*; and *Teaching Sociology*. In addition, a *Rose Series* (funded from the estate of Arnold and Caroline Rose) publishes monographs that are important "small market" books in sociology. That series shifted from very specialized academic monographs to integrative pieces of broad appeal. The ASA's newest journal is a general perspectives journal, aimed at the social science community (including students), and the educated lay public.

The Sydney S. Spivack Program in Applied Social Research and Social Policy (funded from a donation from Spivack's estate) sponsors Congressional seminars and media briefings on timely topics for which there is a body of sociological knowledge. From these events, the ASA has published a series of issue briefs on topics ranging from youth violence to welfare-to-work to immigration to affirmative action. These publications are useful to ASA members but also to a wider public audience.

The teaching of sociology in kindergarten through high school and in undergraduate and graduate schools has received varying degrees of emphasis over the course of the ASA's history. In particular, in the late 1970s and early 1980s, when sociology enrollments and membership in the ASA were at a low point, the ASA Teaching Services Program was developed. Now part of the Academic and Professional Affairs Program (APAP), the Teaching Services Program includes providing opportunities through seminars and workshops to improve classroom teaching and to examine a wide range of new curricula for almost all sociology courses. The Teaching Resources Center in the

ASA's executive office produces over a hundred resources, including syllabi sets and publications on topics such as classroom techniques, curriculum, departmental management, and career information. APAP works concertedly with departments and chairs to build strong departments of sociology and excellent curricula. The ASA sponsors an annual conference for chairs, a meeting of directors of graduate study, and an electronic broadcast, CHAIRLINK, for chairs.

Odd as it may seem, the ASA often did not collect or have access to data on the profession. In 1993, the Research Program on the Discipline and Profession remedied the situation by conducting surveys of members and departments, and a tracking survey of a cohort of Ph.D.s. The program routinely publishes "research briefs" that share these data and aid departments and individuals with planning and trend analysis.

TRANSITION FROM SECRETARIAT TO A PROFESSIONAL ASSOCIATION

The ASA has undergone an organizational transformation over its century of serving the professional interests of sociologists. The shape and mission of the executive office reflects the shifts. In the early years, the office was essentially a secretariat—a place where records were kept, and dues and payments were processed. The first executive officer, Matilda White Riley, appointed in 1963, jokes that the office was a file card box on her kitchen table.

As the American Sociological Society (as it was named until 1959) grew and flourished, it adopted the model of a "learned society," primarily concerned with the production of new disciplinary knowledge. The society/association centered its resources on the annual meeting and the journals. The executive office personnel, primarily clerical, staffed those functions.

The expansion period of the 1960s and 1970s, and the societal context of those times, led the ASA to add many programs and activities (for a detailed description, see Simpson and Simpson 1994). The ASA transformed into a professional association, with a wider range of services and benefits to its members as well as to a broader

1998 Section Totals

		Total	Low Income	Student	Regular
1.	Undergraduate Education	419	12	62	345
2.	Methodology	414	13	118	283
3.	Medical Sociology	1,021	35	306	680
4.	Crime, Law, and Deviance	634	16	236	382
5.	Sociology of Education	579	12	182	385
6.	Family	759	30	216	513
7.	Organizations, Occupations, and Work	1,062	27	346	689
8.	Theory	691	19	180	492
9.	Sex and Gender	1,114	32	405	677
10.	Community and Urban Sociology	553	16	175	362
11.	Social Psychology	666	19	260	387
12.	Peace, War and, Social Conflict	274	7	69	198
13.	Environment and Technology	401	15	126	260
14.	Marxist Sociology	362	11	103	248
15.	Sociological Practice	308	13	36	259
16.	Sociology of Population	406	8	84	314
17.	Political Economy of the World System	416	9	151	256
18.	Aging and the Life Course	563	16	147	400
19.	Mental Health	408	17	116	275
20.	Collective Behavior and Social Movements	568	10	222	336
21.	Racial and Ethnic Minorities	685	15	227	443
22.	Comparative Historical Sociology	522	5	150	367
23.	Political Sociology	580	9	207	364
24.	Asia/Asian America	325	6	117	202
25.	Sociology of Emotions	279	9	96	174
26.	Sociology of Culture	843	27	315	501
27.	Science, Knowledge, and Technology	390	13	147	230
28.	Computers, Sociology and	263	11	67	185
29.	Latino/a Sociology	247	5	86	156
30.	Alcohol and Drugs	247	10	57	180
31.	Sociology of Children	330	10	85	235
32.	Sociology of Law	316	3	123	190
33.	Rational Choice	183	3	37	143
34.	Sociology of Religion	535	19	173	343
35.	International Migration	283	12	83	188
36.	Race, Gender, and Class	830	20	382	428
37.	Mathematical Sociology	206	4	76	126
38.	Section on Sexualities	281	12	137	132
39.	History of Sociology	215	5	42	168
	Totals	**19,178**	**535**	**6,147**	**12,496**

Table 2

public. As Simpson and Simpson (1994) describe the change: "ASA reacted to the pressures of the 1960s and 1970s mainly by absorbing the pressure groups into its structure. A result has been to expand the goals and functions of the association beyond its initial disciplinary objective. Functions are more differentiated now, encompassing more professional and activist interests" (p. 265). The executive office grew slightly, with the growth in Ph.D.-level sociology staff who led these new ventures. In addition to the executive officer, these sociologists had titles (e.g., Staff Sociologist for Minorities, Women, and Careers) that reflected their work.

In the last ten years, some significant organizational changes have occurred. The executive office has been professionalized, with new hires often having at least a B.A. in sociology. The senior sociology staff direct the core programs (see below) and no longer have fixed terms of employment. As such, the office is more programmatic and proactive.

Key changes in the ASA's governance include:

• Passage of an ASA mission and goals statement, with six core programs in the executive office (the six programs are:

Minority Affairs; Academic and Professional Affairs; Public Affairs; Public Information; Research on the Discipline and Profession; and the Spivack Program),

- The launch of the ASA's Spivack Program in applied social research and social policy and a continuous, intentional effort to bring research to bear on public policy issues,

- The beginning, and end, of the ASA's certification program,

- The beginning, and end, of the journal *Sociological Practice Review*,

- The beginning of the MOST program (Minority Opportunities for Summer Training for the first five years and Minority Opportunities through School Transformation, for the next five years, funded by the Ford Foundation),

- Greater autonomy for sections and an increase in the number of sections,

- New policies on ASA resolutions and policymaking,

- Revision of the Code of Ethics, as an educative document, which serves as a model for aligned sociological groups,

- Restructuring of ASA committees to a more targeted "task force" model,

- Addition of a new "perspectives" journal,

- Increased attention to science policy and funding, including collaborations with many other groups,

- Increased attention to sociology departments as units, and to chairs as their leaders, as shown in the Department Affiliates program,

- Active collaboration between the ASA and higher education organizations such as the American Association for Higher Education and the American Association of Colleges and Universities.

Members (and nonmember sociologists) have differing views about the current form of the ASA, which is discussed at the end of this article.

The ASA is but one organization in a network of sociological organizations or associations in which sociologists comprise a significant part of the membership. These groups operate in a complementary way to the ASA; some were formed in juxtaposition to the ASA to fulfill a need the ASA was not serving or to pressure the ASA to change. The genres of these organizations are briefly discussed below.

REGIONAL AND STATE ASSOCIATIONS

In many disciplines, a national association includes state and regional chapters. In sociology, those regional and state groups have always been independent entities, with their own dues, meetings, and journals. Nonetheless, the ASA has worked collaboratively with these associations. The ASA sends staff representatives to their annual meetings, offers to serve on panels and meet with their councils, sends materials and publications, and convenes a meeting of regional and state presidents at the ASA's annual meeting. In the 1960s regional representatives sat on the ASA council. Everett Hughes (1962) provided a sociological critique of this approach to governance, suggesting that the ASA was a disciplinary not a professional association. He argued that the ASA should not be organized as a federation of such representatives, and this regional delegate format ended in 1967. Later, candidates for the Committee on Committees and the Committee on Nominations were nominated by district (not identical to regional associations) to ensure regional representation. That approach ended in 1999.

Twenty-four states (or collaborations among states) have sociological associations. Some are extremely active (e.g., Wisconsin, Minnesota, North Carolina, Illinois, Georgia) and have some special foci that link to their state-based networks. The Georgia Sociological Association, for example, sponsors a workshop for high school teachers; the association also honors a member of the media for the best presentation of sociological work. Wisconsin sociologists used the Wisconsin Sociological Association to organize to defeat a licensure bill that would have prevented sociologists from employment in certain social service jobs. The Minnesota sociologists have made special outreach efforts to practitioners and include these colleagues on their board.

Regional Sociology Associations

Regional Organization	Founding Date	# of Members (1999)	Journal
Eastern Sociological Society	1930	1,000	*Sociological Forum*
Mid-South Sociological Association	1975	293	*Sociological Spectrum*
Midwest Sociological Society	1936	1,250	*The Sociological Quarterly*
New England Sociological Association		250	none
North Central Sociological Association	1925	442	*Sociological Focus*
Pacific Sociological Association	1929	1,350	*Sociological Perspectives*
Southern Sociological Society	1935	1,748	*Social Forces*
Southwestern Sociological Association	1923	507	Supports *Social Science Quarterly*
District of Columbia Sociological Society	1934	200	none

Table 3

ALIGNED ASSOCIATIONS

Many of the aligned associations offer a small, vital intellectual home for sociologists interested in a particular specialty. Over time, a few of these organizations have consciously decided to form a section within the ASA. The various sociology of religion groups did so recently, to have a "place" within the ASA as well as their own meeting and publications. Many of the aligned groups have members from many disciplines including sociology.

INTERDISCIPLINARY TIES

The most significant interdisciplinary organization is the Consortium of Social Science Associations (COSSA), formed in 1980. The budget cutting of the Reagan administration served as a catalyst for the major social science associations to establish this umbrella organization to lobby for funding for social science research. In the 1980s and 1990s, COSSA, with its own professional staff, has become a well-respected voice on social science policy, federal funding, and the professional concerns of social scientists (e.g., data archiving, confidentiality protection, and support for research on controversial topics). COSSA is, of course, an organization of organizations.

In 1997, the ASA offered membership discounts with other societies, so that individuals could join several of these groups. The interdisciplinary discounts now apply to: the American Political Science Association, the American Educational Research Association, the Society for Research in Child Development, and the Academy of Management.

POLITICAL PRESSURES ON AND IN ASA: FEMINISM AND ACTIVISM

Of the many aligned associations, two organizations provide association missions that the ASA does not (or does not sufficiently) satisfy, and have an agenda to change the ASA.

Sociologists for Women in Society (SWS), founded in 1970, has had a two-pronged mission: to use the tools and talents in sociology to improve the lives of women in society; and secondly, to enhance the participation, status, and professional contributions of feminist sociologists. Most SWS members are also ASA members. Originally named the Women's Caucus, the group's 1970 statement of demands summarized the gender issues in the ASA quite clearly: "What we seek is effective and dramatic action; an unbiased policy in the selection of stipend support of students; a concerted commitment to the hiring and promotion of women sociologists to right the imbalance that is represented by the current situation in which 67 percent of the women graduate students in this country do not have a single woman sociology professor of senior rank during the course of their graduate training, and when we participate in an association of sociologists in which NO woman will sit on the 1970 council, NO woman is included among the associate editors of the *American Sociological Review*, and NO woman sits on the thirteen member committee on publications and nominations" (Roby, p. 24). Over time, as the founding mothers of SWS moved through their career trajectories, more and more SWS members became part of the leadership of the ASA. In 2000, nine of twenty ASA council members are women. Since its founding, SWS has sought to pressure the ASA in more feminist directions, and to supplement what the

State and Aligned Sociological Organizations

State Associations
  National Council of State Sociological Associations
  Alabama/Mississippi Sociological Association
  Arkansas Sociological Association
  California Sociological Association
  Florida Sociological Association
  Georgia Sociological Association
  Great Plains Association (North and South Dakota)
  Hawaii Sociological Association
  Illinois Sociological Association
  Iowa Sociological Association
  Kansas Sociological Association
  Anthropologists and Sociologists of Kentucky
  Michigan Sociological Society
  Sociologists of Minnesota
  Missouri State Sociological Association
  Nebraska Sociological Association
  New York State Sociological Association
  North Carolina Sociological Association
  Oklahoma Sociological Association
  Pennsylvania Sociological Society
  South Carolina Sociological Association
  Virginia Social Science Association
  Washington Sociological Association
  West Virginia State Sociological Association
  Wisconsin Sociological Association

Aligned Associations
  Alpha Kappa Delta
  Anabaptist Sociology and Anthropology Association
  Association of Black Sociologists
  Association of Christians Teaching Sociology
  Association for Humanist Sociology
  Association for the Sociology of Religion
  Chicago Sociological Practice Association
  Christian Sociological Society
  North American Society for the Sociology of Sport
  Rural Sociological Society
  Society for the Advancement of Socio-Economics
  Society for Applied Sociology
  Society for the Study of Social Problems
  Society for the Study of Symbolic Interaction
  Sociological Practice Association
  Sociologists' AIDS Network
  Sociologists for Women in Society
  Sociologists' Lesbian, Gay, Bisexual, and Transgender Caucus
  Sociology of Education Association

International Associations
  Asia Pacific Sociological Association
  Australian Sociological Association
  British Sociological Association
  Canadian Sociology & Anthropology Association
  European Society for Rural Sociology
  European Sociological Association
  International Institute of Sociology
  International Network for Social Network Analysis
  International Society for the Sociology of Religion
  International Sociological Association
  International Visual Sociology Association
  Sociological Association of Aotearoa (New Zealand)

Social Science/Interdisciplinary Associations
  Consortium of Social Science Associations
  Academy of Management
  American Association for the Advancement of Science
  American Association for Public Opinion Research
  American Educational Research Association
  American Evaluation Association
  American Society of Criminology
  American Statistical Association
  Association of Gerontology in Higher Education
  Council of Professional Associations on Federal Statistics
  Gerontological Society of America
  Law and Society Association
  Linguistic Society of America
  National Council on Family Relations
  National Council for the Social Studies
  Popular Culture Association
  Population Association of America
  Religious Research Association
  Social Science History Association
  Society for Research in Child Development
  Society for the Scientific Study of Religion
  Society for Social Studies of Science

Commissions
  Commission on Applied and Clinical Sociology

Table 4

ASA seemed not to offer. SWS runs its annual meeting program parallel to the ASA's annual meeting. In the earlier years, many sessions concentrated on work in sex and gender, as well as on informal networking, and mentoring workshops. Over time, as the ASA's section on sex and gender has become the largest in the association, the SWS program has downplayed scholarly papers on sex and gender, and has emphasized instead informal networking, socializing, and political organizing.

SWS proposed that the ASA publish a journal on *Sex & Gender*, but the ASA declined, due to a rather full publication portfolio. SWS entered an agreement with Sage Publishers to start such a journal, which has been a successful intellectual and business venture. At various points in its history, SWS has been explicit in its watchdog role over the ASA. Members came to observe the ASA council meetings; the membership endorsed candidates for ASA offices; and candidates were asked to complete a survey that was sent to all SWS members.

The Society for the Study of Social Problems (SSSP), founded in 1951, pursued the insider-outsider strategy as well. The SSSP meets prior to (often with a day of overlap) the ASA annual meeting. As the name implies, the topics for sessions and for the divisions deal with social problems, what sociologists know about them, and their solutions. The SSSP journal, *Social Problems*, is well regarded and well subscribed.

In the 1950s, the ASA centered on positivism and "objective" scientific pursuits. Twenty years earlier, a group of ASA members had warned that the achievement of scientific status and academic acceptance were hindered by the application of sociology to social problems. The motion read, in part: "The undersigned members, animated by an ideal of scientific quality rather than of heterogeneous quantity, wish to prune the Society of its excrescences and to intensify its scientific activities. This may result in a reduction of the members and revenues of the society, but this is preferable to having many members whose interest is primarily or exclusively other than scientific" (Rhoades 1981, pp. 24–25). The SSSP has been a vital counterpoint to those views, keeping sociology's leftist leanings alive.

THE APPLIED SIDE

In 1978, two new sociological associations formed to meet the needs of sociological practitioners. The Clinical Sociology Association (CSA), now called the Sociological Practice Association (SPA), centered on sociologists engaged in intervention work with small groups (e.g., family counseling) or at a macro-level (e.g., community development). This group emphasized professional training and credentials. Most of the members were employed primarily outside of the academe; many felt they needed additional credentials to meet state licensure requirements or to receive third-party payments, or both. The SPA established a rigorous certification program, where candidates with a Ph.D. in sociology and substantial supervised experience in clinical work, would present their credentials and make a presentation as part of the application for certification. Those who passed this review could use the title Certified Clinical Sociologist.

The Society for Applied Sociology (SAS) was formed by a group of colleagues in Ohio, most of whom are primarily academics, but who engage in extensive consulting and applied work. The core of the SAS centers on applied social research, evaluation research, program development, and other applications of sociological ideas to a variety of organizational settings. The SAS has worked extensively with curriculum and program development to prepare the next generation of applied sociologists. The SAS has also focused on the master's-level sociologist much more than other organizations.

Both of these practice organizations hold an annual meeting and sponsor a journal. At various times in the twenty years of each group, members have advocated a merger to reduce redundancy, strengthen the membership base, and use resources together. One place where the two groups have worked in tandem is through their joint Commission on Applied and Clinical Programs, which accredits sociology programs that meet the extensive criteria set forth by the commission. In this sense, these applied sociology programs (usually a part or a track within a regular sociology department) are modeling professional programs such as social work, which have an accrediting mechanism. Both societies held a joint meeting prior to the ASA meeting in 2000, which may portend future collaboration.

The history of the ASA shows the ebb and flow in interest in applied sociology, certainly going back to President Lester Frank Ward, and evident again with the election of contemporary Presidents William Foote Whyte, Peter Rossi, and Amitai Etzioni. Within the ASA, there is an active, though not large, section on sociological practice, drawing overlapping membership with the SPA and the SAS. The ASA published a journal, *Sociological Practice Review*, as a five-year experiment (1990–1995) but dropped the publication when there were insufficient subscribers and few manuscripts. In the early 1980s, in response to member interest, the ASA began a certification program, through which Ph.D.-level sociologists could be certified in six areas (demography, law and social control, medical sociology, organizational analysis, social policy and evaluation research, and social psychology). At the master's level, sociologists could take an exam; passing the test would result in certification in applied social research. The certification program received few applicants and was terminated by the ASA council in 1998.

Since the 1980s, there have been forces pushing for more involvement of practitioners in the ASA, and thus more membership benefits to serve non-academic members, as the paring down of those benefits (as in the case of the *Sociological Practice Review* and certification) when interest wanes. In part, there is greater "within group" variance among practitioners than "between group" variance between practitioners and academics. Thus while there is clearly a *political constituency* for applied work, it is less clear there is a core intellectual constituency.

In 1981, the ASA held a conference on applied sociology, from which a book of proceedings was published by Jossey-Bass. That event was a springboard for the introduction of applied issues within the ASA. A committee on sociological practice, a section on sociological practice, and an ASA award for a distinguished career in sociological practice were created. In 1999, about 25 percent of ASA members had primary employment in nonacademic positions; the estimate of the number of Ph.D.s (some of whom were nonmembers) in sociological practice was higher. The diversity of the nonacademic membership and their professional needs has been a challenge to the ASA. In a 1984 article in the *American Sociological Review*, Howard Freeman and Peter Rossi wrote of the significant changes that might be needed in departments of sociology and in the reward structure of the profession to reduce the false dichotomy between applied and basic research.

COMMITMENT TO DIVERSITY

The ASA has made concerted efforts to be inclusive of women and minorities in its activities and governance. Since 1976, the ASA has undertaken a biennial report on the representation of women and minorities in the program (invited events and open submissions), on editorial boards, in elections, and in the governance (committees) of the ASA.

In 1987, the ASA appointed a task force on participation designed to identify ways to more fully enfranchise colleagues in two- and four-year colleges. That task force held a number of open hearings and met for five years before issuing a report of recommendations to the council. As a spin-off from the committee on teaching, a task force on community colleges made recommendations to the council in 1997 and 1998 about how to more actively involve these colleagues in ASA affairs.

The ASA council adopted the following policy in 1997:

Much of the vitality of ASA flows from its diverse membership. With this in mind, it is the policy of the ASA to include people of color, women, sociologists from smaller institutions or who work in government, business, or other applied settings, and international scholars in all of its programmatic activities and in the business of the Association.

At the same time, the demographics of the profession have been shifting (Roos and Jones 1993). Over 55 percent of new Ph.D.s are women, and about 45 percent of ASA members are female. The Minority Fellowship Program, begun in 1974, has provided predoctoral funding and mentoring support for minority sociologists. The program boasts an astounding graduation record of 214 Ph.D.s; many of these colleagues from the early cohorts are now senior leaders in departments, organizations, and in the ASA.

DEMOCRATIZATION OR CONSOLIDATION?

The ASA membership has diverse views about the extent to which the current organizational structure and goals are optimal. Simpson and Simpson argue that core disciplinary concerns have taken a back seat at the ASA; they speak of the "disciplinary elite and their dilution" (1994, p. 271). Their analysis of ASA budgets, as a indicator of priorities, shows shifts from disciplinary concerns (e.g., journals and meetings) to professional priorities (e.g., jobs, teaching, applied work, and policy issues). Other segments of the profession allege that the ASA leadership is too elite (Reynolds 1998) and has a falsely rosy view of the field (p. 20). Demographically and programmatically, the ASA has changed in its century of service to sociology. With a solid membership core and generally positive trends in the profession, the ASA will continue to sit at the hub of a network of sections and aligned organizations.

REFERENCES

Collins, Randall 1989 "Future Organizational Trends of the American Sociological Association." *Footnotes* 17:1–5, 9.

Freeman, Howard, and Peter H. Rossi 1984 "Furthering the Applied Side of Sociology." *American Sociological Review*, vol. 49. 4 (August): 571–580.

Hughes, Everett C. 1962 "Association or Federation?" *American Sociological Review* 27:590.

Reynolds, Larry T. 1998 "Two Deadly Diseases and One Nearly Fatal Cure: The Sorry State of American Sociology." *The American Sociologist*. vol. 29. 1:20–37.

Rhoades, Lawrence J. 1981 *A History of the American Sociological Association: 1905–1980*. Washington, D.C.: American Sociological Association.

Roby, Pamela 1992 "Women and the ASA: Degendering Organizational Structures and Processes, 1964–1974." *The American Sociologist* (Spring):18–48.

Roos, Patricia A., and Katharine Jones 1993 "Shifting Gender Boundaries: Women's Inroads into Academic Sociology." *Work and Occupations*, vol. 20. 4 (November): 395–428.

Simpson, Ida Harper, and Richard Simpson 1994 "The Transformation of ASA." *Sociological Forum*, vol. 9. 2 (June):259–278.

CARLA B. HOWERY

ANALYSIS OF VARIANCE AND COVARIANCE

Analysis of variance (ANOVA) and analysis of covariance (ANACOVA) are statistical techniques most suited for the analysis of data collected using experimental methods. As a result, they have been used more frequently in the fields of psychology and medicine and less frequently in sociological studies where survey methods predominate. These techniques can be, and have been, used on survey data, but usually they are performed within the analysis framework of linear regression or the "general linear model." Given their applicability to experimental data, the easiest way to convey the logic and value of these techniques is to first review the basics of experimental design and the analysis of experimental data. Basic concepts and procedures will then be described, summary measures and assumptions reviewed, and the applicability of these techniques for sociological analysis discussed.

EXPERIMENTAL DESIGN AND ANALYSIS

In a classical experimental design, research subjects are randomly assigned in equal numbers to two or more discrete groups. Each of these groups is then given a different treatment or stimulus and observed to determine whether or not the different treatments or stimuli had predicted effects on some outcome variable. In most cases this outcome variable has continuous values rather than discrete categories. In some experiments there are only two groups—one that receives the stimulus (the experimental group) and one that does not (the control group). In other studies, different levels of a stimulus are administered (e.g., studies testing the effectiveness of different levels of drug dosages) or multiple conditions are created by administering multiple stimuli separately and in combination (e.g., exposure to a violent model and reading pacifist literature).

In all experiments, care is taken to eliminate any other confounding influences on subjects' behaviors by randomly assigning subjects to groups. As a result of random assignment, preexisting differences between subjects (such as age, gender, temperament, experience, etc.) are randomly distributed across groups making the groups equal in terms of the potential effects of these preexisting differences. Since each group contains approximately equal numbers of subjects of any given age, gender, temperament, experience, etc., there should be no differences between the groups on the outcome variable that are due to these confounding influences. In addition, experiments are conducted in standardized or "physically controlled" situations (e.g., a laboratory), thus eliminating any extraneous external sources of difference between the groups. Through random assignment and standardization of experimental conditions, the researcher is able to make the qualifying statement "Other things being equal. . ." and assert that any differences found between groups on the outcome measure(s) of interest are due solely to the fact that one or more groups received the experimental stimulus (stimuli) and the other group did not.

Logic of analysis procedures. Analysis of variance detects effects of an experimental stimulus by first computing means on the outcome variable for the experimental and control groups and then comparing those means. If the means are the same, then the stimulus didn't "make a difference" in the outcome variable. If the means are different, then, because of random assignment to groups and standardization of conditions, it is assumed that the stimulus caused the difference. Of course, it is necessary to establish some guidelines for interpreting the size of the difference in order to draw conclusions regarding the strength of the effect of the experimental stimulus. The criterion used by analysis of variance is the amount of random variation that exists in the scores within each group. For example, in a three-group comparison, the group mean scores on some outcome measure may be 3, 6, and 9 on a ten-point scale. The meaningfulness of these differences can only be assessed if we know something about the variation of scores in the three groups. If everyone in group one had scores between 2 and 4, everyone in group two had scores between 5 and 7, and everyone in group three had scores between 8 and 10, then in every instance the variation within each group is low and there is no overlap across the within group distributions. As a result, whenever the outcome score of an individual in one group is compared to the score of an individual in a different group, the result of the comparison will be very similar to the respective group mean score comparison and the conclusions about who scores higher or lower will be the same as that reached when the means were compared. As a result, a great deal of confidence would be placed in the conclusion that group membership makes a difference in one's outcome score. If, on the other hand, there were several individuals in each group who scored as low or as high as individuals in other groups—a condition of high variability in scores—then comparisons of these subjects' scores would lead to a conclusion opposite to that represented by the mean comparisons. For example, if group one scores varied between 1 and 5 and group two scores varied between 3 and 10, then in some cases individuals in group one scored higher than individuals in group two (e.g., 5 vs. 3) even though the mean comparisons show the opposite trend (e.g., 3 vs. 6). As a result, less confidence would be placed in the differences between means.

Although analysis of variance results reflect a comparison of group means, conceptually and computationally this procedure is best understood through a framework of explained variance. Rather than asking "How much difference is there

between group means?," the question becomes "How much of the variation in subjects' scores on the outcome measure can be explained or accounted for by the fact that subjects were exposed to different treatments or stimuli?" To the extent that the experimental stimulus has an effect (i.e., group mean differences exist), individual scores should differ from one another because some have been exposed to the stimulus and others have not. Of course, individuals will differ from one another for other reasons as well, so the procedure involves a comparison of how much of the total variation in scores is due to the stimulus effect (i.e., group differences) and how much is due to extraneous factors. Thus, the total variation in outcome scores is "decomposed" into two elements: variation due to the fact that individuals in the different groups were exposed to different conditions, experiences, or stimuli (explained variance); and variation due to random or chance processes (error variance). Random or chance sources of variation in outcome scores can be such things as measurement error or other causal factors that are randomly distributed across groups through the randomization process. The extent to which variation is due to group differences rather than these extraneous factors is an indication of the effect of the stimulus on the outcome measure. It is this type of comparison of components of variance that provides the foundation for analysis of variance.

BASIC CONCEPTS AND PROCEDURES

The central concept in analysis of variance is that of *variance*. Simply put, variance is the amount of difference in scores on some variable across subjects. For example, one might be interested in the effect of different school environments on the self-esteem of seventh graders. To examine this effect, random samples of students from different school environments could be selected and given questionnaires about their self-esteem. The extent to which the students' self-esteem scores differ from each other both within and across groups is an example of the variance.

Variance can be measured in a number of ways. For example, simply stating the range of scores conveys the degree of variation. Statistically, the most useful measures of variation are based on the notion of the *sums of squares*. The sums of squares is obtained by first characterizing a sample or group of scores by calculating an average or mean. The mean score can be thought of as the score for a "typical" person in the study and can be used as a reference point for calculating the amount of differences in scores across all individuals. The difference between each score and the mean is analogous to the difference of each score from every other score. The variation of scores is calculated, then, by subtracting each score from the mean, squaring it, and summing the squared deviations (squaring the deviations before adding them is necessary because the sum of nonsquared deviations from the mean will always be 0). A large sums of squares indicates that the total amount of deviation of scores from a central point in the distribution of scores is large. In other words, there is a great deal of variation in the scores either because of a few scores that are very different from the rest or because of many scores that are slightly different from each other.

Decomposing the sums of squares. The total amount of variation in a sample on some outcome measure is referred to as the *total sums of squares* (SS$_{\text{total}}$). This is a measure of how much the subjects' scores on the outcome variable differ from one another and it represents the phenomenon that the researcher is trying to explain (e.g., Why do some seventh graders have high self-esteem, while others have low or moderate self-esteem?). The procedure for calculating the total sums of squares is represented by the following equation:

$$\text{SS}_{\text{TOTAL}} = \Sigma_i\Sigma_j(Y_{ij} - \overline{Y}..)^2 \qquad (1)$$

where, $\Sigma_i \, \Sigma_j$ indicates to sum across all individuals (i) in all groups (j), and $(Y_{ij} - Y..)^2$ is the squared difference of the score of each individual (Y_{ij}) from the grand mean of all scores ($\overline{Y}.. = \Sigma_{ij} \, Y_{ij} \, / \, N$). In terms of explaining variance, this is what the researcher is trying to account for or explain.

The total sums of squares can then be "decomposed" or mathematically divided into two components: the *between-groups sums of squares* (SS$_{\text{BETWEEN}}$) and the *within-groups sums of squares* (SS$_{\text{WITHIN}}$).

The between-groups sums of squares is a measure of how much variation in outcome scores exists between groups. It uses the group mean as the best single representation of how each individual in the group scored on the outcome measure. It essentially assigns the group mean score to

every subject in the group and then calculates how much total variation there would be from the grand mean (the average of all scores regardless of group membership) if there was no variation within the groups and the only variation comes from cross-group comparisons. For example, in trying to explain variation in adolescent self-esteem, a researcher might argue that junior high schools place children at risk because of schools' size and impersonal nature. If the school environment is the single most powerful factor in shaping adolescent self-esteem, then when adolescents are compared to each other in terms of their self-esteem, the only comparisons that will create differences will be those occurring between students in different school types, and all comparisons involving children in the same school type will yield no difference. The procedure for calculating the between-groups sums of squares is represented by the following equation:

$$\text{SS}_{\text{BETWEEN}} = \Sigma_j N_j(\overline{Y}._j - \overline{Y}..)^2 \qquad (2)$$

where, Σ_j indicates to sum across all groups (j), and $N_j \, (\overline{Y}._j - \overline{Y}..)^2$ is the number of subjects in each group (N_j) times the difference between the mean of each group ($\overline{Y}_j$) and the grand mean ($\overline{Y}.$).

In terms of the comparison of means, the between-groups sums of squares directly reflects the difference between the group means. If there is no difference between the group means, then the group means will be equal to the grand mean and the between-groups sums of squares will be 0. If the group means are different from one another, then they will also differ from the grand mean and the magnitude of this difference will be reflected in the between-groups sums of squares. In terms of explaining variance, the between-groups sums of squares represents only those differences in scores that come about because the individuals in one group are compared to individuals in a different group (e.g., What if all students in a given type of school had the same level of self-esteem, but students in a different school type had different levels?). By multiplying the group mean difference score by the number of subjects in the group, this component of the total variance assumes that there is no other source of influence on the scores (i.e., that the variance within groups is 0). If this assumption is true, then the SS$_{\text{BETWEEN}}$ will be equal to the SS$_{\text{TOTAL}}$ and the group effect could be said to be extremely strong (i.e., able to overshadow any other source of influence). If, on the other hand, this assumption is not true, then the $SS_{BETWEEN}$ will be small relative to the SS_{TOTAL} because other influences randomly dispersed across groups are generating differences in scores not reflected in mean score differences. This situation indicates that group differences in experimental conditions add little to our ability to predict or explain differences in outcome scores. In the extreme case, when there is no difference in the group means, the $SS_{BETWEEN}$ will equal 0, indicating no effect.

The within-groups sums of squares is a measure of how much variation exists in the outcome scores within the groups. Using the same example as above, adolescents in a given type of school might differ in their self-esteem in spite of the esteem-inflating or -depressing influence of their school environment. For example, elementary school students might feel good about themselves because of the supportive and secure nature of their school environment, but some of these students will feel worse than others because of other factors such as their home environments (e.g., the effects of parental conflict and divorce) or their neighborhood conditions (e.g., wealth vs. poverty). The procedure for calculating the within-groups sums of squares is represented by the following equation:

$$\sum_i \sum_j (Y_{ij} - \overline{Y}_j)^2 \qquad (3)$$

where $\Sigma_i \, \Sigma_j$ indicates to sum across all individuals (i) in all groups (j), and $(Y_{ij} - \bar{Y}_j)^2$ is the squared difference between the individual scores (Y_{ij}) and their respective group mean scores (Y_j).

Both in terms of comparing means and explaining variance, the within-groups sums of squares represents the variance due to other factors or "error"; it is the degree of variation in scores despite the fact that individuals in a given group were exposed to the same influences or stimuli. This component of variance can also serve as an estimate of how much variability in outcome scores occurs in the population from which each group of respondents was drawn. If the within-groups sums of squares is high relative to the between-groups sums of squares (or the difference between the means), then less confidence can be placed in the conclusion that any group differences are meaningful.

SUMMARY MEASURES

Analysis of variance procedures produce two summary statistics. The first of these—ETA^2—is a measure of how much effect the predictor variable or factor has on the outcome variable. The second statistic—F—tests the *null hypothesis* that there is no difference between group means in the larger population from which the sample data was randomly selected.

ETA^2. As noted above, a large between-groups sums of squares is indicative of a large difference in the mean scores between groups. The meaningfulness of this difference, however, can only be judged against the overall variation in the scores. If there is a large amount of variation in scores relative to the variation due exclusively to between-groups differences, then group effects can only explain a small proportion of the total variation in scores (i.e., a weak effect). ETA^2 takes into account the difference between means and the total variation in scores. The general equation for computing ETA^2 is as follows:

$$ETA^2 = \frac{SS_{BETWEEN}}{SS_{TOTAL}} \qquad (4)$$

As can be seen from this equation, ETA^2 is the proportion of the total sums of squares explained by group differences. When all the variance is explained, there will be no within-group variance, leaving $SS_{TOTAL} = SS_{BETWEEN}$ ($SS_{TOTAL} = SS_{BETWEEN} + 0$). Thus, ETA^2 will be equal to 1, indicating a perfect relationship. When there is no effect, there will be no difference in the group means ($SS_{BETWEEN} = 0$) and ETA^2 will be equal to 0.

F Tests. Even if ETA^2 indicates that a sizable proportion of the total variance in the sample scores is explained by group differences, the possibility exists that the sample results do not reflect true differences in the larger population from which the samples were selected. For example, in a study of the effects of cohabitation on marital stability, a researcher might select a sample of the population and find that, among those in his or her sample, previous cohabitors have lower marital satisfaction than those without a history of cohabitation. Before concluding that cohabitation has a negative effect on marriage in the broader population, however, the researcher must assess the probability that, by chance, the sample used in this study included a disproportionate number of unhappy cohabitors or overly satisfied noncohabitors, or both. There is always some probability that the sample will not be representative, and the F statistic utilizes probability theory (under the assumption that the sample was obtained through random selection) to assess that likelihood.

The logic behind the F statistic is that chance fluctuations in sampling are less likely to account for differences in sample means if the differences are large, if the variation in outcome scores in the population from which the sample was drawn is small, if the sample size is large, or if all these situations have occurred. Obviously, large mean differences are unlikely due to chance because they would require many more extremely unrepresentative cases to be selected into the sample. Selecting extreme cases, however, is more likely if there are many extremes in the population (i.e., the variation of scores is great). Large samples, however, reduce the likelihood of unrepresentative samples because any extreme cases are more likely to be counteracted by extremes in the opposite direction or by cases that are more typical.

The general equation for computing F is as follows:

$$F = \frac{MS_{BETWEEN}}{MS_{WITHIN}} \qquad (5)$$

The $MS_{BETWEEN}$ is the mean square for between-group differences. It is an adjusted version of the $SS_{BETWEEN}$ and reflects the degree of difference between group means expressed as individual differences in scores. An adjustment is made to the $SS_{BETWEEN}$ because this value can become artificially high by chance as a function of the number of group comparisons being made. This adjustment factor is called the *degrees of freedom* ($DF_{BETWEEN}$) and is equal to the number of group comparisons ($k-1$, where k is the number of groups). The formula for the $MS_{BETWEEN}$ is:

$$MS_{BETWEEN} = SS_{BETWEEN} / (k-1) \qquad (6)$$

The larger the $MS_{BETWEEN}$ the greater the value of F and the lower the probability that the sample results were due to chance.

The MS_{WITHIN} is the mean square for within-group differences. This is equivalent to the SS_{WITHIN},

with an adjustment made for the size of the sample minus the number of groups (DF_{WITHIN}). Since the SS_{WITHIN} represents the amount of variation in scores within each group, it is used in the F statistic as an estimate of the amount of variation in scores that exists in the populations from which the sample groups were drawn. This is essentially a measure of the potential for error in the sample means. This potential for error is reduced, however, as a function of the sample size. The formula for the MS_{WITHIN} is:

$$MS_{WITHIN} = SS_{WITHIN} / (N\text{-}k) \qquad (7)$$

As can be seen in equations six and seven, when the number of groups is high, the estimate of variation between groups is adjusted downward to account for the greater chance of variation. When the number of cases is high, the estimation of variation within groups is adjusted downward. As a result, the larger the number of cases being analyzed, the higher the F statistic. A high F value reflects greater confidence that any differences in sample means reflect differences in the populations. Using certain assumptions, the possibility that any given F value can be obtained by chance given the number of groups ($DF1$) and the number of cases ($DF2$) can be calculated and compared to the actual F value. If the chance probability is only 5 percent or less, then the null hypothesis is rejected and the sample mean differences are said to be "significant" (i.e., not likely due to chance, but to actual effects in the population).

ADJUSTING FOR COVARIATES

Analysis of variance can be used whenever the predictor variable(s) has a limited number of discrete categories and the outcome variable is continuous. In some cases, however, an additional continuous predictor variable needs to be included in the analysis or some continuous source of extraneous effect needs to be "controlled for" before the group effects can be assessed. In these cases, analysis of covariance can be used as a simple extension of the analysis of variance model.

In the classical experimental design, the variable(s) being controlled for—the covariate(s)—is frequently some background characteristics or pretest scores on the outcome variable that were not adequately randomized across groups. As a result, group differences in outcome scores may be found and erroneously attributed to the effect of the experimental stimulus or group condition, when in fact the differences between groups existed prior to, or independent of, the presence of the stimulus or group condition.

One example of this situation is provided by Roberta Simmons and Dale Blyth (1987). In a study of the effects of different school systems on the changing self-esteem of boys and girls as they make the transition from sixth to seventh grade, these researchers had to account for the fact that boys and girls in these different school systems had different levels of self-esteem in sixth grade. Since those who score high on a measure at one point in time (T1) will have a statistical tendency to score lower at a later time (T2) and vice versa (a negative relationship), these initial differences could lead to erroneous conclusions. In their study, if boys had higher self-esteem than girls in sixth grade, the statistical tendency would be for boys to experience negative change in self-esteem and girls to experience positive change even though seventh-grade girls in certain school systems experience more negative influences on their self-esteem.

The procedure used in adjusting for covariates involves a combination of analysis of variance and linear regression techniques. Prior to comparing group means or sources of variation, the outcome scores are adjusted based upon the effect of the covariate(s). This is done by computing predicted outcome scores based on the equation:

$$\hat{Y} = a + b_1 X_1 \qquad (8)$$

where $\hat{Y}$ is the new adjusted outcome score, a is a constant, and b_1 is the linear effect of the covariate (X_1) on the outcome score (Y). The difference between the actual score and the predicted score ($Y_{ij} - \hat{Y}_{ij}$) is the residual. These residuals represent that part of the individuals' scores that is not explained by the covariate. It is these residuals that are then analyzed using the analysis of variance techniques described above. If the effect of the covariate is negative, then those who scored high on the covariate will have their scores adjusted upward. Those who scored lower on the covariate would have their scores adjusted downward. This would counteract the reverse effect that the covariate

has had. Group differences could then be assessed after the scores have been corrected.

This model can be expanded to include any number of covariates and is particularly useful when analyzing the effects of a discrete independent variable (e.g., gender, race, etc.) on a continuous outcome variable using survey data, where other factors cannot be randomly assigned and where conditions cannot be standardized. In such situations, other preexisting difference between groups (often, variables measured on continuous scales) need to be statistically controlled for. In these cases, researchers often perform analysis of variance and analysis of covariance within the context of what has been termed the "general linear model."

GENERAL LINEAR MODEL

The *general linear model* refers to the application of the linear regression equation to solve analysis problems that initially do not meet the assumptions of linear regression analysis. Specifically, there are three situations where the assumptions of linear regression are violated but regression techniques can still be used: (1) the use of nominal level measures (e.g., race, religion, marital status) as independent variables—a violation of the assumption that all variables be measured at the interval or ratio level; (2) the existence of interaction effects between independent variables—a violation of the assumption of additivity of effects; and (3) the existence of a curvilinear effect of the independent variable on the dependent variable—a violation of the assumption of linearity. The linear regression equation can be applied in all of these situations provided that certain procedures and operations on the variables are carried out. The use of the general linear model for performing analysis of variance and analysis of covariance is described in greater detail below.

Regression with dummy variables. In situations where the dependent variable is measured at the interval level of measurement (ordered values at fixed intervals) but one or more independent variables are measured at the nominal level (no order implied between values), analysis of variance and covariance procedures are usually more appropriate than linear regression. Linear regression analysis can be used in these circumstances, however, as long as the nominal level variables are first "dummy coded." The results will be consistent with those obtained from an analysis of variance and covariance, but can also be interpreted within a regression framework.

Dummy coding is a procedure where a separate dichotomous variable is created for each category of the nominal level variable. For example, in a study of the effects of racial experience, the variable for race can have several values that imply no order or degree. Some of the categories might be white, black, Latino, Indian, Asian, and other. Since these categories imply no order or degree, the variable for race cannot be used in a linear regression analysis.

The alternative is to create five dummy variables—one for each race category except one. Each of these variables measures whether or not the respondent is the particular race or not. For example, the first variable might be for the category "white," where a value of 0 is assigned if the person is any other race but white, and a value of 1 is assigned if the person is white. Similarly, separate variables would be created to identify membership in the black, Latino, Indian, and Asian groups. A dummy variable is not created for the "other" category because its values are completely determined by values on the other dummy variables (e.g., all persons with the racial category "other" will have a score of 0 on all of the dummy variables). This determination is illustrated in the table below.

Since there are only two categories or values for each variable, the variables can be said to have interval-level characteristics and can be entered into a single regression equation such as the following:

$$Y = a + b_1D1 + b_2D2 + b_3D3 + b_4D4 + b_5D5 \quad (9)$$

where Y is the score on the dependent variable, a is the constant or Y-intercept, b_1, b_2, b_3, b_4, and b_5 are the regression coefficients representing the effects of each category of race on the dependent variable, and D1, D2, D3, D4, and D5 are dummy variables representing separate categories of race. If a person is black, then his or her predicted Y score would be equal to $a + b_2$, since D2 would have a value of 1 ($b_2D2 = b_2 * 1 = b_2$) and D1, D3, D4, and D5 would all be 0 (e.g., $b_1D1 = b_1 * 0 = 0$). The effect of race would then be the addition of each of the

Respondent's Race	Values on Dummy Variables				
	D1	D2	D3	D4	D5
White	1	0	0	0	0
Black	0	1	0	0	0
Latino	0	0	1	0	0
Indian	0	0	0	1	0
Asian	0	0	0	0	1
Other	0	0	0	0	0

dummy variable effects. Other dummy or interval-level variables could then be included in the analysis and their effects could be interpreted as "controlling for" the effects of race.

Estimating analysis of variance models. The use of dummy variables in regression makes it possible to estimate analysis of variance models as well. In the example above, the value of a is equal to the mean score on the dependent variable for those who had a score of "other" on the race variable (i.e., the omitted category). The mean scores for the other racial groups can then be calculated by adding the appropriate b value (regression coefficient) to the a value. For example, the mean for the Latino group would be $a + b_3$. In addition, the squared multiple correlation coefficient (R^2) is equivalent to the measure of association used in analysis of variance (ETA^2), and the F test for statistical significance is also equivalent to the one computed using conventional analysis of variance procedures. This general model can be further extended by adding additional terms into the prediction equation for other control variables measured on continuous scales. In effect, such an analysis is equivalent to an analysis of covariance.

APPLICABILITY

In sociological studies, the researcher is rarely able to manipulate the stimulus (or independent variable) and tends to be more interested in behavior in natural settings rather than controlled experimental settings. As a result, randomization of preexisting differences through random assignment of subjects to experimental and control groups is not possible and physical control over more immediate outside influences on behavior cannot be attained. In sociological studies, "other things" are rarely equal and must be ruled out as possible alternative explanations for group differences through "statistical control." This statistical control is best accomplished through correlational techniques, although in certain circumstances the analysis of covariance can be used to statistically control for possible extraneous sources of influence.

Where analysis of variance and covariance are more appropriate in sociological studies is: (1) where the independent variable can be manipulated (e.g., field experiments investigating natural reactions to staged incidences, or studies of the effectiveness of different modes of intervention or teaching styles); (2) analyses of typologies or global variables that capture a set of unspecified, interrelated causes or stimuli (e.g., comparisons of industrialized vs. nonindustrialized countries, or differences between white collar vs. blue collar workers); or (3) where independent (or predictor) variables are used that have a limited number of discrete categories (e.g., race, gender, religion, country, etc.).

REFERENCES

Blalock, Hubert M. 1972 *Social Statistics*, 2nd ed. New York: McGraw-Hill.

Bornstedt, G. W., and D. Knoke 1995 *Statistics for Social Data Analysis*. Itasca, Ill.: F. E. Peacock Publishers, Inc.

McClendon, M. J. 1994 *Multiple Regression and Causal Analysis*. Itasca, Ill.: F. E. Peacock Publishers, Inc.

Nie, Norman H., C. Hadlai Hull, Jean G. Jenkins, Karin Steinbrenner, and Dale H. Bent 1975 *SPSS: Statistical Package for the Social Sciences*, 2nd ed. New York: McGraw-Hill.

Scheffe, H. A. 1959 *The Analysis of Variance*. New York: Wiley.

Simmons, Roberta G., and Dale A. Blyth 1987 *Moving Into Adolescence: The Impact of Pubertal Change and School Context*. New York: Aldine de Gruyter.

Tabachnick, Barbara G., and Linda S. Fidell 1996 *Using Multivariate Statistics*, 3rd ed. New York: Harper-Collins.

RICHARD BULCROFT

ANDROGYNY

See Femininity/Masculinity.

ANOMIE

The concept *anomie* was used by early sociologists to describe changes in society produced by the Industrial Revolution. The demise of traditional communities and the disruption of norms, values, and a familiar way of life were major concerns of nineteenth-century philosophers and sociologists. For sociologists, anomie is most frequently associated with Emile Durkheim, although others used it differently even during his lifetime (Wolff 1988).

Durkheim ([1893] 1956) used the French word *anomie*, meaning "without norms," to describe the disruption that societies experienced in the shift from agrarian, village economies to those based on industry. Anomie is used to describe a state of society, referring to characteristics of the social system, not of individuals, although individuals were affected by this force. Increasingly, this term has taken on a more social psychological meaning. This is not to say that it no longer has uses consistent with the initial definition, but its meaning has been broadened considerably, at times consistent with Durkheim's usage, at times at substantial variance with it.

There are, no doubt, sociologists who cringe at any expanded usage of this and other concepts, but the fact of the matter is that we have no more control over its usage than Thomas Kuhn (1970) has over abominable uses of the concept "paradigm," or than computer engineers have over those who say "interface" when they mean "meet with." Although we cannot completely stop the misappropriation of such terms as anomie we can be careful that sociological extensions of anomie are logically derived from their early uses.

DURKHEIM ON ANOMIE

According to Durkheim, village life based on agriculture had consistent, well-established norms that governed the day-to-day lives of individuals. Norms prescribed patterns of behavior, obligation, and expectations. Durkheim called this pattern of social life mechanical solidarity. Communities characterized by "mechanical solidarity" were self-contained units in which the family and the village provided for all of the needs of their members. With the emergence of industrial capitalism and the beginnings of population shifts from the hinterland to cities, mechanical solidarity could not successfully structure social life. Durkheim believed that a new, "organic solidarity" based on a division of labor would emerge, with a regulating normative structure that would be as functional as mechanical solidarity. The emergence of organic solidarity would take time, however. The transitional period, characterized by normative disorganization, Durkheim described as anomic. By this he did not mean to imply literal normlessness but, rather, a state of *relative* normative disorder (Coser 1977). Compared with communities characterized by mechanical solidarity, developing larger towns and cities would have a less regulated, less structured, less ordered pattern of social life.

Release from the restraining influence of norms was not a liberating circumstance, according to Durkheim. In this state, without adequate normative direction, people did not know what to expect or how to behave. Many of the social problems that Durkheim witnessed in rapidly changing industrializing Europe, he blamed on inadequate normative regulation. In his classic *Suicide*, Durkheim ([1897] 1951) identifies "anomic suicide" as occurring when the values and norms of the group cease to have meaning or serve as anchors for the individual, leading to feelings of isolation, confusion, and personal disorganization.

CONTEMPORARY USES OF "ANOMIE"

Anomie continues to be used as defined by Durkheim, but it has also been extended during the twentieth century. In addition to extensions similar to past uses of this concept, social psychological conceptions of anomie have become widespread. Robert Merton's use of "anomie" is very similar to that described by Durkheim. His application (1949) has been the core theoretical statement in one of the twentieth century's major criminological traditions. "Anomia" is a social psychological derivative used to represent a state of disaffection or disconnectedness.

Merton on Anomie. Merton (1949) used the concept anomie to describe how social structure produced individual deviance. According to Merton, when there existed within a society a disjuncture between the legitimate goals that members of a society were aspiring to and the legitimate means of achieving these goals, then that society was in a state of anomie. For both Durkheim and Merton, frustrated aspirations were an important cause of norm violations, or deviance. They differed in what they saw as the source of aspirations. For Durkheim, it was human nature to have limitless desires, growing from a natural "wellspring" within. Merton argued that desires did not come from

within us, but were advanced by a widely held conception of what constitutes "the good life."

Durkheim believed that when a society was characterized by anomie, there were inadequate normative constraints on the desires and expectations of people. Peasants could come to believe, even expect, that they could rise to live like the aristocracy, or become captains of newly developing industry. Part of mechanical solidarity was the norms that constrained these expectations, that ordered the intercourse between social classes, that checked the natural wellsprings of desires and encouraged peasants to be happy with their lot in life. Without these checks, desires exceeded reasonable hope of attainment, producing frustration and potentially deviance.

Merton's conception of anomie placed the society itself in the position of determining both the legitimate goals that people should aspire to and the legitimate means of pursuing these goals. While this goal has often been expressed by researchers as wealth attainment, Merton (1997) believed that wealth attainment was only one example of many societal goals. Unfortunately, society frequently caused people to have grandiose expectations without providing all of its members with reasonable opportunities to pursue them legitimately. This circumstance, where the goals and the means were not both universally available to the members of a society, Merton called anomie.

When individuals were faced with anomie, they had to choose whether to forgo the socially advanced goals, their society's shared vision of the good life, or to seek these objectives by means not defined as legitimate. Merton described five choices available to these individuals. With "conformity," the individual uses the socially prescribed means to obtain the goals advanced by that society. "Innovation" is the choice to use illegitimate means to achieve the legitimate goals; much criminal behavior is an example of innovation. When a person goes through the motions of using the legitimate means, fully aware that the socially advanced goals are beyond his reach, this is "ritualism." "Retreatism" is the choice neither to use the legitimate means nor to strive for the legitimate goals of a society. Finally, "rebellion" is rejecting the society's means and goals and replacing them with ones defined by the individual as superior.

A common mistake is interpreting Merton as arguing that an individual chooses to live his or her life as a conformist, or innovator, or retreatist. To the contrary, Merton's position is that we all are constantly making choices when faced with behavioral alternatives. At one point during the day one might choose to act as a conformist, but later, when confronted with another choice, one may choose to innovate. For example, a person who engages in robbery, innovation, is not always an innovator; he or she may also have a job, which indicates conformity. While one of these choices may predominate with some people, they should be seen as alternatives that people choose from in deciding how to act in a particular instance, not identities that they assume.

In applying Merton's perspective to Western nations, sociologists have argued that most of these societies are characterized by some degree of anomie, which manifests itself as a lack of equal opportunity. The extent of anomie, the degree of disjuncture between goals and means in a society, can be used to predict the level of crime and deviance that society will experience. The high crime rates of the United States can be linked to great inequalities in income, education, and job opportunities (Loftin and Hill 1974). To explain individual propensity to deviate from norms, one must consider the extent to which individuals have accepted the society's conception of "the good life," and the legitimate means individuals can use to attain it (Cloward and Ohlin 1960). As an explanation of crime, this theory has given way to different approaches, but anomie has been absorbed into larger perspectives to explain the relationship between poverty and crime (Messner 1983).

New Approaches to Anomie. Anomie saw a theoretical resurgence in the late 1980s and 1990s (Agnew and Passas 1997), especially in criminological research. This resurgence first occurred with Agnew's (1985) *general strain theory* and later, with macro-variations such as *institutional anomie* (Messner and Rosenfeld 1994).

Strain Theory. While many have been critical of anomie and strain theories of the past (Hirschi 1969; Kornhauser 1978), Agnew (1985, 1992) argues that research in the areas of medical sociology, social psychology, and psychology can help create new directions for this theory. Agnew (1992)

has proposed a micro-level theory; that "Adolescents are pressured into delinquency by the negative affective states—most notably anger and related emotions—that often result from negative relationships" (p. 48). His extension of traditional strain theories focuses on more than one form of strain or anomie. Agnew (1992) suggests there are three major types of strain that can be experienced by individuals: strain (1) "as the failure to achieve positively valued goals," (2) "as the removal of positively valued stimuli," and (3) "as the presentation of negative stimuli." This extension of anomie or strain theories allows our understanding of the creation of anomie to move even farther away from that first misconception that it *must* be connected to wealth attainment.

Institutional Anomie Theory. Most research on anomie has been at the micro-level (Agnew and Passas 1997). For example, variations such as Agnew's general strain theory have ignored the theoretical implications at the macro-level (Agnew and Passas 1997; see also Bernard 1987; Messner 1988; Messner and Rosenfeld 1994; Rosenfeld 1989). Institutional anomie theory posits that in order to understand any social phenomena we must understand the basics of social organization. These basics are culture and social structure and are best understood by their linking mechanism, social institutions (Messner and Rosenfeld 1994; Rosenfeld and Messner 1997). Rosenfeld and Messner (1994, 1997) suggest that social institutions are both interdependent and in conflict with one another, which leads to a constant, necessary balancing of institutional demands. According to Rosenfeld and Messner (1997) the economy is at the center of this balancing act. Institutional anomie theory helps explain the effect of the domination of the economy over other institutions by suggesting that "economic dominance stimulates the emergence of anomie at the cultural level, and . . . erodes the structural restraints against crime associated with the performance of institutional roles" (Rosenfeld and Messner 1997, p. 213). Institutional anomie theory which, up until this stage, has been used to explain trends in crime, could successfully be extended to other social phenomena.

Social Psychological Conceptions of Anomia. Items designed to measure individual feelings of anomia are now frequently included in surveys such as the General Social Survey, an annual national survey conducted by the National Opinion

Research Center (NORC) at the University of Chicago. Examples of these items illustrate the current uses of the concept, as in the following anomia items from the 1988 NORC survey (respondents were instructed to indicate the extent of their agreement with each statement): "Most public officials (people in public office) are not really interested in the problems of the average man," and "It's hardly fair to bring a child into the world with the way things look for the future" (NORC 1988, pp. 215–216). (Nearly 40 percent of the respondents to the second question agreed, and 68 percent agreed with the first.)

IN SUMMARY

Anomie has been and will continue to be a mainstay concept in sociology. Papers discussing the meanings and uses of this concept continue to be written (see, for example, Adler and Laufer 1995; Bjarnason 1998; Deflem 1989; de Man and Labreche-Gauthier 1993; Hackett 1994; Hilbert 1989; Menard 1995; Passas and Agnew 1997; Wolff 1988). The basic meaning of the term anomie, though—both in its initial usage as a description of society and in its modern extensions—is well established and widely understood within the discipline. Students new to sociology should take care to understand that the definitions of the word may not be as broad for sociologists as for the general public. The utility of the concept for the study of society is best maintained by extending it in ways that are consistent with its original definition.

REFERENCES

Adler, Freda, and William S. Laufer 1995 *Advances in Criminological Theory*, vol. 6: *The Legacy of Anomie*. New Brunswick, N.J.: Transaction.

Agnew, Robert 1992 "Foundations For a General Strain Theory of Crime and Delinquency." *Criminology* 30:47–87.

—— 1985 "A Revised Strain Theory of Delinquency." *Social Forces* 64:151–167.

——, and Nikos Passas 1997 Introduction. In Nikos Passas and Robert Agnew, eds., *The Future of Anomie Theory*, Boston: Northeastern University Press.

Bernard, Thomas J. 1987 "Testing Structural Strain Theories." *Journal of Research in Crime and Delinquency* 24:262–280.

Bjarnason, Thoroddur 1998 "Parents, Religion and Perceived Social Coherence: A Durkheimian Framework of Adolescent Anomie." *Journal for the Scientific Study of Religion* 37:742–755.

Cloward, Richard A., and Lloyd E. Ohlin 1960 *Delinquency and Opportunity: A Theory of Delinquent Gangs*. New York: Free Press.

Coser, Lewis A. 1977 *Masters of Sociological Thought: Ideas in Historical and Social Context*, 2nd ed. New York: Harcourt Brace Jovanovich.

Deflem, Mathiew 1989 "From Anomie to Anomia and Anomic Depression: A Sociological Critique on the Use of Anomie in Psychiatric Research." *Social Science and Medicine* 29:627–634.

de Man, A.F., and L. Labreche-Gauthier 1993 "Correlates of Anomie in French-Canadian Adolescents." *Journal of Social Psychology* 133:141–146.

Durkheim, Emile (1897) 1951 *Suicide*. New York: Free Press.

—— (1893) 1956 *The Division of Labor in Society*. New York: Free Press.

Hackett, Edward J. 1994 "A Social Control Perspective on Scientific Misconduct." *Journal of Higher Education* 65:242–261.

Hilbert, Richard A. 1989 "Durkheim and Merton on Anomie: An Unexplored Contrast and Its Derivatives." *Social Problems* 36:242–250.

Hirschi, Travis 1969 *Causes of Delinquency*. Berkeley: University of California Press.

Kornhauser, Ruth 1978 *Social Sources of Delinquency*. Chicago: University of Chicago Press.

Kuhn, Thomas 1970 *The Structure of Scientific Revolutions*, 2nd ed. Chicago: University of Chicago Press.

Loftin, Colin, and Robert H. Hill 1974 "Regional Subculture and Homicide." *American Sociological Review* 39:714–724.

Menard, Scott 1995 "A Developmental Test of Mertonian Anomie Theory." *Journal of Research in Crime and Delinquency* 32:136–175.

Merton, Robert K. 1997 Forward. In Nikos Passas and Robert Agnew, eds., *The Future of Anomie Theory*. Boston: Northeastern University Press.

—— 1949 *Social Theory and Social Structure: Toward the Codification of Theory and Research*. New York: Free Press.

Messner, Steven F. 1988 "Merton's 'Social Structure and Anomie': The Road Not Taken." *Deviant Behavior* 9:33–53.

—— 1983 "Regional and Racial Effects on the Urban Homicide Rate: The Subculture of Violence Revisited." *American Journal of Sociology* 88:997–1007.

———, and Richard Rosenfeld 1994 *Crime and the American Dream.* Belmont, Calif.: Wadsworth.

National Opinion Research Center 1988 *General Social Surveys, 1972–1988: Cumulative Codebook.* Chicago: National Opinion Research Center, University of Chicago.

Passas, Nikos, and Robert Agnew 1997 *The Future of Anomie.* Boston: Northeastern University Press.

Rosenfeld, Richard 1989 "Robert Merton's Contribution to the Sociology of Deviance." *Sociological Inquiry* 59:453–466.

———, and Steven F. Messner 1997 "Markets, Morality, and an Institutional-Anomie Theory of Crime." In Nikos Passas and Robert Agnew, eds., *The Future of Anomie Theory.* Boston: Northeastern University Press.

Wolff, Kurt H. 1988 "Anomie and the Sociology of Knowledge, in Durkheim and Today." *Philosophy and Social Criticism* 14:53–67.

ROBERT CRUTCHFIELD
KRISTIN A. BATES

ANTI-SEMITISM

See Discrimination; Prejudice; Race.

APARTHEID

See African Studies; Discrimination; Race; Segregation and Desegregation.

APPLIED SOCIOLOGY

Applied sociology is sociology in use. It is policy-oriented, action-directed, and intends to assist people and groups to think reflectively about what it is they do, or how it is they can create more viable social forms capable of adapting to changing external and internal conditions. The roots of applied sociology in the United States go back to the publication in 1883 of Lester Ward's *Dynamic Sociology: or Applied Social Science*, a text in which he laid the groundwork for distinguishing between an understanding of causal processes and how to intervene in them to foster social progress. Today applied sociology has blossomed in every arena of sociological endeavor (Olsen and Micklin 1981).

The nature of applied sociology can more easily be grasped by examining those characteristics that distinguish it from basic sociology. Different audiences are involved (Coleman 1972). Basic sociology is oriented toward those who have a concern for the advancement of sociological knowledge. The quality of such work (quantitative or qualitative,) is evaluated in accordance with agreed-upon standards of scientific merit. Applied sociology is oriented more toward those who are making decisions, developing or monitoring programs, or concerned about the accountability of those who are making decisions and developing programs. The quality of applied work is evaluated in accordance with a dual set of criteria: (1) how useful it is in informing decisions, revealing patterns, improving programs, and increasing accountability; and (2) whether its assumptions and methods are appropriately rigorous for the problems under investigation.

If we were to imagine a continuum between pure research and pure practice, applied sociology would occupy a space in the middle of this continuum. This space is enlarged along one boundary when practitioners and applied sociologists collaborate to explain patterns of behavior or develop causal models for predicting the likely impact of different courses of action. It is enlarged on the other boundary when applied and basic sociologists collaborate in the elaboration of abstract theory so as to make it more useful (Lazersfeld and Reitz 1975). There is always tension between the two, however. In part, the tension is attributable to the analytic distance that should characterize sociological analysis more generally (Lofland 1997). In part, it is attributable to the infusion of an ethical position in applied analysis, a posture which, if nothing else, is sensitive to the operation of power.

The boundaries of applied sociology may also be specified by enumerating the activities that play a central role in what it is that applied sociologists do. Freeman and Rossi (1984) have suggested three activities: (1) mapping and social indicator research, (2) modeling social phenomena, and (3) evaluating purposive action. To this could be added at least one more activity: (4) conceptualizing, studying, and facilitating the adaptability of alternative social forms. Examining these activities also permits considering some of the presumed trade-offs that are commonly thought to distinguish basic from applied sociology.

Mapping and social indicator research. Such studies are primarily descriptive, and designed to provide estimates of the incidence and prevalence of phenomena that are social in nature. There may be interest in how these phenomena are distributed in different social categories (e.g., by ethnic group affiliation, lifestyles, or social classes) or are changing over time. For example, corporations may wish to know how consumption patterns for various goods are changing over time for different groups to facilitate the development of marketing strategies. Federal and state agencies may wish to understand how the incidence and prevalence of diseases for different social groups is changing over time to develop more effective prevention and treatment strategies. Neighborhood groups may wish to know how citizen complaints regarding the police, high school graduation, or cervical cancer rates are distributed in relation to income characteristics of neighborhoods.

It is often assumed that applied sociology is less rigorous than basic sociology. Freeman and Rossi (1984) suggest that it is more appropriate to argue that the norms governing the conduct of basic sociological research are universally rigorous, while the norms governing the conduct of applied sociological research, of which mapping and social indicator research are but two examples, have a sliding scale of rigor. For critical decisions, complex phenomena that are either difficult to measure or disentangle, or where precise projections are needed, sophisticated quantitative or qualitative measures, or both, may be required and sophisticated analytic techniques may be needed, or may need to be developed. But as time and budget constraints increase, and the need for precision decreases, "quick and dirty" measures might be more appropriate. The level of rigor in applied sociology, in short, is driven by the needs of the client and the situation as well as the nature of the problem under investigation.

Modeling social phenomena. The modeling of social phenomena is an activity common to both basic and applied sociology. Sociologists of both persuasions might be interested in modeling the paths by which adolescents develop adaptive or maladaptive coping strategies, or the mechanisms by which social order is maintained in illicit drug networks. The applied sociologist would need to go beyond the development of these causal models. For the adolescents, applied sociologists would

need to understand how various interventions might increase the development and maintenance of adaptive strategies. In the case of drug networks, they might need to understand the relative effectiveness of different crime-control strategies in reducing the capacity of drug networks to protect themselves.

Just as with mapping and social indicator research, while there are norms supporting rigor to which basic researchers should adhere in the development of causal models, there is usually a sliding scale of rigor in applied research. There is not a necessary trade-off between doing applied work and levels of rigor. It usually happens, however, that applied problems are relatively more complex and tap into concepts that are less easy to quantify. In trying to capture more of the complexity, precision in the specification of concepts and elegance of form of the overall model may be traded off against an understanding of dynamics that is sufficient to inform decisions.

For both basic and applied work it is imperative that the mechanisms by which controllable and uncontrollable concepts have an impact on the phenomenon of interest are properly specified. Specification decisions must be made with respect to three aspects of the dynamics of situations (Britt 1997). First, the nature of what concepts are (and what they are not) must be specified with regard to the contextually specific indicators that give them meaning. Second, the concepts that are considered sufficiently important to be included in a model (as well as those that are deemed sufficiently unimportant to be left out) must be specified. Finally, the nature of relationships that exist (and do not exist) among the included concepts must be specified. Since these specification decisions interpenetrate one another (i.e., have implications for one another) over time, it may be prudent to think of models as vehicles for summarizing what we think we know about the dynamics of situations (Britt 1997).

The clients of applied researchers, however, are not interested in how elegant models are, but in how well the implications of these models assist them in reducing the uncertainty associated with decisions that must be made. As time and budget constraints increase, or researchers become more confident in their ability to understand which controllable concepts are having the biggest (or most unanticipated) impact, less formal techniques may be used to develop and evaluate the models under consideration. Elegance must be balanced against usability. Complexity must be balanced against communicability. Theoretical sophistication must be balanced against the capacity of a model to interpret the lives of individuals and groups living through situations.

Evaluating purposive action. Evaluation research is an applied activity in which theories and methods of the social sciences are used to ascertain the extent to which programs are being implemented, services are being delivered, goals are being accomplished, and these efforts are being conducted in a cost-effective manner. These may be relatively small-scale efforts with finite and specific research questions. A manufacturing company may be interested in evaluating the impact of a new marketing program. A drug rehabilitation center may be interested in evaluating the cost-effectiveness of a new treatment modality. A movement organization may be interested in the situational effectiveness of particular strategies for fostering policies that are conducive to the reduction in infant-mortality differentials or the production of higher graduation rates in high-risk areas, or to a more equitable allocation of tax revenues (Maines and McCallion 2000).

These programs may or may not be of national importance, may or may not have large sums of money contingent on the outcomes, and may or may not require an understanding of anything but gross effects. It may be necessary to perform such analyses with limited personnel, time, and money. Under such circumstances, relatively unsophisticated methods are going to be used to conduct the evaluations and reanalysis will not be likely.

On the other hand, programs may involve the lives of many people, and deal with critical and complex social issues. The Coleman report on the equality of educational opportunity was presumably intended to establish once and for all that gross differences in school facilities did exist for black and white children in the United States (Coleman et al. 1966). The report, carried out by a team of sophisticated social scientists in a relatively short time, unleashed a storm of reanalyses and critiques (e.g., Mosteller and Moynihan 1972). These reanalyses attempted to apply the most

sophisticated theoretical and methodological weapons in the sociological arsenal to the task of evaluating the implications of the Coleman report. Similarly, econometric analyses initially conducted to evaluate the impact of capital punishment on the homicide rate spawned very painstaking and sophisticated applied research (e.g., Bowers and Pierce 1975) in an attempt to evaluate the robustness of the conclusions. In these latter two cases, a high level of rigor by any standard was maintained.

Conceptualizing, studying, and facilitating the adaptability of alternative social forms. A legitimate test of applied sociology is whether it can be used as a basis for designing and implementing better social institutions (Street and Weinstein 1975). An element of critical theory is involved here that complicates the distinction between basic and applied sociology, for it challenges applied sociologists and their clients to imagine: (1) alternative social forms that might be more adaptive in the face of changing social, environmental, and technological trends; and (2) alternative environments that must be sought if equitable social forms are to exist. At the level of families, this may mean asking what new role relationships could create more adaptive family structures. Alternatively, it might mean asking in what normative environments egalitarian family roles might exist. Or perhaps, asking what the impact of pressure for reproductive rights might be on the influence of women in families and communities. At the level of work groups faced with changing technologies and dynamic environments, it is appropriate to ask whether flatter organizational structures and more autonomous work groups might better serve both organizational goals and those of its members (e.g., Myers 1985). At the community level, exploring the viability of alternative interorganizational relationships, or how communities respond to the threat of drug dealing are among a host of legitimate questions. Whatever the specific focus of such questions and the role of applied sociologists in working with clients to answer them, questions of power and ethics should never be far away.

In applied sociology, problems drive the development of both theory and method. When problems and their dynamics cannot be explained by existing theories, new assumptions are added (Lazerefeld and Reitz 1975), new ways of thinking about concepts like adaptability are developed (e.g., Britt 1989), or more fundamental theoretical shifts take place in a manner described by Kuhn (1961). When problems cannot be studied using existing methodological and statistical techniques, new techniques are developed. For example, the computer was developed under a contract from the Census Bureau so that the 1950 census could be conducted, and advances in area sampling theory were stimulated by the Department of Commerce needing to get better unemployment estimates (Rossi 1986). Ragin (1987) developed qualitative comparative analysis to permit the rigorous analysis of relatively rare events such as revolutions. Yet the applied implications of being able to study the alternative combinations of conditions that might give rise to particular outcomes has immense applied value (Britt 1998).

The continuing pressure on applied sociology to adapt to the needs of clients has had two important second-order effects beyond the development of theory and method. The nature of graduate training for applied sociologists is changing by virtue of the wider repertoire of skills needed by applied sociologists, and the dilemmas faced by sociologists vis-à-vis their clients are being confronted, and norms regarding the appropriateness of various courses of action are being developed.

A universal component of graduate applied education is the internship. Learning by doing, and experiencing the array of problems associated with designing and conducting research under time and budget constraints, while still having supportive ties with the academic program, are very important. The range and depth of coursework in qualitative and quantitative methods and statistics is increasing in applied programs to prepare students for the prospect of needing to employ techniques as varied as structural equations, focus groups, archival analysis, and participant observation in order to deal with the complexity of the problems requiring analysis.

There have been corresponding changes in the area of theory, with more emphasis given to moving back and forth from theory to applied problem. And there have been increases in courses designed to train students in the other skills required for successful applied work: networking, problem decomposition, and dealing with client-sociologist dilemmas.

REFERENCES

Bowers, W., and G. Pierce 1975 "The Illusion of Deterrence in Isaac Erlich's Research on Capital Punishment." *Yale Law Journal* 85: 187–208.

Coleman, J. G. 1972 *Policy Research in the Social Sciences*. Morristown, N.J.: General Learning Press.

Coleman, J. S., E. Q. Campbell, C. J. Hobson, J. McPartland, A. M. Mood, F. D. Weinfield, R. L. York 1966 *Equality of Educational Opportunity*, 2 vols. Washington, D.C.: U.S. Government Printing Office.

Freeman, H. E., and P. H. Rossi 1984 "Furthering the Applied Side of Sociology." *American Sociological Review* 49:571–580.

Lazersfeld, P. F., and J. G. Reitz 1975 *An Introduction to Applied Sociology*. New York: Elsevier.

Mosteller, F., and D. P. Moynihan 1972 *On Equality of Educational Opportunity*. New York: Random House.

Myers, J. B. "Making Organizations Adaptive to Change: Eliminating Bureaucracy at Shenandoah Life." *National Productivity Review*, (Spring) 131–138.

Olsen, M.E., and M. Micklin 1981 *Handbook of Applied Sociology*. New York: Praeger.

Rossi, P.H. 1986 "How Applied Sociology can Save Basic Sociology." *Journal of Applied Sociology* 3:1–6.

Street, D., and E. Weinstein 1975 "Prologue: Problems and Prospects of Applied Sociology." *The American Sociologist* 10:65–72.

Maives, D. R. and M. J. McCallion (2000) Urban Inequality and the Possibilities of Church–based Intervention. *Studies in Symbolic Interaction* 23, (forthcoming).

DAVID BRITT

ART AND SOCIETY

There is no consensus as to what art is nor, until the 1970s, had sociologists expended much energy on its study or on the development of a sociology of the arts. While in Europe art had longer been of interest to sociologists than in the United States, even there it had not developed into an identifiable field with clear and internationally accepted parameters. As recently as 1968 the term *sociology of art* was not indexed in the *International Encyclopaedia of the Social Sciences*, which sought to sum and assess the thinking and accomplishments in the rapidly expanding social sciences of the post-World War II period. Yet by the end of the century the study of art had moved into the mainstream of sociological theory and was rapidly becoming a favored subject for empirical investigation not only in the countries of Central and Western Europe but also in the United States.

Why should art, as a subject for sociological study, have been so neglected as to have virtually disappeared from mention in American textbooks for half a century after World War I? In large part this reflected the inherent tension between sociology and art, which, as noted by Pierre Bourdieu, make an "odd couple." Artists, believing in the uniqueness of the original creator, resented the social scientist's attempt to demystify their achievements by dissecting the role of the artist in society, by questioning to what extent artists are "born" rather than "made," by conceptualizing artistic works as the products of collective rather than individual action, by anthropologically approaching art institutions, by studying the importance of networks in artistic success, and by investigating the economic correlates of artistic productivity. Many scholars in the humanities were also skeptical. For them the appeal of art is something of a mystery and best left that way; they could hardly relate to the attempts of social scientists who, in their quest for objectivity, sought to eliminate any evaluative component from their own research. This practice of disregarding one's own personal preferences and tastes hardly seemed legitimate to aestheticians. Moreover, in pursuing a rigorous methodology, many sociologists chose to study only those problems that could yield readily to statistical analysis, and art did not seem to be one of those. They also preferred to focus on subjects that were important in the solution of social problems, and, in the United States, the arts were not generally regarded as high on this list.

Nonetheless, there has been—especially since the late 1960s—a slow but steady movement toward the development of a sociology of the arts. This is due, in part, to a narrowing of the intellectual gulf between the humanistic and sociological approaches. On the one hand, art historians have legitimated the study of art within its social context, and, on the other, mainstream sociology has become more hospitable to the use of other than purely "scientific" methodology. In part this progress resulted from the expanded contacts of American sociologists after World War II with their counterparts in other countries where art is regarded as a vital social institution and a public good. And just as art must be understood and studied within its social context, so too the growing sociological interest in the arts reflects the growing importance of the arts within American society and the recognition of this importance by the government. Despite the concerted opposition of those who believe there is no role for government in funding the arts, at every level of government—federal, state, and local—arrangements for the support of grassroots arts have become institutionalized.

A small but dedicated number of scholars can be credited with sparking this postwar advancement of theory and research in the sociology of culture and, more specifically, in the sociology of the arts. The latter term, though not unknown before then, began to surface with some frequency in the 1950s; thus, in 1954 a session on the sociology of art was listed in the program of the annual meeting of the American Sociological Association. In 1957 a symposium on the arts and human behavior at the Center for Advanced Study in the Behavioral Sciences served as a catalyst for the production of a book, based partially on papers presented there. In its preface, the editor, Robert N. Wilson, concluded that a sociology of art, though in the early stages of its development, was not yet ripe for formalization. Nonetheless, Wilson's book included a number of articles based on empirical research that attracted attention. In one, Cynthia White, an art historian, and Harrison White, a Harvard sociologist, reported on their investigation into institutional change in the French painting world and how this affected artistic careers. Later expanded and published in book form as *Canvases and Careers* (1965), this research provides a working example of how a changing art form might best be studied and understood within its historical and social context.

Perhaps the most important step toward the development of the field in these postwar years came with the publication of a collection of readings edited by Milton Albrecht, James Barnett, and Mason Griff (1970). Clearly titled as to subject matter—*The Sociology of Art and Literature*—it was intended to serve a classroom purpose but also to advance an institutional approach to its study. In one article, originally published in 1968, Albrecht oriented the reader to art as an institution, using *art* as a collective term for a wide variety of aesthetic products, including literature, the visual arts, and music. In another ("The Sociology of Art"),

Barnett reprinted his state-of-the-field synthesis as it stood in 1959, and, in yet another, Griff published a seminal article on the recruitment and socialization of artists, drawing in some part on his earlier empirical studies of art students in Chicago. Though here, too, the editors spoke of the sociology of art as being still in its infancy, they helped it to take its first steps by including in their reader a large number of empirically grounded articles—by scholars in the humanities as well as the social sciences. Divided into six subjects—forms and styles, artists, distribution and reward systems, tastemakers and publics, methodology, history and theory—it served for many years as an exemplary resource both for those attempting to set up courses on the arts and society and those embarking on research.

Beginning in the 1970s the sociology of art moved toward formalization and started to come into its own. Speeding this development in the new age of television dominance was a growing sociological interest in the mass media, in visual communications, and in the popular arts. The debate about mass versus popular culture was revitalized by new fears about the effects of commercialization, but some scholars began to wonder about the terms in which the debate was being cast. The assumption that art forms could be categorized as "high" or "low" or, put another way, as "mass" or "elite"—an assumption that had fueled the critiques of Theodor Adorno and other members of the Frankfurt School—came into question as reputable researchers looked more closely at the empirical evidence (Gans 1974). Howard S. Becker's conceptualization of art as collective action (1982) did not so much mute the debate as turn attention away from the circumstances surrounding the production of any particular work—that is, what kind of an artist produced work for what kind of audience under what system of rewards—toward the collective (cooperative) nature of the activity whereby works regarded as art are produced as well as to that collective process itself. As attention turned to the production of culture, the arts came to be widely regarded by sociologists as socially constructed entities whose symbolic meanings reside not in the objects themselves but change as circumstances change.

Recent American studies in the sociology of art have taken varied approaches, both as to subject matter and methodology. Some have focused on genres that are considered marginal to established categories of fine art, including such "outsider art" as that produced by asylum inmates, "naive artists," African primitives, and Australian aborigines. Others have researched the process whereby "outsider artists" may make the transition to being "insiders" while still others, extending their interests to the politics of art, have considered what happens to "insiders" (and the art they have produced) when shifts in the political culture recast them as "outsiders." Sociologists have also extended their inquiries to the economics of art as they have considered the influence of funding and the structure of museums on the creation, production, preservation, and dissemination of art works; case studies of "arts management" abound.

Some inquiries involving genres marginal to established categories of fine art have adopted methodologically unusual approaches. These include Wendy Griswold's studies of the social factors influencing the revival of Renaissance plays (1986); Robert Crane's study of the transformation of art styles in post-World War II New York (1987); Liah Greenfeld's study of taste, choice, and success in the Israeli art worlds (1989); Vera Zolberg's studies of art patronage and new art forms (1990); and Gladys Lang and Kurt Lang's study of the building and survival of artistic reputations (1990).

These and other empirical studies that have already appeared in print or are under way are helping to clarify what is meant by a sociology of art. While there still may be no consensus as to what art is—nor need there be—some consensus is shaping up as to the direction in which the field should be moving. Leading theoreticians—Vera Zolberg, Janet Wolff, Paul DiMaggio, Richard Peterson, and Anne Bowler among them—agree on the need to keep the art itself at the center of theoretical concern but continue to disagree on the proper methodological approach to that "centering." Essentially, this pits the case for focusing on the institutions in which aesthetic objects are produced and received—an analytical approach—against one that emphasizes criticism and textual interpretation of the objects themselves. Zolberg has voiced the need to avoid the narrowness of both social science and aesthetic disciplines, accepting the premise that art should be contextualized in terms of time and place in a general sense as well as in a specific sense, that is, in terms of institutional norms, professional training, reward, and patronage or other support. To approach art as a part of society's culture, Zolberg argues, is no more potentially reductionist than to treat it, as aestheticians do, as an activity that only restricted groups with special interests and knowledge can hope to comprehend. Literature in the field is growing at a rapid rate as intellectual barriers between humanistic and social science approaches to the study of art begin to crumble.

REFERENCES

Adorno, Theodor (1962) 1976 *Introduction to the Sociology of Music*. New York: Seabury Press.

Albrecht, M. C., J. H. Barnett, and M. Griff (eds.) 1970 *The Sociology of Art and Literature: A Reader*. New York: Praeger.

Alexander, Victoria D. 1996 *Museums and Money: The Impact of Funding on Exhibitions, Scholarship, and Management*. Bloomington: Indiana University Press.

Balfe, Judith Huggins (ed.) 1993 *Paying the Piper: Causes and Consequences of Art Patronage*. Urbana: University of Illinois Press.

Becker, Howard S. 1982 *Art Worlds*. Berkeley: University of California Press.

Bourdieu, Pierre (1979) 1984 *Distinction: A Social Critique of the Judgment of Taste*. Cambridge, Mass.: Harvard University Press.

Bowler, Anne 1994 "Methodological Dilemmas in the Sociology of Art." In Diana Crane, ed., *Sociology of Culture*. Oxford: Blackwell.

Crane, Diana 1987 *The Transformation of the AvantGarde: The New York Art World 1940–85*. Chicago: University of Chicago Press.

Foster, Arnold W., and Judith R. Blau (eds.) 1989 *Art and Society: Readings in the Sociology of the Arts*. Albany: State University of New York Press.

Gans, Herbert J. 1974 *Popular Culture and High Culture: An Analysis and Evaluation of Taste*. New York: Basic Books.

Greenfeld, Liah 1989 *Different Worlds: A Sociological Study of Taste, Choice and Success in Art*. Cambridge, England: Cambridge University Press.

Griswold, Wendy 1986 *Renaissance Revivals: City Comedy and Revenge Tragedy in the London Theater, 1576–1980*. Chicago: University of Chicago Press.

Lang, Gladys Engel, and Kurt Lang 1990 *Etched in Memory: The Building and Survival of Artistic Reputation*. Chapel Hill: University of North Carolina Press.

—— 1996 "Banishing the Past: The German Avant-Garde." *Qualitative Sociology* 19:323–343.

Peterson, Richard A. (ed.) 1976 *The Production of Culture*. Beverly Hills, Calif.: Sage Publications.

Rueschemeyer, Marilyn 1993 "State Patronage in the German Democratic Republic." In Judith Higgins Balfe, ed., *Paying the Piper*. Urbana: University of Illinois Press.

White, Harrison C., and Cynthia A. White 1965 *Canvasses and Careers: Institutional Change in the French Painting World*. New York: Wiley.

Wilson, Robert N. (ed.) 1964 *The Arts in Society*. Englewood Cliffs, N.J.: Prentice-Hall.

Wolff, Janet 1992 "Excess and Inhibition: Interdisciplinarity in the Study of Art." In Lawrence Grossberg, Cary Wilson, and Paula A. Treichler, eds., *Cultural Studies*. New York: Routledge Press.

Zolberg, Vera L. 1990 *Constructing a Sociology of the Arts*. New York: Cambridge University Press.

——, and Charbo, Joni M. (eds.) 1997 *Outsider Art*. New York: Cambridge University Press.

GLADYS ENGEL LANG

ASIAN-AMERICAN STUDIES

The term *Asian American* is used in the United States by federal, state, and local governments to designate people of Asian descent, including Pacific Islanders (residents from the Pacific islands that are under U. S. jurisdiction, such as Guam, American Somoa, and the Marshall Islands). Although historically relevant and geographically appropriate, inclusion of the Pacific islands in the generic term *Asian American* stemmed from administrative convenience for the federal government rather than from race or ethnic identifications.

Reflecting deep-seated prejudices against people of color, in 1917 the Congress of the United States created the Asiatic Barred Zone, which stretched from Japan in the east to India in the west. People from within the zone were banned from immigration. The geographic concept was incorporated into the Immigration Act of 1924 (Oriental Exclusion Act), a law that had a profound impact on the demographic structure of Asian-American communities as well as on U.S. foreign policy. Although it is generally assumed that the term *Asian American* has a racial basis, particularly from the perspective of U.S. immigration history, the racial overtone is muted by the inclusion in the 1980 census of people from India in the "Asian and Pacific Islander" category; they had been classified as "white" prior to 1980.

IMMIGRATION AND RESTRICTIONS OF ASIAN AMERICANS

Asian immigration can be divided into two periods: the old and the new. The old immigration period was marked by nonoverlapping waves of distinct Asian populations who came largely in response to the sociopolitical conditions in their homelands and to the shortage of unskilled labor experienced by special-interest groups in the United States. The new immigration was characterized by the simultaneous arrival of people from the Asia-Pacific Triangle, spurred principally by the 1965 legislative reforms in U.S. immigration policy, shortages of certain skilled and professional labor, the involvement of United States in Asia, and the sociopolitical situations in Asia in the context of the Cold War. In between these two waves, there was another wave of Asian immigrants, who came between the end of World War II and the mid 1960s, though the number was small and involved principally Filipinos and their families because of their services in the US military. This group came outside the fifty-person quota allowed for Filipinos as a result of the *Tydings-McDuffie Act of 1935* when the Republic of the Philippines was granted independence.

The year 1848 marked the beginning of Asian immigration to the United States when the coastal Chinese—mostly from Guangdong—responded to the California gold rush and failures in the rural economy of China. Within fewer than thirty-five years, the Chinese became the first group in U.S. history to be legally barred from becoming citizens because of race. The 1882 Anti-Chinese Exclusion Act was followed by an influx of immigrants from the southern prefectures of Japan during the last decade of the nineteenth century—until that flow ended abruptly with the so-called "Gentlemen's Agreement" of 1907–1908. Unlike the termination of Chinese immigration, and reflecting Japan's position as a world power, cessation of entry by Japanese was accomplished through a diplomatic compromise between the two governments rather than through an act of Congress. Without a continuous flow of Japanese farm workers to ease the labor shortage on the Hawaiian plantations, contractors turned to the Philippine Islands—which had been a U.S. possession since 1898—for cheap labor. From 1906 to the independence of the Republic of the Philippines in 1946, over 125,000 (predominantly single) Filipino males, the majority of them from the Ilocos region, labored on Hawaiian sugar plantations.

The exclusions of Asians enacted into the National Origins Act of 1924 essentially remained in effect until 1965. By Act of Congress in 1943, however, 105 Chinese were permitted to immigrate annually, and in 1952, under the McCarran-Walter Act, a token one hundred persons from each Asian country were allowed entry. The symbolic opening of immigration doors to Asians was attributed to Walter Judd, a congressman from Minnesota who had spent many years in China as a medical missionary. The provision of a quota of one hundred persons seemed to be an important moral victory for those who wanted the elimination of the exclusion act, but it was in fact a restatement of the 1924 national origin quota basis for immigration.

The new stream of Asian immigrants to the United States reflected the 1965 legislative reform that allowed an equal number of persons (20,000) from each country outside the Western Hemisphere to immigrate. Furthermore, family unification and needed skills became the major admission criteria, replacing national origin. Besides China and the Philippines, Korea and the Indian sub-continent became, and continue to be, the major countries of origin of many newly arrived Asian immigrants. Refugees from Vietnam, Cambodia, and Laos began to enter the United States in 1975, and by 1990, peoples from the former Indochina (Vietnam, Cambodia and Laos) had become the third-largest Asian group, following Chinese and Filipinos. In contrast, Japan's immigration to the United States practically ceased from 1945 to 1965, when it resumed at a much lower rate than those reported for other Asian countries.

SOCIAL CONSEQUENCES OF IMMIGRATION RESTRICTIONS

Several distinct demographic characteristics illustrate most graphically past restrictions and the

1965 revision of the immigration laws. Earlier immigrants from China and the Philippines were predominantly single males. As a result of racial prejudice that culminated in the passage of antimiscegenation laws directed primarily against people of color in many western and southwestern states, the majority of these earlier Asian immigrants remained unmarried. The lack of family life caused unattached immigrants to depend on one another, creating an apparent great solidarity among people of the same ethnic group. Many of the earlier studies of Chinese and Filipino communities depicted themes of social isolation and loneliness, which did not apply to the Japanese community. Paul Siu (1952) portrayed the extreme social isolation of Chinese laundrymen in Chicago in his doctoral dissertation, that was published at the time only as a paper in the *American Journal of Sociology*, with the title "The Sojourner." Although Siu's work was written under the direction of Robert E. Park and Ernest W. Burgess, it was not included in the Chicago School sociological series published by the University of Chicago Press that focused on urban and ethnic social structure of the time allegedly because Siu argued that the Chinese immigrants did not fit the Park-Burgess assimilation model because of the "race factor." Thus a major piece of Asian-American research, *The Chinese Laundryman: A Study in Social Isolation* (Siu 1987) remained unpublished until after the author's death in the mid-1980s.

The existence of single-gender communities of Filipinos and Chinese is clearly demonstrated in the U.S. censuses between 1860 and 1970. In 1860, the sex ratio for Chinese was 1,858 men for every 100 women. By 1890, following the peak of Chinese immigration during the previous decade, the ratio was 2,678 males for every 100 females—the highest recorded. Skewed sex ratios for the Chinese population later declined steadily as the result of legislative revisions in 1930 (46 U.S. Stat. 581) and 1931 (46 U.S. Stat. 1511) that enabled women from China to enter the United States.

A second factor that helped to balance the sex ratio in the Chinese community, particularly among the younger age cohorts, was the presence of an American-born generation. In 1900, U.S.-born persons constituted only 10 percent of the Chinese-American population. By 1970, the figure was 52 percent. Nevertheless, in the 1980 census, the sex ratio remained high for some age groups within

certain Asian-American subpopulations: among Filipinos, for example, the highest sex ratio was found in those sixty-five and older.

The demographic characteristics of Japanese Americans present yet another unusual feature. Under the "Gentlemen's Agreement" between Japan and the United States, Japanese women were allowed to land on the West Coast to join their men though the immigration of male laborers was curtailed. The majority of the women came as picture brides (Glenn 1986, pp. 31–35) within a narrow span of time. Thus, the years following 1910 were the decade of family building for the first (*issei*) generation of Japanese Americans. Since almost all *issei* were young and their brides were chosen from a cohort of marriageable applicants of about the same age, it was not surprising that issei began their families at about the same time after marriage. The historical accident of controlled migration of brides resulted in a uniform age cohort of the second-generation Japanese Americans (*nisei*). The relatively homogeneous age group of the nisei generation meant that their children, the third generation (known as *sansei*), were also of about the same age. The fourth generation followed the same pattern. The amazingly nonoverlapping age and generational cohorts among Japanese Americans is not known to have had parallels in other population groups.

Fourth, while Asian Americans in general continue to grow in number as a result of new immigration, the size of the Japanese American population increases primarily by the addition of new generations of U.S.-born babies. It is generally believed that the offspring of Japanese women who marry Caucasians have lost their Japanese identity, even though there are no estimates of the impact of intermarriages upon the shrinkage of the Japanese-American community. An educated guess would be that about two-thirds of Japanese Americans marry non-Japanese partners. Given the fact that Japanese immigrants had lower fertility rates than women in Japan during the period prior to and shortly after World War II, and that the number of new immigrants since the war has remained small, Japanese communities have larger percentages of older people than do other ethnic minority populations, including other Asian Americans. In short, Japanese Americans will be a much smaller ethnic minority in the future. The plurality ranking for all Asian groups placed the Japanese at the top of the list in 1970; they dropped to the third place in 1980, are expected to place fourth in 1990, and to be ranked last by the year 2000.

One more demographic fact is worthy of note. Hawaii and the West Coast states continue to draw large numbers of new immigrants from Asia. Through a process known as "chain migration," relatives are likely to follow the immigrants soon after their arrival. This leads to sudden increases in population within the ethnic enclaves. The post-1965 pattern of population growth in many Chinatowns, for instance, is an example of the renewal and revitalization of ethnic communities— which prior to 1965 were experiencing a decline— as are the formation and expansion of Koreantowns, Filipinotowns, and Little Saigons. Moreover, the settlement of post-1965 immigrants from Asia is more dispersed than that of the earlier groups, owing to the fact that the need for professional and skilled manpower is widely distributed throughout the United States. The emergence of Thai, Malaysian, and Vietnamese communities in major metropolitan areas has added a new dimension to the ethnic composition of Asian Americans.

Two separate chains of immigration resulted from the new immigration legislation of 1965. One chain, largely found in Chinese and Filipino communities, is kin-selective in that the process of settlement follows the family ties of earlier immigrants. The other process is occupation-selective, based on skills and professional qualifications. These two processes created significantly different immigrant populations, with clearly discerned bimodal distributions of status characteristics. It is therefore common to find recent immigrants from Asia among the high-income groups as well as among the families living below the poverty level; some find their homes in the ethnic enclaves of central cities while others live in high-income suburban communities. Any attempt to describe Asian Americans by using average measures of social status characteristics, such as income, education, and occupation, can produce a distorted and misleading profile that fits no particular group, which can be misused by researchers and planners. A more useful description would be the use of standard errors to show the polarities or deviations of the immigrant group from the norm of the majority.

In short, the sociodemographic and socioeconomic characteristics of all Asian American communities since 1850 have been greatly influenced by federal immigration legislation. A clear grasp of the structure and change of Asian-American communities must begin with an understanding of the history of immigration legislation.

ASIAN-AMERICAN RESEARCH

Asian-American research may be divided into six periods: (1) the early period before World War II, which was influenced by, and was a part of, the Chicago School of Sociology that focused on the emergence of a multiethnic urban America. (2) the World War II period, which saw a preponderance of Japanese-American studies that also centered around the University of Chicago; (3) the postwar era, with a strong emphasis on culture and personality studies related to Japanese and Japanese Americans; (4) a shift toward "ethnic" experience as a result of the civil rights movement; and the emergence of a new academic course of Asian-American studies and finally (5) the integration of social science theories and concepts of ethnic inequalities and the changing Asian-American vista in the 1980s and 1990s.

The Early Period. The pioneer sociological studies on the assimilation of immigrants in American urban communities may be attributed to the work of Robert E. Park. Although Park had done little empirical investigation, he had supervised a large number of graduate students and had formulated what was known as the theory of race cycle, which stressed the unidirectional process of competition, accommodation, and assimilation as the basis of race relations in urban America. Park later led a group of researchers to study Chinese and Japanese communities on the Pacific Coast. The results failed to prove the race-cycle theory. In defending his views, according to Lyman (1977, p.4), Park employed the Aristotelian doctrine of "obstacles," which suggests that among Chinese and Japanese the assimilation progress in the hypothesized direction was only delayed.

Early published sociological research on Asian Americans included the works of Bogardus (1928, 1930), who attempted to delineate degrees of prejudice against minorities through an operational concept of "social distance." Other topics were chosen randomly such as "Oriental crime" in California (Beach 1932); school achievement of Japanese-American children (Bell 1935); and anti-Asian sentiments (Sandmeyer 1939; Ichihashi 1932). A noted pioneer community study of Japanese Americans conducted by Frank Miyamoto (1939) in Seattle in the late 1930s paved the way for the long and significant bibliography on Japanese-American studies that followed.

Perhaps the most significant and ambitious piece of work during the prewar era was the study of social isolation of Chinese immigrants, which took more than a decade to complete. The author, Paul Siu, working under a condition of extreme poverty for a decade, observed the life of Chinese laundrymen. The product of his research endeavors offers a classic text in the study of "unmeltable" immigrants, from which the concept of "sojourner" independently complemented the earlier work of G. Simmel (Siu 1952, 1987).

World War II and Japanese-American Studies. Large-scale systematic studies on Asian Americans began shortly after the Japanese attack on Pearl Harbor, when the United States declared war on Japan. The U.S. government stripped Japanese Americans of their property, relocated them, and housed them in internment camps for several years. Alexander Leighton, a psychiatrist, recruited nisei social science graduates to assist in his work in the camps, monitoring the morale and loyalty of internees; this perhaps was the pioneer work in assessing their group cohesion and structure. A few of Leighton's nisei assistants completed their doctoral studies after the war, maintaining a close and affectionate relationship with him. All had made their own contributions as social scientists and as Asian-American specialists. Leighton's work on the internment of these civilians (both citizens and non citizens) resulted in the publication of a classic text on loyalty (Leighton 1945).

Thomas and Nishimoto (1946), Thomas (1952), and Broom and Kitsuse (1955) also carefully documented the situation and the people of Japanese-American communities. The focus of these studies was the question of loyalty on the part of Japanese-American citizens and their offspring in spite of their brilliant wartime combat duties on behalf of their adopted country in Europe. It was the American home front conditions had sparked an area of

development in social science research that paralleled some of the classic work on the study of the Polish peasant (Thomas and Znanieki 1946). As a result it increased the general knowledge base on Japanese Americans, including their families and communities, and their sacrifices and contributions to America's wartime efforts.

Culture and Personality Studies in the Postwar Era. During World War II, the U.S. government had reason and the opportunity to question the suitability of Asians as American citizens in regard to loyalty and civic responsibilities. It was also a time to test the myth that Asian immigrants could not assimilate into American society. Social scientists were intrigued by the way culture shapes the personality. Ruth Benedict's classic work on the Japanese personality and society (Benedict 1946) opened a new vista for research. A cohort of young scholars at the University of Chicago, which included Japanese-American graduate students, became known for their pioneer work in studying Japanese behavioral patterns. It had a profound effect on a generation of interested social scientists and resulted in the publication of many classic works on culture and personality (Caudill 1952; Jacobson and Rainwater 1953; Caudill and DeVos 1956; DeVos 1955; Kitano 1961, 1962, 1964; Caudill and Scarr 1961; Babcock and Caudill 1958; Meredith 1966; and Vogel 1961). Similar studies on other Asian-American groups are conspicuously absent.

Ethnic Studies and the Civil Rights Movement. In the 1960s, the civil rights movement, sparked by the death of Martin Luther King, Jr., contributed to the passage of an unprecedented immigration-legislation reform. At the time there existed among Asian Americans on the Pacific Coast, principally in California, a collective search for identity that shared many of the goals and rhetoric of the black movement. Research into the ethnic (Asian) U.S. communities had added two dimensions. The first was the need to raise ethnic consciousness as a part of the social movement. Personal testimonials of experiences as members of an oppressed minority provided insight into the psychology of ethnic minorities. The emphasis on the cathartic, as well as the cathectic quality in much of the writings of the civil-rights era reflected the mood of the period: that there is a need for alternative theories against the early assimilation model in standard texts on racial and ethnic studies. Second, consistent with the radical theme, was the apparent influence of Marxian views on race and ethnic relations, which posited that African-American and other minorities are victims of oppression in a capitalist society.

Expectedly, the civil rights movement began a renewed interest in research on the experiences of the earliest Asian Americans. With time the titles ranged from well-documented academic publication to insightful popular readings for the lay public (Chen 1980; Daniels 1988; Choy 1979; Ichioka 1988; Miller 1969; Nee and de Bary 1973; Saxton 1971; Sung 1971; Takaki 1989; Wilson and Hosokawa 1980).

Asian-American studies was established in the 1970s as an academic discipline in a number of institutions of higher learning, particularly in California, at a time when there were only a few major publications as sources of information for undergraduates (e.g., Kitano 1961–1976; Lyman 1974; Petersen 1971). The birth of an academic specialty was marked by the conspicuous absence of available materials, particularly on Filipinos, Koreans, Vietnamese, and the peoples of the Indian sub continent (Min 1989). In response to this void, the Asian-American Studies Center at the University of California at Los Angeles published two collections of papers *(Roots and Counterpoint)* and a quarterly journal, The *Amerasia*. On the Atlantic Coast, a group of U.S.-born professionals published an intellectual nonacademic monthly, *The Bridge*, for nearly a decade. In the 1970s and 1980s, these publications were recommended as collateral readings for college students interested in Asian-American studies. *Amerasia* has since become more academic in the 1980s and 1990s while *Bridge*, for the lack of funds, quietly folded after nearly one decade. In its place, two new academic publications appeared in the 1990s: the Journal of Asian American Studies, which is a U.S. East Coast complement (at Cornell University) to *Amerasia*; and the *Journal of Asian American Health*, that serves health research readers as well as the general public. In addition, funded research on health and mental health by the U. S. Department of Health and Human Services has greatly enhanced the research productivities on Asian Americans as well as cumulative bibliographies.

The New Age of Asian-American Research: Emerging Theories and Concepts. Stanley Lyman at the University of California at Berkeley, and S. Frank Miyamoto at the University of Washington, are generally acknowledged as pioneers in Asian-American research. Through his numerous papers and books, Lyman has maintained a theoretical relevance and has demonstrated an historical insight into the origin and growth of Asian-American communities, especially those of the Chinese and Japanese. As a social historian, he based his research, by and large, on archival documents (see Lyman 1970b). Miyamoto, on the other hand, belongs to a founding generation of Japanese-American researchers whose long-time association with the University of Washington and his training under Professor Herbert Blumer at the University of Chicago gave him a mix of symbolic interactionist bend and logical positivist approach to the establishment of sound theoretical propositions in the study of Japanese Americans.

In the 1980s and 1990s, a few well-trained sociologists began to emerge, many of them foreign born and foreign educated, with American postgraduate training—the "first-generation new immigrants"—scholars who arrived at a time when America had become sensitive to diverse cultures. The new breed of Asian-American researchers are increasingly more vocal, questioning traditional sociological theories and concepts based on studies of European immigrants in the early 1920s and 1930s. There is also a reflection of the postmodern and world community perspectives that have become influential intellectual trends of the time. These new studies of Asian-American communities have added much to a field that had been underserved by the social sciences. In addition, as Asian-American studies became a new academic discipline in line with the African-American and other ethnic minority and gender studies, the need grew for more social science information. The lack of usable and more accurate estimates on many attributes of Asian Americans based on adequate sample design and culturally appropriate survey instruments employed in federal surveys has frustrated many Asian-American researchers, in spite of the special publication of information on Asian Americans and Pacific Islanders in the 1980 and 1990 censuses. Asian-American researchers constructively point out how such statistics can be improved to the advantage of both legislators and research academicians (see Yu and Liu 1992).

Much information on Asian Americans, particularly new immigrants, still depends on small sample backyard research by individual investigators. In the post–civil rights movement decades, studies on ethnic identities and race and ethnic relations continue to flourish, adding new Asian immigrants into the sample of observations and analyses. The newly arrived Korean businessmen and professionals gave birth to fresh topics in the research literature. Publications on Korean professionals and small businesses provided opportunities to support the old "middleman" theory that argued Asians succeeded in finding business opportunities by being middleman between white and black supplier and customer relations; (see Light and Bonacich 1988) and also advanced an argument that newly emerged Asian-American ethnic business communities can best be understood in the context of a global business community (Min 1987, and 1988; Yu, E.Y. 1983, Light and Sanchaz 1987).

Newer research also includes a collection of refugee studies that involved Vietnamese, Cambodians, and Laotian Hmongs. Publications on the Vietnamese community centered largely on the initial movement of refugees after the withdrawal of American troops from Vietnam on April 25, 1975. Liu and his associates made a survey of the first wave of refugees who were brought in directly from Vietnam to Camp Pendelton in California (Liu, Lamanna, and Murata 1979). He directed the reader's attention to the special status of refugees vis-à-vis immigrants, and the pathway to becoming refugees from previously nonrefugee status as a result of both political and military decisions. The distinction between refugees and immigrants was later further elaborated by Haines (1989a, 1989b). Gold (1992) compared Vietnamese with Jewish refugees' adaptive experience, and showed commonalities of refugee experience in general. Freeman (1984) on the other hand, collected life histories and reported refugees' own accounts of flight and adjustment. Taken together, studies on Vietnamese, Cambodians, and Laotians focused more on their cohort experience as refugees, rather than their transition to an emerging new ethnic community.

The smaller number of Cambodian and Laotian Hmong people, relative to the Vietnamese, is a major reason why they remained as a part of the underserved Asian-American population in the Asian-American literature. Much of the writings on the Hmong people were based on clinical interviews by practicing health providers and academic psychiatrists (Beiser 1987, 1988; Boehnlein 1987; Mollicca et al. 1987). There is also the reflection of a time when the concern was on wartime trauma, refugee experience, and cultural adjustment (see Chan 1994). These publications tend to leave an impression that Hmong people had the most difficult time in America, and are psychologically maladjusted. A popular book that portrayed the experience between American physicians and a Hmong child revealed how culture interfered in clinical judgment, no matter how well intentioned (Fadiman 1997)

There remained a scarcity of systematic studies, except for Agarwal's (1991) work on Indian immigrants. Agarwal's survey on immigrant Asian Indians in America was based on a rather small sample of professionals. Available studies on immigrant Americans from the Indian subcontinent, however, remained inadequate and woefully few.

The arrival of voluminous publications on new immigrants from Asia did not slow down studies of prior to 1965 immigrants. A cumulative bibliography began to focus on the aftermath of Japanese nisei resettlement (Ichioka 1989a; Miyamoto 1989; Warren 1989), and sensei scholars began to search for the Japanese identity of their parents' generation (Ichioka 1989b). A well-publicized book by Ronald Tataki (1989), *Strangers from a Different Shore: A History of Asian Americans*, contained verbatim recorded life histories. The book was well received by the public but was poorly reviewed in the social science literature because it lacks a new conceptual framework for an old topic. However, it did arouse renewed interest in Asian Americans and their American experience, particularly at a time of race consciousness.

While the third-generation Japanese Americans were busy finding their identities, nisei continued to search for the meaning of "being American." In September of 1987, on the campus at the University of California at Berkeley, a group of scholars who belonged to the original Japanese American Evacuation and Resettlement Study

(JERS) at the Berkeley campus convened, and reminisced about lost valuable information of that period (see JERS 1989). Among those who attended include Ichioka, Miyamoto, L.R and J.H. Hirabayashi, Suzuki, Spencer, Kikuchi, Takagi, and Sakoda. Later researchers learned from discussion notes that there was a diary kept by Charles Kikuchi, known as the *Kikuchi Diary*, but it was destroyed. A manuscript entitled *American Betrayed* by Professor Morton Grodzin was suppressed from being published. Furthermore, another manuscript reportedly written by Violet de Christoforo described internees' refusal to leave camps as camps were closed. The book also exposed the harshness of expulsion. The existence of this manuscript, if true, shed additional light on similar experiences reported in Camp Pendelton as the Vietnamese camps were closed, when refugees were labeled as suffering from *campetitis* by the federal administrator in charge of closing all camps that housed refugees from Indochina (see Liu et al. 1979).

Clearly Asian-American research could not be separated from the general field of race and ethnic studies. In the 1980s and 1990s, researchers continued to be fascinated by Asians who had mutual ill feelings in their home countries because of neighboring dominations and the World War II experience, but appeared to be united behind a cause of advancing the status of Asian-Americans as a group. Whether there is a single identity of all Asian-Americans, or multiple subidentities of separate entities depends, of course, on issues. But the persistence of a multiple subidentities seem to be present not only among the first-generation immigrants, which is understandable, it also appears to be real among second- or third-generation ethnics. Fugita and O'Brien's (1991) volume on Japanese Americans is a good illustration; they seemed to have suggested that a single identity of Asian Americans is but an abstract rather than a reality. Among the Asian-American professionals, perhaps this issue is more complex and deep than is commonly expected (see Espirita 1992).

There also had begun some long-awaited new social science contributions to the literature on Filipino immigrants in the 1980s that were absent in the earlier generation. These studies included Filipino-American income levels (Cabezas, Shinagawa, and Kawaguchi 1986–1987), Filipino assimilation (Pido 1986), and Filipino health practices (Montepio 1989).

As more practicing professionals took part in studying Asian immigrants, there appeared in the 1970s and 1980s a bifurcation of writings on Asian Americans: those that catered to an academic audience and those that served as "voices" of the grassroots community (see Radhakrishnan 1996). It is understandable that, when more and more publications contained a whole spectrum of topics, the quality of writings would also vary widely. At the conceptual level, there remained in these writings a contrast between neo-Marxian and neo-classical economic approaches to status attainment, income, and employment opportunities for Asian Americans.

For example, the censuses of 1980 and 1990 confirmed the fact that U.S.-born Japanese and Chinese men came closest to parity with white men with respect to individual income. Japanese and Chinese women have significantly lower income than white women. The rest of those Asian men and women continued to have lower incomes than those of whites, Japanese, and Chinese. One explanation seemed to have suggested that Asians as a group valued education and scholastic achievement or individual effort, known as the *human capital theory* (Becker 1975). But within various Asian subgroups, the disturbing question is why some Asian immigrants attained higher income than others in the same ethnic group. Here both Becker's *human capital* and the *labor market segmentation* explanations are applicable. The Lahei suggests a two tier wage system prevail (see Cabezas, Shinagawa, and Kawaguchi 1986–1987; Bonacich 1975, 1988, 1992).

Perhaps a third explanation of the differential pace of status attainment came from some writings about the Filipino immigrant-labor market structure that related to the manner in which newcomers came to join their kin-relatives. The so-called "network recruitment" tended to form clusters in the same occupation area, resembling the earlier immigration patterns of Chinese in California (who came from four or five villages in Guangdong Province) and Japanese farm workers (who were recruited from southern prefectures of Japan).

Unlike blacks and Native Americans, Asian Americans varied significantly in terms of language proficiency, which had an enormous impact on income and the kinds of occupations in which they tended to cluster together. Barry Chiswick

(1974) has demonstrated that English proficiency is a major factor in income parity. P.G. Min (1986) showed that Filipino and Korean immigrants, an even match for income, engage in quite different occupations. Koreans engage in business but Filipinos do not. Min pointed out that the language barrier forces Koreans to be self-employed, no matter how hazardous their business turns out to be. Furthermore, it was Korean immigrants' linkage to industrial development in Korea that led to the development of some of the Korean communities in the United States. Filipino communities, on the other hand, did not develop similar enterprises to form a visible ethnic enclave in America. Instead, they depended more on ethnic professional societies and trade associations as basis of ethnic cohesion.

The same rationale was also applied in the case of "new" Chinatown studies. The earlier descriptive studies of Chinatown either over-romanticized the exotic quality of an ethnic enclave, or highlighted the worst side of humanity. To see Chinatown as a unique economic system is perhaps a new approach that is not without controversy. Zhou (1992), herself a new immigrant scholar from China, took the conceptual framework of her major advisor A. Portes, and wrote and published her dissertation on New York's Chinatown. She ably showed how a separate economic system had developed and embedded in urban America. Zhou's book on Chinatown is refreshingly different from several other volumes on the same topic published between the latter part of the 1970s to the early part of the 1990s that continued to portray patterns of conflict and cleavage (Wong 1977; Kuo 1977; Kwon 1987; Kinkead 1992).

The rise of Asian-American Studies programs, either as a part of multicultural or ethnic studies, or as an independent program, certainly has been instrumental in the increasing research and number of publications that deal with Asian-American communities. Given the interdisciplinary nature of the field, the multitudes of topics to be covered, and the unusual personal experiences of writers, the uneven quality of these publications is expected and sometimes unavoidable. Among studies on new communities, on income and status attainment, and on racial and ethnic relations, there appeared to be a genuine effort to formulate theoretically applicable concepts, and to use existing theories and models, which compared to fairly

good and important descriptive studies of an earlier era, both before and after World War II. A good example is the analysis of the Korean rotating credit associations in Los Angeles (Light, Kwuon, and Zhong 1990), in which the authors examined the functions of financing and savings groups based on informal trust in Korean business communities.

The most noticeable achievement of the Asian-American Studies programs in the 1970s through the 1990s is the abundant effort to compile important bibliographies, by searching for research materials that are normally scattered through scientific journals, unpublished files, doctoral and masters' dissertations, working papers, diaries, and conference proceedings. The federal government is credited with making bibliographies on Indochinese refugees, either through the U.S. Government Printing Office, or at the University of Minnesota Southeast Asian Refugee Studies Project (see references at the end of this section). Finally, the rise of Asian-American Studies programs increased efforts to establish libraries and documentation centers in a number of universities throughout the country.

REFERENCES

Agarwal, Priya 1991 *Passage from India: Post 1965 Indian Immigrants and Their Children*. Palos Verdes, Calif.: Yavati Publishers.

Becker, G. S. 1975 *Human Capital*. Chicago: University of Chicago Press.

Beiser, Morton 1987, "Changing Time Perspective and Mental Health among Southeast Asian Refugees." *Culture, Medicine & Psychiatry* 11(4):437–464.

—— 1988 "Influence of Time, Ethnicity, and Attachment on Depression in Southeast Asian Refugees." *American Journal of Psychiatry* 145(1):46–51.

Boehnlein, J. K. 1987 "Clinical Relevance of Grief and Mourning Among Cambodian Refugees." *Social Science and Medicine* 25:765–772.

Cabezas, A. L., H. Shinagawa, and G. Kawaguchi 1986–1987 "New Inquiries into the Socioeconomic Status of Filipino Americans in California. *Amerasia* 12(1):21.

Caces, Fe Immigrant Recruitment into the Labor Force: Social Networks Among Filipinos in Hawaii, AA 12:23–38.

Chan, Sucheng (ed.) 1994 *Hmong Means Free: Life in Laos and America*. Philadelphia: Temple University Press.

Chiswick, Barry 1974 *Income Inequality*.

Chuong, Chung Hoang 1987 *The Vietnam Conflict and the Vietnamese in the U.S.: A Bibliography*. Berkeley Calif: University of California Press.

ERIC Clearinghouse on Urban Education 1988 *"Asian/ Pacific American Education. Brief Bibliographies,"* March, 1988.

Espirita, Yen Le 1922 *Asian American Panethnicity: Bridging Institutions and Identities*. Philadelphia: Temple University Press.

Fadiman, Anne *The Spirit Catches You and You Fall Down*. New York: The Noonday Press.

Freeman, James M. 1984 *Hearts of Sorrow: Vietnamese American Lives*. Stanford, Calif.: Stanford University Press.

Fugita, S., and J. O'Brien *Japanese American Ethnicity: The Persistence of a Community*. Seattle: The University of Washington Press.

Gold, Steven J. 1992 *Refugee Communities: A Comparative Study*. Newbury Park, Calif.: Sage Publications.

Haines, D.W. 1989 "Southeast Asian Refugee Resettlement in the United States and Canada." *Amerasia Journal* 15(2):141–156.

—— (ed) 1989b *Refugees as Immigrants: Cambodians, Laotians, and Vietnamese in America*. Totowa, N.J.: Rowman and Littlefield.

Hammond, R. E., and G. L. Hendricks 1988 *Southeast Refugee Youth: An Annotated Bibliography*. Minneapolis University of Minnesota Center for Urban and Regional Affairs.

Ichioka, Juji "Coming of Age: From Rural 30s to Cities." *Amerasia Journal*.

—— "A Study in Dualism: Japanese American Courier: 1928–1942" *Amerasia Journal*.

Japanese American Evacuation and Resettlement Study 1989 *Views from Within*. Los Angeles: UCLA Asian American Studies Center.

Kim, Hyung-chan 1989 *Asian American Studies: An Annotated Bibliography and Research Guide*. Westport, Conn.: Greenwood Press.

Kinkead, Gwen 1992 *Chinatown: A Portrait of a Closed Society*.

Kuo, Chia-liong 1977 *Social and Political Change in New York's Chinatown*. New York: New York University Press.

Kwong, Peter 1987 *New Chinatown*.

Light, Ivan, and Edna Bonacich 1988 *Immigrant Entrepreneurs: Koreans in Los Angeles, 1965–1982*. Berkeley, Calif.: University of California Press.

Light, I. M., J. Kwuon, and D. Zhong "Korean Rotating Credit Association in Los Angeles." *Amerasia* 16(2):35–54.

Light, I., and A. A. Sanchez 1987 "Immigrant Entrepreneurs in 272 SMSAs." *Sociological Perspectives* 30(4):373–399.

Liu, William T., Maryanne Lamanna, and Alice Murata 1979 *Transitions to Nowhere: Vietnamese Refugees in America*. Nashville, Tenn: The Charter House Publishers.

Marston, J. 1987 *An Annotated Bibliography of Cambodia and Cambodian Refugees*. Minneapolis: University of Minnesota Center for Urban and Regional Affairs.

Min, Pyong Gap 1989 "Textbooks for Asian American Studies: A Review Essay." *Amerasia* 15(1):259–266.

—— 1988 *Ethnic Business Enterprise: Korean Small Business in Atlanta*. New York: Center for Migration Studies.

—— 1986–1987 "Filipino and Korean Immigrants in Small Business: A Comparative Analysis." *Amerasia* 12:53–71.

Miyamoto, A. S. 1988 "Problems of Interpersonal Style Among Nisei: From Self Restraint to Self Expression." *Amerasia* 13:29–45.

Mollicca, R. F., G. Wyshak, and J. Lavelle 1987 "The Psychosocial Impact of War Trauma and Torture on Southeast Asian Refugees." *American Journal of Psychiatry* 144(12):1567–1572.

Montepio, S. N. 1989 "Folk Medicine in the Filipino American Experience." *Amerasia* 13(1):151–162.

—— 1987–1988 "Magical Medicine and the Filipino Healer: Floklore and Mythology Studies. 11, 12:36–46.

National/Pacific Asian Resources Center 1988 *On Aging: Annotated Bibliography*. Seattle: National Pacific Asian Resources Center.

Pido, Antonio J. A. 1986 Center for Migration Studies: New York. *The Filipinos in America: Macro/Micro Dimensions of Immigration and Integration*.

Radhakrishnan R. 1996 *Diasporic Mediations: Between Home and Location*. St. Paul: University of Minnesota Press.

Sawada, Mitziko "After the Camps: Seabrook Farms, N.J. and the Resettlement of Japanese Americans, 1944–1947. *Amerasia*.

Shin, H. E., and K. S. Chang 1988 "Peripherization of Immigrant Professionals: The Case of Korean Physicians in the United States."*International Migration Review* 22:4 609–626.

Smith, J. C. 1988 *The Hmong, An Annotated Bibliography, 1983–1987*. Minneapolis University of Minnesota Southeast Asian Refugee Studies Project.

Southeast Asian Asian Refugee Studies Project 1983 *Bibliography of Hmongs*. Minneapolis: University of Minnesota Press.

U.S. Government Printing Office 1989 *An Annotated Bibliography on Refugee Mental Health*. Washington, D.C.: U.S. Government Printing Office.

Warren, W. H. 1989 "Maps: A spacial Approach to Japanese American Communities in Los Angeles." *Amerasia* 13:137–151.

Wong, Bernard 1987 "The Role of Ethnicity in Enclave Enterprises: A Study of the Chinese Garment Factories in New York City." *Human Organization* 46(2):120–130.

—— 1988 *Patronage, Brokerage, Entrepreneurship and the Chinese Community of New York*. New York: AMS Press.

—— 1977 *Chinese American Community*.

Wong, Paul, Meora Manvi, and Takeo Hirota Wong 1998 "Asiacentrism and Asian American Studies?" *Amerasia*. 21 (1, 2):137–147.

Yochum, G., and V. Agarwal 1988 "Permanent Labor Certifications for Alien Professionals, 1975–1982". *International Migration Review* 22(2):365–381.

—— 1983 "Korean Communities in America: Past, Present, and Future." *Amerasia* 10(2):23–51.

Yu, Elena, and William T. Liu 1992 "U.S. National Health Data on Asian/Pacific Islanders: A Research Agenda for the 1990s." *American Journal of Public Health* 82:12.

Zhou, M. 1992 *Chinatown: The Socioeconomic Potentials of An Urban Enclave*. Philadelphia: Temple University Press.

WILLIAM T. LIU
ELENA S. H. YU

ASSIMILATION

See Ethnicity.

ATHEISM

See Religious Orientations.

ATTITUDES

Attitude "is probably the most distinctive and indispensable concept in contemporary American social psychology" (Allport 1985, p. 35). Hundreds of books and thousands of articles have been published on the topic. A review of this literature may be found in Eagly and Chaiken (1998). Despite this popularity, there is considerable disagreement about such basics as terminology. Several terms are frequently used as synonyms for attitude, including *opinion* and *belief*. Contemporary writers often distinguish attitudes from *cognitions*, which is broader and includes attitudes as well as perceptions of one's environment. Most analysts distinguish attitude from *value*, the latter referring to a person's ultimate concerns or preferred modes of conduct.

An attitude is a learned predisposition to respond to a particular object in a generally favorable or unfavorable way. Every attitude is about an object, and the object may be a person, product, idea, or event. Each attitude has three components: (1) a belief, (2) a favorable or unfavorable evaluation, and (3) a behavioral disposition. This definition is used by most contemporary writers. However, a small minority define attitude as consisting only of the positive or negative evaluation of an object.

A *stereotype* is one type of attitude. Originally, the term referred to a rigid and simplistic "picture in the head." In current usage, a stereotype is a belief about the characteristics of members of some specified social group. A stereotype may be positive (Asian Americans are good at math) or negative (women are bad at math). Most stereotypes are resistant to change.

Attitudes link the person to other individuals, groups, and social organizations and institutions. Each person has literally hundreds of attitudes, one for each significant object in the person's physical and social environment. By implication, the individual's attitudes should reflect his or her location in society. Thus, attitudes are influenced by gender, race, religion, education, and social class. Considerable research on the relationship between social position and attitudes has been carried out; this literature is reviewed by Kiecolt (1988).

ATTITUDE FORMATION

Many attitudes are learned through direct experience with the object. Attitudes toward one's school, job, church, and the groups to which one belongs are examples. Attitudes toward the significant persons in one's life are also learned in this way. More often, attitudes are learned through interactions with others. Socialization by parents, explicit teaching in educational and religious settings, and interactions with friends are important sources of attitudes. Research shows that children's attitudes toward a variety of objects, including gender roles and political issues, are similar to those held by their parents.

Another source of attitudes is the person's observations of the world. A topic of continuing interest is the impact of mass media on the attitudes (and behavior) of users. A thorough review of the literature on this topic (Roberts and Maccoby 1985) concludes that television viewing affects both children's and adolescents' attitudes about gender roles. Further, the viewing of programs intentionally designed to teach positive attitudes toward racial or ethnic minorities does increase children's acceptance of such persons. With regard to adults, evidence supports the "agenda setting" hypothesis; the amount and quality of coverage by the media (press, radio, and television) of an issue influences the public's perception of the importance of that issue. The effects of mass media exposure on aggression are discussed by Felson (1996) and Geen (1998).

Stereotypes are also learned. A stereotype may arise out of direct experience with a member of the stereotyped group, for example, a person who encounters a musically talented black person may create a stereotype by overgeneralizing, inferring that all African Americans are gifted musically. More often, however, stereotypes are learned from those with whom we interact such as parents. Other stereotypes may be acquired from books, television, or film. Research indicates that television programming portrays women, the elderly, and members of some ethnic minorities in negative ways and that these portrayals create (or reinforce) misperceptions and negative stereotypes in viewers (McGuire 1985).

Social institutions influence the attitudes one learns in several ways. Adults' ties to particular ethnic, religious, and other institutions influence the attitudes they teach their children. The instruction given in schools reflects the perspectives of the dominant political and economic institutions in society. The amount and quality of media coverage of people and events reflects the interests of particular groups in society. Through these mechanisms, the individual's attitudes reflect the society, institutions, and groups of which she or he is a member.

Each attitude fulfills one or more of four functions for the individual. First, some attitudes serve an instrumental function: An individual develops favorable attitudes toward objects that aid or reward the individual and unfavorable attitudes toward objects that thwart or punish the individual. For example, a person who earns a large salary will have a positive attitude toward the job. Second, attitudes often serve a knowledge function. They provide the person with a meaningful and structured environment. Third, some attitudes express the individual's basic values and reinforce self-image. Whites' attitudes toward black Americans reflect the importance that whites place on the values of freedom and equality. Fourth, some attitudes protect the person from recognizing certain thoughts or feelings that threaten his or her self-image or adjustment.

Stereotypes also serve several functions. The act of classifying oneself as a member of a group (males, Republicans, whites) elicits the image of a contrasting group (females, Democrats, Latinos). Thus, stereotypes contribute to social identity. They also reduce the demands on the perceiver to process information about individual members of a stereotyped group; instead, one can rely on a stereotype. Finally, stereotypes may be used to justify the political and economic status quo.

ATTITUDE MEASUREMENT

Because attitudes are mental states, they cannot be directly observed. Social scientists have developed a variety of methods for measuring attitudes, some direct and some indirect.

Direct Methods. These methods involve asking the person questions and recording the answers. Direct methods include various rating scales and several sophisticated scaling techniques.

The three most frequently used rating scales are single item, Likert scales, and the semantic differential. The *single-item scale* usually consists of a direct positive or negative statement about the object, and the respondent indicates whether he or she agrees, disagrees, or is unsure. Such a measure is easy to score, but is not precise. A *Likert scale* typically involves several statements, and the respondent is asked to indicate the degree to which she or he agrees or disagrees with each. By analyzing differences in the pattern of responses across respondents, the investigator can order individuals from greatest agreement to greatest disagreement. Whereas Likert scales assess the denotative (literal) meaning of an object to a respondent, the *semantic differential* technique assesses the connotative (personal) meaning of the object. Here, an investigator presents the respondent with a series of bipolar adjective scales. Each of these is a scale whose poles are two adjectives having opposite meanings, for example, good–bad, exciting–boring. The respondent rates the attitude object, such as "my job," on each scale. After the data are collected, the researcher can analyze them by various statistical techniques.

A variety of more sophisticated scaling techniques have been developed. These typically involve asking a series of questions about a class of objects, for example, occupations, crimes, or political figures, and then applying various statistical techniques to arrive at a summary measure. These include magnitude techniques (e.g., the Thurstone scale), interlocking techniques (e.g., the Guttman scale), proximity techniques (e.g., smallest space analysis), and the unfolding technique developed by Coombs. None of these has been widely used.

Indirect Methods. Direct methods assume that people will report honestly their attitudes toward the object of interest. But when questions deal with sensitive issues, such as attitudes toward members of minority groups or abortion, respondents may not report accurately. In an attempt to avoid such reactivity, investigators have developed various indirect methods.

Some methods involve keeping respondents unaware of what is being measured. The "lost letter" technique involves dropping letters in public areas and observing the behavior of the person who finds it. The researcher can measure attitudes toward abortion by addressing one-half of the letters to a prochoice group and the other half to a prolife group. If a greater percentage of letters to the latter group are returned, it suggests people have prolife attitudes. Another indirect measure of attitude is pupil dilation, which increases when the person observes an object she or he likes and decreases when the object is disliked.

Some indirect measures involve deceiving respondents. A person may be asked to sort a large number of statements into groups, and the individual's attitude may be inferred from the number or type of categories used. Similarly, a respondent may be asked to write statements characterizing other people's beliefs on an issue, and the content and extremity of the respondent's statements are used to measure his or her own attitude. A third technique is the "bogus pipeline." This involves attaching the person with electrodes to a device and telling the person that the device measures his or her true attitudes. The respondent is told that some signal, such as a blinking light, pointer, or buzzer, will indicate the person's real attitude, then the person is asked direct questions.

While these techniques may reduce inaccurate reporting, some of them yield measures whose meaning is not obvious or is of questionable validity. Does mailing a letter reflect one's attitude toward the addressee or the desire to help? There is also evidence that measures based on these techniques are not reliable. Finally, some researchers believe it is unethical to use techniques that involve deception. Because of the importance of obtaining reliable and valid measures, research has been carried out on how to ask questions. This research is reviewed by Schuman and Presser (1996).

For a comprehensive discussion of attitude measurement techniques and issues, see Dawes and Smith (1985).

ATTITUDE ORGANIZATION

An individual's attitude toward some object usually is not an isolated psychological unit. It is embedded in a cognitive structure and linked with a variety of other attitudes. Several theories of attitude organization are based on the assumption that individuals prefer consistency among the elements of cognitive structure, that is, among attitudes and perceptions. Two of these are balance theory and dissonance theory.

Balance Theory. Balance theory, developed by Heider, is concerned with cognitive systems composed of two or three elements. The elements can be either persons or objects. Consider the statement "I will vote for Mary Sweeney; she supports parental leave legislation." This system contains three elements—the speaker, P; another person (candidate Mary Sweeney), O; and an impersonal object (parental leave legislation), X. According to balance theory, two types of relationships may exist between elements. *Sentiment relations* refer to sentiments or evaluations directed toward objects and people; a sentiment may be either positive (liking, endorsing) or negative (disliking, opposing). *Unit relations* refer to the extent of perceived association between elements. For example, a positive unit relation may result from ownership, a relationship (such as friendship or marriage), or causality. A negative relation indicates dissociation, like that between ex-spouses or members of groups with opposing interests. A null relation exists when there is no association between elements.

Balance theory is concerned with the elements and their interrelations from P's viewpoint. In the example, the speaker favors parental leave legislation, perceives Mary Sweeney as favoring it, and intends to vote for her. This system is balanced. By definition, a *balanced state* is one in which all three relations are positive or in which one is positive and the other two are negative. An *imbalanced state* is one in which two of the relationships between elements are positive and one is negative or in which all three are negative. For example, "I love (+) Jane; Jane loves (+) opera; I hate (-) opera" is imbalanced.

The theory assumes that an imbalanced state is unpleasant and that when one occurs, the person will try to restore balance. There is considerable empirical evidence that people do prefer balanced states and that attitude change often occurs in response to imbalance. Furthermore, people maintain consistency by responding selectively to new information. There is evidence that people accept information consistent with their existing attitudes and reject information inconsistent with their cognitions. This is the major mechanism by which stereotypes are maintained.

Dissonance Theory. Dissonance theory assumes that there are three possible relationships between any two cognitions. Cognitions are consistent, or *consonant*, if one naturally or logically follows from the other; they are *dissonant* when one implies the opposite of the other. The logic involved is psycho logic—logic as it appears to the individual, not logic in a formal sense. Two cognitive elements may also be irrelevant; one may have nothing to do with the other.

Cognitive dissonance is a state of psychological tension induced by dissonant relationships between cognitive elements. There are three situations in which dissonance commonly occurs. First, dissonance occurs following a decision whenever the decision is dissonant with some cognitive elements. Thus, choice between two (or more) attractive alternatives creates dissonance because knowledge that one chose A is dissonant with the positive features of B. The magnitude of the dissonance experienced is a function of the proportion of elements consonant and dissonant with the choice. Second, if a person engages in a behavior that is dissonant with his or her attitudes, dissonance will be created. Third, when events disconfirm an important belief, dissonance will be created if the person had taken action based on that belief. For example, a person who buys an expensive car in anticipation of a large salary increase will experience dissonance if she or he does not receive the expected raise.

Since dissonance is an unpleasant state, the theory predicts that the person will attempt to reduce it. Usually, dissonance reduction involves changes in the person's attitudes. Thus, following a decision, the person may evaluate the chosen alternative more favorably and the unchosen one more negatively. Following behavior that is dissonant with his or her prior attitude, the person's attitude toward the behavior may become more positive. An alternative mode of dissonance reduction is to change the importance one places on one or more of the attitudes. Following a decision, the person may reduce the importance of the cognitions that are dissonant with the choice; this is the well-known "sour grapes" phenomenon. Following disconfirmation of a belief, one may increase the importance attached to the disconfirmed belief. A third way to reduce dissonance is to change behavior. If the dissonance following a choice is great, the person may decide to choose B instead of A. Following disconfirmation, the person may change behaviors that were based on the belief.

Numerous books and hundreds of articles about dissonance theory have been published since it was introduced by Festinger in 1957. There is a substantial body of research evidence that supports various predictions from and elaborations of the theory. Taken together, this literature has produced a detailed taxonomy of situations that produce dissonance and of preferred modes of dissonance reduction in various types of situations.

ATTITUDE STABILITY AND ATTITUDE CHANGE

Both balance and dissonance theories identify the desire for consistency as a major source of stability and change in attitudes. The desire to maintain consistency leads the individual either to interpret new information as congruent with his or her existing cognitions (assimilation) or to reject it if it would challenge existing attitudes (contrast). This process is very important in preserving stability in one's attitudes. At the same time, the desire for consistency will lead to attitude change when imbalance or dissonance occurs. Dissonance theory explicitly considers the link between behavior and attitudes. It predicts that engaging in counterattitudinal behavior may indirectly affect attitudes. This is one mechanism by which social influences on behavior may indirectly affect attitudes. This mechanism comes into play when the person experiences changes in roles and the requirements of the new role are inconsistent with his or her prior attitudes.

The classic perspective in the study of attitude change is the *communication–persuasion paradigm*, which grew out of the work by Hovland and his colleagues at Yale University. *Persuasion* is defined as changing the beliefs or attitudes of a person through the use of information or argument. Attempts at persuasion are widespread in everyday interaction, and the livelihood of advertisers and political consultants. According to the paradigm, each attempt involves source, message, target, and context. Thousands of empirical studies, many of them experiments done in laboratory settings, have investigated the influence of variations in these four components on the outcome of an attempt. In general, if the source is perceived as an expert, trustworthy, or physically attractive, the message is more likely to produce attitude change.

Thus, it is no accident that magazine and television commercials feature young, attractive models. Message variables include the extent of discrepancy from the target's attitude, whether it arouses fear, and whether it presents one or both sides. Under certain conditions, highly discrepant, fear-arousing, and one-sided messages are more effective. Target factors include intelligence, self-esteem, and prior experience and knowledge. The most researched contextual factor is mood. For a review of this research, see Perloff (1993).

In the 1990s considerable work built upon the *elaboration–likelihood model* proposed by Petty and Cacioppo (1986). This model identifies two basic routes through which a message may change a target's attitudes: the central and the peripheral. Persuasion via the *central route* occurs when a target scrutinizes the arguments contained in the message, interprets and evaluates them, and integrates them into a coherent position. This process is termed *elaboration*. In elaboration, attitude change occurs when the arguments are strong, internally coherent, and consistent with known facts. Persuasion via the *peripheral route* occurs when, instead of elaborating the message, the target pays attention primarily to extraneous cues linked to the message. Among these cues are characteristics of the source (expertise, trustworthiness, attractiveness), superficial characteristics of the message such as length, or characteristics of the context such as response of other audience members. Several factors influence whether elaboration occurs. One is the target's involvement with the issue; if the target is highly involved with and cares about the issue addressed by the message, he or she is more likely to elaborate the message. Other factors include whether the target is distracted by noise or some other aspect of the situation, and whether the target is tired. Which route a message elicits in attitude change is important. Attitudes established by the central route tend to be more strongly held and more resistant to change because the target has thought through the issue in more detail.

The literature on attitude change flourished in the 1990s. The effects of many variables have been studied experimentally. A review of the research conducted in 1992 to 1995 concluded that any one variable may have multiple effects, depending upon other aspects of the persuasion attempt (Petty, Wegener, and Fabrigar 1997). For example, consider the effect of mood on attitude change. Assuming that happy people are more open to new information, one might predict that persuasive messages would lead to greater attitude change in happy persons than in sad ones. However, research indicates that happy people spend less time processing persuasive messages than persons in neutral moods, and so may be less influenced by them. The *hedonic contingency* hypothesis states that the effect of mood depends upon the hedonic tone of the message. Happy people want to maintain their happy mood, so they are likely to scrutinize and process happy messages but not sad ones. Sad people often want to change their mood, and most messages will improve it, so their processing is not affected by messages' hedonic tone. The results of two experiments support the hypothesis (Wegener, Petty, and Smith 1995). Thus, the effect of mood on persuasion depends on whether the message is uplifting or depressing.

ATTITUDE–BEHAVIOR RELATION

The attitude–behavior relation has been the focus of considerable research since the early 1970s. This research has identified a number of variables that influence the extent to which one can predict a person's behavior from his or her attitudes.

Some of these variables involve the measurement of the attitude and of the behavior. The correspondence of the two measures is one such variable: one can predict behavior more accurately if the two measures are at the same level of specificity. An opinion poll can predict the outcome of an election because there is high correspondence between the attitude ("Which candidate do you prefer for mayor in next month's election?") and the behavior (voting for a candidate in that election). The length of time between the measure of attitude and the occurrence and measure of the behavior is also an important variable. The shorter the time, the stronger the relationship. The longer the elapsed time, the more likely the person's attitude will change, although some attitudes are stable over long periods, for example, twenty years.

The characteristics of the attitude also influence the degree to which one can predict behavior from it. In order for an attitude to influence behavior, it must be activated, that is, brought from memory into conscious awareness. An attitude is usually activated by a person's exposure to the attitude object. Attitudes vary in *accessibility*, the ease with which they are activated. The more accessible an attitude is, the more likely it is to guide future behavior (Kraus 1995). Another variable is the source of the attitude. Attitudes based on direct experience with the object are more predictive of behavior. The certainty or confidence with which the person holds the attitude also moderates the attitude–behavior relationship.

The attitude–behavior relation is also influenced by situational constraints—the social norms governing behavior in a situation. An attitude is more likely to be expressed in behavior when the behavior is consistent with these norms.

An important attempt to specify the relationship between attitude and behavior is the *theory of reasoned action*, developed by Fishbein and Ajzen (1975). According to this theory, behavior is determined by behavioral intention. Behavioral intention is determined by two factors: attitude and subjective norm. Attitude is one's beliefs about the likely consequences of the behavior and one's evaluation—positive or negative—of each of those outcomes. Subjective norm is the person's belief about other important persons' or groups' reactions to the behavior and the person's motivation to comply with the expectations of each. One of the strengths of the theory is this precise specification of the influences on behavioral intention. It is possible to measure quantitatively each of the four components (likely consequences, evaluation, likely reactions, motivation to comply) and use these to make precise predictions of behavior. Many empirical studies report results consistent with such predictions. The theory applies primarily to behavior that is under conscious, volitional control.

On the other hand, researchers have shown that attitudes can affect behavior without being brought into conscious awareness (Bargh 1996). Attitudes toward objects influence our judgments and behavior toward those objects without conscious awareness or intent. Stereotypes of social groups are often activated automatically, as soon as an individual is perceived as a member of the group. Automatic processing is more likely when the individual experiences information overload, time pressures, or is not interested in engaging in effortful processing.

ATTITUDE AS INDICATOR

Increasingly, attitudes are employed as indicators. Some researchers use attitude measures as indicators of concepts, while others study changes in attitudes over time as indicators of social change.

Indicators of Concepts. Measures of specific attitudes are frequently used as indicators of more general concepts. For example, agreement with the following statement is interpreted as an indicator of powerlessness: "This world is run by the few people in power, and there is not much the little guy can do about it." Powerlessness is considered to be a general orientation toward the social world and is a sense that one has little or no control over events. Feelings of powerlessness may be related to such varied behaviors as vandalism, not voting in elections, and chronic unemployment.

Attitude measures have been used to assess many other concepts used in the analysis of political attitudes and behavior. These include the liberalism–conservatism dimension, political tolerance (of radical or unpopular groups), trust in or disaffection with national institutions, and relative deprivation. (For a review of this literature, see Kinder and Sears 1985.) Attitude measures are used to assess many other characteristics of persons. In the realm of work these include occupational values, job satisfaction, and leadership style.

A major concern when attitudes are employed as indicators is *construct validity*, that is, whether the specific items used are valid measures of the underlying concept. In the powerlessness example, the connection between the content of the item and the concept may seem obvious, but even in cases like this it is important to demonstrate validity. A variety of analytic techniques may be used, including interitem correlations, factor analysis, and LISREL.

Indicators of Social Change. Two methodological developments have made it possible to use attitudes to study social change. The first was the development of probability sampling techniques, which allow the investigator to make inferences about the characteristics of a population from the results obtained by surveying a sample of that population. The second is the use of the same attitude measures in surveys of representative samples at two or more points in time.

A major source of such data is the General Social Survey (GSS), an annual survey of a probability sample of adults. The GSS repeats a core set of items on a roughly annual basis, making possible the study of changes over a period of thirty years. Many of these items were drawn directly from earlier surveys, making comparisons over a forty- or fifty-year timespan possible. A published book describes these items and presents the responses obtained each time the item was used (Niemi, Mueller, and Smith 1989). Other sources of such data include the National Election Studies and the Gallup Polls.

This use of attitude items reflects a general concern with social change at the societal level. The investigator uses aggregate measures of attitudes in the population as an index of changes in cultural values and social institutions. Two areas of particular interest are attitudes toward race and gender roles. In both areas, efforts have been made to improve access to educational programs, jobs, and professions, increase wages and salaries, and provide greater opportunity for advancement. The availability of responses to the same attitude items over time allows us to assess the consistency between these social changes and attitudes in the population. Consider the question "Do you think civil rights leaders are trying to push too fast, are going too slowly, or are moving at about the right speed?" This question was asked in surveys of national samples every two years from 1964 to 1976 and in 1980. The percentage of whites replying "too fast" declined from 74 percent in 1964 to 40 percent in 1980 (Bobo 1988), suggesting increased white support for the black movement. In general, research indicates that both racial and gender-role attitudes became more liberal between 1960 and 1990, and this finding is consistent with the social changes in these areas. Other topics that have been studied include attitudes toward abortion, social class identification, and subjective quality of life.

There are several issues involved in this use of attitude items. The first is the problem of "nonattitudes." Respondents may answer survey questions or endorse statements even though they have no attitude toward the object. In fact, when respondents are questioned about fictional objects or organizations, some of them will express an opinion. Schuman and Kalton (1985) discuss this issue in detail and suggest ways to reduce the extent to which nonattitudes are given by respondents.

The second issue involves the interpretation of responses to items. In the example above, the analyst assumes that white respondents who reply "Too fast" feel threatened by the movement. However, there is evidence that small changes in the wording of survey items can produce substantial changes in aggregate response patterns. This evidence and guidelines for writing survey items are discussed in Schuman and Presser (1996).

Finally, there is the problem of equivalence in meaning over time. In order to make meaningful comparisons across time, the items need to be the same or equivalent. Yet over time the meaning of an item may change. Consider the item "Are you in favor of *desegregation*, strict *segregation*, or something in between?" This question was asked of national samples in 1964 and every two years from 1968 to 1978. From 1964 to 1970, the percentage of white, college-educated adults endorsing desegregation increased; from 1970 to 1978, the percentage decreased steadily. Until 1970, desegregation efforts were focused on the South; after 1970, desegregation efforts focused on school integration in northern cities. Evidence suggests that endorsement of desegregation changed because the meaning of the question for white adults changed (Schuman, Steeh, and Bobo 1985).

REFERENCES

Allport, Gordon W. 1985 "The Historical Background of Social Psychology." In G. Lindzey and E. Aronson, eds., *Handbook of Social Psychology*, 3rd ed. New York: Random House.

Bargh, John A. 1996 "Automaticity in Social Psychology." In E.T. Higgins and A. Kruglanski, eds., *Social Psychology: Handbook of Basic Principles*. New York: The Guilford Press.

Bobo, Lawrence 1988 "Attitudes toward the Black Political Movement: Trends, Meaning, and Effects on Racial Policy Preference." *Social Psychology Quarterly* 51:287–302.

Dawes, Robyn M., and Tom L. Smith 1985 "Attitude and Opinion Measurement." In G.Lindzey and E. Aronson, eds., *Handbook of Social Psychology*, 3rd ed. New York: Random House.

Eagly, Alice, and Shelly Chaiken 1998 "Attitude Structure and Function." In D. T. Gilbert, S. T. Fiske, and G. Lindzey, eds., *Handbook of Social Psychology*, 4th ed. New York: McGraw-Hill.

Felson, Richard B. 1996 "Mass Media Effects on Violent Behavior." In J. Hagen and K. Cook, eds., *Annual Review of Sociology*, vol. 22. Palo Alto, Calif.: Annual Reviews.

Festinger, Leon 1957 *A Theory of Cognitive Dissonance.* Stanford, Calif.: Stanford University Press.

Fishbein, Martin, and Icek Ajzen 1975 *Belief, Attitude, Intention, and Behavior.* Reading, Mass.: Addison-Wesley.

Geen, Russel 1998 "Aggression and Antisocial Behavior." In D. T. Gilbert, S. T. Fiske, and G. Lindzey, eds., *Handboook of Social Psychology*, 4th ed. New York: McGraw-Hill.

Kiecolt, K. Jill 1988 "Recent Developments in Attitudes and Social Structure." In W. R. Scott and J. Blake. eds., *Annual Review of Sociology*, vol. 14. Palo Alto, Calif.: Annual Reviews.

Kinder, Donald R., and David O. Sears 1985 "Public Opinion and Political Action." In G. Lindzey and E. Aronson, eds., *Handbook of Social Psychology*, 3rd ed. New York: Random House.

Kraus, S.J. 1995 "Attitudes and the Prediction of Behavior: A Meta-Analysis of the Emperical Literature." *Personality and Social Psychology Bulletin* 18:152–162.

McGuire, William J. 1985 "Attitudes and Attitude Change." In G. Lindzey and E. Aronson, eds., *Handbook of Social Psychology*, 3rd ed. New York: Random House.

Niemi, Richard G., John Mueller, and Tom W. Smith 1989 *Trends in Public Opinion: A Compendium of Survey Data.* New York: Greenwood Press.

Perloff, R. M. 1993 *The Dynamics of Persuasion.* Hillsdale, N.J.: Lawrence Erlbaum.

Petty, Richard, and John Cacioppo 1986 "The Elaboration–Likelihood Model of Persuasion." *Advances in Experimental Social Psychology* 19:123–205.

Petty, Richard, Duane Wegener, and Leandre Fabrigan 1997 "Attitudes and Attitude Change." *Annual Review of Psychology* 48:609–647.

Roberts, Donald F., and Nathan Maccoby 1985 "Effects of Mass Communication." In G. Lindzey and E. Aronson, eds., *Handbook of Social Psychology*, 3rd ed. New York: Random House.

Schuman, Howard 1995 "Attitudes, Beliefs, and Behavior." In K. S. Cook, G. A. Finc, and J. S. House, eds., *Sociological Perspectives on Social Psychology*. Boston: Allyn and Bacon.

——, and Stanley Presser 1996 *Questions and Answers in Attitude Surveys.* Thousand Oaks, Calif.: Sage Publications.

Schuman, Howard, and Graham Kalton 1985 "Survey Methods." In G. Lindzey and E. Aronson, eds., *Handbook of Social Psychology*, 3rd ed. New York: Random House.

Schuman, Howard, Charlotte Steeh, and Lawrence Bobo 1985 *Racial Attitudes in America*. Cambridge, Mass.: Harvard University Press.

Wegener, Duane T., Richard E. Petty, and Stephen M. Smith 1995 "Positive Mood can Increase or Decrease Message Scrutiny: The Hedonic Contingency View of Mood and Message Processing." *Journal of Personality and Social Psychology* 69:5–15.

JOHN D. DELAMATER

ATTRIBUTION THEORY

Attribution is a cognitive process that entails linking an event to its causes. Attribution is one of a variety of cognitive inferences that are included within social cognition, which is one of several theoretical models within social psychology. Social cognition has been the most dominant social psychological perspective within psychology since the 1960s, and this is evident in the popularity of research on attribution. In the mid-1970s, as much as 50 percent of the articles in major social psychology journals concerned attributional processes, in part because attribution theory is relevant to the study of person perception, event perception, attitude change, the acquisition of self-knowledge, and a host of applied topics including therapeutic interventions, close relationships, legal and medical decision making, and so forth. Although the proportion of published research that focused on this topic declined during the 1980s, attribution remains one of the more popular fields of social psychological research.

DEFINITION

An attribution is an inference about why an event occurred. More generally, "attribution is a process that begins with social perception, progresses through a causal judgment and social inference, and ends with behavioral consequences" (Crittenden 1983, p. 426). Although most theories of and research on attribution focus on causal inference, empirical research has dealt with attributions not only of cause but also of blame and responsibility. Although these types of attributions are closely related, they are not conceptually identical. Furthermore, because personality characteristics constitute a major category of potential causes of behavior, attributions about individuals' traits (both one's own traits and those of others) have received explicit theoretical attention.

MAJOR THEORIES OF ATTRIBUTION

Even though attribution has been one of the most popular social psychological research topics in the social sciences, only a few theories of attribution have been developed. The study of attribution began with Fritz Heider's (1958) original attempt to provide a systematic, conceptual explanation of "naive" psychology. Heider maintained that people strive to understand, predict, and control events in their everyday lives in much the same way as scientists do in their professional lives. On the basis of observation, individuals form theories about their social worlds, and new observations then serve to support, refute, or modify these theories. Because people act on the basis of their beliefs, Heider argued that it is important to understand this layperson's psychology. Although Heider did not develop an explicit theory of attribution, he did assert several principles that have guided all subsequent theorizing on this topic.

Primary among these principles is the notion that people are inclined to attribute actions to stable or enduring causes rather than to transitory factors. Heider also stressed the importance of distinguishing unintentional from intentional behavior, a distinction that has been particularly influential in theories of the attribution of responsibility. He identified environmental and personal factors as two general classes of factors that produce action and hypothesized that an inverse relationship exists between these two sets of causes. He also suggested that the "covariational principle" is fundamental to attribution: An effect is attributed to a factor that is present when the effect is present and to a factor that is absent when the effect is absent. Heider's early analyses of social perception represent a general conceptual framework about common sense, implicit theories people use in understanding events in their daily lives. The two most influential theories of attribution are based on Heider's work but go beyond it in the development of more systematic statements about attributional processes.

Covariational model. Harold Kelley's (1967, 1973) covariational model of attribution addresses the question of whether a given behavior is caused by an actor or, alternatively, by an environmental stimulus with which the actor engages. According to this model, the attribution of cause is based on three types of information: consensus, distinctiveness, and consistency. Consensus refers to the similarity between the actor's behavior and the behavior of other people in similar circumstances. Distinctiveness refers to the generality of the actor's behavior: Does she or he behave in this way toward stimuli in general, or is the behavior specific to this stimulus? Consistency refers to the actor's behavior toward this stimulus across time and modality. There are many possible combinations of these three types of information, but Kelley makes explicit predictions about just three. The combination of high consensus, high distinctiveness, and high consistency supports an attribution to the environmental stimulus, whereas a profile of low consensus, low distinctiveness, and high consistency supports an attribution to the actor. When the behavior is inconsistent, regardless of the level of consensus or distinctiveness, an attribution to circumstances is predicted.

Empirical tests of Kelley's model have focused either on the effects of a particular type of information or, more in keeping with his formulation, on the effects of particular patterns of information (McArthur 1972). In an innovative analysis, Miles Hewstone and Jos Jaspars (1987) proposed a different logic (although one consistent with Kelley's model), suggesting that potential attributers consider whether different causal loci are necessary and sufficient conditions for the occurrence of an effect. They conclude that the notion of causality is flexible and thus assert that there may be some advantage to conceiving of situation-specific notions of causality. More recent work has examined the universality and external validity of Kelley's model. Irina Anderson and Geoffrey Beattie (1998), for example, analyzed actual conversations between men and women talking about rape. They found that men tended to use the reasoning outlined in Kelley's model by making reference to consensus, distinctiveness, and consistency, as well as by using these types of information to formulate

attributions for behavior. Women, on the other hand, made less use of these variables and introduced the variable of "foreseeability" into their analyses.

Correspondent inference. The theory of correspondent inference (Jones and Davis 1965; Jones and McGillis 1976) addresses the attribution of personality traits to actors on the basis of their behavior and focuses on attributions about persons in greater depth than does Kelley's covariational model. These two theories thus address different questions. Kelley asks: When do we attribute an event to an actor or to some stimulus in the environment? Edward Jones asks: When do we attribute a trait to an actor on the basis of her or his behavior? The theory of correspondent inference focuses more narrowly on the actor but also yields more information about the actor in that it specifies what it is about the actor that caused the behavior. Jones and his coauthors predict that two factors guide attributions: (1) the attributer's prior expectancies for behavior, specifically, expectancies based either on knowledge of earlier behaviors of the actor (target-based) or on the actor's social category memberships (category-based), and (2) the profile of effects that follow from the behavioral choices available to the actor.

Edward Jones and Daniel McGillis propose that expectancies determine the degree of confidence with which a particular trait is attributed; the lower the expectancy of behavior, the more confident the attribution. The profile of effects helps the attributer identify what trait might have produced the behavior in question. Noncommon effects—effects that follow from only one of the behavioral options—provide information about the particular disposition. The fewer the noncommon effects, the clearer the attribution. Thus, behavior that contradicts prior expectancies and a profile of behavioral choices with few noncommon effects combine to maximize the possibility of attributing a disposition to the actor (a correspondent inference). Empirical research generally has supported these predictions.

These two models share some attributional principles. Expectancy variables (target-based and category-based) are analogous to Kelley's types of information. Although the predicted effects of consensus information and its analogue, category-based expectancies, are compatible, the predicted effects of consistency and distinctiveness information and their analogue, target-based expectancies, present some incompatibilities. This contradiction has been evaluated both conceptually and empirically (Howard and Allen 1990).

Attribution in achievement situations. Bernard Weiner (1974) and his colleagues have applied attributional principles in the context of achievement situations. According to this model, we make inferences about an individual's success on the basis of the individual's ability to do the task in question, how much effort is expended, how difficult the task is, and to what extent luck may have influenced the outcome. Other possible causal factors have since been added to this list. More important perhaps is Weiner's development of, first, a structure of causal dimensions in terms of which these causal factors can be described and, second, the implications of the dimensional standing of a given causal factor (Weiner, Russell, and Lerman 1978). The major causal dimensions are locus (internal or external to the actor), stability or instability, and intentionality or unintentionality of the factor. Thus, for example, ability is internal, stable, and unintentional. The stability of a causal factor primarily affects judgments about expectancies for future behavior, whereas locus and intentionality primarily affect emotional responses to behavior. This model has been used extensively in educational research and has guided therapeutic educational efforts such as attribution retraining. Cross-cultural research has explored the cultural generalizability of these models. Paul Tuss, Jules Zimmer, and Hsiu-Zu Ho (1995) and Donald Mizokawa and David Rickman (1990) report, for instance, that Asian and Asian American students are more likely to attribute academic failure and success to effort than are European American students, who are more likely to attribute performance to ability. European American students are also more likely to attribute failure to task difficulty. Interestingly, as Asian Americans spend more time in the United States, they place less emphasis on the role of effort in performance.

Attribution biases. The theoretical models described above are based on the assumption that social perceivers follow the dictates of logical or rational models in assessing causality. Empirical research has demonstrated, not surprisingly, that there are systematic patterns in what has been variously conceived of as bias or error in the attribution process (Ross 1977). Prominent among these is what has been called the "fundamental attribution error," the tendency of perceivers to overestimate the role of dispositional factors in shaping behavior and to underestimate the impact of situational factors. One variant of this bias has particular relevance for sociologists. This is the general tendency to make inadequate allowance for the role-based nature of much social behavior. That is, perceivers fail to recognize that behavior often derives from role memberships rather than from individual idiosyncrasy. Again, cross-cultural research has called into question the generalizability of this bias. Joan Miller (1984) shows that the tendency to attribute behavior to persons is markedly more prominent in the United States, among both adults and children, whereas a tendency to attribute behavior to situational factors is more prominent among Indian Hindus, both adults and children, calling into question the "fundamentalness" of this attributional pattern.

A second systematic pattern is the actor-observer difference, in which actors tend to attribute their own behavior to situational factors, whereas observers of the same behavior tend to attribute it to the actor's dispositions. A third pattern concerns what have been called self-serving or egocentric biases, that is, attributions that in some way favor the self. According to the false consensus bias, for example, we tend to see our own behavioral choices and judgments as relatively common and appropriate whereas those that differ from ours are perceived as uncommon and deviant. There has been heated debate about whether these biases derive from truly egotistical motives or reflect simple cognitive and perceptual errors.

METHODOLOGICAL AND MEASUREMENT ISSUES

The prevalent methodologies and measurement strategies within attributional research have been vulnerable to many of the criticisms directed more generally at social cognition and to some directed specifically at attribution. The majority of attributional research has used structured response formats to assess attributions. Heider's original distinction between person and environmental cause has had a major influence on the development of these structured measures. Respondents typically are asked to rate the importance of situational and dispositional causes of events. These ratings have been obtained on ipsative scales as well as on independent rating scales. Ipsative measures pose these causes as two poles on one dimension; thus, an attribution of cause to the actor's disposition is also a statement that situational factors are not causal. This assumed inverse relationship between situational and dispositional causality has been rejected on conceptual and empirical grounds. In more recent studies, therefore, respondents assign each type of causality separately. (Ipsative measures are appropriate for answering some questions, however, such as whether the attribution of cause to one actor comes at the expense of attribution to another actor or to society.) In theory, then, both dispositional and situational variables could be identified as causal factors.

The breadth of these two categories has also been recognized as a problem. Dispositional causes may include a wide variety of factors such as stable traits and attitudes, unstable moods and emotions, and intentional choices. Situational cause is perhaps an even broader category. It is quite possible that these categories are so broad as to render a single measure of each virtually meaningless. Thus, researchers often include both general and more specific, narrower responses as possible choices (e.g., choices of attributing blame to an assailant or to the situation might be refined to the assailant's use of a weapon, physical size, and psychological state, on the one hand, and the location, time of day, and number of people nearby, on the other).

Structured measures of attributions are vulnerable to the criticism that the categories of causes presented to respondents are not those they use in their everyday attributions. Recognizing this limitation, a few researchers have used open-ended measures. Comparative studies of the relative utility of several different types of measures of causal attributions conclude that scale methods perform somewhat better in terms of their inter-test validity and reliability, although open-ended measures are preferable when researchers are exploring causal attributions in new situations. Some researchers have attempted to overcome some of the limitations of existing scales; Curtis McMillen and Susan Zuravin (1997), for example, have developed and refined "Attributions of Responsibility" and "Blame Scales" for use in clinical research that may be useful for other kinds of attributional situations.

The great majority of attribution studies use stimuli of highly limited social meaning. Generally, the behavior is represented with a brief written vignette, often just a single sentence. Some researchers have shifted to the presentation of visual stimuli, typically with videotaped rather than actual behavioral sequences, in order to ensure comparability across experimental conditions. Recognizing the limitations of brief, noncontextualized stimuli, a few researchers have begun to use a greater variety of more extended stimuli including newspaper reports and published short stories. Most of these stimuli, including the videotaped behavioral sequences, rely heavily on language to convey the meaning of behavior. Conceptual attention has turned recently to how attribution relies on language and to the necessity of considering explicitly what that reliance means. Some researchers (Anderson and Beattie 1998; Antaki and Leudar 1992) have attempted to use more naturalistic approaches, incorporating into the study the analysis of spontaneous conversations among study participants.

WHEN DO WE MAKE ATTRIBUTIONS?

Long after attribution had attained its popularity in social psychology, a question that perhaps should have been raised much earlier began to receive attention: When do we make attributions? To what extent are the attributions in this large body of research elicited by the experimental procedures themselves? This is a question that can be directed to any form of social cognition. It is particularly relevant, however, to attribution. Most people, confronted with a form on which they are to answer the question "Why?," do so. There is no way of knowing, within the typical experimental paradigm, whether respondents would make attributions on their own. In a sense there are two questions: Do people make attributions spontaneously, and if they do, under what circumstances do they do so?

In response to the first question, Weiner (1985) has marshaled impressive evidence that people do indeed make attributions spontaneously. Inventive procedures have been developed for assessing the presence of attributional processing that is not directly elicited. This line of evidence has dealt almost entirely with causal attributions. Research suggests that trait attributions may be made spontaneously much more often than causal attributions. In response to the second question, a variety of studies suggest that people are most likely to make attributions when they encounter unexpected events or events that have negative implications for them.

SOCIOLOGICAL SIGNIFICANCE OF ATTRIBUTION

Attribution is a cognitive process of individuals; much of the extant research on attribution is, accordingly, highly individualistic. In the 1980s, however, researchers began to pay increasing attention to the sociological relevance of attribution. The process of attribution itself is fundamentally social. Attribution occurs not only within individuals but also at the interpersonal, intergroup, and societal levels. Moreover, the process of attribution may underlie basic sociological phenomena such as labeling and stratification.

Interpersonal attribution. At the interpersonal level, attribution is basic to social interaction. Interpersonal encounters are shaped in many ways by attributional patterns. Behavioral confirmation, or self-fulfilling prophecies, illustrate the behavioral consequences of attribution in social interaction; attribution of specific characteristics to social actors creates the expectancies that are then confirmed in behavior. Considering attribution at this interpersonal level demonstrates the importance of different social roles and perspectives (actors vs. observers) as well as how attribution is related to evaluation. The self is also important to the attribution process; the evidence for attributional egotism (self-esteem enhancing attributional biases), self-presentation biases, and egocentrism is persuasive. Attributions also affect social interaction through a widespread confirmatory attribution bias that leads perceivers to conclude that their expectancies have been confirmed in social interaction.

Research has challenged the universality of egocentric biases by examining differences in attributional styles according to race, class, and gender. Several studies (Reese and Brown 1995; Wiley and Crittenden 1992; Broman 1992; Andrews and Brewin 1990) have shown that women

are less likely than men to make self-serving dispositions. In a study of academics' accounts of their success in the profession, Mary Glenn Wiley and Kathleen Crittenden (1992) argue that women explain their success in a more modest manner in order to preserve a feminine identity, at the expense of their professional identities. This attributional style may make it more likely for women to blame themselves for various types of negative situations. Consistent with this reasoning, Bernice Andrews and Chris Brewin (1990) found that female victims of marital violence tended to blame themselves for their experience of violence. Childhood experiences of physical or sexual abuse increased women's chances of characterological self-blame when, as adults, they found themselves in abusive relationships. (Other research, however, notes that the relationship between attributions and adjustment is complex and not always so straightforward; see McMillen and Zuravin 1997.)

Race and class characteristics also create distinct attributional patterns; research on these factors has been more likely than research on gender to consider possible interactive effects on attributions. In a study conducted by Fathali Moghaddam and colleagues (1995) on attributional styles of whites, blacks, and Cubans in Miami, for example, middle-class black respondents were more likely to blame negative outcomes on discrimination than were lower-class blacks. Lower-class whites were the only group to attribute failure to themselves personally.

The great preponderance of research on social interaction has been based on relationships between strangers in experimental contexts, which may seem to undermine the claim that attribution is significant for interpersonal interaction. The best evidence of this significance, then, is the increasingly large body of research on the role of attribution in the formation, maintenance, and dissolution of close relationships. There is substantial evidence that attributions are linked to relationship satisfaction and behaviors such as conflict resolution strategies. There is also evidence that distressed and nondistressed couples make differing attributions for significant events in their relationships; these patterns may actually serve to maintain marital distress among troubled couples, thus ultimately influencing marital satisfaction. Attributions also play an important role in relationship dissolution. Attributions are a critical part of the detailed accounts people provide for the dissolution of their relationships, and these accounts go beyond explanation to rationalize and justify the loss of relationships.

Research on interpersonal attribution extends the intrapersonal approach in several ways. When people who interact have substantial knowledge of and feelings about each other, the attribution process involves evaluation as well as cognition. Issues of communication, and hence potential changes in preexisting attributions for recurrent relationship events, also become salient at the interpersonal level. There is very little research on how attributions change through interaction and relationships, but this is clearly a significant topic. Attributions at the interpersonal level also entail greater concern with accountability for action; causality at this level also raises issues of justification.

Intergroup attribution. Intergroup attribution refers to the ways in which members of different social groups explain the behavior of members of their own and other social groups. At this level, social categorization has a direct impact on attribution. Studies using a variety of subjects from different social groups and often different countries show consistent support for an ingroup-serving attributional pattern, for example, a tendency toward more dispositional attributions for positive as opposed to negative behavior for ingroup actors. The evidence for the converse pattern, more dispositional attributions for negative as opposed to positive behavior for outgroup actors, is not as strong. (Moreover, these patterns are stronger in dominant than in dominated groups.) Social desirability biases can counteract this pattern; Steven Little, Robert Sterling, and Daniel Tingstrom (1996), for example, found that white respondents held black actors less responsible for participating in a bar fight than did black respondents. The authors suggest that this finding may be due to the desire of the white sample—undergraduates from a suburban area—to appear racially progressive.

Parallel studies of a group's success and failure show a consistent pattern of ingroup protection. Outgroup failure is attributed more to lack of ability than is ingroup failure. Effects of group membership on attributions about success are not as strong. Interestingly, there is also some evidence of outgroup-favoring and/or ingroup-derogating attributions among widely recognized lower-status, dominated groups such as migrant labor populations (Hewstone 1989). A third form of evidence of intergroup attribution is provided by studies of attributions about social positions occupied by existing groups. In general, these studies, like those cited above, show higher ratings of ingroup-serving as opposed to outgroup-serving attributions.

Societal attribution. At the societal level, those beliefs shared by the members of a given society form the vocabulary for social attributions. The concept of social representations, which has its origins in Durkheim's concept of "representation collectives," was developed by Serge Moscovici (1976) to represent how knowledge is shared by societal members in the form of common-sense theories about that society. Social representations are intimately connected to the process of attribution. Not only are explanation and accountability part of a system of collective representations, but such representations determine when we seek explanations. Social representations serve as categories that influence the perception and processing of social information; moreover, they underscore the emphasis on shared social beliefs and knowledge. Social representations are useful in interpreting research on laypersons' explanations of societal events such as poverty and wealth, unemployment, and racial inequality. Poverty tends to be attributed to individualistic factors, for example, whereas unemployment tends to be attributed to societal factors. Not surprisingly, these patterns may be qualified by attributors' own class backgrounds; although middle-class people attribute poverty more often to internal factors, those who are themselves poor attribute poverty more often to external factors such as governmental policies (Singh 1989). Gender and racial stereotyping can also shape attributions. Cynthia Willis, Marianne Hallinan, and Jeffrey Melby (1996), for example, found that respondents with a traditional sex-role orientation showed a favorable bias toward the male perpetrator in domestic violence situations. When the female victim was African American and married, both egalitarians and traditionalists were less likely to attribute blame to the man.

Moving away from an emphasis on normative stereotyping, research has considered possible effects of counter-stereotyping on attributional patterns, and of attributions on changes in stereotypes. Portrayals of structurally subordinate groups that counter stereotypical expectations can increase the perceived credibility of members of those groups (Power, Murphy, and Coover 1996). Moreover, an attribution of counterstereotypic behavior to dispositional factors of clearly typical outgroup members can modify outgroup stereotypes (Wilder, Simon, and Faith 1996).

Cross-cultural research illustrates another aspect of societal attributions. This work compares the extent and type of attributional activity across cultures. Although there has been some support for the applicability of Western models of attribution among non-Western cultures, most of this research has demonstrated in a variety of ways the cultural specificity of particular patterns of attribution (Bond 1988). As noted above, for example, Joan Miller (1984) provides cross-cultural empirical evidence that the fundamental attribution error, the tendency to attribute cause more to persons than to situations, is characteristic of Western but not non-Western societies. Attributions about the self also vary across cultures; members of some non-Western cultures attribute performance more to effort than to ability; the opposite pattern has been found in the United States. Cultural patterns also shape responsibility attributions; V. Lee Hamilton and Shigeru Hagiwara (1992) found that U.S. (and male) respondents were more likely to deny responsibility for their own inappropriate behaviors than were Japanese (and female) respondents, who were more likely to apologize for the behaviors. Hamilton and Hagiwara argue that the Japanese (and women) were more concerned with maintaining the quality of the interaction between the accuser and the accused.

SOCIOLOGICAL APPLICATIONS

It may be useful to identify several sociological phenomena to which theories of attribution are relevant. A number of scholars have suggested integrating attribution theory and labeling theory (Crittenden 1983). Attribution occurs within an individual; labels are applied by a group. Judith Howard and Randy Levinson (1985) offer empirical evidence that the process of applying a label is directly analogous to attribution. They report that the relationships between attribution information and jury verdicts are consistent with predictions based on a labeling perspective.

Richard Della Fave (1980) demonstrates the importance of attribution for understanding a key but neglected aspect of stratification, namely, how it is that stratification systems become legitimated and accepted by those disadvantaged as well as by those advantaged by those systems. He draws heavily on attribution theory in developing a theory of legitimation and in identifying possible sources of delegitimation.

Attribution is a significant social process that ranges widely from cognitive processes to collective beliefs. The field is still imbalanced; more work has been done at the intrapersonal and interpersonal levels. There is evidence for both intergroup and societal attributions, however, and research at these two levels is steadily increasing (Hewstone 1989). Recent research has demonstrated connections across areas as diverse as social cognition, social interaction, intergroup relations, and social representations; these connections provide increasing evidence of the importance of attribution for sociological phenomena. Indeed, in the next decade it may be that the fruits of attribution theories will be evident more in research on these other topics, than in research on attribution alone.

REFERENCES

Anderson, Irina, and Geoffrey Beattie 1996 "How Important is Kelley's Model of the Attribution Process When Men and Women Discuss Rape in Conversation?" (*Semiotica* 1/2:1–21.

Andrews, Bernice, and Chris R. Brewin 1990 "Attributions of Blame for Marital Violence: A Study of Antecedents and Consequences." *Journal of Marriage and the Family* 52:757–767.

Antaki, Charles, and Ivan Leudar 1992 "Explaining in Conversation: Towards an Argument Model." *European Journal of Social Psychology* 22:181–194.

Bond, Michael H. (ed.) 1988 *The Cross-Cultural Challenge to Social Psychology*. Newbury Park, Calif.: Sage.

Broman, Clifford L. 1992 "The Black Experience: Attributing the Causes of Labor Market Success." *National Journal of Sociology* 6:77–90.

Crittenden, Kathleen S. 1983 "Sociological Aspects of Attribution." *Annual Review of Sociology* 9:425–446.

Della Fave, L. Richard 1980 "The Meek Shall Not Inherit the Earth: Self-Evaluation and the Legitimacy of Stratification." *American Sociological Review* 45:955–971.

Hamilton, V. Lee, and Shigeru Hagiwara 1992 "Roles, Responsibility, and Accounts Across Cultures." *International Journal of Psychology* 27:157–179.

Heider, Fritz 1958 *The Psychology of Interpersonal Relations.* New York: Wiley.

Hewstone, Miles 1989 *Causal Attribution: From Cognitive Processes to Collective Beliefs.* Oxford: Basil Blackwell.

——, and Jos M. F. Jaspars 1987 "Covariation and Causal Attribution: A Logical Model of the Intuitive Analysis of Variance." *Journal of Personality and Social Psychology* 53:663–672.

Howard, Judith A., and Carolyn Allen 1990 "Making Meaning: Revealing Attributions Through Analyses of Readers' Responses." *Social Psychology Quarterly* 52:280–298.

Howard, Judith A., and Randy Levinson 1985 "The Overdue Courtship of Attribution and Labeling." *Social Psychology Quarterly* 48:191–202.

Jones, Edward E., and Keith E. Davis 1965 "From Acts to Dispositions: The Attribution Process in Person Perception." *Advances in Experimental Social Psychology* 2:219–266.

Jones, Edward E., and Daniel McGillis 1976 "Correspondent Inferences and the Attribution Cube: A Comparative Reappraisal." In J. H. Harvey, W. Ickes, and R. F. Kidd, eds., *New Directions in Attribution Research*, Vol. 1. Hillsdale, N.J.: Erlbaum.

Kelley, Harold H. 1967 "Attribution Theory in Social Psychology." *Nebraska Symposium of Motivation* 15:192–238.

——1973 "The Processes of Causal Attribution." *American Psychologist* 28:107–128.

Little, Steven G., Robert C. Sterling, and Daniel H. Tingstrom 1996 "The Influence of Geographic and Racial Cues on Evaluation of Blame." *The Journal of Social Psychology* 136:373–379.

McArthur, Leslie Z. 1972 "The How and What of Why: Some Determinants and Consequences of Causal Attribution." *Journal of Personality and Social Psychology* 22:171–197.

McMillen, Curtis, and Susan Zuravin 1997 "Attributions of Blame and Responsibility for Child Sexual Abuse and Adult Adjustment." *Journal of Interpersonal Violence* 12:30–48.

Miller, Joan G. 1984 "Culture and the Development of Everyday Social Explanation." *Journal of Personality and Social Psychology* 46:961–978.

Mizokawa, Donald T., and David B. Ryckman 1990 "Attributions of Academic Success and Failure: A Comparison of Six Asian-American Ethnic Groups." *Journal of Cross-Cultural Psychology* 21:434–451.

Moghaddam, Fathali M., Donald M. Taylor, Wallace E. Lambert, and Amy E. Schmidt 1995 "Attributions and Discrimination: A Study of Attributions to the Self, the Group, and External Factors among Whites, Blacks, and Cubans in Miami." *Journal of Cross-Cultural Psychology* 26:209–220.

Moscovici, Serge 1976 *La Psychanalyse: Son image et son public*, 2nd ed. Paris: Presses Universitaires de France.

Moskowitz, G. B. 1996 "The Mediational Effects of Attributions and Information Processing in Minority Social Influence." *British Journal of Social Psychology* 35:47–66.

Power, J. Gerard, Sheila T. Murphy, and Gail Coover 1996 "Priming Prejudice: How Stereotypes and Counter-Stereotypes Influence Attribution of Responsibility and Credibility among Ingroups and Outgroups." *Human Communication Research* 23:36–58.

Reese, Laura T., and Ronald E. Brown 1995 "The Effects of Religious Messages on Racial Identity and System Blame among African Americans." *The Journal of Politics* 57:24–43.

Ross, Lee 1977 "The Intuitive Psychologist and His Shortcomings: Distortions in the Attribution Process." *Advances in Experimental Social Psychology* 19:174–220.

Singh, Anup K. 1989 "Attribution Research on Poverty: A Review." *Psychologia* 32:143–148.

Tuss, Paul, Jules Zimmer, and Hsiu-Zu Ho 1995 "Causal Attributions of Underachieving Fourth-Grade Students in China, Japan, and the United States." *Journal of Cross-Cultural Psychology* 26:408–425.

Weiner, Bernard 1974 *Achievement Motivation and Attribution Theory.* Morristown, N.J.: General Learning Press.

——1985 "'Spontaneous' Causal Thinking." *Psychological Bulletin* 97:74–84.

——, Dan Russell, and David Lerman 1978 "Affective Consequences of Causal Ascription." In J. H. Harvey, W. Ickes., and R. F. Kidd, eds., *New Directions in Attribution Research*, Vol. 3. Hillsdale, N.J.: Erlbaum.

Wilder, David A., Andrew F. Simon, and Myles Faith 1996 "Enhancing the Impact of Counterstereotypic Information: Dispositional Attributions for Deviance." *Journal of Personality and Social Psychology* 71:276–287.

Wiley, Mary Glenn, and Kathleen S. Crittenden 1992 "By Your Attributions You Shall Be Known: Consequences of Attributional Accounts for Professional and Gender Identities." *Sex Roles* 27:259–276.

Willis, Cynthia E., Marianne N. Hallinan, and Jeffrey Melby 1996 "Effects of Sex Role Stereotyping among European American Students on Domestic Violence Culpability Attributions." *Sex Roles* 34:475–491.

JUDITH A. HOWARD
DANIELLE KANE

B

BALANCE THEORY

See Attitudes; Cognitive Consistency Theories.

BANKRUPTCY AND CREDIT

Every society must resolve the tension between debtors and creditors, especially if the debtors cannot pay or cannot pay quickly enough. Many of the world's religions have condemned lending money for interest, at least among co-religionists. In traditional societies, money lenders, although necessary for ordinary commerce, were often viewed as morally suspect. The development of a robust capitalism was based upon raising capital by paying interest or dividends, and so it has been important for capitalist societies to develop institutions and mechanisms for handling debt and credit.

The inherent tension between creditors and debtors turns upon the creditor's claim to justice as the property owner and the debtor's interest in fairness in the terms of repayment. To be sure, lenders sometimes used their position to create social control mechanisms such that debtors often could never work their way out of debt. Such arrangements as sharecropping and the use of the company store often tied laborers to employers through the bonds of debt. With some exceptions, states and legal regimes upheld property rights against the claims of the debtors.

Through the years, societies have sanctioned creditors' use of slavery, debt-prison, transportation to debtors' colonies, debt-peonage, seizure of assets or garnishment of wages to control debtors. Most such methods, however, work to the advantage only of the first creditor or the most aggressive creditor to demand payment. Bankruptcy, as used in the United States and a number of other countries, provides a means for resolving not only the debtor-creditor conflict but also the potential conflict among creditors.

Bankruptcy is a very old concept. The word itself comes from an Italian phrase meaning "broken bench," because a bankrupt merchant's work bench would be broken by his creditors if he could not repay the debt. In the United States, each state has laws governing debtor-creditor relations, but the enactment of bankruptcy statutes is reserved to the Congress by the U.S. Constitution. United States bankruptcy occurs in the federal courts and is regulated by statutes enacted by Congress. Special bankruptcy courts are located in each federal judicial district, and specially appointed bankruptcy judges oversee the caseload. Bankruptcy decisions may be appealed to the federal district court and subsequently to the federal appeals court and the U.S. Supreme Court.

Bankruptcy is technically different from insolvency. Insolvency refers to a financial situation in which a person or business has liabilities that exceed assets. To be bankrupt, the debtor must file for bankruptcy protection in the federal court. Although the overwhelming majority of individuals filing for bankruptcy are also insolvent, occasionally a solvent business will file for bankruptcy because of anticipated liabilities that will exceed its assets. An example of such a bankruptcy is that of pharmaceutical manufacturer A. H. Robbins, whose

Dalkon Shield intrauterine device (a contraceptive) was judged the cause of many injuries and some deaths among women who used it. As the financial judgments against the company mounted, its management sought the protection of the bankruptcy courts. Bankruptcy allowed the company to hold its creditors at bay for a period of time to allow the company to propose a financial settlement.

THE ROLE OF THE STATES

Although bankruptcy is a federal matter, states also have laws to govern debtor-creditor relations. Each state's debtor-creditor laws are affected by its history and by the debt conventions that are part of its history. Before becoming a state, for example, Georgia was a debtor's colony. Before the Civil War, debtors in such southern states often fled harsh debt-collection laws by going to Texas, indicated by "G.T.T." in sheriffs' records. Texas has traditionally retained pro-debtor statutory provisions, especially its generous exemption.

An exemption is the property that a debtor may keep despite bankruptcy or a judgment for nonpayment. The federal bankruptcy statutes recognize the right of state law to prescribe exemptions. There is also a federal exemption, but state legislatures may require their citizens to claim only the state exemption, which in some states is smaller than the federal exemption. State exemption laws vary widely, with some states allowing a substantial exemption and other states exempting very little property. Even a generous exemption law, however, is not a guarantee that a debtor will keep a lot of property. A home is not exempt if there is a mortgage on the home, and other goods are similarly not protected from a secured creditor if they have been used as collateral for a debt.

The states with a Spanish heritage often followed the Spanish tradition that a bankrupt's family should have the means to continue to make a living. Thus, the state laws of Florida, Texas, and California, for example, have traditionally been liberal in permitting debtors to keep their homesteads and some other assets, such as the tools of their trade and current wages. Other states exempt items that are believed necessary for the family's well being, such as children's school books, certain farm equipment, sewing machines, and funeral plots. There is a recent trend toward substituting dollar limitations for exemptions instead of listing specific items of property.

The state exemption is the principal determinant of the resources a bankrupt debtor will have following the bankruptcy. The rest of the debtor's postbankruptcy status depends upon the type of bankruptcy the debtor declares.

TYPES OF BANKRUPTCY

Bankruptcy may be entered either on a voluntary or on an involuntary basis. U.S. bankruptcy law arranges several ways by which debtors may voluntarily declare bankruptcy. Either individuals or corporate actors, including incorporated and unincorporated businesses, not-for-profit agencies, and municipalities may declare bankruptcy. The law makes special provision for the bankruptcies of railroads and stockbrokers. Creditors may in some circumstances initiate an involuntary bankruptcy. Only a small proportion of all bankruptcies is involuntary, and nearly all of those cases are targeted toward a business.

The Clerk of the Bankruptcy Court classifies each case filed as a business bankruptcy or a nonbusiness bankruptcy. These distinctions are not always clear-cut. As many as one in every five "nonbusiness" debtors reports currently owning a business or having recently owned a business. Moreover, many of the "business" bankruptcies are small family-owned enterprises. Whether classified as business or nonbusiness, the bankruptcy of a small business owner typically affects the family's welfare as well as that of the business.

Individual, noncorporate debtors typically have two choices in bankruptcy: *Chapter 7 liquidation* or a *Chapter 13 repayment plan*. In a Chapter 7 case, the debtor's assets over and above the exempt property will be sold and the creditors will be paid *pro rata*. Creditors with secured debts (those debts with collateral) will be allowed to have the collateral. All remaining debt will be discharged, or wiped away by the court. The debtor will not be able to file a Chapter 7 bankruptcy again for six years.

The Chapter 13 repayment plan is available only to individual debtors with a regular source of income. There are also other legal limitations, such as maximum limits on the amount of debt owed. The debtor files with the court a plan for repaying debts over a three-to-five year schedule. The debtor must report all income to the court, and must also include a budget that provides the necessities of rent, food, clothing, medical treatment, and so on. The difference between the budgeted amount and the monthly income is the disposable income, which becomes the amount of the monthly payment.

The Chapter 13 petitioner must pay to a trustee, who is appointed by the court, all disposable income for the period of the plan. The debtor gets to keep all property. The trustee disburses the funds to the creditors. For a judge to confirm a Chapter 13 plan, the unsecured creditors must receive more money through the plan payments than they would have received in a Chapter 7 liquidation. At the conclusion of the plan, any remaining debt is discharged. Following this discharge, the Chapter 13 petitioner is also barred from further Chapter 7 bankruptcies for six years.

About two of every three Chapter 13 filers do not complete the proposed plan. Although the Chapter 13 may provide some benefits to the debtor—for example, he might have time to reorganize his finances—once plan payments are missed the court may dismiss the Chapter 13 and the debtor loses the protection of bankruptcy. Repayment plans such as Chapter 13 were begun by bankruptcy judges in northern Alabama before Congress wrote them into law. Even today, Chapter 13 is disproportionately popular in some judicial districts in the South. About one-third of all nonbusiness bankruptcies are filed in Chapter 13.

Some debts survive bankruptcy, regardless of the chapter in which the bankruptcy is filed. Child support, alimony, federally-backed educational loans, and some kinds of taxes are among those effectively nondischargeable in Chapter 7. Creditors may also object to the discharge of a specific debt if the debt arose from certain misbehavior, including fraud and drunkenness. Creditors may also object to the discharge generally on the grounds of debtor misbehavior, including hiding assets, disposing of assets before the bankruptcy, and lying to the court. A judge may object to a debtor filing in Chapter 7 if the judge believes that the filing represents a "substantial abuse." A Chapter 13 plan must be filed in "good faith."

For persons with substantial assets and for businesses there is an additional choice, *Chapter 11*, also called a *reorganization*. In Chapter 11, a debtor business seeks the protection of the court to reorganize itself in such a way that its creditors can be repaid (although perhaps not one hundred cents on the dollar). Creditors are given an opportunity to review the plan and to vote on its acceptability. If a sufficient number of creditors agree, the others may be forced to go along. In large cases, a committee of creditors is often appointed for the duration of the Chapter 11. Reorganizations may provide a means to save jobs while a business reorganizes.

In recent years, critics have charged that undoing business obligations has become an important motive for companies to reorganize under Chapter 11. Various companies have been accused of trying to avoid labor contracts, to avoid product liability, or to insulate management from challenges. These strategic uses of bankruptcy are potentially available to solvent companies. Although strategic uses of bankruptcies by individuals probably occur, most studies have found that the individuals in bankruptcy are in poor financial condition, often with debts in excess of three years' income.

There is also *Chapter 12* bankruptcy, another type of *reorganization* specifically for farmers. It was introduced in 1986 and in most years between one and two thousand cases are filed in Chapter 12.

Federal law permits the fact of a bankruptcy to remain on a credit record for ten years, but the law also prohibits discrimination against bankrupt debtors by governments or private employers.

BANKRUPTCY TRENDS

The number of business bankruptcies remains relatively small, usually fewer than 75,000 in a year, with exceptions in a few years. The number of nonbusiness bankruptcies, however, has generally risen for about two decades, from about 313,000 in 1981 to 811,000 in 1991. Nonbusiness bankruptcies passed the millionmark in 1996, and by 1998 there were more than 1.4 million nonbusiness bankruptcies in the United States.

Embedded within the general increase in bankruptcy are substantial regional variations in filing rates that seem to follow the business cycle. Some analysts believe that bankruptcy is a lagging indicator; that is, some months after an economic slowdown, bankruptcies begin to rise as laid-off workers run out of resources or small business owners find they cannot remain in business.

Each bankruptcy affects at least one household, and one estimate puts the average number of creditors affected at eighteen. Some creditors, such as credit card issuers, are affected by numerous bankruptcies within a single year. Some bankruptcies initiate a chain of events: The bankruptcy of a single business may lead later to the bankruptcies of employees who lost their jobs, of creditors whose accounts receivable were never received, and of suppliers who could not find new customers. Creditors often argue that the rising numbers of bankruptcies cause them costs that are then passed on to all consumers in the form of higher interest rates.

A bankruptcy may be filed either by a single individual or jointly by a couple. Since the early 1980s, there has been a sharp increase in the proportion of bankruptcies filed by adult women. Several studies indicate between one-third and one-half of bankruptcies are now filed by women. Over half of bankrupt debtors are between the ages of thirty and fifty. Their mean occupational prestige is approximately the same as that of the labor force as a whole, and their educational level is also similar to that of the adult population. The proportion of immigrants in the bankrupt population is approximately the same as their proportion in the general population. There are conflicting findings about the extent to which minority populations are overrepresented or underrepresented in bankruptcy. Despite their educational and occupational levels, however, the median incomes of bankrupt debtors are less than half the median income of the general population.

CAUSES OF BANKRUPTCY

Much of what social scientists know about bankruptcy comes from reviewing the bankruptcy petitions filed in courts, and from interviewing judges, lawyers, clerks, and others who work in the bankruptcy courts. Information about the causes of bankruptcy, however, typically comes from interviews with the debtors themselves. Because many

debtors are ashamed of their bankruptcies, and because American debtor populations are geographically mobile, interview studies often have somewhat low response rates. For learning the cause of a bankruptcy, however, there is probably no substitute for asking the debtor.

Debtors often report "inability to manage money" or "too much debt" as the reason for their bankruptcy. In probing a little deeper, however, researchers have found five major issues involved in a large fraction of all bankruptcies: job problems, divorce and related family problems, medical problems, homeowner problems, and credit card debts.

Many debtors have been laid off completely, lost overtime, or had their hours of work or their pay rates reduced. Some debtors have had long periods of unemployment; others have lost their jobs because of the closure of the plant or the store where they worked. The job loss causes an unplanned loss of income, and this fact in turn often creates a mismatch between the petitioner's debt obligations and the ability to meet those obligations. During the recession of the early 1990s, when many industries were downsizing and otherwise restructuring their labor forces, about two in every five bankrupt debtors reported a job-related reason for bankruptcy.

Divorce and other family problems may result in lower incomes for the two ex-spouses (especially the ex-wife). Moreover, in most divorce settlements the debts are also divided, and the debt burden may be too great for one of the ex-spouses. Sometimes an ex-spouse will file bankruptcy knowing that any jointly-incurred debts discharged by the bankrupt spouse will have to be paid by the other ex-spouse. Although alimony and child support cannot be discharged as debts, for custodial parents who do not receive the payments the financial consequences may be grave. Similarly, for parents who must make the payments, a reduction in other debts may make the payments more possible. Finally, it is harder to support two households on the income that used to support just one household. For all of these reasons, the recently divorced may find themselves in bankruptcy.

Medical problems may lead to higher debts if the debtor is uninsured or if insurance is insufficient to pay for needed medical procedures, pharmaceuticals, and professional services. Medical problems may at the same time lead to lower incomes if a person is too ill or injured to work. Either way, a spell of illness or an automobile accident may push a previously solvent person into a situation in which debts are no longer manageable. Medical problems rise in frequency as a reported cause of bankruptcy for adults aged fifty-five to sixty-four, years in which medical problems may increase but before Medicare coverage becomes available.

Earlier efforts to examine medical debts as an indicator of the causes of bankruptcy showed medical debt to be a fairly insignificant cause, whereas direct interviews of debtors are more likely to reveal medical issues as causative. There are reasons to believe that the debt indicators underestimate this reason for bankruptcy. Insurance will often pay medical providers but will not replace income, so that debts to hospitals or physicians might not appear in the records even though the illness or injury is nevertheless the reason that the debtor cannot repay debts. Moreover, some medical providers accept credit cards, so that the medical expenses are hidden within credit card debt. And some debtors will make efforts to pay off their medical creditors first for fear of being denied services. On the other hand, there may be some overestimate of the impact of medical issues in interviews, because respondents may believe a medical reason may be seen as a socially acceptable cause for bankruptcy.

Bankrupt debtors are somewhat less likely to be homeowners than the general population, but a substantial number of homeowners file for bankruptcy, often to prevent the foreclosure of their mortgage. Chapter 13 permits homeowners to pay the arrearages (missed payments) on their mortgage along with their current payments. Home ownership may also be an issue for a worker who is transferred to a different city and buys a second home before the first home is sold. Equity is the portion of the home's value for which the homeowner has made payment. The recent proliferation of home-equity loans, which allow homeowners to use the equity in their homes as collateral, has also put homes at risk even if the payments on the principal mortgage are current. Small business owners are often required to use their homes as collateral for business loans, which means that a failing business may also entail the threat of the family losing its home. Home-equity lending is

being extended to a number of other situations, including college loans and credit cards, with the result that many Americans are risking their homes, often without realizing it.

A final reason for bankruptcy is large credit card debts, often at high rates of interest. All-purpose cards (such as Visa, MasterCard, and American Express) are now used for many consumption purposes, including payment of federal income taxes, payment of college tuition, and many goods and services, with the result that credit card debt is assumed for many different purposes. Most ordinary living expenses can now be charged with a credit card, so that interpreting a high credit card debt is difficult. High rates of interest accelerate the credit card debt quickly. Credit card debt is the fastest-growing reason for bankruptcy being given by debtors.

BANKRUPTCY MYTHS

Empirical studies have refuted a number of myths about bankruptcy. One such myth is that some people file for bankruptcy again and again. Several studies have been unable to confirm this myth, but there are a number of people who are unsuccessful at Chapter 13 who eventually file Chapter 7. These people have not really repeated bankruptcy, because they have never received a discharge from their debts in their Chapter 13 filings.

Another myth is that large numbers of bankrupt debtors have high debts because of alcoholism, drug abuse, and gambling. Although most empirical studies have identified a few isolated cases in which one of these problems plays a role, the great increase in bankruptcy numbers cannot be attributed to a great increase in addictive behavior.

A third myth is that there is widespread abuse of the bankruptcy process because many debtors could allegedly pay all of their debts. Most studies of the repayment possibilities for the debtors find that the debtors are unable to repay their debts, even if their families live on very modest budgets (such as the model low-income budget of the U.S. Bureau of Labor Statistics). The few studies that have found debtors able to repay have often eliminated from repayment whole categories of debt that the debtors themselves cannot eliminate. There are, however, documented cases of fraudulent or abusive use of bankruptcy, some of which are prosecuted by the government as criminal matters.

STRUCTURAL SOURCES OF BANKRUPTCY

Several changes in American financial life have contributed to the imbalance of debt with income and may have increased the numbers of people who file for bankruptcy.

Consumer credit has been available for decades, principally as a means to help households finance a large purchase over a period of time. Individual sellers extended credit, often on the basis of personal knowledge of the borrower and the borrower's ability to repay. Later, banks, credit unions, and personal finance companies helped finance the purchase of homes, cars, and small appliances. These institutional arrangements offered more protection to the seller and made a personal acquaintanceship less important in the lending decision.

The development of credit cards, with preapproved credit limits, allowed consumers to buy a large variety of goods or services on credit, not just large or expensive items. It was not just the invention of the credit card, however, but some later developments in its use that have changed consumer financial patterns in a way that may have influenced higher bankruptcy rates.

First, beginning in the late 1970s, most states repealed their laws making usury an offense, and Congress made state usury laws largely ineffective. Usury, the charging of excessive interest, was formerly regulated by the states, most of which set limits on the maximum amount of interest that could be charged to borrowers. With the repeal of these laws, high rates of interest–some as high as 20 percent or more–could legally be charged. Prior to this time, such high rates of interest were usually defined as criminal and were associated with loan-sharking and the lending practices of organized crime.

Second, credit cards became a major profit center for many banks, especially because of the high interest rates that could be charged. Marketing of credit cards mushroomed. New markets, including relatively low-income families, became the targets of sophisticated mail and telephone campaigns. Even though many of the families might not be able to repay everything they charged,

the large interest payments made the lending profitable. Credit cards are now extensively marketed to young people, especially college students, who are relatively unfamiliar with financial matters.

Third, credit devices proliferated to include gold and platinum levels, cash advances, and many other features that were both profitable to card issuers and attractive to card holders. Sometimes card holders did not understand how these features worked; for example, many card holders did not realize that there is no grace period for repaying a cash advance, and the interest rate on a cash advance is often higher than the rate for purchases.

Fourth, merchants who accepted credit cards enjoyed increased business because the buyers did not have to carry a large supply of cash. Advertising by stores and restaurants increasingly emphasized the acceptability of credit cards, so that the advertising for goods and services reinforced the advertising of the credit card issuers. Meanwhile, the credit card issuers provided protection against nonpayment to the merchant who accepted a credit card, and they also provided some protection for the card-holder against the fraudulent use of the cards.

Fifth, a major restructuring of the U.S. economy occurred at the beginning of the 1990s, in which millions of workers were laid off or could find only contingent jobs. Many of these workers found credit cards to be a convenient way to maintain consumption levels and their family's lifestyle even though their expected income stream was interrupted.

These trends contributed to an increase in the numbers of people who had high debt-to-income ratios. Some people incurred high levels of debt, often at high interest rates, and simultaneously experienced declining or stagnant income. While not every person with a high debt-to-income ratio filed for bankruptcy, those who did file for bankruptcy had very high ratios. Changes in the American economy during the decade of the 1990s probably influenced the increase in the number of bankruptcies. In particular, the increasing indebtedness of Americans closely tracked the rise in bankruptcies.

Rising Indebtedness. The economic changes of the 1990s, in addition to the well-entrenched borrowing for home mortgages, car purchases, and college expenses, have resulted in an increase in consumer credit outstanding from 298 billion dollars in 1980 to 1,025 billion in 1995. Thus, while the U.S. population increased by 16 percent, indebtedness increased by 244 percent. These are nominal dollars, but even accounting for inflation (constant dollars) the debt burden doubled. During this same time frame, mortgage lending increased by 223 percent, from 1,463 billion dollars in 1980 to 4,724 billion dollars in 1995. Credit card debt, which was only 81.2 billion dollars in 1980, had increased by 351 percent to 366.4 dollars in 1995. Thus, while there was an increase in all forms of indebtedness, credit card debt—which began from a smaller base—showed the largest percentage increase.

Industry sources estimate that in 1990 there were 1.03 billion credit cards in circulation in the United States, and that by 2000 a projected 1.34 billion cards will be in circulation. In 1990, these cards accounted for 466 billion dollars of spending and resulted in 236 billion dollars of debt. By 2000, the projected spending is 1,443 billion dollars, with 661 billion dollars as debt.

In its survey of how consumers use credit cards, the Board of Governors of the Federal Reserve System reported that 54.5 percent of the sample always paid off the balance on their credit cards each month. Another 19.1 percent sometimes pay off the balance, and the remaining 26.4 percent hardly ever pay off the balance. It is from this latter group that the credit card issuers run the greatest risk of eventual nonpayment but also have the possibility of earning the greatest amount of interest. About 30 percent of the consumers earning less than $50,000 a year "hardly ever" pay off the balance, compared with only 10.5 percent of those who earn more than $100,000. Over 35 percent of the consumers under the age of thirty-five hardly ever pay off their balance, compared with 10.5 percent of people over the age of seventy-five.

Credit cards alone do not pose a major financial problem for most people, even for those who maintain a balance; the median balance is about $1,000, with a median charge of $200 a month. For those people with larger balances, however, and with interest charges and sometimes penalties and late fees added to the principal, indebtedness may become a serious problem. And although facing this problem can be postponed by making small monthly payments, the balance can quickly become too large ever to be handled on most salaries.

The ubiquity and convenience of credit cards has led to their growing use for additional purposes: as a form of identification, as security for returning rented cars and videotapes, and—perhaps ironically—as an indicator of creditworthiness for additional extensions of credit.

INTERNATIONAL CREDIT ISSUES

Besides the indebtedness of the individuals in a population, there is also growing concern about other forms of indebtedness. Many countries, especially those with less developed economies, have borrowed large sums of money from more developed countries. The repayment of these loans, and the terms that are demanded, have provided a source of tension between the richer nations and the poorer nations. International agencies such as the International Monetary Fund often prescribe austerity measures to help a country meet its repayment obligations.

The development of transnational corporations has also raised issues of which set of debtor-creditor laws govern transactions that may span several countries. Debtor-creditor laws and the laws of insolvency and bankruptcy vary dramatically from country to country, and an important issue in international commerce is how to handle problems of nonpayment. Many of these issues remain highly contested and largely unsettled.

REFERENCES

Caplovitz, David 1974 *Consumers In Trouble: A Study of Debtors in Default*. New York: Free Press.

Delaney, Kevin J. 1992 *Strategic Bankruptcy: How Corporations and Creditors Use Chapter 11 to Their Advantage*. Berkeley: University of California Press.

Jacob, Herbert 1969 *Debtors in Court; The Consumption of Government Services*. Chicago: Rand McNally.

Ritzer, George 1995 *Expressing America: A Critique of the Global Credit Card Society*. Thousand Oaks, Calif.: Pine Forge Press.

Ryan, Martin 1995 *The Last Resort: A Study of Consumer Bankrupts*. Aldershot, Eng.: Avebury.

Stanley, David T., and Marjorie Girth 1971 *Bankruptcy: Problem, Process, Reform*. Washington, D.C.: The Brookings Institution.

Sullivan, Teresa A., Elizabeth Warren, and Jay Lawrence Westbrook 2000 *The Fragile Middle Class*. New Haven, Conn.: Yale University Press.

—— 1999 *As We Forgive Our Debtors: Bankruptcy and Consumer Credit in America*. Reprint. Chevy Chase, Md.: Beard Books.

—— 1995 "Bankruptcy and the Family." *Marriage and Family Review* 21, 3/4 (1995):193–215.

—— 1994 "Consumer Debtors Ten Years Later: A Financial Comparison of Consumer Bankrupts 1981–1991." *American Bankruptcy Law Journal* 68,2 (Spring):121–154.

—— 1994 "The Persistence of Local Legal Culture: Twenty Years of Evidence from the Federal Bankruptcy Courts." *Harvard Journal of Law and Public Policy* 17,3 (Summer):801–865.

TERESA A. SULLIVAN

BEHAVIORISM

Behaviorism is the conceptual framework underlying the science of behavior. The science itself is often referred to as the *experimental analysis of behavior or behavior analysis*. Modern behaviorism emphasizes the analysis of conditions that maintain and change behavior as well as the factors that influence the acquisition or learning of behavior. Behaviorists also offer concepts and analyses that go well beyond the common-sense understanding of reward and punishment. Contemporary behaviorism provides an integrated framework for the study of human behavior, society, and culture.

Within the social sciences, behaviorism has referred to the social-learning perspective that emphasizes the importance of reinforcement principles in regulating social behavior (McLaughlin 1971). In addition, sociologists such as George Homans and Richard Emerson have incorporated the principles of behavior into their theories of elementary social interaction or exchange (Emerson 1972; Homans 1961). The basic idea in social exchange approaches is that humans exchange valued activities (e.g., giving respect and getting help) and that these transactions are "held together" by the principle of reinforcement. That is,

exchange transactions that involve reciprocal reinforcement by the partners increase in frequency or probability; those transactions that are not mutually reinforcing or are costly to the partners decrease in frequency over time. There is a growing body of research literature supporting social exchange theory as a way of understanding a variety of social relationships.

SOME BASIC ISSUES

The roots of behaviorism lie in its philosophical debate with introspectionism—the belief that the mind can be revealed from a person's reports of thoughts, feelings, and perceptions. Behaviorists opposed the use of introspective reports as the basic data of psychology. These researchers argued for a natural-science approach and showed how introspective reports of consciousness were inadequate. Reports of internal states and experiences were said to lack objectivity, were available to only one observer, and were prone to error. Some behaviorists used these arguments and also others to reject cognitive explanations of behavior (Skinner 1974; Pierce and Epling 1984; but see Bandura 1986 for an alternative view).

The natural-science approach of behaviorism emphasizes the search for general laws and principles of behavior. For example, the *quantitative law of effect* is a mathematical statement of how the rate of response increases with the rate of reinforcement (Herrnstein 1970). Under controlled conditions, this equation allows the scientist to predict precisely and to regulate the behavior of organisms. Behavior analysts suggest that this law and other behavior principles will eventually account for complex human behavior (McDowell 1988).

Contemporary behaviorists usually restrict themselves to the study of observable responses and events. Observable events are those that are directly sensed or are made available to our senses by instruments. The general strategy is to manipulate aspects of the environment and measure well-defined responses. If behavior reliably changes with a manipulated condition, the researcher has established an environment-behavior relationship. Analysis of such relationships has often resulted in behavioral laws and principles. For example, the principle of discrimination states that an organism will respond differently to two situations if its behavior is reinforced in one setting but not in the other. You may talk about politics to one person but not to another, because the first person has been interested in such conversation in the past while the second has not. The principle of discrimination and other behavior principles account for many aspects of human behavior.

Although behaviorism usually has been treated as a uniform and consistent philosophy and science, a conceptual reconstruction indicates that there are many branches to the behavioral tree (Zuriff 1985). Most behavior analysts share a set of core assumptions; however, there are internal disputes over less central issues. To illustrate, some behaviorists argue against hypothetical constructs (e.g., memory) while others accept such concepts as an important part of theory construction.

Throughout the intellectual history of behaviorism, a variety of assumptions and concepts has been presented to the scientific community. Some of these ideas have flourished when they were found to further the scientific analysis of behavior. Other formulations were interesting variations of behavioristic ideas, but they became extinct when they served no useful function. For instance, one productive assumption is that a person's knowledge of emotional states is due to a special history of verbal conditioning (Bem 1965, 1972; Skinner 1957). Self-perception and attributional approaches to social psychology have built on this assumption, although researchers in this field seldom acknowledge the impact. In contrast, the assumption that thinking is merely subvocal speech was popular at one time but is now replaced by an analysis of problem solving (Skinner 1953, 1969). In this view, thinking is behavior that precedes and guides the final performance of finding a solution. Generally, it is important to recognize that behaviorism continues to evolve as a philosophy of science, a view of human nature, and an ideology that recommends goals for behavioral science and its applications.

THE STUDY OF BEHAVIOR

Behaviorism requires that a scientist study the behavior of organisms for its own sake. Behaviorists do not study behavior in order to make inferences about mental states or physiological processes. Although most behaviorists emphasize the importance of biology and physiological processes, they focus on the interplay of behavior and environment.

In order to maintain this focus, behaviorists examine the evolutionary history and physiological status of an organism as part of the context for specific environment-behavior interactions. For example, a biological condition that results in blindness may have profound behavioral effects. For a newly sightless individual, visual events, such as watching television or going to a movie no longer support specific interactions, while other sensory events become salient (e.g., reading by braille). The biological condition limits certain kinds of behavioral interactions and, at the same time, augments the regulation of behavior by other aspects of the environment. Contemporary behaviorism therefore emphasizes what organisms are doing, the environmental conditions that regulate their actions, and how biology and evolution constrain or enhance environment-behavior interactions.

Modern behaviorists are interested in voluntary action, and they have developed a way of talking about purpose, volition, and intention within a natural-science approach. They note that the language of intention was pervasive in biology before Darwin's functional analysis of evolution. Although it appears that giraffes grow long necks in order to obtain food at the tops of trees, Darwin made it clear that the process of evolution involved no plan, strategy of design, or purpose. Natural variation ensures that giraffes vary in neck size. As vegetation declines at lower heights, animals with longer necks obtain food, survive to adulthood, and reproduce; those with shorter necks starve to death. In this environment (niche), the frequency of long-necked giraffes increases over generations. Such an increase is called natural selection. Contemporary behaviorists insist that selection, as a causal mode, also accounts for the form and frequency of behavior during the lifetime of an individual. A person's current behavior is therefore composed of performances that have been selected in the past (Skinner 1987).

An important class of behavior is selected by its consequences. The term *operant* refers to behavior that operates upon the environment to produce effects, outcomes, or consequences. Operant behavior is said to be emitted because it does not depend on an eliciting stimulus. Examples of operant behavior include manipulation of objects, talking with others, problem solving, drawing, reading, writing, and many other performances. Consequences select this behavior in the sense that specific operants occur at high frequency in a given setting. To illustrate, driving to the store is operant behavior that is likely to occur when there is little food in the house. In this situation, the operant has a high probability if such behavior has previously resulted in obtaining food (i.e. the store is open). Similarly, the conversation of a person also is selected by its social consequences. At the pub, a student shows high probability of talking to his friends about sports. Presumably, this behavior occurs at high frequency because his friends have previously "shown an interest" in such conversation. The behavior of an individual is therefore adapted to a particular setting by its history of consequences.

A specific operant, such as opening a door, includes many performance variations. The door may be opened by turning the handle, pushing with a foot, or even by asking someone to open it. These variations in performance have a common effect upon the environment in the sense that each one results in the door being opened. Because each variation produces similar consequences, behaviorists talk about an operant as a response class. Operants such as opening a door, talking to others, answering questions, and many other actions are each a response class that includes a multitude of forms, both verbal and nonverbal.

In the laboratory, the study of operant behavior requires a basic measure that is sensitive to changes in the environment. Most behaviorists use an operant's rate of occurrence as the basic data for analysis. Operant rate is measured as the frequency of an operant (class) over a specified period of time. Although operant rate is not directly observable, a cumulative recorder is an instrument that shows the rate of occurrence as changes in the slope (or rise) of a line on moving paper. When an operant is selected by its consequences, the operant rate increases and the slope becomes steeper. Operants that are not appropriate to the requirements of the environment decrease in rate of occurrence (i.e., decline in slope). Changes in operant rate therefore reflect the basic causal process of *selection by consequences* (Skinner 1969).

Behavior analysts continue to use the cumulative recorder to provide an immediate report on a subject's behavior in an experimental situation. However, most researchers are interested in complex settings where there are many alternatives and multiple operants. Today, microcomputers collect and record a variety of behavioral measures that are later examined by complex numerical analysis. Researchers also use computers to arrange environmental events for individual behavior and provide these events in complex patterns and sequences.

CONTINGENCIES OF REINFORCEMENT

Behaviorists often focus on the analysis of environment-behavior relationships. The relationship between operant behavior and its consequences defines a *contingency of reinforcement*. In its simplest form, a two-term contingency of reinforcement may be shown as $R(Sr$. The symbol R represents the operant class, and Sr stands for the reinforcing stimulus or event. The arrow indicates that "if R occurs, then Sr will follow." In the laboratory, the behavior analyst arranges the environment so that a contingency exists between an operant (e.g., pecking a key) and the occurrence of some event (e.g., presentation of food). If the presentation of the event increases operant behavior, the event is defined as a positive reinforcer. The procedure of repeatedly presenting a positive reinforcer contingent on behavior is called positive reinforcement (see Pierce and Epling 1999).

A contingency of reinforcement defines the probability that a reinforcing event will follow operant behavior. When a person turns the ignition key of the car (operant), this behavior usually has resulted in the car starting (reinforcement). Turning the key does not guarantee, however, that the car will start; perhaps it is out of gas, the battery is run down, and so on. Thus, the probability of reinforcement is high for this behavior, but reinforcement is not certain. The behavior analyst is interested in how the probability of reinforcement is related to the rate and form of operant behavior. For example, does the person continue to turn the ignition key even though the car doesn't start? Qualities of behavior such as persistence, depression, and elation reflect the probability of reinforcement.

Reinforcement may depend on the number of responses or the passage of time. A schedule of reinforcement is a procedure that states how consequences are arranged for behavior. When reinforcement is delivered after each response, a continuous schedule of reinforcement is in effect. A child who receives payment each time she mows the lawn is on a continuous schedule of reinforcement. Continuous reinforcement produces a very high and steady rate of response, but as any parent knows, the behavior quickly stops if reinforcement no longer occurs.

Continuous reinforcement is a particular form of ratio schedule. Fixed-ratio schedules state the number of responses per reinforcement. These schedules are called *fixed ratio* since a fixed number of responses are required for reinforcement. In a factory, piece rates of payment are examples of fixed-ratio schedules. Thus, a worker may receive $1 for sewing twenty pieces of elastic wristband. When the ratio of responses to reinforcement is high (value per unit output is low), fixed-ratio schedules produce long pauses following reinforcement: Overall productivity may be low, leading plant managers to complain about "slacking off" by the workers. The problem, however, is the schedule of reinforcement that fixes a high number of responses to payment.

Reinforcement may be arranged on a variable, rather than fixed, basis. The schedule of payoff for a slot machine is a *variable-ratio* schedule of reinforcement. The operant involves putting in a dollar and pulling the handle, and reinforcement is the jackpot. The jackpot occurs after a variable number of responses. Variable-ratio schedules produce a high rate of response that takes a long time to stop when reinforcement is withdrawn. The gambler may continue to put money in the machine even though the jackpot rarely, if ever, occurs. Behavior on a variable-ratio schedule is said to show *negative utility* since people often invest more than they get back.

Behavior may also be reinforced only after an interval of time has passed. A *fixed-interval* schedule stipulates that the first response following a specified interval is reinforced. Looking for a bus is behavior that is reinforced after a fixed time set by the bus schedule. If you just missed a bus, the probability of looking for the next one is quite low. As time passes, the rate of response increases with

the highest rate occurring just before the bus arrives. Thus, the rate of response is initially zero but gradually rises to a peak at the moment of reinforcement. This response pattern is called *scalloping* and is characteristic of fixed-interval reinforcement. In order to eliminate such patterning, a *variable-interval* schedule may be stipulated. In this case, the first response after a variable amount of time is reinforced. If a person knows by experience that bus arrivals are irregular, looking for the next bus will occur at a moderate and steady rate because the passage of time no longer signals reinforcement (i.e., arrival of the bus).

The schedules of reinforcement that regulate human behavior are complex combinations of ratio and interval contingencies. An *adjusting* schedule is one example of a more complex arrangement between behavior and its consequences (Zeiler 1977). When the ratio (or interval) for reinforcement changes on the basis of performance, the schedule is called adjusting. A math teacher who spends more or less time with a student depending on the student's competence (i.e., number of correct solutions) provides reinforcement on an adjusting-ratio basis. When reinforcement is arranged by other people (i.e., social reinforcement), the level of reinforcement is often tied to the level of behavior (i.e., the greater the strength of response the less the reward from others). This adjustment between behavior and socially arranged consequences may account for the flexibility and variability that characterize adult human behavior.

Human behavior is regulated not only by its consequences. Contingencies of reinforcement also involve the events that precede operant behavior. The preceding event is said to "set the occasion" for behavior and is called a discriminative stimulus or *Sd*. The ring of a telephone *(Sd)* may set the occasion for answering it (operant), although the ring does not force one to do so. Similarly, a nudge under the table *(Sd)* may prompt a new topic of conversation (operant) or cause the person to stop speaking. Discriminative stimuli may be private as well as public events. Thus, a headache may result in taking a pill or calling a physician. A mild headache may be discriminative stimulus for taking an aspirin, while more severe pain sets the occasion for telephoning a doctor.

Although discriminative stimuli exert a broad range of influences over human behavior, these events do not stand alone. These stimuli regulate behavior because they are an important part of the contingencies of reinforcement. Behaviorism has therefore emphasized a three-term contingency of reinforcement, symbolized as $Sd:R(r)Sr$. The notation states that a specific event (Sd) sets the occasion for an operant (R) that produces reinforcement (Sr). The discriminative stimulus regulates behavior only because it signals past consequences. Thus, a sign that states "Eat at Joe's" may set the occasion for your stopping at Joe's restaurant because of the great meals received in the past. If Joe hires a new cook, and the meals deteriorate in quality, then Joe's sign will gradually lose its influence. Similarly, posted highway speeds regulate driving on the basis of past consequences. The driver who has been caught by a radar trap is more likely to observe the speed limit.

CONTEXT OF BEHAVIOR

Contingencies of reinforcement, as complex arrangements of discriminative stimuli, operants, and reinforcements, remain a central focus of behavioral research. Contemporary behaviorists are also concerned with the *context of behavior*, and how context affects the regulation of behavior by its consequences (Fantino and Logan 1979). Important aspects of context include the biological and cultural history of an organism, its current physiological status, previous environment—behavior interactions, alternative sources of reinforcement, and a history of deprivation (or satiation) for specific events or stimuli. To illustrate, in the laboratory food is used typically as an effective reinforcer for operant behavior. There are obvious times, however, when food will not function as reinforcement. If a person (or animal) has just eaten a large meal or has an upset stomach, food has little effect upon behavior.

There are less obvious interrelations between reinforcement and context. Recent research indicates that depriving an organism of one reinforcer may increase the effectiveness of a different behavioral consequence. As deprivation for food increased, animals worked harder to obtain an opportunity to run on a wheel. Additionally, animals who were satiated on wheel running no longer pressed a lever to obtain food. These results imply that eating and running are biologically interrelated. Based on this biological history, the supply or

availability of one of these reinforcers alters the effectiveness of the other (Pierce, Epling, and Boer 1986). It is possible that many reinforcers are biologically interrelated. People commonly believe that sex and aggression go together in some unspecified manner. One possibility is that the availability of sexual reinforcement alters the reinforcing effectiveness of an opportunity to inflict harm on others.

CHOICE AND PREFERENCE

The emphasis on context and reinforcement contingencies has allowed modern behaviorists to explore many aspects of behavior that seem to defy a scientific analysis. Most people believe that choice and preference are basic features of human nature. Our customary way of speaking implies that people make decisions on the basis of their knowledge and dispositions. In contrast, behavioral studies of decision making suggest that we choose an option based on its rate of return compared with alternative sources of reinforcement.

Behaviorists have spent the last thirty years studying choice in the laboratory using concurrent schedules of reinforcement. The word *concurrent* means "operating at the same time." Thus, concurrent schedules are two (or more) schedules operating at the same time, each schedule providing reinforcement independently. The experimental setting is arranged so that an organism is free to alternate between two or more alternatives. Each alternative provides a schedule of reinforcement for choosing it over the other possibilities. A person may choose between two (or more) response buttons that have different rates of monetary payoff. Although the experimental setting is abstract, concurrent schedules of reinforcement provide an analogue of choice in everyday life.

People are often faced with a variety of alternatives, and each alternative has its associated benefits (and costs). When a person puts money in the bank rather than spending it on a new car, television, or refrigerator, we speak of the individual choosing to save rather than spend. In everyday life, choice often involves repeated selection of one alternative (e.g. putting money in the bank) over the other alternatives considered as a single option (e.g. buying goods and services). Similarly, the criminal chooses to take the property of others rather than take the socially acceptable route of working for a living or accepting social assistance. The arrangement of consequences for crime and legitimate ways of making a living is conceptually the same as concurrent schedules of reinforcement (Hamblin and Crosbie 1977).

Behaviorists are interested in the distribution or allocation of behavior when a person is faced with different rates of reinforcement from two (or more) alternatives. The distribution of behavior is measured as the relative rate of response to, or relative time spent on, a specific option. For example, a student may go to school twelve days and skip eight days each month (not counting weekends). The relative rate of response to school is the proportion of the number of days at school to the total number of days, or 12/20 = 0.60. Expressed as a percentage, the student allocates 60 percent of her behavior to school. In the laboratory, a person may press the left button twelve times and the right button eight times each minute.

The distribution of reinforcement may also be expressed as a percentage. In everyday life, it is difficult to identify and quantify behavioral consequences, but it is easily accomplished in the laboratory. If the reinforcement schedule on the left button produces $30 an hour and the right button yields $20, 60 percent of the reinforcements are on the left. There is a fundamental relationship between relative rate of reinforcement and relative rate of response. This relationship is called the *matching law*. The law states that the distribution of behavior to two (or more) alternatives matches (equals) the distribution of reinforcement from these alternatives (Herrnstein 1961; de Villiers 1977).

Although it is difficult to identify rates of reinforcement for attending school and skipping, the matching law does suggest some practical solutions (Epling and Pierce 1988). For instance, parents and the school may be able to arrange positive consequences when a child goes to school. This means that the rate of reinforcement for going to school has increased, and therefore the relative rate of reinforcement for school has gone up. According to the matching law, a child will now distribute more behavior to the school.

Unfortunately, there is another possibility. A child may receive social reinforcement from friends for skipping, and as the child begins to spend more time at school, friends may increase their rate of reinforcement for cutting classes. Even though the absolute rate of reinforcement for going to school has increased, the relative rate of reinforcement has remained the same or decreased. The overall effect may be no change in school attendance or even further decline. In order to deal with the problem, the matching law implies that interventions must increase reinforcement for attendance and maintain or reduce reinforcement for skipping, possibly by turning up the cost of this behavior (e.g., withdrawal of privileges).

The matching law has been tested with human and nonhuman subjects under controlled conditions. One interesting study assessed human performance in group discussion sessions. Subjects were assigned to groups discussing attitudes toward drug abuse. Each group was composed of three confederates and a subject. Two confederates acted as listeners and reinforced the subject's talk with brief positive words and phrases, provided on the basis of cue lights. Thus, the rate of reinforcement by each listener could be varied depending on the number of signals arranged by the researchers. A third confederate asked questions but did not reinforce talking. Results were analyzed in terms of the relative time subjects spent talking to the two listeners. Speakers matched their distribution of conversation to the distribution of positive comments from the listeners. Apparently, choosing to speak to others is behavior that is regulated by the matching law (Conger and Kileen 1974).

Researchers have found that exact matching does not always hold between relative rate of reinforcement and relative rate of response. A more general theory of behavioral matching has been tested in order to account for the departures from perfect matching. One source of deviation is called *response bias*. Bias is a systematic preference for an alternative, but the preference is not due to the difference in rate of reinforcement. For example, even though two friends provide similar rates of reinforcement, social characteristics (e.g., status and equity) may affect the distribution of behavior (Sunahara and Pierce 1982). Generalized matching theory is able to address many social factors as sources of bias that affect human choice and preference (Baum 1974; Pierce and Epling 1983; Bradshaw and Szabadi 1988).

A second source of deviation from matching is called *sensitivity to differences* in reinforcement.

Matching implies that an increase of 10 percent (e.g., from 50 to 60 percent) in relative rate of reinforcement for one alternative results in a similar increase in relative rate of response. In many cases, the increase in relative rate of response is less than expected (e.g., only 5 percent). This failure to discriminate changes in relative rate of reinforcement is incorporated within the theory of generalized matching. To illustrate, low sensitivity to changes in rate of reinforcement may occur when an air-traffic controller rapidly switches between two (or more) radar screens. As relative rate of targets increases on one screen, relative rate of detection may be slow to change. Generalized matching theory allows behaviorists to measure the degree of sensitivity and suggests procedures to modify it (e.g., setting a minimal amount of time on a screen before targets can be detected).

Matching theory is an important contribution of modern behaviorism. In contrast to theories of rational choice proposed by economists and other social scientists, matching theory implies that humans may not try to maximize utility (or reinforcement). People (and animals) do not search for the strategy that yields the greatest overall returns; they equalize their behavior to the obtained rates of reinforcement from alternatives. Research suggests that matching (rather than maximizing) occurs because humans focus on the immediate effectiveness of their behavior. A person may receive a per-hour average of $10 and $5 respectively from the left and right handles of a slot machine. Although the left side generally pays twice as much, there are local periods when the left option actually pays less than the right. People respond to these changes in *local rate of reinforcement* by switching to the lean alternative (i.e., the right handle), even though they lose money overall. The general implication is that human impulsiveness ensures that choice is not a rational process of getting the most in the long run but a behavioral process of doing the best at the moment (Herrnstein 1990).

MATHEMATICS AND BEHAVIOR MODIFICATION

The matching law suggests that operant behavior is determined by the rate of reinforcement for one alternative relative to all other sources of reinforcement. Even in situations that involve a single response on a schedule of reinforcement, the behavior of organisms is regulated by alternative sources of reinforcement. A rat that is pressing a lever for food may gain additional reinforcement from exploring the operant chamber, scratching itself, and so on. In a similar fashion, rather than work for teacher attention a pupil may look out the window, talk to a friend, or even daydream. Thus in a single-operant setting, multiple sources of reinforcement are functioning. Herrnstein (1970) argued this point and suggested an equation for the single operant that is now called the *quantitative law of effect*.

Carr and McDowell (1980) applied Herrnstein's equation to a clinically relevant problem. The case involved the treatment of a 10-year-old boy who repeatedly and severely scratched himself. Before treatment the boy had a large number of open sores on his scalp, face, back, arms, and legs. In addition, the boy's body was covered with scabs, scars, and skin discoloration. In their review of this case, Carr and McDowell demonstrated that the boy's scratching was operant behavior. Careful observation showed that the scratching occurred more often when he and other family members were in the living room watching television. This suggested that a specific situation set the occasion for the self-injurious behavior. Further observation showed that family members repeatedly and reliably reprimanded the boy when he engaged in self-injury. Reprimands are seemingly negative events, but adult attention (whether negative or positive) can serve as reinforcement for children's behavior.

In fact, McDowell (1981) showed that the boy's scratching was in accord with Herrnstein's equation (i.e., the quantitative law of effect). He plotted the reprimands per hour on the *x*-axis and scatches per hour on the *y*-axis. When applied to this data, the equation provided an excellent description of the boy's behavior. The quantitative law of effect also suggested how to modify the problem behavior. In order to reduce scratching (or any other problem behavior), one strategy is to increase reinforcement for alternative behavior. As reinforcement is added for alternative behavior, problem behavior must decrease; this is because the reinforcement for problem behavior is decreasing (relative to total reinforcement) as reinforcement is added to other (acceptable) behavior.

APPLIED BEHAVIOR ANALYSIS AND EDUCATION

The application of behavior principles to improve performance and solve social problems is called *applied behavior analysis* (Baer, Wolf, and Risley 1968). Principles of behavior change have been used to improve the performance of university students, increase academic skills in public and high school students, teach self-care to developmentally delayed children, reduce phobic reactions, get people to wear seat belts, prevent industrial accidents, and help individuals stop cocaine abuse, among other things. Behavioral interventions have had an impact on such things as clinical psychology, medicine, education, business, counseling, job effectiveness, sports training, the care and treatment of animals, environmental protection, and so on. Applied behavioral experiments have ranged from investigating the behavior of psychotic individuals to designing contingencies of entire institutions (see Catania and Brigham 1978; Kazdin 1994).

One example of applied behavior analysis in higher education is the method of personalized instruction. Personalized instruction is a self-paced learning system that contrasts with traditional lecture methods that often are used to instruct college students. In a university lecture, a professor stands in front of a number of students and talks about his or her area of expertise. There are variations on this theme (e.g., students are encouraged to be active rather than passive learners), basically the lecture method of teaching is the same as it has been for thousands of years.

Dr. Fred Keller (1968) recognized that the lecture method of teaching was inefficient and in many cases a failure. He reasoned that anyone who had acquired the skills needed to attend college was capable of successfully mastering most or all college courses. Some students might take longer than others to reach expertise in a course, but the overwhelming majority of students would be able to do so. If behavior principles were to be taken seriously, there were no bad students, only ineffective teaching methods.

In a seminal article, titled "Good-bye, teacher...," Keller outlined a college teaching method based on principles of operant conditioning (Keller 1968). Keller's personalized system of instruction (PSI) involves arranging the course material in a sequence of graduated steps (units or modules).

Each student moves through the course material at his or her own pace and the modules are set up to ensure that most students have a high rate of success learning the course content. Some students may finish the course in a few weeks, others require a semester or longer.

Course material is broken down into many small units of reading and (if required) laboratory assignments. Students earn points (conditioned reinforcement) for completing unit tests and lab assignments. Mastery of lab assignments and unit tests is required. If test scores are not close to perfect, the test (in different format) must be taken again after a review of the material for that unit. The assignments and tests build on one another so they must be completed in a specified order.

Comparison studies have evaluated student performance on PSI courses against the performance of students given computer-based instruction, audio-tutorial methods, traditional lectures, visual-based instruction, and other programmed instruction methods. College students instructed by PSI outperform students taught by these other methods when given a common final examination (see Lloyd and Lloyd 1992 for a review). Despite this positive outcome, logistical problems in organizing PSI courses such as teaching to mastery level (most students get an A for the course), and allowing students more time than the allotted semester to complete the course, have worked against widespread adoption of PSI in universities and colleges.

SUMMARY

Modern behaviorism emphasizes the context of behavior and reinforcement. The biological history of an organism favors or constrains specific environment-behavior interactions. This interplay of biology and behavior is a central focus of behavioral research. Another aspect of context concerns alternative sources of reinforcement. An individual selects a specific option based on the relative rate of reinforcement. This means that behavior is regulated not only by its consequences but also by the consequences arranged for alternative actions. As we have seen, the matching law and the quantitative law of effect are major areas of basic research that suggest new intervention strategies for behavior modification. Finally, applied behavior analysis, as a technology of behavior change, is having a wide impact on socially important problems of human behavior. A personalized system of instruction is an example of applied behavior analysis in higher education. Research shows that mastery-based learning is more effective than alternative methods of instruction, but colleges and universities its implementation.

REFERENCES

Baer, D.M., M.M. Wolf, and T. R. Risley 1968 "Some Current Dimensions of Applied Behavioral Analysis." *Journal of Applied Behavior Analysis* 1:91–97.

Bandura, A. 1986 *Social Foundations of Thought and Action*. Englewood Cliffs, N.J.: Prentice Hall.

Baum, W. M. 1974 "On Two Types of Deviation from the Matching Law: Bias and Undermatching." *Journal of the Experimental Analysis of Behavior* 22:231–242.

Bem, D. J. 1965 "An Experimental Analysis of Self-Persuasion." *Journal of Experimental Social Psychology* 1:199–218.

—— 1972 "Self-Perception Theory." In L. Berkowitz, ed., *Advances in Experimental Social Psychology*, Vol. 6. New York: Academic Press.

Bradshaw, C. M., and E. Szabadi 1988 "Quantitative Analysis of Human Operant Behavior." In G. Davey and C. Cullen, eds. *Human Operant Conditioning and Behavior Modification*. New York: Wiley.

Carr, E. G., and J. J. McDowell 1980 "Social Control of Self-Injurious Behavior of Organic Etiology." *Behavior Therapy* 11:402–409.

Catania, C. A., and T. A. Brigham, eds. 1978 *Handbook of Applied Behavior Analysis: Social and Instructional Processes*. New York: Irvington Publishers.

Conger, R., and P. Killeen 1974 "Use of Concurrent Operants in Small Group Research." *Pacific Sociological Review* 17:399–416.

De Villiers, P. A. 1977 "Choice in Concurrent Schedules and a Quantitative Formulation of the Law of Effect." In W. K. Honig and J. E. R. Staddon, eds., *Handbook of Operant Behavior*. Englewood Cliffs, N.J.: Prentice-Hall.

Emerson, R. M. 1972 "Exchange Theory Part 1: A Psychological Basis for Social Exchange." In J. Berger, M. Zelditch, Jr., and B. Anderson, eds. *Sociological Theories in Progress* 38–57. Boston: Houghton Mifflin Co.

Epling, W. F., and W. D. Pierce 1988 "Applied Behavior Analysis: New Directions from the Laboratory." In G. Davey and C. Cullen, eds., *Human Operant Conditioning and Behavior Modification*. New York: Wiley.

Fantino, E., and C.A. Logan 1979 *The Experimental Analysis of Behavior: A Biological Perspective*. San Francisco: W. H. Freeman.

Herrnstein, R. J. 1961 "Relative and Absolute Response Strength as a Function of Frequency of Reinforcement." *Journal of the Experimental Analysis of Behavior* 4:267–272.

—— 1970 "On the Law of Effect." *Journal of the Experimental Analysis of Behavior* 13:243–266.

—— 1990 "Rational Choice Theory: Necessary but Not Sufficient." *American Psychologist* 45:356–367.

Homans, G. C. 1974 *Social Behavior: Its Elementary Forms*, rev. ed. New York: Harcourt Brace Jovanovich.

Kazdin, A. E. 1994 *Behavior Modification in Applied Settings*. New York: Brooks/Cole Publishing.

Keller, F. S. 1968 "Good-bye teacher. . ." *Journal of Applied Behavior Analysis* 1:79–89.

Lloyd, K. E., and M. E. Lloyd 1992 "Behavior Analysis and Technology of Higher Education." In R. P. West and L. A. Hamerlynck, eds., *Designs for Excellence in Education: The Legacy of B. F. Skinner* 147–160. Longmont, Colo.: Spores West, Inc.

McDowell, J. J. 1981 "On the Validity and Utility of Herrnstein's Hyperbola in Applied Behavior Analysis." In C. M. Bradshaw, E. Szabadi and C. F. Lowe, eds., *Quantification of Steady-State Operant Behaviour* 311–324. Amsterdam: Elsevier/North-Holland.

—— 1988 "Matching Theory in Natural Human Environments." *The Behavior Analyst* 11:95–109.

McLaughlin, B. 1971 *Learning and Social Behavior*. New York: Free Press.

Pierce, W. D., and W. F. Epling 1983 "Choice, Matching, and Human Behavior: A Review of the Literature." *The Behavior Analyst* 6:57–76.

—— 1984 "On the Persistence of Cognitive Explanation: Implications for Behavior Analysis." *Behaviorism* 12:15–27.

—— 1999 *Behavior Analysis and Learning*. Upper Saddle River, N.J.: Prentice-Hall.

——, W.F. Epling, and D. Boer 1986 "Deprivation and Satiation: The Interrelations Between Food and Wheel Running." *Journal of the Experimental Analysis of Behavior* 46:199–210.

Skinner, B.F. 1953 *Science and Human Behavior*. New York: Free Press.

—— 1957 *Verbal Behavior*. New York: Appleton Century Crofts.

—— 1969 *Contingencies of Reinforcement: A Theoretical Analysis*. New York: Appleton Century Crofts.

—— 1974 *About Behaviorism*. New York: Knopf.

—— 1987 "Selection by Consequences." In B.F. Skinner, *Upon Further Reflection*. Englewood Cliffs, N.J.: Prentice-Hall.

Sunahara, D., and W. D. Pierce 1982 "The Matching Law and Bias in a Social Exchange Involving Choice Between Alternatives." *Canadian Journal Of Sociology* 7:145–165.

Zeiler, M. 1977 "Schedules of Reinforcement: The Controlling Variables." In W.K. Honig and J.E.R. Staddon, eds., *Handbook of Operant Behavior*. Englewood Cliffs, N.J.: Prentice-Hall.

Zuriff, G.E. 1985 *Behaviorism: A Conceptual Reconstruction*. New York: Columbia University Press.

W. David Pierce

BIRTH AND DEATH RATES

Much of the birth and death information published by governments is in absolute numbers. These raw data are difficult to interpret. For example, a comparison of the 42,087 births in Utah with the 189,392 in Florida in 1996 reveals nothing about the relative levels of fertility because Florida has a larger population (Ventura et al. 1998, p. 42).

To control for the effect of population size, analyses of fertility and mortality usually use rates. A rate measures the number of times an event such as birth occurs in a given period of time divided by the population at risk to that event. The period is usually a year, and the rate is usually expressed per 1,000 people in the population to eliminate the decimal point. Dividing Florida's births by the state's population and multiplying by 1,000 yields a birth rate of 13 per 1,000. A similar calculation for Utah yields 21 per 1,000, evidence that fertility makes a greater contribution to population growth in the state with the large Mormon population.

BIRTH RATES

The crude birth rate calculated in the preceding example,

Crude birth rate per 1,000= (1)

$$\frac{\text{Live births in year } x}{\text{Midyear population in year } x} \times 1,000$$

is the most common measure of fertility because it requires the least amount of data and measures the impact of fertility on population growth. Crude birth rates at the end of the twentieth century range from over 40 per 1,000 in many African countries and a few Asian countries such as Yemen and Afghanistan to less than 12 per 1,000 in the slow-growing or declining countries of Europe and Japan (Population Reference Bureau 1998).

The crude birth rate is aptly named when used to compare childbearing levels between populations. Its estimate of the population at risk to giving birth includes men, children, and postmenopausal women. If women of childbearing age compose different proportions in the populations under consideration or within the same population in a longitudinal analysis, the crude birth rate is an unreliable indicator of the relative level of childbearing. A portion of Utah's 61 percent higher crude birth rate is due to the state's higher proportion of childbearing-age women, 23 percent, versus 20 percent in Florida (U.S. Bureau of the Census 1994). The proportion of childbearing-age women varies more widely between nations, making the crude birth rate a poor choice for international comparisons.

Other rates that more precisely specify the population at risk are better comparative measures of childbearing, although only the crude birth rate measures the impact of fertility on population growth. If the number of women in childbearing ages is known, general fertility rates can be calculated:

General fertility rate per 1,000= (2)

$$\frac{\text{Live births in year } x}{\text{Women 15–44 in year } x} \times 1,000$$

This measure reveals that a thousand women in Utah of childbearing age produce more births in a year than the same number in Florida, 89 versus 64 births per 1,000 women between ages fifteen and forty-four (Ventura et al. 1998, p. 42). The 39 percent difference in the two states' general fertility rates is substantially less than that indicated by

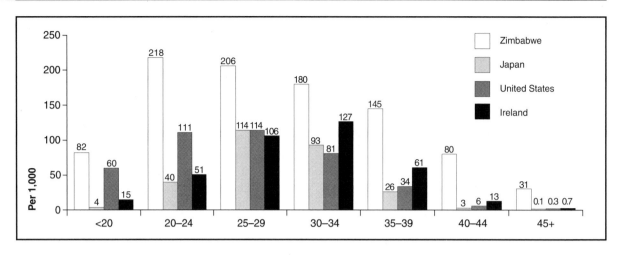

Figure 1. Age-Specific Fertility Rates: Selected Countries, Mid-1990s.

SOURCE: United Nations, *Demographic Yearbook, 1996.*

their crude birth rates which are confounded by age-composition differences.

Although the general fertility rate is a more accurate measure of the relative levels of fertility between populations, it remains sensitive to the distribution of population across women of child-bearing ages. When women are heavily concentrated in the younger, more fecund ages, such as in developing countries today and in the United States in 1980, rather than the less fecund older ages, such as in the United States and other developed countries today, the general fertility rate is not the best choice for fertility analysis. It inflates the relative level of fertility in the former populations and deflates the estimates in the latter populations.

Age-specific fertility rates eliminate potential distortions from age compositions. These rates are calculated for five-year age groups beginning with ages fifteen to nineteen and ending with ages forty-five to forty-nine:

Age-specific fertility rate per 1,000 = (3)

$$\frac{\text{Live births in year } x \text{ to women age } a}{\text{Women age } a \text{ in year } x} \times 1,000$$

Age-specific fertility rates also provide a rudimentary measure of the tempo of childbearing. The four countries in Figure 1 have distinct patterns. Zimbabwe, a less-developed country with high fertility, has higher rates at all ages. At the

other extreme, Japan's low fertility is highly concentrated between the ages of twenty-five and thirty-four, even though the Japanese rates are well below those in Zimbabwe. In contrast, teenage women in the United States continue to have much higher fertility than teenage women in Japan and other industrialized countries, despite declines in the 1990s. The younger pattern of American fertility also is evident in the moderately high rates for women in their early twenties. At the other extreme, Irish women have an older pattern of fertility.

More detailed analyses of the tempo of childbearing require extensive information about live birth order to make fertility rates for each age group specific for first births, second births, third births, and so forth (Shryock and Siegel 1976, p. 280). A comparison of these age-order-specific rates between 1975 and 1996 reveals an on-going shift toward later childbearing in the United States (Ventura et al. 1998, p. 6). The first birth rate increased for women over thirty while it decreased for women ages twenty to twenty-four. As a result, 22 percent of all first births in 1996 occurred to women age thirty and over, compared to only 5 percent in 1975.

When the tempo of fertility is not of interest, the advantages of age-specific fertility rates are outweighed by the cumbersome task comparing many rates between populations. As an alternative, each population's age-specific rates can be condensed in an age–sex adjusted birth rate (Shryock and Siegel 1976, pp. 284–288). The most frequently used age–sex adjusted rate is calculated:

Total fertility rate= (4)

$$\frac{\text{Sum (age-specific fertility rates per 1,000 X 5)}}{1,000}$$

if the age-specific fertility rates are for five-year age groups. Single-year age-specific rates are summed without the five-year adjustment. When expressed per single woman, as in equation (4), the total fertility rate can be interpreted as the average number of births that a hypothetical group would have at the end of their reproduction if they experienced the age-specific fertility observed in a particular year over the course of their childbearing years.

Age-specific rates in real populations that consciously control fertility can be volatile. For example, the fertility rate of American women ages thirty to thirty-four fell to 71 per 1,000 in the middle of the Great Depression and climbed back to 119 during the postwar Baby Boom, only to fall again to 53 in 1975 and rebound to 84 in 1996 (U.S. Bureau of the Census 1975, p. 50; Ventura et al. 1998, p. 32). Consequently, a total fertility rate calculated from one year's observed age-specific rates is not a good estimate of the eventual completed fertility of childbearing-age women. It is, however, an excellent index of the level of fertility observed in a year that is unaffected by age composition.

The total fertility rate also can be interpreted as an estimate of the reproductivity of a population. Reproductivity is the extent to which a generation exactly replaces its eventual deaths. While the total fertility measures the replacement of both sexes, other measures of reproductivity focus only on the replacement of females in the population (Shryock and Siegel 1976, pp. 314–316). The gross reproduction rate is similar to the total fertility rate except that only female births are included in the calculation of the age-specific rates. It is often approximated by multiplying the total fertility rate by the ratio of female births to all births.

Theoretically, women need to average two births, one female and one male, and female newborns need to live long enough to have their own female births at the same ages that their mothers gave birth to them to maintain a constant population size. In real populations some female newborns die before their mothers' ages at their births and the tempo of fertility fluctuates. As a result, both the total fertility rate and the gross reproduction rate overestimate reproductivity. The net reproduction rate adjusts for mortality, although it remains sensitive to shifts in the tempo of childbearing. This measure of reproductivity is calculated by multiplying the age-specific fertility rates for female births by the corresponding life-table survival rates that measure the probability of female children surviving from birth to the age of their mothers, and summing across childbearing ages. If the tempo of fertility is constant, a net reproduction rate of greater than one indicates population growth; less than one indicates decline; and one indicates a stationary population.

Because of the impact of female mortality, the total fertility rate must exceed two for a generation to replace all of its deaths. In industrialized countries with a low risk of dying before age fifty, the total fertility rate needs to be about 2.1 for replacement. Developing countries with higher mortality need a higher total fertility rate for replacement. Malawi, for example, with an infant mortality rate of 140 per 1,000 live births and a life expectancy of only thirty-six needs a rate of about three births per woman for replacement.

The fertility of most industrialized countries has fallen below replacement (Population Reference Bureau 1998). Some, including the United States (Figure 2), Ireland, Iceland, and New Zealand, are barely below replacement. Others have declined to unprecedented low rates. Spain (Figure 2), Portugal, Italy, Greece, Germany, most Eastern European countries, and Japan have total fertility rates of 1.1 to 1.4 births per woman. Some of these populations are already declining. Without constant, substantial net in-migration, all will decline unless their fertility rates rebound to replacement levels or above.

In contrast, the total fertility rates of most developing countries whose economies are still dependent primarily on agriculture exceed replacement (Population Reference Bureau 1998). The highest rates are found in Africa where most countries have rates greater than five births per

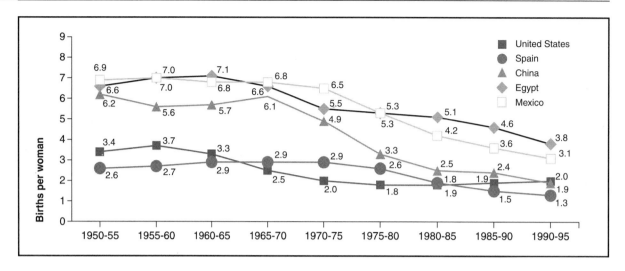

Figure 2. Total Fertility Rates: Selected Countries, 1950–1995.

SOURCE: United Nations, *World Population Prospects, 1996.*

woman. A few, including Ethiopia, Somalia, Niger, and Angola, equal or exceed seven births per woman. As a result, sub-Saharan Africa is growing at about 2.6 percent per year. If unchanged, Africa's population would double in twenty-seven years. Change, however, appears underway in most African countries. The largest fertility declines since 1980 have occurred in North African countries like Egypt (Figure 2) and in Kenya, Zimbabwe, and South Africa. Nevertheless, fertility in all African countries remains well above replacement. The continent's 1998 total fertility rate was 5.6 births per woman.

Fertility has declined to lower levels in other developing regions. Led by three decades of decline in Mexico (Figure 2), Brazil, Ecuador, Peru, and Venezuela, fertility rates for Central and South America have declined to 3.4 and 2.8 births per woman, respectively. Most Caribbean countries have near replacement-level fertility. Haiti, the Dominican Republic, and Jamaica are the major exceptions.

Rapid fertility declines also have occurred throughout much of Asia. China's aggressive birth control policy and nascent economic growth reduced its fertility to 1.8 births per woman (Figure 2), about the same as its Korean and Taiwanese neighbors. A number of other Asian countries, including the large populations of Bangladesh, Iran, Thailand, Vietnam, and Turkey, experienced more than a 50 percent decline in the last two decades of the twentieth century. The even larger populations of India and Indonesia continued their previous slow downward trend, yielding 1998 rates of 3.4 and 2.7 births per woman, respectively. Only a few Asian countries, other than traditional Moslem societies such as Afghanistan, Iraq, and Pakistan, continue to have more than five births per woman.

The fertility measures discussed up to this point are period rates. They are based on data for a particular year and represent the behavior of a cross-section of age groups in the population in that year. Fertility also can be measured over the lifetime of birth cohorts. Cumulative fertility rates can be calculated for each birth cohort of women by summing the age-specific fertility rates that prevailed as they passed through each age (Shryock and Siegel 1976, p. 289). This calculation yields a completed fertility rate for birth cohorts that have reached the end of their reproductive years. It is the cohort equivalent of the period total fertility rate.

DEATH RATES

The measurement of mortality raises many of the same issues discussed with fertility. Rates are more informative than absolute numbers, and those rates that more precisely define the population at risk to dying are more accurate. Unlike fertility, however, the entire population is at risk to dying, and this universal experience happens only once to an individual.

The impact of mortality on population growth can be calculated with a crude death rate:

Crude death rate per 1,000=   (5)

$$\frac{\text{Deaths in year } x}{\text{Midyear population in year } x} \times 1,000$$

Crude death rates vary from over 20 per 1,000 in some African countries to as low as 2 per 1,000 (Population Reference Bureau 1998). The lowest crude death rates are not in the developed countries of Europe, North America, and Oceania, which have rates between 7 and 14 per 1,000. Instead, the lowest crude death rates are found in oil-rich Kuwait, Qatar, and United Arab Emirates, where guest workers inflate the proportion of young adults, and in the young populations of developing countries experiencing declining mortality. Developed countries that underwent industrialization and mortality decline before 1950 have old-age compositions. The proportion of people age sixty-five and over ranges between 11 and 17 percent in these countries compared to less than 5 percent in most African, Asian, and Latin American populations. Although there is a risk of dying at every age, the risk rises with age after childhood. Consequently, older populations have higher crude death rates.

To control for the strong influence of age on mortality, age-specific rates can be calculated for five-year age groups:

Age-specific mortality rate per 1,000=   (6)

$$\frac{\text{Deaths in year } x \text{ to the population age } a}{\text{Population age } a \text{ in year } x} \times$$

1,000

Before age five, the age-specific mortality rate usually is subdivided to capture the higher risk of dying immediately after birth. The rate for one- to four-year olds, like other age-specific rates, is based on the midyear estimate of this population. The conventional infant mortality rate, however, is based on the number of live births:

Infant mortality rate per 1,000=   (7)

$$\frac{\text{Deaths under age 1 in year } x}{\text{Live births in year } x} \times 1,000$$

The infant mortality rate is often disaggregated into the neonatal mortality rate for the first month of life and the postneonatal rate for the rest of the year.

Neonatal mortality rate per 1,000=   (8)

$$\frac{\text{Deaths under 29 days of life in year } x}{\text{Live births in year } x} \times 1,000$$

Postneonatal mortality rate per 1,000=   (9)

$$\frac{\text{Deaths from 29 days to age 1 in year } x}{\text{Live births in year } x} \times 1,000$$

Infant mortality varies widely throughout the world. Iraq, Afghanistan, Cambodia, and many African countries have 1998 rates that still exceed 100 per 1,000 live births, although most have declined (Population Reference Bureau 1998). Infant mortality rates in most other African, Asian, and all other Latin American countries have declined as well. They now range in developing countries from 7 in Cuba to 195 in Sierra Leone. In contrast, developed countries have rates at or below 10, led by Japan with under 4 infant deaths per 1,000 live births.

The declining American infant mortality rate, 7 per 1,000 live births in 1998, continues to lag behind Japan, Australia, New Zealand, Canada, and most Northern and Western European countries due to a higher prevalence of prematurity and low-birth-weight babies which are major causes of infant death (Peters et al. 1998, pp. 12–13). The prematurity and low-birth-weight rates for the country's largest minority, African Americans, are double those of non-Hispanic whites (Ventura 1998, pp. 57–58). Not all minority mothers have higher rates than non-Hispanic whites. Low-birth-weight rates are lower for Americans of Chinese, Mexican, Central and South American origin, about the same for Native Americans and those of Cuban origin, and higher for Puerto Rican, Filipino, and Japanese Americans.

Death Rates per 100,000 for the Fourteen Leading Causes of Death in the Population 45-64 Years of Age, by Sex and Selected Race and Ethnic Categories: United States, 1997

	Males			Females		
	Non-Hispanic			Non-Hispanic		
	Whites	Blacks	Hispanic	Whites	Blacks	Hispanic
Heart diseases	254	469	160	93	231	69
Cancers	254	431	147	219	285	129
Strokes	25	91	32	19	58	20
Respiratory diseases	26	31		24	22	7
Accidents						
Motor vehicle	19	30	21	9	11	9
Other	23	49	26	8	14	6
Pneumonia and flu	11	32	11	8	15	6
Diabetes	20	60	33	16	54	29
HIV	6	72	25		18	5
Suicide	25		12	8		
Liver disease and cirrhosis	26	44	53	10	15	14
Kidney disease						4
Septicemia				4	14	
Homicide and legal intervention		28	12			

Table 1. *Death Rates per 100,000 for the Leading Causes of Death in the Population 45–64 Years of Age, by Sex and Selected Race and Ethnic Categories: United States, 1997.*

SOURCE: Hoyert, D. *Deaths: Final Data for 1997.*

Infant mortality also varies by sex. The rate for male infants born to white mothers in the United States is 6.7 per 1,000 live births, compared to 5.4 for female infants (Peters 1998, p. 80). Similarly, the rate for male infants born to African-American mothers is 16 per 1,000 live births, compared to 13 for female infants.

Like race and ethnic differences, the sex difference in mortality is evident at all ages. The greatest gap is among young adults; American males are two and one-half to three times more likely to die between the ages of fifteen and twenty-nine than females due largely to behavioral causes. These include motor vehicle and other accident fatalities, homicides, and suicides. Higher male death rates from congenital anomalies at younger ages and from heart disease in middle age (Table 1) suggest that biological factors also contribute to the sex difference in mortality. Behavioral causes continue to play a significant role in the sex difference in mortality in middle age with chronic liver disease and cirrhosis and human immunodeficiency virus (HIV) adding premature male mortality.

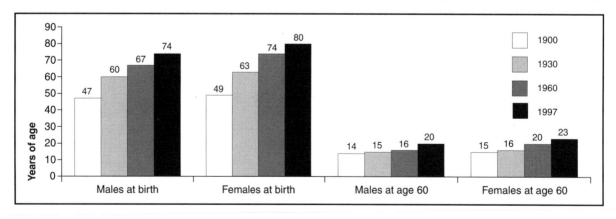

Figure 4. *Life Expectancy for Whites by Sex: United States, 1900–1996.*

SOURCE: U.S. Bureau of the Census, *Historical Statistics of the United States, Colonial Times to 1970,* and D. Hoyert, *Deaths: Final Data for 1997.*

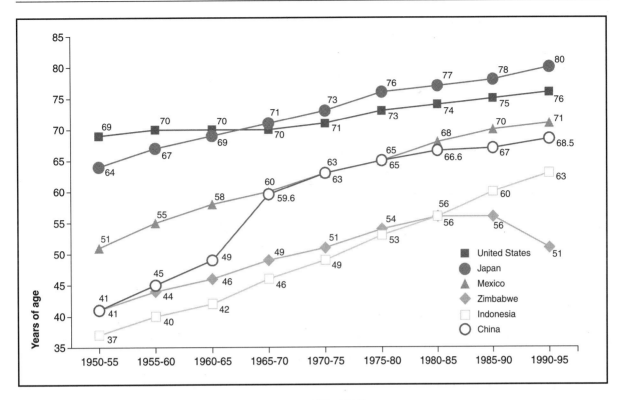

Figure 3. Life Expectancy at Birth: Selected Countries, 1950–1995.

SOURCE:United Nations, *World Population Prospects, 1996.*

Note that cause-specific death rates are calculated per 100,000 population in a specified group, rather than per 1,000 to avoid working with decimals.

Age-specific mortality rates usually are specific for sex and race or ethnicity because of the large differences evident in Table 1. Using five-year age categories results in thirty-eight rates for each racial or ethnic group. Analyses of such data can be unwieldy. When the age pattern of mortality is not of interest, an age-adjusted composite measure is preferable. The most readily available of these for international comparisons is life expectancy.

Life expectancy is the average number of years that members of an age group would live if they were to experience the age-specific death rates prevailing in a given year. It is calculated for each age group in a life table (Shryock and Siegel 1976, pp. 249–268). Life expectancy has increased since the nineteenth century in developed countries like the United States in tandem with economic growth and public health reforms. Japan has the longest

life expectancy at birth, eighty years, due to extremely low infant mortality. With the exception of Russia and some of the other former Soviet-bloc countries of Eastern Europe that have had declines in life expectancy, all other developed countries have life expectancies at birth that equal or exceed seventy years (Population Reference Bureau 1998).

Figure 3 presents trends in life expectancy since World War II in selected countries. Some of the most rapid increases have been in Asia and Latin America. China, Sri Lanka, Malaysia, Mexico, and Venezuela, for example, have 1998 life expectancies at birth of over seventy years. Increases in life expectancy in African countries, in contrast, where there is a relatively high prevalence of poor nutrition, unsanitary conditions, and infectious diseases, generally have lagged behind Asia and Latin America. Most have 1998 life expectancies in the forties or fifties, similar to those of developed countries at the end of the nineteenth century. The future trend in life expectancy in many African countries is uncertain.

Progress made in some is being undermined by the spread of HIV and political conflict. The drug therapies that have reduced mortality from HIV in developed countries have so far proven too costly for widespread use in Africa and political unrest continues.

Declines in infant and child mortality from infectious diseases have been largely responsible for the historical increase in life expectancy around the world. As a result, life expectancy has increased far more at birth than at age sixty (Figure 4). Heart disease, cancer, and cerebrovascular diseases have become the major causes of death in the United States (Peters et al. 1998, p. 7), other developed countries, and some developing countries. Bringing these chronic diseases under control has proven to be difficult. Research suggests that both genetic composition and unhealthy behaviors affect the development of such chronic diseases over time. In the United States where health education campaigns have stressed the link between these diseases and obesity, use of tobacco, and lack of sufficient physical activity, mortality has declined from heart disease since 1950 and from cancer since 1990. If these trends continue, gains in life expectancy at older ages will accelerate.

REFERENCES

Hoyert, D., Kenneth Kochanek, and Sherry Murphy 1999 "Deaths: Final Data for 1997." *National Vital Statistics Reports*, vol. 47, no. 19. Hyattsville, Md.: National Center for Health Statistics.

Population Reference Bureau 1998 *1998 World Population Data Sheet*. Washington, D.C.: Population Reference Bureau.

—— 1980 *1980 World Population Data Sheet*. Washington, D.C.: Population Reference Bureau.

Shryock, Henry, and Jacob Siegel 1976 *The Methods and Materials of Demography*. San Francisco: Academic Press.

United Nations 1998 *Demographic Yearbook, 1996*. New York: United Nations.

—— 1998 *World Population Prospects, 1996*. New York: United Nations.

U.S. Bureau of the Census 1994 "Population Projections for States by Age, Sex, Race, and Hispanic Origin: 1993 to 2020." *Current Population Reports*, series P-25, no. 1111. Washington, D.C.: Government Printing Office.

—— 1975 *Historical Statistics of the United States, Colonial Times to 1970*. Washington D.C.: Government Printing Office.

Ventura, Stephanie, Joyce Martin, Sally Curtin, and T. J. Mathews 1998 "Report of Final Natality Statistics, 1996." *Monthly Vital Statistics Report*, vol. 46, no. 11, Supp. Hyattsville, Md.: National Center for Health Statistics.

DEBORAH A. SULLIVAN
DEPARTMENT OF SOCIOLOGY
ARIZONA STATE UNIVERSITY

BISEXUALITY

See Sexual Orientation, Sexually Transmitted Diseases.

BLACK STUDIES

See African-American Studies; Affirmative Action; Discrimination; Prejudice; Race.

BRITISH SOCIOLOGY

In a global age, the concept of British sociology poses an interesting question with regard to the viability of national sociologies. Neither academic disciplines nor the subjects studied fit easily into national boundaries. An academic's closest colleague may be in New York or Delhi rather than in Lancaster or Birmingham. Key figures in British sociology, such as Dahrendorf, Westergaard, and Bauman are not British but have spent some or all of their careers working in British institutions (Halsey 1989). As sociologists working in Britain they were well placed to investigate questions related to British society. Then there are the British sociologists who have left Britain to research and teach elsewhere; John Goldthorpe to Sweden and Germany, and John Hall and Michael Mann to the United States, for example. British sociologists have often studied other nations too: Ronald Dore focuses on Japan, David Lane on Russia, and John Torrance on Austria to name a few. With all of these international influences exemplifing the present status of sociology in Britain, how "British" then is British sociology? This entry briefly explores the range of sociology that has developed in

Britain from its origins to the present day, and ends by noting possible implications for its future.

FOUNDATION

The discipline of sociology in Great Britain has a history that stretches back to the early 1900s. Martin White and the London School of Economics (LSE) figure prominently in the development of British sociology. In 1907, White effectively founded the study of sociology in Britain by investing about £1,000 to fund a series of lectures at the LSE, as well as to establish the Sociological Society. The first annual report of the society indicated 408 members distributed throughout Great Britain, and thirty-two overseas. Early members of the society included an interesting variety of prominent public and literary figures, such as H.H. Asquith, Hilaire Belloc, and the Bishop of Stepney; British academics including Bertrand Russell, Graham Wallas, and Beatrice Webb; as well as international academics such as Emile Durkheim and Ferdinand Tonnies, among others. Also in 1907, White gave the University of London £10,000 for a permanent chair in sociology to be located at LSE. White also donated additional funds for lectureships, bursaries, and scholarships in sociology. Because of White's prominence in supporting these early initiatives, Dahrendorf has argued that "it is not too much to say that one man, Martin White, established the discipline of sociology in Britain. . . Moreover, sociology came to life at LSE." (Dahrendorf 1995, p. 103).

Despite this promising start, by 1945 the LSE remained the only university with a department of sociology in Britain. Several reasons have been identified for this late development. Among these was the long-standing opposition to the creation of sociology as a university subject by the universities of Oxford and Cambridge, which were at the top of the educational establishment in Britain. In addition, two other disciplines had claims on similar social research that predated the emergence of sociology. Anthropology and political economy both focused on social research that suited the interests of Britain at the time. Studies of foreign shores while Britain was still a major empire was of greater interest than social research focused on issues closer to home. Empirically based scholarship on the political economy was preferable to

the theoretical emphasis of many sociologists because of its perceived lack of application to the real world. The purported lack of credibility of those promoting the study of sociology, many of whom were either located on the outside or on the margins of academe, did not lend a helping hand to the development of sociology either. But, the most persistent obstacle was the hierarchical social structure of British society that prevented the effective interrogation of its social structures (Albrow 1989).

EXPANSION

Following World War II, the fortunes of sociology changed dramatically, in line with the social changes in Britain at this time. In these years there was a general feeling of optimism regarding possible changes in social relationships as well as increasing expectations of education and science to create a better life. In this context the study of sociology represented a commitment to social reorganization. "There was a demand [for sociology]. . . irrespective of what was on offer" (Albrow 1989, p. 202).

Around this same time, Edward Shils moved to London from the University of Chicago. His teaching of classical European sociology has been described "as magnificent a professorial presentation of the social science scenery as could be found in the Western world," and had a great deal to do with shaping and inspiring the first generation of British sociologists (Halsey 1999). This first generation of "career sociologists" in Britain completed their education at the LSE between 1950 and 1952. They included: J.A. Banks, Olive Banks, Michael Banton, Basil Bernstein, Percy Cohen, Norman Dennis, Ralf Dahrendorf, A.H. Halsey, David Lockwood, Cyril Smith, J.H. Smith, Asher Tropp, and John Westergaard. All became prominent sociologists in Britain by the mid-1960s. Members of this cohort have described the sociological analysis they developed as grounded in their own experiences of social inequality and informed by critical reflections on Marx, Parsons, and Popper (Halsey 1985; Dahrendorf 1995). Two of the many publications from members of this group are: David Lockwood's *Some Remarks on The Social System*, published in 1956, and Dahrendorf's *Class and Class Conflict in Industrial Society*, published in 1959. Lockwood's paper is notable because it became the most widely read single paper by a British sociologist at the time. Dahrendorf's book, a critical reflection on Marx and Parsons, argued that Weber's ideas were useful in explaining the positive effects of conflict in Great Britain, and was dedicated to this first cohort at the LSE.

British sociology was further developed in the next decade by the work of John Rex at the University of Leeds. His work *Key Problems in Sociological Theory* (1961) became the most popular British sociological theory textbook in the 1960s. Rex used a Weberian action framework in contrast to the functionalist orthodoxy prominent at the time. In addition to Leeds, departments of sociology had been established at the universities of Leicester, Birmingham, Liverpool, Nottingham, and Hull. In 1967, three important works became available in Britain, Garfinkel's *Studies in Ethnomethodology*, Berger and Luckmann's *The Social Construction of Reality*, and Schutz's *The Phenomenology of the Social World*. These books contained an implicit critique of the kind of sociology that had been pursued in Britain up to this time. They emphasized a qualitative analysis of the ways in which social actors create meaning and acquire social positions in the context of language. The growth of the discipline continued throughout this time with nearly every institution of higher education in Britain housing a department of sociology. This led some to make the observation that it was growing with "explosive force" (Heyworth 1965, p.11). Sociology as a discipline was beginning to come into its own in Britain.

By the 1970s, there were many theoretical currents in British sociology; not only were phenomenological and Marxist arguments being pursued, but also the works of Althusser, the French structuralists, the "Frankfurt School," and Habermas and Gramsci. Links between British sociology and European social theory were becoming stronger. In addition there were important empirical studies being done; the best example is the 1972 Oxford Mobility Studies undertaken by a group of sociologists at Nuffield College, Oxford, and greatly influenced by the work of one of their team, John Goldthorpe. Around this same time a dialogue between the debates in social theory and empirical understanding was initiated by Anthony Giddens

in his analysis of the founders of sociology, *Capitalism and Modern Social Theory* (1971). By 1979 he had developed structuration theory to reconcile the previous theoretical debates. Giddens's systematic analysis of modernity is the most extensive and widely disseminated work of any British sociologist to date.

Starting in the 1980s, the emerging theoretical *zeitgeist* of British sociology was an increasing interest in the study of culture. Cultural studies as developed in the 1960s through the rather different works of Richard Hoggart, E.P. Thompson, and Stuart Hall emphasized the social aspects of culture and led to the specialization in the 1980s and 1990s of the areas of media, feminism, and ethnicity. Cultural analyses were developed as part of an overall analysis of fundamental shifts in modern societies around production, consumption, and social interaction. Influenced by European theories of politics, ideology, and discourse, existing Marxist and functionalist theories were seen as unable to adequately theorize the modern social world.

The work of sociologists based at the Birmingham Centre for Contemporary Cultural Studies represents an example of this analysis. In 1983, the group consisting of John Solomos, Bob Findlay, Simon Jones, and Paul Gilroy outlined a neo-Marxist approach to racism in a series of articles entitled *The Empire Strikes Back*. Gilroy's book, which followed the original articles, *There Ain't No Black in the Union Jack*, developed these themes and stressed the contest over the meaning of "race" that occurs in the public sphere between different social actors. Gilroy's analysis is an example of the wider move in British sociology away from a Marxist analysis of class conflict toward an emphasis on new social movements, such as the women's movement, youth movements, peace movements, green movements, and others they claimed were not easily reducible to class-based politics. There is, of course, a continuing debate between cultural-studies thinkers and Marxists, such as Robert Miles, who argue that class conflict is still far from dead, and remains a central feature in explaining the production of racism. The diversity and pluralism within sociology in Britain at this time has been described as one of its great strengths (Albrow 1989).

CHALLENGES AND OPPORTUNITIES

The growth of sociology in Britain was abruptly impeded by a governmental investigation of higher-education research funding in 1981. One recommendation following the investigation was the withdrawal of funding for any new departments of sociology and those seen as "substandard." Sociologists were also limited in their representation on the Social Science Research Council (SSRC), with only two of the ninety-four members from sociology departments. As a reflection of this change in academic focus, the SSRC was renamed the Economic and Social Research Council in 1984. Albrow (1989) argues that no other academic discipline was singled out in this way.

Governmental scrutiny of sociology programs and departments has become an integral part of British higher education. It is, however, not because it continues to be singled out for special treatment as it was in previous decades but rather it is part of the larger process of fiscal accountability and quality assurance instituted by the government. The first two Research Assessment Exercises (RAE) were conducted in 1992 and 1996 respectively. Each RAE rated every department of every subject on its research output. In 1996, sociology at the universities of Essex and Lancaster received 5* (the highest rank) ratings, while close behind were the universities of Loughborough, Manchester, Oxford, Surrey, Warwick, and Edinburgh, and the college of Goldsmiths, with ratings of 5 each (RAE 1996). Most important about the ratings is that the British government ". . . funding bodies use the ratings to inform the distribution of grants for research to HEIs" (higher education institutions) (RAE 1996). It has been reported that, "Some 20 percent of funding from the Higher Education Funding Council for England is a reward for research excellence, as a measured by the "research assessment exercise" (Wolf 1999). In fact, these funds are extremely important to the day-to-day running of departments and in some cases make them viable or not.

If research was to be assessed, then teaching could not be far behind. The Teaching Quality Assessment (TQA) exercise was instituted in 1993 with various subjects coming up for review in each country of Britain over an eight-year period. In England, sociology was reviewed between 1995 and 1996. At the time of TQA there were approximately 20,000 students studying sociology in eighty-one institutions of higher education in England alone. The Overview Report of all departments reviewed in England noted that, "The overall picture that emerges from the assessment process of the quality of education in sociology is a positive one. . . . On the other hand there is little room for complacency." It was further noted that, "The majority of institutions use a suitable range and variety of teaching, learning and assessment methods. The assessors found considerable evidence of innovative approaches to teaching, which encouraged and enthused students (HEFCE 1996, p. 14).

Funding does not follow from high TQA scores. Instead, high-scoring departments can bid for money from the Fund for the Development of Teaching and Learning. In sociology five consortium projects were funded to a total of over £1,000,000. The five projects publish a regular newsletter and there are plans to launch an online journal for teaching in 2000 (Middleton 1999).

THE NEXT CENTURY

As British sociology enters a global age it is challenged with the ironies and complexities of understanding the current state of modernity that includes the increasing interconnectedness of the world as a whole, the increasing choices each individual has, and the resilience of national identities as evidenced by the increasing number of nations that emerge year after year. Each of these issues has been the subject of research by British sociologists in the past decade. The 1990s saw an "explosion" of interest in studies of culture informed by debates around the high-modern or postmodern condition, albeit influenced by the works of the French sociologists, Pierre Bourdieu, and Michel Foucault (Swingewood 1998). Both the study of nations and trends toward globalization find British sociology in the lead as well. Ernest Gellner (1983) and Anthony Smith (1986) have claimed the territory of nations and nationalism. At the same time, Anthony Giddens (1990), Roland Robertson (British by birth) (1992), Leslie Sklair (1995), and Martin Albrow (1996) have advanced theories of globalization. Emerging from work on globalization is the sociology of human rights. Two examples include: Anthony Woodiwiss's (1998) work on the compatibilities between Asian values and human rights discourses, and Kevin Bales's (1999) study of economic globalization and the development of modern slavery. These seem to highlight some important issues to be debated within sociology (worldwide) in this millennium.

The first century of British sociology saw its ups and downs. At times it was a popular subject to study and at other times it faced significant threats to its existence. Probably there was no threat more dramatic than the former Prime Minister Margaret Thatcher's declaration that, "There is no such thing as society." However, despite the attacks and the loss of funding, sociology as a discipline has managed not only to survive but is poised to lead policy making in Britain. Currently there are increasing numbers of Members of Parliament and Lords who have a sociology background and there are nearly a dozen Vice Chancellors of universities who are sociologists. "Indeed, the subject somehow seems in tune with the times. With a government that not only accepts, but explicitly seeks to understand, and manage society, it is surely no coincidence that Tony Blair's favourite academic, Anthony Giddens. . . is another sociologist-cum-VC (or Director as the position is called at the London School of Economics)" (Brown 1999, p. iii). The reference here is to Giddens's latest contribution to British sociology, his book entitled *The Third Way: The Renewal of Social Democracy* (1998). In many ways sociology has come full circle, with LSE academics once again playing an important role in its resurgence. Despite all attempts to deny its value, sociology in Britain can once again try to fulfill the claim made a century ago and an ocean away, that "Sociology has a foremost place in the thought of modern men [and women]" (Small 1895, p.1).

REFERENCES

Albrow, Martin 1996 *The Global Age*. Cambridge, Eng.: Polity.

—— 1989 "Sociology in the United Kingdom after the Second World War.", In N. Genov, ed., *National Traditions in Sociology*. London: Sage.

Bales, Kevin 1999 *Disposable People: Modern Slavery in the Global Economy*. Berkeley: University of California Press.

Berger, Peter L., and Thomas Luckmann 1967 *The Social Construction of Reality*. London: Allen Lane.

Brown, Matthew 1999 "Time to Take Us Seriously." *Guardian Higher* 19 January, ii–iii.

Centre for Contemporary Cultural Studies (eds.) 1983 *The Empire Strikes Back*. London: Hutchinson.

Dahrendorf, Ralph 1995 *A History of the London School of Economics*. Oxford: Pergamon.

—— 1959 *Class and Class Conflict in Industrial Society*. London: Routledge and Kegan Paul.

Garfinkel, Harold 1967 *Studies in Ethnomethodology*. Englewood Cliffs, N.J.: Prentice-Hall.

Gellner, Ernest 1983 *Nations and Nationalism*. Oxford: Basil Blackwell.

Giddens, Anthony 1998 *The Third Way: The Renewal of Social Democracy*. Cambridge, Eng.: Polity.

—— 1990 *The Consequences of Modernity*. Cambridge, Eng.: Polity.

—— 1971 *Capitalism and Modern Social Theory*. Cambridge, Eng.: Cambridge University Press.

Gilroy, Paul 1987 *There Ain't No Black in the Union Jack*. London: Hutchinson.

Goldthorpe, John H. 1980 *Social Mobility and Class Structure in Modern Britain*. Oxford: Clarendon.

Halsey, Albert H. 1999 "Edward Albert Shils." Personal correspondence, 18 June.

—— 1989 "A Turning of the Tide? The Prospects for Sociology in Britain." *British Journal of Sociology* 40(3):353–373.

—— 1985 "Provincials and Professionals: The British Post-war Sociologists." In Martin Bulmer, ed., *Essays on the History of British Sociological Research*. Cambridge, Eng.: Cambridge University Press.

Heyworth, Lord 1965 *Report of the Committee on Social Studies*. London: HMSO, Cmnd 2660.

Higher Education Funding Council for England 1996 *Subject Overview Report: Quality Assessment of Sociology 1995–1996*. Bristol, Eng.: HEFCE.

Lockwood, David 1956 "Some Remarks on The Social System." *British Journal of Sociology* VII(2):134–145.

Middleton, Chris 1999 Personal correspondence, 9 June.

Research Assessment Exercise 1996 "Unit of Assessment: 42 Sociology." http://www.niss.ac.uk/education/hefc/rae96/1_96t42.html.

—— 1996 "The Outcome." http://www.niss.ac.uk/education/hefc/rae96/cl_96.html.

Rex, John 1961 *Key Problems in Sociological Theory*. London: Routledge and Kegan Paul.

Robertson, Roland 1992 *Globalization: Social Theory and Global Culture*. London: Sage.

Schutz, Alfred 1967 *The Phenomenology of the Social World*. Evanston, Ill.: Northwestern University Press.

Sklair, Leslie 1995 *Sociology of the Global System*. Baltimore, Md.: Johns Hopkins University Press.

Small, Albion 1895 "The Era of Sociology." *American Journal of Sociology*. 1(1):1–15.

Smith, Anthony 1986 *The Ethnic Origins of Nations*. Oxford: Basil Blackwell.

Swingewood, Alan 1998 *Cultural Theory and the Problem of Modernity*. London: Macmillan.

Wolf, Martin 1999 "More Meant Worse." *Financial Times*, 21 June, 22.

Woodiwiss, Anthony 1998 *Globalization, Human Rights and Labour Law in Pacific Asia*. Cambridge, Eng.: Cambridge University Press.

PETER THAYER ROBBINS
VANEETA-MARIE D'ANDREA

BUREAUCRACY

The origin of the term *bureaucracy* can be traced to eighteenth-century French literature (Albrow 1970). The early usage referred to an official workplace (bureau) in which individual activities were routinely determined by explicit rules and regulations. As modern systems of management, supervision, and control, bureaucracies are designed to rationally coordinate the duties and responsibilities of officials and employees of organizations. The delineation of official duties and responsibilities, by means of formal rules and programs of activity (March and Simon 1958), is intended to displace and constrain the otherwise private, idiosyncratic, and uniquely personal interests and actions of individuals. Bureaucratic systems of administration are designed to ensure that the activities of individuals rationally contribute to the goals and interests of the organizations within which they work.

THE CONTRIBUTION OF MAX WEBER

The historical trend toward increasing bureaucratization throughout modern Western Europe, highlighted by the changing structure of military organizations, is documented by the work of Karl Marx ([1852] 1963) and of Alexis de Tocqueville (1877). Michels' (1949) analysis of the dynamics of power distribution within bureaucratic organizations and the concomitant development of oligarchic tendencies (fundamentally detrimental to democratic principles) provided an understanding of one of the more important unintended consequences of bureaucratic processes. However, the study of bureaucratic structure and processes as a prominent sociological topic is based on the intellectual legacy of Max Weber (1864–1920). Although Weber conducted his studies at the turn of the nineteenth century, wide recognition of his work by English-speaking theorists had to await later translations of his work (Weber 1946, 1947).

Weber's thorough and richly informative work included consideration of Chinese, Egyptian, Roman, Prussian, and French administrative systems. In his comparative analysis of this vast array of diverse cultural systems of administration, Weber recognized an inexorable relationship between power and authority, on the one hand, and differing systems of administration on the other. In Weber's analysis, the bureaucratic form of administration reflects one of three ways in which power can be legitimated. To gain a clear appreciation of the unique features of bureaucratic structure and processes, it is necessary to briefly address Weber's proclaimed relationship between power, authority, and systems of administration. *Power*, for Weber, represents the ability or capacity to have other people behave in accordance with certain orders or dictates, irrespective of whether those affected regard its application as rightful or legitimate. *Authority* represents the legitimation of this power by those individuals whose activities are so ordered such that the application of power and its impact on them are perceived to be proper and acceptable. In Weber's historical analysis, three different types of authority are identified: traditional, charismatic, and rational–legal (Weber 1947, p. 328).

Three Types of Authority. *Traditional authority* represents a system in which the use of power is regarded as legitimate when it is predicated upon belief in the sanctity of time-honored traditions and patterns of behavior. By contrast, *charismatic authority* is based on situationally specific acts of personal devotion. Under these circumstances, authority is conferred upon a specific individual who is regarded by the devoted followers to exhibit exceptional, sacred, and/or heroic characteristics. Charismatic authority is therefore limited to a specific setting and time. *Rational–legal* authority derives from the belief in the legitimacy of law, specifically in the legality of rules and the authority of officials and employees to perform certain legally sanctioned and mandated duties to which they have been formally assigned. Official rational–legal authority often permits individuals to perform tasks that otherwise would not be permitted. For example, police officers may engage in certain behaviors in the course of their official duties, such as the use of lethal force, that if performed by an ordinary citizen would expose the citizen to legal liability. Thus, it is not the act or set of behaviors per se that is critical to an understanding of rational–legal authority, but rather who performs the act or behavior and whether the individual performing the act is legally authorized to engage in such behavior.

Three Systems of Administration. Each type of authority is associated with a distinctive system of administration. Over the course of premodern social history, traditional authority was the principal means by which social organization was achieved. This type of authority structure resulted in the development of a wide variety of highly stable but nonetheless particularistic systems of administration, in which personal relations of dependence or loyalty provided the bases for authority. In general, these systems of administration are most clearly exemplified by patrimonial and feudal systems of administration. Unlike traditional authority, charismatic authority results in highly unstable systems of administration, because the foundations of these systems, the profoundly personal relationships between charismatic leaders and followers, are decisively limited in both time and circumstance. Given the tenuous foundation of charismatic authority structures, it is not surprising that the systems of administration that arise in such situations encounter difficulties in generating stable administrative practices. In this regard, problems pertaining to the routinization of authority and leadership succession are particularly salient and acute (Weber 1947, pp. 358–373). Thus, administrative systems predicated upon charismatic authority tend to be inherently transitory and most likely arise during periods of crisis or unprecedented change.

In contrast to the personal bases of authority inherent in both traditional and charismatic systems of administration, rational–legal systems of administration rely on impersonal rules and regulations, culminating in the emergence of highly precise and universalistic systems of administration that are most clearly exemplified by the modern rational bureaucracy. Weber clearly regards such administrative practices to be relatively recent in their development: "Bureaucracy . . . is fully developed in political and ecclesiastical communities only in the modern state, and in the private economy only in the most advanced institutions of capitalism" (Weber 1978, p. 956).

THE FORMAL CHARACTERISTICS OF BUREAUCRACIES

The most distinguishing feature of modern rational bureaucracies is the formal control, prescription, and regulation of individual activity through the enforcement of rules. The explicit intent of enforcing these rules is to efficiently achieve specific organizational goals. In orchestrating individual action, a succinct and unambiguous specification of the official duties and responsibilities is provided to minimize, if not to eliminate, the influence of personal interests and ambitions upon the performance of official duties. The official or employee is then able to concentrate exclusively upon the technical aspects of the work, in particular the efficient and rational completion of assigned tasks. In addition to this attempt to separate individuals' private concerns from their official duties and responsibilities, other distinguishing characteristics of bureaucracies include:

1. The hierarchical ordering of authority relations, limiting the areas of command and responsibility for subordinate as well as superordinate personnel

2. The recruitment and promotion of individuals on the basis of technical expertise and competence

3. A clearly defined division of labor with specialization and training required for assigned tasks

4. A structuring of the work environment to ensure continuous and full-time employment, and the fulfillment of individual career expectations within the organization

5. The impersonality and impartiality of relationships among organization members and with those outside the organization

6. The importance of "official records" in the form of written documents.

THE RATIONALITY OF BUREAUCRATIC RULES

Within a bureaucratic organization, rules serve to direct individual action in ways that promote the technical efficiency of the organization. The distinctive feature of bureaucratic organization is not the use of rules per se but, rather, the type of rules employed within an organization as well as the justification for the use of rules. Rules have been, and continue to be, used in other forms of administration to control individual action; however, the rules used in the other administrative forms (such as rules based on tradition in feudal administration or on dependency in a patrimonial system) are not necessarily based on technical knowledge and the rational achievement of specific goals. By contrast, within a modern bureaucracy explicit rules are designed to assure uniformity of performance in accordance with technical requirements. Bureaucracies denote systems of control that attempt to ensure that the technical abilities of individuals are effectively utilized. A concerted effort is made to systematically exclude any factor or element that would reduce the prospect of an official's or employee's performance being anything other than organizationally focused, affectively neutral, and achievement oriented (Parsons and Shils 1951, pp. 76–91).

THE IDEAL TYPE CONSTRUCT

By underscoring the unique features of modern bureaucratic systems of administration, Weber provides an ideal-type characterization of bureaucracies. Despite subsequent confusion as to the value of the ideal-type portrayal of bureaucracies, Weber did not intend the characterization to represent an accurate empirical description of bureaucracies. As noted in the introduction to one of his edited works, "Situations of such pure type have never existed in history. . . . The ideal types of Weber's sociology are simply mental constructs to serve as categories of thought, the use of which will help us to catch the infinite manifoldness of reality . . . "(Rhinestein 1954, pp. xxix–xxx). The ideal-type characterization is not suggestive of either extreme cases or distinct logical categories of phenomena (Mouzelis 1967). Rather, it provides a simplification and exaggeration of empirical events so that one can appreciate more clearly the features of the phenomena in question. Actual bureaucratic organizations may exhibit only a limited number of these properties or may possess them in varying degrees, a point well understood by Weber.

A GENERAL THEORETICAL PERSPECTIVE ON BUREAUCRATIC ORGANIZATIONS

As a general line of inquiry, the study of bureaucratic structure and processes has tended to represent a "closed" or "rational-system" approach to the study of organizations (Scott 1992). Predicated upon Weber's conception of bureaucracy, the "legal-rational" features of organizations such as the use of formal rules, the creation of specific personnel positions or roles, and personnel policies directed at the efficient achievement of organizational goals have been the focus of study. By directing attention toward the internal properties of bureaucratic organizations, interest in a number of topics has arisen, including the impact of technology on organizational structures (Thompson 1967), the interrelationships among organizational features (Hage et al. 1968), the integration of individuals within organizations (Argyris 1964; Herzberg et al. 1959), and the increase of worker productivity and organizational efficiency (Taylor 1911; Mayo 1933). Across this array of topics, a general theoretical perspective prevails in which the internal properties of bureaucratic organizations are regarded to be of cardinal importance. By directing primary attention toward the internal properties of bureaucratic organizations, the extent to which organizations are embedded in the more global structure and context of society is not fully realized. However, as bureaucratic organizations have grown in function and complexity, assuming an ever-expanding role in society, and displacing previous, more particularistic and personalized forms of administration, management, and control, the vibrant interplay between the internal properties of organizations and the environments in which they are situated has become more salient. Correspondingly, a more "open" theoretical orientation is warranted. Organizations are viewed as "natural systems" (Scott 1992) in which the interaction between an organization and its environment involves a series of potential two-way relationships. While many of the processes within a bureaucracy are designed to insulate the organization from external influences, invariably environmental influences can appreciably impact an organization and its internal operations. Similarly, the bureaucratic organization, with its expanding role in modern society, has unquestionably had a major impact on society.

EMPIRICAL ASSESSMENT

Stanley Udy (1959) was among the first to propose that, rather than regarding the specification of bureaucracies to be strictly a matter of definition, we need to ascertain empirically the extent to which bureaucratic characteristics are associated with one another in actual organizations. In the subsequent efforts at empirical assessment of the extent to which organizations exhibit bureaucratic properties, the works of Richard Hall (1963) and the Aston University research group (Pugh et al. 1968) are especially noteworthy. Hall's (1963) findings suggest that among samples of U.S. organizations, bureaucratic features of organizations may vary independently of one another. As is illustrated by the negative relationship between an emphasis on technical qualifications and other bureaucratic features—in particular hierarchy of authority and rule enforcement—Hall's study suggests that bureaucratic systems of organization may be indicative of multidimensional rather than unitary processes.

The Aston University research group (Pugh et al. 1968) reported similar findings for organizations in Britain. On the basis of their measurements of the bureaucratic characteristics of organizations specified by Weber, these researchers found four mutually independent dimensions of organizational structure rather than a single overarching bureaucratic dimension. With this finding, the authors concluded that bureaucracy is a multidimensional phenomenon and that it ". . . is not unitary, but that organizations may be bureaucratic in any number of ways" (Pugh et al. 1968, p. 101). However, these findings have not been unchallenged. The contentious nature of inquiry into the precise structure of bureaucratic organization is succinctly reflected in the work of

Blau (1970) and of Child (1972), the adoption of a modified position by one of the investigators in the original Aston group (Hickson and McMillan 1981), and the subsequent reply by Pugh (1981).

THE RISE OF BUREAUCRATIC CONTROL

Although bureaucracy existed in imperial Rome and ancient China, as well as in various national monarchies, the complexity of legislative issues arising within the modern state has caused an enormous growth of administrative function within both government and the private sector. Consequently, the power and authority of bureaucratic administrative officials to control policy within an organization as well as the modern state has, over time, increased significantly. The rise to power of bureaucratic officials means that, without expressly intending to achieve power, nonelected officials can and do have a significant impact on a broad spectrum of activities and future developments within society. As Weber noted,

The bureaucratic structure is everywhere a late product of historical development. The further back we trace our steps, the more typical is the absence of bureaucracy and of officialdom in general. Since bureaucracy has a rational character, with rules, means–ends calculus, and matter-of-factness predominating, its rise and expansion has everywhere had revolutionary results. (1978, p. 1002)

Moreover, Weber contended that traditional authority structures have been, and will continue to be, replaced by the rational–legal authority structures of modern bureaucracies, given their "purely technical superiority over any other form of organization" (Weber 1946, p. 214). Regardless of the apparent technical benefit, the increased prominence of bureaucracies in both the public and the private sectors is not without its problems. As Weber acknowledged, certain negative consequences may follow the development of bureaucratic systems of administration to include:

1. The monopolization of information and the creation of "official secrets"

2. The inability to change bureaucratic structure because of vested incentive and reward systems, and the dependency of society on the specialization and expertise provided by the bureaucracy

3. The tendency for bureaucracies to act in an autocratic manner, indifferent to variations or changes not previously articulated or anticipated within the bureaucracy. (Weber 1947, pp. 224–233)

A frequently expressed concern is that bureaucracies are often unresponsive to the individuals and groups they were designed to serve. To exacerbate the situation still further, few, if any, techniques of control are available outside the bureaucracies to make officials more responsive. Additionally, a number of practical problems may arise to potentially undermine bureaucratic efficiency. These difficulties can include the unwarranted application of rules and regulations, the duplication of effort, and an indifferent and even cavalier attitude among officials. Nonetheless, bureaucracies are relatively efficient and technically superior forms of administration proven to be indispensable to large, complex organizations and modern society. As Perrow has noted (1972), criticism of bureaucracies frequently relates to the fact that the actions of officials are not bureaucratic enough and personal interests may not be fully insulated from official duties.

In viewing the operation and function of bureaucracies, it is imperative that the operational efficiency of bureaucratic procedures be recognized but not at the cost of neglecting a more "humanistic" orientation (Kamenka 1989, ch. 5). The situational constraints faced by individuals and groups both within and outside bureaucracies warrant attention. As Martin Albrow has noted, bureaucracy is "a term of strong emotive overtones and elusive connotations" (1970, p. 13), and as such it represents more than a straightforward technical process and deserves an eclectic perspective in order to fully appreciate its complexities.

BUREAUCRATIC DYSFUNCTIONS

The classic works of Merton (1940) and of Gouldner (1954) illustrate how unanticipated developments can adversely impact the intended effectiveness of bureaucratic procedures. Merton notes that, commencing with the need for bureaucratic control, individual compliance with rules is enforced, thereby allowing for the development of routinely prescribed, reliable patterns of activity. However, when

this agenda of rule compliance is implemented in a dynamic and fluctuating environment requiring more spontaneous responses, these prescribed patterns of bureaucratic activity can lead to adverse unintended consequences. Even though the circumstances require a different type of response, prescribed and fixed patterns of response may still be adopted because such responses are legitimated and defensible within the bureaucracy, given the extent to which they enhance individual reliability. Consequently, officials and employees do not accommodate the unique features of the situation, efficiency is undermined, and difficulties with clients and customers may ensue. Eventually, troublesome experiences with customers and clients may contribute to an even greater emphasis on bureaucratically reliable behavior rather than attenuating this encapsulated and counterproductive type of behavior. As Merton (1940) notes, "Adherence to the rules, originally conceived of as a means, becomes transformed into an end in itself; there occurs the familiar process of displacement of goals whereby an instrumental value becomes a terminal value. . ." While more highly adaptive and flexible behavior is required and permitted within a bureaucracy, powerful structural constraints may operate to promote situationally inappropriate rule-bound behavior (Blau and Meyer 1987; Allinson 1984).

Like Merton, Gouldner (1954) is concerned with possible unintended effects of formal rule enforcement. In Gouldner's model, the implications of using general and impersonal rules as a means of enforcing organizational control are investigated. The intention of using such rules is to mask or partially conceal differential power relations between subordinates and their superiors. In societies with egalitarian norms, such as the United States, this serves to enhance the legitimacy of supervisory positions, thereby reducing the prospect of tension between groups with differing power. However, the use of general and impersonal rules also has the unintended consequence of providing only minimal guidelines regarding acceptable organizational behavior. In turn, if only minimum standards of performance are specified and if individuals conform only to these standards, then a disparity arises between the stated goals of the organization, which require a level of performance beyond minimally acceptable and specified standards, and actual individual performance. Since a greater level of individual output and performance is required, more personal and closer forms of supervision need to be employed. This closer supervision increases the visibility of power relations, a consequence that may undermine the effect previously achieved by the use of general and impersonal rules.

The satirical, but nonetheless insightful, work of Peter and Hull (1969) indicates that bureaucratic processes may not always reflect the principle of personal expertise. Peter and Hull contend that even though individual talent and expertise are the formal requisites for recruitment and promotion within a bureaucracy, individuals often are promoted to positions that exceed their level of competence. Since the act of promotion often requires the assumption of new duties, an element of uncertainty over whether individuals will be as efficient in their new positions as they were in their previous positions is ever present. Not until an individual has had the position for a period of time is it apparent if he will be able to perform the newly assigned tasks in an efficient and competent manner. Most individuals are able to achieve an acceptable level of competence in their new duties; but what about those individuals who are unable to perform their new duties competently? Peter and Hull contend that, instead of being relocated to more suitable positions, these individuals remain in the elevated positions due, in all likelihood, to the difficulties and organizational costs associated with removing and reassigning them. Consequently, some individuals may be promoted to and remain in positions that exceed their level of competence, a portrayal clearly at variance with the image of operational efficiency.

THE PERVASIVENESS OF BUREAUCRACY IN SOCIETY

Throughout the nineteenth and twentieth centuries, a notable increase occurred in the number and type of functions performed within or regulated by a bureaucratic organization. Bureaucracies have superceded other more personalized, particularistic operations (ostensibly due to the technical superiority of the bureaucratic process) or, as new processes developed, they developed within the context of a bureaucratic structure. The ubiquitous presence of bureaucracies in modern society is indicated by the common usage of the term "red tape." The term originally denoted unnecessary and prolonged bureaucratic paperwork and procedures, and has since been expanded to encompass a more generic sense of unproductive effort. The level of everyday exposure to bureaucracies is sufficient such that notions of what a bureaucracy is (or perhaps more importantly, what it is not) have become a part of the popular culture of modern society. Fictional settings in which bureaucratic procedures interfere with the good intentions of people, promote an unproductive or unhealthy outcome, or lead to an uninspired work environment are common themes of movies, novels, syndicated cartoon features, and television shows.

The expansion of bureaucratic procedures has clearly impacted developments in the areas of health care and labor. In the area of health care, changes in the technological base of medicine, the methods by which medical services are financed, the regulatory role of government, as well as efforts to enhance the efficiency and accountability of health care providers has culminated in the bureaucratization of medical care (Mechanic 1976). In contrast to past medical practice settings characterized by a private and dyadic relationship between a doctor and a patient, the delivery of medical care in bureaucratized settings, intended to provide broader and more uniform care, increases the likelihood of conflicts of interest and the diminished salience of individualized care. When medical care is delivered in a bureaucratic setting, the specific features of patient care may be based on a number of nonclinical elements in addition to the clinically pertinent factors. Nonclinical criteria such the determination of what services will be provided and the avoidance of "unnecessary" services, patient case management by nonmedical personnel, a predetermined referral protocol and network, and the disclosure of sensitive patient information within the bureaucratic organization all limit the role of the doctor. Each of these nonclinical, bureaucratically derived elements introduce different and potentially conflicting viewpoints in an evaluation of effective patient care and may direct attention more toward resolving organizational conflicts than enhancing patient care. The issues facing bureaucratic medical care will likely become more acute with the "aging" of society and the need to attend to a greater number of patients suffering from debilitating, protracted, and nonrecoverable medical conditions.

The logic underlying the structure of bureaucratic organization is to control and regulate work routines on the basis of formal rules and regulations. In intending to use formal rules to administer workers' duties and responsibilities, it is assumed that key components of a job can be identified to the extent that rules can effectively monitor and be used to evaluate individual performance. The precise specification of work routines for the purpose of enhancing worker productivity and organizational efficiency has been an ongoing interest throughout the twentieth century, as indicated by the time-motion studies and efficiency "experts" of the early part of the century and process evaluation and quality assessments of the later part of the century. In the course of precisely specifying work responsibilities and routines, the de-skilling of the labor force (Taylor 1911) is, if not an intended outcome, a likely development. If a job can be defined in terms of specific component tasks and if the component tasks are rudimentary enough to be regulated by formal rules, then the skill requirements of job are reduced. As this process continues, the skill levels of workers in the labor force may exhibit similar reduction. Organizations can hire an individual with the nominal skill sets needed to adhere to the formally specified rules instead of hiring someone who is capable of displaying individual judgment working effectively in an environment characterized by job variability and uncertainty.

Bureaucracies have become both indispensable and despised fixtures of modern society. In the drive for overall organizational efficiency and accountability, individuals within and outside the bureaucracy often experience the unsettling feeling that they have no influence over a process that may directly impact them. The aggravation of wanting to have a problem solved or question answered but being unable to find anyone who is in the position to respond to the expressed concern fuels criticism of bureaucracies.

While criticism of bureaucratic procedures (or lack of "appropriate" procedures) is frequent, it is also apparent many of the everyday functions in society are possible only because of the operation of bureaucracies. The major institutions of society, with the multitude of diverse projects performed every day, depend on the administrative and regulatory features of bureaucracies. The

faceless bureaucratic official who may be criticized for indifference is nonetheless an essential element in such consequential areas as national defense, public education and welfare, and communications. The assessment of bureaucratic structure and procedures therefore needs to attend to both the overall scope of bureaucratic functions and the manner in which particular tasks are performed.

"Red tape" and inefficiency are two of the most heavily criticized elements of public bureaucracies, and instigate appropriate calls for reform. However, bureaucracies contain complex structures and multifaceted procedures intended to serve a number of purposes. Criticism often reflects common misperceptions rather than the true workings of bureaucracies. Regarding red tape, the bureaucracy does not necessarily create these protracted procedures in an effort to either insulate the organization from competition or to ensure that little if anything gets done without the organization's official approval. Rather, it is more likely the result of disclosure and accountability requirements imposed on the bureaucracy (Kaufman 1977, p. 29). Similarly, inefficiency needs to be placed in the more global perspective of what in addition to the specific task is being accomplished by the bureaucracy. If the focus is limited to a specific task (e.g., construction of a highway), then the process can reasonably be viewed as inefficient if the task could have been completed sooner or cost less if done by someone else. However, there may be a number of additional goals that the bureaucracy is attempting to achieve while completing the specific task in question. In the public sector, a bureaucracy is often required to be responsive to a number of outside interest groups to ensure that its operation is socially fair, accountable, and impartial, in addition to being technically able to complete a particular task (Wilson 1989, pp.315–325). The determination of efficiency is compounded by this collateral concern regarding the attainment of social goals and specific technical goals. Bureaucracies are thus faced with the dual challenge of being socially responsible and technically proficient and therefore have to be assessed on the basis of the extent to which they concurrently achieve these two sets of goals and not just one set at the exclusion of the other.

SEE ALSO: *Complex Organizations; Organizational Effectiveness; Organizational Structure*

REFERENCES

Albrow, Martin 1970 *Bureaucracy*. London: Pall Mall Press.

Allinson, Christopher W. 1984 *Bureaucratic Personality and Organization Structure*. Aldershot, Eng.: Gower.

Argyris, Chris 1964 *Integrating the Individual and the Organization*. New York: Wiley.

Blau, Peter M. 1970 "Decentralization in Bureaucracies." In Mayer N. Zald, ed., *Power in Organizations*. Nashville, Tenn.: Vanderbilt University Press.

——, and Marshall W. Meyer 1987 *Bureaucracy in Modern Society*, 3rd ed. New York: Random House.

Child, John 1972 "Organization, Structure, and Strategies of Control." *Administrative Science Quarterly* 17:163–177.

Gouldner, Alvin W. 1954 *Patterns of Industrial Bureaucracy*. Glencoe, Ill.: Free Press.

Hage, Jerald, Derek Pugh, David Hickson, Robert Hinings, and Chris Turner 1968 "Dimensions of Organizational Structure." *Administrative Science Quarterly* 13:65–104.

Hall, Richard 1963 "The Concept of Bureaucracy: An Empirical Assessment." *American Journal of Sociology* 69:32–40.

Herzberg, Frederick, Bernard Mausner, and Barbara Snyderman 1959 *The Motivation to Work*. New York: Wiley.

Hickson, David, and C. J. McMillan 1981 *Organization and Nation: The Aston Programme IV*. Westmead, Eng.: Gower.

Kamenka, Eugene 1989 *Bureaucracy*. Oxford: Basil Blackwell.

Kaufman, Herbert 1977 *Red Tape*. Washington, D.C.: The Brookings Institute.

March, James G., and Herbert A. Simon 1958 *Organizations>*. New York: Wiley.

Marx, Karl (1852) 1963 *The Eighteenth Brumaire of Louis Bonaparte*. New York: International Publishing Co.

Mayo, Elton 1933 *The Human Problems of Industrial Civilization*. New York: Macmillan.

Mechanic, David 1976 *The Growth of Bureaucratic Medicine: An Inquiry into the Dynamics of Patient Behavior and the Organization of Medical Care*. New York: Wiley.

Merton, Robert K. 1940 "Bureaucratic Structure and Personality." *Social Forces* 18:560–568.

Michels, Robert 1949 *Political Parties: A Sociological Study of the Oligarchial Tendencies of Modern Democracy*. New York: Free Press.

Mouzelis, Nicos P. 1967 *Organization and Bureaucracy*. London: Routledge and Kegan Paul.

Parsons, Talcott, and E. A. Shils 1951 *Toward a General Theory of Action*. Cambridge, Mass.: Harvard University Press.

Perrow, Charles 1972 *Complex Organizations: A Critical Essay*. Glenview, Ill.: Scott Foresman.

Peter, Laurence F., and Raymond Hull 1969 *The Peter Principle*. New York: Morrow.

Pugh, D. S. 1981 "The Aston Programme of Research: Retrospect and Prospect." In Andrew H. Van de Ven and W. F. Joyce, eds., *Perspectives on Organization Design and Behavior*. New York: Wiley.

——, et al. 1968 "Dimensions of Organization Structure." *Administrative Science Quarterly* 13:65–105.

Rhinestein, Max 1954 *Max Weber on Law in Economy and Society*. New York: Simon and Schuster.

Scott, W. Richard 1992 *Organizations: Rational, Natural, and Open Systems*, 3rd ed. Englewood Cliffs, N.J.: Prentice-Hall, Inc.

Taylor, Frederick W. 1911 *Principles of Scientific Management*. New York: Harper and Row.

Thompson, James 1967 *Organizations in Action*. New York: McGraw-Hill.

Tocqueville, Alexis de (1877) 1955 *L'ancien regime and the French Revolution*, J. P. Mayer and A. P. Kerr, eds. Garden City, N.Y.: Doubleday.

Udy, Stanley H. Jr. 1959 "'Bureaucracy' and 'Rationality' in Weber's Organization Theory." *American Sociological Review* 24:591–595.

Weber, Max 1946 *From Max Weber: Essays in Sociology*, H. H. Gerth and C. W. Mills, eds. London: Oxford University Press.

Wilson, James Q. 1989 *Bureaucracy: What Government Agencies Do and Why They Do It*. New York: Basic Books.

—— 1978 *Economy and Society: An Outline of Interpretive Sociology*, Guenther Roth and Claus Wittich, eds. Berkeley: University of California Press.

—— 1947 *The Theory of Social and Economic Organization*, A. M. Henderson and T. Parsons, eds. Glencoe, Ill.: Free Press.

DAVID G. NICKINOVICH

C

CAPITALISM

NOTE: *Although the following article has not been revised for this edition of the Encyclopedia, the substantive coverage is currently appropriate. The editors have provided a list of recent works at the end of the article to facilitate research and exploration of the topic.*

Sociology has no complete, formal consensus on a specific definition of capitalism. The discipline of sociology itself arose as an attempt to understand and explain the emergence and nature of modern capitalist societies. Sociology's founding theorists were very much concerned with the development of capitalism. Émile Durkheim sought to find the bases of new forms of morality and social solidarity in the division of labor, which capitalism both expanded and accelerated (Durkheim 1984). Karl Marx, of course, spent his adult life analyzing and criticizing capitalist society. Marx's project was guided by his hope and expectation that capitalism would be displaced as history moved toward a socialist, and then communist, future. Max Weber, too, devoted considerable attention to the origins of modern capitalism and the historically specific character of Western society under capitalist expansion. Contemporary sociology's treatment of capitalism is grounded in the works of these theorists. The works of Marx and Weber, insofar as they more explicitly focused attention on the dynamics of capitalism, provide a point of departure for discussing modern sociology's approaches to capitalism.

The term *capitalism* is sometimes used to refer to the entire social structure of a capitalist society. Unless otherwise indicated, it is used here with specific reference to a form of economy to which multiple social institutions are effectively bound in relatively compatible ways. Weber used the term *capitalism* in a very general way: "wealth used to gain profit in commerce" (Weber 1976, p. 48). This understanding of capitalism permits the discovery of capitalism in a wide variety of social and historical settings. Weber describes this general form of capitalism in traditional India and China, ancient Babylon, Egypt, and Rome and in medieval and modern Europe. However, Weber also constructs a more specific typology that pertains to the form that capitalism has taken in more contemporary Western society. This form of capitalism is referred to as modern, or Western, capitalism. In *The Protestant Ethic and the Spirit of Capitalism*, Weber (1958 pp. 21–22) contends that this is "a very different form of capitalism which has appeared nowhere else" and that it is unique in its rational "organization of formally free labor." Other important characteristics of modern capitalism, such as the separation of business from the household and rational bookkeeping, derive their significance from this peculiar organization of labor. In this emphasis on the importance of free labor, or the creation of a labor market, Weber's definition of capitalism moves much closer to Marx's use of the term.

For Marx, it is the creation of a market for human labor that is the essence of capitalism. Marx wrote that capitalism can "spring into life only when the owner of the means of production and subsistence meets in the market with the free laborer selling his labor power" (Marx, quoted in Sweezy 1970 pp. 56–57). The emergence of the free laborer represents the destruction of other noncapitalist economic forms. Feudal or slave economies, for example, are not characterized by the recognized right of laborers to sell their own labor power as a commodity. Simple commodity production, or economies in which laborers own their own means of production (tools, equipment, etc.), are not characterized by the need for laborers to sell their labor power as a commodity. In the latter case, Weber concurs with Marx that this freedom is only formal since such laborers are compelled to sell their labor by the "whip of hunger."

The sociological conception of capitalism also varies with particular theoretical understandings of the nature of history. Marxists, guided by an evolutionlike vision of history, tend to see capitalism as a stage in humanity's progressive movement to a communist future. In this manner, Marxist sociology also often refers to various phases of capitalism. Wright (1978 pp. 168–169), for example, describes six stages of capitalist development: primitive accumulation, manufacture, machinofacture, monopoly capital, advanced monopoly capital, and state-directed monopoly capitalism. The implicit assumptions of law-like forces at work in the historical process are evident in the Marxist confidence that capitalism, like all previous socioeconomic orders, will eventually be destroyed by the internal contradictions it generates. References to the current stage of capitalism as "late capitalism" (e.g., Mandel 1978), for instance, reveal a belief in the inevitability of capitalism's demise.

The Weberian tradition, on the other hand, rejects the assumption of history's governance by "iron laws." This leads to a recognition of various types of capitalism but without the presumption that capitalism must eventually be eliminated. The Weberian tradition discovers in the history of Western capitalism a process of rationalization toward depersonalization, improved monetary calculability, increased specialization, and greater technical control over nature as well as over persons (Brubaker 1984). However, while the Weberian tradition can expect the *probability* of continued capitalist rationalization, it does not predict the *inevitability* of such a course for history. It is important to note that, for Weber, a transition from

capitalism to socialism would probably only further this rationalization. Such developments were seen as associated with industrial society and bureaucratic forms of domination rather than with capitalism per se.

This background permits a more detailed examination of contemporary sociology's treatment of capitalism. Already, it can be seen that sociology's understanding of capitalism is more specific than popular conceptions of capitalism as simply "free-market" or "free-enterprise" systems. This is especially so insofar as sociology focuses its attention on modern society. It is the emergence of a "free market" in human labor that sociology tends to recognize as the distinguishing characteristic of modern capitalism. For Durkheimian sociology, this market guides the normal division of labor that is the basis of social solidarity. In this view, the absolute freedom of such a market is necessary to generate the conditions of equal opportunity that are required to guarantee norms by which people come to accept capitalism's highly developed division of labor. Under conditions of a truly free labor market, the stratification system is seen as legitimate since individuals attain their position through their own achievement and not by means of some ascribed status (e.g., caste, gender, race, ethnicity, nepotism) or political patronage. For Marxian sociology, it is in this labor market that the two fundamental and opposing classes of capitalism meet: the owners of the means of production or capitalists (bourgeoisie) and the workers (proletariat). In this view, the struggle between these two classes is the dynamic force behind capitalist development. For Weberian sociology, this market for human labor is necessary for the development of the advanced and superior calculability of capitalist economic action. This calculability is, in turn, a fundamental component of the rationalization process in modern Western society.

This transformation of human labor into a commodity is the force behind both capitalism's internal dynamism as well as its outward expansion. On the one hand, capitalism is constantly driven to enhance its productivity. This compulsion of modern capitalism continuously to develop its technical capacity to produce is not driven simply by competition among capitalists but is related to the unique role that human labor plays in capitalist production. Prior to the emergence of a market for human labor, premodern forms of capitalism exhibited no such pressure constantly to revolutionize the technical means of production. Modern capitalism's dependence on human labor as a commodity, however, demands that this cost of production be kept as low as possible. First, technological development can lower the cost of labor as a commodity by vastly increasing the production of mass consumer goods. The subsequent reduction in the cost of items like food and clothing translates into reductions in the cost of wages to sustain laborers and their families. Another means to this end is automation, the creation of technology that can replace or enhance human labor. Such technological development also permits capitalists to circumvent the natural limits of the human body to labor and the tendency of laborers to organize and demand higher wages, especially important spurs to technological development in capitalist societies characterized by a shortage of labor. However, under such conditions the capitalist's demand for profitability may limit the internal expansion of technology as a means of increasing production (i.e., capital-intensive production) in favor of an outward expansion that draws upon new sources of labor. This expansion of capitalism can take two basic forms. On the one hand, there is a drive toward proletarianization, or the inclusion of more and more of society's population segments that have previously escaped the labor market. On the other hand, there is a tendency to reach outside of the society itself toward other societies, thus incorporating ever larger regions of the world into the sphere of capitalism.

In the early development of capitalist societies, peasants are freed from feudal relations and slaves are freed from slave relations to add to the available pool of labor. This transformation is rarely a smooth one. The great revolutions in Western Europe and the U.S. Civil War forced these precapitalist classes to surrender their workers to the capitalist labor market. Another major source of labor for capitalist expansion has been independent laborers or persons who "work for themselves." Farmers who own their own land and equipment and work without hired labor are a good example of the type of self-employed producer that sociologists commonly refer to as simple commodity producers. There are other occupations in this general classification, of course. Highly skilled laborers have at times been able to

retain independence from capitalist labor markets. However, capitalism has displayed a powerful capacity to bring these laborers into the sphere of capitalist, wage labor relations. For example, carpenters, mechanics, butchers, even doctors and lawyers increasingly find themselves working for wages or a salary in a capitalist firm rather than working for themselves. From time to time, the number of self-employed appears actually to rise in certain capitalist societies (Bechhofer and Elliott 1985). This is usually the result of the introduction of some new technology or new service. Sometimes persons who strongly wish to be their "own bosses" are able to take advantage of specific market conditions or are willing to sacrifice potential income to achieve this status. But clearly, if capitalist societies are examined over the course of the last 200 to 300 years, the tendency is strongly toward increased absorption of persons into the capitalist labor market.

In recent times, labor markets in nations like the United States have found another major source of labor power in women. The traditional role of homemaker impeded the inclusion of women in the labor market. That role of women within the home has changed somewhat, but the role played by women in expanding the pool of labor available to capital has increased tremendously. According to Christensen (1987), for example, in 1960 30 percent of American mothers were employed; in 1986, 62 percent were employed. Ethnic minorities have often performed a similar function in expanding the size of the labor market. Succeeding waves of immigrants have frequently played an initially marginal role in the labor market, only to be gradually absorbed into more routine participation as time passes.

Capitalism's inherent expansionary tendencies also push the capitalist society to reach beyond the borders of the nation. This expansion occurs as capitalism seeks markets for its products but also in the search for raw materials and cheaper labor to produce goods for the home market. Eventually, capitalism may simply seek profitable investment outlets outside the nation of origin. Sociology has analyzed capitalism's transnational expansion with two general but conflicting theoretical approaches. Modernization theory views this expansion in a positive way, seeing it as a means by which undeveloped societies are enabled to begin the process of development that the developed societies have already achieved. This theoretical orientation has been especially important in shaping development policies directed at the "third world" by many Western governments, the World Bank, and even the United Nations (Giddens 1987).

Sociology's other basic approach to the emergence of a world-scale capitalist economy involves a more critical interpretation. This view tends to see capitalist expansion as having actually caused underdevelopment. The underdevelopment approach sees the lack of development in less-developed societies (periphery) as a consequence of systematic exploitation of their people and resources by the advanced societies (core). This process of underdevelopment is generally viewed as having occurred in three stages. The first stage, that of merchant capitalism, persisted from the sixteenth century to the late nineteenth century. Merchant capitalism, supported by military force, transferred vast amounts of wealth from the periphery to the European nations to help finance initial industrial development in what are now the advanced capitalist societies. The second stage, colonialism, persisted until about ten to fifteen years after World War II, when many colonial nations were granted formal independence. In the colonial stage, the developed societies organized economic and political institutions in the less-developed nations to serve the needs of industrial capitalism in the advanced nations. In the postcolonial period, formal political independence has been granted, but the persistent economic inequalities between developed and underdeveloped nations strongly favor the more-developed capitalist societies. Even when raw materials and finished products remain in the lesser-developed nation, the profits derived from such production are taken from the periphery and returned to the advanced core societies. Thus, the pattern of underdevelopment continues in the face of formal independence.

Traditionally, much of sociology's attention to international capitalist expansion has focused on relations between nations. Increasingly, sociology is examining these matters with greater attention to relations between classes. This shift of emphasis reflects the increasing importance of the transnational corporation in recent times. The transnational corporation's greater capacity to use several international sites for component production and the shift of much industrial production to

underdeveloped regions are generating a process of deindustrialization in the advanced capitalist societies. While capitalism has long been a world system, many sociologists contend that the transnational, or "stateless," corporation has significantly less commitment or loyalty to any specific nation. Capital flows ever more rapidly throughout the world, seeking the cheapest source of labor. Modern computer technology has facilitated this trend. Asian, European, and North American capital markets are increasingly interdependent. Sociology's shift of emphasis reflects this tendency for the U.S. capitalist to have more in common, sociologically, with the Japanese or German capitalist than the U.S. investor has in common with the American worker. Sociology's new attention to the internationalization of capital may present a need for rethinking the usefulness of the nation as the typical boundary of a society. The emergence of the "new Europe" and the demise of state socialism in Eastern Europe and the USSR may also lead to a more flexible notion of what constitutes a society.

The preceding discussion has focused on capitalism as a specific form of economy that is defined by the expansion of a labor market in which propertyless workers sell their labor power for money. Capitalist societies are, of course, far more complex than this. There are a number of distinct economic forms that coexist with capitalism in both complementary and conflictual relations. The capitalist economy itself may be broken down into two basic sectors, one representing big business and one representing small business. Sociologists usually refer to these as the monopoly sector and the competitive sector. This dual economy is reflected in a segmented, or dual, labor market. Monopoly sector workers are more likely to be male, unionized, receive better wages and benefits, have greater job security, and work in a more clearly defined hierarchy of authority based on credentials. Competitive sector workers are less likely to possess strong credentials, more likely to be female, receive lower pay, work under more dangerous conditions, and work without union protection, benefits, or job security.

Noncapitalist economic forms also exist alongside this dual capitalist economy. The self-employed reflect a form distinct from modern capitalism that sociologists commonly refer to as simple commodity producers or petite bourgeoisie. These people produce goods and services (commodities) for sale on the market, but they work for themselves and use only their own labor in production. Most capitalist societies also contain cooperative economic organizations that are distinct from capitalist enterprises. Cooperatives are commercial, nonprofit enterprises, owned and democratically controlled by the members. The nonprofit status and democratic distribution of control (one member, one vote) set cooperatives apart. The cooperative is an especially important form of economic organization for those simple commodity producers, like farmers, described above. All capitalist societies today also contain elements of socialist economy. Key social services, such as health care, and even some commodity production are provided by the state in many societies commonly recognized as capitalist. The United States is perhaps among the most resistant to this movement toward mixed economy. Yet even the United States has, to some extent, socialized education, mail delivery, libraries, police and fire protection, scientific research and technological development, transportation networks (e.g., highways, airports, urban transit), military production, industrial infrastructure provision, and so on. The mixed character of this economy is further indicated by the common practice of the government contracting capitalist firms to produce many goods and services. In a related way, the development of welfare has influenced the nature of capitalist society. The increased intervention of government into the economy has generated the notion of the welfare state. While popular conceptions of the welfare state tend to focus on the role that government plays in alleviating the impacts of poverty on individuals, sociology also recognizes that welfare reduces the cost of reproducing the commodity—labor. In this sense, welfare functions, in the long run, as a subsidy to capital. Further, many of the socialized sectors of capitalist economies function to ensure a profitable environment for capitalist firms (O'Connor 1973; Offe 1984). In many instances, such subsidization of capital is biased toward the largest corporations.

Some sociologists have contended that the rise of the large capitalist corporation, with its dispersed stock ownership and bureaucratic form of organization, has eroded the power of individual capitalists to control the corporation in which they have invested their capital. Instead, it is argued, bureaucratic managers have gained control over corporate capital. Such managers are thought to be relatively free of the drive to maximize profits and are willing to accept average rates of profit. In this way, the ruthless character of earlier forms of capitalism are seen as giving way to a capitalism that is managed with broader interests in mind. Further, the dispersal of ownership and control is said to eliminate the misuse of capital in the interests of an elite and wealthy minority. This "managerialist" position complements pluralist political theory by providing greater authority for institutions of representative democracy to control the allocation of society's resources.

This view is challenged in a variety of ways. Other sociologists contend that while management may have gained some formal independence, its job requires devotion to profit maximization, and its performance is assessed on this criteria. In this view, the larger companies' executives and owners are able to use interlocking directorates and their common class background (e.g., elite schools, private clubs, policy-planning organizations) to minimize price competition and thus sustain high profit levels. Others argue that those informal ties are of less consequence than their common dependency on banks. In this view, banks, or finance capital, play a disproportionately powerful role in centralizing control over the allocation of capital resources. This position strongly opposes the managerialist arguments and those who envision an independent corporate elite whose power lies in the control of corporate bureaucracies rather than in personal wealth (Glasberg and Schwartz 1983). Further, to the extent that it is valid, this argument is particularly important given the increasing internationalization of capital discussed above, since a great deal of that development has occurred in the sphere of finance capital.

These sorts of arguments reflect an important shift in sociology's understanding of the relationship between capitalism and democracy. Sociology's Enlightenment roots provided a traditional legacy of viewing capitalism and democracy as intertwined in the process of modernization. While this parallel development is certainly recognizable in early forms of modern capitalism, more recent forms of capitalism call into question the extent to which capitalism and democracy are inevitably bound together. Indeed, recent works suggest that capitalism and democracy are now opposed to one another (e.g., Piven and Cloward 1982). This view holds that the tremendous inequality of wealth generated by modern capitalism impedes the possibility of political equality. Even conservative writers (e.g., Huntington 1975) have noted the problematic relationship between contemporary capitalism and democracy, suggesting a retrenchment of democratic forms in defense of capitalism. The future of capitalism will be shaped by this tension with democracy, but that tension itself is located in an increasingly global economy. At the moment, the politics of capitalist society seem to lag behind the economic changes. The individual is increasingly pressured to sell his or her labor as a commodity on a world market, yet at the same time that individual remains a citizen, not of the world, but of the nation. The transnational capitalist enterprise and the flow of capital, on the other hand, are ever more free of such national borders.

(SEE ALSO: *Marxist Sociology; Postindustrial Society*)

REFERENCES

Bechhofer, F., and B. Elliott 1985 "The Petite Bourgeoisie in Late Capitalism." *Annual Review of Sociology* 11:181–207.

Brubaker, Rogers 1984 *The Limits of Rationality*. London: Allen and Unwin.

Christensen, Kathleen 1987 "Women and Contingent Work." *Social Policy* 17:15–18.

Dicken, Peter 1997 "Transnational Corporations and Nation-States." *International Social Science Journal* 47:77–89.

Durkheim, Emile 1984 *The Division of Labor in Society*. New York: Free Press.

Giddens, Anthony 1987 *Sociology: A Brief but Critical Introduction*, 2d ed. New York: Harcourt Brace Jovanovich.

Glasberg, Davita Silfen, and Michael Schwartz 1983 "Ownership and Control of Corporations." *Annual Review of Sociology* 9:311–332.

Haller, William J., and Vijai P. Singh 1996 "Technology, Producer Services, and the New International Division of Labor." *Journal of Developing Societies* 12:4–18.

Huntington, Samuel P. 1975 "The United States." In Michael Crozier, Samuel P. Huntington, and Joji Watanuki, eds., *The Crisis of Democracy: Report on the Governability of Democracies to the Trilateral Commission*. New York: New York University Press.

London, Bruce, and Robert J. S. Ross 1995 "The Political Sociology of Foreign Direct Investment: Global Capitalism and Capital Mobility, 1965–1980." *International Journal of Comparative Sociology* 36:3–4.

Mandel, Ernest 1978 *Late Capitalism*. London: Verso.

Melling, Joseph 1991 "Industrial Capitalism and the Welfare of the State: The Role of Employers in the Comparative Development of Welfare States: A Review of Recent Research." *Sociology* 25:219–239.

Morss, Elliott R. 1991 "The New Global Players: How They Compete and Collaborate." *World Development* 19:55–64.

O'Connor, James 1973 *The Fiscal Crisis of the State*. New York: St. Martin's Press.

Offe, Claus 1984 *Contradictions of the Welfare State*. Cambridge, Mass.: M.I.T. Press.

Piven, Frances Fox, and Richard A. Cloward 1982 *The New Class War*. New York: Pantheon Books.

Polychroniou, Constantine G. 1990 "Global Capitalism: A Perspective of Convergence." *International Review of Modern Sociology* 20:239–251.

Prashad, Vijay 1994 "Contract Labor: The Latest Stage of Illiberal Capitalism." *Monthly Review* 46:19–26.

Rogers, Hudson P., Alphonso O. Ogbuehi, and C. M. Kochunny 1995 "Ethics and Transnational Corporations in Developing Countries: A Social Contract Perspective." *Journal of Euromarketing* 4:11–38.

Ross, Robert J. S. 1995 "The Theory of Global Capitalism: State Theory and Variants of Capitalism on a World Scale." In D. Smith and B. J. Jozsef, eds., *A New World Order? Global Transformations in the Late Twentieth Century*. Westport, Conn.: Praeger Publishers.

Scott, Alan 1996 "Bureaucratic Revolutions and Free Market Utopias." *Economy and Society* 25:89–110.

Sklair, Leslie 1995 *Sociology of the Global System* 2nd ed. Baltimore, Md.: Johns Hopkins University Press.

Sklair, Leslie 1998 "The Transnational Capitalist Class and Global Capitalism: The Case of the Tobacco Industry." *Political Power and Social Theory* 12:3–43.

Sweezy, Paul M. 1970 *The Theory of Capitalist Development*. New York: Monthly Review Press.

Valocchi, Steve 1990 "The Capitalist State and the Origins of National Welfare Policy in Nineteenth-Century Germany." *Critical Sociology* 17:91–109.

Weber, Max 1958 *The Protestant Ethic and the Spirit of Capitalism*. Talcott Parsons, trans. New York: Scribners.

——1976 *The Agrarian Sociology of Ancient Civilizations*. R. I. Frank, trans. London: New Left Books.

Wright, Erik Olin 1978 *Class, Crisis, and the State*. London: New Left Books.

PATRICK H. MOONEY

CASE STUDIES

There is a sense in which virtually every activity that we associate with sociology might be called "case studies." These activities include the generation of samples (which are made up of individual cases) for statistical analysis, the use of empirical examples (or cases) to illustrate aspects of general sociological theories, and comparative analyses of the interconnected events (again cases) that form historical and cultural patterns. Indeed, Charles Ragin and Howard S. Becker (1992) have edited an anthology dedicated to defining case studies, entitled *What is a Case?* Historically, the answer that sociologists have usually given to this question is that case studies are in-depth analyses of single or a few communities, organizations, or persons' lives. They involve detailed and often subtle understandings of the social organization of everyday life and persons' experiences. Because they focus on naturally occurring events and relationships (not laboratory experiments or survey data), case studies are sometimes described as naturalistic. Case studies usually involve extensive interviews about persons' lives, or direct observation of community or organization members' activities, or both.

The case-study approach is not unique to sociology but is a general approach to social life that is used by social scientists (especially anthropologists and historians), psychotherapists and family therapists, and journalists. All such uses of case studies involve idiographic interpretation that emphasizes how social action and relationships are influenced by their social contexts. Case studies are unique within sociology because they require that researchers immerse themselves in the lives and concerns of the persons, communities, or organizations they study, or all of these. While case studies are based on the general scientific method and are intended to advance the scientific goals of sociology, they are also humanistic because they offer readers insight into the concerns, values, and relationships of persons making up diverse social worlds.

Social scientists use the understandings developed in case studies to introduce the general public to the unique ways of life or problems of communities, or both, to apply and build theories, and to develop policy interventions concerned with individual and social problems. Two classic examples of how case studies may be used to achieve these ends are Elliott Liebow's (1967) *Tally's Corner* and Helen MacGill Hughes's (1961) *Fantastic Lodge*. Liebow's book reports on his experiences as a participant-observer within a poor, male, African-American urban community. Liebow describes the practical problems faced by these men in living their everyday lives, and the practical strategies they used to deal with life's pressing problems. The study challenged many of the prevailing assumptions held by policy makers and academics during the 1960s, and has been used to reassess how the social service and mental health needs of inner city, minority groups are best addressed.

Hughes's study, which is subtitled *The Autobiography of a Drug Addict*, details the life experiences of Janet Clark, a young white woman living in a poor urban area. Hughes describes Ms. Clark as speaking from a marginal urban world made up of drugs and drug addicts, arrest and incarceration, and the urban "sporting" life. The book raises themes that were later systematized by Howard S. Becker (1963)—the person who conducted the interviews of Janet Clark—in developing his version of the labeling approach to the sociology of deviance. The labeling perspective emphasizes that deviance is not just a matter of rule breaking, but is always created through the official responses of others. It has had profound and enduring implications for how sociologists define, study, and analyze societal responses to rule-breaking behavior.

CASE STUDIES AND THE DEVELOPMENT OF SOCIOLOGY IN THE UNITED STATES

Sociological case studies are most associated with the ethnographic traditions established at the University of Chicago during the first half of the twentieth century. The Chicago school's emphasis on case studies partly reflects the influence of Robert E. Park, who joined the Sociology Department in 1916 and later served as department chair. Park taught his students that case studies should emphasize how persons' lives and the organization of communities are shaped by general social processes and structures. For example, Park analyzed the ways in which cities develop as interrelated territories involving distinctive ways of life and opportunities. He described such territories as "natural areas" and stressed that they emerged based on social and economic competition.

Many of the best-known and most influential sociological case studies done in the United States were conducted in the 1920s and 1930s by students and faculty members at the University of Chicago who were interested in the distinctive ways of life in diverse natural areas (e.g., Anderson 1923; Cressey 1932; Shaw 1930; Thomas 1923; Wirth 1928; and Zorbaugh 1929). While it was done later, H. M. Hughes's (1961) study of Janet Clark's life is also an example of the Chicago approach to case studies and urban life. Perhaps the best-known and most influential case study done in the early Chicago school tradition is William Whyte's (1943) *Street Corner Society*, a participant-observer study of a poor Italian-American community. The significance of the study is related to Whyte's use of his observations to identify and explicate some basic sociological issues involving social relations and social control in small groups.

Park's approach to case studies has been modified and refined over the years, particularly by Everett C. Hughes (1970), who developed a comparative approach to work groups and settings. The approach uses case studies to identify and analyze comparatively generalized aspects of work groups and settings, such as work groups' definitions of "dirty work" and their interest in controlling the conditions of their work. Becker's (1963) use of multiple case studies in articulating the labeling perspective is a notable example of how the comparative strategy advocated by E. C. Hughes may be applied to develop sociological theory. Another major contributor to the Chicago school of sociology is Erving Goffman (1959), who used case studies to develop a dramaturgical perspective on social interaction. The perspective treats mundane interactions as quasi-theatrical performances involving scripts, stages, and characters.

Although less influential than the Chicago school, a second source for case studies in American sociology was structural-functionalist theorists who analyzed communities and organizations as stability-seeking social systems. Structural-functional case studies were influenced by anthropological studies of nonindustrial communities and the more abstract theories of Talcott Parsons and Robert Merton. These studies analyze how social systems are maintained and adapt to changing environmental circumstances. For example, structural functionalists have used case studies to analyze the consequences of organizational activities and relationships for maintaining organizational systems (Blau 1955; Gouldner 1954; Sykes 1958).

An exemplary structural-functionalist case study is Rosabeth Moss Kanter's (1977) analysis of a multinational corporation, which she calls Indsco. The study examines how social relations in corporations are shaped by social structures which produce feelings of uncertainty and marginality among managers and secretaries. Kanter uses her case study to illustrate how gender segregation is produced and maintained in Indsco as secretaries and managers cope with the practical problems emergent from corporate power and opportunity structures. She also makes some practical suggestions for altering these structures in order to better address the needs of managers and secretaries, and to produce more egalitarian relations between corporate members. Many of Kanter's suggestions have been adopted by diverse American corporations. This is another way in which case studies may influence social policies.

RECENT DEVELOPMENTS IN CASE-STUDIES RESEARCH

While many qualitative sociologists continue to work within the Chicago school and structural-functional traditions, several important developments have occurred in qualitative sociology in the past twenty-five years. For example, many of the case studies of ethnic communities done by early Chicago school sociologists deal with the problems and social organization of European-American communities. Many more recent case studies, on the other hand, explore these issues within the context of nonEuropean-American communities. Ruth Horowitz's (1983) case study of a Hispanic community and Elijah Anderson's (1990) research in an African-American community are major contributions to this development.

Age-based communities have also emerged as subjects for case studies by sociologists. One focus in this literature involves the distinctive life circumstances and coping strategies of communities of older people. Arlie Hochschild's (1973) study of a group of widowed women as an "unexpected community" is an important example of this focus, as is Jennie Keith's (1977) analysis of the social construction of community in a retirement facility in France. Another approach to case-study research is Jaber Gubrium's (1993) analysis of the life stories told to him by a group of elderly nursing home residents. Equally significant are recent case studies of communities of young people, particularly of communities organized around shared interests in popular culture. A useful example is Sarah Thornton's (1996) case study of dance clubs and raves in London. Thornton's analysis extends traditional analysis of communities as subcultures by showing how this community was created and is maintained through the actions of (not so youthful) members of the London mass media.

A related change has been case studies of experiential communities. That is, social groups that share common social experiences, but not a common territory. For example, Richard Majors and Janet Mancini Billson (1992) analyze African-American males as a racial and gender community that is organized around shared practical problems and strategies for managing them. Using a semiotic perspective, Dick Hedbridge (1979) also analyzes an experiential community in using several case studies to show how young people form a subculture that is organized around the expression of cultural styles, which symbolically resist dominant forces in society. Another focus in this literature is on the distinctive life experiences of members of gay and lesbian communities. A notable example is Carol A. B. Warren's (1974) case study of a gay community in which she raises some important questions about the labeling perspective. Thus, both Warren's and Hedbridge's research show how case studies contribute to theoretical development in sociology.

A different, but complementary, use of the case-study research strategy is auto-ethnography. These are case studies conducted within and about one's own group. The researcher acts as both a sociologist seeking information about a community, and as a subject of the research. A groundbreaking auto-ethnography is David Hayano's (1982) study of professional card players. This case study provides readers with distinctive access to, and insights into, the experiences of professional card players. Two other notable auto-ethnographies are Helen Rose Fuchs Ebaugh's (1977) case study

of her own and others' exit from the social role of Roman Catholic nun, and Thomas Schmid's and Richard S. Jones's (1991) analysis of Jones's and other inmates' adaptations to prison life.

Auto-ethnographers' concern for taking account of their own and others' experiences is extended in another trend in sociological case-studies research. This trend focuses on emotions as a basic and important aspect of social life. Many case studies done by sociologists of emotions deal with other persons' emotional experiences (Hochschild 1983; Katz 1988). Other sociologists, however, adopt a more auto-ethnographic strategy by treating their own lives and feelings as topics for sociological analysis. The sociologist's feelings become the case or part of the case under study. An important example of the latter approach to case studies is David Karp's (1996) discussion of his own experiences with depression, and his linking of them to the emotional experiences reported by other members of this community of sufferers.

In addition to the changes discussed above, three other changes in case-studies research warrant special notice. They are the emergence of radical case studies, a focus on reality construction, and concern for the politics and poetics of writing case studies.

RADICAL CASE STUDIES

While early sociological case studies were sometimes associated with reformist movements, they were seldom intended to advance politically radical causes or to build radical social theory. This orientation may be contrasted with that of radical journalists of the same era (such as Upton Sinclair) who used case studies to highlight social problems and raise questions about the legitimacy of capitalism. Radical sociologists have begun to use case studies to develop their sociological goals. One source for radical case studies is Marxist sociologists concerned with the ways in which worker-management relations are organized in work settings, how social classes are perpetuated, and how capitalism is justified.

Marxist sociologists use their case studies to challenge more conservative case studies that, from the radicals' standpoint, do not take adequate account of the ways in which persons' everyday lives are shaped by political and economic structures. They are also used to analyze historical changes in capitalism and the consequences of the changes for workers. For Marxist theorists, a major change has been the rise of a new of society—monopoly capitalism—dominated by multinational corporations. These theorists use case studies of work settings to illustrate and analyze the effects of monopoly capitalism on workers (Burawoy 1970).

Although it is not as well developed in sociology as in anthropology, another focus of radical case studies involves the social and personal consequences of the international division of labor. The studies are concerned with the ways in which multinational corporations internationalize the production process by exporting aspects of production to Third World countries. Case studies of this trend show the profound impact of global economic changes for gender and family roles in Third World countries (Ong 1987). Finally, radical sociologists have used the case-study method to analyze the ways in which capitalist institutions and relationships are justified and perpetuated by noneconomic institutions such as schools (Willis 1977).

A second source for radical case studies is feminist sociology. While it is diverse and includes members who hold many different political philosophies, all forms of feminist sociology are sensitive to the politics of human relationships. A major theme in feminist case studies involves the ways in which women's contributions to social relationships and institutions go unseen and unacknowledged. Feminist sociologists use case studies to call attention to women's contributions to society and analyze the political implications of their invisibility. A related concern involves analyzing relationships and activities that are typically treated as apolitical and private matters as matters of public concern. One way in which feminist sociologists do so is by treating aspects of their own lives as politically significant and making them matters for sociological analysis (McCall 1993).

The case-study approach is central to the feminist sociology of Dorothy E. Smith (1987). Smith treats case studies as points of entry for studying general social processes that shape persons' experiences and lives. Her approach to case studies emphasizes how the seemingly insignificant activities of everyday life are related by general social processes (such as patriarchy and market relationships) and how they help to perpetuate the processes. Smith describes, for example, how the commonplace activity of dining in a restaurant is organized within, and perpetuates, capitalist commodity relations. Smith's analysis might also be seen as an example of the general analytic strategy, which Michael Burawoy (1998) calls the "extended case method." This approach to case studies involves four major steps:

- Researcher observations of, and immersion in, a social setting,

- Analysis of the researcher's observations as aspects of general social processes that shape life in diverse contemporary social settings,

- Historicizing the observations and social processes by showing how they are embedded in historical forces that guide and structure the evolution of capitalist society, and

- Linking the observations and analyses to formal sociological theories that explain the researcher's initial observations and their larger social and historical contexts.

This is one way in which case studies may be used as a springboard for developing systematic, general, and formal sociological analyses.

CASE STUDIES OF REALITY CONSTRUCTION

Basic to the case-study method and idiographic interpretation is a concern for human values and culture. Beginning in the 1960s, one focus of this concern has been with the ways in which social realities are produced in social interactions. The new focus is generally based on the social phenomenology of Alfred Schutz and ethnomethodology. While different in some ways, both are concerned with the folk methods that people use to construct meanings (Silverman 1975). For example, Harold Garfinkel (1967), the founder of ethnomethodology, used a case study of a patient seeking a sex-change operation to analyze how we orient to ourselves and others as men and women.

Case studies of reality construction emphasize how social realities are created, sustained, and changed through language use. The emphasis has given rise to new orientations to traditional areas of sociological research, such as science. Until recently, sociologists of science have treated scientific work as a simple, noninterpretive process centered in scientists' adherence to the rules of the scientific method, which emphasizes how "facts" and "truth" emerge from observations of the "real" world. Viewed this way, scientific facts are not matters of interpretation or social constructions. This view of science has been challenged by case studies of scientific work that focus on the ways in which scientific facts are socially produced based on scientists' interpretations of their experiments (Latour and Woolgar 1979).

A major branch of ethnomethodology is conversation analysis, which focuses on the turn-by-turn organization of social interactions (Sacks, Schegloff, and Jefferson 1974). For conversation analysts, social reality is collaboratively constructed within turn-taking sequences, which may be organized around such linguistic practices as questions and answers or charges and rebuttals. A major contribution of conversation-analytic studies has been to show how IQ and other test results are shaped by the ways in which test-givers and test-takers interact (Marlaire and Maynard 1990). Also, sociologists influenced by conversation analysis theory have considered how power and dominance are interactionally organized and accomplished.

Some qualitative sociologists have extended and reformulated ethnomethodological case studies by analyzing the relationships between the interpretive methods used by interactants in concrete situations and the distinctive meanings they produce in their interactions. This approach to case studies focuses on the practical and political uses of meanings in social institutions. These ethnographers analyze meanings as rhetorics which interactants use to persuade others and to assign identities to themselves and others. An important contribution to this approach to case-study research is Donileen Loseke's (1992) study of decision making and social relations in a shelter for battered women. Loseke details the practical contexts within which shelter workers, shelter residents, and applicants to the shelters encounter each other and manage their social relationships. It is in these encounters, Loseke states, that shelter workers and residents give concrete meaning to the abstract cultural category of battered women.

Two other important, and related, trends in case studies of reality construction involve comparative analysis of two or more cases, and the use of new theoretical perspectives in analyzing case-study data. One example is Jaber Gubrium's (1992) comparative analysis of two different family therapy sites. Gubrium uses observational data from the sites to show how different therapy approaches are organized to "detect" and remedy different kinds of family and personal problems. He also shows how aspects of Weberian theory may be used in analyzing the sociological significance of family therapy. Gale Miller and David Silverman (1995) have also contributed to this development by comparatively analyzing social interactions in two different counseling centers located in the United States and England. This study is based on the ethnography of institutional discourse perspective (Miller 1994), which is a strategy for developing general theoretical statements from case-study research.

THE POLITICS AND POETICS OF WRITING CASE STUDIES

While some qualitative sociologists focus on the folk methods of description and interpretation used by others in creating realities, other sociologists are reconsidering the reality constructing methods used by sociologists in writing case studies. Their interest centers in the question, How do we do our work? The question raises issues about the relationships between qualitative researchers and the people they study. For example, is it enough that case studies inform the public and sociologists about aspects of contemporary society, or should they also help the persons and communities studied? A related issue involves editorial control over the writing of case studies. That is, should the subjects of case studies have a voice in how they are described and analyzed?

Such questions have given rise to many answers, but most of them involve analyzing case studies as narratives or stories that sociologists tell about themselves and others. For example, John van Maanen (1988) divides ethnographic writing into several types of "tales" involving different orientations to the persons described, readers, and authorship. Other analyses focus on the various rhetorical devices used by ethnographers to write their case studies (Bruyn 1966). Such rhetorical devices include metaphor, irony, paradox, synecdoche, and metonymy, which ethnographers use both to describe others and to cast their descriptions as objective and authoritative.

Qualitative sociologists' interest in writing case studies may be part of a larger interdisciplinary movement involving social scientists and humanists. The movement is concerned with analyzing the rhetorics of social scientific inquiry (Nelson et al. 1987) as well as how to write better narratives. The latter issue is basic to efforts by British sociologists to develop new forms of writing that better reflect the ways in which their case studies are socially constructed (Woolgar 1988) and other sociologists' interest in developing alternatives to the logico-scientific writing style that better express their theoretical perspectives, political philosophies, and experiences (DeVault 1990; Richardson 1990). A related change in this area is some sociologists' interest in using performance art to represent their research data. For example, Carolyn Ellis and Arthur Bochner (1992) have written a play about the experiences and dilemmas faced by women and their male partners in deciding whether to abort the woman's pregnancy. Ellis and Bochner state that this presentational form allows for a wider range of communication devices than does the usual textual approach to reporting case-study findings.

In sum, the case-study method is a dynamic approach to studying social life, which sociologists modify and use to achieve diverse political and theoretical goals. While the popularity of the case-study method waxes and wanes over time, it is likely to always be a major research strategy of humanistically oriented sociologists.

(SEE ALSO: *Ethnomethodology; Field Research Methods; Life Histories; Qualitative Methods*)

REFERENCES

Anderson, Elijah 1990 *Streetwise: Race, Class, and Change in an Urban Community*. Chicago: University of Chicago Press.

Anderson, Nels 1923 *The Hobo*. Chicago: University of Chicago Press.

Becker, Howard S. 1963 *Outsiders: Studies in the Sociology of Deviance*. New York: Free Press.

Blau, Peter M. 1955 *The Dynamics of Bureaucracy*. Chicago: University of Chicago Press.

Bruyn, Severyn T. 1966 *The Human Perspective in Sociology*. Englewood Cliffs, N.J.: Prentice-Hall.

Burawoy, Michael 1970 *Manufacturing Consent*. Chicago: University of Chicago Press.

——1998 "Critical Sociology: A Dialogue Between Two Sciences." *Contemporary Journal of Sociology* 27:12–20.

Cressey, Paul 1932 *The Taxi-Dance Hall*. Chicago: University of Chicago Press.

DeVault, Marjorie L. 1990 "Talking and Listening from Women's Standpoint." *Social Problems* 37:96–116.

Ebaugh, Helen Rose Fuchs 1997 *Out of the Cloister: A Study of Organizational Dilemmas*. Austin: The University of Texas Press.

Ellis, Carolyn and Arthur P. Bochner 1992 "Investigating Subjectivity." In Carolyn Ellis and Michael G. Flaherty, eds., *Telling and Performing Personal Stories*. Newbury Park, Calif.: Sage Publications.

Garfinkel, Harold 1967 *Studies in Ethnomethodology*. Englewood Cliffs, N.J.: Prentice-Hall.

Goffman, Erving 1959 *The Presentation of Self in Everyday Life*. Garden City, N.Y.: Doubleday.

Gouldner, Alvin 1954 *Patterns of Industrial Democracy*. New York: Free Press.

Gubrium, Jaber F. 1992 *Out of Control: Family Therapy and Domestic Disorder*. Newbury Park, Calif.: Sage.

—— 1993 *Speaking of Life: Horizons of Meaning for Nursing Home Residents*. Hawthorne, N.Y.: Aldine de Gruyter.

Hayano, David M. 1982 *Poker Faces: The Life and Work of Professional Card Players*. Berkeley: University of California Press.

Hedbridge, Dick 1979 *Subculture: The Meaning of Style*. New York: London.

Hochschild, Arlie Russell 1973 *The Unexpected Community*. Englewood Cliffs, N.J.: Prentice-Hall.

—— 1983 *The Managed Heart: Commercialization of Human Feeling*. Berkeley: University of California Press.

Horowitz, Ruth 1983 *Honor and the American Dream: Culture and Identity in a Chicano Community*. New Brunswick, N.J.: Rutgers University Press.

Hughes, Everett C. 1970 "The Humble and the Proud." *The Sociological Quarterly* 11:147–156.

Hughes, Helen MacGill 1961 *The Fantastic Lodge: The Autobiography of a Drug Addict*. Greenwich, Conn.: A Fawcett Premier Book.

Kanter, Rosabeth Moss 1977 *Men and Women of the Corporation*. New York: Basic Books.

Katz, Jack 1988 *Seductions of Crime: Moral and Sensual Attractions in Doing Evil*. New York: Basic Books.

Keith, Jennie 1973 *Old People, New Lives: Community Creation in a Retirement Residence*. Chicago: University of Chicago Press.

Latour, Bruno and Steven Woolgar 1979 *Laboratory Life*. Beverly Hills, Calif.: Sage Publications.

Liebow, Elliot 1967 *Tally's Corner: A Study of Negro Streetcorner Men*. Boston: Little, Brown.

Loseke, Donileen R. 1992 *The Battered Woman and Shelters: The Social Construction of Wife Abuse*. Albany, N.Y.: SUNY Press.

Majors, Richard, and Janet Mancini Billson 1992 *Cool Pose: The Dilemmas of Black Manhood in America*. New York: Touchstone Books.

Marlaire, Courtney L., and Douglas W. Maynard 1990 "Standardized Testing as an Interactional Phenomenon." *Sociology of Education* 63:83–101.

McCall, Michal A. 1993 "Social Constructionism and Critical Feminist Theory and Research." In Gale Miller and James A. Holstein, eds., *Constructionist Controversies: Issues in SocialProblems Theory*. Hawthorne, N.Y.: Aldine de Gruyter.

Miller, Gale 1994 "Toward Ethnographies of Institutional Discourse: Proposal and Suggestions." *Journal of Contemporary Ethnography* 23:280–306.

———, and David Silverman 1995 "Troubles Talk and Counseling Discourse: A Comparative Study." *Sociological Quarterly* 36:725–747.

Nelson, John S., Allan Megill, and Donald N. McCloskey (eds.) 1987 *The Rhetoric of the Human Sciences*. Madison: University of Wisconsin Press.

Ong, Aihwa 1987 *Spirits of Resistance and Capitalist Discipline*. Albany, N.Y.: SUNY Press.

Ragin, Charles C. and Howard S. Becker (eds.) 1992 *What is a Case? Exploring the Foundations of Social Inquiry*. Cambridge, UK: Cambridge University Press.

Richardson, Laurel 1990 "Narrative and Sociology." *Journal of Contemporary Ethnography* 19:116–135.

Sacks, Harvey, Emmanuel A. Schegloff, and Gail Jefferson 1974 "A Simplest Systematics for the Organization of Turn-Taking for Conversation." *Language* 50:696–735.

Schmid, Thomas, and Richard S. Jones 1991 "Suspended Identity Dialectic: Identity Transformation in a Maximum Security Prison." *Symbolic Interaction* 14:415–432.

Shaw, Clifford 1930 *The Jack-Roller*. Chicago: University of Chicago Press.

Silverman, David 1975 "Accounts of Organizations: Organizational 'Structures' and the Accounting Process." In John B. McKinlay, ed., *Processing People: Cases in Organizational Behavior*. London: Holt, Rinehart and Winston.

Smith, Dorothy E. 1987 *The Everyday World as Problematic*. Boston: Northeastern University Press.

Sykes, Gresham M. 1958 *The Society of Captives*. Princeton, N.J.: Princeton University Press.

Thomas, W. I. 1923 *The Unadjusted Girl*. Boston: Little, Brown.

Thornton, Sarah 1996 *Club Cultures: Music, Media and Subcultural Capital*. Hanover, N.H. and London: Wesleyan University Press.

Van Maanen, John 1988 *Tales of the Field*. Chicago: University of Chicago Press.

Warren, Carol A. B. 1974 *Identity and Community in the Gay World*. New York: John Wiley & Sons.

Whyte, William Foote 1943 *Street Corner Society: The Social Structure of an Italian Slum*. Chicago: University of Chicago Press.

Willis, Paul 1977 *Learning to Labour*. New York: Columbia University Press.

Wirth, Louis 1928 *The Ghetto*. Chicago: University of Chicago Press.

Woolgar, Steven 1988 *Science, the Very Idea*. New York: Tavistock.

Zorbaugh, Harvey 1929 *The Gold Coast and the Slum*. Chicago: University of Chicago Press.

GALE MILLER
RICHARD S. JONES

CASTE AND INHERITED STATUS

The study of social inequalities is one of the most important areas of sociology as inequalities in property, power, and prestige have long-term consequences on access to the basic necessities of life such as good health, education, and a well-paying job. Unequal resources between groups also influence their interaction with all the basic institutions of society: the economy, the political system, and religion, among others. An understanding of how inequalities arise, their forms and consequences, and the processes that tend to sustain them is essential for the formulation of policies that will improve the well-being of all in society.

All societies in the world are socially stratified (i.e. wealth, power, and honor are unequally distributed among different groups). However, they vary in the ways in which inequality is structured. One of the most frequently used bases for categorizing different forms of stratification systems is the way status is acquired. In some societies, individuals acquire status on the basis of their achievements or merit. In others, status is accorded on the basis of ascribed, not achieved characteristics. One is born into them or inherits them, regardless of individual abilities or skills. A person's position is unalterable during his or her lifetime. The most easily understood example is that of the prince who inherits the status of king because he is the son of a king.

Sociologists who study stratification use the idea of ascribed and achieved status to contrast caste systems with class systems. In class systems one's opportunities in life, at least in theory, are determined by one's actions, allowing a degree of individual mobility that is not possible in caste systems. In caste systems a person's social position is determined by birth, and social intercourse outside one's caste is prohibited.

The term "caste" itself is often used to denote large-scale kinship groups that are hierarchically organized within a rigid system of stratification. Caste systems are to be found among the Hindus in India and among societies where groups are ranked and closed as in South Africa during the apartheid period. Toward the end of this article, examples of caste systems will be given from other non-Hindu societies to illustrate how rigid, ranked systems of inequality, where one's position is fixed for life, are found in other areas that do not share India's religious belief system.

Early Hindu literary classics describe a society divided into four *varnas*: Brahman (poet-priest),

Kshatriya (warrior-chief), Vaishya (traders), and Shudras (menials, servants). The *varnas* formed ranked categories characterized by differential access to spiritual and material privileges. It excluded the Untouchables, who were despised because they engaged in occupations that were considered unclean and polluting.

The *varna* model of social ranking persisted throughout the Hindu subcontinent for over a millennia. The basis of caste ranking was the sacred concept of purity and pollution with Brahmans, because they were engaged in priestly duties considered ritually pure, while those who engaged in manual labor and with ritually polluting objects were regarded as impure. Usually those who had high ritual status also had economic and political power. Beliefs about pollution generally regulated all relations between castes. Members were not allowed to marry outside their caste; there were strict rules about the kind of food and drink one could accept and from what castes; and there were restrictions on approaching and visiting members of another caste. Violations of these rules entailed purifactory rites and sometimes expulsion from the caste (Ghurye 1969).

The *varna* scheme refers only to broad categories of society, for in reality the small endogamous group or subcaste (*jati*) forms the unit of social organization. In each linguistic area there are about two thousand such subcastes. The status of the subcaste, its cultural traditions, and its numerical strength vary from one region to another, often from village to village.

Field studies of local caste structures revealed that the caste system was more dynamic than the earlier works by social scientists had indicated. For example, at the local level, the position of the middle castes, between the Brahmans and the Untouchables, is often not very clear. This is because castes were often able to change their ritual position after they had acquired economic and political power. A low caste would adopt the Brahminic way of life, such as vegetarianism and teetotalism, and in several generations attain a higher position in the hierarchy. Upward mobility occurred for an entire caste, not for an individual or the family. This process of upward mobility, known as Sanskritization (Srinivas 1962), did not however, affect the movement of castes at the extremes. Brahmans in most parts of the country were found at the top, and Untouchables everywhere occupied a degrading status because of their economic dependency and low ritual status.

The operation of this hierarchical society was justified with reference to traditional Hindu religious beliefs about *samsara* (reincarnation) and *karma* (quality of actions). A person's position in this life was determined by his or her actions in previous lives. Persons who were born in a Brahman family must have performed good deeds in their earlier lives. Being born a Shudra or an Untouchable was punishment for the sinful acts committed in previous lives.

Some scholars (Leach 1960; Dumont 1970) saw the caste system as a cooperative, inclusive arrangement where each caste formed an integral part of the local socioeconomic system and had its special privileges. In a *jajmani* system, as this arrangement between castes was known, a village was controlled by a dominant caste, which used its wealth, numerical majority, and high status to dominate the other castes in the village. Most other castes provided services to this caste. Some worked on the land as laborers and tenants. Others provided goods and services to the landowning households and to other castes. A village would thus have a potter, blacksmith, carpenter, tailor, shoemaker, barber, sweeper, and a washerman, with each caste specializing in different occupations. These were hereditary occupations. In return for their services castes would be paid in kind, usually farm produce. These patron-client relationships continued for generations, and it was the religious duty of the *jajman* (patron) to take care of others.

Although the system did provide security for all, it was essentially exploitative and oppressive (Berreman 1981; Beidelman 1959; Freeman 1986), particularly for the Untouchables, who were confined to menial, despised jobs, working as sweepers, gutter and latrine cleaners, scavengers, watchmen, farm laborers, and curers of hides. They were denied access to Hindu temples; were not allowed to read religious Sanskrit books and remained illiterate; could not use village wells and tanks; were forced to live in settlements outside the village; and were forbidden to enter the residential areas of the upper castes.

CHANGES IN THE CASTE SYSTEM

British rule profoundly affected the Indian social order. The ideas of Western culture; the opening of English educational institutions; the legal system, which introduced the principle of equality before the law; and the new economic activities and the kind of employment they generated all brought new opportunities for greater advancement. Although these new developments resulted in greater mobility and opened doors for even the low castes, those castes that benefited most were the ones already in advantageous positions. Thus, Brahmans with a tradition of literacy were the first to avail themselves of English education and occupy administrative positions in the colonial bureaucracy.

The spread of communications enabled local subcastes to link together and form caste associations. These organizations, although initially concerned with raising the caste status in terms of Brahmanical values, later sought educational, economic, and social benefits from the British (Rudolph and Rudolph 1960). When the colonial authorities widened political participation by allowing elections in some provinces, castes organized to make claims for political representation. In some regions, such as the South, the non-Brahman castes were successful in restricting entry of Brahmans in educational institutions and administrative services.

To assuage the fears of communities about upper-caste Hindu rule in independent India and also to weaken the nationalist movement, the British granted special political representation to some groups such as the Untouchables. They had become politically mobilized under the leadership of Dr. B. R. Ambedkar and had learned, like other castes and communities, the use of political means to secure status and power (Zelliot 1970).

After the country became independent from British rule in 1947, the Indian leaders hoped that legislative and legal measures would reorder an entrenched social structure. A new Constitution was adopted, which abolished untouchability and prohibited discrimination in public places. In addition, special places were reserved for Untouchables in higher educational institutions, government services, and in the lower houses of the central and state legislatures.

What progress has the country made toward improving the lives of the Untouchables, who now form 16.48 percent (according to the 1991 Indian Census) of the population? Has the traditional caste system disintegrated?

The movement from a traditional to a modern economy—increase in educational facilities; expansion of white-collar jobs, especially in the state sector; expansion of the transportation and communication networks; increase in agricultural production (known as the Green Revolution)—has had a significant impact on the institution of caste. However, political factors have been equally if not more important in producing changes in the caste system. One is the democratic electoral system. The other is the state's impact on intercaste relations through its policy of preferences for selected disadvantaged castes.

The close association between caste and traditional occupation is breaking down because of the expansion of modern education and the urban-industrial sector. In India, an urban middle class has formed whose members are drawn from various caste groups. This has reduced the structural and cultural differences between castes, as divisions based on income, education, and occupation become more important than caste cleavages for social and economic purposes. However, the reduction is most prominent among the upper socioeconomic strata—the urban, Western-educated, professional, and higher-income groups, whose members share a common lifestyle (Beteille 1969).

For most Indians, especially those who live in rural areas (73 percent of the Indian population is still rural), caste factors are an integral part of their daily lives. In many parts of the country Dalits (the term means "oppressed" and is now preferred by the members of the Untouchable community rather than the government-assigned label "Scheduled Castes") are not allowed inside temples and cannot use village water wells. Marriages are generally arranged between persons of the same caste.

With the support of government scholarships and reservation benefits, a small proportion of Dalits has managed to gain entry into the middle class—as school teachers, clerks, bank tellers, typists, and government officials. Reservation of seats in the legislature has made the political arena somewhat more accessible, although most politicians belonging to the Dalit community have little say in party matters and government policymaking. The majority of Dalits remain landless agricultural laborers, powerless, desperately poor, and illiterate.

Modern economic forces are changing the rural landscape. The increase in cash-crop production, which has made grain payments in exchange for services unprofitable; the introduction of mechanized farming which has displaced manual labor; the preference for manufactured goods to hand-made ones; and the migration to cities and to prosperous agricultural areas for work and better wages have all weakened the traditional patron-client ties and the security it provided. The Dalits and other low castes have been particularly affected as the other sectors of the economy have not grown fast enough to absorb them.

The rural social structure has been transformed in yet another way. The dominant castes are no longer from the higher castes but belong to the middle and lower peasant castes—the profit maximizing "bullock capitalists" (Rudolph and Rudolph 1987) who were the chief beneficiaries of land reform and state subsidies to the agricultural sector (Blair 1980; Brass 1985). They have displaced the high-caste absentee landlords who have moved to cities and taken up modern occupations.

Modern political institutions have also brought about changes in the traditional leadership and power structure of local communities. Relations between castes are now governed by rules of competitive politics, and leaders are selected for their political skills and not because they are members of a particular caste. The role of caste varies at different levels of political action. At the village and district levels caste loyalties are effectively used for political mobilization. But at the state and national levels, caste factors become less important for political parties because one caste rarely commands a majority at these levels. The rise of a Dalit political party, the Bahujan Samaj Party, is evidence that Dalits are finally gaining some political power. They are particularly strong in the northern Indian state of Uttar Pradesh where they received 20.61 percent of the votes in the 1996 general elections. However, at the national level they have fared poorly, capturing only 11 seats (and 3.64 percent of the votes) in the 1996 general elections.

In the 1990s there were numerous instances of confrontations between the middle peasant castes and Dalits in rural areas. Violence and repression against Dalits has increased as they have begun to assert themselves. With the support of Communist and Dalit movements, they are demanding better wages, the right to till government-granted land, and the use of village wells.

In urban areas, caste conflict has mainly centered around the issue of "reservation." The other backward castes (who belong mainly to the Shudra caste and form about 50 percent of the country's population) have demanded from the government benefits similar to those available to Dalits in government service and educational institutions. Under electoral pressures the state governments have extended these reservation benefits to the other backward castes, leading to discontent among the upper castes.

Extension of preferential treatment from Dalits to the more numerous and in some states somewhat better-off backward castes has not only created great resentment among the upper castes but also has reduced public support for the policy of special benefits for the Dalits. In cities they have often been victims during anti-reservation agitations. That this is happening at the very time when the preferential programs have gradually succeeded in improving the educational and economic conditions for Dalits is not accidental (Sheth 1987).

As education and the meaning of the vote and the ideas of equality and justice spread, the rural and urban areas will witness severe intercaste conflicts. What is significant, however, is that these conflicts are not over caste beliefs and values, but like conflicts elsewhere between ethnic groups, have to do with control over political and economic resources.

CASTE IN OTHER SOCIETIES

Do castes exist outside India? Is it a unique social phenomenon distinct from other systems of social stratification? Opinion among scholars is divided over this issue. Castelike systems have been observed in the South Asian subcontinent and beyond (in Japan, Africa, Iran, and Polynesia). Caste has also been used to describe the systems of racial stratification in South Africa and the southern United States.

Whether the term "caste" is applicable to societies outside the South Asian region depends on how the term is defined. Those who focus on its religious foundations argue that caste is a particular species of structural organization found only in the Indian world. Louis Dumont (1970), for example, contends that caste systems are noncomparable to systems of racial stratification because of the differences in ideology—one based on the ideology of hierarchy, the other on an equalitarian ideology.

Cultural differences notwithstanding, caste as a ranked system exists in many societies. In fact, wherever ethnic groups stand in a hierarchical or ranked relationship to each other they resemble castes (Weber 1958; Horowitz 1985; Berreman 1981). As in caste systems, the identity of an ethnic group is regarded as being a consequence of birth or ancestry and hence immutable; mobility opportunities are restricted; and members of the subordinate group retain their low social position in all sectors of society—political, economic, and social. Social interactions between groups remain limited and are suffused with deference. Given these similarities in their social structures and social processes, caste stratification is congruent with race stratification and ranked ethnic systems. Below are some examples of castelike systems in countries outside South Asia.

In Japan, during the Tokugawa period (from the early 1600s to the middle 1800s), the Shogun rulers established a very rigid, hierarchical system that was maintained by force of law and other means. At the top were the *shogunate* warrior-bureaucrats, their *samurai* military elite, and the higher aristocracy. This was followed by peasants, then artisans, and then merchants. At the bottom and separated from the rest of the populace there was a group of outcasts called *eta* (meaning heavily polluted) or *hinin* (meaning nonhuman) who were treated much like the Indian Untouchables described above. Eta were legally barred from marrying outside their group or from living outside their designated hamlets. These hamlets were called *buraku*, and their residents known as *Burakumins*.

Burakumins are indistinguishable in appearance from other Japanese. They faced discrimination because they inherited their status from people whose jobs were considered polluting and undesirable like butchering animals, tanning skins, digging graves, handling corpses, and guarding tombs.

The outcasts were formally emancipated in 1871, by the Meiji government (1868–1912). The descendants of *Burakumins* were identified as "new common people." However, they continued to face discrimination as their identity could be revealed through the household register system that included the ancestry of all Japanese families. Although now the household register is not made available to the public without the permission of the family, the identity of individuals is frequently revealed when families and employers conduct investigations for marriage purposes and hiring (Ishida 1992).

Rwanda, a country just south of the Equator in Africa and which has witnessed violent ethnic conflict is another example of a system of caste stratification. Before European colonization, political power was concentrated in the hands of the king and the pastoral aristocracy (Tutsi). The Tutsis constituted only about 10 percent of the population. Hutus, the lower caste of agriculturalists, formed the vast majority of the population. The lowest caste, known as Twa, were a small minority and worked as potters, court jesters, and hunters. No intermarriage was permitted between the groups. The Tutsis used their political and military power to maintain the hierarchical system (Southall 1970), particularly in central parts of the country. This hierarchical relationship was later reinforced under colonial rule and lasted until it was brought to an end in the 1950s (Newbury 1988).

As Gerald Berreman (1981) has argued, the blacks in America and South Africa, the Burakumin of Japan, the Dalit of India, and the Hutu and Twa of Rwanda, all live in societies that are alike in their structure and in their effect on the life experiences of those most oppressed. However, those at the bottom do not accept their condition willingly. Often too powerless to revolt openly, structurally similar forms of domination create common forms of *infrapolitics*—of surreptitious resistance. Rituals of aggression, tales of revenge, use of carnival symbolism, gossip, and rumor are all examples of the strategic form of resistance the subordinates use for open defiance under severely repressive conditions (Scott 1990). Finally, similarities also exist in the political consequences of preferential policies that culturally distinct societies such as the United States and India have adopted to reduce group disparities (Weiner 1983).

REFERENCES

Beidelman, T. O. 1959 *A Comparative Analysis of the Jajmani System*. Monograph VII of the Association of Asian Studies. Locust Valley, N.Y.: J.J. Augustin.

Berreman, Gerald 1981 *Caste and Other Inequities* Delhi: Manohar.

Beteille, Andre 1969 *Caste: Old and New*. Bombay: Asia Publishing House.

Blair, Harry W. 1980 "Rising Kulaks and Backward Castes in Bihar: Social Change in the Late 1970's." *Economic and Political Weekly* 12 (Jan.):64–73.

Brass, Paul R. 1983 *Caste, Faction and Party in Indian Politics. Faction and Party*, vol.I. Delhi: Chanakya Publications.

—— 1985 *Caste, Faction and Party in Indian Politics. Election Studies*, vol. II. Delhi: Chanakya Publications.

Breman, Jan 1974 *Patronage and Exploitation*. Berkeley: University of California Press.

Dumont, Louis 1970 *Homo Hierarchicus*. Chicago: University of Chicago Press.

Freeman, James M. 1986 "The Consciousness of Freedom Among India's Untouchables." In D. K. Basu and R. Sisson, eds., *Social and Economic Development in India*. Beverly Hills, Calif.: Sage.

Galanter, Marc 1984 *Competing Equalities: Law and the Backward Classes in India*. Berkeley: University of California Press.

Gerth, H. H., and C. Wright Mills 1958 *From Max Weber: Essays in Sociology*. New York: Oxford University Press.

Ghurye, G. S. 1969 *Caste and Race in India*, 5th ed. Bombay: Popular Prakashan.

Gould, Harold A. 1987 *The Hindu Caste System: The Sacralization of a Social Order*. Delhi: Chanakya Publications.

Horowitz, Donald L. 1985 *Ethnic Groups in Conflict*. Berkeley: University of California Press.

Hutton, J. H. 1961 *Caste in India*, 4th ed. Oxford, Eng.: Oxford University Press.

Ishida, Hiroshi 1992 "Stratification and Mobility: The Case of Japan." In Myron L. Cohen, ed., *Asia Case Studies in the Social Sciences*. New York: M.E. Sharpe.

Kolenda, Pauline 1978 *Caste in Contemporary India: Beyond Organic Solidarity*. Menlo Park, Calif.: Benjamin/Cummings.

Kothari, Rajni 1970 *Caste in Indian Politics*. New Delhi: Orient Longman.

Leach, E. R. (ed.) 1960 *Aspects of Caste in South India, Ceylon, and North-West Pakistan*. Cambridge, Eng.: Cambridge University Press.

Mahar, J. M. (ed.) 1972 *The Untouchables in Contemporary India*. Tucson: University of Arizona Press.

Rudolph, L. I., and S. H. Rudolph 1960 "The Political Role of India's Caste Associations." *Pacific Affairs* 33(1):5–22.

—— 1987 *In Pursuit of Laxmi*. Chicago: University of Chicago Press.

Scott, James C. 1990 *Domination And The Arts Of Resistance: Hidden Transcripts*. New Haven, Conn.: Yale University Press.

Sheth, D. L. 1987 "Reservation Policy Revisited." *Economic and Political Weekly*, vol. 22, Nov.14.

Southall, Aidan W. 1970 "Stratification In Africa." In Leonard Plotnicov and Arthur Tuden, eds., *Essays in Comparative Social Stratification*. Pittsburg, Pa.: University of Pittsburg Press.

Srinivas, M.N. 1962 *Caste in Modern India*. London: Asia Publishing House.

—— 1969 *Social Change in Modern India*. Berkeley: University of California Press.

Weiner, Myron 1983 "The Political Consequences of Preferential Policies: A Comparative Perspective." *Comparative Politics* 16(1):35–52.

Zelliot, Eleanor 1970 "Learning the Uses of Political Means: The Mahars of Maharashtra." In Rajni Kothari, ed., *Caste in Indian Politics*. Delhi: Orient Longman.

RITA JALALI

CAUSAL INFERENCE MODELS

NOTE: *Although the following article has not been revised for this edition of the Encyclopedia, the substantive coverage is currently appropriate. The editors have provided a list of recent works at the end of the article to facilitate research and exploration of the topic.*

The notion of causality has been controversial for a very long time, and yet neither scientists, social scientists, nor laypeople have been able to think constructively without using a set of explanatory concepts that, either explicitly or not, have implied causes and effects. Sometimes other words have been substituted, for example, *consequences, results,* or *influences*. Even worse, there are vague terms such as *leads to, reflects, stems from, derives from, articulates with,* or *follows from*, which are often used in sentences that are almost deliberately ambiguous in avoiding causal terminology. Whenever such vague phrases are used throughout a theoretical work, or whenever one merely states that two variables are correlated with one another, it may not be recognized that what purports to be an "explanation" is really not a genuine theoretical explanation at all.

It is, of course, possible to provide a very narrow definition of causation and then to argue that such a notion is totally inadequate in terms of scientific explanations. If, for example, one defines causation in such a way that there can be only a single cause of a given phenomenon, or that a necessary condition, a sufficient condition, or both must be satisfied, or that absolute certainty is required to establish causation, then indeed very few persons would ever be willing to use the term. Indeed, in sociology, causal terminology was almost deliberately avoided before the 1960s, except in reports of experimental research. Since that time, however, the notion of *multivariate causation*, combined with the explicit allowance for impacts of neglected factors, has gradually replaced these more restrictive usages.

There is general agreement that causation can never be proven, and of course in a strict sense *no* statements about the real world can ever be "proven" correct, if only because of indeterminacies produced by measurement errors and the necessity of relying on evidence that has been filtered through imperfect sense organs or fallible measuring instruments. One may accept the fact that, strictly speaking, one is always dealing with causal *models* of real-world processes and that one's inferences concerning the adequacy of such models must inevitably be based on a combination of *empirical evidence* and untested *assumptions*, some of which are about underlying causal processes that can never be subject to empirical verification. This is basically true for all scientific evidence, though the assumptions one may require in making interpretations or explanations of the underlying reality may be more or less plausible in view of supplementary information that may be available. Unfortunately, in the social sciences such supplementary information is likely to be of questionable quality, thereby reducing the degree of faith one has in whatever causal assertions have been made.

In the causal modeling literature, which is basically compatible with the so-called structural equation modeling in econometrics, equation systems are constructed so as to represent as well as possible a presumed real-world situation, given whatever limitations have been imposed in terms of omitted variables that produce unknown biases, possibly incorrect functional forms for one's equations, measurement errors, or in general what are termed *specification errors* in the equations. Since such limitations are always present, any particular equation will contain a disturbance term that is assumed to behave in a certain fashion. One's assumptions about such disturbances are both critical for one's inferences and also (for the most part) inherently untestable with the data at hand. This in turn means that such inferences must always be tentative. One never "finds" effects, for example, but only infers them on the basis of findings about covariances and temporal sequences *and* a set of untested theoretical assumptions. To the degree that such assumptions are hidden from view, both the social scientist and one's readers may therefore be seriously misled to the degree that these assumptions are also incorrect.

In the recursive models commonly in use in sociology, it is assumed that causal influences can be ordered, such that one may designate an X_1 that does not depend on any of the remaining variables in the system but, presumably, varies as a result of exogenous causes that have been ignored in the theory. A second variable, X_2, may then be found that may depend upon X_1 as well as a different set of exogenous factors, but the assumption is that X_2 does *not* affect X_1, either directly or through any other mechanism. One then builds up the system, equation by equation, by locating an X_3 that may depend on either or both of X_1 or X_2, plus still another set of independent variables (referred to as exogenous factors), but with the assumption that neither of the first two X's is affected by X_3. Adding still more variables in this recursive fashion, and for the time being assuming linear and additive relationships, one arrives at the system of equations shown in equation system 1,

$$X_1 = \varepsilon_1$$
$$X_2 = \beta_{21}X_1 + \varepsilon_2$$
$$X_3 = \beta_{31}X_1 + \beta_{32}X_2 + \varepsilon_3 \qquad (1)$$
$$\vdots$$
$$X_k = \beta_{k1}X_1 + \beta_{k2}X_2 + \beta_{k3}X_3 + \cdots + \beta_{k,k-1}X_{k-1} + \varepsilon_k$$

in which the disturbance terms are represented by the ε_i and where for the sake of simplicity the constant terms have been omitted.

The essential property of recursive equations that provides a simple causal interpretation is that changes made in any given equation may affect subsequent ones but will *not* affect any of the prior equations. Thus, if a mysterious demon were to change one of the parameters in the equation for X_3, this would undoubtedly affect not only X_3 but also X_4, X_5, through X_k, but could have no effect on either of the first two equations, which do not depend on X_3 or any of the later variables in the system. As will be discussed below, this special property of recursive systems does not hold in the more general setup involving variables that may be reciprocally interrelated. Indeed, it is this recursive property that justifies one's dealing with the equations separately and sequentially as single equations. The assumptions required for such a system are therefore implicit in all data analyses (e.g., log-linear modeling, analysis of variance, or comparisons among means) that are typically discussed in first and second courses in applied statistics.

Assumptions are always critical in causal analyses or—what is often not recognized—in *any* kind of theoretical interpretation of empirical data. Some such assumptions are implied by the forms of one's equations, in this case linearity and additivity. Fortunately, these types of assumptions can be rather simply modified by, for example, introducing second- or higher-degree terms, log functions, or interaction terms. It is a mistake to claim—as some critics have done—that causal modeling requires one to assume such restrictive functional forms.

Far more important are two other kinds of assumptions—those about measurement errors and those concerning the disturbance terms representing the effects of all omitted variables. Simple causal modeling of the type represented by equation system 1 requires the naive assumption that all variables have been perfectly measured, an assumption that is, unfortunately, frequently ignored in many empirical investigations using path analyses based on exactly this same type of causal system. Measurement errors require one to make an auxiliary set of assumptions regarding both the sources of measurement-error bias and the causal connections between so-called true scores and measured indicators. In principle, however, such measurement-error assumptions can be explicitly built into the equation system and empirical estimates obtained, provided there are a sufficient number of multiple indicators to solve for the unknowns produced by these measurement errors, a possibility that will be discussed in the final section.

In many instances, assumptions about one's disturbance terms are even more problematic but equally critical. In verbal statements of theoretical arguments one often comes across the phrase "other things being equal," or the notion that in the ideal experimental design all causes except one must be literally held constant if causal inferences are to be made. Yet both the phrase "other things being equal" and the restrictive assumption of the perfect experiment beg the question of how one can possibly know that "other things" are in fact equal, that all "relevant" variables have been held constant, or that there are no possible sources of measurement bias. Obviously, an alert critic may always suggest another variable that indeed does vary across settings studied or that has not been held constant in an experiment.

In recursive causal models this highly restrictive notion concerning the constancy of all possible alternative causes is relaxed by allowing for a disturbance term that varies precisely because they are *not* all constant. But if so, can one get by without requiring any other assumptions about their effects? Indeed not. One must assume, essentially, that the omitted variables affecting any one of the X's are uncorrelated with those that affect the others. If so, it can then be shown that the disturbance term in each equation will be uncorrelated with each of the independent variables appearing on the right-hand side, thus justifying the use of ordinary least-squares estimating procedures. In practical terms, this means that if one has had to omit any important causes of a

given variable, one must also be willing to assume that they do not systematically affect any of its presumed causes that have been explicitly included in our model. A skeptic may, of course, be able to identify one or more such disturbing influences, in which case a modified model may need to be constructed and tested. For example, if ε_3 and ε_4 contain a common cause that can be identified and measured, such a variable needs to be introduced explicitly into the model as a cause of both X_3 and X_4.

Perhaps the five-variable model of Figure 1 will help the reader visualize what is involved. To be specific, suppose X_5, the ultimate dependent variable, represents some behavior, say, the actual number of delinquent acts a youth has perpetrated. Let X_3 and X_4, respectively, represent two internal states, say, guilt and self-esteem. Finally, suppose X_1 and X_2 are two setting variables, parental education and delinquency rates within the youth's neighborhood, with the latter variable being influenced by the former through the parents' ability to select among residential areas.

The fact that the disturbance term arrows are unconnected in Figure 1 represents the assumption that they are mutually uncorrelated, or that the omitted variables affecting any given X_i are uncorrelated with any of its explicitly included causes among the remaining X's. If ordinary least squares is used to estimate the parameters in this model, then the empirically obtained residuals e_i will indeed be uncorrelated with the independent X's in their respective equations, but since this automatically occurs as a property of least-squares estimation, it cannot be used as the basis for a test of our a priori assumptions about the true disturbances.

If one is unwilling to accept these assumptions about the behavior of omitted variables, the only way out of this situation is to reformulate the model and to introduce further complexities in the form of additional measured variables. At some point, however, one must stop and make the (untestable) assumption that the revised causal model is "closed" in the sense that omitted variables do not disturb the patterning of relationships among the included variables.

Assuming such theoretical closure, then, one is in a position to estimate the parameters, attach

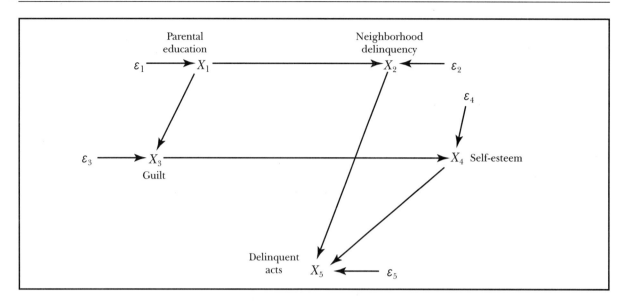

Figure 1. Simple Recursive Model

their numerical values to the diagram, and also evaluate the model in terms of its consistency with the data. In the model of Figure 1, for instance, there are no direct arrows between X_2 and X_3, between X_4 and both X_1 and X_2, and between X_5 and both X_1 and X_3. This means that with controls for all prior or intervening variables, the respective partial correlations can be predicted to be zero, apart from sampling errors. One arrives at the predictions in equation system 2.

$$r_{23.1} = 0 \qquad r_{14.23} = 0 \qquad r_{24.13} = 0$$
$$r_{15.234} = 0 \qquad r_{35.124} = 0 \tag{2}$$

Thus, for each omitted arrow one may write out a specific "zero" prediction. Where arrows have been drawn in, it may have been possible to predict the signs of direct links, and these directional predictions may also be used to evaluate the model. Notice a very important property of recursive models. In relating any pair of variables, say, X_2 and X_3, one expects to control for antecedent or intervening variables, but it is *not* appropriate to introduce as controls any variables that appear as subsequent variables in the model (e.g., X_4 or X_5). The simple phrase "controlling for all relevant variables" should therefore not be construed to mean variables that are presumed to depend on both of the variables being studied. In an experimental setup, one would presumably be unable to

carry out such an absurd operation, but in statistical calculations, which involve pencil-and-paper controlling only, there is nothing to prevent one from doing so.

It is unfortunately the case that controls for dependent variables can sometimes be made inadvertently through one's research design (Blalock 1985). For example, one may select respondents from a list that is based on a dependent variable such as committing a particular crime, entering a given hospital, living in a certain residential area, or being employed in a particular factory. Whenever such improper controls are introduced, whether recognized explicitly or not, our inferences regarding relationships among causally prior variables are likely to be incorrect. If, for example, X_1 and X_2 are totally uncorrelated, but one controls for their common effect, X_3, then even though $r_{12} = 0$, it will turn out that $r_{12.3} \neq 0$.

Recursive models also provide justifications for common-sense rules of thumb regarding the conditions under which it is *not* necessary to control for prior or intervening variables. In the model of Figure 1, for example, it can be shown that although $r_{24.13} = 0$, it would be sufficient to control for *either* X_1 or X_3 but not both in order for the partial to disappear. Similarly, in relating X_3 to X_5, the partial will be reduced to zero if one controls for either X_2 and X_4 or X_1 and X_4. It is not necessary

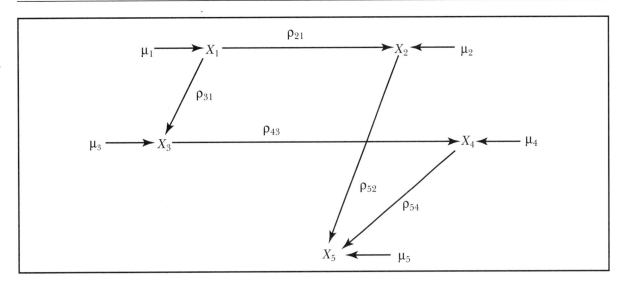

Figure 2. Model of Figure 1, with Path Coefficients and Standardized Variables

to control for all three simultaneously. More generally, a number of simplifications become possible, depending on the patterning of omitted arrows, and these simplifications can be used to justify the omission of certain variables if these cannot be measured. If, for example, one could not measure X_3, one could draw in a direct arrow from X_1 to X_4 without altering the remainder of the model. Without such an explicit causal model in front of us, however, the omission of variables must be justified on completely ad hoc grounds. The important point is that pragmatic reasons for such omissions should not be accepted without *theoretical* justifications.

PATH ANALYSIS AND AN EXAMPLE

Sewall Wright (1934, 1960) introduced a form of causal modeling long before it became fashionable among sociologists. Wright, a population geneticist, worked in terms of standardized variables with unit variances and zero means. Expressing any given equation in terms of what he referred to as path coefficients, which in recursive modeling are equivalent to beta weights, Wright was able to derive a simple formula for decomposing the correlation between any pair of variables x_i and x_j. The equation for any given variable can be written as $x_i = p_{i1}x_1 + p_{i2}x_2 + ... + p_{ik}x_k + u_i$, where the p_{ij} represent standardized regression coefficients and where

the lower-case x's refer to the standardized variables. One may then multiply both sides of the equation by x_j, the variable that is to be correlated with x_i. Therefore, $x_i x_j = p_{i1}x_1 x_j + p_{i2}x_2 x_j + ... + p_{ik}x_k x_j + u_i x_j$. Summing over all cases and dividing by the number of cases N, one has the results in equation system 3.

$$r_{ij} = \frac{\sum x_i x_j}{N} = p_{i1}\frac{\sum x_1 x_j}{N} + p_{i2}\frac{\sum x_2 x_j}{N} + \cdots + p_{ik}\frac{\sum x_k x_j}{N} + \frac{\sum u_i x_j}{N}$$

$$= p_{i1}r_{1j} + p_{i2}r_{2j} + \cdots + p_{ik}r_{kj} + 0 = \sum_{k} p_{ik}r_{kj} \qquad (3)$$

The expression in equation system 3 enables one to decompose or partition any total correlation into a sum of terms, each of which consists of a path coefficient multiplied by a correlation coefficient, which itself may be decomposed in a similar way. In Wright's notation the path coefficients are written without any dots that indicate control variables but are indeed merely the (partial) regression coefficients for the standardized variables. Any given path coefficient, say p_{54}, can be interpreted as the change that would be imparted in the dependent variable x_5, in its standard deviation units, if the other variable x_4 were to change by one of its standard deviation units, with the remaining explicitly included independent variables (here x_1, x_2, and x_3) all held constant. In working with standardized variables one is able to simplify these expressions owing to the fact that r_{ij}

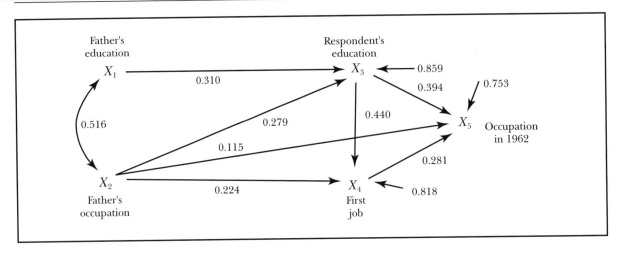

Figure 3. Path Diagram for Blau-Duncan Model

$= \Sigma x_i x_j / N$, but one must pay the price of then having to work with standard deviation units that may vary across samples or populations. This, in turn, means that two sets of path coefficients for different samples, say men and women, cannot easily be compared since the standard deviations (say, in income earned) may be different.

In the case of the model of Figure 2, which is the same causal diagram as Figure 1, but with the relevant p_{ij} inserted, one may write out expressions for each of the r_{ij} as shown in equation system 4.

$$r_{12} = p_{21}r_{11} = p_{21}(1) = p_{21}$$

$$r_{13} = p_{31}r_{11} = p_{31}$$

$$r_{23} = p_{31}r_{12} = p_{31}p_{21} = r_{13}r_{12} \quad (\text{or } r_{23.1} = 0)$$

$$r_{14} = p_{43}r_{13} = p_{43}p_{31}$$

$$r_{24} = p_{43}r_{23} = p_{43}p_{31}p_{21}$$

$$r_{34} = p_{43}r_{33} = p_{43} \tag{4}$$

$$r_{15} = p_{52}r_{21} + p_{54}r_{41} = p_{52}p_{21} + p_{54}p_{43}p_{31}$$

$$r_{25} = p_{52}r_{22} + p_{54}r_{42} = p_{52}p_{54}p_{43}p_{31}p_{21}$$

$$r_{35} = p_{52}r_{23} + p_{54}r_{43} = p_{52}p_{31}p_{21} + p_{54}p_{43}$$

$$r_{45} = p_{52}r_{24} + p_{54}r_{44} = p_{52}p_{43}p_{31}p_{21} + p_{54}$$

In decomposing each of the total correlations, one takes the path coefficients for each of the arrows coming into the appropriate dependent variable and multiplies each of these by the total correlation between the variable at the source of

the arrow and the "independent" variable in which one is interested. In the case of r_{12}, this involves multiplying p_{21} by the correlation of x_1 with itself, namely $r_{11} = 1.0$. Therefore one obtains the simple result that $r_{12} = p_{21}$. Similar results obtain for r_{13} and r_{34}. The decomposition of r_{23}, however, results in the expression $r_{23} = p_{31}r12 = p_{31}p_{21} = r_{12}r_{13}$, which also of course implies that $r_{23.1} = 0$.

When one comes to the decomposition of correlations with x_5, which has two direct paths into it, the expressions become more complex but also demonstrate the heuristic value of path analysis. For example, in the case of r_{35}, this total correlation can be decomposed into two terms, one representing the indirect effects of x_3 via the intervening variable x_4, namely the product $p_{54}p_{43}$, and the other the spurious association produced by the common cause x_1, namely the more complex product $p_{52}p_{31}p_{21}$. In the case of the correlation between x_4 and x_5 one obtains a similar result except that there is a direct effect term represented by the single coefficient p_{54}.

As a numerical substantive example consider the path model of Figure 3, which represents the basic model in Blau and Duncan's classic study, *The American Occupational Structure* (1967, p. 17). Two additional features of the Blau-Duncan model may be noted. A curved, double-headed arrow has been drawn between father's education and father's occupation, indicating that the causal paths between these two exogenous or independent variables have not been specified. This means that there is no p_{21} in the model, so that r_{12} cannot be decomposed. Its value of 0.516 has been inserted into the diagram, however. The implication of a failure to commit oneself on the direction of causation between these two variables is that decompositions of subsequent r_{ij} will involve expressions that are sometimes combinations of the relevant p's *and* the unexplained association between father's education and occupation. This, in turn, means that the indirect effects of one of these variables "through" the other cannot be assessed. One can determine the direct effects of, say, father's occupation on respondent's education, or its indirect effects on occupation in 1962 through first job, but not "through" father's education. If one had, instead, committed oneself to the directional flow from father's education to father's occupation, a not unreasonable assumption, then all indirect effects and spurious connections could be evaluated. Sometimes it is indeed necessary to make use of double-headed arrows when the direction of causation among the most causally prior variables cannot be specified, but one then gives up the ability to trace out those indirect effects or spurious associations that involve these unexplained correlations.

The second feature of the Blau-Duncan diagram worth noting involves the small, unattached arrows coming into each of the "dependent" variables in the model. These of course represent the disturbance terms, which in a correctly specified model are taken to be uncorrelated. But the *magnitudes* of these effects of outside variables are also provided in the diagram to indicate just how much variance remains unexplained by the model. Each of the numerical values of path coefficients coming in from these outside variables, when squared, turns out to be the equivalent of $1 - R^2$, or the variances that remain unexplained by *all* of the included explanatory variables. Thus there is considerable unexplained variance in respondent's education (0.738), first job (0.669), and occupation in 1962 (0.567), indicating, of course, plenty of room for other factors to operate. The challenge then becomes that of locating additional variables to improve the explanatory value of the model. This has, indeed, been an important stimulus to the development of the status attainment literature that the Blau-Duncan study subsequently spawned.

The placement of numerical values in such path diagrams enables the reader to assess, rather easily, the relative magnitudes of the several direct effects. Thus, father's education is inferred to have a moderately strong direct effect on respondent's education, but none on the respondent's occupational status. Father's occupation is estimated to have somewhat weaker direct effects on both respondent's education and first job but a much weaker direct effect on his later occupation. The direct effects of respondent's education on first job are estimated to be only somewhat stronger than those on the subsequent occupation, with first job controlled. In evaluating these numerical values, however, one must keep in mind that all variables have been expressed in standard deviation units rather than some "natural" unit such as years of schooling. This in turn means that if variances for, say, men and women or blacks and whites are not the same, then comparisons across samples should be made in terms of unstandardized, rather than standardized, coefficients.

SIMULTANEOUS EQUATION MODELS

Recursive modeling requires one to make rather strong assumptions about temporal sequences. This does not, in itself, rule out the possibility of reciprocal causation provided that lag periods can be specified. For example, the actions of party A may affect the later behaviors of party B, which in turn affect still later reactions of the first party. Ideally, if one could watch a dynamic interaction process such as that among family members, and accurately record the temporal sequences, one could specify a recursive model in which the behaviors of the same individual could be represented by distinct variables that have been temporally ordered. Indeed Strotz and Wold (1960) have cogently argued that many simultaneous equation models appearing in the econometric literature have been misspecified precisely because they do not capture such dynamic features, which in causal models should ideally involve specified lag periods. For example, prices and quantities of goods do not simply "seek equilibrium." Instead, there are at least three kinds of autonomous actors—producers, customers, and retailers or wholesalers—who react to one another's behaviors with varying lag periods.

In many instances, however, one cannot collect the kinds of data necessary to ascertain these lag periods. Furthermore, especially in the case of aggregated data, the lag periods for different actors may not coincide, so that macro-level changes are for all practical purposes continuous rather than discrete. Population size, literacy levels, urbanization, industrialization, political alienation, and so forth are all changing at once. How can such situations be modeled and what additional complications do they introduce?

In the general case there will be k mutually interdependent variables X_i that may possibly each directly affect the others. These are referred to as endogenous variables, with the entire set having the property that there is no single dependent variable that does not feed back to affect at least one of the others. Given this situation, it turns out that it is not legitimate to break the equations apart in order to estimate the parameters, one equation at a time, as one does in the case of a recursive setup. Since any given variable may affect the others, this also means that its omitted causes, represented by the disturbance terms ε_i will also directly or indirectly affect the remaining endogenous variables, so that it becomes totally unreasonable to assume these disturbances to be uncorrelated with the "independent" variables in their respective equations. Thus, one of the critical assumptions required to justify the use of ordinary least squares cannot legitimately be made, meaning that a wide variety of single equation techniques discussed in the statistical literature must be modified.

There is an even more serious problem, however, which can be seen more readily if one writes out the set of equations, one for each of the k endogenous variables. To this set are added another set of what are called predetermined variables, Z_j, that will play an essential role to be discussed below. Our equation set now becomes as shown in equation system 5.

The regression coefficients (called "structural parameters") that connect the several endogenous variables in equation system 5 are designated as β_{ij} and are distinguished from the γ_{ij} representing the direct effects of the predetermined Z_j on the relevant X_i. This notational distinction is made because the two kinds of variables play different roles

$$x_1 = \beta_{12}x_2 + \beta_{13}x_3 + \cdots + \beta_{1k}x_k + y_{11}z_1 + y_{12}z_2 + \cdots + y_{1m}z_m + \varepsilon_1$$

$$x_2 = \beta_{21}x_1 + \beta_{23}x_3 + \cdots + \beta_{2k}x_k + y_{21}z_1 + y_{22}z_2 + \cdots + y_{2m}z_m + \varepsilon_2$$

$$x_3 = \beta_{31}x_1 + \beta_{32}x_2 + \cdots + \beta_{3k}x_k + y_{31}z_1 + y_{32}z_2 + \cdots + y_{3m}z_m + \varepsilon_3 \tag{5}$$

$$\vdots$$

$$x_k = \beta_{k1}x_1 + \beta_{k2}x_2 + \cdots + \beta_{k,k-1}x_{k-1} + y_{k1}z_1 + y_{k2}z_2 + \cdots + y_{km}z_m + \varepsilon_k$$

in the model. Although it cannot be assumed that the disturbances ε_i are uncorrelated with the endogenous X's that appear on the right-hand sides of their respective equations, one may make the somewhat less restrictive assumption that these disturbances are uncorrelated with the predetermined Z's.

Some Z's may be truly exogenous, or distinct independent variables, that are assumed not to be affected by any of the endogenous variables in the model. Others, however, may be lagged endogenous variables, or prior levels of some of the X's. In a sense, the defining characteristic of these predetermined variables is that they be uncorrelated with any of the omitted causes of the endogenous variables. Such an assumption may be difficult to accept in the case of lagged endogenous variables, given the likelihood of autocorrelated disturbances, but we shall not consider this complication further. The basic assumption regarding the truly exogenous variables, however, is that these are uncorrelated with all omitted causes of the X's, though they may of course be correlated with the X's and also possibly each other.

Clearly, there are more unknown parameters than was the case for the original recursive equation system (1). Turning attention back to the simple recursive system represented in equation system 1, one sees that the matrix of betas in that equation system is triangular, with all such coefficients above the main diagonal being set equal to zero on a priori grounds. That is, in equation system 1, half of the possible betas have been set equal to zero, the remainder being estimated using ordinary least squares. It turns out that in the more general equation system 5, there will be too

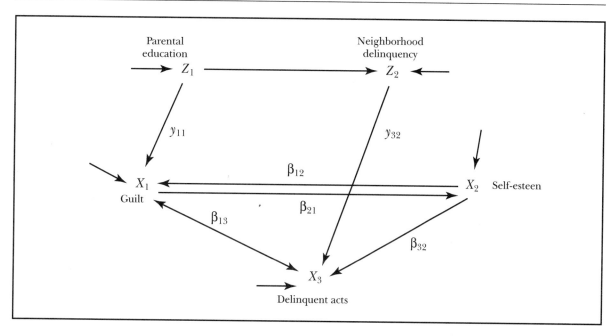

Figure 4. Nonrecursive Modification of Figure 1

many unknowns unless additional restrictive assumptions are made. In particular, in each of the k equations one will have to make a priori assumptions that at least $k - 1$ coefficients have been set equal to zero or some other known value (which cannot be estimated from the data). This is why one needs the predetermined Z_i and the relevant gammas. If one is willing to assume that, for any given endogenous X_i, certain direct arrows are missing, meaning that there are no *direct* effects coming from the relevant X_j or Z variable, then one may indeed estimate the remaining parameters. One does not have to make the very restrictive assumptions required under the recursive setup, namely that if X_j affects X_i, then the reverse cannot hold. As long as one assumes that *some* of the coefficients are zero, there is a chance of being able to identify or estimate the others.

It turns out that the *necessary* condition for identification can be easily specified, as implied in the above discussion. For any given equation, one must leave out at least $k - 1$ of the remaining variables. The necessary *and* sufficient condition is far more complicated to state. In many instances, when the necessary condition has been met, so will the sufficient one as well, unless some of the

equations contain exactly the same sets of variables (i.e., exactly the same combination of omitted variables). But since this will not always be the case, the reader should consult textbooks in econometrics for more complete treatments.

Returning to the substantive example of delinquency, as represented in Figure 1, one may revise the model somewhat by allowing for a feedback from delinquent behavior to guilt, as well as a reciprocal relationship between the two internal states, guilt and self-esteem. One may also relabel parental education as Z_1 and neighborhood delinquency as Z_2 because there is no feedback from any of the three endogenous variables to either of these predetermined ones. Renumbering the endogenous variables as X_1, X_2, and X_3, one may represent the revised model as in Figure 4.

In this kind of application one may question whether a behavior can ever influence an internal state. Keeping in mind, however, that the concern is with *repeated* acts of delinquency, it is entirely reasonable to assume that earlier acts feed back to affect subsequent guilt levels, which in turn affect future acts of delinquency. It is precisely this very frequent type of causal process that is ignored whenever behaviors are taken, rather simply, as "dependent" variables.

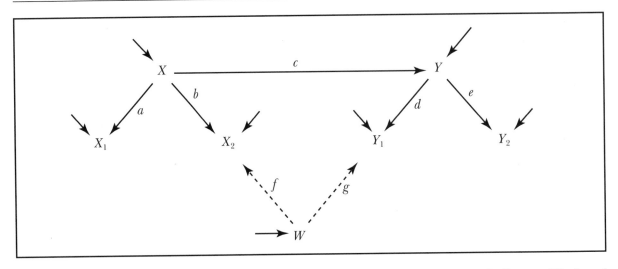

Figure 5. Simple Measurement-Error Model, with Two Unmeasured Variables X and Y, Two Indicators of Each, and Source of Bias W

Here, $k = 3$, so that at least two variables must be left out of each equation, meaning that their respective coefficients have been set equal to zero. One can rather simply check on the necessary condition by counting arrowheads coming to each variable. In this instance there can be no more than two arrows into each variable, whereas in the case of guilt X_1 there are three. The equation for X_1 is referred to as being "underidentified," meaning that the situation is empirically hopeless. The coefficients simply cannot be estimated by *any* empirical means. There are exactly two arrows coming into delinquency X_3, and one refers to this as a situation in which the equation is "exactly identified." With only a single arrow coming into self-esteem X_2, one has an "overidentified" equation for which one actually has an excess of empirical information compared to the number of unknowns to be estimated. It turns out that overidentified equations provide criteria for evaluating goodness of fit, or a test of the model, in much the same way that, for recursive models, one obtains an empirical test of a null hypothesis for each causal arrow that has been deleted.

Since the equation for X_1 is underidentified, one must either remove one of the arrows, on a priori grounds, or search for at least one more predetermined variable that does *not* belong in this equation, that is, a predetermined variable that is assumed not to be a direct cause of level of guilt. Perhaps school performance can be introduced as Z_3 by making the assumption that Z_3 directly affects both self-esteem and delinquency but not guilt level. A check of this revised model indicates that all equations are properly identified, and one may proceed to estimation. Although space does not permit a discussion of alternative estimation methods that enable one to get around the violated assumption required by ordinary least squares, there are various computer programs available to accomplish this task. The simplest such alternative, two-stage least squares (2SLS), will ordinarily be adequate for nearly all sociological applications and turns out to be less sensitive to other kinds of specification errors than many of the more sophisticated alternatives that have been proposed.

CAUSAL APPROACH TO MEASUREMENT ERRORS

Finally, brief mention should be made of a growing body of literature—closely linked to factor analysis—that has been developed in order to attach measurement-error models to structural-equation approaches that presume perfect measurement. The fundamental philosophical starting point of such models involves the assumption that in many if not most instances, measurement errors can be conceived in causal terms. Most often, the indicator or measured variables are taken as *effects* of underlying or "true" variables, plus additional factors that may produce combinations of random measurement errors, which are unrelated to all other variables in the theoretical system, and systematic biases that are explainable in causal terms. Thus, measures of "true guilt" or "true self-esteem" will consist of responses, usually to paper-and-pencil tests, that may be subject to distortions produced by other variables, including some of the variables in the causal system. Perhaps distortions in the guilt measure may be a function of amount of delinquent behavior or parental education. Similarly, measures of behaviors are likely to overestimate or underestimate true frequencies, with biases dependent on qualities of the observer, inaccuracies in official records, or perhaps the ability of the actor to evade detection.

In all such instances, we may be able to construct an "auxiliary measurement theory" (Blalock 1968; Costner 1969) that is itself a causal model that contains a mixture of measured and unmeasured variables, the latter of which constitute the "true" or underlying variables of theoretical interest. The existence of such unmeasured variables, however, may introduce identification problems by using more unknowns than can be estimated from one's data. If so, the situation will once more be hopeless empirically. But if one has available *several* indicators of each of the imperfectly measured constructs, *and* if one is willing to make a sufficient number of simplifying assumptions strategically placed within the overall model, estimates may be obtainable.

Consider the model of Figure 5 (borrowed from Costner 1969), which contains only two theoretical variables of interest, namely, the unmeasured variables X and Y. Suppose one has two indicators each for both X and Y and that one is willing to make the simplifying assumption that X does not affect either of Y's indicators, Y_1 and Y_2, and that Y does not affect either of X's indicators, X_1 and X_2. For the time being ignore the variable W as well as the two dashed arrows drawn from it to the indicators X_2 and Y_1. Without W, the nonexistence of other arrows implies that the remaining causes of the four indicators are assumed to be uncorrelated with all other variables in the system, so that one may assume measurement errors to be strictly random.

If one labels the path coefficients (which all connect measured variables to unmeasured ones) by the simple letters a, b, c, d, and, e, then with $4(3)/2 = 6$ correlations among the four indicators, there will be six pieces of empirical information (equation system 5) with which to estimate the five unknown path coefficients.

$$r_{x_1x_2} = ab \qquad r_{x_1y_2} = ace$$

$$r_{y_1y_2} = de \qquad r_{x_2y_1} = bcd \qquad (6)$$

$$r_{x_1y_1} = acd \qquad r_{x_2y_2} = bce$$

One may now estimate the correlation or path coefficient c between X and Y by an equation derived from equation system 6.

$$c^2 = \frac{abc^2de}{(ab)(de)} = \frac{r_{x_1y_1}r_{x_2y_2}}{r_{x_1x_2}r_{x_1y_2}} = \frac{r_{x_1y_2}r_{x_2y_1}}{r_{x_1x_2}r_{y_1y_2}} \qquad (7)$$

Also notice that there is an excess equation that may be used to check on the consistency of the model with the data, namely the prediction that $r_{x_1y_1} r_{x_2y_2} = r_{x_1y_2} r_{x_2y_1} = abc^2de$.

Suppose next that there is a source of measurement error bias W that is a common cause of one of X's indicators (namely X_2) and one of Y's (namely Y_1). Perhaps these two items have similar wordings based on a social survey, whereas the remaining two indicators involve very different kinds of measures. There is now a different expression for the correlation between X_2 and Y_1, namely $r_{x_2y_1} = bcd + fg$. If one were to use this particular correlation in the estimate of c^2, without being aware of the impact of W, one would obtain a biased estimate. In this instance one would be able to detect this particular kind of departure from randomness because the consistency criterion would no longer be met. That is, $(acd)(bce) \neq (ace)(bcd + fg)$. Had W been a common cause of the two indicators of either X or Y alone, however, it can be seen that one would have been unable to detect the bias even though it would have been present.

Obviously, most of one's measurement-error models will be far more complex than this, with several (usually unmeasured) sources of bias, possible nonlinearities, and linkages between some of the important variables and indicators of *other* variables in the substantive theory. Also, some indicators may be taken as *causes* of the conceptual variables, as for example often occurs when one is attempting to get at experience variables (e.g., exposure to discrimination) by using simple objective indicators such as race, sex, or age. Furthermore, one's substantive models may involve feedback relationships so that simultaneous equation systems must be joined to one's measurement-error models.

In all such instances, there will undoubtedly be numerous specification errors in one's models, so that it becomes necessary to evaluate alternative models in terms of their goodness of fit to the data. Simple path-analytic methods, although heuristically helpful, will no longer be adequate. Fortunately, there are several highly sophisticated computer programs, such as LISREL, that enable social scientists to carry out sophisticated data analyses designed to evaluate these more complex models and to estimate their parameters once it has been decided that the fit to reality is reasonably close. (See Joreskog and Sorbom 1981; Long 1983; and Herting 1985.)

In closing, what needs to be stressed is that causal modeling tools are highly flexible. They may be modified to handle additional complications such as interactions and nonlinearities. Causal modeling in terms of attribute data has been given a firm theoretical underpinning by Suppes (1970), and even ordinal data may be used in an exploratory fashion, provided that one is willing to assume that dichotomization or categorization has not introduced substantial measurement errors that cannot be modeled.

Like all other approaches, however, causal modeling is heavily dependent on the assumptions one is willing to make. Such assumptions need to be made as explicit as possible—a procedure that is unfortunately often not taken sufficiently seriously in the empirical literature. In short, this set of tools, properly used, has been designed to provide precise meaning to the assertion that neither theory nor data can stand alone and that any interpretations of research findings one wishes to provide must inevitably also be based on a set of assumptions, many of which cannot be tested with the data in hand.

Finally, it should be stressed that causal modeling can be very useful in the process of theory *construction*, even in instances where many of the variables contained in the model will remain unmeasured in any given study. It is certainly a mistake to throw out portions of one's theory merely because data to test it are not currently available. Indeed, without a theory as to how missing variables are assumed to operate, it will be impossible to justify one's assumptions regarding the behavior of disturbance terms that will contain such variables, whether explicitly recognized or not. Causal modeling may thus be an important tool for guiding future research and for providing guidelines as to what kinds of neglected variables need to be measured.

(*SEE ALSO*: *Correlation and Regression Analysis; Epistemology; Multiple Indicator Models; Scientific Explanation; Tabular Analysis*)

REFERENCES

Allison, Paul D. 1995 "Exact Variance of Indirect Effects in Recursive Linear Models." *Sociological Methodology* 25:253–266.

Arminger, Gehard 1995 "Specification and Estimation of Mean Structure: Regression Models." In G. Arminger, C. C. Clogg, and M. E. Sobel, eds., *Handbook of Statistical Modeling for the Social and Behavioral Sciences*. New York: Plenum Press.

Blalock, Hubert M. 1968 "The Measurement Problem: A Gap Between the Languages of Theory and Research." In H. M. Blalock and A. B. Blalock, eds., *Methodology in Social Research*. New York: McGraw-Hill.

——1985 "Inadvertent Manipulations of Dependent Variables in Research Designs." In H. M. Blalock, ed., *Causal Models in Panel and Experimental Designs*. New York: Aldine.

Blau, Peter M., and Otis Dudley Duncan 1967 *The American Occupational Structure*. New York: Wiley.

Blossfeld, Hans-Peter, and Gotz Rohwer 1997 "Causal Inference, Time and Observation Plans in the Social Sciences." *Quality and Quantity* 31:361–384.

Bollen, Kenneth A. 1989 *Structural Equations with Latent Variables*. New York: Wiley.

Costner, Herbert L. 1969 "Theory, Deduction, and Rules of Correspondence." *American Journal of Sociology* 75:245–263.

Herting, Jerald R. 1985 "Multiple Indicator Models Using LISREL." In H. M. Blalock, ed., *Causal Models in the Social Sciences*, 2nd ed. New York: Aldine.

Joreskog, Karl G., and Dag Sorbom 1981 *LISREL V: Analysis of Linear Structural Relationships by the Method of Maximum Likelihood; User's Guide*. Uppsala, Sweden: University of Uppsala Press.

Long, J. Scott 1983 *Confirmatory Factor Analysis: A Preface to LISREL*. Beverly Hills, Calif.: Sage.

Pearl, Judea 1998 "Graphs, Causality, and Structural Equation Models." *Sociological Methods and Research* 27:226–284.

Sobel, Michael E. 1995 "Causal Inference in the Social and Behavioral Sciences." In G. Arminger, C. C. Clogg, and M. E. Sobel, eds., *Handbook of Statistical Modeling for the Social and Behavioral Sciences*. New York: Plenum Press.

Sobel, Michael E. 1996 "An Introduction to Causal Inference." *Sociological Methods and Research* 24:353–379.

Spirtes, Peter, Thomas Richardson, Christopher Meek, Richard Scheines, and Clark Glymour 1998 "Using Path Diagrams as a Structural Equation Modeling Tool." *Sociological Methods and Research* 27:182–225.

Strotz, Robert H., and Herman O. A. Wold 1960 "Recursive Versus Nonrecursive Systems." *Econometrica* 28:417–427.

Suppes, Patrick 1970 *A Probabilistic Theory of Causality*. Amsterdam: North-Holland.

Von Eye, Alexander, and Clifford C. Clogg (eds.) 1994 *Latent Variables Analysis: Applications for Developmental Research*. Thousand Oaks, Calif.: Sage Publications.

Wright, Sewall 1934 "The Method of Path Coefficients." *Annals of Mathematical Statistics* 5:161–215.

——1960 "Path Coefficients and Path Regressions: Alternative or Complementary Concepts?" *Biometrics* 16:189–202.

HUBERT M. BLALOCK, JR.

CENSORSHIP AND THE REGULATION OF EXPRESSION

Modern discussions of censorship center on the legitimacy of the regulatory structures and actions through which expression and communication are governed, and the extent to which these structures meet the requirements of democratic societies. In this entry, we first survey prominent historical examples of centralized censorship systems in the West. This history provides a context for a discussion of modern conceptions of censorship and issues associated with the term itself. We then turn to legal structures regulating speech and press in the United States, to government control of political speech, and to some modern-day controversies over the regulation of expression.

EARLY SYSTEMS OF GOVERNMENT CENSORSHIP

Traditional conceptions of censorship are rooted in rigid systems of ecclesiastic and governmental control over discourse and printing. The term itself derives from the office of the census in early Rome, where the censor served as both census taker and as supervisor of public conduct and morals. Before the advent of the printing press in the fifteenth century, most manuscripts in Europe were produced in monasteries, which controlled their production. Centralized systems of control over books developed largely in response to the invention of the printing press, which both church and state perceived as threats to their authority. In the mid-sixteenth century the Catholic Church issued the Index of Forbidden Books, which was enforced through compliance of the faithful, prepublication screening of books, the burning of heretical tracts, and the persecution of heretics. In Protestant countries, the State generally assumed control over the publication of books. The English monarchy published its first list of prohibited books in 1529 and exercised its control through a contractual arrangement with the Stationers' Company, which, in 1557, was granted a monopoly on the production and distribution of printed materials. This charter remained in effect until 1694 when it was allowed to expire, primarily because of difficulties in its administration. These centralized mechanisms of control were replaced by less systematic methods, such as laws against seditious libel, through which speech that merely criticized government policies could be punished.

Although systems similar to these proliferated worldwide and continue to exist in modern-day authoritarian regimes, they are consensually viewed as incompatible with the practice of democracy. The history of free speech principles in the West coincides with the rise of democratic thought, as expressed in the writings of the eighteenth-century Enlightenment philosophers in France and in the influential political philosophies of John Locke, John Milton, and John Stuart Mill in England. The turn of mind that gripped Europe during this period is reflected in Locke's dictum that governments are the servants of the people, not the reverse, and in the insistence by each of these philosophers that self-governance cannot function under regimes where the circulation of ideas is dependent upon the whims of rulers. In modern political theory, Habermas (1989) considers the demise of systematic state censorship to be a precondition of the rise of a "public sphere," an admittedly idealized realm of discourse—independent of both state and market—in which public issues can be deliberated in an environment where reason, not the status of speakers is honored.

THE RHETORIC OF "CENSORSHIP"

The use of language plays a critical role in framing thought and discussion about the legitimate control of speech. The term "censorship" most frequently arises in debates over the desirability of restricting access to one or another form of communicative content. However, the term is fraught with the complexities of multiple meanings, uses, and understandings. These complexities arise from the historical baggage it carries, the multiple contexts—popular, legal, and scholarly—in which it is used, and the highly contested nature of the debates in which it is invoked. Although systematic empirical analyses of the term have yet to be conducted, its meanings appear to differ along two dimensions, connotative and descriptive. Underlying the connotative force of the term is the strong conviction that suppression of speech is at best a necessary evil. As such, the term typically carries with it a highly pejorative connotation and a strong air of illegitimacy. Although First Amendment scholar Smolla (1991) informs us that "censorship was not always a dirty word," this facet of the term is now found in Webster's Dictionary, which states that it refers especially to control that is "exercised repressively."

Descriptive uses of the term differ according to the breadth of the domain covered. Under strict uses of the term, censorship means the prior restraint of information by government. It is this meaning that enables the Federal Communications Commission (FCC) to enact regulations that impose post hoc penalties for some forms of speech while at the same time declaring that "nothing in the Act [that governs the FCC] shall be . . . construed to give the Commission the power of censorship." In a second form of use, censorship refers to any form of government regulations that restrict or disable speech. Fines imposed by the FCC for "indecent" speech on radio fit this use, as the intent is to deter further indecency. In a third, less conventional usage, the term is modified to refer to nongovernmental restrictions on speech. For example, in one of the few instances in which the Supreme Court has applied the term to private concerns (*Red Lion v. FCC*, 395 U.S. 367, 1969), the Court stated that "The First Amendment does not protect private censorship by broadcasters who are licensed by the Government to use a scarce resource which is denied to others."

In each of these three descriptive domains the term "censorship" almost invariably carries its pejorative inflection. In its broadest sense, censorship signifies control over the means of expression; the determination of what content will not be communicated. This sense of the term is found in the work of Bourdieu (1991), for whom censorship is located not only in explicit prohibitions, but also in the everyday practices and power relationships that determine what is and is not said. It includes not only the sixteenth-century Inquisitor who decides which books will be burned, but also the twentieth-century film editor who leaves a scene on the cutting room floor. It includes both the intentional actions of individuals and, as importantly, the de facto results of impersonal forces that lead some ideas not to be expressed. This expansive meaning, which has yet to make significant inroads into popular discourse, is incompatible with the pejorative connotation found in everyday usage: If censorship is an integral part of everyday life, it cannot always, or even typically, be evil.

The prototypical understanding of "censorship" is firmly anchored at the point where the term's pejorative connotation intersects with governmental restrictions on speech. This can be seen in how the term is and is not used in legal and popular discourse. First, there are numerous forms of government restrictions that tend not to be thought of as censorship at all. Examples include punishment for perjury, threats, and libel, and prohibitions on misleading advertising. The core meaning of the term "censorship" tends to be applied to restrictions that are consensually deemed to be illegitimate; it tends not to be applied to restrictions that are consensually deemed to be legitimate, although they fall within the descriptive scope of the term. As such, the term typically serves to label those policies and actions that have been deemed undesirable rather than to describe a set of activities whose legitimacy could then be judged. A thorough sociological understanding of "censorship" would require a mapping of the shifting boundaries around which this legitimacy is withheld or conferred. For example, punishment for blasphemy was once considered legitimate, whereas penalties for inciting hatred against ethnic groups may not be thought of as "censorship" in the future. Second, in areas where the legitimacy of a restriction is under dispute, those who oppose the restriction tend to label it as censorship, whereas those who support the restriction attempt to distance themselves from the term.

This core understanding of the term—as illegitimate government action—leads to a number of consequences, two of which will be mentioned here. First, discussions of the legitimate control of expression are typically framed as battles between censorship, on the one hand, and Free speech, on the other: Free speech is the absence of governmental control. This framing of the communicative needs of a democracy—codified in the First Amendment—places a wholesome burden on governments to justify regulatory action. On the other hand, this framing excludes from discussion the positive role that governments can (and do) play in supporting these needs. It also excludes consideration of the instances in which private concerns and impersonal market forces can produce deleterious effects; ones that exclude particular viewpoints from the marketplace of ideas. The restrictions placed by health maintenance organizations (HMOs) upon what physicians can say to their patients (i.e., "gag rules") are but one of countless areas in which private institutions "censor" valuable speech.

Research is needed to uncover the role that the rhetoric of "censorship" plays in maintaining the conception of free speech as the absence of government regulation. It is apparently with the goal of disabling this entrenched dichotomy that some theorists have used the term—e.g., "soft censorship," "de facto censorship" "private censorship"—to refer to those private and impersonal forces that lead some forms of expression to be systematically excluded from the marketplace of ideas (e.g., Barbur 1996; cf. Post 1998). Barbur, for example, argues that "monopoly is a polite word for uniformity, which is a polite word for virtual censorship—censorship not as a consequence of political choices, but as a consequence of inelastic markets, imperfect competition, and economies of scale..." (1996, pp. 137–138). Similarly, theorists

like Baker (1998) use the term "structural regulation" to refer to government interventions designed to increase viewpoint diversity in the public forum. The goal of such rhetorical interventions is to reframe the discussion of "free speech" in a way that is meticulously sensitive to the threats of government incursions on speech, yet, that at the same time allow this discussion to incorporate both the speech-restricting characteristics of private action and the speech-expanding possibilities of government.

The second consequence of our core understanding of "censorship" is linked primarily to the distaste the term evokes. This pejorative connotation renders the term useful in singling out illegitimate expressive restrictions, and as a persuasive device in popular and legal debate. However, the pejorative nature of the term also disables it as a useful construct in discussions that aim to present a balanced account of contemporary debates over the control of expression. For example, to frame a controversy concerning the legitimacy of restrictions on hate speech as a debate over whether such speech should be censored is to ask, in effect, whether the illegitimate suppression of hate speech is or is not legitimate. This framing, though a popular one, clearly biases the discussion toward one side of the debate.

In this entry we attempt to use less loaded terms to describe the concerns that the term "censorship" evokes and the underlying controversies in which the term is typically used. Correspondingly, we strive to reserve the term "censorship" for those uses in which it is integral to the viewpoint being expressed.

LEGAL PRINCIPLES GOVERNING THE REGULATION OF EXPRESSION IN THE UNITED STATES

The legal principles governing freedom of expression in the United States are based largely on interpretations of the First Amendment to the Constitution, whose "speech" and "press" clauses are combined in the statement that "Congress shall make no law . . . abridging the freedom of speech, or of the press." The amendment refers only to actions taken by the U.S. Congress, and it was not held to apply to laws made by the individual states until 1925 (*Gitlow v. New York*, 2688 U.S.

652, 1925) when the Court ruled that the fourteenth Amendment required that state laws not be in conflict with federal law. In addition to state and constitutional law, other major sources of legal regulation originate in common law (e.g., sedition, privacy) and administrative law (e.g., rulemaking of the FCC).

Despite the apparent clarity of the First Amendment language, both Congress and the states have crafted many laws that regulate freedoms of speech and press. These regulations stem primarily from three sources. First, the First Amendment is subject to widely varying interpretations. Some constitutional scholars conclude that at time the Bill of Rights was drafted, conceptions of freedom of expression referred only to prior restraints on speech. Others note ambiguities in the words "abridge" and "speech," and further question the intent of the framers of the Constitution. For example, do regulation of defamatory tracts, false commercial advertising, perjury, threats, violent obscenity, or nude dancing necessarily count as abridgments of speech (Sunstein 1993)? Some have also argued that the speech clause governs only political speech or that the press clause should not be interpreted to apply to tabloid entertainment that masquerades as news.

Second, the modern world differs from the world of the late eighteenth century. The framers could not have foreseen the technological advances that have brought us telephones, television, and the Internet. Neither could they have had in mind the concentrated corporate ownership or the advertising-driven programming that characterizes today's media. Some argue that government regulation is required in order to achieve the principles embodied in the Constitution.

Third, speech rights do not stand alone. For example, the rights of some to speak may conflict with the rights of others to be let alone or to be treated with dignity and equality. Also, the speech rights asserted by some inevitably conflict with the speech rights claimed by others.

In light of such issues, the clarity and simplicity that at first seem to characterize the First Amendment turn out to be illusory. As a result, scholars have developed theories of the underlying values that they believe free speech should promote in a democracy and should govern interpretation of

the First Amendment. Although no theory is universally accepted as dominant, most agree with the judgment of constitutional scholar Emerson (1973) that the value of free expression lies in its ability to promote participation in the decision-making process by all members of society; to advance knowledge and the pursuit of truth; to promote individual self-fulfillment; and, by allowing dissent to be publicly vented, to promote a balance between stability and change.

Disputes over the role of government in regulating speech turn, in part, on which of these values is given precedence. Those who emphasize the role of speech in promoting deliberative democracy often favor an affirmative role of government to promote viewpoint diversity or to ensure that the distribution of viewpoints in the public sphere is somewhat reflective of their distribution in the community. In practical terms, this may lead to restrictions on the amount of money that corporations can contribute to political campaigns, to the enforcement of rights of access to media by citizens, to the strategic placement of "public forum" spaces on the Internet, to stricter enforcement of the antitrust laws as they pertain to media, or to government subsidies for valued forms of speech (Baker 1998). In many instances, the promotion of viewpoint diversity and balance may require the government to regulate or infringe upon the speech or property rights of some in order to advance the needs of deliberative democracy.

DIFFERENTIAL JUDICIAL TREATMENT OF DIFFERENT FORMS OF EXPRESSION

The corpus of First Amendment decisions shows that all speech is not equal in the protections it is afforded. Political discourse—broadly defined to include speech about social, cultural, and religious issues—is considered speech of the highest value. As a result, the government must demonstrate a "compelling" interest to warrant its restriction. Particularly, political speech cannot be directly restricted unless it is "directed to inciting or producing imminent lawless action and is likely to incite or produce such action." Advertising was long considered outside the purview of First Amendment protections and was subject to strict regulation. Commercial speech has experienced tremendous leaps in its status under the Court as many local restrictions have been declared unconstitutional. Obscenity lies at the lowest rung of speech and receives no protection under the First Amendment. Although the requirements for demonstrating that speech is obscene have become progressively more demanding, Congress and the states are permitted to ban the public dissemination of speech that meets these criteria (see below). Depending upon how they are classified in terms of value to society, other forms of speech receive greater or lesser protection. For example, unlicensed medical advice and misleading advertising can be restricted through a "balancing test" which shows that the harm that stems from suppressing them are fewer than the harm they cause. A "balancing test" which shows that the harm that stems from suppressing them are less than the harm they cause.

Current First Amendment doctrine also reflects a second, cross-cutting mode of classification according to which proposed regulations are categorized as content neutral, content based, or viewpoint based. Of the three, content neutral regulations must pass the lowest constitutional hurdle whereas viewpoint-based regulations must pass the highest. An example of content-neutral regulations might include rules that designate sound-level restrictions on expressive activities, such as music in Central Park. Examples of viewpoint-based restrictions might include a ban on a gay parade or on either Democrat or Republican billboards. Regulations on expression that are content based, but viewpoint neutral face a high, but not insurmountable, constitutional hurdle. For example, in their contractual relations with cable companies, municipalities have been allowed to require the companies to provide local news and sports, and the federal government has been allowed to prohibit all partisan political campaigning on army bases.

The application of First Amendment law is also a function of the technological environment, or medium, in which expression is conveyed. Except through the sporadic use of antitrust laws, the Court has been least likely to permit regulations of print-based news and most likely to allow regulations of broadcast media. Cable television has fallen somewhere in between, with regulations reflecting the monopolistic control that companies exert over cable access to individual households and the fact that municipalities own the property through which television cables are distributed. Telephone companies are classified as "common carriers," which interdicts their editorial control over the information that passes through their wires. The newest form of communication, the Internet, has so far been granted the highest rung of protection from government regulation.

The willingness of the Court to allow government regulation of broadcast media lies largely on three rationales: public ownership of the airwaves, scarcity of the broadcast spectrum, and "pervasiveness" of the broadcast signal. First, the airwaves through which broadcast signals are transmitted are owned by the public and licensed on a renewable basis to radio and television broadcasters. Second, only a limited number of broadcast signals can coexist in any given segment of airspace (scarcity principle). In other words, the broadcast spectrum is a scarce resource, one that has historically required some regulatory body to decide which of the many interested broadcasters will be allotted the frequencies that exist. The management of these tasks is the function of the FCC, which was authorized to regulate broadcasters in the "public convenience, interest, or necessity." In interpreting the "public-interest" clause, the FCC has issued a number of requirements, including, for example, a modicum of public-interest programming such as local news, rights of reply to those attacked in political editorials, and requirements to air political advertisements. Regulations governing the latter are governed by a "no censorship" clause, whereby the FCC deprives stations of editorial rights over political advertisements. Although most of these regulations are aimed to increase viewpoint diversity, broadcasters often argue that FCC rules infringe upon their rights to free speech. Finally, the Supreme Court's judgment that radio and television broadcasts are "pervasive" refers to the assumed inability of viewers and listeners to fully control their own access, or that of their children, to unexpected program content. The susceptibility of audience members to be caught unawares by programming that offends them, or that they deem harmful to their children, has led the court to characterize such broadcasts as an "uninvited intruder" into the privacy of a viewer's abode. Primarily to provide a "safe haven," for children, the Court has allowed time restrictions on the broadcast of "indecent" or "patently offensive" programming.

Given the different levels of protection afforded by the First Amendment for different forms of expression, the determination of which category of speech, which kind of regulation, and which form of media a given case will be deemed to embody, is of critical importance. Levels of protection for different forms of speech have changed over time and there is no reason to think that they will not continue to do so. Movies were long considered a form of crass entertainment, outside of First Amendment protections, and birth control information was once classified as obscene. In the not-distant future, the plethora of programming opportunities on the Internet is likely to result in Supreme Court challenges of the scarcity principle upon which public-interest broadcast regulations are based. Particularly in the area of new media, the difficulties inherent in determining how to categorize a particular speech situation often leads the categorical approach to cede to an approach in which the harms of competing outcomes are less formally "balanced" against each other. Projects for sociology might include examination of the social underpinnings of the origin of these categories, of the application of these categories to different forms of speech, and of the evidentiary criteria used to assess both the harms of speech and the harms of regulation. For instance, a near consensus has been reached in the scientific community that media violence leads to social aggression and violence (e.g., Donnerstein and Smith 1997), whereas evidence of harms done by "indecent" broadcasts is anecdotal. What then are the social and political processes that lead one and not the other to be regulated?

PUBLIC SPEECH, PRIVATE SPACES

As can be seen in the language of the First Amendment, the central concern of the framers of the Constitution was to protect the private realm from domination by the state. The First Amendment itself has little to say about the control that private organizations exert over the expressive rights of individuals, or the control that private media companies exert over the communication of public issues. Examples of private-domain controversies include disputes over the "gag rules" that prohibit physicians from discussing alternate, more expensive treatments; corporate contracts that prevent employees from publicizing questionable employer practices; and control over the correspondence that employees send over company e-mail systems. An evolving legal controversy surrounds the growing replacement of public forums—sidewalks, streets, and public parks—by private ones, such as shopping malls, condominiums, and gated communities. Should the political protesters who once convened in front of the local store be barred from entry to the shopping mall where the store now stands? Should those gathering signatures for political initiatives be excluded from gated communities? These issues pit the property rights of owners against the expressive needs of communities. Supreme Court decisions have given individual states some leeway in deciding which and when one of these interests is the more compelling. Related issues arise in the domain of media, where some point to the growing concentration of media ownership (Bagdikian 1997), the presence of only one daily newspaper in most U.S. cities, and the "skewing" of media content away from the interests of the poor (Baker 1998) as evidence that the marketplace of ideas is not fully served by unregulated economic markets (Sunstein 1993).

A strict reading of the First Amendment suggests that the government has no right to intercede to regulate communication between a corporation and its employees (harassment rules provide an exception) or to intervene when privately owned media fail to meet the needs of a community. Many argue that this is as it should be: employees can always seek employment elsewhere and those whose speech is barred in one forum can always seek another. Others insist that differences between the conditions of modern society and those at the time the Constitution was drafted warrant the extension of communicative rights beyond those provided in the First Amendment.

THE LEGAL SUPPRESSION OF SPEECH DEEMED TO THREATEN THE ESTABLISHED ORDER

A central rationale for laws restricting the expressive activities of people and press is to preserve national security. The chief mechanisms of enforcement under democratic governments have been restrictions on governmentally controlled information, laws prohibiting seditious libel, and, in times of war, systems of prepublication clearance of press dispatches. Most agree that there are some circumstances, particularly in times of war, in which some national security restrictions are necessary. However, a strong proclivity exists to abuse these laws to protect policies or governments that are losing, or have lost, their base of popular support.

The prototypical conception of censorship is firmly rooted in governmental restrictions on speech that is critical of government, yet poses significant threats to security. The law of seditious libel was imported to the United States from England, where, during the eighteenth century, it served as a principal vehicle through which governments attempted to stave off criticism and to control public opinion. The power of seditious libel laws lay largely in their breadth—advocacy of an "ill opinion" of government was considered actionable—and from the selectivity with which they could be enforced. During most of the eighteenth century, these cases were decided by judges rather than juries, and the truth of a charge was not a defense until the nineteenth century.

The climate in which the Constitution's press clause was drafted was one in which a central threat to viewpoint diversity was posed by governments who could use their monopolies on legitimized force to control the marketplace of ideas. The most noted illustration of this in colonial America was the case of John Peter Zenger, whose newspaper, the *New York Weekly* was launched in 1734 as the only voice of opposition to the widely reviled colonial Governor, William Cosby. When the newspaper's opening salvo attacked Cosby's arbitrary exercise of power, Zenger was promptly charged with seditious libel. After spending eight months in jail, Zenger was acquitted by a jury (reluctantly allowed in this case), who ignored the judge's instructions that the truth of a charge was irrelevant. Although many thought the First Amendment would change such abuse, Congress soon passed the Sedition Act, which was used by President John Adams, a Federalist, to silence criticism launched by Republican supporters of Thomas Jefferson.

The Sedition Act was allowed to lapse when Jefferson took the Presidency and would not return until World War I. However, in the years during which the Constitution did not apply to the states, statutory attacks on specific viewpoints could be fierce at the state level. Louisiana's pre-Civil War statute prosecuting speech that sowed "discontent among the free population or insubordination among the slaves" provides just one example of how law could be enlisted in the service of majoritarian predjudices. When the federal government returned to the sedition business with passage of the Espionage and Sedition Acts, the country was characterized by a climate of isolationism and a receptive ear to the tenets of Socialists, who opposed the entry of the United States into World War I. The Sedition Act rendered it illegal to speak against the draft or to advocate strikes that might hinder wartime production. It resulted in more than 800 convictions, including that of Socialist presidential candidate Eugene Debs. Prosecutions for political speech continued after World War II, when provisions of the 1940 Smith Act were used as the legal arm of an extensive and popularly backed campaign to suppress Communist viewpoints in the press, the workplace, and the entertainment media.

A significant judicial outcome of cases stemming from the enforcement of these acts was the evolution of the criteria used to determine whether political speech warrants conviction. Whereas it had previously sufficed that expression result in only a "bad tendency" to cause harm, these cases eventually produced today's criterion of "immanent lawlessness." Had the expressive restrictions of the first part of the century been in place during the civil rights movement and the Vietnam War, much of what was said and written during these periods would have resulted in federally sanctioned jail sentences.

National security interests have also been invoked to justify secrecy classification systems, the labeling of foreign "propaganda," and the use of contract law by agencies including the Central Intelligence Agency and the Voice of America to require prepublication clearance of communications by both current and former employees.

WARTIME RESTRICTIONS

Compulsory systems of prepublication clearance during wartime were first used during the Civil War and, with the notable exception of Vietnam, have continued to be used in all major military conflicts. The exception of Vietnam was prompted by the government's fear that prior review systems would alienate the press and by the fact that readily available nonmilitary air transportation in the area would have rendered enforcement difficult. However, there is credible evidence that military officials systematically misrepresented progress by the United States during the war and that media routines and practices rendered them susceptible to this manipulation (Hallin 1986).

Despite the consensus on the need for some form of press management system to protect the lives of soldiers during wartime, controversies arise over the scope and mechanisms of enforcement. Of particular concern to press and public is the fear that controls ostensibly designed to protect the lives of soldiers are used instead to manage public opinion at home.

PORNOGRAPHY

The term pornography comes from the Greek words for "prostitute" and "write," and originally referred to writings about prostitutes and their activities. Today, pornography is broadly used to mean material with explicit sexual content. Like the word censorship itself, however, the definition of pornographic or obscene material is often contested. For example, feminist writers often draw a distinction between pornography, which combines sexuality with abuse or degradation, and erotica, which is sexually arousing material that respects the human dignity of the participants. A distinction is also sometimes drawn between hard-core pornography, which shows actual sexual intercourse or penetration, and soft-core pornography, which may be only suggestive of these activities. Child pornography is prohibited in most nations, and restrictions on its production and distribution tend to be noncontroversial.

In the United States, the Commission on Obscenity and Pornography (1970) and the Attorney General's Commission on Pornography (1986) have provided recommendations for government action regarding pornography. The first report suggested that pornography should not be regulated by law, while the second rejected the claims that pornographic material was harmless and urged prosecution especially for materials that contained violence or degradation. These differing conclusions highlight the ongoing tensions between individual rights and perceived community needs, as

well as changes in the progress and interpretation of research on the effects of pornography. The uses of the conclusions drawn in these and other social-scientific reports are of particular sociological interest. For example, the Nixon Administration was quick to dismiss the conclusions of a report (which it had itself commissioned) that were contrary to its political goals. Here, as in other contested areas of expression, the political climate in which research findings are interpreted is often the deciding factor in how research is used.

Regarding the related question of obscenity, in 1973 the Supreme Court (*Miller v. California*, 413, U.S. 15, 1973) established three criteria for determining whether a given work was obscene: An average person, applying contemporary local community standards, finds that the work, taken as a whole, appeals to prurient interest; the work depicts in a patently offensive way sexual conduct specifically defined by applicable state law; and the work in question lacks serious literary, artistic, political, or scientific value.

Political struggles over the regulation of pornography have been especially intriguing because they have brought together conservatives and feminists, groups traditionally on opposite sides of the ideological spectrum. Although both sides may support banning pornography, they have different reasons for doing so, and the scope of the material they wish to have regulated differs as well. Feminists focus on the degrading character of pornography, whereas conservatives view pornography as morally corrosive. Antipornography activists such as Catherine MacKinnon have defined pornography as a civil rights issue, arguing that pornography itself is a form of sexual discrimination; by presenting women in dehumanizing ways, pornography subordinates them.

Although there is wide variation in pornographic content, pornography often presents what many consider to be an unrealistic view of sexual relations. Encounters take place most often between strangers, not in the context of enduring relationships; participants are sex objects rather than complete individuals. Sexual activity always results in ecstasy, and consequences (such as pregnancy or disease) are nonexistent.

Empirical research on the effects of pornography has shown a range of negative effects. In typical experimental studies, participants are randomly assigned to pornographic stimuli or nonpornographic stimuli, and their attitudes, behaviors, or physiological reactions are then assessed. There are also paradigms assessing prolonged exposure, including ones in which participants return to the laboratory for multiple sessions of exposure to pornography, to better simulate real-life consumption patterns. Among other effects, studies have shown that after exposure to pornography, participants viewed rape as a less serious crime, overestimated the popularity of less common sexual practices, and showed greater callousness toward women. Furthermore, pornography consumers have shown weaker beliefs in the desirability of marriage and having children, and stronger beliefs in the normality of sexual promiscuity. Ironically, pornography has also been shown to reduce viewers' satisfaction with their own sex lives and partners.

Although these outcomes have been found in a variety of studies using different research procedures, not all studies have confirmed these findings. Some critics of this research argue that rape and other antisocial sexual behavior existed even before pornography became widely available, and that forces besides pornography play a greater causal role in antisocial behavior. Others argue that the increased levels of aggression, hostility, or bias often found in experimental studies of pornography might be traced to differences between the experimental and naturalistic environments in which pornography is viewed: particularly, it is argued that these effects may be due to the lack of opportunity for men to ejaculate in the experimental setting. They also caution that the political biases of investigators may influence the interpretation of results. Others believe that even if the effects research is accurate, the costs of suppressing pornographic material—as measured in state encroachment on individual autonomy—outweigh any benefits that might be gained.

An argument sometimes raised for controlling or eliminating pornography in the form of images (rather than words) is that the individuals pictured in the pornographic photos and films suffered harm or coercion during the creation of the materials. A counterpoint to this argument is provided by Stoller and Levine (1993), who have conducted in-depth ethnographic style interviews with producers, performers, and other employees in the pornography industry. In this work, the researchers allowed the people who create pornography to speak in their own words, providing both defenses of pornography and insight into why individuals choose, for better or for worse, to work in the pornography industry.

HATE SPEECH

From the advent of the printing press onward, most efforts to legally regulate expression have focused on various forms of mass communication. Efforts to restrict speech can also target communication in interpersonal settings. One such example can be found in attempts to place legal limits on hate speech; defined as harassing or intimidating remarks that derogate the hearer's race, gender, religion, or sexual orientation.

Those who support regulating hate speech compare it to "fighting words," a category of speech not protected by the First Amendment, or argue that it creates a "hostile environment," which violates provisions of the Civil Rights Acts of 1964 and 1990. Champions of hate speech regulations cite the harms its victims suffer: these may range from feelings of exclusion from a community, to the experience of debasement that leads students to skip classes or distress that leads them to leave school. In short, the liberty of a speaker to harass may deny the hearer's right to equality. Critics of hate speech codes cite the administrative excesses they allow. For example, the student guide to the University of Michigan code stated that students could be punished for making a comment "in a derogatory way about someone's appearance."

Following an increase in reported incidents of hate speech in the late 1980s and early 1990s, many universities in the United States adopted policies forbidding discriminatory verbal harassment. However, as they affect public institutions, these rules have been declared unconstitutional in the courts, in part for being either too broad—affecting too many forms of speech—or for being viewpoint based (see above).

The problems inherent in drafting laws that affect only the speech these rules target can be seen in comparing the provisions of the University of Michigan code with provisions in the bill advanced by Senator Jesse Helms to limit what kinds of works could receive funding from the National Endowment for the Arts. Among the Helms bill's other planks (aimed at homoerotic art, for example), it sought to prohibit funding of "material which denigrates . . . a person, group, or class of citizens on the basis of race, creed, sex, age . . ." Similarly, the Michigan code sought to bar speech that "stigmatizes or victimizes an individual on the basis of race, ethnicity, religion, sex . . ." and also "creates a hostile environment." The projects targeted by the Helms bill included one with a crucifix immersed in a bottle of urine. This work could also be a violation of the Michigan code if it were to be hung in an area frequented by offended Christians. Difficulties of this sort have prompted those supporting hate speech codes to argue that this is one area in which viewpoint-based speech regulations should be allowed: that, similar to laws in Germany that selectively ban Holocaust denial, speech laws in the United States should be allowed to account for the history of discrimination experienced by some groups, but not others. Critics say that viewpoint discrimination of this sort would open the floodgates for future laws that selectively target viewpoints that happen to be deemed undesirable.

The hate speech debates highlight a fundamental dilemma faced by modern democracies: to what extent are we willing to tolerate speech whose very goal is to silence the speech of others, or to deny their rights to equal education or employment? Efforts continue to craft codes that are narrow in scope and that meet constitutional muster, with even staunch civil libertarians favoring prosecution when hate speech poses a clear and present danger of violence (e.g., Smolla 1992). The hate speech debates also mark a significant turn in the rhetoric of "censorship," one in which advocates of speech codes have attempted to enlist the power of this term in their favor. This rhetorical strategy is exemplified by the argument of Catharine MacKinnon, one of the staunchest code supporters, that "the operative definition of censorship . . . shifts from government silencing what powerless people say, to powerful people violating powerless people into silence and hiding behind state power to do it" (1993, p. 10).

BATTLES FOR CONTROL OVER SCHOOL CURRICULA

Schools are the arena in which the values of open deliberation and the constructive exchange of ideas are most prized in democratic societies. It is with some irony, then, that schools are also the domain in which some of the most concerted efforts to limit the scope of deliberation have been focused. The content of textbooks used by most students in the United States has been selectively tailored to the ideological viewpoints of organized pressure groups, and at least one-third of high school students are not exposed to books and films that parents and pressure groups have successfully purged from their educational experience (Davis 1979).

From the vantage point of most teachers, parental and school board mandates to omit works of literature from the curriculum are viewed as illegitimate challenges to their expertise and infringements on their rights as professionals. In effect, teachers believe that they are in the best positions to judge the educational needs of the students they teach. However, the tradition of academic freedom that characterizes both public and private universities is rarely present in elementary and secondary education. Public school curricula are generally approved by the state or by school boards that actively regulate what is taught and what students read. School board members tend to be elected to their positions and are particularly responsive to what teachers view as unreasonable censorial demands.

Parents, on the other hand, see their interventions in the school curricula as a legitimate exercise of control over what their children read in school. They justify their decision, in part, with respect to the compulsory nature of early schooling, where they see their children as captive audiences. A number of well-funded organizations have exerted strong influences on both school boards and textbook adoption processes to influence what does and does not gain entry to the schoolroom.

In money terms, the largest impact of pressure groups has been on textbook publication and adoptions. Most states place orders for textbooks for schools in the entire state. Because publishers cannot provide multiple versions for different regions or states, texts are geared to the largest markets, usually Texas and California (Del Fattore 1992). As a result, publishers provide their writers with guidelines that govern topics and viewpoints that are currently deemed objectionable (or desirable) in the largest states that engage in statewide adoptions. In this way, pressure groups in one state, such as Texas, often exercise veto power over the entire country's textbook market. Local communities in small and mid-size states exercise a relatively small influence on content.

Community protest and lawsuits are the principal vehicles used to challenge textbooks and reading lists in literature, social studies, and health education. An illustrative controversy—at McClintock High School in Tempe, Arizona in 1996—highlights the susceptibility of teachers and schools to parental and community demands. In this case, a parent of a McClintock High student protested the assignment of Mark Twain's classic *The Adventures of Huckleberry Finn* because the word "nigger" is included in its dialogue. In the ensuing controversy, some held that if schools were forced to shield students from exposure to the term, such intervention would undermine the legitimate authority of teachers and would endorse ignorance of American history and the practice of censorship.

We may ask whether the students grasp the distinctions among Twain's stance on racism, the use of the term "nigger" by a character in the novel, and societal endorsement of the term then and today. Of course the crux of such conflicts also rests upon the educational and social contexts in which sensitive, taboo, or potentially affronting topics that appear in the world of fiction are discussed. For instance, if *The Adventures of Huckleberry Finn* or any other literature is misused to communicate racism, the problem is larger than the choice of which books are read in the classroom.

Unfortunately, the social context of this controversy added complexity. School benches at the same high school were etched with the words "I hate niggers." Of course, there is an important distinction between eliminating the word "nigger" from *The Adventures of Huckleberry Finn* and removing "I hate niggers" from a school bench. The etching creates a hostile educational and social environment in a way that the assignment of book should not do, as long as teachers and schools are doing their jobs well. In controversy after controversy, these distinctions are as important as

they have been difficult to establish. Often teachers simply capitulate to perceptions of the most conservative or protective community elements and use readings that are sure to be "safe" (Davis 1979).

In 1990s most lawsuits were mounted by fundamentalists who condemned many books on school lists as anti-Christian, antiparent, antigovernment, immoral, and obscene. The challenged books change from year to year, but frequently banned books have included *Of Mice and Men* (Steinbeck), *Catch 22* (Heller), and *Catcher in the Rye* (Salinger). Fundamentalists are effective out of all proportion to their numbers because of the intense dedication they bring to their cause.

Research has yet to provide a sound basis for confidently assessing the effects of reading on school children's beliefs. When a story contains a character's arguments against the existence of God, might students question their faith? Qualitative research, particularly, has shown that students take widely divergent readings from stories and that these understandings are frequently critical of the viewpoints adopted by both characters and writers.

Can we maintain that literature gives readers insights into life? That it can change lives? Parents—former pupils, after all—have been encouraged to believe that great works contain great truths. It is not surprising that some of those parents who discern arguments against the social order in their children's readings seek to eliminate the threat from children's lives. Eventually, these ongoing and recurring controversies may be illuminated by scientifically grounded understanding of the social and cognitive foundations of narrative impact (Green, Strange, and Brock 2000).

One of the strongest arguments for keeping school curricula open to ideas to which we currently object or to heinous artifacts of historical prejudices is that one of the important functions of education is the development of critical inquiry. From this perspective, to turn the schoolhouse into an environment where only "safe" ideas are encountered is to do students and society a disservice. This position is rendered more compelling in the context of the current media landscape which makes it certain that students will also encounter these ideas outside the context of a critical learning environment. This argument, of course, rests on the assumption that schools are, in fact, places where critical inquiry is fostered.

THE SOCIAL PSYCHOLOGY OF "CENSORSHIP"

When information (e.g. a book, a film, a speech, etc.) is explicitly "censored" do people desire that information much less—in accordance with the presumed intention of the censoring agents? Are people less likely to be influenced by a point of view when its expression has been prohibited by those in authority? To answer such questions, the impact of the label "censored" can be studied experimentally by exposing people to a communication (or a "taste" of a communication) to which "censored" is affixed and by then observing the consequences of such a juxtaposition of label and communication on their values and beliefs. When this careful experimental work has been done, the answer to both of these questions is "no." Numerous experiments have shown that explicit censorship often *backfires*: the prohibition of communications leads people to covet them and to change their attitudes in the directions the censored material advocates.

A social-commodity theory (Brock 1968) accounts for the backfire effect of censorship in terms of the psychology of supply and demand. All public communications are perceived to have some limits on their distribution, and message recipients usually have some dim awareness of the extent of these limits. However, if the distribution is explicitly limited by government statute, or other overt interventions, awareness of scarcity is sharply heightened and the desirability and impact of the communication are consequently increased. When some information becomes less available, this unavailability augments the information's value. A decrease in supply causes an increase in demand, and perceived censorship invariably entails a perceived decrease in supply.

Experimental social psychology has illuminated the impact of censorship by showing that (a) an individual can be influenced by a censored communication, even without actually receiving it, (b) the backfire effect increases as the penalties for violating censorship are increased; and, somewhat paradoxically, (c) the backfire effect is greater when the prohibition applies selectively to one group of people. For example, for a seventeen year old, a film that was prohibited to persons under eighteen years of age would be more desirable than a film that was prohibited to all persons. In the former case, the censorship has more impact because it is viewed as violating a personal freedom; freedom to view a film is more threatened if there are many other people (all persons over eighteen years, say) who do have that freedom.

The experimentally grounded insights from social psychology—that explicit censorship usually doesn't work as planned, and that it often backfires—is often not factored into the planning and interventions of censoring agents. In some instances this may be good, as it reduces the effectiveness of those who attempt to limit information that is vital to public deliberation. In some instances, public information officers appear to have become aware that perceptions of censorship can hamper their efforts. In the 1970s, the Department of Defense directed that the term be completely dropped. This seemingly cosmetic change affects the way news coverage labels the sources of news reports: what was once attributed to the Office of Censorship, became, during the Gulf War, a report from the Joint Information Bureau.

Research on related forms of content advisory labels, such as "parental discretion advised," "viewer discretion advised," and the more specific codes signaling levels of violence, nudity, sex, and profanity on television, has begun to reveal the extent to which different kinds of labels affect the selection choices of boys and girls of different ages (Cantor and Harrison, 1994–1995). In several cases, these studies have revealed a "backfire" or "forbidden fruit" effect similar to the pattern found in reactions to the censorship label. The finding that restricted materials become more attracted—which depended on age, gender, and the kinds of labels used—have been extended to video game and music advisories.

Advocates of requiring such labels argue that their goal is not to limit communication at its source, but rather to provide parents and children a greater degree of control over their communication choices. Some critics argue that, regardless of intent, these labels lead producers to alter their productions in order to avoid undesirable labeling. As with the "censored" label, the effects on consumption of the targeted content will depend not only on how the label affects desirability of the materials, but also on the ultimate availability of the labeled content. If parents use advisory labels to preselect their children's television viewing choices, these labels will effectively place greater selective control in the hands of parents. The probability that parents will do so is heightened by technologies like the "V-chip," through which parental choices can be automated. Similar labels may have a much different effect on the selection of music and video games, where children are more likely to make their own media selections.

Research has also begun to examine the social and psychological origins of calls to restrict deemed harmful to children or to society at large. Studies of the "third person effect" suggest that support for restrictions on such content may sometimes be grounded in systematic overestimates of the effects of media on other persons. Sociological treatments of the rise of public alarm are particularly relevant here. Nicola Beisel's (1992) account of the late-nineteenth-century attack on obscenity that resulted in the highly suppressive Comstock Laws is one example of a fruitful direction that research might take.

INTERNATIONAL ISSUES

Whereas most democratic nations have codified and enforced protections against the most blatant forms of government suppression of sociopolitical speech, governments around the world continue to engage in harsh repression. The bounty placed on the life of Salman Rushdie in retribution for his book, *The Satanic Verses*, is a well-publicized instance of the most egregious form of government-sanctioned repression. However, a variety of both legal and extra-legal tactics continue to be used worldwide to protect those in power. To cite just two typical examples from 1999: A court in Kazakhstan suspended publication of an opposition newspaper for the three months preceding presidential elections on the pretext that it failed to indicate the place of printing on its masthead; and, shortly after the director of the Cameroon newspaper *Le Messager-Populi* was released from a ten-month prison sentence for spreading "false information," the paper's founder was driven from the country upon threats to his life (see generally, Webb and Bell 1998). Typical extra-legal means of suppressing speech critical of the government include awarding and withdrawing governmental

advertising contracts, the licensing of journalists, controls on distribution of newsprint, and, more generally, government ownership and control of broadcast media.

Controls at the site of reception provide another means of suppressing viewpoints that lack the official stamp of approval. For example, a number of countries pose outright bans on ownership of satellite receiving dishes. However, new technologies, particularly the Internet, pose serious threats to the control of political information by authoritarian regimes. The Internet's impending threat is linked to the growing dependency upon computer-based communications in the marketplace. Authoritarian governments appear to be faced with a Hobson's choice: allow connections to the vast and diverse information resources of the Internet or face economic stagnation.

Particularly when looking beyond suppressive controls on political speech, it is important to recognize the distinction between government-controlled media and government-funded media. The BBC is but one example of the government-funded, public television stations that have developed reputations for independent news coverage that gives voice to diverse perspectives of both majority and minority interests. Publicly-subsidized television in Holland instantiates an intriguing model of "free speech" through a system that allots television channels and channel space on a proportional basis to key institutions and sociocultural groups. Public television stations in many European nations seek independence from the demands of both government and marketplace through nongovernmental boards of trustees and through stable funding mechanisms not subject to annual tampering by politically driven legislatures.

INTERNATIONAL INFORMATION FLOW

A handful of news agencies, led by the Associated Press (AP), Reuters, and Agence-France Presse dominate the news that people around the world read about issues and events originating outside their borders. The dominance of both print and broadcast news by a small group of companies is particularly felt in developing nations, ones lacking the capital to compete with the economies of scale enjoyed by entrenched foreign corporations. The concern generated in developing nations focuses not only on the news they receive from abroad, but also on the images that news agencies project about them. This concern is compounded by news agency values that typically stress large-scale violence and disruption—"coups and earthquakes" as the saying goes—and ignore the cultural achievements and developmental efforts for which these countries would like to be known.

Those who control international news flows view their position of dominance as a desirable and natural outcome of free-market practice. Those in developing nations view the imbalances as a form of de facto neo-imperialism. This view finds its historical roots in the late-nineteenth and early-twentieth centuries, when three European news agencies, Havas (France), Wolff (Germany), and Reuters (England) carved the world into three areas of monopoly control, ones that built upon their respective colonial empires. Some insight into the present-day perspective of developing nations can be gained by examining how news about the United States was communicated in the early part of the century. During those years, the "Ring Cartel" prevented AP from sending news about the United States beyond its borders. According to Kent Cooper, the AP manager who fought to dismantle it, the cartel decided "what the people of each nation would be allowed to know of the people of other nations and in what shade of meaning the news was to be presented." It was Reuters who "told the world about Indians on the war path in the West, lynchings in the South, and bizarre crimes in the North. . . . The charge for years was that nothing credible to America was ever sent" (cited in Frederik 1993, p.39). To those in developing nations, it is the AP who now plays the role of cartel.

Several proposals have been advanced to correct the imbalance in international news flows. Notable are those advanced through the United Nations Educational, Scientific, and Cultural Organization (UNESCO) during the late 1970s and early 1980s. These calls for a "New World Information Order" (NWIO) generated immediate and prolonged controversy, and provoked the United States to withdraw from UNESCO in 1985. The contours of these debates are as intriguing as they are complex, reflecting sharp differences in news values, international economic principles, and the very definition of "free speech." Whereas NWIO supporters liken the values of developmental journalism to current trends in the United States, such

as "civic" journalism, its detractors suggest that the values of developmental journalism cater to the needs of local authority. And whereas NWIO critics argue for a "free flow" of information across international boundaries, NWIO supporters advocate a "balanced flow." Although these issues remain unresolved, promising developments include the rise of regional news agencies, programs such as CNN's World Report, in which locally produced broadcasts gain worldwide exposure; and prospects that the Internet will facilitate the international communication of locally produced news.

The increasing global dominance of U.S. movies and television programming have prompted the European Economic Community and Canada, among other regional and national entities, to seek ceilings on imported cultural goods as exceptions to free trade principles in international trade agreements. These demands reflect the belief that when applied to the area of expression, free market principles support forms of "soft" or "de facto censorship" in which locally produced speech is driven from the marketplace of ideas (cf. Frederik 1993). More generally, these demands reflect the growing tension between the ongoing course of globalization and the threats to cultural sovereignty it entails.

REFERENCES

Bagdikian, B. 1997 *The Media Monopoly*. Boston: Beacon Press.

Baird, R.M., and S.E. Rosenbaum 1991 *Pornography: Private Right or Public Menace?* Buffalo, N.Y.: Prometheus Books.

Baker, C.E. 1998 "The Media that Citizens Need." *University of Pennsylvania Law Review* 147, 317.

Barbur, B. R. 1996 *Jihad vs. McWorld: How Globalism and Tribalism are Reshaping the World*. New York: Ballantine Books.

Beisel, Nicola. 1992 "Constructing a Shifting Moral Boundary: Literature and Obscenity in Nineteenth-Century America." In M. Lamont and M. Fournier, Eds., *Cultivating Differences: Symbolic Boundaries and the Making of Inequality*. Chicago: University of Chicago Press.

Bourdieu, P. 1991. "Censorship and the Imposition of Form." In J.B. Thompson, Ed. *Language and Symbolic Power*. Cambridge, Mass.: Harvard University Press.

Brock, T.C. 1968. "Implications of Commodity Theory for Value Change." In A.G. Greenwald, T.C. Brock, and T.M.Ostrom, eds. *Psychological Foundations of Attitudes*. New York: Academic Press.

Cantor, J., and K. Harrison 1994–1995 Ratings and Advisories for Television Programming." In *National Television Violence Study: Scientific Papers*. Los Angeles: Mediascope Inc.

Christenson, Peter G., and Donald F. Roberts 1998. "*It's Not Only Rock and Roll: Popular Music in the Lives of Adolescents*." Cresswell, N.J.: Hampton Press.

Court Case Citation, Gitlow vs. New York, 268 U.S. 652, 1925.

Court Case Citation, Red Lion Broadcasting vs. FCC, 395 U.S. 367, 1969.

Court Case Citation, Miller vs. California, 413 U.S. 15, 1973.

Curran, J., and M. Gurevitch 1996 *Mass Media and Society*. London: Edward Arnold.

Davis, J. Ed. 1979. *Dealing with Censorship*. Urbana, Ill.: National Council of Teachers of English.

Deetz, S. A. 1992. *Democracy in an Age of Corporate Colonization: Developments in Communication and the Politics of Everyday Life*. New York: State University of New York Press.

Del Fattore, J. 1992. *What Johnny Shouldn't Read: Textbook Censorship in America*. New Haven, Conn.: Yale University Press.

Dennis, E. E., et al. 1991. *The Media at War: The Press and the Persian Gulf Conflict*. New York: Gannett Foundation Media Center.

Donnerstein, E., and S.L. Smith 1997. "Impact of Media Violence on Children, Adolescents, and Adults." In S. Kirschner and D. A. Kirschner, Eds., *Perspectives on Psychology and the Media*. Washington, D.C.: American Psychological Association.

Emerson, T. I. 1973 *The System of Free Expression*. New York: Random House.

Foerstel, H.N. 1997. *Free Expression and Censorship in America: An Encyclopedia*. Westport, Conn.: Greenwood Press.

Frederick, H.H. 1993 *Global Communication and International Relations*. Belmont, Calif.: Wadsworth.

Green, J. 1990 *The Encyclopedia of Censorship*. New York: Facts on file.

Green, M.C., J.J. Strange, and T.C. Brock (eds.) 2000. *Narrative Impact: Social and Cognitive Foundations*. Mahwah, N.J.: Erlbaum Associates.

Habermas, J. 1989 *The Structural Transformation of the Public Sphere*. Cambridge Mass.: Polity.

Hallin, D. C. 1986. *The "Uncensored War": The Media and Vietnam*. New York: Oxford University Press.

Jensen, C. 1997 *20 Years of Censored News*. New York: Seven Stories Press.

MacKinnon, C. A. 1993 *Only Words*. Cambridge, Mass.: Harvard University Press.

Post, R.C. (ed.) 1998 *Censorship and Silencing: Practices of Cultural Regulation*. Los Angeles: The Getty Research Institute for the History of Art and the Humanities.

Shoemaker, P.J., and S.D. Reese 1996 *Mediating the Message: Theories of Influences on Mass Media Content*. New York: Longman.

Smolla, R.A. 1993 *Free Speech in an Open Society*. New York: Vintage Books.

Stoller, R.J, and I.S. Levine 1993 *Coming Attractions: The Making of an X-Rated Video*. New Haven, Conn.: Yale University Press.

Sunstein, C. 1993. *Democracy and the Problem of Free Speech*. New York: Free Press.

Webb, W.L, and R. Bell (eds.) 1998 *An Embarrassment of Tyrannies: Twenty-Five Years of Index on Censorship*. New York: George Braziller.

Zillmann, D., and J. Bryant (eds.) 1989 *Pornography: Research Advances and Policy Considerations*. Hillsdale, NJ: Erlbaum.

JEFFREY J. STRANGE
MELANIE C. GREEN
TIMOTHY C. BROCK

CENSUS

A national census of population is "the total process of collecting, compiling, evaluating, analysing and publishing or otherwise disseminating demographic, economic, and social data pertaining, at a specified time, to all persons in a country" (United Nations 1988, p. 3). The United Nations encourages its members to take regular censuses and provides technical assistance. It also publishes an annual demographic yearbook and maintains a web site with selected census data and other population information for most countries.

A nation may conduct censuses on other subjects such as housing, business firms, agriculture, and local governments. Because of the close link between families and housing units, censuses of population and housing are usually combined.

The actual enumeration for a national population census is usually spread over a period of weeks or months, but an attempt is made to record circumstances as of a designated census day (April 1 for the 2000 U.S. census). In some censuses, persons are reported in their legal or usual place of residence (*a de jure enumeration*). According to the Bible, a census decree issued by the government in Rome ordered that persons be counted and taxed in their home towns. In response, Joseph and his pregnant wife, Mary, traveled from Nazareth to Bethlehem, where Mary gave birth to Jesus. Other censuses record people where they are on the census day (*a de facto enumeration*). Whatever residency rule is followed, all conceivable special circumstances must be anticipated, questionnaires well designed, and census staff thoroughly trained.

The U.S. census uses the concept of "usual residence," where the person lives and sleeps most of the time, but some exceptions are made. A few examples from the 2000 U.S. census illustrate the range of circumstances. Some persons staying in hotels and rooming houses are transients temporarily absent from their usual homes; they completed special census forms that were later compared to the census forms received from their home addresses to confirm that they were properly reported by other household members. An operation called "Service-Based Enumeration" was designed to locate homeless persons and others with no usual residence. College students were presumed to be residents at the place they lived while attending college, even if they were at home on spring break on census day. Efforts were made to avoid having an away-at-college child erroneously double-counted as a member of the home household. Pre-college students at away-from-home schools were assigned to the parental household. Citizens working in another country for the U.S. government, and their families, were enumerated (primarily through the use of administrative records), but other citizens living abroad at the census date were not counted. Short-term tourists, however, were supposed to be reported by other members of their households, or by late enumeration upon their return home. Persons not legally resident in the United States were supposed to be counted, but many feared all contact with authorities and took steps to avoid detection by census procedures.

The total population count is only one result of a modern census. Information is also obtained on many characteristics, such as age, sex, and relationship to others living in the same household, educational level, and occupation. The census then reports on population size and characteristics for provinces, states, counties, cities, villages, and other administrative units. To obtain all this information, the 2000 U.S. census (U.S. Census Bureau 1999) asked every household to complete a "short form" with six questions about each person and one question about each housing unit. A carefully selected sample of one of every six households received a "long form" that included additional questions on fourteen topics for each person and thirteen topics for each housing unit.

Reporting information for the entire country and for the thousands of cities and other subareas results in many volumes of printed reports. Many nations issue additional data on computer-readable files designed for convenient use by national and local governments, organizations, and individuals. Increasing quantities of data are available to anyone with access to the Internet.

In the United States, the idea for a regular census emerged during debates about the problems of creating a representative form of government. The U.S. Constitution (Article I, Section 2) directs that membership in the House of Representatives be based on population: "The actual enumeration shall be made within three years after the first meeting of the Congress of the United States, and within every subsequent term of ten years, in such manner as they shall by law direct."

The questions asked in a census reflect political and social issues of the day and often provoke spirited debates. For example, slavery was a recurrent divisive issue for the Constitutional Convention. One of the two newly created legislative bodies, the House of Representatives, was to have the number of legislators from each state proportional to the population of the state. Including slaves in the population count would increase the legislative power of southern states. A compromise (Article I, Section 2) provided that: "Representatives. . . shall be apportioned among the several states. . . according to their respective numbers, which shall be determined by adding to the whole number of free persons, excluding Indians not taxed, three-fifths of all other persons." The distinction between "free persons" and "all other persons" (slaves) was eliminated after the Civil War (Amendment 14, Section 2).

The 1790 census was modest in scope. Assistants to federal marshals made lists of households, recording for each household the number of persons in five categories: free white males over sixteen and under sixteen, free white females, other free persons, and slaves (Anderson 1988, p. 13).

Censuses from 1790 through 1840 were conducted with little central organization or statistical expertise. A temporary federal census office was established to conduct the 1850 census. The individual rather than the household became the focus of the enumeration, and the content of the census was expanded to include occupation, country or state of birth, and other items. Experienced statisticians were consulted, and the United States participated in the first International Statistical Congress in 1853.

The temporary office for the 1890 census became one of the largest federal agencies, employing 47,000 enumerators and 3,000 clerical workers. To help with the enormous task of tallying data, census officials supported the development by a young inventor, Herman Hollerith, of an electrical tabulating machine. His punched-card system proved effective in census operations and later contributed to the growth of the IBM corporation.

A permanent census office was established in 1902. An increasingly professional staff assumed responsibility for the population censuses and a broad range of other statistical activities. Deficiencies in the federal statistical system became apparent during the 1930s as the nation tried to assess the effects of the Great Depression and to analyze an array of new programs and policies. Several federal agencies successfully advocated expansion of the social and economic content of the 1940 census. New questions in 1940 asked about participation in the labor force, earnings, education, migration (place of residence in 1935), and fertility. A housing census was paired with the population census to provide information about housing values and rents, mortgages, condition of dwellings, water supply, and other property issues. The practice of providing population and housing information for subareas of large cities was greatly expanded.

Governmental statistical agencies are often set in their ways, concerned with continuity rather than innovation and removed from the higher levels of policymaking. For several decades beginning in the late 1930s, the U.S. Census Bureau was extraordinarily creative. Social scientists and statisticians employed by the Census Bureau were active in research and scholarly publication and played leadership roles in professional organizations. Census Bureau personnel pioneered in development of the theory and practice of population sampling. To accommodate large increases in content and geographic scope, the 1940 census questionnaire was divided into two parts. A set of basic questions was asked of everyone, while a set of supplementary questions was asked of a one-in-twenty sample. Subsequent U.S. censuses have continued to use sampling, as with the "long-form" versions of the 1990 and 2000 questionnaires that went to one of every six households. Sampling theory was also applied to the development of periodic sample surveys to provide timely information between censuses and to provide information on additional topics.

For the 1950 census, the Bureau participated actively in the development and utilization of another new technology, the computer. In later censuses, the schedules were microfilmed and optically scanned for direct input of information (without names and addresses) into a computer for error-checking, coding, and tabulating.

Through 1950, census enumeration in the United States was accomplished almost entirely by having an enumerator conduct a personal interview with one or more members of each household and write the information on a special form. By 1990, most census questionnaires were distributed and returned to the Census Bureau by mail, with telephone follow-up replacing many personal visits. Large-scale use of the Internet and other innovative response technologies may be practicable for widespread use in the 2010 census.

National censuses have so far been the best method for obtaining detailed information about the entire population. Only censuses provide counts and characteristics for small administrative and statistical areas, such as villages, voting districts, city blocks, and census tracts. Only censuses provide reliable information on small population groups, such as the income distribution of female plumbers. Only censuses provide the large numbers of cases needed for complex multivariate analyses. But censuses are so large and difficult to process that by the time the data are released they are, for some purposes, out of date, and this problem increases throughout the interval, commonly ten years, until the next census.

To address the timeliness problem, most national statistical agencies conduct a series of large sample surveys that provide select information on key topics at timely intervals. In the United States, for example, the latest unemployment rate, released on the first Friday of each month, is headline news. It is based on the Current Population Survey, a monthly sample survey that provides current information on many social and economic characteristics.

A few countries keep population registers, continuous records of where people live along with some of their characteristics. If reasonably complete and accurate, these may be used to supplement and update some census information. In many nations, administrative records such as social security, national health, tax, and utility company files, may be adapted to provide periodic estimates of population size and a few characteristics, but difficult questions arise about data quality and comparability with census- and survey-based information. Citizens of many nations are wary about letting the government and corporations compile extensive personal data. Legislative restrictions are increasingly being placed on what information may be gathered and stored and how it may be used.

The questions asked in successive censuses typically change more slowly than the procedures. Keeping the same topics and the same wordings of questions help a government measure change from one census to the next. This appeals to researchers and policy analysts, but policymakers and administrators, whose attention is focused mainly on current programs and next year's budget, often plead for new wording to better serve current concepts. Another reason tending to stifle innovation is that the census is an expensive and visible tool. A lengthy review process confronts any agency that seeks to add, delete, or alter a question. In the United States, both the executive branch and the Congress must approve the final census schedule. A question on pet ownership has been regularly proposed but rejected because there is no compelling governmental interest in such a question and private sample surveys can provide the desired information. A third reason the content of the questionnaire changes little is that proponents of new topics and questions must compete for questionnaire space, while questions previously asked tend to already have a network of users who have a vested interest in retaining the topic. This competition spurs extensive lobbying and mobilization of support from federal agencies, congressional committees, and interest groups.

An innovative approach to providing timely data is "continuous measurement" using a "rolling-sample" survey. The *American Community Survey* has been implemented by the U.S. Census Bureau (1999), with plans to expand to three million households a year in 2003. Because the survey uses a small, permanent, well-trained and supervised staff (as compared to the large, temporary, briefly trained staff utilized for a census), data quality may be higher than in a census. Another advantage of a monthly survey over a decennial census is the ease of introducing new topics and testing the effects of changes in the wording of questions.

American Community survey results will be cumulated over a year to provide estimates of numbers and characteristics for the nation, states, and places or groups of 65,000 or more people. For smaller places and groups, or for more reliable and detailed data for larger places, data will be cumulated for periods of up to five years. The five-year cumulated sample is designed to be approximately equivalent to the census "long-form" sample and may eliminate the need for a "long form" in the 2010 census. Moving averages could provide annual updates and be used for time series. There are many issues to be worked through in developing and evaluating this type of survey and in determining how well information averaged over a long period compares to standard statistical measures based on time-specific censuses and surveys.

In many nations, questions on race and ethnicity are a sensitive and contentious topic. In the United States, the groups recognized have changed from each census to the next. For example, special tallies were made from the 1950 and 1960 censuses of persons with Spanish surnames, but only for five southwestern states. Beginning in 1970, and elaborated in later censuses, persons were asked if they were of Spanish/Hispanic origin. Many responses to this question have seemed to be inconsistent with responses to the separate question on race. The Bureau has conducted sample surveys to test various question wordings, and has sponsored field research and in-depth interviews to provide insights into how people interpret and respond to questions about ethnicity. For the 2000 census the basic concepts were retained, but the wording of each was adjusted, provision was made for individuals to report more than one race, and the question on Hispanic ethnicity was placed before the question on race.

In recent decades, extensive social science research has been conducted in many parts of the world on issues of racial and ethnic identity. These identities are almost always more flexible and more complex than can be captured with simple questions. A further complication is that many persons have ancestral or personal links to two or more racial and ethnic groups; how they respond depends on how they perceive the legitimacy and purposes of the census or survey.

In the 1990s, the U.S. Office of Management and Budget conducted an extensive review of its policy statement that specifies the standard race and ethnic classifications to be used by all government agencies, including the Census Bureau (Edmonston and Schulze 1995). Serious methodological problems have arisen as a result of inconsistencies among classifications of individuals on repeated interviews and in different records. A dramatic example occurs with infant mortality rates for race and ethnic groups, which are based on the ratio of counts based on birth registration to counts based on death registration of infants less than one year old. Comparing birth and death certificates for the same person, recorded less than one year apart, revealed large numbers for whom the race/ethnic classification reported at birth differed from that reported at death. The high-level government review also heard from many interest groups, such as Arab-Americans, multiracial persons, and the indigenous people of Hawaii,

who were anxious for the government to enumerate and classify their group appropriately.

In the United Kingdom, controversy about a proposed question on ethnic identity led to the question's omission from the 1981 census schedule, thus hindering analyses of an increasingly diverse population.

The most politically intense and litigious controversy about recent U.S. censuses is not that of content but of accuracy. States, localities, and many interest groups have a stake in the many billions of dollars of government funds that are distributed annually based in part on census numbers.

President George Washington commented about the first census that "our real numbers will exceed, greatly, the official returns of them; because the religious scruples of some would not allow them to give in their lists; the fears of others that it was intended as the foundation of a tax induced them to conceal or diminish theirs; and through the indolence of the people and the negligence of many of the Officers, numbers are omitted" (quoted in Scott 1968, p. 20).

A perfect census of a school, church, or other local organization is sometimes possible, if membership is clearly defined and the organization has up-to-date and accurate records, or if a quick and easily monitored enumeration is feasible. A national census, however, is a large-scale social process that utilizes many organizations and depends on cooperation from masses of individuals. Planning, execution, and tabulation of the 2000 U.S. Census of Population extended over more than ten years. Hundreds of thousands of people were employed at a cost of several billion dollars. A discrepancy between the results of a national census and "our real numbers" is inevitable.

Statisticians, recognizing that error is ubiquitous, have developed many models for identifying, measuring, and adjusting or compensating for error. Census statisticians and demographers around the world have participated in these developments and in trying to put professional insights to practical use.

Following the 1940 U.S. census, studies comparing birth certificates and selective service records to census results documented a sizable net undercount. To provide more information on census coverage and accuracy, a post-enumeration survey was conducted following the 1950 census using specially selected and closely supervised enumerators. One finding from the survey was that the undercount of infants in the census did not arise, as first thought, from a tendency for new parents to forget to mention a new baby to the census enumerator. The problem, rather, was that many young couples and single parents had irregular and difficult-to-find living arrangements, and entire households were missed by census enumerators. Based on this and related findings, much effort was given in subsequent censuses to precensus and postcensus review of lists of dwelling units.

Special surveys preceding, accompanying, and following censuses are increasingly used to provide evidence on magnitude of error, location of error in specific groups or places, and procedural means for reducing error. Techniques of "demographic analysis" have also been developed and continually refined to provide evidence of census error. The basic technique is to analyze the numbers of persons of each age, sex, and race in successive censuses. For example, the number of twenty-eight year-old white women in the 1990 census should be consistent with the number of eighteen-year-olds in 1980 and eight-year-olds in 1970. Information on births, deaths, immigration, and emigration is taken into account. Based on demographic analysis, the estimated net undercount for the total U.S. population was about 5.6 percent in 1940, 1.4 percent in 1980 (Fay, Passel, and Robinson 1988, Table 3.2) and 1.8 percent in 1990. Estimates of net undercount have also been made for specific age, sex, and race groupings.

If the net undercount were uniform for all population groups and geographic regions, it would not affect equity in the distribution of seats in Congress or public funds. But census errors are not uniform. The estimates for 1990 show net undercounts exceeding 10 percent of adult black males and small net overcounts for some age and race groups.

In 1980, the mayor of Detroit, the City of Detroit, New York City, and others sued the federal government, alleging violation of their constitutional rights to equal representation and fair distribution of federal funds (Mitroff, Mason, and

Barabba 1983). More litigation occurred with respect to the 1990 census. In neither case were the initially reported census counts adjusted to reflect estimated errors in enumeration, although in the case of the 1990 census the Census Bureau technical staff and director thought their methodology would improve the accuracy of the counts.

The Census Bureau developed innovative plans for the 2000 census to integrate an evaluation survey with the census, to use sampling to increase quality and reduce costs of enumerating nonresponsive households, and to produce official counts that already incorporate the best available procedures for minimizing error.

These Census Bureau plans engendered major political and budgetary battles between the Republican-controlled Congress and the Democratic administration. Many of the persons hardest to reach using traditional census methods are poor, often minorities. Many members of Congress assumed that a census with near-zero undercount would increase the population reported for states and localities that tend to vote more for Democrats, and hence reduce, relatively, the representation for states and localities that tend to vote more for Republicans. At the national level, this could alter the reapportionment among states of seats in the House of Representatives. Legislatures in states, counties, and cities are also subject to decennial redistricting according to the "one-person, one-vote" rule, and similar shifts in relative political power could occur.

The controversy between legislative and administrative branches over methods for the 2000 census was taken to the Supreme Court, with plaintiffs seeking a ruling that the Bureau's plans to use sample-based estimates would be unconstitutional. The Supreme Court avoided the constitutional argument, but ruled that current law did not permit such use of sampling. The Democrats lacked the power to rewrite that part of the basic census law. The two parties compromised by appropriating additional dollars to cover the extra costs of complete enumeration while retaining funds for many of the methodological innovations that permit preparation of improved estimates. Reapportionment among states of seats in Congress could therefore use the results of traditional complete enumeration. Most scholars, analysts, and other users of census data are likely to consider the adjusted estimates more accurate and hence more useful.

The percentage net undercount understates the total coverage error in the census. If one person is omitted and another person counted twice, the total count is correct but there are two "gross" errors that may affect the counts for specific places and characteristics. Identification of gross errors is receiving increased attention, to improve information on the nature of census error and potential error-reducing methods, and to facilitate development of techniques of data analysis that compensate for known and unknown errors.

One of the difficulties in debates about undercount and other census error arises from confusion between the idea of a knowable true count and the reality that there is no feasible method for determining with perfect accuracy the size and characteristics of any large population. A national census is a set of procedures adopted in a political, economic, and social context to produce population estimates. It is politically convenient if all parties accept these results as the common basis for further action, much as sports contests use decisions by umpires or referees. The more that policy and budgets depend on census results and the more aware that politicians and citizens become of the importance of the census, the more contentious census taking will be.

Every nation confronts political and social problems with its censuses. Regularly scheduled censuses are often postponed or abandoned because of international conflict. The United States and the United Kingdom canceled plans for mid-decade censuses because of national budget constraints. West Germany was unable to take a census for several years because of citizen fears about invasions of privacy. Ethnic conflict has interfered with census taking in India, Lebanon, and other nations.

The processes by which census procedures are determined, the ways in which census figures are used, and the conflicts that occur about these procedures and numbers are not merely "technical" but are embedded in a broader social process. The character of a nation's census and the conflicts that surround it are core topics for the "sociology of official statistics" (Starr 1987).

(SEE ALSO: *Demography*; *Population*)

REFERENCES

Anderson, Margo J. 1988 *The American Census: A Social History*. New Haven: Yale University Press.

—— and Stephen E. Fienberg 1999 *Who Counts? The Politics of Census-Taking in Contemporary America*. New York: Russell Sage Foundation.

Edmonston, Barry, and Charles Schultze 1995 *Modernizing the U.S. Census*. Washington, D.C.: National Academy Press.

Mitroff, Ian I., Richard O. Mason, and Vincent P. Barabba 1983 *The 1980 Census: Policymaking and Turbulence*. Lexington, Mass.: Lexington Books.

Scott, Ann H. 1968 *Census, USA: Fact Finding for the American People, 1790–1970*. New York: Seabury Press.

Starr, Paul 1987 "The Sociology of Official Statistics." In W. Alonso and P. Starr, eds., *The Politics of Numbers*. New York: Russell Sage Foundation.

Steffey, Duane, and Norman Bradburn (eds.) 1994 *Counting People in the Information Age*. Washington, D.C.: National Academy Press.

United Nations 1998 *Principles and Recommendations for Population and Housing Censuses*. ST/ESA/STAT/SER.M/67/Rev.1. New York: United Nations.

United States Census Bureau. *Census Bureau Home Page*. On the Internet at http.//www.census.gov. See links to *Census 2000* and *American Community Survey*.

KARL TAEUBER

CHANGE MEASUREMENT

See Experiments; Longitudinal Research; Quasi-Experimental Research Design; Measurement.

CHILD ABUSE

See Childhood Sexual Abuse; Family Violence; Incest; Sexual Violence.

CHILDBEARING

See Family Planning; Family Size; Fertility Determinants; Pregnancy and Pregnancy Termination.

CHILDHOOD SEXUAL ABUSE

Although child abuse is probably as old as childhood itself, serious research into child abuse arguably began in 1962 with the publication of Kempe and colleagues' seminal paper, "The Battered Child Syndrome" (Kempe, Silverman, Steele, Droegemuller, and Silver 1962). Not long afterwards, health care professionals began to direct their attention to the specific problem of childhood sexual abuse (Cosentino and Collins 1996). In the past few decades, numerous instances have been documented in detailed case histories, and important research into the causes and consequences of childhood sexual abuse has been initiated.

Numerous extensive reviews have been published that summarize what is presently known about childhood sexual abuse, focusing on the following domains.

- Short-term effects (Beitchman et al. 1991; Beitchman et al. 1992; Briere and Elliott 1994; Browne and Finkelhor 1986; Finkelhor 1990; Gomes-Schwartz et al. 1990; Green 1993; Kelley 1995; Kendall-Tackett et al. 1993; Trickett and McBride-Chang, 1995).

- Long-term consequences (Beitchman et al. 1991; Briere 1988; Briere and Elliott 1994; Briere and Runtz 1991; Cahill et al.1991a; Collings 1995; Ferguson 1997; Finkelhor 1987; Gibbons 1996; Glod 1993; Green 1993; Murray 1993; Polusny and Follette 1995; Trickett and McBride-Chang 1995; Wolfe and Birt, 1995).

- Prevention of abuse (Adler and McCain 1994; Berrick and Barth 1992; MacMillan et al. 1994; Olsen and Widom 1993; Wolfe et al. 1995).

- Treatment of both survivors and abusers (Cahill et al. 1991b; Cosentino and Collins 1996; Faller 1993; Finkelhor and Berliner 1995; O'Donohue and Elliot 1993).

Consequently, this chapter is not intended to provide a detailed analysis and review of the literature on childhood sexual abuse. Rather, it is meant to serve as a brief overview of, and introduction to, this area of inquiry.

DEFINITION OF THE PROBLEM

Before delving into the field of childhood sexual abuse, one must first understand what is meant by the term. Indeed, the lack of a standard definition has been a major criticism of the field and controversies abound (Finkelhor 1994a; Gibbons 1996; Gough 1996a; Green 1993). In general, the legal and practical research definitions of child sexual abuse require the following two elements: (1) sexual activities involving a child (sometimes construed as including adolescence), and (2) the existence of an "abuse condition" indicating lack of consensuality (Faller 1993; Finkelhor 1994a). "Sexual activities" refer to behaviors intended for sexual stimulation; such activities need not involve physical contact, however, leading to separate definitions for "contact sexual abuse" and "noncontact sexual abuse." Contact sexual abuse includes both penetrative (e.g., insertion of penis or other object into the vagina or anus) and nonpenetrative (e.g., unwanted touching of genitals) acts. Noncontact sexual abuse refers to activities such as exhibitionism, voyeurism, and child pornography (see Faller 1993 and Finkelhor 1994a for reviews on definitions of childhood sexual abuse).

An abuse condition is said to exist when there is reason to believe that the child either did not, or was incapable of, consenting to sexual activity. Three main conditions can be distinguished: (1) the perpetrator has a large age or maturational advantage over the child; or (2) the perpetrator is in a position of authority or in a caretaking relationship with the child; or (3) activities are carried out against the child's will using force or trickery. As evident from this brief summary, "Childhood Sexual Abuse" covers a wide range of acts and situations, and therefore is open to considerable subjective interpretation.

INCIDENCE AND PREVALENCE OF CHILDHOOD SEXUAL ABUSE

Increasing attention has been directed toward childhood sexual abuse not only because of the psychosocial sequelae associated with its occurrence, but also because it now appears to be more widespread than previously thought (Adler and McCain 1994). However, accurate estimates of the occurrence of childhood sexual abuse are difficult to obtain because many cases are never reported. Thus, available statistics represent only those cases reported to child protection agencies or to law enforcement, and therefore underestimate the true magnitude of the problem.

There are two official sources of incidence data for cases in the United States: The National Incidence Study of Child Abuse and Neglect (NIS), a federally funded research project; and statistics from state child protection agencies (Finkelhor 1994a). The NIS conducted in 1993 documented over 300,000 cases of sexual abuse among children known to professionals in the course of a year, or a rate of approximately forty-five cases per 10,000 children (Sedlak and Broadhurst 1996). Child protective services data suggest that approximately 140,000 cases of childhood sexual abuse occur annually, or twenty-one cases per 10,000 children (Leventhal 1998). An editorial by Finkelhor (1998) suggested that the incidence may be declining. However, this remains to be substantiated. In general, reports suggest that the rate of childhood sexual abuse has increased substantially over the past decades (Sedlak and Broadhurst 1996).

Retrospective surveys provide a second source of information on the occurrence of childhood sexual abuse. Reported rates depend upon how it is defined and operationalized in any given survey. When childhood sexual abuse has been assessed with a single item that narrowly defines it as rape or sexual intercourse, reported prevalence rates tend to be low (e.g., less than 12 percent). Conversely, when it is defined more broadly (e.g., touching genitalia) and assessed using multiple items, prevalence rates tend to be much higher, but with a wide range. The discrepancies observed in the estimated prevalence of childhood sexual abuse points to the need for increased standardization and the use of better assessment instruments in this research.

Because rates of childhood sexual abuse are substantially greater among females than males (e.g., Cosentino and Collins 1996; Finkelhor et al. 1990; Sedlak and Broadhurst 1996), the majority of this research has focused on women. Surveys suggest that anywhere from 18 percent to 30 percent of college women and 8 percent to 33 percent of male and female high school students report having experienced this abuse at some point in their lives (Ferguson 1997; Finkelhor 1994a; Gibbons 1996; Green 1993; Gorey and Leslie 1997). Among the general adult female population, prevalence rates range from 2 percent to 62 percent (Finkelhor 1987; Finkelhor et al. 1990; Saunders et al. 1992). Rates are even higher within various clinical populations, with 35 percent to 75 percent of female clients reporting a history of some form of sexual abuse during childhood (Gibbons 1996; Wurr and Partridge 1996).

The number of males who have been sexually abused is difficult to estimate because it has been the subject of fewer high-quality studies (Holmes and Slap 1998; Watkins and Bentovim 1992). Nonetheless, a few studies have examined this issue among men and estimate that approximately 3 percent to 16 percent of all men in the United States were sexually abused during childhood (Finkelhor et al. 1990; Gibbons 1996; Holmes and Slap 1998). As is the case for women, rates are higher when studying clinical populations, with estimates ranging from 13 percent to 23 percent (Holmes and Slap 1998; Metcalfe et al. 1990).

In sum, based on the evidence available in the literature, Finkelhor (1994a) estimates that 20 percent of adult women and 5 percent to 10 percent of adult men are survivors of childhood sexual abuse. Similarly, a synthesis of sixteen cross-sectional surveys on the prevalence of it among nonclinical populations reported unadjusted estimates of 22.3 percent for women and 8.5 percent for men (Gorey and Leslie 1997).

SEQUELAE

Research conducted over the past decade indicates that a wide range of psychological and interpersonal problems are more prevalent among those people who have been sexually abused than among those who have not been sexually abused. Although a definitive casual relationship between such problems and sexual abuse cannot be established using retrospective or cross-sectional research methodologies (Briere 1992a; Plunkett and Oates 1990), the aggregate of consistent findings in this literature has led many investigators and health care providers to conclude that childhood sexual abuse is a major risk factor for a variety of problems, both in the short-term and in later adulthood (Briere and Elliott 1994; Faller 1993). The various problems and symptoms described in the literature can be categorized as follows: (1) posttraumatic stress; (2) cognitive distortions; (3) emotional distress; (4) impaired sense of self; (5) avoidance phenomena; (6) personality disorders; and (7) interpersonal difficulties. In the remainder of this section, each of these categories is defined and illustrated using examples from the research literature.

Posttraumatic stress refers to certain enduring psychological symptoms that occur in reaction to a highly distressing, psychiatric disruptive event. To be diagnosed with posttraumatic stress disorder (PTSD) an individual must experience not only a traumatic event, but also the following problems: (1) frequent re-experiencing of the event through nightmares or intrusive thoughts; (2) a numbing of general responsiveness to, or avoidance of, current events; and (3) persistent symptoms of increased arousal, such as jumpiness, sleep disturbances, or poor concentration (American Psychiatric Association (APA) 1994). In general, researchers have found that children and adults who have been sexually abused are significantly more likely to receive a PTSD diagnosis than their nonabused peers (McLeer et al. 1992; Murray 1993; Rowan and Foy 1993; Saunders et al. 1992; Wolfe and Birt 1995).

Cognitive distortions are negative perceptions and beliefs held with respect to oneself, others, the environment, and the future. In the abused individual, this type of thought process is reflected in his or her tendency to overestimate the amount of danger or adversity in the world and to underestimate his or her worth (Briere and Elliott 1994; Dutton et al. 1994; Janoff-Bulman 1992). Numerous studies document such feelings and perceptions such as helplessness and hopelessness, impaired trust, self-blame, and low self-esteem among children who have been sexually abused (Oates et al. 1985). Moreover, these cognitive distortions often continue on into adolescence and adulthood (Gold 1986; Shapiro and Dominiak 1990).

Emotional distress or pain, which typically manifests itself as depression, anxiety, anger, or all of these, is reported by many survivors of childhood sexual abuse. Depression is the most commonly reported symptom among adults with a

history of childhood sexual abuse (Beitchman et al. 1992; Browne and Finkelhor 1986; Cahill et al. 1991a; Polusny and Follette 1995). Greater depressive symptomatology is also found among children who have been abused (Lipovsky et al.1989; Yama et al.1993).

Similarly, elevated anxiety levels have been documented in child victims of sexual abuse and adults who have a history of it (Gomes-Schwartz et al. 1990; Mancini et al. 1995; Yama et al. 1993). Adults with a history of childhood sexual abuse are more likely than their nonabused counterparts to meet the criteria for generalized anxiety disorder, phobias, panic disorder, obsessive compulsive disorder, or all of these (Mancini et al. 1995; Mulder et al. 1998; Saunders et al. 1992).

Another common emotional sequel of childhood sexual abuse is anger; specifically, chronic irritability, unexpected or uncontrollable feelings of anger, difficulties associated with expressing anger, or all of these (Briere and Elliott 1994; Van der Kolk et al. 1994). During childhood and adolescence, anger is most likely to be reflected in behavioral problems such as fighting, bullying, or attacking other children (Chaffin et al. 1997; Garnefski and Diekstra 1997).

Sexual abuse also can damage a child's developing sense of self, with adverse long-term consequences. The development of a sense of self is thought to be one of the earliest developmental tasks of the infant and young child, typically unfolding in the context of early relationships (Alexander 1992). Thus, how a child is treated early in life critically influences his or her growing self-awareness. Childhood sexual abuse can interfere with this process, preventing the child from establishing a strong self image (Cole and Putnam 1992). Without a healthy sense of self, the person is unable to soothe or comfort himself or herself adequately, which may lead to overreactions to stressful or painful situations, and to an increased likelihood of re-victimization (Messman and Long 1996). Indeed, numerous studies have found high rates of sexual re-victimization (e.g., rape, coercive sexual experience) among individuals reporting a history of childhood sexual abuse (Fergusson et al. 1997; Urquiza and Goodlin-Jones 1994; Wyatt et al. 1992)

Avoidance is another major response to having been sexually abused. Avoiding activities among victims may be viewed as attempts to cope with the chronic trauma and dysphoria induced by the abuse. Among the dysfunctional activities associated with efforts to avoid recalling or reliving specific memories are: dissociative phenomena, such as losing time, repression of unpleasant memories, detachment, or body numbing (APA 1994; Cloitre et al. 1997; Mulder et al. 1998; Nash et al. 1993); substance abuse and addiction (Arellano 1996; Briere 1988; Wilsnack et al. 1997); suicide or suicidal ideation (Briere and Runtz 1991; Saunders et al. 1992; Van der Kolk et al. 1991); inappropriate, indiscriminate, and/or compulsive sexual behavior (McClellan et al. 1996; Widom and Kuhns, 1996), (for reviews see Friedrich 1993; Kendall-Tackett et al. 1993; Tharinger 1990); eating disorders (Conners and Morse 1993; Douzinas et al. 1994; Schwartz and Cohn 1996; Wonderlich et al. 1997); and self-mutilation (Briere 1988; Briere and Elliott 1994). Each of these behaviors serve to prevent the individual from experiencing the considerable pain of abuse-specific awareness and thus reduces the distress associated with remembrance. However, avoidance and self-destructive methods of coping with the abuse may ultimately lead to higher levels of symptomatology, lower self-esteem, and greater feelings of guilt and anger (Leitenberg et al. 1992).

Numerous investigations have found a greater rate of borderline personality and dissociative identity (formerly multiple personality disorder) disorders among adult female survivors of chilhood sexual abuse (Green 1993; Polusny and Follette 1995; Silk et al. 1997). Borderline personality disorder includes symptoms of impulsiveness associated with intense anger or suicidal, self-mutilating behavior, and affective instability with depression which are typical sequelae in sexually abused children and in adult survivors of sexual abuse (APA 1994). Childhood trauma, especially continued sexual abuse, is an important etiological factor in many cases of dissociative identity disorder, the most extreme type of dissociative reaction (APA 1994).

Finally, interpersonal difficulties and deficient social functioning often are observed among individuals who have been sexually abused (Briere 1992b; Cloitre et al. 1997). Such difficulties stem from the immediate cognitive and conditioned responses to victimization that extend into the longer term (e.g., distrust of others), as well as the accommodation responses to ongoing abuse (e.g., passivity). Often, victims of childhood sexual abuse know the perpetrator, who might be a family member, clergy, or friend of the family. The abuse is thus a violation and betrayal of both personal and interpersonal (relationship) boundaries. Hence, it is not surprising that many children and adults with a history of childhood sexual abuse are found to be less socially competent, more aggressive, and more socially withdrawn than their nonabused peers (Cloitre et al. 1997; Mannarino et al. 1991; Mullen et al. 1994).

Among adults, interpersonal difficulties are manifested in difficulties in establishing and maintaining relationships (Finkelhor et al. 1989; Liem et al. 1996) and in achieving sexual intimacy (Browne and Finkelhor 1986; Mullen et al. 1994). Children who have been sexually abused are more likely to exhibit increased or precocious sexual behavior, such as kissing and inappropriate genital touching (Cosentino et al. 1995).

The consequences of childhood sexual abuse can be quite severe and harmful. However, it is important to note that an estimated 10 to 28 percent of persons with a history of it report no psychological distress (Briere and Elliott 1994; Kendall-Tackett et al. 1993). This raises the question of why some persons exhibit difficulties while others do not. Research addressing this question has found the following to be important mediators of individual reactions to childhood sexual abuse:

- *Age at onset of abuse.* Although further elucidation is needed, the available evidence suggests that postpubertal abuse is associated with greater trauma and more severe adverse sequelae than is prepubertal abuse (Beitchman et al. 1992; Browne and Finkelhor 1986; McClellan et al. 1996; Nash et al. 1993);

- *Gender of the victim.* One of the main findings in this area is that male victims appear to show greater disturbances of adult sexual functioning (Beitchman et al. 1992; Dube and Herbert 1988; Garnefski and Diekstra 1997);

- *Relationship to perpetrator.* Abuse involving a father or father figure (e.g., stepfather), which accounts for an estimated 25 percent of all cases (Sedlak and Broadhurst

1996), is associated with greater long-term harm (Browne and Finkelhor 1986; Gold 1986);

• *Duration and frequency of abuse.* In general, the greater the frequency and duration of abuse, the greater the impact on later psychological and social functioning (Nash et al. 1993);

• *Use of force.* The use of force or threat of force is associated with more negative outcomes (Kendall-Tackett et al. 1993);

• *Penetration or invasiveness.* Penetrative abuse is generally associated with greater long-term harm than are most other forms of abuse (Kendall-Tackett et al. 1993); and

• *Family characteristics and response to abuse disclosure.* Individuals who have been abused are more likely to originate from single-parent families, families with a high level of marital conflict, and families with pathology (e.g., parent is an alcoholic, violence between parents, maternal disbelief, and lack of support); all of which are associated with a poorer outcome and greater levels of distress (Beitchman et al. 1992; Draucker 1996; Green 1996; Romans et al. 1995).

CROSS-CULTURAL ISSUES

This review has focused exclusively on studies done in the United States. This is important to keep in mind because the nature of abuse varies according to one's cultural belief system (Gough 1996). As a result, attempts to compare societies on the basis of their care of children or the extent of violence in family relations are fraught with problems (Gough 1996b; Levinson 1989). In addition, methodological factors, such as the questions asked and how childhood sexual abuse is defined and measured, hamper the ability to make direct comparisons among the rates across different countries. All that can be surmised, to date, is that it is not a phenomena just of the United States, but is an international problem (Finkelhor 1994b). Finkelhor's synthesis indicates that most countries have rates similar to those found in the United States and that females are abused at a greater rater than males.

Nonetheless, cross-cultural studies can shed new light on the origins and impact of sexual abuse (Leventhal 1998; Runyan 1998). Such investigations may enable us to understand better the relative importance of different factors that influence the occurrence of abuse and teach us about societies that have been successful at protecting children. Intercultural comparative investigations can also help us appreciate the range of sexual behaviors that are, or can be considered "normal," and thereby contribute to a better understanding of abnormality in childhood sexual behavior and adult behaviors toward children.

It is not surprising that definitions of abuse not only vary within a culture, but also between cultures. The meaning of "abuse," especially, depends upon ideas of individual rights and roles and responsibilities between people and groups within society (Gough 1996a). How a child is viewed will influence what is evaluated as abuse. Definitions of child abuse would be quite different, for example, in a feudal state in which children are considered to be their parents' possessions. Cultural expectations about sexual interactions among adolescents and between different age groups will also affect whether particular practices are defined as abuse (Abramson and Pinkerton 1995). Among the Sambia people of the highlands of Papua, New Guinea, for example, all young boys are expected to participate in ritualized fellatio with older boys as part of their initiation into manhood (Abramson and Pinkerton 1995). In essence, the younger boys are forced to submit; thus, this practice fulfills the two main criteria for childhood sexual abuse as defined above (coercive sex with a child or adolescent). Nevertheless, the Sambia consider ritualized fellatio to be critical for survival (they believe that semen is the source of manly strength and that it must be obtained through ingestion).

Definitions of abuse can also be expected to change over time to reflect societal changes. For instance, anecdotal evidence suggests that in Victorian England it was considered acceptable for a nurse or nanny to quiet a male infant by putting his penis in her mouth (Abramson and Pinkerton 1995). Today, this practice would clearly be considered childhood sexual abuse. The recent broadening of definitions of abuse has been accompanied by a greater sensitivity to signs of abuse that fit these changing definitions, and a greater willingness for professionals and others to intervene into the private family lives of others, or beyond the walls of institutional life, and so to offer greater visibility of children's experiences (Gough 1996a).

DIRECTIONS FOR FUTURE RESEARCH

Perusal of the literature in this domain suggests several avenues for future studies. First and foremost, large-scale, longitudinal investigations of child victims are needed that examine global functioning, abuse-specific functioning, and attributional and coping strategies along with abuse, child, family, and community factors. Such studies could provide information about both the initial effects of sexual abuse and the factors that influence adjustment at later developmental stages and into adulthood. Because not all victims of childhood sexual abuse develop adjustment problems, a better understanding of who is likely to experience such problems is needed.

Second, further research is needed regarding the efficacy of various approaches for the treatment of related problems (see Cosentino and Collins 1996; O'Donohue and Elliot 1993 for reviews). The utility or effectiveness of any particular treatment modality has yet to be demonstrated using a large-scale, randomized study in which treatment outcomes are measured using standardized instruments and untreated control groups. Consequently, treatment decisions often are made by clinicians without empirically tested guidelines.

Third, greater attention needs to be paid to methodological rigor in the conduct of childhood sexual abuse studies (Green 1993; Plunkett and Oates 1990; Trickett and McBride-Change 1995). In particular, investigators need to: (1) define it clearly and consistently; (2) use instruments with documented psychometric properties; (3) use control or comparison groups, when appropriate; and (4) employ large sample sizes whenever this is feasible. Studies of treatment modalities should also conduct multiple follow-up assessments to determine whether intervention effects are sustained over time. Finally, studies are needed that clearly disentangle the effects of sexual abuse from other forms of abuse or maltreatment.

SUMMARY

Childhood sexual abuse is a significant and widespread problem in our society, no matter how it is defined. Since it was first brought to the public's attention in the 1960s, a vast amount of research has been conducted in an effort to understand its impact on victims. From the various reviews on the topic, several conclusions can be drawn. First, despite the considerable heterogeneity among sexual abuse victims, as a group, sexually abused children and adolescents tend to display significantly higher levels of symptomatology than their nonabused, nonclinic-referred peers. Second, compared to other clinic-referred children, two problem areas appear to differentiate sexually abused children and adolescents: post-traumatic stress disorder symptomatology and sexuality problems. Third, the type and severity of sequelae experienced by victims depends on the specific characteristics of the abuse situation and the perpetrator. Fourth, research on adult survivors suggest that abuse-related problems tend to persist into adulthood. Indeed, childhood sexual abuse histories are common among several clinical populations, including patients initially diagnosed as depressed or as having a borderline personality disorder.

Taken together, these findings suggest that clinicians and health care providers should screen for sexual abuse among children, adolescents, and adults. For instance, questions about childhood sexual abuse could become part of routine intake procedures. Moreover, it is important that a wide range of service providers are sensitive to, and have staff trained to deal with, issues of childhood sexual abuse when it emerges. Service providers' policy and practice guidelines should explicitly acknowledge the prevalence and impact of it on women, men, and children.

Schools also need to have greater involvement in the prevention and diagnosis of childhood sexual abuse, especially since it generally occurs between the ages of six and twelve (Finkelhor 1994a; Sedlak and Broadhurst 1996). School-based education programs may be a useful vehicle for intervention and prevention. Teachers need to be educated and trained about their role in recognizing and reporting suspected cases.

Finally, further community awareness is needed to help prevent it from occurring. Greater community efforts toward providing treatment services for persons with a history of childhood sexual abuse are needed as are programs targeting potential perpetrators. Society must work together to stamp out this abhorrence and to assist its survivors.

Preparation of this article was supported in part by a training grant from the Maternal and Child Health Bureau, U.S. Department of Health and Human Services (MCJ 9040). The author thanks Steven D. Pinkerton, Ph.D. for his helpful comments on this manuscript.

REFERENCES

Abramson, P.R., and S.D. Pinkerton 1995 *With pleasure: Thoughts on the Nature of Human Sexuality.* New York: Oxford University Press.

Adler, N.A., and J.L. McCain 1994 "Prevention of Child Abuse. Issues for the Mental Health Practitioner." *Child and Adolescent Psychiatric Clinics of North America* 3(4):679–693.

Alexander, P.C. 1992 "Application of Attachment Theory to the Study of Sexual Abuse." *Journal of Consulting and Clinical Psychology* 60:185–195.

American Psychiatric Association 1994 *Diagnostic and Statistical Manual of Mental Disorders,* 4th ed. Washington, D.C.: Author.

Arellano, C.M. 1996 "Child Maltreatment and Substance use: A Review of the Literature." *Substance Use and Misuse* 31(7):927–935.

Beitchman, J.H., K.J. Zucker, J.E. Hood, G.A. DaCosta, and D. Akman 1991 "A Review of the Short-term Effects of Childhood Sexual Abuse." *Child Abuse and Neglect* 15:537–556.

——, and E. Cassavia 1992 "A review of the long-term effects of child sexual abuse." *Child Abuse and Neglect* 16:101–118.

Berrick, J.D., and R.P. Barth 1992 "Child Sexual Abuse Prevention: Research Review and Recommendations." *Social Work Research and Abstracts* 28(4):6–15.

Briere, J. 1988 "The Long-term Clinical Correlates of Childhood Sexual Victimization." *Annals of the New York Academy of Sciences* 528:327–334.

—— 1992a "Methodological Issues in the Study of Sexual Abuse Effects." *Journal of Consulting and Clinical Psychology* 60:196–203.

—— 1992b *Child Abuse Trauma: Theory and Treatment of the Lasting Effects.* Newbury Park, Calif.: Sage Publications.

——, and D.M. Elliott 1994 "Immediate and Long-term Impacts of Child Sexual Abuse." *Sexual Abuse of Children* 4(2):54–69.

——, and M. Runtz 1991 "The Long-term Effects of Sexual Abuse: A Review and Synthesis." *New Directions for Mental Health Services* 51:3–13.

Browne, A., and D. Finkelhor 1986 "Impact of Child Sexual Abuse: A Review of the Research." *Psychological Bulletin* 99(1):66–77.

Cahill, C., S.P. Llewelyn, and C. Pearson 1991a "Long-term effects of Sexual Abuse Which Occurred in Childhood: A Review." *British Journal of Clinical Psychology* 30(2):117–130.

—— 1991b "Treatment of sexual abuse which occurred in childhood: A review." *British Journal of Clinical Psychology* 30(1):1–12.

Chaffin, M., J.N. Wherry, and R. Dykman 1997 "School Age Children's Coping with Sexual Abuse: Abuse Stresses and Symptoms Associated with Four Coping Strategies." *Child Abuse and Neglect* 21(2):227–240.

Cloitre, M., P. Scarvalone, and J.A. Difede 1997 "Posttraumatic Stress Disorder, Self- and Interpersonal Dysfunction Among Sexually Retraumatized Women." *Journal of Traumatic Stress* 10(3):437–452.

Cole, P.M., and F.W. Putnam 1992 "Effect of Incest of Self and Social Functioning: A Developmental Psychopathology Perspective." *Journal of Consulting and Clinical Psychology* 60:174–184.

Collings, S.J. 1995 "The Long-term Effects of Contact and Noncontact Forms of Child Sexual Abuse in a Sample of University Men." *Child Abuse and Neglect* 19(1):1–6.

Connors, M.E., and W. Morse 1993 "Sexual Abuse and Eating Disorders: A review." *International Journal of Eating Disorders* 13(1):1–11.

Cosentino, C.E., and M. Collins 1996 "Sexual Abuse of Children: Prevalence, Effects, and Treatment." *Annals of the New York Academy of Sciences* 789:45–65.

Cosentino, C.E., H.F. Meyer-Bahlburg, J.L. Alpert, S.L. Weinberg, and R. Gaines 1995 "Sexual Behavior Problems and Psychopathology Symptoms in Sexually Abused Girls." *Journal of the American Academy of Child and Adolescent Psychiatry* 34(8):1033–1042.

Douzinas, N., V. Fornari, B. Goodman, T. and Sitnick 1994 "Eating Disorders and Abuse." *Child and Adolescent Psychiatric Clinics of North America* 3(4):777–796.

Draucker, C.B. 1996 "Family-of-Origin Variables and Adult Female Survivors of Childhood Sexual Abuse: A review of the Research." *Journal of Child Sexual Abuse* 5(4):35–63.

Dube, R., and M. Hebert 1988 "Sexual Abuse of Children Under 12 Years of Age: A Review of 511 Cases." *Child Abuse and Neglect* 12(3):321–330.

Dutton, M.A., K.J. Burghardt, S.G. Perrin, K.R. Chrestman, and P.M. Halle 1994 "Battered Women's Cognitive Schemata." *Journal of Traumatic Stress* 7(2):237–255.

Faller, K.C. 1993 *Child Sexual Abuse: Intervention and Treatment Issues*. Washington, D.C.: U.S. Dept. of Health and Human Services, Administration for Children and Families, Administration on Children, Youth, and Families, National Center on Child Abuse and Neglect.

Ferguson, A.G. 1997 "How Good is the Evidence Relating to the Frequency of Childhood Sexual Abuse and the Impact Such Abuse has on the Lives of Adult Survivors?" *Public Health* 111(6):387–391.

Fergusson, D.M., L.J. Horwood, and M.T. Lynskey 1997 "Childhood Sexual Abuse, Adolescent Sexual Behaviors and Sexual Revictimization." *Child Abuse and Neglect* 21(8):789–803.

Finkelhor, D. 1987 "The Sexual Abuse of Children: Current Research Reviewed." *Psychiatric Annals* 17:233–241.

—— 1990 "Early and Long-term Effects of Child Sexual Abuse: An Update." *Professional Psychology* 21(5):325–330.

—— 1994a "Current Information on the Scope and Nature of Child Sexual Abuse." *Future of Children* 4(2):31–53.

—— 1994b "The International Epidemiology of Child Sexual Abuse." *Child Abuse and Neglect* 18(5):409–417.

—— 1998 "Improving Research, Policy, and Practice to Understand Child Sexual Abuse." *Journal of the American Medical Association* 280(21):1864–1865.

——, and L. Berliner 1995 "Research on the Treatment of Sexually Abused Children: A Review and Recommendations." *Journal of the American Academy of Child and Adolescent Psychiatry* 34(11):1408–1423.

Finkelhor, D., G. Hotaling, I.A. Lewis, and C. Smith 1990 "Sexual Abuse in a National Survey of Adult Men and Women: Prevalence, Characteristics, and Risk Factors." *Child Abuse and Neglect* 14(1):19–28.

—— 1989 "Sexual Abuse and its Relationship to Later Sexual Satisfaction, Marital Status, Religion, and Attitudes." *Journal of Interpersonal Violence* 4:279–399.

Friedrich, W.N. 1993 "Sexual Victimization and Sexual Behavior in Children: A Review of Recent Literature." *Child Abuse and Neglect* 17(1):59–66.

Garnefski, N., R.F. and Diekstra 1997 "Child Sexual Abuse and Emotional and Behavioral Problems in Adolescence: Gender Differences." *Journal of the American Academy of Child and Adolescent Psychiatry* 36(3):323–329.

Gibbons, J. 1996 "Services for Adults who Have Experienced Child Sexual Assault: Improving Agency Response." *Social Science and Medicine* 43(12):1755–1763.

Glod, C.A. 1993 "Long-term Consequences of Childhood Physical and Sexual Abuse." *Archives of Psychiatric Nursing* 7(3):163–173.

Gold, E.R. 1986 "Long-term Effects of Sexual Victimization in Childhood: An Attributional Approach." *Journal of Consulting and Clinical Psychology* 54:471–471.

Gomes-Schwartz, B., J.M. Horowitz, and A.P. Cardarelli 1990 *Child Sexual Abuse: The Initial Effects*. Newbury Park, Calif.: Sage Publications.

Gorey, K.M., and D.R. Leslie 1997 "The Prevalence of Child Sexual Abuse: Integrative Review Adjustment for Potential Response and Measurement Biases." *Child Abuse and Neglect* 21(4):391–398.

Gough, D. 1996a "Defining the Problem: Comment." *Child Abuse and Neglect* 20(11):993–1002.

—— 1996b "Child Abuse in Japan." *Child Psychology and Psychiatry Review* 1:12–18.

Green, A.H. 1993 "Child Sexual Abuse: Immediate and long-term Effects and Intervention." *Journal of the American Academy of Child and Adolescent Psychiatry* 32(5):890–902.

—— 1996 "Overview of Child Sexual Abuse." In S. J. Kaplan, ed., *Family Violence: A Clinical and Legal Guide*. Washington, D.C.: American Psychiatric Press, Inc.

Holmes, W.C., and G.B. Slap 1998 "Sexual Abuse of Boys. Definition, Prevalence, Correlates, Sequelae, and Management." *Journal of the American Medical Association* 280(21):1855–1862.

Janoff-Bulman, R. 1992 *Shattered Assumptions: Towards a new Psychology of Trauma*. New York: Free Press.

Kelley, S.J. 1995 "Child Sexual Abuse: Initial Effects." *Annual Review of Nursing Research* 13:63–85.

Kempe, C.H., F.N. Silverman, B.F. Steele, W. Droegemuller, and A.K. Silver 1962 "The Battered Child Syndrome." *Journal of the American Medical Association* 187:17–24.

Kendall-Tackett, K.A., L.M. Williams, and D. Finkelhor 1993 "Impact of Sexual Abuse on Children: A Review and Synthesis of Recent Empirical Studies." *Psychological Bulletin* 113:164–180.

Leitenberg, H., E. Greenwald, and S. Cado 1992 "A Retrospective Study of Long-term Methods of Coping with Having Been Sexually Abused During Childhood." *Child Abuse and Neglect* 16(3):399–407.

Leventhal, J.M. 1998 "Epidemiology of Sexual Abuse of Children: Old Problems, New Directions." *Child Abuse and Neglect* 22(6):481–491.

Levinson, D. 1989 *Family Violence in Cross Cultural Perspective.* Newbury Park, Calif.: Sage.

Liem, J.H., J.G. O'Toole, and J.B. James 1996 "Themes of Power and Betrayal in Sexual Abuse Survivors' Characterizations of Interpersonal Relationships." *Journal of Traumatic Stress* 9(4):745–761.

Lipovsky, J.A., B.E. Saunders, and S.M. Murphy 1989 "Depression, Anxiety, and Behavior Problems Among Victims of Father-child Sexual Assault and Nonabused Siblings." *Journal of Interpersonal Violence* 4:452–468.

MacMillan, H.L., J.H. MacMillan, D.R. Offord, L. Griffith, and A. MacMillan 1994 "Primary Prevention of Child Sexual Abuse: A Critical Review: II." *Journal of Child Psychology and Psychiatry and Allied Disciplines* 35(5):857–876.

Mancini, C., M. Van Ameringen, and H. MacMillan 1995 "Relationship of Childhood Sexual and Physical Abuse to Anxiety Disorders." *Journal of Nervous and Mental Disease* 183(5):309–314.

Mannarino, A.P., J.A. Cohen, J.A. Smith, and S. Moore-Motily 1991 "Six- and Twelve-month Follow-up of Sexually Abused Girls." *Journal of Interpersonal Violence* 6:494–511.

McClellan, J., C. McCurry, M. Ronnei, J. Adams, A. Eisner, and M. Storck 1996 "Age of Onset of Sexual Abuse: Relationship to Sexually Inappropriate Behaviors." *Journal of the American Academy of Child and Adolescent Psychiatry* 35(10):1375–1383.

McLeer, S.V., E. Deblinger, D. Henry, and H. Orvaschel 1992 "Sexually Abused Children at High Risk for Post-traumatic Stress Disorder." *Journal of the American Academy of Child and Adolescent Psychiatry* 31:875–879.

Messman, T.L., and P.J. Long 1996 "Child Sexual Abuse and its Relationship to Revictimization in Adult Women: A Review." *Clinical Psychology Review* 16(5):397–420.

Mulder, R.T., A.L. Beautrais, P.R. Joyce, and D.M. Fergusson 1998 "Relationship Between Dissociation, Childhood Sexual Abuse, Childhood Physical Abuse, and Mental Illness in a General Population Sample." *American Journal of Psychiatry* 155(6):806–811.

Mullen, P.E., J.L. Martin, J.C. Anderson, S.E. Romans, and G.P. Herbison 1994 "The Effect of Child Sexual Abuse on Social, Interpersonal and Sexual Function in Adult life." *British Journal of Psychiatry* 165(2):35–47.

Murray, J.B. 1993 "Relationship of Childhood Sexual Abuse to Borderline Personality Disorder, Posttraumatic Stress Disorder, and Multiple Personality Disorder." *Journal of Psychology* 127(6):657–676.

Nash, M.R., O.A. Zivney, and T. Hulsey 1993 "Characteristics of Sexual Abuse Associated with Greater Psychological Impairment Among Children." *Child Abuse and Neglect* 17(3):401–408.

Oates, R.K., D. Forest, and A. Peacock 1985 "Self-esteem of Abused Children." *Child Abuse and Neglect* 9:159–163.

O'Donohue, W., A. and Elliot 1993 "Treatment of the Sexually Abused Child: A review." *Journal of Clinical Child Psychology* 3:218–228.

Olsen, J.L., and C.S. Widom 1993 "Prevention of Child Abuse and Neglect." *Applied and Preventive Psychology* 2(4):217–229.

Plunkett, A., and R.K. Oates 1990 "Methodological Considerations in Research on Child Sexual Abuse." *Pediatric and Perinatal Epidemiology* 4(3):351–360.

Polusny, M.A., and V.M. Follette 1995 "Long-term Correlates of Child Sexual Abuse: Theory and Review of the Empirical Literature." *Applied and Preventive Psychology* 4:143–166.

Romans, S.E., J.L. Martin, J.C. Anderson, M.L. O'Shea, and P.E. Mullen 1995 "Factors that Mediate Between Child Sexual Abuse and Adult Psychological Outcome." *Psychological Medicine* 25(1):127–142.

Rowan, A.B., and D.W. Foy 1993 "Post-traumatic Stress Disorder in Child Sexual Abuse Survivors: A Literature Review." *Journal of Traumatic Stress* 6(1):3–20.

Runyan, D.K. 1998 "Prevalence, Risk, Sensitivity, and Specificity: A Commentary on the Epidemiology of Child Sexual Abuse and the Development of a Research Agenda." *Child Abuse and Neglect* 22(6):493–498.

Saunders, B.E., L.A. Villeponteaux, J.A. Lipovsky, D.G. Kilpatrick, and J.L. Veronen 1992 "Child Sexual Assault as a Risk Factor for Mental Disorders Among Women: A community Survey." *Journal of Interpersonal Violence* 7:189–204.

Schwartz, M.F., and L. Cohn 1996 *Sexual Abuse and Eating Disorders: A Clinical Overview.* New York: Brunner/Mazel.

Sedlak, A.J., and D.D. Broadhurst 1996 *Third national incidence study of child abuse and neglect.* Washington, D.C.: U.S. Dept. of Health and Human Services, Administration for Children and Families, Administration on Children, Youth, and Families, National Center on Child Abuse and Neglect.

Shapiro, S., and G. Dominiak 1990 "Common Psychological Defenses Seen in the Treatment of Sexually Abused Adolescents." *American Journal of Psychotherapy* 44(1):68–74.

Silk, K.R., J.T. Nigg, D. Esten, and N.E. Lohr 1997 "Severity of Childhood Sexual Abuse, Borderline Symptoms, and Familial Environment." In M.C.

Zanarini, ed., *Role of Sexual Abuse in the Etiology of Borderline Personality Disorder* Washington, D.C.: American Psychiatric Press, Inc.

Tharinger, D. 1990 "Impact of Child Sexual Abuse on Developing Sexuality." *Professional Psychology: Research and Practice* 21(5):331–337.

Trickett, P.K., and C. McBride-Chang 1995 "The Developmental Impact of Different Forms of Child Abuse and Neglect." *Developmental Review* 15(3):311–337.

Urquiza, A.J., and B.L. Goodlin-Jones 1994 "Child Sexual Abuse and Adult Revictimization with Women of Color." *Violence and Victims* 9(3):223–232.

Van der Kolk, B.A., J.C. Perry, and J.L. Herman 1991 "Childhood Origins of Self-destructive Behavior." *American Journal of Psychiatry* 148(12):1665–1671.

Van der Kolk, B.A., A. Hostetler, N. Herron, and R.E. Fisler 1994 "Trauma and the Development of Borderline Personality Disorder." *Psychiatric Clinics of North America* 17(4):715–730.

Watkins, B., and A. Bentovim 1992 "The Sexual Abuse of Male Children and Adolescents: A Review of Current Research." *Journal of Child Psychology and Psychiatry and Allied Disciplines* 33(1):197–248.

Widom, C.S., and J.B. Kuhns 1996 "Childhood Victimization and Subsequent Risk for Promiscuity, Prostitution, and Teenage Pregnancy: A Prospective Study." *American Journal of Public Health* 86(11):1607–1612.

Wilsnack, S.C., N.D. Vogeltanz, A.D. Klassen, and T.R. Harris 1997 "Childhood Sexual Abuse and Women's Substance Abuse: National survey findings." *Journal of Studies on Alcohol* 58(3):264–271.

Wolfe, D.A., N.D. Reppucci, and S. Hart 1995 "Child Abuse Prevention: Knowledge and Priorities." *Journal of Clinical Child Psychology* 24(Suppl):5–22.

Wolfe, V.V., and J.A. Birt 1995 "The Psychological Sequelae of Child Sexual Abuse." *Advances in Clinical Child Psychology* 17:233–263.

Wonderlich, S.A., T.D. Brewerton, Z. Jocic, B.S. Dansky, and D.W. Abbott 1997 "Relationship of Childhood Sexual Abuse and Eating Disorders." *Journal of the American Academy of Child and Adolescent Psychiatry* 36(8):1107–1115.

Wurr, C.J., and I.M. Partridge 1996 "The Prevalence of a History of Childhood Sexual Abuse in an Acute Adult Inpatient Population." *Child Abuse and Neglect* 20(9):867–872.

Wyatt, G.E., D. Guthrie, and C.M. Notgrass 1992 "Differential Effects of Women's Child Sexual Abuse and Subsequent Sexual Revictimization." *Journal of Consulting and Clinical Psychology* 60(2):167–173.

Yama, M.F., S.L. Tovey, and B.S. Fogas 1993 "Childhood Family Environment and Sexual Abuse as Predictors of Anxiety and Depression in Adult Women." *American Journal of Orthopsychiatry* 63(1):136–141.

HEATHER CECIL

CHILDREARING

See Parental Roles; Socialization.

CHINA STUDIES

The sociological study of China has a complex history. It could be argued that Confucian thought embodied a native tradition of sociological thinking about such things as the family, bureaucracy, and deviant behavior. However, modern Chinese sociology initially had foreign origins and inspiration. The appearance of the field in China might be dated from the translation of parts of Herbert Spencer's *The Study of Sociology* into Chinese in 1897. The earliest sociology courses and departments in China were established in private, missionary colleges, and Western sociologists such as D. H. Kulp, J. S. Burgess, and Sidney Gamble played central roles in initiating sociology courses and research programs within China (see Wong 1979).

The Chinese Sociological Association was established in 1930, and in the following two decades a process of Sinification progressed. Chinese sociologists, trained both at home and in the West, emerged. Sociology courses and departments began to proliferate in government-run, public colleges. Increasingly, texts using material from Chinese towns and villages displaced ones that focused on Chicago gangs and the assimilation of Polish immigrants into America. As this process of setting down domestic roots continued, Chinese sociology developed some distinctive contours. Inspiration for the field came as much from British social anthropology as from sociology. The crisis atmosphere of the 1930s and 1940s fostered a strong emphasis on applied, problem-solving research. As a result of these developments, Chinese sociology in those years came to include what in the United States might be considered social anthropology and social work. Within these broad contours, Chinese sociologists/anthropologists produced some of the finest early ethnographies of "nonprimitive" communities—Chinese peasant villages (see Fei 1939; Yang 1944; Lin 1948).

Although many of the earliest leaders in establishing Chinese sociology were foreigners, by the time of the Chinese communist victory in 1949, its leading practitioners were Chinese. There were only a small number of Western sociologists who concentrated their research on Chinese society (see Lang 1946; Levy 1949), and their methods, problems, and data were not distinctive from those being employed by their Chinese counterparts. Originally a foreign transplant, Chinese sociology had become a thriving enterprise with increasingly strong domestic roots.

When the Chinese Communist Party (CCP) swept to national power in 1949, some Chinese sociologists left the country but most remained. (The development of sociology in the Republic of China on Taiwan after 1949 will not be dealt with here.) Initially, those who remained were optimistic that their skills would be useful to the new government. Experience in community fieldwork and an orientation toward studying social problems seemed to make Chinese sociologists natural allies of those constructing a planned social order. These hopes were dashed in 1952 when the CCP abolished the field of sociology. That decision was motivated by the CCP's desire to follow the Soviet model. Joseph Stalin had earlier denounced sociology as a "bourgeois pseudo-science" and banned the field from Soviet academe. More to the point, there was no room in the People's Republic of China (PRC) for two rival sciences of society, Marxism-Leninism-Maoism and sociology. The CCP argued that it had developed its own methods of "social investigations" during the revolutionary process, with Mao Zedong playing a leading role in this development (see Mao [1927] 1971; Thompson 1990). This approach stressed grass roots investigations designed to further official revolutionary or economic goals of the CCP rather than any sort of attempted value-free search for objective truth. Chinese sociologists, trained in a different tradition and able to use professional claims to raise questions about CCP policies, were seen as a threat to the ideological hegemony of the new regime.

The ban on sociology in China was to last twenty-seven years, until 1979. One major attempt was made by Chinese sociologists in 1956 and 1957 to get the ban lifted. In the more relaxed political atmosphere prevailing at that time, ushered in by the CCP's slogan "let 100 flowers bloom and 100 schools of thought contend" and encouraged by the revival of sociology in the Soviet Union, leading figures such as Fei Xiaotong, Pan Guangdan, Wu Jingchao, and Chen Da wrote articles and made speeches arguing that sociology could be useful to socialist China in the study of social change and social problems— precisely the same rationale used prior to 1952. When the political atmosphere turned harsh again in the latter part of 1957, with the launching of the "anti-rightist campaign," Fei and many of the other leaders of this revival effort were branded "rightist elements" and disappeared from view.

From 1952 to 1979 some of those trained in sociology were assigned to work that had some links to their abolished field. Throughout this period ethnology remained an established discipline, devoted to the study of China's various ethnic minorities. When Fei Xiaotong emerged from his political purgatory in 1972, it was as a leading figure in ethnology. But Fei and others could not do research on the 94 percent of the population that is Han Chinese, and they also had to renounce publicly all their former work and ideas as "bourgeois." Psychology survived better than sociology by becoming defined as a natural, rather than a social, science. Some areas of social psychology (for example, educational psychology) remained at least somewhat active through the 1960s and 1970s (see Chin and Chin 1969). Other components of sociology disappeared in 1952 but reappeared prior to 1979. Demography was established as a separate field in the early 1970s and remains a separate discipline in Chinese academe today. With these partial exceptions, however, Chinese sociology ceased to exist for these twenty-seven years.

While sociology was banned in China, the sociological study of that society developed gradually in the West. Starting in the late 1950s, American foundations and government agencies, and to some extent their European and Japanese counterparts, provided funds for the development of the study of contemporary China—for fellowships, research centers, journals, language training facilities, and other basic infrastructure for the field. Within this developmental effort, sociology was targeted as an underdeveloped discipline (compared to, say, history, literature, and political science) deserving of special priority. Stimulated by this developmental effort, during the 1960s and 1970s the number of Western sociologists active in the study of China increased from a handful to perhaps two dozen.

Prior to the early 1970s, with a few minor exceptions (e.g., Geddes 1963), it was impossible for foreign sociologists to travel to China, much less to do research there. Even when such travel became possible during the 1970s, it was initially restricted to very superficial "academic tourism." In this highly constrained situation, foreign sociologists studying China developed distinctive research methods.

Much research was based on detailed culling of Chinese mass media reports. Special translation series of Chinese newspapers and magazines and of monitored radio broadcasts developed in the 1950s and became the mainstays of such research. The Chinese media provided fairly clear statements about official policy and social change campaigns. By conveying details about local "positive and negative models" in the implementation of official goals, the media also provided some clues about the difficulties and resistance being encountered in introducing social change. In a few instances the media even yielded apparently "hard" statistical data about social trends. A minor industry developed around scanning local press and radio reports for population totals, and these were pieced together to yield national population estimates (typically plus or minus 100 million).

Some researchers developed elaborate schemes to code and subject to content analysis such media reports (see, for example, Andors 1977; Cell 1977). However, this reliance on media reports to study Chinese social trends had severe limits. Such reports revealed much more about official goals than they did about social reality, and the researcher might erroneously conclude that an effort to produce major changes was actually producing them. The sorts of unanticipated consequences that sociologists love to uncover were for the most part invisible in the highly didactic Chinese media. It was also very difficult to use media reports to analyze variations across individuals and communities, the staple of sociological analysis elsewhere. Studies based on media reports tended to convey an unrealistic impression of uniformity, thus reinforcing the prevailing stereotype of China as a totalitarian society.

Partly in reaction to these limitations, a second primary method of research on China from the outside developed—the refugee interview. Scholars in sociology and related fields spent extended periods of time in Hong Kong interviewing individuals who had left the PRC for the British colony. Typically, these individuals were used not as respondents in a survey but as ethnographic informants "at a distance" about the corners of the Chinese social world from which they had come. Although the individuals interviewed obviously were not typical of the population remaining in the PRC, for some topics these refugees provided a rich and textured picture of social reality that contrasted with the unidimensional view conveyed by Chinese mass media. Elaborate techniques were developed by researchers to cope with the problems of atypicality and potential bias among refugee informants (see Whyte 1983).

By combining these methods with brief visits to China, sociologists and others produced a large number of useful studies of contemporary mainland society (Whyte, Vogel, and Parish 1977). Even though the arcane methods they used often seemed to nonspecialists akin to Chinese tea-leaf reading, the best of these studies have stood the test of time and have been confirmed by new research made possible by changes in China since 1979. However, the exclusion from meaningful field research in China did have unfortunate effects on the intellectual agendas of researchers. Much energy was focused on examining the "Maoist model" of development and whether or not China was succeeding in becoming a revolutionary new type of social order. Since the reality of Chinese social organizations in the Maoist period was quite different from the slogans and ideals upon which such constructions were based, this effort appears to have been a waste of scarce intellectual resources. Both this unusual intellectual agenda and the distinctive research methods sociologists studying China were forced to use reinforced the isolation of these researchers from "mainstream" work in sociology.

The year 1979 was significant in two ways for the sociological study of China. First, as already noted, that was the year in which China's leaders gave approval for the "rehabilitation" of sociology. After the death of Mao Zedong in 1976, and given the authority crisis that followed in the wake of the Cultural Revolution, the post-Mao leadership reopened many issues. China faced a number of serious social problems that had been ignored previously, and in this situation long-standing arguments about the utility of sociology for the study of social problems could be raised once again.

The second major change that occurred in 1979 was the "normalization" of diplomatic relations between the United States and China. That development led to approval for American and other Western researchers to conduct extended field research in China for the first time since 1949. The days of frustrating confinement to research from outside and academic tourism were over. It also became possible for U.S. sociologists to meet Chinese counterparts and to begin to discuss common research interests and plans for collaboration. Westerners began coming to China to teach sociology courses, Chinese began to be sent abroad for training in sociology, and collaborative conferences and publications were initiated. Leading figures in the West, including Peter Blau, Alex Inkeles, Nan Lin, W. J. Goode, Hubert Blalock, and Jeffrey Alexander, lectured in China and recruited Chinese counterparts for collaborative research and for training in their home institutions. All of the kinds of intellectual interchange between Chinese sociologists and their foreign counterparts that had been impossible for a generation were resumed.

The dangerous political aura surrounding sociology in the Mao era and the lesson of the abortive 1957 attempt to revive the field might have been expected to make it difficult to attract talented people to Chinese sociology after 1979. However, the field revived very rapidly and showed surprising intellectual vigor. A number of surviving pre-1949 sociologists reappeared to play leading roles in the revival, considerable numbers of middle-aged individuals trained in related fields were recruited (or ordered) to become sociologists, and many young people expressed eagerness to be selected for training in the field. The Chinese Sociological Association was formally revived, with Fei Xiaotong as its head. (Fei "unrenounced" his pre-1949 works, weakened his ties with ethnology, and resumed advocacy of the program of Chinese

rural development he had championed a generation earlier.) A number of departments of sociology were established in leading universities, and new sociological journals and a large number of monographs and textbooks began to appear. Institutes of sociology were established within the Chinese Academy of Social Science in Peking as well as in many provincial and city academies. Apparently, the novelty of the field, the chance to make a place for oneself, and perhaps even the chance to study abroad without having to face competition from layers of senior people more than compensated for the checkered political past of sociology. In any case, the speed and vigor with which the field revived surprised the skeptics (see Whyte and Pasternak 1980).

The intellectual focus of the revived sociology was fairly broad. Social problems and the sociology of development were two major foci. Within these and other realms, two sets of issues loomed large. One was the study of the after-effects of the Cultural Revolution and the radical policies pursued under Mao Zedong in the period 1966 to 1976. The other major issue concerned the impact of the opening to the outside world, decollectivization of agriculture, and the market-oriented reforms launched in 1978. A large number of studies began on these and other issues, and by the end of the 1980s the problem facing foreign sociologists studying China was not so much the scarcity of data on their object of study but its abundance. The publication of large amounts of statistical material, the availability of census and survey data dealing with demographic and other matters, and the mushrooming of social science publications threatened to overwhelm those who tried to keep track of Chinese social trends.

In pursuing their new intellectual agendas, Chinese sociologists easily found common ground with Western specialists. The latter were no longer so entranced with the Maoist model and shared a fascination with the social impact of the post-Mao changes. Many Western specialists readily adapted to the chance to conduct research in China and to collaborate with Chinese colleagues. Hong Kong did not die out as a research site and remained vital for some topics, but work from outside China was increasingly seen as supplementary to research conducted within the country. (After 1997 and Hong Kong's reversion to China this was still the case, as the special autonomy enjoyed by the former British colony produced a freer research atmosphere than in the rest of the country.) China specialists now had to share the stage with many sociologists who did not have area studies training. With data more readily available and collaboration with Chinese counterparts possible, area studies training and familiarity with the arcane techniques developed in the 1960s and 1970s were no longer so important. Many non-China specialists found the opportunity to study the world's most populous society increasingly attractive. These changes have been beneficial for China specialists within sociology. Given their small numbers and the complexity of Chinese society, there is more than enough "turf" to be shared with sociologists not trained in China studies. And these changes have reduced the intellectual isolation of the specialists, from both colleagues in China and those in their own departments.

As a result of these changes, Chinese sociologists ended their isolation from world sociology, and Western sociologists conducting research on China escaped from a highly constrained environment and began to produce work that was less idiosyncratic. It should be noted, however, that sociological research in China is not without limits, either for foreign researchers or for Chinese. Even in the most liberal phases of the initial reform decade from 1979 to 1989, some topics remained taboo, some locales were off limits, and bureaucratic obstruction and interference were constant facts of life. Nonetheless, even for foreigners it became possible to conduct extended ethnographic studies, carry out probability sample surveys, and gain access for secondary analysis to the raw data from census and survey studies conducted by Chinese, experiences that those who were studying the Soviet Union before its collapse could only envy. The result was a new spurt of research activity and publication that enriched our knowledge of Chinese social life immensely. (For a review of Western research during the decade after 1979, see Walder 1989. For an overview of developments within Chinese sociology during that period, see Lu 1989.)

However, the political fallout from the 1989 Tiananmen massacre raised new problems for the sociological study of China. At least some conservatives within the Chinese leadership used the crackdown following the massacre to attack sociology and other newly revived social sciences in terms reminiscent of 1952 and 1957. The field was once again accused of being an ideological Trojan horse designed to spread doubts about socialist orthodoxy. Some sociology departments were not allowed to enroll new students, while others had their enrollment targets cut. While these restrictions eased after a year or two, new and serious threats to collaborative research projects continued through the 1990s. Edicts designed to restrict and maintain strict political control over survey projects involving foreign collaboration were passed in secret in 1990 and 1995, resulting in the confiscation of survey data already collected in one instance and delays and torpedoing of projects in others. (The data confiscated after the 1990 secret edict were eventually released to the researchers involved, and other stalled projects resumed, but only after several years of tense negotiations.) In 1998 an international collaborative survey project in social gerontology was publicly attacked within China for allegedly endangering the health of China's elderly and having a concealed aim of enabling foreigners to profit from the "genetic secrets" of the Chinese people. Only after a vigorous public defense from both foreign and Chinese researchers was the disputed project saved. These developments mean that researchers who embark on sociological research within China on even quite nonpolitical topics face some risk that they will not be able to complete their projects due to political interference.

Despite the unpredictable political environment, Chinese and foreign sociologists pressed ahead with a wide-ranging variety of research activities during the 1990s. The success of this effort is a testament to the increasingly robust ties linking Chinese and foreign sociologists. During the 1980s large numbers of aspiring young Chinese sociologists were sent abroad for doctoral training, primarily to the United States. By the latter part of that decade and into the 1990s, a majority of the Western sociology doctoral theses dealing with China were being produced by students from China. After the 1989 Tiananmen massacre most of these newly minted specialists on Chinese society did not return to China, but instead embarked on research careers in the West. However, mindful of the desirability of leaving the door open for their eventual return, China did not treat this decision as disloyalty, but instead in most instances encouraged and invited these foreign-based Chinese sociologists to visit China to assist in the development of the discipline there and to undertake collaborative research projects. These young, foreign-trained sociologists are able to come and go and to navigate the complex political and bureaucratic terrain surrounding sociological research within China much more easily than their non-Chinese counterparts. Furthermore, the relatively smaller number of Chinese sociologists trained abroad who have returned to the PRC usually have found their new skills and contacts valued and rewarded, rather than treated with envy and suspicion. Many of these individuals are moving up rapidly into positions of responsibility and leadership within Chinese research institutes and universities, where they are generally able to keep research projects moving ahead despite bureaucratic obstacles. As a result of these trends, an increasing share of the new sociological research initiatives and publications that are having an impact on China studies in the West involve sociologists from China, whether currently based abroad or within China.

The changing sources of funding for research on Chinese society also are having an impact. Whereas in the past most research by Chinese social scientists was funded by the Chinese government and was responsive to state priorities and concerns, in the reform era Chinese sociologists and others in China face increasing constraints on government funding of research. New competitive peer review procedures are being introduced to determine who gets scarce research funds, and Chinese authorities encourage research institutes and researchers to find ways to raise or obtain funds on their own to support their research. In this altered environment a variety of Western and international sources of funding—from United Nations agencies, the World Bank, the Ford Foundation, foreign nongovernmental organizations, etc.—have become important in financing research that Chinese sociologists otherwise could not carry out. This changed funding picture thus reinforces other trends that are strengthening the links between sociology within China and abroad.

While the topics pursued within the sociological study of China in the 1990s were varied, the dominant focus was still on the process of market reforms. Some of the impetus for this focus came from a comparison with developments in the former Soviet Union and its satellites. Sociologists have joined others in trying to understand why to date the dismantling of central planning and the introduction of market reforms have generally been much more successful in China than in Eastern Europe (see, for example, Rozman 1992; Walder 1996a). The bulk of this research, however, looks not at the causes, but at the social consequences of the reforms, and here the concerns are varied and wide-ranging. For example, spirited debates have arisen about whether or in what respects the reforms are contributing to increased inequality within China, and about whether preform political elites are largely monopolizing the gains produced by the reforms or are being displaced increasingly by new elites (see, for example, Nee 1996; Xie and Hannum 1996; Walder 1996b; Bian and Logan 1996; Zhou, Tuma, and Moen 1996; Buckley 1997). Sociologists and others are also examining the new entrepreneurial class arising within China as a result of market reforms to determine what sorts of social origins they have, and researchers on this topic debate whether these entrepreneurs are a force for political change or are, instead, co-opted and controlled as a result of their dependence upon the state (see, for example, Unger 1996; Nevitt 1999). Research on the latter theme is part of a larger exploration of whether China's reforms are leading to the development of institutions of a "civil society" that might eventually lead to the democratization of China's political system (see Whyte 1992; White 1993). Within research on Chinese stratification there is also a growing body of work considering whether, on balance, the reforms have been harmful or beneficial in terms of the quest for gender equality (see Bauer et al. 1992; Croll 1994; Lee 1998; Entwisle and Henderson forthcoming). Another major focus of research concerns changes in Chinese family life, with the investigation of topics such as rising divorce and premarital sex rates and whether such trends indicate that Chinese family patterns are increasingly "converging" toward the patterns found in other societies (e.g. Xu and Whyte 1990; Davis and Harrell 1993; Logan, Bian, and Bian forthcoming). Still another major focus is on tracing the impact of particular reform changes—for example, the relaxation of migration restrictions that have allowed tens of millions of rural migrants to flood into China's cities, the attempt to revive labor markets as a way of distributing jobs, and the layoffs and unemployment being generated by reforms of China's inefficient state-owned enterprises (e.g. Bian 1994; Guthrie 1997; Matthews 1998)Solinger 1995; Sensenbrenner 1996.

Another primary research focus of China sociologists, in addition to the causes and consequences of the post-1978 economic reforms, involves China's dramatic fertility decline and its social consequences. The transformation of China from a society with moderately high fertility (total fertility rates of 5+) to extraordinarily low rates (total fertility rates under 2) has occurred in roughly the same time period as China's economic reforms (from the 1970s through the 1990s), but these two fundamental changes have been produced by contradictory processes. Whereas in economic affairs the state has increasingly withdrawn from bureaucratic management and has allowed markets to govern distribution, in regard to population the state has shifted away from indirect management and persuasion in favor of direct bureaucratic mandating of fertility quotas. The high national priority of this fertility reduction program has complex implications, in terms of sociological research. High priority, combined with recurring foreign criticism of China's human rights record in the realm of family planning (see Whyte 1998), produce political sensitivities that often obstruct and constrain research on this topic. However, that same priority has made research on topics related to fertility so important that foreign as well as Chinese demographers and others have been recruited to help plan and carry out a large number of high-quality surveys of China's demographic dynamics. These data have also in most instances been made available for examination by foreign as well as Chinese researchers. On balance the result has been a boom in research on China's population and a much better understanding of current trends in fertility, mortality, and other demographic domains than existed prior to the 1980s (see, for example, Banister 1987; Coale 1984; Feeney and Yuan 1994; Riley and Riley 1997).

In sum, recurring political turbulence in China has in some cases obstructed and delayed sociological research, but both the field and its practitioners have continued to forge ahead despite the uncertainties involved. The rapid and complex social changes that have occurred in China in the 1980s and 1990s have provided many new research questions for sociologists to explore, and a maturing network of Chinese sociologists and foreign China specialists (and nonspecialist sociologists interested in studying the world's most populous and most rapidly developing society) have taken advantage of new research opportunities. As a result of these changes the sociological study of China at the end of the 1990s was much better established than it was two decades earlier, with a wide variety of social processes and trends better studied and more fully understood.

REFERENCES

Andors, Stephen 1977 *China's Industrial Revolution: Politics, Planning, and Management, 1949 to the Present.* New York: Pantheon.

Banister, Judith 1987 *China's Changing Population.* Stanford, Calif.: Stanford University Press.

Bauer, J., Wang Feng, N. Riley, and Zhao Xiaohua 1992 "Gender Inequality in Urban China." *Modern China* 18:333–369.

Bian, Yanjie 1994 *Work and Inequality in Urban China.* Albany, N.Y.: SUNY Press.

——, and John Logan 1996 "Market Transition and the Persistence of Power: The Changing Stratification System in Urban China." *American Sociological Review* 61:739–758.

Buckley, Christopher 1997 Social mobility and stratification in urban China from Maoism through reform. Ph.D. diss. Australian National University.

Cell, Charles P. 1977 *Revolution at Work.* New York: Academic Press.

Chin, R., and A. Chin 1969 *Psychological Research in Communist China 1949–1966.* Cambridge, Mass.: MIT Press.

Coale, Ansley 1984 *Rapid Population Change in China, 1952–1982.* Washington, D.C.: National Academy Press.

Croll, Elisabeth 1994 *From Heaven to Earth: Images and Experiences of Development in China.* London: Routledge.

Davis, Deborah, and Stevan Harrell (eds.) 1993 *Chinese Families in the Post-Mao Era.* Berkeley: University of California Press.

Entwisle, Barbara, and Gail Henderson (eds.) forthcoming *Redrawing Boundaries: Work, Household, and Gender in China.* Berkeley: University of California Press.

Feeney, Griffith, and Yuan Jianhua 1994 "Below Replacement Fertility in China? A Close Look at Recent Evidence." *Population Studies* 48:381–394.

Fei Xiaotong [Fei Hsiao-t'ung] 1939 *Peasant Life in China.* London: G. Routledge.

Geddes, W. R. 1963 *Peasant Life in Communist China.* Ithaca, N.Y.: Society for Applied Anthropology.

Guthrie, Douglas 1997 Strategy and structure in Chinese firms: Organizational action and institutional change in Shanghai. Ph.D. diss. University of California, Berkeley.

Lang, Olga 1946 *Chinese Family and Society.* New Haven, Conn.: Yale University Press.

Lee, Ching Kuan 1998 *Gender and the South China Miracle.* Berkeley: University of California Press.

Levy, Marion J., Jr. 1949 *The Family Revolution in Modern China.* Cambridge, Mass.: Harvard University Press.

Lin Yaohua [Lin Yüeh-hwa] 1948 *The Golden Wing: A Sociological Study of Chinese Familism.* New York: Oxford University Press.

Logan, John, Bian Fuqin, and Bian Yanjie forthcoming "Tradition and Change in the Urban Chinese Family: The Case of Living Arrangements." *Social Forces.*

Lu Xueyi 1989 *China Yearbook of Sociology, 1979–1989* (in Chinese). Peking: Chinese Encyclopedia Press.

Mao Zedong (1927) 1971 "Report on an Investigation of the Peasant Movement in Hunan." In Mao Tsetung, *Selected Readings from the Works of Mao Tsetung.* Peking: Foreign Languages Press.

Matthews, Rebecca 1998 Where do labor markets come from? The emergence of urban labor markets in the People's Republic of China. Ph.D. diss. Cornell University, Ithaca, N.Y.

Nee, Victor 1996 "The Emergence of a Market Society: Changing Mechanisms of Stratification in China." *American Journal of Sociology* 101:908–949.

Parris, Kristen 1999 "Entrepreneurs and Citizenship in China." *Problems of Post-Communism* 46:43–61.

Riley, Nancy, and Robert Riley 1997 *China's Population: A Review of the Literature.* Liege: International Union for the Scientific Study of Population.

Rozman, Gilbert (ed.) 1992 *Dismantling Communism: Common Causes and Regional Variations.* Washington, D.C.: Woodrow Wilson Center Press.

Sensenbrenner, Julia 1996 Rust in the iron rice bowl: Labor reforms in Shanghai state enterprises, 1992–93. Ph.D. diss. Johns Hopkins University.

Solinger, Dorothy 1995 "China's Urban Transients in the Transition from Socialism and the Collapse of the Urban Public Goods Regime." *Comparative Politics* 27:127–147.

Thompson, Roger 1990 *Mao Zedong: Report from Xunwu.* Stanford, Calif.: Stanford University Press.

Unger, Jonathan 1996 "'Bridges': Private Business, the Chinese Government, and the Rise of New Associations." *The China Quarterly* 147:795–819.

Walder, Andrew (ed.) 1996a *China's Transitional Economy.* London: Oxford University Press.

—— 1996b "Markets and Inequality in Transitional Economies: Toward Testable Theories." *American Journal of Sociology* 101:1060–1073.

—— 1989 "Social Change in Post-Revolution China." *Annual Review of Sociology* 15:405–424.

White, Gordon 1993 "Prospects for Civil Society in China: A Case Study of Xiaoshan City." *Australian Journal of Chinese Affairs* 29:63–87.

Whyte, Martin King 1998 "Human Rights Trends and Coercive Family Planning in the PRC." *Issues and Studies* 34:1–29.

—— 1992 "Urban China: A Civil Society in the Making?" In A. Rosenbaum, ed., *State and Society in China.* Boulder, Colo.: Westview Press.

—— 1983 "On Studying China at a Distance." In Anne Thurston and Burton Pasternak, eds., *The Social Sciences and Fieldwork in China.* Boulder, Colo.: Westview.

——, and Burton Pasternak 1980 "Sociology and Anthropology." In Anne Thurston and Jason Parker, eds., *Humanistic and Social Science Research in China.* New York: Social Science Research Council.

Whyte, Martin K., Ezra F. Vogel, and William L. Parish, Jr. 1977 "Social Structure of World Regions: Mainland China." *Annual Review of Sociology* 3:179–207.

Wong, Siu-lun 1979 *Sociology and Socialism in Contemporary China.* London: Routledge and Kegan Paul.

Xie, Yu, and Emily Hannum 1996 "Regional Variation in Earnings Inequality in Reform-Era Urban China." *American Journal of Sociology* 101: 950–992.

Xu, Xiaohe, and Martin King Whyte 1990 "Love Matches and Arranged Marriages: A Chinese Replication." *Journal of Marriage and the Family* 52:709–722.

Yang, C. K. 1944 *A North China Local Market Economy.* New York: Institute of Pacific Relations.

Zhou, Xueguang, Nancy Tuma, and Phyllis Moen 1996 "Stratification Dynamics under State Socialism: The Case of Urban China, 1949–1993." *Social Forces* 74:759–796.

MARTIN KING WHYTE

CITIES

A *city* is a relatively large, dense, permanent, heterogeneous, and politically autonomous settlement whose population engages in a range of nonagricultural occupations. Definitions of cities and their associated phenomena vary by time and place, and by population size, area, and function (Shryock, Siegel, and associates 1976, pp. 85–104). The city is often defined in terms of administrative area, which may be larger than, smaller than, or equal to the area of relatively dense settlement that comprises what is otherwise known as the city proper. The suburb is a less dense but permanent settlement that is located outside the city proper and contains populations that usually have social and economic ties to the city.

Definitions of urban vary by nation; in the United States the term refers to populations of 2,500 or more living in towns or cities and to populations living in urbanized areas, including suburbs. In other nations, the lower limits for settlements defined as urban vary between 200 and 50,000 persons. United Nations definitions of urban areas emphasize a population of 20,000 or more, and cities a population of 100,000 or more. *Urbanization* refers to the economic and social changes that accompany population concentration in urban areas and the growth of cities and their surrounding areas.

Cities reflect other areas with which they are linked and the civilizations of which they are a part. Cities are centers of markets, governments, religion, and culture (Weber 1958, pp. 65–89). A *community* is a population sharing a physical environment and leading a common and interdependent life. The size, density, and heterogeneity of the urban community have been described as leading to "urbanism as a way of life," which includes organizational, attitudinal, and ecological components different from those of rural areas (Wirth 1938).

THE CITY IN HISTORY

Town and city development has been described as tied to a technological revolution in agriculture that increased food production, thereby freeing agriculturalists to engage in nonagricultural occupations. This resulted in an evolution to urban living and eventually to industrial production (Childe 1950). A second view is that some towns and cities first developed as trade centers, and were then nourished by agricultural activity in their hinterlands (Jacobs 1970).

Increasing complexity of social organization, environmental adaptation, and technology led to the emergence of cities (Child 1950; Duncan 1964). Excluding preagricultural settlements, towns and then cities were first established in the fourth to third millennium B.C. in ancient Mesopotamia within the Tigris and Euphrates river valleys, in the Harappa civilization in the valleys of the Indus River and its tributaries, and in the Egyptian Old Kingdom in the lower Nile valley. Other centers appeared in the Huang Ho basin on the east coast of China and the Peruvian Andes in the second to first millennium B.C., and in Mesoamerica in the first millennium B.C. (Phillips 1997, pp. 82–85).

Small agricultural surpluses and limits on transportation meant that the first towns were small and few in number, and contained only a small proportion of the populations of their regions. Economic activities of the earliest towns were tied largely to their surrounding areas. After the rise of towns in the Middle East, trading centers appeared on the shores and islands of the Mediterranean; some, such as Athens, became city-states. After developing more effective communication and social organization, some Western city-states expanded and acquired empires, such as those of Alexander the Great and of Rome. Following the decline of Rome, complex city life continued in the East and in the West in the Byzantine and Muslim empires, while the population of Europe declined and reverted, for the most part, to subsistence agriculture and organized into small territories held together by the Catholic Church (Hawley 1981, pp. 1–35).

Sjoberg (1960) has described preindustrial cities as feudal in nature and sharing social, ecological, economic, family, class, political, religious, and educational characteristics different from those in modern industrial cities. In the former, the city center, with its government and religious and economic activities, dominated the remainder of the city and was the locale of the upper social classes. Homogeneous residential areas were found throughout the city, but nonresidential activities were not confined to distinct neighborhoods (Sjoberg 1960).

Beginning in the tenth century, further town development in the West was facilitated by increases in agricultural technology, population, trade, and communication; the rise of an entrepreneurial class; and an expanding web of social norms regarding economic activity. Communication and manufacturing were revived, which led to the growth of towns with local autonomy and public administration, and eventually to networks of cities. Surplus rural populations migrated to towns and cities, which grew because of their specialization and larger markets, becoming focal points of European societies (Hawley 1981, pp. 37–83).

The emergence of a global economy structured city development (Lo and Yeung 1996, pp. 1–13). In the thirteenth and fourteenth centuries, some European central place and port cities, such as those of the Hanseatic League of Northern Europe, established commercial links with others. Meanwhile, other cities in the Eastern Hemisphere and some cities in the Western Hemisphere were linked together by long-distance trade routes transcending the boundaries of empires and states (Wolfe 1982, p. 250). Military-commercial alliances facilitated the incorporation of territories into states. Commercial ties expanded during the late-fifteenth and the sixteenth centuries, as Europeans developed merchant capitalism, and traded with and colonized peoples on other continents. European and North American states developed more complex economies during the next three centuries, facilitating development of a "European world economy" with a global market, a global division of labor, and a global system of cities (Wallerstein 1974).

WESTERN CITIES SINCE THE INDUSTRIAL REVOLUTION

In most regions of the more developed world, urban growth and urbanization have occurred at an increasing rate since the beginning of the Industrial Revolution. After 1820, the numbers and sizes of urban areas and cities in the United States increased as a result of employment concentration in construction and manufacturing, so urban areas began to grow more rapidly than rural ones.

The population classified as urban by the U.S. Census Bureau (based on aggregations of 2,500 or more and including the surrounding densely populated territories) increased from 5 percent in 1790 to 75 percent in 1990. In 1790 the largest urban place in the United States had fewer than 50,000 inhabitants. As late as 1840, not a single urban place in the United States had more than half a million inhabitants. There were four such places in 1890, fourteen in 1940, twenty-two in 1980, and twenty-three in 1990 (U.S. Bureau of the Census 1997, p. 44).

City growth in the United States during the nineteenth century was driven by migration, since there were sometimes excesses of urban deaths over births in the early part of that century and lower birthrates in the last part of that century. Population concentration facilitated greater divisions of labor within and among families and individuals, as well as increasing numbers of voluntary associations centered on new urban interests and problems. At first, cities were compact, growth was vertical, and workers resided near their workplaces. The outward expansion of the residential population was facilitated in the last part of the century by steam and electric railways, the outward expansion of industry, and the increasing role of the central business district in integrating economic activities (Hawley 1981, pp. 61–145).

The increasing scale of production in the United States led to the development of a system of cities that organized activities in their hinterlands. Cities were differentiated from each other by their degree of dominance over or subordination to other cities, some of which were engaged in centralized manufacturing, others of which depended on transportation, commercial, administrative, or other functions. According to Hawley (1986), cities may have certain key functions that dominate other cities, that is, integrating, controlling, or coordinating activities with these cities. Examples of key functions are administration, commerce, finance, transportation, and communication (Duncan et al. 1960). Since each city exists within its own organizational environment, the expansion of linkages of urban organizations has accompanied the development of a system of cities (Turk 1977).

In the United States, the nature of key functions in city systems changed with the expansion of settlements westward, as colonial seaports, river ports, Midwestern railway towns, central places on the Great Plains, extractive centers, and government centers were integrated into an urban system. A nationwide manufacturing base was established by 1900, as were commercial and financial centers. By 1960 a fully developed system of differentiated urban centers existed within the United States (Duncan and Lieberson 1970).

METROPOLITAN AREAS

In the United States, metropolitan areas are defined as being of two kinds. *Metropolitan statistical areas* (MSAs) are areas including one or more central cities with a population of 50,000 or more, or areas with a less densely populated central city but with a combined urban population of at least 100,000 (75,000 in New England), including surrounding counties or towns. *Consolidated metropolitan statistical areas* (CMSAs) contain at least one million population and may have subareas called *primary metropolitan statistical areas* (PMSAs) (Frey 1990, p. 6). In 1990 a majority of the population of the United States resided in the thirty-nine major metropolitan areas: those with more than one million population (Frey 1995, p. 276).

New urban-population-density patterns appeared in the United States with the development of metropolitan areas. Growth was characterized by increases in population density in central cities, followed by increases in density in the metropolitan ring. Transport and communication technologies facilitated linkages of diverse neighborhoods into metropolitan communities dominated by more densely populated central cities. These linkages in turn organized relationships between central cities and less densely populated hinterlands and subcenters. Older metropolitan areas became the centers of CMSAs, while newer areas were the frontiers of expansion, growing by natural increase and especially by net migration. Metropolitan sprawl extended beyond many former nonurban functions, as well as more centrally located older features of the cityscape.

The interior of large Western metropolitan areas represents a merging of urban neighborhoods into complex overlapping spatial patterns, which reflect to some extent the dates when urban neighborhoods were settled and built-up. The blurring of neighborhood distinctions, facilitated by

freeway and mass transit networks, facilitate interaction among "social circles" of people who are not neighborhood-based. Meanwhile, urban neighborhoods organized around such factors as status, ethnicity, or lifestyle, also persist. As the city ages, so does suburban as well as centrally located housing—a delayed consequence of the spread of urban settlement.

Kasarda (1995, p. 239) states that major cities in the United States have been transformed from centers of manufacturing and wholesale and retail trade, to centers of finance, administration, and information processing. Frey (1995, p.272) indicates that during the 1970s and 1980s populations concentrated in metropolitan areas with diverse economies that emphasized service and knowledge industries, as well as in recreation and retirement areas. In the 1970s there was a metropolitan and nonmetropolitan population turnaround. Populations in smaller metropolitan areas grew more rapidly than did those in larger metropolitan areas and population in developing countries grew more rapidly than in developed countries. In the 1980s, metropolitan population shifts, enhanced by international and internal migration, led to an urban revival, increasing regional racial, skill, and age divisions, the suburban dominance of growth and employment and more isolation of the urban core (Frey 1995, pp. 272–275).

Residential moves—the individual counterpart of population redistribution processes—are affected by population characteristics and other factors. Elements that influence mobility decisions are socioeconomic and psychological factors pertaining to the family and the family life cycle, housing and the local environment, and occupational and social mobility (Sabagh et al. 1969). For each of these factors, conditions may restrain persons from moving, or push or pull them to new locations. Information concerning new housing opportunities, the state of the housing market, and the availability of resources may impede or facilitate moves; subsequent moves may stem from recent migration or residential turnover in the metropolitan areas (Long 1988, pp. 219–224).

TRADITIONAL EXPLANATIONS OF CITIES

During the nineteenth century the character of the Western city was seen as different from that of noncity areas. Beginning with the public-health movement and concerns with urban housing, social scientists documented "pathologies" of urban life through the use of social surveys, the purpose of which was to provide policy-relevant findings. But since "urbanism as a way of life" has permeated the United States, many of the social and economic problems of cities have spread into smaller towns and rural areas, thus rendering the notion of unique urban pathologies less valid than when it was formulated.

In the first six decades of the twentieth century, explanations of city development were based largely on Western human ecology perspectives, and disagreements have arisen (Sjoberg 1968, p. 455). Theories based on Social Darwinism (Park [1916–1939] 1952) and economics (Burgess 1925, pp. 47–52) were first used to explain the internal structures of cities. "Subsocial" aspects of social and economic organization—which did not involve direct interpersonal interaction—were viewed as generating population aggregation and expansion. Market related competitive-cooperative processes—including aggregation-thinning out, expansion-contraction, centralization, displacement, segregation, migration, and mobility—were believed to determine the structures and patterns of urban neighborhoods (Quinn 1950). The competition of differing urban populations and activities for optimal locations was described as creating relatively homogeneous communities, labeled "natural areas," which display gradient patterns of decreasing densities of social and economic activities and problems with increasing distance from the city center.

On the basis of competitive-cooperative processes, city growth was assumed to result in characteristic urban shapes. The Burgess hypothesis specifies that in the absence of countervailing factors, the American city takes the form of a series of concentric zones, ranging from the organizing central business district to a commuters' zone (Burgess 1925, pp. 47–52). Other scholars emphasized star-shaped, multiple-nuclei, or cluster patterns of development. These views were descriptive rather than theoretical; assumed a Western capitalist commercial-industrial city; were distorted by topography, and street and transportation networks; and generally failed to take into account use of land for industrial purposes, which is found in most city zones.

Theodorson (1982) and Michaelson (1976, pp. 3–32) have described research on American cities as reflecting neo-orthodox, social-area analysis, and sociocultural approaches, each with its own frame of reference and methods. Neo-orthodox approaches have emphasized the interdependence of components of an ecological system, including population, organization, technology, and environment (Duncan 1964). This view has been applied to larger ecological systems that can extend beyond the urban community. Sustenance organization is an important focus of study (Hawley 1986). While neo-orthodox ecologists did not integrate the notion of Social Darwinism into their work, the economic aspects of their approach have helped to guide studies of population phenomena, including population shifts and urban differentiation (Frey 1995, pp. 271–336; White 1987), residence changes (Long 1988, pp. 189–251), racial and ethnic diversity (Harrison and Bennett 1995, pp. 141–210), segregation (Farley and Allen 1987, pp. 103–159; Lieberson and Waters 1988, pp. 51–93), housing status (Myers and Wolch 1995, pp. 269–334), and industrial restructuring and the changing locations of jobs (Kasarda 1995, pp. 215–268).

Social-area analysis, in contrast, regards modern industrial society as based on increasing scale, which represents "increased rates and intensities of social relation," "increased functional differentiation," and "increased complexity of social organization" (Shevky and Bell 1955). These concepts are related to neighborhood dimensions of social rank, urbanization, and segregation, which are delimited by the factor analysis of neighborhood or census tract measures. "Factorial ecology" has been widely used for classifying census tracts, sometimes for planning purposes. There are disagreements concerning whether factor-analysis studies of urban neighborhood social structure, which are associated with social-area analysis and similar approaches, result in theoretically useful generalizations (Janson 1980, p. 454; White 1987, pp. 64–66)

Sociocultural ecology has used social values such as sentiment and symbolism to explain land use in central Boston (Firey 1947) and other aspects of city life. While values and culture are relevant to explanations of city phenomena, this perspective has not led to a fully developed line of investigation.

Michaelson (1976, pp. 17–32) has argued that none of these aforementioned ecological approaches to the city explicitly study the relationship between the physical and the social environment, for the following reasons: (1) their incomplete view of the environment; (2) their focus on population aggregates; (3) their failure to consider contributions of other fields of study; and (4) the newness of the field. Since Michaelson wrote his critique, sociologists have given more attention to the urban environment.

NEW EXPLANATIONS OF CITIES

Traditional explanations of cities did not adequately account for the economic, political, racial and social upheavals in U.S. cities during the 1960s. Further, urbanization in less developed regions does not necessarily follow the Western pattern. City growth may absorb national population increments and reflect a lack of rural employment, a migration of the rural unemployed to the city, and a lack of urban industrial development. Increasing concentration of population in larger cities in less developed regions may be followed by the emergence of more "Western-style" hierarchies of cities, functions, and interorganizational relationships. Many cities in less developed regions experience the environmental hazards of Western cities, a compartmentalization of life, persistent poverty and unemployment, a rapidly worsening housing situation, and other symptoms of Western social disorganization. The juxtaposition of local urbanism and some degree of Western urbanization may vitiate a number of traditional Western solutions to urban problems.

Kasarda and Crenshaw (1991, pp. 467–500) have summarized and compared theoretical perspectives concerning how urbanization occurs in less developed regions. Modernization-human ecology perspectives portray city building as the result of changes in social organization and applications of technology. Rural-urban migration, resulting from urban industrialization and excess rural fertility, can eventually lead to the reduction of rural-urban economic and social differences (Hawley 1981). Dependency-world-system perspectives describe the capitalist world-system as guiding change in the less developed regions so as to maintain the dominance of the more developed core (Wallerstein 1974). Urban bias perspectives emphasize the role of the state, sometimes governed by urban elites, which relys on urban resources, and favors urban over rural development (Lipton 1977). Kasarda and Crenshaw (1991) regard these perspectives as underspecified and as lacking empirical confirmation.

Political economy perspectives explain city growth in more developed as well as less developed regions as a product of globalization, including capital accumulation and nation-state formation (Tilly 1975). Europe and the United States colonized non-European peoples and obtained raw materials from the colonies which they processed and exchanged with their colonies as manufactured products. Colonial areas gained political independence after World War II. Economic restructuring then resulted in the globalization of economic and cultural life, and changes in the international division of labor between cities.

Sassen (1991) indicates that following World War II communications technology facilitated the dispersion of manufacturing by multinational corporations to low-wage cities, some in former colonial areas. A globally integrated organization of economic activity then supplanted world economic domination by the United States. Economic activities were integrated beyond national urban hierarchies into a small number of key global cities, which are now international banking centers, with transnational corporate headquarters, sophisticated business services, information processing, and telecommunications. These cities (London, New York, and to a lesser degree Tokyo) command the global economy and are supported by worldwide hierarchies of decentralized specialized cities (Sassen 1991). International networks of cities sometimes provide opportunities for multinational corporations from less developed regions to penetrate more developed regions (Lo and Yeoung 1998, p. 2).

Feagan and Smith (1987, pp. 3–33) describe economic restructuring in U.S. cities in the 1980's as including plant closures and start-ups, the development and expansion of corporate centers, and corporate movement to outlying areas, all of which impact different groupings of cities. They portray economic restructuring as a product of interactions between governmental components of nation-states; multinational, national, and local corporations and businesses; and nongovernment organizations. These interactions guide policies affecting local taxation, regulation, implementation, and public-private partnerships. Some city neighborhoods have become expendable locations for rapidly shifting economic activity. Policies to accommodate to shifting sites of economic activity influence international and intranational migration, family life, as well as the use of urban, suburban, and rural space.

Aspects of political-economy perspectives have been taken into account in more traditional studies of cities (Frey 1995, pp. 271–336; Kasarda 1995, pp. 215–268). Walton (1993, pp. 301–320) maintains that political-economy perspectives have made the following contributions to the study of cities: (1) showing that urbanization and urbanism are contingent upon the development of social and economic systems; (2) generating comparative studies, particularly in developing countries; (3) elucidating the operation of the informal economy in cities; (4) outlining a political economy of place; (5) showing how globalization relates to ethnicity and community; and (6) relating urban political movements to changes in the global economy.

RETROSPECT AND PROSPECT

Globalization of economic and cultural life is associated with new urban trends. While cities in less developed regions lack resources when compared with those in more developed regions, cities in both types of regions are becoming more responsive to changes in worldwide conditions.

During the twenty-first century the majority of human population is expected to be urban residents (United Nations 1998). In 1995 approximately 46 percent (2.6 billion) of the world's population lived in urban areas. By the year 2005, approximately half of the population is projected to be urban, compared with fewer than one of every three persons in 1950. By 2030 approximately six-tenths (5.1 billion) of the population is projected to be urban.

Urban areas in less developed areas are projected to dominate the growth of the less developed regions and of the world during the twenty-first century. Reasons are the high population growth rates and high numerical population growth of less developed regions, and high rural-urban migration to cities in these regions. In 1995, only

38 percent of the populations in the less developed regions were urban dwellers, compared with 75 percent of the populations in the more developed regions. Urban areas in less developed areas are expected to account for approximately 90 percent (2.4 billion) of the total of 2.7 billion persons that the United Nations projects will be added to the earth's population from 1995 to 2030 (United Nations 1998). (Cities in more developed regions are expected to account for only 140 million of the population increase in the same period.)

There will continue to be significant differences in urbanization between the less developed regions. About three fourths of Latin-American population was urban in 1995, roughly the average level of industrialized regions in Europe, Japan, Australia, New Zealand, the United States and Canada. The most extensive future urban growth will be in Asia and Africa, which are now only about one-third urban (O'Mera 1999; United Nations 1998).

An increasing portion of urban population is residing in giant urban agglomerations. An *urban agglomeration*, according to the United Nations (1998), is the population within a contiguous territory inhabited at urban levels without regard to administered boundaries. In 1995 the fifteen largest ranged in size from 27 million (Tokyo) to 9.9 million (Delhi). Less developed countries are sometimes characterized by primate cities, that is, the largest city in a country dominates other cities and are larger than would be expected on the basis of a "rank-size" rule, which indicates that the rank of a population aggregation times its size equals a constant (Shryock, Siegel, and associates 1976), thus resulting in an inadequate supporting hierarchy of smaller cities. Primate cities often appear in small countries, and in countries with a dual economy, but are not as apparent in large countries or those with long urban histories (Berry 1964).

Megacities, defined by the United Nations (1998) as those cities with 10 million or more inhabitants, are increasing in number and are concentrated in less developed regions. There were fourteen megacities in 1995, including ten in less developed regions. Twenty-six megacities are projected in 2015, including twenty-two in less developed regions, of which sixteen will be in Asia. Megacities have both assets and liabilities. Brockerhoff and

Brennan (1998, pp. 75–114) have suggested that cities' size and rates of population growth are inversely related to welfare. Kasarda and Crenshaw (1991, pp. 471–474) note that megacities, which may have serious social and economic problems, can be driving engines for industrial production in developing regions, and contribute disproportionately to their countries' economies (Kasarda and Crenshaw 1991, pp. 467–501).

Berry (1978) indicates that urbanization may be accompanied by "counter-urbanization" or decreasing city size and density. City growth sometimes occurs in cycles, which begin with rapid growth in the urban core, followed by rapid growth in the suburban ring, a decline in growth in both the core and the ring, and then rapid growth in the core (United Nations 1998). These cycles—of urbanization, suburbanization, counter-urbanization, and reurbanization—appear to be associated with concentrations of services in city centers, followed by improvements in commuting by the labor force and increased suburban home ownership by urban labor forces. The 1970s deurbanization (metropolitan turnaround) in the United States was followed by reurbanization in the 1980s, and the start of another period of deurbanization in the 1990s (United Nations 1998). During the 1970s and 1980s counter-urbanization occurred in other more developed regions and in less developed regions, including a slow-down of population growth rates in some megacities in developing regions, particularly in Latin America (United Nations 1998).

Changes in the global economy and in the aforementioned city growth cycles are associated with new forms of urban land use in the United States, which are laid over preexisting urban patterns. Businesses, which provide the economic base for cities, move between optimum locations in different cities (Wilson 1997, p. 8). Globalization has enhanced the growth of suburbs and "edge cities" organized around outlying business and high-technology centers linked by telecommunications networks to other cities (Castells, 1989; Muller 1997). Unregulated informal sectors of the economy develop in a variety of intraurban locations. High-income native and immigrant populations, which profit from the new global economy, sometimes cluster in protected enclaves. Low-income immigrant and ethnic populations often occupy areas inhabited by earlier cohorts of the urban poor. Such trends may be related to a spread of ghetto-underclass neighborhoods and to increasingly polarized intracity neighborhood differences of poverty and affluence (Morenoff and Tienda 1997, pp. 59–72).

Trans-border cites are new urban forms that transcend the boundaries of nation-states and reflect increasingly borderless economies. They result from globalization trends, including the economic integration of regions, reductions of trade barriers, and the establishment of multinational free trade zones. They link cities adjacent to a border, and sometimes metamorphose into trans-border systems, complete with specialized functions and populations, and extensive cross-border social and economic ties (Rubin-Kurtzman et al. 1993). Examples are Southern California (U.S.)-Baja California (Mexico), the Singapore-Johore (Malysia)-Riau (Indonesia) region, and the Beijing (China)-Pyongyang (North Korea)-Seoul (South Korea)-Tokyo (Japan) urban corridor. Trans-border cities pose questions regarding the limits of national sovereignty, but can also integrate human and economic resources and thus enhance international stability.

Cities will continue to exhibit extremes of affluence and poverty, but the extent and consequences of these extremes are unclear. Massey (1996, pp. 395–412) has argued that both the affluent and the poor are concentrating in cities in the United States; consequences may include increased densities of crime, addictions, diseases, and environmental degradation, the emergence of oppositional subcultures, and enhanced violence. Massey assumes these trends apply to less developed regions as well as to the United States. Farley (1996, pp. 417–420) has advanced a counterargument that while economic inequality is increasing in the United States, as may be the geographic segregation of the poor, the continuing (1996) rise in prosperity increases welfare at all income levels. Firebaugh and Beck (1994, pp. 631–653) maintain that economic growth, even in dependent less developed countries, may eventually increase welfare. Hout et al. (1998) state that political institutions, which are partially responsible for growing inequality, can provide appropriate remedies.

As cities account for increasing shares of the earth's population, they will consume increasing shares of the earth's resources, produce increasing shares of pollution, and their populations will be more subject to negative feedbacks from human impacts on the environment. O'Mera (1999, p. 137) estimates that populations of cities, while occupying only two percent of the earth's surface, consume 75 percent of the earth's resources. Cities are often sited on areas that contain prime agricultural land; urban expansion then inhibits and degrades crop production. Conversion of rural land to urban use intensifies natural hazards including floods, forest and brush fires, and earth slides. Further development concentrates and then disburses to outlying locations such artificial hazards as air pollution, land and water pollution, and motor vehicle and air traffic noise. Cities are also sited on the shorelines of oceans, thus increasing numbers of city residents are subject to the impacts of storm surges and erosion. Lowry (1992) argues that environmental impacts attributed to cities reflect population growth, industrialization and prosperity rather than city growth itself.

Some of the aforementioned trends are apparent, for example, in Los Angeles and Mexico City, which ranked seventh and second in size, respectively, among the world's largest megacities in 1995. After World War II and until the 1970s, Los Angeles's industrial and population growth and suburban sprawl made it a prototype for urban development that brought with it many inner-city, energy, suburban, environmental, state-management, ethnic, and capital-accumulation problems.

Since the early 1970s, Los Angeles has become a radically changed global megacity based on accumulation of global capital, economic restructuring, communications, and access to new international markets. The reorganization of Los Angeles has affected labor-force demands and the character of both native and immigrant populations. Immigration transformed Los Angeles into a multicultural metropolis (Waldinger and Bozorgmehr 1996, pp. 3–37). The area's economy emphasizes high-income service-sector jobs and low-income service-sector and industrial-sector jobs. Los Angeles has a great concentration of industrial technology and great international cultural importance, is dependent on the private automobile, has environmental hazards (earthquakes, brush fires, and air pollution), limited water supplies, housing shortages, crime, and has experienced uncontrolled intergroup conflicts in 1965 and 1992.

Mexico City, while not commanding the same global economic stature as Los Angeles, is the primate city of Mexico. Mexico City shares many of Los Angeles's problems, including environmental hazards (earthquakes, and air pollution), water shortages, lack of housing and services, expansion of low-income settlements, dependence on the private automobile, lack of sufficient transportation, earthquakes, crime, and rising ethnic violence. Effects of policy responses to these problems have been dampened by economic reversals (Ward 1998).

These illustrations suggest that cities at somewhat similar levels of influence within their respective countries share similar characteristics, whether in the more developed or in the less developed regions. This would support a view that determinants of city development are rooted in the global economy and are influenced by similar trends, but vary according to the city's place in the system.

REFERENCES

Berry, Brian J. L. 1978 "The Counter-Urbanization Process: How General?" In Niles M. Hansen, ed., *Human Settlement Systems: International Perspectives on Structure, Change and Public Policy*. Cambridge, Mass.: Ballinger.

—— 1964 "Cities as Systems Within Systems of Cities." In J. Friedman and W. Alonso, eds., *Regional Development and Planning*. Cambridge, Mass.: MIT Press.

Brockerhoff, Martin, and Ellen Brennan 1998 "The Poverty of Cities in Developing Regions." *Population and Development Review* 241:75–114.

Burgess, Ernest W. (1924) 1925 "The Growth of the City, an Introduction to a Research Project." In Robert E. Park, Ernest W. Burgess, and R. D. McKenzie, eds., *The City*. Chicago: University of Chicago Press.

Castells, Manual 1989 *The Informational City: Information Technology, Economic Restructuring, and the Urban-Regional Process*. Cambridge, Mass.: Basil Blackwell, Ltd.

Childe, V. Gordon 1950 "The Urban Revolution." *Town Planning Review* 21:3–17.

Duncan, Beverly, and Stanley Lieberson 1970 *Metropolis and Region in Transition*. Beverly Hills, Calif.: Sage.

Duncan, Otis D. 1964 "Social Organization and the Ecosystem." In Robert E. L. Faris, ed., *Handbook of Modern Sociology*. Chicago: Rand McNally.

——, William R. Scott, Stanley Lieberson, Beverly Duncan, and Haliman H. Winsborough 1960 *Metropolis and Region*. Baltimore: Johns Hopkins University Press.

Farley, Reynolds 1996 "The Age of Extremes: A Revisionist Perspective." *Demography* 37:417–420.

——, and Walter R. Allen 1987 *The Color Line and the Quality of Life in America*. New York: Russell Sage Foundation.

Feagin, Joe R., and Michael Peter Smith 1987 "Cities and the New International Division of Labor: An Overview." In Michael Peter Smith and Joe R. Feagin, eds., *The Capitalist City*. New York: Basil Blackwell, Ltd.

Firebaugh, Glen, and Frank D. Beck 1994 "Does Economic Growth Benefit the Masses? Growth Dependence and Welfare in the Third World." *American Sociological Review* 59:631–653.

Firey, Walter 1947 *Land Use in Central Boston*. Cambridge, Mass.: Harvard University Press.

Frey, William 1995 "The New Geography of Population Shifts." In Reynolds Farley, ed., *State of the Union: America in the 1990s, Volume Two: Social Trends*. New York: Russell Sage Foundation.

—— 1990 "Metropolitan America: Beyond the Transition." *Population Bulletin* 45, 2:1–53.

—— 1987 "Migration and Depopulation of the Metropolis: Regional Restructuring or Rural Renaissance?" *American Sociological Review* 52:240–257.

Harrison, Roderick, and Claudette E. Bennett 1995 "Racial and Ethnic Diversity." In Reynolds Farley, ed., *State of the Union: America in the 1990s, Volume Two: Social Trends*. New York: Russell Sage Foundation.

Hawley, Amos H 1986 *Human Ecology: A Theoretical Essay*. Chicago: University of Chicago Press.

—— 1981 *Urban Society: An Ecological Approach*, 2nd ed. New York: Wiley.

Hout, Michael, Richard Arons, and Kim Voss 1996 "The Political Economy of Inequality in the 'Age of Extremes.'" *Demography* 33:421–425.

Jacobs, Jane 1970 *The Economy of Cities*. New York: Vintage.

Janson, Carl-Gunnar 1980 "Factorial Social Ecology: An Attempt at Summary and Evaluation." In A. Inkeles, N. J. Smelser, and R. H. Turner, eds., *Annual Review of Sociology*, vol. 6. Palo Alto, Calif.: Annual Reviews.

Kasarda, John 1995 "Industrial Restructuring and the Changing Nature of Jobs." In Reynolds Farley, ed., *State of the Union: America in the 1990s, Volume One: Economic Trends*. New York: Russell Sage Foundation.

——, and Edward M. Crenshaw 1991 "Third World Urbanization: Dimensions, Theories, and Determinants." In W. Richard Scott, ed., *Annual Review of Sociology* 17:467–500.

Lieberson, Stanley, and Mary C. Waters 1988 *From Many Strands: Ethnic and Racial Groups in Contemporary America*. New York: Russell Sage Foundation.

Lipton M. 1977 *Why Poor People Stay Poor: Urban Bias in World Development*. Cambridge, Mass.: Harvard University Press.

Lo, Fu-chen, and Yoe-Man Yeung 1996 "Introduction." In Fu-chen Lo and Yoe-Man Yeung, eds., *Emerging World Cities in Pacific Asia*. Tokyo: United Nations University Press.

Long, Larry 1988 *Migration and Residential Mobility in the United States*. New York: Russell Sage Foundation.

Lowry, Ira S. 1991 "World Urbanization in Perspective." In Kingsley Davis and Mikhail S. Bernstram, eds., *Resources, Environment, and Population: Present Knowledge: Future Options, Population and Development Review, a supplement to Volume 16, 1990*.

Massey, Douglas S. 1996 "The Age of Extremes: Concentrated Affluence and Poverty in the Twenty-first Century." *Demography* 33:395–412.

Michaelson, William 1976 *Man and His Urban Environment: A Sociological Approach*. Reading, Mass.: Addison-Wesley.

Morenoff, Jeffrey, and Marta Tienda 1997 "Underclass Neighborhoods in Temporal and Ecological Perspective." In Alan W. Heston, ed., David Wilson, special ed., *The Annals of the American Academy of Political and Social Science Globalization and the American City* 551:59–72.

Muller, Peter O. 1997 "The Suburban Transformation of the Globalizing American City." In Alan W. Heston, ed., David Wilson, special ed., *The Annals of the American Academy of Political and Social Science: Globalization and the Changing American City* 551:44–50.

Myers, Dowell, and Jennifer R. Wolch 1995 "The Polarization of Housing Status." In Reynolds Farley, ed., *State of the Union: America in the 1990s, Volume Two: Social Trends*. New York: Russell Sage Foundation.

O'Mera, Molly 1999 "Exploring a New Vision for Cities." In Linda Stack, ed., *State of the World 1999*. New York: W.W. Norton and Company.

Park, R. E. (1916–1939) 1952 "Human Communities: The City and Human Ecology." *Collected Papers*, vol. 2. Glencoe, Ill.: Free Press.

Phillips, E. Barbara 1996 *City Lights: Urban-Suburban Life in the Global Society*. New York: Oxford University Press.

Quinn, James 1950 *Human Ecology*. New York: Prentice-Hall.

Rubin-Kurtzman, Jane R., Roberto Ham Chande, and Maurice D. Van Arsdol, Jr. 1993 "Population in Trans-Border Regions: The Southern California-Baja, California Urban System." *International Migration Review* 30:1020–1045.

Sabagh, Georges, Maurice D. Van Arsdol, Jr., and Edgar W. Butler 1969 "Determinants of Intrametropolitan Residential Mobility: Conceptual Considerations." *Social Forces* 48, 1:88–97.

Sassen, Saskia 1991 *The Global City*. Princeton, N.J.: Princeton University Press.

Shevky, Eshref, and Wendell Bell 1955 *Social Area Analysis: Theory, Illustrative Applications and Computational Procedures*. Stanford Sociological Series, no. 1. Stanford, Calif.: Stanford University Press.

Shryock, Henry S., Jacob S. Siegel, and associates 1976 *The Materials and Methods of Demography*, condensed edition ed. by Edward G. Stockwell. San Diego: Academic Press/Harcourt Brace Jovanovich.

Sjoberg, Gideon 1968 "The Modern City." In David L. Sills, ed., *International Encyclopedia of the Social Sciences, vol. 1*. New York: MacMillan and Free Press.

—— 1960 *The Pre-Industrial City: Past and Present*. New York: Free Press.

Theodorson, George A. 1982 *Urban Patterns: Studies in Human Ecology*. University Park: Pennsylvania State University Press.

Tilly, Charles 1974 *The Formation of National States in Western Europe*. Princeton, N.J.: Princeton University Press.

Turk, Herman 1977 *Organizations in Modern Life: Cities and Other Large Networks*. San Francisco: Jossey-Bass.

United Nations 1998 *World Urbanization Prospects: The 1996 Revision*. New York: United Nations.

U.S. Bureau of the Census 1997 *Statistical Abstract of the United States*. Washington, D.C.: Government Printing Office.

Waldinger, Roger, and Mehdi Bozorgmehr 1996 "The Making of a Multicultural Metropolis." In Roger Waldinger and Mehdi Bozorgmehr, eds., *Ethnic Los Angeles*. New York: Russell Sage Foundation.

Wallerstein, Immanuael 1974 *The Modern World System: Capitalist Agriculture and the Origin of the European World Economy in the Sixteenth Century*. New York: Academic Press.

Walton, John 1993 "Urban Sociology: The Contribution and Limits of Political Economy." In Judith Blake, ed., *Annual Review of Sociology*. Palo Alto, Calif.: Annual Reviews Inc.

Ward, Peter M. 1998 *Mexico City: Revised Second Edition*. Chichester, N.Y.: John Wiley.

Weber, M. 1958 "The Nature of the City." In Don Martindale and Gertrude Neuwirth, eds., *The City*. New York: Free Press.

White, Michael J. 1987 *American Neighborhoods and Residential Differentiation*. New York: Russell Sage Foundation.

Wilson, David 1997 "Preface." In Alan W. Heston, ed., David O. Wilson, special ed., *The Annals of the American Academy of Political and Social Science: Globalization and the Changing U.S. City*, 551: 8–16.

Wirth, Louis 1938 "Urbanism as a Way of Life." *American Journal of Sociology* 44:1–24.

Wolf, Eric R. 1982 *Europe and the People Without History*. Berkeley: University of California Press.

MAURICE D. VAN ARSDOL, JR.

CIVIL DISOBEDIENCE

See Protest Movements; Student Movements.

CIVIL LIBERTIES

Civil liberties and associated controversies reflect the basic sociological issue of what may comprise the requirements of a free yet sustainable society. Classical interests of social thought directly or indirectly concern civil liberties because they address the degree to which individuals may exercise autonomy within the bounds of enduring social relations and community needs. Some of sociology's most venerable research has focused directly on civil liberties. Stouffer's *Communism, Conformity, and Civil Liberties* (1955) served as an intellectual punctuation mark on the McCarthy era, the period during which public discord over civil liberties reached its most intense state in the post–World War II world. Sociological thinking and research has helped American intellectuals and policy makers frame the issues associated with civil liberties and understand the implications of decisions regarding civil liberties for the well-being of society.

Civil liberties may be understood as legally protected areas in which the individual may function without interference by the state or the broader community of citizens. "Civil liberties" are analytically distinct from "civil rights." Civil liberties concern the individual's freedom from the broader society and its laws. Civil rights derive from the individual's claim on society and the state to give him or her equal protection through the state's police power and equal rights regarding public facilities, services, and largesse. Civil liberties concern the individual's rights to think, speak, and act outside the state's apparatus and jurisdiction. Civil rights address the individual's claim on equal access to public resources such as buses and schools, protection from harm by state agencies, and participation in government and politics.

Sociology offers several core capabilities to promote the citizens' and policy makers' understanding of civil liberties and the implications of related public decisions. Classical and contemporary work by sociologists has pertinence in three areas. First, sociological theory and commentary informed by theory helps specify the central dilemmas raised by civil liberties. Second, sociological research enables observers to discover the state of public opinion regarding civil liberties, the dynamics by which public opinion has developed and changed in the past, and the manner in which public opinion may unfold in the future. Finally, sociological thinking and research serves as a resource for understanding the potential consequences of public decisions regarding civil liberties in the years to come. This last capability can aid public decision making and help lay groundwork for achieving the broadest range of civil liberty in society while maintaining the social cohesion necessary to ensure stability, continuity, and affirmation of individual life by core social institutions.

Debate regarding civil liberties has traditionally concerned freedom of expression and due process. Positions regarding freedom of expression have sought to protect the right of individuals to publicly support politically unpopular causes or to display or publish material others may view as objectionable (e.g., pornography). Due process issues have focused on the rights of defendants in criminal cases and claimants in civil and administrative proceedings. Civil liberties advocates have drawn core support from the Bill of Rights and subsequent amendments to the U.S. Constitution

safeguarding free speech, prohibiting unreasonable search and seizure, and limiting the criminal justice system's ability to require citizens to give self-incriminating testimony. Civil liberties advocates depend heavily on legal doctrines and devices derivative of the Bill of Rights such as fairness, equal protection of the law, and the right of privacy.

The late twentieth century saw a vast extension of activities to which the status of a civil liberty was applied. The 1998 edition of the American Civil Liberties Union's (ACLU) *The Year in Civil Liberties*, for example, reports challenges by ACLU units to practices and policies such as:

- Religious celebration in public settings (viz. school prayer and holiday displays),

- Youth curfews,

- Prohibition of marijuana use for medical purposes,

- School vouchers,

- Wrongful dismissal from employment due to politics or sexual preference,

- Restraint and corporal punishment of prisoners and "high-risk" legal defendants,

- The death penalty,

- Prohibition of public funding for abortions,

- Legal barriers to adoption of children by lesbian or gay individuals or couples,

- Restriction of legal marriage to heterosexuals only,

- "Sodomy" laws.

According to the ACLU document, these laws and policies belong to a common category of threats to "fairness, freedom of expression, equality, and keeping the government out of our private lives."

The ACLU does not unilaterally speak for those concerned with civil liberties. But controversy surrounding the ACLU's extended definition of civil liberties recapitulates central issues in sociological theory, social thought, and public policy. Early social theorists emerging from free-market economics and utilitarianism encountered (wittingly or by implication) the question of what holds society together, given that individuals "naturally" behave in an atomized manner. Modern participants in civil liberties controversies confront (again wittingly or by implication) a tension between unrestricted individual liberty and the needs of the community and requirements for viable social institutions.

Etzioni, in an essay commenting on the ACLU's expansion of concerns, emphasizes contradictions between individual liberties and community needs (Etzioni 1991). He stresses the necessity of modifying constitutionally protected individual rights in instances of compelling social exigency. Examples of such modification in the late twentieth century included x-raying of luggage at airports, conducting voluntary fingerprinting of children to facilitate their identification if kidnapped, contact-tracking for people infected with HIV, and mandatory drug testing of workers whose impairment endangers others, such as train engineers. Although these measures have enjoyed public support and none has materially affected the basic rights of the general population, each has been the focus of civil liberties controversies and actions.

Etzioni characterizes opposition to measures such as these as "radical individualism," encouraged at late century by an imbalance between "excessive individual rights and insufficient social responsibility." His analysis characterizes the U.S. Constitution as broader than a code of legal provisions to protect the individual from government. The law of the land is also a reflection of "public morality, social values, and civic virtue." Eclipse of these elements of civil society, Etzioni implies, precludes even marginal modification of legal traditions in the face of compelling social need. He warns that resulting governmental paralysis may ultimately give rise to popular disillusionment, social distress, and abandonment of safeguards to personal liberty on a far greater scale than the marginal modifications initially proposed.

Another critic of ACLU positions alleges that the imbalance between one-sided civil liberties protection and community needs has already affected American social institutions adversely and to a significant degree. Siegel (1991) writes that "the libertarians and their allies in the courts have . . . reshaped virtually every American public institution in the light of their understanding of due

process and equal protection under the Fourteenth Amendment." This reshaping has had an "elitist" quality, proceeding through abstract legal reasoning and argument but materially harmful, particularly to the economically disadvantaged. According to Siegel's argument, civil liberties victories in court place burdens on social institutions and prevent them from responding to social reality. Siegel writes:

Civil liberties have become an economic issue as those who can afford it either flee the cities or buy out of public institutions. For those who can't afford to pay for private school, or private vacations, and are left with junkie infested parks, who can't afford the private buses which compete with public transportation, and are unable to pay for private police protection, the rights revolution has become a hollow victory. The imposition of formal equality, the sort that makes it almost impossible, for instance, to expel violent high school students, has produced great substantive inequality as would-be achievers are left stranded in procedurally purified, but failing institutions. (Siegel 1991)

Both Etzioni's and Siegel's critique of the civil liberties movement reflect sociology's core perspective and concern, the essential tension between individualistic and social forces. More concretely, sociology's traditional concern with civil liberties has focused on the citizen's thinking regarding tolerance of deviation. Survey research has served as the primary source of such information.

Stouffer's above-referenced classic sounded an optimistic note at the conclusion of the McCarthy era. His study focused on tolerance of people espousing communism and atheism, "nonconformist" ideologies that excited widespread public hostility at the time. In separate surveys conducted by the National Opinion Research Center (NORC) and the Gallup organization, Stouffer asked respondents whether communists and atheists should be allowed to speak in their communities, whether they should be allowed to teach in colleges or universities, and whether their books should be removed from public libraries.

The Stouffer study is remembered largely for reporting relationships between two focuses of social distinction and tolerance for the noncon-formist ideologies. Community leaders and people with advanced education were more likely to score in the "more tolerant" range than the national cross section. On this basis, Stouffer concluded that Americans would become more tolerant of nonconformity in the decades to follow, since the average American was receiving more years of education than his or her parents. Level of education correlated strongly with tolerance in every age group except sixty and over.

A subtheme in the heritage left by Stouffer was evidence for personality-based causes of intolerance regarding civil liberties for deviants. Experience with European totalitarianism had led psychologists to develop the theory of the "authoritarian personality." Measured according to a device known as the "F scale," personalities of this kind were distinguished by a simplistic world view, respect for power, and obedience to authority (Adorno 1950). Statistically significant relationships were found between F scale items and intolerance in the Stouffer data. Consistent with these findings, sociologists such as Lipset (1981) claimed that authoritarianism was more likely to be found in the working rather than the middle or upper classes. It is tempting to conclude that a negative relationship between education and basic authoritarianism explains the greater willingness of educated people to extend civil liberties to the politically unpopular, and to speculate that greater education will reduce, if it has not reduced already, personality-related proclivities toward intolerance.

Later research, though, has shown the sociology of public opinion regarding civil liberties to be more complex. Early critics pointed out technical flaws in the F scale. The scale's items, for example, were all worded in the same direction, encouraging positive responses. Critics raised the possibility that reported relationships between F scale scores and education merely reflected a positive response bias which was particularly strong among working-class respondents. Members of the working class, it was theorized, have a tendency to acquiesce to strong, positive assertions, particularly when these are presented by higher-status individuals such as pollsters.

Reanalysis of the Stouffer data and analysis of data from NORC's 1990 General Social Survey (GSS) by Schuman, Bobo, and Krysan (1992) casts doubt upon the causal chain implied above: that low social status (indicated by education) "causes" authoritarian personality, and that authoritarian personality subsequently "causes" intolerance of civil liberties for nonconformists and deviates. Reanalyzing Stouffer's data, these investigators found relationships between authoritarianism and intolerance of communists and atheists only among the more highly educated. In the 1990 GSS data, they found relationships between authoritarianism and intolerance for blacks and Jews again confined to the educated. The investigators conclude that there is no substantive relationship between class and authoritarianism. Evidence does emerge for a relationship between personality factors and both support for civil liberties for nonconformists and tolerance of minorities. But the roots of these personality factors are unknown and presumably much more complex than class-based socialization.

Changes in public concerns since the 1950s make it risky to apply the findings of Adorno, Stouffer, and others of their era to today's citizens and social issues. By the end of the twentieth century, communism and atheism had ceased to be mainstream public concerns in the United States. Analysis of civil liberties issues regarding crime had risen to prominence. Remedies such as permanent incarceration of habitual criminals and community notification regarding sex offenders ("Megan's Law") had been widely adopted. Increased latitude by police for searching and surveillance of citizens was widely discussed.

Public attitudes favoring compromise of civil liberties in the interests of aggressive law enforcement seemed stable during the 1980s and 1990s. Comparison over time of poll results on the trade-off between aggressive policing and civil liberties indicates growing support for warrantless police searches of cars and drivers. Decided majorities of respondents to Roper and Gallup polls in 1985 and 1986 approved of school officials' searching students' belongings for drugs or weapons, again without a warrant. The late twentieth century, though, saw no large-scale support for abandonment of civil liberties in pursuit of greater security. One trend showed a modest rise in support for surveillance of citizens, but another indicated just the opposite: the public did not think it was necessary to "give up some civil liberties" to prevent terrorism (Shaw 1998).

Civil libertarians might feel more alarmed by the polls' findings regarding public ignorance about constitutional rights. According to one survey, only 56 percent of Americans were aware of the innocent-until-proven-guilty principle (Parisi 1979). In another study, only one-third of the respondents correctly indicated the truth or falsehood of a statement regarding double jeopardy (McGarrell and Flanagan 1985).

Review of the studies cited above implies two major conclusions about public opinion regarding civil liberties. First, social determinants of support for civil liberties are likely to be complex and to change over time. Second, the specific focus of concern surrounding civil liberties—for example, the rights of communists versus those of crooks—may predominantly affect their support among citizens. Continual exercise of pertinent sociological research tools is required to maintain awareness of civil liberties-related attitudes and trends; associated theories appear in periodic need of reconstruction.

There is good evidence that sociological thinking and research techniques can promote understanding of the consequences of public decisions regarding civil liberties and help balance civil liberties and community needs. Etzioni's critique includes a recommendation for "limited adjustment" of civil liberties in the interests of society. Criteria for activation of limited adjustment include a "clear and present danger" of sufficient gravity to "endanger large numbers of lives, if not the very existence of our society," and a "direct link between cause and effect." As illustrations, Etzioni cites nuclear weapons, crack cocaine, and AIDS. He recommends minimal interference with constitutional rights, seeking remedies whenever possible that do not actually involve civil liberties.

Even the most measured approach to "adjustment" of civil liberties, though, raises issues for social theory and research. Designation of "clear and present danger" is as much a social fact as one of nuclear physics, pharmacology, and epidemiology. Civil libertarians may justifiably ask what makes crack cocaine a potential threat to society while other narcotics, while causing significant human misery, have not brought society down. Similar issues may be raised regarding AIDS, a biologically less-contagious disease than the traditional scourges of syphilis and gonorrhea. To what extent, researchers should ask, may the objective significance of these threats have been exaggerated by public emotion?

The impacts of small modifications of civil liberties on the problems these measures are intended to ameliorate should also be viewed as empirical issues. Does contact-tracking of people with AIDS actually drive some underground, making their disease invisible to society and hence more dangerous? If so, how many go underground, for how long, and by what means? Research on likely behavior of people with AIDS and other stigmatized diseases is an essential adjunct to related public decision making.

Finally, the degree to which minor adjustment may ultimately weaken the fabric of civil liberties is a necessary direction for research. Etzioni puts aside the notion that minor modification may initiate a slide down the "slippery slope" toward government or communitarian domination by citing the innocuous nature of procedures such as child fingerprinting. But systematic examination of many seemingly small adjustments may indicate that some indeed result in cascades of increasingly pernicious modifications. Study of the conditions under which the minor modification of traditions has in fact led to their eventual collapse could form the basis of a relevant theory.

REFERENCES

Adorno, Theodore W. et al. 1950 *The Authoritarian Personality*. New York: Harper.

Etzioni, Amitai 1991 "Too Many Rights, Too Few Responsibilities." *Society* 28:41–48.

Lipset, Seymour M. 1981 *Political Man*. New York: Doubleday.

McGarrell, E.F., and T. Flanagan (eds.) 1985 *Sourcebook of Criminal Justice Statistics–1984*. Washington, D.C.: Department of Justice.

Parisi, Nicolette et al. (eds) 1979 *Sourcebook of Criminal Justice Statistics–1978*. Washington, D.C.: Department of Justice.

Schuman, Howard, Lawrence Bobo, and Maria Krysan 1992 "Authoritarianism in the General Population: The Education Interaction Hypothesis." *Social Psychology Quarterly* 55:379–387.

Shaw, Greg M. et al. 1998 "Crime, the Police and Civil Liberties." *Public Opinion Quarterly* 62:405–426.

Siegel, Fred 1991 "Individualism, Etatism, and the ACLU." *Society* 28:20–22.

Stouffer, Samuel A. 1955 *Communism, Conformity, and Civil Liberties*. Garden City, N.Y.: Doubleday.

Whitfield, Emily, and Amy Weil 1998 *The Year in Civil Liberties: 1998*. New York: American Civil Liberties Union.

HOWARD P. GREENWALD

CIVIL RIGHTS

See Protest Movements; Student Movements.

CLANS

See Indigenous Peoples.

CLASS AND RACE

There is considerable debate in the sociology of race relations over how social inequality based on class and that based on race intertwine or intersect. Are these separate dimensions of inequality that simply coexist? Or are they part of the same reality?

Efforts to develop an understanding of the relationship between class and race have a long history in sociology. In the 1930s and 1940s it was common to conceptualize the issue as "caste and class" (Davis, Gardner, and Gardner 1941). Studies were conducted in southern towns of the United States, and a parallel was drawn between the southern racial order and the Indian caste system. Class differentiation was observed within each of the two racial "castes," but a caste line divided them, severely limiting the social status of upper-class African Americans. This view, while descriptively illuminating, was challenged by Cox (1948), who saw U.S. race relations as only superficially similar to caste and based on a very different dynamic.

The relationship between class and race remains hotly debated today. Wilson (1980, 1987) has argued that class has superceded race as a factor in the continuing disadvantage of black

inner-city communities. Wilson argues that economic forces, including the exodus of major industries, have more to do with the social problems of the inner city than do race-based feelings and actions. On the other hand, Omi and Winant (1986) assert the independence of race from class and resist the reduction of race to class forces. They claim that the United States is organized along racial lines from top to bottom and that race is a more primary category than class.

For most Marxist sociologists of race relations, class and race cannot be treated as separate dimensions of inequality that somehow intersect. Rather, they argue that race and class are both part of the same system and need to be understood through an analysis of the system as a whole. Modern race relations are seen as distinctive products of the development of world capitalism. Both racism and capitalism developed together reinforcing one another in a single, exploitative system. The central question then becomes: How has capitalism, as a system based on class exploitation, shaped the phenomena of race and racism?

CAPITALISM AND RACISM

Conventional thinking tends to follow the line that the development of capitalism should eliminate racism. People holding this position argue that racism is an unfortunate leftover from more traditional social systems. Capitalism, based on rational criteria such as efficiency, should gradually eliminate the irrational features of the past. The market is "colorblind," it should only select on the basis of merit. For example, in the area of job allocation, selecting on the basis of such irrelevant criteria as skin color or the race of one's great grandparents, would lead those firms that so choose to perform less well than those that select purely on the basis of ability, and they would go out of business. Only the rational, colorblind firms would survive and racism would disappear in the labor market.

Unfortunately, this idealized theoretical model of the way capitalism works has not proved true in practice. We continue to live in a highly segregated society, with a continuing racial division of labor, and with a high degree of racial inequality on every social and economic dimension. White families, on average, control much higher levels of wealth than African-American families, for example (Oliver and Shapiro 1995). The continuation of racism within advanced capitalist societies requires further explanation.

Whereas cultural differences have served as a basis for intergroup conflicts for the entire history of humanity, the expansion of Europe, starting in the sixteenth century, set the stage for a new form of intergroup relations. Never before was conquest so widespread and thorough. Nor was it ever associated with such a total ideology of biological and cultural inferiority. Modern racism, with its peudoscientific claims of inferiority, is a unique phenomenon.

An understanding of European expansion, and its impact on people of color, begins with an analysis of capitalism as it developed in Europe. Capitalism is a system that depends on the private ownership of productive property. In order to earn profits on property, the owners depend on the existence of a nonowning class that has no alternative but to sell its labor-power to the owners. The owners accumulate wealth through profit, that is, the surplus they extract from labor. Hence, a class struggle develops between capitalists and workers over the rights of capitalists to the surplus.

In Europe, labor came to be "free," that is, people were no longer bound by serfdom or other forms of servitude but were free to sell their labor-power on an open market to the highest bidder. Being free in this sense gave European workers a certain political capacity, even though they were often driven to conditions of poverty and misery.

Capitalism is an expansionary system. Not only does it unleash great economic growth, but it also tends to move beyond national boundaries. The expansionist tendencies lie in a need for new markets and raw materials, a search for investment opportunities, and a pursuit of cheaper labor in the face of political advances by national labor forces. European capitalism thus developed into an imperialistic system (Lenin 1939).

European imperialism led to a virtually total conquest of the globe. Europe carved up the entire world into spheres of influence and colonial domination. The idea and ideology of race and racism emerged from this cauldron. Europeans constructed a kind of folk-scientific view of human differences, dividing the world's human population into semi-species or "races." Of course, this division

has no basis in fact, and racial categorization has been completely discredited. Nevertheless, the idea of race, and its use in structuring societies along hierarchical lines, remains exceedingly robust. In sum, race is strictly a social construction, but one with profound implications for the way society is organized.

European domination took multiple forms, from unequal treaties, unfair trade relations, conquest, and the establishment of alien rule to annihilation and white settlement in places where once other peoples had thrived. Imperialism received ideological justification in beliefs that non-European cultures were primitive, uncivilized, barbaric, and savage, and their religions were pagan and superstitious. Europeans were convinced that they had the true religion in Christianity and that all other peoples needed to be "saved." The denigration of other cultures was accompanied by beliefs in natural, biological inferiority. Dark skin color was a mark of such inferiority, while white skin was viewed as more highly evolved. Africans, in particular, were seen as closer to the apes. These kinds of ideas received pseudoscientific support in the form of studies of cranial capacity and culturally biased intelligence tests (Gould 1981). The totalizing oppression and dehumanization of colonial domination is well captured in Memmi's *The Colonizer and the Colonized* (1967).

European economic domination had many aspects, but a major feature was the exploitation of colonized workers. Unlike white labor, which was free (in the sense of unbound), colonial labor was typically subjected to various forms of coercion. As conquered peoples, colonized nations could be denied any political rights and were treated openly as beings whose sole purpose was to enhance white wealth. Throughout the colonial world, various forms of slavery, serfdom, forced migrant labor, indentured servitude, and contract labor were common.

Not only did European imperialists exploit colonized workers in their homelands, but they also moved many people around to other areas of the colonial world where they were needed. The most notorious instance was the African slave trade, under which Africans were brought in bondage to the Caribbean area and sections of North and South America. However, other examples include the movement of contract workers from China and India all over the colonial world. Britain, as the chief imperialist power, moved Indians to southern Africa, Fiji, Trinidad, Mauritius, and other places to serve as laborers in remote areas of the British Empire. These movements created "internal colonies" (Blauner 1972), where workers of color were again subject to special coercion.

Even seemingly free immigrants of color have been subject to special constraints. For example, Chinese immigrants to the United States in the late nineteenth century were denied naturalization rights, in contrast to European immigrants, and as a result, were subjected to special legal disabilities. In the United States, Australia, Canada, and elsewhere, Chinese were singled out for "exclusion" legislation, limiting their access as free immigrants.

African slavery had the most profound effects on the shaping of racial thought and racial oppression. Even though slavery contradicted the basic premise of capitalism as based on a free labor market, it nevertheless flourished within world capitalism, and was an essential feature of it. In a seminal book, Williams (1944; 1966) argued that capitalism could not have developed without slavery, a position elaborated upon by Blackburn (1997). The coerced labor of African slaves enabled the western European nations to accumulate capital and import cheap raw materials that served as a basis for industrialization.

WORKING CLASS DIVISIONS

Within the United States, the coexistence of free labor in the North and slavery in the South, proved to be disastrous, drawing an especially harsh race line between blacks and whites. The very concept of whiteness became associated with the notion of freedom and free labor, while blacks were seen as naturally servile (Roediger 1991). White workers divided themselves from blacks (and other racially defined workers), believing that capitalists could use coerced and politically disabled workers to undermine their interests. Thus a deep division emerged in the working class, along racial lines. The racism of the white working class can be seen as a secondary phenomenon, arising from the ability of capitalists to engage in the super-exploitation of workers of color.

The sections of the world with the worst racial conflicts are the "white settler colonies." In the British Empire, these include the United States, South Africa, Zimbabwe (Rhodesia), Canada, Australia, and New Zealand. These societies established large white working classes that came into conflict with colonial capitalists over the use of coerced labor (Harris 1964).

From the point of view of workers of color, the distinction between white property owners and white workers seems minimal. Although class conflict raged within the white community, people of color experienced the effects as a uniform system of white domination. All whites appeared to benefit from racism, and all whites appeared to collude in maintaining segregation, job discrimination, and the disenfranchisement of people of color. In this sense, race appears to override class. Nevertheless, it should be recognized that people of color were and are exploited as *labor*, in order to enhance capitalist profits. Thus their relationship to capital includes both race and class elements. Racial oppression intensifies their class oppression as workers.

MIDDLE CLASSES

So far we have talked only of the relations between white capital, white labor, and colonized labor. The colonial world was, of course, more complex than this. Not only did colonized people have their own middle or upper classes, but sometimes outside peoples immigrated or were brought in and served as indirect rulers of the colonized.

Middle strata from among the colonized peoples can play a dualistic role in the system. On the one hand, they can help the imperialists exploit more effectively. Examples include labor contractors, police, or small business owners who make use of ethnic ties to exploit members of their own group. In these types of situations, the dominant white group can benefit by having members of the colonized population help to control the workers primarily for the dominant whites while taking a cut of the surplus for themselves. On the other hand, middle strata can also be the leaders of nationalist movements to rid their people of the colonial yoke.

Outside middle strata, sometimes known as middleman minorities, can be invaluable to the colonial ruling class. As strangers to the colonized, they have no ambivalence about the aspirations of the colonized for self-determination. They take their cut of profits while not seriously threatening to take over from the Europeans. Because middleman groups tend to serve as the chief interactors with the colonized, they often become a major butt of hostility, deflecting the hostility that would otherwise be directed at the colonial elite. Thus the class and race relations resulting from the development of European capitalism and imperialism have been complex and world-shaping.

CONTEMPORARY RACE RELATIONS

Even though formal colonialism as outright political domination has been successfully challenged by national liberation movements, and even though the most oppressive forms of coerced labor have been legally banned in most of the world, neocolonialism and racial oppression continue in various guises.

For example, African Americans in the United States remain a relatively disenfranchised and impoverished population. Although illegal, racial discrimination persists in everyday practice, and racist ideology and attitudes pervade the society. Many whites continue to believe that blacks are innately inferior and object to social integration in the schools or through intermarriage. African Americans are almost totally absent from positions of power in any of the major political, economic, and social institutions of the society. Meanwhile, they suffer from every imaginable social deprivation in such areas as housing, health care, and education.

The capitalist system maintains racism in part because racially oppressed populations are profitable. Racial oppression is a mechanism for obtaining cheap labor. It allows private owners of capital to reduce labor costs and increase their share of the surplus derived from social production. This is very evident in Southern California today, where the large, immigrant Latino population provides virtually all the hard labor at exceptionally low wages. Their political status as noncitizens, a typical feature of racist social systems, makes them especially vulnerable to the dehumanization of sweatshops and other forms of super-exploitation.

With an increasingly globalized world capitalism, these processes have taken an international dimension. Not only do capitalists take advantage of oppressed groups in their own nation-states, but they seek them out wherever in the world they can be found. Such people are, once again, of color. Of course, the rise of Japan as a major capitalist power has changed the complexion of the ruling capitalist elite, but the oppressed remain primarily African, Latin American, and Asian.

It is common today for people to assume that racism goes both ways and that everyone is equally racist, that African Americans have just as much animosity toward whites as whites have toward blacks. According to this thinking, whites should not be singled out for special blame because racism against those who are different is a universal human trait: We are all equally guilty of racism. This view denies the importance of the history described above. To the extent that peoples of color are antiwhite, it is a reaction to a long history of abuse. Claiming that the antiwhite sentiments of blacks are equally racist and on the same level as white racism is an attempt to negate the responsibility of Europeans and their descendents for a system of domination that has tried to crush many peoples.

At the foundation of the problem of race and class lies the value system of capitalism, which asserts that pursuit of self-interest in a competitive marketplace will lead to social enhancement for all and that therefore the social welfare need not be attended to directly. This assumption is patently untrue. The United States, perhaps the worst offender, has let this social philosophy run amok, resulting in the creation of a vast chasm between excessive wealth and grinding poverty, both heavily correlated with color. Without severe intervention in "free market" processes, the United States is heading toward increased racial polarization and even possible violence.

Movements for social change need to address racial oppression and disadvantage directly. Changing the system of capitalist exploitation will not eliminate racism, since the power and resources available to white workers are so much greater than those of workers of color. The whole system of inequality based on appropriation of surplus wealth by a few, mainly white, private property owners needs to be challenged, along with its racial aspects. Major redistribution, based on racial disadvantage, would be required. Neither class-based nor racial inequality can be attacked alone. They are linked with each other and must be overthrown together.

REFERENCES

Blackburn, Robin 1997 *The Making of New World Slavery: From the Baroque to the Modern, 1492–1800.* London: Verso.

Blauner, Robert 1972 *Racial Oppression in America.* New York: Harper and Row.

Cox, Oliver Cromwell 1948 *Caste, Class, and Race.* New York: Modern Reader.

Davis, Alliso, Burleigh B. Gardner, and Mary R. Gardner 1941 *Deep South.* Chicago: University of Chicago Press.

Gould, Stephen Jay 1981 *The Mismeasure of Man.* New York: W.W. Norton.

Harris, Marvin 1964 *Patterns of Race in the Americas.* New York: Walker.

Lenin, V. I. 1939 *Imperialism: The Highest Stage of Capitalism.* New York: International.

Memmi, Albert 1967 *The Colonizer and the Colonized.* Boston: Beacon Press.

Oliver, Melvin L., and Thomas M. Shapiro 1985 *Black Wealth/White Wealth: A New Perspective on Racial Inequality.* New York: Routledge.

Omi, Michael, and Howard Winant 1986 *Racial Formation in the United States.* New York: Routledge and Kegan Paul.

Roediger, David R. 1991 *The Wages of Whiteness: Race and the Making of the American Working Class.* London: Verso.

Williams, Eric 1966 *Capitalism and Slavery.* New York: Capricorn.

Wilson, William J. 1987 *The Truly Disadvantaged: The Inner City, the Underclass, and Public Policy.* Chicago: University of Chicago Press.

—— 1980 *The Declining Significance of Race: Blacks and Changing American Institutions.* Chicago: University of Chicago Press.

EDNA BONACICH

CLASSIFICATION

See Tabular Analysis; Typologies.

CLINICAL SOCIOLOGY

Clinical sociology is a humanistic, multidisciplinary specialization that seeks to improve the quality of people's lives. Clinical sociologists assess situations and reduce problems through analysis and intervention. Clinical analysis is the critical assessment of beliefs, policies, and/or practices with an interest in improving a situation. Intervention, the creation of new systems as well as the change of existing systems, is based on continuing analysis.

Clinical sociologists have different areas of expertise—such as health promotion, sustainable communities, social conflict, or cultural competence—and work in many capacities. They are, for example, community organizers, sociotherapists, mediators, focus group facilitators, social policy implementers, action researchers, and administrators. Many clinical sociologists are full-time or part-time university professors, and these clinical sociologists undertake intervention work in addition to their teaching and research.

The role of the clinical sociologist can be at one or more levels of focus from the individual to the intersocietal. Even though the clinical sociologist specializes in one or two levels of intervention (e.g., marriage counseling, community consulting), the practitioner will move among a number of levels (e.g., individual, organization, community) in order to analyze or intervene or both.

THE HISTORY OF AMERICAN CLINICAL SOCIOLOGY

When sociology emerged as a discipline in the 1890s, the nation was struggling with issues of democracy and social justice. There was rural and urban poverty, women were still without the vote, and there were lynchings. Farmers and workers in the late 1800s were frustrated because they could see the centralization of economic and political power in the hands of limited groups of people. This kind of frustration led to public protests and the development of reform organizations. In this climate, it is not surprising that many of the early sociologists were scholar-practitioners interested in reducing or solving the pressing social problems that confronted their communities.

The First University Courses. While many of the early sociologists were interested in practice, the earliest known proposal using the words "clinical sociology" was by Milton C. Winternitz (1885–1959), a physician who was dean of the Yale School of Medicine from 1920 through 1935. At least as early as 1929, Winternitz began developing a plan to establish a department of clinical sociology within Yale's medical school. Winternitz wanted each medical student to have a chance to analyze cases based on a medical specialty as well as a specialty in clinical sociology.

Winternitz vigorously sought financial support for his proposal from the Rosenwald Fund, but he was unable to obtain the necessary funds for a department of clinical sociology. He did note, however, the success of a course in the medical school's section on public health that was based on the clinical sociology plan.

The first course using the words "clinical sociology" in the title was taught by Ernest W. Burgess (1886–1966) at the University of Chicago. Burgess taught the course in 1928 and then offered it twice in 1929. During these years, the course was considered to be a "special" course and did not appear in the university's catalog. Burgess offered the clinical sociology course, as a regular course, five times from 1931 through 1933. The course continued to be listed in the catalog for the next several years but was not taught after 1933.

The University of Chicago catalogs did not include a description of the clinical sociology course, but the course always was listed under the social pathology grouping. All courses in this section dealt with topics such as criminality, punishment, criminal law, organized crime, and personal disorganization. Several of the students enrolled in these first clinical sociology courses were placed in child guidance clinics. Clarence E. Glick, for instance, was the staff sociologist at Chicago's Lower North Side Child Guidance Clinic and Leonard Cottrell was the clinical sociologist at the South Side Child Guidance Clinic.

Two other universities offered clinical courses in the 1930s—Tulane University in Louisiana and New York University. The Tulane University course was designed to give students the opportunity to learn about behavior problems and social therapy by conferences and fieldwork in a child guidance clinic. Louis Wirth (1897–1952), a full-time faculty member and director of the New Orleans Child Guidance Clinic, was scheduled to teach the course

in the spring of 1930. Wirth was unable to teach the course because he accepted a one-year Social Science Research Council Fellowship to work in Europe. The course was taught in his absence, but the university's course information does not identify the professor who took Wirth's place.

When Wirth returned to the United States in 1931, he joined the faculty of the University of Chicago. In the spring of 1932 he taught a "minor" course in clinical sociology but by then he no longer was working with child guidance clinics.

New York University also offered clinical sociology courses in the early 1930s. Harvey Warren Zorbaugh (1896–1965) was a faculty member there in the School of Education which provided undergraduate and graduate preparation for visiting teachers, educational counselors, clinicians, social workers, and school guidance administrators. The major focus of the program was the solution of educational problems and other social dilemmas.

Zorbaugh, along with Agnes Conklin, offered "Seminar in Clinical Practice" in 1930. The course was intended to qualify students as counselors or advisers to deal with behavioral difficulties in schools. From 1931 through 1933 the clinical practice course was called "Seminar in Clinical Sociology." The course was one of the highest numbered courses in educational sociology and was offered both terms of each year. The course was open to graduate students who were writing theses or engaged in research projects in the fields of educational guidance and social work.

Zorbaugh, author of *The Gold Coast and the Slum: A Sociological Study of Chicago's Near North Side*, had been involved with clinics at least since 1924. That was the year Zorbaugh and Clifford Shaw organized two sociological clinics in Chicago—the Lower North and South Side Child Guidance Clinics. Zorbaugh was associate director of the Lower North Side Child Guidance Clinic in 1925.

Zorbaugh was a founder, in 1928, of the Clinic for the Social Adjustment of the Gifted at New York University. He was director of this clinic at its inception and was actively involved in its work for over fifteen years. The clinic was for intellectually gifted and talented preadolescents. The clinic gave graduate students the opportunity to have supervised experiences in teaching, clinical diagnosing and treating of children with behavioral problems.

During the 1953–54 academic year, Alvin W. Gouldner (1920–1980) was teaching in the Department of Sociology and Anthropology at Antioch College in Ohio. Before joining the faculty, Gouldner had been a university teacher for four years and then worked, for one year, as a consultant to Standard Oil of New Jersey.

Gouldner offered "Foundations of Clinical Sociology" at Antioch. The course was taught at the highest undergraduate level, and students who enrolled in the course were expected to have completed the department's course in social pathology. The college bulletin provided the following description of the course:

A sociological counterpart to clinical psychology with the group as the unit of diagnosis and therapy. Emphasis on developing skills useful in the diagnosis and therapy of group tenstions. Principles of functional analysis, group dynamics, and organizational and small group analysis examined and applied to case histories. Representative research in the area assessed.

The term "clinical sociology" first appears in print . The first known published linking of the words *clinical* and *sociology* was in 1930 when Milton C. Winternitz, a pathologist and dean of the Yale Medical School, wanted to establish a department of clinical sociology. After working on the idea at least as early as 1929, he wrote about it in a report to the president of the Yale Medical School and the report was published in the 1930 Yale University *Bulletin*. That same year saw the publication of a speech Winternitz had given at the dedication of the University of Chicago's new social science building. The speech also mentioned clinical sociology.

Abraham Flexner, a prominent critic of medical education and director of the Institute for Advanced Study at Princeton, mentioned clinical sociology in 1930 in his *Universities: American, English, German*. Flexner did not approve of the Institute of Human Relations that Winternitz was establishing at Yale. In the pages of criticism devoted to the institute, Flexner briefly mentioned clinical sociology: "Only one apparent novelty is proposed: a professor of clinical sociology" (Flexner 1930).

Winternitz continued to write about the value of clinical sociology until 1936 when his last report as dean was filed. One of Winternitz's (1932) most forceful statements in support of the field was the contemporary-sounding statement that appeared in his 1930–1931 annual report:

The field for clinical sociology does not seem by any means to be confined to medicine. Within the year it has become more and more evident that a similar development may well be the means of bringing about aid so sorely needed to change the basis of court action in relation to crime. . .

Not only in medicine and in law, but probably in many other fields of activity, the broad preparation of the clinical sociologist is essential. . .

The first discussion of clinical sociology by a sociologist was Louis Wirth's 1931 article, "Clinical Sociology," in *The American Journal of Sociology*. Wirth wrote at length about the possibility of sociologists working in child development clinics, though he did not specifically mention his own clinical work in New Orleans. Wirth wrote "it may not be an exaggeration of the facts to speak of the genesis of a new division of sociology in the form of clinical sociology" (Wirth 1930).

In 1931, Wirth also wrote a career development pamphlet, which stated:

The various activities that have grown up around child-guidance clinics, penal and correctional institutions, the courts, police systems, and similar facilities designed to deal with problems of misconduct have increasingly turned to sociologists to become members of their professional staffs (Wirth 1931).

Wirth "urged (sociology students) to become specialists in one of the major divisions of sociology, such as social psychology, urban sociology. . . or clinical sociology" (Wirth 1931).

In 1931, Saul Alinsky was a University of Chicago student who was enrolled in Burgess's clinical sociology course. Three years later, Alinsky's article, "A Sociological Technique in Clinical Criminology," appeared in the *Proceedings of the Sixty-Fourth Annual Congress of the American Prison Association*. Alinsky, best known now for his work in community organizing, was, in 1934, a staff sociologist and member of the classification board of the Illinois State Penitentiary.

In 1944 the first formal definition of clinical sociology appeared in H.P. Fairchild's *Dictionary of Sociology*. Alfred McClung Lee, the author of that definition, was known as one of the founders of the Society for the Study of Social Problems, the Association for Humanist Sociology, and the Sociological Practice Association. Lee later used the word "clinical" in the title of two articles—his 1945 "Analysis of Propaganda: A Clinical Summary" and the 1955 article "The Clinical Study of Society."

Also appearing in 1944 was Edward McDonagh's "An Approach to Clinical Sociology." McDonagh had read Lee's definition of clinical sociology but had not seen Wirth's 1931 article. McDonagh, in his *Sociology and Social Research* article, proposed establishing social research clinics that had "a group way of studying and solving problems" (McDonagh 1944).

In 1946 George Edmund Haynes's "Clinical Methods in Interracial and Intercultural Relations" appeared in *The Journal of Educational Sociology*. Haynes was a cofounder of the National Urban League (1910) and the first African American to hold a U.S. government subcabinet post. His 1946 article, written while he was executive secretary of the Department of Race Relations at the Federal Council of the Churches of Christ in America, discussed the department's urban clinics. The clinics were designed to deal with interracial tensions and conflicts by developing limited, concrete programs of action.

Contemporary contributions . While publications mentioning clinical sociology appeared at least every few years after the 1930s, the number of publications increased substantially after the founding of the Clinical Sociology Association in 1978. The association, now called the Sociological Practice Association, made publications a high priority. Individuals were encouraged to publish and identify their work as clinical sociology, and the association established publication possibilities for its members. The *Clinical Sociology Review* and the theme journal *Sociological Practice* were published by the association beginning in the early 1980s. These annual journals were replaced in the 1990's by *Sociological Practice: A Journal of Clinical and Applied Sociology*, a quarterly publication.

The Sociological Practice Association has had a central role in the development of American clinical sociology. The association helped make available the world's most extensive collection of teaching, research, and intervention literature under the label of clinical sociology and it introduced the only clinical sociology certification process.

The Sociological Practice Association's rigorous certification process for clinical sociologists is available at the Ph.D. and M.A. levels. The Ph.D.-level process was adopted in 1983 and certification was first awarded in 1984. The association began to offer M.A.-level certification in 1986. Successful candidates at both the doctoral and master's level are awarded the same designation—C.C.S. (Certified Clinical Sociologist).

Experienced clinical sociologists are encouraged to apply for certification. which is given for intervention work (assessing and changing social systems). As part of the application process, a candidate is required to identify her or his area of specialization (e.g., community, family counseling) and level of intervention (e.g., organization, individual). The certification process requires membership in the Sociological Practice Association, documentation of appropriate education and supervised training, documentation of interdisciplinary training, essays about ethics and theory, and a demonstration before peers and a reviewing committee.

The Sociological Practice Association, along with the Society for Applied Sociology, also has put in place a Commission on Applied and Clinical Sociology. The commission has set standards for the accreditation of clinical and applied sociology programs at the baccalaureate level and intends to do the same for graduate programs.

CLINICAL SOCIOLOGY AND SOCIOLOGICAL PRACTICE

The practical sociology of the 1890s and early 1900s is now referred to as sociological practice. This general term *sociological practice* involves two areas, clinical sociology and applied sociology. Clinical sociology emphasizes hands-on intervention while applied sociology emphasizes research for practical purposes. Both specialties require different kinds of specialized training.

Some sociological practitioners are "clinical" in that they only or primarily do intervention work; others are "applied" in that they only or primarily conduct research that is of practical interest. Some practitioners do both. Clinical sociologists, for instance, may conduct research before beginning an intervention project to assess the existing state of affairs, during an intervention (e.g., to study the process of adaptation), and/or after the completion of the intervention to evaluate the outcome of that intervention. For some clinical sociologists, the research activity is an important part of their own clinical work. These sociologists have appropriate research training and look for opportunities to conduct research. Other clinical sociologists prefer to concentrate on the interventions and leave any research to other team members. Those clinical sociologists who decide not to engage in research may have research skills but prefer to conduct interventions, may not have enough expertise in the conduct of research, or may know that other team members have more expertise in research.

THEORIES, METHODS, AND INTERVENTION STRATEGIES

Clinical sociologists are expected to have education and training in at least one area in addition to sociology. This means that not only are clinical sociologists exposed to the range of theories (e.g., symbolic interaction, structural-functionalism, conflict, social exchange) and quantitative and qualitative research methods generally taught in sociology programs, but they also have additional influences from outside of their own programs. The result is that clinical sociologists integrate and use a broad range of theoretical and methodological approaches.

Clinical sociologists use existing theory to formulate models that will be helpful in identifying and understanding problems and also to identify strategies to reduce or solve these problems. Clinical sociologists also have shown that practice can have an influence on existing theories and help in the development of new ones.

While clinical sociologists use a wide variety of research methods and techniques (e.g., participatory action research, geographic information systems, focus group analysis, surveys), they probably are best known for their case studies. Case studies involve systematically assembling and analyzing detailed, in-depth information about a person, place, event, or group. This methodological approach involves many data-gathering techniques such as document analysis, life histories, in-depth interviews, and participant observation.

Clinical sociologists who have been in the field for ten or twenty years probably learned about intervention strategies primarily through courses and workshops given outside of sociology departments as well as through their work and community experiences. Clinical sociologists who have more recently entered the field also may have learned intervention techniques as part of their sociology programs. These sociology programs might include courses, for instance, on focus groups, mediation, or administration, as well as require supervised residencies or internships.

CLINICAL SOCIOLOGY IN INTERNATIONAL SETTINGS

Clinical sociology is as old as the field of sociology and its roots are found in many parts of the world. The clinical sociology specialization, for instance, often is traced back to the fourteenth-century work of the Arab scholar and statesperson Abd-al-Rahman ibn Khaldun (1332–1406). Ibn Khaldun provided numerous clinical observations based on his varied work experiences such as Secretary of State to the rule of Morocco and Chief Judge of Egypt.

Auguste Comte (1798–1857) and Emile Durkheim (1858–1917) are among those whose work frequently is mentioned as precursors to the field. Comte, the French scholar who coined the term "sociology", believed that the scientific study of societies would provide the basis for social action. Emile Durkheim's work on the relation between levels of influence (e.g., social compared to individual factors) led Alvin Gouldner (1965, p.19) to write that "more than any other classical sociologist (he) used a clinical model."

Interest in clinical sociology has been growing in a number of countries. For example, French is the predominant language of many, if not most, of the current international clinical sociology conferences, and books and articles have appeared with clinical sociology in the title in France and French-speaking Canada. The French-language clinical sociologists emphasize clinical analysis. They have a solid international network and have done an excellent job of attracting nonsociologists to that network. Their literature is substantial. Particularly notable is the work of Jacques van Bockstaele and Maria van Bockstaele; Robert Sevigny, Eugene Enriquez, Vincent de Gaulejac, and Jacques Rheaume.

Beginning in the mid-1990's, Italians hosted clinical sociology conferences, published clinical sociology books and articles and ran numerous clinical sociology training workshops. If one is interested in learning about clinical sociology in Italy, one would want to review the work of Michelina Tosi, Francesco Battisti, and Lucio Luison. Luison's 1998 book, *Introduzione alla Sociologia clinica* (Introduction to Clinical Sociology), contains thirteen articles written by Americans. One is an original article written for the volume but all the others are translations of articles that appeared in the Sociological Practice Association's *Clinical Sociology Review* or *Sociological Practice*. The volume concludes with the Sociological Practice Association's code of ethics.

Clinical sociology also is found in other parts of the world. Of particular interest would be developments in Greece, Brazil, Mexico, Uruguay, and South Africa. In South Africa, for instance, one university's sociology department has put a sociological clinic in place and another sociology department has developed a graduate specialization in counseling.

The international development of clinical sociology has been supported primarily by two organizations. The clinical sociology division of the International Sociological Association (ISA) was organized in 1982 at the ISA World Congress in Mexico City. The other major influence is the clinical sociology section of the Association internationale des Sociologues de Langue Francaise (International Association of French Language Sociologists).

It is clear that a global clinical sociology is beginning to emerge. American clinical sociology had a strong role in the early development of the global specialization but now it is only one of many influences. It will be interesting to see if the thrust of the international field will be as explicitly humanistic and intervention-oriented as American clinical sociology.

REFERENCES

Bruhn, John G., and Howard M. Rebach 1996 *Clinical Sociology: An Agenda for Action.* New York: Plenum.

Clark, Elizabeth J., Jan Marie Fritz, and P.P. Rieker (eds.) 1990 *Clinical Sociological Perspectives on Illness & Loss: The Linkage of Theory and Practice.* Philadelphia: The Charles Press.

Enriquez, Eugene 1997 "The Clinical Approach: Genesis and Development in Western Europe." *International Sociology.* 12/2(June):151–164.

—— 1992 "Remarques Terminales Vers une Sociologie Clinique d'Inspiration Psychanalytique." *L'Organisation en Analyse.* Fevrier. Paris: P.U.F.

——, Gilles Houle, Jacques Rheaume, and Robert Sevigny (eds.) 1993 *L'Analyse Clinique dans les Sciences Humaines.* Montreal: Editions Saint-Martin.

Fritz, Jan Marie (ed.) 1996 *The Clinical Sociology Resource Book.* 4th ed. Washington, D.C.: American Sociological Association Teaching Resources Center and the Sociological Practice Association.

Fritz, Jan Marie 1991a "The History of American Clinical Sociology: The First Courses." *Clinical Sociology Review* 9:5–26.

Fritz, Jan Marie 1991b "The Emergence of American Clinical Sociology." Pp. 17–32 In H. Rebach and J. Bruhn, eds., *Handbook of Clinical Sociology.* New York: Plenum.

Fritz, Jan Marie 1985 *The Clinical Sociology Handbook.* New York: Garland.

Gaulejac, Vincent de and Shirley Roy (ed.), 1993 *Sociologies Cliniques.* Paris: Hommes et Perspectives.

Giorgino, Enzo 1998 "Per un Ridefinizione del Lavoro Professionale in Sociologia." *Sociologia e Professione.* 29 (Marzo):8–23.

Glassner, Barry, and Jonathan A. Freedman 1979 *Clinical Sociology.* New York: Longman.

Gouldner, Alvin 1965 "Explorations in Applied Social Science." *Social Problems.* 3/3(January):169–181. Reprinted 1965 in Alvin Gouldner and S.M. Miller, eds., *Applied Sociology.* 5–22 New York: Free Press.

Luison, Lucio (ed.) 1998 *Introduzione alla Sociologia Clinica: Teorie, Metodi e Tecniche di Intervento.* Milano: FrancoAngeli.

Rebach, Howard M., and John G. Bruhn (eds.), 1991 *Handbook of Clinical Sociology.* New York: Plenum

Rheaume, Jacques 1997 "The Project of Clinical Sociology in Quebec." *International Sociology.* 12/2(June):165–174.

Sevigny, Robert 1997 "The Clinical Approach in the Social Sciences." *International Sociology.* 12/2(June):135–150.

Straus, Roger A. (ed.), 1999 *Using Sociology: An Introduction from the Applied and Clinical Perspectives.* Third edition. New York: General Hall.

Straus, Roger A. (ed.), 1979 "Special Issue on Clinical Sociology." *The American Behavioral Scientist.* March/April.

Tosi, Michelina, and Francesco Battisti (eds.) 1995 *Sociologia Clinica e Sistemi Socio-Sanitari: Dalle Premesse Epistemologiche Allo Studio di Casi e Interventi.* Milano: FrancoAngeli.

van Bockstaele, Jacques, Maria van Bockstaele, Colette Barrot, and Cl. Magny 1963 "Travaux de Sociologie Clinique: Quelques Conditions d'une Intervention de Type Analytique en Sociologie." *L'Année Sociologique.* Paris: Presses Universitaires de France.

van Bockstaele, Jacques, Maria van Bockstaele, Colette Barrot, Jacques Malbos, and Pierrette Schein 1968 "Problemes de la Sociologie Clinique: Nouvelles Observations sur la Definition de la Socioanalyse." *L'Année Sociologique.* Paris: Presses Universitaires de France.

Winternitz, Milton Charles 1932 "Clincal Sociology." In Report of the dean of the School of Medicine, *Bulletin of Yale University.*

Wirth, Louis 1931a "Clinical Sociology." *American Journal of Sociology,* 37:49–66.

—— 1931b Sociology: Vocations for those Interested in It. Pamphlet.Vocational Guidance Series, No. 1. Chicago: University of Chicago. Louis Wirth Collection, University of Chicago, Department of Special Collections. Box LVI, Folder 6.

JAN MARIE FRITZ

CLUSTER ANALYSIS

See Correlation and Regression Analysis; Factor Analysis.

COALITIONS

Originally a word for union or fusion, the term *coalition* came in the eighteenth century to mean a temporary alliance of political parties. In modern social science, the meaning has broadened to include any combination of two or more social actors formed for mutual advantage in contention with other actors in the same social system. In most contemporary theories of coalition formation, it is taken for granted that the principles governing coalition formation are not much affected by the size of the actors, who may be small children or large nations, but are significantly affected by the number of actors in the system. In the sociological and social-psychological literature, interest has focused on coalition formation in social systems containing three actors, commonly known as *triads*, and on the factors that influence the formation of coalitions in that configuration. Coalitions in triads have certain properties that are very useful in the analysis of power relationships in and among organizations. Moreover, tetrads, pentads, and higher-order social systems can be viewed for analytical purposes as clusters of linked triads. In the literature of political science, the principal topic has been the formation of electoral and legislative coalitions in multi-party and two-party systems.

The social science perspective on coalitions derives from two major sources: the formal sociology of Georg Simmel (1902) and the *n*-person game theory of John Von Neumann and Oskar Morgenstern (1944). Simmel had the fundamental insight that conflict and cooperation are opposite sides of the same coin so that no functioning social system can be free of internal conflicts or of internal coalitions. Simmel also proposed that the geometry of social relationships is independent of the size of the actors in a social system but heavily influenced by their number; that social systems are held together by internal differentiation; that relationships between superiors and subordinates are intrinsically ambivalent; that groups of three tend to develop coalitions of two against one; and that, in stable social systems, coalitions shift continually from one situation to another.

While the basic ideas are attributable to Simmel, the analytical framework for most of the empirical research on coalitions that has been undertaken so far is that of Von Neumann (and his collaborator Oskar Morgenstern). Any social interaction involving costs and rewards can be described as an *n*-person game. In two-person games, the problem for each player is to find a winning strategy, but in games with three or more players, the formation of a winning coalition is likely to be the major strategic objective. The theory distinguishes between zero-sum games, in which one side loses whatever the other side gains, and non-zero-sum games with more complex payoff schedules. And it provides a mathematical argument for the equal division of gains among coalition partners, the gist of which is that any essential member of a winning coalition who is offered less than an equal share of the joint winnings can be induced to desert the coalition and join an adversary who offers more favorable terms. In the various experimental and real-life settings in which coalitions are studied, this solution has only limited application, but game theory continues to furnish the vocabulary of observation.

Some recent writers identify coaliton theory as that branch of game theory involving zero-sum games with more than two players and game theory as a branch of rational choice theory (Wood and McLean 1995). The basic assumption of rational choice—by voters, lobbyists, legislators, and managers—has been vigorously attacked (see Green and Shapiro 1994) and as strongly defended (Nicholson 1992, among many others). The critics argue that rational choice theory is essentially self-contained; its elaborate intellectual apparatus does not provide a clear view of political action. The defenders say, in effect, that judgment should be withheld.

Meanwhile, game theory (and its coalition branch) have been developing new ideas, largely based on the key concept of equilibrium. Equilibrium in a game is that condition in which none of the players have incentives to deviate from their chosen strategies. It is called *Nash equilibrium*, after its formulator (Nash 1951), and has been extended to include two interesting varieties: subgame perfect equilibrium and Bayesian equilibrium. The former requires that rational players refrain from incredible threats. The latter replaces the players' initial knowledge about payoff schedules with a set of probabilistic statements, subject to change by additional information. Another interesting innovation is the concept of *nested games* (Tsebelis 1990), in which the apparent irrationality of players' moves in a given game is a rational consequence of their concurrent involvement in other games.

Modern empirical work on coalitions falls into two major categories: (1) experimental studies of outcomes in games played by small groups—games that have been devised by the experimenter to test hypotheses about the choice of coalition partners and the division of coalition winnings under specified conditions, and (2) observational studies of coalitions in the real world. Stimulated by the publication of divergent theories of coalition formation (Mills 1953; Caplow 1956; Gamson 1961) in the *American Sociological Review*, coalition experiments became part of the standard repertory of social psychology in the 1960s and continue to be so to this day (Bottom, Eavey, and Miller 1996). A great deal has been learned about how the choice of coalition partners and the division of coalition winnings are affected by variations in game rules and player attributes. Much, although by no means all, of this work has focused on three-player games in which the players have unequal resources and any coalition is a winning coalition, the distribution of resources falling into one of three types: (1) A>B>C, A<B+C; (2) A=B, B>C, A<B+C; and (3) A>B, B=C, A<B+C. With respect to the choice of coalition partners, the central question has been whether subjects will consistently choose the partner with whom they can form the minimum winning coalition, or the stronger partner, or the partner who offers the more favorable terms, or the partner who resembles themselves in attributes or ideology. The general finding is that each of these results can be produced with fair consistency by varying the rules of the experimental game. The division of winnings between coalition partners has attracted even more attention than the choice of partners. The question has been whether winnings will be divided on the principle of *equality*, as suggested by game theory; or of *parity*, proportionate to the contribution of each partner, as suggested by exchange theory; or at an intermediate ratio established by *bargaining*. Although many experimenters have claimed that one or the other of these principles is primary, their collective results seem to show that all three modes of division occur spontaneously and that subjects may be tilted one way or another by appropriate instructions. Additional nuances of coalition formation have been explored in games having more than three players, variable payoffs, or incomplete information. Non-zero-sum games and sequential games with continually changing weights have been particularly instructive. The findings readily lend themselves to mathematical

expression (Kahan and Rapoport 1984; Prasnikar and Roth 1992).

The explicit application of coalition analysis to real-life situations began with William Riker's (1962) study of political coalitions in legislative bodies; he discerned a consistent preference for minimal winning coalitions and emphasized the pivotal role of weak factions. Theodore Caplow (1968) showed how the developing theory of coalitions in triads could be used to analyze conflict and competition in nuclear and extended families, organizational hierarchies, primate groups, revolutionary movements, international relations, and other contexts. The initial development of observational studies was relatively slow, compared with the proliferation of laboratory studies, but there were some notable achievements, particularly in family dynamics and international relations, where coalition models fit gracefully into earlier lines of investigation. Coalition theory was also applied, albeit in a more tentative way, to work groups, intra- and interorganizational relationships, litigation and criminal justice, class and ethnic conflict, and military strategy. However, the bulk of empirical research after 1980 was undertaken by political scientists and focused on international relations, with particular emphasis on nuclear deterrence (Powell 1990) and on the formation of legislative coalitions (Laver and Schofield 1990; Shepsle 1991; Krebbiel 1991; Cox and McCubbins 1993). Some investigators have shifted their focus from coalition formation to coalition breaking (Lupia and Strom 1995; Horowitz and Just 1995; Mershon 1996), which appears to follow a quite different dynamic. Economists have studied customs unions, trading blocs, and other forms of economic combination (Burbidge et al. 1995; Yi 1996). But with a few notable exceptions (e. g. Lemieux 1997), sociologists have tended to neglect the study of coalitions since the promising beginnings of the 1970s.

Whatever the field of application, the examination of coalitions, especially the simple coalition of two against one, provides a key to the social geometry of innumerable situations involving conflict, competition, and cooperation. In nearly every conflict, each of the contending parties seeks the support of relevant third parties, and the side that gains that support is likely to prevail. In very many competitive situations, the outcome is eventually decided by the formation of a winning coalition. And any system of cooperation that involves

a status order must rely on the routine formation of coalitions of superiors against subordinates and be able to counter coalitions of subordinates against superiors.

All of these situations are susceptible to coalitions of two against one, which tend to transform strength into weakness and weakness into strength. Under many conditions, in the first of the triads mentioned above (A>B>C, A<B+C), both A and B will prefer C as a coalition partner; his initial weakness ensures his inclusion in the winning coalition. When A>B, B=C, A<B+C, B and C will often prefer each other as coalition partners; A's initial strength ensures his exclusion from the winning coalition. When A=B, A>C, C's initial weakness again makes him a likely winner. The first purpose of any hierarchy must be to restrain in one way or another the inherent tendency of subordinates to combine against superiors. Although force and ritual are often deployed for this purpose, the stability of complex status orders depends on certain interactive effects that appear in triads with overlapping membership, called *linked triads*. In such clusters, the choice of coalition partners in one triad influences the choices made in other triads. The natural rules that seem to govern the formation of coalitions in linked hierarchical triads are that a coalition adversary in one triad may not be chosen as a coalition partner in another triad, and that actors offered a choice between incompatible winning coalitions will choose the one in the higher-ranking triad. The net effect favors conservative coalitions of superiors against subordinates without entirely suppressing revolutionary coalitions of subordinates against superiors.

Cross-cutting the coalition preferences that arise from unequal distributions of power and resources are preferences based on affinity, compatibility, and prior experience with potential partners. These other bases of coalition formation are conspicuous in intimate groups such as the family, where same-sex coalitions alternate with same-generation coalitions.

The study of coalitions in nuclear families is particularly rewarding because the distribution of power in the triad of mother-father-child changes so dramatically as the child grows, and because same-sex coalitions are differently valued than cross-sex coalitions. The initial distribution of power between husband and wife is always transformed by the arrival of children; most cultures encourage certain patterns, such as the Oedipus and Electra complexes dear to Freudians: coalitions of mother and son against father and of father and daughter against mother. Research on the contemporary American family suggests that parental coalitions are quite durable, both mother-daughter and mother-son coalitions against the father are very common, father-daughter coalitions against the mother much less so, and father-son coalitions against the mother comparatively rare. Sibling coalitions are most likely among same-sex siblings adjacent in age. Sibling aggression is endemic in families of this type, especially in the presence of parents. An interesting study by Richard Felson and Natalie Russo (1988) suggests that parents usually take side with the weaker child in these incidents, and this leads to more frequent aggression by the excluded child. There are very few family conflicts that cannot be instructively described by a coalition model.

The application of coalition theory to international relations was particularly rewarding with respect to the "strategic triangle" of the United States, China, and the Soviet Union during the Cold War era of 1950–1985. In one of the many studies that have examined the internal dynamics of this triad, James Hsiung (1987) concluded that China as the weak player in this triad benefitted much more than either of the superpowers from the various coalitional shifts that occurred over time, as would be theoretically expected in a triad of this type (A=B, B>C, A<B+C). A study by Caplow (1989) explained the failure of peace planning in 1815, 1919, and 1945, by showing how efforts to put an end to the international war system were undermined by the formation of coalitions to prevent the domination of the peacekeeping organization by the strongest of the victorious powers. Many older studies of international balances of power visualize international relations as a game in which the first priority of every major player is to block the domination of the entire system by any other player. Frank C. Zagare's (1984) analysis of the Geneva Conference on Vietnam in 1954 as a three-player game compared the preference schedules of the three players and showed how they combined to produce the unexpected outcome of the negotiations.

Both family dynamics and international relations in peacetime exemplify situations of continuous conflict, wherein relationships have long histories and are expected to persist indefinitely, and the opposition of interests is qualified by the necessity for cooperation. The choice of coalition partners and the division of winnings is strongly influenced by the past transactions of the parties and by the fact that payoffs are not completely predictable. Continuous conflict triads with $A>B>C$, $A<B+C$ often alternate the three possible coalitions according to circumstances: the *conservative coalition* AB reinforces the existing status order; the *revolutionary coalition* BC challenges it; and the *improper coalition* AC subverts it.

Episodic conflicts, by contrast, involve discrete zero-sum games played under strict rules. The passage of any measure in a legislative body necessarily involves the formation of a coalition. Even when one party has a solid majority, its members will seldom be in complete agreement on an issue. The formation of a coalition for the passage of a specific measure usually involves hard bargaining and payoffs negotiated in advance. Under these conditions, the tendency to minimize costs by forming the minimal winning coalitions is very strong. When $A>B>C$, $A<B+C$, a BC coalition is highly probable. Empirical studies of legislative voting bear this out, although more than minimal coalitions also occur, for various reasons.

The resolution of disputes by civil and criminal litigation is another variety of episodic conflict that can be studied as a coalition process. Donald Black (1989) explored the triad of judge and courtroom adversaries and discovered a clear tendency for judges to favor the litigant to whom they are socially closer, ordinarily the litigant of higher status—a tacit conservative coalition. But in forms of dispute resolution where the third party is less authoritative, the weaker adversary may be favored. Marital counselors, for example, often side with wives against husbands, and ombudsmen and other relatively powerless mediators normally incline toward the weaker party.

In terminal conflicts, the object is the permanent destruction of adversaries, and the formation of coalitions is a delicate matter. In the triad where $A>B>C$, $A<B+C$, a successful BC coalition that destroys A leaves C at the mercy of B. Indeed, any winning coalition is hazardous for the weaker

partner. A fragile peace can be maintained if A>B>C and A=B+C; the BC coalition forms as a matter of course, creating what is known as a balance of power. This has been the key configuration in European affairs for the past several centuries. The balance breaks down with any significant shift in the relative power of the parties; for example, if A grows stronger than the BC coalition, it will be tempted to conquer them. If B becomes equal to A, an AB coalition may be tempted to attack and partition C. If C grows stronger and the triad assumes the form A>B, B=C, B+C>A, the formation of a BC coalition to overthrow A is likely. In the eighteenth century, the breakdown of a balance of power led to war without delay. Under current conditions, the breakdown of a balance of power among major industrialized states does not involve an automatic resort to arms, but in several regional arenas, such as the Middle East, the old mechanism is still intact.

Terminal conflicts occur also within nations as coups, resistance movements, and revolutions. One common pattern is the urban uprising against a dictatorial regime, in which the players are the government, the army, and the populace. If the army continues to support the government and is willing to fire on the populace, the uprising fails, as in China in 1989. If the army sides with the populace, the government is overthrown, as in Indonesia in 1998. Often the issue is undecided until the moment when the troops confront the demonstrators. At a more fundamental level, successful revolutions require a coalition of formerly separate factions against the ruling group.

Every organization generates both internal and boundary coalitions. Internal coalitions are activated whenever persons or groups of unequal status interact before witnesses. In general, the presence of a high-status witness reinforces the authority of a superior, while the presence of a low-status witness reduces it; examined in detail, these catalytic effects are delicate and precise. Boundary coalitions occur whenever one organization has permanent relations with another. Their respective agents must form a coalition with each other to perform their functions, and that coalition pits them both against their own colleagues, always with interesting consequences.

In a long-term perspective, the three bodies of coalition studies, theoretical, experimental, and observational, have developed unevenly. The theories are elaborate and elegant. The experimental studies have explored nearly every possibility suggested by the theories, run down every lead, manipulated every variable. But in sociology, as distinct from political science and economics, the observational studies have scarcely tapped the rich possibilities suggested by the available theories. The most important work remains to be done.

(SEE ALSO: *Decision-Making Theory and Research*)

REFERENCES

Adams, Wesley J. 1985 "The Missing Triad: The Case of Two-Child Families." *Family Process* 24:409–413.

Black, Donald 1989 *Sociological Justice*. New York: Oxford University Press.

Bonacich, Phillip, Oscar Grusky, and Mark Peyrot 1985 "Family Coalitions: A New Approach and Method." *Social Psychological Quarterly* 44:42–50.

Bottom, William P., Cheryl L. Eavey, and Gary J. Miller 1996 "Coalitional Integrity as a Constraint on the Power of Agenda Setters," *Journal of Conflict Resolution* 40:2:298–319.

Burbidge, John B., James A. DePater, Gordon M. Myers, and Abhjit Sengupta 1997 "A Coalition-Formation Approach to Equilibrium Federations and Trading Blocs" *American Economic Review* 87:940–56.

Caplow, Theodore 1956 "A Theory of Coalitions in the Triad." *American Sociological Review* 21:480–493.

—— 1968 *Two Against One: Coalitions in Triads*. Englewood Cliffs, N.J.: Prentice-Hall.

—— 1989 *Peace Games*. Middletown, Conn.: Wesleyan University Press.

Felsen, Richard B. and Natalie Russo 1988 "Parental Punishment and Sibling Aggression." *Social Psychology Quarterly* 51:1:11–18.

Gamson, William A. 1961 "A Theory of Coalition Formation." *American Sociological Review* 26:565–573.

Green, D.P. and I. Shapiro 1994 *Pathologies of Rational Choice Theory*. New Haven, Conn.: Yale University Press.

Horowitz, John K. and Richard E. Just 1995 "Political Coalition Breaking and Sustainability of Policy Reform." *Journal of Development Economics* 47:271–286.

Hsiung, James C. 1987 "Internal Dynamics in the Sino-Soviet-U.S. Triad," In I.J. Kim, ed., *The Strategic Triangle*. New York: Paragon.

Kahan, James P., and Amnon Rapoport 1984 *Theories of Coalition Formation.* Hillsdale, NJ: Lawrence Erlbaum Associates.

Komorita, S.S., and Charles E. Miller 1986 "Bargaining Strength as a Function of Coalition Alternatives." *Journal of Personality and Social Psychology* 51:325–332.

Lemieux, Vincent 1997 "Reseaux et Coalitions." *L'Annee Sociologique* 47:1:55–71.

Lupia, Arthur, and Kaare Strom 1995 "Coalition Termination and the Strategic Timing of Parliamentary Elections." *American Political Science Review* 89:648–665.

Mershon, Carol 1996 "The Costs of Coalition: Coalition Theories and Italian Governments." *American Political Science Review* 90:3:534–554.

Miller, Charles E., and R. Crandall 1980 "Experimental Research on the Social Psychology of Bargaining and Coalition Formation." In R. Paulus, ed., *Psychology of Group Influence.* Hillsdale, N.J.: Lawrence Erlbaum Associates.

Mills, Theodore M. 1953 "Power Relations in Three-Person Groups." *American Sociological Review* 18:351–357.

Murnighan, J. Keith 1978 "Models of Coalition Behavior: Game Theoretic, Social Psychological, and Political Perspectives." *Psychological Bulletin* 85:1130–1153.

Nail, Paul, and Steven G. Cole 1985 "Three Theories of Coalition Behavior: A Probabilistic Extension." *British Journal of Social Psychology* 24:181–190.

Nash, John 1951 "Non-cooperative games." *Annals of Mathematics* 54:286–95.

Nicholson, Michael 1992 *Rationality and the Analysis of International Conflict.* Cambridge, U.K.: Cambridge University Press.

Prasnikar, V., and A. E. Roth 1992 "Considerations of fairness and strategy: Experimental evidence from sequential games." *Quarterly Journal of Economics* 107:865–868.

Riker, William H. 1962 *The Theory of Political Coalitions.* New Haven, CT: Yale University Press.

Rodgers, Joseph Lee, and Vaida D. Thompson 1986 "Towards a General Framework of Family Structure: A Review of Theory-Based Empirical Research." *Population and Environment* 8:143–171.

Rose, Irene Kathryn 1986 "Testing Coalition Theory in the Great Gatsby and the Rabbit Trilogy." Ph.D. diss., University of Oklahoma.

Russo, Richard B., and Natalie Russo 1988 "Parental Punishment and Sibling Aggression." *Social Psychological Quarterly* 51:11–18.

Sened, Itai 1996 "A Model of Coalition Formation: Theory and Evidence." *Journal of Politics* 58:2:350–372.

Simmel, Georg 1902 "The Number of Members as Determining the Sociological Form of the Group." *American Journal of Sociology* 8:1–46; 158–196.

Tsebilis, G. 1990 *Nested Games; Rational Choice in Comparative Politics.* Berkeley: University of California Press.

Von Neumann, John and Oskar Morgenstern 1944 *Theory of Games and Economic Behavior.* 2d ed. Princeton, N.J.: Princeton University Press.

Wood, Stewart, and Iain McLean 1995 "Recent Work in Game Theory and Coalition Theory." *Political Studies* 43:703–717.

Yi, Sang-Seung 1996 "Endogenous Formation of Customs Unions under Imperfect Competition." *Journal of International Economics* 41:1–2; 153–177.

Zagare, Frank C. 1984 *Game Theory: Concepts and Applications.* Beverly Hills, Calif.: Sage Publications.

THEODORE CAPLOW

COGNITIVE CONSISTENCY THEORIES

Cognitive consistency theories have their origins in the principles of Gestalt psychology, which suggests that people seek to perceive the environment in ways that are simple and coherent (Köhler 1929). Cognitive consistency theories have their beginnings in a number of seemingly unrelated research areas (Eagly and Chaiken 1993). Early consistency theorists drew upon theories of conflict (Lewin 1935; Miller 1944), memory (Miller 1956), and the intolerance for ambiguity by those with an authoritarian personality (Adorno, Frenkel-Brunswick, Levinson, and Stanford 1950). According to Newcomb (1968a), social scientists should not have been surprised at the rise of cognitive consistency theories. He points to a truism that in any field of scientific inquiry, there is an inevitable movement from description of the elements of the field, to understanding the relationships between them. At the heart of cognitive consistency theories is the assumption that people are motivated to seek coherent attitudes, thoughts, beliefs, values, behaviors, and feelings. If these are inconsistent, they will produce a "tension state" in the individual, and motivate the individual to reduce this tension. Individuals reduce this tension, according to consistency theories, by making their relevant cognitions consistent.

Cognitive consistency theories gained tremendous popularity in the social sciences in the 1950s, and generated hundreds of studies. Toward the end of the 1960s, however, research interest waned. In 1968, Abelson and collegues published a massive handbook, entitled *Theories of Cognitive Consistency: A Sourcebook*. The book was a thorough chronicle of cognitive consistency theories, and it addressed these theories from virtually any angle the reader could imagine. Ironically, the scholarly detail in which the editors and authors carefully described their research seemed to have been the death knell of cognitive consistency theories. Virtually no research on cognitive consistency theories took place during the 1970s.

With the end of the 1960s, theories of behavior that centered around motivational and affective forces (which certainly described cognitive consistency theories) were "out of vogue" with researchers. Many point to the simultaneous rise of social cognition approaches in general, and attribution theory in particular as helping to divert interest from cognitive consistency theories. Research on cognitive consistency theories was supplanted by more complex (some believed) "cold cognition" approaches that strictly dealt with how cognitive processes work together, not accounting for "hot" forces such as feelings and motivation.

Theories of cognitive consistency theory did not die, they just went away for a while. Abelson (1983) noted the reemergence of cognitive consistency theories in the early 1980s with the observation that authors were beginning to write about social cognition theories in light of the renewed interest in the nature of affect (e.g., Fiske 1982; Hamilton 1981). Toward the end of the 1980s, researchers began to take a closer look at the influence of affect on cognitive processes (e.g., Forgas 1990; Isen 1987; Schwarz 1990). This change was precipitated by the development of several theoretical perspectives concerning the nature and structure of emotion (e.g., Frijda 1988; Ortony, Clore, and Collins 1988). In an influential article, Zanna and Rempel (1988) argued that attitudes toward different attitude objects may be more or less determined by affective, rather than cognitive, sources. Consistency theories were not only back, they were thriving (Harary 1983).

This chapter will discuss five major theories of cognitive consistency that have had the most impact on the behavioral sciences. They are (in no particular order) balance theory (Heider 1946, 1958), strain toward symmetry (Newcomb 1953, 1968b), congruency theory (Osgood and Tannenbaum 1955), affective-cognitive consistency model (Rosenberg 1956), and finally, what Eagly and Chaiken (1993) refer to as the "jewel in the consistency family crown," (p. 456) cognitive dissonance theory (Festinger 1957).

BALANCE THEORY

The earliest consistency theory is Heider's balance theory (1946, 1958). This approach is concerned with an individual's perceptions of the relationships between himself (p) and (typically) two other elements in a triadic structure. In Heider's formulation, the other elements are often another person (o) and another object (e.g., an issue, object, a value). The attitudes in the structure are designated as either positive or negative. The goal of assessing the structure of a triad is to ascertain whether the relationships (attitudes) between the actors and the other elements are balanced, or consistent. According to Heider (1958), a balanced triad occurs when all the relationships are positive, or two are negative and one is positive (i.e., two people have a negative attitude toward an issue, but they like each other), and the elements in the triad fit together with no stress. Imbalance occurs when these outcomes are not achieved (i.e., all three relationships are negative, or you have a negative attitude toward an issue that your friend favors). Heider assumed that people prefer balanced states to imbalanced ones, because imbalance results in tension and feelings of unpleasantness. Balance, according to Heider, is rewarding.

Interestingly, imbalanced states can also be rewarding and exciting. Heider said that sometimes balance can be "boring" and that "The tension produced by unbalanced situations often has a pleasing effect on our thinking and aesthetic feelings" (1958, p. 180). In other words, imbalance stimulates us to think further, to solve the problem, to imagine, and to understand the mystery of the imbalance. According to balance theory, there are three ways to restore balance to an imbalanced triad: (1) one may change one's attitude toward either the object or the other person, in order to restore balance; (2) one might distort reality to perceive that the relationships are balanced (e.g., your friend doesn't really favor something you dislike, she really dislikes it); and (3) one might cognitively differentiate the relationship one has with a friend, so that the friend's opposing attitude toward something one favors is separated from one's positive attitude toward the friend as a person (e.g., you might compartmentalize a friend's opposite political views apart from your attitude toward her, in order to maintain your friendship and maintain balance, in most other areas where she is concerned) (Eagly and Chaiken 1993).

A limitation of Heider's balance theory is that it did not account for the strength of attitudes between persons and objects in the triad. It merely categorized the relationships as either positive or negative, and it therefore assumed that tension that is produced by imbalance was objectively of the same strength and effect on the individuals in the triad. Because some attitudes are held with more conviction and are more meaningful and important to us, it stands to reason that triads that involve imbalance with such strongly-held attitudes ought to evoke more tension (Eagly and Chaiken 1993). Another shortcoming of the theory is that it only deals with relationships between three entities. To address this latter concern, Cartwright and Harary (1956) published a paper that nicely generalized Heider's theory to account for structures of any size.

STRAIN TOWARD SYMMETRY MODEL

Newcomb (1953, 1968b) suggested that there are three, rather than two types of balance relationships in a triad. First, a structure that does not motivate modification (or acceptance) is termed a "nonbalanced" structure. These situations are characterized by indifference. Here, disagreement with another individual about an issue or object does not arouse tension if that other individual is devalued (or otherwise not important). However, when the other person is valued (i.e., a friend or significant other), then agreement with him or her about an object results in a "positively balanced" structure, while disagreement results in a "positively imbalanced" structure. The term "positive" in the latter two types of structure denotes the valence of the relationship between p and o, who is a valued other. The important focus in Newcomb's approach is the relationship of o to p, and p's view of o as a valued person, and "suitability as a source of information, or support, or of influence concerning the object" (Newcomb 1968b, p. 50). Newcomb's experiments supported his idea that the tension that is aroused when p and o have strong attitudes in the structure is much greater than when their attitudes are held with little conviction. He also found that positively balanced situations are the most preferred structures, followed by nonbalanced structures, with the positively imbalanced situations being the least preferred.

CONGRUENCY THEORY

A particular advantage of Osgood and Tannenbaum's (1955; Tannenbaum 1968) congruency theory is its precision in assessing: 1) the strength of the relationships between p and o, 2) the strength of the motivation to change an incongruent triad, and 3) the degree of attitude change that is necessary to balance a triad. Another advantage of this theory is that, like Newcomb's approach, it takes into account the strength of the attitudes of p and o in evaluating the degree of incongruity in the structure. Osgood and Tannenbaum discuss the Heider triad in terms of p, another individual, termed the source (s) and s's attitude (termed an "assertion") toward another object or concept (x). According to the theory, attitudes can be quantified along a seven-unit evaluative scale, from extremely negative (-3) to neutral (0) to extremely positive ($+3$).

When p's attitude toward s and x are positive, and s's assertion is equally strong and of the same valence, there is a "congruous" structure to the triad. There is no motivation to change one's attitude toward the object or toward the source. When p's attitude toward s is positive, and p has an equally positive attitude toward x that s later negatively evaluates, an incongruous structure is established. In this situation, p is motivated to change his or her attitude toward s, or x, or both, in the direction of congruity. Consider the following example. If p's attitude toward s is a $+2$, and p's attitude toward x is a -2, the structure would be congruent if s's assessment is a -2. If, however, the assessment is a $+2$, the structure is imbalanced. In this case, p's attitude toward either x or s needs to change four units to make the triad congruent. Of course, if the relationships are weaker, the degree of attitude change to make the triad congruent is that much less (by the exact amount denoted in the quantitative calculation of all the relations of p, s, and x). Osgood and Tannenbaum also argued that strongly held attitudes would be less likely to be modified in incongruent triads. This was supported in subsequent research (Tannenbaum 1968).

AFFECTIVE-COGNITIVE CONSISTENCY MODEL

This approach suggests that people seek consistency in order to satisfy a general motivation toward simplicity in cognition, and/or to adhere to norms, traditions, customs, or values that reinforce consistency in one's cognitions and behavior (Rosenberg 1956, 1968). Another interesting twist on the consistency approach is that in the affective-cognitive consistency model, Rosenberg (1956, 1968) proposed that people are more motivated to maintain cognitive consistency so that *other people* perceive that they are consistent. In other words, while the individual may occasionally feel some tension as a result of inconsistency, other people find the inconsistency more aversive, because it represents a conflict for those around the individual. Specifically, if o has a positive attitude toward p, but p dislikes x, which o likes, o is caught between being friendly with, and avoiding, p. In this model, o feels tension at this conflict, and must reduce the tension by changing attitudes toward p (e.g., increasing attraction toward p, which would thereby outweigh any conflict with p's negative attitude toward x) or toward x (e.g., o devalues x, so that p's dislike of x does not result in o feeling conflicted).

Rosenberg's model also considers the relationship between the individual, his or her values, and an attitude object. For example, consider that p also has various other important values, denoted as y1, y2, y3, etc. Rosenberg suggests that the p-x-y triad is just as important in understanding cognitive consistency as the traditional p-o-x triad. In the affective-cognitive consistency approach, we must consider p's attitudes toward each of his or her values, how p feels about x, and p's perception of the relationship between x and each of the values. When all or most of the p-x-y triads are consistent, the individual has achieved cognitive consistency. When most or all of the p-x-y triads are inconsistent, the individual experiences cognitive inconsistency.

The reason Rosenberg's approach is called the affective-cognitive consistency model is that it proposes that inconsistency results when one's feelings are inconsistent with one's beliefs. That is, when the way we think and feel about an object or person are at odds, we will modify one or both to make the attitude consistent. Thus, this model attempts to address consistency within one's own attitudes toward other people and objects, but also consistency in how one's value system relates to other people and objects. The model is also unique in suggesting that other people experience more tension as a result of one's own inconsistency. Generally speaking, the model has been supported by experiments (Rosenberg 1964), and is considered a very useful addition to the family of cognitive consistency theories.

COGNITIVE DISSONANCE THEORY

Of all the cognitive consistency theories, none has had more influence on researchers and subsequent theories than cognitive dissonance theory (Festinger 1957). A conservative estimate suggests that at least 1,000 articles have been published in which researchers present data bearing upon the theory and their own revisions of the theory (Cooper and Fazio 1984). Many agree with Jones's (1976) assessment that cognitive dissonance theory is "the most important development in social psychology to date" (p. x). Along the way, the theory has been hailed for its elegant simplicity, and its powerful range of utility (Collins 1992). It has also been criticized for its lack of specificity (Lord 1992; Schlenker 1992).

In formal terms, Festinger's theory states that two elements (behaviors or thoughts, or both) "...are in a dissonant relation if, considering these two alone, the obverse of one element would follow from the other" (1957, p. 13). Dissonance, then, refers to a negative arousal brought about by one's inconsistent thoughts or actions, or both. Essentially, this translates into the following assumptions. If one has opposing thoughts or behaviors, or both, this brings about an aversive state of tension, akin to a drive state like hunger or thirst. This tension motivates the individual to seek relief by eliminating the tension. The tension can be dissipated by changing: 1) either a thought or attitude to make it consonant with the opposing thought or behavior, or 2) one's behavior, to make it consonant with the opposing behavior or thought. Because it is often much easier to change one's thoughts rather than one's behaviors, these are typically the elements that get modified by the person in dissonance reduction.

As an example, Festinger (1957) talked about the dissonance experienced by most smokers at some point in their lives. Smokers engage in behavior (smoking) that is harmful to their health. This is at odds with our desire to avoid harming ourselves. This arouses tension in the individual. The smoker could reduce it by changing his or her behavior (quit smoking) or changing the way he or she thinks about the smoking behavior. As mentioned above, changing behavior is often more difficult than changing cognitions, and, as most smokers will affirm, quitting smoking is certainly no exception to this axiom. In this instance, Festinger suggests, smokers eliminate their dissonance by changing their thoughts about smoking. They may: 1) disbelieve the validity of the health consequences of smoking, or distort the information about smoking by thinking that smoking is only harmful if you smoke so many packs a day, or if you inhale cigar smoke, etc., or more fatalistically, 2) convince themselves that "we all die of something, and I might as well die doing something I enjoy." All of these changes in thoughts eliminate the dissonance for the smoker.

It should be noted that Festinger was not talking about logical inconsistencies. There are certainly conditions under which people think and do logically inconsistent things, yet feel no dissonance, or they feel dissonance, yet are not in a situation where a logical inconsistency is present. Festinger recognized what has become a truism in psychology, that a person's reaction to a stimulus is not a function of the objective properties of the stimulus itself, but rather the individual's *construal, or perception of*, that stimulus. This explains why the presence or absence of logical inconsistencies may or may not be accompanied by dissonance in an individual. The most important and reliable way to predict a person's behavior in a dissonance situation is to understand how he or she construes the potential dissonance arousing thoughts or behaviors, or both.

History. Cognitive dissonance theory came onto the scene in the 1950s when reinforcement theories of behavior were very dominant in virtually all areas of inquiry in psychology. According to reinforcement principles, behavior that is followed by a reward is more likely to be repeated. Behavior that is followed by a strong reward should be more likely to be learned and repeated than behavior followed by a weak (or no) reward. Reinforcement theory was such a simple yet very powerful principle that it seemed to explain virtually all behavior in any context. For that reason, it was extremely popular among behavioral scientists. An experiment by Festinger and Carlsmith (1959) showed that reinforcement theory was not the all-purpose theory it appeared to be. In their experiment, Festinger and Carlsmith (1959) had participants do boring tasks (i.e., turning pegs one-quarter turn on a cribbage board) for an hour. Participants randomly assigned to a control group were then given a short questionnaire in which they were asked to rate how much they enjoyed the task. In other conditions, the experimenter then told participants that his research assistant had not yet arrived for a different version of the experiment, and he asked the participant if he would do the research assistant's job of telling the next participant (in the hall, who was in reality a confederate) that he enjoyed the experiment tasks. This was, of course, a lie, because the tasks were boring. These participants were assigned to one of two conditions. Some were given $1 to tell the lie, and others were given $20 to tell the lie. After participants had told the lie and were leaving, the experimenter ran up to the participant, explaining that he forgot to have the participant complete the ratings of the attitudes toward the experiment tasks.

The experiment pitted reinforcement theory against the predictions made from dissonance theory. Reinforcement theory suggests that the participants who were given $20 should find the tasks more rewarding (pleasant), and should have a more positive attitude toward the tasks (and the experiment) than those only given a weak (or no) reward. Dissonance theory suggests that those in the control condition would feel no dissonance because they did a boring task, and would rate the tasks as such on the questionnaire. However, counter to intuition (and reinforcement theory) those in the $20 condition should feel little (or no) dissonance, because although they did boring tasks, and disliked the tasks, saying that the tasks were fun is not an inconsistent behavior if one has adequate justification ($20) for doing so. They could attribute their lying to the incentive, and they would not feel hypocritical. The $1 participants experienced significant dissonance because they did boring tasks, but yet they said they thought the tasks were fun. As Festinger and Carlsmith predicted, the $1 was an insufficient justification for the lie, so the dissonance remained unless the participants changed their attitudes toward the task, and convinced themselves (as shown in their ratings of the tasks) that maybe the tasks were *not* boring, and in fact, they rather enjoyed them! The results were precisely as predicted, and this paved the way for a flurry of research that tested the exciting, often dramatic, and counterintuitive predictions that arose from cognitive dissonance theory.

Alternate Versions of Dissonance Theory. Very soon after the publication of Festinger's theory, research revealed that the theory might need to be revised somewhat, to account for more of the data that were being published, which didn't quite fit with the theory. In one notable revision, one of Festinger's protegés, Aronson (1969) posited that the theory would be strengthened if it stated that dissonance would be most clearly aroused when the self-concept of the person is engaged. In other words, dissonance is stronger and more clearly evoked when the way we think about ourselves is at odds with our cognitions or behavior. This modification was supported by much subsequent research (Aronson 1980). Less an alternate version and more of a theoretical competitor, Bem's (1967) self-perception theory was the first major theory that offered a plausible account of the dissonance data, and pointed to different causal mechanisms. Unlike cognitive dissonance theory, Bem's approach did not invoke reference to hypothetical motivational processes, but rather tried to account for the person's behavior in terms of the stimuli present in the individual's environment and his or her related behavior. Bem's theory proposed that attitudinal change in dissonance experiments happens not due to an aversive tension (or other motivation), but due to a person's perceptions of his or her own behavior. Specifically, Bem said that people infer their attitudes from their actions, in much the same way that observers of our behavior infer the nature of our attitudes from our behavior. Attitude change occurs when their most recent behavior is different from their previous attitudes.

This behavioral approach to dissonance phenomena recasts the Festinger and Carlsmith experiment in a very different light. In a replication of the Festinger and Carlsmith study, Bem asked participants to listen to a tape describing a person named Bob, who did some boring motor tasks. Control condition participants then were asked to assess Bob's attitude toward the tasks. Other subjects then learned that Bob was given $1 or $20 to say to the next participant that the motor tasks were fun. Participants then listened to a recording of Bob enthusiastically telling a subsequent woman participant how enjoyable the motor tasks were. Participants were then asked to evaluate Bob's attitude toward the motor tasks. Those who were told that Bob was given $20 to tell the lie inferred that the only reason he told the lie was because he was paid a lot of money. They assumed that he didn't really have a positive attitude toward the motor tasks. Those who were told that Bob received $1 didn't think Bob had a good reason for lying, so his behavior (lying) told participants that Bob must really feel positively about the motor tasks. Control condition participants inferred that Bob negatively evaluated the motor tasks. As can be seen, these results are virtually identical to those obtained in the Festinger and Carlsmith experiment. Thus, according to self-perception, the Festinger and Carlsmith participants inferred their attitudes toward the boring tasks based on their recent behavior.

Subsequent research on self-perception theory was aimed at testing the self-perception theory contention that no arousal exists as a result of the dissonance situation. Zanna and Cooper (1976) found that arousal did indeed accompany counterattitudinal advocacy, so it was apparent that self-perception did not apply to all dissonance situations. Fazio, Zanna, and Cooper (1977) suggested that dissonance accounted for attitude change when behavior is truly counterattitudinal, but that self-perception can account for situations where behavior is only mildly counterattitudinal. For most researchers, this seems to have settled the debate about the situations to which each theory may be applied (Abelson 1983).

A final major revision was proposed by Cooper and Fazio (1984). They suggested that dissonance does not result from mere cognitive inconsistency, but only is evoked when the person feels personally responsible for causing an aversive event.

The theory suggests, then, that aversive consequences are necessary for dissonance to occur. In subsequent experiments, however, Aronson and his colleagues (Aronson, Fried, and Stone 1991) induced participants to make an educational video advocating the use of condoms for safe sex, to be shown in high schools. Then, the participant was subsequently reminded of situations in which he or she had not used condoms in the past. According to Cooper and Fazio, there should be no dissonance because the participant had not produced an aversive event, but rather, a positive one (advocating safe sex in an educational video). According to Aronson, however, the participant should feel dissonance because he or she was saying one thing and doing another (acting like a hypocrite). Aronson predicted that if dissonance was aroused in those hypocrites, they should be more likely to (if given the opportunity) take more free pamphlets and condoms at the end of the study, as a way of regaining consistency with their advocated position (i.e. they were making an effort to change their behavior to be consistent with their advocated message). Results showed that this is precisely what occurred. Subsequent research has demonstrated strong support for Aronson and colleagues' (1991) contention that the production of aversive consequences is not necessary to create dissonance (Harmon-Jones, Brehm, Greenberg, Simon, and Nelson 1996).

CURRENT STATUS OF COGNITIVE CONSISTENCY THEORIES

In the 1990s, cognitive consistency theories experienced a rebirth, primarily through renewed interest in cognitive dissonance theory (Aronson 1992). With the renewed interest in motivation, and the interaction of cognition and affect, researchers are once again taking up the questions (and there are many) left unanswered by earlier cognitive dissonance researchers. For example, while research has shown that dissonance evokes (as Festinger theorized) psychological discomfort (in comparison to physiological arousal), researchers know little about what occurs between the onset of the psychological discomfort and the start of the discomfort reduction process (Elliot and Devine 1994). Some have called for an effort to more fully explicate the conditions under which dissonance occurs, and when it does not occur (Aronson 1992), and researchers are beginning to

do just that (Shultz and Lepper 1996). Cognitive consistency theories have been a cornerstone of psychology for over four decades, and while they receded into the background in the 1970s, they are experiencing a strong resurgence of empirical and theoretical interest.

REFERENCES

Abelson, R. P. 1983 "Whatever Became of Consistency Theory?" *Personality and Social Psychology Bulletin* 9:37–54.

——, E. Aronson, W. J. McGuire, T. M. Newcomb, M. J. Rosenberg, and P. H. Tannenbaum (eds.) 1968 *Cognitive Consistency Theories: A Sourcebook.* Chicago, Ill.: Rand McNally.

Adorno, T. W., E. Frenkel-Brunswick, D. J. Levinson, and R. N. Sanford 1950 *The Authoritarian Personality.* New York: Harper and Row.

Aronson, E. 1969 "The Theory of Cognitive Dissonance: A Current Perspective." In L.Berkowitz, ed., *Advances in Experimental Social Psychology*, Vol. 4. New York: Academic Press.

—— 1980 "Persuasion via Self-Justification: Large Commitments for Small Rewards." In L. Festinger, ed., *Retrospections on Social Psychology*. New York: Oxford University Press.

—— 1992 "The Return of the Repressed: Dissonance Theory Makes a Comeback."*Psychological Inquiry* 3 (4):303–311.

——, C. Fried, and J. Stone 1991 "AIDS Prevention and Dissonance: A New Twist on an Old Theory." *American Journal of Public Health* 81:1636–1638.

Bem, D. J. 1967 "Self-perception: An Alternative Interpretation of Cognitive Dissonance Phenomena." *Psychological Review* 74 (3):183–200.

Cartwright, D., and F. Harary 1956 "Structural Balance: A Generalization of Heider's Theory." *Psychological Review* 63:277–293.

Collins, B. 1992 "Texts and Subtexts." *Psychological Inquiry* 3 (4):315–320.

Cooper, J., and R. H. Fazio 1984 "A New Look at Dissonance Theory." In L. Berkowitz, ed., *Advances in Experimental Social Psychology*, Vol. 17. New York: Academic Press.

Eagly, A. H., and S. Chaiken 1993 *The Psychology of Attitudes.* New York: Harcourt, Brace, Jovanovich.

Elliot, A. J., and P. G. Devine 1994 "On the Motivational Nature of Cognitive Dissonance: Dissonance as Psychological Discomfort." *Journal of Personality and Social Psychology* 67(3):382–394.

Fazio, R. H., M. P. Zanna, and J. Cooper 1977 "Dissonance and Self-Perception: An Integrative View of Each Theory's Proper Domain of Application." *Journal of Experimental Social Psychology* 13:464–479.

Festinger, L. 1957 *A Theory of Cognitive Dissonance*. Palo Alto, Calif.: Stanford University Press.

——, and M. Carlsmith 1959 "Cognitive Consequences of Forced Compliance." *Journal of Abnormal and Social Psychology* 58:203–210.

Fiske, S. T. 1982 "Schema-Triggered Affect: Applications to Social Perception." In M. S. Clark and S. T. Fiske, eds., *Affect and Cognition*. Hillsdale, N.J.: Erlbaum.

Forgas, J. P. 1990 "Affect and Social Judgments: An Introductory Review." In J. P. Forgas, ed., *Emotion and Social Judgments*. Oxford: Pergamon Press.

Frijda, N. H. 1988 "The Laws of Emotion." *American Psychologist* 43:349–358.

Hamilton, D. L. 1981 "Illusory Correlation as a Basis for Stereotyping." In D. L. Hamilton, ed., *Cognitive Processes in Stereotyping and Intergroup Behavior*. Hillsdale, N.J.: Erlbaum.

Harary, F. 1983 "Consistency Theory is Alive and Well." *Personality and Social Psychology Bulletin* 9:60–64.

Harman-Jones, E., J. Brehm, J. Greenberg, L. Simon, and D. E. Nelson 1996 "Evidence that the Production of Dissonance is Not Necessary to Create Cognitive Dissonance." *Journal of Personality and Social Psychology* 70:5–16.

Heider, F. 1946 "Attitudes and Cognitive Organizations." *Journal of Psychology* 21:107–112.

—— 1958 *The Psychology of Interpersonal Relations*. Hillsdale, N.J.: Erlbaum.

Isen, A. M. 1987 "Positive Affect, Cognitive Processes, and Social Behavior." In L. Berkowitz, ed., *Advances in Experimental Social Psychology*, Vol. 20. New York: Academic Press.

Köhler, W. 1929 *Gestalt Psychology*. New York: Liveright.

Lewin, K. 1935 *A Dynamic Theory of Personality*. New York: McGraw-Hill.

Lord, C. G. 1992 "Was Cognitive Dissonance Theory a Mistake?" *Psychological Inquiry* 3 (4):339–342.

Miller, G. A. 1956 "The Magical Number Seven Plus or Minus Two: Some Limits on Our Capacity for Processing Information." *Psychological Review* 63:81–97.

Miller, N. E. 1944 "Experimental Studies of Conflict." In J. Hunt, ed., *Personality and the Behavioral Disorders*, Vol. 1. New York: Ronald Press.

Newcomb, T. M. 1953 "An Approach to the Study of Communicative Acts." *Psychological Review* 60:393–404.

—— 1968a "Introduction." In R. P. Abelson, E. Aronson, W. J. McGuire, T. M. Newcomb, M. J. Rosenberg, and P. H. Tannenbaum, eds., *Cognitive Consistency Theories: A Sourcebook*. Chicago, Ill.: Rand McNally.

—— 1968b "Interpersonal Balance." In R. P. Abelson, E. Aronson, W. J. McGuire, T. M. Newcomb, M. J. Rosenberg, and P. H. Tannenbaum, eds., *Cognitive Consistency Theories: A Sourcebook*. Chicago, Ill.: Rand McNally.

Ortony, A., G. L. Clore, and A. Collins 1988 *The Cognitive Structure of Emotions*. New York: Cambridge University Press.

Osgood, C. E., and P. H. Tannenbaum 1955 "The Principle of Congruity in the Prediction of Attitude Change." *Psychological Review* 62:42–55.

Rosenberg, M. J. 1956 "Cognitive Structure and Attitudinal Affect." *Journal of Abnormal and Social Psychology* 53:367–372.

—— 1964 "A Structural Theory of Attitude Dynamics." In E. E. Sampson, ed., *Approaches, Contexts, and Problems of Social Psychology*. Englewood Cliffs, N.J.: Prentice-Hall.

—— 1968 "Hedonism, Inauthenticity, and Other Goads Toward Expansion of a Consistency Theory." In R. P. Abelson, E. Aronson, W. J. McGuire, T. M. Newcomb, M. J. Rosenberg, and P. H. Tannenbaum, eds., *Cognitive Consistency Theories: A Sourcebook*. Chicago, Ill.: Rand McNally.

Schlenker, B. R. 1992 "Of Shape Shifters and Theories." *Psychological Inquiry* 3 (4):342–344.

Schultz, T. R., and M. R. Lepper 1996 "Cognitive Dissonance Reduction as Constraint Satisfaction." *Psychological Review* 103 (2):219–240.

Schwarz, N. 1990 "Feelings as Information: Informational and Motivational Functions of Affective States." In R. Sorrentino and E. T. Higgins, eds., *Handbook of Motivation and Cognition*, Vol. 2. New York: Guilford.

Tannenbaum, P. H. 1968 "The Congruity Principle: Retrospective Reflections and Recent Research." In R. P. Abelson, E. Aronson, W. J. McGuire, T. M. Newcomb, M. J. Rosenberg, and P. H. Tannenbaum, eds., *Cognitive Consistency Theories: A Sourcebook*. Chicago, Ill.: Rand McNally.

Zanna, M. P., and J. Cooper 1976 "Dissonance and the Attribution Process." In J. H. Harvey, W. J. Ickes, and R. F. Kidd, eds., *New Directions in Attribution Research*. Hillsdale, N.J.: Erlbaum.

Zanna, M.P., and J. K. Rempel, 1988 "Attitudes: A New Look at an Old Concept." In D. Bar-Tal and A.

Kruglanski, eds., *The Social Psychology of Knowledge*. Cambridge, Eng.: Cambridge University Press.

TODD D. NELSON

COGNITIVE DISSONANCE THEORY

See Cognitive Consistency Theories; Social Psychology.

COHABITATION

See Alternative Life-Styles; Courtship.

COHORT ANALYSIS

See Cohort Perspectives; Longitudinal Research; Quasi-Experimental Research Design.

COHORT PERSPECTIVES

The birth cohort, or set of people born in approximately the same period of time, has a triple reference as an analytical tool in sociology: (1) to cohorts of people who are *aging* and succeeding each other in particular eras of history; (2) to the *age composition* of the population and its changes; and (3) to the interplay between cohorts of people and the age-differentiated *roles and structures* of society. Diverse sociological studies illustrate the use of these cohort perspectives (i.e., both theoretical and empirical approaches) to investigate varied aspects of aging and cohort succession, population composition, and the reciprocal relationships between cohorts and social structures.

CONCEPTUAL FRAMEWORK

Figure 1 is a rough schematization of the major conceptual elements implicated in these interrelated cohort perspectives as they have relevance for sociology (for an overview, see Riley, Johnson, and Foner 1972; Riley, Foner and Riley 1999).

Aging and Cohort Succession. The *diagonal bars* represent cohorts of people born at particular time periods who are aging from birth to death—that is, moving across time and upward with age. As they age, the people in each cohort are changing socially and psychologically as well as biologically; they are actively participating with other people; and they are accumulating knowledge, attitudes, and experiences. The series of diagonal bars (as in the selected cohorts A, B, and C) denote how successive cohorts of people are continually being born, grow older through different eras of time, and eventually die.

Age Composition of the Population. The *perpendicular* lines direct attention to the people simultaneously alive in the society at particular dates. A single cross-sectional slice through the many coexisting cohorts (as in 1990) demonstrates how people who differ in cohort membership also differ in age—they are stratified by age from the youngest at the bottom to the oldest at the top. Over time, while society moves through historical events and changes, this vertical line should be seen as moving across the space from one period to the next. At different time periods the people in particular age strata are no longer the same people; inevitably, they have been replaced by younger entrants from more recent cohorts with more recent life experiences.

Cohorts and Social Structures. Corresponding to the age strata in the population, the perpendicular lines also denote the age-related role opportunities and normative expectations available in the various social structures (e.g., in schools for the young, in work organizations for those in the middle years, in nursing homes for the old, in families for all ages, etc.). People and structures are interdependent: changes in one influence changes in the other. Yet the two are often out of alignment, causing problems for both individuals and society.

This three-fold heuristic schematization, though highly oversimplified, aids interpretation and design of sociological work that takes cohort perspectives into account. (For simplicity, the discussion is limited here to cohorts in the larger society, with entry into the system indexed by date of birth. Parallel conceptualization refers also to studies of cohorts entering other systems, such as hospitals, with entry indexed by date of admission, or the community of scientists, with entry indexed by date of the doctoral degree—e.g., Zuckerman and

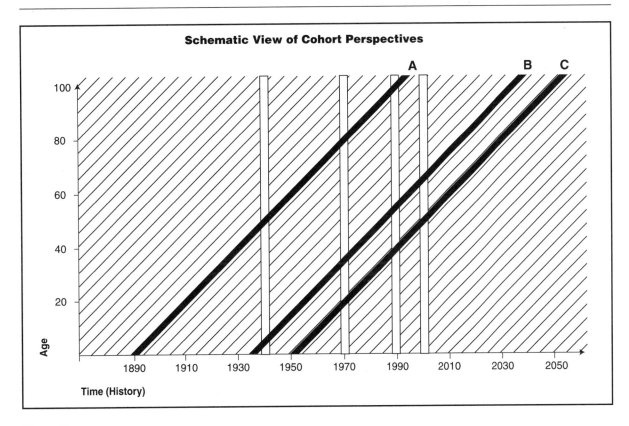

Figure 1

SOURCE: Riley, Foner, and Waring, 1998, p. 245 (adapted).

Merton 1972; here "aging" refers to duration in the particular system.)

AGING PERSPECTIVES

Research on the processes of aging within and across cohorts illuminates the interrelated aspects of people's lives and the particular characteristics and historical backgrounds of the cohorts to which they belong.

Intracohort Perspectives. Many empirical studies and much conceptual work uses the "life-course approach" to trace over time the lives of members of a single cohort (e.g., Clausen 1986). As one familiar example, studies of "status attainment" investigate lifelong trajectories of achievement behaviors, using longitudinal and causal modeling to examine the interconnections among such variables as family background, scholastic achievement, succession of jobs, and employment and unemployment (cf. Featherman 1981). The intracohort perspective is used in many forms—micro-

and macro-level, objective and subjective—in a range of studies on how people as they develop and grow older move through diverse paths in the changing society (Dannefer 1987), how sequences of role transitions are experienced, and how aging people relate to the changing environment. Psychologists as well as sociologists study interindividual changes in performance over the life course (e.g., Schaie 1996), while Nesselroade (1991) looks at intra-individual fluctuations over shorter periods of time.

Longitudinal studies of aging in a single cohort can contribute importantly to causal analysis by establishing the time order of correlated aspects of people's lives and environmental events. However, this perspective is vulnerable to possible misinterpretation through the *fallacy of "cohort-centrism,"* that is, erroneously assuming that members of all cohorts will age in exactly the same fashion as members of the cohort under study (Riley 1978). Yet in fact, members of different cohorts, as they respond to different periods of history, usually age in different ways. For example, the enjoyment of "midlife" experienced at around age 50 by cohort members studied in the 1990s may not be felt by some future cohort until age 85.

Intercohort Perspectives. Broader than the intracohort focus, is a focus on the lives of members of two or more successive cohorts who are growing older under differing historical or socio-cultural conditions. Studies of intercohort differences in the late-twentieth century demonstrated for other sciences what sociologists had learned early: the central principle that the process of aging is not immutable or fixed for all time, but varies across and within cohorts as society changes (Riley 1978). Such studies have shown that members of cohorts already old differ markedly from those in cohorts not yet old in such respects as standard of living, education, work history, age of menarche, experience with acute vs. chronic diseases, and perhaps most importantly the number of years they can expect to live. These cohort differences cannot be explained by evolutionary changes in the human genome, which remains much the same from cohort to cohort; instead, they result from a relatively unchanging genetic background combined with a continually changing society (Riley and Abeles 1990, p.iii). Thus the finding of cohort differences has pointed to possible linkages of lives with particular social or cultural changes over historical time, or with particular "period" events such as epidemics, wars, or depressions (e.g., Elder and Rockwell 1979). These linkages are useful in postulating explanations for changes—or absence of changes—in the process of aging.

Studies of cohort differences focus on aging processes at either the individual or the collective level. At the individual level, cohort membership is treated as a *contextual characteristic* of the individual, and then analyzed together with education, religion, and other personal characteristics to investigate how history and other factors affect the heterogeneous ways individuals grow older (e.g., Messeri 1988; but see Riley 1998). At the collective level, the lives of members are aggregated within each cohort to examine alterations in average patterns of aging. Striking advances have recently been made in the data banks available for intercohort comparisons. Archived data from many large-scale studies now cover long periods of history, multiple societies, and multidisciplinary aspects of the life

course; and repeated longitudinal studies are being launched, such as the National Institute on Aging's Health and Retirement Study (HRS) and Asset and Health Dynamics Among the Oldest Old (AHEAD) (cf. Campbell 1994; O'Rand and Campbell 1999).

Cohort perspectives are useful, not only in explaining past changes in aging processes, but also in improving forecasts of future changes. Unlike the more usual straight projections of cross-sectional information, forecasts based on cohorts can be informed by established facts about the past lives of people in each of the cohorts already alive (e.g., Manton 1989). Thus, if cohorts of teenagers today are on the average less healthy, less cared for, or less prepared for life than their parents were at the same age (National Association of State Boards of Education 1990), the lives of both offspring and parents will predictably also differ in the future when both have grown older.

COMPOSITIONAL PERSPECTIVES.

Complementing sociological work on cohort differences (or similarities) in the aging process are studies of how cohort succession contributes to formation and change in the age composition of the population. Thus in Figure 1, the perpendicular lines indicate how cohorts of people fit together at given historical periods to form the cross-sectional *age strata* of society; and how, as society changes, new cohorts of people are continually aging and entering these strata, replacing the previous incumbents.

Single Period of Time. In Figure 1, as indicated above, a single vertical line at a given period (as in 1990) is a cross-sectional slice through all the coexisting cohorts, each with its unique size, composition, earlier life experiences, and historical background. This familiar cross-sectional view of all the age strata is often denigrated because its misinterpretation is the source of the *life-course fallacy*—that is, the erroneous assumption that cross-sectional age differences refer directly to the process of aging, hence disregarding the cohort differences that may also be implicated (Riley 1973). That people who are differentially located in the age composition of society differ not only in age but also in cohort membership was dramatized early by Mannheim ([1928] 1952) and Ryder

(1968); yet persistent failure to comprehend this duality has perpetuated numerous false stereotypes (e.g., that intelligence or physical functioning begin inevitable declines at very early ages).

Properly interpreted, of course, a cross-sectional perspective has its special uses: for describing current differences and similarities, social relationships, and interactions among coexisting people who differ in age-cum-cohort membership. Thus, for example, issues of "intergenerational equity" require explication by both age and cohort, as a larger share of the federal budget is reportedly spent on cohorts of people now old than on cohorts of children (Duncan, Hill, and Rodgers 1986; Preston 1984).

Across Time. Comprehension of the underlying dynamics of the age strata requires going beyond the single cross-sectional snapshot to a sequence of cross-sections (the moving perpendicular line in Figure 1), as successive cohorts interact with historical trends in the society (Ryder 1965; Riley 1982). Historical change means not only that new cohorts are continually entering the system through birth or immigration, while others are leaving it through death or emigration (e.g., men tend to die earlier than women, and blacks earlier than whites). Historical change also means that the members of *all* existing cohorts are simultaneously aging and thus moving from younger to older strata. As successive cohorts move concurrently through the system, they affect the age strata in several ways. They can alter the numbers and kinds of people in particular strata, as each cohort starts the life course with a characteristic size, genetic makeup, sex ratio, racial and ethnic background, and other properties that are subsequently modified through migration, mortality, and environmental contact. The succession of cohorts can also affect the capacities, attitudes, and actions of people in particular strata as the members of each cohort bring to society their experiences with the social and environmental events spanned by their respective lifetimes.

The most significant alterations in the age composition of modern societies stem from the dramatic and unprecedented increases in the longevity of successive cohorts. Age pyramids diagramming the age composition of the United States in 2010 compared with 1955, for example, demonstrate that entirely new strata have been added at the oldest ages (Taeuber 1992)—strata of old people who are healthier and more competent than their predecessors (Manton, Corder, and Stallard 1997). The advent of these "new" old people is already having untold consequences: Individuals now have time to spread education, work, family activities, and leisure more evenly over their long lives, and wider structural opportunities are needed in society for the age-heterogenous population.

SOCIAL STRUCTURAL PERSPECTIVES

Cohorts, as described above, are composed of people, who age and fit together in strata to form the composition of the population; but cohorts also shape, and are shaped by social structures—the surrounding families, communities, work organizations, educational institutions, and the like. Against the backdrop of history, social structures, like lives, tend to change, and two "dynamisms"—changing structures and changing lives—are in continuing interplay, as each influences the other. Thus full understanding of cohorts requires understanding their reciprocal relations with structures (as in Foner and Kertzer 1978; Mayer 1988). Toward this end, some studies examine how the processes of aging and cohort flow relate to structures, while other studies examine the congruence—or lack of congruence—between age composition and social structures.

Aging and Structures. Because cohorts differ in size and character, and because their members age in new ways (the diagonal lines in Figure 1), they exert collective pressures for adjustments—not only in people's ideas, values, and beliefs—but also in role opportunities throughout the social institutions.

As one example, the influences of cohort differences in *size* were defined early by Joan Waring's (1975) powerful analysis of "disordered cohort flow." This disordered flow has been dramatically brought to attention as the Baby Boom cohorts first pressed for expansions in the school systems and the labor force, and will become the twenty-first century "senior boom" that will exacerbate the inadequacy of roles for the elderly. Later, as large cohorts were followed by smaller successors, ways were sought to reduce these expanded structures again. Meanwhile, as structures changed, the lives of people moving through these structures also changed.

In another example, the influences of cohort differences in *norms* has been analyzed as the process of "cohort norm formation" (Riley 1978). As members of a cohort respond to shared historical experiences, they gradually and subtly develop common patterns of response, common definitions, and common beliefs, that crystallize into new norms and become institutionalized in altered social structures. For instance, over the past century many individual women in successive cohorts have responded to common social changes by making many millions of separate but similar personal decisions to move in new directions: to go to college, have a career, or form their families in innovative ways. Such decisions, beginning in one cohort and transmitted from cohort to cohort, can feed back into the social structures and gradually pervade entire segments of society. Thus, many new age norms have become expectations that women should work, and have stimulated the demand for new role opportunities at work and in the family for people of all ages.

Age Composition and Structures. At any given period of history, the coexisting cohorts of people that form the age strata coincide with the existing role structures (both indicated by the perpendicular lines in Figure 1). People who differ in age and experience confront the available age-related opportunities, or lack of opportunities, in work, education, recreation, the family, and elsewhere. However, people and structures rarely fit together smoothly: there is a mismatch or "lag" of one dynamism behind the other.

Structural Lag. While people sometimes lag behind structures as technology advances, more frequent in modern society is the failure of structural changes to keep pace with the increasing numbers of long-lived and competent people (Riley, Kahn, and Foner 1994). Cohorts of those who are young today have few "real-world" opportunities; those in the middle years are stressed by the combined demands of work and family; and those who have reached old age are restive in the prolonged "roleless role" of retirement. Cohorts of people now old are more numerous, better educated, and more vigorous than their predecessors were in 1920 or 1950; but few changes in the places for them in society have been made. Capable people and empty role structures cannot long coexist. Thus, implicit in the lag are perpetual pressures toward structural change.

Age Integration. Among societal responses to structural lag are current tendencies toward "age integration" (Riley, Foner, and Riley 1999, p.338). With pressures from the expanded numbers of age strata, many age barriers dividing education, work and family, and retirement are gradually becoming more flexible. People of different ages are more often brought together, as lifelong education means that old and young study together, as new entrepreneurships hire employees of mixed ages, as in many families four generations are alive at the same time, or as the age segregation of nursing homes is replaced by home health care with wide access to others. Where such tendencies may lead in the future is not yet known. But the interdependence between cohorts and structure is clear.

RESEARCH METHODS.

When aspects of these broad cohort perspectives are translated into empirical studies, a variety of research methods are required for specific objectives: from analyses of historical documents and subjective reports, to panel analyses and mathematical modeling, to rigorous tests of specific hypotheses. This brief overview can only hint at the diverse research designs involved in analyses of the multiple factors affecting lives of people in particular cohorts; or in the shifting role opportunities for cohort members confronting economic, religious, political, and other social institutions (for one example, see Hendricks and Cutler 1990).

Cohort Analysis. The tool most widely used in large-scale studies is "cohort analysis," which takes the intercohort aging perspective—in contrast to "period analysis" (Susser 1969), which takes the cross-sectional perspective. (The difference is illustrated in Figure 1 by comparison of the diagonal cohort lines, in contrast to comparison of a sequence of vertical compositional slices). In his 1992 formulation of the technical aspects of cohort analysis, Ryder defines the term as "the parameterization of the life cycle behavior of individuals over personal time, considered in the aggregate, and the study of change in those parameters over historical time" (p. 230). He conceptualizes the cohort as "providing a macro-analytic link between movements of individuals from one to another status, and movements of the population composition from one period to the next."

His classic work on "demographic translation" sets out the mathematical procedure for moving between the cohort and the period "modes of temporal aggregation" (Ryder 1963, 1983).

Central to this method is the *identification problem* confounding many attempts at cohort analysis. This problem occurs from efforts to interpret the separate effects of three concepts—cohort, period, and age (C, P, and A)—when only two variables, such as date and years of age, are indexed. Apart from various procedures that assume one of the parameters is zero, the most appropriate solution to this problem is to specify and measure directly the three concepts used in the particular analysis (Cohn 1972; Rodgers 1982; Riley, Foner, and Waring 1988, pp. 260–261). After all, as Ryder puts it (1992, p. 228), the cohort (C) is a set of actors, the age (A) is their age, and the period (P) stands for the social context at the time of observation..

Wide Range of Methods. Ryder's exegesis of this particular method illustrates, through its strengths and limitations, the utility of the tripartite conceptualization of cohort perspectives as a heuristic guide. The strengths in Ryder's formulation focus exclusively on the significance of cohorts as a macro-analytic vehicle for social change. In the broader cohort perspectives outlined here, many other methods are useful for specific objectives where cohort analysis is inappropriate. Some employ a cross-sectional approach. Others utilize intercohort comparisons to focus on aging processes at the individual as well as the collective levels. Still others complement demographic analyses of populations with examination of the related structures of social roles and institutions.

Thus, despite its signal contributions, neither cohort analysis nor any other single method can comprehend the full power of cohorts as ingredients of aging processes, age composition, and the complex interplay with social structure.

(SEE ALSO: *Structural Lag)*

REFERENCES

Campbell, Richard T. 1994 "A Data-Based Revolution in the Social Sciences." *ICPSR Bulletin*, XIV, 1–4.

Clausen, John A. 1986 *The Life Course: A Sociological Perspective.* Englewood Cliffs, N.J.: Prentice-Hall.

Cohn Richard 1972 "On Interpretation of Cohort and Period Analyses: A Mathematical Note." In Matilda White Riley, Marilyn Johnson, and Anne Foner, eds., *Aging and Society: A Sociology of Age Stratification*, Vol. III. New York: Russell Sage Foundation.

Dannefer, Dale 1987 "Aging as Intracohort Differentiation: Accentuation, the Matthew Effect, and the Life Course." *Sociological Forum* 2 (spring):211–236.

Duncan, Greg J., Martha Hill, and Willard Rodgers 1986 "The Changing Fortunes of Young and Old." *American Demographics* 8:26–34.

Elder, Glenn H., Jr., and R. C. Rockwell 1979 "Economic Depression and Postwar Opportunity in Men's Lives: A Study of Life Patterns and Mental Health." In R. G. Simmons, ed., *Research in Community and Mental Health*, Vol. 1. Greenwich, Conn.: JAI Press.

Featherman, David L. 1981 "The Life-Span Perspective." In *The National Science Foundation's 5-Year Outlook on Science and Technology*, Vol. 2. Washington, D.C.: Government Printing Office.

Foner, Anne and David I. Kertzer 1978 "Transitions Over the Life Course: Lessons from Age-Set Societies." *American Journal of Sociology* 83:1081–1104.

Hendricks, Jon, and Stephen J. Cutler 1990 "Leisure and the Structure of our Life Worlds." *Aging and Society* 10:85–94.

Mannheim, Karl (1928) 1952 "The Problem of Generations." In Paul Kecskemeti, ed., *Essays on the Sociology of Knowledge.* London: Routledge & Kegan Paul.

Manton, Kenneth G. 1989 "Life-Style Risk Factors." In M. W. Riley and J. W. Riley, Jr., eds., *The Quality of Aging: Strategies for Interventions*, Special issue of *The Annals* (503). Newbury Park, Calif.: Sage.

——, Larry Corder, and Eric Stallard 1997 "Chronic Disability Trends in Elderly United States Populations: 1982–1994." *Proceedings of the National Academy of Sciences* 94:2593–2598

Mayer, Karl Ulrich 1988 "German Survivors of World War II: The Impact of the Life Course of the Collective Experiences of Birth Cohorts." In M. W. Riley, B. J. Huber, and B. B. Hess, eds., *Social Structures and Human Lives.* Newbury Park, Calif.: Sage.

Messeri, Peter 1988 "Age, Theory Choice, and the Complexity of Social Structure." In M. W. Riley, B. J. Huber, and B. B. Hess, eds., *Social Structures and Human Lives.* Newbury Park, Calif.: Sage.

National Association of State Boards of Education 1990 *Code Blue: Uniting for Healthier Youth.* Alexandria, Va.: National Association of State Boards of Education.

Nesselroade, John R. 1991 "The Warp and the Woof of the Development Fabric." In R. M. Downs, L. S.

Liben, and D. S. Palermo, eds., *Visions Of Aesthetics.* Hillsdale, N.J.: Lawrence Erlbaum.

O'Rand, Angela M. and Richard T. Campbell 1999 "On Reestablishing the Phenomenon and Specifying Ignorance: Theory Development and Research Design in Aging." In Vern L. Bengtson and K. Warner Schaie, eds., *Handbook of Theories of Aging.* New York: Springer.

Preston, Samuel 1984 "Children and the Elderly: Diverse Paths for America's Dependents." *Demography* 21:435–457.

Riley, Matilda White 1973 "Aging and Cohort Succession: Interpretations and Misinterpretation." *Public Opinion Quarterly* 37:35–49.

—— 1978 "Aging, Social Change, and the Power of Ideas." *Daedalus* 107:39–52.

—— 1982 "Aging and Social Change." In M. W. Riley, R. P. Abeles, and M. S. Teitelbaum, eds., *Aging from Birth to Death: Sociotemporal Perspectives*, Vol. II, AAAS Selected Symposium 79. Boulder, Colo.: Westview Press.

—— 1988 "The Aging Society: Problems and Prospects." In *Proceedings of the American Philosophical Society*, Vol. 132, No. 2, 148–153.

—— 1994 "A Life Course Approach." In J. Z. Giele and G. H. Elder, Jr., eds., *Methods of Life Course Research.* Thousand Oaks: Sage.

——, and Ronald P. Abeles 1990 *The Behavioral and Social Research Program at the National Institute of Aging: History of a Decade.* Bethesda, Md.: National Institute on Aging, National Institutes of Health.

Riley, Matilda White, Anne Foner, and John W. Riley, Jr. 1999 In Vern L. Bengtson and K. Warner Schaie, eds., *Handbook of Theories of Aging.* New York: Springer.

Riley, Matilda White, Robert L. Kahn, and Anne Foner 1994 *Age and Structural Lag: Society's Failure to Provide Meaningful Opportunities in Work, Family, and Leisure.* New York: Wiley.

Riley, Matilda White, Anne Foner, and Joan Waring 1988 "Sociology of Age." In Neil J. Smelser, ed., *Handbook of Sociology.* Newbury Park, Calif.: Sage Publications.

Riley, Matilda White, Marilyn Johnson, and Anne Foner 1972 *Aging and Society, Vol. III: A Sociology of Age Stratification.* New York: Russell Sage Foundation.

Rodgers, Willard L. 1982 "Estimable Functions of Age, Period, and Cohort Effects." *American Sociological Review* 47:774–787.

Ryder, Norman B. 1963 "The Translation Model of Demographic Change." In Norman B. Ryder, ed., *Emerging Techniques in Population Research.* New York: Milbank Memorial Fund.

—— 1965 "The Cohort as a Concept in the Study of Social Change." *American Sociological Review* 30:843–861.

—— 1968 "Cohort Analysis." *International Encyclopedia of the Social Sciences* 5:546–550.

—— 1983 "Cohort and Period Measures of Changing Fertility." In Rodolfo A. Bulatao and Ronald D. Lee, eds., *Determinants of Fertility in Developing Countries.* New York: Academic Press.

—— 1992 "Cohort Analysis." In E. F. Borgatta and M. L. Borgatta, eds., *Encyclopedia of Sociology*, Vol. 1,. New York: MacMillan.

Schaie, K. Warner 1996 *Intellectual Development in Adulthood: The Seattle Longitudinal Study.* New York: Cambridge University Press.

Susser, Mervyn 1969 "Aging and the Field of Public Health." In M. W. Riley, J. W. Riley, Jr., and M. E. Johnson, eds., *Aging and Society, Vol. II, Aging and the Professions.* New York: Russell Sage Foundation.

Taeuber, Cynthia M. 1992 "Sixty-five Plus in America." *Current Population Reports*, P23-178RV. Washington, D.C.: U.S. Bureau of the Census.

Waring, Joan M. 1975 "Social Replenishment and Social Change." *American Behavioral Scientist* 19:237–256.

Zuckerman, Harriet and Robert K. Merton 1972 "Age, Aging and Age Structure in Science." In M. W. Riley, M. Johnson, and A. Foner, eds., *Aging and Society: Volume II, A Sociology of Age Stratification.* New York: Russell Sage Foundation.

Matilda White Riley

COLLECTIVE BEHAVIOR

Collective behavior consists of those forms of social behavior in which the usual conventions cease to guide social action and people collectively transcend, bypass, or subvert established institutional patterns and structures. As the name indicates, the behavior is collective rather than individual. Unlike small group behavior, it is not principally coordinated by each-to-each personal relationships, though such relationships do play an important part. Unlike organizational behavior, it is not coordinated by formally established goals, authority, roles, and membership designations, though emergent leadership and an informal role structure are important components. The best known forms of collective behavior are rumor, spontaneous collective responses to crises such as natural disasters; crowds, collective panics, crazes, fads, fashions, publics (participants in forming public opinion), cults, followings; and reform and revolutionary movements. Social movements are sometimes treated as forms of collective behavior, but are often viewed as a different order of phenomena because of the degree of organization necessary to sustain social action. This essay will include only those social movement theories that also have relevance for the more elementary forms of collective behavior.

Theories of collective behavior can be classified broadly as focusing on the behavior itself (microlevel) or on the larger social and cultural settings within which the behavior occurs (macrolevel or structural). An adequate theory at the microlevel must answer three questions, namely: How is it that people come to transcend, bypass, or subvert institutional patterns and structures in their activity; how do people come to translate their attitudes into significant overt action; and how do people come to act collectively rather than singly? Structural theories identify the processes and conditions in culture and social structure that are conducive to the development of collective behavior. Microlevel theories can be further divided into *action* or *convergence* theories and *interaction* theories.

MICROLEVEL CONVERGENCE THEORIES

Convergence theories assume that when a critical mass of individuals with the same disposition to act in a situation come together, collective action occurs almost automatically. In all convergence theories it is assumed that: "The individual in the crowd behaves just as he would behave alone, *only more so*," (Allport 1924, p. 295), meaning that individuals in collective behavior are doing what they wanted to do anyway, but could not or feared to do without the "facilitating" effect of similar behavior by others. The psychological hypothesis that frustration leads to aggression has been widely applied in this way to explain racial lynchings and riots, rebellion and revolution, and other forms of collective violence. Collective behavior has been conceived as a collective pursuit of meaning and personal identity when strains and imbalances in social institutions have made meaning and identity problematic (Klapp 1972). In order to explain the convergence of a critical mass of people experiencing similar frustrations, investigators

posit deprivation shared by members of a social class, ethnic group, gender group, age group, or other social category. Because empirical evidence has shown consistently that the most deprived are not the most likely to engage in collective protest, more sophisticated investigators assume a condition of *relative deprivation* (Gurr 1970), based on a discrepancy between expectations and actual conditions. Relative deprivation frequently follows a period of rising expectations brought on by improving conditions, interrupted by a setback, as in the J-curve hypothesis of revolution (Davies 1962). Early explanations for collective behavior, generally contradicted by empirical evidence and repudiated by serious scholars, characterized much crowd behavior and many social movements as the work of criminals, the mentally disturbed, persons suffering from personal identity problems, and other deviants.

Rational decision theories. Several recent convergence theories assume that people make rational decisions to participate or not to participate in collective behavior on the basis of selfinterest. Two important theories of this sort are those of Richard Berk and Mark Granovetter.

Berk (1974) defines collective behavior as the behavior of people in crowds, which means activity that is transitory, not well planned in advance, involving face-to-face contact among participants, and considerable cooperation, though he also includes panic as competitive collective behavior. Fundamental to his theory is the assumption that crowd activity involves rational, goal-directed action, in which possible rewards and costs are considered along with the chances of support from others in the crowd. Rational decision making means reviewing viable options, forecasting events that may occur, arranging information and choices in chronological order, evaluating the possible consequences of alternative courses of action, judging the chances that uncertain events will occur, and choosing actions that minimize costs and maximize benefits. Since the best outcome for an individual in collective behavior depends fundamentally on what other people will do, participants attempt to advance their own interests by recruiting others and through negotiation. Berk's theory does not explain the origin and nature of the proposals for action that are heard in the crowd, but describes the process by which these proposals are sifted as the crowd moves toward collaborative action, usually involving a division of labor. To explain decision making, he offers a simple equation in which the probability of a person beginning to act (e.g., to loot) is a function of the product of the net anticipated personal payoff for acting (e.g., equipment or liquor pilfered) and the probability of group support in that action (e.g., bystanders condoning or joining in the looting.)

Granovetter's (1978) application of rational decision theory focuses on the concept of *threshold*. He assumes that each person, in a given situation, has a threshold number or percentage of other people who must already be engaging in a particular action before he or she will join in. Since it can be less risky for the individual to engage in collective behavior (riotous behavior, for example) when many others are doing so than when few are involved, the benefit-to-cost ratio improves as participation increases. Based on the personal importance of the action in question, individual estimation of risk, and a host of other conditions, individual thresholds will vary widely in any situation. Collective behavior cannot develop without low-threshold individuals to get it started, and development will stop when there is no one with the threshold necessary for the next escalation step. Collective behavior reaches an equilibrium, which can be ascertained in advance from knowing the distribution of thresholds, when this point is reached. Like Berk, Granovetter makes no effort to explain what actions people will value. Furthermore, intuitively appealing as the theory may be, operationalizing and measuring individual thresholds may be, for all practical purposes, impossible.

MICRO-LEVEL INTERACTION THEORIES

Contagion Theories. Early interaction theories, which lay more emphasis on what happens to people in the context of a crowd or other collectivity than on the dispositions people bring to the collectivity, stressed either the emergence of a group mind or processes of imitation, suggestion, or social contagion. Serge Moscovici (1985a, 1985b) is a defender of these early views, stressing that normal people suffer a lowering of intellectual faculties, an intensification of emotional reactions, and a disregard for personal profit in a crowd. The fundamental crowd process is suggestion, emanating from charismatic leaders. During the twentieth

century, the breakdown of social ties has created masses who form larger and larger crowds that are controlled by a few national and international leaders, creating an historically new politics or appeal to the masses.

Herbert Blumer (1939) developed a version of the contagion approach that has been the starting point for theories of collective behavior for most American scholars. Blumer explains that the fitting together of individual actions in most group behavior is based on shared understandings under the influence of custom, tradition, conventions, rules, or institutional regulations. In contrast, collective behavior is group behavior that arises spontaneously, and not under the guidance of preestablished understandings, traditions, or rules of any kind. If sociology in general studies the social order, collective behavior consists of the processes by which that order comes into existence. While coordination in publics and social movements and involving more complex cognitive processes called *interpretation interaction*, coordination in the crowd and other elementary forms of collective behavior is accomplished through a process of *circular reaction*. Circular reaction is a type of interstimulation in which the response by others to one individual's expression of feeling simply reproduces that feeling, thereby reinforcing the first individual's feeling, which in turn reinforces the feelings of the others, setting in motion an escalating spiral of emotion. Circular reaction begins with individual restlessness, when people have a blocked impulse to act. When many people share such restlessness, and are already sensitized to one another, circular reaction can set in and create a process of *social unrest* in which the restless state is mutually intensified into a state of *milling*. In milling, people move or shift their attention aimlessly among each other, thereby becoming preoccupied with each other and decreasingly responsive to ordinary objects and events. In the state of *rapport*, collective excitement readily takes over, leading to a final stage of *social contagion*, the "relatively rapid, unwitting, and non-rational dissemination of a mood, impulse, or form of conduct."(Blumer 1939) Social unrest is also a prelude to the formation of publics and social movements. In the case of the public, the identification of an issue rather than a mood or point of view converts the interaction into discussion rather than circular reaction. Social movements begin with circular reaction, but with persisting concerns they acquire organization and programs, and interpretative interaction prevails.

Emergent Norm Theory. Ralph Turner and Lewis Killian [(1957) 1989] criticize convergence theories for underemphasizing the contribution of interaction processes in the development of collective behavior, and found both convergence and contagion theories at fault for assuming that participants in collective behavior become homogeneous in their moods and attitudes. Instead of emotional contagion, it is the emergence of a norm or norms in collective behavior that facilitates coordinated action and creates the illusion of unanimity. The emergent norm is characteristically based on established norms, but transforms or applies those norms in ways that would not ordinarily be acceptable. What the emergent norm permits or requires people to believe, feel, and do corresponds to a disposition that is prevalent but not universal among the participants. In contrast to convergence theories, however, it is assumed that participants are usually somewhat ambivalent, so that people could have felt and acted in quite different ways if the emergent norm had been different. For example, many rioters also have beliefs in law and order and fair play that might have been converted into action had the emergent norm been different. Striking events, symbols, and keynoting—a gesture or symbolic utterance that crystallizes sentiment in an undecided and ambivalent audience—shape the norm and supply the normative power, introducing an element of unpredictability into the development and direction of all collective behavior.

Emergent norm theory differs from contagion theories in at least six important and empirically testable ways. First, the appearance of unanimity in crowds, social movements, and other forms of collective behavior is an illusion, produced by the effect of the emergent norm in silencing dissent. Second, while the collectivity's mood and definition of the situation are spontaneously induced in some of the participants, many participants experience group pressure first and only later, if at all, come to share the collectivity's mood and definition of the situation. Third, unlike collective excitement and contagion, normative pressure is as applicable to quiet states such as dread and sorrow as it is to excited states. Fourth,

according to emergent norm theory, a conspicuous component in the symbolic exchange connected with the development of collective behavior should consist of seeking and supplying justifications for the collectivity's definition of the situation and action, whereas there should be no need for justifications if the feelings were spontaneously induced through contagion. Fifth, a norm not only requires or permits certain definitions and behaviors; it also sets acceptable limits, while limits are difficult to explain in terms of a circular reaction spiral. Finally, while contagion theories stress anonymity within the collectivity as facilitating the diffusion of definitions and behavior that deviate from conventional norms, emergent norm theory asserts that familiarity among participants in collective behavior enhances the controlling effect of the emergent norm.

Emergent norm theory has been broadened to make explicit the answers to all three of the key questions microlevel theories must answer: The emergent normative process as just described provides the principal answer to the question, why people adopt definitions and behavior that transcend, bypass, or contravene established social norms; participants translate their attitudes into overt action rather than remaining passive principally because they see action as feasible and timely; and action is collective rather than individual primarily because of preexisting groupings and networks and because an event or events that challenge conventional understandings impel people to turn to others for help in fashioning a convincing definition of the problematic situation. In addition, these three sets of processes interact and are mutually reinforcing in the development and maintenance of collective behavior. This elaboration of the emergent norm approach is presented as equally applicable to elementary forms of collective behavior such as crowds and to highly developed and organized forms such as social movements.

Other Interaction Theories. Although all interactional theories presume that collective behavior develops through a cumulative process, Max Heirich (1964) makes this central to his theory of collective conflict, formulated to explain the 1964–1965 year of spiraling conflict between students and the administration at the University of California, Berkeley. Common action occurs when observers perceive a situation as critical, with limited time for action, with the crisis having a simple cause and being susceptible to influence by simple acts. Heirich specifies determinants of the process by which such common perceptions are created and the process by which successive redefinitions of the situation take place. Under organizational conditions that create unbridged cleavages between groups that must interact regularly, conflict escalates through successive encounters in which cleavages become wider, issues shift, and new participants join the fray, until the conflict becomes focused around the major points of structural strain in the organization.

Also studying collective conflict as a cumulative process, Bert Useem and Peter Kimball (1989) developed a sequence of stages for prison riots, proceeding from pre-riot conditions, to initiation, expansion, siege, and finally termination. While they identify disorganization of the governing body as the key causative factor, they stress that what happens at any one stage is important in determining what happens at the next stage.

Clark McPhail (1991), in an extensive critique of all prior work, rejects the concept of collective behavior as useless because it denotes too little and fails to recognize variation and alternation within assemblages. Instead of studying collective behavior or crowds, he proposes the study of *temporary gatherings*, defined as two or more persons in a common space and time frame. Gatherings are analyzed in three stages, namely, assembling, gathering, and dispersing. Rather than positing an overarching principle such as contagion or norm emergence, this approach uses detailed observation of individual actions and interactions within gatherings and seeks explanations at this level. Larger events such as campaigns and large gatherings are to be explained as the "repetition and/or combination of individual and collective sequences of actions."(McPhail 1991, p. 221). These elementary actions consist of simple observable actions such as clustering, booing, chanting, collective gesticulation, "locomotion," synchroclapping, and many others. The approach has been implemented by precise behavioral observation of people assembling for demonstrations and other preplanned gatherings. A promised further work will help determine how much this approach will contribute to the understanding of those fairly frequent events usually encompassed by the term collective behavior.

MACROLEVEL OR STRUCTURAL THEORIES

Microlevel theories attempt first to understand the internal dynamics of collective behavior, then use that understanding to infer the nature of conditions in the society most likely to give rise to collective behavior. In contrast, macrolevel or structural theories depend primarily on an understanding of the dynamics of society as the basis for developing propositions concerning when and where collective behavior will occur. Historically, most theories of elementary collective behavior have been microlevel theories, while most theories of social movements have been structural. Neil Smelser's 1993 *value-added* theory is primarily structural but encompasses the full range from panic and crazes to social movements.

Smelser attempted to integrate major elements from the Blumer and Turner/Killian tradition of microtheory into an action and structural theory derived from the work of Talcott Parsons. Smelser describes the normal flow of social action as proceeding from values to norms to mobilization into social roles and finally to situational facilities. Values are the more general guides to behavior; norms specify more precisely how values are to be applied. Mobilization into roles is organization for action in terms of the relevant values and norms. Situational facilities are the means and obstacles that facilitate and hinder attainment of concrete goals. The four "components of social action" are hierarchized in the sense that any redefinition of a component requires readjustment in the components below it, but not necessarily in those above. Each of the four components in turn has seven levels of specificity with the same hierarchical ordering as the components. Types of collective behavior differ in the level of the action components they aim to restructure. Social movements address either values, in the case of most revolutionary movements, or norms, in the case of most reform movements. Elementary collective behavior is focused at either the mobilization or the situational facilities level. Collective behavior is characterized formally as "an uninstitutionalized mobilization for action in order to modify one or more kinds of strain on the basis of a generalized reconstitution of a component of action." (Smelser 1963 p. 71). The distinguishing feature of this action is a shortcircuiting of the normal flow of action from the general to the specific. There is a jump from extremely high levels of generality to specific, concrete situations, without attention to the intervening components and their levels of specificity. Thus, in Smelser's view, collective behavior is intrinsically irrational.

In order for collective behavior to occur, six conditions must be met, each of which is necessary but insufficient without the others. Smelser likens the relationship among the six determinants to the value-added process in economics, with each adding an essential component to the finished product. The first determinant is *structural conduciveness*, meaning that the social structure is organized in a way that makes the particular pattern of action feasible. The second determinant is *structural strain*, consisting of ambiguities, deprivations, conflicts, and discrepancies experienced by particular population segments. Third (and central in Smelser's theorizing), is the growth and spread of a *generalized belief* that identifies and characterizes the supposed source of strain and specifies appropriate responses. The generalized belief incorporates the short-circuiting of the components of action that is a distinctive feature of collective behavior. Fourth are *precipitating factors*, usually a dramatic event or series of events that give the generalized belief concrete and immediate substance and provide a concrete setting toward which collective action can be directed. The fifth determinant is *mobilization of participants for action*, in which leadership behavior is critical. The final determinant is the *operation of social control*. Controls may serve to minimize conduciveness and strain, thus preventing the occurrence of an episode of collective behavior, or they may come into action only after collective behavior has begun to materialize, either dampening or intensifying the action by the way controls are applied. These determinants need not occur in any particular order.

Addressing a more limited range of phenomena, David Waddington, Karen Jones, and Chas Critcher (1989) have formulated a *flashpoint* model to explain public disorders that bears some resemblance to the value-added component of Smelser's theory. Public disorders typically begin when some ostensibly trivial incident becomes a flashpoint. The flashpoint model is a theory of the conditions that give a minor incident grave significance. Explanatory conditions exist at six levels. At the *structural* level are conflicts inherent in material and ideological differences between social groups that are not easily resolvable within the existing social structure, meaning especially the state. At the *political/ideological* level, dissenting groups are unable to express their dissent through established channels, and their declared ends and means are considered illegitimate. At the *cultural* level, the existence of groups with incompatible definitions of the situation, appropriate behavior, or legitimate rights can lead to conflict. At the *contextual* level, a history of past conflicts between a dissenting group and police or other authorities enhances the likelihood that a minor incident will become a flashpoint. At the *situational* level, immediate spatial and social conditions can make public control and effective negotiation difficult. Finally, at the *interactional* level, the dynamics of interaction between police and protesters, as influenced by meanings derived from the other five levels, ultimately determine whether there will or will not be public disorder and how severe it will be. Unlike Smelser, Waddington and associates make no assumption that all levels of determinants must be operative. Also, they make no explicit assumption that disorderly behavior is irrational, though their goal is to formulate public policy that will minimize the incidence of public disorders.

Resource mobilization theories have been advanced as alternatives to Smelser's value-added theory and to most microlevel theories. Although they have generally been formulated to explain social movements and usually disavow continuity between social movements and elementary collective behavior, they have some obvious implications for most forms of collective behavior. There are now several versions of resource mobilization theory, but certain core assumptions can be identified. Resource mobilization theorists are critical of prior collective behavior and social movement theories for placing too much emphasis on "structural strain," social unrest, or grievances; on "generalized beliefs," values, ideologies, or ideas of any kind; and on grass-roots spontaneity in accounting for the development and characteristics of collective behavior. They assume that there is always sufficient grievance and unrest in society to serve as the basis for collective protest (McCarthy and Zald 1977), and that the ideas and beliefs exploited in protest are readily available in the culture (Oberschall 1973). They see collective protest as centrally organized, with the bulk of the participants "mobilized" much as soldiers in an army are mobilized and directed by their commanders. In explaining the rise of collective protest they emphasize the availability of essential resources, such as money, skills, disposable time, media access, and access to power centers, and prior organization as the base for effectively mobilizing the resources. Resource mobilization theorists favor the use of rational decision models to explain the formulation of strategy and tactics, and emphasize the role of social movement professionals in directing protest.

There has been some convergence between resource mobilization theorists and the theorists they criticize. The broadened formulation of emergent norm theory to incorporate resources (under "feasibility") and prior organization as determinants of collective behavior takes account of the resource mobilization contribution without, however, giving primacy to these elements. Similarly, many resource mobilization theorists have incorporated social psychological variables in their models.

Alberto Melucci (1989) offers a *constructivist* view of collective action which combines macro- and micro-orientations. Collective action is the product of purposeful negotiations whereby a plurality of perspectives, meanings, and relationships crystallize into a pattern of action. Action is constructed to take account of the goals of action, the means to be utilized, and the environment within which action takes place, which remain in a continual state of tension. The critical process is the negotiation of collective identities for the participants. In the current post-industrial era, conflicts leading to collective action develop in those areas of communities and complex organizations in which there is greatest pressure on individuals to conform to the institutions that produce and circulate information and symbolic codes.

REFERENCES

Allport, Floyd H. 1924 *Social Psychology*. Boston: Houghton Mifflin.

Berk, Richard A. 1974 "A Gaming Approach to Crowd Behavior." *American Sociological Review* 39:355–73.

Blumer, Herbert 1939 "Collective Behavior." in Robert E. Park ed., *An Outline of the Principles of Sociology* 221–280. New York: Barnes & Noble.

Davies, James C. 1962 "Toward a Theory of Revolution." *American Journal of Sociology* 27:5–19.

Granovetter, Mark 1978 "Threshold Models of Collective Behavior." *American Journal of Sociology* 83:1420–43.

Gurr, Ted R. 1970 *Why Men Rebel*. Princeton: Princeton University Press.

Heirich, Max 1971 *The Spiral of Conflict: Berkeley, 1964*. Berkeley: University of California Press.

Klapp, Orrin E. 1972 *Currents of Unrest: An Introduction to Collective Behavior*. New York: Holt, Rinehart, & Winston.

McPhail, Clark 1991 *The Myth of the Madding Crowd* New York: Aldine de Gruyter.

Melucci, Alberto 1989 *Nomads of the Present: Social Movements and Individual Needs in Contemporary Society*. Philadelphia: Temple University Press.

Moscovici, Serge 1985a *The Age of the Crowd: A Historical Treatise on Mass Psychology*. Cambridge: Cambridge University Press.

—— 1985b "The Discovery of the Masses," In C. F. Graumann and Moscovici, eds., *Changing Conceptions of Crowd Mind and Behavior*, 5–25 New York: Springer-Verlag.

Smelser, Neil J. 1963 *Theory of Collective Behavior*. New York: Free Press.

Turner, Ralph H., and Lewis M. Killian (1957) 1987 *Collective Behavior*. Englewood Cliffs, N. J.: Prentice-Hall.

Turner. Ralph H. 1994 "Race Riots Past and Present: A Cultural-Collective Behavior Approach." *Symbolic Interaction* 17:309–24.

—— 1996 "Normative Emergence in Collective Behavior and Action" *Solidarity: Research in Social Movements*. 1:1–16.

Useem, Bert, and Peter Kimball 1989 *States of Siege: U. S. Prison Riots, 1971–1986*. New York: Oxford University Press.

Waddington, David, Karen Jones, and Chas Critcher 1989 *Flashpoints: Studies in Public Disorder*. London: Routledge.

RALPH H. TURNER

COLONIZATION

See Imperialism, Colonialism, and Decolonization.

COMMUNES

See Alternative Life-Styles.

COMMUNISM

See Socialism and Communism.

COMMUNITARIANISM

Communitarianism is a social philosophy that core assumption is the required shared ("social") formulations of the good. The assumption is both empirical (social life exhibits shared values) and normative (shared values ought to be formulated). While many sociologists may consider such an assumption as subject to little controversy, communitarianism is in effect a highly contested social philosophy. It is often contrasted with liberalism (based on the works of John Locke, Adam Smith, and John Stuart Mill, not to be confused with liberalism as the term is used in contemporary American politics). Liberalism's core assumption is that what people consider right or wrong, their values, should strictly be a matter for each individual to determine. To the extent that social arrangements and public policies are needed, these should not be driven by shared values but by voluntary arrangements and contracts among the individuals involved, thus reflecting their values and interests. Communitarians, in contrast, see social institutions and policies as affected by tradition and hence by values passed from generation to generation. These become part of the self through nonrational processes, especially internalization, and are changed by other processes such as persuasion, religious or political indoctrination, leadership, and moral dialogues.

In addition, communitarianism emphasizes particularism, the special moral obligations people have to their families, kin, communities, and societies. In contrast, liberalism stresses the universal rights of all individuals, regardless of their particular membership. Indeed, liberal philosopher Jeremy Bentham declared that the very notion of a society is a fiction.

Until 1990, sociological and social psychological researchers and theorists and communitarian philosophers often ignored one another's works, despite the fact that they dealt with closely related issues. It should be noted, though, that communitarians were much more inclined to be openly and systematically normative than many social scientists.

HISTORY

Like many other schools of thought, communitarianism has changed considerably throughout its history, and has various existing camps that differentiate significantly. As far as can be determined, the term "communitarian" was not used until 1841, when Goodwyn Barmby, an official of the Communist Church, founded the Universal Communitarian Association.

Communitarian issues were addressed long before that date, however, for instance in Aristotle's comparison of the isolated lives of people in the big metropolis to close relationships in the smaller city. Both the Old and the New Testament deal with various issues one would consider communitarian today, for instance the obligations to one's community. The social teaching of the Catholic Church (for instance, concerning subsidiarity) and of early utopian socialism (for example, regarding communal life and solidarity), all contain strong communitarian *elements*, although these works are not comprehensive communitarian statements and are not usually considered as communitarian works per se.

Among early sociologists whose work is strongly communitarian, although this fact is as a rule overlooked by social philosophers, are Ferdinand Tönnies, especially his comparison of the *Gemeinschaft* and *Gessellschaft*, (or community and society); Emile Durkheim, especially his concerns about the integrating role of social values and the relations between the individual and society; and George Herbert Mead. These works are extensively examined elsewhere in this encyclopedia and hence are not discussed here.

A communitarian who combined social philosophy and sociology Martin Buber. Especially relevant are Buber's contrast between I-It and I-Thou relations, his interest in dialogue, and his distinction between genuine communal relationships and objectified ones.

Other sociologists whose work contains communitarian elements are Robert E. Park, William Kornhauser, and Robert Nisbet. Philip Selznick, Robert Bellah and his associates, and Amitai Etzioni wrote books that laid the foundations for new (or responsive) communitarianism, which Etzioni launched as a "school" and somewhat of a social movement in 1990.

Selznick's *The Moral Commonwealth* is especially key in forming a strong intellectual grounding for new communitarian thinking, and presents an integration of moral and social theory in a synthesis of "communitarian liberalism." According to Selznick, communitarianism does not reject basic liberal ideals and achievements; it seeks reconstruction of liberal perspectives to mitigate the excesses of individualism and rationalism, and to encourage an ethic of responsibility (in contrast to liberalism, where the concept of responsibility has no major role). In a community there is an irrepressible tension between exclusion and inclusion, and between civility and piety. Thus community is not a restful idea, a realm of peace and harmony. On the contrary, competing principles must be recognized and dealt with.

AUTHORITARIAN, POLITICAL THEORETICAL, AND RESPONSIVE COMMUNITARIANISM

Different communitarian camps are no closer to one another than National Socialists (Nazis) are to Scandinavian Social Democrats (also considered socialists). It is hence important to keep in mind which camp one is considering. The differences concern the normative relations between social order and liberty, and the relations between the community and the individual.

Authoritarian Communitarians. Authoritarian communitarians(some of whom are often referred to as "Asian" or "East Asian" communitarians) are those who argue that to maintain social order and harmony, individual rights and political liberties must be curtailed. Some believe in the strong arm of the state (such as former Singapore Prime Minister Lee Kuan Yew and Malaysian head of state Mahathir Bin Mohamad), and some in strong social bonds and the voice of the family and community (especially the kind of society Japan had, at

least until 1990). Among the arguments made by authoritarian communitarians is that social order is important to people, while what the West calls "liberty" actually amounts to social, political, and moral anarchy; that curbing legal and political rights is essential for rapid economic development; and that legal and political rights are a Western idea, which the West uses to harshly judge other cultures that have their own inherent values. The extent to which early sociological works, for instance, by Tönnies and *Community and Power* by Robert Nisbet, include authoritarian elements, is open to question.

Political Theoreticians . In the 1980s communitarian thinking became largely associated with three scholars: Charles Taylor, Michael Sandel, and Michael Walzer. They criticized liberalism for its failure to realize that people are socially "situated" or contextualized, and its negligence of the greater common good in favor of individualistic self-interests. In addition, as Chandran Kukathas relates in *The Communitarian Challenge to Liberalism* (Paul, Miller, Paul, eds. 1990, p.90), communitarians argue that political community is an important value which is neglected by liberal political theory. Liberalism, they contend, views political society as a supposedly neutral framework of rules within which a diversity of moral traditions coexist. . . .[Such a view] neglects the fact that people have, or can have, a strong and 'deep' attachment to their societies—to their nations.

While for many outside sociology, especially until 1990, these three scholars were considered the founding fathers of communitarian thinking, none of them uses the term in their work, possibly to avoid being confused with authoritarian communitarians. These scholars almost completely ignored sociological works that preceded them, and were largely ignored by sociologists.

New or Responsive Communitarians. Early in 1990, a school of communitarianism was founded in which sociologists played a key role, although it included scholars from other disciplines such as William A. Galston (political theory), Mary Ann Glendon (law), Thomas Spragens, Jr. (political science), and Alan Ehrenhalt (writer) to mention but a few. The group, founded by Amitai Etzioni, took communitarianism from a small and somewhat esoteric academic discipline and introduced it into public life, and recast its academic content. Its tools were *The Responsive Communitarian Platform: Rights and Responsibilities*, a joint manifesto summarizing the guiding principles of the group; an intellectual quarterly, *The Responsive Community*, whose editors include several sociologists; several books; position papers on issues ranging from a communitarian view of the family to organ donation and to bicultural education; and numerous public conferences, op-eds, and a web site (www.gwu.edu/~ccps).

Key Assumptions and Concepts. Responsive communitarianism methodologically is based on the macro-sociological assumption that societies have multiple and not wholly compatible needs and values, in contrast to philosophies that derive their core assumptions from one overarching principle, for instance liberty for libertarianism. Responsive communitarianism assumes that a "good society" is based on a carefully crafted balance between liberty and social order, between individual rights and social responsibilities, between particularistic (ethnic, racial, communal) and society-wide values and bonds. In that sense, far from representing a Western model, the communitarian good society combines 'Asian' values (also reflecting tenets of Islam and Judaism that stress social responsibilities) with a Western concern with political liberty and individual rights.

While the model of the good society is applicable to all societies, communitarianism stresses that different societies, during various historical periods, may be off balance in rather contrasting ways and hence may need to move in *different* directions in order to approximate the *same* balance. Thus, contemporary East Asian societies require much greater tolerance for individual and communal differences, while in the American society—especially at the end of the 1980s—excessive individualism needs to be reigned in. To put it differently, communitarianism suggests that the specific normative directives that flow from the good society model are historically and culturally contingent.

Responsive communitarians stress that the relationship between liberty and social order is not a zero-sum situation; up to a point they are mutually supportive. Thus, in situations such as those prevailing in late-1990s Moscow, where liberty and social order are neglected, increasing order might well also enhance people's autonomy and life

choices. The same might be said about reducing crime in American cities when it reached the point where people did not venture into parks, and were reluctant to ride the subway or walk the streets after dark. Moreover, totalitarian regimes, the ultimate loss of freedom, are said to arise when order is minimized.

While up to a point social order and liberty enhance one another, if the level of social order is increased further and further, responsive communitarians expect it to reach a level where it will erode people's liberty. And, if the scope of liberty is extended ever more, it will reach a point where it will undermine the social order. This idea is expressed in the term *inverting symbiosis*, which indicates that up to a point liberty and order nourish one another, and beyond it they turn antagonistic.

The same point applies to the relationship between the self and the community. Political theorists have tended to depict the self as "encumbered," "situated," or "contextualized," all of which imply that it is constrained by social order. Responsive communitarians stress that individuals within communities are able to be more reasonable and productive than isolated individuals, but if social pressure to conform reaches a high level, such pressures undermine the development and expression of the self.

The next question is: Under what conditions can the zone of symbiosis be expanded, and that of antagonism between liberty and order be minimized? To answer that question the communitarian view of human nature must be introduced. While sociologists tend to avoid this term, on the grounds that it is not testible and can lead to racism (as evident in the notion that some groups of people are more intelligent by nature), communitarians use the term with less reluctance.

The view of human nature most compatible with responsive communitarian thinking is a *dynamic* (developmental) view, which holds that people at birth are akin to animals. But unlike social conservatives, who tend to embrace a dour view of human nature, and tend to view even adults after socialization as impulsive, irrational, dangerous, or sinful—communitarians maintain that people can become increasingly virtuous if the proper processes of value-internalization and reinforcement of undergirding social institutions, the "moral infrastructure," are in place. At the same time, communitarians do not presume that people can be made as virtuous as liberals assume them to be from the onset. (Liberals tend to assume that crime and forms of deviant behavior reflect social conditions, especially government interventions that pervert good people, rather than criminals' innate nature.)

The moral infrastructure, an essential foundation of a good society, draws on four social formations: families, schools, communities, and the community of communities. The four core elements of the moral infrastructure are arranged like Chinese nesting boxes, one within the other, and in a sociological progression. Infants are born into *families*, which communitarians stress have been entrusted throughout human history with beginning the process of instilling values and launching the moral self. *Schools* join the process as children grow older, further developing the moral self ("character"), or trying to remedy character neglect suffered under family care. Schools are hence viewed not merely or even primarily as places of teaching, where the passing of knowledge and skills occur, but as educational institutions in the broadest sense of the term.

Human nature, communitarians note, is such that even if children are reared in families dedicated to child raising and moral education, and children graduate from strong and dedicated schools, these youngsters are still not sufficiently equipped for a good, communitarian society. This is a point ignored by social philosophers who often assume that once people have acquired virtue and are habituated, they will be guided by their inner moral compass. The very concept of "conscience" assumes the formation of a perpetual inner gyroscope.

In contrast, communitarians—following standard sociological positions—assume that the good character of those who have acquired it tends to degrade. If left to their own devices, individuals gradually lose much of their commitments to their values, unless these are continuously reinforced. A major function of the *community*, as a building block of the moral infrastructure, is to reinforce the character of its members. This is achieved by the community's "moral voice," the informal sanction of others, built into a web of informal affect-laden relationships, which communities provide.

In general, the weaker the community—because of high population turnover, few shared core values, high heterogeneity, etc.—the thinner the social web and the slacker the moral voice. The strength of the moral voice and the values it speaks for have been studied using a series of questions such as, Should one speak up if child abuse is witnessed? Or if children are seen painting swastikas? What about less dire situations, such as insisting that friends wear their seatbelts, or admonishing a nondisabled person one witnesses parking in a handicap space?

Informal surveys show that Americans in the 1980s were very reluctant to raise their moral voice; many accepted the liberal ideology that what is morally sound is to be determined by each individual, and one should not pass judgments over others. Alan Wolfe's study, *One Nation After All*, found that Americans, even in conservative parts of the country, have grown very tolerant of a great variety of social behavior. Increase in tolerance is of course by itself virtuous; communitarians, though, raise the question: At which point does such increased tolerance engendering an amoral culture where spousal abuse, discrimination, child neglect, drunk drivers, obsessive materialism, and other forms of antisocial behavior become matters the community should ignore, leaving them to individual discretion or the law.

More specifically, communitarians inquire various elements of the moral infrastructure whether they reinforce, neglect, or undermine it. In this context, the special communitarian perspective of voluntary associations is especially important. Previously, the significance of these associations has been highlighted as protecting individuals from the state (a protection they would not have if they faced the state as isolated or "atomized" individuals), and as intermediating bodies that aggregate, transmit, and underwrite individual signals to the state.

Communitarians argue that, in addition, the very same voluntary associations often fulfill a rather different role: They serve as social spaces in which members of communities reinforce their social webs and articulate their moral voice. That is, voluntary associations often constitute a basis of communal relationships. Thus, the members of a local chapter of the Masons, Elks, or Lions care about one another and reinforce each other's particular brand of conservative views. Similarly, the members of the New York City Reform Clubs, Americans for Democratic Action, and local chapters of the ACLU reinforce one another's particular brand of liberal views.

Communitarians pay special attention to the condition of public spaces as places communities happen (as distinct from private places like homes and cars). Even though one may carpool with friends or have them over for a visit, these are mainly activities of small friendship groups (what Robert Putnam calls "bowling alone"). Communities need more encompassing webs, and those are formed and reinforced in public gathering places—from school assembly halls to parks, from plazas to promenades. To the extent that these spaces become unsafe, communities lose one of their major sources of reinforcement; recapturing them for community use is hence a major element of community regeneration.

Most important, drawing again on sociology, and particularly on what has been called the "consensus" rather then the "conflict") model, communitarians tend to maintain that if in addition to strong families and schools that build character, a society has communities, where social webs are intact and thats moral voice is clearly articulate, that society will be able to base its social order largely on moral commitments rather than the forces of the state. This is the case, communitarians argue, drawing on sociological assumptions and studies, because once moral commitments are internalized and reinforced they help shape people's preferences in favor of prosocial behavior—thus reducing the need for coercion by the state and diminishing the tension between liberty and social order.

Many discussions of community and of the moral infrastructure stop at this point, having explored the moral agency of family, school, and community. However, social and moral communities are not freestanding; they are often parts of more encompassing social entities. Moreover, communitarians note that unless communities are bound socially and morally into more encompassing entities, they may war with one another. Hence, the importance of *communities of communities*, the society.

Communitarians argue that one should not view society as composed of millions of individuals, but as pluralism within unity. They further maintain that subcultures and loyalties are not a threat to the integrity of society as long as a core of shared values and institutions (such as the Constitution and its Bill of Rights, the democratic way of life, and mutual tolerance) are respected.

Communitarians draw on the four elements of the moral infrastructure—families, schools, communities, and communities of communities—as a sort of a checklist to help determine the state of the moral infrastructure in a given society. They argue that the decline of the two-parent family (due to high divorce rates, growing legitimation of single-parent families, and psychological disinvestment of parents in children), the deterioration of schools (due to automatic promotions and deterioration of social order in schools), the decline of communities (due to modernization), and the decline of the community of communities (as a result of excessive emphasis on diversity without parallel concern over shared bonds) resulted in the decline of moral and social order in the American society during the 1970s and 1980s. This was evidenced by the sharp rise in violent crime, drug abuse, teen pregnancy, and in the decline of voluntarism, among other factors. The fact that some of these trends slowed down and reversed in the 1990s is viewed in part by communitarians as a reflection of changes in social thinking and practices they helped champion.

Here lies a great difference between the communitarian position and that of various religious social conservatives. Both groups recognize the need to regenerate the moral infrastructure, but conservatives favor returning to traditional social formations while communitarians point to new ways of shoring up society's ethical framework. For instance, many social conservatives favor women "graciously submitting to their husbands" and returning to homemaking, while communitarians argue for peer marriage, a concept introduced by Pepper Schwartz. Peer marriage suggests equal rights and responsibilities for mothers and fathers, but favors marriages that last, as compared to the liberal argument that single-parent families or child care centers can socialize children as well if not better than two-parent families. (Among the sociologists who have struck a communitarian position in this matter are Linda Waite, Glen Elder, Alice Rossi, and David Popenoe).

The communitarian argument over the role of communities in maintaining social order is strongly supported by sociological research of the kind conducted by Robert Sampson on the role of communities in fighting crime and drug abuse. David Karp and Todd Clear have also studied community involvement in criminal justice, focusing on ideas of restorative justice and policies that are concerned more with reintegrating offenders into their communities than merely punishing them.

Other communitarian themes examined by sociologists include topics explored by Edward W. Lehman, especially his writing on macro-sociology; Martin Whyte's work on the family; and Richard Coughlin's comparison of communitarian thinking to socioeconomics.

CIVIL SOCIETY, THE THIRD WAY, AND THE GOOD SOCIETY

Much of the normative debate in the West, at least since the middle of the nineteenth century, has focused on the merit of the free market (or capitalism) versus the role of the state in securing the citizens' well-being. Communitarians have basically leapfrogged this debate, focusing instead on the importance of the third element of social life, that of the civic society, which is neither state nor market. Communitarians have played a key role in the debate over the condition of civic society in the West, such as examining whether participation in voluntary associations, voting, and trust in institutions have declined, and to what effect. The work of Robert Bellah and his associates has been particularly influential here, demonstrating the rise of first expressive and then instrumental individualism, and their ill effects.

Communitarians have argued that rather than dumping people (often the most vulnerable members of society) into the marketplace as the welfare state is curtailed, civic society's various institutions can empower these individuals to help one another in attending to some of their social needs. Communal institutions (including places of worship) can shoulder important parts of care previously provided by state agencies, although the state will have to continue to shoulder an important part of the burden.

Communitarians stress that mutuality, rather than charity, is the basis for community-wide action that is not solely limited to helping one particular vulnerable group or another. The CPR training of some 400,000 Seattle citizens, who are thus able to help one another without public costs or private charges, is held up as a key case in point. Other examples include voluntary recycling programs, crime watch patrols, and above all the massive assistance given to immigrants by members of their own ethnic group. Communitarians have also pointed to the importance of a culture of civility in maintaining a society's ability to work out differences without excessive conflict.

Communitarians have argued that a civic society is good, but not good enough. Civic society tends to be morally neutral on many matters other than values concerning its own inherent virtue and the attributes citizens need to make them into effective members of a civic society, for instance, to be able to think critically. Thus, all voluntary associations, from the KKK to the Urban League, from militias to Hadassah, are considered to have the same basic standing. In contrast, a good society seeks to promote a core of substantive values, and thus views some social associations and activities as more virtuous than others. In the same vein, communitarians have stressed that while everyone's legal right to free speech should be respected, there is no denying that some speech—seen from the community's viewpoint—is morally sound while other speech is abhorrent. For instance, the (legal) right to speak does not make hate speech (morally) right. Communitarians would not seek to suppress hate speech by legal means, however, but they urge communities to draw on their moral voice to chastise those who speak in ways that are offensive.

CRITICS AND RESPONSES

Critics of responsive communitarianism argue that the concept of community is vague; indeed that the term "community" itself cannot be well defined. In response, *community* has been defined as a combination of two elements: a) A web of affect-laden relationships among a group of individuals, relationships that often crisscross and reinforce one another (rather than merely one-on-one or chainlike individual relationships)and b) A measure of commitment to a set of shared values, norms, and meanings, and a shared history and identity to a particular culture.

Some critics also contend that the quest for community is anachronistic, that contemporary societies are urban and populations geographically highly mobile, and thus bereft of community. Communitarians respond that communities exist in contemporary societies in small towns, suburbs, campuses and within city neighborhoods, often based on ethnic ties in places such as Korea Town in Los Angeles, Little Italy in New York City, the Irish section of South Boston, and so on. Moreover, communitarians point out that communities need not be geographic, members can be spread among nonmembers. For instance, homosexual groups often constitute communities even if they are not all neighbors.

Critics maintain that communities are authoritarian and oppressive, and have charged communitarians with seeking "Salem without witches." Communitarians respond that communities vary regarding this assessment. Contemporary communities tend to be relatively freer, given the relative ease of intercommunity mobility as well as shifting loyalties and psychic investments among various groups of which the same person is a member.

Critics also maintain that communities are exclusionary, and hence bigoted. Communitarians respond that communities must respect the laws of the society in which they are situated, but do tend to thrive on a measure of homogeneity and on people's desire to be with others of their own kind. Moreover, given the human benefit of community membership, a measure of self-segregation should be tolerated.

Critics of responsive communitarianism claim that communitarians ignore matters of power and injustice as well as economic considerations, and are generally inclined to adopt a consensus rather than a conflict model. Communitarians agree that they ought to pay more attention to the effects of these factors on communities. However, they do envision the possibilities of conflict within communities, and responsive communitarians do propose that one should not treat conflict and community as mutually exclusive. Extending this idea to the treatment of diversity and multiculturalism, communitarians argue in favor of a society in which many differences can be celebrated as long

as a set of commitments to the overarching society is upheld.

VALUES AND VIRTUES

While sociologists greatly altered and enriched communitarian thinking, communitarian thinking's main contribution to sociology is the challenge of facing issues raised by the moral standing of various values, and the related question of cross-cultural moral judgments. Sociologists tend to treat all values as conceptually equal; a sociologist may refer to racist Afrikaners' beliefs and to humanitarian beliefs using the same "neutral" term, calling both "values." Communitarians use the term virtue to denote that some values (or belief systems) have a higher standing than others because they are compatible with the good society, while other values are not (and hence aberrant).

In the same vein, communitarians do not shy away from passing cross-cultural moral judgments, rejecting cultural relativism's claim that all cultures have basically equal moral standing. Thus, they view female circumcision, sex slaves, and *hudud* (chopping off the right hand of thieves) as violations of liberty and individual rights, and abandoning children, violating implicit contracts built into communal mutuality, or neglecting the environment, as evidence of a lack of commitment to social order and neglect of social responsibilities.

IMPACT

So far this examination has focused on the place of communitarian thinking in academic, conceptual, theoretical, and imperial works. Responsive communitarians have also been playing a considerable public role, presenting themselves as the founders of a new kind of environmental movement, one dedicated to shoring up society (not the state) rather than nature. Like environmentalism, communitarianism appeals to audiences across the political spectrum, although it has found greater acceptance with some groups rather than others. British Prime Minister Tony Blair is reported to have adopted the communitarian platform, and German Social Democrat Rudolf Scharping has suggested that his party should meet the communitarians "half way." President Bill Clinton and his wife Hillary Rodham Clinton (author of *It*

Takes a Village) have combined communitarian with welfare-liberal themes. Among conservatives, Jack Kemp, a group of Tory members of the British parliament (especially David Willet), and German governor Kurt Biedenkopf are often listed as influenced by communitarianism. While this is only a partial list, it serves to illustrate the scope of communitarianism's influence and its cross over traditional ideological lines.

Communitarian terms have become part of the public vocabulary in the 1990s, especially references to "assuming responsibilities to match rights," while "communitarianism" itself is used much less often. The number of articles about communitarian thinking in the popular press increased twelvefold during the last decade of the twentieth century. The increase in the number of books, articles, and Ph.D. dissertations in academia for the same period, has been about eightfold. Interestingly, taking communitarianism from academia to the "streets" in the early 1990s resulted in the middle and late 1990s into a significant increase in acasemic interest. In the process, bridges have been built between social philosophers, sociologists, and community members and leaders, although they still sometimes travel on parallel rather than convergent pathways.

An extensive bibliography of communitarian works is also listed on The Communitarian Network's website, http:www.gwu.edu/~ccps.

REFERENCES

Bellah, Robert et al.1991 *The Good Society*. New York: Knopf.

—— 1986 *Habits of the Heart*. New York: Harper & Row.

Coughlin, Richard 1991 *Morality, Rationality, and Efficiency: New Perspectives on Socio-economics*. Armonk. N.Y.: M.E. Sharpe.

Etzioni, Amitai 1998 *The Essential Communitarian Reader*. New York: Roman & Littlefield.

—— 1996 *The New Golden Rule*. New York: Basic Books.

—— 1995 *New Communitarian Thinking*. Charlottesville, Va.: The University of Virginia Press.

—— 1993 *The Spirit of Community*. New York: Touchstone.

Paul, Ellen Franken, Fred Miller, Jr., and Jeffrey Paul (eds.) 1996 *The Communitarian Challenge to Liberalism*. New York: Cambridge University Press.

Selznick, Philip 1992 *The Moral Commonwealth*. Berkeley: University of California Press.

The Responsive Community: Rights and Responsibilities, a quarterly journal.

AMITAI ETZIONI

COMMUNITY

The sociology of community has been a dominant source of sociological inquiry since the earliest days of the discipline. Each of the three most influential nineteenth century sociologists (Marx, Durkheim, and Weber) regarded the social transformation of community in its various forms to be a fundamental problem of sociology and sociological theory. Thomas Bender (1978) suggests that as early social thinkers observed the disruption of the traditional social order and traditional patterns of social life associated with industrialization, urbanization, and the rise of capitalism, significant attention was focused on the social transformation of community and communal life. It should be emphasized that contemporary sociology remains, at its core, a discipline largely concerned with the definition and persistence of community as a form of social organization, social existence, and social experience.

The definition of community in sociology has been problematic for several reasons, not the least of which has been nostalgic attachment to the idealized notion that community is embodied in the village or small town where human associations are characterized as *Gemeinschaft*: that is, associations that are intimate, familiar, sympathetic, mutually interdependent, and reflective of a shared social consciousness (in contrast to relationships that are *Gesellschaft*—casual, transitory, without emotional investment, and based on self-interest). According to this traditional concept of community, the requirements of community or communal existence can be met only in the context of a certain quality of human association occurring within the confines of limited, shared physical territory.

The classic perspective on community offered by Carle Zimmerman (1938) is consistent with this theme, in that the basic four characteristics argued by Zimmerman to define community (social fact, specification, association, and limited area) require a territorial context. George Hillary (1955), in a content analysis of ninety-four definitions of community advanced in sociological literature, discovered basic consensus on only three definitional elements: social interaction between people, one or more shared ties, and an area context. However, Hillary noted that area context was the least required of these three definitional elements. Others (e.g., Lindeman 1930; Bender 1978; McMillan and Chavis 1986) argue that community can be achieved independently of territorial context where social networks exist sufficiently to sustain a *Gemeinschaft* quality of interaction and association. According to this point of view, territory is neither a necessary nor a sufficient condition to define the existence of community. In this vein, David McMillan and David Chavis suggest a state of community exists when four elements co-exist: membership, influence, integration and fulfillment of needs, and shared emotional connections. They argue that communities can be defined either in relational terms or territorial terms as long as these four elements are present together.

MAJOR QUESTIONS IN THE SOCIOLOGY OF COMMUNITY

The major questions that concern the sociology of community include the distinguishing characteristics and definition of community, the bases of communal experience and integration, the unique functions and tasks of community, the units of social structure within the community and the relationships and interactions between structural units, the economic and social bases of the community social structure, the relationship and distinction between internal community social structure and macrosocial structures external to the community, the relationship between individual experience and behavior and communal experience and behavior, the causes and processes of transformation from *Gemeinschaft* to *Gesellschaft* states of social existence, and processes of community persistence and adaptation in the face of social change.

COMMUNITY STUDIES

Community studies undertaken by sociologists over the past sixty years have to a large extent

sought to address some if not all of these issues. The most famous and controversial include Robert and Helen Lynd's Middletown studies (1929, 1937) and the Yankee City series by W. Lloyd Warner and his associates (1963). The more well-known studies that have focused on the problem of community within large cities have included William Whyte's *Street Corner Society* and Gerald Suttles's *The Social Order of the Slum*, which themselves are aligned with earlier Robert Park and Ernest Burgess conceptions of the "natural community" arising within the confines of a seemingly faceless, anonymous, large city (Suttles 1972, pp. 7–9). Descriptive studies that emphasize field work and examine social structure as a spatial phenomenon are the hallmark of the highly influential Chicago School that arose and flourished under Robert Park and Ernest Burgess of the University of Chicago Department of Sociology during the 1920s and 1930s.

Robert and Helen Lynd carried out two studies (1929, 1937) involving extensive personal field work on the town of Muncie, Indiana: *Middletown* (1929) and *Middletown in Transition* (1937). In the first Middletown study, the Lynds spent the years 1924–1925 participating in and observing the community life of Middletown (population 36,500), and performing extensive survey work. Their objective was to address all aspects of social life and social structure of the community. A fundamental focus of the Lynds' earlier analysis concerned the consequences of technological change (industrialization) on the social structure of Middletown, in particular the emergence of social class conflicts subsequent to turn-of-the-century industrialization.

Although the Lynds found distinctions between the living conditions and opportunity structures of business and working-class families that were consistent with their Marxist expectations (i.e., children of the working class were more likely to drop out of school to help support the family, working-class families labored longer hours for less pay and less financial security, and living conditions in general were more harsh for working-class families), they failed to discover a disparate value structure or alienation among the working class. At all levels of social class, the Middletown of 1925 shared a common conservative value structure that entailed self-reliance, faith in the future, and a belief in hard work. The subsequent study, undertaken in 1935 by Robert Lynd and a staff of five assistants, addressed the effects on Muncie of certain events during the period between 1925 and 1935, some of which were economic boom times, a thirty-seven percent population increase, and the emergence of the Great Depression. The Lynds' fundamental questions in the later study addressed the persistence of the social fabric and culture of the community in the face of the "hard times" and other aspects of social change, the stability of community values concerning self-reliance and faith in the future when confronted by structurally-induced poverty and dependence, whether the Depression promoted a sense of community, or undermined community solidarity by introducing new social cleavages, and the outcomes of latent conflicts observed in the mid-1920s (Lynd and Lynd 1937, p. 4).

The conclusion reached by the Lynds was that the years of depression did little to diminish or otherwise change the essentially bourgeois value structure and way of life in Middletown, and that in almost all fundamental respects the community culture of Middletown remained much as it did a tumultuous decade earlier: "In the main, a Rip Van Winkle, fallen asleep in 1925 while addressing Rotary or the Central Labor Union, could have awakened in 1935 and gone right on with his interrupted address to the same people with much the same ideas" (Lynd and Lynd 1937, p. 490). Although this remark seems to reflect some amount of disappointment on the Lynds' part that Middletown's bourgeois value system and class structure remained so unchanged in the face of widespread and unprecedented destitution, the Lynds still remained convinced that the Middletown family was in jeopardy, as evidenced by (among other things) an ever-widening generation gap. The Lynds' apprehensions concerning the survival of the American family were (and are) in keeping with the popular belief concerning the decline of the American family as its socialization functions are assumed by other formal social institutions external to the family.

The Middletown III study undertaken from 1976 to 1978 by Theodore Caplow, Howard M. Bahr, and Bruce A. Chadwick, attempted to closely replicate the methodology of the Lynds. However, their findings were at odds with the more pessimistic predictions of the Lynds. In contrast to the Lynds' foreboding in 1935 and popular sociology since that time, Caplow and his associates

contend that Middletown's families of the 1970s have "increased family solidarity, a smaller generation gap, closer marital communication, more religion, and less mobility" (Caplow et al. 1982, p. 323). The conclusions derived from the third Middletown studies also reject similar assumptions concerning consistent linear trends in equalization, secularization, bureaucratization, and depersonalization consistent with the relentless *Gemeinschaft* to *Gesellschaft* theme (Bahr, Caplow, and Chadwick 1983).

Although many of the Lynds' predictions concerning the social transformation of Middletown failed to pan out as history unfolded, their work and remarkable powers of observation remain unparalleled in many respects. Of equal importance, the early Middletown studies helped to inspire such other works as *Street Corner Society* and the Yankee City studies, and they remain the standard by which all other community studies are judged.

The largest scale community study undertaken remains W. Lloyd Warner's Yankee City, published in a five volume series from 1941 through 1959 (W. Lloyd Warner and Paul S. Lund, *The Social Life of a Modern Community* 1941; W. Lloyd Warner and Paul S. Lund, *The Status System of a Modern Community* 1942; W. Lloyd Warner and Leo Srole, *The Social Systems of American Ethnic Groups* 1945; W. Lloyd Warner and J. O. Low, *The Social System of the Modern Factory* 1947; and W. Lloyd Warner *The Living and the Dead* 1959). The Yankee City project was undertaken by Warner and his associates in Newburyport, Massachusetts during the late 1930s. Warner, an anthropologist, attempted to obtain a complete ethnographic account of a "representative" American small community with a population range from 10,000 to 20,000. To accomplish this task, Warner's staff (numbering in the thirties) conducted aerial surveys of Newburyport and its surrounding communities, gathered some 17,000 "social personality" cards on every member of the community, gathered data on the professed and de facto reading preferences of its citizens, and even subjected plots of local plays to content analysis (Thernstrom 1964).

Warner's conception of Yankee City was that of a stable, rather closed community with a social structure being transformed in very negative ways by the latter stages of industrialization. According to Warner's vision of Yankee City, the loss of local economic control over its industries through a factory system controlled by "outsiders" disrupted traditional management—labor relations and communal identification with local leadership. Moreover, the factory system was seen by Warner as promoting an increasingly rigid class structure and decreased opportunities for social mobility. In particular, Warner's discussion of the loss of local economic control through horizontal and vertical affiliation, orientation, and delegation of authority seems to have offered a prophetic glimpse into the future for many American communities.

Although the Yankee City study produced a voluminous ethnographic record of an American city that has remained untouched in scale, Warner found little support for his contention that the ethnographic portrait of Newburyport produced by the Yankee City series could be generalized to other small American communities. Moreover, Warner's contention that social mobility is reduced by industrial change was not supported by the quality of his data and was less true in Warner's time than it probably is today. Other critiques of Warner's Yankee City study primarily concern his nearly exclusive reliance on ethnographic information as the basis for all measures of social structure and his disdain for historical data (Thernstrom 1964).

Both Gerald Suttles's *The Social Order of the Slum* (1968) and William Whyte's *Street Corner Society* (1943) provide sociology with unparalleled ethnographic accounts of neighborhood social structure and communal life in urban environs. Suttles's work focuses on the territorial relationships, neighborhood social structure, and communal life among Italian, Latino, and African American inhabitants of the slums of Chicago's Near West Side in the 1960s. Whyte's *Street Corner Society,* based on Whyte's residence in a Chicago Italian slum district a generation earlier, provides sociology with an understanding of the complex and stable social organization that existed within slum neighborhoods conventionally believed to have epitomized social disorganization. Whyte's observations and keen insights concerning small group behavior are pioneering contributions to that area of sociology. Both studies, in method, theory, and substance are classic examples of Chicago School

sociology. More contemporary community studies, while they draw heavily on Chicago School sociological traditions in theory and method, have as their primary concern aspects of community that relate to poverty, juvenile delinquency, and violence. For example, Robert Sampson and his colleagues conducted a large-scale study of Chicago neighborhoods that linked subjective definitions of neighborhood with social cohesion and violence inhibiting actions on the part of neighbors (Sampson 1997a, 1997b). Theoretically, Sampson's work draws heavily on Robert Park's conception of the social cohesion that exists within the "natural areas" of the city that are defined by both physical and sentimental boundaries (Park 1925), while methodologically Sampson and his colleagues employed the classic Chicago School preference for field observation—albeit with the modern advantages of a video camera located within a slowly moving van in place of the shoe leather sociology of their predecessors.

COMMUNITY IN THE CONTEXT OF SOCIAL REFORM

Efforts to enhance the social context of human existence continuously take place at all levels of social organization, from the microcontext of the nuclear family to the macrocontext of relationships between nation-states. No unit of social organization has received more attention in theories and activities linked to social reform than the human community, however it is defined and measured. Community in the context of social reform is typically viewed or employed in one of the following four ways: as a unit of analysis for the purpose of broad generalization, as a critical mediating influence between the organization of mass society and individual outcomes, as a specific target of social reform efforts, or as a symbolic conception of whatever is "right" or "wrong" with society at large.

The use of rural and urban communities as the basis for reform-motivated generalization emerged in the United States during the Progressive era, when social activists affiliated with Chicago's famous settlement house, Hull House, and the newly formed Department of Sociology at the University of Chicago shared a common geographically-rooted conception of social science and concern for the living conditions of Chicago's urban poor (Sklar 1998). *Hull House Maps and Papers*, published in 1895, provides a remarkably detailed description of the lives and living conditions within Chicago's ethnic neighborhoods based on the field research of university students and full-time residents of Hull House. In fact, the beginnings of Chicago School sociology were clearly rooted in the methods if not the concerns of Hull House social reformers, despite the fact that as women they were excluded from holding academic appointments until the creation of the Chicago School of Civics and Philanthropy in 1907 (Muncy 1991).

In later years, small towns and neighborhoods within larger towns became a common unit of analysis as community studies conducted by the federal Children's Bureau tried to assess the incidence and causes of infant mortality. The first of these studies, conducted in Johnstown, Pennsylvania in 1913, was the earliest scientific study of the incidence of infant mortality by social class, education, occupation, and specific living conditions conducted in the United States (Duke 1915). Reform-driven community studies since then have addressed such social issues as child labor, juvenile delinquency, education, industrial working conditions, and adequate housing. Although single communities are still used by social reformers as a basis for broad generalization, such studies are enormously expensive to conduct, often of limited use for generalization, and altogether less frequent with the availability of national survey data.

Despite the conceptual ambiguities involved, the geographically-bounded community (e.g., census tract, city ward, resident defined neighborhood) is generally viewed by liberal and conservative social reformers alike as the critical mediating social context between the well-being of individuals, the effective functioning and stability of families, and society at large. Robert Hauser and his associates identify such factors as the physical infrastructure, the quality and quantity of neighborhood institutions, the demographic composition, and the degree of "social capital" present as measurable aspects of neighborhoods that are critical to the well-being of children and families (Hauser, Brown, and Prosser 1997). The concept of social capital, introduced by James Coleman, refers to the beneficial normative context that arises in some neighborhoods based on the social ties among neighboring households and local institutions (Coleman 1988). In this vein, Robert

Sampson demonstrates that neighborhoods with evidence of more social capital are more effective in inhibiting adolescent delinquency (Sampson, 1997b). Speaking from the opposite perspective of social disorganization, William Julius Wilson (1987, 1996), and Douglas Massey and Nancy Denton (1993) emphasize the deleterious effects on the normative context within communities created by such macrolevel exogenous factors as economic restructuring, concentrated poverty, and racial segregation. A related concern is the extent to which increased spatial stratification by social class may be promoting neighborhoods and larger communities, which function as distinct social worlds with ever more divergent values and opportunity structures (Massey 1996).

Efforts to effect social reform at the community level have a long tradition of sentiment, failure, and mixed success. There are a variety of reasons for failure, not the least of which is that communities, like individuals, both mirror and are shaped by complex exogenous social processes. Contemporary issues include conceptual differences in the measures used for community, the fact that community effects on individual outcomes are difficult to isolate and often weaker than popular theory would suggest (Plotnick and Hoffman 1999; Brooks-Gunn, Duncan, and Aber 1997), and the limiting effect of macrolevel processes on community-level reform efforts (Wallace and Wallace 1990; Halpern 1991). Recent efforts at community-level social reform have placed more emphasis on understanding the unique social context within a target community before applying social prescriptions that appear logically appealing or may have worked elsewhere. For example, David Hawkins and Richard Catalano, in their work on juvenile drug and alcohol abuse, focus on a community assessment process that considers the risk and protective factors that are unique to each community before deciding upon specific community-level interventions (Hawkins and Catalano 1992).

SOCIAL THEORY AND THE TRANSFORMATION OF COMMUNITY

Every generation of sociologists since the time of Durkheim have concerned themselves with the social transformation and meaning of community in the face of industrial change and urbanization.

Roland Warren (1978) describes the modern social transformation of community as a change of orientation by the local community units toward the extracommunity systems of which they are a part, with a corresponding decrease in community cohesion and autonomy (Warren 1978, pp. 52–53). Warren identifies seven areas through which social transformation can be analyzed: division of labor, differentiation of interests and association, increasing systemic relationships to the larger society, bureaucratization and impersonalization, transfer of functions to profit enterprise and government, urbanization and suburbanization, and changing value.

Bender (1978) proposes that the observations by various community scholars at different points in historical time, each suggesting that theirs is the historical tipping point from community to mass society, contradict linear decline or an interpretation of history that stresses the collapse of community. He suggests that a "bifurcation of social experience" or sharpening of the distinction between *Gemeinschaft* and *Gesellschaft* realms of social interaction is a more accurate interpretation of the historical transformation of community than that provided by the linear *Gemeinschaft-to-gesellschaft* framework.

Barry Wellman and Barry Leighton (1979) suggest that there are three essential arguments concerning the fate of community in mass society: community "lost," community "saved," and community "liberated." The community "lost" argument emerged during the Industrial Revolution, as traditional communal modes of production and interaction gave way to centralized, industrialized sources of production and dependence. According to this hypothesis and its variations, the intimate, sustained, and mutually interdependent human associations based on shared fate and shared consciousness observed in traditional communal society are relentlessly giving way to the casual, impersonal, transitory, and instrumental relationships based on self-interest that are characteristic of social existence in modern industrial society.

The classic essay in the community "lost" tradition is Louis Wirth's "Urbanism as a Way of Life" (1938). Wirth's eloquent essay presents a perspective of urban existence that continues to capture sociological thinking about the emergence of a heterogeneous urban mass society characterized by a breakdown of informal, communal ways of meeting human need and the rise of human relationships that are best characterized as "largely anonymous, superficial, and transitory" (Wirth 1938, p. 1). Another important contribution in the decline of community tradition is the "community of limited liability" thesis (Janowitz 1952; Greer 1962). According to this thesis, networks of human association and interdependence exist at various levels of social organization, and there are social status characteristics associated with differentiated levels of participation in community life (e.g., family life-cycle phase). The idea of "limited liability" poses the argument that, in a highly mobile society, the attachments to community tend to be based on rationalism rather than on sentiment and that even those "invested" in the community are limited in their sense of personal commitment.

In direct contrast to the community "lost" perspective, the community "saved" argument suggests that communities and communal relationships continue to exist within industrialized bureaucratic urban societies as people are increasingly motivated to seek "safe communal havens" (William and Lieghton 1979, p. 373). For example, Bahr, Caplow, and Chadwick (1983), forty years after the Lynds' *Middletown in Transition* study, failed to find the singular trends in bureaucratization, secularization, mobility, and depersonalization that would be predicted from a linear decline of community hypothesis. Their observation of Middletown in the 1970s was more consistent with the perspective proposed by Robert Redfield (1955); that both urban ways and folkways coexist within contemporary small towns and cities: "In every isolated little community there is civilization; in every city there is the folk society" (Redfield 1955, p. 146).

The community "liberated" argument concedes and to some extent qualifies key aspects of both the community "lost" and community "saved" perspectives. While it acknowledges that neighborhood-level communal ties have been weakened in the face of urbanization, it argues that communal ties and folkways still flourish, albeit in alternative non-spatial forms. The community "liberated" argument suggests that the spatial dependence of communal ties have been replaced by ease of mobility and communication across boundaries of both geographic and social distance. Although the community "liberated" argument preceeded the development of the Internet and cyberspace "chatrooms" by decades, it emphasizes the role of communication technology in the creation of such future manifestations of community and in that sense was strikingly prophetic.

Despite the fact that the decline of community or the community "lost" perspective continues to hold broad appeal (e.g., Robert Putnam's "The Strange Disappearance of Civic America," *The American Prospect*, Winter, 1996), the empirical evidence for a real decline in community is far from conclusive. A time trend analysis of national surveys concerning the persistence of community in American society by Avery Guest and Susan Wierzbicki (1999) suggests that while traditional intra-neighborhood forms of socializing have slowly declined over the past two decades, they have been largely replaced by communal ties outside the local neighborhood. Moreover, Guest and Wierzbicki's findings also suggest that spatial "within neigborhood" communal ties continue to be important to a large segment of the population. Their findings imply that the major questions about the place of community in mass society should not be about whether communal forms of relationships will continue to exist, but rather under what conditions and in what form.

REFERENCES

Bahr, Howard M., Theodore Caplow, and Bruce Chadwick 1983 "Middletown III: Problems of Replication, Longitudinal Measurement, and Triangulation." *Annual Review of Sociology* 9:249–258.

Bender, Thomas 1978 *Community and Social Change in America*. New Brunswick, N.J.: Rutgers University Press.

Brooks-Gunn, Jeanne, Greg Duncan, and Lawrence Aber 1997 *Neighborhood Poverty: Context and Consequences for Children, Volume I*. New York: Russell Sage Foundation.

Caplow, Theodore, Howard M. Bahr, Bruce A. Chadwick, Reuben Hill, and Margaret Holmes Williamson 1982 *Middletown Families: Fifty Years of Change and Continuity*. Minneapolis: University of Minnesota Press.

Coleman, James 1988 "Social Capital in the Creation of Human Capital." *American Journal of Sociology*, 94 (supp): S95–S120.

Duke, Emma 1914 *Infant Mortality: Results of a Field Study in Johnstown, P.A., Based on Births in One Calendar Year*. U.S.D.L. Children's Bureau Publication No. 9. Washington D.C.: U.S. Government Printing Office.

Greer, Scott 1962 *The Emerging City: Myth and Reality*. New York: Free Press of Glencoe.

Guest, Avery, and Susan Wierzbicki 1999 "Social Ties at the Neighborhood Level: Two Decades of GSS Evidence." *Urban Affairs Review* 35: forthcoming.

Halpern, Robert 1991 "Supportive Services for Families in Poverty: Dilemmas of Reform." *Social Service Review* 65 (3):343–365.

Hauser, Robert, Brett Brown, and William Prosser 1997 *Indicators of Children's Well-Being*. New York: Russell Sage Foundation.

Hillary, George A., Jr. 1955 "Definitions of Community: Areas of Agreement." *Rural Sociology* 20:111–123.

Janowitz, Morris 1952 *The Community Press in an Urban Setting: The Social Elements of Urbanism*. Chicago: University of Chicago Press.

Jencks, Christopher and Susan Mayer 1996 "The Social Consequences of Growing Up in a Poor Neighborhood." In Lynn Le and McGeary MGH, eds., *Inner-city Poverty in the United States*. Washington D.C.: National Academy Press.

Lindeman, E. C. 1930 "Community." In Edwin R. A. Seligman, ed., *The Encyclopedia of Social Sciences*. New York: Macmillan.

Lynd, Robert, and Helen Lynd 1929 *Middletown: A Study in American Culture*. New York: Harcourt, Brace and Company.

—— 1937 *Middletown in Transition: A Study in Cultural Conflicts*. New York: Harcourt, Brace and Company.

Massey, Douglas 1996 "The Age of Extremes: Concentrated Affluence and Poverty in the Twenty-First Century." *Demography* 33 (4):395–413.

—— and Nancy Denton 1993 *American Apartheid: Segregation and the Making of the Underclass*. Cambridge, Mass.: Harvard University Press.

McMillan, David and David Chavis 1986 "Sense of Community: A Definition and Theory." *Journal of Community Psychology* 14:6–23.

Muncy, Robyn 1991 *Creating a Female Dominion in American Reform 1890–1935*. New York: Oxford University Press.

Park, Robert 1925 "The City: Suggestions for the Investigation of Human Behavior in the Urban Environment." In Robert Park, Ernest Burgess, and Roderick McKenzie, eds., *The City*. Chicago: University of Chicago Press.

Plotnick, Robert and Saul Hoffman 1999 "The Effect of Neighborhood Characteristics on Young Adult Outcomes: Alternative Estimates." *Social Science Quarterly* 80 (1):forthcoming.

Putnam, Robert 1996 "The Strange Disppearance of Civic America." *The American Prospect.* Winter, 1996: 34–48.

Redfield, Robert 1955 *The Little Community.* Chicago: University of Chicago Press.

Sampson, Robert 1997a "Neighborhoods and Violent Crime: A Multilevel Study of Collective Efficacy." *Science* 277:918–925.

——— 1997b "Collective Regulation of Adolescent Misbehavior: Validation Results from Eighty Chicago Neighborhoods." *Journal of Adolescent Research* 12 (2):227–244.

Sklar, Kathryn 1998 "Hull-House Maps and Papers: Social Science as Women's Work in the 1890's." In Helene Silverberg, ed., *Gender and American Social Science: The Formative Years.* Princeton, N.J.: Princeton University Press.

Suttles, Gerald 1972 *The Social Construction of Communities.* Chicago: University of Chicago Press.

——— 1968 *The Social Order of the Slum: Ethnicity and Territory in the Inner City.* Chicago: The University of Chicago Press.

Thernstrom, Stephen 1964 *Poverty and Progress.* Cambridge, Mass.: Harvard University Press.

Wallace, Roderick, and Deborah Wallace 1990 "Origins of Public Health Collapse in New York City: The Dynamics of Planned Shrinkage, Contagious Urban Decay, and Social Disintegration." *Bulletin of the New York Academy of Medicine* 66:391–434.

Warner, W. Lloyd 1959 *The Living and the Dead: A Study of the Symbolic Life of Americans.* New Haven: Yale University Press.

———, and J.O. Low 1947 *The Social System of the Modern Factory: The Strike, A Social Analysis.* New Haven: Yale University Press.

———, Paul S. Lund, and Leo Srole 1963 *Yankee City.* New Haven: Yale University Press.

Warner, W. Lloyd, and Leo Srole 1945 *The Social Systems of American Ethnic Groups.* New Haven: Yale University Press.

Warner, W. Lloyd, and Paul S. Lund 1941 *The Social Life of a Modern Community.* New Haven: Yale University Press.

——— 1942 *The Status System of a Modern Community.* New Haven: Yale University Press.

Warren, Roland 1978 *The Community in America.* Chicago: Rand McNally.

Wellman, Barry, and Barry Leighton 1979 "Networks, Neighborhoods, and Community: Approaches to the Study of the Community Question." *Urban Affairs Quarterly* 14 (3):363–390.

Whyte, William Foote 1943 *Street Corner Society: The Social Structure of an Italian Slum.* Chicago: University of Chicago Press.

Wilson, William 1996 *When Work Disappears: The World of the New Urban Poor.* New York: Knopf.

——— 1987 *The Truly Disadvantaged: The Inner City, the Underclass, and Public Policy.* Chicago: University of Chicago Press.

Wirth, Louis 1938 "Urbanism as a Way of Life." *American Journal of Sociology* 44:1–24.

Zimmerman, Carle C. 1938 *The Changing Community.* New York: Harper and Brothers.

GUNNAR ALMGREN

COMMUNITY HEALTH

See Community; Comparative Health-Care Systems; Health Promotion and Health Status; Medical Sociology.

COMPARABLE WORTH

"Comparable worth" is one approach to increasing pay equity between jobs done primarily by women and minorities and those done primarily by majority men. It refers to equalizing compensation for jobs requiring comparable levels of effort, skill, and responsibility. The concept of comparable worth defines "equal work" as "work of equivalent value," a broader concept than limiting "equal work" to meaning the "same work." Comparable worth uses job-evaluation methods to establish equivalencies of different jobs in order to identify and correct disparities in pay between jobs held primarily by women and minority men and jobs held primarily by nonminority men. It is worth noting that the term *pay equity* is often used in conjunction with discussions of comparable worth; it usually refers not only to comparable worth but also to other approaches to achieving equity and justice in wages. Pay equity is the best subject heading or "key word" to use when doing further research on the topic of comparable worth.

Proponents of using comparable worth to establish pay equity argue that 1) at least some part of the lower wages in female-dominated jobs and occupations is due to pay discrimination against women, and 2) job evaluation systems can determine the equivalency of different jobs and thus identify the jobs and occupations where this form of discrimination exists.

The issue of comparable worth arose in response to obvious differences in the rewards for jobs held primarily by women and those held primarily by men—even when those jobs required the same or similar levels of education, skill, and responsibility. Advocates of comparable worth and pay equity argue that these wage differences are based on historical and current discrimination in the setting of wages for jobs held primarily by women and minorities. That is, jobs in which workers are primarily women and minorities have been, and remain, systematically undervalued relative to equivalent jobs held by majority men. This undervaluation depresses the wages in jobs done by women and minorities relative to the wages for jobs historically performed by white men. Thus, discrimination is embedded in the current wage structure of jobs (Remick 1984; Marini 1989). Continued job and occupational segregation by sex, combined with the continued systematic undervaluation of jobs held by women and minorities, is thereby a cause of continued inequality and a form of labor market discrimination.

The argument that discrimination is the basis for the inequality of wages between men's and women's jobs is not new. In the 1922 presidential address to the British Association of Economists, F.Y. Edgeworth spoke on "Equal Pay to Men and Women for Equal Work." Edgeworth outlined three major conclusions regarding wage inequality between men and women. First, that men and women work in different jobs, albeit jobs that often require similar levels of effort and skill. Second, that jobs held by women are paid far less than those held by men. Third, that removing overt discrimination would be unlikely to equalize wages for men and women fully (Edgeworth 1922). The findings of recent empirical studies have generally supported these three conclusions.

There is considerable evidence demonstrating that men and women work in different occupations. Comparisons of occupational segregation by sex in the United States since 1900 show that levels of segregation have been persistent through the 1960s and 1980s (Gross 1968; Jacobs 1989). During the 1980s more than half of the workers of one sex would have had to change occupations in order to equalize the distribution of men and women across all occupations (Jacobs 1989). Researchers using more specific job titles within firms have found that almost no men and women work together in the same job in the same firm (Bielby and Baron 1986).

On average, women continue to earn substantially less than men. Women earned 62 percent of what men earned in 1975 and just over 75 percent of what men earned in 1995 (Figart and Kahn 1997). The concentration of women in low-paying, female-dominated occupations has been found to account for a substantial portion of this income difference. The amount of the income gap between men and women explained by the sex segregation of occupations varies from 25 percent to over 33 percent across many studies of this issue (Sorensen 1986; Figart and Kahn 1997). The remainder of the difference between men's and women's average earnings is due to other factors, such as differences in the overall skills and experience individual men and women bring with them to the labor market.

Empirical studies have examined whether the gap in wages between female-dominated and male-dominated occupations is based on differences in the occupations with regard to the skills required or the work environments. Treiman and colleagues (1984), in an evaluation of the effects of differences in characteristics of male and female occupations on wages, found that "about 40 percent of the earnings gap between male- and female-dominated occupations can be attributed to differences in job characteristics and 60 percent to differences in the rate of return on these characteristics." That is, he found that the premium paid for skills in male-dominated occupations was higher than that paid for the same skills in female-dominated occupations. Other research has confirmed the findings that specific skills (such as dealing with the public) or requirements (such as having a high school diploma) increase wages more in a male-dominated occupation than in a female-dominated occupation (McLaughlin 1978; Beck and Kemp 1986). Other possible explanations for differences in wages between male-dominated and female-dominated occupations—such as that female-dominated occupations have greater nonmonetary compensations (such as vacation, sick leave, flexibility in working hours) (Jencks, Perman and Rainwater 1988) or that they are more accommodating to intermittent careers (England 1982)—have not been supported by empirical studies.

The conclusion of J.S. Mill in 1865, as quoted by Edgeworth in 1922—"The remuneration of the peculiar employments of women is always, I believe, greatly below that of employments of equal skill and equal disagreeableness carried on by men."—is similar to the conclusion reached by the National Research Council/National Academy of Sciences committee report in 1981:

"[Such] differential earnings patterns have existed for many decades. They may arise in part because women and minority men are paid less than white men for doing the same (or very similar) jobs within the same firm, or in part because the job structure is substantially segregated by sex, race, and ethnicity and the jobs held mainly by women and minority men pay less than the jobs held mainly by non-minority men" (Treiman and Hartmann 1981, p.92).

The evidence is fairly conclusive that occupational-level wage discrimination exists—that is, that skills and requirements are less well rewarded in jobs held primarily by women than they are in jobs held primarily by men. Comparable worth advocates argue that applying job-evaluation methods is a viable method for reducing this form of wage discrimination. This is clarified in Helen Remick's proposed working definition of comparable worth as "the application of a single, bias-free point factor job evaluation system within a given establishment, across job families, both to rank-order jobs and to set salaries"(1984, p.99).

Job-evaluation methods are well established and have been used for decades to establish equivalencies across jobs. Actual methods of job evaluation differ, but the usual approach is to start by describing all jobs within a given organization. Next, a list of important job requirements is developed and jobs are rated on each requirement. For example, one requirement could be the use of mathematics. In this case each job would be rated from "low" (e.g. addition and subtraction of whole numbers) to "high" (e.g., the use of differential equations). Most job-evaluation methods include job requirements such as level of education, skills, level of responsibility, and the environment in which the work is performed. Some job-evaluation methods also include such characteristics of job incumbents as average education, training, and experience. More complex job-evaluation systems also consider how jobs rank with regard to fringe benefits (e.g. sick leave), hours (e.g. shift work), training and promotion opportunities, hazards, autonomy (e.g. can leave work without permission), authority (e.g. supervises others), and organizational setting (e.g. organizational size) (see Jencks et al. 1988). After each job is rated and given a certain number of "points" for each requirement, the points are then added into an overall "score" for each job. These scores are then weighted based on the importance assigned to a particular job attribute. Each job then receives a total number of points based on all of the appropiate factors in order to compare the value to the firm of different jobs. These composite scores are then used to rank jobs in order to help determine appropriate wages (Blau and Ferber 1986). This makes it possible to compare wages paid for jobs with very different—but comparable—content. In addition to considering the training and work requirements for jobs within the firm, systems of job evaluation often also take into account whatever information is available on prevailing wages for different types of labor. The use of job evaluation is neither new nor unusual, and currently job evaluation is often used to determine pay scales by governments and by many businesses. Job evaluations are primarily used when employers cannot rely on the market to establish wages. (See Spilerman 1986, for a discussion of the types of organizations that determine wages based on nonmarket mechanisms.) Employers must determine wages, for example, when positions are filled entirely from within an organizational unit (e.g. through promotion of an existing workforce) or when they fill jobs that are unique to a particular firm. In these cases, "going rates" for all jobs are not always available in local labor markets.

There are at least two critical limitations to using job-evaluation methods in establishing comparable worth. First, it is difficult to eliminate the effects of past practices on the identification and the weighting of important job characteristics.

Existing job-evaluation schemes have been criticized for undervaluing, or not even considering, the skills and abilities that are emphasized in some female jobs (Beatty and Beatty 1984; Stienberg 1992). For example, at one time the coding in the job-evaluation system used in the Dictionary of Occupational Titles rated the primarily male occupation "Dog Pound Attendant" as requiring a higher level of complexity with regard to working with data, people, and things than the primarily female occupations of "Nursery School Teacher" and "Practical Nurse"—which were rated as having minimal or no relationship with data, people, or things (Miller et al. 1980). Second, because job-evaluation methods are used within a particular firm or organization, they do not address wage inequalities *across* firms or organizations. This particularly limits the scope of comparable worth because, with the exception of governments (which often employ individuals across a wide range of occupational categories), most organizations are staffed by individuals in a relatively narrow span of occupations. For example, jobs in the textile and poultry-processing industries, usually held by women, and jobs in the lumber industry, usually held by men, could have the same overall scores in terms of job characteristics. However, because these jobs are usually not in the same organization, it is unlikely that job-evaluation methods could be used to equalize wages for these jobs.

Comparable-worth methods have been used in a number of legal actions in attempts to increase the equivalencies of wages for jobs held primarily by women and those held primarily by men. The outcomes of these cases have been mixed (see Remick 1984; Heen 1984; Steinberg 1987; and Figart and Kahn 1997 for reviews and discussions of cases). In the United States, the right of "equal pay for equal work" is provided by Title VII of the Civil Rights Act of 1964. An important legal action based on the premise of comparable worth was the Supreme Court ruling in the *County of Washington v Gunther*, 452 U.S. 161 (1981). This ruling removed a major legal obstacle to comparable worth as the basis of equalizing wages. Although it did not endorse the comparable worth approach, it did rule that a man and woman need not do "equal work" in order to establish pay discrimination under Title VII (Heen 1984). Subsequent lower court rulings have not resulted in clear-cut decisions regarding comparable worth, and at present

it seems unlikely that, in the United States, court decisions will mandate the comparable-worth approach. Legal and legislative actions based on comparable worth and pay equity also have emerged in countries other than the United States. Canada included a provision for equal pay for work of equal value in the Canadian Human Rights Act of 1977 (see Cadieux 1984; and Ontario Pay Equity Commission 1998). The implementation of this legislation has resulted in significant decisions regarding the need to increase wages in female-dominated occupations—both in private industry and in the government. However, the implementation of these decisions has not been without difficulty. For example, the government and the government-workers union of the Northwest Territories were, in early 1998, in disagreement with regard to whether the evaluation system used by the government to establish comparable worth was biased (Government of the Northwest Territories 1998).

Despite its limitations and difficulties in implementation, the concept of comparable worth as a basis for pay equity remains important in public policy initiatives. The National Committee on Pay Equity (1999), the American Federation of State, County, and Municipal Employees (1999), and other organizations provide information and support for advocates of comparable worth. As one approach to increasing pay equity, comparable-worth applications have the potential for identifying and correcting one of the most persistent bases for the disparity between earnings for majority men and earnings for women and minorities.

REFERENCES

Beatty, R. W., and J. R. Beatty 1984 "Some Problems with Contemporary Job Evaluation Systems." In H. Remick, ed., *Comparable Worth and Wage Discrimination: Technical Possibilities and Political Realities*. Philadelphia: Temple University Press.

Bielby, W. T., and J. N. Baron 1986 "Men and Women at Work: Sex Segregation and Statistical Discrimination." *American Journal of Sociology* 91:759–99.

Blau, F. D., and M. A. Ferber 1986 *The Economics of Women, Men and Work*. New York: Prentice-Hall.

Cadieux, Rita 1984 "Canada's Equal Pay for Work of Equal Value Law." In H. Remick, ed., *Comparable Worth and Wage Discrimination: Technical Possibilities and Political Realities*. Philadelphia: Temple University Press.

Edgeworth, F. Y. 1922 "Equal Pay to Men and Women for Equal Work." *The Economic Journal* 32:431–56.

Fngland, P. 1982 "The Failure of Human Capital Theory to Explain Occupational Sex Segregation." *Journal of Human Resources* 17:358–70.

Figart, Sarah M., and Peggy Kahn 1997 *Contesting the Market: Pay Equity and the Politics of Economic Restructuring*. Detroit, Mich.: Wayne State University Press.

Government of the Northwest Territories http://www.gov.nt.ca/Executive/Pay_Equity, last edited April, 1998.

Gross, E. 1968 "Plus ça change. . . ? The Sexual Structure of Occupations Over Time." *Social Problems* 16:198–208.

Heen, M. 1984 "A Review of Federal Court Decisions Under Title VII of the Civil Rights Act of 1964." In H. Remick, ed., *Comparable Worth and Wage Discrimination: Technical Possibilities and Political Realities*. Philadelphia: Temple University Press.

Jacobs, J. A. 1989 "Long Term Trends in Occupational Segregation by Sex." *American Journal of Sociology* 95:160–73.

Jencks, C., L. Perman, and L. Rainwater 1988 "What is a Good Job? A New Measure of Labor-Market Success." *American Journal of Sociology* 93:132–257.

Kemp, A. A., and E. M. Beck 1986 "Equal Work, Unequal Pay: Gender Discrimination Within Work-similar Occupations." *Work and Occupations* 13:324–347.

Marini, M. M. 1989 "Sex Differences in Earnings in the U.S." In W. R. Scott, ed., *Annual Review of Sociology*, vol. 15. Palo Alto, Calif.: Annual Reviews.

McLaughlin, S. 1978 "Occupational Sex Identification and the Assessment of Male and Female Earnings Inequality." *American Sociological Review* 43:909–921.

Miller, Ann R., D. J. Treiman, P. S. Cain, and P. A. Roos 1980 *Work, Jobs, and Occupations: A Critical Review of the Dictionary of Occupational Titles*. Washington, D.C.: National Academy Press.

National Committee on Pay Equity, http://www.feminist.com/fairpay.htm, as of February, 1999.

Ontario Pay Equity Commission, http://www.gov.on.ca/LAB/pec/acte.htm, last modified December 28, 1998.

Remick, H. (ed.) 1984 *Comparable Worth and Wage Discrimination: Technical Possibilities and Political Realities*. Philadelphia: Temple University Press.

—— 1984 "Major Issues in *a priori* Applications." In H. Remick, ed., *Comparable Worth and Wage Discrimination: Technical Possibilities and Political Realities* 99–117. Philadelphia: Temple University Press.

Sorensen, E. 1986 "Implementing Comparable Worth: A Survey of Recent Job Evaluation Studies." *American Economic Review Papers and Proceedings* 76:364–367.

Spilerman, S. 1986 "Organizational Rules and the Features of Work Careers." *Research in Social Stratification and Mobility* 5:41–102.

Steinberg, Ronnie, et al. 1985 *The New York State Comparable Worth Study: Final Report*. New York: Center for Women in Government.

Treiman, D. J., and H. I. Hartman 1981 *Woman, Work and Wages: Equal Pay for Jobs of Equal Value*. Washington, D.C.: National Academy Press.

U.S. Bureau of the Census 1987 *Male-Female Differences in Work Experience Occupation and Earnings: 1984*. Current Population Report P–70, no. 10. Washington, D.C.: U.S. Government Printing Office.

—— 1986 *Statistical Abstract of the United States: 1987*, 107th ed. Washington, D.C.: U.S. Government Printing Office.

Nancy E. Durbin
Barbara Melber

COMPARATIVE HEALTH-CARE SYSTEMS

At the dawn of the twenty-first century, access to health-care services, their cost and quality constitute key social, political, and economic issues for virtually every country in the world. Identifying the conditions under which health-care systems function most effectively has become a vital, albeit elusive, goal. One point is certain: It is impossible to fully understand the dynamics of health-care systems without comparative health-care research. Knowledge of systems other than one's own provides the observer with multiple vantage points from which to gain a fresh perspective on strengths and weaknesses at home. Studying other systems, including their successful as well as failed health-reform efforts, provides a global laboratory for health-systems development. While some countries have been quick to draw upon the health-care innovations of their neighbors, the United States has been relatively slow to look internationally for health-reform ideas. Fortunately, the proliferation of comparative health-care studies promises that such insularity will be much less likely in the future.

The comparative study of health-care systems focuses on two broad types of issues. The first involves *describing* the range of health-care services in populations or societies, particularly their organization and functioning. By far the most common type of research, descriptive studies, brings together statistical indicators and factual explanations about how various national systems operate (van Atteveld et al. 1987). Some of this work incorporates an analytical dimension by categorizing systems in terms of conceptual schemes or typologies. Less attention has been paid to the second type of research, which looks more closely at the dynamics of how health-care systems behave. The intent in this type of research is to *analyze* the patterns among system characteristics, especially with the idea of anticipating the outcomes that are likely with specific types of system arrangements. Still in its infancy, this work promises an in-depth yet practical understanding of how health-care can be organized and financed to achieve desirable levels of both quality and access.

Interest in cross-national studies of health-care systems increased dramatically in the early 1990s as a result of national debates over reorganizing American health-care. Rapidly aging populations in many advanced, capitalistic countries, in combination with the expanding scope of high technology medicine, resulted in increased public demand for health-care. At the same time, poverty and other forms of social inequality as well as ineffective societal institutions created major public health problems in many developing countries, such as hazardous water, inadequate or harmful food supplies, poor air quality, unsafe homes and workplaces, and the swift spread of infectious diseases. In both cases, health-care systems have been severely challenged and often cannot meet the needs of citizens. Because of these problems and also due to enhanced global cooperation, social scientists and policy makers are increasingly turning their attention to the experience of other countries.

KEY CHARACTERISTICS FOR THE COMPARISON OF HEALTH-CARE SYSTEMS

Drawing on the work of Anderson (1989) and Frenk (1994), a health-care system can be defined as the combination of health-care institutions, supporting human resources, financing mechanisms, information systems, organizational structures that link institutions and resources, and management structures that collectively culminate in the delivery of health services to patients. Within this broad framework, the methodology for comparing health-care systems can vary widely. A standard approach would include some or all of the dimensions outlined below.

The most fundamental comparative dimension is the *organization, financing, and control* of a health-care system. This involves comparing which health services are provided; how they are paid for; how they are configured, planned, and regulated; and how citizens gain access to them. Among countries with advanced economies, health-care services today look much the same to the casual observer; however, the financing arrangements and policy-making mechanisms that underlie them vary widely. The role of government is perhaps the most significant organizational variable in international health-care. All governments, with the notable exception of the U.S. government, accept responsibility for the health-care of citizens (Evans 1997). Some governments take it upon themselves to actually provide health services and, therefore, own their own clinics and hospitals and hire their own physicians and staff—examples are Sweden and Denmark. Within the U.S., the Veteran's Administration operates its own healthcare system this way. In a variation of this model, the government acts as the purchaser (but not the owner) of health-care services, obtaining services from private providers on behalf of patients, such as in Canada or the reformed health-care system in Britain. In Finland, local governments can purchase from either public or private providers. In another model, illustrated by Germany and Japan, the government avoids acting as the major payer, and instead takes the role of an overseer, setting mandates for health coverage, including the type and level of coverage, and regulating the terms of what is largely a private system. Due to economic pressures, national governments in both Germany and Japan provided increasing subsidies to support their systems in the 1990s.

It is important also to compare health-care systems in terms of *physician characteristics and provider arrangements for primary care and prevention*. The supply of medical personnel (e.g., the number of physicians per unit of population) is a key comparative indicator. Interestingly, there is significant variation in the number of physicians in advanced economy nations, ranging per 10,000 population from fifty-five in Italy to thirty-four in Germany to twenty-six in the United States, which is more typical, to seventeen in the United Kingdom (Anderson and Poullier 1999). Equally interesting is that there is no apparent corresponding variation in the health status of these populations. A more complex issue is how different systems organize and divide medical work between various professions and occupations. In some countries, such as Sweden, Finland, and the Netherlands, midwives or nurse midwives have primary responsibility for normal prenatal care and childbirth; in others, such as the United States, physicians have responsibility for these tasks and midwives are relatively rare. Practice arrangements between generalist and specialist physicians are another point of comparison. The United States is unique among its peers because primary care physicians working in ambulatory settings also have hospital privileges, and, therefore, have the right to admit patients and to treat hospitalized patients. In Britain, Sweden, Germany, and many other countries, on the other hand, only specialists comprise the hospital medical staff and only they can treat patients there.

Hospitals and long-term care arrangements constitute another dimension in comparing health-care systems. Countries vary widely in how they use hospitals, as well as in how and where citizens with chronic illnesses and other debilitating conditions receive ongoing, nonacute care. Many Western countries today are in the process of shifting from institutional to community-based care. There are many factors affecting this transition, including whether alternatives to institutional care, such as home health and support programs, are readily available. In countries such as Japan and Germany, that through the 1990s have relied on informal family caregiving arrangements rather than institutions or community-based services, sociodemographic changes (elders living longer as well as changes in the work force participation of caregivers) are producing a long-term care crisis.

Health-systems also can be compared according to the degree to which care is *integrated and coordinated* between various sectors and levels of services. Systems that have rigid boundaries between ambulatory and hospital services, or between general medical and mental health services and that are so highly specialized that patients are required to transfer among multiple providers, illustrate arrangements where communication

across "borders" is vital for optimal patient care. The Nordic countries, in particular, have been highly conscious of gaps in the coordination and continuity of care, and have developed reforms to bridge them. Finland has adopted a model that integrates the basic education of both health-care and social care personnel, a strategy intended to link the biomedical and social aspects of health and health-care at the very beginning of professional education.

Perhaps the most common basis for comparing countries' health-care systems is various outcome statistics such as *economic characteristics, personnel resources, utilization rates, and population health status measures*. The proportion of the population covered by government-assured health insurance stands as the indicator with the least international variation. Of the twenty-nine countries analyzed by the Organization for Economic Cooperation and Development in 1998, governments in twenty-four countries assured coverage to 99 percent to 100 percent of their population. The five exceptions were Germany with 92 percent coverage, Mexico and the Netherlands with 72 percent, Turkey with 66 percent, and the U.S. with 33 percent (Anderson and Poullier 1999). Other indicators in the same report vary widely. In per capita health-care spending, the United States spends just less than $4,000, an amount that is substantially more than for the other nations, which range from Switzerland's $2547 to Turkey's $260. Contrary to what one might think, the amount a country spends on health-care is not reflected in the longevity of its population. Men in twenty-one countries live longer than do men in the United States (up to an average of 77 years in Japan compared to 72.7 in the United States). Similarly, women in nineteen countries live longer than American women (up to an average of 83.6 years in Japan versus 79.4 in the United States). In fact, relatively few of the high-spending countries appear among those with the greatest longevity.

Detailed comparisons of statistical characteristics have limited value when neither issues of measurement nor the contextual meanings associated with each measure are immediately clear. Each country has its own distinctive set of *sociohistorical and cultural characteristics*; these should be considered in comparative research, since they often play an important role in explaining the origin and development of health-care systems (Payer 1996). For example, Starr (1982) has posed and explored the question of why the United States ignored national health insurance at the same time most European countries were adopting such programs. National insurance, he argues, was a form of social protectionism and was, therefore, most likely to be enacted by paternalistic regimes such as Germany and only later by more liberal states such as France and the United Kingdom. In addition, the United States' long history of rejecting national health insurance reflects its decentralized government, the relative lack of domestic unrest, and the failure of major interest groups (labor, business, and medicine) to provide support. Regarding the same issue, Steinmo and Watts (1995) contend that the structure of American political institutions creates conditions that work against the adoption of national health insurance.

A final means of comparing health-care systems is on the basis of *specific problems*, including assessments of citizen satisfaction (Donelan et al. 1999). Closely related comparisons focus on the various *strategies for reform* that countries have implemented in an attempt to address their problems (Graig 1993). Much can be learned by studying and comparing which solutions seem to work best for certain types of problems, as well as observing patterns of failure across multiple systems.

FRAMEWORKS FOR COMPARING HEALTH-CARE SYSTEMS

While it is useful to compare health-care systems on the basis of a series of characteristics, in-depth understanding of the variation in systems requires a more analytical approach. Most frameworks proposed by comparative health-system researchers can be characterized as typologies that, though they add a conceptual basis for distinguishing among systems, offer limited analytical complexity or depth. These typologies typically emphasize political or economic criteria, and several of the more complex schemes attempt to integrate the two. Graig (1993) organized the six countries she analyzed on a continuum with public systems (e.g., the United Kingdom) at one end, private systems (the United States) at the other, and mixed or "convergence" systems, such as Japan, Germany, and the Netherlands, in the middle. Roemer

(1991) developed a sixteen-cell typology that combines political and economic elements, describing systems in relation to government policies (entrepreneurial/permissive, welfare oriented, universal/comprehensive, and socialist/centrally planned) as they intersect with economic conditions (affluent, developing, poor and resource rich). These and similar approaches offered by Anderson (1989) and Light (1990) offer descriptive distinctions, but do not emphasize the theoretical basis for the particular category schemes.

Mechanic (1996) hypothesizes that health-systems internationally are converging, based on the idea that medicine forms a world culture in which knowledge and health-care ideas are quickly disseminated. He proposes six areas of convergence: nations' concerns with controlling cost and improving the efficiency and effectiveness of health-care, nations' realization that population health outcomes are largely a product of circumstances outside the medical care system, nations' concern and attempts to address inequalities in health outcomes and access to care, nations' growing interest in patient satisfaction and consumer choice, and the increasing attention nations are placing on the linkage between medical and social factors in health-care, and the struggle all nations are having between technology, specialization, and the need to develop primary care. Field (1980) also theorizes a progression of health-system development with a scheme placing systems along a continuum according to the extent to which health-care is seen as a social good. He identifies five system types in order of their progression toward a socialized system: anomic, pluralistic, insurance/social security, national health service, and socialized health-care.

Elling (1994) takes issue with the notion of "automatic convergence" and with typologies that posit unidirectional evolution or change, pointing out that countries are involved in ongoing, dynamic class struggles in the development of health-systems. His neo-Marxist framework, influenced by Wallerstein's world-systems theory, allows for countries to move back and forth among five types: core capitalist (e.g., the United States and Germany), core capitalist/social welfare (e.g., Canada, Japan, Sweden, United Kingdom), industrialized socialist-oriented (e.g., pre-1990s Soviet and eastern European systems), capitalist dependencies in the periphery and semi-periphery (e.g., Brazil and India), and socialist-oriented, quasi-independent of the world system (e.g., China and Cuba).

In 1990, Esping-Andersen (1990) contributed an important theoretical framework to the field of comparative welfare states research, that can also be useful in distinguishing among health-care systems in advanced capitalist nations. Esping-Andersen conceptualizes all welfare activities, including health-care, as a product of a state-market-family nexus. His typology organizes "welfare regimes" around this nexus, specifically as it results in the decommodification of workers in a country; that is, the degree to which a citizen can obtain basic health and social welfare services outside of the market. In terms of health-care, this would mean a citizen's ability to access health-care services without having to purchase them "out-of-pocket." Esping-Andersen identifies three types of systems: conservative or corporatist, liberal, and socialist or social democratic. In *The Three Worlds of Welfare Capitalism*, he constructs measures of decommodification that he applies to data from eighteen nations in order to assess where each nation's welfare regime ranks according to the three types. Under Esping-Andersen's scheme, social democratic systems include the Nordic countries and the Netherlands; liberal systems include Canada, Japan, and the United States; and the conservative or corporatist welfare states include France, Germany, and Italy. These placements appear similar to what Graig proposed using a much simpler public-private dimension; however, Esping-Andersen's methodology is unique in its theoretical approach and because it can be operationalized quantitatively to allow precise distinctions among a large number of nations.

Reviewing various health-care system frameworks shows a wide variety of approaches and scholarly emphases. Comparative research is in the process of moving beyond simple typologies to focus on the conditions under which different types of systems emerge and under which they change. This work demonstrates the value of a broad approach, integrating the key aspects that affect the development of health-care systems, including historical, cultural, political, and economic factors.

REVIEW OF SELECTED HEALTH-CARE SYSTEMS

Comparative international research on health-care systems requires information that is both detailed and current. Obtaining data is complicated by the fact that health-systems throughout the world operate in a state of constant flux. These summaries present the most recent information available for the health-care systems of selected countries. Among countries with advanced economies, Sweden and the United States often occupy opposite extremes when it comes to health-care organization and financing. For this reason, Sweden is the first country discussed along with three countries that have similar systems—Finland, the United Kingdom, and Canada—followed next by Germany, Japan, Russia, and China, with additional discussions of France, Mexico, Argentina, Chile, Colombia, and Ghana.

Swedish health-care reflects three basic principles: *equality* among citizens in access to health-care; *universality* in the nature of services (the idea that everyone should receive the same quality of services); and *solidarity*, the concept of one social group sacrificing for another group in the interest of the whole society (Zimmerman and Halpert 1997). Solidarity in this context refers to taxing those who use fewer services at the same rate as those who use more—for example, similar health-care taxation for younger persons or affluent persons versus the elderly or the poor). The Swedish health-care system is predominantly a publicly owned and funded system; thus, approximately 85 percent of Swedish health-care is publicly funded, whereas in the United States the public portion is just under 50 percent (Lassey, Lassey, and Jinks 1997). The differences between the two systems are more startling in terms of the growth of overall spending. In the early 1980s, both countries were spending approximately 9.5 percent of their Gross Domestic Product on health-care. By the end of the century, the situation had changed dramatically; in 1999, Sweden was spending 8.6 percent ($1728 per capita) compared to 13.5 percent ($3924 per capita) in the United States (Anderson and Poullier 1999). Populations in the two nations also differ markedly on several basic health status indicators. Infant mortality Sweden is four deaths per thousand live births compared to 7.8 in the United States. Swedish men live nearly four years longer on average than American men, and Swedish women live two years longer than their American counterparts. These favorable statistical indicators compel a closer look into how the Swedish health-care system is organized.

The Swedish welfare state, including health-care and social services, is one of the most comprehensive and universal in the world. Health-care in Sweden is the responsibility of the state, which delegates it, in turn, to each of Sweden's twenty-one county councils (Swedish Institute 1999). Elected officials in each county are charged with providing comprehensive health services for residents, and with levying the taxes to finance them. The system is decentralized; each county by law must provide the same generous common core of services to all residents, although just how they decide to do it can vary. In the 1990s, Sweden embarked on a series of reforms in order to increase health-care quality and efficiency. As a result, Swedish citizens now have greater freedom in choosing their own primary care physicians. The vast majority of these doctors are employed by the county councils to practice in small group clinics and health centers distributed geographically throughout the country. Specialist physicians practice in hospitals where they also see outpatients on both a referral and self-referral basis. The medical division of labor also includes district nurses, physical therapists, and midwives, all of whom are used extensively to deliver care through local health centers (maternity clinics in the case of midwives). Midwives also work in hospitals where they have responsibility for normal cases of labor and delivery. Sweden's elderly constitute an increasing proportion of the population, creating significant challenges for both current and future health and social services. Sweden's social policy emphasizes that citizens should be able to live in their own homes for as long as possible, meaning that nursing home placement occurs only when absolutely necessary. Services for the elderly may involve as many as five or six home nursing visits per day in order for the disabled and elderly to remain at home in the community.

Swedish citizens are taxed heavily to maintain the quality and level of services they expect; at the same time, they have shown high levels of political support for maintaining their expensive system. In the 1980s, many services were entirely free; however, today there typically is a modest copayment.

The copayment for a primary care physician visit, for example, currently ranges from $12 to $17 depending on the county council. For specialist physician visits the copayment ranges from $15 to $31, and for hospital stays it is fixed at $10/day. The Swedish system includes a high-cost ceiling so that, after a person spends approximately $113 out-of-pocket each year, health-care services are free. Medications must be purchased by the individual until they have reached a threshold of a little more than $100. Prescriptions are then discounted until the patient has spent $225, at which point medications become free (Swedish Institute 1999). These amounts have increased somewhat during the 1990s, but due to Swedens already high taxation rate, county councils were hesitant to ask patients to pay more. Reforms during the same period included establishing internal performance incentives or "public competition" (Saltman and Von Otter 1992), a structural arrangement that arguably enabled Sweden to maintain the basic features of its health-care system without large tax or out-of-pocket increases. Some have expressed concern that the system is stretched to its limits. Regardless of which view is correct, the Swedish system requires a healthy economy in order to continue, given continuing cost pressures and an increasingly aged population.

The Swedish model of a publicly owned and financed health-care system shares common features with systems in several other countries, including the United Kingdom, Finland, and Canada. The British National Health Service (NHS), like its Swedish counterpart, provides publicly funded, comprehensive health-care to the population, and enjoys a solid base of citizen support, albeit under ongoing criticism. What distinguishes the NHS from health-care systems in other Western countries is its frugality. Characterized by long waiting lists and what Klein (1998) refers to as "rationing by professionally defined need," Britain runs the cheapest health-care system in Europe, outside of Spain and Portugal. In the early 1990s, the NHS went through a series of dramatic changes, creating "internal markets," a system of inside competition intended to increase productivity and further decentralize its historically large and unwieldy bureaucracy. These reforms—several of which were adopted by Sweden—reorganized primary care practices and shifted physician payment from fixed salary to capitation. NHS hospitals also entered into new arrangements where they have greater structural independence and compete among themselves. In 1997, the British government introduced new proposals that changed course yet again. The direction of the NHS in the twenty-first century is unclear (Klein 1998).

Finland's health-care system also is publicly owned, financed through general taxation, and decentralized. In fact, Finland operates with more health-care decentralization than Sweden. Since 1993, Finnish funding for health-care has been incorporated into block grants from the national government that are given annually to each of the country's 455 municipalities, some of which form partnerships for purposes of delivering health-care (Hermanson, Aro, and Bennett 1994). Within the parameters of national guidelines, elected officials in each of these jurisdictions (similar to the county councils in Sweden) have the responsibility to obtain and deliver health-care services to the population. High standards, a comprehensive array of services, as well as modest out-of-pocket payments, make the Finnish system comparable to the Swedish system. Canada also provides health-care to its entire population. The Canadian system is administered by the provinces and is financed largely by public taxation, roughly three-quarters of which is from the provincial government. While basic services remain constant, some specific provisions of health-care in Canada vary considerably from province to province. Unlike in Sweden, Finland, and the United Kingdom, Canadian physicians are paid on a fee-for-service basis. Furthermore, Canadian primary care physicians act as gatekeepers to specialists and hospitals (much as they do in Finland and the United Kingdom, but not in Sweden). As is the case with all the countries in this group of four, Canadians have extreme pride in their health-care system. They appear resolute in maintaining it, although a number of controversial cost-cutting measures and as yet unsolved problems raise considerable concern about the future (Lassey, Lassey, and Jinks 1997).

Germany and Japan, as well as France, have achieved comprehensive and universal coverage (92 percent in the case of Germany) with a model that is closer to that of the United States than the social democratic model of Sweden discussed above (U.S. General Accounting Office 1991). In all three of these countries, medical care is provided by private physicians, by both private and public hospitals, and patients can choose their physicians. Benefits are comprehensive and mandated by the national government, which also regulates enrollment, premiums, and reimbursement of providers. In contrast to the four countries discussed earlier, financing in Germany, Japan, and France is predominantly private with multiple payers. Workplace-based insurance (financed typically through payroll deductions) covers most employees and their dependents while other payers cover the remainder of the population. Patients make copayments for physician visits and hospital stays, ranging from a nominal amount in Germany to as much as 20 percent or 30 percent of the fee in France and Japan. There is national regulation to ensure consistency. Coverage and care conditions vary from fund to fund, resulting in greater inequalities of benefits compared to the public systems of Sweden, Finland, Canada, and the United Kingdom. Arguing that such systems actually help maintain social divisions and inequality, Esping-Andersen (1990) refers to them as conservative or corporatist.

Although Germany privately finances much of its health-care system, the national government plays a strong role. All but the most wealthy of German citizens are required by law to join one of Germany's 750 insuring organizations, called "sickness funds." In practice, all but about 10 percent of the population opt to join the system, encouraged to participate by the great difficulty of getting back in later on. Sickness funds are private, nonprofit organizations that collect premiums or "contributions" for each member—half paid by the individual and half by the employer—and, in turn, contract for health services with physician organizations and hospitals. One of the biggest problems for the German system is continuing cost pressures, exacerbated by the reunification of East and West Germany in 1991. The system uses fixed budgets for hospitals and strict fee schedules for physicians, with punitive measures for inordinate increases in volume, to combat the problem. These were tightened in a major 1993 reform that imposed strict three-year budgets on all major sectors of the system as well as longer-term structural reforms. Early results have been positive (U.S. General Accounting Office 1994).

Japanese health-care follows much the same private, multi-payer model as in Germany, with health-care provided to all citizens through 5,000 independent insurance plans. The plans fall into three major groups, each enrolling about a third of the population: large-firm employees, small-firm employees, and self-employed persons and pensioners. In the case of the first two plans, as is the case with the German sickness funds, the employer pays approximately half of the premium and the employee pays the remaining portion. The similarity to the German system is no accident; Japan has consciously patterned its health-care syatem after Germany's, dating back to its modernization in the late nineteenth and early twentieth centuries (Lassey, Lassey, and Jinks 1997). Despite these similarities, Japan's health-care system presents some unique and somewhat startling features compared to the other systems discussed here.

Compared to other systems with a significant private component, the Japanese system costs considerably less (Andersen and Poullier 1999). In 1997, for example, per capita health-care spending in Japan was $1741, less than in the United States, Canada, France, Germany, and many other European countries. Of the nations discussed here, only the austere British system ($1347 per capita) and efficiency-conscious Finnish system ($1492 per capita) spent less. Japan's economical approach to delivering health-care raises two paradoxes. First, the low levels of spending would seem to contradict the fact that Japan currently has the longest life expectancy and the lowest infant mortality in the world. In addition, utilization rates in Japan are high, which some would argue indicates a sicker rather than a healthier population. Specifically, the Japanese visit physicians two to three times more frequently, stay in the hospital three to four times longer, and devote considerably more health spending to pharmaceuticals than the other nations discussed here. How can these contradictions be explained? Ikegami and Campbell (1999) argue that, in part, the paradox can be explained by the country's much lower incidence of social problems related to health, such as crime, drug use, high-speed motor vehicle accidents, teen-age births, and HIV infections. Less aggressive medicine and lower hospital staffing and amenities also are thought to keep down costs in Japan.

Health-care arrangements in nations where the political economy is neither "advanced" nor a stronghold of capitalistic democracy can also be instructive. During the latter part of the twentieth century and until today, both China and Russia have been faced with the monumental challenge of providing health-care with very limited financial resources to huge, diverse populations, many of which live under poor social conditions. Their health-care systems, however, are quite different and their current problems reflect the distinctive political and economic trajectories of the two countries. Russian health-care at the dawn of the twenty-first century is a system in crisis. Based on socialist principles of universal and free access, the old Soviet system included a primary care network of local clinics ("polyclinics") typically connected to a general hospital, as well as more specialized hospitals. This means that a regional city might have separate hospitals for emergencies, maternity, children, and various infectious diseases (Albrecht and Salmon 1992). Funding came directly from the central government until 1993 when a new health insurance law was approved, shifting the source of financing to employer payroll deductions. There are major questions, however, as to whether such a system can be effective during the current period of resource scarcity and instability in major social institutions (Lassey, Lassey, and Jinks 1997).

Chinese health-care, for most Westerners, evokes images of acupuncture and other forms of Eastern medicine, as well as the idealized "barefoot doctors" of the 1960s and 1970s, practitioners with basic medical training who provided primary care in rural areas. In reality, traditional Chinese medicine exists alongside an increasingly dominant Western medical establishment, and the barefoot doctors have all but disappeared. Since new leadership took over the Communist Party in the late 1970s, China has encouraged privatization and decentralization in health-care. By the 1990s, nearly half of all village health-care was provided by private practitioners (Lassey, Lassey, and Jinks 1997). These changes reportedly have been accompanied by a decline in preventive care and public health efforts in rural areas. At the same time, the situation in urban areas seems to have improved. China's revolutionary-era network of local and regional clinics and hospitals has been modernized, although resource shortages continue to limit the level of technological advancement. The most significant change in China is the growing impact of privatization, which appears to be bringing China many of the same problems that have plagued privatized systems elsewhere: lack of insurance coverage, increasing costs, maldistribution of providers, and inequalities in the overall quality of care (Liu, Liu, and Meng 1994). As in the United States, the gap between the health-care received by the rich and that received by the poor is growing (Shi 1993).

Huge disparities between the rich and poor are characteristic of Latin America where they constitute a significant barrier to universal health coverage. Latin-American health-systems vary considerably, reflecting socioeconomic differences between countries as well as historical and political contingencies. The Mexican system illustrates many of the obstacles faced by developing nations, whether in Latin America or elsewhere. The Mexican constitution established federal responsibility for health-care in 1917, along with a centralized administrative tradition that still exists; yet, to date, the two major government insurance schemes cover only about 47 percent of the population, with another 7 percent insured privately. Ostensibly, there are programs for the remaining 46 percent of the population, most of whom are low income, but in reality, many low income areas and impoverished communities are poorly served. Some have argued that a basic health-care infrastructure is in place and that there are sufficient numbers of well-trained health-care professionals available (Lassey, Lassey, and Jinks 1997). They contend that, had it not been for several national crises in the 1980s and 1990s, coupled with a lack of political will, more of the Mexican population would now be covered by the health-care system.

Bertranou (1999) has compared Argentina, Chile, and Columbia, all of which have employed various ways to reform health insurance arrangements in recent years. Chile's reforms date back to its military dictatorship in the early 1980s. At that time, private health insurers were allowed to compete for worker payroll contributions. There was little regulation of the system which encouraged adverse selection, resulting in significant inequities within the system. Even so, approximately 70 percent of the Chilean population today is covered by insurance, compared to 64 percent in Argentina and only 43 percent in Colombia. Argentina faces numerous obstacles in reforming its complex and confusing system of three types of health-care arrangements (social insurance organizations,

private health insurers and providers, and the public health-system). Its goals include universal coverage and a standard benefits package. In the case of Columbia, reform goals are more related to the relative poverty in the country and the fact that large segments of the population cannot afford health insurance. Per capita expenditures for health-care in Columbia are 42 percent of what they are in Chile and 20 percent of the expenditure level in Argentina. Instead of giving free access to public facilities, Columbia's reforms involve providing vouchers that allow low-income families to join the health organization of their choice. To be successful, all these reform efforts require social equilibrium where governments are able to maintain political and economic stability.

The political instability and socioeconomic inequality that have characterized Latin America are also a hindrance to health-care systems in Africa. An even more fundamental problem in Africa, however, is the formidable lack of resources to address overwhelming health-care needs (Schieber and Maeda 1999). Even where clinics, hospitals, and medical personnel exist, there is likely to be a lack of the required equipment and medicines. In Africa as a whole, 80 percent of the physicians live and practice in the cities where less than 20 percent of the population lives. According to Sanneh (1999), this continuing situation supports the prominent role of traditional healers, 85 percent of whom live in rural areas. The difficulties encountered by Ghana in implementing a system of primary care illustrate the situation affecting many African nations. In 1983, soon after the primary care system was adopted, the government attempted cost containment by introducing "user fees" in all public health facilities, clinics as well as hospitals. Two years later the fees were increased and, subsequently, a health insurance program was instituted. One must question the practical significance of these developments in a country where over half of rural residents and nearly half of those in urban areas live below poverty (Anyinam 1989). These circumstances are a reminder that developing countries contain 84 percent of the world's population, yet account for only 11 percent of global health-care spending (Schieber and Maeda 1999), making the task of designing strategies for effective health-care delivery in the developing world the true challenge for comparative health-care system researchers.

Comparing health-care systems entails a vast array of information, including historical background, cultural patterns and beliefs, geographic considerations, as well as social, economic, and political factors. It involves detailed descriptions of policies and procedures, complex statistical profiles, as well as an understanding of conceptual frameworks, theory, and comparative methods. The potential rewards of comparative work, however, balance the challenges. Whether there is convergence in the structure and functioning of health-care systems or not, many of the problems faced by nations in delivering health-care to citizens are similar. There are lessons to be learned from comparing health-care systems internationally that can only aid in addressing these problems.

REFERENCES

Albrecht, Gary L., and J. Warren Salmon 1992 "Soviet Health-care in the Glastnost Era." In Marilyn Rosenthal and Marcel Frenkel, eds., *Health-care Systems and their Patients: An International Perspective*. Boulder, Co: Westview Press.

Anderson, Gerard F., and Jean-Pierre Poullier 1999 "Health Spending, Access, and Outcomes: Trends in Industrialized Countries." *Health Affairs* 18:178–192.

Anderson, Odin W. 1989 *The Health Service Continuum in Democratic States: An Inquiry into Solvable Problems*. Ann Arbor, Mich.: Health Administration Press.

Anyinam, C. A. 1989 "The Social Costs of the International Monetary Fund's Adjustment Programs for Poverty: The Case of Health-Care Development in Ghana." *International Journal of Health Services* 19:531–547.

Bertranou, Fabio M. 1999 "Are Market-Oriented Health Insurance Reforms Possible in Latin America? The Cases of Argentina, Chile and Colombia." *Health Policy* 47:19–36.

Donelan, Karen, Robert J. Blendon, Cathy Schoen, Karen Davis, and Katherine Binns 1999 "The Cost of Health-System Change: Public Discontent in Five Nations." *Health Affairs* 18:206–216.

Elling, Ray H. 1994 "Theory and Method for the Cross-National Study of Health Systems" *International Journal of Health Services* 24:285–309.

Esping-Andersen, Gosta 1990 *The Three Worlds of Welfare Capitalism*. Princeton, N.J.: Princeton University Press.

Evans, Robert G. 1997 "Going for the Gold: The Redistributive Agenda behind Market-Based HealthCare Reform." *Journal of Health Politics, Policy and Law* 22:427–465.

Field, Mark G. "The Health-System and the Polity: A Contemporary American Dialectic." *Social Science and Medicine* 14:397–413.

Frenk, Julio 1994 "Dimensions of Health-System Reform." *Health Policy* 27:19–34.

Graig, Laurene A. 1993 *Health of Nations: An International Perspective on U.S. Health Care Reform*. 2nd Ed. Washington, D.C.: Congressional Quarterly.

Hermanson, Terhi, Seppo Aro, and Charles L. Bennett 1994 "Finland's Health-Care System: Universal Access to Health-Care in a Capitalistic Democracy." *Journal of the American Medical Association* 271:1957–1962.

Ikegami, Naoki, and John Creighton Campbell 1999 "Health-Care Reform in Japan: The Virtues of Muddling Through." *Health Affairs* 18:56–75.

Klein, Rudolf 1998 "Why Britain is Reorganizing Its National Health Service—Yet Again." *Health Affairs* 17:111–125.

Lassey, Marie L., William R. Lassey, and Martin J. Jinks 1997 *Health-Care Systems Around the World: Characteristics, Issues, Reforms*. Upper Saddle River, N.J.: Prentice Hall.

Light, Donald W. 1990 "Comparing Health-Care Systems: Lessons from East and West Germany." In P. Conrad and R. Kern eds., *The Sociology of Health & Illness: Critical Perspectives*, 3rd ed. New York: St. Martin's Press.

Liu, Gordon, Xingszhu Liu, and Qingyue Meng 1994 "Privatization of the Medical Market in Socialist China: A Historical Approach." *Health Policy* 27:157–174.

Mechanic, David, and David A. Rochefort 1996 "Comparative Medical Systems." *Annual Review of Sociology* 22:239–270.

Payer, Lynn 1996 *Medicine and Culture*, 2nd ed. New York: Owl Books/Henry Holt.

Roemer, Milton I. 1991 *National Health-Systems of the World*, vols. 1 and 2 New York: Oxford University Press.

Saltman, Richard B., and Casten Von Otter 1992 *Planned Markets and Public Competition: Strategic Reform in Northern European Health Systems*. Philadelphia: Open University Press.

Sanneh, Kanja B. A. S. 1999 "The Role of Traditional Healers in Primary Health-Care: Roadblocks to Health Education in Africa." Unpublished paper. Department of Health Policy and Management, University of Kansas.

Schieber, George, and Akiko Maeda 1999 "Health-Care Financing and Delivery in Developing Countries." *Health Affairs* 18:193–205.

Shi, Leiyu 1993 "Health-Care in China: A Rural-Urban Comparison After the Reforms." *Bulletin of the World Health Organization* 71:723–736.

Starr, Paul 1982 *The Social Transformation of American Medicine*. New York: Basic Books.

Steinmo, Sven, and Jon Watts 1995 "It's the Institutions, Stupid! Why Comprehensive National Health Insurance Always Fails in America." *Journal of Health Politics, Policy and Law* 20:329–372.

Swedish Institute 1999 "Fact Sheet on Health Care." Stockholm, Sweden: Swedish Institute

U.S. General Accounting Office 1991 "Health-Care Spending Control: The Experience of France, Germany, and Japan." GAO/HRD–92–9 Washington, D.C.: U.S. General Accounting Office.

U.S. General Accounting Office 1994 "German Health-reforms: Changes Result in Lower Health Costs in 1993." GAO/HEHS–95–27 Washington, D. C.: U.S. General Accounting Office.

Van Atteveld, L., C. Broeders, and R. Lapre 1987 "International Comparative Research in Health-Care: A Study of the Literature." *Health Policy* 8:105–136.

Zimmerman, Mary K., and Burton Halpert 1997 "Health and Welfare Reforms in Sweden: 1990–1996: How Safe is the Safety Net?" Paper presented at the annual meeting of the Midwest Sociological Society Des Moines, Ia.

MARY KO ZIMMERMAN

COMPARATIVE-HISTORICAL SOCIOLOGY

Explicit analytic attention to time and space as the context, cause, or outcome of fundamental social processes distinguishes comparative-historical analysis from other forms of social research. Historical processes occurring in or across geographic, political, or economic units (e.g., regions, nation-states, multi-state alliances, or entire world systems) are systematically compared for the purposes of more generally understanding patterns of social stability and social change (Abrams 1982; Skocpol 1984a; Tilly 1984; Mahoney 1999). Three very different and influential studies illustrate both the kinds of questions comparative-historical sociolgists address and the approaches they use.

First is the classic study by Reinhard Bendix ([1956] 1974) on work and authority in industry. Bendix initially observed that all industrial societies must authoritatively coordinate productive activities. Yet by systematically comparing how this was done in four countries during particular historical periods—pre-1917 Russia, post-World War II East Germany, and England and United States during epochs of intense industrialization—he showed that national variation in ideologies of workplace dominance were related to differences in the social structures of the countries studied.

Second is the analysis of the historical origins and development of the modern world system by Immanuel Wallerstein (1974). Wallerstein took as his unit of analysis the entire sixteenth-century capitalist world economy. Through comparing instances of the geographic division of labor, and especially the increasing bifurcation of global economic activity into "core" and "peripheral" areas, Wallerstein suggested that the economic interdependence of nation-states likely conditions their developmental trajectories.

Third is the analysis of social revolutions by Theda Skocpol (1979). Skocpol compared the histories of revolution in three ancient regime states: pre-1789 France, czarist Russia, and imperial China, and found that revolutionary situations emerged in these states because international crises exacerbated problems induced by their agrarian class structures and political institutions. She then buttressed her causal generalizations by comparing similar agrarian societies—Meiji Japan, Germany in 1806 and 1848, and seventeenth century England—that witnessed failed revolutions.

Each of these influential studies combined theoretical concepts and nonexperimental research methods to compare and contrast historical processes occurring within and across a number of geographic cases or instances. By using such research methods, Bendix, Wallerstein, Skocpol, and many others are following in the footsteps of the founders of sociology. In their attempts to understand and explain the sweeping transformations of nineteenth-century Europe, Alexis de Tocqueville, Karl Marx, Emile Durkheim, and Max Weber all employed and contributed to the formulation of this broad analytic frame (Smelser 1976; Abrams

1982). Comparative-historical analysis in sociology—and, as we shall see, debate over how it should be conducted—thus is as old as sociology itself.

PURPOSES, PROMISE, ACHIEVEMENTS

The analytic power of comparative-historical strategies stems from the uniquely paradoxical quality of the perspectives, data, and procedures in comparative-historical research. On the one hand, historical comparisons have the potential to harness and exploit the huge variation in social processes and institutions. Some scholars believe this essential to the development of truly general theory and to transcultural/transhistorical explanation (Przeworski and Tuene 1970; Kiser and Hechter 1991). On the other hand, historical comparisons have the potential to exploit the "time-space boundedness" of social life and its historical antecedents and specificity. Others view this as equally essential to theoretical development and to concrete, "real world" explanation (Moore 1966; Skocpol 1984b; Tilly 1984; Stryker 1996). Most comparative-historical sociologists capitalize in some fashion on this paradox, finding diversity in the midst of uniformity and producing regularities from differences.

One of the great advantages of historical comparisons is that they reduce bias induced by culturally and historically limited analyses and interpretations of the social world. Social structures and processes in the past were generally quite different from those observed today, and contemporary institutional arrangements and social relations differ substantially across cultures, regions, and states. Patterns of historical change and continuity, moreover, have varied from one country or culture to another. Some scholars, such as Bendix (1963, [1956] 1974), relish this diversity and use historical comparisons to emphasize and interpret the peculiarities of each case. Even seeming uniformities across cases may mask important differences, and comparative-historical inquiry may be used to detect these "false similarities" (Bloch [1928] 1969).

Examination of historical or national differences also can lead to the detection of previously unknown facts that may suggest a research problem or pose a hypothesis amenable to empirical exploration. Marc Bloch ([1928] 1969), for example, tells of how his knowledge of the English land enclosures led him to discover similar events in France. Comparing histories also aids in the formation of concepts and the construction of "ideal types" (Weber 1949; Bendix 1963; Smelser 1976). For example, Weber's ([1904] 1958) concepts of "the Protestant ethic" and "the spirit of capitalism" and Wallerstein's (1974) notion of the "world system" derive from comparative-historical inquiry. Linking apparently disparate historical and geographical phenomena, as Karl Polanyi ([1944] 1957) does when he relates the gold standard to the relative geopolitical tranquility throughout much of the nineteenth century, also is one of the fruits of comparative-historical analysis. New information, conceptual development and the discovery of unlikely commonalties, linkages, and previously unappreciated differences are necessary for the generation, elaboration, and historical grounding of social theory.

The analysis of comparative-historical patterns can allow for more adequate testing of established theory than does study of a single nation, culture, or time period. Plausible theories of large-scale social change, for example, are intrinsically processual and so require historical analysis for a genuine elaboration or examination of their hypotheses (Tilly 1984). Historical comparisons also can be used to assess the generality of putative "universal" explanations for social structure and social action (e.g., functionalism, Marxism). Abstract propositions thought operative across time and space, for example, can be directly confronted through the analysis of parallel cases that should display the same theoretical process (Skocpol and Summers 1980), thereby specifying a theory's generality and empirical scope.

Comparative-historical analysis sometimes is directed toward developing explanations that explicitly are "relative" to space and time (Beer 1963) or that represent historically or culturally "limited generalizations" (Joynt and Rescher 1960). Skocpol's (1979) analysis of social revolutions in France, Russia, and China, for example, resulted in limited causal generalizations deemed valid for these three cases only. Exceptions to theoretical and empirical generality, moreover, can be conceptualized as deviant cases—anomalies or puzzles. For example, Werner Sombart ([1906] 1976) posed the question "Why is there no socialism in the United States?" precisely because the United

States, when contrasted to the European experience and stacked up against available explanations for the development of class-conscious labor politics, appeared both historically and theoretically anomalous. To explain such puzzles, the original theory is modified and new concepts and theories with greater explanatory power are formulated. The improved theory then serves as the new starting point for subsequent inquiry, so that cumulation of knowledge is facilitated (Stryker 1996). Thus historical patterns are comparatively situated, the "inexplicable" residue of time and place therefore is potentially "explicable" (Sewell 1967), and sociological theory is further developed.

ANALYTIC TYPES OF HISTORICAL COMPARISONS

Contemporary comparative-historical research practice rests upon diverse, even contradictory, epistemologies and research strategies (Bonnell 1980, Skocpol 1984b, Tilly 1984; Ragin 1987; McMichael 1990; Kiser and Hechter 1991; Griffin 1992; Sewell 1996; Stryker 1996; Mahoney 1999). These can be initially grouped into two basic approaches, labeled here "analytical formalism" and "interpretivism." Each displays considerable internal diversity, and the two can overlap and be combined in practice. Moreover, they can be synthesized in creative ways, thereby capitalizing on the strengths of each approach and reducing their respective weaknesses. The synthesis, "causal interpretivism," is sufficiently distinct as to constitute a third approach to the analysis of comparative history.

Analytically formal comparison. *Formal comparison* conforms generally to conventional scientific practice in that causal explanation is the goal. It is therefore generally characterized by the development and empirical examination or testing of falsifiable theory of wide historical scope, by the assumption of the preexistence of discrete and identifiable cases, and by the use of formal logical or statistical tools and replicable analytic procedures. Historical narration and the "unities of time and place" (Skocpol 1984b, p. 383) are deliberately replaced by the language of causal analysis. Analytic formal comparison can be used to generalize across time and space, to uncover or produce limited causal regularities among a set of carefully

chosen cases, and to establish a theory's scope conditions. There are two major procedural subtypes in this genre, statistical comparisons and formal qualitative comparisons.

Statistical analyses of comparative-historical phenomena are logically and inferentially identical to statistical analyses of any other social phenomena. Thus, they rely on numerical counts, theoretical models, and techniques of statistical inference to assess the effects of theoretically salient variables, to test the validity of causal arguments, and to develop parsimonious, mathematically precise generalizations and explanations. One important way in which the statistical method appears in comparative-historical inquiry is in the form of "comparative time-series" analysis, in which statistical series charting historical change are systematically compared across countries. Charles, Louise, and Richard Tilly (1978) and Bruce Western (1994), for example, first use statistical time-series procedures to map and explain historical variation in working-class activity within European nations. They then compare, either qualitatively (the Tillys) or quantitatively (Western), these national statistical patterns to detect and explain historical differences and similarities across these countries. The second major use of statistical procedures relies on quantitative data from many social units for only one or a few time points. Emphasis in this "cross-national" tradition (e.g., Chase-Dunn 1979; Jackman 1984; Korpi 1989) is on detecting causal generalizations that are valid for a large sample or even an entire population of countries. Though the results of such studies typically resemble a static, cross sectional snapshot of historical process, this analytic strategy sometimes is necessitated because complete time-series data do not exist for very many nations, especially those now undergoing economic and social development (e.g., Pampel and Williamson 1989). Due both to their data limitations and to their focus on statistical regularities and theory testing, cross-national studies typically slight historical processes and homogenize cultural differences across cases. The understanding of cases as real social units deserving of explanation in their own right consequently is sometimes lost (Tilly 1984; Skocpol 1984b; Ragin 1987; Stryker 1996). In the 1990s, however, some cross-national statistical analysts, though continuing their search for general patterns, began to incorporate a more thorough appreciation of history and cultural difference into their analyses (e.g., Western 1994).

Formal qualitative comparison, by way of contrast, views cases "holistically," as qualitatively distinct and independent units that cannot (or should not) be decomposed into scores on quantitative variables as in statistical analysis. This strategy adopts a "case-oriented" approach that pervades the entire research process (Ragin 1987). The explanation of a few carefully chosen cases, for example, generally is the rationale for and product of the analysis, and explicit strategies have been designed to select proper instances to be compared and analyzed (Przeworski and Teune 1970; Frendreis 1983; Lijphart 1971; Stryker 1996). Detection of causal regularities is often inferred through the application of John Stuart Mill's ([1843] 1967) inductive canons or "method of agreement" and "method of difference" to comparative data (Skocpol 1984b; Ragin 1987). Using the method of agreement, analysts select cases that have positive outcomes on the phenomenon under study but that differ on putative explanatory conditions. These cases are then compared to see what causal factor they share. Alternative explanations are eliminated if antecedent conditions representing those claims do not occur in all cases with positive outcomes. The "method of difference" is used to guard against false inferences adduced from the method of agreement. Here analysis is conducted with cases instancing both positive and negative outcomes but that are as similar as possible on the putative causal factors. The objective of Mill's methods is to find the one condition that is present in all positive cases and absent in all negative cases (Skocpol 1984b; Ragin 1987).

Mill's methods are marred because they presuppose that one causal factor or configuration holds for all cases with positive instances. Historical patterns displaying "causal heterogeneity" or "multiple causal conjunctures"—two or more distinct combinations of causal forces generating the same outcome (Ragin 1987)—are therefore logically ruled out. This shortcoming results from the excessive weight Mill's canons give negative cases: Because exceptions exist to almost any general process, the inability to find causal universals that are doubly confirmed by the twin logics of agreement and difference can rule out virtually any nontrivial explanation (Lijphart 1971; Ragin 1987;

Mahoney 1999). However, Charles Ragin's (1987) alternative comparative algorithm—"qualitative comparative analysis" (QCA)—allows for the detection of causal heterogeneity in a large number of cases. QCA uses a data reduction strategy rooted in Boolean algebra to search for similarities among positive instances and to exploit the inferential utility of negative cases. Negative or "deviant" cases may be explained by, or give rise to, an alternative causal process, but they are not allowed to invalidate all causal generalizations. Ragin argues that QCA's Boolean logic most closely approximates the mode of reasoning—including the use of logically possible "historical hypotheticals" and "historical counterfactuals"—employed by Weber (1949) and Barrington Moore (1966) in their powerful but less formalized comparative-historical studies.

Formal qualitative comparison can provide both historically grounded explanation and theoretical generalization. QCA is especially useful because it permits multiple causal configurations to emerge from comparative historical data and largely removes the inferential problems induced by the analysis of a small number of cases of unknown representativeness. Nonetheless, detractors—who otherwise disagree about preferred research strategies—believe that formal comparison via either Mill's methods or QCA often is fraught with hidden substantive assumptions, unable to exert sufficient analytical control over the multitude of competing explanations, and compromised by its roots in inductive logic (Burawoy 1989; Kiser and Hechter 1991). Moreover, formal comparisons rest on a key assumption that is seriously challenged by proponents of holistic interpretive comparison—that the historical cases themselves are not systematically interrelated (Wallerstein 1974; McMichael 1990).

Interpretive comparisons. . Interpretive comparisons are most concerned with developing a meaningful understanding of broad cultural or historical patterns (Skocpol 1984b). Two very different comparative logics, "holistic" and "individualizing," are used to construct historical interpretations. Although neither logic relies extensively on formal analytic procedures, nor is geared toward testing theory, interpretive comparisons are not necessarily atheoretical or lacking in rigor. Indeed, concepts and theories, often of sweeping scope and grandeur, are extensively developed and deployed, but for the most part as interpretive and organizing frames, or as lenses through which history is understood and represented. Interpretive comparisons often are thought impressive, but sometimes of questionable validity due either to their self-validating logic or to their lack of explicit scientific criteria for evaluating the truth content of the interpretation (Bonnell 1980; Skocpol 1984b; Tilly 1984; Stryker 1996; Mahoney 1999).

Holistic comparisons usually are tied to particular theories and are used when a "social whole" such as a world system (Wallerstein 1974) is methodologically posited. Conceptualizing the entire world system in this manner suggests that there is but one theoretical unit of analysis, and that unit is the world system. What are considered to be separate "units of analysis" or "cases" in most comparative-historical strategies are, in the holistic methodological frame, really only interrelated and interdependent historical realizations of a singular emergent process or social system. Whether nation-states, regions, or cultures, these "moments" therefore are not the discrete and independent units demanded by analytic formalism. Analysts using holistic historical comparisons in this manner often depend on an "encompassing" functional logic that explains similarities or differences among parts of a whole by the relationship the parts have to the whole (Tilly 1984). Thus, Wallerstein's (1974) comparisons explain the differential development of temporally and spatially specific (though interdependent) economic units in the world system—the core, periphery, and semi-periphery—by their differential positions and roles in the world economy. Such explanations are often circular in their reasoning and always difficult to test, but they may serve as useful illustrations of the workings of a social whole or of the inner logic of a theory (Bonnell 1980; Skocpol 1984b).

Philip McMichael (1990) suggests "incorporated comparison" as an alternative to purge holistic comparison of its mechanistic and self-validating logic. Here a kind of social whole is posited, but it does not preexist and regulate its parts, as does the world system. Instead, it is analytically "reconstituted" by conceptualizing different historical instances as interdependent moments, which, when cumulated and connected through time and space, "form" the whole as a general but empirically diverse historical process. Thus the very definition and selection of "cases" becomes

the object of theorizing and research and not its point of departure or merely the vehicle conveying data for analysis. Karl Polanyi's ([1944] 1957) analysis of the emergence and decline of laissez-faire capitalism is a compelling example of this form of holistic comparison.

Individualizing interpretive analysts use historical comparison to demonstrate the historical and cultural particularity of individual cases. Analysts in this tradition often choose research questions and cases on the basis of their recurrent moral and historical significance rather than scientific representativeness or comprehensiveness. They also tend self-consciously to eschew general theory, quantification, and the methodology of causal analysis. Rather, interpretation is grounded in rich historical narration, in anthropological sensitivity to the import of cultural practice, in the culturally embedded meanings in social action, and in the use of persuasive concepts that crystallize or resonate with significant social values and themes (Bendix 1963; Geertz 1973; Bonnell 1980; Tilly 1984; Skocpol 1984b). Bendix's ([1956] 1974) research on work and authority in industry is an exemplar of this strategy, and Daniel Goldhagen's (1996) recent study, *Hitler's Willing Executioners*, is another much more controversial example.

Casual Interpretivism. Historical comparisons rooted in *causal interpretivism* synthesize aspects of both analytical-formal and interpretive-historical comparisons. Inspired in part by Weber's (1949) formulation of "causal interpretation" (and anthropologist Clifford Geertz's [1980] similar idea of "interpretive explanation"), this strategy is stamped by explicit causal reasoning, the potential for explanatory generality across comparable instances, and the use of methodological procedures allowing for strict replication, on the one hand, and attention to historical narrative, cultural particularity, and subjective meaning, on the other.

Causal interpretivism has been most fruitfully developed and applied in the analysis of historical narratives (Sewell 1996; Griffin 1992, 1993; Quadagno and Knapp 1992; Somers 1998). Narratives are "sequential accounts" organizing information into "chronological order to tell stories about what happened. . ." and why it happened as it did, and, as such, are "tools for joining sequentiality, contingency, and generalizability" (Stryker 1996, p.305, 307). Narrativists conceptualize historical time so that it is "eventful:" Any given moment in a historical chain of unfolding sequences is both a repository of past actions and a harbinger of future possibilities (Thompson 1978). Temporal order and the causal relationships among actions that make up events therefore become the major object of inquiry in comparative narrative analysis.

Narrative focuses squarely on the import of human agency in reproducing or changing societal arrangements, thereby complementing the attentiveness comparative-historical sociologists have traditionally given social structural constraints and opportunities (Stryker 1996). Channeling analytical attention in this fashion directs narrativists both to transformative historical happenings (the French Revolution, for instance [Sewell 1996]) and to the development and deployment of decidedly temporal concepts, such as path dependence, sequential unfolding, temporally cumulative causation, and the pace of social action (Abrams 1982; Aminzade 1992). The structure of action underpinning particular historical narratives, moreover, can also be strictly compared with an eye toward both showing general patterns across events and individual exceptions to those generalizations (Abbott 1992; Griffin 1993). Dietrich Rueschemeyer and John Stephens (1997), for example, demonstrate how "eventful time, including the order and sequence of key actions, can both be incorporated into causal generalizations for such large scale processes as democratization and capitalist economic development and [be] exploited to ascertain where those generalizations break down.

Comparative narrativists have developed a variety of procedures to enhance the theoretical payoff and replicability of their research: (1) event-structure analysis (Griffin 1993), which allows explicit codification of reasons for inferences and for cross-level generalization; (2) semantic grammar analysis, which uses linguistic rules to convert text, such as newspaper accounts of strikes In Italy, into numbers for subsequent statistical analysis (Franzosi 1995, 1998); and (3) systematizing electronic means to collect, store, code, and analyze diverse types of historical texts, from newspaper articles to court opinions and legislative hearings (Stryker 1996; Pedriana and Stryker 1997). Robin Stryker (1996) has also developed the useful notion of "strategic narrative" as a guide to case selection in comparative-historical analysis: Strategic narrative suggests

that some historical events and ways of constructing stories will promote theory-building more than will others, thus facilitating cumulation of knowledge.

Regardless of precisely how analytical formalism is incorporated, unpacking a narrative and reconstituting it as an explicit causal account—that is, comprehending and explaining the logical within the chronological, and the general within the particular—often requires that analysts imaginatively reconstruct participants' cultural understandings (interpretation), as well as systematically harness theoretical abstractions, comparative generalizations, and replicable research methods. In effect, then, analysts explain because they are compelled to interpret, and they interpret because causal explanation is demanded (Beer 1963; Griffin 1993; Mahoney 1999).

METHODOLOGICAL ISSUES AND DIFFICULTIES

Though comparative-historical analysis is neither necessarily cross-national or cross-cultural, nor always confronting the same obstacles as narrative history, it does share many of the methodological problems (and solutions) and dilemmas traditionally associated with both types of research. These include, among others: (1) defining and selecting comparable analytical units; (2) case interdependence; (3) the nonrepresentativeness of cases; (4) determining conceptual equivalence and measurement reliability and validity across time and space; (5) the paucity of data, especially that which is quantitative, over long periods of time, and for newly emerging nations; (6) the selectivity and general unsoundness of the historical record; (7) the use of spatially and temporally aggregated data, and, more generally, the distance between what can be collected and systematically measured and what the theory or research question actually calls for; and (8) fruitful ways to wed historical narration and cultural specificity, on the one hand, to the development of general sociological theory and cumulative, replicable results, on the other. Some of these difficulties especially plague analytically formal comparisons (e.g., the artificiality and interdependence of cases; the paucity of systematic, quantifiable data at the proper theoretical level of analysis; and the excessive generality at the cost of important historical and cultural specificity);

others haunt with more force interpretive comparisons (e.g., nonrepresentative cases; analytical looseness and non replicability; and excessive particularity at the expense of generalization and theoretical development).

Granting their very real import, these difficulties are not normally intractable. As we have shown, methodologically self-conscious comparative-historical scholars, both qualitative and quantitative, have devised strategies to: construct and select the most relevant cases for analysis; exploit cross-level data (e.g., within and between nation-states) and make causal inferences across levels of analysis; guard against logically false or self-validating inferences; infuse the analysis of historical narrative with greater theoretical and analytical rigor; and increase the number and representativeness of their cases. They have also devised or imported useful ways to ensure maximum measurement equivalence across cultures; sample historical records; estimate data missing from statistical series and to correct for truncated data; capitalize on case interdependence with new statistical methods; historically ground time-series analysis; etc. (see Bloch [1928] 1969; Carr 1961; Przeworski and Teune 1970; Zelditch 1971; Tuma and Hannan 1984; Skocpol 1984b; Ragin 1987; Kohn 1989; Isaac and Griffin 1989; McMichael 1990; Kiser and Hechter 1991; Griffin 1993; Western 1994; Deane, Beck, and Tolnay 1998).

Some problems, admittedly, have no satisfactory solution, and nothing can compensate for the utter dearth of valid information on particular happenings or variables. This, though, is hardly different from any other form of social research. The litany of methodological difficulties discussed above, in fact, afflict all social research. Survey analysts, for example, deal with questionnaire responses of dubious accuracy and unknown meaning taken from geographically and temporally limited samples, and scholars working with institutional records of any sort must deal with information collected by institutionally self-interested actors.

It is important to recognize that although comparative-historical inquiry is no more "error-prone" or unreliable than are other forms of social research, it often adopts a very different underlying "working philosophy" from most theory-driven quantitative analysis. Usually in highly deductive and statistical analysis (including comparative

strategies), theory construction and theory testing are two clearly defined and quite separate phases of a research program (Kiser and Hechter 1991; Stryker 1996). Segmenting research practice in this way is thought necessary to ensure that hypothesis testing produces a fair empirical test, unbiased by prior analysis, or even intimate foreknowledge of the data. Given these rules and objectives, then, concepts, indicators, hypotheses, and theory are not usually changed in the middle of analysis; that would invalidate the statistical or logical test.

In contrast, comparative-historical inquiry that is qualitative and inductive, though often also analytically formal, establishes a continual dialogue between social theory and empirical evidence, so that conceptual abstraction and comparative history are mutually defined and constructed in reference to each other. In *The Protestant Ethic and the Spirit of Capitalism*, for example, Weber ([1904] 1958) used historical evidence on economic and religious practices and beliefs to refine his ideal types and his hypotheses and, simultaneously, conceptually frame that empirical data to render it intelligible and explicable. Many comparative-historical sociologists follow Weber's general strategy, that is, they start their inquiry with one set of concepts, indicators, or hypotheses, or all three, and end with another, modified set because they mutually adjust data and theory, ensuring a good "fit" between the two as analysis progresses. In their study of capitalist economic development and democratic political practice in many nations, for example, Rueschemeyer, John Stephens, and Evelyne Huber Stephens (1992) amended their theoretical definition of democracy, both broadening its historical scope and specifying more precisely its meaning, as they moved in their analysis from Europe to Latin America. Thus what may look like scientific "cheating" to a deductive or quantitative scholar is an appropriate, fruitful strategy for comparative-historical sociologists whose goals are concept formulation and reformulation, theory construction, and empirical understanding, rather than strict hypothesis testing.

Analytic rigor does not rest with the mechanistic application of technique per se, but, instead, with a systematic and methodologically self-disciplined stance toward both data collection and analysis and the use of evidence to advance inferences. Most comparative-historical scholars adhere to explicit decision rules, permitting others to replicate, critically judge, and constructively critique the research. To help ensure the validity and reliability of measures in this sort of inquiry, and while also maintaining the needed flexibility to improve key concepts and measures during the analysis, for instance, Stryker (1996) has shown how researchers can adapt traditional content-analytic coding techniques to capture time and space as explanatory context. Context can be conceptualized and measured as a conjunction of "values" on general theoretical constructs, and, at the same time, researchers can develop what she terms "action coding" to construct more systematically the who, what, when, where, how, and why of action and event sequences. With enhanced systematization—that is, the use of precise concepts, measures, and coding techniques, and the clear communication of these—comes enhanced reliability and replicability (Stryker 1996).

THE FUTURE OF COMPARATIVE-HISTORICAL ANALYSIS

Jack Goldstone (1997, p. 119) has stated that comparative-historical inquiry has produced "many of the greatest achievements of macro-sociological scholarship." At the end of the twentieth century, these achievements were severely tested by a series of interdependent, large-scale social transformations of every bit the historical magnitude and moral significance of those motivating sociology's founders: economic and cultural globalization; the growth of transnational "super states" brought about by strategic military and economic alliances among sovereign nation-states; post-communist marketization and democratization in former Soviet-bloc nations; and armed nationalist struggles and resurgent ethnic conflicts. Broad interest in, and need for, illuminating comparative-historical analysis therefore is only likely to increase.

The utility of research in this tradition rests more on the creative use of good theory than it does on its methodology. But "creative use" of theory is itself largely a matter of how theory is combined with research strategy. On this score, the future of comparative-historical sociology would seem bright.

One encouraging trend is the increasing use of statistical techniques developed explicitly to analyze temporal (Tuma and Hanna 1984; Isaac and Griffin 1989; Abbott 1992; McCammon 1998) and spatial processes (Deane et al. 1998). Time-series and spatial analyses are not always subject to the same limitations as are cross-national statistical analyses, and quantitative spatial techniques are particularly apt given heightened global interdependence. Spatial analysis, for instance, can uncover how historical processes move from place to place (country, region, etc.), and it can ascertain whether structures or practices in one country are diffused into other countries or deterred from entering them (Deane et al. 1998).

Another very positive trend that probably will become more widespread is combining and synthesizing different kinds of comparative logics. Both Jeffrey Paige (1975) and John Stephens (1980) combined cross-national quantitative analysis of a large number of nation-states with qualitative, case-oriented work on a small, but theoretically strategic subset of their cases. Paige combined his statistical generalizations with three parallel case studies, finding differences in the nature of agrarian revolts. Stephens, on the other hand, systematically compared a subset of four countries to show how the historical processes of welfare-state development differed from one nation to another. He therefore used both generalizing and individualizing comparative logics. Goldstone (1991) followed a similar strategy, combining "within-case" quantitative analyses with case-oriented comparisons to show how long-term population growth contributed to state breakdown in the early modern world. Combining diverse comparative-historical approaches in this way, and synthesizing analytical formalism and interpretation in causal interpretivism, yield insights that simply are not possible with any single methodological strategy.

Even if the differences among diverse approaches prove too great to overcome completely—a possibility suggested by the debate over the utility of highly deductive explanatory schemas such as rational choice theory in comparative-historical research (Quadagno and Knapp 1992; Kiser and Hechter 1991, 1998; Somers 1998)—diversity in goals, strategies, and procedures has spurred methodological innovation and the cross-fertilization of scholarship from divergent methodological strategies (Beer 1963; Rueschemeyer and Stephens 1997; Goldstone 1997). It thereby provides the continued promise of enhanced knowledge and richly textured, multi-voiced portrayals and understandings of perennial questions of fundamental human significance.

REFERENCES

Abbott, Andrew 1992 "From Causes to Events: Notes on Narrative Positivism." *Sociological Methods and Research* 20:428–55.

Abrams, Philip 1982 *Historical Sociology*. Ithaca, N.Y.: Cornell University Press.

Aminzade, Ron 1992 "Historical Sociology and Time." *Sociological Methods and Research* 20:456–480.

Beer, Samuel 1963 "Causal Explanation and Imaginative Reenactment." *History and Theory* 3:6–29.

Bendix, Reinhard (1956) 1974 *Work and Authority in Industry: Ideologies of Management in the Course of Industrialization*. Berkeley: University of California Press.

—— 1963 "Concepts and Generalizations in Comparative Sociological Studies." *American Sociological Review* 28:532–539.

Bloch, Marc (1928) 1969 "A Contribution Towards Comparative History of European Societies." In M. Bloch, ed., *Life and Work in Medieval Europe: Selected Papers of Marc Bloch*. New York: Harper Torchbooks.

Bonnell, Victoria 1980 "On the Uses of Theory, Concepts and Comparison in Historical Sociology." *Comparative Studies in Society and History* 22:156–173.

Burawoy, Michael 1989 "Two Methods in Search of Science: Skocpol versus Trotsky." *Theory and Society* 18:759–805.

Carr, E. H. 1961. *What is History?* New York: Vintage.

Chase-Dunn, Christopher 1979 "Comparative Research on World System Characteristics." *International Studies Quarterly* 23:601–625.

Deane, Glenn, E.M. Beck, and Stewart E. Tolnay 1998 "Incorporating Space into Social Histories: How Spatial Processes Operate and How we Observe Them." *International Review of Social History* 43:57–80.

Franzosi, Roberto 1998 "Narrative as Data: Linguistic and Statistical tools for the Quantitative Study of Historical Events. *International Journal of Social History* 43:81–104.

Frendreis, James 1983 "Explanation of Variation and Detection of Covariation: The Purpose and Logic of Comparative Analysis." *Comparative Political Studies* 16:255–272.

Geertz, Clifford 1980 "Blurred Genres: The Reconfiguration of Social Thought." *American Scholar* 49:165–179.

—— 1973 *The Interpretation of Cultures*. New York.: Basic Books.

Goldhagen, Daniel 1996 *Hitler's Willing Executors: Ordinary Germans and the Holocaust*. New York: Knopf.

Goldstone, Jack 1997 "Methodological Issues in Comparative Macrosociology." *Comparative Social Research* 16:107–120.

—— 1991 *Revolution and Rebellion in the Early Modern World*. Berkeley and Los Angeles: University of California Press.

Griffin, Larry J. 1993 "Narrative, Event-Structure, and Causal Interpretation in Historical Sociology." *American Journal of Sociology* 98:1094–1133.

—— 1992 "Temporality, Events and Explanation in Historical Sociology: An Introduction." *Sociological Methods and Research* 20:403–27.

Hibbs, Douglas 1978 "On the Political Economy of Long-run Trends in Strike Activity." *British Journal of Political Science* 8:51–75.

Isaac, Larry, and Larry J. Griffin 1989 "Ahistoricism in Times Series Analysis of Historical Process: Critique, Redirection and Illustrations from U.S. Labor History." *American Sociological Review* 54:873–890.

Jackman, Robert 1984 "Cross National Statistical Research and the Study of Comparative Politics." *American Journal of Political Science* 28:161–182.

Joynt, Cary, and Nicholas Rescher 1960 "The Problem of Uniqueness in History." *History and Theory* 1:150–162.

Kiser, Edgar, and Michael Hechter 1998 "The Debate on Historical Sociology: Rational Choice Theory and Its Critics." *American Journal of Sociology* 104:785–816.

—— 1991 "The Role of General Theory in Comparative-Historical Sociology." *American Journal of Sociology* 97:1–30.

Kohn, Melvin (ed.) 1989 *Cross-National Research in Sociology*. Beverly Hills, Calif.: Sage.

Korpi, Walter 1989 "Power, Politics and State Autonomy in the Development of Social Citizenship: Social Rights During Sickness in Eighteen OECD Countries Since 1930." *American Sociological Review* 54:309–328.

Lijphart, Arend 1971 "Comparative Politics and the Comparative Method." *American Political Science Review* 65:682–93.

Mahoney, James 1999 "Nominal, Ordinal, and Narrative Appraisal in Macrocausal Analysis" *American Journal of Sociology* 104:1154–1196.

McCammon. Holly 1998 "Using Event History Analysis in Historical Research: With Illustrations from a Study of the Passage of Women's Protective Legislation." *International Review of Social History* 43:33–55.

McMichael, Philip 1990 "Incorporating Comparison within a World-Historical Perspective: An Alternative Comparative Method." *American Sociological Review* 55:385–397.

Mill, John Stuart (1843) 1967 *A System of Logic: Ratiocinative and Inductive*. Toronto: University of Toronto Press.

Moore, Barrington 1966 *The Social Origins of Dictatorship and Democracy*. Boston: Beacon Press.

Paige, Jeffrey 1975 *Agrarian Revolt: Social Movements and Export Agriculture in the Underdeveloped World*. New York: Free Press.

Pampel, Fred, and John Williamson 1989 *Age, Class, Politics and the Welfare State*. Cambridge: Cambridge University Press.

Pedriana, Nicholas, and Robin Stryker. 1997. "Political Culture Wars 1960s Style: Equal Employment Opportunity, Affirmative Action Law and the Philadelphia Plan." *American journal of Sociology* 103:633–691.

Polanyi, Karl (1944) 1957 *The Great Transformation: The Political and Economic Origins of Our Times*. Boston: Beacon Press.

Przeworski, Adam, and Henry Teune 1970 *The Logic of Comparative Social Inquiry*. New York: Wiley.

Quadagno, Jill, and Stan Knapp 1992 "Have Historical Sociologists Forsaken Theory? Thoughts on the History/Theory Relationship." *Sociological Methods and Research* 20:481–507.

Ragin, Charles 1987 *The Comparative Method*. Berkeley: University of California Press.

Rueschemeyer, Dietrich, and John Stephens 1997 "Comparing Historical Sequences: A Powerful Tool for Causal Analysis." *Comparative Social Research* 17:55–72.

——, and Evelyne Huber Stephens 1992 *Capitalist Development and Democracy*. Chicago: University of Chicago Press.

Sewell, William, Jr. 1996. "Three Temporalities: Toward an Eventful Sociology." In, T. J. McDonald, ed., *The Historic Turn in the Human Sciences*. Ann Arbor: University of Michigan Press.

—— 1967 "Marc Bloch and the Logic of Comparative History." *History and Society* 6:208–218.

Skocpol, Theda (ed.) 1984a *Vision and Method in Historical Sociology*. New York: Cambridge University Press.

—— 1984b "Emerging Agendas and Recurrent Strategies in Historical Sociology." In T. Skocpol, ed., *Vision and Method in Historical Sociology*, New York: Cambridge University Press.

—— 1979 *States and Social Revolutions*. Cambridge: Cambridge University Press.

——, and Margaret Somers 1980 "The Uses of Comparative History in Macrosocial Inquiry." *Comparative Study of Society and History* 22:174–197.

Smelser, Neil 1976 *Comparative Methods in the Social Sciences*. Englewood Cliffs, N.J.: Prentice-Hall.

Sombart, Werner (1906) 1976 *Why Is There No Socialism in the United States?* White Plains, N.Y.: M.E. Sharpe.

Somers, Margaret 1998 "We're No Angels": Realism, Rationality Choice and Relationality in Social Science." *American Journal of Sociology* 104:722–784.

Stephens, John 1980 *The Transition from Capitalism to Socialism*. Atlantic Highlands, N.J.: Humanities Press.

Stryker, Robin 1996 "Beyond History vs. Theory: Strategic Narrative and Sociological Explanation." *Sociological Methods and Research* 24:304–352.

Thompson. Edward P. 1978 *The Poverty of Theory and Other Essays*. London: Merlin.

Tilly, Charles 1984 *Big Structures, Large Processes, Huge Comparisons*. New York: Russell Sage Foundation.

——, Louise Tilly, and Richard Tilly 1975 *The Rebellious Century 1830–1930*. Cambridge, Mass.: Harvard University Press.

Tuma, Nancy, and Michael Hannan 1984 *Social Dynamics*. New York: Academic Press.

Wallerstein, Immanuel 1974 *The Modern World System*. New York: Academic Press.

Weber, Max (1904) 1958 *The Protestant Ethic and the Spirit of Capitalism*. New York: Scribners.

—— 1949 *The Methodology of the Social Sciences*. New York: Free Press.

Western, Bruce 1994 "Unionization and Labor Market Institutions in Advanced Capitalism, 1950–85." *American Journal of Sociology* 99:1314–1341.

Zelditch, Morris 1971 "Intelligible Comparisons." In I. Vallier, ed., *Comparative Methods in Sociology,*. Berkeley: University of California Press.

LARRY J. GRIFFIN
ROBIN STRYKER

COMPLEX ORGANIZATIONS

Organizations, as a class, are socially constructed innovations, deliberately designed as solutions to problems. Although some forms of organization, such as churches and armies, have been around for centuries, only since the Industrial Revolution have complex organizations assumed the form people take for granted today. Because they are shaped by the contexts or environments in which they are established, contemporary organizations reflect the impact of their historical origins in societies characterized by growing affluence and conflicts over the control and distribution of wealth. Organizations come in a bewildering variety of forms because they have been explicitly designed to deal with a wide range of problems and because they have emerged under widely varying environmental conditions.

THE IMPORTANCE OF ORGANIZATIONS

Why are complex organizations important? Organizations, which produce goods, deliver services, maintain order, and challenge the established order are the fundamental building blocks of modern societies, and the basic vehicles through which collective action is undertaken. The prominence of organizations in contemporary society is apparent when we consider some consequences of their actions.

Organizations coordinate the actions of people in pursuit of activities too broad in scope to be accomplished by individuals alone. Railroads were the first large corporations in the United States, arising because small autonomous merchants and traders could not effectively coordinate the passage of long-distance shipments. In the twentieth century, the production of mass-market consumption goods, such as automobiles and electric appliances, was made possible by the rise of large, vertically integrated manufacturing firms. Similarly, in the public sector, the implementation of government social policies has necessitated the development of large government agencies that process thousands of cases on a universalistic, impersonal basis.

The concentration of power in organizations contributes not only to the attainment of large-scale goals in modern societies, but also to some major social problems. When organizations focus on attaining specific goals, such as making profits for shareholders, they may neglect the side effects or externalities of their actions. Examples include air and water pollution and the careless disposal of unwanted hazardous materials by large manufacturers. The manufacture of unsafe consumer products and instances of large-scale fraud and collusion also illustrate the capacity of organizations to do harm as well as good.

Increasingly, major tasks in society are addressed not by single organizations but instead by networks of interdependent organizations. Interorganizational arrangements pool the efforts of numerous specialized organizations in pursuit of a common end. For example, automobiles are produced in *vertical* production networks centered on assemblers that maintain ongoing relationships with multiple tiers of suppliers responsible for the manufacture and delivery of components. However, in the industrial districts of northern Italy, textile production occurs within *horizontal* production networks consisting of small and specialized firms that employ flexible machinery and temporarily cooperate with one another for particular projects. Cooperation enables them to adapt to changing market demands and to learn from one another. Likewise, services for the severely mentally ill are delivered by independent but interrelated agencies providing specific medical and social services. Many large-scale motion pictures are produced not by self-contained studios, but rather by combinations of producers, directors, cinematographers, and other personnel assembled only for the duration of a particular project. Ongoing arrangements involving hospitals, doctors, and university laboratories have been created by the National Cancer Institute to coordinate cancer research and treatment. As these examples demonstrate, interorganizational arrangements give organizations the flexibility to address the unique features of specific cases, while avoiding the rigidities sometimes found in very large organizations.

DEFINITIONS OF ORGANIZATIONS

What are complex organizations? A simple definition is that organizations are goal-directed, boundary-maintaining, socially-constructed systems of human activity. Some definitions add other criteria, such as deliberateness of design, the existence of status structures, patterned understandings between participants, orientation to an environment, possession of a technical system for accomplishing tasks, and substitutability of personnel (Scott 1998).

Goal orientation and deliberate design of activity systems are distinctive features discriminating between organizations and other collectivities, such as families and small groups. Organizations are purposive systems in which members behave as if they are committed to the organization's goals, although individual participants might personally feel indifferent toward those goals or even alienated from their organizations. Concerted collective action toward an apparent common purpose also distinguishes organizations from social units such as friendship circles, audiences, and mass publics. Because many organizational forms are now institutionalized in modern societies, people readily turn to them or construct them when a task or objective exceeds their own personal abilities and resources (Meyer and Rowan 1977; Zucker 1988).

Organizations have activity systems—or technologies—for accomplishing work, which can include processing raw materials, information, or people. Activity systems consist of bounded sets of interdependent role behaviors; the nature of the interdependencies is often contingent upon the techniques used.

Other key elements of organizations, such as socially constructed boundaries, are shared with other types of collectivities. The establishment of an "organization" implies a distinction between members and nonmembers, thus marking off organizations from their environments. Maintaining this distinction requires boundary-maintenance activity, because boundaries may be permeable, and thus some organizations establish an authoritative process to enforce membership distinctions. For example, businesses have human resource management departments that select, socialize, and monitor employees, and voluntary associations have membership committees that perform similar functions. Distinctive symbols of membership may include unique modes of dress and special vocabularies.

Within organizations, goal attainment and boundary maintenance manifest themselves as issues of coordination and control, as authorities construct arrangements for allocating resources or integrating workflows. These internal structures affect the perceived meaning and satisfaction of individual participants by, for example, differentially allocating power and affecting the characteristics of jobs. Control structures, which shape the way participants are directed, evaluated, and rewarded are constrained by participants' multiple external social roles, some complementing, but others conflicting with organizational roles.

ENVIRONMENTS

Organizations, with few exceptions, are incomplete social systems that are not self-sufficient and thus depend on interchanges with their environments. Therefore, goal setting by owners or leaders must take into account the sometimes contrary preferences of organizations and other actors, because activity systems are fueled by resources obtained from outsiders. For example, participants must be enticed or coerced into contributing to the organization's activities: businesses pay people to work for them, while voluntary nonprofit organizations may offer more intangible benefits, such as sociable occasions.

Over the past few decades, organizational sociology has gradually expanded its scope to include more of the external elements associated with organizational life. Initially, theorists emphasized relatively tangible features: environments were seen as stocks of resources (such as raw materials, capital, or personnel) and information. To the degree that resources are scarce or concentrated in a few hands, organizations are more dependent on their environments and may be vulnerable to exploitation or external control by outsiders (Pfeffer and Salancik 1978). To the degree that information is dispersed, heterogeneous, or subject to change, organizations confront problems of uncertainty.

Much research has been devoted to understanding how organizations deal with the problems of dependence and uncertainty that environments pose. Some organizations respond internally, by developing specialized structures and processes. For example, boundary-spanning personnel are charged with dealing with actors outside the organization, acquiring resources, and disposing of products; they thereby enable others in the technical core to work under more certain conditions. Some organizations respond externally, by building bridges that stabilize their ties to environments. They use interorganizational devices such as long-term contracts and working agreements, joint programs or alliances, and interlocking directorates (Mizruchi and Galaskiewicz 1993).

More recent scholarship has stressed the socially constructed, *institutional* aspects of environments. Organizations must be attentive to these external aspects to acquire and maintain legitimacy and social standing. Scott (1995) distinguished between regulative, normative, and cognitive-cultural understandings of institutions. Regulative institutions are external systems of rules, often established by states, to which organizations must conform. External rules may be prescriptive, such as when a law requires that publicly traded corporations have boards of directors with at least three members. Rules may also be proscriptive, such as when regulatory bodies or courts prohibit particular trade practices and ownership patterns.

Normative institutions are sets of beliefs and values shared by organizations and their participants about the morally appropriate way in which to organize activities. Professional associations are common sources of normative prescriptions, enforced through processes such as certification. Cognitive institutions are cultural frames or scripts that constitute the social forms seen as natural and taken for granted in a given society. In contemporary society, the idea of organizations itself is institutionalized; legitimate pursuit of an activity often requires the formation of an organization because of the widespread belief that this is an efficient, effective, and fair manner in which to proceed (Meyer and Rowan 1977).

ORGANIZATIONAL DEMOGRAPHICS

The number of organizations in industrial societies is very large. Over five million businesses with at least one employee existed in the United States in 1998, and there were thousands of governmental agencies, nonprofit organizations, and voluntary associations (Aldrich 1999). Social scientists have developed various schemes to describe the diversity of organizations. For example, the North American Industry Classification System (Office of Management and the Budget 1997) classifies establishments by their products and the processes used to make them. Organizations can also be classified according to their goals or the social functions they serve (Parsons 1960), or on the basis of the prime beneficiaries of organizational actions: owners, members, clients, or the general public (Blau and Scott 1962). Another classification contrasts generalist and specialist organizations and hypothesizes that each type thrives in a different kind of environment (Hannan and Freeman 1989).

Industrial societies contain a large number of organizations, with three characteristics of special note. First, the size distribution of businesses and nonprofit organizations is highly skewed, with a large number of very small organizations. In 1990, approximately 90 percent of the five million firms in the United States with employees employed fewer than twenty people. Over 98 percent employed fewer than one hundred workers (Small Business Administration 1994). Employment statistics were very similar in the European Union (ENSR 1993), with about 93 percent of firms employing fewer than ten workers, although the figure varied by nation. In 1994, most of the 4.3 million corporations in the United States had fewer than $one hundred,000 in assets, and they accounted for less than 0.3 percent of all corporate assets. Thus, most organizations are fairly vulnerable to environmental forces and must adapt to them or disband.

Second, although the number of large organizations is small, they have achieved a dominant share of revenues and assets. Business organizations are highly stratified by size, and large firms have more resources with which to resist and counter environmental pressures. In 1994, the top 0.002 percent of corporations, each with a quarter-billion or more in assets, held about 83 percent of all corporate assets. In 1992, the fifty largest manufacturing firms in the United States accounted for about 24 percent of value added and about 13 percent of employment, and the two hundred largest firms accounted for 42 percent of value added and around 25 percent of employment (U.S. Bureau of the Census 1996).

Third, smaller organizations still employ a relatively large share of all workers. In the United States, about 39 percent of all employees work in firms that employ fewer than one hundred workers. In particular industries, such as agriculture and construction, substantially more than half the work force is employed in organizations with fewer than one hundred workers. In the European Union, firms with fewer than one hundred workers employ about 55 percent of the labor force, although variation across nations is substantial. For example, in Germany and the United Kingdom, firms larger than one hundred employ more than half the labor force, whereas in Greece and Italy, such firms employ only about 20 percent of the labor force (ESNR 1993).

Populations of organizations in modern societies are constantly undergoing processes of expansion, contraction, and change. Some organizations are founded in a flash of creative energy and then disband almost immediately, whereas others emerge slowly and then last for decades. Some organizations adapt readily to every environmental challenge, whereas others succumb to the first traumatic event they face. Sociologists have turned their attention to these vital events surrounding the reproduction and renewal of organizational populations, focusing on three processes: foundings, transformations, and disbandings (Aldrich 1999; Hannan and Freeman 1989).

New organizations are established fairly frequently, although systematic data on founding rates are available only for businesses. Studies in the United States and other Western industrialized nations show that about ten businesses are founded per year for every one hundred businesses active at the start of the year. In the United States, approximately 4 to 6 percent of the adult population in the mid-1990s has engaged in some activities with an intent to start a business, and about half of them actually succeeded in their initial efforts (Reynolds and White 1997). Explanations for variations in rates of organizational foundings have stressed the characteristics of opportunity structures, the organizing capacities of groups, and strategies adopted by entrepreneurs as they take account of opportunities and resources available to them (Aldrich and Wiedenmayer 1991).

Societal demands for special-purpose organizations increased with urbanization and with economic, political, and social differentiation, while the resources required to construct organizations grew more abundant with the development of a money economy and the spread of literacy (Stinchcombe 1965). The spread of facilitative legal, political, and other institutions also played a major role, by creating a stable, predictable context within which entrepreneurs could look forward to appropriating the gains from organizational foundings. Occasional periods of political upheaval and revolution stimulate foundings by freeing resources from previous uses, and thus massive changes occurred in the organizational populations of Eastern Europe in the 1990s. For example, centralized health care systems were disbanded with the demise of state socialist regimes, and there is a good deal of flux in the organizations within this sector (Mechanic and Rochefort 1996).

Transformations occur when existing organizations adapt their structures to changing conditions. The issue of how frequently and under what conditions organizations change has provoked some of the most spirited debates in organizational sociology. Strategic choice-theorists have argued for managerial autonomy and adaptability, whereas ecological and institutional theorists have tended to stress organizational inertia and dependence. Research has moved away from polarizing debates and reframed the question of transformation, asking about the conditions under which organizations change and whether changes occur more frequently in core or peripheral features (Singh and Lumsden 1990).

In the 1980s and 1990s, growing awareness of techniques for performing dynamic analyses have produced some useful studies of transformation, such as those on diversification, top executive changes, and changes in corporate form (Fligstein 1991). These studies tell us that changes *do* occur, although they do not report whether rates of change go up or down over an organization's life cycle. Most of these studies are of the very largest business firms, for which data are publicly available, and not for representative samples.

If all newly founded organizations lived forever, the study of organizational change would be confined to issues of founding, adaptation, and inertia. Research has shown that organizations disband at a fairly high rate, however, and a sizable literature has grown up on organizational mortality (Baum 1996; Singh 1990). Organizations can cease to exist as separate entities in two ways: by completely dissolving—the process by which the vast majority of organizations disband—or by becoming part of a different entity through merger or acquisition. Throughout the 1990s, between two and six thousand mergers and acquisitions a year took place, amounting to less than 1 percent of the incorporated firm population in any given year (Aldrich 1999). For example, in 1994, mergers and acquisitions involved about one-tenth of one percent of all corporate assets. By contrast, between 1976 and 1984, the annual rate of dissolution in the business population of the United States was about 10 percent (Small Business Administration 1994).

Age and size are the strongest predictors of how long an organization will survive. Young organizations disband at a substantially higher rate than older ones; a conservative estimate is that only half of new organizations survive more than five years. Internally, new organizations depend upon the cooperation of strangers who must be taught new routines, some of which are unique to particular organizations (Stinchcombe 1965). Externally, new organizations must penetrate niches in potentially hostile environments, overcoming competitors and establishing their legitimacy with potential members, customers, suppliers, and others. Survival beyond infancy is easier when an organization adopts a form that has already been institutionalized and is widely regarded as legitimate and proper (Zucker 1988). Population ecologists have given special attention to the density of an organizational form—the number of organizations of a given kind—in their analyses of vital rates. Density is thought to be an indicator both of the acceptance or legitimacy of a form (which raises foundings and decreases disbandings) and of the number of competitors attempting to survive within a given environmental niche (which reduces foundings and increases disbandings). The life chances of an organization initially increase— though not smoothly—as density rises, and then decrease as competition intensifies.

SOURCES OF INTERNAL DIVERSITY AMONG ORGANIZATIONS

All models of organizations as coherent entities can be reduced to two basic views. The systemic view sees organizations as social systems, sustained by the roles allocated to their participants, whereas an associative perspective treats organizations as associations of self-interested parties, sustained by the rewards the participants derive from their association with the organization (Swanson 1971). These two views each have a venerable heritage in the social sciences. Despite subtle variations, all perspectives on organizations ultimately use one or both of these models.

Institutional, functionalist, and ecological perspectives rely on a systemic model, viewing organizations as relatively coherent, stable entities. Such models emphasize the activity systems in organizations that are deliberately designed to accomplish specific goals. Formal structures of organizations, including a division of labor, authority relationships, and prescribed communication channels, are treated as fulfilling a purposeful design. For example, an institutional approach emphasizes member socialization and other processes that make the transmission of shared meanings easier. Ecological models usually treat organizations as units that are being selected for or against by their environments, and thus assume that organizations cohere as units.

Interpretive and more micro analytic views rely more on an associative model, leading to the expectation that organizations are constantly at risk of dissolution (March and Olsen 1976). For example, in the interpretive view, the reproduction of organizational structure depends on participants resubscribing to, or continually negotiating, a shared understanding of what they jointly are doing. Some cultural theories of organization emphasize the different, conflicting views that coexist within one organization (Martin 1992).

Views of organizations as marketplaces of incentives (Dow 1988), bundles of transactions (Williamson 1981), or arenas of class conflict (Clegg 1989), are in harmony with the associative view, insofar as they focus on actors' contributions to sustaining interaction. Indeed, organizational economics views organizations primarily as mechanisms for mediating exchanges among individuals, arguing that they arise only when market coordination has proven inadequate (Williamson 1981). One variant on this approach, agency theory, focuses on the relationships between self-interested principals (such as owners or stockholders) and the self-interested agents (such as workers or managers) engaged on behalf of principals. The self-interests of these actors may be divergent, and hence agency theory examines how systems of incentives, monitoring, and coordination can be designed to align the activities of agents with the objectives of principals, at minimal cost.

These complementary views of organizations— the associative and the systemic—highlight the sources of two fundamental problems of social organization, those of differentiation and integration. Some differentiation occurs through the division of labor among different roles and subunits; for example, employees may be divided into departments such as sales, finance, and manufacturing. Differentiation pressures also arise because participants sometimes bring widely varying expectations to the same organization. Differentiation is thus a centrifugal force threatening the coherence of social units. Integration, by contrast, refers to procedures for maintaining coherence, as diverse roles are linked and activities coordinated to sustain an organization as a coherent entity. Examples of integrative processes include the holding of weekly departmental meetings or the circulation of inter office memos.

Differentiation increases organizational complexity because it increases the extent and nature of specialization (Blau 1972). Complexity increases with the number of different components, and may be horizontal (tasks spread over many roles or units), vertical (many levels in a hierarchy of authority), or spatial (many operating sites). Complexity also increases when tasks are grouped by product/market (soap, paper products, or foods) or by function (finance, production, or marketing).

Problems of coordination are present for any activity system, but especially for a complex one. Many concepts used to describe organization structure involve alternative processes used in attempts to achieve integration. One scheme, for example, identified five coordinating mechanisms: direct supervision, three forms of standardization, and mutual adjustment (Mintzberg 1983). With direct supervision, or simple control, decision making is highly centralized: persons at the top of a hierarchy make decisions that lower level personnel simply carry out. This coordination pattern was prevalent in preindustrial organizations, and today is especially likely within small organizations (Edwards 1979).

Coordination also can be attained through standardizing work processes, skills, or outputs. Work processes may be standardized through formalization, that is, the development of rules and procedures. Examples include rules for processing orders, for assembling and packaging products, or for conducting screening interviews for clients. A formalized organization may appear decentralized, since few explicit commands are given, and lower-level participants have freedom in making decisions within the rules. The rules may, however, be so restrictive as to leave little room for discretion. A variant on process standardization is technical control; here, rules and procedures—and thereby coordination and control—are built into the design of machinery, as in an assembly line. Most worker discretion is eliminated by the structure of the technical system, and what remains is centralized in the upper echelons of the organization.

Standardization of skills involves considerable training and indoctrination of personnel, so that participants will carry out organizational policies with minimal oversight. Organizations employing large numbers of professionals are likely to rely on this coordination strategy (Von Glinow 1988). Professional participants enjoy considerable autonomy in making decisions, but their prior socialization sets most decision premises for them.

By producing products with standard properties, subunits of an organization are able to work independently of one another; if they use each other's outputs, the standards tell them what to anticipate. For example, large clothing firms produce massive runs of identical garments, and thus the various departments within firms know precisely what to expect from one another as they follow daily routines. Similar purposes are served by precise tolerances for parts used in manufacturing machinery and information systems designed to permit easy sharing of data within offices.

In small, young organizations, coordination is achieved by the simple mutual adjustment of personnel to one another. This form of coordination is also found in larger organizations working on complex, novel tasks, for which innovation is at a premium, such as consulting firms or research and development units. In such organizations, the activities of participants are reciprocally contingent, rather than sequentially ordered as in an assembly line. Formal structural devices have been advocated as ways of facilitating mutual adjustment under complex circumstances, such as integrating managers and project teams into matrix-management structures.

Standardization, bureaucratization, and formalization have done much to enable organizations to perform repetitive work efficiently. The same phenomena contribute to some well-known organizational pathologies; in particular, these coordination devices tend to reduce flexibility. In the 1990s, organizations struggled to develop less rigid structures for accomplishing work. Efforts to achieve flexibility included reductions in size, expansion of the scope of employee responsibilities through cross-training and broadened job descriptions, reductions in layers of management, and maintenance of long-term relationships with suppliers as an alternative to vertical integration. Many of these devices rely on strengthening the internal social networks that link an organization's personnel as well as the external ones linking it to the environment. Such linkages enable organizations to remain adaptable, cope with market uncertainties, and take advantage of opportunities for learning.

CONCLUSION

Complex organizations are the building blocks of industrial and post industrial societies, enabling people to accomplish tasks otherwise beyond their individual competencies. Organizations also help create and sustain structures of opportunities and constraints that affect nearly every aspect of societies. Sociologists and other social scientists are grappling with a variety of complementary and conflicting perspectives on organizations, ranging from microanalytic interpretive views to macroevolutionary institutional and ecological views. Regardless of perspective, research on organizations has shown its capacity to interest, inform, and provoke us, as sociologists investigate these social constructions that figure so prominently in our lives.

REFERENCES

Aldrich, Howard E. 1999 *Organizations Evolving*. London: Sage.

——, and Gabriele Wiedenmayer 1991 "From Traits to Rates: An Ecological Perspective on Organizational Foundings." In Jerome Katz and Robert Brockhaus, eds., *Advances in Entrepreneurship, Firm Emergence, and Growth*, vol. 1, 145–114 Greenwich, Conn.: JAI.

Baum, Joel A.C. 1996 "Organizational Ecology." in Stewart R. Clegg, Cynthia Hardy, and Walter Nord, eds., *Handbook of Organization Studies* 77–114 London: Sage.

Blau, Peter M. 1972 "Interdependence and Hierarchy in Organizations." *Social Science Research* 1:1–24.

——, and W. Richard Scott 1962 *Formal Organizations*. San Francisco: Chandler.

Clegg, Stewart 1989 "Radical Revisions: Power, Discipline and Organizations." *Organization Studies* 10:97–115.

Dow, Gregory K. 1988 "Configurational and Coactivational Views of Organizational Structure." *Academy of Management Review* 13:53–64.

Edwards, Richard C. 1979 *Contested Terrain: The Transformation of the Workplace in the Twentieth Century*. New York: Basic Books.

ENSR 1993 *The European Observatory for SMEs: First Annual Report*. Zoetermeer, The Netherlands: European Observatory for SME Research and EIM Small Business Research and Consultancy.

Fligstein, Neil 1991 *The Transformation of Corporate Control*. Cambridge, Mass.: Harvard University Press.

Hannan, Michael T., and John H. Freeman 1989 *Organizational Ecology*. Cambridge, Mass: Harvard University Press.

March, James G., and Johan P. Olsen 1976 *Ambiguity and Choice in Organizations*. Bergen, Norway: Universitetsforlaget.

Martin, Joanne 1992 *Cultures in Organizations: Three Perspectives*. New York: Oxford University Press.

Mechanic, David, and David A. Rochefort 1996 "Comparative Medical Systems." *Annual Review of Sociology* 22:239–270.

Meyer, John W., and Brian Rowan 1977 "Institutionalized Organizations: Formal Structure as Myth and Ceremony." *American Journal of Sociology* 83:340–363.

Mintzberg, Henry 1983 *Structure in Fives: Designing Effective Organizations*. Englewood Cliffs, N.J.: Prentice-Hall.

Mizruchi, Mark S., and Joseph Galaskiewicz 1993 "Networks of Interorganizational Relations." *Sociological Methods & Research* 22:46–70.

Office of Management and Budget, Statistical Policy Division 1997 *North American Industry Classification System*. Washington, D.C.: U.S. Government Printing Office.

Parsons, Talcott 1960 *Structure and Process in Modern Societies*. New York: Free Press.

Pfeffer, Jeffrey, and Gerald R. Salancik 1978 *The External Control of Organizations*. New York: Harper and Row.

Reynolds, Paul D., and Sammis B. White 1997 *The Entrepreneurial Process: Economic Growth, Men, Women, and Minorities*. Westport, Conn.: Quorum Books.

Scott, W. Richard 1998 *Organizations: Rational, Natural, and Open Systems*, 4th ed. Englewood Cliffs, N.J.: Prentice-Hall.

—— 1995 *Institutions and Organizations*. Thousand Oaks, Calif.: Sage.

Singh, Jitendra (ed.) 1990 *Organizational Evolution*. Beverly Hills, Calif.: Sage.

——, and Charles Lumsden 1990 "Theory and Research in Organizational Ecology." *Annual Review of Sociology* 16:161–195.

Small Business Administration 1994 *Handbook of Small Business Data*. Washington, D.C.: U.S. Government Printing Office and Office of Advocacy, Small Business Administration.

Stinchcombe, Arthur 1965 "Social Structure and Organizations." In J. G. March, ed., *Handbook of Organizations*. 142–193 Chicago: Rand-McNally.

Swanson, Guy E. 1971 "An Organizational Analysis of Collectivities." *American Sociological Review* 36:607–614.

U.S. Bureau of the Census 1996 Selected statistics from the 1992 Census of Manufactures report MC92–S–2 "Concentration Ratios in Manufacturing." http://www.census.gov.mcd/mancen/download/mc92cr.sum (21 Jan. 1999)

Von Glinow, Mary Ann 1988 *The New Professionals: Managing Today's High-Tech Employees*. Cambridge, Mass.: Ballinger.

Williamson, Oliver 1981 "The Economics of Organization: The Transaction Cost Approach." *American Journal of Sociology* 87:548–577.

Zucker, Lynne G. (ed.) 1988 *Institutional Patterns and Organizations: Culture and Environment*. Cambridge, Mass.: Ballinger.

HOWARD E. ALDRICH
PETER V. MARSDEN

COMPLIANCE AND CONFORMITY

Conformity is a change in behavior or belief toward a group standard as a result of the group's influence on an individual. As this definition indicates, conformity is a type of social influence through which group members come to share similar beliefs and standards of behavior. It includes the processes by which group members converge on a given standard of belief or behavior as well as the pressures they exert on one another to uphold such standards. *Compliance* is behavioral conformity in order to achieve rewards or avoid punishments (Kelman 1958). Since one can behaviorally adhere to a group standard without personally believing in it, the term is often used to indicate conformity that is merely public rather than private as well. Compliance can also refer to behavioral conformity to the request or demand of another, especially an authority.

In an individualistic society such as the United States, conformity has a negative connotation (Markus and Kitiyama 1994). Yet conformity is a fundamental social process without which people would be unable to organize into groups and take effective action as a collectivity. For people to coordinate their behavior so that they can organize and work together as a group, they must develop and adhere to standards of behavior that make each other's actions mutually predictable. Simply driving down a street would be nearly impossible if most people did not conform to group norms that organize driving.

Conformity is also the process that establishes boundaries between groups. Through the conformity process, the members of one group become similar to one another and different from those of another group. This, in turn, creates a shared social identity for people as the members of a distinctive group. Given the pressure of ever-changing circumstances, social groups such as families, peer groups, business firms, and nations, only maintain their distinctive cultural beliefs and moderately stable social structures through the constant operation of conformity processes.

Perhaps because it is essential for social organization, conformity appears to be a universal human phenomenon. The level of conformity varies by culture, however. Collectivist cultures (e.g., Japan) that emphasize the interdependence of individuals show higher levels of conformity than individualistic cultures (e.g., the United States) that focus on the independence of individuals (Bond and Smith 1996).

Although essential, conformity always entails a conflict between a group standard and an alternative belief or behavior (Asch 1951; Moscovici 1985). For their physical and psychological survival, people need and want to belong to social groups. Yet to do so, they must curb the diversity and independence of their beliefs and behavior. Without even being aware of it, people usually willingly adopt the group position. Occasionally, however, individuals believe an alternative to be superior to the group standard and suffer painful conflict when pressured to conform.

Sometimes a nonconforming, deviate alternative is indeed superior to the group standard in that it offers a better response to the group circumstances. Innovation and change is as important to a group's ability to adjust and survive as is conformity. In fact, a nonconforming member can influence the majority opinion even as the majority pressures the deviate to conform. As Irving Janis (1972) points out in his analysis of "groupthink," however, conformity pressures can grow so strong that they silence alternative opinions and strangle a group's ability to critically analyze and respond to the problems it faces. Thus, conformity is a double-edged sword. It enables people to unify for collective endeavors but it exacts a cost in potential innovation.

CLASSIC EXPERIMENTS

The social scientific investigation of conformity began with the pioneering experiments of Muzafer Sherif (1936). They beautifully illustrate the easy, almost unconscious way people in groups influence one another to become similar. Sherif made use of the autokinetic effect, which is a visual illusion that makes a stationary pinpoint of light in a dark room appear to move. Sherif asked subjects in his experiments to estimate how far the light moved.

When individuals estimated the light alone, their estimates were often quite divergent. In one condition of the experiment, however, subjects viewed the light with two or three others, giving their estimates out loud, allowing them to hear each other's judgments. In this group setting, individuals gave initial estimates that were similar to one another and rapidly converged on a single group estimate. Different groups settled on very different estimates but all groups developed a consensus judgment that remained stable over time.

After three sessions together, group members were split up. When tested alone they continued to use their group standard to guide their personal estimates. This indicates that the group members had not merely induced one another to conform in outward behavior. They had influenced one another's very perception of the light so that they believed the group estimate to be the most accurate judgment of reality.

In another condition, Sherif first tested subjects alone so that they developed personal standards for their estimates. He then put together two or three people with widely divergent personal standards and tested them in a group setting. Over three group sessions, individual estimates merged into a group standard. Thus, even when participants had well-established personal standards for judging, mere exposure to the differing judgments of others influenced them to gradually abandon their divergent points of view for a uniform group standard. This occurred despite a setting where the subjects, all strangers, had no power over one another and were only minimally organized as a group.

The Sherif experiment suggests that conformity pressures in groups are subtle and extremely powerful. But critics quickly noted that the extreme ambiguity of the autokinetic situation might be responsible for Sherif's results. In such an ambiguous situation, participants have little to base their personal judgments on, so perhaps it is not surprising that they turn to others to help them decide what to think. Do people conform when the task is clear and unambiguous? Will they yield to a group consensus if it is obvious that the consensus is wrong? These are the questions Solomon Asch (1951, 1956) addressed in his classic experiments.

To eliminate ambiguity, Asch employed clearcut judgment tasks where subjects chose which of three comparison lines was the same length as a standard line. The correct answers were so obvious that individuals working alone reached 98 percent accuracy. Similar to the Sherif experiment, Asch's subjects gave their judgments in the presence of seven to nine of their peers (all participants were male college students). Unknown to the single naive subject in each group, all other group members were confederates of the experimenter. On seven of twelve trials, as the confederates announced their judgments one by one, they unanimously gave the wrong answer. It was arranged so that the naive subject always gave his judgment after the confederates.

The subject here was placed in a position of absolute conflict. Should he abide by what he knows to be true or go along with the unanimous opinion of others? A third of the time subjects violated the evidence of their own senses to agree with the group.

The Asch experiments clearly demonstrated that people feel pressure to conform to group standards even when they know the standards are wrong. It is striking that Asch, like Sherif, obtained these results with a minimal group situation. The group members were strangers who meant little to one another. Yet they exerted substantial influence over one another simply by being in the same situation together. Because of the dramatic way it highlights the conflict inherent in conformity between individuals and groups, Asch's experimental design has become the paradigm for studying conformity.

NORMATIVE AND INFORMATION INFLUENCE

Sherif's and Asch's striking results stimulated an explosion of research to explain how conformity occurs (see Kiesler and Kiesler 1976, Cialdini and Trost 1998 for reviews). It is now clear that two analytically distinct influence processes are involved. Either or both can produce conformity in a given situation. Morton Deutsch and Harold Gerard (1955) labelled these *informational influence* and *normative influence*.

In informational influence, the group defines perceptual reality for the individual. Sherif's experiment is a good illustration of this. The best explanation derives from Leon Festinger's (1954) social comparison theory. According to the theory, people form judgments about ambiguous events by comparing their perceptions with those of similar others and constructing shared, socially validated definitions of the "reality" of the event. These consensual definitions constitute the social reality of the situation (Festinger 1950). Because people want the support of others to assure them of the validity of their beliefs, disagreeing with the majority is uncomfortable. People in such situations doubt their own judgment. They change to agree with the majority because they assume that the majority view is more likely to be accurate.

As this indicates, conformity as a result of informational influence is not unwilling compliance with the demands of others. Rather, the individual adopts the group standard as a matter of private belief as well as public behavior. Informational influence is especially powerful in regard to social beliefs, opinions, and situations since these are inherently ambiguous and socially constructed.

Normative influence occurs when people go along with the group majority in order to gain rewards or avoid unpleasant costs. Thus it is normative influence that is behind compliance. People depend on others for many valued outcomes, such as inclusion in social relationships, a sense of shared identity, and social approval. Because of this dependency, even strangers have some power to reward and punish one another. Asch's results are a good example. Although a few of Asch's participants actually doubted their judgment (informational influence), most conformed in order to avoid the implicit rejection of being the odd person out. Studies show that fears of rejection for nonconformity are not unfounded (see Levine 1980 for a review). While nonconformists are sometimes admired, they are rarely liked. Furthermore, they are subject to intense persuasive pressure and criticism from the majority.

FACTORS THAT INCREASE CONFORMITY

Anything that increases vulnerability to informational and normative influence increases conformity. Although there may be personality traits that incline people to conform, the evidence for this is conflicting (Crowne and Marlowe 1969; Moscovici 1985). Situational factors seem to be the most important determinants of conformity. Research indicates that conformity is increased by a) the ambiguity or difficulty of the task, b) the relative unimportance of the issue to the person, c) the necessity of making a public rather than private response, d) the similarity of group members, e) high interdependence among the group members, f) the attractiveness and cohesiveness of the group, and g) the unanimity of the majority (see Kiesler and Kiesler 1976; Cialdini and Trost 1998 for reviews).

When a task or situation is ambiguous or difficult, it is not easy to tell what the best response to it would be. As a result, much as in Sherif's experiments, group members rely heavily on each other's opinions to decide what is best, increasing their susceptibility to informational influence. When decision-making groups in government or business face complex, difficult decisions where the right choice is uncertain, informational influence increases the members' tendency to agree and can affect their critical analysis of the situation (Janis 1972). Tastes and beliefs about matters, such as clothing style or music, about which there are no objectively right choices are subject to sudden fads or fashions for similar reasons. Powerful conformity processes take over as group standards define for the individual what the "right" clothes or music are.

The less people care about an issue, the more open they are to both informational and normative influence. Without the motivation to examine an issue personally, people usually accept the group standard about it, both because the agreement of others makes the standard seem right and because there are more rewards and fewer costs in going along with the group. Because of such rewards and costs, people are especially likely to go along when their response must be public rather than private.

Since people compare their perceptions and views most closely to those of people who are socially similar to them, similarity increases group members' informational influence on one another. Similarity also increases liking and, when people like one another, they have more power to reward or punish each other, so normative influence increases as well. Because of the increased power of both informational and normative influence, conformity pressures are often especially strong in peer groups.

When members are highly dependent on one another for something they value, conformity pressure increases because the members have more power to reward or frustrate one another (normative influence). Similarly, when a group is very attractive to an individual, its members have more power to normatively influence the individual. Gangs, fraternities, and professional societies all use this principle to induce new members to adopt their groups' distinctive standards. Also, when a group is very tight knit and cohesive, members' commitment to the group gives it more power over their behavior, increasing the forces of conformity.

The unanimity of the majority in a group is an especially important factor in the conformity process. In his studies, Asch (1951) found that as long as it was unanimous, a majority of three was as effective in inducing conformity as one of sixteen. Subsequent research generally confirms that the size of a majority past three is not a crucial factor in conformity. It is unanimity that counts (see Allen 1975 for a review). When Asch (1951) had one confederate give the correct answer to the line task, the naive subjects' conformity to the majority dropped from a third to only 5 percent. One fellow dissenter shows an individual that nonconformity is possible and provides much needed social support for an alternate construction of social reality. Interestingly, a dissenter need not agree with an individual to encourage nonconformity. It is only necessary that the dissenter also break with the majority.

Another factor that affects conformity is the sex composition of the group. Although the results of studies are inconsistent, statistical summaries of them, called meta-analyses, indicate that there is an overall tendency for women to conform slightly more than men (Becker 1986; Eagly and Wood 1985). Sex differences in conformity are most likely when behavior is under the surveillance of others. The evidence suggests two explanations (see Eagly 1987 for a review). First, sex carries status value in interaction, which creates social expectations for women to be less competent and influential in the situation than men (Ridgeway 1993). Second, sex stereotypes pressure men to display independence when they are being observed.

THE INFLUENCE OF THE MINORITY ON THE MAJORITY

Conformity arises out of a social influence process between an individual and the group majority. The influence process is not always one way, however. As Serge Moscovici (1976) points out, a dissenting group member is not just a recipient of pressure from the majority, but also someone who, by breaking consensus, challenges the validity of the majority view, creating conflict, doubt, and the possibility of opinion change in the group. Dissenters sometimes modify the opinion of the majority in a process called *minority influence*. Research shows that for a minority opinion to affect the majority it must be presented consistently and clearly without wavering and it helps if there are two such dissenters in the group rather than one (see Moscovici 1985; Moscovici, Mucchi-Faina, and Maass 1994; Wood et al. 1994, for reviews). A dissenting minority increases divergent thinking among group members that can enhance the likelihood that they will arrive at creative solutions to the problems the group faces (Nemeth 1986).

CONFORMITY AND STATUS

Research in the Asch and Sherif paradigms focuses on conformity pressures among peers. However, when group members differ in status, it affects the group's tolerance of their nonconformity. Higher status members receive fewer sanctions for nonconformity than lower status members (Gerson 1975). As long as they adhere to central group norms, high status members' nonconformity can actually increase their influence in the group (Berkowitz and Macauley 1961). Edwin Hollander (1958) argues that, because high status members are valued by the group, they are accorded "idiosyncrasy credits" that allow them to nonconform and innovate without penalty as long as they stay within certain bounds. It is middle status members who actually conform the most (Harvey and Consalvi 1960). They have fewer idiosyncrasy credits than high status members and more investment in the group than low status members.

Nonconformity can also affect the position of status and influence a person achieves in the group. Hollander (1958, 1960) proposed that individuals earn status and idiosyncrasy credits by initially conforming to group norms, but replications of his study do not support this conclusion (see Ridgeway 1981 for a review). Conformity tends to make a person "invisible" in a group and so does little to gain status. Nonconformity attracts attention and gives the appearance of confidence and competence which can enhance status. But it also appears self-interested, which detracts from status (Ridgeway 1981). Consequently, moderate levels of nonconformity are most likely to facilitate status attainment.

COMPLIANCE WITH AUTHORITY

Reacting to the Nazi phenomenon of World War II, studies of compliance to authority have focused on explaining people's obedience even when ordered to engage in extreme or immoral behavior. Compliance in this situation is comparable to conformity in the Asch paradigm in that individuals must go against their own standards of conduct to obey. The power of a legitimate authority to compel obedience was dramatically demonstrated in the Milgram (1963, 1974) experiments. As part of an apparent learning study, a scientist-experimenter ordered subjects to give increasingly strong electric shocks to another person. The shock generator used by the subject labelled increasing levels as "danger-severe shock" and "XXX" (at 450 volts). The victim (a confederate who received no actual shocks) protested, cried out, and complained of heart trouble. Despite this, 65 percent of the subjects complied with the scientist-experimenter and shocked the victim all the way to the 450 volt maximum. It is clear that most of the time, people do as they are told by legitimate authorities.

Uncertainty over their responsibilities in the situation (a definition of social reality issue) and concern for the authority's ability to punish or reward them seem to be the principle causes for people's compliance in such circumstances. Note the comparability of these factors to informational and normative influence. Situational factors that socially define the responsibility question as a duty to obey rather than to disobey increase compliance (Kelman and Hamilton 1989), as do factors that increase the authority's ability to sanction.

Research has demonstrated several such factors. Compliance is increased by the legitimacy of the authority figure and his or her surveillance of the individual's behavior (Milgram 1974; Zelditch and Walker 1984). When others in the situation obey or when the individual's position in the chain of command removes direct contact with the victim, compliance increases (Milgram 1974). On the other hand, when others present resist the authority, compliance drops dramatically. Stanley Milgram (1974) found that when two confederates working with the subject refused to obey the experimenter, only 10 percent of subjects complied fully themselves. As with a fellow dissenter from a unanimous majority, other resisters define disobedience as appropriate and provide support for resisting. In an analysis of "crimes of obedience" in many government and military settings, Herbert Kelman and Lee Hamilton (1989) show how such factors lead to compliance to illegal or immoral commands from authority.

Conformity and compliance are fundamental to the development of norms, social organization, group culture, and people's shared social identities. As a result, research on conformity and compliance continues to develop in several directions. Efforts are underway to develop broader models of the social influence process that can incorporate both conformity and compliance (see Cialdini and Trost 1998). These efforts give added emphasis to people's dependence on social relationships and groups and address questions such as whether minority and majority influence work through different or similar processes. Also, new, more systematic cross-cultural research attempts to understand both what is universal and what is culturally variable about conformity and compliance (Markus and Kitiyama 1994; Smith and Bond 1996).

REFERENCES

Allen, Vernon L. 1975 "Social Support for Nonconformity." In L. Berkowitz, ed., *Advances in Experimental Social Psychology*, vol. 8, 2–43. New York: Academic Press.

Asch, Solomon E. 1951 "Effects of Group Pressure Upon the Modification and Distortion of Judgments." In H. Guetzkow, ed., *Groups, Leadership, and Men*. Pittsburgh: Carnegie Press.

—— 1956 "Studies of Independence and Submission to Group Pressure: I. A Minority of One Against a Unanimous Majority." *Psychological Monographs* 70 (9, whole no. 416).

Becker, B. J. 1986 "Influence Again: Another Look at Studies of Gender Differences in Social Influence." In Janet Shibley Hyde and Marci C. Lynn, eds., *The Psychology of Gender: Advances Through Meta-Analysis*. Baltimore: Johns Hopkins University Press.

Berkowitz, Leonard, and J. R. Macaulay 1961 "Some Effects of Differences in Status Level and Status Stability." *Human Relations* 14:135–147.

Bond, M. H. and P. B. Smith 1996 "Culture and Conformity: A Meta-Analysis of Studies Using Asch's Line Judgment Task." *Psychological Bulletin* 119:111–137.

Cialdini, Robert B., and Melanie R. Trost 1998 "Social Influence: Social Norms, Conformity, and Compliance." In D. T. Gilbert, S. T. Fiske, and G. Lindzey, eds., *The Handbook of Social Psychology*, 4th ed., vol. 2. New York: McGraw-Hill.

Crowne, D. P., and D. Marlowe 1964 *The Approval Motive: Studies in Evaluative Dependence*. New York: Wiley.

Eagly, Alice H. 1987 *Sex Differences in Social Behavior: A Social-Role Interpretation*. Hillsdale, N.J.: Earlbaum.

——, and Wendy Wood 1985 "Gender and Influenceability: Stereotype vs. Behavior." In V. E. O'Leary, R. K. Unger, and B. S. Walson, eds., *Women, Gender and Social Psychology*. Hillsdale, N.J.: Earlbaum.

Festinger, Leon 1950 "Informal Social Communication." *Psychological Review* 57:217–282.

—— 1954 "A Theory of Social Comparison Processes." *Human Relations* 7:117–140.

Gerson, Lowell W. 1975 "Punishment and Position: The Sanctioning of Deviants in Small Groups." In P. V. Crosbie, ed., *Interaction in Small Groups*. New York: Macmillan.

Harvey, O. J., and Conrad Consalvi 1960 "Status and Conformity to Pressures in Informal Groups." *Journal of Abnormal and Social Psychology* 60:182–187.

Hollander, Edwin P. 1958 "Conformity, Status, and Idiosyncrasy Credit." *Psychological Review* 65:117–127.

—— 1960 "Competence and Conformity in the Acceptance of Influence." *Journal of Abnormal and Social Psychology* 61:365–369.

Janis, Irving L. 1972 *Victims of Groupthink: A Psychological Study of Foreign-Policy Decisions and Fiascoes*. Boston: Houghton-Mifflin.

Kelman, Herbert C. 1958 "Compliance, Identification, and Internalization: Three Processes of Attitude Change." *Journal of Conflict Resolution* 2:51–60.

——, and V. Lee Hamilton 1989 *Crimes of Obedience*. New Haven, Conn.: Yale University Press.

Kiesler, Charles A. and Sara B. Kiesler 1976 *Conformity*. 2d ed. Reading, Mass.: Addison-Wesley.

Levine, John M. 1980 "Reaction to Opinion Deviance in Small Groups." In P. Paulus, ed., *Psychology of Group Influence*. Hillsdale, N.J.: Earlbaum.

Markus, Hazel R., and S. Kitiyama 1994 "A Collective Fear of the Collective: Implications for Selves and Theories of Selves." *Personality and Social Psychology Bulletin* 20:568–579.

Milgram, Stanley 1963 "Behavioral Study of Obedience." *Journal of Abnormal and Social Psychology* 67:371–378.

—— 1974 *Obedience to Authority: An Experimental View*. New York: Harper and Row.

Moscovici, Serge 1976 *Social Influence and Social Change*. London: Academic Press.

—— 1985 "Social Influence and Conformity." In G. Lindzey and E. Aronson, eds., *The Handbook of Social Psychology*. 3d ed., vol. 2. New York: Random House.

——, A. Mucchi-Faina, and A. Maass 1994 *Minority Influence*. Chicago: Nelson-Hall.

Nemeth, Charlan 1986 "Differential Contributions of Majority and Minority Influence." *Psychological Review* 93:23–32.

Ridgeway, Cecilia L. 1981 "Nonconformity, Competence, and Influence in Groups: A Test of Two Theories." *American Sociological Review* 46:333–347.

—— 1993 "Gender, Status, and the Social Psychology of Expectations." In P. England, ed., *Theory on Gender/Feminism on Theory*. New York: Aldine.

Sherif, Muzafer 1936 *The Psychology of Social Norms*. New York: Harper and Row.

Wood, Wendy, S. Lundgren, J. A. Ouelette, S. Busceme, and T. Blackstone 1994 "Minority Influence: A Meta-Analytic Review of Social Influence Processes." *Psychological Bulletin* 115:323–345.

Zelditch, Morris, Jr., and Henry A. Walker 1984 "Legitimacy and the Stability of Authority." In E. Lawler, ed., *Advances in Group Processes*, vol. 1. Greenwich, Conn.: JAI Press.

CECILIA L. RIDGEWAY

COMPLEMENTARITY

See Mate Selection Theories.

COMPUTER APPLICATIONS IN SOCIOLOGY

Most sociologists, both professionals and students, now have their own computer with direct access to a printer for writing and to the Internet for electronic mail (e-mail). Beyond the basic tasks of writing and e-mailing are a variety of other computer-supported research applications, both quantitative and qualitative. This article describes how sociologists and other social scientists use these applications and what resources are available.

The data and modeling requirements of social research have united sociologists with computers for over a hundred years. It was the 1890 U. S. census that inspired Herman Hollerith, a census researcher, to construct the first automated data processing machinery. Hollerith's punchcard system, while not a true computer by today's definitions, provided the foundation for contemporary computer-based data management.

In 1948 the U. S. Bureau of the Census, anticipating the voluminous tabulating requirements of the 1950 census, contracted for the building of Univac I, the first commercially produced electronic computer. The need to count, sort, and analyze the 1950 census data on this milestone computer led to the development of the first high-speed magnetic tape storage system, the first sort-merge software package, and the first statistical package, a set of matrix algebra programs.

Only a decade later many social scientists were exploring ways to use computers in their research. In the early 1960s, the first book devoted entirely to computer applications in social science research (Borko 1962) was published. Not only were social scientists writing about how to apply computers, they were designing and developing new software. Some of the most popular statistical software packages, e.g., SPSS (Nie, Bent, and Hull 1975), were developed by social scientists.

During the 1980s, universities and colleges began to acquire microcomputers, accepting the premise that all researchers needed their own desktop computing equipment. The American Council of Learned Societies (ACLS) survey in 1985 (Morton and Price 1986) reported that 50 percent of sociologists had a computer for exclusive use. A survey of academic departments supported by the American Sociological Association (Koppel, Dowdall, and Shostak 1985) found that slightly less than half of the sociology faculty reported to have immediate access to microcomputers. To put these findings into a more complete perspective, of the approximately 9,000 sociologists in 1985, about 4,500 had their own computers and about 5,200 reported routine computer use. Now, it is hard to find a sociologist's office without at least one computer. And in many countries most students in sociology have a computer for writing papers and accessing online resources.

Sociology and the Web. The Internet may be one of the largest and probably the most rapidly growing peaceful social movements in history. It is not just a technology, or a family of technologies, but a rapidly evolving socio-cultural phenomena often called "cyberspace" or "cyberculture." No matter how this phenomena is defined, it is changing the way sociologists conduct their work.

By the mid-1990s sociology, like most other academic disciplines, had come to depend upon e-mail. In addition, a rapidly growing number had begun to use the World Wide Web (WWW), commonly called the Web (Babbie 1996). Bainbridge (1995) claimed that the Web is "a significant medium of communication for sociologists, and extrapolation of present trends suggests it may swiftly become the essential fabric of sociology's existence." In January 1999, the author searched Web sites with the Alta Vista search engine for the word "sociology" and found 750,000 instances. Two years earlier a search yielded only 250,000. Sociology is indeed rapidly building its presence on the Web.

The Internet and the Web are often described as a medium of communication because e-mail, electronic conferencing, online chats (synchronous discussion), groupware, and data exchange imply social interaction. Another major metaphor of the Web is that of a database for information search and retrieval. However, new roles are emerging for the Web. For the individual, the Web has become an important "presentation of self," an opportunity for publishing personal and professional resumes and other such information. For the organization, the Web has become an opportunity for advertising, recruiting, communicating with the public, and conducting commerce itself. The rapid proliferation of personal Web sites in the form of various home pages suggests that many now see the Web primarily as a medium for personal and organizational impression management.

An appendix to this article provides a number of sources of sociological activity and information on the Internet, especially the Web. Not only does the appendix serve as a resource for information about sociology, but it also portrays the diverse, complex state of the institutionalization of sociology on the Web.

In the next few years the Web and its technologies will offer many new opportunities for conducting research. Already there are software packages developed for Web-assisted surveys and other types of data collection. The amount of data accumulating on the Web is enormous. And the graphical content of the Web is indeed a challenge to sociologists conducting computerized content analyses. The pace of these new developments will continue to challenge sociologists to not only to stay current with the new tools for research but to conduct research on the rapidly growing cultures of the Internet.

Publications on Sociological Computing. The primary source for articles on social science computer applications is the *Social Science Computer Review*, a quarterly publication of Sage Publications, Inc., which also regularly offers book and software reviews. Other relevant software reviews periodically appear in such journals as *Educational*

and Psychological Measurement, the *Journal of Marketing Research*, *The American Statistician*, and *Simulation and Games*. In addition, JAI Press publishes an occasional series volume on "Computers and the Social Sciences."

In the late 1980s, the American Sociological Association (ASA) formed a "Section on Microcomputing." Over 350 sociologists joined this new section in 1990, making it the fastest-growing new section in the history of the ASA. The section publishes a quarterly newsletter and organizes sessions at annual meetings. In 1993, the section name was officially changed to "Sociology and Computers." A regular newsletter called *SCAN (Sociology and Computers: A Newsletter)* is published by members.

Another indicator of growing involvement in computing was the first annual conference, "Computing in the Social Sciences," held in 1990 at Williamsburg, Virginia. From this conference emerged a professional association, the Social Science Computing Association. The official journal of this association is the *Social Science Computer Review*, and they still hold an annual conference.

Computer Applications in Sociology. The practice of computing in sociology has evolved rapidly. Computers have been applied to practically every research task, including such unlikely ones as field note-taking, interviewing, and hundreds of other tasks (Brent and Anderson 1990). The many diverse uses of computing technology in social research are difficult to categorize because applications overlap and evolve unpredictably. Nonetheless, it is necessary to discuss different categories of applications in order to describe the state of the art of computing in sociology. Since 1987, the Winter issue of the *Social Science Computer Review* has been devoted to an annual symposium on the "State of the Art of Social Science Computing." The categorization of computer applications in this article reflects these discussions. First, some major types of applications are summarized in order of descending popularity. Then some of the challenges of computing for sociological research are noted.

Writing and Publishing. Once equated with the secretarial pool, word processing now is an activity of nearly every graduate student and professional in sociology. It consists not only of writing but preparing tables, "typesetting" mathematical equations, and resizing objects, such as three-dimensional graphs embedded within text. Social researchers are using such capabilities and moving rapidly toward workstation environments that obscure the transition between data analysis and manuscript preparation (Steiger and Fouladi 1990). Not only do researchers use their computers for writing papers, but word processing software plays a central role in the refinement of data collection instruments, especially questionnaires and codebooks, which allows for rapid production of alternative forms and multiple drafts.

Trends in text production that blur traditional distinctions between writing and publishing (Lyman 1989) may in the long term have the most impact on what sociologists do. The growing body of articles and books in electronic-text form propel scholarship toward *hypertext*, which is a document system that provides for nonsequential reading of text using links that automatically access other documents. Contemporary word processors contain the capacity to easily produce documents in HTML (Hypertext Markup Language) that are ready for installation as sites on the Web. HTML can contain hypertext links, which with a single click of the mouse can bring up a totally different document from anywhere in the world, making it a truly new form of publishing.

There are several major forms of text entry that may also change the nature of writing and publishing. These forms include scanning for optical character recognition (OCR), voice recognition, and automated language translation. The technology for scanning text documents and producing computer text files has been in use for some years and requires only a scanning device and OCR software. This technology will continue to improve and its use will yield fewer errors and require considerably less effort in the future.

Likewise it is now possible to use voice recognition software to automatically transcribe dictation, interviews, and field notes into computer text files. One of the remaining problems in this approach is that all voice recognition software now requires considerable "training" time where the errors made in recognizing a speaker's word-sound pattern are corrected. The software is thus "taught"

to make refined guesses in translating vocalized sounds into electronic text. Even the best voice recognition software now makes a moderate number of errors, so it is not yet a panacea for manual transcription of either the spoken word or audio recordings.

It is possible now to find software that will translate text into many different languages. However, like voice recognition software, translation software still requires considerable time to manually check, decipher, and make judgments about the text produced by such programs. Future software may yield significantly improved results, automating nearly all of the voice recognition and translation process.

Communicating Electronically (E-mail, etc.). Networks for computer-mediated communication (CMC) continue to expand internationally following the traditional logistic diffusion curve (Gurbaxani 1990). Electronic networks now supplement most other forms of social communication. E-mail, which is asynchronous or nonsimultaneous, is still the most common form of electronic interaction, but Internet-based, synchronous (simultaneous) "mailing lists" and "newsgroups" are also popular, as are "chat rooms" or "discussion groups." With improvements in transmitting digital audio and video files on the Internet, it is expected that some new forms of video conferencing will become commonplace. At the turn of the millennium, desktop video conferencing is available "off the shelf," but suffers from extraneous noise and rough motion. While individual sociologists vary greatly in how they utilize e-mail, nearly all sociologists in economically developed countries depend upon it for certain types of communication.

While e-mail messages are generally written in plain text, "attachments" to e-mail now make it possible for formatted documents, even those including graphics and multimedia, to be shared with others around the world in a matter of minutes. This remarkable technology makes co-authoring, and other forms of collaboration, far more feasible due to reduced time and cost.

As e-mail systems continue to expand, they offer social researchers new opportunities for conducting studies using electronic networks. For instance, Gaiser (1997) explored issues of running online focus groups. Online surveys have become quite common in various forms: e-mail texts, e-mail attachments, entry forms on the Web, and as programs in external storage devices like diskettes and CD-ROMs. Sampling problems and low completion rates pose the greatest challenges. Ongoing methodological investigations will be necessary to determine the implications of this new mode of research.

Statistics. Hundreds of computer programs and articles have been written to address the needs of statistical computing in social research. Prior to the 1980s, all statistical work was performed on large or medium-size, mainframe computers. But advances in both hardware and software for microcomputers now make it possible to conduct the statistical data analysis of most small or moderate-size research studies on microcomputers. A large share of ongoing social data analysis, like analysis of massive census files, would never get done without computer technology. For example, one use of LISREL, a computer procedure which analyzes linear structural relationships by the method of maximum likelihood, would consume weeks or months without a computer.

Not only does statistical computing save time but it offers unique views of the patterns in one's data. Without the ability to quickly reorganize data and display it in a variety of forms, social researchers neglect important patterns and subtle relationships within complex data. Some patterns cannot be observed without special software tools. For example, Heise's (1988) computer program called Ethno gives the researcher a framework for conceptualizing, examining, and analyzing data containing event sequences. In addition, several general-purpose statistical packages offer powerful exploratory data analysis capabilities with bidirectionality through dynamic data links (Steiger and Fouladi 1990). One type of bidirectionality puts a graph in one window and frequency distributions in another, and when the user adjusts the data in one window, it automatically changes in the other.

Finding a statistical program tailored to a particular problem or technique is often challenging as the potential "user community" may be quite small. The best sources for such software are the notices and reviews in journals such as the *Social Science Computer Review, Educational and Psychological Measurement, Journal of Marketing Research,*

and *The American Statistician.* Another important source is the annual *Sociological Methodology* and it's software list on the Web (http://weber.u.washington.edu/~socmeth2/software.html). Some of the software noted in these sources can be obtained at no cost or very low cost. No matter what the cost, one cannot assume that any complex program is free of errors. Thus is it important to run test data and to apply data to multiple programs in order to check for inaccuracies.

Accessing, Retrieving and Managing Data. While years ago students and researchers had to use a library or similar institution to gain access to bibliographic data files, now such services are available from one's desktop using the Web or external storage units such as CD-ROM or DVD-ROM. Large bibliographic databases including Sociological Abstracts and Psychological Abstracts are available in these forms, as is a vast amount of data in the form of statistical tables and maps. Now that devices for "writing" onto CD-ROMs have become inexpensive, it is expected that data from even small research projects will be disseminated in this medium.

One major development is interactive access to data by means of the Web. A variety of models are used for interactive access to both preformatted text files and precoded data files. Among the systems are GSSDIRS from ICPSR at the University of Michigan (http://www.ICPSR.umich.edu/gss), IPUMS at the University of Minnesota (http://www.hist.umn.edu/~ipums), QSERVE from Queens College-CUNY (http://www.soc.qc.edu/qserve), and SDA Archive from the University of California at Berkeley (http://csa.berkeley.edu:7502/archive.htm).

The software technology for archiving and analyzing social data is less than a half-century old. But it is very plausible to expect many advancements in the next fifty years. Interactive data analysis sites of the Web hint about what these advancements might be. For instance, using the SDA Archive Web site (see http address above), one can get a large crosstabulation table for any three variables in the full General Social Survey of over 35,000 respondents in less time than it takes to type in the variable names.

The refinement of such systems faces issues such as how to balance functionality with ease of use, the plausibility of standardizing interfaces for many numeric data files, and the use of gateways between the Web and third-party software such as statistical packages. It will take considerable research and development to sort out the feasibility of providing many different analytical facilities in the Web environment. A major challenge is determining the amount and type of data documentation necessary for typical users to get meaningful results in a reasonable amount of time. A considerable challenge is created when a variety of types of materials are necessary for retrieving useful data-related information. The main types are text, graphics, meta databases (data about databases), fielded text/data (such as bibliographic databases), and multimedia (audio and video) clips.

Qualitative Computing. Computer-based content analysis began with Stone (1966) and associates, and now plays an important role in the social sciences (Weber 1984; Kelle 1995). A survey of 110 qualitative-oriented researchers found three-fourths regularly used computers (Brent, Scott, and Spencer 1987). Ragin and Becker (1989, p. 54) persuasively claimed that qualitative research using these computing tools yields more systematic attention to diversity, for example, by encouraging a "more thorough examination of comparative contrasts among cases."

This type of computing became much more common as researchers combined content analysis with other tasks associated with qualitative analysis. Several general-purpose programs for qualitative analysis have been widely distributed (Tesch 1989; Fielding and Lee 1991). These tools make the analysis of large amounts of text more accurate and efficient, and potentially direct the focus of attention to analytic procedures. The general tasks of text entry, code assignment, counting, and data organization have been extended to include special routines for improving the quality of coding and code management (Carley 1988). Hesse-Biber, Dupuis, and Kinder (1997) technically extended this methodology to include the management and analysis of audio and video segments as well as text.

Simulating and Modeling. Early in the history of sociological computing, Coleman (1962) and McPhee and Glaser (1962) designed computer simulation models and showed how they could be used to identify elusive implications of different theoretical assumptions. Other social scientists followed in their footsteps but the excitement of the pioneers was lost and few simulations and formal computer models were developed in the 1970s. With the emergence of artificial intelligence and other modeling methodologies, social researchers demonstrated renewed interest in formal computer-supported models of social processes (cf. Feinberg and Johnson 1995; Hanneman 1988; Markovsky, Lovaglia, and Thye 1997). New computer simulations for social policy analysis as well as pedagogy or instruction have emerged as well (Brent and Anderson 1990, pp. 188–210).

Neural networks combined with other techniques of artificial intelligence and expert systems have excited a number of social scientists (Garson 1990). Neural nets organize computer memory in ways that model human brain cells and their ability to process many things in parallel. Systems that use neural nets are especially good when pattern matching is required, however, the computations require high-performance computers.

Computer-Assisted Data Collection. CATI (Computer-Assisted Telephone Interviewing) is a computing system with online questionnaires or entry screens for telephone interviewers. It has become very common in sociological research, although its impact is not fully understood (Groves et al. 1988). It is used on free-standing PCs, networked PCs, or larger computers. These systems generally, but not always, have the following characteristics: centralized facilities for monitoring individual interviewer stations, instantaneous edit-checks with feedback for invalid responses, and automatic branching to different questions depending upon the respondents' answers. Other major forms of computer-supported data collection include (1) CAPI (Computer-Assisted Personal Interviewing), the acronym used in survey research to refer to face-to-face interviewing assisted with a laptop or hand-held computing device; (2) Computerized Self-Administered Questionnaires (CSAQ), online programs designed for direct input from respondents; and (3) data-entry programs to facilitate the entry of data collected manually at a prior time.

A related innovation is software built for designing online questionnaires. For example, the Questionnaire Programming Language (QPL), developed by Dooley (1989), allows the researcher to draft a questionnaire with any word processor. From embedded branching commands within the questionnaire document, the QPL software package simultaneously produces two versions of the questionnaire: one for computer administration and the other for interviewer- or self-administration. An additional bonus of the program is that it automatically produces data definition commands for SPSS or SAS to use for data analysis.

Visualization and Graphics. Many social researchers have come to rely on computer graphic systems to produce maps, charts summarizing statistical data, network diagrams, and to retrieve data from GIS (Geographic Information Systems) databases. GIS data contain coordinates to associate a specific spatial point or area with any attribute, e.g., social density, associated with that point or collection of points. Because of the complexities of these data structures, the integration of these techniques onto sociologists' desktops has been slow. Another constraint is the paucity of techniques for analyzing such data. Work such as that of Cleveland (1993) for analyzing and visualizing data graphically may increase the utilization of such data by sociologists. In addition, techniques for storing and delivering interactive audio and video by means of the Web may stimulate sociologists to investigate multimedia data containing sounds and moving images.

Teaching and Learning. During the 1970s long before the microcomputer, a small group of social science instructors began to explore how to utilize computer technology in teaching (Bailey 1978). Now it has become quite common, and several sociologically-oriented instructional packages are widely used. The most popular have been Chipendale, designed by James Davis (1990), and MicroCase, developed by Roberts and Stark (cf. Roberts and Corbett 1996). These two packages have served as the basis for the exercises contained in at least a dozen published textbooks and workbooks. A variety of instructional approaches and software tools are described regularly in *Teaching Sociology* and the *Social Science Computer Review*.

ISSUES AND CHALLENGES

The practice of computing in social research has evolved rapidly. Computers have been applied to practically every research task, including such unlikely ones as interviewing, and hundreds of other tasks (Brent and Anderson 1990). This variety of computer applications will continue to evolve with the newer Internet-based technologies.

The application of computing to sociology is not without problems. Errors in data and software abound yet rarely do social scientists check their results by running more than one program on the same data. Data and software tend to be very costly, but there are many impediments to the sharing of these critical resources. Better software is needed but graduate students often are discouraged from programming new software. Nonetheless, new breakthroughs in computer technology will continue, and major new opportunities will emerge. Many of the advances in sociological computing during the next few years undoubtedly will follow the lines of progress already described: hypertext networks; integrated, high performance, graphic data analysis stations; software for computer-supported cooperative work; and neural networks for complex models of social systems.

Perhaps the most exciting challenge for the future involves a concert of these innovations directed at the problem of modeling and analyzing vast amounts of social data. One solution would incorporate three-dimensional, multicolored, dynamic graphical representations of complex social data structures. But new techniques for analyzing these data will require new models of dynamic social structures as well as parallel social processes. Computer representations of these models tend to require extremely fast processing. Access to such models on the Web, supplemented with audio and video displays, may evolve into an important part of the sociologist's tool kit of the future.

REFERENCES

Anderson, Ronald E. 1981 "Instructional computing in sociology: current status and future prospects." *Teaching Sociology.* 8,2 (Jan):171–195.

—— 1997 "A Research Agenda for Computing and the Social Sciences." *Social Science Computer Review* 14, 1 (Summer):123–134.

——, and Edward Brent 1989 "Computing in Sociology: Promise and Practice." *Social Science Computer Review* 7,4 (Winter).

—— 1991 "Sociological Computing: An Opportunity Missed?" *The American Sociologist* 22,11 (Spring):65–77.

Babbie, Earl 1996 "We Am a Virtual Community." *The American Sociologist* 27,1 (Spring):65-71.

Bailey, D. (ed.) 1978 *Computer Science in Social and Behavioral Science Education.* Englewood Cliffs, N.J.: Educational Technology Press.

Bainbridge, William Sims 1995 "Sociology on the World Wide Web." *Social Science Computer Review* 13,4 (Winter):508-523.

Borko, Harold (ed.) 1962 *Computer Applications in the Behavioral Sciences.* Santa Monica, Calif.: System Development Corporation.

Brent, Edward, and Ronald E. Anderson 1990 *Computer Applications in the Social Sciences.* New York: McGraw-Hill.

Brent, Edward, James Scott, and John Spencer 1987 "The use of computers by qualitative researchers." *Qualitative Sociology* 10(3):309-313.

Carley, Kathleen 1988 "Formalizing the Social Expert's Knowledge." *Sociological Methods & Research* 17, 2:165-232.

Cleveland, William S. 1993 *Visualizing Data.* Summit, N.J.: Hobart Press.

Coleman, J. S. 1962 "Analysis of social structures and simulation of social processes with electronic computers." In H. Guetzkow, H., ed., *Simulation in Social Science: Readings*, 61-69 Englewood Cliffs, N.J.: Prentice-Hall.

Davis, James 1990 CHIPendale. Zeda Data, 25 Haskins Rd. Hanover, NH.

Dooley, Kevin 1989 QPL Data Collection Program. Washington D.C.: Human Resources Division, U. S. General Accounting Office.

Fan, David 1996 Use of the Press to Predict Time Trends in Public Opinions and Behaviors. Paper presented at the 1996 Conference on Computing for the Social Sciences at the University of Minnesota.

Feinberg, William E., and Norris R. Johnson 1995 "FIRESCAP: A Computer Simulation Model of Reaction to a Fire Alarm." *Journal of Mathematical Sociology* 20, 2-3:257-269.

Fielding, Nigel G., and Raymond M. Lee (eds.) 1991 *Using Computers in Qualitative Research.* Newbury Park, Calif.: Sage Publications, Inc.

Gaiser, Ted J. 1997 "Conducting On-Line Focus Groups" *Social Science Computer Review* 15,2 (Summer):135-144.

Garson, G. David 1990 "Expert Systems: An Overview for Social Scientists." *Social Science Computer Review* 8,3 (Fall):387-410.

Groves, Robert M., P. P. Biemer, L. E. Lyberg, J. T. Massey, W. L. Nicholls, and J. Waksberg (eds.) 1988 *Telephone Survey Methodology.* New York: John Wiley and Sons.

Gurbaxani, Vijay 1990 "Diffusion in Computing Networks: BITNET." *Communications of the ACM* 33,12 (Dec):65-75.

Hanneman, Robert A. 1988 *Computer-Assisted Theory Building.* Newbury Park, Calif.: Sage Publications, Inc.

Heise, David 1988 "Computer analysis of cultural structures." *Social Science Computer Review* 6:183-196.

Hesse-Biber, Sharlene, Paul Dupuis, and Scott Kinder 1997 "Anthropology: New Developments in Video Ethnography and Visual Sociology—Analyzing Multimedia Data Qualitatively." *Social Science Computer Review* 15, 1 (Spring):5-12.

Kelle, Udo 1995 *Computer-Aided Qualitative Data Analysis.* Newbury Park, Calif.: Sage Publications, Inc.

Kiesler, Sarah, and Lee S. Sproull 1986 "Response effects in the electronic survey.", *Public Opinion Quarterly* 50:402-413.

Koppel, R, G. Dowdall, and A. Shostak 1985 "Using computers to teach sociology: A departmental survey." *Footnotes* 13,8 (November):4.

Lyman, Peter 1989 "The Future of Sociological Literature in an Age of Computerized Texts." In G. Blank, J. L. McCartney, and E. Brent, eds., *New Technology in Sociology: Practical Applications in Research and Work*, 17-32 New Brunswick, N.J.:

Markovsky, Barry, Michael Lovaglia, and Shane Thye 1997 "Sociology: Computer-Aided Research at the Iowa Center for the Study of Group Processes." *Science Computer Review* 15, 1 (Spring):48-64.

McPhee, W. N., and W. A. Glaser (eds.) 1962 *Public Opinion and Congressional Election.* New York: Free Press.

Morton, H. C., and A. J. Price 1986 "The ACLS survey of scholars: views on publications, computers, libraries." EDUCOM Bulletin 21,3 (Winter):8-21.

Nie, N., D. Bent, and W. Hull 1975 *Statistical Package for the Social Sciences.* New York: McGraw-Hill.

Ragin, Charles C. and Howard S. Becker 1989 "How the Microcomputer is Changing our Analytic Habits." In G. Blank, J. L. McCartney, and E. Brent, eds., *New Technology in Sociology: Practical Applications in Research and Work.* New Brunswick, N.J.: Transaction.

Roberts, Lynne and Michael Corbett 1996 *Social Research Using MicroCase.* Bellevue, Wash.: MicroCase Corporation.

Steiger, James H., and Rachel T. Fouladi 1990 "Some Key Emerging Trends in Statistical and Graphical Software for the Social Scientist." *Social Science Computer Review* 8,4 (Winter):627-664.

Stone, Philip et al. 1966 *The General Inquirer.* Cambridge, Mass.: MIT Press.

Tesch, Renata 1989 "Computer Software and Qualitative Analysis: A Reassessment." In G. Blank, J. L. McCartney, and E. Brent, eds., *New Technology in Sociology: Practical Applications in Research and Work.* New Brunswick, N.J.: Transaction.

Weber, R. P. 1984 "Computer-Aided Content Analysis, A Short Primer." *Qualitative Sociology,* 7 (1/2):126–147.

Wellman, Barry 1996 "Computer Networks as Social Networks." *Annual Review of Sociology* 22.2/3:Annual Reviews, Inc.

APPENDIX: SOCIOLOGY WEB/INTERNET SITES

These lists of Web and other Internet sites include electronic addresses for some of sociology's professional associations and some special interest groups, several resource referral sites giving many additional links, several sites giving access to sociological data, and lists of Internet Mailing Lists on "listservs." The addresses given were all current as of January 1, 1999. While many of the addresses have been stable for several years, there is no guarantee that they will remain accessible. Nonetheless, these addresses profile sociology's presence or representation on the Internet, especially the Web, and serve as entry points to sociology-related information in "cyberspace."

PROFESSIONAL ASSOCIATIONS OF SOCIOLOGISTS

American Sociological Association (ASA)
http://www.asanet.org/

International Sociological Association (ISA)
http://www.ucm.es/OTROS/isa/

Midwest Sociological Society
http:///www.drake.edu/MSS/

Pacific Sociological Association
http://www.csus.edu/psa/

Society for Applied Sociology
http://www.appliedsoc.org/

Society for the Study of Symbolic Interaction
http://www.soci.niu.edu/~sssi/

Society for the Study of Social Problems (SSSP)

http://itc.utk.edu/sssp/

SOCIOLOGY INTEREST GROUPS

ASA Section on Sociology and Computers
http://www.asanet.org/Sections/computer.html
(see also http://www.princeton.edu/~soccomp/links.html)

ASA Section on Organizations, Occupations, and Work
http://www.northpark.edu/acad/soc/oow/

International Network for Social Network Analysis
http://www.heinz.cmu.edu/project/INSNA/

ELECTRONIC JOURNALS ON SOCIOLOGY

The Electronic Journal of Sociology
http://www.sociology.org/

Sociological Research Online (A quarterly "refereed" electronic journal of sociology from the United Kingdom)
http://www.socresonline.org.uk/socresonline/

Current Research in Social Psychology (CRISP)
http://www.uiowa.edu/~grpproc/crisp/crisp.html

Journal of World-Systems Research
http://csf.colorado.edu/wsystems/jwsr.html

MAJOR SOCIOLOGY DATA SOURCES

Inter-University Consortium for Political and Social Research (ICPSR)
http://www.icpsr.umich.edu/

General Social Survey Data and Information Retrieval System (GSSDIRS)
http://www.icpsr.umich.edu/gss

Council of European Social Sciences Data Archives (CESSDA)
http://www.nsd.uib.no/cessda/europe.html

Integrated Public Use Microdata Series (IPUMS)
http://www.ipums.umn.edu

Social Indicators of Development (World Bank's data on social effects of economic development)
http://www.ciesin.org/IC/wbank/sid-home.html

MAJOR REFERRAL SITES FOR SOCIOLOGY RESOURCES

Demography and Population Studies WWW Virtual Library
http://coombs.anu.edu.au/ResFacilities/DemographyPage.html

WWW Virtual Library: Sociology—SOCNET—Courses, Resources
http://www.mcmaster.ca/socscidocs/w3virtsoclib/socnet.htm

SOCIOWEB A Sociology Resource Center
http://www.socioweb.com/~markbl/socioweb/

Research engines for the social sciences
http://tile.net/">tile.net

WeacTies (for Sociology of the Internet)
http://www.princeton.edu//~soccomp/weacties/

SELECTED NONELECTRONIC PERIODICALS IN SOCIOLOGY

Sociological Methodology: An Annual Volume
http://weber.u.washington.edu/~socmeth2/software.html

Social Science Computer Review
http://sagepub.com

The Information Society
http://www.ics.uci.edu/~kling/tis.html

INTERNET MAILING LISTS (LIST SERVERS) ON SOCIOLOGICAL TOPICS

This list of List Servers, or Listserv discussion groups, indicate the popularity of such communication vehicles. The format for each entry is: List-Name followed by a brief one-phrase description. The second line is the Internet subscription address. Unless otherwise noted, anyone can subscribe by sending a one-line message to these addresses. The one-line message should say "subscribe" followed by the List-Name.

ASASCAN Section on Sociology and Computing (ASA)
listserv@vm.temple.edu

FAMLYSCI Family studies
listserv@ukcc.uky.edu

IVSA International Visual Sociology Association
listserv@pdomain.uwindsor.ca

MATHSOC Mathematical Sociology
listserv@listserv.dartmouth.edu

RURSOC-L Rural Sociology Discussion List
listserv@lsv.uky.edu

SOCIOLOGY-L Sociology Faculty Information
listserv@american.edu

SOCNET Social Networks
listserv@lists.ufl.edu

SOCIOLOGY USENET NEWSGROUPS

In contrast to Internet Mailing Lists, UseNet Newsgroups do not broadcast a message to all those included on the list. Internet users must specifically access the postings (messages) for any such newsgroup. While on any given day, "sociology" will be mentioned in a variety of newsgroup discussions, the only newsgroup where academic sociological topics are regularly discussed is: alt.sci.sociology. Generally a few messages are added to this discussion area every day.

RONALD E. ANDERSON

CONFIDENCE INTERVALS

See Statistical Inference.

CONFLICT THEORY

NOTE: *Although the following article has not been revised for this edition of the Encyclopedia, the substantive coverage is currently appropriate. The editors have provided a list of recent works at the end of the article to facilitate research and exploration of the topic.*

Conflict theory explains social structure and changes in it by arguing that actors pursue their interests in conflict with others and according to their resources for social organization. Conflict theory builds upon Marxist analysis of class conflicts, but it is detached from any ideological commitment to socialism. Max Weber generalized conflict to the arenas of power and status as well as economic class, and this multidimensional approach has become widespread since the 1950s.

WHAT CONSTITUTES A CONFLICT GROUP?

For Marx and Engels, a society's conflicting interests derive from the division between owners and nonowners of property. Dahrendorf (1959) proposed that conflicts are based on power, dividing order-givers, who have an interest in maintaining the status quo, from order-takers, who have an interest in changing it. Property is only one of the bases of power conflict, and conflicts can be expected inside any type of organization, including socialist ones. In the Weberian model there are even more types of conflict, since every cultural group (such as ethnic, religious, or intellectual groups) can also struggle for advantage. In addition, economic conflict takes place in three different types of market relations, pitting employers against workers, producers against consumers, and lenders against borrowers (Wiley 1967). Gender stratification produces yet another dimension of conflict.

THE PROCESS OF CONFLICT

Conflicting interests remain latent until a group becomes mobilized for active struggle. This occurs when its members are physically concentrated, have material resources for communicating among themselves, and share a similar culture. The higher social classes are typically more mobilized than lower classes, and most struggles over power take place among different factions of the higher classes. Lower classes tend to be fragmented into localized groups and are most easily mobilized when they are a homogeneous ethnic or religious group concentrated in a particular place. The better organized a conflict group is, the longer and more intensely it can struggle; such struggles become routinized, as in the case of entrenched labor unions or political parties. Less organized conflict groups that become temporarily mobilized are more likely to be violent but unable to sustain the conflict.

Overt conflict increases the solidarity of groups on both sides. Coser (1956), elaborating the theory of Georg Simmel, points out that conflict leads to a centralization of power within each group and motivates groups to seek allies. A conflict thus tends to polarize a society into two factions, or a world of warring states into two alliances. This process is limited when there are cross-cutting memberships among groups, for instance, if class, ethnic, and religious categories overlap. In these cases, mobilization of one line of conflict (e.g., class conflict) puts a strain on other dimensions of conflict (e.g., ethnic identity). Thus, cross-cutting conflicts tend to neutralize each other. Conversely, when multiple lines of group membership are superimposed, conflicts are more extreme.

Conflicts escalate as each group retaliates against offenses received from the other. How long this process of escalation continues depends on how much resources a group can draw upon: its numbers of supporters, its weapons, and its economic goods. If one group has many more resources than the other, the conflict ends when the mobilizing capacity of the weaker side is exhausted. When both sides have further resources they have not yet mobilized, escalation continues. This is especially likely when one or both sides have sustained enough damage to outrage and mobilize their supporters but not great enough damage to destroy their organizational resources for struggle.

Deescalation of conflict occurs in two very different ways. If one side has overwhelming superiority over the other, it can destroy opposition by breaking the other group's organizational capacity to fight. The result is not harmony but an uneasy peace, in which the defeated party has been turned back into an unmobilized latent interest. If neither side is able to break up the other's organization, conflict eventually deescalates when resources are eaten up and the prospects of winning become dimmer. Although wars usually arouse popular solidarity at first, costs and casualties reduce enthusiasm and bring most wars to an end within a few years. Civilian uprisings, strikes, and other small-scale conflicts typically have fewer resources to sustain them; these conflicts deescalate more quickly. During a deescalation, the points of contention among the opponents modulate from extreme demands toward compromises and piecemeal negotiation of smaller issues (Kriesberg 1982). Very destructive levels of conflict tend to end more rapidly than moderate conflicts in which resources are continuously replenished.

COERCIVE POWER AND REVOLUTION

In a highly coercive state, such as a traditional aristocracy or a military dictatorship, power is organized as an enforcement coalition (Collins 1988; Schelling 1962). Members of the ruling organization monitor each other to ensure loyalty. A change in power is possible only when a majority of the enforcers disobey orders simultaneously. Revolts occur in a rapid "bandwagon effect," during which most members scramble to become part of the winning coalition. The more coercive the state, the more extreme the swings between long periods of tyrannical stability and brief moments of political upheaval.

Since the state claims a monopoly on the instruments of violence, revolutionary changes in power occur through the reorganization of coercive coalitions. Revolts from below are almost always unsuccessful as long as the state's military organization stays intact. For this reason, revolutions typically are preceded by a disintegration of the military, due to defeat in war, depletion of economic resources in previous conflicts, and splits within the ruling group (Skocpol 1979). These breakdowns of military power in turn are determined by geopolitical processes affecting the expansion or contraction of states in the surrounding world (Stinchcombe 1968; Collins 1986).

WHO WINS WHAT?

Conflict shapes the distribution of power, wealth, and prestige in a society. The victorious side is generally the group that is better mobilized to act in its collective interest. In many cases, the dominant group is well organized, while the opposing interest group remains latent. The result is a stable structure of stratification, in which overt conflict rarely occurs.

Lenski (1966) showed that concentration of wealth throughout world history is determined by the interaction of two factors. The higher the production of economic surplus (beyond what is necessary to keep people alive), the greater the potential for stratification. This surplus in turn is appropriated according to the distribution of power.

Turner (1984) theorizes that the concentration of power is unequal to the extent that there is external military threat to the society or there is a high level of internal conflict among social groups. Both external and internal conflict tend to centralize power, providing that the government wins

these conflicts; hence, another condition must also be present, that the society is relatively productive and organizationally well integrated. If the state has high resources relative to its enemies, conflict is the route by which it concentrates power in its own hands.

Prestige is determined by the concentration of power and wealth. Groups that have these resources can invest them in material possessions that make them impressive in social encounters. In addition, they can invest their resources in culture-producing organizations such as education, entertainment, and art, which give them cultural domination. According to Pierre Bourdieu's research (1984), the realm of culture is stratified along the same lines as the stratification of the surrounding society.

EFFECTS OF CONFLICT GROUPS UPON INDIVIDUALS

The latent lines of conflict in a society divide people into distinctive styles of belief and emotion. Collins (1975) proposed that the differences among stratified groups are due to the microinteractions of daily experience, which can occur along the two dimensions of vertical power and horizontal solidarity. Persons who give orders take the initiative in the interaction rituals described by Goffman (1959). These persons who enact the rituals of power identify with their front-stage selves and with the official symbols of the organizations they control; whereas persons who take orders are alienated from official rituals and identify with their private, backstage selves. Individuals who belong to tightly enclosed, localized groups emphasize conformity to the group's traditions; persons in such positions are suspicious of outsiders and react violently and emotionally against insiders who are disrespectful of the group's symbols. Loosely organized networks have less solidarity and exert less pressure for conformity. Individuals build up emotional energy by microexperiences that give them power or solidarity, and they lose emotional energy when they are subordinated to power or lack experiences of solidarity (Collins 1988). Both emotions and beliefs reproduce the stratification of society in everyday life.

(SEE ALSO: *Coalitions; Game Theory and Strategic Interaction; Interpersonal Power*)

REFERENCES

Bailey, Kenneth D. 1997 "System and Conflict: Toward a Symbiotic Reconciliation." *Quality and Quantity* 31:425–442.

Bourdieu, Pierre 1984 *Distinction*. Cambridge, Mass.: Harvard University Press.

Briggs, E. Donald 1992 "New Directions in Conflict Theory: Conflict Resolution and Conflict Transformation." *Canadian Journal of Political Science / Revue canadienne de science politique* 25:430–431.

Chapin, Mark 1994 "Functional Conflict Theory, the Alcohol Beverage Industry, and the Alcoholism Treatment Industry." *Journal of Applied Social Sciences* 18:169–182.

Collins, Randall 1975 *Conflict Sociology*. New York: Academic Press.

—— 1986 *Weberian Sociological Theory*. Cambridge: Cambridge University Press.

—— 1988 *Theoretical Sociology*. San Diego: Harcourt Brace Jovanovich.

Collins, Randall 1993 "What Does Conflict Theory Predict about America's Future?" *Sociological Perspectives* 36:289–313.

Coser, Lewis A. 1956 *The Functions of Social Conflict*. New York: Free Press.

Dahrendorf, Ralf 1959 *Class and Class Conflict in Industrial Society*. Stanford, Calif.: Stanford University Press.

Gagnon, V. P., Jr. 1995 "Ethnic Conflict as an Intra-Group Phenomenon: A Preliminary Framework." *Revija za Sociologiju* 26:1–2.

Glaser, James M. 1994 "Back to the Black Belt: Racial Environment and White Racial Attitudes in the South." *Journal of Politics* 56:21–41.

Goffman, Erving 1959 *The Presentation of Self in Everyday Life*. New York: Doubleday.

Hanneman, Robert A., Randall Collins, and Gabriele Mordt 1995 "Discovering Theory Dynamics by Computer Simulation: Experiments on State Legitimacy and Imperialist Capitalism." *Sociological Methodology* 25:1–46.

Haugaard, Mark 1997 "The Consensual Basis of Conflictual Power: A Critical Response to 'Using Power, Fighting Power' by Jane Mansbridge." *Constellations* 3:401–406.

Kriesberg, Louis 1982 *Social Conflicts*. Englewood Cliffs, N.J.: Prentice-Hall.

Lenski, Gerhard E. 1966 *Power and Privilege: A Theory of Stratification*. New York: McGraw-Hill.

Schelling, Thomas C. 1962 *The Strategy of Conflict*. Cambridge, Mass.: Harvard University Press.

Skocpol, Theda 1979 *States and Social Revolutions*. New York: Cambridge University Press.

Stinchcombe, Arthur L. 1968 *Constructing Social Theories*. New York: Harcourt.

Turner, Jonathan H. 1984 *Societal Stratification: A Theoretical Analysis*. New York: Columbia University Press.

—— 1993 *Classical Sociological Theory: A Positivist's Perspective*. Chicago, Ill.: Nelson-Hall Publishers.

Van-Huyssteen, Elsa F. 1994 "Interpretation of the South African Legal System in Terms of the Analytical Conflict Perspective." *Suid Afrikaanse Tydskrif vir Sosiologie / South African Journal of Sociology* 25:87–94.

Wiley, Norbert F. 1967 "America's Unique Class Politics: The Interplay of the Labor, Credit, and Commodity Markets." *American Sociological Review* 32:529–540.

RANDALL COLLINS

CONSISTENCY THEORY

See Cognitive Consistency Theories.

CONTENT ANALYSIS

"Content analysis" has evolved into an umbrella label that includes various procedures for making reliable, valid inferences from qualitative data, including text, speech, and images. These procedures have improved and expanded due to numerous developments in recent years since this encyclopedia's first edition.

Traditionally, "content analysis" has referred to systematic procedures for assigning prespecified codes to text, such as interviews, newspaper editorials, open-ended survey answers, or focus-group transcripts, and then analyzing patterns in the codings. Some projects will count each specific occurrence within a text, while others will have coders tally the number of column inches assigned a code. Either way, the procedure usually employs a "top down" strategy, beginning with a theory and hypotheses to be tested, developing reliable coding categories, applying these to coding-specified bodies of text, and finally testing the hypotheses by statistically comparing code indexes across documents.

With the increasing popularity of qualitative sociology, content analysis has also come to refer to "grounded" inductive procedures for identifying patterns in various kinds of qualitative data including text, illustrations, and videos. For example, the data might include observers' detailed notes of children's behaviors under different forms of supervision, possibly supplemented with videotapes of those same behaviors. While traditional content analysis usually enlisted statistical analyses to test hypotheses, many of these researchers do not start with hypotheses, but carefully search for patterns in their data.

However, rather than just produce statistical analyses or search for patterns, investigators should also situate the results of a content analysis in terms of the contexts in which the documents were produced. A content-analysis comparison of letters to stockholders, for example, should take into consideration the particular business sectors covered and the prevailing economic climates in which they were written. An analysis of American presidential nomination acceptance speeches should consider that they changed dramatically in form once they started to be broadcast live on national radio. A content analysis may have reliable coding, but the inferences drawn from that coding may have little validity unless the researcher factors in such shaping forces.

Like any expanding domain, there has been a tendency for content analysis to segment into specialized topics. For example, Roberts (1997) focuses on drawing statistical inferences from text, including Carley's networking strategies and Gottschalk's clinical diagnostic tools. There also has been a stream of instructional books, including several series published by Sage, that focus on particular kinds of qualitative data such as focus-group transcripts. A technical literature also has developed addressing specialized computer software and video-analysis techniques. Nevertheless the common agenda is analyzing the content of qualitative data. Inasmuch as our lives are shaped by different forms of media, and inasmuch as different analytic procedures can complement one another in uncovering important insights, it makes sense to strive toward an integration, rather than fragmentation.

Many advances in content-analysis procedures have been made possible by the convenience and power of desktop and laptop computers. In addition, an overwhelming proportion of text documents are now generated on computers, making their text files computer accessible for content analysis. And a revolution in hand-held analogue and digital video cameras, together with computer-based technology for editing and analyzing videotapes, makes new research procedures feasible.

Consider, for example, new possibilities for analyzing responses to open-ended questions in survey research. For years, survey researchers have been well aware that closed-ended questions require respondents to frame how they think about an issue in terms of a question's multiple choices, even when the choice options had little to do with how a respondent views an issue. But the costs and time involved in analyzing open-ended responses resulted in such questions rarely being used. Even when they were included in a survey, the interviewers usually just recorded capsule summaries of the responses that omitted most nuances of what was said.

Contrast this then with survey research using today's audio information-capturing technologies. Telephone survey interviewers are guided by instructions appearing on a computer screen. Whenever an open-ended question appears, the interviewer no longer needs to type short summaries of the responses. Instead, a computer digitally captures an audio recording of each open-ended response, labels it, and files it as a computer record. Any audio response can later be easily fetched and replayed, allowing a researcher, for example, to identify a "leaky voice," that is, one indicative of the respondent's underlying emotion or attitude. And the full audio responses are then available to be transcribed to text, including, if desired, notations indicating hesitations and voice inflections. Until computer voice recognition is completely reliable, transcribing usually remains a manual task. But with spreadsheet software (such as *Excel*) no longer restrictively limiting the amount of text in any one cell, the text of each individual's entire response to a question can be placed in a spreadsheet cell, thus capturing both the closed-ended and open-ended data for a survey into a convenient, single spreadsheet for researchers to analyze.

With the survey data in this convenient form, researchers can then code open-ended responses manually, putting their assigned codes in additional spreadsheet columns. As a teaching exercise, it is instructive to assign students a task such as identifying gender differences among a thousand responses to a broad open-ended question, such as a question asking respondents' views about peace or family values. Students first might sort the spreadsheet by gender in order to read separately samples of male responses and female responses and obtain a sense of what possible gender differences exist. They then develop coding instructions that capture these differences and apply the codes to the entire set of responses. This coding, of course, is better done without knowledge of the respondents' genders, with responses in a random order, and on different respondents than those used to develop the codes. After coding several hundred responses, however, students usually begin to glaze over and soon the most ardent humanist student is asking whether the computer could possibly be of help in assigning codes.

For some kinds of coding, computer help is indeed available in the form of computer programs that assign codes. Such codings can be treated as advisory and then manually confirmed, augmented perhaps by also assigning a weight. Or they may be used as is after being spot-checked for accuracy. Not only can a computer complete huge amounts of tedious coding in minutes, possibly assigning many different types of codings to each text, but these codings may uncover statistically significant frequency differences that human coders would not uncover, if only because computer analysis is so even-handed and untiring. The static created by occasional miscodings may be more than offset by gains from a reliable consistency in making many codings.

Computer coding assignments are usually based on the occurrence of words, particular senses of words, or multiword idioms appearing in the text. For example, the word "father" in a text might be coded as "male," "family member," etc. as well as

possibly "authority-role." Computer content-analysis software may search the contexts of words in the text to ferret out and correctly code common word senses. For example, for a national study of people's perceptions of African-American young males on several open-ended questions, it was particularly important for the computer to identify correctly each respondent's usages of such multi-meaning words as "race," "white," "black," and "color."

In addition to developing their own coding categories, researchers may enlist existing computer-scored categories that are relevant to the task at hand. For example, it might be hypothesized that one group being studied is more optimistic and its responses will reflect more "positive thinking" while another is more negative or pessimistic. To code "positive thinking" a researcher may want the computer to apply an existing content-analysis category that includes over 1200 words, word roots, word senses, phrasal verbs, and idioms, thus essentially covering most expressions of "positive-thinking" that occur as infrequently as three times per million words of ordinary English text. A similar category exists for negative-thinking, allowing the investigator to check whether the groups being studied differ in their coded positive thinking, negative thinking, or both. And by enlisting such standard categories, the results obtained in one study can be readily compared with results found in other studies.

Once data has been captured in a convenient format for computer use, they can be repeatedly analyzed. For example, should our now glazed-over students have any energy left after analyzing the responses by gender, they could be given an additional assignment of identifying and coding rural-urban differences in these same open-ended responses. Given so many analyses that can be made, it makes sense to let the computer do what it can, saving manual labor for those types of codings that would be hard to have a computer assign. Even multimedia qualitative-analysis software such as *HyperResearch* includes some rudimentary tools for automatic assignments.

Moreover, desktop computer software has also become available that identifies patterns in text without having to develop coding categories. For example, SPSS's *TextSmart* uses an algorithm that groups respondents into clusters based on word-use co-occurrences within responses and then maps these clusters into a two-dimensional grid that uses colors to represent each cluster group. If such an automated inductive procedure can produce additional valid insights that other techniques are likely to overlook, then why not use it too?

Pioneering work in inductive automatic categorizing, such as Iker's (1969), usually enlisted procedures based upon correlation matrixes, such as factor analysis. These procedures tended not to be particularly suited to analyzing text both because of the shape of word-usage frequency distributions as well as the limited number of words that a correlation matrix could feasibly handle. *TextSmart*, based upon a word-distance measure, provides much more suitable solutions. Further automatic categorizing procedures may be expected from artificial intelligence, as well as from categorizing techniques being developed for Internet search engines.

Content-analysis research strategies can thus now easily be multipronged, spanning from completely automatic inductive procedures to manual coding. But even manual coding these days is likely to utilize computer software to help coders manage information. Consider these changes in costs and convenience: Unlike mainframe computing of the 1960s and 1970s, when the cost of an hour of computer time was about the same as a coder's wage for several weeks, the marginal cost of using a desktop computer is essentially the electricity it uses. Today's desktop computer is likely to be more than fivefold faster at content-analysis coding than those mainframe computers ever were. They also can access much larger dictionaries and other information in their RAM than was ever feasible on a user partition of a mainframe computer, thus making their coding more accurate and comprehensive. Moreover, a single CD-ROM full of text to be analyzed is easily popped into a desktop computer, whereas in the days of mainframe computing, a comparable amount of text would have to be keypunched on over 3,000 boxes of IBM cards.

Given today's convenience and low cost of computer-based procedures, there is no reason to limit an analysis to one approach, especially if insights gained from one approach will differ and often complement those gained from another. Instead of being limited by technology, the limits now may lie in the skills, proclivities, and comfort zones of the researchers. Research teams, rather than individual researchers, may prove the best solution, for only in a team made up of people with complementary strengths is one likely to find the full range of statistical, conceptual, intuitive, experiential, and perhaps clinical strengths needed to carry out penetrating, comprehensive content-analysis projects. Moreover, some researchers will prefer to learn from the main trends while others will learn more from studying outlying cases. Some will learn from bottom-line numbers while others will learn more from innovative graphics that highlight information patterns. Some will focus on current data while others will contextualize data historically by comparing them with data in archives. Data that has been gathered and assembled at considerable cost, especially data-gathering that imposed on many respondents, merit as thorough and comprehensive analyses as these various procedures collectively offer.

Unfortunately, however, an "either-or" assumption about how to do content analysis has continued to be supported both by books and computer software. Authors who do an excellent job of describing one approach to content analysis, such as Boyatzis (1998), give an impression that an either-or decision has to be made about which approach to use. Some software—especially that ported from mainframe computers or developed for early desktop computers—still may steer or even limit researchers who use it to just one approach. For example, some software packages create specialized data formats such as "classification trees" that then in effect constrain the user to analyses that can be readily derived from that format. Software reviews such as Lewis's (1998) excellent comparison of *ATLAS/ti* and *NUD-IST* software have been explicit about what assumptions a researcher buys into when utilizing each package.

Additional leverage in analyzing qualitative information has stemmed from computer-based tools, such as newer versions of *HyperResearch* and *ATLAS/ti*, that integrate the handling of multiple media (text, illustrations, and video). Especially as more software comes from countries where there are expert programming skills and programming labor is relatively inexpensive, we can expect ambitious content-analysis software, of which *TextAnalyst* from Russia (www.megaputer.com) may be a forerunner.

Given continuing content-analysis software developments, those who would like to learn what is currently available are advised search Internet sites rather than rely upon even recently published materials. One recommended starting point is the Georgia State University content-analysis site (www.gsu.edu/~wwwcom/content.html), which gives links to software web sites (including software mentioned in this article), indexes recent content-analysis publications, and has a mailing list of more than 700 members. Technical reviews of relevant language-analysis tools, such as Berleant's (1995), occasionally appear in computational linguistics journals and web sites. For training, the University of Essex Summer School in Social Science Data Analysis and Collection (www.essex.ac.uk), as part of a program of a European consortium, has been offering a content-analysis module for years as part of its program.

Given the developments described here, some of the contributions that content analysis should be able to make to sociological research include:

1. A major shift from reliance upon closed-ended questions to an appropriate use of open-ended questions that lets people be heard in the ways they frame issues, as well as the way they think and feel about them, as discussed in detail by Stone (1997)

2. A better understanding of both print and television media and its impact on public opinion, both in setting agendas and in influencing opinion intensity, as laid out in Neuman (1989). This will involve research that compares the content of media with the content of opinions. Not only will survey research data be archived and accessible from Internet servers, but full-display media will be accessible from Lexis-Nexis and on-line editions supplied by media providers, as well as television news archives such as those at Vanderbilt University

3. Better use of historical qualitative data, including both text and graphic materials, to address such issues as how economic cycles impact ideology, as examined by Namenwirth and Weber (1987), or to uncover cycles of creativity, as demonstrated by Martindale (1990)

4. Investigations, several of which are already underway, of both intranet communication patterns within organizations as well as Internet communications, including analyses of the content of communications over those networks.

There is also, however, good reason for caution. Never before in history has so much qualitative information been available electronically. High-volume image scanning will also further increase the amount of information that can be electronically accessed and content-analyzed. Quite understandably, those agencies responsible for limiting terrorist activities may look on content-analysis procedures as possibly providing early warnings that could save lives. But these procedures can also become tools for a "big-brother" monitoring society. Sociologists have an important role in anticipating these problems and helping resolve them.

REFERENCES

Berleant, Daniel 1995 "Engineering 'Word Experts' for Word Disambiguation." *Natural Language Engineering* 1 (4):339–362.

Boyatzis, Richard E. 1998 *Transforming Qualitative Information: Thematic Analysis and Code Development.* Thousand Oaks, Calif.: Sage.

Iker, Howard, and Norman Harway 1969 "A Computer Systems Approach Toward the Recognition and Analysis of Content." In George Gerbner, Ole Hosti, Klaus Krippendorff, William Paisley, and Philip Stone, eds., *The Analysis of Communication Content.* New York: Wiley.

Lewis, R. Berry 1998 "*ATLAS/ti* and *NUD-IST*: A Comparative Review of Two Leading Qualitative Data Analysis Packages." *Cultural Anthropology Methods* 10 (3):41–47.

Martindale, Colin 1990 *The Clockword Muse: The Predictability of Artistic Change.* New York: Basic Books.

Namenwirth, J. Zvi, and Robert Philip Weber 1987 *Dynamics of Culture.* Winchester, Mass.: Allen and Unwin.

Neuman, Richard 1989 "Parallel Content Analysis: Old Paradigms and New Proposals." *Public Communication and Behavior* 2:205–289.

Roberts, Carl W. (ed.) 1997 *Text Analysis for the Social Sciences: Methods for Drawing Statistical Inferences from Texts and Transcripts.* Mahwah, N.J.: Lawrence Erlbaum.

Stone, Philip J. 1997 "Thematic Text Analysis: New Agendas for Analyzing Text Content." In Carl W. Roberts, ed., *Text Analysis for the Social Sciences: Methods for Drawing Statistical Inferences from Texts and Transcripts.* Mahwah, N.J.: Lawrence Erlbaum.

PHILIP STONE

CONTINGENCY TABLES

See Tabular Analysis; Typologies.

CONVERGENCE THEORIES

The idea that societies move toward a condition of similarity—that they converge in one or more respects—is a common feature of various theories of social change. The notion that differences among societies will decrease over time can be found in many works of eighteenth and nineteenth century social thinkers, from the prerevolutionary French *philosophes* and the Scottish moral philosophers through de Tocqueville, Toennies, Maine, Marx, Spencer, Weber, and Durkheim (Weinberg 1969; Baum 1974). More recently, the study of "postindustrial" society and the debate over "postmodernist" aspects of contemporary society also reflect to some degree the idea that there is a tendency for broadly similar conditions or attributes to emerge among otherwise distinct and dissimilar societies.

In sociological discourse since the 1960s, the term *convergence theory* has carried a more specific connotation, referring to the hypothesized link between economic development and concomitant changes in social organization, particularly work and industrial organization, class structure, demographic patterns, characteristics of the family, education, and the role of government in assuring basic social and economic security. The core notion of convergence theory is that as nations achieve similar levels of economic development they will become more alike in terms of these (and other) aspects of social life. In the 1950s and 1960s, predictions of societal convergence were most closely associated with modernization theories, which generally held that developing societies will follow a path of economic development similar to that followed by developed societies of the West. Structural-functionalist theorists, such as Parsons (1951) and Davis (1948), while not actually employing the terminology of convergence theory, paved the way for its development and use in modernization studies through their efforts to develop a systematic statement of the functional prerequisites and structural imperatives of modern industrial society; these include an occupational structure based on achievement rather than ascription, and the common application of universalistic rather than particularistic evaluative criteria. Also, beginning in the 1960s, convergence theory was invoked to account for apparent similarities in industrial organization and patterns of stratification found in both capitalist and communist nations (Sorokin 1960; Goldthorpe 1964; Galbraith 1967).

CONVERGENCE THEORY AND MODERNIZATION

The conventional and most controversial application of convergence theory has been in the study of modernization, where it is associated with the idea that the experience of developing nations will follow the path charted by Western industrialized nations. Related to this idea is the notion of a relatively fixed pattern of development through which developing nations must pass as they modernize (Rostow 1960). Inkeles (1966), Inkeles and Smith (1974), and Kahl (1968) pursued the idea of convergence at the level of individual attitudes, values, and beliefs, arguing that the emergence of a "modern" psychosocial orientation accompanies national modernization (see Armer and Schnaiberg 1972 for a critique).

Kerr and colleagues' *Industrialism and Industrial Man* (1960) offers the classic statement of the "logic of industrialism" thesis, which the authors proposed as a response to Marxian theory's equation of industrial society with capitalism. More specifically, Kerr et al. sought to identify the "inherent tendencies and implications of industrialization for the work place," hoping to construct from this a portrait of the "principal features of the new society" (p. 33). The features common to industrial society, they argued, include rapid changes in science, technology, and methods of production; a high degree of occupational mobility, with continual training and retraining of the work force; increasing emphasis on formal education, particularly in the natural sciences, engineering, medicine, managerial training, and administrative law; a workforce highly differentiated in terms of occupational titles and job classifications; the increasing importance of urban areas as centers of economic activity; and the increasing role of government in providing expanded public services, orchestrating the varied activities of a large and complex economy, and administering the "web of rules" of industrial society. Importantly, Kerr et al. envisioned these developments as cutting across categories of political ideology and political systems.

Although the "logic of industrialism" argument is often cited as a prime example of convergence theory (see Form 1979; Moore 1979; Goldthorpe 1971), Kerr et al. never explicitly made this claim for their study. While mentioning convergence at various points in their study, the authors pay equal attention to important countercurrents leading toward diverse outcomes among industrial societies. The concluding chapter of *Industrialism and Industrial Man* is, in fact, entitled "Pluralistic Industrialism," and addresses the sources of diversity as well as uniformity among industrial societies. Among sources of diversity identified are the persistence of existing national institutions, enduring cultural differences, variations in the timing of industrialization (late versus early), the nature of a nation's dominant industry, and the size and density of population. Counterposed against these factors are various sources of uniformity, such as technological change, exposure to the industrial world, and a worldwide trend toward increased access to education leading to an attenuation of social and economic inequality.

The critique of convergence theory in the study of modernization recalls critiques of earlier theories of societal evolution advanced under the rubric of social Darwinism in the nineteenth century and structural functionalism in the mid-twentieth century. The use of convergence theory to analyze modernization has been attacked for its alleged assumptions of unilinearity and determinism (i.e., a single path of development that all societies must follow), its teleological or historicist

character (Goldthorpe 1971), its Western ideological bias (Portes 1973), and for ignoring the structurally dependent position of less-developed countries in the world economy (Wallerstein 1974). Yet a careful review of the literature suggests that many criticisms have often tended to caricature convergence theory rather than addressing its application in actual research studies. Since the 1960s few if any researchers have explicitly claimed convergence theory, at least in its unreconstructed form, as their own. For example, Moore (1979), an exponent of the "conventional" view of modernization, subtitled his book, *World Modernization*, "the limits of convergence," and went to great pains to distance himself from the "model modernized society" position associated with early versions of convergence theory (see Moore 1979, pp. 26–28, 150–153). And Parsons (1966), whose name is virtually synonymous with structural functionalism, concluded one of his later writings on comparative sociology with the statement that "any linear theory of societal evolution" is "untenable" (p. 114). As Form (1979) observes, convergence theory passed through a cycle typical of social science theories: a burst of initial interest and enthusiasm, followed by intense criticism and controversy, finally giving way to neglect. The major challenge to those wishing to revive convergence theory and rescue it from its critics is to specify its theoretical underpinnings more precisely, to develop appropriate empirical studies, and finally account for variation as well as similarity among observed cases.

FORMS OF CONVERGENCE AND DIVERGENCE

In recent years Inkeles (1980, 1981; also Inkeles and Sirowy 1983) has made the most systematic attempt to reformulate convergence theory and respecify its core hypotheses and propositions. Inkeles (1981) argues that earlier versions of convergence theory failed to distinguish adequately between different elements of the social system, which is problematic because these elements not only change at different speeds, but may move in opposite directions. He proposes dividing the social system into a minimum of five elements for purposes of assessing convergence: modes of production and patterns of resource utilization; institutional arrays and institutional forms; structures or patterns of social relationships; systems of popular attitudes, values, and behavior; and systems of political and economic control. Finally, he specifies the different forms convergence and divergence may take: (1) simple convergence involving the movement from diversity to uniformity; (2) convergence from different directions involving movement toward a common point by an increase for some cases and a decrease for others; (3) convergence via the crossing of thresholds rather than changes in absolute differences; (4) divergent paths toward convergence, where short-term fluctuations eventually fall into line or a "deviant" case that eventually defines the norm for other cases (for example, France's move toward small family size in the late eighteenth century); and (5) convergence in the form of parallel change, where nations all moving in the same direction along some dimension of change continue to remain separated by a gap. Although parallel change of this sort does not represent true convergence, it is consistent with the key assumption of convergence theory, namely, that "insofar as they face comparable situations of action . . . nations and individuals will respond in broadly comparable ways" (p. 21).

Inkeles (1981) also describes various forms that divergence may take: (1) simple divergence, the mirror image of simple convergence, in which movement occurs away from a common point toward new points further apart than the original condition; (2) convergence with crossover, where lines intersect and then proceed to spread apart; and (3) convergent trends masking underlying diversity (for example, although the United States, Great Britain, and Sweden all experienced large increases in public assistance programs from 1950 to the early 1970s, the social groups receiving benefits were quite different among the three nations, as were the political dynamics associated with the spending increases within each nation). Finally, Inkeles (1981) notes the importance of selecting appropriate units of analysis, levels of analysis, and the time span for which convergence, divergence, or parallel change can be assessed. These comments echo earlier sentiments expressed by Weinberg (1969) and Baum (1974) about how to salvage the useful elements of standard convergence theory while avoiding the pitfalls of a simplistic functionalist-evolutionary approach. Common to these attempts to revive convergence theory is the exhortation to develop more and better

empirical research on specific institutional spheres and social processes. As the following sections demonstrate, a good deal of work along these lines is already being done across a wide range of substantive questions and topical concerns that can aptly be described in the plural as *convergence theories*, indicating their revisionist and more pluralistic approach.

INDUSTRIAL SOCIOLOGY

Despite criticisms of Kerr and colleagues' (1960) concept of the logic of industrialism, the question of convergent trends in industrial organization has remained the focus of active debate and much research. The large research literature related on this question, reviewed by Form (1979), has produced mixed evidence with respect to convergence. Studies by Shiba (1973, cited in Form 1979), Form (1976), and Form and Kyu Han (1988), covering a range of industrializing and advanced industrial societies found empirical support for convergence in workers' adaptation to industrial and related social systems, while Gallie's (1977, cited in Form 1979) study of oil refineries in Great Britain and France found consistent differences in workers' attitudes toward systems of authority. On the question of sectoral and occupational shifts, Gibbs and Browning's (1966) twelve-nation study of industrial and occupational division of labor found both similarities—consistent with the convergence hypothesis—as well as differences. Studies across nations varying in levels of industrial development revealed only "small and unsystematic differences" in worker commitment (Form 1979, p. 9), thus providing some support for the convergence hypothesis. Japan has been regarded as an exceptional case among industrialized nations because of its strong cultural traditions based on mutual obligation between employers and employees. These characteristics led Dore (1973), for example, to argue vigorously against the convergence hypothesis for Japan. A more recent study by Lincoln and Kalleberg (1990) "stands convergence on its head," arguing that patterns of work organization in the United States are being impelled in the direction of the Japanese model. Finally, with respect to women in the labor force, the evidence of convergence is mixed. Some studies found no relationship between female labor-force participation and level of industrialization

(Ferber and Lowry 1977; Safilios-Rothchild 1971), though there is strong evidence of a trend toward increasing female participation in nonagricultural employment among advanced industrial societies (Paydarfar 1967; Wilensky 1968) along with the existence of dual labor markets stratified by sex, a pattern found in both communist and capitalist nations in the 1970s (Cooney 1975; Bibb and Form 1977; Lapidus 1976).

STRATIFICATION

Closely related to the study of industrial organization is the question of converging patterns of stratification and mobility. The attempt to discover common features of the class structure across advanced industrial societies is a central concern for social theorists of many stripes. The question has inspired intense debate among both neo-Weberian and Marxist sociologists, although the latter, for obvious ideological reasons, tend to eschew the language of convergence theory. An early statement of the class convergence thesis was made by Lipset and Zetterberg (1959), to the effect that observed rates of mobility between social classes tend to be similar from one industrial society to another. Erikson et al. (1983) conducted a detailed test of the class mobility convergence hypothesis in England, France, and Sweden, and found little support for it. They conclude that the "process of industrialization is associated with very variable patterns . . . of the social division of labour" (p. 339).

A subcategory of comparative stratification research concerns the evidence of convergence in occupational prestige. A study published in 1956 by Inkeles and Rossi, based on data from six industrialized societies, concluded that the prestige hierarchy of occupations was "relatively invariable" and tended to support the hypothesis that modern industrial systems are "highly coherent. . . relatively impervious to the influence of traditional culture patterns" (p. 329). Although the authors did not specifically mention convergence, their conclusions were fully consistent with the idea of emergent similarities. A subsequent study by Treiman (1977) extended the comparison of occupational prestige to some sixty nations, ranging from the least developed to the most developed. The study found that occupational-prestige rankings were markedly similar across all

societies, raising the question of whether convergence theory or an explanation based on the functional imperatives of social structure of all complex societies, past or present, was most consistent with the empirical findings. The conclusion was that both explanations had some merit, since although all complex societies—whether developed, undeveloped, or developing—showed similar occupational-prestige rankings, there was also evidence that the more similar societies were in levels of industrialization, the more similar their patterns of occupational-prestige evaluation appeared to be.

DEMOGRAPHIC PATTERNS

The theory of demographic transition provides one of the most straightforward examples of convergence. The essence of the theory is that fertility and mortality rates covary over time in a predictable and highly uniform manner. Moreover, these changes are directly linked to broad developmental patterns, such as the move from a rural, agriculturally based economy to an urban-industrial one, increases in per capita income, and adult literacy (Berelson 1978). In the first stage of the demographic transition, both fertility rates and death rates are high, with population remaining fairly constant. In the second stage, death rates drop (as a result of improvements in living conditions and medical care) while fertility rates remain high, and population levels increase rapidly. In the third stage, fertility rates begin to decline, with total size of the population leveling off or even decreasing. This simple model works remarkably well in accounting for demographic patterns observed among all industrialized (and many industrializing) societies during the post-World War II period. A large spread in fertility rates among nations at the beginning of the 1950s gave way to declining rates of fertility ending with a nearly uniform pattern of zero population growth in the 1970s.

The convergent tendencies predicted by the theory of demographic transition have not gone unchallenged, however. Freedman (1979), for example, suggests that cultural factors mediate the effects of social structural factors central to transition theory. Coale (1973) and Teitelbaum (1975) note that demographic transition theory has not provided much explanatory or predictive power with regard to the timing of population changes or the regional variations observed within nations undergoing change.

FAMILY

Inkeles (1980) explored the effects of putative convergent tendencies discussed above for family patterns. While he found evidence of convergence in some aspects of family life, other patterns continue "to be remarkably stable in the face of great variation in their surrounding socio-economic conditions" (p. 34). Aspects of family life that show clear convergent patterns include the trend toward falling fertility rates and a shift in relative power and resource control in the direction of increasing autonomy of women and declining authority of parents. Other aspects of the family, such as age at first marriage, appear to present a more complex picture, with short-term fluctuations obscuring long-term changes, and great variation from one culture to another. Still other characteristics of family life seem resistant to change; cited as examples in Inkeles (1980) are cultural patterns such as veneration of elders in many Asian societies, basic human needs for companionship and psychological support, and the role of husbands helping wives with housework. In all, Inkeles (1980) estimates that only about half the indicators of family life he examined showed any convergence, and even then not always of a linear nature.

EDUCATION

Following Inkeles' (1981) reformulation of convergence theory, Inkeles and Sirowy (1983) studied the educational systems of seventy-three rich and poor nations. Among thirty different "patterns of change" in educational systems examined, they found evidence of marked convergence in fourteen, moderate convergence in four, considerable variability in nine, mixed results in two, and divergence in only one. Based on these findings, they conclude that the tendency toward convergence on common structures is "pervasive and deep. It is manifested at all levels of the educational system, and affects virtually every major aspect of that system" (p. 326). Also worthy of note is that while the authors take the conventional position that convergence is a response to pressures arising from a complex, technologically advanced social and economic system, they also identify diffusion via integration of networks through which ideas, standards, and practices in education are shared. These networks operate largely through international organizations, such as UNESCO and the OECD; their role as mediating structures in a process leading toward cross-national similarities in education constitutes an important addition to convergence theory, with wide-ranging implications for convergence in other institutions.

THE WELFARE STATE

The development of the welfare state has inspired active theoretical debate and empirical research on convergence theory, with researchers divided over the nature and extent of convergence found across nations. On the one hand, there is indisputable evidence that extensive social security, health care, and related benefit programs is restricted to nations that have reached a level of economic development where a sufficient surplus exists to support such efforts. Moreover, the development of programs of the welfare state appears to be empirically correlated with distinct bureaucratic and demographic patterns that are in turn grounded in economic development. For example, Wilensky (1975) found that among sixty nations studied the proportion of the population sixty-five years of age and older and the age of social security programs were the major determinants of levels of total welfare-state spending as a percent of gross national product. Since levels of economic development and growth of the elderly population both represent areas of convergence among advanced societies, it is reasonable to expect that patterns of welfare-state development will also tend to converge. Indeed, in such respects as the development of large and expensive pension and health-care programs, of which the elderly are the major clientele, this is the case (Coughlin and Armour 1982; Hage et al. 1989). Other empirical studies have found evidence of convergence in public attitudes toward constituent programs of the welfare state (Coughlin 1980), in egalitarian political movements affecting welfare effort across nations (Williamson and Weiss 1979), and in levels of spending (Pryor 1968), normative patterns (Mishra 1976), and social control functions of welfare-state programs across capitalist and communist nations (Armour and Coughlin 1985).

Other researchers have challenged the idea of convergence in the welfare state. In a historical study of unemployment programs in thirteen Western European nations, Alber (1981) found no evidence that programs had become more alike in eligibility criteria, methods of financing, or generosity of benefits, although he did find some evidence of convergence in duration of unemployment benefits in nations with compulsory systems. A study conducted by O'Connor (1988) testing the convergence hypothesis with respect to trends in welfare spending from 1960 to 1980 concluded that "despite the adoption of apparently similar welfare programmes in economically developed countries there is not only diversity but divergence in welfare effort. Further, the level of divergence is increasing" (p. 295). A much broader challenge to the convergence hypothesis comes from studies focusing on variations in welfare-state development among western capitalist democracies. Hewitt (1977), Castles (1978, 1982), and Korpi (1983), to cite a few leading examples, argue that variations across nations in the strength and reformist character of labor unions and social democratic parties account for large differences in the levels of spending for and redistributive impact of welfare-state programs. However, the disagreement among these studies and scholars arguing for convergence may be simply a function of case selection. For example, in a study of nineteen rich nations, Wilensky (1976, 1981) linked cross-national diversity in the welfare state to differences in "democratic corporatism," and secondarily to the presence of Catholic political parties, thus rejecting the simplistic idea that the convergence observed across many nations at widely different levels of economic development extends to the often divergent policy developments in the relatively small number of advanced capitalist societies.

The debate over convergence in the welfare state is certain to continue. A major obstacle in resolving the question involves disagreement on the nations chosen for study, selection and construction of measures (see Uusitalo 1984), and judgments about the time frame appropriate for a definitive test of the convergence hypothesis. Wilensky et al. (1985, pp. 11–12) sum up the mixed status of current research on convergence in welfare-state development as follows:

Convergence theorists are surely on solid ground when they assert that programs to protect against the seven or eight basic risks of industrial life are primarily responses to economic development . . . . However, showing that societies have adopted the same basic programs. . . is only a partial demonstration of convergence insofar as it does not demonstrate convergence in substantive features of the programs or in the amount of variation among affluent countries compared to poor countries.

GLOBALIZATION

Growing attention to a variety of large-scale changes in economic relations, technology, and cultural relations, broadly subsumed under the description "globalization," has inspired renewed interest in the ideas of convergence and modernity (see Robertson 1992 for a critical account). The literature on globalization has several threads. One approach focuses on the economic and cultural impact of transnational capitalist enterprises that are judged to be responsible for the spread of a pervasive ideology and culture of consumerism (Sklair 1995). Ritzer (1993) summarizes this phenomenon as the "McDonaldization of society"—a broad reference to the ubiquity and influence of the consumer brand names (and the large corporate interests behind them) that are instantly recognizable in virtually every country in the world today. The main implication of this perspective is that indigenous industries, habits, and culture are rapidly being driven aside or even into extinction by the "juggernaut" of the world capitalist economy dominated by a relatively few powerful interests.

Meyer et al. (1997) provide a different interpretation of globalization in their work on "world society." Although they argue that "many features of the contemporary nation-state derive from a worldwide model constructed and propagated through global cultural and associational processes" (pp. 144–145), the essence of their position is that nations are drawn toward a model that is "surprisingly consensual. . .in virtually all the domains of rationalized social life" (p. 145). Meyer et al. contend that various core principles, such as those legitimating human rights and favoring environmentalism, do not emerge spontaneously as an imperative of modernity, but rather diffuse rapidly among nations worldwide through the agency of international organizations, networks of scientists and professionals, and other forms of association. Although not referring specifically to convergence theory, this world society and culture approach makes a strong case for the emergence of widely shared structural and cultural similarities, many of which hold out the promise of improvement, among otherwise diverse nation-states.

The rapid growth of telecommunications and computing technology, especially apparent in the emergence of the Internet as a major social and economic phenomenon of the 1990s, presents yet another aspect of globalization that holds profound implications for possible societal convergence. However important and wide-ranging, the precise patterns that will ultimately emerge from these technological innovations are not yet clear. While new computing and communication technologies compress the time and space dimensions of social interaction (Giddens 1990), and have the potential to undercut national identities and cultural differences along the lines envisioned by McLuhan's (1960) "global village," the same forces of advanced technology that can level traditional differences may ultimately reinforce the boundaries of nation, culture, and social class. For example, even as the computers and related communication technologies become more ever more widely disseminated, access to and benefits from the new technologies appear to be disproportionately concentrated among the "haves," leaving the "have nots" more and more excluded from participation (Wresch 1996). Over time, such disparities might well serve to widen differences both across and within nations, thus leading toward divergence rather than convergence.

Finally, interest in convergence has also been given a boost by various political developments in the 1990s. In particular, the twin developments of the collapse of communism in Eastern Europe and the Soviet Union and the progressive weakening of economic and political barriers in Europe are notable in this regard. The demise of state socialism has revived interest in the possibilities of global economic and political convergence among advanced industrial societies (see, for example, Lenski et al. 1991, p. 261; Fukuyama 1992). Although ongoing economic and political turmoil in the "transition to capitalism" in the former Soviet Union during the 1990s may cast serious doubt on the long-term prospects for convergence, developments have clearly moved in that direction with astonishing speed.

The continuing movement toward unification in Europe associated with the European Union (EU, formerly the European Community) represents another significant case of political and economic convergence on a regional scale. The gradual abolition of restrictions on trade, the movement of labor, and travel among EU nations (and not least of all the establishment of a single currency in 1999), and the harmonization of social policies throughout the EU, all signal profound changes toward growing convergence in the region that promises to continue into the twenty-first century.

CONCLUSION

The idea of convergence is both powerful and intuitively attractive to sociologists across a range of backgrounds and interests (Form 1979). It is difficult to conceive of an acceptable macro theory of social change that does not refer to the idea of convergence in one way or another. Despite the controversy over, and subsequent disillusionment with, early versions of convergence theory in the study of modernization, and the often mixed results of empirical studies discussed above, it is clear that the concept of societal convergence (and convergence theories that allow for the possibility of divergence and invariance) provides a useful and potentially powerful analytical framework within which to conduct cross-national studies across a broad range of social phenomena. Even where the convergence hypothesis ultimately ends up being rejected, the perspective offered by convergence theories can provide a useful point of departure for research. Appropriately reformulated, focused on elements of the social system amenable to empirical study, and stripped of the ideological baggage associated with its earlier versions, convergence theories hold promise to advance the understanding of the fundamental processes and regularities of social change.

REFERENCES

Alber, Jens 1981 "Government Responses to the Challenge of Unemployment: The Development of Unemployment Insurance in Western Europe. In Peter

Flora and Arnold J. Heidenheimer, eds., *The Development of Welfare States in Europe and America*. New Brunswick, N.J.: Transaction Books.

Armer, Michael, and Allan Schnaiberg 1972 "Measuring Individual Modernity: A Near Myth." *American Sociological Review* 37:301–316.

Armour, Philip K., and Richard M. Coughlin 1985 "Social Control and Social Security: Theory and Research on Capitalist and Communist Nations." *Social Science Quarterly* 66:770–788.

Aron, Raymond 1967 *The Industrial Society*. New York: Simon and Schuster.

Baum, Rainer C. 1974 "Beyond Convergence: Toward Theoretical Relevance in Quantitative Modernization Research." *Sociological Inquiry* 44:225–240.

Bendix, Reinhard 1967 "Tradition and Modernity Reconsidered." *Comparative Studies in Society and History* 9:292–346.

Berelson, B. 1978 "Prospects and Programs for Fertility Reduction: What? Where?" *Population and Development Review* 4:579–616.

Bibb, R. and W.H. Form 1977 "The Effects of Industrial, Occupational, and Sex Stratification in Blue-Collar Markets." *Social Forces* 55:974–996.

Castles, Francis 1982 "The Impact of Parties on Public Expenditure." In Frances Castles, ed., *The Impact of Parties: Politics and Policies in Democratic Capitalist States*. Beverly Hills, Calif.: Sage.

—— 1978 *The Social Democratic Image of Society*. London: Routledge and Kegan Paul.

Coale, Ansley J. 1973 "The Demographic Transition." In *The International Population Conference, Liège*. Liège, Belgium: International Union for the Scientific Study of Population.

Cooney, R.S. 1975 "Female Professional Work Opportunities: A Cross-National Study." *Demography* 12:107–120.

Coughlin, Richard M. 1980 *Ideology, Public Opinion and Welfare Policy*. Berkeley: University of California, Institute of International Studies.

——, and Philip K. Armour 1982 "Sectoral Differentiation in Social Security Spending in the OECD Nations." *Comparative Social Research* 6:175–199.

Davis, Kingsley 1948 *Human Society*. New York: Macmillan.

Dore, Ronald 1973 *British Factory-Japanese Factory*. Berkeley: University of California Press.

Erikson, Robert, John H. Goldthorpe, and Lucienne Portocarero 1983 "Intergenerational Class Mobility and the Convergence Thesis: England, France, and Sweden." *British Journal of Sociology* 34:303–343.

Ferber, M., and H. Lowry 1977 "Women's Place: National Differences in the Occupational Mosaic." *Journal of Marketing* 41:23–30.

Form, William 1979 "Comparative Industrial Sociology and the Convergence Hypothesis." *Annual Review of Sociology* 4:1–25.

—— 1976 *Blue-Collar Stratification*. Princeton, N.J.: Princeton University Press.

——, and Bae Kyu Han 1988 "Convergence Theory and the Korean Connection." *Social Forces* 66:618–644.

Fox, William S., and William W. Philliber 1980 "Class Convergence: An Empirical Test." *Sociology and Social Research* 64:236–248.

Freedman, Ronald 1979 "Theories of Fertility Decline: A Reappraisal. *Social Forces* 58:1–17.

Fukuyama, Francis 1992 *The End of History and the Last Man*. New York: Free Press.

Galbraith, John Kenneth 1967 *The New Industrial State*. Houghton-Mifflin.

Gibbs, J.P., and H.L. Browning 1966 "The Division of Labor, Technology, and the Organization of Production in Twelve Countries." *American Sociological Review* 31:81–92.

Giddens, Anthony 1990 *The Consequences of Modernity*. Stanford, Calif.: Stanford University Press.

Goldthorpe, John H. 1971 "Theories of Industrial Society: Reflections on the Recrudescence of Historicism and the Future of Futurology." *Archives of European Sociology* 12:263–288.

—— 1964 "Social Stratification in Industrial Society." In P. Halmos, ed., *The Development of Industrial Societies*, 97–123. Keele, Eng.: University of Keele.

Hage, Jerald, Robert Hanneman, and Edward T. Gargan 1989 *State Responsiveness and State Activism*. London: Unwin Hyman.

Hewitt, Christopher 1977 "The Effect of Political Democracy and Social Democracy on Equality in Industrial Societies: A Cross-National Comparison." *American Sociological Review* 42:450–464.

Inkeles, Alex 1981 "Convergence and Divergence in Industrial Societies." In M.O. Attir, B.H. Holzner, and Z. Suda, eds., *Directions of Change: Modernization Theory, Research, and Realities*, 3–38. Boulder, Colo.: Westview Press.

—— 1980 "Modernization and Family Patterns: A Test of Convergence Theory." In D.W. Hoover and J.T.A. Koumoulides, eds., *Conspectus of History*, 31–64. Cambridge, Eng.: Cambridge University Press.

—— 1966 "The Modernization of Man." In M. Weiner, ed., *Modernization* New York: Basic Books.

——, and Larry Sirowy 1983 "Convergent and Divergent Trends in National Educational Systems." *Social Forces* 62:303–333.

Inkeles, Alex, and David E. Smith 1974 *Becoming Modern.* Cambridge, Mass.: Harvard University Press.

Inkeles, Alex, and Peter H. Rossi 1956 "National Comparisons of Occupational Prestige." *American Journal of Sociology* 61:329–339.

Kahl, J.A. 1968 *The Measurement of Modernization: A Study of Values in Brazil and Mexico.* Austin: University of Texas Press.

Kerr, Clark, John T. Dunlap, Frederick H. Harbison, and Charles A. Myers 1960 *Industrialism and Industrial Man.* Cambridge, Mass.: Harvard University Press.

Korpi, Walter 1983 *The Democratic Class Struggle.* London: Routledge and Kegan Paul.

Lapidus, Gail W. 1976 "Occupational Segregation and Public Policy: A Comparative Analysis of American and Soviet Patterns." In M. Blaxell and B. Reagan, eds., *Women and the Workplace* Chicago: University of Chicago Press.

Lenski, Gerhard, Jean Lenski, and Patrick Nolan 1991 *Human Societies,* 6th ed. New York: McGraw-Hill.

Lincoln, James R., and Arne L. Kalleberg 1990 *Culture, Control, and Commitment: A Study of Work Organization and Work Attitudes in the United States and Japan.* Cambridge, Eng.: Cambridge University Press.

Lipset, Seymour M., and Hans Zetterberg 1959 "Social Mobility in Industrial Societies." In S.M. Lipset and R. Bendix, eds., *Social Mobility in Industrial Society.* London: Heinemann.

McLuhan, Marshall 1960 *Exploration in Communications.* Boston: Beacon Press.

Meyer, John W., John Boli, George M. Thomas, and Francisco O. Ramirez 1997 "World Society and the Nation-State." *American Journal of Sociology* 103:144–181.

Mishra, Ramesh 1976 "Convergence Theory and Social Change: The Development of Welfare in Britain and the Soviet Union." *Comparative Studies in Society and History* 18:28–56.

Moore, Wilbert E. 1979 *World Modernization: The Limits of Convergence.* New York: Elsevier.

O'Connor, Julia S. 1988 "Convergence or Divergence?: Change in Welfare Effort in OECD Countries 1960–1980." *European Journal of Political Research* 16:277–299.

Parsons, Talcott 1966 *Societies: Evolutionary and Comparative Perspectives.* Englewood Cliffs, N.J.: Prentice Hall.

Parsons, Talcott 1951 *The Social System.* Glencoe, Ill.: The Free Press.

Paydarfar, A.A. 1967 "Modernization Process and Demographic Changes." *Sociological Review* 15:141–153.

Portes, Alejandro 1973 "Modernity and Development: A Critique." *Comparative International Development* 8:247–279.

Pryor, Frederick 1968 *Public Expenditure in Capitalist and Communist Nations.* Homewood, Ill.: Irwin.

Ritzer, George 1993 *The McDonaldization of Society.* Newbury Park, Calif.: Sage.

Robertson, Roland 1992 *Globalization: Social Theory and Global Culture.* London and Newbury Park, Calif.: Sage.

Rostow, Walt W. 1960 *The Stages of Economic Growth.* Cambridge, Eng.: Cambridge University Press.

Safilios-Rothchild, C. 1971 "A Cross-Cultural Examination of Women's Marital, Educational and Occupational Aspirations." *Acta Sociologica* 14:96–113.

Sklair, Leslie 1995 *Sociology of the Global System.* Baltimore, Md.: Johns Hopkins University Press.

Sorokin, Pitirim A. 1960 "Mutual Convergence of the United States and the U.S.S.R. to the Mixed Sociocultural Type." *International Journal of Comparative Sociology.* 1:143–176.

Teitelbaum, M.S. 1975 "Relevance of Demographic Transition for Developing Countries." *Science* 188:420–425.

Treiman, Donald J. 1977 *Occupational Prestige in Comparative Perspective.* New York: Academic Press.

Uusitalo, Hannu 1984 "Comparative Research on the Determinants of the Welfare State: The State of the Art." *European Journal of Political Research* 12:403–442.

Wallerstein, Immanuel 1974 "The Rise and Future Demise of the World Capitalist System: Concepts for Comparative Analysis." *Comparative Studies in Social History* 16:287–415.

Weed, Frank J. 1979 "Industrialization and Welfare Systems: A Critical Evaluation of the Convergence Hypothesis." *International Journal of Comparative Sociology* 20:282–292.

Weinberg, Ian 1969 "The Problem of the Convergence of Industrial Societies: A Critical Look at the State of the Theory." *Comparative Studies in Society and History* 11:1–15.

Wilensky, Harold L. 1981 "Leftism, Catholicism, and Democratic Corporatism: The Role of Political Parties in Recent Welfare State Development." In Peter Flora and Arnold J. Heidenheimer, eds., *The Development of Welfare States in Europe and America,* 345–382. New Brunswick, N.J.: Transaction Books.

—— 1976 *The "New Corporatism": Centralization and the Welfare State.* Beverly Hills, Calif.: Sage.

—— 1975 *The Welfare State and Equality*. Berkeley: University of California Press.

—— 1968 "Women's Work: Economic Growth, Ideology, Structure." *Industrial Relations* 7:235–248.

——, Gregory M. Luebbert, Susan Reed Hahn, and Adrienne M. Jamieson 1985 *Comparative Social Policy: Theory, Methods, Findings*. Berkeley: University of California, Institute of International Studies.

Williamson, John B., and Joseph W. Weiss 1979 "Egalitarian Political Movements, Social Welfare Effort and Convergence Theory: A Cross-National Analysis." *Comparative Social Research* 2:289–302.

Williamson, John B., and Jeanne J. Fleming 1977 "Convergence Theory and the Social Welfare Sector: A Cross-National Analysis." *International Journal of Comparative Sociology* 18:242–253.

Wresch, William 1996 *Disconnected: Haves and Have Nots in the Information Age*. New Brunswick, N.J.: Rutgers University Press.

RICHARD M. COUGHLIN

CONVERSATION ANALYSIS

Conversation analysis has evolved over several decades as a distinct variant of ethnomethodology. Its beginnings can be traced to the mid-1960s, to the doctoral research and the unpublished but widely circulated lectures of Harvey Sacks. Sacks was a University of California sociologist who had studied with Harold Garfinkel, the founder of the ethnomethodological movement, as well as with Erving Goffman. While not an ethnomethodologist, Goffman's proposal that face-to-face interaction could be an analytically independent domain of inquiry certainly helped inspire Sacks's work. Two other key figures whose writings (separately and together with Sacks) contributed to the emergence of conversation analysis were Gail Jefferson, one of Sacks's first students, and Emanuel A. Schegloff, another sociologist trained in the University of California system who was decisively influenced by Garfinkel and, in much the same manner as Sacks, by Goffman (Schegloff 1988).

Sacks, like Garfinkel, was preoccupied with discovering the methods or procedures by which humans coordinate and organize their activities, and thus with the procedures of practical, common-sense reasoning in and through which "social

order" is locally constituted (Garfinkel [1967] 1984). In addressing this problem, he devised a remarkably innovative approach. Working with tapes and transcripts of telephone calls to a suicide prevention center (and with recordings of other, somewhat more mundane sorts of conversations), Sacks began examining the talk as an object in its own right, as a fundamental type of social action, rather than primarily as a resource for documenting other social processes. In short, Sacks came to recognize that the talk itself was the action. It was in the details of the talk that we could discover just how what was getting done in the activity was accomplished, systematically and procedurally, then and there, by the coparticipants themselves. This appeared to be an especially fruitful way of investigating the local production of social order.

As Schegloff (1989, p. 199) later wrote in a memoir of these first years, Sacks's strategy in his pioneering studies was to first take note of how members of society, in some actual occasion of interaction, achieved some interactional effect—for example, in the suicide center calls, how to exhibit (and have others appreciate) that one has reasonably, accountably, arrived at the finding "I have no one to turn to"—and then to ask: Was this outcome accomplished methodically? Can we describe it as the product of a method of conduct, such that we can find other enactments of that method that will yield the same outcome, the same recognizable effect? This approach provided, Sacks suggested, an opportunity to develop formal accounts of "members' methods" for conducting social life.

In this way, Sacks sought to address the basic question of (as he put it in one of his early manuscripts) "what it is that sociology can aim to do, and . . . how it can proceed" (Sacks [1964–1968] 1984, p. 21). Sociology, he argued, could be a "natural observational science," concerned with the methodic organization of naturally occurring events, rather than with behavior that was manipulated through experimental techniques or other interventions such as surveys, interviews, and the like. And it could be committed to direct observation of this organization *in situ*, rather than dependent upon analytic theorizing and a concomitant reliance on idealized models of action.

Naturalistic observation also met the ethnomethodological mandate that all evidence for the use of members' methods, and for members' orientation to or tacit knowledge of them, was to be derived exclusively from the observed behavior of the coparticipants in an interactional event. As Schegloff and Sacks (1973, p. 290) subsequently summarized the logic of this stance, if the event, the recorded conversational encounter, exhibited a methodically achieved orderliness, it "did so not only to us [the observing analysts], indeed not in the first place for us, but for the co-participants who had produced" it. After all, the task was to discover members' methods for coordinating and ordering conversational events, and these could not in any way be determined by analysts' conceptual stipulations or deduced from inventive theories.

The contrast with other methods and approaches for studying interactional processes could not be sharper, particularly with those methods adopted by Bales (1950) and Homans (1961) and their many followers, with their commitment to theoretically derived and precise operational definitions of social phenomena as a prerequisite to any scientific investigation (see Sacks 1992, vol. 1, p. 28 and p. 105, for his thinking on Bales and Homans). But Sacks's methodological stance contrasts even with those traditions usually regarded as neighbors of conversation analysis, such as symbolic interactionism and Goffman's "micro-Durkheimian" approach. These approaches assume that without an analytically stipulated conceptual scheme, there is no orderliness (or the orderliness cannot be seen) in what Garfinkel (1991) terms "the plenum"—the plentitude of members' lived experience.

Sacks was also making a well-reasoned argument for the importance of studying mundane conversation, directly confronting the belief that sociology's overriding concern should be the study of "big issues"; that is, the belief that the search for social order should center on the analysis of large-scale, massive institutions. Social order, he insisted, can be found "at all points," and the close study of what from conventional sociology's point of view seemed like small (and trivial) phenomena—the details of conversation's organization—might actually give us an enormous understanding of the way humans do things and the kinds of methods they use to order their affairs (Sacks [1964–1968] 1984, p. 24).

This last proposition bears special emphasis, for Sacks felt that these details went unnoticed,

and perhaps could not even be imagined, by conventional analytic sociology. When had sociologists concerned themselves with the profoundly methodic character of things like how to avoid giving your name without refusing to give it, he argued, or with how to get help for suicidalness without requesting it? Or with members' methods for things like "doing describing" and "recognizing a description," methods that provide for hearing the first two sentences from a story told by a young child—"The baby cried. The mommy picked it up."—as saying: The mommy who picked up the baby is the baby's mommy, and she picked it up because it was crying. Though apparently mundane, this observation provided the basis for a series of investigations regarding members' categorization methods and eventually came to provide for an entirely different approach to studies of social institutions and phenomena like race and gender. Sacks noted that since every person can be categorized at any time in various ways (for example, in terms of age, gender, or stage of life), a person's use of, or reliance on, one category rather than another to guide his or her actions with others must be grounded in one of a multitude of discoverable systems of relevance, some of which are potentially applicable in any situation, such as age, race, and gender, and others that are more limited in their use, such as occupationally defined categories or those made relevant by the organization of conversation itself, such as speaker/hearer, caller/called, and the like.

As these last examples of categories suggest, "membership analysis"—making sense of who someone is for the purpose of appropriately designing some next action—is an unremitting problem for members of a society, one that has to be solved in real time, and for which there is no single solution. Furthermore, who a person relevantly "is" for the purposes of some next action can change from moment to moment. As a consequence, Sacks pointed out that sociologists can no longer innocently categorize populations whatever way they (and their theories) see fit. Instead, analysts must similarly demonstrate the relevance of a category *to the participants* in any scene, as well as its consequentiality for them in terms of how the action proceeds, in order to ground its use in any sociological investigation (see Silverman 1998 for a useful summary of this argument).

Such grounding would stand in contrast to the epidemiological uses of categorization that underpin standard social scientific research. Sacks's colleague, anthropologist Michael Moerman (1974, pp. 67–68), once noted that social scientists "have an apparent inability to distinguish between warm . . . human bodies and one kind of identification device which some of those bodies sometimes use." Further, since Sacks was primarily concerned with categorization as a thoroughly practical, procedural activity for members he was not much interested in the content of categories, with drawing the cultural grids that preoccupied cognitive anthropologists and many social psychologists. Instead, Sacks believed that by starting with the close study of actual events—such as members' observable use of categories *in situ*—and showing that they happened in an endogenously, socially organized manner, a much sounder basis for studying and understanding social life could be established.

It should be evident, then, that the appellation *conversation analysis* does not really capture the enterprise's commitment to addressing the most basic problem for the social sciences: the underlying character and structure of social action. As the title of one of Sacks's first publications, "An Initial Investigation of the Usability of Conversational Data for Doing Sociology," makes clear, the use of recorded conversational materials was more of an opportunistic research strategy than a commitment to studying talk per se (Sacks 1972). Tape recordings of conversations constituted a record of the details of actual, singular events that could be replayed and studied extensively, and would permit other researchers direct access to exactly these same details. Still, for these identical reasons, it is conversation's organization—its detectable, orderly properties—that has remained the concrete object of study for the enterprise.

During years since the "initial investigations," conversation analysis has given rise to a substantial research literature. Pursuing the lines of analysis first identified in the early studies while simultaneously opening up many new avenues of inquiry, researchers working in this tradition have produced findings that are, in the words of one contemporary practitioner, "strikingly cumulative and interlocking" (Heritage 1987, p. 256). Important collections of papers include those of Sudnow (1972), Schenkein (1978), Atkinson and Heritage (1984), Button and Lee (1987), and ten Have and

Psathas (1995). Sacks's lectures have now been edited and published in complete form (Sacks 1992). Special issues of *Sociological Inquiry*, *Social Psychology Quarterly*, *Human Studies*, *Social Problems*, *Research on Language and Social Interaction*, *Text*, and the *Western Journal of Speech Communication* have also been devoted to ethnomethodological and conversation-analytic topics.

Three major domains in conversation's organization identified in this literature are the organization of sequences, of turn taking, and of repair. These organizations can be described as systems of naturally organized activity, systems known and used by members as courses of practical action and practical reasoning, and designed to resolve generic problems of coordination that confront any conversationalist (and perhaps members of all social species). A sketch of some research findings with respect to these organizations should serve to illustrate how they function in this fashion, as well as the interlocking nature of their domains.

Consider first the organization of sequences. Begin with the fact that even the most cursory inspection of conversational materials reveals that talk-in-interaction has a serial arrangement to it. For example, in a conversation between two parties, party A will talk first, then party B, then A, then B, and so forth. Accordingly, in two-party conversations, turns at talk constitute a series of alternately produced utterances: ABABAB. But overlaying this serial arrangement of utterances are distinctly characterizable conversational sequences, where turns at talk do not simply happen to occur one after the other but rather "belong together" as a socio-organizational unit, and where there is thus a methodic relationship between the various turns or parts.

This methodic, structurally linked relationship between sequence parts is central to how sequences work in resolving coordination problems in conversation. This point can be demonstrated by briefly focusing on one of the earliest studies of sequence organization by Schegloff (1968), an investigation into how the initiation of conversational interactions is coordinated. Schegloff directed attention to a frequently occurring initial exchange, which was called a "summons–answer sequence." This sequence is composed, he discovered, of closely linked parts. The production of the first turn in the sequence, the summons, projected a relevant next action, an answer, to be accomplished by the recipient of the summons in the very next turn. Moreover, the occurrence of the expected answer cannot properly be the final turn in the exchange. The summons–answer exchange is therefore nonterminal: Upon production of the answer, the summoner is then expected to speak again, to provide the reason for the summons. This provides for a coordinated entry into conversation, and for the possibility of an extended spate of talk.

Observe that a set of mutual obligations is established by the structural relationships between these sequence parts, with each current action projecting some "next." In the strongest form of these obligations (sequence classes vary in this regard), the property of "conditional relevance" holds between the parts of a sequence unit. A "summons–answer" sequence is but one type of a large class of utterance units, known as "adjacency pairs," that are characterized by this property. Examples here include "greeting–greeting," "question–answer," and "invitation–acceptance/declination." In adjacency pairs, when one utterance or action is conditionally relevant on another, the production of the first provides for the occurrence of the second. It could be said, then, using the example above, that the issuance of a summons is an action that selects a particular next action, an answer, for its recipient. If this action does not occur, its nonoccurrence will be a noticeable event. That is to say, it is not only nonoccurring, it is notably, "officially" absent; accordingly, this would warrant various inferences and actions. For instance, the summoner might infer that a recipient "didn't hear me," which would provide for the relevance and grounds of a repetition of the summons.

The discovery that human activities like conversation were coordinated and organized in a very fundamental way by such methodic relationships between actions, with some current or "first" action projecting and providing for some appropriate "second," led to investigations into the various methods by which the recipient of a first may accomplish a second, or recognizably hold its accomplishment in abeyance until issues relevant to its performance are clarified or resolved, or avoid its accomplishment altogether by undertaking some other activity. Researchers learned, for

example, that for some firsts, there was not a single appropriate second but rather a range of alternative seconds. Note that in the examples of adjacency pair structures listed just above, invitations project either an acceptance or a declination as a course of action available to the recipient. In this case, and in others like "request–granting/denial" and "compliment–acceptance/rejection," it was found that the alternative second parts are not generally of equal status; rather, some second parts are preferred and others dispreferred, these properties being distinct from the desires or motivations of the coparticipants. "Preference" thus refers to a structural rather than dispositional relationship between alternative but nonequivalent courses of action. Evidence for this includes distributional data across a wide range of speakers and settings, and, more important, the fact that preferred and dispreferred alternatives are regularly performed in distinctively different ways. The preference status of an action is therefore exhibited in how it is done.

Related to this, conversation analytic researchers observed that the producers of a first action often dealt in systematic, methodic ways with these properties of preference organization. To take one example, the producer of a request can and often does analyze the recipient silence that follows as displaying or implicating a denial—a denial as-yet-unstated, but nevertheless projected—and seeks to preempt the occurrence of this dispreferred action by issuing a subsequent version of the request, before the recipient starts to speak. Subsequent versions attempt to make the request more acceptable and provide another opportunity for a favorable response (Davidson 1984).

Moreover, members were observed to orient to the properties of preference organization through their performance of actions plainly meant to be understood as specifically preliminary to some adjacency pair first action. Such "pre"-type actions are designed to explore the likelihood that producing that first part of some pair will not be responded to in a dispreferred way. For instance, an utterance like "Are you doing anything tonight?" provides, in a methodical way, an opportunity for its producer to determine, without yet having to actually issue the invitation, whether it would most likely be declined. Similarly, this provides an opportunity for the recipient of the "pre" to indicate that a dispreferred action would be forthcoming without ever having to perform that action. Additionally, because "pre" actions themselves engender sequences by making some response to them a relevant next action, they constitute the first part of a "pre-sequence." It follows that since these and other features of preference organization together maximize the likelihood of preferred actions and minimize the likelihood of dispreferred ones, they serve as important structural resources for maintaining social solidarity and "preserving face."

These interrelated observations on the organization of sequences were generalized outward in conversation analytic research from the relatively simple adjacency pair organization by the recognition that virtually every utterance occurs at some sequentially relevant, structurally defined place in talk (see especially Atkinson and Heritage 1984, pp. 5-9). Moreover, it is this placement that provides the primary context for an utterance's intelligibility and understanding. Put another way, utterances are in the first place contextually understood by reference to their placement and participation within sequences of action, and it is therefore sequences of action, rather than single utterances or actions, that have become the primary units of analysis for the conversation-analytic enterprise. Accordingly, researchers in this tradition have not restricted themselves to studying only especially "tight" sequence units, but have instead broadened their investigations to (mentioning just a few) the sequencing of laughter, disputes, story and joke telling, political oratory, and the initiation and closing of topics. In addition, the sequential organization of gaze and body movement in relation to turns at talk has been the focus of some truly pathbreaking research using video recordings (see, for example, Goodwin 1981, 1994; Heath 1986).

Now let us consider the organization of turn taking, surely a central feature of virtually all talk-in-interaction. Recall that the prior discussion on the organization of sequences frequently made reference to sequence parts as "turns," implicitly trading on the understanding that talk in conversation is produced in and built for turns, with recurring speaker change and a consequent serial ordering of utterances. In conversation, this turn ordering, as well as the size and content of each

turn, is not predetermined or allocated in advance. Instead, it is locally determined, moment-by-moment, by the coparticipants in the talk. In fact, this completely local determination of who speaks when, how long they speak, and what they might say or do in their turn, is what provides for talk being hearable as a "conversation," rather than as, say, a debate or a ceremony of some kind. But this does not tell us just how—*methodically*—speaker change is achieved such that, ordinarily, one party talks at a time and there is little or no silence (or "gap") between turns. Clearly, this requires close coordination among coparticipants in any conversational encounter. The systematic practices by which this is accomplished are analyzed by Sacks, Schegloff, and Jefferson in a 1974 paper that remains one of the most important in the conversation-analysis literature.

Basic to the accomplishment of turn taking is the practice of changing speakers at possible utterance completion places, what Sacks, Schegloff, and Jefferson term *transition relevance places*. How are such places, where speaker change may relevantly occur but is in no way guaranteed or required, discernable by members? A key feature of the units by and through which turns are constructed offers one resource here: For an utterance to be usable as a turn constructional unit, it must have a recognizable completion, and that completion must be recognizable prior to its occurrence (Sacks, Schegloff, and Jefferson [1974] 1978, p. 12). That is to say, its completion is projectable, and a coparticipant in the conversation who wishes to speak next can therefore begin his or her turn just at the place where the current speaker projects completion.

Of course, this does not preclude this coparticipant, or any other, from starting to speak elsewhere in the course of a current speaker's turn. (Indeed, what actually constitutes a "turn at talk" is as locally and mutually determined as any other aspect of conversation's organization, even as the resources for doing so are general ones.) There are various interactional moves that could involve, as one way they might be accomplished, this sort of action. At the same time, however, research on turn-taking has revealed that turns beginning elsewhere may well be met with procedures systematically designed to enforce the practice of starting at possible completion places. Further, features of the turn taking system such as that described just above account for a great deal of the overlapping speech that can occasionally be observed. For instance, a speaker might append a tag question like "you know?" to his or her turn, while a coparticipant, having no resources available to project such an action, starts to speak just prior to or at the beginning of that appended tag, at the place that was projectably the "first possible completion" of the turn. This would result in overlapping speech, with both parties talking simultaneously. This was just one example; studies of "more than one party at a time" speech have uncovered massive evidence that its occurrence and its resolution (the restoration of one party at a time), as well as the solution to the problem of which overlapping action should then be consequential for next action, is methodically organized.

Having described the function of turn constructional practices in turn taking, Sacks, Schegloff, and Jefferson still faced the issue of how coparticipants, at possible completion places, determine just who will be the "next speaker" (note in this regard that conversation can involve more than two parties) or even if there will be a next speaker, given that a current speaker might want to continue talking. They discovered that to deal with this problem, members have available a "turn allocational component" for the system. This component consists of a set of ordered rules that come into play at transition relevance places and which provide for the methodic allocation of the right to produce a next turn, or more accurately, a turn constructional unit. In related research, methods for securing the temporary suspension of turn-taking procedures (to tell an extended story, for example) and for coordinating exit from the system (to end the conversation) have been documented.

Finally there is the entire set of procedures by which any troubles in speaking, hearing, and understanding talk are systematically handled and "repaired." As Schegloff (1979, p. 269) points out, insofar as "any of the systems and contingencies implicated in the production and reception of talk—articulatory, memory, sequential, syntactic, auditory, ambient noise, etc.—can fail," any piece of talk is susceptible to, or can reveal, troubles in speaking, hearing, or understanding. As a consequence, members of society must have some systematically organized set of methods for managing such trouble when it arises. Further, in order for interaction to serve as a primary site for the

coordination of social activity, any such troubles must be located and dealt with as quickly as possible to avoid whole stretches of talk developing on a problematic basis. Finally, this set of methods must provide the opportunity to discover and display trouble in speaking, hearing, or understanding by any of the ratified coparticipants to the interaction, while simultaneously managing such trouble from the variety of quarters from which it might arise, whether the trouble is noticed or produced by the current speaker or her recipient, and whether its source is endogenous to the interaction or impinges on it from outside.

When Schegloff, Sacks, and Jefferson (1977) began examining the related set of practices through which speakers managed such troubles they discovered two important features. First, they noticed that participants in interaction treat the initiation of repair as a separate matter from the actual accomplishment of a solution. That is, they distinguish between the various practices for locating a trouble source and making it the focus of the interaction and the set of practices for implementing a solution. Second, they observed that these two activities were not distributed evenly among the parties: The organization of repair exhibited a preference for self-repair and a preference for self-initiation of repair. And they went on to show that this latter feature is primarily a product of the way that the organization of repair relies on, and is fitted to, the system for distributing turns.

The organization of repair initiation operates in a restricted "repair initiation opportunity space" that is organized around the trouble source or "repairable." Within this repair initiation opportunity space each party to an interaction moves through a series of discrete opportunities to locate and indicate potential and actual troubles. In turn, these discrete opportunities to initiate repair shape where (relative to the trouble source) a repair is effected, and by whom. The current speaker has the first opportunity to initiate repair on any trouble source within his or her own turn while still in the midst of it, or just after it is complete but before a next speaker starts. If they do initiate repair during (or immediately following the possible completion of) their own turn, such speakers also have the first opportunity to effect repair as well.

Of course, as we noted above, conversation is characterized by the alternation between current and next, thus once a current speaker completes her turn a next speaker begins, typically by addressing herself to that just-prior talk. Accordingly, if a next speaker has some trouble with the prior speaker's turn, the next turn is the place where she can initiate repair (using a variety of forms, including "what?" and "huh?" and other designs that vary in the degree to which they specify the exact source of trouble). By initiating repair using one of these methods, that speaker selects the speaker of the trouble source to speak next, and to offer a solution to the trouble indicated. If the next speaker has no trouble with the prior turn, and she uses it to move the action forward (instead of stopping it to initiate repair), her turn will display a variety of understandings regarding the talk it follows. In doing so, her turn may also reveal some type of misunderstanding (from the point of view of the speaker of the prior turn). If that occurs the speaker of the prior turn can then initiate repair in "turn after next" (or "third position") and offer a solution immediately. Perhaps the recurrent and recognizable format for this is "I don't mean x, I mean y."

Thus, the movement of talk through these three positions—current, next turn, and turn after next—systematically provides the various parties to the interaction the opportunity to detect any trouble in speaking, hearing, and understanding, whatever its source, and initiate repair on it. As a consequence almost all instances of repair are initiated in one of these adjacent locations. The localization of repair initiation opportunities, and the distribution of them over three turns, has several consequences for the organization of social life. First, the localization of repair within a finite, and relatively restricted, space ensures that trouble is dealt with swiftly. Second, and related to this, given the systematic relevance of repair, if speakers move through these three positions without any party initiating repair, a shared understanding of the talk is thereby confirmed *en passant*.

Finally, as with sequence organization, the issue of preference is best grasped as a structural property of the organization of talk-in-interaction (rather than being a product of concerns regarding the private desires of the parties). The two preferences observed by Schegloff, Sacks, and Jefferson are a product of the distribution of opportunities to initiate and effect repair that systematically favors the speaker of the trouble source over others. As Sacks, Schegloff, and Jefferson ([1974] 1978, p. 40) put it, the organization of turn taking and the organization of repair "are thus 'made for each other' in a double sense." It is worth noting in this regard that insofar as interaction provides the primary site for the achievement of intersubjectivity, for what makes sociality possible, the organization of repair constitutes its last line of defense (Schegloff 1994).

Taken together, the operation of the turn-taking system and the practices involved in the organization of sequences and repair account for many of the detectable, orderly features of conversation. This orderliness was shown to be locally organized and managed, the product of members' methods. It will be useful to make note once again of the research strategy that enabled such findings. Because the data consisted of recordings of naturally occurring activity, a scientific account of the phenomenon under investigation could be empirically grounded in the details of actual occurrences. The investigation began with a set of observable outcomes of these occurrences—in the case of turn taking, for example, speaker change overwhelmingly recurred; overwhelmingly, one party talked at a time; turn order, size, and content were not fixed, but varied; and so on. It was then asked: Could these outcomes be described as products of certain social organized practices, of methods of conduct? At the same time, if members of society did in fact use such formal methods, how were they systematically employed to produce just those outcomes, in just those occurrences, in all their specificity? In addressing the problem in this way, then, conversation analysis was able to discover how cardinal forms of social order were locally constituted.

The research on turn taking in conversation has provided one starting point for more recent studies of interaction in "institutional" settings, such as news interviews, doctor-patient and other clinical consultations, courtrooms, plea bargaining sessions, job interviews, and citizen calls to emergency services. In many of these studies, researchers pursued Sacks, Schegloff, and Jefferson's ([1974] 1978, pp. 45–47) suggestion that the practices underlying the management of ordinary conversation are the "base" or primary ones (for an example, see Heritage and Maynard in press).

Other forms of interaction—in this case, so-called "institutional" forms—are in part constituted and recognizable through systematic variations from conversational turn taking, or through the narrowing and respecification of particular conversational practices involved in the organization of sequences, repair, and other activities.

Take the case of courtroom interaction. The turn-taking system operative in these encounters places restrictions on turn construction and allocation: Coparticipants ordinarily restrict themselves to producing turns that are at least minimally recognizable as "questions" and "answers," and these turn types are pre-allocated to different parties rather than locally determined. The relatively restricted patterns of conduct observable in these settings is, in large part, the product of this form of turn taking. Accordingly, variation in turn taking in such settings has been shown to have a "pervasive influence both on the range and design of the interactional activities which the different parties routinely undertake and on the detailed management of such encounters" (Heritage 1987, p. 261; Atkinson and Drew 1979).

Note that throughout the above discussion, the term "institutional" has been presented with quotation marks around it. This was done to emphasize ethnomethodology's preoccupation with the local production of social order. From this view, that some activity or encounter is recognizably either an "ordinary conversation" or more "institutional" in nature—for example, is recognizably a "cross-examination," a "call to the police," a "clinical consultation," or whatever—is something that the coparticipants can and do realize, procedurally, at each and every moment of the encounter. The task for the analyst is to demonstrate how they actually do this; how, for example, they construct their conduct, turn by turn, so as to progressively constitute and thus jointly and collaboratively realize the occasion of their encounter, together with their own social roles in it, as having some distinctively institutional sense (Heritage and Greatbatch 1991). Conversation analytic research on "institutional" interaction has therefore undertaken, through its investigations into the methodic practices by which this gets done, a systematic study of a wide range of human activities.

This mode of research, with its commitment to understanding precisely how any activity becomes what it recognizably and accountably is—that is to say, how it acquires its social facticity-has tended to focus in the 1990s on work activities and settings, under the rubric of "workplace studies." The scope of investigation has expanded to encompass all forms of "embodied action" (that is, not only the talk), with extensive use of video recordings and, influenced by Suchman's (1987) pioneering study of human-machine interaction, with careful attention to how the machines, technologies, and other artifacts that saturate the modern work site are taken up and enter into the endogenous organization of work tasks (see, for example, Whalen (1995), and the papers collected in Luff, Hindmarsh, and Heath in press).

Research into conversation's organization also continues to evolve. While there has been relatively little work that attempts to fundamentally deepen the original account of the turn-taking system developed by Sacks, Schegloff, and Jefferson (for a notable exception see Lerner 1996), there has been important research at the intersection of grammar and interaction—recognizing that talk-in-interaction is in fact the natural home of human language. This work demonstrates that the approach to language taken Chomsky's Transformational Grammar could be supplanted by one based on naturalistic study of the "grammar for conversation." Given that Chomsky's approach has decisively shaped, both directly and indirectly, the understanding of language in cognitive science, psychology, computational linguistics, and the other disciplines that rely on a model of grammatical organization for their own research, these findings are plainly significant.

Conversation analytic work on graamar and interaction was launched by Schegloff's (1979) paper on the "relevance of repair for a syntax for conversation." This line of work has underscored the need for studies of language to draw on naturally occurring spates of talk. As Schegloff observed, while nearly every episode of ordinary talk contains instances of repair within the "sentences" (or sentential turn constructional units) out of which it is built, the entire view of language developed by linguists is based on imagined (or what might as well be imagined) instances of language that are free of such repair. Schegloff went on to show that most instances of talk-in-interaction, at least in English, are organized by reference to the systematic relevance of repair, whether an instance of it actually occurs in the sentence or not.

Of course repair is not the only organization relevant for grammar, and so more recently scholars have begun to examine what more might be learned about language by studying it as produced in naturally occurring interaction. With respect to this problem, conversation analysts have argued that insofar as language most likely evolved in face-to-face encounters by members of our species, its structure and organization must have evolved, at least in part, to manage the basic exigencies confronted by speakers and hearers. Thus, in addition to the systematic relevance of repair, the structure and organization of grammar most likely evolved as resources that shape, and are shaped by, how opportunities to speak are distributed, what constraints are introduced by a current turn on subsequent ones, and how speakers' formulations of the events, persons, and objects are organized. Perhaps most developed are a series of findings that link the organization of grammar and the system for distributing turns at talk briefly described above.

As we stated earlier regarding turn-constructional units, one of their key features is that each sentence, or utterance, projects from its beginning roughly what it will take for it to be possibly complete. And over its course, each utterance projects in finer and finer detail the exact moment that a speaker may end her utterance. Thus, instead of expressing logical predicates or cognitive states, grammar may be best understood, in the first instance, as a sequentially sensitive resource that progressively projects the course and duration of turns at talk (Ford and Thompson 1996).

One of the most striking consequences of such a view of grammar is that the locus of its organization is transformed. While most approaches to grammar rely on the sentence as the basic unit of organization (with occasional nods to the organization of "discourse"), the grammatical units produced in interaction are fundamentally organized relative to their sequential environment, most proximally the just prior, current, and next turns. Thus, rather than the sentence, or even discourse, being the fundamental unit or environment of

analysis, interaction and sequences of turns appear to be that within which grammar is most proximally organized. This appears to be true even at levels beneath the turn whether a sentence, clause, or phrase. As Schegloff (1996) shows, turn beginnings and turn endings, as well as what happens in between, are sites of strategic manipulation. Through this manipulation, both grammatical and prosodic, speakers fit their utterances to prior talk, launch new actions, and shape when they will be heard as possibly complete. Any scientific analysis of language, then, must take into account this central function.

Thus, as the collection of papers assembled in Ochs, Schegloff, and Thompson (1996) suggest, rather than viewing grammar as an independent, clearly delineated, and internally coherent structure, it is best approached as one more of the interrelated set of resources through which interaction, and social life more broadly, is organized.

REFERENCES

Atkinson, J. Maxwell, and Paul Drew 1979 *Order in Court: The Organization of Verbal Interaction in Judicial Settings*. London: Macmillan.

Atkinson, J. Maxwell, and John Heritage (eds.) 1984 *Structures of Social Action: Studies in Conversation Analysis*. Cambridge, Eng.: Cambridge University Press.

—— 1984 "Introduction." In J. Maxwell Atkinson and John Heritage, eds., *Structures of Social Action: Studies in Conversation Analysis*. Cambridge, Eng.: Cambridge University Press.

Bales, Robert F. 1950 *Interaction Process Analysis*. Cambridge, Mass.: Addison-Wesley.

Button, Graham, and John R. E. Lee (eds.) 1987 *Talk and Social Organization*. Clevedon, Eng.: Multilingual Matters.

Davidson, Judy 1984 "Subsequent Versions of Invitations, Offers, Requests, and Proposals Dealing with Potential or Actual Rejection." In J. Maxwell Atkinson and John Heritage, eds., *Structures of Social Action: Studies in Conversation Analysis*. Cambridge, Eng.: Cambridge University Press.

Ford, Cecilia E., and Sandra A. Thompson 1996 "Interactional Units in Conversation: Syntactic, Intonational, and Pragmatic Resources for the Management of Turns." In Elinor Ochs, Emanuel A. Schegloff and Sandra A. Thompson, eds., *Interaction and Grammar.* Cambridge, Eng.: Cambridge University Press.

Garfinkel, Harold 1991 "Respecification: Evidence for Locally Produced, Naturally Accountable Phenomena of Order, Logic, Reason, Meaning, Method, etc. in and as of the Essential Haecceity of Immortal Ordinary Society (I)–An Announcement of Studies." In Graham Button, ed., *Ethnomethodology and the Human Sciences.* Cambridge, Eng.: Cambridge University Press.

—— (1967) 1984 *Studies in Ethnomethodology.* Cambridge: Polity Press.

Goodwin, Charles 1994 "Professional Vision." *American Anthropologist* 96:606–633.

—— 1981 *Conversational Organization: Interaction Between Speakers and Hearers.* New York: Academic Press.

Heath, Christian C. 1986 *Body Movement and Speech in Medical Interaction.* Cambridge, Eng.: Cambridge University Press.

Heritage, John 1987 "Ethnomethodology." In Anthony Giddens and Jonathan H. Turner, eds., *Social Theory Today.* Stanford, Calif.: Stanford University Press.

——, and David Greatbatch 1991 "On the Institutional Character of Institutional Talk: The Case of News Interviews." In Deirdre Boden and Don H. Zimmerman, eds., *Talk and Social Structure.* Cambridge: Polity Press.

Heritage, John, and Douglas W. Maynard (eds.) In press *Practicing Medicine: Talk and Action in Primary Care Encounters.* Cambridge, Eng.: Cambridge University Press.

Homans, George C. 1961 *Social Behavior: Its Elementary Forms.* New York: Harcourt Brace.

Lerner, Gene H. 1996 "On the 'Semi-Permeable' Character of Grammatical Units in Conversation: Conditional Entry into the Turn Space of Another Speaker." In Elinor Ochs, Emanuel A. Schegloff, and Sandra A. Thompson, eds., *Interaction and Grammar.* Cambridge, Eng.: Cambridge University Press.

Luff, Paul, John Hindmarsh, and Christian Heath (eds.) In press *Workplace Studies: Recovering Work Practice and Informing Systems Design.* Cambridge, Eng.: Cambridge University Press.

Maynard, Douglas W. 1997 "The News Delivery Sequence: Bad News and Good News in Conversational Interaction." *Research on Language and Social Interaction* 30:93–130.

Ochs, Elinor, Emanuel A. Schegloff, and Sandra A. Thompson (eds.) 1996 *Interaction and Grammar.* Cambridge, Eng.: Cambridge University Press.

Sacks, Harvey 1992. *Lectures on Conversation.* 2 vols. Oxford: Blackwell.

—— (1964–1968) 1984 "Notes on Methodology." In J. Maxwell Atkinson and John Heritage, eds., *Structures of Social Action: Studies in Conversation Analysis.* Cambridge, Eng.: Cambridge University Press.

—— 1972 "An Initial Investigation into the Usability of Conversational Data for Doing Sociology." In David Sudnow, ed., *Studies in Social Interaction.* New York: Free Press.

——, Emanuel A. Schegloff, and Gail Jefferson (1974) 1978 "A Simplest Systematics for the Organization of Turn-Taking for Conversation." In Jim Schenkein, ed., *Studies in the Organization of Conversational Interaction.* New York: Academic Press.

Schegloff, Emanuel A. 1996 "Turn Organization: One Intersection of Grammar and Interaction." In Elinor Ochs, Emanuel A. Schegloff, and Sandra A. Thompson, eds., *Interaction and Grammar.* Cambridge, Eng.: Cambridge University Press.

—— 1989 "Harvey Sacks–Lectures 1964–1965. An Introduction/Memoir." *Human Studies* 12:185–209.

—— 1988 "Goffman and the Analysis of Conversation." In Paul Drew and Anthony Wootton, eds., *Erving Goffman: Exploring the Interaction Order.* Boston: Northeastern University Press.

—— 1979 "The Relevance of Repair for Syntax-for-Conversation." In T. Givon, ed., *Syntax and Semantics 12: Discourse and Syntax.* New York: Academic Press.

—— 1968 "Sequencing in Conversational Openings." *American Anthropologist* 70:1075–1095.

——, Gail Jefferson, and Harvey Sacks 1977 "The Preference for Self-Correction in the Organization of Repair in Conversation." *Language* 53:361–382.

Schegloff, Emanuel A., and Harvey Sacks 1973 "Opening Up Closings." *Semiotica* 7:289–327.

Schenkein, Jim (ed.) 1978 *Studies in the Organization of Conversational Interaction.* New York: Academic Press.

Silverman, David 1998 *Harvey Sacks: Social Science and Conversation Analysis.* New York: Oxford University Press.

Suchman, Lucy A. 1987 *Plans and Situated Actions: The Problem of Human-Machine Communication.* Cambridge, Eng.: Cambridge University Press.

Sudnow, David (ed.) 1972 *Studies in Social Interaction.* New York: Free Press.

ten Have, Paul, and George Psathas 1995 *Situated Order: Studies in the Social Organization of Talk and Embodied Activities.* Washington, D.C.: University Press of America.

Whalen, Jack 1995 "A Technology of Order Production: Computer-Aided Dispatch in 9-1-1 Communications." In Paul ten Have and George Psathas, eds.,

Situated Order: Studies in the Social Organization of Talk and Embodied Activities. Washington, D.C.: University Press of America.

JACK WHALEN
GEOFF RAYMOND

COOPERATION AND COMPETITION

See Small Groups.

CORPORATE ORGANIZATIONS

NOTE: *Although the following article has not been revised for this edition of the Encyclopedia, the substantive coverage is currently appropriate. The editors have provided a list of recent works at the end of the article to facilitate research and exploration of the topic.*

Societies carry out many of their activities through formal organizations. Organizations are units in which offices, or positions, have distinct but interdependent duties. Organizations—hospitals, schools, governments, business firms—share certain features. Usually, at least one of the offices serves as the linchpin: It coordinates the separate duties within the organization. The key office has ultimate authority in that the orders it issues constrain the actions of lower-level offices.

But organizations also differ from one another. In some, the assets belong to particular individuals. In others, ownership resides in a collectivity. The latter represents a corporate organization or *corporation*. Three features describe the modern corporation. First, it has certain legal rights and privileges. By law, a corporation can sue and be sued in the courts, make contracts, and purchase and receive property. Second, it usually exists in perpetuity: It outlasts the individuals who set it up. Ownership rests with stockholders, whose numbers and makeup can change from one time to another. Third, the owners have only a limited responsibility for the obligations the corporation makes.

These features distinguish the corporate organization from two other forms of ownership: the *proprietorship* and the *partnership*. In a proprietorship a particular person owns the property of the organization; in a partnership, two or more persons share it. The right to handle the property and affairs of the organization rests with a designated proprietor or set of partners. Significantly, proprietors and partners bear personal responsibility for the debts of the organization.

The corporation constitutes a social invention. The form evolved to handle problems that arose within religious, political, and other kinds of communities. It holds a place of importance in contemporary Western societies. Because it is the product of social conditions and an influence on them, the corporation represents a topic of substantial interest in sociology.

At present, the corporation appears commonly within the world of business. But when the corporation began to take shape during the Middle Ages, the questions to be resolved lay outside that realm. One of these questions had to do with church ownership. In medieval Germany, landowners often set up churches on their estates and placed a priest in charge of them. As priests gained authority over their charges, they argued that the church and the land surrounding it no longer belonged to the donor. Deciding the true owner proved to be difficult. A given priest could die or be replaced; hence, any particular priest seemed to have no claim to ownership. One practice regarded the owner to be the saint whose name the church bore. Eventually, the idea developed that ownership inhered in the church, and that the church constituted a body independent of its current leaders or members (Coleman 1974; Stone 1975).

Thorny problems also arose as medieval settlements formed into towns. A town required someone to manage its affairs such as collecting tolls and transacting other business. But the laws that prevailed at the time applied only to individuals. Any actions individuals took obligated them personally. By this principle, managers would have to meet any commitments they made on behalf of the town. To eliminate the dilemmas that the principle situation posed, new laws made the town a corporate person. The corporate person would have all the rights and privileges of any human being. This action reduced the risks that public service might otherwise entail. For many of the same reasons that the church and town became corporate persons, the university of the Middle Ages moved towards the corporate form.

The early corporations played rather passive roles. Essentially, they held property for a collective, whose members might change from time to time. Contrastingly, the corporations of the twentieth century constitute spirited forces. They hire multitudes of employees. They produce goods and services and mold ideals and tastes. The decisions their leaders make about where to locate often determine which locales will prosper and which will languish.

The influence that corporations have produces concerns about the control of them. Much of the work on corporations that sociologists have undertaken highlights these concerns. The work on control and corporations covers three topics: the means through which corporations control their employees; the allocation of control between owners and managers; and the extent to which societies control corporations. For all three topics, control implies command over the affairs of and operations within the corporate organization.

CONTROL OVER EMPLOYEES

The corporate form has a long history, yet it did not typify the early factories that manufacturers established in the United States. Before the early 1900s, most factories operated as small operations under the control of a single entrepreneur. The entrepreneur hired an overseer who might in turn choose a foreman to hire, discipline, and fire workers. Through consolidation and merger, the economic landscape of the 1920s revealed far more large organizations than had the tableau of a half-century earlier.

More changed over the years of the late nineteenth and early twentieth centuries than just the size of organizations. The corporate form spread; the faceless corporation replaced the corporeal entrepreneur. Corporations moved towards professional management. Factories that businessmen once controlled personally now operated through abstract rules and procedures. The people whom the workers now contacted on a regular basis consisted of staff for the corporation and not the corporate owners themselves. Bureaucratic tenets took root.

A bureaucracy constitutes a particular mode that organizations can take. Consistent with all organizations, bureaucratic ones divide up duties. Two features separate a bureaucracy from other modes, however. First, a system of ranks or levels operates. Second, fixed rules and procedures govern actions. The rules define the tasks, responsibilities, and authority for each office and each level.

Few of the factories in nineteenth-century America operated as bureaucracies. Instead, the individuals who made the products decided how the work would be done. A minimum number of levels existed. Supervisors or foremen hired and fired workers, but workers made the rules on the work itself. The workers were craftsmen or artisans, and they contended that only those who possessed the skills that the work demands should decide how or if it should be divided. Gradually, machinery took over the skilled work. Machines and not workers controlled the pace. By the end of the 1920s, neither the laborers nor the machinery shaped the work. Professional managers did. These managers enforced rules and oversaw an organization where specialized tasks and graded authority prevailed (Nelson 1975; Clawson 1980; and Jacoby 1985).

The corporation of the late twentieth century continues to operate as a bureaucracy. Some sources argue that efficiency explains the adoption of the bureaucratic model (see especially Chandler 1980, 1984). Others challenge the emphasis on efficiency, charging it with being overly rational or too apolitical. The first challenge appears most notably in the work on organizations as institutions. This literature regards survival as the premier goal for any organization. The closer an organization approximates an institution—an element taken for granted in the society—the greater its chances for survival.

According to the institutional perspective, organizations adopt practices that appear to be reasonable. Myths develop about which patterns prove most useful and efficient, and any organization that does not adopt a pattern that the myth favors courts failure (Meyer and Rowan 1977; DiMaggio 1988; DiMaggio and Powell 1983; Tolbert and Zucker 1983; also see Scott 1987 for a review of the different branches of institutional theory).

A different argument maintains that the emphasis on efficiency fails to capture the politics of corporations. This perspective treats corporations as systems in which the interests of owners clash with those of workers. Owners, it asserts, seek to reduce uncertainties and to eliminate the vagaries that can plague organizations. From this angle, bureaucracy serves the interests of owners primarily because it reduces the influence that workers exercise and thereby removes a source of uncertainty (Braverman 1974; Edwards 1979).

Workers need not have formal authority in order to affect outcomes within organizations. Studies document the creative ways in which employees enliven monotonous jobs and pursue their own ends (Roy 1952; Mechanic 1962; Burawoy 1979, 1985). Yet, officially, the higher levels have greater power than have the lower levels. This is the consequence of the bureaucratic nature of corporations, not of their pattern of ownership. The bureaucratic mode is not unique to corporations. Proprietorships and partnerships can display the traits of bureaucracy. The diffuseness of ownership that one finds in the corporation possibly makes formal control less obvious than obtains when ownership resides in identifiable persons.

OWNER VERSUS MANAGERIAL CONTROL

Managers occupy important places in the contemporary organization. One argument regards managers as more powerful than stockholders. Adolph Berle and Gardiner Means offered this argument in the 1930s. As Berle and Means saw the situation, stockholding had become too widely dispersed for any individual holder or even group of holders to command corporations. Managers, they contended, filled the void (Berle and Means 1932). Later discussions echoed the thesis that the expansion of the corporate form had raised the power of corporate managers (Berg and Zald 1978; also see Chandler 1962, 1977).

Critics contend that the thesis overstates the role and power of managers. They base their criticism on studies of the influence that corporate leaders wield. Maurice Zeitlin (1974) helped launch this line of research when he argued that few scholars had tested the Berle and Means thesis and that the handful of extant studies showed owners to be less fractious and fractionated than the thesis supposed. Michael Useem (1984), among others,

heeded the call from Zeitlin for research on the networks that link shareholders. Useem concluded from his study on contacts and networks among large shareholders that a corporate community operated, held together by an inner circle whose interests transcended company, region, and industry lines. Beth Mintz and Michael Schwartz (1985) examined the connections between financial institutions and other corporations and decided that control over corporate directions rested disproportionately in the world of finance. The work from the critics cautions us against the assumption that a multiplicity of owners implies control by managers.

SOCIAL CONTROL OVER CORPORATIONS

The corporate form constitutes a remarkable innovation. But as the corporation has become ever more active and entrenched, it has generated problems for society. Corporations have at times engaged in criminal behavior (Sutherland 1949; Clinard and Yeager 1980). At other times, their actions have violated no law but have put the well-being of the public at risk. Both situations often show the inadequacy of the mechanisms through which society attempts to control corporations.

Corporations are creatures of the state. Ostensibly, then, they operate only at the indulgence of the state. But myriad corporations now have greater resources than do the states that chartered them. Moreover, the laws that states have at their disposal often fit individuals better than they do corporations. Corporations can be sued for wrongdoing; but a fine that would bankrupt an individual might be a mere pittance for a large corporation. Both James Coleman (1974) and Christopher Stone (1975) have argued that the law can never be the sole means for controlling corporations; a sense of responsibility to the public must prevail within corporations.

Even if the law were shown to be effective in constraining corporations within a state, it might prove rather impotent in the case of multinational organizations. A multinational or transnational corporation holds a charter from one nation-state but transacts business in at least one other. The governmental entity that issues the charter cannot alter the policies the corporation pursues in its other locales. In addition, the very size of many multinationals restricts the pressure that either the home or the host country can impose.

Through various actions corporations demonstrate that they are attentive to the societies they inhabit. Corporate leaders serve on the boards of social service agencies; corporate foundations provide funds for community programs; employees donate their time to local causes. The agenda of corporations long have included these and similar activities. Increasingly, the agenda organize such actions around the idea of corporate social responsibility. Acting responsibly means taking steps to promote the commonweal (Steckmest 1982).

Some corporations strive more consistently to advance social ends than do others. Differences in norms and values apparently explain the contrast. Norms, or maxims for behavior, indicate the culture of the organization (Deal and Kennedy 1982). The culture of some settings gives the highest priority to actions that protect the health, safety, and welfare of citizens and their heirs. Elsewhere, those are not what the culture emphasizes (Clinard 1983; Victor and Cullen 1988).

The large corporation had become such a dominant force by the 1980s that no one envisioned a return to an era of small, diffuse organizations. Yet, during that decade some sectors had started to move from growth to contraction. At times, the shift resulted from legislative action. When the Bell Telephone System divided in 1984, by order of the courts, the change marked a sharp reversal. For more than a century the system had glided toward integration and standardization (Barnett and Carroll 1987; Barnett 1990).

Whether through fiat or choice, corporations contract (Whetten 1987; Hambrick and D'Aveni 1988). Two perspectives associate the rise and fall in the fortunes of corporations to changes in the social context. The first perspective, resource dependence, centers on the idea that organizations must secure their resources from their environs (McCarthy and Zald 1977; Jenkins 1983). When those environs contain a wealth of resources—personnel in the numbers and with the qualifications the organization requires, funds to finance operations—the corporation can thrive. When hard times plague the environs, the corporation escapes that fate only with great difficulty.

The perspective known as population ecology likewise connects the destiny of organizations to conditions in their surroundings. Population ecologists think of organizations as members of a population. Changing social conditions can enrich or impoverish a population. Individual units within it can do little to offset the tide of events that threatens to envelop the entire population. (Hannan and Freeman 1988; Wholey and Brittain 1989; for a critique of the approach see Young 1988).

Neither resource dependency theory nor population ecology theory focuses explicitly on the corporate form. But just as analyses of corporations inform the discussions sociologists have undertaken on formal organizations, models drawn from studies of organizations have proved useful as scholars have tracked the progress of corporations.

The corporation clearly constitutes a power to be reckoned with. As with its precursors, the modern corporation serves needs that collectivities develop. In fact, the corporation rests on an assumption that is fundamental in sociology: A collectivity has an identity of its own. But the corporation of the twentieth century touches more than those persons who own its assets or produce its goods. This social instrument of the Middle Ages is now a social fixture.

(SEE ALSO: *Capitalism; Organizational Effectiveness; Organizational Structure; Transnational Corporations*)

REFERENCES

Antai, Ariane-Berthoin 1992 *Corporate Social Performance: Rediscovering Actors in Their Organizational Contexts.* Boulder, Colo.: Westview Press.

Barnett, William P. 1990 "The Organizational Ecology of a Technological System." *Administrative Science Quarterly* 35:31–60.

Barnett, William P., and Glenn Carroll 1987 "Competition and Mutualism Among Early Telephone Companies." *Administrative Science Quarterly* 32:400–421.

Berg, Ivar, and Mayer N. Zald 1978 "Business and Society." *Annual Review of Sociology* 4:115–143.

Berle, Adolph A., and Gardiner C. Means 1932 *The Modern Corporation and Private Property.* New York: Macmillan.

Braverman, Harry 1974 *Labor and Monopoly Capital: The Degradation of Work in the Twentieth Century.* New York: Monthly Review.

Breedlove, William L., and J. Michael Armer 1996 "Economic Disarticulation and Social Development in Less-Developed Nations: A Cross-National Study of Intervening Structures." *Sociological Focus* 29:359–378.

Burawoy, Michael 1979 *Manufacturing Consent: Changes in the Labor Process under Monopoly Capitalism.* Chicago: University of Chicago Press.

——1985 *The Politics of Production: Factory Regimes under Capitalism and Socialism.* London: Verso.

Chandler, Alfred D., Jr. 1962 *Strategy and Structure.* Cambridge, Mass.: MIT Press.

——1977 *The Visible Hand.* Cambridge, Mass.: Harvard University Press.

——1980 "The United States: Seedbed of Managerial Capitalism." In A. D. Chandler, Jr., and Herman Daems, eds., *Managerial Hierarchies.* Cambridge, Mass.: Harvard University Press.

——1984 "The Emergence of Managerial Capitalism." *Business History Review* 58:484–504.

Clawson, Dan 1980 *Bureaucracy and the Labor Process.* New York: Monthly Labor Review.

Clinard, Marshall B. 1983 *Corporate Ethics and Crime.* Beverly Hills, Calif.: Sage.

——, and Peter C. Yeager 1980 *Corporate Crime.* New York: Free Press.

Coleman, James S. 1974 *Power and the Structure of Society.* New York: Norton.

Coleman, James S. 1996 "The Asymmetric Society: Organizational Actors, Corporate Power, and the Irrelevance of Persons." In M. David Ermann, and Richard J. Lundman, eds., *Corporate and Governmental Deviance: Problems of Organizational Behavior in Contemporary Society.* New York: Oxford University Press.

Cuthbert, Alexander R., and Keith G. McKinnell 1997 "Ambiguous Space, Ambiguous Rights-Corporate Power and Social Control in Hong Kong." *Cities* 14: 295–311.

Davis, Gerald F. 1994 "The Corporate Elite and the Politics of Corporate Control." *Current Perspectives in Social Theory* 1: 215–238.

Davis, Gerald F., Kristina A. Diekmann, and Catherine H. Tinsley. 1994. "The Decline and Fall of the Conglomerate Firm in the 1980s: The Deinstitutionalization of an Organizational Form." *American Sociological Review* 59: 547–570.

Deal, Terrence, and Allen Kennedy 1982 *Corporate Culture.* Reading, Mass.: Addison-Wesley.

DiMaggio, Paul 1988 "Interest and Agency in Institutional Theory." In Lynne G. Zucker, ed., *Research on Institutional Patterns: Environment and Culture.* Cambridge, Mass.: Ballinger.

——, and Walter Powell 1983 "The Iron Cage Revisited: Institutional Isomorphism and Collective Rationality in Organizational Fields." *American Sociological Review* 48:147–160.

Donaldson, Thomas 1992 "Individual Rights and Multinational Corporate Responsibilities." *National Forum* 72: 7–9.

Dunford, Louise, and Ann Ridley 1996 "No Soul to Be Damned, No Body to Be Kicked: Responsibility, Blame and Corporate Punishment." *International Journal of the Sociology of Law* 24:1–19.

Dunworth, Terence, and Joel Rogers 1996 "Corporations in Court: Big Business Litigation in U.S. Federal Courts, 1971–1991." *Law and Social Inquiry* 21: 497–592.

Edwards, Richard 1979 *Contested Terrain: The Transformation of the Workplace in the Twentieth Century.* New York: Basic Books.

Etzioni, Amitai 1993 "The U.S. Sentencing Commission on Corporate Crime: A Critique." *Annals of the American Academy of Political and Social Science* 525: 147–156.

Hambrick, Donald C., and Richard A. D'Aveni 1988 "Large Corporate Failures as Downward Spirals." *Administrative Science Quarterly* 33:1–23.

Hannan, Michael, and John Freeman 1988 *Organizational Ecology.* Cambridge, Mass.: Harvard University Press.

Hawley, James P. 1995 "Political Voice, Fiduciary Activism, and the Institutional Ownership of U.S. Corporations: The Role of Public and Noncorporate Pension Funds." *Sociological Perspectives* 38:415–435.

Ireland, Paddy 1996 "Corporate Governance, Stakeholding, and the Company: Towards a Less Degenerate Capitalism?" *Journal of Law and Society* 23:287–320.

Jacoby, Sanford 1985 *Employing Bureaucracy: Managers, Unions and the Transformation of Work in American Industry, 1900–1945.* New York: Columbia University Press.

Jenkins, J. Craig 1983 "Resource Mobilization Theory and the Study of Social Movements." *Annual Review of Sociology* 42:249–268.

Jones, Marc T. 1996 "The Poverty of Corporate Social Responsibility." *Quarterly Journal of Ideology* 19:1–2.

Lofquist, William S. 1993 "Legislating Organizational Probation: State Capacity, Business Power, and Corporate Crime Control." *Law and Society Review* 27: 741–783.

Luchansky, Bill, and Gregory Hooks 1996 "Corporate Beneficiaries of the Mid-Century Wars: Respecifying

Models of Corporate Growth, 1939–1959." *Social Science Quarterly* 77:301–313.

McCarthy, John D., and Mayer N. Zald 1977 "Resource Mobilization and Social Movements: A Partial Theory." *American Journal of Sociology* 82:1212–1241.

McKinlay, Alan, and Ken Starkey 1998 *Foucalt, Management and Organizations Theory: From Panopticion to Technologies of Self.* London: Sage Publications.

Mechanic, David 1962 "Sources of Power of Lower Participants in Complex Organizations."*Administrative Science Quarterly* 7:349–364.

Meyer, John, and Brian Rowan 1977 "Institutionalized Organizations: Formal Structure as Myth and Ceremony." *American Sociological Review* 83:340–363.

Mintz, Beth, and Michael Schwartz 1985 *The Power Structure of American Business.* Chicago: University of Chicago Press.

Nelson, Daniel 1975 *Managers and Workers.* Madison: University of Wisconsin Press.

Parker-Gwin, Rachel, and William G. Roy 1996 "Corporate Law and the Organization of Property in the United States: The Origin and Institutionalization of New Jersey Corporation Law, 1888–1903." *Politics and Society* 24:111–135.

Prechel, Harland 1994 "Economic Crisis and the Centralization of Control over the Managerial Process: Corporate Restructuring and Neo-Fordist Decision-Making." *American Sociological Review* 59:723–745.

Ridley, Ann, and Louise Dunford 1994 "Corporate Liability for Manslaughter: Reform and the Art of the Possible." *International Journal of the Sociology of Law* 22:309–328.

Rodman, Kenneth A. 1995 "Sanctions at Bay? Hegemonic Decline, Multinational Corporations, and U.S. Economic Sanctions since the Pipeline Case." *International Organization* 49:105–137.

Roy, Donald 1952 "Restriction of Output in a Piecework Machine Shop." Ph.D. diss., University of Chicago, Chicago.

Sanders, Joseph, and V. Lee Hamilton 1996 "Distributing Responsibility for Wrongdoing inside Corporate Hierarchies: Public Judgments in Three Societies." *Law and Social Inquiry* 21:815–855.

Scott, W. Richard 1987 "The Adolescence of Institutional Theory." *Administrative Science Quarterly* 32:493–511.

Steckmest, Francis W. 1982 *Corporate Performance: The Key to Public Trust.* New York: McGraw-Hill.

Stone, Christopher D. 1975 *Where the Law Ends: The Social Control of Corporate Behavior.* New York: Harper.

Sutherland, Edwin H. 1949 *White Collar Crime.* New York: Holt, Rinehart, and Winston.

Tolbert, Pamela S., and Lynne G. Zucker 1983 "Institutional Sources of Change in the Formal Structure of Organizations: The Diffusion of Civil Service Reform, 1880–1935." *Administrative Science Quarterly* 28:22–39.

Useem, Michael 1984 *The Inner Circle: Large Corporations and the Rise of Political Activity in the U.S. and U.K.* New York: Oxford University Press.

Victor, Bart, and John B. Cullen 1988 "The Organizational Bases of Ethical Work Climates." *Administrative Science Quarterly* 33:101–125.

Westphal, James D., and Edward J. Zajac 1997 "Defections from the Inner Circle: Social Exchange, Reciprocity, and the Diffusion of Board Independence in U.S. Corporations." *Administrative Science Quarterly* 42:161–183.

Whetten, David A. 1987 "Organizational Growth and Decline Processes." *Annual Review of Sociology* 13:335–358.

Wholey, Douglas, and Jack Brittain 1989 "Characterizing Environmental Variation." *Academy of Management Journal* 32:867–882.

Wilks, Stephen 1992 "Science, Technology and the Large Corporation." *Government and Opposition* 27:190–212.

Young, Ruth 1988 "Is Population Ecology a Useful Paradigm for the Study of Organizations?" *American Journal of Sociology* 94:1–24.

Zeitlin, Maurice 1974 "Corporate Ownership and Control: The Large Corporation and the Capitalist Class." *American Journal of Sociology* 79:1073–1119.

Zey, Mary, and Brande Camp 1996 "The Transformation from Multidimensional Form to Corporate Groups of Subsidies in the 1980s: Capital Crisis Theory." *Sociological Quarterly* 37:327–351.

CORA B. MARRETT

CORRECTIONS SYSTEMS

See Penology; Criminal Sanctions; Criminology.

CORRELATION AND REGRESSION ANALYSIS

In 1885, Francis Galton, a British biologist, published a paper in which he demonstrated with graphs and tables that the children of very tall parents were, on average, shorter than their parents, while the children of very short parents tended to exceed their parents in height (cited in Walker 1929). Galton referred to this as "reversion" or the "law of regression" (i.e., regression to the average height of the species). Galton also saw in his graphs and tables a feature that he named the "co-relation" between variables. The stature of kinsmen are "co-related" variables, Galton stated, meaning, for example, that when the father was taller than average, his son was likely also to be taller than average. Although Galton devised a way of summarizing in a single figure the degree of "co-relation" between two variables, it was Galton's associate Karl Pearson who developed the "coefficient of correlation," as it is now applied. Galton's original interest, the phenomenon of regression toward the mean, is no longer germane to contemporary correlation and regression analysis, but the term "regression" has been retained with a modified meaning.

Although Galton and Pearson originally focused their attention on bivariate (two variables) correlation and regression, in current applications more than two variables are typically incorporated into the analysis to yield partial correlation coefficients, multiple regression analysis, and several related techniques that facilitate the informed interpretation of the linkages between pairs of variables. This summary begins with two variables and then moves to the consideration of more than two variables.

Consider a very large sample of cases, with a measure of some variable, X, and another variable, Y, for each case. To make the illustration more concrete, consider a large number of adults and, for each, a measure of their education (years of school completed = X) and their income (dollars earned over the past twelve months = Y). Subdivide these adults by years of school completed, and for each such subset compute a mean income for a given level of education. Each such mean is called a *conditional mean* and is represented by $\bar{Y}|X$, that is, the mean of Y for a given value of X.

Imagine now an ordered arrangement of the subsets from left to right according to the years of school completed, with zero years of school on the left, followed by one year of school, and so on through the maximum number of years of school completed in this set of cases, as shown in Figure 1.

Assume that each of the $\bar{Y}|X$ values (i.e., the mean income for each level of education) falls on a straight line, as in Figure 1. This straight line is the *regression line of Y on X*. Thus the regression line of Y on X is the line that passes through the mean Y for each value of X—for example, the mean income for each educational level.

If this regression line is a straight line, as shown in Figure 1, then the income associated with each additional year of school completed is the same whether that additional year of school represents an increase, for example, from six to seven years of school completed or from twelve to thirteen years. While one can analyze curvilinear regression, a straight regression line greatly simplifies the analysis. Some (but not all) curvilinear regressions can be made into straight-line regressions by a relatively simple transformation of one of the variables (e.g., taking a logarithm). The common assumption that the regression line is a straight line is known as the *assumption of rectilinearity*, or more commonly (even if less precisely) as the *assumption of linearity*.

The slope of the regression line reflects one feature of the relationship between two variables. If the regression line slopes "uphill," as in Figure 1, then Y increases as X increases, and the steeper the slope, the more Y increases for each unit increase in X. In contrast, if the regression line slopes "downhill" as one moves from left to right, Y *decreases* as X increases, and the steeper the slope, the more Y decreases for each unit increase in X. If the regression line doesn't slope at all but is perfectly horizontal, then there is no relationship between the variables. But the slope does not tell how closely the two variables are "co-related" (i.e., how closely the values of Y cluster around the regression line).

A regression line may be represented by a simple mathematical formula for a straight line. Thus:

$$\bar{Y}|X = a_{yx} + b_{yx}X \qquad (1)$$

where $\bar{Y}|X$ = the mean Y for a given value of X, or the regression line values of Y given X; a_{yx} = the Y intercept (i.e., the predicted value of $\bar{Y}|X$ when X = 0); and b_{yx} = the slope of the regression of Y on X (i.e., the amount by which $\bar{Y}|X$ increases or decreases—depending on whether b is positive or negative—for each one-unit increase in X).

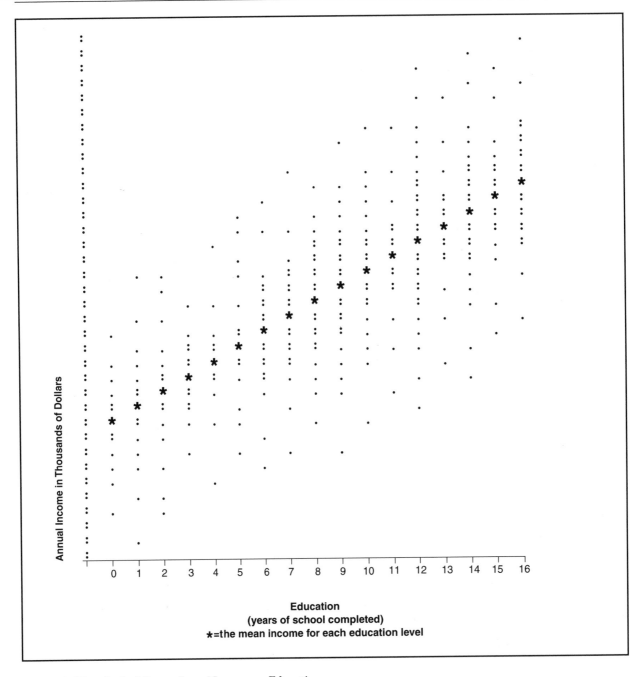

Figure 1. Hypothetical Regression of Income on Education

Equation 1 is commonly written in a slightly different form:

$$\hat{Y} = a_{yx} + b_{yx}X \qquad (2)$$

where $\hat{Y}$ = the regression prediction for Y for a given value of X, and a_{yx} and b_{yx} are as defined above, with $\hat{Y}$ substituted for $\bar{Y}|X$.

Equations 1 and 2 are theoretically equivalent. Equation 1 highlights the fact that the points on the regression line are assumed to represent conditional means (i.e., the mean Y for a given X). Equation 2 highlights the fact that points on the regression line are not ordinarily found by computing a series of conditional means, but are found by alternative computational procedures.

Typically the number of cases is insufficient to yield a stable estimate of each of a series of conditional means, one for each level of X. Means based on a relatively small number of cases are inaccurate because of sampling variation, and a line connecting such unstable conditional means may not be straight even though the true regression line is. Hence, one assumes that the regression line is a straight line unless there are compelling reasons for assuming otherwise; one can then use the X and Y values for all cases together to estimate the Y intercept, a_{yx}, and the slope, b_{yx}, of the regression line that is best fit by the *criterion of least squares*. This criterion requires predicted values for Y that will minimize the sum of squared deviations between the predicted values and the observed values. Hence, a "least squares" regression line is the straight line that yields a lower sum of squared deviations between the predicted (regression line) values and the observed values than does any other straight line. One can find the parameters of the "least squares" regression line for a given set of X and Y values by computing

$$b_{yx} = \frac{\sum (X - \overline{X})(Y - \overline{Y})}{\sum (X - \overline{X})^2} \qquad (3)$$

$$a_{yx} = \overline{Y} - b_{yx}\overline{X} \qquad (4)$$

These parameters (substituted in equation 2) describe the straight regression line that best fits by the criterion of least squares. By substituting the X value for a given case into equation 2, one can then find $\hat{Y}$ for that case. Otherwise stated, once a_{yx} and b_{yx} have been computed, equation 2 will yield a precise predicted income level ($\hat{Y}$) for each education level.

These predicted values may be relatively good or relatively poor predictions, depending on whether the actual values of Y cluster closely around the predicted values on the regression line or spread themselves widely around that line. The *variance* of the Y values (income levels in this illustration) around the regression line will be relatively small if the Y values cluster closely around the predicted values (i.e., when the regression line provides relatively good predictions). On the other hand, the variance of Y values around the regression line will be relatively large if the Y values are spread widely around the predicted values (i.e., when the regression line provides relatively poor predictions). The variance of the Y values around the regression predictions is defined as the mean of the squared deviations between them. The variances around each of the values along the regression line are assumed to be equal. This is known as the assumption of *homoscedasticity* (homogeneous scatter or variance). When the variances of the Y values around the regression predictions are larger for some values of X than for others (i.e., when homoscedasticity is not present), then X serves as a better predictor of Y in one part of its range than in another. The homoscedasticity assumption is usually at least approximately true.

The variance around the regression line is a measure of the accuracy of the regression predictions. But it is not an easily interpreted measure of the degree of correlation because it has not been "normed" to vary within a limited range. Two other measures, closely related to each other, provide such a normed measure. These measures, which are always between zero and one in absolute value (i.e., sign disregarded) are: (a) the correlation coefficient, r, which is the measure devised by Karl Pearson; and (b) the square of that coefficient, r^2, which, unlike r, can be interpreted as a percentage.

Pearson's correlation coefficient, r, can be computed using the following formula:

$$r_{yx} = r_{xy} = \frac{\dfrac{\sum (X - \overline{X})(Y - \overline{Y})}{N}}{\sqrt{\left(\dfrac{\sum (X - \overline{X})^2}{N}\right)\left(\dfrac{\sum (Y - \overline{Y})^2}{N}\right)}} \qquad (5)$$

The numerator in equation 5 is known as the *covariance* of X and Y. The denominator is the square root of the product of the variances of X and Y. Hence, equation 5 may be rewritten:

$$r_{yx} = r_{xy} = \frac{\text{Covariance }(X, Y)}{\sqrt{[\text{Variance }(X)][\text{Variance }(Y)]}} \qquad (6)$$

While equation 5 may serve as a computing guide, neither equation 5 nor equation 6 tells why it describes the degree to which two variables covary. Such understanding may be enhanced by stating that r is the slope of the least squares regression line when both X and Y have been transformed into "standard deviates" or "z measures." Each value in a distribution may be transformed into a "z measure" by finding its deviation from the mean of the distribution and dividing by the standard deviation (the square root of the variance) of that distribution. Thus

$$Z_x = \frac{X - \overline{X}}{\sqrt{\dfrac{\sum (X - \overline{X})^2}{N}}} \qquad (7)$$

When both the X and Y measures have been thus standardized, $r_{yx} = r_{xy}$ is the slope of the regression of Y on X, and of X on Y. For standard deviates, the Y intercept is necessarily 0, and the following equation holds:

$$\hat{Z}_y = r_{yx} Z_x \qquad (8)$$

where $\hat{Z}_y$ = the regression prediction for the "Z measure" of Y, given X; Z_x = the standard deviates of X; and $r_{yx} = r_{xy}$ = the Pearsonian correlation between X and Y.

Like the slope b_{yx}, for unstandardized measures, the slope for standardized measures, r, may be positive or negative. But unlike b_{yx}, r is always between 0 and 1.0 in absolute value. The correlation coefficient, r, will be 0 when the standardized regression line is horizontal so that the two variables do not covary at all—and, incidentally, when the regression toward the mean, which was Galton's original interest, is complete. On the other hand, r will be 1.0 or − 1.0 when all values of Z_y fall precisely on the regression line rZ_x. This means that when r = + 1.0, for every case $Z_x = Z_y$—that is, each case deviates from the mean on X by exactly as much and in the same direction as it deviates from the mean on Y, when those deviations are measured in their respective standard deviation units. And when r = − 1.0, the deviations from the mean measured in standard deviation units are exactly equal, but they are in opposite directions. (It is also true that when r = 1.0, there is no regression toward the mean, although this is very rarely of any interest in contemporary applications.) More commonly, r will be neither 0 nor 1.0 in absolute value but will fall between these extremes, closer to 1.0 in absolute value when the Z_y values cluster closely around the regression line, which, in this standardized form, implies that the slope will be near 1.0, and closer to 0 when they scatter widely around the regression line.

But while r has a precise meaning—it is the slope of the regression line for standardized measures—that meaning is not intuitively understandable as a measure of the degree to which one variable can be accurately predicted from the other. The square of the correlation coefficient, r^2, does have such an intuitive meaning. Briefly stated, r^2 indicates the percent of the possible reduction in prediction error (measured by the variance of actual values around predicted values) that is achieved by shifting from (a) $\overline{Y}$ as the prediction, to (b) the regression line values as the prediction. Otherwise stated,

$$r^2 = \frac{\begin{array}{c}\text{Variance of Y values} \\ \text{around } \overline{Y}\end{array} - \begin{array}{c}\text{Variance of Y values} \\ \text{around } \hat{Y}\end{array}}{\begin{array}{c}\text{Variance of Y values} \\ \text{Around } \overline{Y}\end{array}} \qquad (9)$$

The denominator of Equation 9 is called the *total variance* of Y. It is the sum of two components: (1) the variance of the Y values around $\hat{Y}$, and (2) the variance of the $\hat{Y}$ around $\overline{Y}$. Hence the numerator of equation 9 is equal to the variance of the $\hat{Y}$ values (regression values) around $\overline{Y}$. Therefore

$$r^2 = \frac{\begin{array}{c}\text{Variance of } \hat{Y} \text{ values} \\ \text{around } \overline{Y}\end{array}}{\begin{array}{c}\text{Variance of Y values} \\ \text{around } \overline{Y}\end{array}} \qquad (10)$$

= proportion of variance explained

Even though it has become common to refer to r^2 as the proportion of variance "explained," such terminology should be used with caution. There are several possible reasons for two variables to be correlated, and some of these reasons are inconsistent with the connotations ordinarily attached to terms such as "explanation" or "explained." One possible reason for the correlation between two variables is that X influences Y. This is presumably the reason for the positive correlation between education and income; higher education facilitates earning a higher income, and it is appropriate to refer to a part of the variation in income as being "explained" by variation in education. But there is also the possibility that two variables are correlated because both are measures of the same dimension. For example, among twentieth-century nation-states, there is a high correlation between the energy consumption per capita and the gross national product per capita. These two variables are presumably correlated because both are indicators of the degree of industrial development. Hence, one variable does not "explain" variation in the other, if "explain" has any of its usual meanings. And two variables may be correlated because both are influenced by a common cause, in which case the two variables are "spuriously correlated." For example, among elementary-school children, reading ability is positively correlated with shoe size. This correlation appears not because large feet facilitate learning, and not because both are measures of the same underlying dimension, but because both are influenced by age. As they grow older, schoolchildren learn to read better *and* their feet grow larger. Hence, shoe size and reading ability are "spuriously correlated" because of the dependence of both on age. It would therefore be misleading to conclude from the correlation between shoe size and reading ability that part of the variation in reading ability is "explained" by variation in shoe size, or vice versa.

In the attempt to discover the reasons for the correlation between two variables, it is often useful to include additional variables in the analysis. Several techniques are available for doing so.

PARTIAL CORRELATION

One may wish to explore the correlation between two variables with a third variable "held constant." The *partial correlation coefficient* may be used for this purpose. If the only reason for the correlation between shoe size and reading ability is because both are influenced by variation in age, then the correlation should disappear when the influence of variation in age is made nil—that is, when age is held constant. Given a sufficiently large number of cases, age could be held constant by considering each age grouping separately—that is, one could examine the correlation between shoe size and reading ability among children who are six years old, among children who are seven years old, eight years old, etc. (And one presumes that there would be no correlation between reading ability and shoe size among children who are homogeneous in age.) But such a procedure requires a relatively large number of children in each age grouping.

Lacking such a large sample, one may hold age constant by "statistical adjustment."

To understand the underlying logic of partial correlation, one considers the *regression residuals* (i.e., for each case, the discrepancy between the regression line value and the observed value of the predicted variable). For example, the regression residual of reading ability on age for a given case is the discrepancy between the actual reading ability and the predicted reading ability based on age. Each residual will be either positive or negative (depending on whether the observed reading ability is higher or lower than the regression prediction). Each residual will also have a specific value, indicating how much higher or lower than the age-specific mean (i.e., regression line values) the reading ability is for each person. The complete set of these regression residuals, each being a deviation from the age-specific mean, describes the pattern of variation in reading abilities that would obtain if all of these schoolchildren were identical in age. Similarly, the regression residuals for shoe size on age describe the pattern of variation that would obtain if all of these schoolchildren were identical in age. Hence, the correlation between the two sets of residuals—(1) the regression residuals of shoe size on age and (2) the regression residuals of reading ability on age—is the correlation between shoe size and reading ability, with age "held constant." In practice, it is not necessary to find each regression residual to compute the partial correlation, because shorter computational procedures have been developed. Hence,

$$r_{xy \cdot x} = \frac{r_{xy} - r_{xz} r_{yz}}{\sqrt{(1 - r^2_{xz})(1 - r^2_{yz})}} \qquad (11)$$

where $r_{xy} \cdot z$; = the partial coefficient between X and Y, holding Z constant; r_{xy} = the bivariate correlation coefficient between X and Y; r_{xz} = the bivariate correlation coefficient between X and Z; and r_{yz} = the bivariate correlation coefficient between Y and Z.

It should be evident from equation 11 that if Z is unrelated to both X and Y, controlling for Z will yield a partial correlation that does not differ from the bivariate correlation. If all correlations are positive, each increase in the correlation between the control variable, Z, and each of the focal variables, X and Y, will move the partial, $r_{xy.z}$, closer to 0, and in some circumstances a positive bivariate correlation may become negative after controlling for a third variable. When r_{xy} is positive and the algebraic sign of r_{yz} differs from the sign of r_{xz} (so that their product is negative), the partial will be *larger* than the bivariate correlation, indicating that Z is a *suppressor variable*—that is, a variable that diminishes the correlation between X and Y unless it is controlled. Further discussion of partial correlation and its interpretation will be found in Simon 1954; Mueller, Schuessler, and Costner 1977; and Blalock 1979.

Any correlation between two sets of regression residuals is called a *partial correlation coefficient*. The illustration immediately above is called a *first-order partial*, meaning that one and only one variable has been held constant. A *second-order partial* means that two variables have been held constant. More generally, an *nth-order partial* is one in which precisely n variables have been "controlled" or held constant by statistical adjustment.

When only one of the variables being correlated is a regression residual (e.g., X is correlated with the residuals of Y on Z), the correlation is called a *part correlation*. Although part correlations are rarely used, they are appropriate when it seems implausible to residualize one variable. Generally, part correlations are smaller in absolute value than the corresponding partial correlation.

MULTIPLE REGRESSION

Earned income level is influenced not simply by one's education but also by work experience, skills developed outside of school and work, the prevailing compensation for the occupation or profession in which one works, the nature of the regional economy where one is employed, and numerous other factors. Hence it should not be surprising that education alone does not predict income with high accuracy. The deviations between actual income and income predicted on the basis of education are presumably due to the influence of all the other factors that have an effect, great or small, on one's income level. By including some of these other variables as additional predictors, the accuracy of prediction should be increased. Otherwise stated, one expects to predict Y better using both

X_1 and X_2 (assuming both influence Y) than with either of these alone.

A regression equation including more than a single predictor of Y is called a *multiple regression equation*. For two predictors, the multiple regression equation is:

$$\hat{Y} = a_{y.12} + b_{y1.2}X_1 + b_{y2.1}X_2 \qquad (12)$$

where $\hat{Y}$ = the least squares prediction of Y based on X_1 and X_2; $a_{y.12}$ = the Y intercept (i.e., the predicted value of Y when both X_1 and X_2 are 0); $b_{y1.2}$ = the (unstandardized) regression slope of Y on X_1, holding X_2 constant; and $b_{y2.1}$ = the (unstandardized) regression slope of Y on X_2, holding X_1 constant. In multiple regression analysis, the predicted variable (Y in equation 12) is commonly known as the *criterion variable*, and the X's are called predictors. As in a bivariate regression equation (equation 2), one assumes both rectilinearity and homoscedasticity, and one finds the Y intercept ($a_{y.12}$ in equation 12) and the regression slopes (one for each predictor; they are $b_{y1.2}$ and $b_{y2.1}$ in equation 12) that best fit by the criterion of least squares. The b's or regression slopes are *partial regression coefficients*. The correlation between the resulting regression predictions ($\hat{Y}$) and the observed values of Y is called the *multiple correlation coefficient*, symbolized by R.

In contemporary applications of multiple regression, the partial regression coefficients are typically the primary focus of attention. These coefficients describe the regression of the criterion variable on each predictor, holding constant all other predictors in the equation. The b's in equation 12 are *unstandardized* coefficients. The analogous multiple regression equation for all variables expressed in standardized form is

$$\hat{Z}_y = b^*_{y1.2} Z_1 + b^*_{y2.1} Z_2 \qquad (13)$$

where $\hat{Z}$ = the regression prediction for the "z measure" of Y, given X_1 and X_2 Z_1 = the standard deviate of X_1 Z_2 = the standard deviate of X_2 $b^*_{y1.2}$ = the standardized slope of Y on X_1, holding X_2 constant; and $b^*_{y2.1}$ = the standardized slope of Y on X_2, holding X_1 constant.

The standardized regression coefficients in an equation with two predictors may be calculated from the bivariate correlations as follows:

$$b^*_{y1.2} = \frac{r_{y1} - r_{y2}r_{y12}}{1 - r^2_{12}} \qquad (14)$$

$$b^*_{y2.1} = \frac{r_{y2} - r_{y1}r_{y12}}{1 - r^2_{12}} \qquad (15)$$

where $b^*_{y1.2}$ = the standardized partial regression coefficient of Y on X_1, controlling for X_2; and $b^*_{y2.1}$ = the standardized partial regression coefficient of Y on X_2, controlling for X_1.

Standardized partial regression coefficients, here symbolized by b^* (read "b star"), are frequently symbolized by the Greek letter beta, and they are commonly referred to as "betas," "beta coefficients," or "beta weights." While this is common usage, it violates the established practice of using Greek letters to refer to population parameters instead of sample statistics.

A comparison of equation 14, describing the standardized partial regression coefficient, $b^*_{y1.2}$, with equation 11, describing the partial correlation coefficient, $r_{y1.2}$, will make it evident that these two coefficients are closely related. They have identical numerators but different denominators. The similarity can be succinctly expressed by

$$r^2_{y1.2} = b^*_{y1.2} \, b^*_{1y.2} \qquad (16)$$

If any one of the quantities in equation 16 is 0, all are 0, and if the partial correlation is 1.0 in absolute value, both of the standardized partial regression coefficients in equation 16 must also be 1.0 in absolute value. For absolute values between 0 and 1.0, the partial correlation coefficient and the standardized partial regression coefficient will have somewhat different values, although the general interpretation of two corresponding coefficients is the same in the sense that both coefficients represent the relationship between two variables, with one or more other variables held constant. The difference between them is rather subtle and rarely of major substantive import. Briefly stated, the partial correlation coefficient—e.g., $r_{y1.2}$—is the regression of one standardized residual on another standardized residual. The corresponding standardized partial regression coefficient, $b^*_{y1.2}$, is the regression of one residual on another, but the residuals are standard measure discrepancies from standard measure predictions, rather than the residuals themselves having been expressed in the form of standard deviates.

A standardized partial regression coefficient can be transformed into an unstandardized partial regression coefficient by

$$b_{y1.2} = b^*_{y1.2} \, \frac{s_y}{s_1} \qquad (17)$$

$$b_{y2.1} = b^*_{y2.1} \, \frac{s_y}{s_2} \qquad (18)$$

where $b_{y1.2}$ = the unstandardized partial regression coefficient of Y on X_1, controlling for X_2; $b_{y2.1}$ = the unstandardized partial regression coefficient of Y on X_2, controlling for X_1; $b^*_{y2.1}$ and $b^*_{y2.1}$ are standardized partial regression coefficients, as defined above; s_y = the standard deviation of Y; s_1 = the standard deviation of X_1; and s_2 = the standard deviation of X_2.

Under all but exceptional circumstances, standardized partial regression coefficients fall between −1.0 and +1.0. The relative magnitude of the *standardized* coefficients in a given regression equation indicates the relative magnitude of the relationship between the criterion variable and the predictor in question, after holding constant all the other predictors in that regression equation. Hence, the *standardized* partial regression coefficients in a given equation can be compared to infer which predictor has the strongest relationship to the criterion, after holding all other variables in that equation constant. The comparison of *unstandardized* partial regression coefficients for different predictors in the same equation does not ordinarily yield useful information because these coefficients are affected by the units of measure. On the other hand, it is frequently useful to compare *unstandardized* partial regression coefficients across equations. For example, in separate regression equations predicting income from education and work experience for the United States and Great Britain, if the unstandardized regression coefficient for education in the equation for Great Britain is greater than the unstandardized regression coefficient for education in the equation for the United States, the implication is that education has a greater influence on income in Great Britain than in the United States. It would be hazardous to draw any such conclusion from the comparison of *standardized* coefficients for Great Britain and the United

States because such coefficients are affected by the variances in the two populations.

The multiple correlation coefficient, R, is defined as the correlation between the observed values of Y and the values of Y predicted by the multiple regression equation. It would be unnecessarily tedious to calculate the multiple correlation coefficient in that way. The more convenient computational procedure is to compute R^2 (for two predictors, and analogously for more than two predictors) by the following:

$$R^2 = b^*_{y1.2}r_{y1} + b^*_{y2.1}r_{y2} \qquad (19)$$

Like r^2, R^2 varies from 0 to 1.0 and indicates the proportion of variance in the criterion that is "explained" by the predictors. Alternatively stated, R^2 is the percent of the possible reduction in prediction error (measured by the variance of actual values around predicted values) that is achieved by shifting from (a) $\bar{Y}$ as the prediction to (b) the multiple regression values, $\hat{Y}$, as the prediction.

VARIETIES OF MULTIPLE REGRESSION

The basic concept of multiple regression has been adapted to a variety of purposes other than those for which the technique was originally developed. The following paragraphs provide a brief summary of some of these adaptations.

Dummy Variable Analysis. As originally conceived, the correlation coefficient was designed to describe the relationship between continuous, normally distributed variables. Dichotomized predictors such as gender (male and female) were introduced early in bivariate regression and correlation, which led to the "point biserial correlation coefficient" (Walker and Lev 1953). For example, if one wishes to examine the correlation between gender and income, one may assign a "0" to each instance of male and a "1" to each instance of female to have numbers representing the two categories of the dichotomy. The unstandardized regression coefficient, computed as specified above in equation 3, is then the difference between the mean income for the two categories of the dichotomous predictor, and the computational formula for r (equation 5), will yield the point biserial correlation coefficient, which can be interpreted much like any other r. It was then only a small step to the

inclusion of dichotomies as predictors in multiple regression analysis, and then to the creation of a set of dichotomies from a categorical variable with more than two subdivisions—that is, to *dummy variable analysis* (Cohen 1968; Bohrnstedt and Knoke 1988; Hardy 1993).

Religious denomination—e.g., Protestant, Catholic, and Jewish—serves as an illustration. From these three categories, one forms two dichotomies, called "dummy variables." In the first of these, for example, cases are classified as "1" if they are Catholic, and "0" otherwise (i.e., if Protestant or Jewish). In the second of the dichotomies, cases are classified as "1" if they are Jewish, and "0" otherwise (i.e., if Protestant or Catholic). In this illustration, Protestant is the "omitted" or "reference" category (but Protestants can be identified as those who are classified "0" on both of the other dichotomies). The resulting two dichotomized "dummy variables" can serve as the only predictors in a multiple regression equation, or they may be combined with other predictors. When the dummy variables mentioned are the only predictors, the unstandardized regression coefficient for the predictor in which Catholics are classified "1" is the difference between the mean Y for Catholics and Protestants (the "omitted" or "reference" category). Similarly, the unstandardized regression coefficient for the predictor in which Jews are classified "1" is the difference between the mean Y for Jews and Protestants. When the dummy variables are included with other predictors, the unstandardized regression coefficients are the same except that the difference of each mean from the mean of the "reference" category has been statistically adjusted to control for each of the other predictors in the regression equation.

The development of "dummy variable analysis" allowed multiple regression analysis to be linked to the experimental statistics developed by R. A. Fisher, including the analysis of variance and covariance. (See Cohen 1968.)

Logistic Regression. Early students of correlation anticipated the need for a measure of correlation when the predicted or dependent variable was dichotomous. Out of this came (a) the phi coefficient, which can be computed by applying the computational formula for r (equation 5) to two dichotomies, each coded "0" or "1," and (b) the tetrachoric correlation coefficient, which uses information in the form of two dichotomies to estimate the Pearsonian correlation for the corresponding continuous variables, assuming the dichotomies result from dividing two continuous and normally distributed variables by arbitrary cutting points (Kelley 1947; Walker and Lev 1953; Carroll 1961).

These early developments readily suggested use of a dichotomous predicted variable, coded "0" or "1," as the predicted variable in a multiple regression analysis. The predicted value is then the conditional proportion, which is the conditional mean for a dichotomized predicted variable. But this was not completely satisfactory in some circumstances because the regression predictions are, under some conditions, proportions greater than 1 or less than 0. *Logistic regression* (Retherford 1993; Kleinman 1994; Menard 1995) is responsive to this problem. After coding the predicted variable "0" or "1," the predicted variable is transformed to a logistic—that is, the logarithm of the "odds," which is to say the logarithm of the ratio of the number of 1's to the number of 0's. With the logistic as the predicted variable, impossible regression predictions do not result, but the unstandardized logistic regression coefficients, describing changes in the logarithm of the "odds," lack the intuitive meaning of ordinary regression coefficients. An additional computation is required to be able to describe the change in the predicted proportion for a given one-unit change in a predictor, with all other predictors in the equation held constant.

Path Analysis. The interpretation of multiple regression coefficients can be difficult or impossible when the predictors include an undifferentiated set of causes, consequences, or spurious correlates of the predicted variable. Path analysis was developed by Sewell Wright (1934) to facilitate the interpretation of multiple regression coefficients by making explicit assumptions about causal structure and including as predictors of a given variable only those variables that precede that given variable in the assumed causal structure. For example, if one assumes that Y is influenced by X_1 and X_2, and X_1 and X_2 are, in turn, both influenced by Z_1, Z_2, and Z_3, this specifies the assumed causal structure. One may then proceed to write multiple regression equations to predict X_1, X_2, and Y, including in each equation only those variables that come prior in the assumed causal order. For example, the Z variables are appropriate predictors in the equation predicting X_1 because they are assumed causes of X_1. But X_2 is not an appropriate predictor of X_1 because it is assumed to be a spurious correlate of X_1 (i.e., X_1 and X_2 are presumed to be correlated only because they are both influenced by the Z variables, not because one influences the other). And Y is not an appropriate predictor of X_1 because Y is assumed to be an effect of X_1, not one of its causes. When the assumptions about the causal structure linking a set of variables have been made explicit, the appropriate predictors for each variable have been identified from this assumed causal structure, and the resulting equations have been estimated by the techniques of regression analysis, the result is a path analysis, and each of the resulting coefficients is said to be a "path coefficient" (if expressed in standardized form) or a "path regression coefficient" (if expressed in unstandardized form).

If the assumed causal structure is correct, a path analysis allows one to "decompose" a correlation between two variables into "direct effects"; "indirect effects"; and, potentially, a "spurious component" as well (Land 1969; Bohrnstedt and Knoke 1988; McClendon 1994).

For example, we may consider the correlation between the occupational achievement of a set of fathers and the occupational achievement of their sons. Some of this correlation may occur because the father's occupational achievement influences the educational attainment of the son, and the son's educational attainment, in turn, influences his occupational achievement. This is an "indirect effect" of the father's occupational achievement on the son's occupational achievement "through" (or "mediated by") the son's education. A "direct effect," on the other hand, is an effect that is not mediated by any variable included in the analysis. Such mediating variables could probably be found, but if they have not been identified and included in this particular analysis, then the effects mediated through them are grouped together as the "direct effect"—that is, an effect not mediated by variables included in the analysis. If the father's occupational achievement and the son's occupational achievement are also correlated, in part, because both are influenced by a common cause (e.g., a common hereditary variable), then that part of the correlation that is attributable to that common cause constitutes the "spurious component" of the correlation. If the variables responsible for the "spurious component" of a correlation have been included in the path analysis, the "spurious component" can be estimated; otherwise such a "spurious component" is merged into the "direct effect," which, despite the connotations of the name, absorbs all omitted indirect effects and all omitted spurious components.

"Stepwise" Regression Analysis. The interpretation of regression results can sometimes be facilitated without specifying completely the presumed causal structure among a set of predictors. If the purpose of the analysis is to enhance understanding of the variation in a single dependent variable, and if the various predictors presumed to contribute to that variation can be grouped, for example, into proximate causes and distant causes, a *stepwise regression analysis* may be useful. Depending on one's primary interest, one may proceed in two different ways. For example, one may begin by regressing the criterion variable on the distant causes, and then, in a second step, introduce the proximate causes into the regression equation. Comparison of the coefficients at each step will reveal the degree to which the effects of the distant causes are mediated by the proximate causes included in the analysis. Alternatively, one may begin by regressing the criterion variable on the proximate causes, and then introduce the distant causes into the regression equation in a second step. Comparing the coefficients at each step, one can infer the degree to which the first-step regression of the criterion variable on the proximate causes is spurious because of the dependence of both on the distant causes. A stepwise regression analysis may proceed with more than two stages if one wishes to distinguish more than two sets of predictors. One may think of a stepwise regression analysis of this kind as analogous to a path analysis but without a complete specification of the causal structure.

Nonadditive Effects in Multiple Regression. In the illustrative regression equations preceding this section, each predictor has appeared only once, and never in a "multiplicative" term. We now consider the following regression equation, which includes such a multiplicative term:

$$\hat{Y} = a_{y.12} + b_{y1.2}X_1 + b_{y2.1}X_2 + b_{y.12}X_1X_2 \quad (20)$$

In this equation, Y is said to be predicted, not simply by an additive combination of X_1 and X_2 but also by their product, X_1X_2. Although it may not be intuitively evident from the equation itself, the presence of a multiplicative effect (i.e., the regression coefficient for the multiplicative term, $b_{y.12}$, is not 0) implies that the effect of X_1 on Y depends on the level of X_2, and vice versa. This is commonly called an *interaction effect* (Allison 1977; Blalock 1979; Jaccard, Turrisi and Wan 1990; Aiken and West 1991; McClendon 1994). The inclusion of multiplicative terms in a regression equation is especially appropriate when there are sound reasons for assuming that the effect of one variable differs for different levels of another variable. For example, if one assumes that the "return to education" (i.e., the annual income added by each additional year of schooling) will be greater for men than for women, this assumption can be explored by including all three predictors: education, gender, and the product of gender and education.

When product terms have been included in a regression equation, the interpretation of the resulting partial regression coefficients may become complex. For example, unless all predictors are "ratio variables" (i.e., variables measured in uniform units from an absolute 0), the inclusion of a product term in a regression equation renders the coefficients for the additive terms uninterpretable (see Allison 1977).

SAMPLING VARIATION AND TESTS AGAINST THE NULL HYPOTHESIS

Descriptions based on incomplete information will be inaccurate because of "sampling variation." Otherwise stated, different samplings of information will yield different results. This is true of sample regression and correlation coefficients, as it is for other descriptors. Assuming a random selection of observed information, the "shape" of the distribution of such sampling variation is often known by mathematical reasoning, and the magnitude of such variation can be estimated. For example, if the true correlation between X and Y is 0, a series of randomly selected observations will rarely yield a correlation that is precisely 0. Instead, the observed correlation will fluctuate around 0 in the "shape" of a normal distribution, and the standard deviation of that normal sampling distribution—called the *standard error* of r—will be

$$\sigma_r = \frac{1}{\sqrt{N-1}} \qquad (21)$$

where σ_r = the standard error of r (i.e. the standard deviation of the sampling distribution of r, given that the true correlation is 0); and N = the sample size (i.e., the number of randomly selected cases used in the calculation of r). For example, if the true correlation were 0, a correlation coefficient based on a random selection of 400 cases will have a standard error of approximately 1/20 or .05. An observed correlation of .15 or greater in absolute value would thus be at least three standard errors away from 0 and hence very unlikely to have appeared simply because of random fluctuations around a true value of 0. This kind of conclusion is commonly expressed by saying that the observed correlation is "significantly different from 0" at a given level of significance (in this instance, the level of significance cited could appropriately be .01). Or the same conclusion may be more simply (but less precisely) stated by saying that the observed correlation is "significant."

The standard error for an unstandardized bivariate regression coefficient, and for an unstandardized partial regression coefficient, may also be estimated (Cohen and Cohen 1983; Kleinman, Kupper and Muller 1988; Hamilton 1992; McClendon 1994; Fox 1997). Other things being equal, the standard error for the regression of the criterion on a given predictor will decrease as (1) the number of observations (N) increases; (2) the variance of observed values around predicted values decreases; (3) the variance of the predictor increases; and (4) the correlation between the predictor and other predictors in the regression equation decreases.

PROBLEMS IN REGRESSION ANALYSIS

Multiple regression is a special case of a very general and adaptable model of data analysis known as the *general linear model* (Cohen 1968; Fennessey 1968; Blalock 1979). Although the assumptions underlying multiple regression seem relatively demanding (see Berry 1993), the technique is remarkably "robust," which is to say that the technique yields valid conclusions even when the assumptions are met only approximately (Bohrnstedt and Carter 1971). Even so, restricted or biased samples may lead to conclusions that are misleading if they are inappropriately generalized. Furthermore, regression results may be misinterpreted if interpretation rests on an implicit causal model that is misspecified. For this reason it is advisable to make the causal model explicit, as in path analysis or structural equation modeling and to use regression equations that are appropriate for the model as specified. "Outliers" and "deviant cases" (i.e., cases extremely divergent from most) may have an excessive impact on regression coefficients, and hence may lead to erroneous conclusions. (See Berry and Feldman 1985; Fox 1991; Hamilton 1992.) A ubiquitous but still not widely recognized source of misleading results in regression analysis is measurement error (both random and non-random) in the variables (Stouffer 1936; Kahneman 1965; Gordon 1968; Bohrnstedt and Carter 1971; Fuller and Hidiroglou 1978; Berry and Feldman 1985). In *bivariate* correlation and regression, the effect of measurement error can be readily anticipated: on the average, random measurement error in the *predicted* variable attenuates (moves toward zero) the correlation coefficient (i.e., the standardized regression coefficient) but not the unstandardized regression coefficient, while random measurement error in the *predictor* variable will, on the average, attenuate both the standardized and the unstandardized coefficients. In multiple regression analysis, the effect of random measurement error is more complex. The unstandardized partial regression coefficient for a given predictor will be biased, not simply by random measurement error in that predictor, but also by other features. When random measurement error is entailed in a given predictor, X, that predictor is not completely controlled in a regression analysis. Consequently, the unstandardized partial regression coefficient for every other predictor that is correlated with X will be biased by random measurement error in X. Measurement error may be non-random as well as random, and anticipating the effect of non-random measurement error on regression results is even more challenging than anticipating the effect of random error. Non-random measurement errors may be correlated errors (i.e., errors that are correlated with other variables in the system being analyzed), and therefore they have the potential to distort greatly the estimates of both standardized and unstandardized partial regression coefficients. Thus, if the measures used in regression analysis are relatively crude, lack high reliability, or include distortions (errors) likely to be correlated with other variables in the regression equation (or with measurement errors in those variables), regression analysis may yield misleading results. In these circumstances, the prudent investigator should interpret the results with considerable caution, or, preferably, shift from regression analysis to the analysis of structural equation models with multiple indicators. (See Herting 1985; Schumacker and Lomax 1996.) This alternative mode of analysis is well suited to correct for random measurement error and to help locate and correct for nonrandom measurement error.

REFERENCES

Agresti, Alan and Barbara Finlay 1997 *Statistical Methods for the Social Sciences*, 3rd ed. Upper Saddle River, N.J.: Prentice Hall.

Aiken, Leona S., and Stephen G. West 1991 *Multiple Regression: Testing and Interpreting Interactions*. Newbury Park, Calif.: Sage.

Allen, Michael Patrick 1997 *Understanding Regression Analysis*. New York: Plenum Press.

Allison, Paul 1977 "Testing for Interaction in Multiple Regression." *American Journal of Sociology* 83:144–153.

Berry, William D. 1993 *Understanding Regression Assumptions*. Newbury Park, Calif.: Sage.

——, and Stanley Feldman 1985 *Multiple Regression in Practice*. Beverly Hills, Calif.: Sage.

Blalock, Hubert M., Jr. 1979 *Social Statistics*, 2nd ed. New York: McGraw-Hill.

Bohrnstedt, George W., and T. Michael Carter 1971 "Robustness in Regression Analysis." In Herbert L. Costner, ed., *Sociological Methodology 1971*. San Francisco: Jossey-Bass.

——, and David Knoke 1988 *Statistics for Social Data Analysis*, 2nd ed. Itasca, Ill.: F. E. Peacock.

Carroll, John B. 1961 "The Nature of the Data, or How to Choose a Correlation Coefficient." *Psychometrica* 26:347–372.

Cohen, Jacob 1968 "Multiple Regression as a General Data Analytic System." *Psychological Bulletin* 70:426–443.

——, and Patricia Cohen 1983 *Applied Multiple Regression/Correlation Analysis for the Behavioral Sciences*, 2nd ed. Hillsdale, N.J.: Lawrence Erlbaum Associates.

Fennessey, James 1968 "The General Linear Model: A New Perspective on Some Familiar Topics." *American Journal of Sociology* 74:1–27.

Fox, John 1991 *Regression Diagnostics*. Newbury Park, Calif.: Sage.

——, 1997 *Applied Regression Analysis, Linear Models and Related Methods*. Beverly Hills, Calif.: Sage.

Fuller, W. A., and M. A. Hidiroglou 1978 "Regression Estimates after Correcting for Attenuation." *Journal of the American Statistical Association* 73:99–104.

Gordon, Robert 1968 "Issues in Multiple Regression." *American Journal of Sociology* 73:592–616.

Hamilton, Lawrence C. 1992 *Regression with Graphics: A Second Course in Applied Statistics*. Pacific Grove, Calif.: Brookes-Cole.

Hardy, Melissa A. 1993 *Regression with Dummy Variables*. Newbury Park, Calif.: Sage.

Heise, David R. 1969 "Problems in Path Analysis and Causal Inference." In Edgar Borgatta and George W. Bohrnstedt, eds., *Sociological Methodology 1969*. San Francisco: Jossey-Bass.

Herting, Gerald 1985 "Multiple Indicator Models Using LISREL." In H. M. Blalock, Jr., ed., *Causal Models in the Social Sciences*. New York: Aldine.

Jaccard, James, Robert Turrisi, and Choi K. Wan 1990 *Interaction Effects in Multiple Regression*. Newbury Park, Calif.: Sage.

Kahneman, D. 1965 "Control of Spurious Association and the Reliability of the Controlled Variable." *Psychological Bulletin* 64:326–329.

Kelley, Truman Lee 1947 *Fundamentals of Statistics*. Cambridge, Mass.: Harvard University Press.

Kleinman, David G. 1994 *Logistic Regression: A Self Learning Text*. New York: Springer.

——, Lawrence L. Kupper, and Keith E. Muller 1988 *Applied Regression Analysis and Other Multivariable Methods*. Boston: PWS-Kent.

Land, Kenneth C. 1969 "Principles of Path Analysis." In Edgar Borgatta and George W. Bohrnstedt, eds., *Sociological Methodology 1969*. San Francisco: Jossey-Bass.

McClendon, McKee J. 1994 *Multiple Regression and Causal Analysis*. Itasca, Ill.: F. E. Peacock.

Menard, Scott 1995 *Applied Logistic Regression Analysis*. Beverly Hills, Calif.: Sage.

Mueller, John H., Karl F. Schuessler, and Herbert L. Costner 1977 *Statistical Reasoning in Sociology*, 3rd ed. Boston: Houghton Mifflin.

Retherford, Robert D. and Minju Kim Choe 1993 *Statistical Models for Causal Analysis*. New York: Wiley.

Schroeder, Larry P., David L. Sjoquist and Paula E. Stephan 1986 *Understanding Regression Analysis: An Introductory Guide*. Beverly Hills, Calif.: Sage.

Schumacker, Randall E., and Richard G. Lomax 1996 *A Beginner's Guide to Structural Equation Modeling*. Mahwah, N.J.: Lawrence Erlbaum Associates.

Stouffer, Samuel A. 1936 "Evaluating the Effects of Inadequately Measured Variables in Partial Correlation Analysis." *Journal of the American Statistical Association* 31:348–360.

Walker, Helen M. 1929 *Studies in the History of Statistical Method*. Baltimore: Williams and Wilkins.

——, and Joseph Lev 1953 *Statistical Inference*. New York: Holt.

Weisberg, Sanford 1985 *Applied Linear Regression*. New York: Wiley.

Wright, Sewell 1934 "The Method of Path Coefficients." *The Annals of Mathematical Statistics* 5:161–215.

HERBERT L. COSTNER

COUNTERCULTURES

The enclaves in which people of the modern era live no longer resemble the small, integrated, and homogeneous communities of earlier times; rather, these have been replaced by large societies that are complex and diverse in their composition. The United States, a prime exemplar, is composed of multiple smaller groups holding characteristics, beliefs, customs, and interests that vary from the rest of society. While there are many cultural universals binding such groups to the mainstream, they also exhibit significant cultural diversity. Some of these groups display no clear boundaries demarcating them from the rest of society and fail to achieve any degree of permanence. Yet those that do, and that also share a distinctive set of norms, values, and behavior setting them off from the dominant culture, are considered *subcultures*. Subcultures can be organized around age, ethnicity, occupation, social class, religion, or lifestyle and usually contain specific knowledge, expressions, ways of dressing, and systems of stratification that serve and guide its members (Thornton 1997). Distinctive subcultures within the United States include jazz musicians, gangs, Chicanos, gay, college athletes, and drug dealers. While it was once hypothesized that these subcultures would merge together in a "melting pot," incorporating a mix

of the remnants of former subcultures (Irwin 1970), trends suggest that they resist total assimilation and retain their cultural diversity and distinct identity.

Some subcultures diverge from the dominant culture without morally rejecting the norms and values with which they differ. Others are more adamant in their condemnation, clearly conflicting with or opposing features of the larger society. Milton Yinger first proposed, in 1960, to call these *contracultures*, envisioning them as a subset of subcultures, specifically, those having an element of conflict with dominant norms, values, or both (Yinger 1960). Indeed, the feature he identified as most compelling about a contraculture is its specific organization in opposition to some cultural belief(s) or expression(s). Contracultures often arise, he noted, where there are conflicts of standards or values between subcultural groups and the larger society. Factors strengthening the conflict then strengthen the contracultural response. Contraculture members, especially from such groups as delinquent gangs, may be driven by their experiences of frustration, deprivation, or discrimination within society.

Yinger's conceptualization, although abstract and academic at first, came to enjoy widespread popularity with the advent of the 1960s and the student movement. Here was the kind of contraculture he had forecast, and his ideas were widely applied to the trends of the time, albeit under another label. Most analysts of contracultures preferred the term *counterculture*, and this soon overtook its predecessor as the predominant expression. In 1969 historian Theodore Roszak published his *The Making of a Counter Culture*, claiming that a large group of young people (ages fifteen to thirty) had arisen who adamantly rejected the technological and scientific outlook characteristic of Western industrialized culture, replacing this, instead, with a humanistic/mysticist alternative. In a more recent update, Roszak (1995) reflected back on that time, further locating the counterculture phenomenon as an historical aberration that arose out of the affluence of post-World War II America. Kenneth Keniston (1971) described this counterculture as composed of distinct subgroups (radicals, dropouts, hippies, drug users, communards, or those living in communes) rising from the most privileged children of the world's wealthiest nation. Jack Douglas (1970) also discussed the social, political, and economic background to this movement and its roots in members' entrenchment in the welfare state and the existing youth and student cultures. While this movement was clearly political as well, Douglas outlined some of its social dimensions, including rejection of the workaday world and its idealization of leisure, feeling, openness, and antimaterialism. Richard Flacks (1971) and Fred Davis (1971) followed with descriptions of the counterculture's overarching lifestyles, values, political beliefs, and ideologies. Ralph Turner (1976), Nathan Adler (1972), and Erik Erikson (1968) explored the social psychological implications of this counterculture, positing, respectively, a transformation in the self from "institution" to "impulse," the rise of an antinomian personality, where individuals oppose the obligatoriness of the moral law, and the formation of the *negative identity*. John Rothchild and Susan Berns Wolf (1976) documented the vast extension of countercultural outposts around the country and their innovations in child rearing. Charles Reich (1970) emphatically stated that this counterculture, consisting mostly of students, was being reinforced by merging with nonstudent youth, educated labor, and the women's movement, already effecting a major transformation in Western laws, institutions, and social structure. There was strong belief that this movement would significantly and permanently alter both society and its consciousness (Wuthnow 1976). After researching one commune in depth, Berger (1981) later mused about the survival of the counterculture, acknowledging its failure to meet earlier expectations, yet examining how its ideals and values become incorporated into the mainstream culture (cf. Spates 1976).

Other subcultural analysts noted more broadly that these groups are typically popular among youth, who have the least investment in the existing culture, and that, lacking power within society, they are likely to feel the forces of social control swiftly moving against them, from the mass media to police action. Countercultures were further differentiated from subcultures by the fact that their particular norms and values, were not well integrated into the dominant culture, generally known among group members, and other mainstream subcultures.

Yinger reclaimed theoretical command of the counterculture concept with his reflective expansions on the term in a presidential address for the American Sociological Association (Yinger 1977) and a book that serves as the definitive statement on the topic (1982). He asserted the fundamental import of studying these sharp contradictions to the dominant norms and values of a society as a means of gaining insight into social order. Countercultures, through their oppositional culture (polarity, reversal, inversion, and diametric opposition), attempt to reorganize drastically the normative bases of social order. These alternatives may range from rejecting a norm or value entirely to exaggerating its emphasis in their construction of countervalues. As a result, some countercultures fade rapidly while others become incorporated into the broader cultural value system. Examples of countercultural groups would include the 1960s student counterculture (in both its political and social dimensions); youth gangs (especially delinquent groups); motorcycle gangs (such as the Hell's Angels); revolutionary groups (the Weathermen of the Students for a Democratic Society, the Black Panthers, millenialists [Williams 1996]); terrorist organizations (such as the Symbionese Liberation Army); extremist racist groups (the Ku Klux Klan, skinheads [Baron 1997; Hamm 1995; Young and Craig 1997], the Aryan Nation); survivalists (Branch Davidians); punkers; bohemian Beats; "straight edgers;" Rainbow family; Earth First! (Lange 1990; Short 1991) and some extreme religious sects (such as the Amish and the Hare Krishnas [see Saliba 1996]).

VARIETIES OF COUNTERCULTURES

Yinger believed that countercultural groups could take several forms. The *radical activist* counterculture "preaches, creates, or demands new obligations" (Yinger 1977, p. 838). They are intimately involved with the larger culture in their attempts to transform it. Members of the *communitarian utopian* counterculture live as ascetics, withdrawing into an isolated community forged under the guidelines of their new values. *Mystical* countercultures search for the truth and for themselves, turning inward toward consciousness to realize their values. Theirs is more a disregard of society than an effort to change it. These three forms are not necessarily intended to describe particular groups. Rather, they are ideal types, offered to shed insights into characteristics or tendencies groups may combine or approximate in their formation. Hippie communities or bohemian Beat groups combined the mystical and utopian features of countercultures in their withdrawal from conventional society and their search for a higher transcendence. Revolutionary youth gangs, such as the 1960s radicals, the Hell's Angels, and the punkers, fuse the mystical search for new experiences and insights (often through drug use) with an activist attack on the dominant culture and its institutional expressions. Survivalists, Amish, and Hare Krishnas fuse the radical critique of conventional values and lifestyles with a withdrawal into an isolated and protected community.

Countercultures can be differentiated by their primary breaks with the dominant culture. Some take odds with its *epistemology*, or the way society contends that it knows the truth. Hippies and other mystics, for example, have tended to seek insight in homespun wisdom, meditation, sensory deprivation, or drugs, rejecting the rationality of science and technology. Others assert an alternative system of *ethics*, or the values pursued in defining good or striving for the good life. Some, like skinheads or KKK members, may be quite conservative in their definition of the good life; others are libertarian, advocating for people to "do their own thing." Still other countercultures offer alternative *aesthetic standards* by which fashion, taste, and beauty are judged. Punk or acid rock musical movements, performance or postmodernist art movements, and bohemian or hippie fashion movements were all aesthetic statements that incorporated a radical rejection of the standards of conventional taste and its connection to conventional values. Thus, entire countercultural movements may be based on their advocacy of these competing beliefs.

COUNTERCULTURES AND SOCIAL CHANGE

Due to their intense opposition to the dominant culture, countercultures are variously regarded as "engines of social change, symbols and effects of change, or mere faddist epiphenomena" (Yinger 1982, p. 285). Examining these in reverse order, countercultures are often considered *mutations* of the normative social order, encompassing such drastic lifestyle changes that they invoke deep ambivalence and persecution. Most major countercultural mutations appear in the form of religious movements. Other countercultures arise out of underlying or developing societal stress: rapid political or economic change; demographic transformations in the population (age, gender, location); a swift influx of new ideas; drastic escalation or diminishment of hopes or aspirations; weakening of ties to primary support circles (families, neighborhoods, work groups); and the erosion of meaning in the deepest symbols and rituals of society. These factors are then augmented by communication among people sharing such experiences or beliefs, leading them to coalesce into normatively and ideologically integrated groups. Countercultures can also precipitate social change if the norms and values they champion are incorporated into the mainstream. In commenting on the 1960s student movement, Chief Justice Warren Burger of the United States Supreme Court stated that "the turbulent American youth, whose disorderly acts [I] once 'resented,' actually had pointed the way to higher spiritual values" (cited in Yinger 1977, p. 848). Lasting influence may not always result from major countercultural movements, as witnessed by the rapid erosion in influence of Mao's cultural revolution after his death, yet it is possible. This occurs through a cultural dialectic, wherein each existing system, containing antithetical, contradictory ideas, gives rise to the oppositional values of a counterculture. These are ultimately incorporated into a future new order.

COUNTERCULTURE CASE STUDIES

While the student movement of the 1960s was undoubtedly the largest and most influential counterculture to arise in the United States, a review of three more contemporary American countercultures may yield further insight into the parameters and character of these movements. Let us focus on the Hare Krishnas, punks, and survivalists.

The Hare Krishna movement, also known as the International Society for Krishna Consciousness (ISKCON), is one of the religious movements that became popular in the United States during the great "cult" period of the 1970s (Judah 1974; Rochford 1985). Its rise after the decline of the 1960s student movement is not coincidental, for many people who were former hippies or who were influenced by or seeking the ideals and values of the 1960s turned toward new religions (Tipton

1982) in search of the same features of community, idealism, antimaterialism, mysticism, transcendence to a higher plane, and "a spiritual way of life, which stands outside the traditional institutions found in America" (Rochford 1985, p. 44). Its primary values conflicting with mainstream culture include the rejection of (1) material success through competitive labor; (2) education to promote that end; (3) possessions for sense gratification; (4) authority favoring the status quo; (5) imperialistic aggression; and (6) the hypocrisy of racial discrimination (Judah 1974, p. 16). After the death of its American spiritual master, Srila Prabhupada, in 1977, however, the movement peaked and became more commercialized, transferring its emphasis from self-expression and uniqueness perpetuation of the sect, thereby becoming more of a mass phenomenon.

In contrast to the religious and value components of the Hare Krishnas' rejection of mainstream culture, the punk or punk rock counterculture of the late 1970s and early 1980s was more of a style movement (Hebdige 1981). As Fox (1987, p. 349) has noted, "The punks created a new aesthetic that revealed their lack of hope, cynicism, and rejection of societal norms." This was expressed in both their appearance and their lifestyle. The punk belief system was antiestablishment and anarchistic, celebrating chaos, cynicism, and distrust of authority. Punks disdained the conventional system, with its bureaucracies, power structures, and competition for scarce goods (Fox 1987). Members lived outside the system, unemployed, in old abandoned houses or with friends, and engaged in heavy use of drugs such as heroin and glue. Hardcore commitment was usually associated with semipermanent alteration of members' appearance through tattoos, shaven heads, or Mohawk hairstyles (Brake 1985). The musical scene associated with punks was contrary to established tastes as well and often involved self-abandonment characterized by "crash dancing" (Street 1986).

In contrast to the hippies, Krishnas, and punks, the survivalist counterculture was grounded in exaggeration of right-wing beliefs and values. While some of the former groups preached love, survivalists were characterized by hate. Formed out of extremist coalition splinter groups such as neo-Nazis, the *KKK*, the John Birch Society, fundamentalist Mormon Freemen, the White Aryan Resistance, and tax protesters from Posse Comitatus,

survivalists drew on long-standing convictions that an international conspiracy of Jews was taking over everything from banking, real estate, and the press to the Soviet Politburo, and that the white race was being "mongrelized" by civil-rights legislation. A cleansing nuclear war or act of God, with "secular" assistance, would soon bring the Armageddon, eradicating the "Beast" in their midst (Coates 1987). Members thus set about producing and distributing survivalist literature, stockpiling machine guns, fuel, food, and medical supplies on remote farms and in underground bunkers, joining survivalist retreat groups, and attending survivalist training courses (Peterson 1984). Within their retreat communities they rejected the rationalization, technologization, secularization, and commodification of society, creating an environment of creative self-expression where an individual could accomplish meaningful work with a few simple tools. In their withdrawn communities and "utopian" future scenario, men would reclaim their roles as heads of the family; women would regain mastery over crafts and nurturance. Theirs is thus a celebration of fantasy and irrationality (Mitchell, n.d.). Yet while they isolate themselves in countercultures composed of like-minded individuals, they try to influence mainstream society through activism in radical right-wing politics as well. Their actions and beliefs, although rejecting the directions and trends in contemporary society, arise out of and represent frustrations felt by embattled segments of the Moral Majority (mainly fundamentalist Christian, white groups).

Scholarly treatment of counterculture movements is not limited to the United States. In the field of new social movements research, many European scholars have looked at organizations that are designed to mobilize forces against nationalistic cultures. These studies, ranging in topics from nuclear weapons, ecology, squatters' rights, gays, women, and other countercultural groups (i.e., Autonomen or terrorist organizations), have explored the common denominators inherent in all new social movements. Using quantitative data from protest events collected from newspaper sources in France, the Netherlands, Germany, and Switzerland, Hanspeter Kriesi and others (1995) outlined the "new cleavage" that exists in these Western European societies.

Countercultures thus stand on the periphery of culture, spawned by and spawning social trends and changes [by their opposition to dominant culture]. As Yinger (1977, p. 850) noted, "Every society gets the countercultures it deserves, for they do not simply contradict, they also express the situation from which they emerge. . . . Countercultures borrow from the dominant culture even as they oppose it."

(SEE ALSO: *Alternative Lifestyles*; *Social Movements*; *Student Movements*)

REFERENCES

Adler, Nathan 1972 *The Underground Stream: New Life Styles and the Antinomian Personality.* New York: Harper.

Baron, Stephen W. 1997 "Canadian Male Street Skinheads: Street Gang or Street Terrorists?" *Canadian Review of Sociology and Anthropology* 34:151–174.

Berger, Bennett 1981 *The Survival of a Counterculture.* Berkeley, Calif.: University of California Press.

Brake, Michael 1985 *Comparative Youth Culture: The Sociology of Youth Culture and Subcultures in America, Britain, and Canada.* London: Routledge.

Coates, James 1987 *Armed and Dangerous.* New York: Hill and Wang.

Davis, Fred 1971 *On Youth Subcultures: The Hippie Variant.* New York: General Learning Press.

Douglas, Jack D. 1970 *Youth in Turmoil.* Chevy Chase, Md.: National Institute of Mental Health.

Erikson, Erik 1968 *Identity: Youth and Crisis.* New York: W. W. Norton.

Flacks, Richard 1971 *Youth and Social Change.* Chicago: Markham.

Fox, Kathryn J. 1987 "Real Punks and Pretenders: The Social Organization of a Counterculture." *Journal of Contemporary Ethnography* 16:344–370.

Hamm, Mark 1993 *American Skinheads.* Westport, Conn.: Praeger.

Hebdige, Dick 1981 *Subcultures: The Meaning of Style.* New York: Methuen.

Irwin, John 1970 "Notes on the Present Status of the Concept Subculture." In D.O. Arnold, ed., *The Sociology of Subcultures.* Berkeley, Calif.: Glendessary Press.

Judah, J. Stillson 1974 *Hare Krishna and the Counterculture.* New York: Wiley.

Keniston, Kenneth 1971 *Youth and Dissent: The Rise of a New Opposition.* New York: Harcourt Brace Jovanovich.

Kriesi, Hanspeter, Ruud Koopmans, Jan Willem Dyvendak, and Marco G. Giugni 1995 *New Social Movements in Western Europe.* Minneapolis: University of Minnesota Press.

Lange, Jonathan I. 1990 "Refusal to Compromise: The Case of Earth First!" *Western Journal of Communication* 54:473–494.

Mitchell, Richard n.d. *Dancing at Armageddon: Doomsday and Survivalists in America.* Unpublished paper, Oregon State University.

—— 1991 "Secrecy and Disclosure in Fieldwork." In W. Shaffir and R. Stebbins, eds., *Experiencing Fieldwork.* Newbury Park, Calif.: Sage.

Peterson, Richard G. 1984 "Preparing for Apocalypse: Survivalist Strategies." *Free Inquiry in Creative Sociology* 12:44–46.

Reich, Charles A. 1970 *The Greening of America.* New York: Random House.

Rochford, E. Burke 1985 *Hare Krishna in America.* New Brunswick, N.J.: Rutgers University Press.

Roszak, Theodore 1969 *The Making of a Counter Culture.* New York: Doubleday.

—— 1995 "Introduction to the 1995 Edition." In Theodore Roszak *The Making of a Counter Culture.* Berkeley, Calif.: University of California Press.

Rothchild, John, and Susan Berns Wolf 1976 *The Children of the Counter-Culture.* New York: Doubleday.

Saliba, John A. *Understanding New Religious Movements.* Grand Rapids, Mich.: William B. Eerdmans Press.

Short, Brant 1991 "Earth First! And the Rhetorics of Moral Confrontation." *Communication Studies* 42:172–198.

Spates, James L. 1976 "Counterculture and Dominant Culture Values: A Cross-National Analysis of the Underground Press and Dominant Culture Magazines." *American Sociological Review* 41:868–883.

Street, J. 1986 *Rebel Rock: The Politics of Popular Music.* Oxford: Basil Blackwell.

Thornton, Sarah 1997 "General Introduction." In Ken Gelder and Sarah Thornton, eds., *The Subcultures Reader.* London: Routledge.

Tipton, Steven M. 1982 *Getting Saved from the Sixties.* Berkeley, Calif.: University of California Press.

Turner, Ralph 1976 "The Real Self: From Institutions to Impulse." *American Journal of Sociology* 81:989–1016.

Williams, Rhys H. "Politics, Religion and the Analysis of Culture." *Theory and Society* 25:883–900.

Wuthnow, Robert 1976 *The Consciousness Revolution.* Berkeley, Calif.: University of California Press.

Yinger, J. Milton 1960 "Contraculture and Subculture." *American Sociological Review* 25: 625–635.

—— 1977 "Countercultures and Social Change." *American Sociological Review* 42:833–853.

—— 1982 *Countercultures*. New York: Free Press.

Young, Kevin, and Laura Craig 1997 "Beyond White Pride: Identity, Meaning, and Contradiction in the Canadian Skinhead Subculture." *Canadian Review of Sociology and Anthropology* 34:175–206.

PATRICIA A. ADLER
PETER ADLER

COURT SYSTEMS AND LAW

Most sociological discussions of law begin with Weber's definition in which a specific staff is charged with avenging norm violation or ensuring compliance (*Economy and Society* 1968, p. 34). Weber's goal was to distinguish law from morality and convention, by which a whole community may act to impose sanctions. He also developed his now classic typology of formal legal systems (those limited only to legal as opposed to those legal systems he called "substantive," based on religious, economic, or moral criteria) and rational (those legal systems based on rules as opposed to those involving use of oracles, oaths, and ordeals, for example). Although he was careful to call these distinctions "ideal-types," that caution has not stopped persons from offering specific examples that are actually mixed types, as in speaking of "khadi justice" (a term, unfortunately, used by Weber himself) as a prime example of substantively irrational decision making in which a Moslem khadi sits under a palm tree and dispenses justice according to his personal feelings or inspiration. As Rosen (1989, ch. 1) shows, in actual cases he observed, the khadi does not exclude any evidence but relies on witnesses, notaries, documents, and any relevant evidence as well as testimony from interested parties. His goal, as in Islamic law generally, is to "put people back in the position of being able to negotiate their own permissible relationships . . ." (p. 17; see Nader 1969; Starr 1992). He follows a careful procedure, although the conduct of persons in his court may appear to Westerners to be more informal and more disorderly than that allowed in a typical Western court.

While anthropological studies of tribal societies have been shown to exhibit the whole panoply of Weberian categories (cf. Gluckman 1954; Bohannan 1957, 1967; Howell 1954; Kuper and Kuper 1965), even the classic moot (eg. Gibbs 1963; Gulliver 1969), while classifiable as substantively irrational since it subjects disputes to discussion by a whole village of involved or even merely curious onlookers, still follows definite procedures and is guided by a mediator or authorized persons. See also Stone (1979) on miners' meetings in the gold rush Yukon; MacLachland (1974) on the tribunal of the Acordada in eighteenth-century Mexico; and the People's Courts in postrevolutionary Russia (Feifer 1964). The goal of the moot, as Gibbs notes, is not solely legal but is at least what he calls therapeutic since the end sought is restoration of relationships and harmony. It turns out that goal is quite consonant with what we find in formally rational systems in the Western world. In any case, bases of all legal systems include: first, a reasonable certainty and predictability on which persons can depend, which, in practice, means no retroactive laws (as Fuller 1969 notes); second, fairness, which comes down to treating like cases alike; and third, justice should not only be done but be seen to be done, which means that there are no secret decisions, and decisions are in accord with generally agreed values, assuming they exist. These similarities are more important than the many variations in detail that can be found in different legal systems (cf. Pospisil 1958).

In what follows, we shall focus on the two main systems of law, *common law* and *Civil law*, which are found widely in much of the world. In so doing, we can give only passing reference to such systems as Islamic, Jewish, or Tibetan law, or to the many subtle differences found in tribal law. To further complicate matters, many national legal systems are blends of other systems, especially as the result of conquest (as is the case in Japan, which took over a German code but then had common-law features of public law grafted onto it after its occupation by the United States in the 1940s). In modern society, legal systems have become identified with the nation-state so that Canadian law differs from American law, as does Scotch from French law. Nevertheless, many can be said to share one of the two traditions we are considering. Although the two systems have been converging in many respects, each is distinctive in outlook as well as in court organization and the kinds of legal careers likely to be found.

The *Civil law* is by far the older, going back at least to the *Corpus Juris Civilis* of the Emperor Justinian in the sixth century C. E., though some scholars would trace it back to the 12 Tables of Rome, said to have been put together in 450 B. C. E. This system is found throughout Western and now Eastern Europe, most of Central as well as South America, and in many other areas in Africa as well as Asia, plus the state of Louisiana (for an example see *Williams vs. Employers Liability Assurance Corporation, Limited*, 296 F.2d 569 (1961) U.S), the Canadian province of Quebec (Magnet 1980), and Scotland. The *common law* system is often dated from the Norman conquest of England in the eleventh century, when the Normans sought to impose a single system on the country, hence the name "common law." Common law is now found not only in Great Britain but in those countries that made up the British Empire, such as Canada, Australia, New Zealand, Ireland, India, as well as the United States, and is influential in many countries of Africa and Asia. During colonialism, the common law countries preserved legal ties with England through Privy Council appeal, a process largely abolished or greatly attenuated today. Comparable appeals or ties to a single place were largely unknown to the civil law system. Whether the European Community will establish some form of tie remains to be seen.

THE BASIC COURT PARADIGM: THE TRIADIC DILEMMA

When persons with a grievance decide to take action, they may: (1) act separately from each other as in direct attacks, seizure of property, etc. (see Black 1993, chs. 2, 5); (2) confront the other party; or (3) enlist the participation of a third party to help settle the dispute. Courts are preeminently concerned with this third option, what we call "the triadic dilemma." Although courts deal with matters other than dispute settlement, such as law making (when judges make a new policy in decision making) as well, of course, as social control, they all employ a variant of a triad. Two persons or collectivities who have been unable to settle their differences or who have accused others of public harm have in all societies sought the help or guidance of a third party. The hope of each party is that the third party will side with them. Although each may think it fairest if the third party is neutral, in practice each hopes for a decision in his or her favor. As Simmel (1902; Wolff 1950; Caplow 1968) shows, parties of three are inherently unstable, being liable to break down when two of the three form a coalition to defeat the third, a phenomenon well-known to parents of small children.

The third party may be simply a go-between who offers his services unasked in the interest of preserving or restoring good relations. Or he or she may, as Shapiro (1986, ch. 1) notes, take a more active role as a mediator, though only with the consent of the two disputing parties. While mediators may seek to preserve their neutrality, in fact he may, as in the case of real estate agents, make proposals of their own and may shade the decision by how they handle the facts each shares with them. Less consent from the disputants is involved when an arbitrator appears who may be persons agreed to by the parties or persons imposed by the state or the terms of a labor contract, for example. Arbitrators are under no obligation of coming up with a solution agreeable to both, but they will usually try for such a solution. The most coercive situation of all is the appearance of a judge, either as required by law or by decision of a governmental body. Here the parties may have no say at all either in his appointment or on the body of rules he applies, which may be the terms of a contract or the rules of law.

The dilemma in all these triadic situations is, as noted, preventing the breakdown into two against one. Whatever the outcome, those who lose are likely to feel the other two have somehow combined against them or that they were defeated from the start. In common law systems, the myth of the neutral judge is much celebrated, although since judges are political figures who owe their position to their political activities and may even have been rewarded with the judgeship for their services, it is not surprising the loser feels he never had a chance. In Civil law systems, there is no pretence of neutrality. The judge is a member of the civil service and hence a part of government itself. With the prosecutor in criminal cases being also a member of the administration, the dice are loaded as two against one. On the other hand, this does not mean the civil law system is less fair or just.

Indeed, because of the many protections offered to the accused in common law systems, one author commented that if he were guilty, he would rather be tried in the United States but if innocent, then he would prefer the Civil law system because, for reasons we shall explain, judges have far less power than they do in the United States, and the system is far less adversarial. The Civil law judge assumes a more neutral role in searching for "truth," rather than winners or losers. Attempts are made in both systems to produce an outcome that each will feel is "just." Disputants may be asked to submit voluntarily, and if they do, they will be felt to have offered at least a modicum of consent to the outcome. Alternatively, attempts are made to avoid an all-or-none outcome. For example, in auto accident cases, one party may be felt to be 70 percent at fault and the other 30 percent, with a division of property in that proportion. In criminal situations, as in the United States, a plea bargain may enable the accused to walk away with a much lesser penalty than he or she might otherwise have suffered.

Actually, although plea bargaining is thought of as peculiar to criminal proceeding, negotiation is equally common in what are called "civil situations" (involving actions between two or more persons) where, as in criminal proceedings, an estimated 90 percent of cases are settled without trial. Such resort to negotiation places a special strain on the triadic model, particularly where the judge may himself participate, at least to the point of interviewing the accused in case of crime, or the parties in civil law, to provide assurance, at least in his own mind, that the accused or the plaintiff is aware of what is happening and has voluntarily entered into the "deal." (Klein 1976). What one needs to understand is that the ubiquity of negotiation in American law is an organizational model. Lawyers, both defending and prosecuting, as well as lawyers in other courtroom situations become "repeat players" (Galanter 1974), who deal routinely with one another as well as with judges, clerks, and others in the court. Gradually, their work becomes routinized, with all focusing on getting things moving and coming out with cases settled. The goal of the system, then, becomes one of efficiently moving cases through, with participants seeing themselves, however unwittingly, as agents of the system. As that takes place, the triad can be seen as disappearing altogether and being replaced by a work group consisting of three or more players who have an interest in the outcome of the game (see Eisenstein and Jacob 1977; Jacob 1983).

We proceed to a detailed examination of the two systems, beginning with the common law system as most familiar to American readers. But that very familiarity is likely to blind us to the assumptions of the system that contrast so sharply with the equally hidden assumptions of the civil law system.

THE COMMON LAW SYSTEM

Although most persons are taken with the image of justice as a "blind lady" who acts on the basis of the facts and the inherent justice of the situation, as Jacob (1996) points out, courts in common law systems are ridden with policy assumptions, no more so in the United States than in other places. While courts go about their business of settling disputes and ensuring orderly procedures, their procedures send symbolic messages (see Nelken 1997; Sarat and Kearns 1988). This is especially the case for appellate courts where, in contrast to European courts, judges are fond of wrapping up their decisions in opinions that are often more widely cited and influential than the decision itself. While conservatives are usually at pains to insist that judges confine themselves to being "strict constructionists," their opinions resonate with what the legal scholar Dworkin (1977) calls "principles." In the classic case of *Riggs vs Palmer* (115 N.Y. 506, 22 N.E. 188, 190, 1889), a presumptive heir on becoming alarmed at the possibility that his grandfather might change his will proceeded to eliminate that possibility by murdering him. The grandson was properly tried, but defended his right to his inheritance. The court refused to award the inheritance to him, leading a dissenting judge in the case to ask for the court's reasoning for this decision. After all, wrote the dissenter, the will was in order, was it not? There were the required witnesses, and there was no question that it was the intent of the testator that the young man should receive the bulk of the estate. With barely a reference to those issues, the majority awarded the bulk of the estate to the deceased's daughters, who, under the will, were to receive only token amounts. In sum, the majority proceeded to rewrite the will in direct contravention of the deceased's clearly expressed wishes. Although the majority hunted mightily for a source for their decision, turning variously to Aristotle, the Bible, an ancient case from Bologna, the Napoleonic Code, Roman law and, finally, to a rather desperate assumption that no specific law was really needed, anyhow. In the end they asserted that there is a "fundamental maxim" found in all "civilized countries," namely:

No one shall be permitted to profit by his own fraud, or to take advantage of his own wrong, or to found any claim upon his own iniquity, or to acquire property by his own crime. (Riggs vs. Palmer *1889*)

But the dissenter asked: What is the legal source of this "maxim?" It could not be found in any case previously decided, nor in any statute (such is no longer the case in most jurisdictions). Although he agreed that the principle had intuitive appeal and might be found in most religious and moral systems, the law, at least Western secular law, is not simply a set of religious or moral principles. In the United States, the Constitution specifically erects a wall between church and state. Since that case, the principle, once announced by the court, has been cited and is indeed now a part of U. S. (and most other common law countries) law. But we must not go too far and declare that common law is simply a set of principles. Rather, the law is informed by policy assumptions, often hidden, but influential nonetheless. Although civil law is equally political, attempts are much stronger to hide the policy assumptions with an insistence that only a legislature can make law. All judges are supposed to do is apply it with as little innovation or interpretation as possible, let alone enunciating "principles." The overall issue of how much politics and governmental policy is reflected in judicial decision making clearly affects the triadic system's functioning to produce or not produce a sense of justice done and seen to be done. It is this feature that has been seized upon by Marxists and proponents of socialist law who see both common law and civil law as simply disguised systems whereby bourgeois ideologies are foisted on a powerless proletariat by capitalist exploiters, whether governmental or private. Their answer to the triadic dilemma is that there never can be neutral third parties, with the result that the only reality is endless strife between parties with temporary truces as victors seek to pick up the spoils.

In addition to taking policy positions, courts in common law systems can have massive effects on society by judicial review of legislative acts, a phenomenon severely limited in civil law systems as we shall note. Courts also provide a major

alternate route to persons who lack funds or who have been stymied by attempts to influence legislation. Persons can convert a private grievance into a public cause (Savat and Scheingold 1998) by, for example, deciding that severe burns from hot coffee served at McDonald's requires court action to impose punitive damages as a warning to all companies serving the public that consumer safety must be a part of the design even in private firms. So too, persons suffering from lung cancer who have been unable to get protective legislation against cigarette companies have turned to the courts, not simply for financial awards, but for vindication of what they feel are violations of their rights, as citizens, to life. When added up, the damage awards in such suits as well as those even in routine automobile accidents, violations of privacy, and tort and contractual disputes have never been totaled but constitute a huge shift in resources comparable to that involved in taxation. Nor have we touched on the part that lawyers' fees play in such cases.

Finally, unlike judges in civil law jurisdictions who are part of the civil service from the start (judges in France, for example, even go to special schools), judges especially in the United States, often come to their judgeships in mid-life, after serving in political positions, business or other areas of life. Jacob points out that:

. . . between 1963 and 1992, between 58 and 73 percent of federal appeals judges had a record of party activism before their appointments; among federal district judges, between 49 and 61 percent had such a background. (1996, p.19)

Yet such a background should not lead to cynicism that judges are necessarily biased or pro-big business or pro-party. Their background in ordinary society helps ensure a commitment to the importance of the rule of law, of procedural fairness, and of individual rights as a legitimate expectation of ordinary citizens.

A special characteristic of common law court is often the source of surprise and some envy on the part of those schooled in civil law systems. American courts are often perceived as a jumble, with multiple urban, country, and state systems, so that what is actionable in Montana may not be actionable in Idaho and that if one is not happy with treatments in a state court, one can, with some issues, move to a federal court. Such "forum shopping" seems a travesty to those accustomed to single systems. Yet the United States has more a single system than have many European countries. In those countries, there are often two sets of courts—ordinary courts that try the vast majority of civil cases, and a second set of administrative courts for those who have quarrels with the government or administration. In the United States most regular courts can handle any case that comes before them (though there are many specializations), and ultimately, the U. S. Supreme Court sits at the top as the final arbiter of law (considering constitutional questions especially important and above all). Nor, it should be added, are courts entirely separate systems. They are dependent for salary and other resources on what Congress and legislatures will provide, and they do not appoint their own numbers. The U. S. Supreme Court is indeed supreme on law, but it is in no sense the apex of a bureaucracy that can appoint and discipline members of lower courts. Further, it is basically passive, waiting for cases to be brought to it when there is a "case or controversy," thus severely limiting its ability to act autonomously as a conscience of the nation. Often citizens gnash their teeth as the U. S. Supreme Court refuses to hear a case or decides it on the narrow issue that happens to have been presented to it. In that sense, the entire legal system is the property of the lawyers and what they choose to present to the courts, a situation vastly different from what we find in civil law systems.

The impact of lawyers in common law systems is greater than in civil law and indeed in any other system known to the world. Two major factors help account for lawyer dominance. One is the dependence on case law. Although legislation and statutes are basic sources of law, the necessity for interpretation and application to particular cases places enormous power in the hands of courts. If all legal systems require a strong sense of certainty, then that certainty is provided in common law systems by the majestic procession of cases, whether simply confirming one another, adding details, or overruling contradictory cases. To argue a case in an American court is to recite cases, and if there are enough of them, lawyers and judges feel the outcome can be considered settled. On the other hand, civil law systems depend on codes as enacted by revolutionary regimes, which codes are felt to

be the ultimate source of law, supplemented by legislation that is still felt to be a kind of supplement to the code. In a sense, the code is thought to settle the matter of certainty with little need for lawyers to interpret it. (This is less true in Germany where lawyers play a larger role.)

But in addition, especially in America, the model of the triad is felt to be basic. A court case consists of two adversaries who argue before a (one hopes, neutral and just) judge. The emphasis is on the adversarial process itself, a situation that produces not necessarily "truth" but rather a victory for one side. Lawyers play the key role, a matter that often leaves the outcome to the skill of the lawyers as much as to other features of the case. The judge is felt, if not to be neutral, at least to be passive, waiting for lawyers to present objections or evidence as they wish. If a lawyer chooses not to present a piece of evidence or simply sloppily forgets to do so, the judge cannot intervene to instruct the lawyer on what he has left out. In civil law systems, the judge, while a mere civil servant, has more power to direct the course of the trial, assuming what is often spoken of as an "inquisitorial style." Given the major role that lawyers play in common law systems, it is important to give attention to how that role is played out. Since data are more complete, we shall use U.S. sources. However, comparable rates of increase for most categories are found in Canada and Great Britain (see Galanter 1992). This is not meant to deny the differences, especially cultural variations, in those countries (see Atiyah and Summers 1987).

DOMINANCE OF LAWYERS IN COMMON LAW SYSTEMS

In spite of their widespread influence and frequently very high income, lawyers in America are not a happy lot. They are not esteemed (a Gallup Poll found that 46 percent of respondents rated lawyers "low" or "very low" in honesty and ethical standards, just barely above used-car salesmen). A survey by the California Bar Association in 1992 reported that 70 percent of those polled said they would choose another career if they could. Even more—75 percent—confessed that they would not want their children to become lawyers. Other studies report that lawyer job satisfaction is dropping, along with much higher levels of alcoholism, drug abuse, and symptoms of depression than those found in the general population.

In spite of such indices of self-destruction, the number of lawyers in the United States has been rising, especially in the 1990s. From 374,000 in 1975, the number of lawyers will soon top one million as 31,000+ new lawyers are admitted to the bar every year. The field is proving attractive to minorities and women. From a low of only about 3 percent in 1971, female lawyers now make up over one-quarter of the total of practicing lawyers, and nearly one-half of students in entering law school classes. Female lawyers, as a group, are younger, with only 7 percent being over 50 compared to 30 percent of their male colleagues.

The location of practice has, however, not changed significantly. Private practice is dominant, even increasing, so that by 1991, 73 percent of lawyers were in private practice, with only 8.8 percent found in private industry, and 8.2 percent in government. But private practice has been undergoing profound changes. Solo practitioners have become scarcer as lawyers move increasingly to firms. The increase is mainly in larger firms (those with at least eleven lawyers). In 1980, the very large firms (one hundred or more lawyers) accounted for only 7 percent of firm employment. By 1991, that percent jumped to twenty-three. The large firms are the more common locus for men, with women being more likely to be found in government, legal aid, and in public defender's offices. Some of these differences are declining as more women enter the profession and attain experience. On the other hand, more women, proportionally, are leaving the profession.

It is the large firms that attract more and more of the new lawyers who seek distinguished and lucrative careers. The largest—often called "mega firms"—range from the Washington, D. C., firm of Williams & Connolly with 127 lawyers (sixty-one partners) producing revenues of $78 million, to true giants, such as the New York firm of Skadden, Arps, Slate, Meagher & Flom, with over 1,000 lawyers (236 partners) earning well over half-a-billion dollars in gross revenue. Some firms are even larger. They are not, of course, all under one roof but scattered in different cities as well as in foreign countries. Not only are these the places where the largest salaries are found, but they are also the platforms from which government and

other influential careers are launched, including leading positions on major committees and boards, as well as ambassadorships and presidencies. Twenty-five of the forty-one U. S. presidents have been lawyers, as well as half of U. S. senators and nearly half of all members of Congress. Lawyers are widely found in governorships and state legislatures as well. If these are not the most esteemed members of society, they certainly are among the most powerful and perhaps the most feared.

Although most persons in common law systems are aware of the presence of lawyers in those settings, it is not the image most have when they think of lawyers, and it is not the setting in which they see them in television drama. Instead, it is the lawyer, often solo or in a small firm, arguing for his or her client in a courtroom before a jury. The television image runs counter to the image of real lawyers in the news, leading to charges that the United States is a "litigious" society, in which large awards are given for burns suffered from spills of hot coffee, and there are suits against arrest for breast-feeding in public or for recovery of expenses on being stood up for a date. Though most such cases are thrown out immediately by disgusted judges or settled out of court for modest sums, critics person who may never hear of those outcomes continue to demand that we follow the lead of the nonlitigious Japanese, for example, who make do with very few lawyers. Actually, the number of lawyers in Japan is deliberately kept low by the governing elite to preserve a hierarchical social order. Nor are the Japanese devoid of a taste for litigation by any means (Haley 1978, 1991, ch. 5).

Nor has the United States had a "litigation explosion" nearly as great as some have claimed. There was only a moderate increase at the state level in the 1990s. It is true that there has been a large increase in the number of federal cases, not of the trivial sort noted above but rather of big businesses suing each other. The news of most of those ends up on the back pages of the *Wall Street Journal*. Other federal cases deal with asbestos and similar injuries as well as other suits by government (Galanter 1983; Galanter and Palay 1991). The reason it seems that the U.S. is experiencing a litigation explosion is that there is an increasing prominence of what have been called "mega" cases, in which large masses of lawyers and experts pursue a single case, sometimes for years on end. Although most involve business, a few involve highly prominent individuals who have the resources and will to fight, intimidate, and otherwise bring up issues, subsidiary issues, and more of what Damaska (1978, p. 240) has called "companion litigation" where, along with the main case, separate suits are filed on discovery, on legal fees, on standing, and on other issues, which lengthen proceedings and often do little more than harass the other side or both sides into exhaustion. Such cases take the form of a "prolonged clinch and. . . settlement" (Galanter 1983, p. 163) while rarely ever ending up in court. Meanwhile, such cases contribute to the image of the United States as a "litigious" society.

Yet, even granting all such cases, very few lawyers are involved in doing such things. Only a small minority of all dealings of U. S. lawyers ever result in a contested court action. Most legal practice takes place in offices for the benefit of business firms, and only a small minority deal with individual clients at all. Even in those cases, lawyers spend much of their time persuading suit-eager clients not to go to court but to work out a settlement. Lawyers generally limit themselves to cases they think they can win. Often filing a case is symbolic of seriousness of intent, forcing a response from the other party; but the cases are settled, sometimes on the very eve of the court date or even as the trial, if there is one, is in process.

What all this amounts to is that the legal profession in the United States is "split." Most lawyers quietly carry on the journeymen work of settling disputes and assisting persons to compromise so that they can carry on with their lives. A very, very few carry out the courtroom battles of the O. J. Simpson type that dominate the front pages of the nation's newspapers. In such cases, lawyers are not seen as settling disputes but they are seen by many people as "getting people off," leading to cynicism or to despising lawyers, even when or even because they win. Many cases take place outside the large law firm, but the reputation of lawyers created by the sensational cases affects the public image of all lawyers, wherever located.

One special feature of the split deserves attention; namely, income. Solo and small-firm lawyers carry out much of the work of helping persons set up partnerships, get a divorce or settlement from an insurance company, draw up wills, and deal with persons who are in minor trouble with the law. On the other hand, work in a large law office is carried out by specialists who do the complex work of big business. Large businesses often make use of their own "in-house counsel" for the routine work of contracts, labor-management negotiation, and other repetitive legal activities. The company turns to outside law firms for the unusual, once-only activity, such as mergers and acquisitions, floating new securities, takeovers, and bankruptcies. Such activities call for the highest degree of expertise and knowledge, far beyond what a solo lawyer might be called upon to have. A major study of Chicago lawyers (Heinz and Laumann 1982) asked them to rank legal specialties in prestige. At the top were securities, tax, antitrust, patents, banking, and public utilities—the activities in which large law firms are involved. At the bottom were criminal defense and prosecution, personal injury, consumer debt, landlord-tenant, divorce, and family—the concerns of the solo and small-firm lawyer. The income differentials between the two clusters are equally impressive. A major study reported salaries from large firms in Indianapolis and New York to average around $300,000 per partner for the year, but many make much more. A New York law firm reported that each of its 121 lawyers (sixty-one equity partners) earned over $1 million. Many others were not far behind. Lawyers in solo and small firms are not poor but make a good deal less. A 1995 survey reported that those lawyers earn somewhere between $75,000 and $100,000 a year, assuming they work a full two-thousand billable hours, which some do not. Associates (that is, nonpartners) start out, according to a 1996 study, from lows of $40,000 to as high as $70,000, but then rise with each year in the larger firms to $150,000 and up, plus bonuses. Stories of such incomes add little to offset the low esteem in which lawyers are held, especially since most persons who deal with lawyers find the lawyer wants money "up front" or on a retainer basis, unless a contingency arrangement is made, and often even then. (Note: The preceding section draws from the author's paper, Gross 1998.)

TOO MANY LAWYERS?

A final issue that troubles many observers both in common law and civil law countries is

Judges, Lawyers, and Civil Litigation in Selected Countries

Country	Judges		Lawyers		Civil Cases	
	Date	Number per Million	Date	Number per Million	Date	Number per Million
Australia	1977	41.6	1975	911.6	1975	62.06
Belgium	1975	105.7	1972	389.7	1969	28.31
Canada	1970	59.3	1972	890.1	1981-2	46.58
Denmark					1970	41.04
England/Wales	1973	50.9	1973	606.4	1973	41.1
France	1973	84.0	1973	206.4	1975	30.67
Italy	1973	100.8	1973	792.6	1973	9.66
Japan	1974	22.7	1973	91.2	1978	11.68
Netherlands	1975	39.8	1972	170.8	1970	8.25
New Zealand	1976	26.8	1975	1081.3	1978	53.32
Norway	1977	60.8	1977	450.0	1976	20.32
Spain	1970	31.0	1972	893.4	1970	3.45
Sweden	1973	99.6	1973	192.4	1973	35.0
United States	1980	94.9	1980	2348.7	1975	44.0
W. Germany	1973	213.4	1973	417.2	1977	23.35

Table 1

whether the United States, in particular, is "over-lawyered." Some even see this question as helping account for the so-called litigiousness of American law. Whatever the numbers, an increasing number of civil cases are settled either during or after trial. Lawyers play their role in filing cases, but most of their work is done outside the court, which, of course, means lots of work for lawyers. Further, although cases may never reach court, as Mnookin and Kornhauser (1979) put it, much negotiation takes place in the "shadow of law." That is, lawyers, well or poorly acquainted with actual court cases, call attention to what is "likely" to happen if they go to court, not to speak of the delay and expense. So law, or at least imagined law, plays a dominant role even when never specifically called into play (Ewick and Silbey 1998).

A useful table (table 1), if read with caution, is provided after careful research by Galanter (1983, p. 53).

Although we do not provide the sources, the results differ in dependability and the care with which they have been calculated. Still, the contrasts, however crude, are revealing. As to civil cases, the United States is seen to stand toward the middle, exceeded by Australia, New Zealand, and Canada, with many others being much lower. The United States is at the lower end in judges, being exceeded by W. Germany, Belgium, Italy, and

Sweden. But when we come to lawyers, the United States far exceeds other countries, though Australia, New Zealand, Canada, and Spain are also richly supplied. As we note later in the discussion of civil law countries, many others not called "lawyers" do what the United States would call "law." Such persons include notaries, government officials of many kinds, law clerks in private firms, and, in Japan, the very high proportion of those who take the exam but are not allowed to practice (they do just about everything lawyers in the United States do except represent clients in court).

In making such international or intercultural comparisons, one should bear in mind differences in conceptions of what is worth disputing over and indeed what a dispute is in the first place. The studies by Felstiner, Abel, and Sarat (1980–81) suggest that a great many, perhaps most, injurious experiences are never perceived as such, but rather thought of as simply part of the risks of living. Some proportion of these are seen as violations of some right, but even many of those are simply "lumped," that is, borne with equanimity or tolerated as not worth pursuing because of time or costs. A small proportion are, however, charged to a specific causal agent, and if a person or collectivity, then become what are called "grievances." Some small proportion of those in turn, if voiced, turn into claims that, if rejected, become "disputes." In turn, most (90 percent approximately) disputes brought to lawyers are settled with varying degrees of satisfaction, lawyers often functioning to persuade the aggrieved that they should accept a settlement and move along with their lives. Whether persons are willing to pursue a grievance depends on technology and the ability to find a causal agent, as well as the existence of such legal devices as no-fault automobile insurance or divorce, which have the effect of diverting cases out of the legal system (see Kritzer, Bogart, and Vidmar 1991). Some countries, such as many on the European continent, have special labor tribunals and other systems that also divert cases out of what would, in the United States, be a legal case. The United States has fewer such alternative forums than is the case in the civil law world.

Jacob (1996, p. 52) speculates that the United States is, perhaps, more a nation of strangers, leading to a greater willingness to pursue disputes than is the case in countries with a stronger sense of community. In general, it may be said that the closer persons are, whether as family, neighbors or co-religionists, the less likely are they to sue one another. On the other hand, that does not mean there are fewer conflicts in such groups. Rather, there are internal mechanisms for settling them *within* such groups.

A final point about common law systems that contrasts with civil law systems is the widespread availability of appeal, particularly within the judicial systems. Although much of this is perfunctory and may involve little more than an attempt to satisfy clients with the appeals court routinely affirming the lower court, still appeal is possible, much more so than in civil law countries. Appellate judges often lack experience and are not required to have experience as trial judges. In some cases, judges have discretion on whether to hear an appeal, leading to selection of cases that may be controversial or present novel points of law. The extreme is presented by the U. S. Supreme Court which, in the 1990s, has elected to consider around 100 out of some 5,000 cases presented to it, usually reserving to hear constitutional cases and conflicts between the states or foreign governments. It is difficult to assess the impact of appeals on the civil or criminal process. Unlike trial judges, appeals judges do not merely decide cases but also give reasons. Such reasons are often examined by elite lawyers and are now routinely discussed in the "legal" columns of popular magazines. It is not clear that the reasons affect policy in any obvious way. But the language of the court enters common discourse and affects thinking. School boards, church councils, Boy Scout boards, and even teachers' decisions on classroom discipline become legalistic, with persons being given notice of charges, given chances to answer, and allowed to bring witnesses in their defense. In the United States, as in common law countries, the law seems to be everywhere (Galanter 1983), even if not formally invoked.

THE CIVIL LAW TRADITION

In drawing comparisons between the common law and civil law traditions, it is important not to dismiss variations as due simply to "historical experience" or to even vaguer influence of "culture." History and culture are, of course, operative at all times, but we seek not simply a description but a sociological explanation. We must begin with the recognition of what Zweigert and Kotz (1987) call "functionalism." By that they mean that all legal systems deal with generally similar problems as, say, medical systems do. Whether the society employs witchcraft, herbs, appeals to the gods, leeches, hot baths, or Western-style x-rays and surgery, they all deal with illnesses of the body. So, too, legal systems concern themselves with trouble presented by the fact that humans live in society and must deal with each other. In Chiangmai, Thailand, for example, it is not surprising to find that three main classes of law suits appear: crimes as offenses against public order or the state, which are dealt with seriously by the courts; private wrongs, such as those arising from marital disputes, which are settled by negotiation; and those conflicts involving contracts and property rights, which are settled by careful examination of written and especially certified documents (Engel 1978). The details are indeed "cultural," involving what Watson (1977) speaks of as "legal transplants," by which a society adopts some procedure borrowed from another society because it is accessible, written in a language the elite can read (such as Latin for Roman law), or more commonly simply the law of a conquering power as with England or India. One wastes one's time if one looks for rational reasons or tries to account for such transplants on grounds of "efficiency," although often people come to believe in the superior efficiency of the system of law they happen to use.

On the other hand, a close examination of legal procedures can have much to teach about the assumptions taken for granted in the culture (Ross 1993; Nelken 1997). In a report on a personal experience in Indonesia, Lev (1972) tells of an accident in a hotel in which a toilet tank, affixed high up on a wall, fell, nearly hitting a friend. To Lev's amazement, the hotel presented him and his friend with a bill for repairs. Lev refused, turning for help to a local judge, who was also a friend, for support for what Lev felt were his legal rights. The judge, while agreeing that those were indeed his legal rights, proposed that Lev make a token payment as evidence of "good will." With reluctance, Lev did so since compromise or peace was, the judge reminded him, after all, more important than vindication of rights. An even more obvious example is presented in a Mexican case in which the supreme court absolved a court for liability for the theft of money and jewels left in the care of the court pending settlement of the case. After all, said the court, Mexico is a poor country that cannot afford safe deposit boxes or secure storage places, but they do the best they can. The court then quotes what it clearly sees as a universal "principle of law," "*impossibilium nulla obligatio est*," which the court translates simply as "No one is obligated to do the impossible" (quoted in Merryman, Clark, and Haley 1994, p. 684). These considerations are spoken of by Glendon (1987) as the "hortatory" function of law in civil law systems. She contrasts that with a view that American and British law usually involve a command backed up by punishment. Yet, whatever the system, laws, whether self-consciously doing so (as in civil law systems) or inadvertently (as in common law systems), always teach lessons as persons observe their operations.

Understanding of the civil law systems requires recognition that they come to us in two widely separated parts. The first is what is owed (and that is a great deal) to Roman law as codified in the sixth century under the Emperor Justinian as the *Corpus Juris Civilis*. This magnificent collection includes the law of persons, family, inheritance, property, contracts, and remedies, all of which the juriconsults (the legal experts) of the day saw as forming a unified body of law and which has been largely seen that way ever since. The influence was not simply on the Civil law system as such but has had a strong effect on civil law (narrowly conceived) in common law countries as well. Basic principles the Roman jurists developed echo through the ages up to the present.

With the invasions of Rome that followed, much of this law fell into disuse or was united with the local laws of German tribes. However, *canon law*, as developed by the Catholic Church for its own uses, came to be widely adopted and grafted onto classic Roman law, influencing family law and civil procedure as well as much else, though not public law for the most part. Then, with the Renaissance, classic Justinian law was revived, especially in Bologna, where scholars gathered from all over Europe to study it, in Latin of course, and then spread it, where it came to be known as the *jus commune*. However, as it spread, it was inevitably influenced by local laws and customs that were often simply added to it in the interests of utility for solutions of local problems. A third development was *commercial law*, also from Italy, at about the time of Crusades, when there was much transport of goods and persons. The guilds and towns that developed this law were, for the most part, only tangentially influenced by Roman law since the focus was on rules merchants developed for their own use. Such rules spread even more widely than the *jus commune* up to the present day, where much of it can be found in admiralty law and related fields. It is quite clear, for example, that when two ships approach one another on the high seas there had better be a clear understanding as whether they both keep to the right or to the left, and that understanding must be clear whatever the differences in language, culture, or tradition. It is the nearest thing law offers to a truly international and intercultural system.

But there is more to modern civil law than a revival and Renaissance enrichment. The system was almost totally transformed by the ideas that gave birth to the political revolutions that began in the seventeenth century and are far from over at the present day. The revolutions were, of course, the American and French Revolutions, the military and ideological events associated with the unification of Italy and Germany, the coming new nations as the Turkish Empire disintegrated, the movements for freedom from Spanish and Portuguese domination in the Americas, as well as the chaos that followed the great wars of the nineteenth and twentieth centuries. While the word "chaos" may be useful in a strictly descriptive sense, it is better to speak of these changes in the term employed by Schumpeter (1976) as winds of "creative destruction," for they did not simply destroy but created what we speak of as the modern world. What they destroyed was basically feudalism and the concept of status fixed at birth as well as the conception of a divinely ordained, and hence unchangeable, social universe. In Weber's classic phrase, we witnessed a "disenchantment of the world" which left humans, in the words of the existentialists, fated to create their own world and take responsibility for it. This meant that law was secular, torn loose from any religious basis, but focused instead on what came to be called "positive law," that is law enacted by legislatures and parliaments. The transformation was not merely procedural but involved substantive changes in the assumptions of legal rights. These were the now-familiar rights stated in the American and French revolutionary documents—rights to liberty and property, the opportunity to change one's status through one's own efforts, the right to own land in one's own person rather than merely, as in feudalism, as a serf or dependant of a feudal lord. Along with these changes came fundamental changes in loyalty and allegiance. Instead of fealty and subordination to lord or guild master, allegiance came to be narrowed to a single, overarching focus on the nation-state. The power of the church was similarly destroyed or greatly attenuated, as in England, and with that decline went the jurisdiction of ecclesiastical courts as well, though some of the traditions of canon law as, for example, in civil procedure (where courts make use of written records of proceedings and much less, than in common law systems, of oral testimony in trials), were retained.

Although the state and the law created by legislators came to make up the substance of law, it should be noted that in time it became evident that some controls were necessary on the state itself. In the United States, this control is institutionalized in the doctrine of the separation of powers, especially the ability of the courts to rule on the constitutionality of legislative enactments as well as the authority and legality of administrative acts and regulations. The civil law countries also elaborated a separation of powers but a very different one. The concern there was the enormous power judges had during the feudal period to act, usually in support of the landed classes and the aristocracy. As Stone (1986) points out, the French *parlements* (panels of judges) had almost limitless power—they could arrest seditious persons, ban public gatherings, evaluate regulations of all kinds, supervise guilds and universities, and act as censors of public morals. Somewhat similar powers were enjoyed by the *audiencia* as representatives of royal power by the Spanish conquerors of Latin America. Such power led to their becoming wealthy and powerful, which led, in the case of France, ironically, to their own undoing. Although their vast powers might (and did occasionally) act as a break on royal powers, instead in a final act of defiance of the royal power, they threatened to resign on the very eve of the French Revolution. The Constituent Assembly voted to place them on indefinite vacation and then abolished them altogether. In a sense, their very arrogance and posturing led to a recognition that they would be a permanent obstacle to the new freedoms the revolutionaries wished to establish. A result was that there was a serious attempt to reduce the judge forever to a mechanical figure who would simply carry out the expressed will of the parliament in the name of the people. As such, the judge would have no inherent powers at all but would become a clerk or servant. He was not to presume even to interpret the will of the parliament. But how was that to be achieved?

The answer was to create a code that could answer all legal questions for the judge. In terms of the triadic model, two adversaries would argue before a neutral third who would simply delve into the code, find the answer, and impose the solution on them. In practice, as we can see from our vantage point, matters could never be so simple. As time went on, the concept of a legislative or code monopoly of law gave way to systems whereby the judge could declare legislative or administrative acts unconstitutional, but the process involved much hedging by being careful, at first, at least to locate the places in which such review could take place outside the ordinary court systems in special constitutional courts (often not even called courts) as in France, Germany, Italy, and Spain, and in most Latin American countries, though in the latter, more influenced by U. S. practice, they were less reluctant to call them courts. There was little of this problem in England, which changed more slowly, retained more feudal practices, and, most important, did not go through a bloody revolution to achieve the doctrine of parliamentary superiority (though the British did cut off at least one head and became, for a time, a republic).

Although one often speaks of common law systems as made up of cumulative, judge-dominated case systems, and Civil law countries as code systems, Merryman (1985, ch. v) reminds us that the contrast is overdrawn and misleading. All American law students are forced to master the Uniform Commercial Code, and many states routinely refer to their laws as "codes." So too, there are code nations, such as Hungary, that actually did not enact a code until it became a socialist state, although it was a Civil law country before then. Instead, what is distinctive of codes in civil law systems is that they are unified documents that seek to express the spirit, ideology, and goals of the new state the revolution has created. Thus, the French code, the *Code Napolèon* of 1984, sought to express the ideology of the French Revolution—liberty, equality, and fraternity—in every clause. It was intended to be a blueprint for a utopia. Thus, every attempt was made to abolish or at least hide any earlier statutes or laws that were inconsistent with it and try to make a fresh start. Law would now begin with the *Code Napolèon*.

Further, in lines with the French *Declaration Rights of Man and of the Citizen*, the *Code Napolèon* must be one that the average Frenchman could read and interpret for himself without "humiliating" himself by going through clerks, officials, and other overlords to get to the courts. As such, lawyers would be unnecessary. For this to be possible, the code must be complete—without gaps. Everything would be covered. Although manifestly impossible, the Germans did make a valiant attempt to do so in the Prussian *Landrecht* of 1794, which laid out some 17,000 detailed "fact situations" that were felt to cover everything that could come up, thus eliminating any need for lawyers or interpreters. It failed, but it is a striking illustration of how persuasive was the ideology of the French Revolution, which created the belief that it could be done. In the *Code Napolèon* and others following it, the goal of completeness is achieved but only by broad statements that practically invite judicial interpretation. (For example, the Italian Civil Code of 1942 tells judges to follow the intention of the legislature, and if it is not entirely clear, then to reason by "analogy.")

Germany, under Bismarck, did enact a code in the full sense but in what can only be seen as a very Germanic manner. The *Code Napolèon* began with certain assumptions about human nature (equality, liberty, etc.) and tried to produce a humanistic code that would, presumably, have universal application. Under the influence of Savigny, a major German historian, that approach was felt to be inappropriate. Instead, he insisted (in the face of heated controversy) that the German code (and he did agree that a code was necessary), since it was intended to represent the spirit of German society, must be based on the German *volkgeist* (folk spirit). But it was first necessary to decide what that was. To that end, and with help of German romantic writers, he felt it necessary to plumb German history for the basic elements of the *volkgeist* and build the code up from those elements. That code would then be not only historically oriented but also scientific (in being built up by logical and empirical deduction from basic principles) and professional. This code would not be revolutionary—quite the contrary—but would be a true code in being built up, paragraph by paragraph, from principles that could stand on their own as a legal document and manifesto of the new Germany. One difference from the French code was that with its complexity and its dependence on the many historical details that went into the *volkgeist*, it would require lawyers to explain and interpret it. Nevertheless, it was careful, like the French, to make sure judges would have little power, perhaps even less than was the case in France. For answers, the German litigant, with the help of his lawyers, was to go to the code and, above all, not to seek answers as American and common law lawyers do. That would just return power to the judges again.

Codes were also enacted in the many countries in Europe and elsewhere that followed the French or German systems (Japan tried doing both, with a dollop of the U. S. model thrown in as well (Haley 1991), though the German model eventually triumphed). When a code was shown to have gaps, scholars (in keeping with the tradition of drawing on the juriconsults in Roman law) would develop a new principle, as in an example provided by Watson (1981), wherein a doctrine similar to the British concept of *estoppel* was developed to cover cases where a person had acted contrary to his usual practice but others had come to rely on this new behavior. But when a new interpretation (rather than a gap) was the problem, the court would draw on similar cases, not as precedents but to use as a basis for a new principle that would be held to govern the case at hand. In this manner, the spirit of a code based on permanent principles would be maintained.

The German approach to codification had a lasting effect in emphasizing the dominant role of the scholar in civil law systems generally. Although the scholars were everywhere evident, in the case of Germany, Savigny and his followers felt that in creating what they considered to be a code based on "scientific" principles they were creating a body of law that was indeed scientific in a sense not unlike that of the physical sciences. It was built up from empirical elements, could be found to be true or false, subject, as any science is, to modification as new facts came in. It came to be called "legal science," which remains the dominant school of thought even up to the present, however much criticized. It had its own concepts, such as a "juridical act," and was systematic in structure and therefore an infinite distance from such American schools of thought as "legal realism." Above all, the Pandectists (as they came to be known, from the Latin word for Justinian's *Digest–pandectae*) felt their great strength was their purity in being divorced from politics and everyday life.

Actually, as Merryman (1985, pp. 65) points out, the Pandectists were far from being value free. The doctrine was shot through and through with the basic assumptions of nineteenth-century European liberalism—private property, liberty of contract and, above all, individualism. They were most limited in their concept of law as a matter of transactions between private individuals, an assumption that was to collapse in the growth of giant collectivities, such as corporations and labor federations and, most important, the increased role of the state in managing economic and social life. Although civil law systems recognize the distinction between private and public law, even dividing up law in just that way, they hardly anticipated, nor could they, the merging of the two systems as states began to manage private life, and as private relations became imbued with public consequences as with pollution, the spilling over of populations across borders and, still later, the emergence of new national groups or even nations and new communities such as the European Community (cf. Gessner, Hoeland, and Varga 1996).

It is clear from the above that the Uniform Commercial Code in the United States, though called a code, has nothing in common with the civil law codes. It is not animated by any underlying utopian principles, it makes no claim to answer all questions, and it makes no attempt to supersede any laws. Instead, it is a collection that seeks to bring some order into the many elements of commercial law. States are free to ignore it (though few do so), and new laws can be tacked onto it at any time. It remains judge-made law, with judges being free to draw on it or not for precedent as they please.

Legal science did leave one imprint on American law, though a minor one. *Case law*, as taught in American law schools, was thought of as a kind of science, with cases as the raw materials. Conclusions from case accumulations might generate principles with wide applications. An attempt to state these principles took the form of what were called *restatements*, which are, from time to time, quoted by judges as they go about making law.

JUDGES

As we have noted, the position of judges in civil law countries is vastly different from that in common law countries, especially the United States. Merryman (1985) points out that judges are not only respected in the United States but that some, such as Marshall, Holmes, Brandeis, and Cardozo, are culture heroes. The opinions of U. S. Supreme Court judges are studied carefully, as noted earlier, for hints of policy changes and guidance on how to proceed in deciding on difficult issues such as euthanasia, product safety, and whether schools may require bilingualism of its teachers. There seems no limit to areas into which judges may wander. Nor do judges hesitate in passing judgment on any law (if appropriate, of course) or even on the private life of the President of the United States. As has often been noted, American law is judge-made law built up from cases that lawyers have presented for decision (and, note, the judge must limit himself to such presentations, since he is very limited in his power to bring up issues on his own initiative). The supreme doctrine is that of *stare decisis*, whereby judges are required to follow decided cases; new cases must be compared to those already decided. If similar facts, then a similar decision. If the facts are significantly different, then there is a different decision. As noted by

Clark (Merryman 1991, p. 898), this need to do such case research, which falls on the shoulders of lawyers, helps explain (though only partly) the fact that the United States has more lawyers per capita than any other country for which we have reliable statistics.

Nothing could be further from that image among civil law judges. To begin with, the status of "judge" is usually much lower than is the case for common law judges. A civil law judge is a government employee, a civil servant, appointed to his position, whose career will follow that of other civil servants in rising by seniority and merit. His prestige is not necessarily low but reflects the prestige of civil servants at his level. He likely identifies with other civil servants, though more closely with judges, resulting in a certain insularity from the general public and its concerns. He is particularly isolated from any creative role in decision making. In line with the continuing suspicion of the dangers of judicial power going back to the *parlements* of pre-Revolutionary France (as well as similar excesses in other countries), he must not interpret the law or review legislation. As noted, he is a kind of expert in the application of the law to particular cases. More recently, constitutional review has begun to make its appearance in Austria, Spain, Italy, and Germany, but this goal is achieved not through giving judges in the ordinary courts new powers but rather through the creation of special constitutional review bodies that often are not called "courts" but that in time perform court functions.

This is not to say that appeal from judicial decisions was or is impossible. Quite the contrary, appeal is common but still dominated by attempts, at least in form, to restrict the power of judges. Thus, in France, appeal for what is claimed to be a misinterpretation of a law may be made to the Court (originally called a tribunal) of Cassation which could quash an incorrect interpretation by a lower court. It would indicate the correct interpretation but then remand it to the lower court to modify its ruling. The courts could ignore this decision but in practice would rarely do so. The process was time-consuming, and, in the case of Germany, the higher court would not only quash the lower decision but go ahead and revise the decision itself. It was also possible to appeal administrative rulings, though not, as in the American case, by declaring a law unconstitutional or lacking in validity because of vagueness or for being over-broad. Instead, another body outside the court system was created. These might be what would amount to administrative courts, with a council of state at the top, a process seen not only in France but also in Italy and Belgium, as well as in Germany and Austria, where they were actually called administrative courts. Such attempts to counter state power were not necessary in a country such as England, where courts have the power of *quo warranto* (questioning the legality of an act by a public official) and *mandamus* (the ability to order a public official to perform as required by law). As noted, similar powers are possessed by ordinary American courts, though it is difficult for courts to use them.

The attempts to control the power and initiative of judges was tied up with another concern of civil law traditions; namely, the search for certainty. As long as judges had interpretive powers, the law was a tool in their hands that could be twisted to suit particular interests. Instead, the hope was that if the code plus legislation was clear and complete the judge would not need to exercise any initiative. Such a concern with certainty is not foreign to common law, either—persons need to know what the law says for law to be a guide to behavior. However, in civil law there is little that resembles the concept of equity at law. *Equity*—the power of a judge to limit the harshness of a law or to adapt the law to fit particular situations—gives him great powers. In England, equity reached its greatest development in the creation of chancery courts as a way of appealing to the king against what was felt to be an unjust rule of law. Civil law countries, though occasionally, and grudgingly, conceding a place for equity, preferred to confine it to the legislature, which might grant equitable powers to a court for a particular case or might make what amounts to an equitable grant of power to a court by telling it that, when the law is unclear, the court is to see to it that the parties acted "in good faith." But the suspicion of judicial discretion remains and is not always a simple prejudice. Thus, the Nazi regime in Germany was able to make use of such discretion by using the courts to provide a patina of legality to its racist decrees, a process more difficult in Mussolini's Italy, where discretion was more restricted.

One other important difference is that the English and American courts include in equitable powers that of *contempt*. A litigant or witness who refuses to follow court processes or who refuses to carry out the will of the court may be subject to the contempt power, which can include fines and imprisonment. This degree of power is quite unknown in civil law countries where it is felt to give the judge what amounts to discretion to impose criminal penalties in civil cases. The civil law judge must, in comparable cases, limit himself to drawing on the person's property which may, of course, be felt by the person, as no less painful than a period in prison might be for others.

THE LEGAL PROFESSIONS

In the United States, lawyers, as well as the general public, think of the legal profession in the singular, though specialties are recognized. This is especially the case, as noted earlier, since such a high proportion are in private practice (well over 70 percent) as compared, for example, to only 33 percent in Germany, 42 percent in Colombia and only 23 percent in Chile. The United States also has a very low proportion of the profession acting as judges (only 3 percent) compared to 17 percent in Germany, 23 percent in Chile, and 42 percent in Colombia. (Clark 1982, figures are for the 1960s and 1970s). In Germany, 70 percent of positions in general administration are filled by persons trained in law.

Apart from differences in distribution, the path to a legal career is very dissimilar in different cultures. In the United States, aspiring lawyers go to a graduate law school, then sit for the bar exam (often after an intensive cram course that prepares them for that exam), then after passing the bar (in most states, the success-rate percentage is over 60 percent, and higher for first-time exam takers) he or she enters directly into practice in a firm, in a small-firm partnership, or as a solo. There they learn as they go along. Persons may, and many do, shift around from service in a government department to a public prosecutor office to the corporate law office of a private firm, or elsewhere. They may run for political office and may end up being rewarded for service by appointment or election as judge of a lower-level court and, for a few, high judicial office in a circuit or even a supreme court.

In England, the distinction between solicitor and barrister, though less rigid than in the past, continues. The would-be barrister takes his pupilage under a barrister in one of the Inns of Court where he may, under good conditions, receive an apprenticeship and possible appointment after passing an examination. Only barristers may argue cases in the higher courts. Solicitors maintain direct contact with clients, collect fees, and assist barristers in their work. Solicitors are now being allowed to argue cases in some lower courts. Some barristers may develop honored reputations, a few being chosen as judges as the culmination of a distinguished career. There is almost no shifting to other careers on the part of barristers and very little among solicitors. In that respect, they resemble the lawyers in civil law countries.

In civil law countries, a young lawyer must make an early choice as to whether he wishes to be a judge, a government lawyer, a regular lawyer in private practice, a public prosecutor, or a notary. If he finds later he made a mistake, exit to another legal career is difficult, and does his experience in one does not translate into credits in another. He spends his whole career in the one field, a process that often leads to rivalry and conflict between the fields. An attempt to deal with this problem is made in Germany (and some other countries) in the *referendarzeit*, where a lawyer spends two or so years of practical training as a government lawyer, a judge, and in private practice. If lawyers choose to be judgse, they will begin their career in a low-level court but may move up as openings occur. Although this career process isolates the judges who take on guild-like characteristics as civil servants, it also means that judges are often better trained than is frequently the case in the United States (where it is not uncommon for judges to have had no judicial experience whatsoever). Further, the quality of judging may be higher since candidates are chosen from among the best law school graduates. At the top in constitutional courts, for example, the quality of decision making is the equal of that found anywhere.

Public prosecutor in Civil law countries are much like U. S. district attorneys, but they also are required to represent the public interest in proceedings between private persons in court situations. In Italy and France, the prosecutor is also a member of the judiciary, allowing some shifting back and forth from prosecutor to judge. Some degree of shifting back and forth also takes place in Germany. Those lawyers working for the government in administrative positions are career bureaucrats. Closest to the U. S. lawyer in private practice is the French *avocat* (distinctions such as those between the *avoues*, who acted as solicitors in appeals courts, and the *conseil juridiques*, who give general advice and represent clients before commercial courts, are gradually being eliminated or reduced in significance), the German *anwalt* or Italian *avvocato* (Merryman et al., p. 918). Much different from that known in the United States is the notary who receives legal training and is an important person. He drafts important legal instruments, such as corporate charters, wills, and instruments transferring land, as well as contracts. Most important, he authenticates documents. Once he does so, the instrument is accepted in court without further question. They also have monopolistic control over assigned territories. In Germany the services of a notary are required to validate legal documents for purchase, sale, and mortgage of land, for official records of decisions of company meetings, and for sale of shares in a private company (Merryman et al., p 911). Academic lawyers are found in a law school where they carry on the tradition of the old Roman juriconsult. However, most academic lawyers work for a professor with little or no pay, and wait for a vacancy that may never come. In Latin American countries, such persons may hardly earn a living, having to take on regular work as a lawyer in private practice or in public office.

CIVIL AND CRIMINAL PROCEDURE

Something should be said, in brief, about variations in procedure between the two systems. Here, the word "civil" is used in contrast to criminal. There is no trial or jury in civil cases, as may often be the case in the United States, though not in England. The entire process is different. The presence of a jury in the United States forces an acceleration of the entire process because of the difficulty and expense of getting the jury assembled and empanelled. Once that is the case, the court proceeds immediately with the trial in an attempt to conclude as quickly as possible.

In Civil law jurisdictions, civil cases go much more slowly. There is a brief preliminary stage when pleadings are submitted to a hearing judge. Next follows an evidence-taking, where the hearing judge takes notes and prepares a written record. That is later submitted to the deciding judge

who receives briefs from the counsel and listens to arguments. All of this takes the form of a series of meetings as each issue is brought to the attention of the hearing judge. There is little surprise as each lawyer is notified of each issue as it comes up, and, without a jury, there is no cross-examination. Generally, questions are passed to the judge who may conduct the investigation. There are fewer of the rules of evidence familiar to American lawyers (such as the exclusionary rule whereby illegally gathered information is excluded from trial), though a number of rules are employed, such as excluding biased persons from testifying, as well as taking what is called a "decisory oath" in some countries. There is in many countries a "loser pays" rule, referring mostly to legal fees, though the amounts are usually limited by a court schedule. Contingent fees are usually considered illegal (France) or unethical (Germany) but are found in Japan, Indonesia, and Thailand (Merryman et al., p. 1026). Many foreign legal authorities are appalled by its prevalence in the United States, feeling that a lawyer should not be personally given a stake in the outcome of a case.

Although substantive criminal law is similar in both systems, civil law jurisdictions, in line with the revolutionary principle of limiting the power of judges, reject the American practice, which gives the judge power to award penal and general damages in criminal cases, not to speak of the contempt power (which is very rare), instead insisting the judge be limited to what is provided for in legislation. The contrast is often drawn (or overdrawn) between what is called the "accusatory" model in the United States and the "inquisitorial" model in civil law countries. Historically, the accusatory procedure is felt to have been a development from that of private vengeance in which the interested parties would be the main participants. Instead of settling their dispute by direct conflict or feud, a legal procedure would involve a neutral third party who would seek to secure a settlement. In such a triadic situation, as noted at the outset, the object was to secure an outcome that would settle the matter by leaving each party feeling justice had been done. In earlier times, when trial was by battle, ordeal, or other ways, although seeming to be a throwback to a time of "barbarous" cruelty, these methods, apart from their presumed psychological effects (the guilty party feeling he would be caught and so offering confession at once), had the virtue that they brought the conflict to an end, and prevented further acts of vengeance that would disturb the peace of the community. With the accusatory practice, presumably conflict would also be terminated but might go on if each party felt justice had not been done.

The inquisitorial model introduced the state as an active participant in the trial. Now the judge, who is after all a representative of government, is in a coalition with the prosecution against the third party, the defendant. Although this biases the process, in practice, the introduction of the jury, the fact that proceedings are oral, as well as limitations on the power of the judge all combine to make the system fair, though excesses did and continue to exist.

The criminal trial is in three parts: the investigative phase, with the public prosecutor assuming an active role; the examining phase, presided over by a judge who assumes an active role in examining the evidence; and preparing a record and the trial. Judges may, if warranted, end the proceedings if they feel the evidence is not conclusive, or they may decide the case should go to trial. The accused is entitled to legal representation as well as the right to inspect the material the judge has collected. He can be questioned, but not sworn, and he or she may refuse to answer. Unlike the American system in which a defendant, if sworn, may then be cross-examined, no comparable procedure exists, though a refusal to answer by the accused may be taken into account by the jury. British judges assume a more active role in the trial process than is the case in the United States. However, this is not "inquisitorial" in a narrow sense but rather a reflection of the fact that in the English procedure the judge determines the relevancy of evidence, rather than the strict exclusionary and other rules emphasized in American courts. To do their jobs, English judges are much more willing to question witnesses or even raise issues (Glendon et al., 1982, ch.. 10).

Until the 1980s, plea bargaining was considered to be undesirable practice, only possible in America. But judicial scholars increasingly asked how could civil law jurisdictions possibly handle all the criminal cases they had to decide without some form of plea bargaining? After a spirited debate and careful research, it was finally concluded that

plea bargaining, though not exactly like that used in America, was in fact being used in European countries. In the case of Germany, Hermann (1991) reports that some kind of plea bargaining takes place in from 20 to 30 percent of all cases. While far from the American percentage of 90 percent, that is still considerable, particularly since it is accompanied by other forms of sentence reduction and mitigation of offenses. It is widely employed in complex cases, such as white-collar crimes, tax evasion, and drug offenses, which present nearly impossible evidentiary problems, as well as less serious crimes, which are settled with a fine. It is rare in cases involving violent crimes, however. Bargaining occurs at all stages of a criminal proceeding, often with the active participation of the judge, who may even take the initiative. A settlement may take the form of the accused agreeing to pay a sum of money to a charitable organization. Other alternatives include penal orders that are similar to *nolo contendere* pleas in which the accused agrees to a fine—usually for minor misdemeanor cases, such as traffic cases. Pleas also occur if the accused makes a confession. Normally, a confession does not lead to avoidance of a trial, as is the case in America. Instead, it usually leads to a reduction in the sentence. Other countries are also beginning to allow plea bargaining as many had been doing, but are now doing more openly. The most striking example is that of Italy, which even uses the term *patteggiamento*, the Italian word for bargain (Piazzi and Marafioti 1992; Merryman et al., pp. 1100 ff). However, there is no reduction of the charge, as in the American system, but there is a maximum reduction of one-third of the normal sentence, which may not exceed two years, which has the effect of limiting the practice to cases with shorter normal sentences. In Italy, as is the case in other civil law countries, the trial decision is made by a panel of judges, a practice which, however costly, is defended as superior to the American practice, which places what is felt to be excessive power in the hands of a single judge.

WILL COMMON LAW AND CIVIL LAW SYSTEMS PERSIST?

Although we have focused on differences between the two systems, and the differences are indeed substantial, there is considerable movement toward the convergence of common and Civil law systems. The attempts to severely limit the power of judges have, over the years, been recognized as excessive and more a holdover from fears of arbitrary and class-based favoritism of judges. From the refusal to place limits on the power of legislatures, Civil law countries have developed constitutional limitations, even in the form of courts, though often hidden under other names. Historically, Civil law countries divided the field between private and public law, with most of the concern historically being with civil law (law of persons, marriage, contracts, torts, etc.). Public law was felt to be the concern of legislatures or the sovereign. However, the coming of the modern state has led to an enormous growth of administrative law, along with appropriate court systems, leading to situations not much different in essence from those found in developed common law countries.

Civil codes have receded in significance as state legislatures and parliaments enact more far-reaching laws never contemplated in earlier times, particularly those associated with large-scale industry, the welfare role of governments, complex bodies of labor law, and especially with the emergence of the government as an economic participant in national affairs. Perhaps of greatest significance is the emergence of new international entities, especially the European Community, before which national codes have been slowly giving way. Of course, that tendency may be reversed, but it seems strongly in process. On the other hand, common law countries have recognized the advantages of classic civil law procedures, such as the importance of certainty in legal decision making, though such certainty is sought not through a code but by a succession of cases. The power of judges to make decisions has been the object of attempts by the U. S. Congress to place caps on awards for injury, as well as the attempt of persons to bypass courts and seek justice through changes in legislation, as in cases of pollution, abortion, and other public issues.

Is one system better than the other? The question is unanswerable in that form. Even though civil law authorities continue to be suspicious of lawyers, they discover they must have them and grant them powers they would prefer not to. That is, of course, a well-known problem in the United States as well. Each system must be understood in the context of the culture and social structure of the country that employs it. Ultimately, any question of superiority must be answered in terms of

how well the system serves the legal needs of the country. Most countries, in fact, employ a mix of systems in which one finds bits and pieces of both common law and civil law systems.

REFERENCES

Atiyah, P.S., and Robert S. Summers 1987 *Form and Substance in Anglo-American Law.* Oxford: Clarendon Press.

Black, Donald 1993 *The Social Structure of Right and Wrong.* San Diego, Calif.: Academic Press.

Bohannon, Paul J. (ed.) 1967 *Law and Warfare: Studies in the Anthropology of Conflict.* Garden City, N.J.: Natural History Press.

—— 1957 *Justice and Judgment Along the Tiv,* London: Oxford University Press.

Boigeol, Ann 1998 "The French Bar: The Difficulties of Unifying a Divided Profession." In Richard L. Abel and Philip S. C. Lewis, eds., *Lawyers in Society: The Civil Law World,* vol. 2, 258 ff.

Caplow, Theodore 1968 *Two Against One,* Englewood Cliffs, N.J.: Prentice-Hall.

Clark, David S. 1975 "Judicial Protection of the Constitution in Latin America." *Hastings Constitution Law Quarterly* 2:405–442.

—— 1982 "The Legal Profession in Comparative Perspective: Growth and Specialization." *American Journal of Comparative Law* 30, Supp.:163, 169.

Damaska, M. 1978 "A Foreign Perspective on the American Judicial System." In T. J. Fetter, ed., *State Courts: A Blueprint for the Future.* Williamsburg, Va.: National Center for State Courts.

Dworkin, Ronald 1977 *Taking Rights Seriously.* London: Duckworth.

Eisenstein, James, and Herbert Jacob 1977 *Felony Justice: An Organizational Analysis of Criminal Courts.* Boston: Littel, Brown.

Engel, David M. 1978 *Code and Custom in a Thai Provincial Court: The Interaction of Formal and Informal Systems of Justice.* Tucson: University of Arizona Press.

Ewick, Patricia, and Susan S. Silbey 1998 *The Common Place of Law.* Chicago: University of Chicago Press.

Feifer, George 1964 *Justice in Moscow.* New York: Simon and Schuster.

Felstiner, William, Richard L. Abel, and Austin Sarat 1980–1981 "The Emergence and Transformation of Disputes: Naming, Blaming and Claiming. . ." *Law and Society Review* 15:631–654.

Fuller, Leon 1969 *The Morality of Law*. New Haven, Conn.: Yale University Press.

Galanter, Marc 1992 "Law Abounding: Legalization Around the North Atlantic." *Modern Law Review* 55:1–24.

—— 1983a "Mega-Law and Mega-Lawyering in the Contemporary United States." In Robert Dingwall and Philip Lewis, eds., *The Sociology of the Professions*. London: Macmillan.

—— 1983b "Reading the Landscape of Disputes: What We Know and Don't Know (and Think We Know) About Our Allegedly Contentious and Litigious Society." *UCLA Law Review* 31:5–71.

—— 1983c "The Radiating Effects of Courts." In Keith O. Boyum and Lynn Mather, eds., *Empirical Theories About Courts*. New York: Longman.

—— 1974 "Why the Haves Come Out Ahead: Speculations on the Limits of Legal Change." *Law and Society Review* 9:95–125.

——, and Thomas Palay 1991 *Tournament of Lawyers*. Chicago: University of Chicago Press.

Gessner, Volkmar, Armin Hoeland, and Csaba Varga (eds.) 1996 *European Legal Cultures*. Dartmouth: Aldershot.

Gibbs, James L., Jr. 1963 "The Kpelle Moot: A Therapeutic Model for the Informal Settlement of Disputes." *Africa* 33 (Jan.):1–11.

Glendon, Mary Ann 1987 *Abortion and Divorce in Western Law*. Cambridge, Mass.: Harvard University Press.

——, Michael Wallace Gordon, and Christopher Osakwe 1982 *Comparative Legal Traditions in a Nutshell*. St. Paul, Minn.: West Publishing Co.

Gluckman, Max 1954 *The Judicial Process Among the Barotse of Northern Rhodesia*. Manchester, Eng.: Manchester University Press.

Gross, Edward 1998 "Lawyers and Their Discontents." *Society* 36 (Nov./Dec.):26–31.

Gulliver, P. H. 1969 "Dispute Settlement Without Courts: The Ndendeuli of Southern Tanzania." In Laura Nader, ed., *Law in Culture and Society*. Chicago: Aldine.

Haley, John Owen 1991 *Authority without Power*. New York: Oxford University Press.

—— 1978 "The Myth of the Reluctant Litigant." *Journal of Japanese Studies* 4:359–396.

Heinz, John P., and Edward O. Laumann 1982 *Chicago Lawyers: The Social Structure of the Bar*. New York: Basic Books.

Hermann, Joachim 1992 "Bargaining Justice—A Bargain for German Criminal Justice?" *University of Pittsburgh Law Review* 53:755–776.

Howell, P. O. 1954 *A Handbook of Nuer Law*. London: Oxford University Press.

Jacob, Herbert 1996 "Courts and Politics in the United States." In Herbert Jacob et al., ed., *Courts: Law & Politics in Comparative Perspective*. New Haven, Conn.: Yale University Press.

—— 1983 "Courts as Organizations." In Keith O. Boyum and Lynn Mather, eds., *Empirical Theories About Courts*. New York: Longman.

Klein, John F. 1976 *Let's Make a Deal*. Lexington, Mass.: Lexington Books.

Kritzer, Herbert M., W. A. Bogart, and Neil Vidmar 1991 "The Aftermath of Injury: Cultural Factors in Compensation Seeking in Canada and the United States." *Law and Society Review* 25:499–543.

Lev, Daniel S. 1972 "Judicial Institutions and Legal Culture in Indonesia." In Holt Claire, ed., *Culture and Politics in Indonesia*. Ithaca, N.Y.: Cornell University Press.

Levasseur, Alain 1970 "On the Structure of a Civil Code." *Tulane Law Review* 44:693–719.

MacLachland, Colin M. 1974 *Criminal Justice in Eighteenth Century Mexico: A Study of the Tribunal of the Acordada*. Berkeley: University of California Press.

Magnet, S. Rodgers 1980 "The Right to Emergency Medical Assistance in the Province of Quebec." *Revue du Barreau*, Tome 40, Numero 3, Mai-Juin, 373–447.

Merryman, John Henry 1985 *The Civil Law Tradition>*. Stanford, Calif.: Stanford University Press.

——, Davis S. Clark, and John O. Haley 1994 *The Civil Law Tradition: Europe, Latin America and East Asia*. Charlottesville, Va.: Michie.

Mnookin, Robert, and Lewis Kornhauser 1979 "Bargaining in the Shadow of Law: The Case of Divorce." *Yale Law Journal* 88:950–997.

Nader, Laura 1969 "Styles of Court Procedure: To Make the Balance.: In Laura Nader, ed., *Law in Culture and Society*. Chicago: Aldine.

Nelken, David (ed.) 1997 *Comparing Legal Cultures*. Dartmouth: Aldershot.

Pospisil, Leopold 1958 *Kapauka Papuans and Their Law*. New Haven, Conn.: Yale University Publications in Anthropology, No. 54.

Rosen, Lawrence 1989 *The Anthropology of Justice*. New York: Cambridge University Press.

Rosenn, Keith S. 1992 "A Comparison of the Protection of Individual Rights in the New Constitutions of Colombia and Brazil." *University of Miami Inter-American Law Review* 23:659–691.

Ross Marc Howard 1993 *The Culture of Conflict*. New haven, Conn.: Yale University Press.

G. Roth, and C. Witticg 1978 *Economy and Society*. Berkeley: University of California Press.

Rouland, Norbert 1994 *Legal Anthropology*. Stanford, Calif.: Stanford University Press.

Sarat, Austin, and Thomas R. Kearns (eds.) 1998 *Law in the Domains of Culture*. Ann Arbor: University of Michigan Press.

——, and Stuart Scheingold (eds.) 1998 *Cause Lawyering*. New York: Oxford University Press.

Schumpeter, Joseph A. 1976 *Capitalism, Socialism and Democracy*. New York: Harper and Row.

Shapiro, Martin 1986 *Courts: A Comparative and Political Analysis*. Chicago: University of Chicago Press.

Simmel, Georg 1902 "The Number of Members as Determining the Sociological Form of the Group." *American Journal of Sociology* 8:1–46, and 158–196.

Starr, June 1992 *Law as Metaphor: From Islamic Courts to the Palace of Justice*. Albany, N.Y.: State University of New York Press.

Stone, Bailey 1986 *The French Parlements and the Crisis of the Old Regime*. (excerpted from Merryman et al., eds., 436–437).

Stone, Thomas 1979 "The Mounties as Vigilantes: Perceptions of Community and the Transformation of Law in the Yukon, 1885–1897." *Law and Society Review* 14:83–114.

Watson, Alan 1977 *Society and Legal Change*.

Wolff, Kurt H. (trans., ed., and Introd.) 1950 *The Sociology of Georg Simmel*. New York: Glencoe Press.

Zamudio, Hector Fix 1979 "A Brief Introduction to the Mexican Writ of *Amparo*." *California Western International Law Journal* 9:306–348.

Zweigert, Konrad, and Hein Kotz 1987 *Introduction to Comparative Law* (trans. Tony Weir). Oxford: Clarendon Press.

EDWARD GROSS

COURTSHIP

Given the social centrality of the family institution and the role of courtship in the family formation process, it is not surprising that the study of courtship has received attention from several disciplines. Anthropologists have described practices in primitive and other societies, historians have traced courtship patterns in America from colonial to contemporary times, psychologists and social psychologists have examined intra- and interpersonal components of relationships, and sociologists have developed research-based theories explaining the process of mate selection, and have investigated various courtships dynamics. Here, some attention will be given to each of these approaches, along the way selectively noting scholars who have made major contributions.

Historically, according to Rothman, the term *courtship* applied to situations where the intention to marry was explicit (if not formally—and mutually—stated). *Courting* was the broader term used to describe socializing between unmarried men and women" (Rothman 1984, p. 23, italics in original).

Scholars have disagreed as to whether dating—a twentieth-century term for a primarily recreational aspect of courting—should be considered a part of courtship since, according to Waller (1938) and others, dating may be merely thrill-seeking and exploitative, and not marriage oriented (but see Gordon 1981 for an opposing view). However, wooing (that is, seeking favor, affection, love, or any of these) may be integral to courtship and yet not result in marriage. For present purposes, then, courtship will be understood in its broadest sense—as a continuum from casual to serious. Thus, "the unattached flirt, the engaged college seniors, the eighth-grade 'steadies,' and the mismatched couple on a blind date are all engaging in courtship" (Bailey 1988, p. 6).

Queen, Habenstein, and Quadagno's (1985) classic text provides much of the basis for the following brief and highly generalized overview of some mate-selection patterns unlike those found in contemporary America. Some of these systems involved little or no courtship. For example, among the ancient Chinese, Hebrews, and Romans, marriage was arranged by male heads of kin groups. Among the ancient Greeks and until recently among the Chinese, many brides and grooms did not meet until their wedding day. Around the turn of the century (1900), infant marriages were the rule among the Toda of south India, and the bride was deflowered at about age ten by a man who was not of her clan and not her husband. In medieval England, contrary to the literature of chivalry, love had little to do with mate selection in any social class because marriages were arranged by lords or by parents with primary regard to the acquisition of property.

In societies where romantic love is not a basis for mate choice, such sentiments are seen as dangerous to the formation and stability of desirable marital unions—those that maintain stratification systems (see Goode 1969). Queen, Habenstein, and Quadagno (1985) describe still other mate-selection patterns that do involve some form of love, including the systems found on Israeli kibbutzim at midcentury, among ethnic immigrant groups in the United States, and among African-Americans during slavery (see also Ramu 1989). In the twentieth century, however, and especially since the 1920s, courtship in Western societies has been participant-run and based on ideas of romantic love. In the United States today, it is not uncommon for a couple to meet, woo, and wed almost without the knowledge of their respective kin. "Compared with other cultures, ours offers a wide range of choices and a minimum of control" (Queen, Habenstein, and Quadagno 1986, pp. 8–9).

In colonial America, practices differed somewhat between the North and South. In the North, mate choice was participant run, but a suitor's father had control over the timing of marriage since he could delay the release of an adequate section of family land to his son while the son's labor was still needed. Conjugal (but not romantic) love was thought to be the *sine qua non* of marriage, and couples came to know and trust one another during often lengthy courtships. In the South, a custom of chivalry developed, closely guarding the purity of (at least upper-class) women, but condoning promiscuity among men. Parental consent was required for the beginning of courtship and for marriage and open bargaining about property arrangements was commonplace. Unlike the colonial North, where marriage was considered a civil ceremony, in most parts of the South, Anglican church ministers were required to officiate at weddings. In both regions, banns were published prior to weddings.

During the 1800s, mate choice became more autonomous with the growth of cities and the spread of industrial employment. Choices were affected less by considerations of wealth than by personal qualities—especially morality, spirituality, and "character." Wooing was rather formal, with each participant carefully evaluating the qualities of the other. Courtship tended to be exclusive and directed toward marriage.

Then, from about 1900 to World War II, a system evolved in which there was much "playing the field" (casual dating), gradually more exclusive dating ("going steady"), engagement, and finally, wedding—a relatively fixed sequence. Following the war, stages of courtship were typically marked by symbols (e.g., wearing a fraternity pin, then an engagement ring), each stage implying increased commitment between the partners. By the 1950s, a separate youth culture had developed. Ages at first marriage declined dramatically, and dating started earlier than ever before. The sexual exploration that had previously been a part of the last stage of courtship now occurred earlier, even in very young couples.

During the 1960s, a time of "sexual revolution," nonmarital cohabitation increased—not substituting for marriage but delaying it. In the post World War II. period and since, among the young especially, demands for both freedom and dependence (i.e., the right to sexual freedom without assuming responsibility for its multifaceted consequences) have been relatively widespread. Concurrently, rates of nonmarital pregnancy rose dramatically.

In general, every society attempts to control sexual activity among unmarried (and married) persons, but the forms of control (e.g., chaperonage) and the degree of enforcement have varied. Virginity, especially in women, is highly prized and guarded in some cultures but has no special value in others. Similarly, all societies attempt to limit the pool of those eligible to marry, but the precise constraints have differences across societies and from time to time. Typically, blood kin and relatives by marriage (and in some cases, baptismal relatives such as godparents) are delimited to greater or lesser degrees from the eligibility pool.

Where male elders have arranged marriages for their offspring (generally in ascription-based societies), the accumulation of family power and prestige has been of primary concern, with dowrys, bride prices, or both figuring prominently in prenuptial arrangements. In participant-run mate selection (generally in achievement-based societies), the power and prestige of a dating partner (although defined in terms other than land, cattle, and the like) is still valuable. Good looks (however defined) in women, for instance, are a status symbol for men, and conspicuous consumption in men (cars, clothing, spending habits) provides status for women. Thus, within the field of eligibles is a smaller field of desirables. Unfortunately, the qualities that are valued in dates (from among whom a mate may be chosen) are not necessarily those one would want in a spouse.

Even in participant-run "free choice" systems, there is a tendency toward homogamy in the selection of partners, whether conscious or not. As a society becomes more varied in its mix of persons within residential, educational, religious, or work-related settings, the tendency toward heterogamy increases. That is, the field of eligibles and desirables broadens. Heterogeneity leads to a prediction of "universal availability" (Farber 1964) as the salience of social categories (such as race, age, religion and class) declines. For example, interracial relationships, once unthinkable (e.g., in the colonial American South), increased with urbanization, industrialization, and a general movement toward educational and income equality. Social class endogamy, however, is the general preference, although women are encouraged with varying degrees of subtlety to "marry up," and a dating differential exists such that men tend to court women who are slightly younger, physically smaller, and somewhat less well educated or affluent than themselves.

Contemporary courtship, marked as it is by freedom of choice, has been likened to a market in which the buyer must be wary and in which there is no necessary truth in advertising. Persons compete, given their own assets, for the best marital "catch" or the most status-conferring date. Waller and Hill (1951) warned about the potential for exploitation in both casual and serious courtship and indeed, critics of conventional dating have decried it as a sexist bargaining arrangement in which men are exploited for money and women for sexual favors. The superficiality of dating, its commercialization, the deceit involved (given contradictory motives), and the high levels of anxiety provoked by fears of rejection (especially in men), are additional drawbacks. Since status differentials still characterize the sexes, dating may also be seen as a contest in which a struggle for power and control between partners is part of the game. Thus, courtship's emphasis on individualism, freedom, commercialism, competitive spirit, and success reflects the larger social system within which it functions. One may well ask whether such a system can prepare participants for marriage which, unlike courtship, requires cooperation and compromise for its successful survival.

Efforts to predict who marries whom and why, to delineate the courtship process itself, or both, have interested a number of scholars. Based on a large body of theoretical and empirical work, Adams (1979) developed a propositional theory to explain how courtship moves from initial acquaintance toward (or away from) marriage in an achievement-oriented society. The propositions, in slightly modified language, are as follows:

1. Proximity, which facilitates contact, is a precondition for courtship and marriage.

2. As time passes, marriage is increasingly more likely to be with a currently propinquitous than with a formerly propinquitous partner.

3. Propinquity increases the likelihood that one will meet, be attracted to, and marry someone of the same social categories as oneself.

4. Early attraction is a result of immediate stimuli such as physical attractiveness, valued surface behaviors, and similar interests.

5. The more favorable the reactions of significant others to an early relationship, the more likely the relationship will progress beyond the early attraction stage.

6. The more positive the reaction of the partners to self-disclosures, the better the rapport between them.

7. The better the rapport between the partners, the more likely the relationship will be perpetuated beyond the early attraction stage.

8. The greater the value compatibility—consensus between partners, the more likely that the relationship will progress to a deeper level of attraction.

9. The greater the similarity in physical attractiveness between the partners, the more likely that the relationship will progress to a deeper level of attraction.

10. The more the partners' personalities are similar, the more likely that the relationship will progress to a deeper level of attraction.

11. The more salient the categorical homogeneity of the partners, the more likely that the relationship will progress to a deeper level of attraction.

12. The more salient the categorial heterogeneity of the partners, the more likely that the relationship will terminate either before or after reaching a deeper level of attraction.

13. The greater the unfavorable parental intrusion, the more likely that the relationship will terminate either before or after reaching a deeper level of attraction.

14. An alternative attraction to the current partner may arise at any stage of a couple's relationship. The stronger that alternative attraction to either partner, the more likely that the original couple's relationship will terminate.

15. The greater the role compatibility of the partners, the more likely that the relationship will be perpetuated.

16. The greater the empathy between the partners, the more likely that the relationship will be perpetuated.

17. The more each partner defines the other as "right" or as "the best I can get," the less likely that the relationship will terminate short of marriage.

18. The more a relationship moves to the level of pair communality, the less likely it is that the relationship will terminate short of marriage.

19. The more a relationship moves through a series of formal and informal escalators, the less likely it is to terminate short of marriage (Adams 1979, pp. 260–267).

Adams (1979) also provides some warnings about these propositions. First, some factors (such as partner's good looks) have greater salience for men than for women, while some (such as partner's empathic capacity) have greater salience for women than for men. Second, some factors such as parental interference may have different outcomes in the long run compared to the short run. Third, the timing of courtship may bring different considerations into play, e.g., courtship in later life such as following divorce or widowhood, or when children from previous marriages must be considered (see Bulcroft and O'Connor 1986). Finally, social class factors may affect the predictive value of the propositions. There is also a difference between traditional (male-dominated) and egalitarian relationships—the former more often found in the working class and among certain ethnic groups, the latter more likely to characterize the middle class. Thus, the kind of marriage one anticipates (traditional/egalitarian) may influence the mate-selection process. (See also Aronson 1972 for specifications of the conditions under which various interpersonal attraction predictors such as propinquity and similar interests operate).

Further, as courtship has moved away from the fixed-stage sequence of development, it may be viewed best from a circular-causal perspective (Stephen 1985) in which progress is strongly influenced by communication within the couple, leading to increased or decreased movement toward marriage.

The timing of marriage may be influenced by such factors as meaningful employment opportunities for women (which may diminish their motivation to marry), the increasing acceptability of nonmarital cohabitation and adult singlehood (see Stein 1981), and the effects of nonmarital pregnancy or of various intolerable conditions (such as violence) in the family of origin. Currently, a number of scholars are studying each of these topics. They affect not only the timing of marriage but also how we define courtship.

Regarding premarital factors that contribute to later marital adjustment, no scholar has presented evidence to refute Kirkpatrick's ([1955] 1963) conclusions: The happiness of parents' marriage; adequate length of courtship; adequate sex information in childhood; a happy childhood including a harmonious relationship with parents; approval of the courtship relationship by significant others; good premarital adjustment of the couple and strong motivation to marry; homogamy along age, racial-ethnic, and religious lines; and, later age at marriage.

Murstein (1980) reviewed mate-selection scholarship from the 1970s and predicted that researchers would focus less on the "old standby" variables such as race, class, and religion and more on the dynamic aspects of courtship. He was correct. Some of the major themes that have interested scholars in recent years are identified below.

Studies of cohabitation included early efforts to identify its several types (both structural and motivational). Later studies focused on the effects of cohabitation on subsequent marital happiness, satisfaction, and stability. The general finding across such research is that living with someone prior to marriage has little or no positive effect. Instead, most studies show negative effects in terms of happiness, satisfaction, and stability. This research has been carried out in the United States, Canada, and other countries, and although the rates vary, they are quite uniform in showing that there is a greater tendency to divorce among those who have lived with someone (i.e., the future spouse or any other partner) prior to marriage than among those who did not previously cohabit. Most scholars point out that either or both of two factors are probably at work here; first, the less-than-full acceptance of cohabitation as a lifestyle (implying less or no social support for those who cohabit), and second, the kind of persons who choose a "deviant" lifestyle—persons who are risk-takers, and who are less commitment-oriented. (However, see Popenoe 1987 for a different view of cohabitation in a setting where it is more normative.)

As rates of sexual activity outside of marriage rose, and as sex was to some extent disengaged from procreation (since the arrival of the birth control pill in the 1960s), research and theoretical interest focused on changes in sexual behavior and values in courtship. (See Schur 1988 for a highly negative view of the "Americanization of sex.") It should be noted that cohabitation appears to be a "sexier" arrangement than marriage (Call, Sprecher, and Schwartz 1955), which may account for why prior cohabitants' marriages do not meet their expectations and thus, may be more divorce-prone.

Also on the negative side of the ledger, there is concern about the spread of sexually transmitted diseases, including AIDS, and on factors related to the use or nonuse of "safe" sexual practices. Research continues to examine variations in premarital sexual activity rates and their effects. Frazier (1994) points out that the AIDS epidemic has not sidetracked the sexual revolution that began in the 1960s. This is because the forces that fueled the revolution are still in place, and some are intensifying—"mobility, democratization, urbanization, women in the workplace, birth control and other reproductive interventions, and media proliferation of sexual images, ideas, and variation" (p. 32). Moreover, cohabitation is increasing as are the single-person household and single parenthood. The pursuit of individuality and freedom continues. Many studies show that women are more sexual today than at any previous time in this century, says Frazier. On the positive side, a greater openness about sexuality-related information has occurred. The trend, as Frazier sees it, is away from the illusions of traditional ideas about romance and toward a more reality-based understanding between men and women. Also positive, and part of the same revolution, are expanded definitions of masculinity and femininity as the trend toward egalitarianism continues.

Unmarried households (i.e., single parenthood) have lost much of their past stigma, and increased numbers of women are choosing to remain single over the (potentially illusory) financial security of marriage, notes Frazier. This is largely a function of women's increased earning capacities in an expanded set of labor market opportunities.

Along with the strong trend toward later marriages has come declining family size. The U. S. Department of Commerce (1992) tells us that the median age at marriage has been rising and in the 1990s was higher than it had been a century earlier. One outcome of this is, as noted earlier, a rise in nonmarital births. Related to this is a rise in the now considerable rate of child poverty, since women's (i.e., single mothers) earnings are not as high as single fathers or of men in general.

Frazier, Arikian, Benson, Losoff, and Maurer (1996) report that, among unmarried singles over age thirty, reasons for remaining single have to do with barriers as well as choices and that men would like to marry more than would women. (This situation is reversed among younger adults, where women are more interested in marriage than are men.) Never-married adults want to marry more than do divorced adults, and divorced women have the least desire for marriage. Again, this may have to do with the greater options (if not economic parity with men) open to women in recent years. Both men and women state their primary reasons for wanting to marry as love, the desire for a family, what they see as the "romantic" nature of marriage, a desire for economic security (which, as noted, may be illusory), and the opportunity for regular sexual activity. However, the desire to remain single—for both men and women—is linked to having unrestricted career opportunities, to the desire for an "exciting" lifestyle, and to having the freedom to change and experiment. Men also identify the restrictive nature of marriage and the limits on mobility and experiences as reasons to remain single, but women mention the desire to be self-sufficient and the possibility of poor communication in marriage as among their top reasons for choosing singlehood over marriage.

Around the world, childbearing by unwed women has increased, accounting for about one-third of all births in America and northern Europe in the mid-1990s. Despite the fact that there has been a recent decline in teen births in the United States, teen pregnancies are much higher in America than in other industrialized nations, for which our poor (or absent) sexuality education is often blamed (Ventura, Matthews, and Curtin 1998).

The rising age at marriage and its effects have interested scholars not only in developed countries (e.g., East Germany) but also in developing countries such as Sri Lanka, Java, and sub-Saharan Africa. One effect is the relatively large numbers of young adults still living in the parental home. Living arrangements and other family influences such as parental divorce or having had alcoholic parents have been studied for their effects on dating behavior, premarital pregnancy, violence in courtship, and on drinking behaviors of young adults.

Research shows that expectations of marriage among those of courting age are inflated, when compared to the expectations of persons with marital experience. Inflated expectations may be another of the causes of subsequent divorce. Moreover, scholars who study conduct on dates have uncovered the seeming paradox of egalitarian daters who behave traditionally during the earliest stages of courtship. Behavior that does not reflect

beliefs gives false impressions, and has obvious implications for the spontenaiety and honesty (or lack of them) of the conditions under which courting partners get to know one another. In this era when dating/courtship has lost much of its coherence, we find advice books for young adults with names such as *Dating for Dummies* (1996) and *The Complete Idiot's Guide to Dating* (1996). The titles alone tell a story. Still other writers attempt to capitalize on the old notion of a war between the sexes, implying that in addition to knowing little about how to date/court, we know very little about one another since "men are from Mars and women are from Venus"—unless we study such guides as *Mars and Venus on a Date* (Gray 1988). Under the guise of assisting daters to communicate with one another, they present half-traditional, half-egalitarian versions of how to get along with persons who are seen as each others' "opposites." These popular books rest on the idea that by following their prescriptions, as in *The Rules* (Fein and Schneider 1996), our courtships will be successful and their outcomes happy. (*The Rules*, interestingly, is highly traditionalistic, and reads like a guide for 1950s "dating success.")

In contrast to these for-profit offerings, scholars continue to study "close" or "intimate" premarital relationships as these have changed from stylized conventional dating to the more informal "hanging out" and "hooking up," the latter an almost only just-for-sexual-purposes arrangement. These shifts follow in part from a weakened normative imperative to marry (Thorton 1989) and in part from the trend toward more egalitarian relationships between the sexes. However, in almost all research, male/female similarities and differences continue to form part of the data analysis. Recent studies have examined attraction in an effort to identify its bases, and, less broadly, have investigated "opening lines" used for meeting potential partners. Which lines work, which do not, and why are unsuccessful lines still in use? These are among the kinds of questions that are asked and answered by such investigations. Scholars working in criminal justice-related areas have provided information about the use of Rohypnol, a central nervous system depressant that is "abused throughout the United States by high school and college students, rave and nightclub attendees, and drug addicts and alcohol abusers." Its use facilitates sexual assaults (Office of National Drug

Control Policy 1998). Other investigations examine dating among herpes- and HIV-infected persons. On the more positive and more conventional side, some of the standard variables such as age and education have been reexamined for their impact on mate choice patterns (Qian 1998).

Earlier, the trend toward expanded gender roles was noted. Considerable research interest has been devoted to identifying the components of conventional (traditional) masculinity and femininity and their effects, and on resistance to change in these stereotypes—for example, because of ongoing conventional socialization practices and, as communications experts have documented, because of the effects of various media portrayals supporting the *status quo ante*. Scholars have also noted the greater likelihood of relational success among androgynous than among conventionally masculine men and feminine women.

Research on courtship has extended to the study of "taboo" conversational topics, degrees and forms of honesty and deception, communication style differences between the sexes (one result of differential socialization), and methods of conflict resolution that enhance relationship survival or that presage relationship dissolution. Interest in failed relationships has attempted to identify factors at both individual and dyadic levels that might have predicted which pairings would last and which would not. In ongoing relationships, scholars have investigated the positive and negative effects of outside influences such as parental or peer pressure, and the parts played by same- and cross-sex friends. Other topics of interest have included barriers to the development of trust and the effect of its loss, the meanings of commitment, and the effects of self-disclosure, self-esteem, self-awareness, and jealousy on close relationships.

We have witnessed a virtual explosion in the study of love—attempts to identify its forms, its properties, and its distribution of types across women and men as well as the effects of all of these, especially in terms of romantic love. On the negative side, a number of studies of violence in courtship have shown relatively high rates of this kind of activity, especially between cohabitors—and also reveal that a sizable minority of those who have experienced violence in close relationships identify it with a loving motive. This seemingly odd

justification is explained by the practices of parents who, when using violence against their children, often indicate that they hit or spank "out of love." Thus, the lesson (i.e., the rationalization) is learned early. Other negative aspects of courtship include the study of "mind games" and other facets of competition between partners, sexual aggression including date/acquaintance rape, and the effects of contrasts between idealized images and courtship realities.

As courtship itself has expanded, researchers have taken a interest in an expanded range of relationship types. For example, the romantic involvements between lesbian women and between gay men have been studied in their own right, and also for comparative purposes with heterosexual partnerships. A predictable area for future study is the legalization of marital relationships between same-sex partners.

Other innovations such as video- and computer-matching and personal advertisements in print media have also captured researchers' attention, as has using the internet to make romantic contacts (sometimes called "cyberdating"). Scholars can be expected to pursue the study of the impact of prenuptial agreements on relationships. To a lesser extent, older lines of research have continued to probe the purported decline of, or changes in, the double standard, the "principle of least interest" (Waller 1938) as related to changes in gender roles, the dimensions of intimacy, and on desired traits in dating partners as these may differ between premarital partners and permanent mates.

As society grows more complex and the rate of change is increasingly rapid, confusion over the mate-selection process in all of its dimensions appears to be rife. A study of college student dating shows that these young adults have questions about virtually every aspect of the process and about the choices they make (Laner 1995). High divorce rates have produced a backlash of insecurity as the marriage decision approaches. This is reflected in the frequently asked question, "How can I be *sure* of making the right choice in a partner?" Sociologists and scholars in related disciplines continue to study a growing set of factors that shed light on the answer.

(SEE ALSO: *Alternative Lifestyles; Love; Mate-Selection Theories*)

REFERENCES

Adams, Bert N. 1979 "Mate Selection in the United States: A Theoretical Summarization." In W. R. Burr, R. Hill, F. I. Nye, and I. L. Reiss, eds., *Contemporary Theories About the Family*. New York: Free Press.

Aronson, Elliot 1972 *The Social Animal*. New York:Viking.

Bailey, Beth L. 1988 *From Front Porch to Back Seat: Courtship in Twentieth Century America*. Baltimore: Johns Hopkins University Press.

Browne, Judy 1996 *Dating for Dummies*. Foster City, Calif.: IDG Books.

Bulcroft, Kris, and Margaret O'Connor 1986 "The Importance of Dating Relationships on Quality of Life for Older Persons." *Family Relations* 35:397–401.

Call, Vaughn, Susan Sprecher, and Pepper Schwartz 1995 "The Incidence and Frequency of Marital Sex in a National Sample." *Journal of Marriage and the Family* 57:639–652.

Farber, Bernard 1964 *Family Organization and Interaction*. San Francisco: Chandler.

Fein, Ellen, and Sherrie Schneider 1995 *The Rules: Time-Tested Secrets for Capturing the Heart of Mr. Right*. New York: Warner.

Frazier, Patricia, Nancy Arikian, Sonja Benson, Ann Losoff, and Steven Maurer 1996 "Desire for Marriage and Life Satisfaction among Unmarried Heterosexual Adults." *Journal of Social and Personal Relationships* 13(2):225–239.

Frazier, Shervert H. 1994 "Psychotrends: What Kind of People Are We Becoming?" *Psychology Today* January/February:32–37, 64, 66.

Goode, William J. 1969 "The Theoretical Importance of Love." *American Sociological Review* 34:38–47.

Gordon, Michael 1981 "Was Waller Ever Right? The Rating and Dating Complex Reconsidered." *Journal of Marriage and the Family* 43:67–76.

Gray, John 1998 *Mars and Venus on a Date*. New York: Harper-Collins.

Kirkpatrick, Clifford (1955) 1963 *The Family as Process and Institution*, 2nd ed. New York: Ronald.

Kuriansky, Judy 1996 *The Complete Idiot's Guide to Dating*. New York: Alpha Books.

Laner, Mary R. 1995 *Dating: Delights, Discontents, and Dilemmas*. Salem, Wisc.: Sheffield.

Murstein, Bernard I. 1980 "Mate Selection in the 1970s." *Journal of Marriage and the Family* 42:777–792.

Office of National Drug Control Policy 1998 "Fact Sheet: Rohypnol." Washington, D.C.: Drug Policy Information Clearing House.

Popenoe, David 1987 "Beyond the Nuclear Family: A Statistical Portrait of the Changing Family in Sweden." *Journal of Marriage and the Family* 49:173–183.

Qian, Zhenchao 1998 "Changes in Assortative Mating: The Impact of Age and Education, 1970–1990." *Demography* 35(3):279–292.

Queen, Stuart A., Robert W. Habenstein, and Jill S. Quadagno 1985 *The Family in Various Cultures*, 5th ed. New York: Harper and Row.

Ramu, G. N. 1989 "Patterns in Mate Selection." In K. Ishwaran, ed., *Family and Marriage: Cross-Cultural Perspectives*. Toronto: Wall and Thompson.

Rothman, Ellen K. 1984 *Hands and Hearts: A History of Courtship in America*. New York: Basic Books.

Schur, Edwin M. 1988 *The Americanization of Sex*. Philadelphia: Temple University Press.

Stein, Peter J. (ed.) 1981 *Single Life: Unmarried Adults in Social Context*. New York: St. Martin's.

Stephen, Timothy D. 1985 "Fixed-Sequence and Circular-Causal Models of Relationship Development: Divergent Views on the Role of Communication in Intimacy." *Journal of Marriage and the Family* 47:955–963.

Thornton, Arland 1989 "Changing Attitudes toward Family Issues in the United States." *Journal of Marriage and Family* 51:873–893.

U.S. Bureau of the Census 1992 Statistical Brief 92–13, Family Life Today. . . and How It Has Changed.

Ventura, S. J., T. J. Matthews, and S. C. Curtin 1998 "Declines in Teenage Birth Rates, 1991–97; National and State Patterns." National Vital Statistics Reports 47(12). Hyattsville, Md: National Center for Health Statistics.

Waller, Willard 1938 "The Rating and Dating Complex." *American Sociological Review* 2:727–734.

——, and Reuben Hill 1951 *The Family: A Dynamic Interpretation*, rev. ed. New York: Dryden.

MARY REIGE LANER

CRIME DETERRENCE

See Criminal Sanctions; Criminology; Social Control.

CRIME RATES

The interpretation of crime rates seems unproblematic, but those sociologists who study crime know that is not the case. Even simple counts of crime raise difficult issues. To imagine the difficulties consider two men at a bar. One of them makes a rude comment to the other and the other person shoves him. The person shoved strikes the other person on the jaw before the fight is broken up. The person hit on the jaw calls the police to the scene and wants to press charges, but the person shoved claims self-defense and that the person who shoved him is guilty of an assault. The two men may decide that the matter is not worth pressing and the police may agree. On the other hand, the police may file a report that results in an arrest. If a grand jury thinks the evidence warrants it, the case may go to trial. Even if the case reaches trial, the jury may acquit the accused. Other possible steps in the process exist, but determining whether a crime occurred is often difficult. The process contains many decision points. Will the individuals involved report the incident to the police? Will the police determine that a crime occurred? Now imagine that an interviewer asks one of these men about their history of criminal offending or victimization. Would the individual report this incident to the interviewer? Would one of the individuals admit to an interviewer that he committed an assault? Crime counts constitute an important element in the calculation of crime rates, but they are only one factor.

Rather than report simple crime counts, social scientists often calculate crime rates. Depending on the context, they may do this because crime rates: (1) allow for the comparison of crime patterns across groupings of different sizes, (2) make possible the comparison of the relative frequency of crime over time, or (3) help in the assessment of the risk of victimization. In terms of comparability of patterns across groupings of different sizes, simply reporting the number of crimes in cities with 100,000 or more residents produces unsatisfactory results. Forty homicides may not represent a large number for New York City, but twenty homicides represent a large number in Eugene, Oregon. The calculation of homicide rates per 100,000 residents for New York City and Eugene makes comparisons between the two cities easier. Similar calculations of rates for different years facilitate comparisons over time. The number of homicides may have doubled in Los Angeles from 1920 to 1990 while the rate per 100,000 residents has decreased. In terms of the risk of motor vehicle theft, a rate based on the number of motor vehicle thefts per 10,000 registered motor vehicles may be more helpful than the number of motor vehicles stolen.

Equation (1) represents the general formula for calculating a crime rate:

$$\text{Crime Rate Per Base} = \left(\frac{\text{Number of Incidents}}{\text{Relevant Population Size}}\right) \times \text{Base} \quad (1)$$

Each of the components in this formula: Base, Relevant Population Size, and Number of Incidents, represents an important decision point when calculating a crime rate. Determining the most appropriate measure for each component is not as straightforward as it might first appear.

Selecting a Base: If the base is 100,000, then the interpretation of the rate is the number of incidents per 100,000. With a base of 100 the interpretation is in terms of the number of incidents per 100 (a percent). Reports of crime rates often appear as rates per 100,000 or per 10,000. One reason for this is the relative infrequency of some crimes. For example, in 1997 the number of murders in the United States was 18,210 and the population of the United States was 268 million. If we choose 100 for the base, we find that the homicide rate per 100 is .0068 or .0068 percent. This figure challenges the intuition of most people. We should choose the base to make the rate easier to interpret. If we choose 100,000 for the base, we find that the homicide rate is 6.8 per 100,000; a much easier figure for most people to understand.

Relevant Population Size: The choice of the relevant population size depends upon the selection of an appropriate "relevant population." The Uniform Crime Reports (UCR) typically chooses the number of residents as the relevant population. This number is used to calculate crime rates for cities or for the United States as a whole in the UCR. The National Crime and Victimization Survey (NCVS) often uses the number of residents who are twelve years of age or older as the relevant population, since the survey only asks about crime incidents involving those in that age range. At other times households represent the relevant population as when victimization surveys calculate rates for households touched by crime.

General Definitions of Part I Offenses in the Uniform Crime Reports

Criminal Homicide	Murder and nonnegligent manslaughter: the willful (nonnegligent) killing of one human being by another. Deaths caused by negligence and justifiable homicide are excluded.
Forcible Rape	The carnal knowledge of a female forcibly and against her will. Included are rapes by force and attempts or assaults to rape. Statutory offenses (no force used and victim under age of consent) are excluded.
Robbery	The taking or attempting to take anything of value from the care, custody, or control of a person or persons by force or threat of force or violence or by putting the victim in fear.
Aggravated Assault	An unlawful attack by one person on another for the purpose of inflicting severe or aggravated bodily injury. This type of assault is usually accompanied by the use of a weapon or by means likely to produce death or great bodily harm. Simple assaults are excluded.
Burglary	Breaking or Entering: The unlawful entry of a structure to commit a felony or a theft. Attempted forcible entry is included.
Larceny	Theft (Except Motor Vehicle Theft): The unlawful taking, carrying, leading, or riding away of property from the possession or constructive possession of another. Attempted larcenies are included. Embezzlement, con games, forgery, worthless checks, etc., are excluded.
Motor Vehicle Theft	The theft or attempted theft of a motor vehicle. A motor vehicle is self-propelled and runs on the surface and not on rails. Specifically excluded from this category are motorboats, construction equipment, airplanes, and farming equipment.
Arson	Any willful or malicious burning or attempt to burn, with or without intent to defraud, a dwelling house, public building, motor vehicle or aircraft, personal property of another, etc.

Table 1

SOURCE: Federal Bureau of Investigation, 1998. *Crime in the United States–1997* (Appendix II).

Thus, the total number of people may not be the most appropriate "relevant population." In the case of rape incidents, it might be more appropriate to compute rape rates using women as the relevant population. For motor vehicle theft, the relevant population might be the number of registered motor vehicles. For commercial burglaries, the relevant population might be the number of commercial establishments. Social scientists should choose these populations carefully.

Number of Incidents: Determining the value for the numerator of the crime rate formula raises particularly difficult issues. The UCR, for example, employs a complicated set of rules for counting the number of incidents. For example, the UCR "hierarchy rule" ensures that for Part I crimes (the most serious street crimes) only the *most* serious crime is recorded. Thus, if a person breaks into a store, is confronted by the owner and threatens the owner with a gun, and then kills the owner, the offense is recorded as a homicide, but not as a burglary or robbery or assault. The "hotel rule" is invoked when a burglar breaks into several units in an apartment or hotel and only one burglary is counted. Researchers draw a distinction between an incident rate and a prevalence rate. This involves a distinction between the number of criminal incidents per some relevant population and the number of offenders per some relevant population. Using the number of offenders per some relevant population produces a prevalence rate.

Thus, many decisions help determine the most appropriate crime rate for a particular purpose. These decisions need to be considered when interpreting a particular rate or when attempting to compare one crime rate with another.

SOURCES OF CRIME DATA IN THE UNITED STATES

There are three major sources of crime data in the United States, and knowing the strengths and weaknesses of these data sources helps explain why crime rates derived from them often vary.

Crimes and Crime Indexes For the United States, 1997

Offenses	Number	Rate per 100,000 Inhabitants	Percent Change in the Rate From 1988 to 1997
Crime index total	13,175,100	4,922.7	-13.1
Violent crime index	1,634,770	610.8	-4.1
Homicide	18,210	6.8	-19.0
Forcible rape	96,120	35.9	-4.5
Robbery	497,950	186.1	-15.8
Aggravated assault	1,022,490	382.0	-3.2
Property crime index	11,540,300	4,311.9	-14.2
Burglary	2,461,100	919.6	-29.8
Larceny-theft	7,725,500	2,886.5	-7.9
Motor vehicle theft	1,353,700	505.8	-13.2

Table 2

SOURCE: Data are from *Crime in the United States–1997* (Federal Bureau of Investigation 1998, Table 1)

These three methods are similar to those used to collect crime data internationally: (1) official data collected by law enforcement agencies, (2) surveys of the victims of crimes, and (3) self-report studies based on offenders. Other sources also are available, but less commonly used (e.g., vital statistics, hospital records, and insurance records).

The Uniform Crime Reports. During the later half of the 1920s the International Association of Chiefs of Police (IACP) developed uniform crime definitions and counting rules that would allow it to collect more comparable data from different law enforcement agencies. The IACP initiated the UCR in January of 1930. During the latter part of 1930 the Bureau of Investigation took over the UCR program, and it has remained a function of that bureau (renamed the Federal Bureau of Investigation, or FBI).

The general definitions of the UCR Part I offenses appear in Table 1, but more detailed definitions appear in the *Uniform Crime Reporting Handbook* (FBI 1985). As an example, the Uniform Crime Reporting System defines burglary as the unlawful entry of any fixed structure, vehicle, or vessel used for a regular residence, industry, or business, with or without force, with the intent to commit a felony, or larceny. Without uniform definitions, jurisdictions in which state law defines theft from a storage-shed as a burglary would report such an incident as a burglary to the FBI. In another jurisdiction, breaking and entering might be required for an incident to be classified as a burglary. In such a jurisdiction an incident in which an offender entered a house through an open window in order to steal a stereo would be coded as unlawful entry with intent to commit a crime for the purposes of the state's law, but as a burglary for UCR purposes.

Participation in the UCR is voluntary. Local law-enforcement agencies send their data to the FBI or to state-level UCR programs that forward the data to the FBI. In the early years only the largest law enforcement agencies in the United States participated. But by the 1980s and 1990s, agencies representing about 97 percent of the population of the entire United States participated. The FBI reports two types of crime: Part I crimes and Part II crimes. For Part I crimes, data on crimes known to the police and on arrests are reported; for Part II crimes, only data on arrests are reported. Part I crimes include violent crimes (murder and non-negligent homicide, forcible rape, robbery, and aggravated assault), property crimes (burglary, larceny-theft, and motor vehicle theft), and arson. Each year the news media report crime rates derived from the FBI data and a summary of these data appear annually in *Crime in the United States*. This FBI publication provides crime rates for states, metropolitan statistical areas, counties, cities, other geographical subdivisions, and the nation as a whole.

Table 2 presents Part I crime data from the publication *Crime in the United States–1997* (FBI 1998). The second column presents the number of incidents of a specific type, the third column reports the rate per 100,000 residents, and the final column indicates the change in the rate over a ten year period. In 1997, for example, 1,634,770 violent crimes were known to the police. The rate of violent crimes was 610.8 per 100,000 persons, which represents a decrease in the rate of violent crimes from 1988 to 1997 of 4.1 percent. Officially reported crime rates fell in all Part I categories from 1988 to 1997.

Crimes reported or discovered by the police and found through investigation to have occurred are labeled "crimes known to the police." A crime found not to have occurred is "unfounded," and does not appear as a crime known to the police. Although occasionally police discover a crime being committed (e.g., they happen upon a burglary in progress, or they arrest someone for resisting a police officer) they are highly dependent on citizen reports of criminal incidents.

The UCR also provides data on arrests for Part I and Part II crimes, and reports these crimes on the basis of the geographical divisions described above. Since these data are for arrests, the rates calculated from them should be labeled "arrest rates." Part II crimes include: other assaults (not including aggravated assaults), forgery and counterfeiting, fraud, embezzlement, stolen property (buying, receiving, and possessing), vandalism, weapons (carrying, possessing, etc.), prostitution and commercialized vice, sex offenses (except forcible rape and prostitution), drug abuse violations, gambling, offenses against family and children, driving under the influence, liquor law violations, drunkenness, disorderly conduct, vagrancy, curfew and loitering law violations, and runaways.

National Crime and Victimization Survey (NCVS). The NCVS data come from large surveys using probability samples of respondents. Since 1973 a national-level program has surveyed a probability sample of U.S. households. The U.S. Census Bureau conducts the survey, and during the 1990s the sample contained some 60,000 households and approximately 100,000 respondents. The results of this survey have been published annually since 1973 by The U.S. Department of Justice in *Criminal Victimization in the United States*.

The NCVS collects data on a much smaller number of crimes than the UCR. Since it is a survey of the victims of crime, it does not record homicides, but it does record forcible rapes and sexual assaults, robberies, aggravated assaults, simple assaults, burglaries, larceny-thefts, and motor-vehicle thefts. It also provides details about the victims of crime not available in the UCR. These include the household income of the victim, any injuries sustained by the victim, insurance coverage, length of any hospitalization due to injuries, what protective measures the victim employed, and so on.

Careful field-testing preceded the initiation of data collection for NCVS in 1973 and before any changes made to its design since that time. An early decision involved the length of the reference period (the period the interviewers referred to when they asked whether victimizations occurred during the past period). Researchers chose a six-month reference period on the basis of the costs of doing more frequent surveys and studies that showed the effect of memory decay on remembering whether an event occurred. Respondents tend to telescope events into the reference period, and this can cause substantial increases in the number of victimizations reported during the past six months. To overcome this problem, each respondent remains in the sample for three years with interviews repeated every six months. Victimizations reported to the interviewer the first time a respondent is interviewed do not contribute to estimates of the crime rates. That first interview and subsequent interviews provide bounds for the six-month reference period. The interviewer asks about victimizations occurring since the last interview and has a list of incidents reported in the last interview to make sure that those incidents are not telescoped into the reference period.

To estimate rates for the entire nation from the NCVS data, researchers use the samples to estimate the number of victimizations occurring in the entire nation. They then use these estimates to calculate victimization rates. The derived estimates often contain large sampling errors, since they are based on only a "small" sample of the total population of the United States. These large sampling errors are greatest for the crimes least frequently reported by the respondents, for example, victimization rates for rapes involve more sampling error than rates for aggravated assault (O'Brien 1986).

Self-Reports. Unlike the UCR and NCVS, self-report studies refer to a collection of studies conducted by different researchers using a variety of methodologies. The basic methodology, however, involves sampling respondents and questioning them about criminal or delinquent acts. Although some isolated self-report studies occurred in the 1940s, the technique gained popularity with the work of Short and Nye (1957, 1958).

Perhaps the most ambitious self-report study is the National Youth Survey, or NYS (Elliott et al. 1983). This survey involves a national panel sample. When first instituted in 1976, the panel members were aged eleven to seventeen. Estimates of national-level crime rates for the age groups covered in this survey can be computed because the sample of respondents is a national one. These rates, unlike UCR- and NCVS-based rates, result from respondents answering questions about their offenses.

The NYS, and other self-report surveys, calculate two types of crime rates: "prevalence rates" and "incidence rates." To calculate these crime rates, the NYS uses the general formula represented in Equation (1). The prevalence rate uses the number of respondents who claimed they committed an offense for the numerator, the number of respondents for the relevant population size, and (we choose) 100 for the base. This yields the percentage of respondents who have committed a particular act. In the NYS in 1980, when the respondents were fifteen to twenty-one years old, the prevalence rate for robbery was 2. The incidence rate uses the number of times individuals claimed they committed a particular act as the numerator, the number of respondents as the relevant population size, and typically uses 100, 1000, or 10,000 for the base. We again use 100 for the base and find that in the 1980 NYS the incident rate for robbery was 10. Thus, there was an average of ten robberies per 100 respondents in this age group in 1980, with only two out of 100 respondents claiming involvement in a robbery.

As with the NCVS, self-report studies depend upon the accuracy of respondent reports. Therefore, issues such as telescoping, recall, and embarrassment are consequential for self-reports of criminal activities. In comparison to the UCR and NCVS, many of the crimes reported in self-report surveys are trivial crimes or not crimes at all (e.g., lying to parents or cheating on a test). The sample sizes, even in the largest of such surveys, are not nearly as large as sample sizes in the NCVS. Therefore, given the relative infrequency of serious crimes, the rates for serious crimes are not very precisely measured by self-report surveys; that is, the estimates have large standard errors. Nonetheless, crime rates derived from self-report studies provide much of the data used to investigate the determinants of individual criminal offending.

SOME PROBLEMS WITH UCR, NCVS, AND SELF-REPORT DATA

Using information from official data (UCR), victimization surveys (NCVS), and self-report surveys helps us to gauge the accuracy of crime rates. Crime rates vary depending upon whether they derive from UCR, NCVS, or self-report data. To understand why crime-rate estimates vary depending upon their source, we briefly outline some problematic aspects of these three data sources.

UCR Data. The most obvious problem with UCR data involves underreporting of crimes to the police. The NCVS interviewers ask respondents whether they reported a particular incident to the police. In 1994, 78 percent of the respondents who reported a motor vehicle theft to the interviewer said they reported that crime to the police, 50 percent of the burglaries were reported, 50 percent of the robberies, and only 32 percent of rapes and sexual assaults (U.S. Department of Justice 1997).

Once an incident comes to the attention of the police a number of factors influence whether the incident is recorded as a crime or whether an arrest is made. There may be organizational pressures to raise or lower the crime rate (e.g., Bell 1960; Chambliss 1984; DeFleur 1975; McCleary et al. 1982; Selke and Pepinsky 1982; Sheley and Hanlon 1978; Wheeler 1967). The professional styles of particular police departments may affect the recorded crime rates (Beattie 1960; Skogan 1976; Wilson 1967, 1978). The interactions between officers and offenders also help determine the classification of an incident as a crime and whether an arrest is made (Black 1970; Smith and Visher 1981; Visher 1983). Given these and other problems, it is not surprising that crime rates recorded by the UCR are known to contain substantial errors.

NCVS Data. The NCVS may well provide a more accurate picture of crime rate trends and comparative crime rates than the UCR. As Sellin's (1931, p. 346) dictum suggests, "the value of a crime for index purposes decreases as the distance from the crime itself in terms of procedure increases." Further, the NCVS standardizes the procedures it uses in compiling crime incidents. When the NCVS changes its procedures, careful methodological studies evaluate the changes.

Although the incidents reported to NCVS interviewers need not depend upon a respondent contacting the police, the police responding to the contact, and eventually police recording of the incident as founded, respondents do need to respond appropriately in an interview situation in order for an incident to be recorded as a victimization in the NCVS. In this context, note that the interview situation is a social interaction. The interviewers have little to offer respondentd for their time. Respondents may be reluctant to share embarrassing information with the interviewer, such as a fight at a bar, an assault by a relative, or a sexual assault. As noted earlier, sometimes respondents may forget about incidents or telescope the incidents into or out of the reference period.

Turner (1972) used "reverse record" checks to investigate 206 cases of robbery, assault, and rape found in police records. Interviewers interviewed these "known victims" using an NCVS-like technique. Only 63.1 percent of these "known incidents" were reported to interviewers. The percentage reporting these incidents to the interviewer was strongly related to the relationship of the offender to the victim. Respondents reported 76.3 percent of the incidents involving a stranger; 56.9 percent of the incidents involving known offenders; and only 22.2 percent of the incidents involving a relative.

Not all of this underreporting of incidents to the interviewers is attributable to embarrassment. Turner (1972) found a strong relationship between the number of months between the interview and the incident and the respondents' reporting of the incident to the interviewer. Respondents recalled 69 percent of the incidents occurring one to three months before the interview, 50 percent of those occurring four to six months before, 46 percent of those occurring six to nine months

before, and only 30 percent of those occurring ten to twelve months before.

Self-Report Data. Like UCR and NCVS data, self-report data contain their own weaknesses. As with the NCVS data, the survey research situation raises questions of honesty, forgetting, bounding the reference period, and so on. Some problems are more severe than those encountered by the NCVS. One of these problems is sample size; even the best-financed surveys—like the National Youth Survey (Elliot et al. 1983)—have samples of less than 2,000. Such small samples almost guarantee large sampling errors associated with the resulting crime rates (especially for serious crimes). Small sample size further limits the usefulness of these data for conducting regional analyses (e.g., estimating the crime rates for states or cities). Similarly, it limits the accuracy of these estimates for comparing the crime rates for groups such as Hispanics or Asian females. Unlike the NCVS, many self-report surveys do not involve panels in which respondents are reinterviewed over an extended period of time (the NYS is an exception) so that the interviews cannot be bounded. Often the response rates are quite low. In the NYS (Elliot et al. 1983), a sample of 2,360 eligible youth originally were selected and of these 73 percent agreed to participate in the first wave of data collection in 1976. By 1980 the sample size dropped to 1,494 or 63 percent of the original sample. This contrasts with initial response rates well in excess of 90 percent for the NCVS.

Two other issues need mention. First, self-report studies concentrate on relatively trivial behaviors, such as lying to parents, defying authority, or cheating on tests. One reason for concentrating on such behaviors is that they are more commonly reported. Given the small sample sizes typical of self-report studies, these behaviors may be more reliably measured. Second, some studies do not accurately gauge the frequency of "delinquent behaviors." They use response sets such as "no," "once or twice," or "several times." Experienced researchers now ask about a wide range of behaviors and more specifically ask about the frequency of these behaviors. In the NYS, Elliot et al. (1983) ask about "arson," "prostitution," and "physical threat for sex" as well as "skipped class" and "didn't return change." They use response categories such as "2–3 times a day," "once a day," "2–3 time a week," "once a week," "once every 2–3 weeks," and "once a month," as well as asking the exact number of times respondents offended during the past year.

COMPARISONS OF CRIME RATES GENERATED FROM UCR, NCVS, AND SELF-REPORTS

Fortunately, the problems outlined above do not mean that crime rates based on UCR, NCVS, and self-reports are not useful. Homicide rates, for example, are probably reasonably accurate in terms of absolute rates and in terms of homicide trends over the past sixty-five years. They also are appropriate for comparisons of homicide rates across large cities. When we judge the usefulness and accuracy of crime rates, the type of crime considered is important (e.g., homicide or rape). Further, even if a crime rate is inaccurate in terms of the absolute amount of crime it represents, it may be an accurate measure of the relative amount of that crime in different areas or across time. This would be the case if exactly half or some other proportion of the aggravated assaults were reported in different jurisdictions (or across time). Then we could perfectly compare the relative amount of crime across jurisdictions (or crime trends over time). If only approximately the same proportion of cases were reported across jurisdictions, then comparisons of the relative amount of crime would only be approximate.

Measuring Absolute Crime Rates. The most accurately measured UCR Part I crime almost certainly is homicide. The reasons for this include the seriousness of the crime and the physical evidence it produces (e.g., a body, weapon, or missing person), which make it unlikely that once detected this crime will be ignored. Cantor and Cohen (1980) compared homicide rates based on the U.S. Department of Health, Education, and Welfare's *Annual Vital Health Statistics Report* with those from the UCR for the years 1935–1975 and found a very close correspondence. Using a different approach, O'Brien (1996) found evidence that fluctuations in the homicide rate closely paralleled fluctuations in the rate of other violent crimes from 1973 to 1992.

Motor vehicle theft is the other Part I crime that appears to be well estimated in terms of

absolute rates. In 1994, for example, the NCVS estimated 1,764,000 motor vehicle thefts based on respondents' answers, while the UCR reported 1,539,100 motor vehicle thefts known to the police. Thus the NCVS estimate exceeded the UCR estimate by only 28 percent. When NCVS respondents report a motor vehicle theft they are asked if they reported the theft to the police. Based on their responses one would calculate that the police receive reports of only 1,379,448 motor vehicle thefts, which is fewer motor vehicle thefts than appear in the UCR records. This probably occurs because motor vehicle thefts from private citizens constitute only 80 to 85 percent of the total number of such thefts known to the police (Biderman and Lynch 1991). For the remaining Part I crimes covered by both the UCR and NCVS (personal robbery, aggravated assault, residential burglary, and rape), the NCVS and UCR data show greater differences in absolute rates. The smallest ratio of NCVS incidents to UCR incidents is 1.62 for rape and the largest 3.01 for residential burglary.

Difficulties arise when comparing the self-report rates to UCR and NCVS rates, because self-report studies typically only involve a sample of young people. The estimated crime rates for these young people, however, are so high that we may conclude that the rates generated by self-reports are far greater than those generated by either the NCVS or the UCR. The 1976 NYS produced an estimated incident rate for eleven to seventeen year-olds for aggravated assault of 170 per 1000 and for robbery a rate of 290 per 1000. This compares with rates for those twelve year-olds and over of 7.90 and 6.48 based on the NCVS and rates for all ages of 2.29 and 1.96 based on the UCR. Some part of this discrepancy results from differences in the age groups compared, but not all of it. In 1976 eleven to seventeen year-olds comprised 13.38 percent of the population. Thus, even if it were assumed that no assaults or robberies were committed by other age groups, the aggravated assault rate based on the NYS would be [.1338 × 170 =] 22.75 and the rate for robbery would be [.1338 × 290 =] 38.80.

Measuring Relative Crime Rates. If absolute rates are well measured, then relative rates of crimes across cities or other units probably are well measured. This means that both homicide rates and motor vehicle theft rates should be good measures of the relative rate of crime. In the mid-1970s the NCVS conducted victimization studies with reasonably large size samples; 10,000 or more households containing some 22,000 respondents, in each of twenty-six large U.S. cities. The same cities, of course, reported UCR crime rates for Part I crimes. This provided the opportunity to compare the consistency of these estimates in terms of the relative crime rates measured by the NCVS and the UCR by correlating the two crime-rate measures across the twenty-six cities. The closer these correlations are to 1.00, the greater the degree to which cities with relatively high rates (low rates) on one of the measures have relatively high rates (low rates) on the other. Across these cities, the correlation of UCR and NCVS motor vehicle theft rates was .90 or higher (Nelson 1978, 1979; O'Brien, Shichor, and Decker 1980). The correlations were close to zero for rape, negative for aggravated assault, and positive and moderately strong for burglary and robbery. This indicates that for burglary and robbery the relative rates of crime in these cities are similar whether the UCR or NCVS measures are used, but they are not similar for rape and aggravated assault.

Overall, the use of homicide rates and motor vehicle theft rates to measure the relative amount of these crimes across cities is supported by the above findings. The use of burglary and robbery rates receives weaker support, and the use of rape and aggravated assault rates to compare the relative amount of these crimes across cities does not receive support.

Gender and Race Composition of Offenders. Hindelang (1978, 1979) addressed the issue of whether the UCR and victim reports (NCVS) produce similar percentages of offenders identified as African American or white or as male or female. O'Brien (1995, 2000) replicated these finding using more recent data. These comparisons indicate that for those crimes in which the victim and offender come into contact (which enables the victim to identify the race and sex of the offender), the percentages based on the UCR and NCVS are fairly similar. For example, O'Brien (2000) aggregates data for the years 1992 to 1994 and finds that the percentages of males involved in these crimes, according to the UCR and NCVS, never differ by more than 3 percent. For race of the offender, rape produces the largest difference with victims

stating that 33.2 percent of the offenders are African American and the UCR arrest data indicating that 42.7 percent of those arrested are African American. For robbery, aggravated assault, and simple assault the differences do not exceed 5 percent.

Self-report data at one time were considered to be inconsistent with UCR data, which indicated that males committed crimes at a much higher rate than females and that African Americans also committed crimes at a much higher rate than whites. These large differences between males and females and African Americans and whites, however, are not found when self-report studies ask about more serious crimes and ask more carefully about the frequency of offending (Elliot and Ageton 1980; Hindelang, Hirschi, and Weis 1979).

These comparisons only touch on the issue of the appropriate uses of UCR, NCVS, and self-report data. The appropriate uses depend upon the type of crime and the type of comparison. (For helpful information on which to judge the appropriate uses of these data see Biderman and Lynch 1991; Gove Hughes and Geerken 1985; O'Brien 1985, 2000).

INTERNATIONAL DATA

Many nations collect data from law enforcement agencies, survey victims, and conduct self-report surveys. Difficulties arise, however, when comparing these data, since the definitions of crimes and the counting rules differ from nation to nation. In this section we note some of these problems and cautiously present crime-rate data for two nations. In addition, for a larger number of nations, we present homicide rates.

Perhaps the most comparable large national victimization surveys are the NCVS (conducted in the United States) and the British Crime Survey (conducted in England and Wales). But even in this case, there are important differences—the British Crime Survey (BCS) uses a twelve-month reference period and unbounded interviews, while the NCVS uses a six-month reference period and bounded interviews. The former difference should decrease the estimated victimization rates in the BCS due to "memory decay," but the latter should increase these rates due to "telescoping." The BCS does not ask about crimes involving victims under the age of sixteen, while the NCVS does not ask about crimes involving victims under age twelve.

Further problems arise with the definitions of offenses. In the United States, for example, aggravated assaults include attempted murders and almost any assault in which a weapon is used or assaults for the purpose of inflicting severe or aggravated injury. In England attempted murders receive separate treatment while the assaults most similar to Part I aggravated assaults are "woundings." Woundings require some kind of cut or wound where the skin or a bone is broken, or medical attention is needed, whereas common assault occurs if the victim is punched, kicked or jostled, with negligible or no injury.

Since 1981 definitions of rape have changed substantially in England. Until 1981, to be classified as a rape an incident required a male offender and female victim and the penetration of the vagina by the penis. Husbands could not be convicted of raping their wives, and males under age fourteen could be convicted of a rape. By 1996 rapes could involve offenders as young as ten, spousal victims, male victims, and anal intercourse. In the United States, the UCR definition of rape includes male victims, male or female offenders, spousal victims, anal intercourse, and other sexual acts. With these nontrivial problems in mind, we compare crime rates (based both on surveys and police records) in England and the United States.

Table 3 presents victimization rates for robbery, assault, burglary, and motor vehicle theft in the United States and England (based on the NCVS and the BCS) for the years 1981 and 1995 (Langan and Farrington 1998). Perhaps the most surprising result is that the estimated victimization rates in England are higher than in the United States for these crimes in 1995. The surveys also indicate substantial increases in robbery, assault, burglary, and motor vehicle theft from 1981 to 1995 in England and decreases for all but motor vehicle theft in the United States. The cross-country comparisons of these absolute rates may be more problematic than over-time comparisons within the countries—given that the victimization survey methods and the definitions of these four crimes changed little in these countries over this period.

Table 4 presents crime rates based on police records (Langan and Farrington 1998). In this

Victim Survey Crime Rates per 1,000 in the United States and England: 1981 and 1995

	1981		1995	
	U.S.	England	U.S.	England
Robbery	7.4	4.2	5.3	7.6
Assault	12.0	13.1	8.8	20.0
Burglary	105.9	40.9	47.5	82.9
Motor Vehicle Theft	10.6	15.6	10.8	23.6

Table 3

SOURCE: Langan and Farrington 1998.

table, we report rates per 100,000 residents because of the relatively low rates for homicide and rape. The rates in Table 4 reinforce the patterns reported in Table 3, which showed a substantial increase in crime rates from 1981 to the mid-1990s in England for robbery, assault, burglary, and motor vehicle theft. Table 4 also shows higher rates for these crimes (except for robbery) in England than in the United States in 1996. Two new crimes appear in this table: Homicide, for which the rate in the United States is several times higher than in England, for both 1981 and 1996 (most criminologists agree that homicide rates in the United States are very high by international standards) and rape, which shows a dramatic increase from 4.19 to 21.77 per 100,00 in England (this results, at least in part, from changes in the legal definition of rape that occurred in England between 1981 and 1996).

Although we could attempt other comparisons, most such comparisons involve even greater difficulties than those between the United States and England. Some countries do not differentiate between simple and aggravated assaults; others do not record any but the most severe assaults when the assault occurs within the family. As noted, legal definitions of rape may differ widely (even over time within the same country), reports of burglaries may require breaking and entering into a business or residence, only entering, or even breaking into an outbuilding.

Homicide represents the crime with the most consistent definition across countries: the intentional taking of another person's life without legal justification. Even here some countries may not separate justifiable from unjustifiable homicides.

Police Recorded Crime Rates per 100,000 in the United States and England: 1981 and 1996

	1981		1996	
	U.S.	England	U.S.	England
Homicide	9.83	1.13	7.41	1.31
Rape	70.59	4.19	70.79	21.77
Robbery	258.75	40.86	202.44	142.35
Assault	289.73	197.49	388.19	439.60
Burglary	1649.47	1447.36	942.95	2239.15
Motor Vehicle Theft	474.72	670.09	525.93	948.83

Table 4

SOURCE: Langan and Farrington 1998.

Intentional Homicide Rates per 100,000 in Selected Nations in 1990

Austria	.52	Italy	3.11
Barbados	11.76	Japan	.50
Botswana	.46	Madagascar	1.31
Bulgaria	2.52	Norway	.99
Canada	2.22	Spain	.71
Denmark	.80	Sri Lanka	2.17
Egypt	1.07	Sweden	1.41
Fed. Rep. of Germany	2.13	Switzerland	1.64
India	4.24	Turkey	1.64
Israel	2.30	United States	9.4

Table 5

SOURCE: United Nations Crime and Justice Information Network 1998. http://www.ifs.unvie.ac.at/ uncjin/mosaic/at.inthom/ txt.

The legal justifications for killing a spouse or even a person committing a crime may vary from country to country, as may the reporting and recording of homicides. Still, the data for this crime rate almost certainly are more accurate for international comparisons than those for rape, robbery, burglary, assault, theft, or arson.

Table 5 presents data for 1990 from the United Nations (United Nations Crime and Justice Network 1998) on intentional homicide rates per 100,000 for a selected set of countries. The rate for the United States was taken from the UCR (FBI 1991). Note the wide range of homicide rates, with Barbados and the United States with relatively high rates and Austria, Botswana, Denmark, Japan, Norway, and Spain with relatively low rates. There probably are real differences between these two sets of countries in terms of homicide rates. It is less clear that smaller differences across countries with rather different legal systems, levels of development, and cultural histories, represent differences in the unjustifiable intentional taking of another person's life. To reiterate the difficulty in making cross-national comparisons, we note that INTERPOL's international crime statistics come with the warning: "the information given is in no way intended for use as a basis for comparisons between different countries."

CONCLUSIONS

At the beginning of this article we noted that the computation of a crime rate might seem straightforward, but designating the most appropriate term for each component in equation (1) often is

difficult. Designating the base represents the easiest decision. This choice does not greatly change the interpretation of the rate, although it may make the interpretation more or less intuitive for the reader. Choice of the appropriate relevant population size is more difficult; for example, basing rape rates on the number of females rather than the number of people or the motor vehicle theft rate on the number of registered motor vehicles rather than the number of people. Determining the number of incidents constitutes the most problematic component of calculating crime rates. Here, the differing definitions of crimes, varying counting rules, response rates, rates of reporting incidents to the police or interviewers, response categories, bounding of interviews, memory decay, police discretion in recording crimes, and so on, can greatly affect the estimated crime rate. These factors differentially affect estimates of the number of incidents based on self-reports, UCR, and NCVS data. Even so, within the United States for certain crimes and comparisons, data from these different sources lead to similar conclusions. Comparisons of crime rates across nations, with the possible exception of homicide, is extremely risky.

REFERENCES

Beattie, Ronald H. 1960 "Criminal Statistics in the United States—1960." *Journal of Criminal Law, Criminology, and Police Science* 51:49–65.

Bell, Daniel 1960 "The Myth of Crime Waves." In Daniel Bell, ed., *The End of Ideology: On the Exhaustion of Political Ideas in the Fifties*. New York: Free Press.

Biderman, Albert D., and James P. Lynch 1991 *Understanding Crime Incidence Statistics: Why the UCR Diverges From the NCS.* New York: Springer-Verlag.

Black, Donald J. 1970 "The Production of Crime Rates." *American Sociological Review* 35:733–748.

Cantor, David, and Lawrence E. Cohen 1980 "Comparing Measures of Homicide Trends: Methodological and Substantive Differences in Vital Statistics and Uniform Crime Report Time Series (1935–1975)." *Social Science Research* 9:121–145.

Chambliss, William J. 1984 "Crime Rates and Crime Myths." In William J. Chambliss, ed., *Criminal Law in Action.* New York: John Wiley.

Defleur, Lois B. 1975 "Biasing Influences on Drug Arrest Records: Implications for Deviance Research." *American Sociological Review* 40:88–103.

Elliott, Delbert S., and Suzanne S. Ageton 1980 "Reconciling Race and Class Differences in Self-Reported and Official Estimates of Delinquency." *American Sociological Review* 45:95–110.

——, David Huizinga, Brian A. Knowles, and Rachelle J. Canter 1983 *The Prevalence and Incidence of Delinquent Behavior: 1976–1980: National Estimates of Delinquent Behavior by Sex, Race, Social Class and Other Selected Variables.* Boulder, Colo.: Behavioral Research Institute.

Federal Bureau of Investigation 1985 *Uniform Crime Reporting Handbook.* Washington, D.C.: U.S. Government Printing Office.

—— 1991 *Crime in the United States–1990.* Washington, D.C.: U.S. Government Printing Office.

—— 1998 *Crime in the United States–1997.* Washington, D.C.: U.S. Government Printing Office.

Gove, Walter R., Michael Hughes, and Michael Geerken 1985 "Are Uniform Crime Reports a Valid Indicator of the Index Crimes? An Affirmative Answer with Minor Qualifications." *Criminology* 23:451–491.

Hindelang, Michael J. 1978 "Race and Involvement in Common Law Personal Crimes." *American Sociological Review* 43:93–109.

—— 1979 "Sex Differences in Criminal Activity." *Social Problems* 27:143–156.

——, Travis Hirschi, and Joseph G. Weis 1979 "Correlates of Delinquency: The Illusion of Discrepancy Between Self-Report and Official Measures." *American Sociological Review* 44:995–1014.

Langan, Patrick A., and David Farrington 1998 *Crime and Justice in the United States and In England and Wales, 1981–96.* Washington, D.C.: U.S. Department of Justice.

McCleary, Richard, Barbara C. Nienstedt, and James M. Erven 1982 "Uniform Crime Reports as Organizational Outcomes: Three Time Series Experiments." *Social Problems* 29:361–372.

Nelson, James F. 1978 *"Alternative Measures of Crime: A Comparison of the Uniform Crime Report and the National Crime Survey in 26 American Cities."* Presented at the American Society of Criminology, Dallas, Tex.

—— 1979 "Implications for the Ecological Study of Crime: A Research Note." In William H. Parsonage, ed., *Perspectives on Victimology.* Beverly Hills, Calif.: Sage.

O'Brien, Robert M. 1985 *Crime and Victimization Data.* Beverly Hills, Calif.: Sage.

—— 1986 "Rare Events, Sample Size, and Statistical Problems in the Analysis of NCS (National Crime Survey) City Surveys." *Journal of Criminal Justice* 14:441–448.

—— 1996 "Police Productivity and Crime Rates: 1973–1992." *Criminology* 34:183–207.

—— 2000 "Crime and Victimization Data." In Joseph F. Sheley, ed., *Criminology.* New York: Wadsworth.

——, David Shichor, and David L. Decker 1980 "An Empirical Comparison of the Validity of UCR and NCS Crime Rates." *Sociological Quarterly* 21:301–401.

Selke, William L., and Harold E. Pepinsky 1982 "The Politics of Police Reporting in Indianapolis, 1948–1978." *Law and Human Behavior* 6:327–347.

Sellin, Thorsten 1931 "The Bias of a Crime Index" *Journal of the Institute of Criminal Law and Criminology* 22:335–356.

Sheley, Joseph F., and John J. Hanlon 1978 "Unintended Effects of Police Decisions to Actively Enforce Laws: Implications for Analysis of Crime Trends." *Contemporary Crises* 2:265–275.

Short, James F., and F. Ivan Nye 1957 "Reported Behavior as a Criterion of Deviant Behavior." *Social Problems* 5:207–213.

—— 1958 "Extent of Unrecorded Juvenile Delinquency: Tentative Conclusions." *Journal of Criminal Law and Criminology* 49:296–302.

Skogan, Wesley G. 1976 "Crime and Crime Rates." In Wesley G. Skogan, ed., *Sample Surveys of the Victims of Crime.* Cambridge, Mass.: Ballinger.

Smith, Douglas A., and Christy A. Visher 1981 "Street Level Justice: Situational Determinants of Police Arrest Decisions." *Social Problems* 29:167–177.

Turner, Anthony G. 1972 *The San Jose Methods Test of Known Crime Victims.* Washington, D.C.: U.S. Government Printing Office. National Criminal Justice Information and Statistics Service, Law Enforcement Assistance Administration.

United Nations Crime and Justice Information Network 1998 http://www.ifs.unvie.ac.at/ uncjin/mosaic/ at.inthom/txt.

U.S. Department of Justice 1997 *Criminal Victimization in the United States, 1994.* Washington, D.C.: U.S. Government Printing Office.

Visher, Christy A. 1983 "Gender, Police, Arrest Decisions, and Notions of Chivalry." *Criminology* 21:5–28.

Wheeler, Stanton 1967 "Criminal Statistics: A Reformulation of the Problem." *Journal of Criminal Law, Criminology, and Police Science* 58:317–324.

Wilson, James Q. 1967 "The Police and Delinquents in Two Cities." In Stanton Wheeler and H. M. Hughes, eds., *Controlling Delinquents.* New York: John Wiley.

—— 1978 *Varieties of Police Behavior: The Management of Law and Order in Eight Communities.* Cambridge, Mass.: Harvard University Press.

ROBERT M. O'BRIEN

CRIME, THEORIES OF

Most accounts of the rise of criminological inquiry indicate that it had its beginnings in mid-nineteenth-century developments in Europe, including the work of Cesare Lombroso, an Italian prison physician, who argued that many criminals are atavists, that is, biological throwbacks to a human type, *homo delinquens*, that allegedly existed prior to the appearance of *homo sapiens*. Since the time of Lombroso and other early figures in criminology, the field has grown markedly, both in terms of the variety of scholars who have tried to uncover the causes of crime and also in terms of the diverse theories that have been produced by these persons (Gibbons 1994). Currently legal theorists, psychologists, economists, geographers, and representatives of other scholarly fields engage in criminological theorizing and research. There has also been renewed interest in sociobiological theorizing and investigation regarding criminality. Even so, the largest share of work has been and continues to be carried on by sociologists. Thus, criminology is frequently identified as a subfield of sociology (Gibbons 1979, 1994).

Although a few scholars have argued that crime should be defined as consisting of violations of basic human rights or for some other "social" conception, most criminologists opt for the legalistic view that crime and criminal behavior are identified by the criminal laws of nations, states, and local jurisdictions. Acts that are not prohibited or required by the criminal law are not crimes, however much they may offend some members of the community. Also, the reach of the criminal law in modern societies is very broad, involving a wide range of behavioral acts that vary not only in form but in severity as well. The criminal laws of various states and nations prohibit morally repugnant acts such as murder or incest, but they also prohibit less serious offenses such as vandalism, petty theft, and myriad other acts. Parenthetically, there is considerable controversy in modern America, both among criminologists and among members of the general public, as to whether certain kinds of behavior, such as marijuana use, various consensual sex acts between adults, or abortion, ought to be expunged from or brought into the criminal codes.

Persons of all ages violate criminal laws, although a number of forms of criminality are most frequent among persons in their teens or early twenties. Except for "status offense" violations such as running away, truancy, and the like, which apply only to juveniles (usually defined as persons under eighteen years of age), juvenile delinquency and adult criminality are defined by the same body of criminal statutes. However, criminologists have often constructed theories about delinquency separate from explanations of adult criminality. Although many theories of delinquency closely resemble those dealing with adult crime, some of the former are not paralleled by theories of adult criminality. In the discussion to follow, most attention is upon explanatory arguments about adult lawbreaking, but some mention is also made of causal arguments about juvenile crime.

CRIMINOLOGICAL QUESTIONS AND CAUSAL THEORIES

Given the broad compass of the criminal law, and given the variety of different perspectives from which the phenomenon of crime has been addressed, it is little wonder that there are many theories of crime. Most of these theories center on the explanation of crime patterns and crime rates, or what might be termed "crime in the aggregate," or are pitched at the individual level and endeavor to identify factors that account for the involvement of specific individuals in lawbreaking conduct (Cressey 1951; Gibbons 1992, pp. 35–39)

These are related but analytically separate questions about the causes of crime. As Donald Cressey (1951) argued many years ago, an adequate account of criminality should contain two distinct but consistent aspects: First, a statement that explains the statistical distribution of criminal behavior in time and space (epidemiology), and second, a statement that identifies the process or processes by which persons come to engage in criminal behavior.

Statistical distributions of criminal behavior in time and space are usually presented in the form of crime rates of one kind or another. One of the most familiar of these is the *index crime rate* reported annually for cities, states, and other jurisdictions by the Federal Bureau of Investigation. The index crime rate is comprised of the number of reported cases of murder, non-negligent manslaughter, forcible rape, aggravated assault, robbery, burglary, larceny, auto theft, and arson per jurisdiction, expressed as a rate per 100,000 persons in that jurisdiction's population.

Many crime rate patterns are well known, including relatively high rates of violence in the United States as compared to other nations, state-by-state variations in forcible rape rates, regional variations in homicide and other crimes within the United States, and so forth. However, criminological scholars continue to be hampered in their efforts to account for variations in crime across various nations in the world by the lack of detailed data about lawbreaking in nations and regions other than the United States (although see van Dijk, Mayhew, and Killias 1990).

Criminologists have developed a number of theories or explanations for many crime rate variations. One case in point is Larry Baron and Murray Straus's (1987) investigation of rape rates for the fifty American states, in which they hypothesized that state-to-state variations in gender inequality, social disorganization (high divorce rates, low church attendance, and the like), pornography readership, and "cultural spillover" (authorized paddling of school children, etc.) are major influences on forcible rape. Steven Messner and Richard Rosenfeld's (1994) *institutional anomie theory* is another example of theorizing that focuses on crime rate variations. They argued that in present-day America, cultural pressures to accumulate money and other forms of wealth are joined to

weak social controls arising from noneconomic elements of the social structure, principally the political system, along with religion, education, and family patterns. According to Messner and Rosenfeld, this pronounced emphasis on the accumulation of wealth and weak social restraints promotes high rates of instrumental criminal activity such as robbery, burglary, larceny, and auto theft.

Crime rates are important social indicators that reflect the quality of life in different regions, states, or areas. Additionally, theories that link various social factors to those rates provide considerable insight into the causes of lawbreaking. But, it is well to keep in mind that crime rates are the summary expression of illegal acts of individuals. Much of the time, the precise number of offenders who have carried out the reported offenses is unknown because individual law violators engage in varying numbers of crimes per year. Even so, crime rates summarize the illegal actions of individuals. Accordingly, theories of crime must ultimately deal with the processes by which these specific persons come to exhibit criminal behavior.

In practice, criminological theories that focus on crime rates and patterns often have had relatively little to say about the causes of individual behavior. For example, variations in income inequality from one place to another have been identified by criminologists as being related to rates of predatory property crime such as burglary, automobile theft, and larceny. Many of the studies that have reported this finding have had little to say about how income inequality, defined as the unequal distribution of income among an entire population of an area or locale, affects individuals. In short, explanations of crime rate variations often have failed to indicate how the explanatory variables they identify "get inside the heads of offenders," so to speak.

Although criminological theories about crime rates and crime patterns have often been developed independently of theories related to the processes by which specific persons come to exhibit criminal conduct, valid theories of these processes ought to have implications for the task of understanding the realities of individual criminal conduct. For example, if variations in gender inequality and levels of pornography are related to rates of forcible rape, it may be that males who carry out sexual assaults are also the individuals who most strongly approve of discrimination against women and who are avid consumers of pornography. In the same way, if income inequality bears a consistent relationship to rates of predatory crime, it may be that individual predators express strong feelings of "relative deprivation," that is, perceptions that they are economically disadvantaged and distressed about their situation. However, some additional factors may also have to be identified that determine which of the persons who oppose women's rights or who feel relatively deprived become involved in illegal conduct and which do not.

PERSPECTIVES, THEORIES, AND HYPOTHESES

A number of arguments about crime patterns and the processes through which individuals get involved in lawbreaking are examined below. Before moving to these specific theories, however, two other general observations are in order. First, in criminology, as in sociology more generally, there is considerable disagreement regarding the nature of perspectives, theories, and hypotheses (as well as paradigms, frameworks, and other theoretical constructions). Even so, *perspectives* are often identified as broad and relatively unsystematic arguments; while *theories* are often described as sets of concepts, along with interconnected propositions that link the concepts together into an "explanatory package"; and *hypotheses* are specific research propositions derived from theories. In practice, however, many causal explanations that have been described as theories have been incomplete and also conceptually imprecise. Jack Gibbs (1985) has labeled such "theories" as being in "the discursive mode" rather than as formal theories. Discursive arguments are stated in everyday language and their underlying logic is often difficult to identify. According to Gibbs, because many criminological theories are discursive, precise predictions cannot be deduced from them, nor is it possible to subject predictions to empirical test, that is, to validation through research.

Many criminological theories involve relatively vague concepts, faulty underlying logic, and other problems. At the same time, it is possible to identify a number of general theoretical perspectives in criminology and to differentiate these from relatively formalized and precise theories. For example, many criminologists contend that

American society is *criminogenic* because it involves social and economic features that appear to contribute heavily to criminality. However, this is a general perspective rather than a theory of crime in that it does not identify the full range of factors that contribute to lawbreaking, and it also lacks a set of explicit and interrelated propositions. By contrast, the income inequality argument more clearly qualifies as a causal theory, as does the formulation that links gender inequality, pornography readership, and certain other influences to forcible rape.

A few other comments are in order on theoretical perspectives in criminology. During most of the developmental history of criminology in the United States, from the early 1900s to the present, sociological criminologists voiced support for the criminogenic culture thesis that directs attention to social-structural factors thought to be responsible for criminality. Thus, this view might also be referred to as "mainstream criminology." Most criminologists have linked lawbreaking to major "rents and tears" in societal structure at the same time that most of them have assumed that these crime-producing features can be remedied or lessened through social and economic reforms of one kind or another (Gibbons 1992, 1994; Currie 1985).

In the 1970s, a markedly different perspective competed for attention. Often referred to as "radical-Marxist" or "critical" criminology, it asserted that the causes of crime arise out of societal characteristics that are inherent in corporate capitalism (Gibbons 1992, pp.122–130; Chambliss 1975; Quinney 1974, 1977). According to radical-Marxist criminologists, criminal laws serve the interests of the capitalist ruling class. In turn, the system of corporate capitalism over which the ruling class presides depends for its survival on the exploitation of the resources and people of other countries and the economic oppression of citizens within capitalist nations. These conditions create economic strains for many persons, contribute to the deterioration of family life, and drive many individuals into desperate acts of lawbreaking.

The radical-Marxist perspective received considerable attention in the 1970s. Those who criticized it claimed that it presented a one-dimensional, oversimplified account of the social sources of criminality. For example, while some criminal laws favor the interests of the owners of capital, many others serve broader social interests. Similarly, while some forms of crime may be related to economic problems, others are not.

A number of other alternative perspectives began to appear in criminology in the 1980s and 1990s, so that theorizing about crime and criminality has become even more diversified. These "new criminologies" (Gibbons 1994, pp. 151–175) include postmodernist viewpoints, feminist arguments, and a number of other strains of thought, all of which differ in a number of ways from "mainstream" criminology.

Although broad theorizing has continued to proliferate in criminology, another major trend in recent years has taken criminology in a different direction, toward relatively detailed theories specific to one or another form of crime and toward research investigations of those theories. Baron and Straus's (1987) formulation that links gender inequality, pornography, and specific flaws in the social control system is a case in point, as is Kenneth Polk's (1994) theorizing and research regarding the various "scenarios" of social interaction that culminate in lethal violence. Indeed, contemporary criminology has a rich accumulation of empirical evidence that can be drawn upon by those who seek to understand the nature and causes of criminality in modern societies.

FORMS OF CRIME AND TYPES OF OFFENDERS

The legal codes of the various states and of the federal government include hundreds of specific offenses, but the explanatory task is to develop a relatively small set of theories that make sense of this diverse collection of illegal activities.

In their response to this task, Michael Gottfredson and Travis Hirschi (1990) have argued that virtually all forms of criminal activity, and many kinds of deviant behavior as well, share certain features in common: they are spontaneous, unplanned actions requiring little or no skill for their commission. Further, Gottfredson and Hirschi have claimed that lawbreakers rarely specialize in specific acts of criminality. They concluded that virtually all of these varying criminal and deviant acts can be accounted for by a single, general theory that asserts they are the work of persons who are

characterized by low self-control. Accordingly, in their view, there is no need for schemes that classify types of crime or kinds of offenders or for separate theories to account for them.

However, many criminologists contend that there are relatively distinct forms of crime that differ from each other and also that the behavior of many criminals is relatively patterned. For example, some offenders concentrate their efforts upon larcenous acts while others of them are mainly involved in acts of violence.

A number of criminologists have tried to sort the diverse collection of illegal activities into a smaller number of sociologically meaningful groupings or crime forms (Farr and Gibbons 1990; Gibbons 1994). Some have singled out crude property crime, consisting of larceny, burglary, robbery, and kindred offenses, as one type of crime; others have placed homicide and assaultive acts into another crime type; while still others have treated forcible rape and other sexual offenses as yet another broad form of lawbreaking. Then, too, "white-collar" or organizational crime has often been singled out as a crime pattern (Sutherland 1949; Schrager and Short 1978; Coleman 1987), consisting in large part of criminal acts such as antitrust violations, financial fraud, and the like, carried on by corporations and other large organizations. "Organized crime" is still another type that has received a good deal of criminological attention. Some persons have also pointed to a collection of offenses that receive little visibility in the mass media and elsewhere and have termed these "folk crimes" (Ross 1960–1961, 1973) or "mundane crimes" (Gibbons 1983). Finally, "political crime" has been identified as a major pattern of lawbreaking (Turk 1982).

Although these groupings identify forms of lawbreaking that may differ from each other in important ways, it is also true that they are relatively crude in form in that the underlying dimensions or variables on which they are based have not been spelled out. Further, there is disagreement among criminologists as to the specific crimes that should be identified as instances of white-collar crime, mundane crime, or some other category.

Criminologists have also developed systems for sorting individual offenders into behavioral types (Gibbons 1965). Although related to crime classification efforts, categorization of lawbreakers into types is a separate activity. While it may be possible to identify groupings such as predatory property crime, it many not be true that individual offenders specialize in that form of crime, hence it may be incorrect to speak of "predatory offenders" as a type of criminal. Most offender classification systems have been deficient in one respect or another (Gibbons 1985), but the most serious flaw is that they are oversimplified. Researchers have discovered that many offenders engage in a fairly diverse collection of offenses over their criminal "careers" rather than being crime specialists such as "burglars," "robbers," or "drug dealers" (Chaiken and Chaiken 1982).

THEORIES OF CRIME

The number of theories regarding particular forms of crime is extensive, thus they cannot all be reviewed here (for a review of many of them, see Gibbons 1994). Additional to those theories mentioned previously, a sampling of the more important ones would include the *routine activities* explanation of predatory property crime. Lawrence Cohen and Marcus Felson (1979) contend that predatory property crime involves three major elements: the supply of motivated offenders, the supply of suitable targets, and the absence of capable guardians. In other words, these crimes are carried out by persons with criminal motives, but the incidence of such offenses also depends upon the number of opportunities to burglarize homes or to rob persons. Also, the number of burglaries from one community to another is influenced by the degree to which residents in local areas act as guardians by maintaining surveillance over homes in their neighborhoods or by taking other crime-control steps. This theory takes note of the fact that criminal opportunities have increased in the United States in recent decades at the same time that capable guardianship has declined, due principally to changes in employment patterns. In particular, the number of families in which both adult members work during the day has grown markedly, as has the number of employed, single-parent families. Research evidence lends considerable support to this theory (Cohen and Felson 1979).

Research evidence also indicates that income inequality is related to predatory property crime

(Braithwaite 1979; Carroll and Jackson 1983). Further, Leo Carroll and Pamela Jackson (1983) argue that the routine activities and income inequality arguments are interrelated. They suggest that the labor market trends identified in the former have led to increased crime opportunities, declines in guardianship, and heightened levels of income inequality.

THEORIES OF CRIMINAL BEHAVIOR

While theories about crime patterns and rates have been developed principally by sociological criminologists, representatives of a number of disciplines have endeavored to identify factors and processes that explain the involvement or noninvolvement of specific individuals in lawbreaking. Three basic approaches can be noted: the biogenic-sociobiogenic, psychogenic, and sociogenic orientations. *Biogenic-sociobiogenic views* attribute the genesis or causes of lawbreaking, entirely or in part, to constitutional and hereditary factors, while *psychogenic perspectives* often contend that lawbreakers exhibit personality problems to which their illegal conduct is a response. By contrast, sociologists have most often advanced *sociological theories*, arguing that criminal behavior is learned in a socialization process by individuals who are neither biologically nor psychologically flawed. Also, some persons have constructed theories that combine or integrate elements of these three approaches, one case being James Wilson and Richard Herrnstein's (1985) argument that the behavior of criminals has genetic and constitutional roots and that offenders tend to be more mesomorphic in body build, less intelligent, and more burdened with personality defects than their noncriminal peers. Wilson and Herrnstein also contend that various social factors such as unemployment, community influences, and the like play some part in criminality.

Three generalizations can be made about biological theories: First, conclusive evidence supporting these arguments has not yet been produced; second, biological factors cannot be ruled out on the basis of the empirical evidence currently on hand; and third, if biological factors are involved in criminality, they are probably intertwined with social and psychological influences (Trasler 1987; Fishbein 1990).

In the first half of the twentieth century, psychological arguments about criminals centered on claims that these persons were feebleminded, or somewhat later, that many of them were suffering from serious mental pathology of one sort or another. However, a number of reviews of the evidence, particularly that having to do with the alleged role of low intelligence or personality defects in criminality, turned up little or no support for such claims (Schuessler and Cressey 1950; Waldo and Dinitz 1967; Tennenbaum 1977).

Even so, there is a lingering suspicion among a number of criminologists that the criminal acts of at least some lawbreakers, including certain kinds of sexual offenders, can be attributed to faulty socialization and abberant personality patterns (Gibbons 1994). Additionally, some psychologists have argued that even though the broad theory that criminality is due to marked personality defects on the part of lawbreakers lacks support, it is nonetheless true that individual differences in the form of personality patterns must be incorporated into criminological theories (Andrews and Wormith 1989; Blackburn 1993; Andrews and Bonta 1998). Moreover, in the opinion of a number of sociological criminologists, the argument that individual differences make a difference, both in accounting for criminality and for conformity, is persuasive (Gibbons 1989, 1994). Personality dynamics play a part in the behavior patterns that individuals exhibit, thus such concepts as role and status are often not entirely adequate to account for the behavior of individuals. Lawbreaking is quite probably related to the psychic needs of individuals as well as social and economic influences that play upon them. On this point, Jack Katz (1988) has explored the personal meanings of homicidal acts, shoplifting, and a number of other kinds of criminality to the persons who have engaged in these acts.

Sutherland's theory of *differential association* (Sutherland, Cressey, and Luckenbill 1992, pp.88–90) has been one of the most influential sociological theories about the processes through which persons come to engage in criminality. Sutherland maintained that criminal behavior, including techniques of committing crime and conduct definitions favorable to lawbreaking activity, is learned in association with other persons. Many of the associations of persons involve face-to-face contact, but conduct definitions favoring criminality can be acquired indirectly from reference groups, that is, from persons who are important to individuals but with whom they do not directly associate. Sutherland also contended that associations vary in frequency, duration, priority, and intensity (the personal meaning or significance to individuals of particular social ties).

A very different theory, directed mainly at the explanation of juvenile delinquency, is that if, through faulty socialization, individuals fail to become bonded or connected to others (that is, if they do not develop positive attachments to adult persons such as parents or teachers), they will then be unlikely to refrain from misbehavior (Hirschi 1969). The emphasis in this argument is on the failure to acquire prosocial, nondelinquent sentiments rather than on the learning of antisocial ones. In this view, delinquency is the result of defective socialization rather than of socialization patterns through which criminal attitudes are learned. A more recent but related version of this argument, noted earlier in this essay, is that of Gottfredson and Hirschi (1990), who have claimed that criminality and other forms of deviance are most often engaged in by persons who are low on self-control.

THEORETICAL INTEGRATION

Clearly, there is a wealth of differing arguments about the causes of crime and individual lawbreaking now in existence. Not surprisingly, then, a number of scholars have begun to ask whether it might be possible to amalgamate some or all of these varied lines of explanation into an integrated theory and thereby to develop a more powerful causal argument. Some criminologists have suggested that biological, psychological, and sociological contentions about crime all have some part to play in explaining crime and that, therefore, they should be integrated (Barak 1998). Others have proposed more limited forms of integration in which, for example, several sociological arguments might be merged into a single formulation (e.g., Tittle 1995; Braithwaite 1989) or in which psychological claims about lawbreaking might be linked or integrated with sociological ones. But to date, criminological investigators have not moved very far in the direction of sophisticated theoretical integrations. Further research on the interconnections between biological, psychological, and social factors in crime and criminal conduct will probably be required if integrative efforts are to bear fruit.

(SEE ALSO: *Criminology; Juvenile Delinquency Theories; Social Control*)

REFERENCES

Andrews, D.A., and James Bonta 1998 *The Psychology of Criminal Conduct*, 2d ed. Cincinnati: Anderson.

——, and J. Stephen Wormith 1989 "Personality and Crime: Knowledge Destruction and Construction." *Justice Quarterly* 6:289–309.

Barak, Gregg 1998 *Integrating Criminologies*. Boston: Allyn and Bacon.

Baron, Larry, and Murray A. Straus 1987 "Four Theories of Rape: A Macrosociological Analysis." *Social Problems* 34:467–489.

Blackburn, Ronald 1993 *The Psychology of Criminal Conduct*. New York: Wiley.

Braithwaite, John 1979 *Inequality, Crime and Public Policy*. London: Routledge and Kegan Paul.

—— 1989 *Crime, Shame, and Reintegration*. Cambridge, Eng.: Cambridge University Press.

Carroll, Leo, and Pamela Irving Jackson 1983 "Inequality, Opportunity, and Crime Rates in Central Cities." *Criminology* 21:178–194.

Chaiken, Jan, and Marcia Chaiken 1982 *Varieties of Criminal Behavior*. Santa Monica, Calif.: Rand.

Chambliss, William 1975 "Toward a Political Economy of Crime." *Theory and Society* 2:148–155.

Cohen, Lawrence E., and Marcus Felson 1979 "Social Change and Crime Rate Trends: A Routine Activities Approach." *American Sociological Review* 44:588–607.

Coleman, James W. 1987 "Toward an Integrated Theory of White-Collar Crime." *American Journal of Sociology* 93:406–439.

Cressey, Donald R. 1951 "Epidemiology and Individual Conduct: A Case From Criminology." *Pacific Sociological Review* 3:47–58.

Currie, Elliott 1985 *Confronting Crime*. New York: Pantheon.

Farr, Kathryn Ann, and Don C. Gibbons 1990 "Observations on the Development of Crime Categories." *International Journal of Offender Therapy and Comparative Criminology* 34:223–237.

Fishbein, Diana H. 1990 "Biological Perspectives in Criminology." *Criminology* 28:27–72.

Gibbons, Don C. 1965 *Changing the Lawbreaker*. Englewood Cliffs, N.J.: Prentice-Hall.

—— 1979 *The Criminological Enterprise*. Englewood Cliffs, N.J.: Prentice-Hall.

—— 1983 "Mundane Crime." *Crime and Delinquency* 29:213–227.

—— 1985 "The Assumption of the Efficacy of Middle-Range Explanations: Typologies." In R.F. Meier, ed., *Theoretical Methods in Criminology* .Beverly Hills, Calif.: Sage.

—— 1989 "Comment-Personality and Crime: Non-Issues, Real Issues, and a Theory and Research Agenda." *Justice Quarterly* 6:311–323.

—— 1992 *Society, Crime, and Criminal Behavior*, 6th ed. Englewood Cliffs, N.J.: Prentice-Hall.

—— 1994 *Talking About Crime and Criminals*. Englewood Cliffs, N.J.: Prentice-Hall.

Gibbs, Jack P. 1985 "The Methodology of Theory Construction in Criminology," In R.F. Meier, ed., *Theoretical Methods in Criminology*. Beverly Hills, Calif.: Sage.

Gottfredson, Michael R., and Travis Hirschi 1990 *A General Theory of Crime*. Stanford, Calif.: Stanford University Press.

Hirschi, Travis 1969 *Causes of Delinquency*. Berkeley: University of California Press.

Katz, Jack 1988 *Seductions of Crime*. New York: Basic Books.

Messner, Steven F., and Richard Rosenfeld 1994 *Crime and the American Dream*. Belmont, Calif.: Wadsworth.

Polk, Kenneth 1994 *When Men Kill*. Cambridge, Eng.: Cambridge University Press.

Quinney, Richard 1974 *Critique of Legal Order*. Boston: Little, Brown.

—— 1977 *Class, State, and Crime*. New York: McKay.

Ross, H. Laurence 1960-61 "Traffic Law Violation: A Folk Crime." *Social Problems* 9:231–241.

—— 1973 "Folk Crime Revisited." *Criminology* 11:41–85.

Schrager, Laura Shill, and James F. Short, Jr. 1978 "Toward a Sociology of Organizational Crime." *Social Problems* 25:407–419.

Schuessler, Karl F., and Donald R. Cressey 1950 "Personality Characteristicsof Criminals." *American Journal of Sociology* 55:476–484.

Sutherland, Edwin H. 1949 *White Collar Crime*. New York: Dryden.

——, Donald R. Cressey, and David F. Luckenbill 1992 *Principles of Criminology*, 11th ed. Dix Hills, N.Y.: General Hall.

Tennenbaum, D. J. 1977 "Personality and Criminality: A Summary and Implications of the Literature." *Journal of Criminal Justice* 5:225–235.

Tittle, Charles R. 1995 *Control Balance*. Boulder, Colo.: Westview.

Trasler, Gordon 1987 "Biogenetic Factors." In Herbert C. Quay, ed., *Handbook of Juvenile Delinquency*. New York: Wiley.

Turk, Austin T. 1982 *Political Criminality*. Beverly Hills, Calif.: Sage.

van Dijk, Jan J., Pat Mayhew, and Martin Killias 1990 *Experiences of Crime Across the World*. Deventer, The Netherlands: Kluwer Law and Taxation Publishers.

DON C. GIBBONS

CRIMINAL AND DELINQUENT SUBCULTURES

A subculture is derivative of, but different from, some larger referential culture. The term is used loosely to denote shared systems of norms, values, or interests that set apart some individuals, groups, or other aggregation of people from larger societies and from broader cultural systems. Common examples include youth subcultures, ethnic subcultures, regional subcultures, subcultures associated with particular occupations, and subcultures that develop among people who share special interests such as bird-watching, stamp collecting, or a criminal or delinquent behavior pattern.

Neither membership in a particular category (age, ethnicity, place of residence, occupation) nor behavior (bird-watching, stamp collecting, crime, or delinquency) is sufficient to define a subculture, however. The critical elements are, rather, (1) the degree to which values, norms, and identities associated with membership in a category or types of behaviors are shared, and (2) the nature of relationships, within some larger cultural system, between those who share these elements and those who do not.

In these terms, criminal or delinquent subcultures denote systems of norms, values, or interests that support criminal or delinquent behavior. The many behaviors specified in law as criminal or delinquent are associated with many criminal and delinquent subcultures. The norms, values, or interests of these subcultures may support particular criminal acts, a limited set of such acts (e.g., a subculture of pickpockets vs. a subculture of hustlers). "Professional criminals," for example, take pride in their craft, organize themselves for the safe and efficient performance of the crimes in which they specialize, and generally avoid other types of criminal involvement that might bring them to the attention of the authorities (see Sutherland 1937; Cressey 1983). Not all criminal subcultures are this specific, however. Some are simply opportunistic, embracing several types of criminal behavior as opportunities arise. So it is with delinquent subcultures, where specialization is rare.

While delinquent subcultures typically are associated with a broad range of illegal behaviors, among delinquent groups and subcultures there is great variation in the nature and strength of group norms, values, and interests. Moreover, the extent to which delinquent behavior is attributable to these factors is problematic. Much delinquent behavior of highly delinquent gangs, for example, results from the operation of group processes rather than group norms per se (see Short 1997). The normative properties of groups vary greatly, but even the most delinquent gang devotes relatively little of its group life to the pursuit of delinquent behaviors. Further, when gangs do participate in delinquent episodes, some members of the gang typically do not become involved. This is so, in part, because subcultures typically consist of *collections of normative orders*—rules and practices related to a common value (Herbert 1998)—rather than norms oriented around a single value (such as being "macho," "cool," or exceptionally gifted in some way). In addition, individuals who are associated with a particular subculture tend also to be associated with other subcultures. Simply being associated with a subculture thus is unlikely to be a good predictor of the behavior of a particular individual.

For analytical purposes it is important to distinguish between subcultures and the particular individuals and groups who share the norms, values, and interests of the subculture. While members of a delinquent gang may be the sole carriers of a particular subculture in a particular location, some subcultures are shared by many gangs. Conflict subcultures, for example, are shared by rival fighting gangs among whom individual and group status involves values related to the defense of "turf" (territory) and "rep" (reputation) and norms supportive of these values. Subcultures oriented to theft and other forms of property crime vary in the extent to which they are associated with particular groups. Some types of property crimes require organization and coordination of activities in order to be successful. Some also necessarily involve the efforts of others, such as "fences," in addition to members of a criminally organized gang (see Klockars 1974). Others, such as mugging and other types of robbery, may be carried out by individual offenders, who nevertheless share a subculture supportive of such behavior. Most drug-using subcultures tend to be less oriented toward particular groups than are conflict subcultures because the subcultural orientation is toward drug consumption, and this orientation can be shared with other drug users in many types of group situations. To the extent that a subculture is oriented to experiences associated with a particular group, however, a drug-using subculture may also be unique to that group.

As this analysis suggests, cultures, subcultures, and the groups associated with them typically overlap, often in multiple and complex ways. To speak of youth culture, for example, is to denote a subculture of the larger adult-dominated and institutionally defined culture. Similarly, delinquent subcultures contain elements of both youth and adult cultures. Terry Williams's (1989) lower class, minority, "cocaine kids," for example, were entrepreneurial, worked long hours, and maintained self-discipline—all important elements in the achievement ideology of the American Dream (see Messner and Rosenfeld 1994; also Fagan 1996; Hagan, et al. 1998). Most saw their involvement in the drug trade as a way to get started in legitimate business or to pursue other conventional goals, and a few succeeded at least temporarily in doing so. The criminal subculture with which they identified shared a symbiotic relationship with their customers (including many middle- and upper-class persons), who shared subcultural values approving drug use but who participated in the subculture of drug distribution only as consumers. For the young drug dealers, selling drugs was a way to "be somebody," to get ahead in life, and to acquire such things as jewelry, clothing, and cars—the symbols of wealth, power, and respect.

The nature of relationships between delinquent subcultures and larger cultural systems is further illustrated by Mercer Sullivan's study of cliques of young men in Brooklyn, among whom the "cultural meaning of crime" was "constructed

in . . . interaction out of materials supplied from two sources: the local area in which they spend their time almost totally unsupervised and undirected by adults, and the consumerist youth culture promoted in the mass media" (1989, p. 249). In other words, crime becomes meaningful to young men when they interact with one another and when they participate in youth culture, with its highly commercialized messages. The research literature on criminal and delinquent subcultures is devoted largely to describing and accounting for these types of varied and complex relationships.

THEORY AND RESEARCH

Despite efforts to define the theoretical construct, "subculture"—and related constructs—more precisely and to describe and account for the empirical reality they represent, no general theory of subcultures has emerged (Yinger 1960, 1977). Instead, research has continued to reveal enormous variation in subcultures, and theory has proceeded by illustration and analogy, with little progress in measurement or formal theoretical development. Despite this scientifically primitive situation, principles of subcultural formation have been identified, and knowledge of it has advanced.

It is a "fundamental law of sociology and anthropology," noted Daniel Glaser, that "social separation produces cultural differentiation" (1971, p. 90). More formally, and more cautiously, social separation is a necessary but not sufficient condition for the formation of subcultures. To the extent that groups or categories of persons are socially separated from one another, subcultural formation is likely to occur.

Albert Cohen argued that a "crucial" (perhaps necessary) "condition for the emergence of new cultural forms is the existence, in effective interaction with one another, of a number of actors with similar problems of adjustment" (1955, p. 59). While the notion of "similar problems of adjustment" can be interpreted to include problems faced by quite conventional people with special interests who find themselves "in the same boat" with others who have these same interests (let us say, bird-watchers), this condition seems especially appropriate to subcultures that embrace vandalism, "hell raising," and other types of nonutilitarian delinquent behavior. Observing that this type of behavior occurs most frequently among working-class boys, Cohen hypothesized that this type of delinquent subculture was formed in reaction to status problems experienced by working-class boys in middle-class institutions such as schools. Many working-class boys are inadequately prepared for either the educational demands or the discipline of formal education, and they are evaluated poorly in terms of this "middle-class measuring rod." Working-class girls are less pressured in these terms, Cohen argued, because they are judged according to criteria associated with traditional female roles, and they are subject to closer controls in the family.

The solution to their status problems, as some working-class boys see it, according to Cohen's theory, is to reject the performance and status criteria of middle-class institutions, in effect turning middle-class values upside down. The theory thus seeks to account for the highly expressive and hedonistic quality of much delinquency and for the malicious and negativistic quality of vandalism.

Cohen did not attempt to account for the delinquent behavior of particular individuals or for the behavior of all working-class boys. Most of the latter do not become delinquent—at least not seriously so. They choose instead—or are channeled into—alternative adaptations such as the essentially nondelinquent "corner boys" or the high-achieving "college boys" described by William Foote Whyte (1943).

The forces propelling youngsters into alternative adaptations such as these are not completely understood. Clearly, however, working-class and lower-class boys and girls tend to be devalued in middle-class institutional contexts. Their marginality sets the stage for subcultural adaptations. Delinquents and criminals occupy even more marginal positions. This is particularly true of persistent delinquents and criminals who commit serious crimes, in contrast to those who only rarely transgress the law and with little consequence. When marginality is reinforced by labeling, stigmatization, or prejudicial treatment in schools and job markets, "problems of adjustment" magnify. The common ecological location of many delinquents, in the inner-city slums of large cities, and their coming together in schools, provides the setting for

"effective interaction." The result often is the formation of delinquent youth gangs, an increasingly common organizational form taken by delinquent subcultures (see Thrasher 1927; Klein, 1995; Short 1997).

There is no universally agreed-upon definition of youth gangs. For theoretical purposes, however, it is useful to define gangs as groups whose members meet together with some regularity over time and whose membership is group-selected, based on group-defined criteria. Similarly, organizational characteristics are group determined. Most importantly, gangs are not adult-sponsored groups. The nature of relationships between young people and conventional adults is the most critical difference between gangs and other youth groups (see Schwartz 1987). Gang members are less closely tied to conventional institutions and therefore less constrained by institutional controls than are nongang youth. Group processes of status achievement, allocation, and defense are more likely to result in delinquent behavior among gangs than is the case among adult-sponsored groups.

HOW DO CRIMINAL AND DELINQUENT SUBCULTURES GET STARTED?

Delinquent and criminal subcultures have a long history in industrialized societies (Cressey 1983). Herman and Julia Schwendinger (1985) trace the origins of adolescent subcultures, including delinquent varieties, to social changes that began in the sixteenth century. Traditional economic and social relationships were greatly altered with the advent of capitalism and the Industrial Revolution in Western Europe, leaving in their wake large numbers of unemployed persons and disrupting communities, families, and other primordial groups. Cut adrift from traditional crafts and communities, thousands roamed the countryside, subsisting as best they could off the land or by victimizing travelers. The "dangerous classes" eventually settled in cities, again to survive by whatever means were available, including crime. Criminal subcultures and organizational networks often developed under these circumstances.

The Schwendingers emphasize that criminal subcultures developed as a result of structural changes associated with capitalist values and their accompanying norms and interests—individualism and competitiveness, acquisitiveness and exploitativeness—and the relationships that developed during this period between capitalists and emerging nation-states. While many of the facts upon which this Marxist interpretation is based are generally accepted, careful historical analysis of economic and political systems and their consequences cautions against any simple or straightforward interpretation (see Chirot 1985). The connection between global phenomena and crime and delinquency always is mediated by historical, cultural, and local circumstances—by the historically concrete (see Tilly 1981).

James Coleman and his associates (1974) identified more recent social changes that were associated with the rise and spread of youth culture throughout the United States: the Baby Boom following World War II and the increased affluence of young people associated with post-World War II economic prosperity combined to create a huge youth market with great economic power. At the same time, young people were spending more time in school and therefore delaying their entrance into the labor force; growing numbers of women entered the work force, further separating mothers from youth in homes and neighborhoods; adults increasingly were employed in large organizations where young people were not present; and mass media, catering more and more to the youth market, were greatly expanded. At the close of the twentieth century, each of these broad social changes was more pronounced—and their influence was more widespread throughout the world—than was the case when these observations were made.

In contrast to accounts of the origins of Western European youth cultures, and of youth culture in the United States, Ko-lin Chin (1996) traces the development of Chinese youth gangs in the United States to ancient secret society traditions, and to the more recent Triad societies that formed in the late seventeenth century in China, and their counterpart tongs in the United States. Formed as political groups representing disfavored Chinese officials and the alienated poor, these groups initially stressed patriotism, righteousness, and brotherhood as primary values. However, their secret nature was conducive to clandestine activities such as gambling, prostitution, and running opium dens.

Competition among Triad societies in these activities often led to violence. Failure to achieve political power led to their further transformation into criminal organizations involved in extortion, robbery, drug trafficking, and other serious crimes.

Street gangs comprised of Chinese adolescents did not form in the United States until the late 1950s, but their numbers increased dramatically during the following decade, when changed immigration laws permitted more Chinese to enter the country. Conflict between foreign- and American-born youths led to the emergence of gangs, some seriously delinquent. Chin attributes this development to alienating problems experienced by immigrant Chinese youth in their families, schools, and communities, in dramatic contrast to their American-born counterparts. From the beginning, many Chinese youth gangs have been associated in a variety of ways with established adult secret societies in the United States, Hong Kong, or Taiwan, or in all three places. The existence of "Triad-influenced" organizations has been critical to the types of gangs that have emerged in Chinese communities and to the nature of their criminal activities.

While the origins of delinquent subcultures may reside in antiquity, the formation and evolution of modern variations of them can be explained in terms of more immediate macro-level developments. Some of these developments relate primarily to the ongoing activities and interests of gang members rather than to racial or ethnic changes, or to sweeping social changes. The nature of these influences is illustrated by a drug-using group studied by James Short, Fred Strodtbeck, and their associates (Short and Strodtbeck 1965; see also Short 1997, 1998). This gang was observed as it developed its own unique subculture. The subculture of the "Pill Poppers," as they became known to the research team, evolved from their relationship with a larger, conflict-oriented gang of which they had previously been a part. The Pill Poppers' preoccupation with drugs and their refusal to participate in the more bellicose activities of the larger gang led to their withdrawal and increasing isolation, by mutual agreement. The researchers were able to observe the evolution of this subculture, which was characterized by normative approval of drug consumption, an elevated value on "getting high," and mutual interest in the "crazy" things that happened to them when they were under the influence of drugs. The latter, in particular, became legendary within the group, being told and retold with nostalgia and humor when members of the gang were together. The subculture of this gang contrasted sharply with that of other gangs that were participating in a well-developed conflict subculture.

LEVELS OF EXPLANATION OF CRIMINAL AND DELINQUENT SUBCULTURES

The theories of criminal and delinquent subcultures are macro-level theories (Short 1998). Their purpose is to identify what it is about political, economic, and other social systems that explain the emergence and the social distribution of these phenomena. Other theories at this level focus on the impact of local and broader community opportunities on delinquent subcultures and on youth subcultures generally. Walter Miller (1958) related lower-class culture to gang delinquency, while Richard Cloward and Lloyd Ohlin (1960) found that different delinquent subcultures were associated with the availability of legitimate and illegitimate economic opportunities in local communities. Gary Schwartz (1987) stressed the importance of local community youth-adult authority relationships in determining the nature of youth subcultures, including the extent and the nature of delinquent activities associated with them. Mercer Sullivan (1989) related gang adaptations to more global economic developments such as the transfer of manufacturing jobs from the United States to other countries and an increasingly segmented labor market, which has resulted in the concentration of low-wage and surplus labor in inner-city minority communities (see also Hagedorn 1987, 1998).

William Julius Wilson (1987) provided the most compelling theoretical argument relating economic changes to crime and delinquency among the "truly disadvantaged." Wilson argued that a permanent underclass emerged in the United States during the 1960s and 1970s. Research on delinquent subcultures supports this argument and documents related changes in gang membership. Because fewer good jobs were available to poor, minority young men, more gang members continued their association with gangs as they entered

adulthood. In the past, gang members typically "grew out of" the gang to take jobs, get married, and often become associated with adult social clubs in stable, ethnically-based communities. These options have become less viable among the poor of all races, but minorities have increasingly become the truly disadvantaged. Gang organization has been affected by this change, as older members assume or continue leadership roles. The result often has been that gang involvement in criminal activities has become more sophisticated and instrumental, and younger members have been exploited in criminal enterprise. Relationships between young people and conventional adults also suffer, as older, stable role models and monitors of youthful behavior are replaced by young adult, often criminal, role models for the young (see Anderson 1990, 1999).

Sullivan's study of groups and young males in three Brooklyn communities—black, predominantly Latino, and white—is particularly significant in this regard. The young men in Hamilton Park, the white group, were able to find better jobs than were the others at all ages. More important, because "they had become more familiar with the discipline of the workplace," as they grew older they were able to secure better-quality jobs and to hold on to them, compared to the minority youth studied by Sullivan. Familiarity with the discipline of the workplace is a type of *human capital* that was made possible by an important type of *social capital*—the superior personal networks that the Hamilton Park youth shared with the adult community (Sullivan 1989, pp. 105, 226). The minority youth were disadvantaged, with respect to both human and social capital, in the family and in other ways (see Coleman 1988). Thus, while individual human and social capital are acquired through personal experience, communities and neighborhoods also vary in their stock of human and social capital, qualitatively and quantitatively—yet another way in which delinquent and criminal subcultures reflect aspects of their "parent" (larger) cultures.

All macro-level theories make certain assumptions about the individual level of explanation. The most prominent of these assumptions is that individuals learn subcultural norms, values, and the behaviors they encourage, by interacting with others in their environment. The general processes of learning have been well established by research and theory (see Bandura 1986; Eron 1987).

The child's most important early learning experiences take place in the family, but other influences quickly assert themselves, especially as children associate with age and gender peers. With the beginning of adolescence, the latter become especially powerful as young people experience important biological and social changes. It is at this point that youth subcultures become especially significant.

Subcultures are dynamic and ever changing, influenced by both external and internal forces and processes. Substantial knowledge gaps exist at each level of explanation; precisely how they relate to each other is not well understood, however. By documenting the ongoing interaction among gang members and between gang members and others, group processes help to inform the nature of the relationship in ways that are consistent with what is known at the individual and macro levels of explanation. Both intragang and intergang fighting often serve group purposes, for example, by demonstrating personal qualities that are highly valued by the gang or by reinforcing group solidarity (see Miller, Geertz, and Cutter 1961; Jansyn 1966). Gang conflict often occurs when a gang believes its "rep," its "turf," or its resources (for example, its share of a drug market) are threatened by another gang. Threats to individual or group status often result in violent or other types of criminal behavior (Short 1997).

CONCLUSION

The rich research materials that have accumulated regarding criminal and delinquent subcultures suggest two conclusions: (1) there is a great variety of such adaptive phenomena, and (2) they are of an ever-changing nature. Because they both effect social change and adapt to it, subcultures—including criminal and delinquent subcultures—continue to be important theoretically, empirically, and practically (that is, as a matter of social policy). Robert Sampson and his colleagues (1997) find that willingness to intervene on behalf of the common good, together with collective efficacy (social cohesion among neighbors), is associated with lower rates of violent crime in Chicago neighborhoods. This suggests that developing ways to encourage identification of neighbors with each other and encouraging them to help one another in their common interests will enhance local social

control and help weaken the influence of subcultures that encourage criminal and delinquent behavior.

(SEE ALSO: *Crime, Theories of*; *Criminology*; *Juvenile Delinquency and Juvenile Crime*; *Juvenile Delinquency, Theories of*)

REFERENCES

Anderson, Elijah 1999 *The Code of the Streets*. New York: W.W. Norton.

—— 1990 *Streetwise: Race, Class, and Change in an Urban Community*. Chicago: University of Chicago Press.

Bandura, Albert 1986 *Social Foundations of Thought and Action: A Social Cognitive Theory*. Englewood Cliffs, N.J.: Prentice-Hall.

Chin, Ko-lin 1996 *Chinatown Gangs: Extortion, Enterprise, and Ethnicity*. New York: Oxford University Press.

Chirot, Daniel 1985 "The Rise of the West." *American Sociological Review* 50:181–195.

Cloward, Richard A., and Lloyd E. Ohlin 1960 *Delinquency and Opportunity: A Theory of Delinquent Gangs*. New York: Free Press.

Cohen, Albert K. 1955 *Delinquent Boys: The Culture of the Gang*. New York: Free Press.

Coleman, James S. 1988 "Social Capital in the Creation of Human Capital." *American Journal of Sociology* 94 (Suppl.):S95–S120.

——, Robert H. Bremner, Burton R. Clark, John B. Davis, Doroty H. Eichorn, Zvi Griliches, Joseph F. Kett, Norman B. Ryder, Zahava Blum Doering, and John M. Mays 1974 *Youth Transition to Adulthood*. Report of the Panel of the President's Science Advisory Committee. Chicago: University of Chicago Press.

Cressey, Donald R. 1983 "Delinquent and Criminal Subcultures." In S. E. Kadish, ed., *Encyclopedia of Crime and Justice*. New York: Free Press.

Eron, Leonard D. 1987 "The Development of Aggressive Behavior from the Perspective of a Developing Behaviorism." *American Psychologist* 42:435–442.

Fagan, Jeffrey 1996 "Gangs, Drugs, and Neighborhood Change." In C. Ronald Huff, ed., *Gangs in America*, 2d ed. Newbury Park, Calif.: Sage.

Glaser, Daniel 1971 *Social Deviance*. Chicago: Markham.

Hagan, John, Gerd Hefler, Gabriele Classen, Klaus Boehnke, and Hans Merkens 1998 "Subterranean Sources of Subcultural Delinquency Beyond the American Dream." *Criminology* 36:309–341.

Hagedorn, John M. 1998 "Gang Violence in the Post-Industrial Era." In Michael Tonry and Mark H. Moore, eds., *Youth Violence*, vol. 24, *Crime and Justice*. Chicago: University of Chicago Press.

———, with Perry Macon 1987 *People and Folks: Gangs, Crime, and the Underclass in a Rustbelt City*. Chicago: Lake View Press.

Herbert, Steve 1998 "Police Subculture Reconsidered." *Criminology* 36:343–369.

Jansyn, Leon R. 1966 "Solidarity and Delinquency in a Street-Corner Group." *American Sociological Review* 31:600–614.

Klein, Malcolm W. 1995 *The American Street Gang*. New York: Oxford University Press.

Klockars, Carl B. 1974 *The Professional Fence*. New York: Free Press.

Messner, Steven F., and Richard Rosenfeld 1994 *Crime and the American Dream*. Belmont, Calif.: Wadsworth.

Miller, Walter B. 1958 "Lower Class Culture as a Generating Milieu of Gang Delinquency." *Journal of Social Issues* 14:5–19.

———, Hildred Geertz, Henry S. G. Cutter 1961 "Aggression in a Boys' Street-Corner Group." *Psychiatry* 24:283–298.

Sampson, Robert J., S.W. Raudenbush, and F. Earls 1997 "Neighborhoods and Violent Crime: A Multilevel Study of Collective Efficacy." *Science* 277:918–924.

Schwartz, Gary 1987 *Beyond Conformity or Rebellion: Youth and Authority in America*. Chicago: University of Chicago Press.

Schwendinger, Herman, and Julia Siegel Schwendinger 1985 *Adolescent Subcultures and Delinquency*. New York: Praeger.

Short, James F., Jr. 1998 "The Level of Explanation Problem Revisited—The American Society of Criminology 1997 Presidential Address." *Criminology* 36:3–36.

——— 1997 *Poverty, Ethnicity, and Violent Crime*. Boulder, Colo.: Westview.

———, and Fred L. Strodtbeck 1965 *Group Process and Gang Delinquency*. Chicago: University of Chicago Press.

Sullivan, Mercer L. 1989 *"Getting Paid": Youth Crime and Work in the Inner City*. Ithaca, N.Y.: Cornell University Press.

Sutherland, Edwin H. 1937 *The Professional Thief*. Chicago: University of Chicago Press.

Thrasher, Frederic M. 1927 *The Gang: A Study of 1,313 Gangs in Chicago*. Chicago: University of Chicago Press.

Tilly, Charles 1981 *As Sociology Meets History*. New York: Academic Press.

Whyte, William Foote 1943 *Street Corner Society*. Chicago: University of Chicago Press.

Williams, Terry 1989 *The Cocaine Kids: The Inside Story of a Teenage Drug Ring*. Menlo Park, Calif.: Addison-Wesley.

Wilson, William Julius 1987 *The Truly Disadvantaged: The Inner City, the Underclass, and Public Policy*. Chicago: University of Chicago Press.

Yinger, Milton 1960 "Contraculture and Subculture." *American Sociological Review* 23:625–635.

——— 1977 "Countercultures and Social Change." *American Sociological Review* 42:833–853.

JAMES F. SHORT, JR.

CRIMINAL SANCTIONS

The quality and quantity of normative sanctions have been viewed as a reflection of the nature of social solidarity (Durkheim 1964; Black 1976). In simple societies where the level of willing conformity is high, normative sanctions tend to be informal in nature, substantive in application, and limited in use. In complex societies where levels of willing conformity are lower, normative sanctions are more likely to be formal in nature, procedural in application, and frequent in use (Michalowski 1985). The increasing stratification, morphology, and bureaucracy of modern society have given rise to the predominance of formal justice in the form of criminal law and criminal sanctions (Black 1976). Consequently, the nature of crime has been transformed from an offense committed by one individual against another in the context of community to an offense committed against the society as a whole (Christie 1977). Behaviors considered harmful to the moral, political, economic, or social well-being of society are defined as criminal and thereby worthy of formal state sanctions (Walker 1980). Criminal behaviors include transgressions of both the prohibitions and obligations that define a particular society. Behaviors come to be defined as crimes through the process of criminalization, which includes the calculation of proportional sanctions for each crime.

Criminal sanctions include capital punishment, imprisonment, corporal punishment, banishment, house arrest, community supervision, fines, restitution, and community service. The type and severity of criminal sanctions are prescribed by criminal law (Walker 1980). The quality and quantity of criminal penalties are determined by both the perceived seriousness of the offense and the underlying philosophy of punishment. Punishment by the state on behalf of society has traditionally been justified on either consequential or nonconsequential grounds (Garland 1994). Consequentialism justifies punishment as a means to the prevention of future crime. The utilitarian approach, for example, allows society to inflict harm (by punishment) in order to prevent greater harms that would be caused by future crimes. The utilitarian approach to criminal sanctions is governed by a set of limiting principles (Beccaria 1980). According to utilitarianism criminal sanctions should not be used to penalize behavior that does not harm, the severity of the penalty should only slightly outweigh the benefit derived from the criminal behavior, and alternatives to punishment should be utilized when they prove to be as effective (Bentham 1995).

Nonconsequentialism, on the other hand, justifies punishment as an intrinsically appropriate response to crime (Duff and Garland 1994). The retributive approach, for example, mandates punishment as a way of removing the advantage originally gained by the criminal behavior or as a means of restoring the moral balance that was lost as a result of a crime. According to the retributivist perspective crime separates the offender from the community and it is only through punishment that the separation can be repaired (Morris 1981). While the utilitarian and retributivist justifications have dominated the philosophical discussion of punishment, more recent justifications such as rehabilitation (Rotman 1990) and incapacitation (Morris 1982) have also been viewed in terms of their consequential and nonconsequential nature. From a sociological perspective these philosophies of punishment represent ideal types against which the actual practice of punishment must be examined.

THE SOCIOLOGY OF CRIMINAL SANCTIONS

Several lines of inquiry comprise the sociology of criminal sanctions including the examination of the criminalizing process, the empirical assessment of the effectiveness of particular sanctions, and the analysis of the relationship between social structural changes and the evolution of criminal law.

Critique of the Criminalization Process. The question of which behaviors become defined as criminal and deemed worthy of punitive sanctions has been central to the study of crime and law. The *functional perspective* of criminal law suggests that the criminalization of a particular behavior is the result of a consensus among members of a society (Durkheim 1964). In the *consensus view* criminal law encompasses the behaviors that have been determined to be most threatening to the social structure of society and the well-being of its members (Wilson 1979).

According to the functionalist perspective, criminal law adapts to changes in the normative consensus of society. As society evolves, behaviors once considered criminal may be decriminalized while behaviors that had previously been acceptable may become criminalized. In this context criminal law and its accompanying sanctions are viewed as the collective moral will of society. Punishment is viewed as serving the essential function of creating a sense of moral superiority among the law-abiding members of society, thereby strengthening their social solidarity (Durkheim 1964). Therefore, crime is considered to be inevitable in the functionalist view because the pressure exerted against those who do not conform to normative expectations is necessary to reinforce the willing conformity among members of society. Solidarity results from the social forces directed against transgressors, with the most powerful of these forces being criminal sanctions (Vold 1958). Criminal sanctions enable societies to distinguish between behaviors that are simply considered unacceptable and those behaviors that are considered truly harmful.

Conversely, the conflict perspective suggests that the designation of behaviors as criminal is determined within a context of unequal power. Although various forms of the conflict perspective identify different sources for this power imbalance, they are in general agreement as to the results of the criminalizing process. According to the conflict view, society is made up of groups with conflicting needs, values, and interests that are mediated by an organized state that represents the needs, values, and interests of groups that possess the power to control the state. Such control includes the capacity to determine which behaviors are considered to be criminal and which behaviors are not. As a result behaviors more likely to be committed by the less powerful are defined as criminal while behaviors more likely committed by the powerful are not defined as criminal (Bernard 1983; Reiman 1998). Furthermore, the conflict view suggests that the application of both criminal law and criminal sanctions are skewed in favor of those with power. Within the conflict perspective various theories are differentiated according to their identified source of group conflict. Among the major conflict theories are those that identify a conflict of cultural groups (Sellin 1938), those that identify a conflict of norms (Vold 1958), those that identify a conflict of socioeconomic interests (Marx 1964), and those that identify a conflict of bureaucratic interests (Turk 1969). Despite their different origins, conflict theories are united in their assessment that criminal law and criminal sanctions are utilized to support the average best interest of those with power. As a result the state is assumed to apply criminal sanctions in such a manner that they are not perceived as overly coercive while at the same time preserving the existing power arrangements thereby maintaining the legitimacy of criminal law (Turk 1969).

An Empirical Context for Criminal Sanctions. Empirical assessments of criminal sanctions have been primarily carried out within the contexts of *penology* and the *sociology of punishment.* Penology is a practically oriented form of social science that traces and evaluates various practices of penal institutions and other punitively oriented institutions of the modern criminal justice system (Duff and Garland 1994). Penology began as an extension of the prison itself thats sole purpose was to evaluate the objectives of the institution and develop more efficient ways of achieving these institutional objectives. More recently penology has expanded its inquiry to include the assessment of the entire criminal sanctioning process (studying the prosecution, the court process, as well as alternative sanctions such as probation, fines, electric monitoring, community service, and restitution). Increasingly, penology has been guided by the major theories of crime causation thus becoming a recognized area of study within the discipline of criminology. Contemporary, penological research serves as the empirical foundation for policy development (Bottomley 1989). Despite its more recent criminological grounding, penological research is still viewed as primarily evaluative rather than critical. Penology assumes an exclusively punitive perspective toward transgressions of criminal law, therefore, it is primarily concerned with the relative effectiveness of the various punitive responses to criminal transgressions. The critical dimension of penology is limited to identifying problems within existing institutions and suggesting ways to more efficiently achieve the goal of punishment. Because penology is limited to the study of punishment systems any questions concerning alternative models of crime control such as compensation or conciliation are addressed by the sociological study of punishment (Garland 1990).

Unlike penology, the sociology of punishment raises more fundamental questions concerning the relative effectiveness of both punitive and nonpunitive responses to normative transgressions. Within the context of the sociology of punishment special attention is directed to the way in which society organizes and deploys its power to respond to transgressions (Duff and Garland 1994). It is primarily concerned with the relationship between punishment and society. Punishment is examined as a social institution that reflects the nature of social life. The sociology of punishment is fundamentally interested in why particular types of societies employ particular types of criminal sanctions (Garland 1990). In addition, the sociological analysis of punishment examines the social conditions that necessitate certain styles of normative sanctioning such as the use of penal sanctions in social situations that are characterized by high levels of inequality, heterogeneity, and bureaucratic interaction (Black 1976). The sociology of punishment also includes the study of correlations between the application of various sanctions (e.g. imprisonment, probation, fines, etc.) and demographic variables such as class, race, gender, occupation, and education (Reiman 1998; Zimring and Hawkins 1990). Because of the dominance of imprisonment as the preferred sanction for serious criminal transgressions in Western societies much attention has been directed to the effect of penal confinement on prisoners. Sociological inquiries into the inner world of the prison have examined the social adaptation of prisoners to the unique requirements and relationships that characterized "The total institution" (Goffman 1961; Sykes 1958). The sociological study of punishment suggests that the adoption and application of criminal sanctions are better understood as a reflection of social, political, and economic reality than as the product of moral consensus (Garland 1990).

The Evolution of Criminal Sanctions. Sociologists have paid considerable attention to the qualitative evolution of criminal sanctions. Special attention has been directed to the relationship between changes in the socioeconomic structure and the evolution of criminal law in modern Western societies (Mellosi and Pavarini 1981). Within the more general discussion of law and society, the study of punishment and social structure emerged (Rusche and Kirchheimer 1939). The sociology of penal systems argues that the transformation of penal systems cannot primarily be explained by the changing needs of crime control. Instead, the sociological analysis of shifts in the systems of punishment and criminal law are best understood in terms of their relationship to the prevailing system of production (Sellen 1976). Each society generates criminal law practices and types of punishments that correspond to the nature of its productive relationships. Research on punishment and social structure has focused attention on the origin and evolution of penal systems, the use or avoidance of specific punishments, and the intensity of penal practices in terms of larger social forces—particularly economic and fiscal forces (Rusche and Kirchheimer 1939). For example, in slave economies where the supply of slaves was inadequate, penal slavery emerged; the emergence of the factory system decreased the demand for convict labor, which in turn led to the rise of reformatories and industrial prisons (Melossi and Pavarini 1981). Although the economic analysis of criminal sanctions dominated the early literature on the sociology of punishment, later analysis has focused more broadly on all five aspects of social life (i.e., stratification, morphology, bureaucracy, culture, and social control).

CRIMINAL SANCTIONS AND THE ASPECTS OF SOCIAL LIFE

The comparative study of law has identified criminal law and criminal sanctions as quantifiable variables (Black 1976). By quantifying criminal law and criminal sanctions it is possible to compare both the type and the amount of law utilized by one society versus another. The quantification of law can then be correlated to the nature of social life. The type and amount of criminal law can either be correlated to individual aspects of social life or the collective integration of all the variables of social life. Social life consists of five variable aspects: *stratification* is the vertical aspect of social life (the hierarchy of people relative to their power), *morphology* is the horizontal aspect of social life (the distribution of people in relation to each other), *bureaucracy* is the corporate aspect of social life (the capacity for collective action), *culture* is the symbolic aspect of social life (the representation of ideas, beliefs, and values), and *social control* is the normative aspect of social life (the definition of deviance and the response to it). The first four aspects of social life collectively determine the style of social control.

Comparative legal studies have identified five styles of social control; *penal control, compensatory control, therapeutic control, educative control* and *conciliatory control* (Fogel 1975). The response to normative transgressions under each style is consistent with the general standard of behavior recognized by society at large. Transgressions of the prohibition standard of the penal style of control require a punitive solution in order to absolve the guilt of the transgressor. Violation of the obligation standard of the compensatory style requires payment in order to eliminate the debt incurred by the violation. Behaviors that fall outside the standard of normality that characterizes the therapeutic style require treatment to restore predictability to social interaction. Failure to meet the knowledge standard of the educative style requires reeducation in order to attain a full understanding of society's norms and underlying values. Disruption of the harmony standard of the conciliatory style requires resolution in order to reestablish the relationships among members of the community (Fogel 1975).

Criminal law and punitive sanctions are inversely correlated to other forms of social control. In addition to law, social control is found in many intermediate social institutions, including family, churches, schools, occupations, neighborhoods, and friendships. In societies where such intermediate institutions are dominant, the need for law and formal criminal sanctions is limited. Conversely, in societies where intermediate institutions are less dominant informal social control is less effective, thereby necessitating the expansion of formal social control that typically takes the form of criminal law and punitive sanctions. The quantity of criminal law increases as the quantity of informal social control decreases (Black 1976). The primary measurement of the quantity of criminal law is the frequency and severity of criminal sanctions.

The relative quantity of criminal law and other forms of social control have been linked to the relative presence or absence of the other aspects of social life. At the extremes, societies characterized by significant stratification, morphological diversity, bureaucratic interaction, and cultural multiplicity will employ a more penal style of social control while societies characterized by general equality, homogeneity, face-to-face interaction, and cultural consensus will employ a more conciliatory style of social control. The therapeutic, educative, and compensatory styles of social control are to be found in societies somewhere between the extremes. In Western societies the increase in stratification, morphology, bureaucracy, and cultural multiplicity have combined to lower the level of willing conformity and diminish the effectiveness of informal mechanisms of social control (Garland 1990). The decline of informal social control has been traced to the less efficient use of shaming. Literature on the effectiveness of various normative sanctions has suggested that shame can be either reintegrative or disintegrative in nature depending on the strength of intermediate institutions and the level of willing conformity (Braithwaite 1994). Although the phenomenon of shame is found in both formal and informal systems of social control it is a more central feature of informal social control.

FORMAL VERSUS INFORMAL SANCTIONS

Shaming is the central deterrent element of most informal mechanisms of social control. Its use in formal mechanisms of social control has until the 1990s been limited due to the concerns related to labeling (Becker 1963; Braithwaite 1994). Deterrence research has shown a much stronger shaming effect for informal sanctions than for formal legal

sanctions (Paternoster and Iovanni 1986). It has been suggested that sanctions imposed by groups with emotional and social ties to the transgressor are more effective in deterring criminal behavior than sanctions that are imposed by a bureaucratic legal authority (Christie 1977). Although the empirical evidence comparing the deterrent effect of informal versus formal sanctions is limited, it has consistently shown that there is a greater concern among transgressors for the social impact of their arrest than for the punishment they may receive (Sherman and Berk 1984). Perceptions of the certainty and severity of formal criminal sanctions appear to have little effect on the considerations that lead to criminal behavior. Whatever effect formal criminal sanctions do have on deterring future criminal behavior is primarily dependent on the transgressor's perception of informal sanctions (Tittle 1980).

Deterrence theory is predicated on the assumption of fear (Zimring and Hawkes 1973). It has been assumed that deviants and especially criminal offenders fear the loss directly related to formal sanctions (e.g. loss of liberty, loss of material possessions, etc.). Research on formal sanctions that are coupled with informal sanctions suggests to the contrary that to the extent transgressors would be deterred by fear, the fear that is most relevant is that their transgression will result in a loss of respect or status among their family, friends, or associates (Tittle 1980). In the cost-benefit analysis that is central to the "rational actor" model of crime causation, loss of respect and status weighs much more heavily for most individuals than the direct loss of liberty or material.

Deterrence is considered to be irrelevant to the majority of the populace, therefore, most people are believed to comply with the law because of their internalization of the norms and values of society (Toby 1964). For the majority of the populace failure to abide by the norms and values would call into question their commitment to that society. For the well-socialized individual, moral conscience serves as the primary deterrent. The conscience delivers an anxiety response each time an individual transgresses the moral boundaries of society. The anxiety response fulfills the three requirements of deterrence: it is immediate, it is certain, and it is severe. Formal criminal sanctions on the other hand may be severe but they are not always certain nor swift (Braithwaite 1994).

Criminal sanctions represent a denial of confidence in the morality of the transgressor. In a criminal law system norm compliance is reduced to the calculus of cost versus benefit. Conversely, informal sanctions can be a reaffirmation of the morality of the transgressor by showing disappointment in the transgressor for acting out of character. The shaming associated with the disappointment is reintegrative because its ultimate goal is the restoration of the transgressor to full membership in the group, community, or society. Shaming in the informal context is reintegrative because of its view of the transgressor as a whole and valued member of society and its goal of social restoration. Criminal sanctions, on the other hand, define the transgressor strictly in terms of his or her transgression thus causing a disconnection between the transgressor and society (Garfinkel 1965). Criminal sanctions lack both the incentive and mechanism for reintegration. Without reintegrative potential, criminal sanctions stigmatize rather than shame. Stigmatization is exclusively concerned with labeling while reintegrative shaming is equally concerned with delabeling. In the context of most informal sanctions community disapproval is coupled with gestures of reacceptance. The reintegrative character of informal sanctions ensures that the deviant label be directed to the behavior rather than the person thus avoiding the assignment of a master status to the person (Braithwaite 1994).

In the study of criminal sanctions much attention has been directed to the effects of labeling on the sanctioned transgressor. *Labeling theory* argues that the deviant characteristic (e.g., drug addict, criminal, etc.) assigned to a person may become a status such that the 'label' will dominate all positive characteristics (e.g. parent, teacher, church member, etc.) that might otherwise characterize the person. Such a deviant master status is believed to limit and in some cases preclude the reintegration of the transgressor. For those prevented from reintegrating, the label becomes a self-fulfilling prophecy eventually leading to secondary deviance, namely deviance caused by the label itself (Becker 1963). The possibility of secondary deviance as a result of the stigmatization of the transgressor has been included by some labeling theorists in their assessment of the relative effectiveness of criminal sanctions (Gove 1980). However, it has been alternatively suggested that

stigmatization might enhance crime control because the thought of being a social outcast serves as a stronger sanction and more effective deterrent than being shamed and eventually reintegrated (Silberman 1976). The potential effectiveness of sanctions is dependent upon whether deterrence is more effectively achieved through the fear of social marginalization associated with formal sanctions or the fear of community disapproval associated with informal sanctions (Braithwaite 1994).

CRIMINAL SANCTIONS AND DUE PROCESS

Despite the lack of conclusive evidence in support of the deterrent effect of criminal sanctions, the frequency and severity of such sanctions have significantly increased over the past quarter-century (Stafford and Warr 1993). The dramatic rise in both the prison population and persons under probationary supervision is a reflection of the increase in the age of the population most at risk to engage in criminal acts as well as a renewed commitment to the nonconsequential philosophy of punishment. A number of observers have pointed to the growing use of criminal sanctions as a sign of an increased emphasis on crime control; however, the increasing use of criminal sanctions has coincided with the expansion of legal protections for the accused. The limitations of criminal sanctions in the form of due process guarantees have produced a hybrid criminal process that legitimates the widespread use of punitive responses to normative transgressions by constraining the power of state-sponsored agents of control. The criminal process in the West includes both a strong crime-control component and a strong due process component (Packer 1968). The process is perceived as a contest between relatively equal actors, which helps to legitimate the pain associated with the imposition of criminal sanctions. The criminal process satisfies both society's demand for crime control and its desire to protect the liberty of the individual. Criminal sanctions are shaped by these competing demands of society. On the one hand the crime-control component is based on the assumption that the suppression of criminal conduct is by far the most important function of the criminal process, while the due process component is based on the assumption that ensuring that only the guilty are punished is the most important function of the criminal process.

The crime-control model suggests that the failure to provide an adequate level of security for the general public will undermine the legitimacy of criminal law. In contrast, the due process model suggests that the wrongful punishment of an individual is a greater threat to the legitimacy of law (Turk 1969). Therefore, criminal sanctions must be severe enough to contribute to crime control and their application must be fair and consistent in order to satisfy due process requirements (Packer 1968). The additional constraint on criminal sanctions that they be applied only in cases where genuine intent can be conclusively determined has contributed to the rise of alternative systems of social controls.

SOCIAL CONTROL BEYOND CRIMINAL SANCTIONS

As the definition of what constitutes criminal behavior is narrowed, the social control of noncriminal normative transgression is transferred from the jurisdiction of criminal law to the jurisdictions of medicine and public health. Both public health and psychiatry have long been concerned with social control (Foucault 1965), but what is more significant is the dramatic expansion of their influence and control over the past half-century. Much of what was considered "badness" (and in some cases criminal) and thereby worthy of punishment has been redefined as sickness that requires a therapeutic response. Though the response is quite different, the objective of social control is fundamentally the same (Conrad and Schneider 1992). Some forms of normative transgressions have long been within the medical and public health domain (e.g., mental illness). Research has shown, however, that an increasing number of behaviors that had been punished in the past are now being treated within the medical jurisdiction (e.g., suicide, alcoholism, drug addiction, child abuse, violence, etc.). The most important implication in the shift of the locus of social control from law to medicine is the determination of individual responsibility. In the context of criminal law the full responsibility for normative transgressions is vested in the individual. In the medical context transgressors are not considered responsible for their

actions (or their responsibility is significantly mitigated), therefore, they cannot be punished for actions that are beyond their control. The societal response to behaviors so defined is therapeutic rather than punitive (Conrad and Schneider 1992).

The trend toward the decriminalization of normative transgressions can be traced to the emergence of *deterministic criminology*, which shifted the study of crime causation from rational action to biological, psychological, and sociological sources (Kittrie 1971). The deterministic perspective was initially applied to juvenile delinquency. The influence of deterministic criminology grew in proportion to the expansion of the juvenile justice system. As more questions were raised about the ability of criminal law and criminal sanctions to effectively deal with transgressors such as juvenile delinquents, alternative methods of control became more widely accepted. It has been suggested that the shift from simple to complex societies has necessitated an accompanying shift from punitive to therapeutic methods of social control (Kittrie 1971). For example, the strength of criminal sanctions is believed to be declining because of the increase in residential mobility coupled with the decrease in the influence of primary institutions such as family, church, and school (Braithwaite 1994). As the influence of primary institutions has waned, their ability to command conformity has declined. With the decline of informal social control and the perceived ineffectiveness of criminal sanctions society has increasingly turned to the promise of therapeutic social control as a means of responding to normative transgressions (Conrad and Schneider 1992).

REFERENCES

Beccaria, Cesare (1764) 1980 *On Crime and Punishment.* Indianapolis, Ind.: Bobbs-Merrill.

Becker, Howard 1973 *Outsiders.* New York: The Free Press.

Bentham, Jeremy (1823) 1995 "Punishment and Utility." In Jeffrie Murphy, ed., *Punishment and Rehabilitation.* Belmont, Calif.: Wadsworth.

Bernard, Thomas 1983 *The Consensus–Conflict Debate: Form and Content in Social Theories.* New York: Columbia University Press.

Black, Donald 1976 *The Behavior of Law.* New York: Academic Press.

Bottomley, A. 1989 *Crime and Penal Politics: The Criminologist's Dilemma.* Hull, Eng.: Hull University Press.

Braithwaite, John 1994 *Crime, Shame and Reintegration.* Cambridge, Eng.: Cambridge University Press.

Christie, Nils 1977 "Conflicts as Property." *British Journal of Criminology* 17:1–15.

Conrad, Peter, and Joseph Schneider 1992 *Deviance and Medicalization: From Badness to Sickness.* Philadelphia: Temple University Press.

Duff, Anthony, and David Garland 1994 "Introduction: Thinking About Punishment." In R.A. Duff and D. Garland, eds., *A Reader on Punishment.* New York: Oxford University Press.

Durkheim, Emile (1893) 1964 *The Division of Labor in Society.* New York: Free Press.

Fogel, David 1975 *We Are Living Proof: The Justice Model of Corrections.* Cincinnati, Oh.: W.H. Anderson.

Foucault, Michael 1965 *Madness and Civilization.* New York: Random House.

Garfinkel, Harold 1965 "Conditions of Successful Degradation Ceremonies." *American Journal of Sociology* 61:420–424.

Garland, David 1990 *Punishment and Modern Society: A Study in Social Theory.* Chicago: University of Chicago Press.

Goffman, Erving 1961 *Asylums.* Garden City, N.Y.: Anchor Press.

Gove, William 1980 *The Labeling of Deviance: Evaluating a Perspective.* Beverly Hills, Calif.: Sage.

Kittrie, Nicholas 1971 *The Right to be Different: Deviance and Enforced Therapy.* Baltimore, Md.: Johns Hopkins University Press.

Marx, Karl 1964 "Theories of Surplus Value." In T.B. Bottomore and M. Rubel, eds., *Karl Marx: Selected Writings in Sociology and Social Philosophy.* New York: McGraw-Hill.

Melossi, Dario, and M. Pavarini 1981 *Prison and the Factory: Origins of the Penitentiary System.* Totowa, N.J.: Barnes & Noble Books.

Michalowski, Raymond 1985 *Order, Law and Crime.* New York: Random House.

Morris, Herbert 1981 "A Paternalistic Theory of Punishment." *American Philosophical Quarterly* 18:263–271.

Morris, Norval 1982 "'Dangerousness and Incapacitation' Record of the Association of the Bar in the City of New York" 34:102–128. In A. Duff and D. Garland, eds., *1994 Reader on Punishment.* New York: Oxford University Press.

Packer, Herbert 1968 *The Limits of the Criminal Sanction.* Palo Alto, Calif.: Stanford University Press.

Paternoster, Ray, and Leeann Iovanni 1986 "The Deterrent Threat of Perceived Severity: A Reexamination." *Social Forces* 64:751–777.

Reiman, Jeffrey 1998 *The Rich Get Richer and the Poor Get Prison.* New York: Wiley.

Rotman, Edgardo 1990 *Beyond Punishment: A New View of the Rehabilitation of Offenders.* Westport, Conn.: Greenwood Press.

Rusche, George, and Otto Kirchheimer 1939 *Punishment and Social Structure.* New York: Columbia University Press.

Sellen, Thorsten 1976 *Slavery and the Penal System.* New York: Elsevier.

—— 1938 *Culture, Conflict and Crime.* New York: Social Science Research Council.

Sherman, Lawrence, and Richard Berk 1984 "The Special Deterrent Effect of Arrest for Domestic Assault." *American Sociological Review* 49:261–272.

Silberman, Charles 1978 *Criminal Violence, Criminal Justice.* New York: Vintage.

Stafford Mark, and Mark Warr 1993 "A Reconceptualization of General and Specific Deterrence." *Journal of Research on Crime and Delinquency* 30:123–135.

Sykes, Gresham 1958 *The Society of Captives.* Princeton, N.J.: Princeton University Press.

Tittle, Charles 1980 *Sanctions and Social Deviance.* New York: Praeger.

Toby, Jackson 1964 "Is Punishment Necessary?" *Journal of Criminal Law, Criminology and Political Science* 55:332–337.

Turk, Austin 1969 *Criminality and Legal Order.* Chicago: Rand McNally.

Vold, George 1958 *Theoretical Criminology.* New York: Oxford University Press.

Walker, Nigel 1980 *Punishment, Danger and Stigma: The Morality of Criminal Justice.* Oxford, Eng.: Basil Blackwell.

Wilson, James Q. 1979 *Thinking About Crime.* New York: Basic Books.

Zimring, Franklin, and Gordon Hawkins 1990 *The Scale of Imprisonment.* Chicago: University of Chicago Press.

—— 1973 *Deterrence: The Legal Threat in Crime Control.* Chicago: University of Chicago Press.

PETER CORDELLA

CRIMINALIZATION OF DEVIANCE

A 1996 household survey dealing with drug abuse revealed that 13 percent of persons eighteen to twenty-five, 6 percent of persons twenty-six to thirty-four, and 2 percent of persons thirty-five years or older had smoked marijuana within the last thirty days (Maguire and Pastore 1998, p. 246). The same survey showed that nearly a quarter of persons eighteen to twenty-five had smoked marijuana within the past year and about half of persons eighteen to thirty-four had smoked marijuana at least once during their lifetimes. (The prevalence of marijuana use is considerably greater among males than among females, so these statistics understate marijuana use among young adult males.) A different population survey, also conducted in 1996, revealed that the legalization of marijuana use enjoys considerable support among young adults: 38 percent among respondents eighteen to twenty, 30 percent among respondents twenty-one to twenty-nine, and 28 percent among respondents thirty to forty-nine (Maguire and Pastore 1998, p. 151). Males are much more supportive of legalization than females, and those who claim no religion are most supportive of all.

A reasonable interpretation of these data is that no clear consensus exists that smoking marijuana is wrong. Rather, American society contains a large group, probably a majority, that considers smoking marijuana wrong and a smaller group (but a substantial proportion of young adult males) that uses marijuana, considers it harmless, and is probably indignant at societal interference. Since a nonconformist is immensely strengthened by having even one ally, as the social psychologist Solomon Asch demonstrated in laboratory experiments (Asch 1955), such sizable support for marijuana use means that controlling its use is no easy task. Many other kinds of behavior in contemporary societies resemble marijuana use in that some people disapprove of the behaviors strongly and others are tolerant or supportive. In short, modern societies, being large and heterogeneous, are likely to provide allies even for behavior that the majority condemns.

Yet moral ambiguity does not characterize American society on every issue. Consensus exists that persons who force others to participate unwillingly in sexual relations and persons with body odor are reprehensible. Body odor and rape seem an incongruous combination. What they have in common is that both are strongly disapproved of by the overwhelming majority of Americans. Where they differ is that only one (rape) is a statutory crime that can result in police arrest, a court trial, and a prison sentence. The other, smelling bad, although deviant, is not criminalized. When deviance is criminalized, the organized collectivity channels the indignant response of individuals into public condemnation and, possibly, punishment.

Some sociologists maintain that when sufficient consensus exists about the wrongfulness of an act, the act gets criminalized. This is usually the case but not always. Despite consensus that failing to bathe for three months is reprehensible, body odor has not been criminalized. And acts *have* become criminalized, for example, patent infringement and other white-collar crimes that do not arouse much public indignation. In short, the correlation between what is deviant and what is criminal, though positive, is not perfect.

For a clue to an explanation of how and why deviance gets criminalized, note how difficult it is for members of a society to know with certainty what is deviant. Conceptually, deviance refers to the purposive evasion or defiance of a normative consensus. Defiant deviance is fairly obvious. If Joe, a high school student, is asked a question in class by his English teacher pertaining to the lesson, and he replies, "I won't tell you, asshole," most Americans would probably agree that he is violating the role expectations for high school students in this society. Evasive deviance is less confrontational, albeit more common than defiant deviance, and therefore more ambiguous. If Joe never does the assigned homework or frequently comes late without a good explanation, many Americans would agree that he is not doing what he is supposed to do, although the point at which he steps over the line into outright deviance is fuzzy. Both evasive and defiant deviance require other members of the society to make a judgment that indignation is the appropriate response to the behavior in question. Such a judgment is difficult to make in a heterogeneous society because members of the society cannot be sure how closely other people share their values.

To be sure, from living in a society the individual has a pretty good idea what sorts of behavior will trigger indignant reactions, but not with great confidence. The issue is blurred by subgroup variation and because norms change with the passage of time. Bathing suits that were entirely proper in 1999 in the United States would have been scandalous in 1929. A survey might find that a large percentage of the population disapproves now of nudity on a public beach. The survey cannot reveal for how long the population will continue to disapprove of public nudity. Nor can the survey help much with the crucial problem of deciding how large a proportion of the population that disapproves strongly of a behavior is enough to justify categorizing public nudity as "deviant."

In short, the scientific observer can decide that a normative consensus has been violated only after first establishing that a consensus exists on that issue at this moment of time, and that is not easy. To determine this, individual normative judgments must somehow be aggregated, say, by conducting a survey that would enable a representative sample of the population to express reactions to various kinds of behavior. Ideally, these responses differ only by degree, but in a large society there are often qualitatively different conceptions of right and wrong in different subgroups.

In practice, then, in modern societies neither the potential perpetrator nor the onlooker can be certain what is deviant. Consequently the social response to an act that is on the borderline between deviance and acceptability is unpredictable. This unpredictability may tempt the individual to engage in behavior he would not engage in if he knew that the response would be widespread disapproval (Toby 1998a). It may also restrain onlookers from taking action against the behavior—or at least expressing disapproval—against persons violating the informal rules.

WHAT CRIME INVOLVES: A COLLECTIVE RESPONSE

Crime is clearer. The ordinary citizen may not know precisely which acts are illegal in a particular jurisdiction. But a definite answer is possible. A lawyer familiar with the criminal code of the State of New Jersey can explain exactly what has to be proved in order to convict a person of drunken driving in New Jersey. The codification of an act as criminal does not depend on its intrinsic danger to the society but on what societal leaders *perceive* as dangerous. For example, Cuba has the following provision in its criminal code:

> *Article 108. (1) There will be a sanction of deprivation of freedom of from one to eight years imposed on anyone who: (a) incites against the social order, international solidarity or the socialist State by means of oral or written propaganda, or in any other form; (b) makes, distributes or possesses propaganda of the character mentioned in the preceding clause. (2) Anyone who spreads false news or malicious predictions liable to cause alarm or discontent in the population, or public disorder, is subject to a sanction of from three to four years imprisonment. (3) If the mass media are used for the execution of the actions described in the previous paragraphs, the sanction will be a deprivation of freedom from seven to fifteen years* (Ripoll 1985, p. 20).

In other words, mere possession of a mimeograph machine in Cuba is a very serious crime because Fidel Castro considers the dissemination of critical ideas a threat to his "socialist State," and in Cuba Castro's opinions are literally law. Hence, possession of a mimeograph machine is a punishable offense. Members of Jehovah's Witnesses who used mimeograph machines to reproduce religious tracts have been given long prison sentences. On the other hand, reproducing religious tracts may not arouse indignation in the Cuban population. It is criminal but not necessarily deviant.

In California or New Jersey, as in Cuba, a crime is behavior punishable by the state. But the difference is that in the fifty states, as in all democratic societies, the legislators and judges who enact and interpret criminal laws do not simply codify their own moral sentiments; they criminalize behavior in response to influences brought to bear on them by members of their constituencies. True, women, children, members of ethnic and racial minorities, and the poorly educated may not have as much political input as affluent, middle-aged, white male professionals. But less influence does not mean they don't count at all. In a dictatorship, on the other hand, the political process is closed;

few people count when it comes to deciding what is a crime.

WHEN DEVIANCE IS CRIMINALIZED: POLITICIZATION

As was mentioned earlier, what is deviant is intrinsically ambiguous in a complex society whose norms are changing and whose ethnic mix has varied values. Criminalization solves the problem of predictability of response by transferring the obligation to respond to deviance from the individual members of society to agents of the state (the police). But criminalization means that some members of society are better able than others to persuade the state to enforce *their* moral sentiments. Criminalization implies the politicization of the social control of deviance. In every society, a political process occurs in the course of which deviant acts get criminalized. Generally, the political leadership of a society criminalizes an act when it becomes persuaded that without criminalization the deviant "contagion" will spread, thereby undermining social order (Toby 1996). The leaders may be wrong. Fidel Castro might be able to retain control of Cuban society even if Cubans were allowed access to mimeograph machines and word-processors. Nevertheless, leaders decide on crimes based on their perception of what is a threat to the collectivity. According to legal scholars (Packer 1968), the tendency in politically organized societies is to overcriminalize, that is, to involve the state excessively in the response to deviance. Political authorities, even in democracies, find it difficult to resist the temptation to perceive threats in what may only be harmless diversity and to attempt to stamp it out by state punishment.

Sociology's labeling perspective on deviance (Becker 1963; Lemert 1983) goes further; it suggests that overcriminalization may *increase* deviance by changing the self-concept of the stigmatized individual. Pinning the official label of "criminal" on someone stigmatizes him and thereby amplifies his criminal tendencies. Furthermore, an advantage of ignoring the deviance is that it may be ephemeral and will disappear on its own; thus in 1974 American society virtually ignored "streaking" instead of imprisoning streakers in large numbers for indecent exposure (Toby 1980),

and by 1975 streaking had become a historical curiosity. But whether deviance is self-limiting is an empirical question. The labeling perspective ignores the logical possibility that stigmatizing the deviant may be necessary to deter future deviance by bringing home to the offender (as well as potential offenders) the danger of antagonizing the community. In point of fact, the empirical evidence supports the deterrence possibility more than it does the amplification assumption (Gove 1980; Gibbs 1975). At its most extreme, the labeling perspective denies the desirability of any kind of criminalization:

> "The task [of radical reform] is to create a society in which the facts of human diversity, whether personal, organic, or social, are not subject to the power to criminalize" (Taylor, Walton, and Young 1973, p. 282).

Thus, the labeling perspective flirts with philosophical anarchism. More reasonably, the issue is: which forms of deviance can be regarded as harmless diversity and which threaten societal cohesiveness sufficiently that they require criminalization in order to be contained within tolerable limits? Experience has taught us that the body odor of other people, though objectionable to most Americans, is tolerable. But what about consuming alcohol or cocaine to the point of chronic intoxication? What about sexual practices that shock most people such as sado-masochism or intercourse with a sheep? One way to finesse these thorny questions is to define such acts as the product of mental illness and therefore beyond the control of the individual. Instead of regarding drug abuse or alcoholism or bestiality as deviant choices in the face of temptations, society may choose to regard them as "addictions," that is to say, involuntary (Toby 1998b). Since the ill person is by definition unenviable, he is not a role model, and therefore the deviant contagion does not spread (Toby 1964). But suppose consensus does not exist that these acts are compulsive; suppose that many people feel that the perpetrators are perversely *choosing* to engage in these behaviors. Average citizens may become demoralized when they see their norms flouted or they may be tempted to engage in the deviant behavior themselves. This is why criminalization (and state-sponsored punishment) may be necessary. Punishment serves to deprive the deviant of the benefits of his nonconformity, and therefore he becomes unenviable in the eyes of conformists.

Yes, society may stigmatize and perhaps imprison perpetrators, amid hope that imitators will be rare. But criminalization arouses opposition. Libertarians lean toward permitting almost any nonviolent behavior except the exploitation of children. Mental-health advocates perceive stealing to feed a passion for gambling as a symptom of illness; they may perceive even predatory violence as symptomatic of a sick personality for which the individual cannot be considered responsible. Pragmatists point out that when large numbers of people want to do something, such as gamble or use drugs, it is not practical to attempt to stop them by criminalizing the behavior. They argue that deviants cannot all be punished, certainly not by imprisonment; they corrupt police forces through bribes and deflect police efforts into tasks that cannot be accomplished instead of more feasible deviance-control activities; and the criminal organizations that emerge to cater to these forbidden pleasures promote crimes that would not have occurred in the absence of criminalization.

On the other side of the ledger is the tendency for the absence of criminalization to encourage individuals to engage in a behavior they would not have engaged in when faced with possible criminal sanctions. The Prohibition experiment of the 1920s, despite its perception as a failure, did succeed in reducing the incidence of alcoholism, as reflected in reduced incidence of alcoholic psychosis and of cirrhosis of the liver. But the social cost of criminalizing alcohol consumption was not only the proliferation of criminal enterprises to supply the demand of social drinkers; criminalization also prevented many people who wished to be social drinkers from having the freedom to do so. True, some of these would go on to become alcoholics, but most would not. Thus, the criminalization issue always involves a tradeoff between partially legitimating possibly harmful behavior, such as smoking cigarettes, or curtailing freedom by criminalizing the behavior. This judgment has to be made on a case by case basis. Most people who drink socially do not become alcoholics and most people who smoke do not get lung cancer; hence it is difficult to justify criminalizing drinking and

smoking despite the likelihood that more people become alcoholics and get lung cancer than would if smoking and drinking were criminalized. On the other hand, the tradeoff goes the other way with "hard" drugs; the main argument against decriminalizing the sale of heroin is that the health costs to the general population would be too great; decriminalization would inevitably increase experimentation with the drug and ultimately the number of addicts (Kaplan 1983).

OTHER CONSEQUENCES OF CRIMINALIZATION

The absence of criminal law—and consequently of state-imposed sanctions for violations—is no threat to small primitive communities: Informal social controls can be counted on to prevent most deviance and to punish what deviance cannot be prevented. In heterogeneous modern societies, however, the lack of some criminalization would make moral unity difficult to achieve. When Emile Durkheim spoke of the collective conscience of a society, he was writing metaphorically; he knew that he was abstracting from the differing consciences of thousands of individuals. Nevertheless, the criminal law serves to resolve these differences and achieve a contrived—and indeed precarious—moral unity. In democratic societies, the unity is achieved by political compromise. In authoritarian or totalitarian societies the power wielders unify the society by imposing their own values on the population at large. In both cases law is a unifying force; large societies could not function without a legal system because universalistic rules, including the rules of the criminal law, meld in this way ethnic, regional, and class versions of what is deviant (Parsons 1977, pp. 138–139).

The unifying effect of the criminal law has unintended consequences. One major consequence is the development of a large bureaucracy devoted to enforcing criminal laws: police, judges, prosecutors, jailers, probation officers, parole officers, prison guards, and assorted professionals like psychologists and social workers who attempt to rehabilitate convicted offenders. Ideally, these employees of the state should perform their roles dispassionately, not favoring some accused persons or discriminating against others. In practice, however, members of the criminal justice bureaucracy bring to their jobs the parochial sentiments of their social groups as well as a personal interest in financial gain or professional advancement. This helps to explain why police are often more enthusiastic about enforcing some criminal laws than they are about enforcing others.

Another consequence of criminalization is that the criminal law, being universal in its reach, cannot make allowances for subgroup variation in sentiments about what is right and what is wrong. Thus, some people are imprisoned for behavior that neither they nor members of their social group regard as reprehensible, as in Northern Ireland where members of the Irish Republican Army convicted of assassinating British soldiers considered themselves political prisoners. They went on hunger strikes—in some cases to the point of death—rather than wear the prison uniform of ordinary criminals.

CONCLUSION

The more heterogeneous the culture and the more swiftly its norms are changing, the less consensus about right and wrong exists within the society. In the United States, moral values differ to some extent in various regions, occupations, religions, social classes, and ethnic groups. This sociocultural value pluralism means that it is difficult to identify behavior that everyone considers deviant. It is much easier to identify crime, which is codified in politically organized societies. The criminalization of deviance makes it clear when collective reprisals will be taken against those who violate rules.

Deviance exists in smaller social systems, too: in families, universities, and corporations. In addition to being subjected to the informal disapproval of other members of these collectivities, the deviant in the family, the university, or the work organization can be subjected to formally organized sanctioning procedures like a disciplinary hearing at a university. However, the worst sanction that these nonsocietal social systems can visit upon deviants is expulsion. A university cannot imprison a student who cheats on a final exam. Even in the larger society, however, not all deviance is criminalized, sometimes for cultural reasons as in the American refusal to criminalize the expression of political dissent, but also for pragmatic reasons as in the American failure to criminalize body odor, lying to one's friends, or smoking in church.

REFERENCES

Asch, Solomon E. 1955 "Opinions and Social Pressure." *Scientific American* 193, November.

Becker, Howard S. 1963 *Outsiders. Studies in the Sociology of Deviance.* New York: Free Press.

Gibbs, Jack P. 1975 *Crime, Punishment, and Deterrence.* New York: Elsevier.

Gove, Walter R. 1980 *The Labelling of Deviance: Evaluation of a Perspective*, 2nd ed. Beverly Hills, Calif.: Sage.

Kaplan, John 1983 *The Hardest Drug: Heroin and Public Policy.* Chicago: University of Chicago Press.

Lemert, Edwin M. 1983 "Deviance." In Sanford H. Kadish, ed., *Encyclopedia of Crime and Justice.* New York: Free Press.

Maguire, Kathleen, and Ann L. Pastore (eds.) *Sourcebook of Criminal Justice Statistics 1997.* Washington, D.C.: U.S. Government Printing Office. U. S. Department of Justice, Bureau of Justice Statistics.

Packer, Herbert L. 1968 *The Limits of the Criminal Sanction.* Stanford, Calif.: Stanford University Press.

Parsons, Talcott 1977 *The Evolution of Societies.* Englewood Cliffs, N.J.: Prentice-Hall.

Ripoll, Carlos 1985 *Harnessing the Intellectual: Censoring Writers and Artists in Today's Cuba.* Washington, D.C.: Cuban American National Foundation.

Taylor, Ian, Paul Walton, and Jock Young 1973 *The New Criminology.* London: Routledge and Kegan Paul.

Toby, Jackson 1964 "Is Punishment Necessary?" *Journal of Criminal Law, Criminology, and Police Science*, 55, September.

——— 1980 "Where are the Streakers Now?" In Hubert M. Blalock, ed., *Sociological Theory and Research*, pp. 304–313. New York: Free Press.

——— 1996 "Reducing Crime: New York's Example," *Washington Post*, July 23.

——— 1998a "Getting Serious about School Discipline." *The Public Interest*, 133, Fall.

——— 1998b "Medicalizing Temptation." *The Public Interest*, 130, Fall.

JACKSON TOBY

CRIMINOLOGY

The roots of modern criminology can be found in the writings of social philosophers, who addressed Hobbes's question: "How is society possible?" Locke and Rousseau believed that humans are endowed with free will and are self-interested. If this is so, the very existence of society is problematic. If we are all free to maximize our own self-interest we cannot live together. Those who want more and are powerful can simply take from the less powerful. The question then, as now, focuses on how is it possible for us to live together. Criminologists are concerned with discovering answers to this basic question.

Locke and Rousseau, philosophers who are not considered criminologists, argued that society is possible because we all enter into a "social contract" in which we choose to give up some of our freedom to act in our own self-interest for the privilege of living in society. What happens though to those who do not make, or choose to break, this covenant? Societies enforce the contract by punishing those who violate it. Early societies punished violations of the social contract by removing the privilege of living in society through banishment or death. In the event of minor violations, sanctions such as ostracism or limited participation in the community for a time were administered. The history of sanctions clearly demonstrates the extreme and frequently arbitrary and capricious nature of sanctions (Foucault 1979).

The Classical School of criminology (Beccaria 1764; Bentham 1765) began as an attempt to bring order and reasonableness to the enforcement of the social contract. Beccaria in *On Crimes and Punishments* (1768) made an appeal for a system of "justice" that would define the appropriate amount of punishment for a violation as just that much that was needed to counter the pleasure and benefit from the wrong. In contemporary terms, this would shift the balance in a cost/benefit calculation, and would perhaps deter some crime. Bentham's writings (1765) provided the philosophical foundation for the penitentiary movement that introduced a new and divisible form of sanction: incarceration. With the capacity to finally decide which punishment fits which crime, classical school criminologists believed that deterrence could be maximized and the cost to societal legitimacy of harsh, capricious, and excessive punishment could be avoided. In their tracts calling for reforms in how society sanctions rule-violators, we see the earliest attempts to explain two focal questions of criminology: Why do people commit crimes? How do societies try to control crime? The "classical school" of criminology's answer to the first question is that individuals act rationally, and when the

benefits to violating the laws outweigh the cost then they are likely to choose to violate those laws. Their answer to the second question is deterrence. The use of sanctions was meant to discourage criminals from committing future crimes and at the same time send the message to noncriminals that crime does not pay. Beccaria and Bentham believed that a "just desserts" model of criminal justice would fix specific punishments for specific crimes.

In the mid-nineteenth century the early "scientific study" of human behavior turned to the question of why some people violate the law. The positivists, those who believed that the scientific means was the preeminent method of answering this and other questions, also believed that human behavior was not a product of choice nor individual free will. Instead they argued that human behavior was "determined behavior," that is, the product of forces simply not in the control of the individual. The earliest positivistic criminologists believed that much crime could be traced to biological sources. Gall (Leek 1970), referred to by some as the "father of the bumps and grunts school of criminology," studied convicts and concluded that observable physical features, such as cranial deformities and protuberances, could be used to identify "born criminals." Lombroso (1876) and his students, Ferri and Garofalo, also embraced the notion that some were born with criminal constitutions, but they also advanced the idea that social forces were an additional source of criminal causation. These early positivists were critics of the Classical School. They did not go so far as to argue that punishment should not be used to respond to crime, but they did advance the notion that punishment was insufficient to prevent crime. Simply raising the cost of crime will not prevent violations if individuals are not freely choosing their behavior. The early positivists believed that effective crime control would have to confront the root causes of violations, be they biological or social in nature.

Around 1900, Ferri gave a series of lectures critiquing social control policies derived from classical and neo-classical theory. What is most remarkable about those lectures is that, considered from the vantage point of scholars at the end of the twentieth century, the arguments then were little different from public debates today about what are the most effective means of controlling crime.

Then, as now, the main alternatives were "get tough" deterrence strategies that assumed that potential criminals could be frightened into compliance with the law, versus strategies that would reduce the number of offenses by addressing the root causes of crime. We know far more about crime and criminals today than criminologists of the late nineteenth and early twentieth century knew, yet we continue the same debate, little changed from the one in which Ferri participated in.

The debates today pit those espousing *rational choice theories* of crime (control and deterrence theories being the most popular versions) against what still might best be called *positivistic theories*. To be sure, contemporary positivistic criminology is considerably different from the theories of Gall and Lombroso. Modern criminologists do not explain law-violating behavior using the shapes of heads and body forms. Yet there are still those who argue that biological traits can explain criminal behavior (Wilson and Herrenstein 1985; Mednick 1977), and still others who focus on psychological characteristics. But most modern criminologists are sociologists who focus on how social structures and culture explain criminal behavior. What all of these modern positivists have in common with their predecessors Gall, Lombroso, and company, is that they share a belief that human behavior, including crime, is not simply a consequence of individual choices. Behavior, they argue, is "determined" at least in part by biological, psychological, or social forces. The goal of modern positivist criminologists is to unravel the combination of forces that make some people more likely than others to commit crimes.

Today the research of sociological criminologists focuses on three questions: What is the nature of crime? How do we explain crime? What are the effects of societies' attempts to control crime? Approaches to answering these questions vary greatly, as do the answers offered by criminologists. For example the first question, what is the nature of crime, can be answered by detailing the characteristics of people who commit crimes. Alternatively, one can challenge the very definition of what crime, and consequently criminals, are. In an attempt to answer this question, some criminologists focus on how much crime there is. But of course, even this is a difficult question to answer because there are many ways to count crime, with each type offering different and sometimes seemingly conflicting answers.

WHAT IS THE NATURE OF CRIME?

Simply defining crime can be problematic. We can easily define crime legally: Crime is a violation of the criminal law. The simplicity of this definition is its virtue, but also its weakness. On the positive side, a legalistic definition clearly demarcates what will be counted as crime—those actions defined by the state as a violation. However, it is not as clear as to whom will be defined as criminals. Do we count as criminals those who violate the law and are not arrested? What about those who are arrested and not convicted? Some criminologists would argue that even an act that may appear to be criminal cannot be called "crime" until a response or evaluation has been made of that act. For example, how can we know if an offensive act is a crime if there has been no evaluation of the intent of the perpetrator? In Anglo-American law, without criminal intent, an offensive action is not considered a criminal action. Other critics of a legalistic definition of crime argue that it is an overly limited conception that too narrowly truncates criminological inquiry; a legalistic definition of crime accepts the state's definition of "legal" and equates that with "legitimate." Critical criminologists (Quinney 1974; Chambliss 1975; Taylor, Walton, and Young 1973) argue that we should ask questions about the creation of law such as whose interests are being served by classifying a particular behavior as "illegal." Questions such as these tend to be ignored if we simply accept a legalistic definition. Indeed, the particular definition used influences the kind of questions criminologists ask. When a legalistic definition is used, criminologists tend to ask questions such as: "How much crime occurs?" "Who commits rime?" "Why are some people criminal?" If a broader conception of crime is the focus (i.e., one that addresses the rule-makers as well as the rule-breakers), then one might ask these same questions, but add others: "Where does the law come from?" "Why are some offensive acts considered crimes while others are not?" "Whose interests do the laws serve?" This is not a debate that will ever be resolved. Students of criminology should understand however, that the definition of crime they employ will have important implications for the kinds of questions they will ask, the kinds of data they will use to study crime, and the kinds of explanations and theories they will apply to understand crime and criminal behavior.

HOW IS CRIME STUDIED?

Having made choices about definitions, criminologists are then faced with an array of data and methodologies that can be brought to bear on criminological questions. The data and methodological approach used should be dictated by the definition of crime and the research question being asked. Some very interesting research problems require analysis of quantitative data while others require that the researcher use qualitative approaches to study crime or a criminal justice process. For example, if one is trying to describe the socio-demographic characteristics of criminals then one of several means of counting crimes and people who engage in them might be used. On the other hand, in his book *On The Take* (1978), because Chambliss was interested in the source and nature of organized crime, it was clearly more appropriate for him to spend time in the field observing and interviewing, rather than simply counting.

Methods of Criminological Research. For the most part, criminologists use the same types of research methods as do other sociologists. But a unique quality of crime is its "hiddenness." The character of crime means that those who do it hide it. As a result, the criminologist must be a bit of a detective even while engaged in social science research. To do this criminologists use observational studies such as those conducted by Chambliss (1978) in studying organized crime, or Fisse and Braithwaite (1987) in studies of white-collar crime, or Sanchez-Jankowski (1992) in his studies of gang crime.

Those who use quantitative methods frequently use data generated by the criminal justice system, victimization surveys, or self-reports. All of these data collection procedures have strengths and weaknesses, and they are best used by criminologists who have an appreciation of both. The most widely used criminal justice data are produced by police departments and published by the Federal Bureau Investigation each year in their *Uniform Crime Reports* (UCR). The UCR contains counts of the crimes reported to police, arrest data (including some characteristics of those arrested), police

manpower statistics, and other data potentially of interest to researchers. Victimization surveys may be conducted by individuals or teams of researchers. The National Crime Victimization Survey (NCVS) is conducted annually by the federal government and, as a consequence, is widely used. The virtue of victimization surveys is that they include criminal acts that are never reported to the police. As their name indicates, self-report studies simply ask a sample of people about their involvement in criminal activity. If done correctly, it is quite surprising what people will report to researchers.

Characteristics of criminals. It is always risky to speak of the characteristics of criminals because of the problems with crime data mentioned above. Also, one must take care to specify the types of crimes included in any description of those characteristics correlated with criminal involvement. For example, those engaging in white-collar crime have very different characteristics than perpetrators of what might be called "common crimes" or "street crime." In order to engage in white-collar crime, one has to be old enough to have a white-collar job, and possess those characteristics (such as education) requisite for those jobs. Without these same requirements, the perpetrators of street crime can reasonably be expected to look different from white-collar criminals.

Criminologists frequently speak of "the big four correlates of crime": age, sex, race, and social class. The first two are rather uncomplicated. Crime is, for the most part, a young person's activity (Hirschi and Gottfredson 1983). Probable involvement escalates in the teen years reaching a peak at between ages 15 and 17 and then drops. Most people stop participating in criminal activity by their mid to late twenties, even if they have not been arrested, punished, or rehabilitated. The correlation between sex and crime is also quite straightforward. Males are more likely to engage in crime than females. Criminologists have not found a society where this pattern does not hold.

The correlation between race, or ethnicity, and crime is complex. Most Americans when asked state that they believe that minorities commit more crimes than whites. This oversimplification is not only inaccurate, but it obscures important patterns. First, some nonwhites in the United States are from groups with lower crime rates than whites (e.g. Chinese and Japanese Americans), but even this pattern is more complex. Chinese Americans whose families have been in the United States for generations seem to have lower crime rates than white Americans, but more recent Chinese immigrants have higher rates than white Americans. The category "Asian Americans" is too diverse to make generalizations about the larger group's perpetration of crime. The same is true of Latinos and Latinas. African Americans have disproportionately high crime rates, but Africans and people of Caribbean island descent have lower crime rates than black Americans. To simply describe the correlations between broad racial categories and crime misses an important sociological point: The criminality associated with each group appears to be more a product of their experience in America than simply their membership in that racial/ethnic category. This point is buttressed by patterns of race, ethnicity, and crime in other countries. Visible minorities and immigrants are more likely to have higher crime rates and to be more frequently arrested in countries where they are subordinated (see Tonry 1997 for a collection of studies of race, ethnicity, crime, and criminal justice in several countries).

For decades, in fact probably for centuries, researchers assumed that people from the lower classes committed more crime than those of higher status. In fact, most sociological theories used to explain common crime are based on this assumption. In the mid-1970s several criminologists argued that there really is not a substantial correlation between social class and crime (Tittle, Villemez, and Smith 1978). Many criminologists today believe that if we are simply considering the likelihood of breaking the law then there probably is not much difference by social class. But if the criminal domain being studied is serious violent offenses, then there probably is a negative association between social class and crime. Still, the correlation between social class and violent crime is not as strong as most people would assume (Hindelang, Hirschi, and Weis 1981).

Where crime occurs. A very sociological way of describing crime is to examine the crime patterns that exist for different types of areas. The social "ecological" literature that does this usually focuses on states, metropolitan areas, cities, and neighborhoods. When this occurs, we find that those areas with relatively large numbers of residents who are poor, African American, immigrants, young, and living in crowded conditions have higher crime rates. One must be very careful when interpreting these patterns. Because an area with relatively large numbers of people with these characteristics has a high crime rate, we cannot conclude that they are necessarily the people committing the crimes. For example, high poverty areas have high crime rates. The high crime rates found in poor neighborhoods however, could be produced by their victimization by the nonpoor. The interesting thing about these correlations, as well as patterns of individual crime correlations, are not the observed patterns themselves but rather the questions that arise from these observations.

Victims of crime. One of the more interesting things that we have learned from victimization studies is how similar the victims of crimes are to the offenders. Victims of crime tend to be young, male, and minority group members. In fact, the prototypical victim of violent crime in America is a young, African-American male. The poor and those with limited education are disproportionately the victims of crime as well. These patterns are obviously inconsistent with popular images of crime and victimization, but they are quite predictable when we examine what we know about crime.

CRIMINOLOGY THEORIES

Three theoretical traditions in sociology dominated the study of crime from the early and mid-twentieth century. Contemporary versions of these theories continue to be used today. The "Chicago School" tradition, or *social disorganization theory*, was the earliest of the three. The other two are *differential association strain theories* or *anomie theory* (including subculture theories).

Sociologists working in the Chicago School tradition have focused on how rapid or dramatic social change causes increases in crime. Just as Durkheim, Marx, Toennies, and other European sociologists thought that the rapid changes produced by industrialization and urbanization produced crime and disorder, so too did the Chicago School theorists. The location of the University of Chicago provided an excellent opportunity for

Park, Burgess, and McKenzie to study the social ecology of the city. Shaw and McKay found (1931) that areas of the city characterized by high levels of social disorganization had higher rates of crime and delinquency.

In the 1920s and 1930s Chicago, like many American cities, experienced considerable immigration. Rapid population growth is a disorganizing influence, but growth resulting from in-migration of very different people is particularly disruptive. Chicago's in-migrants were both native-born whites and blacks from rural areas and small towns, and foreign immigrants. The heavy industry of cities like Chicago, Detroit, and Pittsburgh drew those seeking opportunities and new lives. Farmers and villagers from America's hinterland, like their European cousins of whom Durkheim wrote, moved in large numbers into cities. At the start of the twentieth century Americans were predominately a rural population, but by the century's mid-point most lived in urban areas. The social lives of these migrants, as well as those already living in the cities they moved to, were disrupted by the differences between urban and rural life. According to social disorganization theory, until the social ecology of the "new place" can adapt, this rapid change is a criminogenic influence. But most rural migrants, and even many of the foreign immigrants to the city, looked like and eventually spoke the same language as the natives of the cities into which they moved. These similarities allowed for more rapid social integration for these migrants than was the case for African Americans and most foreign immigrants.

In these same decades America experienced what has been called "the great migration": the massive movement of African Americans out of the rural South and into northern (and some southern) cities. The scale of this migration is one of the most dramatic in human history. These migrants, unlike their white counterparts, were not integrated into the cities they now called home. In fact, most American cities at the end of the twentieth century were characterized by high levels of racial residential segregation (Massey and Denton 1993). Failure to integrate these migrants, coupled with other forces of social disorganization such as crowding, poverty, and illness, caused crime rates to climb in the cities, particularly in the segregated wards and neighborhoods where the migrants were forced to live.

Foreign immigrants during this period did not look as dramatically different from the rest of the population as blacks did, but the migrants from eastern and southern Europe who came to American cities did not speak English, and were frequently Catholic, while the native born were mostly Protestant. The combination of rapid population growth with the diversity of those moving into the cities created what the Chicago School sociologists called social disorganization. More specifically, the disorganized areas and neighborhoods where the unintegrated migrants lived were unable to exercise the social control that characterized organized, integrated communities. Here crime could flourish. Crime was not a consequence of who happened to live in a particular neighborhood, but rather of the character of the *social ecology* in which they lived. That is, the crime rate was a function of the area itself and not of the people who lived there. When members of an immigrant or ethnic group moved out of that area (usually in succeeding generations), that group's crime rate would go down. But, the old neighborhood, with its cheaper housing and disorganized conditions, would attract another, more recent group migrating to the city. Those groups settled there because that is where they could afford to live. When they became more integrated in American urban life, like those who came before them, they would move to better neighborhoods and as a result have lower crime rates. Chicago School sociologists called the process of one ethnic group moving out to be replaced by a newly arriving group (with the first group passing on to newcomers both the neighborhood and its high crime) "ethnic succession." This pattern seems to have worked for most ethnic groups except African Americans. For African Americans, residential segregation and racial discrimination prohibited the move to better, more organized neighborhoods.

Contemporary social disorganization theorists (Sampson and Groves 1989) are less concerned with the effects of ethnic migration. The disorganizing effects of urban poverty (Sampson and Wilson 1994), racial residential segregation (Massey and Denton 1993), and the social isolation of the urban poor (Wilson 1987), and the consequent effect on crime is the focus of current research. This line of research has developed intriguing answers to the question of why some racial or ethnic groups have higher crime rates.

Both the anomie and differential association traditions grew out of critiques of the Chicago School version of social disorganization theory. The latter was developed by Sutherland (1924), himself a member of the University of Chicago faculty. Sutherland believed that a theory of crime should explain not only how bad behavior is produced in bad living conditions, but also how bad behavior arises from good living circumstances. This theory should also explain why most residents of disorganized neighborhoods do not become criminals or delinquents. Sutherland explained this by arguing that crime is more likely to occur when a person has a greater number of deviant associations, relative to non-deviant associations.

Differential association occurs when a person has internalized an excess of definitions favorable to violations of the law. Sutherland believed that we all experience a variety of forms of exposure to definitions favorable to violation of the law—"It is OK to steal this because the insurance company will pay for it"—and definitions unfavorable to violation of the law—"It is not OK to steal from stores, because all of us are hurt when prices go up to pay the stores' higher insurance premiums." Sutherland was very careful to point out what differential association was not. It is not a simple count of favorable and unfavorable definitions. Differential association theory is not a theory that focuses on who a person associates with. Indeed Sutherland argued that it is possible to receive definitions favorable to violation from the law-abiding. Of course those spending time with delinquent peers will be exposed to more criminal definitions, but the theory should not be reduced to simply a peer group theory of crime and delinquency (Sutherland and Cressey 1974). As Cressey has pointed out, if crime were simply a consequence of prolonged proximity with criminals, then prison guards would be the most criminal group in the population. Differential association theory continues to be of influence in contemporary sociology, but it does not occupy as central a role as it did in the 1940s and 1950s. Matsueda

(1988), the theory's major contemporary proponent, has emphasized the interactive quality (similar to labeling theory) of differential association theory. Matsueda has suggested new ways to operationalize the key concepts of differential association, and the theory is "evolving" in his writings to bring in aspects of both *interactionist* and *rational choice theory*.

Anomie theory's roots are in the work of Durkheim, who used the concept *anomie* to describe the disruption of regulating norms resulting from rapid social change. Strain theories, including anomie theory, focus on social structural strains, inequalities, and dislocations, which cause crime and delinquency. Durkheim stressed that societal norms that restrained the aspirations of individuals were important for preventing deviance. However, unrealistically high aspirations would be frustrated by a harsh social reality, leading to adaptations such as suicide, crime, and addiction. Merton adapted Durkheim's notion of anomie by combining this idea with the observation that not only do societal norms affect the likelihood of achieving aspirations, but they also determine to a large degree what we aspire to (1938). In other words, society helps determine the goals that we internalize by defining which of them are legitimate but it also defines the legitimate means of achieving these goals. American society, for example, defines material comfort as legitimate goals, and taking a well-paid job as a legitimate means of achieving them. Yet legitimate means such as these and economic success are not universally available. When a society is characterized by a disjunction between its legitimate goals and the legitimate means available to achieve them, crime is more likely.

This conceptualization led a number of criminologists to focus on these "opportunity structure" strains (Cloward and Ohlin 1960), as well as cultural strains (Cohen 1955), to explain why crime would be higher in lower social class neighborhoods. Contemporary strain theorists have moved in two directions. Some have proceeded in ways that are quite consistent with Merton's original conceptualization, while others have set forward a more social psychological conception of strain (Agnew 1992). What ties these contemporary versions of anomie theory to the earlier tradition is the notion that there are individual adaptations to social strain, or structurally based unequal opportunity, and that some of these adaptations can result in crime.

Subcultural explanations of crime are similar to both differential association and anomie theories. Like differential association, *subculture theories* have an important learning component. Both types of theories emphasize that crime, the behavior, accompanying attitudes, justifications, etc., are learned by individuals within the context of the social environment in which they live. And, as anomie and other versions of strain theory emphasize, subcultural explanations of crime tend to focus on lower-class life as a generating milieu in which procriminal norms and values thrive. Cohen's book *Delinquent Boys* (1955) describes delinquency as a product of class-based social strains, which lead to a gang subculture conducive to delinquency. Miller (1958) argued that a prodelinquency value system springs from situations where young boys grow up in poor, female-headed households. He felt that adherence to these values, which he called "the focal concerns of the lower class," made it more likely that boys would join gangs and involve themselves in delinquency. This idea enjoys recurring popularity in explanations of behavior in poor, and especially urban, minority neighborhoods (Banfield 1968; Murray 1984) even though it is notoriously difficult to test empirically.

A different version of subculture theory has been championed by Wolfgang (Wolfgang and Ferracuti 1967). Wolfgang and his colleagues argued that people in some segments of communities internalized, carried, and intergenerationally transferred values that were proviolence. Accordingly, members of this subculture of violence would more frequently resort to violence in circumstances where others probably would not. Critics of this thesis have argued that it is difficult to assess who carries "subculture of violence values" except via the behavior that is being predicted.

Along with most other institutions and traditions, mainstream criminology was challenged in the 1960s. Critics raised questions about the theories, data, methods, and even the definitions of crime used in criminology. The early challenges came from *labeling* theorists. This group used a variant of symbolic interaction to argue that law-violating behavior was widespread in the general population, and the official labeling of a selected subset of violators was more a consequence of who the person was than of what the person had done (Becker 1963). Consequently, crime should not be defined as behavior that violates the law, because many people violate the law and are never arrested, prosecuted, or convicted. Rather, crime is a behavior that is selectively sanctioned, depending on who is engaging in it. It follows then that when criminologists use data produced by the criminal justice system, we are not studying crime but the criminal justice system itself. These data only tell us about the people selected for sanctioning, not about all of those who break the law. And, labeling theorists argued, most of our theories have been trying to explain why lower-class people engage disproportionately in crime, but since they do not—they are simply disproportionately sanctioned—the theories are pointless. What should be explained, labeling theorists argued, is why some people are more likely to be labeled and sanctioned as criminals than are others who engage in the same or similar behavior. The answer they offered was that those with sufficient resources—enough money, the right racial or gender status, etc.—to fend off labeling by the criminal justice system are simply less likely to be arrested.

A further contribution by labeling theorists is the idea that the labeling process actually creates deviance. The act of labeling people as criminals sets in motion processes that marginalize them from the mainstream, create in them the self-identification as "criminal," which in turn affects their behavior. In other words, the act of sanctioning causes more of the behavior the criminal justice system wishes to extinguish.

Marxist criminology actually began in 1916 with the publication of Bonger's *Criminality and Economic Conditions*, but it became central to criminological discourse in the late 1960s and 1970s (Chambliss 1975; Platt 1969; Quinney 1974; Taylor, Walton, and Young 1973). The Marxist critique of mainstream criminology can be summarized by focusing on the argument that it tends to ask three types of questions: Who commits crimes? How much crime is there? Why do people break the law? The Marxist perspective argues that these may be important questions, but more important are those that do not reify the law itself. Marxists argue that in addition to the above questions, criminologists should ask: Where does the law come from? Whose interest does the law serve? Why are the laws structured and enforced in particular ways? Their answers to these questions are based on a class-conflict analysis. Power in social systems is allocated according to social class, and the powerful use the law to protect their interests and the status quo that perpetuates their superordinate status. So the law and criminal justice system practices primarily serve the interest of elites; while they at times serve the interests of other classes, their *raison d'être* is the interests of the powerful. Law is structured to protect the current status arrangements.

Both the labeling and Marxist perspectives experienced broad popularity among students of criminology. Many scholars responded to their critiques not by joining them, but by taking some lessons from the debate and moving forward to develop theories consistent with traditional directions and research methods that were not as dependent on data generated by the criminal justice system. Victimization surveys and self-report studies of crime have become more widely used, in part as a consequence of these critiques.

All of the theories mentioned so far have had significant empirical challenges. Most of the initial statements have been falsified or their proponents have had to revise the perspective in the face of evidence that did not support it. Several of these explanations of crime, or how societies control their members, are used today in a modified form, while others have evolved into contemporary theories that are being tested by researchers. No doubt when someone writes about criminology in the future, some or all of the more recent theories will have joined those that have been falsified or modified as a result of empirical analyses. Contemporary criminological theories tend to be in the control theory, rational choice, or conflict traditions. However, these are not mutually exclusive (e.g. some control theories are very much rational choice theories).

Control theorists begin by saying that we ask the wrong question when we seek to understand why some people commit crimes. We should instead seek to explain why most people do *not* violate the rules. Control theorists reason that we do not need to explain why someone who is hungry or has less will steal from those who have what they want or

need. We do not need to explain why the frustrated and angry among us will express their feelings violently. The interesting question is: Why *don't* most people who have less or have grievances engage in property or violent crime? Other versions of control theory (Nye 1958; Reckless 1961) preceded his, but Hirschi's (1969) classic answer to this question is that those who are "socially bonded" to critical institutions such as families, schools, conventional norms, etc., are less likely to violate the law. The bonds give them a "stake in conformity," something they value and would risk losing should they violate important rules. Though not initially stated in rational choice terms of classical school ideas, one can see similarities between Hirschi's notions of "stakes in conformity" and the Classical School of criminology's concept of the "social contract."

Control theory has evolved in a number of directions. Gottfredson and Hirschi (1990) have argued that crime and deviance are a consequence of the failure of some to develop adequate self-control. Self-control is developed, if at all, early in life—by the age of eight or ten. Those who do not develop self-control will, they argue, exhibit various forms (depending on their age) of deviance throughout their lives. These people will commit crimes disproportionately during the crime-prone ages, between adolescence and the late twenties. Sampson and Laub's (1993) "life-course" perspective argues that social bonds change for people at different stages of their lives. Bonds to families are important early, to schools and law-abiding peers later, and eventually bonds to spouses, one's own children, and jobs and careers ultimately tie people to conventional norms and prevent crime and deviance. Tittle (1995) has offered a *control balance theory* of deviance. He believes that those who balance control exerted by self with control by others that they are subjected to are the least likely to commit acts of crime and deviance. Those whose "control ratio" is out of balance, with too much or too little regulation by the self or others, have a higher probability of breaking rules.

The contemporary rational choice perspective of crime has been most explicitly articulated by economists (Becker 1968; Ehrlich 1973). Becker described the choices people make in social behavior, including crime, as much like those made in economic behavior. Before a purchase we weigh the cost of an item against the utility, or benefit to be gained by owning that item. Likewise, before engaging in crime, a person weighs the cost—prison, loss of prestige, relationships, or even life—against the benefits to crime–pleasure, expression of anger, or material gain. Becker argued that when the benefits outweigh the cost individuals would be more likely to commit criminal actions.

Control theory can also be thought of as a rational choice theory. The "bonded" among us have a stake in conformity, or something to weigh on the "to be lost" side of a cost-benefit analysis. To engage in crime is to risk the loss of valued bonds to family, teachers, or employers. The bond in control theory, thought of in this way, is an informal deterrent. *Deterrence theory* (Geerken and Gove 1975) is ordinarily written of in terms of a formal system of deterrence provided by the criminal justice system. As originally conceived by Classical School criminologists, police, prosecutors, and the courts endeavor to raise the cost of committing crime so that those costs outweigh the benefits from illegal behavior. In the case of those convicted, the courts attempt to do this by varying the sentence so that those convicted become convinced that they must avoid crime in the future. This deterrence aimed at those already in violation is referred to as "specific" or "special" deterrence. The noncriminal public is persuaded by general deterrence to avoid crime. They perceive that crime does not pay when they see others sanctioned. So, when considering criminal options, they weigh the utility of illegal action against the potential cost in the forms of sanctions. According to deterrence theory, when those positive utilities are outweighed by the perceived cost—effective deterrence—they choose not to engage in crime.

A number of contemporary *conflict theories* of criminology are legacies of 1960s and 1970s-era critical perspectives. Most prominent among these is *feminist criminological theory* (Simpson 1989). Contemporary conflict theories, like earlier Marxist theory, address important questions about interest groups. They begin with the position that to understand social life, including crime and responses to crime, the social, political, and economic interests of contesting parties and groups must be taken into account (Marxists, of course, focus on economic conflict). Feminist criminology focuses on gender conflict in society. These criminologists argue that to understand crimes by women, against women, and the reaction to both, we must consider the subordinate status of women. If poverty is one of the root causes of crime, then we should recognize first that the largest impoverished group in American society, and in most western industrialized societies, is children. Increasingly, children are raised in female-headed households whose poverty can be traced to the lower earnings of women, a consequence of gender stratification.

Other conflict analyses of crime focus on income inequality (Blau and Blau 1982), racial inequality (Sampson and Wilson 1994), and labor-market stratification (Crutchfield and Pitchford 1997). What these approaches share is the idea that to understand why individuals engage in crime, or why some groups or geographic areas have higher crime rates, or why patterns of criminal justice are the way they are, consideration of important social conflicts and cleavages must be brought into the analysis. Blau and Blau (1982) illustrated how income inequality, especially inequality based on race, is correlated with higher rates of violent crime. Those metropolitan areas with relatively high levels of inequality tend also to have more violence. Others (Williams 1984; Messener 1989) have argued that it is not so much relative inequality that leads to higher violent crime rates, but rather high levels of poverty. Sampson and Wilson (1994) argue that racial stratification is linked to economic stratification and this complex association accounts for higher levels of crime participation among blacks. Crutchfield and Pitchford (1997), studying a particular form of institutional stratification that was produced by segmented labor markets, found that those marginalized in the work force under some circumstances are more likely to engage in crime.

Hagan, Gillis, and Simpson (1985) developed what they call a "power control theory of delinquency." They combine elements of social control theory and conflict theory to explain class and gender patterns of delinquency. They argue that because of gender stratification, parents seek to control their daughters more and because of class stratification, those in the higher classes have more capacity (because they have the available resources) to monitor (control) their children. Yet, children of the upper classes are actually free to commit more delinquency by virtue of their social-class standing. Consequently, upper-class girls will be more controlled than their lower-class counterparts, but their brothers will have minor delinquency rates resembling those of lower-class boys.

SOCIETY'S ATTEMPT TO CONTROL CRIME

While the theories discussed above focus on the causes of crime, they are also important for describing how social systems control crime. Societies attempt to control the behavior of people living within their borders with a combination of formal and informal systems of control. Social disorganization theory and anomie theory are examples of how crime is produced when normative control breaks down. Differential association and subcultural explanations describe how informal social control is subverted by socialization that supports criminal behavior rather than compliant behavior. Control theories focus specifically on how weak systems of informal social control fail. The obvious exception to this last statement is that portion of control theories that are also deterrence theory. Deterrence theory does consider informal systems of control, but an important part of this thesis is aimed at explaining how formal systems, or the criminal justice system in western societies, attempt to control criminal behavior. Most criminologists believe that informal systems of control are considerably more efficient than formal systems. This makes sense if one remembers that police cannot regulate us as much as we ourselves can when we have internalized conventional norms, and similarly, police cannot watch our behavior nearly as much as our families, friends, teachers, and neighbors can. The criminal justice system then is reduced to supporting informal systems of control (thus the interest in block-watch programs by police departments), engaging in community policing and patrol patterns that discourage crime, or reacting after violations have occurred.

CONCLUSION

Criminologists are interested in answering questions about how crime should be defined, why crime occurs, and how societies seek to control crime. The history of modern criminology, which can be traced to the early nineteenth century, has not produced definitive answers to these questions. To some students that is a source of frustration. To many of us the resulting ambiguity is the source of continuing interesting debate. More importantly, the disagreement among criminologists captures the complexity of social life. Oversimplification to achieve artificial closure on these debates will not produce quality answers to these questions, nor will it, to the consternation of some politicians, lead to workable solutions to crime problems. Most criminologists recognize that the complex debates about the answers to these three seemingly simple questions will ultimately be a more productive route to understanding crime and to finding effective means to address crime problems.

REFERENCES

Agnew, Robert 1992 "Foundations for a General Strain Theory of Crime and Delinquency." *Criminology* 30:47–87.

Banfield, Edward 1968 *The Unheavenly City*. Boston: Little, Brown.

Beccaria, Cesare (1764) 1963 *On Crimes and Punishments*. Translated by Henry Paolucci. Indianapolis, Ind.: Bobbs-Merrill.

Becker, Gary S. 1968 "Crime and Punishment: An Economic Approach." *Journal of Political Economy* 76:169–217.

Becker, Howard 1963 *Outsiders: Studies in the Sociology of Deviance*. New York: Free Press.

Bentham, Jeremy (1765) 1970 *An Introduction to the Principles of Morals and Legislation*. London: Athlone Press.

Blau, Judith, and Peter Blau 1982 "The Cost of Inequality: Metropolitan Structure and Violent Crime." *American Sociological Review* 47:114–128.

Bonger, William 1916 *Criminality and Economic Conditions*. Boston: Little, Brown.

Chambliss, William J. 1978 *On the Take: From Petty Crooks to Presidents*. Bloomington: Indiana University Press.

—— 1975 "Toward a Political Economy of Crime." *Theory and Society* 2:149–170.

Cloward, Richard, and Lloyd Ohlin 1960 *Delinquency and Opportunity: A Theory of Delinquent Gangs*. New York: Free Press of Glencoe.

Cohen, Albert 1955 *Delinquent Boys*. New York: Free Press of Glencoe.

Crutchfield, Robert D., and Susan R. Pitchford 1997 "Work and Crime: The Effects of Labor Stratification." *Social Forces* 76:93–118.

Ehrlich, Isaac 1973 "Participation in Illegitimate Activities: A Theoretical and Empirical Investigation." *Journal of Political Economy* 81:521–565.

Fisse, Brent, and John Braithwaite 1987 "The Impact of Publicity on Corporate Offenders: Ford Motor Company and the Pinto Papers." In M. David Ermann and Richard J. Lundmann, eds., *Corporate and Governmental Deviance*. Oxford: Oxford University Press.

Foucault, Michel 1979 *Discipline and Punish: The Birth of the Prison*. New York: Vintage Books.

Geerken, Michael, and Walter Gove1975 "Deterrence: Some Theoretical Considerations." *Law and Society Review* 9:497–514.

Gottfredson, Michael, and Travis Hirschi 1990 *A General Theory of Crime*. Stanford, Calif.: Stanford University Press.

Hagan, John, A. R. Gillis, and John Simpson 1985 "The Class Structure of Gender and Delinquency: Toward a Power-Control Theory of Common Delinquent Behavior." *American Journal of Sociology* 90:1151–1178.

Hindelang, Michael, Travis Hirschi, and Joseph Weis 1981 *Measuring Delinquency*. Newbury Park, Calif.: Sage.

Hirschi, Travis 1969 *Causes of Delinquency*. Berkeley: University of California Press.

——, and Michael Gottfredson 1983 "Age and the Explanation of Crime." *American Journal of Sociology* 89:552–584.

Leek, Sybill 1970 *Phrenology*. New York: Macmillan.

Lombroso, Cesare 1876 *L'Uomo Delinquente*. Milan: Hoepli.

Massey, Douglas, and Nancy Denton 1993 *American Apartheid: Segregation and the Making of the Underclass*. Cambridge, Mass.: Harvard University Press.

Matsueda, Ross L. 1988 "The Current State of Differential Association Theory." *Crime and Delinquency* 34:277–306.

Mednick, Sarnoff A. 1977 "A Bio-Social Theory of Learning of Law-Abiding Behavior." In Sarnoff A. Mednick and Karl O. Christiansen, eds., *Biosocial Bases of Criminal Behavior*. New York: Gardner.

Merton, Robert K. 1938 "Social Structure and Anomie." *American Sociological Review* 3:672–682.

Messener, Steven 1989 "Economic Discrimination and Societal Homicide Rates: Further Evidence on the Cost of Inequality." *American Sociological Review* 54:597–611.

Miller, Walter 1958 "Lower Class Culture as a Generating Milieu of Gang Delinquency." *Journal of Social Issues* 14:5–19.

Murray, Charles 1984 *Losing Ground: American Social Policy 1950–1980*. New York: Basic Books.

Nye, Ivan F. 1958 *Family Relationships and Delinquent Behavior*. New York: John Wiley.

Platt, Anthony 1969 *The Child Savers: The Invention of Delinquency*. Chicago: University of Chicago Press.

Quinney, Richard 1974 *Critique of the Legal Order: Crime Control in a Capitalist Society*. Boston: Little, Brown.

Reckless, Walter C. 1961 "A New Theory of Delinquency and Crime." *Federal Probation* 25:42–46.

Sampson, Robert, and W. Byron Groves 1989 "Community Structure and Crime: Testing Social Disorganization Theory of Crime." *American Journal of Sociology* 94:774–802.

Sampson, Robert, and John Laub 1993 *Crime in the Making*. Cambridge, Mass.: Harvard University Press.

Sampson, Robert, and William J. Wilson 1994 "Toward a Theory of Race, Crime and Urban Inequality." In John Hagan and Ruth Peterson, eds., *Crime and Inequality*. Stanford, Calif.: Stanford University Press.

Sanchez-Jankowski, Martí 1992 *Islands in the Street*. Los Angeles: University of California Press.

Shaw, Clifford, and Henry McKay 1931 *Social Factors in Juvenile Delinquency*. Washington, D.C.: National Commission of Law Observance and Enforcement.

Simpson, Sally S. 1989 "Feminist Theory, Crime, and Justice." *Criminology* 27:705–631.

Sutherland, Edwin 1924 *Criminology*. Philadelphia: Lippincott.

——, and Donald R. Cressey 1974 *Criminology*, 9th ed. Philadelphia: Lippincott.

Taylor, Ian, Paul Walton, and Jock Young 1973 *The New Criminology: For a Social Theory of Deviance*. London: Routledge and Kegan Paul.

Tittle, Charles 1995 *Control Balance: Toward a General Theory of Deviance*. Boulder, Colo.: Westview Press.

——, W. J. Villemez, and Douglas Smith 1978 "The Myth of Social Class and Criminality: An Empirical Assessment of the Empirical Evidence." *American Sociological Review* 47:505–518.

Tonry, Michael (ed.) 1997 *Ethnicity, Crime, and Immigration: Comparative and Cross-National Perspectives*. Chicago: University of Chicago Press.

Williams, Kirk R. 1984 "Economic Sources of Homicide: Reestimating the Effects of Poverty and Inequality." *American Sociological Review* 20:545–572.

Wilson, James Q., and Richard Herrenstein 1985 *Crime and Human Nature*. New York: Simon and Schuster.

Wilson, William J. 1987 *The Truly Disadvantaged: The Inner City, the Underclass, and Public Policy*. Chicago: University of Chicago Press.

Wolfgang, Marvin E., and Franco Ferracuti 1967 *The Subculture of Violence*. London: Tavistock Publishers.

ROBERT D. CRUTCHFIELD
CHARIS KUBRIN

CRITICAL THEORY

The term *critical theory* was used originally by members of the Institute for Social Research in Frankfurt, Germany, after they emigrated to the United States in the late 1930s, following the rise of Hitler. The term served as a code word for their version of Marxist social theory and research (Kellner 1990a). The term now refers primarily to Marxist studies done or inspired by this so-called Frankfurt School and its contemporary representatives such as Jurgen Habermas. Critical sociologists working in this tradition share several common tenets including a rejection of sociological positivism and its separation of facts from values; a commitment to the emancipation of humanity from all forms of exploitation, domination, or oppression; and a stress on the importance of human agency in social relations.

THE FRANKFURT SCHOOL OF CRITICAL THEORY

The Institute for Social Research was founded in 1923 as a center for Marxist studies and was loosely affiliated with the university at Frankfurt, Germany. It remained independent of political party ties. Max Horkheimer became its director in 1931. Theodor Adorno, Erich Fromm, Leo Lowenthal, Herbert Marcuse, and, more distantly, Karl Korsch and Walter Benjamin were among the prominent theorists and researchers associated with the institute (Jay 1973). Initially, institute scholars sought to update Marxist theory by studying new social developments such as the expanding role of the

state in social planning and control. The rise of fascism and the collapse of effective opposition by workers' parties, however, prompted them to investigate new sources and forms of authoritarianism in culture, ideology, and personality development and to search for new oppositional forces. By stressing the importance and semiautonomy of culture, consciousness, and activism, they developed an innovative, humanistic, and open-ended version of Marxist theory that avoided the determinism and class reductionism of much of the Marxist theory that characterized their era (Held 1980).

"Immanent critique," a method of description and evaluation derived from Karl Marx and Georg W. F. Hegel, formed the core of the Frankfurt School's interdisciplinary approach to social research (Antonio 1981). As Marxists, members of the Frankfurt School were committed to a revolutionary project of human emancipation. Rather than critique existing social arrangements in terms of a set of ethical values imposed from "outside," however, they sought to judge social institutions by those institutions' own internal (i.e., "immanent") values and self-espoused ideological claims. (An example of the practical application of such an approach is the southern civil rights movement of the 1960s, which judged the South's racial caste system in light of professed American values of democracy, equality, and justice.) Immanent critique thus provided members of the Frankfurt School with a nonarbitrary standpoint for the critical examination of social institutions while it sensitized them to contradictions between social appearances and the deeper levels of social reality.

Immanent critique, or what Adorno (1973) termed "non-identity thinking," is possible because, as Horkheimer (1972, p. 27) put it, there is always "an irreducible tension between concept and being." That is, in any social organization, contradictions inevitably exist between what social practices are called—for example, "democracy" or "freedom" or "workers' parties"—and what, in their full complexity, they really are. This gap between existence and essence or appearance and reality, according to Adorno (1973, p. 5), "indicates the untruth of identity, the fact that the concept does not exhaust the thing conceived." The point of immanent critique is thus to probe empirically whether a given social reality negates its own claims—as, for example, to represent a "just" or "equal" situation—as well as to uncover internal tendencies with a potential for change including new sources of resistance and opposition to repressive institutions.

Frankfurt School theorists found a paradigmatic example of immanent critique in the works of Karl Marx, including both his early writings on alienation and his later analyses of industrial capitalism. Best articulated by Marcuse (1941), their reading of *Capital* interpreted Marx's text as operating on two levels. On one level, *Capital* was read as a historical analysis of social institutions' progressive evolution, which resulted from conflicts between "forces" (such as technology) and "relations" (such as class conflicts) in economic production. Scientist readings of Marx, however—especially by the generation of Marxist theorists immediately after the death of Marx—essentialized this dimension into a dogma that tended to neglect the role of human agency and stressed economic determinism in social history. But the Frankfurt School also read *Capital* as a "negative" or "immanent" critique of an important form of ideology, the bourgeois pseudo-science of economics. Here, Marx showed that the essence of capitalism as the exploitation of wage slavery contradicts its ideological representation or appearance as being a free exchange among equal parties (e.g., laborers and employers).

Members of the Frankfurt School interpreted the efforts that Marx devoted to the critique of ideology as an indication of his belief that freeing the consciousness of social actors from ideological illusion is an important form of political practice that potentially contributes to the expansion of human agency. Thus, they interpreted Marx's theory of the production and exploitation of economic values as an empirical effort to understand the historically specific "laws of motion" of market-driven, capitalist societies. At the same time, however, it was also interpreted as an effort—motivated by faith in the potential efficacy of active opposition—to see through capitalism's objectified processes that made a humanly created social world appear to be the product of inevitable, autonomous, and "natural" forces and to call for forms of revolutionary activism to defeat such forces of "alienation."

Members of the Frankfurt School attempted to honor both dimensions of the Marxian legacy.

On the one hand, they sought to understand diverse social phenomena holistically as parts of an innerconnected "totality" structured primarily by such capitalistic principles as the commodity form of exchange relations and bureaucratic rationality. On the other hand, they avoided reducing complex social factors to a predetermined existence as shadowlike reflections of these basic tendencies (Jay 1984). Thus, the methodology of immanent critique propelled a provisional, antifoundationalist, and inductive approach to "truth" that allowed for the open-endedness of social action and referred the ultimate verification of sociological insights to the efficacy of historical struggles rather than to the immediate observation of empirical facts (Horkheimer 1972). In effect, they were saying that social "facts" are never fixed once and for all, as in the world of nature, but rather are subject to constant revisions by both the conscious aims and unintended consequences of collective action.

In their concrete studies, members of the Frankfurt School concentrated on the sources of social conformism that, by the 1930s, had undermined the Left's faith in the revolutionary potential of the working class. They were among the first Marxists to relate Freud's insights into personality development to widespread changes in family and socialization patterns that they believed had weakened the ego boundary between self and society and reduced personal autonomy (Fromm 1941). After they emigrated to the United States, these studies culminated in a series of survey research efforts, directed by Adorno and carried out by social scientists at the University of California, that investigated the relation between prejudice, especially anti-Semitism, and "the authoritarian personality" (Adorno et al. 1950). Later, in a more radical interpretation of Freud, Marcuse (1955) questioned whether conflicts between social constraints and bodily needs and desires might provide an impetus for revolt against capitalist repression if such conflicts were mediated by progressively oriented politics.

Once in the United States, members of the Frankfurt School emphasized another important source of conformism, the mass media. Holding that the best of "authentic art" contains a critical dimension that negates the status quo by pointing in utopian directions, they argued that commercialized and popular culture, shaped predominantly by market and bureaucratic imperatives, is merely "mimetic" or imitative of the surrounding world of appearances. Making no demands on its audience to think for itself, the highly standardized products of the "culture industry" reinforce conformism by presenting idealized and reified images of contemporary society as the best of all possible worlds (see Kellner 1984–1985).

The most important contribution of the Frankfurt School was its investigation of the "dialectic of enlightenment" (Horkheimer and Adorno [1947] 1972). During the European Enlightenment, scientific reason had played a partisan role in the advance of freedom by challenging religious dogmatism and political absolutism. But according to the Frankfurt School, a particular form of reason, the instrumental rationality of efficiency and technology, has become a source of unfreedom in both capitalist and socialist societies during the modern era. Science and technology no longer play a liberating role in the critique of social institutions but have become new forms of domination. Dogmatic ideologies of scientism and operationalism absolutize the status quo and treat the social world as a "second nature" composed of law-governed facts, subject to manipulation but not to revolutionary transformation. Thus, under the sway of positivism, social thought becomes increasingly "one-dimensional" (Marcuse 1964). Consequently, the dimension of critique, the rational reflection on societal values and directions, and the ability to see alternative possibilities and new sources of opposition are increasingly suppressed by the hegemony of an eviscerated form of thinking. One-dimensional thinking, as an instrument of the totally "administered society," thus reinforces the conformist tendencies promoted by family socialization and the culture industry and threatens both to close off and absorb dissent.

The Frankfurt School's interpretation of the domination of culture by instrumental reason was indebted to Georg Lukacs's ([1923] 1971) theory of reification and to Max Weber's theory of rationalization. In the case of Lukacs, "reification" was understood to be the principal manifestation of the "commodity form" of social life whereby human activities, such as labor, are bought and sold as objects. Under such circumstances, social actors come to view the world of their own making as an objectified entity beyond their control at the same time that they attribute human powers to things.

For Lukacs, however, this form of life was historically unique to the capitalist mode of production and would be abolished with socialism.

In the 1950s, as they grew more pessimistic about the prospects for change, Horkheimer and Adorno, especially, came to accept Weber's belief that rationalization was more fundamental than capitalism as the primary source of human oppression. Thus, they located the roots of instrumental rationality in a drive to dominate nature that they traced back to the origins of Western thought in Greek and Hebrew myths. This historical drive toward destructive domination extended from nature to society and the self. At the same time, Horkheimer and Adorno moved closer to Weber's pessimistic depiction of the modern world as one of no exit from the "iron cage" of rationalization. In the context of this totalizing view of the destructive tendencies of Western culture—the images for which were Auschwitz and Hiroshima—the only acts of defiance that seemed feasible were purely intellectual "negations," or what Marcuse (1964) termed "the great refusal" of intellectuals to go along with the one-dimensional society. Consequently, their interest in empirical sociological investigations, along with their faith in the efficacy of mass political movements, withdrew to a distant horizon of their concerns. Marcuse, like Benjamin before him, remained somewhat optimistic. Marcuse continued to investigate and support sources of opposition in racial, sexual, and Third World liberation movements.

Benjamin's *Passagen-Werk* (Arcades project), originally titled *Dialectical Fairy Scene*, was an unfinished project of the 1930s that culminated in a collection of notes on nineteenth-century industrial culture in Paris. The Paris Arcade was an early precursor to the modern department store, a structure of passages displaying commodities in window showcases; it reached its height in the world expositions (e.g., the Paris Exposition in 1900). Through an interpretation of Benjamin's notes, Susan Buck-Morss (1995) has brought this unfinished project to life. Benjamin drew on allegory as a method for analyzing the content and form of cultural images. In contrast to Horkheimer and Adorno's "iron cage" view of mass culture, his dialectical approach held out hope for the revolutionary potential of mass-produced culture. Anticipating aspects of Symbolic Interactionism and feminist theories of performativity, Benjamin explored the relationship between mass production as form (e.g., montage as a form of film production) and political subversion. In contrast to Horkheimer and Adorno who lamented the loss of authority in art and the family, Benjamin welcomed the abolition of traditional sources of authority and hailed the rapidity of technological change in mass production as potentially positive. He interpreted mass production as a form of mimicry that reproduced existing relations of authority and domination while lending itself to potentially subversive reinterpretations and reenactments of existing social relations and social meanings (Buck-Morss 1995).

While retaining an analysis of instrumental reason as a source of domination, Benjamin's allegorical approach worked to unveil the forces of contradiction that were crystallized as promise, progress, and ruin in mythical modern images. These images bore the revolutionary potential of the new to fulfill collective wishes for an unrealized social utopia contained in a more distant past. At the same time, they represented progress as the unrealized potential of capitalism to satisfy material needs and desires. For Benjamin, images of ruin represented the transitoriness, fragility, and destructiveness of capitalism as well as the potential for reawakening and a critical retelling of history (Buck-Morss 1995).

Even though some of the most prominent founders of the Frankfurt School abandoned radical social research in favor of an immanent critique of philosophy (as in Adorno 1973), the legacy of their sociological thought has inspired a vigorous tradition of empirical research among contemporary American social scientists. In large measure, this trend can be seen as a result of the popularization of Frankfurt School themes in the 1960s, when the New Left stressed liberation and consciousness raising, themes that continue to influence sociological practice. Stanley Aronowitz (1973), for example, along with Richard Sennet and Jonathan Cobb (1973), have rekindled the Frankfurt School's original interests in working-class culture in the context of consumer society. Henry Braverman (1974) has directed attention to processes of reification in work settings by focusing on scientific management and the separation of conception from labor in modern industry. Penetrating analyses also have been made of the

impact of commodification and instrumental rationalization on the family and socialization (Lasch 1977), law (Balbus 1977), education (Giroux 1988), advertising culture (Haug 1986), and mass media (Kellner 1990b), as well as other institutional areas. Feminist theorists have contributed a "doubled vision" to critical theory by showing the "systematic connectedness" of gender, class, and race relations (Kelly 1979) and by criticizing critical theory itself for its neglect of gender as a fundamental category of social analysis (Benjamin 1978; Fraser 1989). Among the most far-reaching and innovative contemporary studies are those of the contemporary German sociologist and philosopher Jurgen Habermas.

THE CRITICAL THEORY OF JURGEN HABERMAS

Perhaps no social theorist since Max Weber has combined as comprehensive an understanding of modern social life with as deeply reflective an approach to the implications of theory and methods as Jurgen Habermas. Habermas has attempted to further the emancipatory project of the Frankfurt School by steering critical theory away from the pessimism that characterized the closing decades of Frankfurt School thought. At the same time, he has resumed the dialogue between empirical social science and critical theory to the mutual benefit of both. Further, he has given critical theory a new ethical and empirical grounding by moving its focus away from the relationship between consciousness and society and toward the philosophical and sociological implications of a critical theory of communicative action.

In sharp contrast to the Frankfurt School's increasing pessimism about the "dialectic of enlightenment," Habermas has attempted to defend the liberative potential of reason in the continuing struggle for freedom. While agreeing with the Frankfurt School's assessment of the destruction caused by instrumental rationality's unbridled domination of social life, he nonetheless recognizes the potential benefits of modern science and technology. The solution he offers to one-dimensional thought is thus not to abandon the "project of modernity" but rather to expand rational discourse about the *ends* of modern society. In order to further this goal, he has tried to unite science and ethics (fact and values) by recovering the inherently rational component in symbolic inter-action as well as developing an empirical political sociology that helps to critique the political effects of positivism as well as to identify the progressive potential of contemporary social movements.

From the beginning, Habermas (1970) has agreed with the classical Frankfurt School's con-tention that science and technology have become legitimating rhetorics for domination in modern society. At the same time, he has argued that alternative ways of knowing are mutually legiti-mate by showing that they have complementary roles to play in human affairs, even though their forms of validity and realms of appropriate appli-cation are distinct. That is, plural forms of knowl-edge represent different but complementary "knowl-edge interests" (Habermas 1971).

"Instrumental knowledge," based on the abili-ty to predict, represents an interest in the technical control or mastery of nature. "Hermeneutical knowledge" represents an interest in the clarifica-tion of intersubjective understanding. Finally, "emancipatory knowledge" is best typified in the self-clarification that occurs freely in the nondirective communicative context provided by psychoanaly-sis. In the context of a democratic "public sphere," such self-clarification would have a macro-social parallel in the form of ideology critique had this space not been severely eroded by elite domina-tion and technocratic decision making (Habermas 1989). Emancipatory knowledge thus has an inter-est in overcoming the illusions of reification, wheth-er in the form of neurosis at the level of psychology or ideology at the level of society. In contrast to testable empirical hypotheses about objectified processes, the validity of emancipatory knowledge can be determined only by its beneficiaries. Its validity rests on the extent to which its subjects find themselves increasingly free from compul-sion. Thus, a central problem of modern society is the hegemony of instrumental knowledge that, though appropriate in the realm of nature, is used to objectify and manipulate social relations. In-strumental knowledge thus eclipses the interpretive and emancipatory forms of knowledge that are also essential for guiding social life.

When sufficient attention is paid to interper-sonal communication, Habermas (1979) contends that every act of speech can be seen as implying a universal demand that interpersonal understand-ing be based on the free exchange and clarification of meanings. In other words, an immanent cri-tique of language performance (which Habermas terms "universal pragmatics") reveals the presump-tion that communication not be distorted by dif-ferences in power between speakers. Thus, human communication is implicitly a demand for free-dom and equality. By this form of immanent cri-tique—consistent with the methodological stan-dards of the Frankfurt School—Habermas attempts to demonstrate the potential validity of emancipatory knowledge so that it can be seen as a compelling challenge to the hegemony of instrumental knowl-edge. The purpose of Habermas's communication theory is thus highly partisan. By showing that no forms of knowledge are "value free" but always "interested," and that human communication in-herently demands to occur freely without distor-tions caused by social power differentials, Habermas seeks politically to delegitimate conventions that confine social science to investigations of the means rather than the rational ends of social life.

In his subsequent works, Habermas has tried to reformulate this philosophical position in terms of a political sociology. To do so, he has profound-ly redirected "historical materialism," the Marxist project to which he remains committed (see Habermas 1979). Habermas contends that Marx gave insufficient attention to communicative ac-tion by restricting it to the social class relations of work. This restriction, he argues, inclined the Marxist tradition toward an uncritical attitude to-ward technological domination as well as toward forms of scientism that contribute to the suppres-sion of critique in regimes legitimated by Marxist ideology. Habermas relates his immanent critique of language performance to historical materialism by showing that sociocultural evolution occurs not only through the increasing rationality of techni-cal control over nature (as Marx recognized) but also through advances in communicative rationali-ty, that is, nondistorted communication. Thus, instrumental rationality and communicative ra-tionality are complementary forms of societal "learning mechanisms." The problem of moderni-ty is not science and technology in and of them-selves, because they promise increased control over the environment, but rather the fact that instrumental rationality has eclipsed communica-tive rationality in social life. In other words, in advanced industrial society, technical forms of control are no longer guided by consensually derived societal values. Democratic decision making is diminished under circumstances in which technical experts manipulate an objectified world, in which citizens are displaced from political decision making, and in which "reason"—identified exclusively with the "value free" prediction of isolated "facts"—is disqualified from reflection about the ends of social life.

More recently, Habermas (1987) has restated this theory sociologically to describe an uneven process of institutional development governed by opposing principles of "system" and "lifeworld." In this formulation, the cultural lifeworld—the source of cultural meanings, social solidarity, and personal identity—is increasingly subject to "colonization" by the objectivistic "steering mechanisms" of the marketplace (money) and bureaucracy (power). On the levels of culture, society, and personality, such colonization tends to produce political crises resulting from the loss of meaning, increase of anomie, and loss of motivation. At the same time, however, objectivistic steering mechanisms remain indispensable because large-scale social systems cannot be guided by the face-to-face interactions that characterize the lifeworld. Thus, the state becomes a battleground for struggles involving the balance between the structuring principles of systems and lifeworlds. Habermas contends that it is in response to such crises that the forces of conservatism and the "new social movements" such as feminism and ecology are embattled and that it is here that the struggle for human liberation at present is being contested most directly. As formulated by Habermas, a critical theory of society aims at clarifying such struggles in order to contribute to the progressive democratization of modern society.

CURRENT DEBATES: CRITICAL THEORY AND POSTSTRUCTURALISM

In the late 1980s and early 1990s, the heightened influence of poststructuralism sparked intense debate between critical theorists and poststructuralists. Theorists staked out positions that tended to collapse distinct theories into oppositional categories (critical theory *or* poststructuralism) yet they agreed on several points. Both critical and poststructural theorists critiqued the transcendental claims of

Enlightenment thought (e.g., that truth transcends the particular and exists "out there" in its universality), understood knowledge and consciousness to be shaped by culture and history, and attacked disciplinary boundaries by calling for supra-disciplinary approaches to knowledge construction. Polarization, nonetheless, worked to emphasize differences, underplay points of agreement, and restrict awareness of how these approaches might complement one another (Best and Kellner 1991; Fraser 1997).

Because critical theory aspires to understand semiautonomous social systems (e.g., capital, science and technology, the state, and the family) as interconnected in an overarching matrix of domination (Best and Kellner 1991, p. 220), poststructuralists charge that it is a "grand theory" still mired in Enlightenment traditions that seek to understand society as a totality. In viewing the path to emancipation as the recovery of reason through a critical analysis of instrumentalism, scientism, and late capitalism, critical theory is seen as promoting a centralized view of power as emitting from a macro-system of domination. That is, by promoting a view of social subjects as overdetermined by class, critical theory is said to reduce subjectivity to social relations of domination that hover in an orbit of capitalist imperatives. By theorizing that subjectivity is formed through social interaction (e.g., intersubjectivity), Habermas departs from Horkheimer and Adorno's view of the social subject as ego centered—as a self-reflexive critical subject (Best and Kellner 1991). Nonetheless, poststructuralists contend that Habermas, like his predecessors, essentializes knowledge. In other words, the capacity to recover reason either through critical reflexivity (Horkheimer, Adorno, and Marcuse) or through a form of communicative action that appeals to a normative order (Habermas) promotes a false understanding of subjectivity as "quasi-transcendental."

In rebuttal, critical theorists argue that poststructuralist views of power as decentralized and diffuse uncouple power from systems of domination (Best and Kellner 1991). Poststructuralists view social subjectivity as a cultural construction that is formed in, and through, multiple and diffuse webs of language and power. Critics charge that such a diffuse understanding of power promotes a vision of society as a "view from everywhere" (Bordo 1993). Social identities are seen as indeterminate and social differences as differences of equivalency (Flax 1990). This perspective results in analyses that focus on identity to the exclusion of systemic forms of domination. Thus, for example, while feminists who adhere to critical theory tend to analyze gender as a system of patriarchal domination, poststructuralist feminists, by contrast, tend to focus on the cultural production of gendered subjects, that is, on representation and identity. Habermas ([1980] 1997) and others argue that the avoidance of analyses of systems in favor of more fragmentary micro-analyses of discrete institutions, discourses, or practices is an antimodern movement that obscures the emancipatory potential of modernity (Best and Kellner 1991).

Although this debate is still stirring, some scholars are moving away from oppositional positions in favor of more complex readings of both traditions in order to synthesize or forge alliances between approaches (Best and Kellner 1991; Kellner 1995; Fraser 1997). Thus poststructuralism may serve as a corrective to the totalizing tendencies in critical theory while the latter prevents the neglect of social systems and calls attention to the relationship between multiple systems of domination and social subjectivities. In other words, critical theory points to the need to understand systemic forms of domination while poststructuralism warns against the reduction of social subjectivity to macro-overarching systems of domination. Thus drawing on both traditions, Nancy Fraser (1997, p. 219) suggests that a more accurate picture of social complexity "might conceive subjectivity as endowed with critical capacities and as culturally constructed" while viewing "critique as simultaneously situated and amenable to self-reflection."

Theoretical and empirical applications of such a "both/and approach" abound. For instance, in recognizing that all knowledge is partial, black feminist theorists such as Patricia Hill Collins (1990) articulate both critical theoretical tenets and poststructuralist sensibilities by conceptualizing identity as socially constructed, historically specific, and culturally located while stressing systemic forms of domination without reducing identities to single systems of oppression (also see Agger 1998). Postcolonial theories likewise draw on both traditions in order to understand the fluid relationships among culture, systems of domination, social subjectivity, the process of "othering," and

identity formation (see Williams and Chrisman 1993). Douglas Kellner's (1997) empirical work on media culture likewise employs a multiperspectival approach that combines insights from cultural studies and poststructuralism with critical theory in order to understand mass media as a source of both domination and resistance, and as a way to account for the formation and communicative positionality of social subjects constituted through multiple systems of race, class, and gender. Habermas's (1996) current theorizing on procedural democracy reflects a move toward the poststructuralism of Ernesto Laclau and Chantal Mouffe's (1985) theory of radical democracy that stresses the potential collaboration of diverse agents in progressive social movements that aim at defending and expanding citizen participation in public life.

(SEE ALSO: *Marxist Sociology*)

REFERENCES

Adorno, Theodor 1973 *Negative Dialectics*. New York: Seabury Press.

——, E. Frenkel-Brunswick, D. Levinson, and R. N. Sanford 1950 *The Authoritarian Personality*. New York: Harper.

Agger, Ben 1998 *Critical Social Theory: An Introduction*. Boulder. Colo.: Westview Press.

Antonio, Robert J. 1981 "Immanent Critique as the Core of Critical Theory." *British Journal of Sociology* 32:330–345.

Aronowitz, Stanley 1973 *False Promises*. New York: McGraw-Hill.

Balbus, Isaac 1977 "Commodity Form and Legal Form: An Essay on 'Relative Autonomy'." *Law and Society Review* 11:571–588.

Benjamin, Jessica 1978 "Authority and the Family Revisited: Or, A World without Fathers?" *New German Critique* 13 (Winter):35–57.

Best, Steven, and Douglas Kellner 1991 *Postmodern Theory: Critical Interrogations*. New York: The Guilford Press.

Bordo, Susan 1993 *Unbearable Weight: Feminism, Western Culture, and the Body*. Berkeley: University of California Press.

Braverman, Harry 1974 *Labor and Monopoly Capital*. New York: Monthly Review Press.

Buck-Morss, Susan 1995 *The Dialectics of Seeing: Walter Benjamin and the Arcades Project*. Cambridge, Mass.: The MIT Press.

Flax, Jane 1990 *Thinking Fragments: Psychoanalysis, Feminism, and Postmodernism in the Contemporary West.* Los Angeles: University of California Press.

Fraser, Nancy 1997 *Justice Interruptus: Critical Reflections on the "Postsocialist" Condition.* New York: Routledge.

—— 1989 *Unruly Practices: Power, Discourse, and Gender in Contemporary Social Theory.* Minneapolis: University of Minnesota Press.

Fromm, Erich 1941 *Escape from Freedom.* New York: Avon.

Giroux, Henry A. 1988 *Schooling and the Struggle for Public Life.* Minneapolis: University of Minnesota Press.

Habermas, Jurgen 1996 *Between Facts and Norms: Contributions to a Discourse Theory of Law and Democracy.* Cambridge, Mass.: The MIT Press.

—— 1989 *The Structural Transformation of the Public Sphere.* Cambridge, Mass.: The MIT Press.

—— 1987 *The Theory of Communicative Action II: Lifeworld and System–A Critique of Functionalist Reason.* Boston: Beacon Press.

—— 1986 "Three Normative Models of Democracy." In Seyla Benhabib, ed., *Democracy and Difference.* Princeton, N.J.: Princeton University Press.

—— (1980) 1997 "Modernity: An Unfinished Project." In d' Entregrave;ves, Maurizio Passerin and Seyla Benhabib, eds., *Habermas and the Unfinished Project of Modernity.* Cambridge, Mass.: The MIT Press.

—— 1979 *Communication and the Evolution of Society.* Boston: Beacon Press.

—— 1971 *Knowledge and Human Interests.* Boston: Beacon Press.

—— 1970 *Toward a Rational Society.* Boston: Beacon Press.

Haug, W. F. 1986 *Critique of Commodity Aesthetics.* Minneapolis: University of Minnesota Press.

Held, David 1980 *Introduction to Critical Theory.* Berkeley: University of California Press.

Hill Collins, Patricia 1990 *Black Feminist Thought: Knowledge, Consciousness, and the Politics of Empowerment.* New York: Routledge.

Horkheimer, Max 1972 *Critical Theory: Selected Essays.* New York: Herder and Herder.

——, and Theodor Adorno (1947) 1972 *Dialectic of Enlightenment.* New York: Seabury Press.

Jay, Martin 1984 *Marxism and Totality.* Berkeley: University of California Press.

—— 1973 *The Dialectical Imagination.* Boston: Little, Brown.

Kellner, Douglas 1995 *Media Culture: Cultural Studies, Identity, and Politics Between the Modern and the Postmodern.* New York: Routledge.

—— 1984–85 "Critical Theory and the Culture Industries: A Reassessment." *Telos* 62:196–209.

—— 1990a "Critical Theory and the Crisis of Social Theory." *Sociological Perspectives* 33:11–33.

—— 1990b *Television and the Crisis of Democracy.* Boulder, Colo.: Westview Press.

Kelly, Joan 1979 "The Doubled Vision of Feminist Theory." *Feminist Studies* 5:216–227.

Laclau, Ernesto, and Chantal Mouffe 1985 *Hegemony and Socialist Strategy: Towards a Radical Democratic Politics.* London: Verso.

Lasch, Christopher 1977 *Haven in a Heartless World.* New York: Basic Books.

Lukacs, Georg (1923) 1971 *History and Class Consciousness.* Cambridge, Mass.: The MIT Press.

Marcuse, Herbert 1964 *One-Dimensional Man.* Boston: Beacon Press.

—— 1955 *Eros and Civilization.* Boston: Beacon Press.

—— 1941 *Reason and Revolution.* New York: Oxford University Press.

Sennett, Richard, and Jonathan Cobb 1973 *The Hidden Injuries of Class.* New York: Vintage Books.

Williams, Patrick, and Laura Chrisman 1993 *Colonial Discourse and Post Colonial Theory: A Reader.* New York: Columbia University Press.

DWIGHT B. BILLINGS
PATRICIA JENNINGS

CROSS-CULTURAL ANALYSIS

Cross-cultural research has a long history in sociology (Armer and Grimshaw 1973; Kohn 1989; Miller-Loessi 1995). It most generally involves social research across societies or ethnic and subcultural groups within a society. Because a discussion of macro-level comparative historical research appears in another chapter of this encyclopedia, the focus here is primarily on cross-cultural analysis of social psychological processes. These include communicative and interactive processes within social institutions and more generally the relation between the individual and society and its institutions.

Although all sociological research is seen as comparative in nature, comparisons across subcultural or cultural groups have distinct advantages for generating and testing sociological theory. Specifically, cross-cultural research can help "distinguish between those regularities in social behavior that are system specific and those that are universal" (Grimshaw 1973, p. 5). In this way, sociologists can distinguish between generalizations that are true of all cultural groups and those that apply for one group at one point in time. The lack of cross-cultural research has often led to the inappropriate universal application of sociological concepts that imply an intermediate (one cultural group at one point in time) level (Bendix 1963).

In addition to documenting universal and system-specific patterns in social behavior, cross-cultural analysis can provide researchers with experimental treatments (independent variables) unavailable in their own culture. Thus, specific propositions can be investigated experimentally that would be impossible to establish in a laboratory in the researcher's own country (Strodtbeck 1964). Finally, cross-cultural analysis is beneficial for theory building in at least two respects. First, the documentation of differences in processes across cultures is often the first step in the refinement of existing theory and the generation of novel theoretical models. Second, cross-cultural analysis can lead to the discovery of unknown facts (behavioral patterns or interactive processes) that suggest new research problems that are the basis for theory refinement and construction.

INTERPRETIVE AND INFERENTIAL PROBLEMS

Cross-cultural researchers face a number of challenging interpretive and inferential problems that are related to the methodological strategies they employ (Bollen, Entwisle, and Alderson 1993). For example, Charles Ragin (1989) argues that most cross-cultural research at the macro level involves either intensive studies of one or a small group of representative or theoretically decisive cases or the extensive analysis of a large number of cases. Not surprisingly, extensive studies tend to emphasize statistical regularities while intensive studies search for generalizations that are interpreted within a cultural or historical context. This same pattern also appears in most micro-level cross-cultural research, and it is clearly related to both theoretical orientation and methodological preferences.

Some scholars take the position that cultural regularities must always be interpreted in cultural and historical context, while others argue that what appear to be cross-cultural differences may really be explained by lawful regularities at a more general level of analysis. Those in the first group most often employ primarily qualitative research strategies (intensive ethnographic and historical analysis of a few cases), while those in the second usually rely on quantitative techniques (multivariate or other forms of statistical analysis of large data sets).

METHODOLOGICAL TECHNIQUES AND AVAILABLE DATA SOURCES

The wide variety of techniques employed in cross-cultural analysis reflect the training and disciplinary interests of their practitioners. We discuss the methods of anthropologists, psychologists, and sociologists in turn. Anthropologists generally rely on different types of ethnographic tools for data collection, analysis, and reporting. Ethnographic research has the dual task of cultural description and cultural interpretation. The first involves uncovering the "native's point of view" or the criteria the people under study use "to discriminate among things and how they respond to them and assign them meaning, including everything in their physical, behavioral, and social environments" (Goodenough 1980, pp. 31–32); while the second involves "stating, as explicitly as we can manage, what the knowledge thus attained demonstrates about the society in which it is found and, beyond that, about social life as such" (Geertz 1973, p. 27).

Three types of ethnographic approaches and methodological tools are generally employed in cross-cultural research. The first involves long-term participant observation and the thick description of the culture under study in line with Clifford Geertz's (1973) interpretive perspective of culture. From this perspective, culture is seen as "layered multiple networks of meaning carried by words, acts, conceptions and other symbolic forms" (Marcus and Fisher 1986, p. 29). Thus the metaphor of culture in the interpretive approach is that of a text to be discovered, described, and interpreted. The second involves methods of ethnoscience including elicitation tasks and interviews with key informants that yield data amenable to logical and statistical analysis to generate the "organizing principles underlying behavior" (Tyler 1969; also see

Werner and Schoepfle 1987). Ethnoscience views these organizing principles as the "grammar of the culture" that is part of the mental competence of members. The final type of ethnographic research is more positivistic and comparative in orientation. In this approach cross-cultural analysis is specifically defined as the use of "data collected by anthropologists concerning the customs and characteristics of various peoples throughout the world to test hypotheses concerning human behavior" (Whiting 1968, p. 693).

All three types of ethnographic research generate data preserved in research monographs or data archives such as the Human Relations Area Files, the *Ethnographic Atlas*, and the ever-expanding World Cultures data set that has been constructed around George Murdock and Douglas White's (1968) *Standard Cross Cultural Sample*. A number of scholars (Barry 1980; Lagacé 1977; Murdock 1967; Whiting 1968; Levinson and Malone 1980) have provided detailed discussions of the contents, coding schemes, and methodological strengths and weaknesses of these archives as well as data analysis strategies and overviews of the variety of studies utilizing such data.

Most cross-cultural research in psychology involves the use of quasi-experimental methods. These include classical experimentation, clinical tests and projective techniques, systematic observation, and unobtrusive methods (see Berry, Poortinga, and Pandey, 1996; Triandis and Berry 1980). However, a number of psychologists have recently turned to observational and ethnographic methods in what has been termed "cultural psychology" (Shweder 1990). Much of the recent research in this area focuses on culture and human development and spans disciplinary boundaries and involves a wide variety of interpretive research methods (Greenfield and Suzuki 1998; Shweder et al. 1998).

Sociologists have made good use of intensive interviewing (Bertaux 1990) and ethnography (Corsaro 1988, 1994; Corsaro and Heise 1992) in cross-cultural analysis. However, they more frequently rely on the survey method in cross-cultural research and have contributed to the development of a number of archives of survey data (Kohn 1987; Lane 1990). The growth of such international surveys in recent years has been impressive. The World Fertility Survey (WFS) is an early example.

In one of the first efforts of its kind, women in forty-two developing countries were interviewed between 1974 and 1982 about their fertility behavior, marital and work history, and other aspects of their background. The WFS spawned hundreds of comparative studies that have contributed greatly to the understanding of human fertility (see, for example, Bohgaarts and Watkins 1996; Kirk and Pillet 1998). The Demographic and Health Survey (DHS) largely took up where the WFS left off. In this ongoing project, begun in 1984, nationally representative samples of women aged 15–49 in forty-seven countries have been surveyed regarding lifetime reproduction, fertility preferences, family planning practices, and the health of their children. For some countries, detailed data are available for husbands also and, for a few countries, in-depth interview data are also available.

Less specialized is the international counterpart to the U.S. General Social Survey (GSS); the International Social Survey Program (ISSP). The ISSP got its start in 1984 as researchers in the United States, Germany, Britain, and Australia agreed to field common topical modules in the course of conducting their regular national surveys. Beginning 1985 with a survey of attitudes toward government in the four founding countries, the ISSP has expanded to include surveys on topics as diverse as social networks and social support and attitudes regarding family, religion, work, the environment, gender relations, and national identity. Some specific modules have been replicated and, overall, a large proportion of the items from earlier surveys are carried over to new modules, giving the ISSP both a cross-cultural and longitudinal dimension. At present, thirty-one nations are participating in the ISSP. A number of non-member nations have also replicated specific modules. An interesting offshoot of the ISSP is the International Survey of Economic Attitudes (ISEA). Building on an ISSP module concerning beliefs regarding social inequality, the ISEA collects a wide array of information on attitudes regarding income inequality, social class, and economic policy. The first round was carried out between 1991–1993 in three countries. A second round was carried out in five countries over the 1994–1997 period, and a third round is currently under way. Some of the important reports based on data from these surveys include Jones and Broyfield (1997), Kelley and Evans (1995), and Western (1994).

Also of general interest are the surveys undertaken under the auspices of the World Values Survey Group and Eurobarometer. The World Values Survey (WVS) (originally termed the "European Values Survey") began in 1981 as social scientists in nine Western European countries administered a common survey of social, political, moral, and religious values in their respective countries. Between 1981 and 1984, this survey was replicated in fourteen additional countries, including a number of non-European countries. In 1990–1993, a second wave of the World Values Survey was conducted in a broader group of forty-three nations and a third wave was undertaken in 1995–1996. In terms of content, the WVS is broadly organized around values and norms regarding work, family, the meaning and purpose of life, and topical social issues. Specifically, respondents are queried on everything from their views on good and evil to their general state of health, from their associational memberships to their opinions of the value of scientific discoveries (see Inglehart 1997; MacIntosh 1998). The Eurobarometer surveys began in 1974 as an extension of an earlier series of European Community surveys. Designed primarily to gauge public attitudes toward the Common Market and other EU institutions, the Eurobarometer surveys, carried out every Fall and Spring, have expanded to include a variety of special topics of interest to sociologists, ranging from attitudes regarding AIDS to beliefs about the role of women (see Pettigrew 1998; Quillian 1995).

Finally, there are two more specialized projects that are deserving of note for their scale and scope. Of interest to students of crime and deviance is the International Crime (Victim) Survey (IC(V)S). Begun in 1989 and carried out again in 1992 and 1996, the IC(V)S gathers reports of crime, in addition to surveying attitudes regarding the police and the criminal justice system, fear of crime, and crime prevention (see Alvazzi del Frate and Patrignani 1995; Zvekic 1996). At present, over fifty countries have participated in the IC(V)S. Scholars interested in cross-cultural dimensions of poverty and development have benefitted from the Living Standards Measurement Study (LSMS). In this World Bank-directed program of research, surveys have been conducted in over two dozen developing countries since 1980 with the aim of gauging the welfare of households, understanding household behavior, and assessing the impact of government policy on standards of living. The central instrument is a household questionnaire that details patterns of consumption. Other modules, collecting information regarding the local community, pricing, and schools and health facilities, have also been administered in a number of cases (see Grosh and Glewwe 1998; Stecklov 1997).

CHALLENGES AND PROBLEMS IN CROSS-CULTURAL RESEARCH

There are numerous methodological problems in cross-cultural research including: acquiring the needed linguistic and cultural skills and research funds; gaining access to field sites and data archives; defining and selecting comparable units; ensuring the representativeness of selected cases; and determining conceptual equivalence and measurement reliability and validity. These first two sets of problems are obvious, but not easily resolved. Cross-cultural analysis is costly in terms of time and money, and it usually demands at least a minimal level (and often much more) of education in the history, language, and culture of groups of people foreign to the researcher. The difficulties of gaining access to, and cooperation from, individuals and groups in cross-cultural research "are always experienced but rarely acknowledged by comparative researchers" (Armer 1973, pp. 58–59). Specific discussions of, and development of strategies for, gaining access are crucial because research can not begin without such access. Additionally, casual, insensitive, or ethnocentric presentation of self and research goals to foreign gatekeepers (officials, scholars, and those individuals directly studied) not only negatively affects the original study, but can also cause serious problems for others who plan future cross-cultural research (Form 1973; Portes 1973). Given the cultural isolation of many social scientists in the United States, it is not surprising that these practical problems have contributed to the lack of cross-cultural research in American sociology. However, the internationalization of the social sciences and the globalization of social and environmental issues are contributing to the gradual elimination of many of these practical problems (Sztompka 1988).

For the cross-cultural analysis of social psychological processes the unit of analysis is most often interactive events or individuals that are sampled from whole cultures or subunits such as communities or institutions (e.g., family, school, or workplace). The appropriateness of individuals as the basic unit of analysis has been a hotly debated issue in sociology. The problem is even more acute in cross-cultural analysis, especially in cultures "that lack the individualistic, participatory characteristics of Western societies" (Armer 1983, p. 62). In addition to the special difficulties of representative, theoretical, or random sampling of cases (Elder 1973; Van Meter 1990), cross-cultural researchers must also deal with "Galton's problem." According to the British statistician, Sir Francis Galton, "valid comparison requires mutually independent and isolated cases, and therefore cultural diffusion, cultural contact, culture clash or outright conquest—with their consequent borrowing, imitation, migrations etc.—invalidates the results of comparative studies" (Sztompka 1988, p. 213). Although several researchers have presented strategies for dealing with Galton's problem for correlational studies of data archives (see Naroll, Michik, and Naroll 1980), the problem of cultural diffusion is often overlooked in many quantitative and qualitative cross-cultural studies.

Undoubtedly, ensuring conceptual equivalence and achieving valid measures are the most challenging methodological problems of cross-cultural research. Central to these problems is the wide variation in language and meaning systems across cultural groups. Anthropologists have attempted to address the problem of conceptual equivalence with the distinction between "emic" and "etic." Emics refer to local (single culture) meaning, function and structure, while etics are culture-free (or at least operate in more than one culture) aspects of the world (Pike 1966). A major problem in cross-cultural analysis is the use of emic concepts of one culture to explain characteristics of another culture. In fact, many cross-cultural studies involve the use of "imposed etics," that is Euro-American emics that are "imposed blindly and even ethnocentrically on a set of phenomena which occur in other cultural systems" (Berry 1980, p. 12). A number of procedures have been developed to ensure emic-etic distinctions and to estimate the validity of such measures (Brislin 1980; Naroll, Michik, and Naroll 1980).

Addressing conceptual relevance in cross-cultural research does not, of course, ensure valid measures. All forms of data collection and analysis are dependent on implicit theories of language and communication (Cicourel 1964). As social scientists have come to learn more about communicative systems within and across cultures, there has been a growing awareness that problems related to language in cross-cultural analysis are not easily resolved. There is also a recognition that these problems go beyond the accurate translation of measurement instruments (Brislin 1970; Grimshaw 1973), to the incorporation of findings from studies on communicative competence across cultural groups into cross-cultural research (Briggs 1986; Gumperz 1982).

THE FUTURE OF CROSS-CULTURAL ANALYSIS

There is a solid basis for optimism regarding the future of cross-cultural analysis. Over the last twenty years there has been remarkable growth in international organizations and cooperation among international scholars in the social sciences. These developments have not only resulted in an increase in cross-cultural research, but also have led to necessary debates about the theoretical and methodological state of cross-cultural analysis (Øyen 1990; Kohn 1989).

Cooperation among international scholars in cross-cultural analysis has also contributed to the breaking down of disciplinary boundaries. In the area of childhood socialization and the sociology of childhood, for example, there have been a number of cross-cultural contributions to what can be termed "development in sociocultural context" by anthropologists (Heath 1983), psychologists (Rogoff 1990), sociologists (Corsaro 1997), and linguists (Ochs 1988). Developing interest in children and childhood in sociology has resulted in the establishment of a new research committee ("Sociology of Childhood") in the International Sociological Association (ISA) and a new journal titled *Childhood: A Global Journal of Child Research*, as well as the publication of several international reports and edited volumes (see Qvortrup, Bardy, Sgritta, and Wintersberger 1994). Less interdisciplinary, perhaps, but no less impressive, has been the degree of international cooperation that has developed around a number of other research committees of the ISA. The ISA Research Committee on Stratification, for instance, has had a long history of such collaboration. This has involved the development of a common agenda (official and unofficial) and the pursuit of a common program of research by scholars around the globe (Ganzeboom, Treiman, and Ultee 1991). In addition to these developments, the growth of international data sets and their ready availability due to the new technologies such as the Internet are also grounds for optimism regarding cross-cultural research.

Despite growing international and multi-discipline cooperation and recognition of the importance of comparative research, it is still fair to say that cross-cultural analysis remains at the periphery of American sociology and social psychology. Although there has been some reversal of the growing trend toward narrow specialization over the last ten years, such specialization is still apparent in the nature of publications and the training of graduate students in these disciplines. There is a clear need to instill a healthy skepticism regarding the cultural relativity of a great deal of theory and method in social psychology in future scholars. Only then will future sociologists and social psychologists come to appreciate fully the potential of cross-cultural analysis.

REFERENCES

Alvazzi del Frate, Anna and Angela Patrignani 1995 "Women's Victimisation in Developing Countries." *Issues and Reports* (UNIRI) 5:1–16.

Armer, Michael 1973 "Methodological Problems and Possibilities in Comparative Research." In M. Armer and A. Grimshaw, eds., *Comparative Social Research: Methodological Problems and Strategies*. New York: Wiley.

——, and Allen Grimshaw, (eds.) 1973 *Comparative Social Research: Methodological Problems and Strategies*. New York: Wiley.

Barry, Herbert 1980 "Description and Uses of the Human Relations Area Files." In H. Triandis and J. Berry, eds., *Handbook of Cross Cultural Methodology, Volume 2 Methodology*. Boston: Allyn and Bacon.

Bendix, 1963 "Concepts and Generalizations in Comparative Sociological Studies." *American Sociological Review* 28:532–539.

Berry, J. W. 1980 "Introduction to Methodology." In H. Triandis and J. Berry, eds., *Handbook of Cross Cultural Methodology*. Boston: Allyn and Bacon.

——, Y. H. Poortinga, and J. Pandey, (eds.) 1996 *Handbook of Cross-Cultural Psychology: Theory and Method*, 2nd edition. Boston: Allyn and Bacon.

Bertaux, Daniel 1990 "Oral History Approaches to an International Social Movement." In E. Øyen, ed., *Comparative Methodology: Theory and Practice in International Social Research*. Newbury Park, Calif.: Sage.

Bollen, Kenneth A., Barbara Entwisle, and Arthur S. Alderson 1993 "Macrocomparative Research Methods." *Annual Review of Sociolology* 19:321–351.

Bongaarts, John, and Susan Cotts Watkins 1996 "Social Interactions and Contemporary Fertility Transitions." *Population and Development Review* 22:639–682.

Briggs, Charles 1986 *Learning How to Ask*. New York: Cambridge.

Brislin, Richard 1970 "Back-Translation for Cross-Cultural Research." *Journal of Cross-Cultural Psychology* 1:185–216.

—— 1980 "Translation and Content Analysis of Oral and Written Materials." In H. Triandis and J. Berry, eds., *Handbook of Cross Cultural Methodology*. Boston: Allyn and Bacon.

Cicourel, Aaron 1964 *Method and Measurement in Sociology*. New York: Free Press.

Corsaro, William 1988 "Routines in the Peer Culture of American and Italian Nursery School Children." *Sociology of Education* 61:1–14.

—— 1994 "Discussion, Debate, and Friendship: Peer Discourse in Nursery Schools in the U.S. and Italy." *Sociology of Education* 67:1–26.

——, and David Heise 1990 "Event Structure Models From Ethnographic Data." *Sociological Methodology* 20:1–57.

Elder, Joseph 1973 "Problems of Cross-Cultural Methodology: Instrumentation and Interviewing in India." In M. Armer and A. Grimshaw, eds., *Comparative Social Research: Methodological Problems and Strategies*. New York: Wiley.

Form, William 1973 "Field Problems in Comparative Research: The Politics of Distrust." In M. Armer and A. Grimshaw, eds., *Comparative Social Research: Methodological Problems and Strategies*. New York: Wiley.

Ganzeboom, Harry B. G., Donald J. Treiman, and Wout C. Ultee 1991 "Comparative Intergenerational Stratification Research: Three Generations and Beyond." *Annual Review of Sociology* 17:277–302.

Geertz, Clifford 1973 *The Interpretation of Cultures*. New York: Basic Books.

Goodenough, Ward 1980 "Ethnographic Field Techniques." In H. Triandis and J. Berry, eds., *Handbook of Cross Cultural Methodology*. Boston: Allyn and Bacon.

Greenfield, Patricia and Lalita Suzuki 1998 "Culture and Human Development: Implications for Parenting, Education, Pediatrics, and Mental Health." In W. Damon, I. Siegel, K. Anne Renninger and K. Ann Renninger, eds., *Handbook of Child Psychology: Volume 4, Child Psychology in Practice*. New York: Wiley.

Grimshaw, Allen 1973 "Comparative Sociology: In What Ways Different from Other Sociologies?" In M. Armer and A. Grimshaw, eds., *Comparative Social Research: Methodological Problems and Strategies*. New York: Wiley.

Grosh, Margaret E., and Paul Glewwe 1998 "Data Watch: The World Bank's Living Standards Measurement Study Household Surveys." *Journal of Economic Perspectives* 12:187–196.

Gumperz, John J. 1982 *Discourse Strategies*. New York: Cambridge University Press.

Heath, Shirley 1989 "Oral and Literate Traditions Among Black Americans Living in Poverty." *American Psychologist* 44:45–56.

Inglehart, Ronald 1997 "Modernization, Postmodernization and Changing Perceptions of Risk." *International Review of Sociology* 7:449–459.

Jones, Rachel K., and April Brayfield 1997 "Life's Greatest Joy: European Attitudes Towards the Centrality of Children." *Social Forces* 75:1239–1270.

Kelley, Jonathan and M. D. R. Evans 1995 "Class Conflict in Six Western Nations." *American Sociological Review* 60:157–178.

Kirk, Dudley, and Bernard Pillet 1998 "Fertility Levels, Trends, and Differentials in Sub-Saharan Africa in the 1980s and 1990s." *Studies in Family Planning* 29:1–22.

Kohn, Melvin 1987 "Cross-National Research as an Analytic Strategy." *American Sociological Review* 52:713–731.

—— (ed.) 1989 *Cross-National Research in Sociology*. Newbury Park: Calif.: Sage.

Lagacé, R. O. (ed.) 1977 *Sixty Cultures: A Guide to the HRAF Probability Sample Files*. New Haven, Conn.: HRAF.

Lane, Jan-Erik 1990 "Data Archives as an Instrument for Comparative Research." In E. Øyen, ed., *Comparative Methodology: Theory and Practice in International Social Research*. Newbury Park, Calif.: Sage.

Levinson, David and Martin J. Malone 1980 *Toward Explaining Human Culture: A Critical Review of the Findings of Worldwide Cross-Cultural Research*. New Haven, Conn.: HRAF Press.

MacIntosh, Randall 1998 "Global Attitude Measurement: An Assessment of the World Values Survey Postmaterialism Scale." *American Sociological Review* 63:452–464.

Miller-Loessi, Karen 1995 "Comparative Social Psychology: Cross-Cultural and Cross-National." In K. Cook, G. A. Fine, and J. House, eds., *Sociological Perspectives on Social Psychology*. Boston: Allyn and Bacon.

Murdock, G. P. 1967 *Ethnographic Atlas*. Pittsburgh.: University of Pittsburgh Press.

——, and Douglas White 1969 "Standard Cross-Cultural Sample." *Ethnography* 8:329–369.

Naroll, Raoul, Gary Michik, and Frada Naroll 1980 "Holocultural Research." In H. Triandis and J. Berry, eds., *Handbook of Cross Cultural Methodology*. Boston: Allyn and Bacon.

Ochs, Elinor 1988 *Culture and Language Development: Language Acquisition and Language Socialization in a Samoan Village*. New York: Cambridge University Press.

Øyen, Else 1990 "The Imperfection of Comparisons." In E. Øyen, ed., *Comparative Methodology: Theory and Practice in International Social Research*. Newbury Park, Calif.: Sage.

Pettigrew, Thomas 1998 "Reactions toward the New Minorities of Western Europe." *Annual Review of Sociology* 24:77–103.

Pike, R. 1966 *Language in Relation to a United Theory of the Structure of Human Behavior*. The Hague: Mouton.

Portes, Alejandro 1973 "Perception of the U.S. Sociologist and Its Impact on Cross-National Research." In M. Armer and A. Grimshaw, eds., *Comparative Social Research: Methodological Problems and Strategies*. New York: Wiley.

Quillian, Lincoln 1995 "Prejudice as a Response to Perceived Group Threat: Population Composition and Anti-Immigrant and Racial Prejudice in Europe." *American Sociological Review* 60:586–611.

Qvortrup, Jens, Marjatta Bardy, Sgritta Giovanni, and Helmut Wintersberger (eds.) 1994 *Childhood Matters: Social Theory, Practice, and Politics*. Aldershot, England: Avebury.

Ragin, Charles 1989 "New Directions in Comparative Research." In M. Kohn, ed., *Cross-National Research in Socioloogy*. Newbury Park, Calif.: Sage.

Rogoff, Barbara 1990 *Apprenticeship in Thinking: Cognitive Development in Social Context*. New York: Oxford University Press.

Shweder, Richard 1990 "Cultural Psychology: What Is It?" In J. Stigler, R. Shweder, and G. Herdt, eds., *Cultural Psychology: Essays on Comparative Human Development*. New York: Cambridge University Press.

——, J. Goodnow, G. Hatano, R. LeVine, H. Marcus, and P. Miller 1998 "The Cultural Psychology of Development: One Mine Many Mentalities." In W.

Damon and R. Lerner, eds., *Handbook of Child Psychology: Volume 1, Theoretical Models of Human Development*. New York: Wiley.

Stecklov, Guy 1997 "Intergenerational Resource Flows in Côte d'Ivoire: Empirical Analysis of Aggregate Flows." *Population and Development Review* 23: 525–553.

Strodtbeck, Fred 1964 "Considerations of Meta-Method in Cross-Cultural Studies." *American Anthropologist* 66:223–229.

Sztompka, Piotr 1988 "Conceptual Frameworks in Comparative Inquiry: Divergent or Convergent?" *International Sociology* 3:207–219.

Triandis, Harry, and John Berry 1980 *Handbook of Cross-Cultural Psychology Volume 2, Methodology*. Boston: Allyn and Bacon.

Tyler, Stephen 1969 "Introduction." In S. Tyler, ed., *Cognitive Anthropology*. New York: Holt, Rinehart and Winston.

Van Meter, Karl 1990 "Sampling and Cross-Classification Analysis in International Social Research." In E. Øyen, ed., *Comparative Methodology: Theory and Practice in International Social Research*. Newbury Park, Calif.: Sage.

Werner, O, and G. M. Schoepfle 1987 *Systematic Fieldwork: Foundations of Ethnography and Interviewing*. Beverly Hills, Calif.: Sage.

Western, Bruce 1994 "Institutional Mechanism for Unionization in Sixteen OECD Countries: An Analysis of Social Survey Data." *Social Forces* 73:497–520.

Whiting, John 1968 "Methods and Problems in Cross-Cultural Research." In G. Lindzey and E. Aronson, eds., *The Handbook of Social Psychology, Volume 2*. Reading, Mass.: Addison-Wesley.

Zvekic, Ugljesa 1996. "The International Crime (Victim) Survey: Issues of Comparative Advantages and Disadvantages." *International Criminal Justice Review* 6:1–21.

ARTHUR S. ALDERSON
WILLIAM A. CORSARO

CROWDS AND RIOTS

Crowds are a ubiquitous feature of everyday life. People have long assembled collectively to observe, to celebrate, and to protest various happenings in their everyday lives, be they natural events, such as a solar eclipse, or the result of human contrivance, such as the introduction of machinery into the production process. The historical record is replete with examples of crowds functioning as important textual markers, helping to shape and define a particular event, as well as strategic precipitants and carriers of the events themselves. The storming of the Bastille and the sit-ins and marches associated with the civil rights movement are examples of crowds functioning as both important markers and carriers of some larger historical happening. Not all crowds function so significantly, of course. Most are mere sideshows to the flow of history. Nonetheless, the collective assemblages or gatherings called crowds are ongoing features of the social world and, as a consequence, have long been the object of theorizing and inquiry, ranging from the psychologistic renderings of Gustav LeBon (1895) and Sigmund Freud (1921) to the more sociological accounts of Neil Smelser (1963) and Ralph Turner and Lewis Killian (1987) to the highly systematic and empirically grounded observations of Clark McPhail and his associates (1983, 1991).

Crowds have traditionally been analyzed as a variant of the broader category of social phenomena called collective behavior. Broadly conceived, collective behavior refers to group problem solving behavior that encompasses crowds, mass phenomena, issue-specific publics, and social movements. More narrowly, collective behavior refers to "two or more persons engaged in one or more behaviors (e.g., orientation, locomotion, gesticulation, tactile manipulation, and/or vocalization) that can be judged common or convergent on one or more dimensions (e.g., direction, velocity tempo, and/or substantive content)"(McPhail and Wohlstein 1983, pp. 580–581). Implicit in both conceptions is a continuum on which collective behavior can vary in terms of the extent to which its participants are in close proximity or diffused in time and space. Instances of collective behavior in which individuals are in close physical proximity, such that they can monitor one another by being visible to, or within earshot of, one another, are constitutive of crowds. Examples include protest demonstrations, victory celebrations, riots, and the dispersal processes associated with flight from burning buildings. In contrast are forms of collective behavior that occur among individuals who are not physically proximate but who still share a common focus of attention and engage in some parallel or common behaviors without developing the debate characteristic of the public or the organization of social movements, and who are linked together by social networks, the media, or both. Examples of this form of collective behavior, referred to as diffuse collective behavior (Turner and Killian 1987) or the mass (Lofland 1981), include fads and crazes, deviant epidemics, mass hysteria, and collective blaming. Although crowds and diffuse collective behavior are not mutually exclusive phenomena, they are analytically distinct and tend to generate somewhat different literatures—thus, the focus on crowds in this selection.

Understanding crowds and the kindred collective phenomenon called "riots" requires consideration of five questions: (1) How do these forms of collective behavior differ from the crowd forms typically associated with everyday behavior, such as audiences and queues? (2) What are the distinctive features of crowds as collective behavior? (3) What are the conditions underlying the emergence of crowds? (4) What accounts for the coordination of crowd behavior? and (5) What are the correlates and/or predictors of individual participation?

DISTINGUISHING BETWEEN THE CROWDS OF COLLECTIVE BEHAVIOR AND EVERYDAY BEHAVIOR

There has been increasing recognition of the continuity between collective behavior and everyday behavior, yet the existence of collective behavior as an area of sociological analysis rests in part on the assumption of significant differences between collective behavior and everyday institutionalized behavior. In the case of crowds, those commonly associated with everyday life, such as at sports events and holiday parades, tend to be highly conventionalized in at least two or three ways. Such gatherings are recurrent affairs that are scheduled for a definite place at a definite time; they are calendarized both temporally and spatially. Second, associated behaviors and emotional states are typically routinized in the sense that they are normatively regularized and anticipated. And third, they tend to be sponsored and orchestrated by the state, a community, or a societal institution, as in the case of most holiday parades and electoral political rallies. Accordingly, they are typically socially approved affairs that function to reaffirm rather than challenge some institutional arrangement or the larger social order itself.

In contrast, crowds commonly associated with collective behavior, such as protest demonstrations, victory celebrations, and riots, usually challenge or disrupt the existing order. This is due in part to the fact that these crowds are neither temporally nor spatially routinized. Instead, as David Snow, Louis Zurcher, and Robert Peters (1981) have noted, they are more likely to be unscheduled and staged in spatial areas (streets, parks, malls) or physical structures (office buildings, theaters, lunch counters) that were designed for institutionalized, everyday behavior rather than contentious or celebratory crowds. Such crowd activities are also extrainstitutional, and thus unconventional, in the sense that they are frequently based on normative guidelines that are emergent and ephemeral rather than enduring (Turner and Killian 1987), on the appropriation and redefinition of existing networks or social relationships (Weller and Quarantelli 1973), or on both.

Crowd behavior has long been described as "extraordinary" in the sense that its occurrence indicates that something unusual is happening. Precisely what it is that gives rise to the sense that something "outside the ordinary" is occurring is rarely specified unambiguously, however. John Lofland (1981) suggests that it is increased levels of emotional arousal, but such arousal is not peculiar to crowd episodes. The conceptualization offered here suggests several possibilities: It is the appropriation and use of spatial areas, physical structures, or social networks and relations for purposes other than those for which they were intended or designed that indicates something extraordinary is happening.

THE CHARACTERISTIC FEATURES OF CROWDS

Crowds have been portrayed historically and journalistically as if they are monolithic entities characterized by participant and behavioral homogeneity. Turner and Killian (1987, p. 26) called this image into question, referring to it as "the illusion of unanimity," but not until the turn toward more systematic empirical examination of crowds was it firmly established that crowd behaviors are typically quite varied and highly differentiated, and that crowd participants are generally quite heterogeneous in terms of orientation and behavior.

Variation in Crowd Behaviors and "Riots." Based on extensive field observation of crowds, Sam Wright (1978) differentiated between two broad categories of crowd behaviors: crowd activities and task activities. "Crowd activities" refer to the redundant behavior seemingly common to all incidents of crowd behavior, such as assemblage, milling, and divergence. In their overview of empirical research on behaviors within crowds, McPhail and Ronald Wohlstein (1983) include collective locomotion, collective orientation, collective gesticulation, and collective vocalization among the types of crowd behaviors "repeatedly observed across a variety of gatherings, demonstrations, and some riots" (p. 595).

Taking these observations together, one can identify the following "crowd activities" (Wright 1978) or "elementary forms" of crowd behavior (McPhail and Wohlstein 1983): assemblage/convergence; milling; collective orientation (e.g., common or convergent gaze, focus, or attention); collective locomotion (e.g., common or convergent movement or surges); collective gesticulation (e.g., common or convergent nonverbal signaling); collective vocalization (e.g., chanting, singing, booing, cheering); and divergence/dispersal. Given the recurrent and seemingly universal character of these basic crowd behaviors, it is clear that they do not distinguish between types of crowds, that is, between demonstrations, celebrations, and riots.

To get at the variation in types of crowds, attention must be turned to what Wright conceptualized as "task activities" (1978). These refer to joint activities that are particular to and necessary for the attainment of a specific goal or the resolution of a specific problem. It is these goal-directed and problem-oriented activities that constitute the primary object of attention and thus help give meaning to the larger collective episode. Examples of task activities include parading or mass marching, mass assembly with speechmaking, picketing, proselytizing, temporary occupation of premises, lynching, taunting and harassment, property destruction, looting, and sniping.

Several caveats should be kept in mind with respect to crowd task activities. First, any listing of task activities is unlikely to be exhaustive, because they vary historically and culturally. Charles Tilly's (1978) concept of "repertoires of collective action" underscores this variation. Tilly has stressed that while there are innumerable ways in which people could pursue collective ends, alternatives are in fact limited by sociohistorical forces. His research suggests, for example, that the massed march, mass assembly, and temporary occupation of premises are all collective task activities specific to the twentieth century.

Second, crowd task activities are not mutually exclusive but are typically combined in an interactive fashion during the history of a crowd episode. The mass assembly, for example, is often preceded by the massed march, and property destruction and looting often occur together. Indeed, whether a crowd episode is constitutive of a protest demonstration, a celebration, or a riot depends, in part, on the particular configuration of task activities and, in part, on who or what is the object of protest, celebration, or violence. Both of these points can be illustrated with riots.

It is generally agreed that riots involve some level of collective violence against persons or property, but that not all incidents of collective violence are equally likely to be labeled riots. Collective violence against the state or its social control agents is more likely to be labeled riotous, for example, than violence perpetrated by the police against protesting demonstrators. Traditionally, what gets defined as a riot involves interpretive discretion, particularly by the state. But even when there is agreement that riots are constituted by some segment of a crowd or gathering engaging in violence against person(s) or property, distinctions are often made between types of riots, as evidenced by Morris Janowitz's (1979) distinction between "communal riots" and "commodity riots," Gary Marx's (1972) distinction between "protest riots" and "issueless riots," and the Walker Report's (1968) reference to "police riots." Communal riots involve religious, ethnic, and/or racial intergroup violence in which the members or property of one group are violently assaulted by members of another group, as occurred in the United States in Miami in 1980 (Porter and Dunn 1984) and in South Central Los Angeles in 1992 (Bergesen and Herman 1998). Commodity or property riots, in contrast, typically involve looting, arson, and vandalism against property, which has generally been posited as one of the defining features of the many urban riots that occurred across major U.S. cities in the 1960s. But it has been argued that many of these riots, such as those that occurred following the assassination of Martin Luther King, Jr. in 1968, were also protest riots, or at least had elements of protest associated with them (Fogelson 1971). Even though there has been some effort to identify the conditions that lead to the designation of elements of crowd behavior as protest (Turner 1969), it is clear that communal, commodity, and protest riots are overlapping rather than mutually exclusive crowd phenomena and that distinguishing among them therefore involves some interpretive discretion (Turner 1994). The same is true, as well, with the category of issueless riots, such as the sporting victory celebrations that sometimes take on the flavor of property riots among some of the celebrants. Even in the case of police riots, which involve a loss of discipline and control among the ranks, as occurred during the 1968 Democratic National Convention in Chicago, there is often debate as to whether the assaultive behavior of the police is justified. That there is some level of ambiguity and debate associated with categorizing and distinguishing any crowd episode as not only a riot, but as particular kind of riot, is not surprising considering that all crowd episodes share various task activities or elementary forms even when they differ in terms of their defining task activities.

Following from these observations is a final caveat: The task activities associated with any given crowd episode vary in the degree to which they are the focus of attention. Not all are equally attended to by spectators, social control agents, or the media. Consequently, task activities can be classified according to the amount of attention they receive. One that is the major focus of attention and thus provides the phenomenal basis for defining the episode constitutes "the main task activity," whereas those subordinate to the main task activity are "subordinate or side activities." The main task activity is on center stage and typically is the focus of media attention, as illustrated by the extensive media coverage of property vandalism and looting associated with commodity riots. In contrast, the remaining task activities are sideshows, occasioned by and often parasitic to the focal task activity. Examples of subordinate task activity in the case of property or communal riots, or both, include spectating or observing, informal, unofficial attempts at social control, and even the work of the media.

Variation in Participation Units. Just as empirical research on crowds has discerned considerable heterogeneity in behavior, so there is corresponding variation in terms of participants. Some are engaged in various task activities, some are observing, and still others are involved in the containment and control of the other participants and their interactions. Indeed, most of the individuals who make up a crowd fall into one of three categories of actors: task performers, spectators or bystanders, and social control agents. Task performers include the individuals performing both main and subordinate tasks. In the case of an antiwar march, for example, the main task performers would include the protesting marchers, with counterdemonstrators, peace marshals, and the press or media constituting the subordinate task performers.

Spectators or bystanders, who constitute the second set of actors relevant to most instances of crowd behavior, have been differentiated into proximal and distal groupings according to proximity to the collective encounter and the nature of their response. Proximal spectators, who are physically co-present and can thus monitor firsthand the activities of task performers, have generally been treated as relatively passive and nonessential elements of crowd behavior. However, research on a series of victory celebrations shows that some spectators do not merely respond passively to the main task performance and accept the activity as given, but can actively influence the character of the activity as well (Snow, Zurcher, and Peters 1981). Accordingly, proximal spectators can vary in terms of whether they are passive or animated and aggressive. "Distal spectators" refer to individuals who take note of episodes of crowd behavior even though they are not physically present during the episodes themselves. Also referred to as "bystander publics" (Turner and Killian 1987), they indirectly monitor an instance of crowd behavior and respond to it, either favorably or unfavorably, by registering their respective views with the media and community officials. Although distal spectators may not affect the course of a single episode of crowd behavior, they can clearly have an impact on the career and character of a series of interconnected crowd episodes.

Social control agents, consisting primarily of police officers and military personnel, constitute the final set of participants relevant to most instances of crowd behavior. Since they are the guardians of public order, their primary aim with respect to crowds is to maintain that order by controlling crowd behavior both spatially and temporally or by suppressing its occurrence. Given this aim, social control agents can clearly have a significant impact on the course and character of crowd behavior. This is evident in most protest demonstrations and victory celebrations, but it is particularly clear in the case of riots, which are often triggered by overzealous police activity and often involve considerable interpersonal violence perpetrated by the police. The urban riots of the 1960s in the United States illustrate both tendencies: police-citizen scuffles occasioned by traffic citation encounters or arrests sometimes functioned as a triggering event (Kerner 1968); and the vast majority of riot-associated deaths were attributed to social control agents (Bergesen 1980; Kerner 1968). This was not the case, however, with the riots in Miami in 1980 and in South Central Los Angeles in 1992, in which the clear majority of deaths were at the hands of civilians (McPhail 1994; Porter and Dunn 1984). Although these different sets of findings caution against premature generalization regarding the attribution of responsibility for riot-related deaths, they do not belie the important role of social control agents in affecting the course and character of crowd episodes (Della Porta and Reiter 1998).

Although there is no consensual taxonomy of crowd behaviors and interacting participation units, the foregoing observations indicate that behavioral and participant heterogeneity are characteristic features of most crowd episodes. In turn, the research on which these observations are based lays to rest the traditional image of crowds as monolithic entities composed of like-minded people engaged in undifferentiated behavior.

CONDITIONS OF EMERGENCE

Under what conditions do individuals come together collectively to engage in crowd task activities constitutive of protest or celebration, and why do these occurrences sometimes turn violent or riotous? Three sets of interacting conditions are discernible in the literature: (1) conditions of conduciveness; (2) precipitating ambiguities or grievances; and (3) conditions for mobilization.

Conditions of Conduciveness. The concept of conduciveness directs attention to structural and cultural factors that make crowd behavior physically and socially possible (Smelser 1963). Conditions of conduciveness constitute the raw material for crowd behavior and include three sets of factors: ecological, technological, and social control. Ecological factors affect the arrangement and distribution of people in space so as to facilitate interaction and communication. One such factor found to be particularly conducive is the existence of large, spatially concentrated populations. The vast majority of campus protest demonstrations in the 1960s occurred on large universities, for example. Similarly, the urban riots of the 1960s typically occurred in densely populated residential areas, where there were large, easily mobilizable black populations. Seymour Spilerman's (1976) aggregate-level research on the occurrence of these riots found an almost linear relationship between the size of a city's black population and the likelihood and number of disorders experienced, thus suggesting that there was a threshold population size below which riots were unlikely. More recent analyses of the 1960 riots have found that "the propensity to riot was a function of far more than simply the number of Blacks available for rioting in a particular city" (Myers 1997, p. 108; Olzak, Shanahan, and McEneaney 1996), but such findings do not suggest that concentrated population density and the prospect of rioting are unrelated. Thus, these findings, in conjunction with the earlier observations, provide support for the hypothesis that, all other things being equal, the greater the population density, the greater the probability of crowd behavior.

The heightened prospect of interpersonal interaction and communication associated with population concentration can also be facilitated by the diffusion of communication technology, namely telephone, radio, television, and Internet access. But neither the diffusion of such technology nor population density guarantee the emergence of crowd behavior in the absence of a system of social control that allows for freedom of assembly and speech. It has been found repeatedly that incidence of public protest against the state diminishes considerably in political systems that prohibit and deal harshly with such crowd behavior, whereas the development of a more permissive attitude toward public protest and a corresponding relaxation of measures of social control is frequently conducive to the development of protest behavior. Two concrete examples of this political-opportunity principle include the proliferation of public protest throughout Eastern Europe in 1989 and 1990 following the break-up of the Soviet Union, and prison riots, which research reveals are sparked in part by the erosion of prison security systems and the increased physical vulnerability of those systems (Useem and Kimball 1989).

Precipitating Events and Conditions. However conducive conditions might be for crowd behavior, it will not occur in the absence of some precipitating event or condition. Although the specific precipitants underlying the emergence of crowd behavior may be quite varied, most are variants of two generic conditions: (1) ambiguity; and (2) grievances against corporate entities, typically the state or some governmental, administrative unit, or against communal or status groups such as ethnic, racial, and religious groups.

Ambiguity is generated by the disruption or breakdown of everyday routines or expectancies, and has long been linked theoretically to the emergence of crowd behavior (Johnson and Feinberg 1990; Turner and Killian 1987). Evidence of its empirical linkage to the emergence of crowd behavior is abundant, as with the materialization of crowds of onlookers at the scene of accidents and fires; the celebrations that sometimes follow high-stakes, unanticipated athletic victories; the collective revelry sometimes associated with the disruption of interdependent networks of institutionalized roles, as in the case of power blackouts and police strikes; and prison riots that frequently follow on the heels of unanticipated change in administrative personnel, procedures, and control.

The existence of grievances against the state or some governmental, administrative unit, or against communal or status groups, can be equally facilitative of crowd behavior, particularly of the protest variety. Grievances against the state or other corporate actors are typically associated with the existence of economic and political inequities that are perceived as unjust or political decisions and policies that are seen as morally bankrupt or advantaging some interests to the exclusion of others. Examples of protest crowds triggered in

part by such grievances include the hostile gatherings of hungry citizens and displaced workers in industrializing Europe; the striking crowds of workers associated with the labor movement; and the mass demonstrations (marching, rallying, picketing, vigiling) associated with the civil rights, student, antiwar, and women's movements of the 1960s and 1970s.

Grievances against communal or status groups appear to occur most often in a context of competition and conflict between two or more ethnic or racial groups. A second generation of quantitative research on urban racial rioting in the United States has shown it to be associated with increasing intergroup competition sparked by patterns of hypersegregation of blacks (Olzak, Shanahan, and McEneaney 1996), heightened nonwhite unemployment (Myers 1997), and rapid ethnic succession (Bergesen and Herman 1998). Indeed, if there is a single structural-based source of grievance associated with intergroup rioting throughout much of modern history, it is probably intergroup competition triggered by ethnic/racial displacement and succession.

Crowd violence—"riotous" task activities such as property destruction, looting, fighting, and sniping—has been an occasional corollary of protest crowds, but it is not peculiar to such crowds. Moreover, the occurrence of crowd violence, whether in association with protest demonstrations or celebrations, is relatively infrequent in comparison to other crowd behaviors (Eisinger 1973; Gamson 1990; Lewis 1982). When it does occur, however, there are two discernible tendencies: interpersonal violence most often results from the dynamic interaction of protestors and police (Kritzer 1977; MacCannell 1973); and property violence, as in the case of riot looting, often tends to be more selective and semi-organized than random and chaotic (Berk and Aldrich 1972; Quarantelli and Dynes 1968; Tierney 1994).

Conditions for Mobilization. A precipitating condition coupled with a high degree of conduciveness is rarely sufficient to produce an instance of crowd behavior. In addition, people have to be assembled or brought into contact with one another, and attention must be focused on the accomplishment of some task. On some occasions in everyday life the condition of assemblage is already met, as in the case of the pedestrian crowd and conventional audience. More often than not, however, protest crowds, large-scale victory celebrations, and riots do not grow out of conventional gatherings but require the rapid convergence of people in time and space. McPhail and David Miller (1973) found this assembling process to be contingent on the receipt of assembling instructions; ready access, either by foot or by other transportation, to the scene of the action; schedule congruence; and relatively free or discretionary time. It can also be facilitated by lifestyle circumstances and social networks. Again, the ghetto riots of the 1960s are a case in point. They typically occurred on weekday evenings or weekends in the summer, times when people were at home, were more readily available to receive instructions, and had ample discretionary time (Kerner 1968).

The focusing of attention typically occurs through some "keynoting" or "framing" process whereby the interpretive gesture or utterance of one or more individuals provides a resonant account or stimulus for action. It can occur spontaneously, as when someone yells "Cops!" or "Fire!"; it can be an unintended consequence of media broadcasts; or it can be the product of prior planning, thus implying the operation of a social movement.

COORDINATION OF CROWD BEHAVIOR

Examination of protest demonstrations, celebratory crowds, and riots reveals in each case that the behaviors in question are patterned and collective rather than random and individualistic. Identification of the sources of coordination has thus been one of the central tasks confronting students of crowd behavior.

Earlier theorists attributed the coordination either to the rapid spread of emotional states and behavior in a contagion-like manner due to the presumably heightened suggestibility of crowd members (LeBon [1895] 1960; Blumer 1951) or to the convergence of individuals who are predisposed to behave in a similar fashion because of common dispositions or background characteristics (Allport 1924; Dollard et al. 1939). Both views are empirically off the mark. They assume a uniformity of action that glosses the existence of various categories of actors, variation in their behaviors, ongoing interaction among them, and the

role this interaction plays in determining the direction and character of crowd behavior. These oversights are primarily due to the perceptual trap of taking the behaviors of the most conspicuous element of the episode—the main task performers—as typifying all categories of actors, thus giving rise to the previously mentioned "illusion of unanimity" (Turner and Killian 1987).

A more modern variant of the convergence argument attributes coordination to a rational calculus in which individuals reach parallel assessments regarding the benefits of engaging in a particular task activity (Berk 1974; Granovetter 1978). Blending elements of this logic with strands of theorizing seemingly borrowed from LeBon and Freud, James Coleman (1990) argues that crowd behavior occurs when individuals make a unilateral transfer of control over their actions. Such accounts are no less troublesome than the earlier ones in that they remain highly individualistic and psychologistic, ignoring the extent to which crowd behavior is the product of collective decision making involving the "framing" and "reframing" of probable costs and benefits and the extent to which this collective decision making frequently has a history involving prior negotiation between various sets of crowd participants.

A sociologically more palatable view holds that crowd behavior is coordinated by definition of the situation that functions in normative fashion by encouraging behavior in accordance with the definition. The collective definition may be situationally emergent (Turner and Killian 1987) or preestablished by prior policing strategies or negotiation among the relevant sets of actors (Della Porta and Reiter 1998; Snow and Anderson 1985). When one or more sets of actors cease to adjust their behaviors to this normative understanding, violence is more likely, especially if the police seek to reestablish normative control, and the episode is likely to be labeled as riotous or mob-like.

Today it is generally conceded that most instances of crowd behavior are normatively regulated, but the dynamics underlying the emergence of such regulations are still not well understood empirically. Consequently, there is growing research interest in detailing the interactional dynamics underlying the process by which coordinating understandings emerge and change. Distinctive to this research is the view that social interaction among relevant sets of actors, rather than the background characteristics and cognitive states of individuals, holds the key to understanding the course and character of crowd behavior (Snow and Anderson 1985; Turner 1994; Waddington, Jones, and Critcher 1989).

THE CORRELATES AND PREDICTORS OF PARTICIPATION

Crowd phenomena associated with collective behavior have been distinguished from everyday, conventionalized crowds, the characteristic features of crowds have been elaborated, the major sets of conditions that facilitate the emergence or occurrence of crowds and riots have been identified, and the issue of behavioral coordination in crowd contexts has been explored. In addressing these orienting issues, only passing reference has been made to factors that make some individuals more likely than other individuals to participate in crowd episodes. For example, it is clear that the odds of participating in some crowd episodes are greater with increasing spatial proximity and access to those episodes, schedule congruence, and discretionary time (McPhail and Miller 1973). As well, individuals whose daily routines and expectancies have been rendered ambiguous or who share grievances that are linked to the occurrence of a crowd episode would appear to be more likely candidates for participation. But both of these sets of conditions typically hold for a far greater number of individuals than those who end up participating in a crowd episode in some capacity other than a social control agent or media representative. So what can be said about the personal and interpersonal correlates or predictors of participation?

There is no simple answer to this question or standard formula for predicting crowd participation. However, research on this question suggests at least four general, sensitizing observations, particularly with respect to participation in protest crowds and riots. The first general observation is that commonsensical psychological indicators of protest and riot participation, such as intense frustration or strong feelings of deprivation, have not been found to be valid or reliable predictors. For example, studies of individual riot participation, which have been numerous, have failed to find consistently significant empirical correlations between measures of frustration or deprivation and participation (McPhail 1994). This is not to suggest that riot or protest participants may not sometimes feel deeply frustrated or deprived as compared to others, but that these psychological states do not reliably explain their participation or typically differentiate them from nonparticipants. Such findings are consistent with the second general observation: There are a diversity of motivations for participation in crowd episodes, ranging from curiosity to exploitation of the situation for personal gain (e.g., fun, material goods) to sympathy with the issue for which the episode is a marker or carrier to embracement of and identification with the cause from either a self-interested or altruistic standpoint (Turner and Killian 1987). That neither a distinctive psychological state or deficit nor a dominant motive have been found to be associated with crowd and riot participation does not mean that psychological or personality factors are without relevance to this issue. To the contrary, one such factor that appears to be consistently associated with participation as a main task performer in protest crowds and riots is the existence of a sense of "personal efficacy"—the belief that one's participation will make a difference, the confidence that one's efforts will contribute to the larger cause (Snow and Oliver 1995). This finding, which constitutes the third general observation regarding participation correlates, makes good sense when considered in conjunction with the fourth general observation: Participants in crowd episodes—whether they are victory celebrations, protest events, or riots—seldom participate alone. Instead, rather than being isolates or loners, they are typically in the company of friends or acquaintances; they are, in other words, part of a social network. Additionally, recruitment into many crowd episodes occurs through the very same social networks (Snow and Oliver 1995). Thus, participation in crowd episodes, particularly planned ones such as protest events, tends to be embedded in social networks, which also function to nurture a greater sense of both personal and collective efficacy. When these factors are coupled with the previously mentioned conditions for assemblage, and either ambiguity or target-specific grievances, participation becomes more likely and perhaps even more predictable.

REFERENCES

Allport, Floyd H. 1924 *Social Psychology*. Boston: Houghton Mifflin.

Bergesen, Albert 1980 "Official Violence During the Watts, Newark, and Detroit Race Riots of the 1960s." In Pat Lauderdale, ed., *A Political Analysis of Deviance*. Minneapolis: University of Minnesota Press.

——, and Max Herman 1998 "Immigration, Race, and Riot: The 1992 Los Angeles Uprising." *American Sociological Review* 63:39–54.

Berk, Richard 1974 "A Gaming Approach to Crowd Behavior." *American Sociological Review* 39:355–373.

——, and Howard Aldrich 1972 "Patterns of Vandalism During Civil Disorders as an Indicator of Selection of Targets." *American Sociological Review* 37:533–547.

Blumer, Herbert 1951 "Collective Behavior." In Alfred McClung Lee, ed., *Principles of Sociology*. New York: Barnes and Noble.

Coleman, James S. 1990 *Foundations of Social Theory*. Cambridge, Mass.: Harvard University Press.

Della Porta, Donatella, and Herbert Reiter (eds.) 1998 *Policing Protest: The Control of Mass Demonstrations in Western Democracies*. Minneapolis: University of Minnesota Press.

Dollard, John, Leonard Doob, Neal Miller, Herbert Mowrer, and Robert Sears 1939 *Frustration and Aggression*. New Haven, Conn.: Yale University Press.

Eisinger, Peter 1973 "The Conditions of Protest Behavior in American Cities." *American Political Science Review* 67:11–28.

Fogelson, Robert M. 1971 *Violence as Protest: A Study of Riots and Ghettos*. New York: Doubleday.

Freud, Sigmund 1921 *Group Psychology and Analysis of the Ego*. London: International Psychoanalytical Press.

Gamson, William 1990 The Strategy of Social Protest, 2nd ed., rev. Homewood, Ill.: Dorsey.

Granovetter, Mark 1978 "Threshold Models of Collective Behavior." *American Journal of Sociology* 83:1420–1443.

Janowitz, Morris 1979 "Collective Racial Violence: A Contemporary History." In Hugh Davis Graham and Ted Gurr, eds., *Violence in America: Historical and Comparative Perspectives*, rev. Beverly Hills, Calif.: Sage.

Johnson, Norris R., and William E. Feinberg 1990 "Ambiguity and Crowds: Results From A Computer Simulation Model." *Research in Social Movements, Conflict and Change* 12:35–66.

Kerner, Otto 1968 *Report of the National Advisory Commission on Civil Disorders*. New York: E.P. Dutton.

Kritzer, Herbert M. 1977 "Political Protest and Political Violence: A Nonrecursive Causal Model." *Social Forces* 55:630–640.

LeBon, Gustave (1895) 1960 *The Crowd: A Study of the Popular Mind*. New York: Viking Press.

Lewis, Jerry 1982 "Fan Violence: An American Social Problem." *Research on Social Problems and Public Policy* 2:175–206.

Lofland, John 1981 "Collective Behavior: The Elementary Forms." In Morris Rosenberg and Ralph Turne, eds., *Social Psychology: Sociological Perspectives*. New York: Basic Books.

MacCannell, Dean 1973 "Nonviolent Action as Theater." Nonviolent Action Research Project Series No. 10, Haverford College Center for Nonviolent Conflict Resolution, Haverford, Pa.

Marx, Gary 1972 "Issueless Riots." In James F. Short and Marvin E. Wolfgang, eds., *Collective Violence*. Chicago: Aldine-Atherton.

McPhail, Clark 1994 "The Dark Side of Purpose: Individual and Collective Violence in Riots." *Sociological Quarterly* 35:1–32.

—— 1991 *The Myth of the Madding Crowd*. New York: Aldine de Gruyter.

——, and David L. Miller 1973 "The Assembling Process: A Theoretical and Empirical Examination." *American Sociological Review* 38:721–735.

McPhail, Clark, and Ronald T. Wohlstein 1983 "Individual and Collective Behaviors Within Gatherings, Demonstrations, and Riots." *Annual Review of Sociology* 9:579–600.

Myers, Daniel J. 1997 "Racial Rioting in the 1960s: An Event History Analysis of Local Conditions." *American Sociological Review* 62:94–112.

Olzak, Susan, Suzanne Shanahan, and Elizabeth H. McEneaney 1996 "Poverty, Segregation, and Race Riots: 1960–1993." *American Sociological Review* 61:590–613.

Porter, Bruce, and Marvin Dunn 1984 *The Miami Riot of 1980: Crossing the Bounds*. Lexington, Mass.: Lexington Books.

Quarantelli, Enrico L., and Russell Dynes 1968 "Looting in Civil Disorders: An Index of Social Change." In Louis Masotti and Don R. Bowen, eds., *Riots and Rebellion*. Beverly Hills, Calif.: Sage.

Smelser, Neil 1963 *Theory of Collective Behavior*. New York: Free Press.

Snow, David A., and Leon Anderson 1985 "Field Methods and Conceptual Advances in Crowd Research." Paper presented at Conference on Research Methods in Collective Behavior and Social Movements,

Collective Behavior/Social Movements Section of the American Sociological Association, Bowling Green State University.

Snow David A., and Pamela E. Oliver 1995 "Social Movements and Collective Behavior: Social Psychological Dimensions and Considerations." In Karen S. Cook, Gary Alan Fine, James S. House, eds., *Sociological Perspectives on Social Psychology*. Boston: Allyn and Bacon.

Snow, David A., Louis A. Zurcher, and Robert Peters 1981 "Victory Celebrations as Theater: A Dramaturgical Approach to Crowd Behavior." *Symbolic Interaction* 4:21–42.

Spilerman, Seymour 1976 "Structural Characteristics of Cities and the Severity of Racial Disorders." *American Sociological Review* 35:627–649.

Tierney, Kathleen J. 1994 "Property Damage and Violence: A Collective Behavior Analysis. In Mark Baldassare, ed., *The Los Angeles Riots: Lessons for the Urban Future*. Boulder, Colo.: Westwood Press.

Tilly, Charles 1978 *From Mobilization to Revolution*. Reading, Mass.: Addison-Wesley.

Turner, Ralph H. 1994 "Race Riots Past and Present: A Culture-Collective Behavior Approach." *Symbolic Interaction* 17:309–324.

—— 1969 "The Public Perception of Protest." *American Sociological Review* 34:815–831.

——, and Lewis Killian (1957, 1972) 1987 *Collective Behavior*, 3rd ed. Englewood Cliffs, N.J.: Prentice-Hall.

Useem, Bert, and Peter Kimball 1989 *States of Siege: U.S. Prison Riots 1971–1986*. New York: Oxford University Press.

Waddington, David, Karen Jones, and Chas Critcher 1989 *Flashpoints: Studies in Public Disorder*. London: Routledge.

Walker, Daniel (ed.) 1968 *Rights in Conflict*. New York: Grossett and Dunlop.

Weller, Jack, and Enrico L. Quarantelli 1973 "Neglected Characteristics of Collective Behavior." *American Journal of Sociology* 79:665–685.

Wright, Sam 1978 *Crowds and Riots: A Study in Social Organization*. Beverly Hills, Calif.: Sage.

DAVID A. SNOW
RONNELLE PAULSEN

CULTS

See Religious Organizations; Religious Orientations; Religious Movements.

CULTURE

To produce a definition of culture, one can examine the concept in the abstract, that is, explore the concept theoretically from a variety of standpoints and then justify the definition that emerges through deductive logic. Or one can explore how the concept is used in practice, that is, describe how sociologists, both individually and collectively, define culture in the research process and analyze how they inductively construct a shared definition. This essay takes the latter collective-inductive approach to defining culture. Such an approach is inherently sociological and does not presume to produce an independent definition for the field, rather it seeks to document how successful participants in the field have been in producing a shared definition for themselves. To produce such a "working" definition of culture, one starts by examining the social science roots that have helped determine the current status of the sociology of culture.

The focus on culture in sociology has flourished over the past twenty years, as evidenced by the fact that the Culture Section in the American Sociological Association has become one of the largest and is still one of the fastest-growing sections in the discipline. The growth of interest in culture is also nicely documented by the number of survey review articles and books written during this period (e.g., Denzin 1996; Crane 1994, 1992; Hall and Neitz 1993; Munch and Smelser 1992; Peterson 1990, 1989, 1979; Alexander and Seidman 1990; Wuthnow and Witten 1988; Blau 1988; Mukerji and Schudson 1986). As is clear from the reviews, interest in cultural analysis has grown significantly. The focus on culture in all spheres of research has increased tremendously; and culture is now readily accepted as a level of explanation in its own right. Even in traditionally materialist-oriented research arenas, such as stratification and Marxist studies, cultural activities and interests are not treated as subordinate to economic explanations in current research (e.g., Halle 1994; Nelson and Grossberg 1988; Bourdieu 1984; Williams 1981, 1977). Cultural studies and analysis have become one of the most fertile areas in sociology.

The rapid growth in the focus on culture and cultural explanation has produced some definitional boundary problems. The term *culture* has been used in contemporary sociological research to describe everything from elite artistic activities (Becker 1982) to the values, styles, and ideology of day-to-day conduct (Swidler 1986). Along with art and everyday conduct, included among the "mixed bag" of research that takes place under the auspices of the sociology of culture is work in science (Latour 1987; Star 1989), religion (Neitz 1987), law (Katz 1988), media (Schudson 1978; Gitlin 1985; Tuchman 1978), popular culture (Peterson 1997; Weinstein 1991; Chambers 1986), and work organization (Fine 1996; Lincoln and Kalleberg 1990).

With such an extensive variety in the empirical focus of research in culture, the question for many participants in the field is how to translate this eclecticism into a coherent research field. This goal has not yet been reached, but while a coherent concept of culture is still evolving and the boundaries of the current field of sociology of culture are still fluid and expanding, it is possible to explore how different types of researchers in the social sciences, both currently and historically, have approached the concept of culture. In this inventory process, a better understanding of the concept of culture will emerge, that is, what different researchers believe the concept of culture includes, what the concept excludes, and how the distinction between categories has been made. This essay will provide a historical overview of the two major debates on the appropriate focus and limitations of the definition of culture, and then turn to the contemporary social context in an effort to clarify the issues underlying the current concept of culture.

THE CULTURE–SOCIAL STRUCTURE DEBATE

From the turn of the century until the 1950s, the definition of culture was embroiled in a dialogue that sought to distinguish the concepts of culture and social structure. This distinction was a major bone of contention among social scientists, most noticeably among anthropologists divided between the cultural and social traditions of anthropology. Researchers in the cultural or ethnological tradition, such as Franz Boas (1896/1940), Bronislaw Malinowski (1927, 1931), Margaret Mead (1928, 1935), Alfred Kroeber (1923/1948, 1952), and Ruth Benedict (1934) believed culture was the central concept in social science. "Culturalists"

maintained that culture is primary in guiding all patterns of behavior, including who interacts with whom, and should therefore be given priority in theories about the organization of society. This position was countered by researchers in the structural tradition, such as A.R. Radcliffe-Brown ([1952] 1961) and E. E. Evans-Pritchard (1937, 1940) from the British school of social anthropology, and Claude Levi-Strauss ([1953] 1963) in French structuralism. "Structuralists" contended that social structure was the primary focus of social science and should be given priority in theories about society because social structure (e.g., kinship) determines patterns of social interaction and thought. Both schools had influential and large numbers of adherents.

The culturalists took a holistic approach to the concept of culture. Stemming from Edward Tylor's classic definition, culture was ". . . that complex whole which includes knowledge, belief, art, morals, law, custom, and any other capabilities and habits acquired by man as a member of society" ([1871] 1924, p.1). This definition leaves little out, but the orientation of the late nineteenth century intended the concept of culture to be as inclusive as possible. Culture is what distinguishes man as a species from other species. Therefore culture consists of all that is produced by human collectivities, that is, all of social life. The focus here stems from the "nature" vs. "nurture" disputes common during this period. Anything that differentiates man's accomplishments from biological and evolutionary origins was relevant to the concept of culture. That includes religion as well as kinship structures, language as well as nation-states.

Following Boas, the study of culture was used to examine different types of society. All societies have cultures, and variations in cultural patterns helped further the argument that culture, not nature, played the most significant role in governing human behavior. In addition, the cultural variances observed in different societies helped break down the nineteenth-century anthropological notion of "the psychic unity of mankind, the unity of human history, and the unity of culture" (Singer 1968, p. 527). The pluralistic and relativistic approaches to culture that followed emphasized a more limited, localized conception. Culture was what produced a distinctive identity for a society, socializing members for greater internal homogeneity and identifying outsiders. Culture is thus treated as differentiating concept, providing recognition factors for internal cohesion and external discrimination.

Although this tradition of ethnographic research on culture tended to be internal and localized, what is termed an "emic" approach in cognitive anthropology (Goodenough 1956), by the 1940s there emerged a strong desire among many anthropologists to develop a comparative "etic" approach to culture, that is, construct a generalized theory of cultural patterns. In the comparison of hundreds of ethnographies written in this period, A.L. Kroeber and Clyde Kluckhohn sought to build such a general definition of culture. They wrote,

> *Culture consists of patterns, explicit and implicit, of and for behavior acquired and transmitted by symbols, constituting the distinctive achievement of human groups, including their embodiments in artifacts; the essential core of culture consists of traditional (i.e., historically derived and selected) ideas and especially their attached values; culture systems may, on the one hand, be considered as products of action, on the other as conditioning elements of further action* ([1952] 1963, p. 181).

Milton Singer (1968) characterized this "pattern theory" definition as a condensation of what most American anthropologists in the 1940s and 1950s called culture. It includes behavior, cultural objects, and cognitive predispositions as part of the concept, thus emphasizing that culture is both a product of social action and a process that guides future action. The pattern theory stated simply that behavior follows a relatively stable routine, from the simplest levels of custom in dress and diet to more complex levels of organization in political, economic, and religious life. The persistence of specific patterns is variable in different arenas and different societies, but larger configurations tend to be more stable, changing incrementally unless redirected by external forces. In addition, the theory emphasized that the culture from any given society can be formally described, that is, it can be placed in formal categories representing different spheres of social life to facilitate comparison between societies. As such, universal patterns of culture can be constructed.

In comparison, anthropological structuralists in this period conceive of culture less comprehensively. The structuralists' concept of culture is made distinct through emphasis on a new concept of social structure. Largely through the efforts of Radcliffe-Brown, a theory emerged that argues social structure is more appropriately represented by a network or system of social relations than a set of norms. The structuralist argument is intended to clarify how actors in a society actively produce and are socially produced by their cultural context. By distinguishing the actors and interaction in a social system from the behavioral norms, structuralists seek to establish a referent for social structure that is analytically independent of the culture and artifacts produced in that system. The production of culture is thus grounded clearly in an international framework. Norms of interaction are also produced by interacting participants, but the question of causal primacy between culture and social structure can be considered separately. The initial effort here is simply not to reify the origins of culture.

The exact relationship of culture and social structure, however, becomes the central issue of the structuralist/culturalist debate. For example, how to identify the boundaries of a society one is researching is problematic when the society is not an isolate. Structuralists tend to give social relations, that is, the extent of a network, priority in identifying boundaries, while culturalists focus on the extent of particular types of cultural knowledge or practices. Since both elements are obviously operating interdependently, the efforts to disentangle these concepts make little headway. The arguments to establish causal priority for one concept vis-à-vis the other settle into a fairly predictable exchange. Structuralists base their priority claims on the fact that the interaction of actors in a society is empirically preliminary to the development and application of cultural elements. Culturalists respond that interaction itself is at least partially cultural phenomenon, and that in most complex societies cultural patterns have been well established prior to ongoing social relationships.

By the late 1950s, the concept of culture was becoming increasingly important to sociologists. To help resolve the now tired debate over cultural and structural foci and precedence, A.L. Kroeber and Talcott Parsons published a report in the

American Sociological Review titled "The Concepts of Culture and Social System" (1958), which seeks to establish some ground rules for differentiating the two concepts. At least for sociologists, many of whom identify explicitly with the structural-functional theories of the anthropological structuralists, acknowledgement of a separate social system component that delimits the scope of culture is not difficult. More difficult is ascertaining where the appropriate limits for the concept of culture lie within this domain. Kroeber and Parsons suggest restricting the usage of culture to, "transmitted and created content and patterns of values, ideas, and other symbolic-meaningful systems as factors in the shaping of human behavior and the artifacts produced behavior" (1958, p. 583). This definition emphasized the predispositional aspect of a cultural referent, limiting the scope of culture to a cognitive perspective, and concentrates on a carefully worded description of "symbolic-meaningful systems" as the appropriate referent for culture. While no longer the omnibus conception of a traditional, Tylor-derived approach, this type of cultural analysis is still potentially applicable to any realm of social activity.

THE HIGH-MASS CULTURE DEBATE

In the 1950s and early 1960s, the concept of culture became enmeshed in a new debate that like the previously documented dialogue has both influential and significant numbers of participants on each side of the dispute. Sociologists, however, are more central to the discussion, pitting those who support a broadly conceived, anthropological interpretation of culture that places both commonplace and elite activities in the same category, against a humanities oriented conception of culture that equates the identification of cultural activity with a value statement. This debate attempts to do two things: to classify different types of cultural activity, and to distinguish a purely descriptive approach to the concept of culture from an axiological approach that defines culture through an evaluative process.

That an axiological approach to culture can be considered legitimate by a "scientific" enterprise is perhaps surprising to contemporary sociologists entrenched in the positivistic interpretation of science, yet a central issue for many sociologists in

this period was how and whether to approach questions of moral values. For example, the critical theorist Leo Lowenthal (1950) characterized this period of social science as "applied ascetism" and stated that the moral or aesthetic evaluation of cultural products and activities is not only sociologically possible, but also should be a useful tool in the sociological analysis of cultural differentiation.

These evaluative questions certainly play a part in the analysis of "mass culture," a term that the critic Dwight McDonald explains is used to identify articles of culture that are produced for mass consumption, "like chewing gum" (McDonald 1953, p. 59). A number of commentators, including both sociologists and humanists, observe the growth of mass culture production in the post-World War II United Stated with a mixture of distaste and alarm. The concern of McDonald and critics like him is the decline of intrinsic value in cultural artifacts, a decline in quality that stems from, or is at least attributed to, a combination of economic and social factors associated with the growth of capitalism. For example, mass culture critics argue that the unchecked growth of capitalism in the production and distribution phases of culture industries leads to a "massification" of consumption patterns. Formerly localized, highly differentiated, and competitive markets become dominated by a single corporate actor who merges different sectors of the consumer landscape and monopolizes production resources and distribution outlets. Within these giant culture industry organizations the demand for greater efficiency and the vertical integration of production lead to a bureaucratically focused standardization of output. Both processes function to stamp out cultural differences and create greater homogeneity in moral and aesthetic values, all at the lowest common denominator.

Regardless of the causes of the mass culture phenomena, the critics of mass culture believe it to be a potentially revolutionary force that will transform the values of society. One critic states that "mass culture is a dynamic, revolutionary force, breaking down the old barriers of class, tradition, taste, and dissolving all cultural distinctions. It mixes and scrambles everything together, producing what might be called homogenized culture. . . It thus destroys all values, since value judgements imply discrimination" (McDonald 1953, p. 62).

In launching this attack, mass culture opponents see themselves as the saviors of a "true" or "high" culture (e.g., McDonald, Greenberg, Berelson, and Howe; see Rosenberg and White 1957). They argue that the consumption of mass culture undermines the very existence of legitimate high culture, that is, the elite arts and folk cultures. Without the ability to differentiate between increasingly blurred lines of cultural production, the average consumer turns toward mass culture due to its immediate accessibility. Further, simply through its creation, mass culture devalues elite art and folk cultures by borrowing the themes and devices of different cultural traditions and converting them into mechanical, formulaic systems (Greenberg 1946). Thus critics of mass culture argue that it is critical for the health of society to discriminate between types of culture.

Defenders of mass culture, or at least those who feel the attack on mass culture is too extreme, respond that mass culture critics seek to limit the production and appreciation of culture to an elitist minority. They contend that the elitist criticism of culture is ethnocentric and that not only is mass, popular, or public culture more diverse than given credit for (e.g., Lang 1957; Kracuer 1949), but also the benefits of mass cultural participation far outweigh the limitations of a mass media distribution system (White 1956; Seldes 1957). Post-World War II America experienced an economic boom that sent its citizens searching for a variety of new cultural outlets. The increase in cultural participation certainly included what some critics might call "vulgar" activities, but it also included a tremendous increase in audiences for the arts across the board. Essentially mass culture defenders assert that the argument over the legitimacy of mass culture comes down to a matter of ideology, one that positions the elitist minority against the growing democratization of culture.

To extricate themselves from this axiological conundrum, many sociologists of culture retreated from a morally evaluative stance to a normative one. As presented by Gertrude Jaeger and Philip Selznick (1964), the normative sociological approach to culture, while still evaluative, seeks to combine anthropological and humanist conceptions of culture through a diagnostic analysis of cultural experience. The emphasis here is on elaborating the nature of "symbolically meaningful" experience, the same focus for culture that Kroeber and Parsons (1958) take in their differentiation of culture and social system. To do this, Jager and Selznick adopt a pragmatist perspective (Dewey 1958) that accords symbolic status to cultural objects or events through a social signification process. Interacting individuals create symbols through the communication of meaningful experience, using both denotative and connotative processes. By creating symbols, interacting individuals create culture. Thus the definition of culture becomes: "Culture consists of everything that is produced by, and is capable of sustaining, shared symbolic experience" (Jaeger and Selznick 1964, p. 663). In establishing this sociological definition of culture emphasizing the shared symbolic experience, Jaeger and Selznick also seek to maintain a humanist-oriented capability to distinguish between high and mass culture without marginalizing the focus on high culture. Following Dewey, they argue that the experience of art takes place on a continuum of cultural experience that differs in intensity from ordinary symbolic activities, but has essentially the same basis for the appreciation of meaning. Art or high culture is simply a more "effective" symbol, combining "economy of statement with richness of expression" (Jaeger and Selznick 1964, p. 664). As such, art, like all culture, is identified through the normative evaluation of experience.

In sum, the high culture-mass culture debate shifted the focus on the concept of culture from a question of appropriate scope to a question of appropriate values. From a functionalist point of view, the health of a society's culture is not simply an issue of what type of values are advocated, but of how culture serves a moral and integrative function. Yet the mass culture critique was often unable to distinguish the cultural values of elite intellectuals from the effect of these values on society. To escape from this ethnocentric quagmire, contemporary sociologists have generally turned away from an evaluative position toward culture.

THE CONTEMPORARY APPROACH TO CULTURE: MAPPING THE TERRAIN

As mentioned at the beginning of this essay, the contemporary approach to culture is quite eclectic. Despite the elaborate historical lineage of the concept, there is no current, widely accepted, composite resolution for the definition of culture.

Instead, culture is still currently defined through an extensive variety of perspectives, sanctioning a broad, historically validated range of options. While the omnibus definition from the cultural anthropology tradition has been generally relegated to introductory texts, and the elitist attack on mass culture has been largely replaced by an antiethnocentric, relativist position open to a wide spectrum of symbolic arenas and perspectives, many of the elements of these old debates still appear in new cultural analyses.

For example, as categorized by Richard Peterson introducing a review of new studies in cultural analysis at the beginning of the 1990s, culture tends to be used two ways in sociological research; as a "code of conduct embedded in or constitutive of social life," and as symbolic products of group activity" (Peterson 1990, p. 498). The first perspective is clearly indebted to the traditional cultural anthropology approach and indeed is used to analyze and characterize social units ranging from whole societies (e.g., Cerulo 1995; Bellah et al. 1985) to specific subcultures (e.g., Hebdige 1990, 1979; Willis 1977). Empirical applications using this perspective are also made to geographically dispersed social worlds that organize collective activities (e.g., Lofland 1993 on the peace movement; Fine 1987 on Little League baseball; Latour and Woolgar 1979 on scientific research in biology; Traweek 1988 on scientific research in physics). The second perspective takes the more concrete course of treating culture as specific socially constructed symbols and emphasizes the production and meaning of these specific forms of cultural expression. Most examples of this latter form of cultural research are conducted in substantive arenas collectively known as the "production of culture" (Peterson 1979; Crane 1992), however, the range of empirical focus for this perspective is considerable and includes research in such areas as the moral discourse on the abortion issue (Luker 1984), the politics and aesthetics of artistic evaluation and reception (DeNora 1995; Lang and Lang 1990; Griswold 1986), and the motivational and ideological context of organizational, professional, and work cultures (e.g., Fine 1996; Martin 1992; Katz 1999; Fantasia 1988; Harper 1987; Burawoy 1979).

From the array of activities mentioned above, it is clear that the contemporary concept of culture in sociology does not exclude any particular empirical forms of activity, except perhaps through an emphasis on shared or collective practices, thus discounting purely individual foci. Since all collective social practices are potentially symbolic and therefore culturally expressive, any collective activity can be reasonably studied under the rubric of the sociology of culture. This "open borders" philosophy has at times made it difficult for participants in the sociology of culture to establish any kind of nomothetic perspective for cultural theory. The vast differentiation and sheer complexity of the expression of culture in various forms of social life resists ready categorization. Instead, participants in the sociology of culture have usually opted for the preliminary step of surveying and mapping the terrain of research in the sociology of culture with the goal of helping to define emerging theoretical perspectives in the field. Two particularly informative efforts are the contributions of John Hall and Mary Jo Neitz (1993) and Diana Crane (1992, 1994).

In *Culture: Sociological Perspectives* (1993), Hall and Neitz provide an excellent overview of the substantive and theoretical directions in which research in the sociology of culture has proliferated. They identify five "analytic frames" (p. 17) through which researchers can focus on particular aspects of culture and that emphasize associated processes of inquiry. The first frame is a focus on "institutional structures": that is, research on culture specifically linked with social institutions and such issues as the construction of social and personal identity and conventional or moral conduct (e.g., Bellah et al. 1985; Gilligan 1982; Warner 1988). In the second analytic frame, Hall and Neitz describe "cultural history" and the influence of past cultural practices on the present. Research in this area includes a focus on the significance of rituals (e.g., Douglas 1973; Goffman 1968, 1971; Neitz 1987), the effects of rationalization on social processes and cultural consumption (e.g., Foucault 1965; Mukerji 1983; Born 1995), and the creation of mass culture (e.g., Ewen 1976; Schudson 1984). In the third analytic frame, Hall and Neitz focus on "the production and distribution of culture" with a special emphasis on stratification and power issues. Research in this area includes work on the socioeconomic differentiation of cultural strata (e.g., Gans 1974; Bourdieu 1984; Lamont 1992), gender and ethnic cultural differentiation and their effect on inequality (e.g., Radway 1984; Lamont and Fournier 1992), and the production of culture (e.g., Becker 1982; Gilmore 1987; Hirsch 1972; Coser, Kadushin, and Powell 1982; Faulkner 1983; Crane 1987). The fourth analytic frame, "audience effects," looks at how cultural objects affect the people who consume them and the precise patterns of shared meaning and interpretive ideology that provide a compatible environment for the popular and critical success of particular cultural forms (e.g., Wuthnow 1987; Baxandall 1985; Long 1985). Finally the fifth analytic frame, "meaning and social action," refers to how actors in varied mainstream and subcultural settings use culture to guide behavior and establish social identity. In a range of ethnic, political, and ideological contexts, participants use visible expressive symbols and styles to assert cultural difference and communicate the social and personal significance of cultural objects (e.g., Rushing 1988; Ginsberg 1990; Schwartz 1991; Fine 1987).

These frames serve different purposes. For the nonsociologist or for sociologists from outside the field of culture, they provide a guide to current cultural research and a reasonably accurate descriptive picture of research segmentation within the field. For the sociologist of culture, however, these frames represent not only a "division of labor in sociohistorical inquiry, in the sense that any particular frame seems to generate boundaries. . . "(within in the field), as Hall and Neitz claim (1993, p. 19), but a strategy to bring analytic coherence to a field that has experienced remarkable growth and empirical diffusion over a relatively short period. As such, in the future these frames may emerge through collective activity as problem areas within the field of culture that will guide empirical and methodological tendencies within particular research communities and influence theoretical interaction, that is, co-citation among researchers. The precise impact in the field, however, still remains to be seen.

A somewhat different mapping, primarily in terms of theoretical emphasis, is offered by Diana Crane in her book *The Production of Culture* (1992) and through her efforts as editor of *The Sociology of Culture: Emerging Theoretical Perspectives* (1994). Like Hall and Neitz, Crane seeks to help codify research segmentation in the field of culture, but she does not try to accomplish this daunting task simply by producing a comprehensive survey of current research in the field. Instead, she attempts to give the reader a guide to theoretical issues in the sociology of culture, particularly the place of the concept of culture in the discipline of sociology as a whole, and how the centrality of culture as a variable in mainstream sociological models will determine the significance of future research in the field.

To start, Crane argues that culture has traditionally been regarded as "peripheral" to mainstream concerns in American sociology because of its relationship to classical theory (i.e., Marx, Weber, Durkheim). In comparison to the emphasis by these theorists on social structure, organization, and market forces, cultural elements have been consistently treated as secondary in their impact on peoples' behavior and attitudes, particularly surrounding significant life issues (e.g., economic considerations). One reason for this secondary status may be the difficulty classical and mainstream theorists have in conceptualizing and documenting everyday cultural practices. Crane states, "To American and some British structuralists, culture as a concept lacks a suitably rigorous definition" (Crane 1994, p. 2). And from Archer (1988, p. 1), "the notion of culture remains inordinately vague. . . In every way, 'culture' is the poor relation of 'structure.'" Thus culture, approached as the values, norms, beliefs, and attitudes of a population or subgroup, is treated as "an implicit feature of social life. . ." (Wuthnow and Witten 1988, p. 50–51), difficult to put one's finger on, and therefore difficult to document through specific empirical referents.

But Crane argues that culture in contemporary society is much more than implicit features. She states, "Culture today is expressed and negotiated almost entirely through culture as explicit social constructions or products, in other words, through *recorded culture*, culture that is recorded either in print, film, artifacts or, most recently, electronic media" (Crane 1994, p. 2). Further, contemporary sociologists of culture have tended to focus on this "recorded culture" as the principal empirical referent through which various types of contemporary culture are expressed and thus can easily be explored. Not surprisingly then, the primary direction through which the new sociology of culture has proliferated is in areas like art, science, popular culture, religion, media, technology, and other social worlds where recorded forms of culture are readily accessible. These culture subfields have become the central substantive foci through which the field as a whole has undertaken to build theoretical coherence.

At the same time outside the boundaries of the field of culture per se, it is also clear from recent research in the 1990s that the concept of culture has gained significant relevance in many mainstream areas of the discipline that have traditionally been dominated by macrostructuralist approaches. For example, in both Ewa Morawska and Willfried Spohn's (1994), and Mabel Berezin's (1994) contributions to Crane's *The Sociology of Culture: Emerging Theoretical Perspectives*, the impact of cultural forces are discussed in a variety of macroinstitutional contexts. Morawska and Spohn's focus on examples from the historical perspective includes research on the effect of ideology in the macrostructural analysis of revolution and social change (e.g., Sewell 1985; Skocpol 1985; Goldstone 1991), issues of working-class consciousness and capitalist development (e.g., Aminzade 1981; Calhoun 1982), and the articulation of new forms of religious and ideological doctrines in a social-institutional context (e.g., Wuthnow 1989; Zaret 1985). Berezin's chapter examines the relationship of culture and politics in macromodels of political development and state formation (e.g., Greenfeld 1992; Mitchell 1991). Additional examples in organizational or economic contexts (e.g., Dobbin 1994; Granovetter 1985) only further emphasize the point, that the expanding application of cultural analysis to mainstream models means that for many sociologists, culture is more an explanatory perspective than a substantive area of study. As such, future limitations on the explanatory potential of cultural analysis in sociology will likely be conceptual, not empirical, and the above research suggests a broadly fertile spectrum of empirical possibilities.

Finally, a significant elaboration of the explanatory potential of cultural analysis has taken place in a field organized largely outside the discipline of sociology. "Cultural studies," identifying a loosely connected, interdisciplinary network of scholars from a wide spectrum of perspectives, including the humanities, the social sciences, the arts, and various status-specific programs (e.g., ethnic studies, feminist studies, gay and lesbian studies), has produced a tremendous number of new kinds of cultural analyses that have implications for the sociology of culture. The approach to cultural analysis, however, is often radically different, both empirically and theoretically, than that conventionally used by sociologists. Cultural studies approaches range from a cultural text-based analysis that interprets meaning and sources of social influence directly from cultural objects (e.g., Hooks 1994; Giroux 1992; see Fiske 1994), to complex interpretative decodings of narratives around issues such as identity politics (e.g., Trinh 1989; Hall 1992) and postcolonial repression and resistance (e.g., Appadurai 1990; Grossberg et al. 1992). As a consequence, the history and emerging relationship of cultural studies to sociology is rather piecemeal. Indeed, Norman Denzin (1996) characterizes the potential association to be one of "colonization"; that is, "the attempt to locate and place cultural studies on the boundaries and margins of academic, cultural sociology" (Denzin 1996, p. XV). Others see the possibility of more reciprocal exchange with the possibility of a "revitalization" for sociological cultural perspectives (Seidman 1996). Whichever way the relationship develops, it is clear that efforts to rethink the concept of culture, the impact of cultural values, and approaches to cultural analysis that take place outside of sociology and even outside of academia will have an invigorating effect on the sociological conceptualization of culture. These battles (i.e., "culture wars") already have had important consequences for policy and resource allocation in education (e.g., Nolan 1996; Hunter 1991). There is no reason to think that sociology will or should be immune to these external influences.

In sum, there is a new appreciation of the salience of culture as an explanatory perspective in contemporary sociological research. Whether it involves the convention-setting influence of art worlds, the moral authority of organizational cultures, or the facilitation of class privileges through habitus, the concept of culture is used to explain behavior and social structure from a distinct and powerful perspective. The future elaboration of this perspective in sociology looks very promising.

REFERENCES

Alexander, Jeffrey C., and Steve Seidman (eds.) 1990 *Culture and Society*. Cambridge, Eng./New York: Cambridge University Press.

Aminzade, Ronald 1981 *Class, Politics and Early Industrial Capitalism*. Albany: SUNY Press.

Appadurai, A. 1990 "Disjuncture and Difference in the Global Cultural Economy." *Public Culture* 2:1–24.

Archer, Margaret 1988 *Culture and Agency*. New York: Cambridge University Press.

Baxandall, Michael 1985 *Patterns of Intention*. New Haven: Yale University Press.

Becker, Howard S. 1982 *Art Worlds*. Berkeley: University of California Press.

Bellah, Robert, Richard Madsen, William Sullivan, Ann Swidler, and Steven Tipton 1985 *Habits of the Heart*. Berkeley: University of California Press.

Benedict, Ruth 1934 *Patterns of Culture*. Boston: Houghton Mifflin.

Berezin, Mabel 1994 "Fissured Terrain: Methodological Approaches and Research Styles in Culture and Politics." In Diana Crane, ed., *The Sociology of Culture: Emerging Theoretical Perspectives*. Oxford: Basil Blackwell.

Blau, Judith 1988 "Study of the Arts: A Reappraisal." *Annual Review of Sociology* 14:269–292.

Boas, Franz (1896) 1940 "The Limitations of the Comparative Method of Anthropology." Reprinted in Boas, *Race, Language, and Culture*. New York: Macmillan.

Born, Georgina 1995 *Rationalizing Culture*. Berkeley: University of California Press.

Bourdieu, Pierre 1984 *Distinction*. Cambridge, Mass.: Harvard University Press.

Burawoy, Michael 1979 *Manufacturing Consent*. Chicago: University of Chicago Press.

Calhoun, Craig 1982 *The Question of Class Struggle*. Chicago: University of Chicago Press.

Cerulo, Karen 1995 *Identity Designs: The Sights and Sounds of a Nation*. New Brunswick, N.J.: Rutgers University Press.

Chambers, Iain 1986 *Popular Culture*. London: Methuen.

Coser, Lewis, Charles Kadushin, and Walter Powell 1982. *Books: The Culture and Commerce of Publishing*. New York: Basic Books.

Crane, Diana (ed.) 1994 *The Sociology of Culture: Emerging Theoretical Perspective*. Oxford: Basil Blackwell.

—— 1992 *The Production of Culture*. Newbury Park, Calif.: Sage.

—— 1987 *The Transformation of the Avant-Garde*. Chicago: University of Chicago Press.

Denzin, Norman 1996 *Cultural Studies: A Research Volume*. Greenwich, Conn.: JAI Press.

DeNora, Tia 1995 *Beethoven and the Construction of Genius*. Berkeley: University of California Press.

Dewey, John 1958 *Art as Experience*. New York: Capricorn Books.

Dobbin, Frank 1994 *Forging Industrial Policy: The United States, France, and Britain in the Railway Age*. New York: Cambridge University Press.

Douglas, Mary 1973 *Natural Symbols: Explorations in Cosmology*. New York: Vintage Books.

Dubin, Steve 1992 *Arresting Images: Impolitic Art and Uncivil Action*. New York: Routledge.

Evans-Prichard, E. E. 1940 *The Nuer*. London: Oxford University Press.

—— 1937 *Witchcraft, Oracles and Magic Among the Azande*. Oxford: Clarendon Press.

Ewen, Stuart 1976 *Captains of Consciousness: Advertising and the Social Roots of the Consumer Culture*. New York: McGraw Hill.

Fantasia, Rick 1988 *Cultures of Solidarity*. Berkeley: University of California Press.

Faulkner, Robert 1983 *Music on Demand*. New Brunswick, NJ: Transaction.

Fine, Gary Alan 1996 *Kitchens*. Berkeley: University of California Press.

—— 1987 *With the Boys*. Chicago: University of Chicago Press.

Fiske, John 1994 "Audiencing: Cultural Practices and Cultural Studies." In Norman Denzin and Yvonne Lincoln, eds., *Handbook of Qualitative Research*. Thousand Oaks, Calif.: Sage.

Foucault, Michel 1965 *Madness and Civilization*. New York: Pantheon.

Gans, Herbert J. 1974 *Popular Culture and High Culture*. New York: Basic Books.

Gilligan, Carol 1982 *In a Different Voice*. Cambridge, Mass.: Harvard University Press.

Gilmore, Samuel 1987 "Coordination and Convention: The Organization of the Concert Art World." *Symbolic Interaction* 10:209–227.

Ginsberg, Faye 1990 *Contested Lives*. Berkeley: University of California Press.

Giroux, Henry 1992 "Resisting Difference: Cultural Studies and the Discourse of Critical Pedagogy." In Larry Grossberg et al., eds., *Cultural Studies*. New York: Routledge.

Gitlin, Todd 1985 *Inside Prime Time*. New York: Pantheon.

Goffman, Erving 1971 *Relations in Public*. New York: Harper and Row.

—— 1968 *Interaction Ritual*. Garden City, N.Y.: Anchor Books.

Goldstone, Jack 1991 *Revolution and Rebellion in the Early Modern World*. Berkeley: University of California Press.

Goodenough, Ward 1956 "Componential Analysis and the Study of Meaning." *Language* 32:22–37.

Granovetter, Mark 1985 "Economic Action and Social Structure: The Problem of Embeddedness." *American Journal of Sociology* 91:481–510.

Greenberg, Clement 1946 "Avant-Garde and Kitsch." *The Partisan Reader* 378–389.

Greenfeld, Liah 1992 *Nationalism: Five Roads to Modernity* Cambridge, Mass.: Harvard University Press.

Griswold, Wendy 1986 *Renaissance Revivals*. Chicago: University of Chicago Press.

Grossberg, Larry, et al. 1992. *Cultural Studies*. New York: Routledge.

Hall, John, and Mary Jo Neitz 1993 *Culture: Sociological Perspectives*. Englewood Cliffs, N.J.: Prentice-Hall.

Hall, Stuart 1992 "Cultural Studies and its Theoretical Legacies." In Larry Grossberg, et al., eds., *Cultural Studies*. New York: Routledge.

Halle, David 1994 *Inside Culture: Class, Culture and Everyday Life in Modern America*. Chicago: University of Chicago Press.

Harper, Douglas 1987 *Working Knowledge: Skill and Community in a Small Shop*. Chicago: University of Chicago Press.

Hebdige, Dick 1990 *Cut 'N Mix: Culture, Identity, and Caribbean Music*. London: Routledge.

—— 1979 *Subculture: The Meaning of Style*. London: Routledge.

Hirsch, Paul 1972 "Processing Fads and Fashions: An Organization Set Analysis of the Cultural Industry System." *American Journal of Sociology* 77:639–659.

Hooks, Bell 1994 *Outlaw Culture: Resisting Representations*. New York: Routledge.

Hunter, James D. 1991 *Culture Wars: The Struggle to Define America*. New York: Basic Books.

Jaeger, Gertrude, and Philip Selznick 1964 "A Normative Theory of Culture." *American Sociological Review* 29:653–669.

Katz, Jack 1988 *Seductions of Crime: Moral and Sensual Attractions of Doing Evil*. New York: Basic Books.

Katz, Pearl 1999 *The Scalpel's Edge*. Boston: Allyn and Bacon.

Kracauer, Seigfried 1949 "National Types as Hollywood Presents Them." *Public Opinion Quarterly* 13:53–72.

Kroeber, Alfred 1952 *The Nature of Culture*. Chicago: University of Chicago Press.

—— (1923) 1948 *Anthropology*. New York: Harcourt.

——, and Clyde Kluckhohn (1952) 1963 *Culture: A Critical Review of Concepts and Definitions*. New York: Vintage Books.

——, and Talcott Parsons 1958 "The Concepts of Culture and Social System." *American Sociological Review* 23:582–583.

Lamont, Michele 1992 *Money, Morals, and Manners*. Chicago: University of Chicago Press.

——, and Marcel Fournier (eds.) 1992 *Cultivating Differences: Symbolic Boundaries and the Making of Inequality*. Chicago: University of Chicago Press.

Lang, Gladys Engel, and Kurt Lang 1990 *Etched in Memory: The Building and Survival of Artistic Reputation*. Chapel Hill/London: University of North Carolina Press.

Lang, Kurt 1957 "Mass Appeal and Minority Tastes." In Bernard Rosenberg and David Manning White, eds., *Mass Culture*. New York: Free Press.

Latour, Bruno 1987 *Science in Action: How to Follow Scientists and Engineers Through Society*. Cambridge, Mass.: Harvard University Press.

——, and Steve Woolgar 1979 *Laboratory Life*. Beverly Hills, Calif.: Sage.

Levi-Strauss, Claude (1953) 1963 *Structural Anthropology*. New York: Basic Books.

Lincoln, James, and Arne Kalleberg 1990 *Culture, Control and Commitment: A Study of Work Organization and Work Attitudes in the United States and Japan*. Cambridge, Eng.: Cambridge University Press.

Lofland, John 1993 *Polite Protesters: The American Peace Movement of the 1980s*. Syracuse, N.Y.: Syracuse University Press.

Long, Elizabeth 1985 *The American Dream and the Popular Novel*. Boston: Routledge and Kegan Paul.

Lowenthal, Leo 1950 "Historical Perspectives of Popular Culture." *American Journal of Sociology* 55:323–332.

Luker, Kristen 1984 *Abortion and the Politics of Motherhood*. Berkeley: University of California Press.

Malinowski, Bronislaw 1931 "Culture." *Encyclopedia of the Social Sciences* 4:621–646.

—— 1927 *Sex and Repression in Savage Society*. London: Routledge.

Martin, Joanne 1992 *Cultures in Organizations: Three Perspectives*. New York: Oxford University Press.

McDonald, Dwight 1953 "A Theory of Mass Culture." *Diogenes* 3:1–17.

Mead, Margaret 1935 *Sex and Temperament in Three Primitive Societies*. New York: Morrow.

—— 1928 *Coming of Age in Samoa*. New York: Morrow.

Mitchell, Timothy 1991 *Colonizing Egypt*. Berkeley: University of California Press.

Morawska, Ewa, and Willfried Spohn 1994 "'Cultural Pluralism' in Historical Sociology: Recent Theoretical Directions." In Diana Crane, ed., *The Sociology of Culture: Emerging Theoretical Perspectives*. Oxford: Basil Blackwell.

Mukerji, Chandra 1983 *From Graven Images*. New York: Columbia University Press.

——, and Michael Schudson 1986 "Popular Culture." *Annual Review of Sociology* 12:47–66.

Munch, Richard, and Neil J. Smelser (eds.) *The Theory of Culture*. Berkeley: University of California Press.

Neitz, Mary Jo 1987 *Charisma and Community: A Study of Religious Commitment Within the Charismatic Renewal*. New Brunswick, N.J.: Transaction Books.

Nelson, Cary, and Lawrence Grossberg (eds.) 1988 *Marxism and the Interpretation of Culture*. Urbana: University of Illinois Press.

Nolan, James (ed.) 1996 *The American Culture Wars: Current Contests and Future Prospects*. Charlottesville: University of West Virginia Press.

Peterson, Richard 1997 *Creating Country Music: Fabricating Authenticity*. Chicago: University of Chicago Press.

—— 1990 "Symbols and Social Life: The Growth of Culture Studies." *Contemporary Sociology* 19:498–500.

—— 1989 "La Sociologique de l'Art et de la Culture aux Etats-Unis." *L'Annegrave;e sociologique* 39:153–179.

—— 1979 "Revitalizing the Culture Concept." *Annual Review of Sociology* 5:137–166.

Radcliffe-Brown, A. R. (1952) 1961 *Structure and Function in Primitive Society: Essays and Addresses*. New York: Free Press.

Radway, Janice 1984 *Reading the Romance*. Chapel Hill: University of North Carolina Press.

Rosenberg, Bernard, and David Manning White (eds.) 1957 *Mass Culture*. New York: Free Press.

Rushing, Andrea Benton 1988 "Hair-Raising." *Feminist Studies* 14:325–336.

Schudson, Michael 1984 *Advertising the Uneasy Persuasion*. New York: Basic Books.

—— 1978 *Discovering the News: A Social History of American Newspapers*. New York: Basic Books.

Schwartz, Barry 1991 "Social Change and Collective Memory: The Democratization of George Washington." *American Sociological Review* 56:221–236.

Seidman, Steven 1996 "Revitalizing Sociology: The Challenge of Cultural Studies." In Norman Denzin, ed., *Cultural Studies*. Greenwich, Conn.: JAI Press.

Seldes, Gilbert 1957 "The Public Arts." In Bernard Rosenberg and David Manning White, eds., *Mass Culture*. New York: Free Press.

Sewell, William 1985 "Ideologies and Social Revolutions: Reflections on the French Case." *The Journal of Modern History* 57:57–85.

Singer, Milton 1968 "Culture: The Concept of Culture." In David L. Sills, ed., *International Encyclopedia of the Social Sciences*. New York: Macmillan and Free Press.

Skocpol, Theda 1985 "Cultural Idioms and Political Ideologies in the Revolutionary Reconstruction of State Power: A Rejoinder to Sewell." *The Journal of Modern History* 57:86–96.

Star, Susan Leigh 1989 *Regions of the Mind: Brain Research and the Quest for Scientific Certainty*. Stanford, Calif.: Stanford University Press.

Swidler, Ann 1986 "Culture in Action." *American Sociological Review* 51:273–286.

D

DATA BANKS AND DEPOSITORIES

CONCEPT AND HISTORY OF DATA-BANKS

The tradition of thought that gave rise to the social sciences was based on the quest to understand the laws or regularities governing the emerging industrial societies with democratic political regimes. The political and economic revolutions that were shaking the world substituted the relative predictability of the traditional ways of handling power and production with the disconcerting uncertainties of political consensus and the new market of commodities.

Finding such laws was not easy. The model for scientific inquiry established by the successful endeavors in the various fields of physical and natural sciences was not applicable to social science research. For a period social scientists believed that the complexity of the social object and the immaturity of the field were responsible for the failure of the natural science model. Social scientists gradually became aware, however, that the epistemological foundations of the social sciences were different: in practical terms, because creating an experimental situation in social matters is extremely difficult; and in theoretical terms, because society is a moving target, readily reacting to changes in circumstances. In the end, mainstream social scientists learned to live with these difficulties.

The Newtonian challenge of formulating hypotheses, collecting the relevant data, and accepting only those hypotheses that fit observational data, has been in one way or another the stimulus and the standard of advances in knowledge in the many fields that later composed the social sciences. The systematic collection of empirical observations has been the ballast that has kept modern social sciences from drowning in second-rate philosophy or outright ideology. Numerous social researchers and thinkers have stood up to the challenge of providing reliable observations on the social world. (Since every observer is also a member of society, it is not easy to stand aside and look at it from a fixed point of view.)

In retrospect it is understandable that different paths to the common goal of collecting systematic reliable data were tested with various methodological and technical tools, not always being understood as part of the same endeavor. In the latest bout of cultural dominance of Marxist theories, Karl Marx and his school were viewed as "grand theorists" squarely opposed to the "abstract empiricism" of contemporary sociology. But this was a misconception that completely overlooked the many years spent by Marx painstakingly collecting data on industrial society, and by desire to be a scientist like Charles Darwin—to whom he dedicated the book produced by his gigantic research effort, *Das Kapital*.

Despite the apparent confusion and turmoil, there was an underlying paradigm. Social sciences had to be empirical. No matter how radically critical and antipositivistic have been the epistemological conclusions of the various *Methodenstreiten*, the mainstream has resisted the idea of a data-free social science. Altogether such theoretical orientation has provided this disciplinary area with a fairly resilient ballast against ideological nebulosities. And this can be said safely without underestimating the humongous and repetitive production of irrelevant trivia in tabular or graphic form produced over the years by the low-brows of "abstract empiricism". Data, however, are a peculiar commodity insofar that they have to be produced. Which means most of the time it is costly, painstaking, and time consuming to produce data. By and large, data belong to one of two families. *Primary data* are collected by the researcher himself. *Secondary data* are collected by other agencies, mainly public and private large-scale organizations, in which case the researcher can only perform what is known as *secondary analysis*, and he obviously has no control over the collection of this data. In the latter case it is also useful to further distinguish between data collected for analytical purposes by agencies like the various census bureaus, and those collected for administrative purposes, such as data on health collected by hospitals, or data on education collected by educational institutions, or mortality data collected by governments and other agencies. These are *process-produced data*; data created as by-products of administrative activities.

There are disciplinary areas that have a high degree of institutional stability and control over their data such as physics, but also engineering, medicine or law. The latter two fields, of course, provided the original kernel for the development of universities and *studia generalia*, in Bologna, Padova, or Salerno. Other fields are less stable, usually in the area of the humanities and the social sciences. But in all cases the organized character of the type of knowledge provided by academic disciplines is predominant.

Organized knowledge is the practical rather than speculative knowledge accumulated by governments and their administrative apparatuses, by corporations, political parties, trade unions, churches, and other institutions. Thomas Kuhn has been the leading figure in analyzing innovation processes in the institutions of *organized* knowledge (Kuhn 1962). These types of secondary data are essential for social scientists, and in fact, as noticed long ago by Paul F. Lazarsfeld and Stein Rokkan, among others (Rokkan 1976), the work of sociologists,

especially in Europe, is largely based on interactions with the institutions in charge of this type of knowledge.

Le Suicide by Emile Durkheim is an excellent example of the advantages and drawbacks of secondary analysis of process-produced data. This masterpiece of sociological research gave empirical evidence of the theoretical tenet that a cogent collective agent can influence individual behavior even to the extreme gesture of annihilating the genetic commandment. It could not have been written without access and a hard sweated one at that, to secondary data. No individual scientific actor could collect data on events that are so numerous, and so highly dispersed in time and space. On the other hand, relying on data collected by other agencies means that the researcher relies on somebody else's definition of events. One of the most damaging critiques to Durkheim's work is that his sophisticated theoretical definition of suicides, is nullified by the fact that the cases of suicides in the data used were defined by officers or judges according to completely different, and uncontrollably variable, criteria.

The work of historians, too, would probably not be possible without access to the *organized* knowledge embodied in the archives of agencies of all kind. The early development of economics as a quantitative discipline was greatly favored by the availability of organized knowledge collected by public administrations. The same applies to demography, which could base itself also on data accumulated by the church, and in general to the whole field of statistics, which could today be defined as policy sciences (Cavalli 1972).

The Durkheim syndrome, the need to use data not collected by scholars, but by public employees, is a constant problem for social scientists using information coming from the realm of organizational knowledge. At the beginning of the nineteenth century Melchiorre Gioja expresses the irritation of a scholar dependent on low-quality public data. He took issue with "the many questions that various inept busybodies called secretaries send from the capital to the province. Questions that never produced other than the following three effects:

1. fear that the Government seeks the basis for some aggravation, and therefore opportunistically false answers;

2. ridicule resulting by the silliness, inconsistency, and imprecision of the questions, and thus answers biased by contempt;

3. heaps of paper uselessly encumbering archives, if the government mistrust them, or very serious mistakes if it uses them, not to speak of the time stolen from the municipal or provincial administrators who must prepare the answers." (Gioja 1852, p. 5)

A powerful answer to these problems came from the development of *survey research*, particularly from the 1940s on by American sociologists who developed the "art of asking why"; namely the inquiry into the rational motivations of individual behavior. It is not surprising that these new methods originally developed in two crucial areas of behavior: the choice of candidates in an electoral process, and the choice of a product in consumption behavior. There has been much criticism of mercantile attitudes in voting, and of course it is quite clear that some of the value motivations that are mobilized in choosing a candidate are evidently not the same as those that are mobilized in picking up one granola package rather than another from a shelf. But the critics miss the point. The two areas of behavior are similar, and the inquiry into behavioral motivations should not be diverted by undue considerations of political or ethical correctness. Little wonder that scholars had to develop new data collection tools on this type of behavior. And equally not surprising is that political and economic elites are willing to invest resources in the arduous enterprise of predicting the aggregate outcome of individual behavior. A prudent politician today constantly monitors the opinion of the electorate. And economists make use not only of large-scale models of the behavior of macroeconomic systems, but also of assessments of consumer behavior. Politicians, bureaucrats, entrepreneurs, and managers would have a hard time doing without the tools provided by the social sciences.

Survey data collection methods, however, presented the social scientist and his institutions with novel problems. Pollsters and survey people in general produce huge quantities of individually uninteresting questionnaires. Punched cards were developed to hold data; at first the cards were processed manually as the "McBee cards," but

soon after machine-readable cards were developed, such as those punched with the Hollerith code (universally known as IBM card). Cards were easier to store than questionnaires, but it was easy, in a routine research process, to lose the "codebook" of the research so that in many cases the cards were useless, even if they contained relevant information (Rokkan 1976). Thus the storing, handling, processing, and redistributing of punched cards required specific skills. Furthermore, the traditional institutional structure of universities and research centers is not well adapted to take on these tasks. Originally social scientists turned to libraries to store their data (Lucci and Rokkan 1957), but in the late 1950s and early 1960s libraries were not equipped to handle large masses of data requiring mainframe computers. The big machines were housed in separate structures and tended by IBM technicians. Social scientists had limited access to the mainframe computers and therefore, the data, until the scientists developed their own separate institutions on the model of the Inter University Consortium for Political Research at Ann Arbor, Michigan (ICPR, later turned into ICPSR when social research was added). In Europe the vision and farsightedness of scholars such as Philip Abrams in the United Kingdom, Stein Rokkan in Norway, and Erwin Scheuch in Germany, helped establish the first archives in Essex, the Social Science Research Center, in Bergen, the Norwegian Data Service, and in Koeln, the Zentralarchiv fur Empirische Sozialforschung. Later on these archives developed their own organizations, first IFDO, International Federation of Data Organizations, and later on CESSDA, Council of European Social Science Data Archives. Archives developed in Italy at the Istituto Superiore di Sociologia of Milano (ADPSS), in Denmark (DDA), in the Netherlands (the Steinmetz archive), in Belgium (BASS), and in France (BDSP in Grenoble and in several other places).

SOCIAL SCIENCE DATA ARCHIVES

Cultural and technological changes led to the creation of Social Science Data Archives (SSDA). SSDA are scientific institutions that retrieve, store, and distribute large amounts of data on social science. The oldest and the most important SSDA were established in the United States—where an emphasis on quantitative social research is deeply rooted—when there was growing attention by both public administration and the scientific community to the use of social indicators as standards for the population welfare level. These social actors turned to social indicators for help in planning, applying, and the evaluating public-assistance programs when it became apparent that using economic indicators alone was insufficient and inappropriate.

The first major contribution of social indicators is the *Recent Social Trends* study, supervised by the sociologist William Ogburn and prescribed by the U.S. Government toward the end of the 1920s (Bauer 1966). In 1946 the *Employment Act* was published, which was a systematic collection of information on economy intended to affect policies and programs that would sustain employment rates. Most of the studies and undertakings of the 1960s described a "great society," which could overcome the widening economic and social gap.

The consciousness of social problems, together with the necessity of endowing a collection of social data, prompted the publication of *Towards a Social Report* at the end of the 1960s (Olson 1974). This publication was intended to be "a first step toward the evolution of a regular system in social reporting;" but still, like other similar and contemporary writings, data were used just as illustrations supplementing the text.

Technological developments that contributed to the establishment of SSDA include previously unseen data collection techniques and new quantitative methods to organize and analyze those same data. Throughout the 1960s improvements in computing technologies, specifically in data gathering and storing, allowed researchers to do previously unthinkable levels of analysis (Deutsch 1970).

The first SSDA were born autonomously, unrestricted by publicly administered archives or by the institutions traditionally related to the collection and promotion of data (libraries, museums, and data archives). The earliest SSDA were created in the United States, where in 1947 the Roper Public Opinion Research Center opened, followed by the Inter-University Consortium for Political and Social Research (ICPSR) in 1962 at the University of Michigan in Ann Arbor. In 1960, the University of Koln in Germany developed the Zentralarchiv fur Empirische Sozialforschung (ZA). A few years later, in 1964, the Steinmetzarchief settled in at the

Amsterdam Arts and Sciences Real Academy. The Economic and Social Research Council Data Archive (ESRC-DA) was created at the University of Essex in 1967. These archives specialized in public opinion surveys and social research, but they also focused attention on the great amount of data complied by statistical bureaus and public agencies (Herichsen 1989).

SSDA developed a culture of data sharing; data exchange and the repeated use of available data for new research projects intensified with the introduction of statistical packages for the social sciences and more compact media for data transfer. As data production and SSDA grew, more systematic acquisition policies were implemented, and transborder cooperation resulted in the exchange of data processing tools and of emerging archiving and service standards (Mochmann 1998).

In the early 1970s SSDA were created: in Norway in 1971, in Denmark in 1973, and in the United States (at the University of Wisconsin in Madison, U.C.L.A., and the University of North Carolina in Chapel Hill). In the 1980s SSDA were created in Sweden (1980), France (1981), Austria (1985), and then Canada, Hungary, Israel, Australia, New Zealand, and Switzerland (1993).

Currently, the most important SSDA is the ICPSR at the University of Michigan, which has over 40,000 data files and gathers information from more than 300 institutions. Besides data retrieval, processing, researching, and transferring, it publishes an annual catalog and a four-monthly bulletin, cooperates in great projects concerning data collection (e.g. the *General Social Surveys* and the *Panel Study on Income Dynamics*), conducts formative training (it organizes a summer school on methodology and statistics for social science), and offers educational activities. The ICPSR has been open to foreign institutions since the early 1970s.

SSDA differ on budget and staff size, functions, amount of data files in acrhives, and technical characteristics (e.g. type of hardware and software used, online data accessibility) (IFDO 1991). The SSDA network is tied, however, by international associations such as the Council of European Social Science Data Archives (CESSDA was instituted in 1976 to facilitate cooperation between the most important European SSDA), and the International Federation of Data Organizations (IFDO was founded in 1977 to enhance the cooperation already started by CESSDA).

CESSDA promoted the acquisition, archiving, and distribution of data for social research throughout Europe, facilitated the exchange of data and technology among data organizations, and supported the development of standards for study description schemes to inform users about the archival holdings, classification schemes for access to variables by subject and continuity guides for coherent data collections. In the 1970s and 1980s, European membership grew continuously and CESSDA started to associate and cooperate with other international organizations sharing similar objectives. Today Europe has a good coverage of CESSDA member archives, while planning processes are under way in several more countries that still lack a social science infrastructure.

Recent trends reveal a type of limitation to the growth and proliferation of national SSDA. This occurs partly through the opening of decentralized bureaus and partly through more specialized data file collections—ones with more well-defined inquiry areas. Exemplary regarding this last issue is the *Rural Data Base* of the ESRC, or even the CESSDA internal agreement aiming at a study field subdivision between the different European SSDA (Tannenbaum 1986).

SSDA have been useful not only in their specific field (especially retrieving, storing, gathering, and making available data) but also have improved general quantitative research techniques, secondary analysis, statistical and administrative software packages, and have made available the best hardware in social research. Most of the SSDA publish their own bulletins, organize methodology schools for social science, hold updating seminars, and cooperate in research projects. In the second half of the 1980s SSDA were particularly active in defining the standards for the information system to be used among these institutions. More recently, SSDA have been working on international access practices on two levels: developing standard study description procedures (to define each data file) and promoting access to online archives.

SOCIAL SURVEY INSTRUMENTS

Major social survey instruments are those institutionalized initiatives that have produced some of the most interesting results from the autonomous research applied to problems of general interest. The *General Social Surveys*, the *Continuous National Surveys*, and the *U.S. National Surveys* are the most interesting examples of longitudinal studies. Eurobarometers and the International Social Survey Program (ISSP) are discussed here because, although not strictly comparable to general social surveys, they are two of the most comprehensive and continuous academic survey programs. Although it is not discussed here, a student of the social sciences should examine the *European Household Panels*. This project integrated national household panels from Germany (since 1984), Sweden (since 1984), Luxembourg (since 1985), France (since 1985), Poland (since 1987), Great Britain (since 1991), and Belgium and Hungary (since 1992). These panels include variables on household composition, employment, earnings, occupational biographies, health, and satisfaction indicators. (In order to create an international comparative database for microdata from these projects, the Panel Comparability Project (PACO) was formed).

General Social Surveys. General Social Surveys (GSS) were developed to set out data on demographic, social, and economic characteristics of the population, as well as opinion data on social life (e.g. family, politics, institutions, relationships). This important survey instrument improved over time. In the mid 1940s the Survey Research Center of the University of Michigan conducted panel studies on a national level on specific issues, such as political behavior, socioeconomic status, and consumers' attitudes. In the early 1970s, the National Opinion Research Center (NORC) of the University of Chicago organized the first GSS, which was immediately followed by the Continuous National Surveys program.

Following the consolidation of the research method based on enlarged quantitative surveys on a national level, some institutions committed to the transfer of the results, both within the U.S. academic community and toward universities and research centers worldwide. One should note that data provided by the GSS are given a particular treatment inside the ICPSR, which, besides transferring the data, gathers the sociologists interested in the study and the arrangement of social indicators. The importance of the GSS in U.S. social research is exemplified by the more than 1,000 publications related to GSS data analysis listed in the catalog prepared by NORC.

The GSS is done through interviews of a representative sample of U.S. residents who are over 18 years old and are not institutionalized. Representativeness is guaranteed by a complex sampling mechanism, which relies on a multilevel selection over metropolitan areas, municipalities, regions, and individuals. Sampling criteria have been modified throughout the course of different GSS, but to keep the results comparable between one edition and the following ones correctors have been added to allow for these adjustments.

The GSS questionnaire consists of standard questions that are asked each time, and sometimes groups of questions on specific themes are included. The topics treated are the ones most interesting in the study of society and its trends, with a particular focus on family, economic and social status, gender and ethnic group relationships, and moral questions. Political behavior and working activity are not included because the former is already studied in detail through surveys organized by the Institute for Social Research of the University of Michigan, and the latter is well described in the research on labor forces arranged by the U.S. Bureau of the Census.

Given that one of the fundamental aims of the GSS is to provide a general view of time trends, not only in population characteristics, but also and overall in opinions, evaluations, and behaviors over the most important topics describing the social scenery, these questions are included only from time to time, so the questionnaire is not weighted excessively. Some questions are included only two years in three, others every 10 years, and some only after particular and significant events. Over 100 sociologists worked on the first draft of the questionnaire (in 1972). These sociologists devised a final, definite version by voting for each single question. Every year the selection of questions is done by an ad hoc committee, selected by American Sociological Association members.

Some questions utilized in the GSS come from the national surveys run before 1972 that were promoted by commercial research institutes (e.g.

Gallup, Harris), university research institutes (especially ICPSR), and also federal commissions organized to study particular phenomena. Data comparability is assured by the question scheme, which is the same of the original study.

Continuous National Surveys. The *Continuous National Surveys* (CNS) are national studies (the first one dates back to 1973) conducted monthly, with the aim of supplying the various governmental agencies with the necessary data (e.g. welfare indicators) to schedule social programs. The sample plan consists of persons selected on the basis of their living groups. On this regard, the NORC has carefully prepared a master probability sample of households, that is, a multi-stage sample to collect on a first stage municipalities or else groups of municipalities. From them, all districts or block groups are selected, and then the proper cohabitational groups in which to choose the individuals to interview are selected.

U.S. National Surveys. U.S. national surveys on representative samples of U.S. population have been held since 1974 by the Survey Research Center of the University of Michigan. Some of these studies are held regularly (e.g. the *Surveys of Consumer Finances*, the *Survey of Consumer Attitudes and Behavior*, and the *Panel Studies of Income Dynamics*). In particular, the yearly *Panel Study of Income Dynamics* is one of the most interesting surveys on income trends, and, specifically, on the possible causes for changes in the economic status both of households and single individuals.

The representative sample initially extracted consisted of 2,930 households, to which has been added 1,872 households that were already survey subjects by the U.S. Bureau of the Census on the income topic in the two previous years. Each year these households are re-interviewed, and the sample has grown as members of the original sample established new households. For the first time ever, phone interviews were tested in these researches, and since then the telephone has become broadly used in social research and panel studies.

Eurobarometers. Eurobarometers are opinion studies that have been held twice a year since 1973 in what are now the European Union countries. These studies sample about 1,000 individuals for each country, which represents the population over 15 years-old. The aim of these comparative surveys is to learn about the attitudes of European citizens on some broad interest topics. Questions regard public attitudes toward European integration, but sometimes also address specific problems of a single country or more generally economic, political, and social conditions. Two important functions of Eurobarometers are: being cross-national and easily comparable surveys, they helped integrate social research throughout Western Europe; and, they allowed (and still allow) analysis on social changes in Western Europe. As a matter of fact, there is no survey similar to eurobarometers in what concerns a regular check over time (more than 20 years to date) and space (every single European country). Eurobarometers are now at the disposal of the academic community thanks to the ICPSR and the ZA of Koln.

The International Social Survey Program. The International Social Survey Program (ISSP) combines a cross-national survey with a longitudinal time dimension by replicating particular question modules, ideally in five year intervals. The first survey on the "role of government" started in 1985 in four countries (the United States, Great Britain, West Germany, and Australia). Since then the ISSP has grown rapidly and now covers more than 30 countries around the world, including Bulgaria, the Czech Republic, Hungary, Latvia, Poland, Russia, and Slovenia. Topics of the ISSP have included social networks (1986), social inequality (1987, 1992), family and changing gender roles (1988, 1994), work orientations (1989, 1997), religion (1991), and environment (1993). Role of government was replicated in 1990 and 1996. The official data archive of the ISSP is the ZA, which makes the integrated data sets available via the archival network.

DEPOSITED, ACCESS PROCEDURES AND USE

The existence of SSDA in Europe and in the United States has had a positive effect on the scientific community because SSDA allow access to some data that is particularly useful in secondary analysis. In other words, researchers can collect and use data from different surveys (with particular hypothesis and conceptual frames) to support their own works.

SSDA vary on the type and volume of data that is held and delivered and on the exact services offered. The data differ within and between SSDA in terms of subject matter, time period, and geographical area covered. The data may be individual or aggregate, and the variables may be cross-sectional or time series and suitable for comparative or longitudinal analysis, or both. Charging policies differ from one SSDA to the next and depend upon the type of service being provided, the specific data set demanded, and the institutional affiliation of the requester.

Many data formats are used by SSDA to preserve and deliver the data that is increasingly required to be machine readable, and there is also an increasing demand for the archiving and disseminating of machine-readable metadata.

Despite the heterogeneity of SSDA, there are common goals and tasks. Although we know more about the SSDA in Western Europe, we hope to represent all SSDA in the following list of goals and tasks:

- To promote the acquisition, archiving, and distribution of electronic data for social science teaching and research and to exchange data and technology;

- To exploit the potential of the Internet by the expansion of web-based services and the improvement of dissemination to allow users more direct and immediate access to the data;

- To develop and use metadata standards for the management of data;

- To provide users access to comparative data and to multiple data sources across national boundaries;

- To allow users to receive all or subsets of data via download or on portable media in one of a number of formats;

- To extend the users' base beyond traditional boundaries;

- To better serve the needs of an increasing number of novice users, particularly in terms of data analysis software and improved searching aids through the development and use of social science thesauri and user-friendly interfaces.

The technological changes that contributed to the creation of SSDA have had far-reaching significance for social scientists. The changes throughout the 1990s were considerable: from simple writing (word processing) to data production (especially computer assisted interviewing technique); from archiving (from punch cards to floppy disks and CD-ROMs) to data analysis (the creation of various new software); from bibliographic reference (online access to bibliographic databases) to communication (e-mail) (Cooley and Ryan 1985). The boundaries of technological innovations are not yet clear. The compound archive of integrated data, text, images, and sounds (Garvel 1989), and the Geographical Information System, by which we can analyze data concerning space are examples of previously unimagined products that are possible because of computers (Unwin 1991). These instruments require high-level storing proceedings so that data can be a real resource in the development of empirical knowledge.

While social research in earlier decades lamented the lack of reliable data (in the 1960s the social sciences were considered data poor, and infrastructural support for social research was lacking) the situation has changed. Thousands and thousands of data sets, some of them dating back to the 1940s, are stored for secondary analysis in SSDA. These data sets represent a vast potential for comparative research on historical developments and social change.

PROSPECTS FOR THE FUTURE

In 1994, the European Commission recognized Social Science Data Archives as legitimate institutions to be considered as applicants to the large-scale facility program for scientific research. This is tantamount to recognizing that the social sciences have infrastructure needs equal to those of the "hard" sciences. This goal was originally pursued through the work of a study panel created by the General Directorate for Science and Technology of the European Commission and particularly its Training and Mobility of Researchers program. The study panel met twice, and was entrusted with the tasks of: a) identifying the future priorities of European scientists concerning access to large installations in the social sciences, both in the short and in the medium term (i.e. in the period 1994–2004); b) suggesting ways to meet these priorities—with an indication of their respective costs and benefits—in light of the present and expected availability of large installations, taking into account existing and planned future international cooperations, both within the community and outside as well as the particular needs of researchers working in regions where such installations do not exist; and c) consulting representatives from member states and reporting on what facilities, if any, might be available for possible support in the frame of successor programs. A large-scale facility has, to date, been defined as a large research installation that is rare or unparalleled in Europe and that is necessary for high-level good-quality research. Such facilities tend to have high initial costs of investment and comparatively high operating costs. The large-scale facilities program is intended to provide scientists with access to large installations within and especially outside their own countries, thereby promoting the mobility of researchers and encouraging the creation of a Europe-wide research community. And likewise, these installations are better utilized when their services, facilities, and knowledge are available to a wider community of users. Thus the beneficiaries of the large-scale facilities program are researchers who are provided with access to the facilities and the organizations that receive support for the use and improvement of their equipment. The level of support for such facilities has, to date, been based on the quality and unique features of the facility and the value—particularly in advanced training—to potential users.

As a sequel to the work and recommendations of the study panel, between 1994 and 1999 three Social Science Data Archives, the SSRC Essex archive, the German ZA, and the NSD in Bergen have been included in the large-scale facilities program together with other social science institutions. In addition the General Directorate for Science and Technology created a round table on large-scale facilities in the social sciences. This round table was constituted by the European Union commission to suggest actions needed to support a given field of scientific activity. The prospects of Social Science Data Archives are thus quite positive, and for the first time they have been given a tool capable of furthering their original aims.

REFERENCES

Bauer, R. A. (ed.) 1966 *Social Indicators*. Cambridge, Mass.: MIT Press.

Cavalli, A. 1972 "La Sociologia e le Altre Scienze Sociali. Prospettive di Integrazione Interdisciplinare." In P. Rossi, ed., *Ricerca Sociologica e Ruolo del Sociologo*. Bologna: Il Mulino.

Cooley, R. E., and N. S. Ryn 1985 "An Information Technology Strategy for Social Scientists." *University Computing* 7.

Deutsch, K. 1970 "The Impact of Complex Data Bases on the Social Sciences." In R. L. Bisco, ed., *Data Bases, Computers and the Social Sciences*. New York: Wiley.

Garvel, S. 1989 "National Archives and Electronic Records: Where Are We Going?" *IASSIST Quarterly* 3–4.

Gioja, M. 1852 *Filosofia Della Statistica*. Torino.

Henrichsen, B. 1989 "Data from the Central Bureau of Statistics to the Social Science Community: The Norwegian Experience." *IASSIST Quarterly* fall–winter.

IFDO 1991 "IFDO Survey of Computerized Catalogues." *IFDO News* September.

Kuhn, T. 1962 *The Structure of Scientific Revolutions*. Chicago: University of Chicago Press.

Lucci, T., and S. Rokkan (eds.) 1957 *A Library Center of Survey Research Data*. New York: Columbia University Press.

Mochmann, E. 1998 "European Cooperation in Social Science Data Dissemination." Working paper, round table meeting on infrastructures for social economic research. Koln, 29–30 June.

Rokkan, S. 1976 "Data Services in Western Europe." *American Behavioral Scientist* 19:443–454.

Tannenbaum, E. 1989 "Sharing Information Begets Information." *IASSIST Quarterly*, Summer.

Unwin, D. 1991 "Geographical Information Systems and the Social Science Research." *ESRC Data Archive Bulletin* 48.

GUIDO MARTINOTTI
SONIA STEFANIZZI

DEATH AND DYING

This essay asks three questions about death and dying: 1) Why should an entry on such phenomena, which are clearly of interdisciplinary interest, appear in an encyclopedia of sociology? 2) What related topics have been studied by sociology? 3) What issues are currently pending that call for sociological attention?

DEATH AND DYING AS A FIELD OF SOCIOLOGICAL INQUIRY

The answer to the first question is not readily found in the history of sociological thought, although Victor Marshall once bemoaned the fact that Georg Simmel in 1908 had identified but had not pursued the topic as suitable for sociological inquiry, and a half century later the topic was thought to be a neglected area for sociology (Faunce and Fulton 1958). On other hand, Fulton reminds us that "sociological interest in death is coexistent with the history of sociology" (Fulton and Bendiksen 1994; Fulton and Owen 1988). Both Marshall and Fulton are correct in that the "interest" has typically been peripheral. Herbert Spencer had noted that social progress depended on the separation of the world of the living from the world of the dead, but that was hardly his central theory. Emile Durkheim's *Suicide* depends on an elaborate theory of "anomie," not on any theory of death. Max Weber deals with the fact of death in that it interrupts the pursuit of one's calling—a basic observation later developed by Talcott Parsons. William Graham Sumner wrote widely about such death-related topics as fear of ghosts, mortuary rituals, widowhood, infanticide, war, and even the right to die, but all such references were illustrative of some more general point. In 1956 Herman Feifel chaired a conference on death for the American Psychological Association.

There may well be other precursors, but a bit of history suggests how and when sociology may have staked out its disciplinary claim in a field that had long been cultivated by medicine, theology, ethics, philosophy, law, and psychology.

In May 1967, as part of a new program on "Death Education" at the University of Minnesota, Robert Fulton, a sociologist, arranged perhaps the first interdisciplinary conference on death and dying in the United States. Fulton had just published his ground-breaking book *Death and Identity* (1965), the purpose of which was to help in "preserving rather than losing . . . personal identity . . ." when facing death. It was a time of broad and diverse interest in the subject. Examples had been popping up in many domains: Jay Lifton's notes on the Hiroshima bombing; Eric Lindemann's report on the psychiatric effects of the disastrous Coconut Grove fire in Boston; Avery Weisman's clinical studies of dying patients; Lloyd Warner's interpretation of the meaning of ceremonial events that honor the dead; Herman Feifel's work on social taboos; Richard Kalish's early essays on teaching; Parsons' emerging theory of the relationship of social action to death, and so on. Fulton, clearly aware of these varying expressions of interest, was prompted to try to interpret the diversity and "get it all together." What Fulton did in *Death and Identity* (1965) was to piece together some three dozen edited excerpts from the works of a wide range of experts who had written on an equally wide range of death-related topics. He found American society to be essentially death denying.

The Minnesota Conference, 1967. At the Minnesota Conference of 1967, Alber Sullivan of the Minnesota Medical School and Jacques Choron of the New School of Social Research spoke to various medical and philosophical issues; Jeanne Quint from the University of California reported on the role of the nurse in dealing with terminal patients; Eric Lindemann of Harvard Medical School discussed the symptomatology of acute grief; Herman Feifel of the Veterans Administration, famous for his work on taboos, emphasized that death always carries many meanings; and Talcott Parsons from Harvard probed the topic in broad theoretical terms.

It was a heady agenda but there were some strange omissions. Elizabeth Kubler-Ross, then known to be working on the "stages" of dying (*On Death and Dying*, 1969) was scarcely mentioned, nor was much made of the equally influential work of Barney Glaser and Anselm Strauss (1965), whose book *Awareness of Dying* had been published two years earlier. The participants in the Minnesota Conference were intrigued by various sociological questions. They wrestled with Karl Mannheim's thought experiment of what society would be like if there were no death (Mannheim 1928, 1959). They wondered what mortality and fertility rates had been historically and how they are related (cf. Riley and Riley 1986). They debated Robert Blauner's thesis (Blauner 1966) that death in all known societies imposes imperatives (a corpse must be looked after, property must be reallocated, vacated roles must be reassigned, the solidarity of the

deceased's group must be reaffirmed). They attacked hospital regimens that depersonalized terminal patients, and they challenged the medical profession for treating death as "the enemy" and prolonging life at any cost.

The conference produced extravagant results in anticipating two critical issues: the norms and arrangements for dealing with dying persons were both confused and hazy; and the greater attention paid to caregivers than to dying persons. But the fact that the conference was consistent in insisting that dying always involves at least two persons turned out to be its most important message for the future agenda. Sociological interest in death and dying, of course, did not start with the Minnesota Conference, but what the conference did was to underscore the often overlooked sociological proposition that the dying process is essentially social in nature.

A REVIEW OF SOCIOLOGICAL INQUIRIES

The answer to the second question about related research is more straightforward. A bit of American history shows the range of topics that has received sociological attention. In the 1930s sociological interest in death and dying had focused mainly on the economic plight of the bereaved family (Eliot 1932). In the 1950s attention turned to the high cost of dying and the commercialization of funerals (Bowman 1959). Twenty years later, it shifted to a medley of popular topics of peripheral sociological interest, with many books written on various aspects of death and dying, such as *On the Side of Life*; *On Dying and Denying*; *After the Flowers Have Gone*; *Widow*; *Caretaker of the Dead*; *Death in the American Experience*; *Last Rights*; *Someone You Love is Dying*; *The Practice of Death*; *Grief and Mourning*; *No More Dying*; *Life After Life*; *The Way We Die*; *Death as a Fact of Life*; *The Immortality Factor*; *Facing Death*; *Death and Obscenity*; and *Living Your Dying*. One sociologist termed that burst of literature a "collective bustle," and characterized the "discovery" of death during the 1970s as "the happy death movement" (Lofland 1978). There can be no argument that the topic had become more open. Furthermore, the increasing use of life-sustaining technologies dictated that the circumstances of dying became more controllable and negotiable, even as increasing proportions of all deaths were occurring in the later years.

Little Theoretical Work. Interest in death and dying was varied and diverse during the 1970s and 1980s, and no widely accepted conceptual framework for its study emerged, except that Kathy Charmaz published a seminal book titled *The Social Reality of Death* in 1980. Sociologists had been critical both of the title and content of Kubler-Ross's widely read book *On Death and Dying* (1969) but they recognized the appeal of the subject matter (Riley 1968, 1983). In earlier decades death had been typically viewed as a social transition, as a "rite de passage," but new threads running through the literature were emerging. Formal "arrangements" were being negotiated prior to death, dying persons were generally more concerned about their survivors than they were about themselves, dying individuals were able to exercise a significant degree of control over the timing of their deaths, tensions typically existed between the requirements of formal care and the wishes of dying patients, and similar tensions almost always existed between formal and informal caregivers—between hospital bureaucracies and those significant others who were soon to be bereaved (Kalish 1985a, 1985b; Riley 1970, 1983).

Little systematic attention from sociologists, however, had emerged. *The Encyclopedia of the Social Sciences* (1968) contained but two entries, both on the social meanings of death. Similarly, there are only two indexed references in the 1988 *Handbook of Sociology* (Smelser 1988): one to poverty resulting from the death of breadwinners, the other to the role of death in popular religion. Sociologists had failed to generate any overarching theory. There have been, however, many attempts. Several kernels illustrate the broad range of these theoretical efforts. Parsons (1963) related the changing meanings of death to basic social values; Mannheim (1928, 1952) used mortality to explain social change; Renee Fox (1980, 1981) found that "life and death were coming to be viewed less as absolute . . . entities. . . and more as different points on a meta-spectrum..a new theodicity"; Dorothy and David Counts (1985) specified the role of death in the various social transformations from preliterate to modern societies; Paul Baker (1990), following Lloyd Warner (1959) and others (e.g. Kearl and Rinaldi 1983) elaborated the long-recognized theory that images of the dead exert profound influences on the living, and Michael Kearl wrote a more general statement in 1989. And

more recently, Fulton has published an essay on "Society and the Imperative of Death" (1994) in which he discusses the role of such customs and rituals as the Mardi Gras, the bullfight, the "Dani" of primitive societies, and other symbolic events in which either societal survival or individual salvation is at stake.

One exception to these various theoretical efforts is found in the sustained work of Marshall and collaborators. Starting in 1975 with a seminal article in *The American Journal of Sociology*, followed by his book *Last Chapters* (1980), he collaborated with Judith Levy in a review titled "Aging and Dying" (Marshall and Levy 1990). Marshall began his work with an empirical field study of socialization for impending death in a retirement village, followed by a compelling theoretical essay on age and awareness of finitude in developmental gerontology, and has been consistently engaged in such theoretical efforts. His basic postulate is that "awareness of finitude" operates as a trigger that permits socialization to death.

Empirical Research Largely Topical. In contrast to theoretical work, the empirical literature shows that sociological research on death and dying has been, and largely continues to be, essentially topical. Studies range widely, from the taboo on death to funerals and the social "causes" of death (Riley 1983; Marshall and Levy 1990). They include the following examples:

Planning for Death. A national survey conducted in the late 1960s showed that the great majority of Americans (85 percent) are quite realistic and consider it important to "try to make some plans about death," and to talk about it with those closest to them (Riley 1970). In addition, bereavement practices, once highly structured, are becoming increasingly varied and individually therapeutic; dying is feared primarily because it eliminates opportunities for self-fulfillment; and active adaptations to death tend to increase as one approaches the end of the life course (i.e. the making of wills, leaving instructions, negotiating conflicts).

Death and Dying in a Hospital. Among such studies, a detailed account of the "social organization" of death in a public hospital describes rules for dealing with the corpse (the body must be washed, catalogued, and ticketed). Dignity and bureaucratic efficiency are typically found to be at odds (Sudnow 1967). A contrasting account of hospital rules governing disposition of the body in contemporary Ireland is even more sociological in its emphasis (Prior 1989). In another hospital study the "caring issue" has been seen as the main social problem. The selfhood of the dying person is found to be at risk since the hospital is essentially dedicated to efficiency (Kalish 1985b). However, studies suggest that an increasing proportion of deaths may now be occurring at home or under hospice care, which "mediates between the families and formal institutions that constitute the social organization of death and dying" (Marshall and Levy 1990; see also Bass 1985).

The Funeral. The funeral as a social institution has long been of sociological concern (cf. Habenstein 1968). For example, a massive cross-cultural study attests to its worldwide function in marking a major social transition (Habenstein and Lamers 1963; Howarth 1996). Durkheim had emphasized its ceremonial role in facilitating social regrouping. Later sociologists have shown that elaborate and extravagant funeral rites may be more reflective of commercial interests than of human grief or mourning (Parsons and Lidz 1967).

The Bereaved Family. The now classic study (Eliot 1932) of the economic consequences of death on the family stimulated a large literature that documents the general proposition that survivors—particularly significant others—require various types of social supports to "get through" the period of intense personal grief and the more publicly expressed mourning. In today's societies, the time devoted to bereavement activities is generally shorter (Pratt 1981). This is consistent with Parsons's (1963) position that in societies characterized by an "active" orientation, the bereaved are expected to carry out their grief work quickly and privately.

Social Stressors as "Causes" of Death. Sociologists and psychologists have investigated a range of individually experienced "social stressors" as causes of death, such as bereavement and retirement. The hypothesis that a bereaved spouse is at higher risk of death (the "broken heart" syndrome, or "death causes death") has been widely investigated but with no conclusive results. Similarly, retirees in some longitudinal studies have been shown to experience excess mortality, whereas other investigations have reported opposite results. Retirement is a complex process, not a simple or single event, and the mortality impact of retirement is moot.

In an era in which nursing homes play an important role in the lives of many older people, the mortality consequences of relocation have come under critical scrutiny. Several studies have reported that the "warehousing" of the frail elderly results in increased mortality while in other studies feelings of security in the new "home" are shown to enhance a sense of well-being resulting in lower mortality. Similar caveats apply to macro-level studies that attempt to relate such collectively experienced stressors as economic depressions, wars, and technological revolutions to trends in mortality. Advances in mathematical modelling and the increasing availability of large and relevant data sets make this problem an attractive area for continuing sociological research (see Riley 1983 for details and sources).

Self-Motivated Death. Durkheim's studies of suicide spawned a wide, diverse, and sometimes confusing research literature. In most such studies social integration is the operative concept. If the theoretical relationship is believed to be unambiguous, the empirical relationship is far from tidy. The literature is vast and well beyond the reach of this review. Apart from suicide, it is a sociological truism that individuals are often socially motivated to influence the time of their own deaths. It has long been noted, for example, that both Thomas Jefferson and John Adams delayed their dying in order to participate in Independence Day celebrations. Several empirical studies have explored this so-called "anniversary effect" in which social events of significance are preceded by lower-than-expected mortality (Phillips and Feldman 1973). Such studies rest on Durkheim's insight that if some people are so detached from society that they commit suicide, others may be so attached that they postpone their deaths in order to participate in social events of great significance (Phillips and Smith 1990). An example of the mortality impact of personal and local events is seen in studies of the "birthday dip." One year-long study, in a test area, coded all obituaries for birthdates. The results were striking. Fewer than 10 percent of the deaths occurred during the three months prior to the birth date, whereas nearly half were reported during the following three months. Along similar lines, several sociological investigations have explored the proposition that some people die socially before they die biologically. These studies center on the notion of "levels of awareness" of death (Glaser and Strauss 1965). When both the dying person and his or her significant others are cognizant of death as a soon-to-be-experienced event, the ensuing "open" awareness may enable them to negotiate various aspects of the final phase of life. Other research on "dying trajectories" involves certainties and uncertainties as to the time of death (Glaser and Strauss 1968).

"The Right to Die." As a final and critical example in this review of disparate empirical work, a basic and far-reaching question is being asked: Does the individual, in a society deeply committed to the preservation of life, have a "right" to die? This has become one of the most profound, complex, and pressing issues of our time (Glick 1992). It involves the "rights" and wishes of the dying person, the "rights" and responsibilities of his or her survivors, the "rights" and obligations of attending physicians, and the "rights" and constraints of the law. The human side of such issues is producing a tidal wave of expressions of public interest in television documentaries, opinion surveys, editorials, pamphleteering, and radio talk shows. The issue of euthanasia is openly debated in leading medical journals, an unthinkable topic only a few years ago. Hospital rules, in which do not resuscitate (DNR) orders were written on blackboards then quickly erased, are being changed. Certain aspects of the issue have reached the Supreme Court. A major book has proposed the rationing of medical resources (Callahan 1987). Radical movements have sprung up that advocate active euthanasia and offer recipes for self-deliverance. *Final Exit*, the Hemlock Society's handbook, was an instant best-seller (Humphry 1991). The costs of the last days of life have been dramatized, sometimes spoofed as a myth (Alliance for Aging Research 1996), and sometimes reported with great care (Congressional Research Service). Jack Kevorkian, often referred to as "Dr. Death," has become both hero and despised public enemy. In short, the problems and dilemmas inherent in the "management" of death have captured both popular and scientific attention (see various issues of the Hastings Center Reports). In both instances doctors and lawyers play ambiguous but critical

roles. It is, however, the "negotiation" that is of sociological interest. Norms designed to reduce the perplexities in wrenching decisions or to reassure the decision makers (including dying persons) are generally lacking (Wetle 1994). The need for relevant norms governing "the dying process" has been noted earlier (Riley and Riley 1986), and the main considerations have been specified (Logue 1989). The U. S. Office of Technology Assessment (1987) and the Hastings Center (1987) have issued medical and ethical guidelines, respectively, on the use of life-sustaining procedures. Many years ago sociologists developed research models for studying the social aspects of heroic operations and the treatment of nonsalvageable terminal patients (Fox and Swazey 1974; Crane 1975). Yet models necessary to the formation of norms capable of handling the "rights" and wishes of the various parties to the process of dying are still clearly needed. Furthermore, the conceptual problem of distinguishing between the two actors in the dying process, which the Minnesota Conference had emphasized, has not been resolved.

CURRENT ISSUES

With roots in these diverse studies, a set of three issue-laden topics cry out for more research and understanding: 1) dying individuals want a clearer voice in how their last days are to be treated; 2) policy questions are being raised that call attention to potential conflicts between the rights of individuals and the imperatives of society; and 3) programs and campaigns designed to reduce the difficulties of dying are demanding wide social action. These issues can be grouped under three shorthand labels: the living will; assisted suicide; and the quality of dying. While these issues are of great sociological interest, they are only now beginning to be framed in terms for sociological inquiry. The following discussions, consequently, rely largely on commission reports, conferences, public forums, social commentary in the media, brief reports in such journals as *Omega, Issues in Law and Medicine, Journal of the American Geriatrics Society, Hospice Journal,* and various unpublished materials.

The Living Will. As noted above, one of the most easily understood and practical developments in response to the dilemmas of dying in America is the "living will," the so-called durable power of attorney, or some other form of advance directive. These are quasi-legal instruments, signed by the patient, that instruct attending physicians (or surrogates) as to the patient's preferred treatment at the end of life. Such directives are widely varied as to their specificity and the conditions of application, and it is currently impossible to know how many and what types of directives have been executed. There is, however, ample evidence that they are in widespread use. Simple do-it-yourself forms are available in stationery stores, and countless specialized directives have been developed to cover a wide variety of conditions and contingencies. But both the effectiveness and the ethics of such directives have become subject to wide debate: When and under what conditions is the withdrawal of food or fluids legally and medically permissible? When may guardians or surrogates act for incompetent patients? When does the constitutional right to privacy prevail? Under what conditions may the patient refuse treatment or take the initiative and disconnect respirators or tubes? When do oral directives, if ever, take precedence over written ones? The answers to such questions tend to be moot, although a broad legal doctrine has been promulgated that bears on the availability and use of advance directives. There must be "clear and convincing evidence" that the directive accurately reflects the patient's precise intentions— or would in cases of incompetency. This legal dictum, however, has proved to be both burdensome and murky. The well-known Karen Anne Quinlan case is illustrative. This young woman "existed" in a persistent vegetative state for ten years while the legal process could determine whether Karen's parents had met the "clear and convincing evidence" test (Karen's parents had testified that they knew their daughter well enough to be certain that she would not wish to live in such circumstances). In another widely cited case, Nancy Cruzan "lived" in a similar state for seven years while the intricacies of the law were being debated. These and other such cases point to the need for more useful and practical evidentiary tests. The Hastings Center published a special supplement titled "Advance Care Planning" in 1993.

In 1990, the Patient Self-Determination Act (PSDA) raised a set of new questions. The PSDA requires hospitals, nursing homes, and health providers to inform patients of their right to prepare a living will or some document of end-of-life preferences. The significance of the PSDA was underscored by an occasionally distributed joint statement by the American Medical Association and the Harvard Medical School:

Modern medicine can keep one alive long after any reasonable prospect of mental, spiritual, or emotional life is gone. The only way for a person to retain autonomy in such a situation is to record his or her preferences for medical care before they are needed. (Published in The Harvard Health Letter and elsewhere.)

The force of the PSDA, however, has not been great and today it is generally believed that its lasting importance will be found in its power to enhance understanding of the still-developing and changing doctor-patient relationship. Indeed, the drama of that relationship has now been moved to a larger stage that involves both assisted suicide and the quality of dying.

Assisted Suicide. The role of law in cases where patients or their surrogates seek to control end-of-life decisions has always been debated. The early cases in the 1950s and 1960s had revolved around "informed consent." This rule surfaced when medical treatments resulted in unanticipated negative consequences, and when it could be shown that the patient had not been informed of the risks. Not surprisingly, this rule led to more complicated ones and, during the 1970s, the increasing demand for patient control resulted in an implied "right" to die by refusing treatment. Of sociological interest, it was popular experience— not statutory law or court decisions—that was bringing about social change (see M. W. Riley 1978 for a theoretical statement). Nor was it long before demands for the "right" to receive treatments specifically designed to hasten death were seriously being discussed and in some states actually outlawed. As these events unfolded they have been reported by major news services, and analyzed by Hastings Center reports beginning in 1995.

In 1996 the U.S. Court of Appeals for the Ninth Circuit struck down a Washington state statute that had been passed specifically to deny such a right. The presiding judge included this noteworthy statement:

A competent, terminally ill adult, having lived nearly the full measure of his life, has a strong liberty interest in choosing a dignified and humane death rather than being reduced at the end of his existence to a childlike state of helplessness–diapered, sedated, incompetent.

The case was striking not only for its human interest but also because it invoked the guarantee of personal liberty in the Fourteenth Amendment to the U.S. Constitution. Shortly thereafter a New York statute was struck down by the U.S. Court of Appeals for the Second Circuit (Quill 1996), which had argued that if physicians were allowed to help people die it would put society on a slippery slope leading inevitably to abuse. The court pointed out, however, that physicians are not killers if they prescribe drugs to hasten death any more than they are killers when they discontinue life supports.

As expected, both cases were sent to the U.S. Supreme Court which has, at this writing, let stand state laws that prohibit any form of physician-assisted suicide. But the issue is far from settled. The Court's decision concluded with this surprising statement by Chief Justice Rehnquist:

Throughout the nation, Americans are engaged in an earnest and profound debate about the morality, legality and practicality of physician-assisted suicide. Our holding permits this debate to continue.

This statement was all the more remarkable since the chief justice, in his long opinion, rejected both the "liberty" and "due process" constitutional arguments, but came far short of putting the matter to rest. Indeed, continuing developments indicate that the question of physician-assisted suicide is not likely to go away soon. For example, the State of Oregon has passed two voter referenda, the most recent in 1998 with a 60 percent majority support which makes Oregon the only state (as of 1998) to permit, under strict conditions, physician-assisted suicide. The State of Michigan has rejected an Oregon-type statute and has finally convicted Dr. Kevorkian of second degree murder. Several other states are reported to be experimenting with alternatives that enhance the "right" of the individual to choose to die (for details of these developments see The Hastings Center reports). It may be that the law is overreaching its capacity to deal with such a basic and philosophical issue. The question is profound. Is there any logical (or sociological) difference between the right to refuse treatment designed to prolong life and a parallel right to receive treatment designed to hasten death? Sociologists would ask: What is the distinction between the acceptance of death and its acceleration? Is the question so abstract that it defies empirical inquiry? Both the medical and legal answers to the issue are ambiguous and have been discussed in a book by a physician who publicly admitted helping a patient to die. Dr. Timothy Quill not only was the main plaintiff in the New York case, but he has become the leading medical voice on issues of assisted suicide. He writes with authority and sensitivity: "Death seems antithetical to modern medicine—no longer a natural and inevitable part of the life cycle, but a medical failure to be fought off, ignored, and minimized. The dark side of this desperate battle has patients spending their last days in the intensive care units of acute hospitals, tubes inserted into every body part, vainly trying to forestall death's inevitability. No one wants to die, but if we have to, there must be a better way" (for an account of the issues see Quill 1996).

The Quality of Dying. Sociological concern with assisted suicide has been paralleled with concern for how people die. It had been hoped that the PSDA not only would make advance directives more effective, but would also bring about better communications between doctors and terminal patients. The act, however, was deemed a failure even before it was formally put in place. An impressive experiment, of great sociological interest, was designed to solve these basic issues. Funded and launched by the Robert Wood Johnson Foundation, it was the advance directive problem cast in research terms. The "Study to Understand Prognoses and Preferences in Risks of Treatment" carried such an unwieldy title that it was quickly shortened to the acronym SUPPORT (for a detailed account see The Hastings Center special supplement that carries the subtitle "The Lessons of SUPPORT" 1995). Five teaching hospitals were invited to participate in this multimillion dollar project. Phase One called for baseline data on the end-of-life experiences of some 9,000 dying patients. When the data were analyzed, the researchers were not surprised to find much to criticize in various regimens of hospital care. Their main finding, however, was that doctors and attending nurses must attend not only to the physical comfort and pain management needs of patients but, more importantly, to their psychosocial needs.

Phase Two, consequently, called for experimentation. The 9,000 cases were randomized and an experimental intervention consisting of a protocol designed to sensitize doctors to attend more closely to psychosocial needs was administered to one-half of the cases and withheld from the other half, which had served as a control group. The experiment was continued for two years and expectations were high. Much to the chagrin of the study directors, when the two groups were compared, no differences were found! The experimental intervention showed no effects. This negative finding was so shocking that a number of evaluation panels were enlisted to reanalyze the data and scrutinize the research design. Their efforts, however, only served to corroborate the original analysis and Daniel Callahan (1995), then president of The Hastings Center, concluded with this statement, "This painstaking scrutiny into how people die only goes to show how difficult it is to make the process any better. . . We thought that the care of dying patients could be set right by . . . some good talk between doctor and patient . . . we thought that we just needed reform . . . it is now obvious that we need a revolution" (Callahan 1995).

Callahan's dramatic statement had the effect of nourishing a spate of organizations and proposals that had sprung up to improve the care of dying patients. For example "Project Death in America" (PDIA), centered at Sloan Kettering Hospital in New York was funded by the billionaire George Soros; the "Center to Improve Care of the Dying" (CICD), based in the George Washington Medical School and originally funded by the Retirement Research Foundation in 1995, enjoys wide institutional support and in 1997 launched a program for individual advocacy, "Americans for Better Care of the Dying" (ABCD); the American Board of Internal Medicine (ABIM) began publishing educational materials on techniques to improve care of the dying in 1996; and the American Medical Association (AMA) began alerting its members to the most recent developments in end-of-life care. And finally, the Robert Wood Johnson Foundation, which has long served as the collective voice for issues on dying, launched "Last Acts" in 1997, which is designed to involve the public through such participating organizations as the Institute of Medicine, the American Hospital Association, the Health Care Financing Administration, the National Hospice Organization, the Veterans Health

Administration, the American College of Physicians, and a host of specialized associations such as the American Pain Society, the American Cancer Society, Choice in Dying, Partnership for Organ Donation, Memorial Societies of America, Wellness Councils of America, and on and on. Former First Lady Roslyn Carter, in a nationally broadcast speech, proclaimed that, "We need this coalition so that fewer people will die alone, in pain, and attached to machines, with the result that more people. . . can experience dying for what it ought to be. . . the last act in the journey of life." The President of the Robert Wood Johnson Foundation was both optimistic and enthusiastic:

With all that is going on. . . we are seizing the moment, "Last Acts" will be much more than platitudes about a good death. . . it will undertake to improve care at the end of life. . . If the campaign succeeds . . . we will find a significant decrease in the number of people dying in pain, an increase in referrals to hospice, more people dying at home outside the hospital, and fewer requests for physician-assisted suicide (1997).

If, however, the campaign does not live up to expectations, the foundation will work with the American Medical Association "on helping physicians to work with patients on advance care planning, and providing opportunities for physicians to increase their skills in palliative medicine and comfort care." It is too early to estimate the long-term effects of this blizzard of efforts to improve the way people die, but it is not too early to predict that any improvements in the quality of dying based only on comfort care are likely to be short term. But change is in the air. Dying persons are pressing for more participation in when and how they die, and caregivers are coming under increasing criticism of the limitations of their caring regimens.

AN EVOLVING PERSPECTIVE

As indicated by this review of past research and current issues, the limitations of both legal and medical approaches to the problems of dying in contemporary society mean that the perspectives of sociology will be brought to bear. Perhaps future sociological attention will focus on the uniquely sociological principle that the dying process is not understandable in individual terms. This, in turn, provokes a series of predictions: Sociologists will focus on how dying persons are defined by their survivors and caregivers as well as on the sociological hypothesis that dying persons are more concerned for others than they are for themselves. Sociologists will be required to disentangle the concatenation of forces that has produced today's caregiving regimens in which terminal patients tend to be treated more as objects than as persons. Sociologists will be asked to explain how the process of socialization has seemingly been reversed, with the individual being figuratively stripped of years of social experience and defined as a nonperson. In effect, sociologists will be asked to explain the historical alchemy whereby dying persons themselves have been conned into believing that all they needed was palliation and comfort care.

REFERENCES

Alliance for Aging Research 1996 *Uncovering the Facts about the Cost of the Last Year of Life*. Washington, D.C.: AAR.

Baker, Paul M. 1990 "Socialization after Death: the Might of the Living Dead." In Beth Hess and Elizabeth Markson, eds.,*Growing Old in America*. Rutgers: Trasaction Books.

Bass, David M. 1985 "The Hospice Ideology and Success of Hospice Care." *Research on Aging* 7:1.

Blauner, Robert 1966 "Death and Social Structure." *Psychiatry* 29:378–94.

Bowman, L. 1959 *The American Funeral: A Study in Guilt, Extravagance, and Sublimity*. Washington D.C.: Public Affairs Press.

Callahan, D. 1995 "Dying Well in the Hospital." *Hastings Center Report*. Briarcliff Manor, N.Y.: Hastings Center.

—— 1987 *Setting Limits; Medical Goals in an Aging Society*. New York: Simon and Schuster.

Charmaz, K. C. 1980 *Social Reality of Death*. Reading, Mass.: Addison-Wesley.

Counts, D.A., and D.C. Counts 1985 *Aging and Its Transformations: Moving Toward Death in Pacific Societies*. Lanham, Md: University Press of America.

Crane, D. 1975 *The Sanctity of Social Life: Physicians' Treatment of Critically Ill Patients*. New York: Russell Sage Foundation.

Eliot, T. 1932 "The Bereaved Family." Special issue, *The Annals*160.

Fox, R.C., and T.P. Swazey 1981 "The Sting of Death in American Society." *Social Service Review*. March:42–59.

—— 1980 "The Social Meaning of Death." *The Annals* 447.

——1974 *The Courage to Fail: A Social View of Organ Transplantation and Dialysis*. Chicago: University of Chicago Press.

Fulton, R. 1994 "Society and the Imperative of Death." In I. Corless et al., eds., *Dying, Death and Bereavement*. Boston: Jones and Bartlett.

—— 1965 *Death and Identity*. New York: John Wiley and Sons.

Fulton, R., and R. Bendiksen 1994 *Death and Identity*, 3rd ed. Philadelphia: The Charles Press.

Fulton, R., and G. Owen 1988 "Death and Society in Contemporary Society." *Omega* 18(4).

Glaser, B.G., and A.L. Strauss 1965 *Awareness of Dying*. Chicago: Aldine.

—— 1968 *Time for Dying*. Chicago: Aldine.

Glick, H.R. 1992 *The Right to Die: Policy Innovation and its Consequences*. New York: Columbia University Press.

Habenstein, R.W. 1968 "The Social Organization of Death."*The International Encyclopedia of the Social Sciences*. New York: Macmillan and Free Press.

——, and M.W. Lamers 1963 *Funeral Customs the World Over*. Milwaukee: Bulfin.

Hastings Center 1987 *Guidelines on the Termination of Life-Sustaining Treatment and the Care of the Dying*. Bloomington, Ind.: Indiana University Press.

Howarth, G. 1996 *Last Rites: The Work of the Modern Funeral Director*. Amityville N.Y.: Baywood Publishing Co.

Humphry, Derek 1991 *Final Exit: the Practicalities of Self-Deliverance and Assisted Suicide*. Eugene Oreg.: The Hemlock Society.

Kalish, R.A. 1985a *Death, Grief and Caring Relationships*. Monterey, Calif.: Brooks/Cole.

—— 1985b "The Social Context of Death and Dying." In R.H. Binstock and E. Shanas, eds., *Handbook of Aging and the Social Sciences*. New York: Van Nostrand Reinhold Co.

Kearl, Michael C. *1989 Endings: A Sociology of Death and Dying*. Oxford: Oxford University Press.

——, and A. Rinaldi 1983 "The Political Uses of the Dead as Symbols in Contemporary Civil Religions." *Social Forces*61:3.

Kubler-Ross, E. 1969 *On Death and Dying*. New York: Macmillan.

Lofland, L. 1978 *The Craft of Dying: The Modern Face of Death*. Beverly Hills, Calif.: Sage.

Logue, B. 1989 *Death Control and the Elderly: The Growing Acceptability of Euthanasia.* Providence: Population Studies and Training Center, Brown University.

Mannheim, K. 1928, 1959 "The Problem of Generations." In P. Keeskemeti, ed., *Essays in Sociological Knowledge.* London: Routledge and Kegan Paul.

Marshall, V.W. 1980 *Last Chapters: A Sociology of Aging and Dying.* Belmont Calif.: Wordsworth.

——, and J. A. Levy 1990 "Aging and Dying." In R. H. Binstock and L. George, eds., *Handbook of Aging and the Social Sciences*, 3rd ed. San Diego: Academic Press.

Parsons, T. 1963 "Death in American Society: A Brief Working Paper." *American Behavioral Scientist.*

——, and V. W. Lidz 1967 "Death in American Society." In E.S. Shneidman, ed., *Essays in Self Destruction.* New York: Science House.

Phillips, D.P., and K.A. Feldman 1973 "A Dip in Deaths before Ceremonial Occasions: Some New Relationships between Integration and Mortality." *American Journal of Sociology* 87.

——, and D.G. Smith 1990 "Postponement of Death Until Symbolically Meaningful Occasions." *Journal of the American Medical Association*, vol. 203(14).

Pratt, L.V. 1981 "Business Temporal Norms and Bereavement Behavior." *American Sociological Review* 4:317–333.

Prior, Lindsay 1989 *The Social Organization of Death: Medical Discourses and Social Practices in Belfast.* New York: St.Martin's Press.

Quill, T.E. 1996 *A Midwife through the Dying Process.* Baltimore, Md.: The Johns Hopkins University Press.

Riley, J.W., Jr. 1983 "Dying and the Meanings of Death: Sociological Inquiries." *Annual Review of Sociology* 9:191–216.

—— 1970 "What People Think about Death." In O. G. Brim, Jr. et al., eds., *The Dying Patient.* New York: Russell Sage Foundation.

—— 1968 "Death and Bereavements." In D.L. Sills, ed., *International Encyclopedia of the Social Sciences.* New York: Macmillan and Free Press.

Riley, M. W., and J.W. Riley, Jr. 1986 "Longevity and Social Structure: the Added Years." *Daedalus* 115:51–75.

Sudnow, D. 1967 *Passing On: The Social Organization of Dying.* Englewood Cliffs, N.J.: Prentice-Hall.

U. S. Congress, Office of Technology Assessment 1987 *Life-Sustaining Technologies and the Elderly.* Washington D.C.: U.S. Government Printing Office.

Warner, W.L. 1959 *The Living and the Dead.* New Haven, Conn.: Yale University Press.

Wetle, T. 1994 "Individual Preferences and Advance Planning." *Hastings Center Report.* Briarcliff Manor, N.Y.: Hastings Center.

JOHN W. RILEY, JR.

DECISION-MAKING THEORY AND RESEARCH

Decision making must be considered in any explanation of individual behavior, because behaviors are based on decisions or judgments people have made. Thus, decision-making theory and research is of interest in many fields that examine behavior, including cognitive psychology (e.g., Busemeyer, Medin, and Hastie 1995), social psychology (e.g., Ajzen 1996), industrial and organizational psychology (e.g., Stevenson, Busemeyer, and Naylor 1990), economics (e.g., Lopes 1994), management (e.g., Shapira 1995), and philosophy (e.g., Manktelow and Over 1993), as well as sociology. This section will be an overview of decision-making theory and research. Several excellent sources of further information include: Baron (1994), Dawes (1997), Gilovich (1993), and Hammond (1998).

DECISION-MAKING THEORIES

Most decision-making theory has been developed in the twentieth century. The recency of this development is surprising considering that gambling has existed for millennia, so humans have a long history of making judgments of probabilistic events. Indeed, insurance, which is in effect a form of gambling (as it involves betting on the likelihood of an event happening, or, more often, not happening), was sold as early as the fifteenth and sixteenth centuries. Selling insurance prior to the development of probability theory, and in many early cases without any statistics for, or even frequencies of, the events being insured led to bankruptcy for many of the first insurance sellers (for more information about the history of probability and decision making see Hacking 1975, 1990; Gigerenzer et al. 1989).

Bayes's Theorem. One of the earliest theories about probability was *Bayes's Theorem* (1764/1958). This theorem was developed to relate the probability of one event to another; specifically, the probability of one event occurring given the probability of another event occurring. These events are sometimes called the cause and effect, or the hypothesis and the data. Using H and D (hypothesis and data) as the two events, Bayes's Theorem is: P(H|D) = P(H)P(D|H)/P(D) [1] or P(H|D) = P(D|H)P(H)/[P(D|H)P(H)+P(D|−H)P(−H)] [2] That is, the probability of H given D has occurred is equal to [1] the probability of H occurring multiplied by the probability of D occurring given H has occurred divided by the probability of D occurring, or [2] the probability of D given H has occurred multiplied by the probability of H then divided by the probability of D given H has occurred multiplied by the probability of H plus the probability that D occurs given H has not occurred multiplied by the probability that H does not occur.

The cab problem (introduced in Kahneman and Tversky 1972) has been used in several studies as a measure of whether people's judgments are consistent with Bayes's Theorem. The problem is as follows: A cab was involved in a hit-and-run accident at night. Two cab companies, the Green and the Blue, operate in the city. You are given the following data: (a) 85 percent of the cabs in the city are Green and 15 percent are Blue. (b) a witness identified the cab as Blue. The court tested the reliability of the witness under the same circumstances that existed on the night of the accident and concluded that the witness correctly identified each one of the two colors 80 percent of the time and failed 20 percent of the time. What is the probability that the cab involved in the accident was Blue rather than Green? Using the provided information and formula [2] above, P(Blue Cab|Witness says "Blue") = P(Witness says "Blue"|Blue Cab)P(Blue Cab)/[P(Witness says "Blue"|Blue Cab)P(Blue Cab) + P(Witness says "Blue"|Green Cab)P(Green Cab)] or P(Blue Cab|Witness says "Blue") = (.80)(.15)/[(.80)(.15)+(.20)(.85)] = (.12)/ [(.12)+(.17)] = .41

Thus, according to Bayes's Theorem, the probability that the cab involved in the accident was Blue, given the witness testifying it was Blue, is 0.41. So, despite the witness's testimony that the cab was Blue, it is more likely that the cab was Green (0.59 probability), because the probabilities for the base rates (85 percent of cabs are Green and 15 percent Blue) are more extreme than those for the witness's accuracy (80 percent accuracy).

Generally, people will rate the likelihood that the cab was Blue to be much higher than .41, and often the response will be .80—the witness's accuracy rate (Tversky and Kahneman 1982).

That finding has been used to argue that people often ignore base rate information (the proportions of each type of cab, in this case; Tversky and Kahneman 1982), which is irrational. However, other analyses of this situation are possible (cf. Birnbaum 1983; Gigerenzer and Hoffrage 1995), which suggest that people are not irrationally ignoring base rate information. The issue of rationality will be discussed further below.

Expected Utility (EU) Theory. Bayes's Theorem is useful, but often we are faced with decisions to choose one of several alternatives that have uncertain outcomes. The best choice would be the one that maximizes the outcome, as measured by utility (i.e., how useful something is to a person). Utility is not equal to money (high-priced goods may be less useful than lower-priced goods), although money may be used as a substitute measure of utility. EU Theory (von Neumann and Morganstern 1947) states that people should maximize their EU when choosing among a set of alternatives, as in: EU = ([Ui * Pi]; where Ui is the utility for each alternative, i, and Pi is the probability associated with that alternative.

The earlier version of this theory (Expected Value Theory, or EV) used money to measure the worth of the alternatives, but utility recognizes people may use more than money to evaluate the alternatives. Regardless, in both EU and EV, the probabilities are regarded similarly, so people only need consider total EU/EV, not the probability involved in arriving at the total.

However, research suggests that people consider certain probabilities to be special, as their judgments involving these probabilities are often inconsistent with EU predictions. That is, people seem to consider events that have probabilities of 1.0 or 0.0 differently than events that are uncertain (probabilities other than 1.0 or 0.0). The special consideration given to certain probabilities is called the *certainty effect* (Kahneman and Tversky 1979). To illustrate this effect, which of these two options do you prefer? A. Winning $50 with probability .5 B. Winning $30 with probability .7 Now which of these next two options do you prefer? C. Winning

$50 with probability .8 D. Winning $30 with probability 1.0

Perhaps you preferred A and D, which many people do. However, according to EU, those choices are inconsistent, because D does not have a higher EU than C (for D, EU = $30 = (1.0 * $30); for C, EU = $40 = (.8 * $50)). Recognize that A and B differ from C and D by a .3 increase in probability, and EU prescribes selecting the option with the highest EU. The certainty effect may also be seen in the following pair of options. E. Winning $1,000,000 with probability 1.0 F. Winning $2,000,000 with probability .5

According to EU, people should be indifferent between E and F, because they both have the same EU ($1,000,000 * 1.0 = $2,000,000 * .5). However, people tend to prefer E to F. As the cliche goes, a bird in the hand is worth two in the bush. These results (choosing D and E) suggest that people are risk averse, because those are the certain options, and choosing them avoids risk or uncertainty. But risk aversion does not completely capture the issue. Consider this pair of options: G. Losing $50 with probability .8 H. Losing $30 with probability 1.0

If people were risk averse, then most would choose H, which has no risk; $30 will be lost for sure. However, most people choose G, because they want to avoid a certain loss, even though it means risking a greater loss. In this case, people are risk seeking.

The tendency to treat certain probabilities differently from uncertain probabilities led to the development of decision-making theories that focused on explaining how people make choices, rather than how they should make choices.

Prospect Theory and Rank-Dependent Theories. Changing from EV to EU acknowledged that people do not simply assess the worth of alternatives on the basis of money. The certainty effect illustrates that people do not simply assess the likelihood of alternatives, so decision theories must take that into account. The first theory to do so was prospect theory (Kahneman and Tversky 1979).

Prospect theory proposes that people choose among prospects (alternatives) by assigning each prospect a subjective value and a decision weight (a value between 0.0 and 1.0), which may be functionally equal to monetary value and probability,

respectively, but need not be actually equal to them. The prospect with the highest value as calculated by multiplying the subjective value and the decision weight is chosen. Prospect theory assumes that losses have greater weight than gains, which explains why people tend to be risk seeking for losses but not for gains. Also, prospect theory assumes that people make judgments from a subjective reference point rather than an objective position of gaining or losing.

Prospect theory is similar to EU in that the decision weight is independent of the context. However, recent decision theories suggest weights are created within the context of the available alternatives based on a ranking of the alternatives (see Birnbaum, Coffey, Mellers, and Weiss 1992; Luce and Fishburn 1991; Tversky and Kahneman 1992). The need for a rank-dependent mechanism within decision theories is generally accepted (Mellers, Schwartz, and Cooke 1998), but the specifics of the mechanism are still debated (see Birnbaum and McIntosh 1996).

Improper Linear Models. Distinguishing between alternatives based on some factor (e.g., value, importance, etc.) and weighting the alternatives based on those distinctions has been suggested as a method for decision making (Dawes 1979). The idea is to create a linear model for the decision situation. Linear models are statistically derived weighted averages of the relevant predictors. For example: L(lung cancer) = w1*age + w2*smoking + w3*family history, where L(lung cancer) is the likelihood of getting lung cancer, and wx is the weight for each factor. Any number of factors could be included in the model, although only factors that are relevant to the decision should be included. Optimally, the weights for each factor should be constructed from examining relevant data for the decision.

However, Dawes (1979) has demonstrated that linear models using equal weighting are almost as good as models with optimal weights, although they require less work, because no weight calculations need be made; factors that make the event more likely are weighted +1, and those that make it less likely are weighted −1.

Furthermore, linear models are often better than a person's intuition, even when the person is an expert. Several studies of clinical judgment (including medical doctors and clinical psychologists) have found that linear models always do as well as, if not better than, the clinical experts (see Einhorn 1972). Similarly, bank loan officers asked to judge which businesses will go bankrupt within three years of opening was about 75 percent accurate, but a statistical model was 82 percent accurate (Libby 1976).

Arkes, Dawes, and Christensen (1986) demonstrated this point with people knowledgeable about baseball. Participants were asked to identify "which of. . . three players won the MVP [most valuable player] award for that year." Each player's season statistics were provided. One of the three players was from the World Series winning team, and subjects were told that 70 percent of the time the MVP came from the World Series winning team, so if they were uncertain, they could use that decision rule.

Participants moderately knowledgeable of baseball did better than the participants highly knowledgeable, although the highly knowledgeable participants were more confident. The moderately knowledgeable group did better because they used the decision rule more. Yet, neither group did as well as they could have, if they had used the decision rule for every judgment. How a little knowledge can influence judgment will be further explained in the next section on how people make decisions.

DECISION PROCESSING

Decision theories changed because studies revealed that people often do not make judgments that are consistent with how the theories said they should be making judgments. This section will describe evidence about how people make judgments. Specifically, several *heuristics* will be discussed, which are short cuts that people may use to process information when making a judgment (Kahneman, Slovic, and Tversky 1982, is a classic collection of papers on this topic).

Availability. Consider the following questions: What is the first digit that comes to mind?, What is the first one-digit number that comes to mind?, and What is the first digit, such as one, that comes to mind? Kubovy (1977) found that the second statement, which mentions "1" in passing, resulted in more "1" responses than either of the other

two statements. The explanation is that mentioning "1" made it more available in memory. People are using *availability*, when they make a judgment on the basis of what first comes to mind.

Interestingly, the third statement, which mentions "1" in an explicit manner, resulted in fewer "1" responses than the first statement, which does not mention "1" at all. Kubovy suggests there are fewer "1" responses, because people have an explanation of why they are thinking of "1" following that statement (it mentions "1"), so they do not choose it, because "1" has not been thought of at random. Thus, information must not only be available, but it must be perceived as relevant also.

Mood. Information that is available and may seem relevant to a judgment is a person's present mood (for a review of mood and judgment research see Clore, Schwarz, and Conway 1994). Schwarz and Clore (1983) suggest that people will use their mood state in the judgment process, if it seems relevant to that judgment. They contacted people by phone on cloudy or sunny days, and predicted that people would be happier on the sunny days than on the cloudy days. That prediction was verified. However, if people were first asked what the weather was like, then there was no difference in people's happiness on sunny and cloudy days. Schwarz and Clore suggested that asking people about the weather gave them a reason for their mood, so they did not use their mood in making the happiness judgment, because it did not seem relevant. Thus, according to Schwarz and Clore, people will use their mood as a heuristic for judgment, when the situation elicits actions from people as if they ask themselves, how do I feel about this?

Quantity and Numerosity. An effect that is also similar to availability was demonstrated in a series of experiments by Josephs, Giesler, and Silvera (1994). They found that subjects relied on observable quantity information when making personal performance judgments. They called this effect the *quantity principle*, because people seemed to use the size or quantity of material available to make their judgment. The experimenters had participants proofread text that was either attached to the source from which it came (e.g., a book or journal) or not, which was an unfamiliar task for the participants. They found that performance estimations on an unfamiliar task were affected by the quantity of the task work completed. Participants whose work resulted in a large pile of material rated their performance higher than participants whose work resulted in small pile. However, the amount of actual work done was the same. Moreover, if the pile was not in sight at the time of judgment, then performance estimates did not differ.

Pelham, Sumarta, and Myaskovsky (1994) demonstrated an effect similar to the quantity principle, which they called the *numerosity heuristic*. This heuristic refers to the use of the number of units as a cue for judgment. For example, the researchers found that participants rated the area of a circle as larger when the circle was presented as pieces that were difficult to imagine as a whole circle than if the pieces were presented so that it was easy to imagine, and larger than the undivided circle. This result suggests that dividing a whole into pieces will lead to those pieces being thought of as larger than the whole, and this will be especially so when it is hard to imagine the pieces as the whole. That is, the numerosity of the stimulus to be rated can affect the rating of that stimulus.

Anchoring. *Anchoring* is similar to availability and quantity heuristics, because it involves making a judgment using some stimulus as a starting point, and adjusting from that point. For example, Sherif, Taub, and Hovland (1958) had people make estimates of weight on a six-point scale. Prior to each estimation, subjects held an "anchor" weight that was said to represent "6" on the scale. When the anchor's weight was close to the other weights, then subjects' judgments were also quite close to the anchor, with a modal response of 6 on the six-point scale. However, heavier anchors resulted in lower responses. The heaviest anchor produced a modal response of 2.

However, anchoring need not involve the direct experience of a stimulus. Simply mentioning a stimulus can lead to an anchoring effect. Kahneman and Tversky (1972) assigned people the number 10 or 65 by means of a seemingly random process (a wheel of fortune). These people then estimated the percentage of African countries in the United Nations. Those assigned the number 10 estimated 25 percent, and those assigned the number 65 estimated 45 percent (at the time the actual percentage was 35). This indicates the psychological

impact of one's starting point (or anchor), when making a judgment.

An anecdotal example of someone trying to fight the anchoring phenomenon is a writer who tears up a draft of what she is working on, and throws it away, rather than trying to work with that draft. It may seem wasteful to have created something, only to throw it out. However, at times, writers may feel that what they have produced is holding them in a place that they do not want to be. Thus, it could be better to throw out that draft, rather than trying to rework it, which is akin to pulling up anchor.

Endowment Effect. Related to anchoring is the tendency people have to stay where they are. This tendency is known as the *endowment effect* (Thaler 1980) or the *status quo bias* (Samuelson and Zeckhauser 1988). This tendency results in people wanting more for something they already have than they would be willing to pay to acquire that same thing. In economic terms, this would be described as a discrepancy between what people are willing to pay (WTP) and what they are willing to accept (WTA). Kahneman, Knetsch, and Thaler (1990) found WTA amounts much higher for an item already possessed than WTP amounts to obtain that item. In their study, half of the people in a university class were given a university coffee mug, and half were not. A short time later, the people with the mugs were asked how much money they wanted for their mug (their WTA amount), and those without the mug were asked how much they would pay to get a mug (their WTP amount). The median WTA amount was about twice the median WTP amount: WTA = $7.12, WTP = $2.87. Thus, few trades were made, and this is consistent with the idea that people often seem to prefer what they have to what they could have.

Representativeness. People may make judgments using *representativeness*, which is the tendency to judge events as more likely if they represent the typical or expected features for that class of events. Thus, representativeness occurs when people judge an event using an impression of the event rather than a systematic analysis of it. Two examples of representativeness misleading people are the gambler's fallacy and the conjunction fallacy.

The gambler's fallacy is the confusion of independent and dependent events. Independent events are not causally related to each other (e.g., coin flips, spins of a roulette wheel, etc.). Dependent events are causally related; what happened in the past has some bearing on what happens in the present (e.g., the amount of practice has some bearing on how well someone will perform in a competition). The confusion arises when people's expectations for independent events are violated. For example, if a roulette wheel comes up black eighteen times in a row, some people might think that red must be the result of the next spin. However, the likelihood of red on the next spin is the same as it is each and every spin, and the same as it would be if red, instead of black, had resulted on each of the previous eighteen spins. Each and every roulette wheel spin is an independent event.

The conjunction fallacy (Tversky and Kahneman 1983) occurs when people judge the conjunction of two events as more likely than (at least) one of the two events. The "Linda scenario" has been frequently studied: Linda is thirty-one years old, single, outspoken, and very bright. She majored in philosophy. As a student, she was deeply concerned with issues of discrimination and social justice, and also participated in anti-nuclear demonstrations. Following that description, subjects are asked to rank order in terms of probability several statements including the following: Linda is active in the feminist movement. [F] Linda is a bank teller. [B] Linda is a bank teller and is active in the feminist movement. [B&F]

The conjunction fallacy is committed if people rank the B&F statement higher (so more likely) than either the B or F statement alone, because that is logically impossible. The likelihood of B&F may be equal to B or F, but it cannot be greater than either of them, because B&F is a subset of the set of B events and the set of F events.

People find events with multiple parts (such as B&F) more plausible than separate events (such as B or F alone), but plausibility is not equal to likelihood. Making an event more plausible might make it a better story, which could be misleading and result in erroneous inferences (Markovits and Nantel 1989). Indeed, some have suggested that people act as if they are constructing stories in their minds and then make judgments based on the stories they construct (Pennington and Hastie 1993). But of course good stories are not always true, or even likely.

INDIVIDUAL DIFFERENCES

Another question about decision processing is whether there are individual differences between people in their susceptibility to erroneous decision making. For example, do some people tend to inappropriately use the heuristics outlined above, and if so, is there a factor that accounts for that inappropriate use?

Stanovich and West (1998) had participants do several judgment tasks and related the performance on those tasks to assessments of cognitive ability and thinking styles. They found that cognitive capacity does account for some performance on some judgment tasks, which suggests that computational limitations could be a partial explanation of non-normative responding (i.e., judgment errors). Also, independent of cognitive ability, thinking styles accounted for some of the participants' performance on some judgment tasks.

A similar suggestion is that some erroneous judgments are the result of participants' conversational ability. For example, Slugoski and Wilson (1998) show that six errors in social judgment are related to people's conversational skills. They suggest that judgment errors may not be errors, because participants may be interpreting the information presented to them differently than the researcher intends (see also Hilton and Slugoski 1999).

Finally, experience affects decision-making ability. Nisbett, Krantz, Jepson, and Kunda (1983) found that participants with experience in the domain in question preferred explanations that reflected statistical inferences. Similarly, Fong, Krantz, and Nisbett (1986) found that statistical explanations were used more often by people with more statistical training. These results suggest that decision-making ability can improve through relevant domain experience, as well as through statistical training that is not domain specific.

GROUP DECISION MAKING

Social Dilemmas. *Social dilemmas* occur when the goals of individuals conflict with the goals of their group; individuals face the dilemma of choosing between doing what is best for them personally and what is best for the group as a whole (Lopes 1994). Hardin (1965) was one of the first to write about these dilemmas in describing the "tragedy of the commons." The tragedy was that individuals tried to maximize what they could get from the common and, or the "commons," which resulted in the commons being overused, thereby becoming depleted. If each individual had only used his allotted share of the commons, then it would have continued to be available to everyone.

Prisoner's Dilemma. The best-known social dilemma is the prisoner's dilemma (PD), which involves two individuals (most often, although formulations with more than two people are possible). The original PD involved two convicts' decision whether or not to confess to a crime (Rapoport and Chammah 1965). But the following example is functionally equivalent.

Imagine you are selling an item to another person, but you cannot meet to make the exchange. You agree to make the exchange by post. You will send the other person the item, and receive the money in return. If you both do so, then you each get 3 units (arbitrary amount, but amounts received for each combination of choices is important). However, you imagine that you could simply not put the item in the post, yet still receive the money. Imagine doing so results in you getting 5 units and the other person -1 units. However, the other person similarly thinks that not posting the money would result in getting the item for free, which would result in 5 units for the other person and -1 for you. If you both do not put anything in the post, although you agreed to do so, you would be at the status quo (0 units each).

Do you post the item (i.e., cooperate) or not? Regardless of what the other person does, you will get more out of not cooperating (5 v. 3, when the other person cooperates, and 0 v. -1, when other does not). However, if you both do not cooperate, that produces an inferior group outcome, compared to cooperating (0 [0+0] v. 6 [3+3], respectively). Thus, the dilemma is that each individual has an incentive to not cooperate, but the best outcome for the group is obtained when each person cooperates. Can cooperation develop from such a situation?

Axelrod (1984; cf. Hofstader 1985) investigated that question by soliciting people to participate in a series of PD games (social dilemmas are often referred to as games). Each person submitted a strategy for choosing to cooperate or not over a series of interactions with the other strategies. Each interaction would result in points being awarded to each strategy, and the strategy that generated the most points won. The winning strategy was Tit for Tat. It was also the simplest strategy. The Tit for Tat strategy is to cooperate on the first turn, and then do whatever the other person just did (i.e., on turn x, Tit for Tat will do whatever its opponent did on turn x-1).

Axelrod suggested that four qualities led to Tit for Tat's success. First, it was a *nice* strategy, because it first cooperates, and Tit for Tat will cooperate as long as the other person cooperates. But when the other person does not cooperate, then it immediately retaliates. That is, it responds to noncooperation with noncooperation, which illustrates its second good quality. Tit for Tat is *provocable*, because it immediately reacts to noncooperation, rather than waiting to see what will happen next, or ignore the noncooperation. However, if the opponent goes back to cooperating, then Tit for Tat will also go back to cooperating. That is quality three: *forgiveness*. Tit for Tat will not continue punishing the other player for previous noncooperations. All that counts for Tit for Tat is what just happened, not the total amount of noncooperation that has happened. Finally, Tit for Tat has *clarity*, because it is simple to understand. A complex strategy can be confusing, so it may be misunderstood by opponents. If the opponent's intentions are unclear, then noncooperation is best, because if or when a complex strategy is going to be cooperative cannot be predicted.

Thus, a cooperative strategy can be effective even when there are clear incentives for noncooperation. Furthermore, Axelrod did another computer simulation in which strategies were rewarded by reproducing themselves, rather than simply accumulating points. Thus, success meant that the strategy had more of its kind to interact with. Again, Tit for Tat was best, which further suggests that a cooperative strategy can be effective and can flourish in situations that seem to be designed for noncooperation.

Bargaining and Fairness. Bargaining and negotiation have received increasing attention in decision theory and research (e.g., Pruitt and Carnevale 1993), as has the issue of justice or fairness (e.g., Mellers and Baron 1993). These issues are involved in the "ultimatum game," which involves two people and a resource (often a sum of money). The rules of the game are that one person proposes a division of the resource between them (a bargain), and the other person accepts or rejects the proposal. If the proposal is rejected, then both people get nothing, so the bargain is an ultimatum: this or nothing.

Expected utility (EU) theory suggests that the person dividing the resource should offer the other person just enough to get him to accept the bargain, but no more. Furthermore, EU suggests the person should accept any division, because any division will be more than zero, which is what the person will receive if the bargain is refused. However, typically the bargain is a fifty-fifty split (half of the resource to each person). Indeed, if people are offered anything less than a fifty-fifty split, they will often reject the offer, although that will mean they get nothing, rather than what they were offered, because that seems unfair.

In studies, people have evaluated these bargains in two ways. People can rate how attractive a bargain is (e.g., on a 1–7 scale). Possible divisions to be rated might be: $40 for you, $40 for the other person; $50 for you, $70 for the other person, and so on. Thus, bargains are presented in isolation, one after another, as if each was an individual case unrelated to anything else. This type of presentation is generally referred to as "absolute judgment" (Wever and Zener 1928).

Alternatively, people may evaluate bargains in pairs, and choose one. For example, do you prefer a bargain where you get $40, and the other person gets $40, or a bargain where you get $50, and the other person gets $70? Thus, the bargains are presented such that they can be compared, so people can see the relative outcomes. This type of presentation is generally referred to as "comparative judgment."

Absolute and comparative judgment have different results in the "ultimate" bargaining game.

Blount and Bazerman (1996) gave pairs of participants $10 to be divided between them. In absolute judgment (i.e., is this bargain acceptable?), the money holder accepted a minimum division of $4 for him and $6 for the other person. But asked in a comparative judgment format (i.e., do you prefer this bargain or nothing?), participants were willing to accept less (a minimum division of $2.33 for the money holder and $7.67 for the other person). This result suggests that considering situations involving the division or distribution of resources on a case-by-case basis (absolute judgment) may result in sub-optimal choices (relative to those resulting from comparative judgment) for each person involved, as well as the group as a whole.

Comparative and absolute judgment can be applied to social issues as adoption. There has been controversy about adoption, when the adopting parents have a different cultural heritage than the child being adopted. Some argue that a child should be adopted only by parents of the same cultural heritage as the child to preserve the child's connection to his or her culture. That argument views this situation as an absolute judgment: should children be adopted by parents of a different cultural heritage or not?

However, there is an imbalance between the cultural heritages of the children to be adopted and those of the parents wanting to adopt. That imbalance creates the dilemma of what to do with children who would like to be adopted when there are no parents of the same cultural heritage wanting to adopt them. That dilemma suggests this comparative judgment: should children be adopted by parents of a different cultural heritage than their own, or should children be left unadopted (e.g., be brought up in a group home)?

The answers to these absolute and comparative judgments may differ, because the answer may be that a child should not be adopted by parents of a different cultural heritage as an absolute judgment, but as a comparative judgment the answer may be that a child should be adopted by such parents, despite the cultural differences, because having parents is better than not having parents. Thus, the best answer may differ depending on how the situation is characterized. Such situations may involve more than one value (in this case, the values are providing parents for a child and preserving the cultural heritage that the child was born into). Typically, absolute judgements reflect an acceptance or rejection of one value, while comparative judgments reflect more than one value.

GENERAL JUDGMENT AND DECISION-MAKING ISSUES

That the best solution for a situation can seem different if the situation is characterized differently is one of the most important issues in judgment and decision making. The theories mentioned above (Bayes's, EU, prospect, and rank-dependent) assume problem invariance. That is, they assume that people's judgments will not vary with how the problem is characterized. However, because the characterization of the problem affects how people frame the problem, people's decisions often do vary. (Tversky and Kahneman 1981).

An implication of this variability is that eliciting people's values becomes difficult (Baron 1997; 1998). However, different methods can produce contradictory results. For example, choice and matching tasks often reveal different values preferences. Choice tasks are comparative judgments: Do you prefer A or B? Matching tasks require participants to estimate one dimension of an alternative so that its attractiveness matches that of another alternative (e.g., program A will cure 60 percent of patients at a cost of $5 million, what should B cost if it will cure 85 percent of patients?).

The difference produced by these tasks has been extensively examined in studies of *preference reversals* (Slovic and Lichtenstein 1983). Tversky, Sattath, and Slovic (1988) have suggested that the dimension of elicitation (e.g., probability or value) will be weighted most, so reversals can result from changing the elicitation dimension. Fischer and Hawkins (1993) suggested that preference reversals were the result of the compatibility between people's strategy for analyzing the problem and the elicitation mode. Preference reversals clearly occur, but the cause of them continues to be debated (cf. Payne, Bettman, and Johnson 1992).

Ideas about rationality have also been influenced by the variability of people's judgments. Generally, the idea of rationality originated with a theory and then examined whether people behaved in that way, rather than examining how people behave and then suggesting what is rational. That is, rationality has typically been examined based on a prescriptive theory, such as Bayes's or EU, about how people should make decisions rather than a descriptive theory based on how people actually process information. When studies resulted in judgments that were inconsistent with those prescriptive theories of decision making, researchers concluded that people often acted irrationally.

However, there is growing recognition that study participants may be thinking of situations differently than researchers have assumed (Chase, Hertwig, and Gigerenzer 1998), which has led several researchers to create theories about decision processing (e.g., Dougherty, Gettys, and Ogden in press; Gigerenzer, Hoffrage, and Kleinbolting 1991) and use those theories to address rationality issues rather than the reverse. Approaches that focus on processing have been present in decision theory for some time (cf. Brunswick 1952; Hammond 1955), but they have not been dominant in the field. The acknowledgement of multiple views of rationality coupled with the poor explanations of prescriptive theories for people's actual decision behavior may shift the emphasis to processing models.

Further consideration of the decision-making process has led to other questions that are garnering increased attention. For example, how do people make decisions within dynamic environments? Generally, people make decisions in a dynamic world (Brehmer 1990; Busemeyer and Townsend 1993; Diehl and Sterman 1995), but many decision-making theories (such as those reviewed above) do not account for the dynamics of the environment. Also, how do people's emotions affect the decision-making process? Decisions can involve topics that evoke emotion or have emotional consequences (such as regret, Gilovich and Medvec 1995). Some decision theories have tried to include emotional considerations in decision making (e.g., Bell 1982), but this topic deserves more attention. These questions, as well as the issues discussed above, will make decision theory and research an area of continued interest and relevance.

REFERENCES

Ajzen, I. 1996 "The Social Psychology of Decision Making." In E. T. Higgins and A. W. Kruglanski, *Social Psychology: Handbook of Basic Principles*. New York: Guilford.

Arkes, H. R., R. Dawes, and C. Christensen 1986 "Factors Influencing the Use of a Decision Rule in a Probabilistic Task." *Organizational Behavior and Human Decision Making*, 37:93–110.

Axelrod, R. 1984 *The Evolution of Cooperation*. New York: Basic Books.

Baron, J. 1994 *Thinking And Deciding*, 2d ed. Cambridge, U.K.: Cambridge University Press.

—— 1997 "Biases in the Quantitative Measurement of Values for Public Decisions." *Psychological Bulletin* 122:72–88.

—— 1998 *Judgment Misguided: Intuition and Error in Public Decision Making*. Oxford: Oxford University Press.

Bayes, T. (1764) 1958 "An Essay Towards Solving a Problem in the Doctrine of Chances." *Biometrika* 45:293–315.

Bell, D. 1982 "Regret in Decision Making Under Uncertainty." *Operations Research* 30:961–981.

Birnbaum, M. H. 1983 "Base Rates in Bayesian Inference: Signal Detection Analysis of the Cab Problem." *American Journal of Psychology* 96:85–94.

Birnbaum, M. H., G. Coffey, B. A. Mellers, and R. Weiss 1992 "Utility Measurement: Configural-Weight Theory and the Judge's Point of View." *Journal of Experimental Psychology: Human Perception And Performance* 18:331–346.

Birnbaum, M. H., and W. R. Mcintosh 1996 "Violations of Branch Independence in Choices Between Gambles." *Organizational Behavior And Human Decision Processes* 67:91–110.

Blount, S., and M. H. Bazerman 1996 "The Inconsistent Evaluation of Absolute Versus Comparative Payoffs in Labor Supply and Bargaining." *Journal of Economic Behavior and Organization* 30:227–240.

Brehmer, B. 1990 "Strategies in Real-Time, Dynamic Decision Making." In R. M. Hogarth, ed., *Insights in Decision Making: A Tribute To Hillel J. Einhorn* 262–279. Chicago: University of Chicago Press.

Brunswick, E. 1952 *The Conceptual Framework of Psychology*. Chicago: University of Chicago Press.

Busemeyer, J., D. L. Medin, and R. Hastie 1995 *Decision Making From a Cognitive Perspective*. San Diego: Academic.

——, and J. T. Townsend 1993 "Decision-Field Theory: A Dynamic-Cognitive Approach to Decision-Making in an Uncertain Environment." *Psychological Review* 100:432–459.

Chase, V. M., R. Hertwig, and G. Gigerenzer 1998 "Visions of Rationality." *Trends in Cognitive Sciences*, 2:206–214.

Clore, G. L., N. Schwarz, and M. Conway 1994 "Affective Causes and Consequences of Social Information Processing." In R. S. Wyer and T. K. Srull, eds., *Handbook of Social Cognition: 2nd Edition*. Hillsdale, N.J.: Erlbaum.

Dawes, R. M. 1979 "The Robust Beauty of Improper Linear Models." *American Psychologist* 34:571–582.

—— 1998 "Behavioral Decision Making and Judgment." In D. T. Gilbert, S. T. Fiske, and G. Lindzey, eds., *The Handbook of Social Psychology*, 4th ed. Boston: Mcgraw-Hill.

Diehl, E., and J. D. Sterman 1995 "Effects of Feedback Complexity on Dynamic Decision Making." *Organizational Behavior and Human Decision Processes* 62:198–215.

Dougherty, M. R. P., C. F. Gettys, and E. E. Ogden (in press) "MINERVA-DM: A Memory Processes Model for Judgments of Likelihood." *Psychological Review* 106:180–209.

Einhorn, H. J. 1972 "Expert Measurement and Mechanical Combination." *Organizational Behavior and Human Performance* 13:171–192.

Fischer, G. W., and S. A. Hawkins 1993 "Strategy Compatibility, Scale Compatibility, and the Prominence Effect." *Journal of Experimental Psychology: Human Perception and Performance* 19:580–597.

Fong, G. T., D. H. Krantz, and R. E. Nisbett 1986 "The Effects of Statistical Training on Thinking About Everyday Problems." *Cognitive Psychology* 18:253–292.

Gigerenzer, G., and U. Hoffrage 1995 "How to Improve Bayesian Reasoning without Instruction: Frequency Formats." *Psychological Review* 102:684–704.

——, and H. Kleinbolting 1991 "Probabilistic Mental Models: A Brunswickian Theory of Confidence." *Psychological Review* 98:506–528.

Gigerenzer, G., Z. Swijtink, T. Porter, L. Daston, J. Beatty, and L. Kruger 1989 *The Empire of Chance: How Probability Changed Science and Everyday Life*. Cambridge, U.K.: Cambridge University Press.

Gilovich, T., and V. H. Medvec 1995 "The Experience of Regret: What, Why, and When." *Psychological Review* 102:379–395.

Hacking, I. 1975 *The Emergence of Probability*. Cambridge, U.K.: Cambridge University Press.

—— 1990 *The Taming of Chance*. Cambridge, U.K.: Cambridge University Press.

Hammond, K. R. 1955 "Probabilistic Functioning and the Clinical Method." *Psychological Review* 62:255–262.

—— 1998 *Human Judgment and Social Policy: Irreducible Uncertainty, Inevitable Error, Unavoidable Justice*. New York: Oxford.

Hardin, G. R. 1968 "The Tragedy of the Commons." *Science* 162:1243–1248.

Hastie, R., and N. Pennington 1991 "Cognitive and Social Processes in Decision Making." In L. B. Resnick, J. M. Levine, and S. D. Teasley, eds., *Perspectives on Socially Shared Cognition*, 308–327. Washington, D.C.: APA.

Hilton, D. J., and B. R. Slugoski 1999 "Judgment and Decision-Making in Social Context: Discourse Processes and Rational Inference." In T. Connolly, ed., *Judgment and Decision-Making: An Interdisciplinary Reader* 2d ed. Cambridge, U.K.: Cambridge University Press.

Hofstadter, D. R. 1985 "The Prisoner's Dilemma Computer Tournaments and the Evolution of Cooperation." In D. R. Hofstadter, *Metamagical Themas: Questing for the Essence of Mind and Pattern*, 715–734. New York: Basic Books.

Josephs, R. A., R. B. Giesler, and D. H. Silvera 1994 "Judgment By Quantity." *Journal of Experimental Psychology: General* 123:21–32.

Kahneman, D., J. L. Knetsch, and R. H. Thaler 1990 "Experimental Tests of the Endowment Effect and the Coase Theorem." *Journal of Political Economy* 98:1325–1348.

——, P. Slovic, and A. Tversky 1982 *Heuristics and Biases: Judgments Under Uncertainty*. Cambridge, U.K.: Cambridge University Press.

——, and A. Tversky 1972 "On Prediction and Judgment." *ORI Research Monograph*, 12.

—— 1979 "Prospect Theory: An Analysis of Decisions Under Risk." *Econometrica* 47:263–291.

Kubovy, M. 1977 "Response Availability and the Apparent Spontaneity of Numerical Choices." *Journal of Experimental Psychology: Human Perception and Performance* 3:359–364.

Libby, R. 1976 "Man Versus Model of Man: Some Conflicting Evidence." *Organizational Behavior and Human Performance* 16:1–12.

Lopes, L. L. 1994 "Psychology and Economics: Perspectives on Risk, Cooperation, and the Marketplace." *Annual Review of Psychology* 45:197–227.

Luce, R. D., and P. C. Fishburn 1991 "Rank- and Sign-Dependent Linear Utility Models for Finite First-Order Gambles." *Journal of Risk and Uncertainty* 4:29–59.

Manktelow, K. I., and D. E. Over 1993 *Rationality: Psychological and Philosophical Perspectives*. London: Routledge.

Markovits, H., and G. Nantel 1989 "The Belief-Bias Effect in the Production and Evaluation of Logical Conclusions." *Memory & Cognition* 17:11–17.

Mellers, B. A., and J. Baron 1993 *Psychological Perspectives on Justice: Theory and Applications*. New York: Cambridge University Press.

Mellers, B. A., A. Schwartz, and A. D. J. Cooke 1998 "Judgment and Decision Making." *Annual Review of Psychology* 49:447–477.

Nisbett, R. E., D. H. Krantz, D. Jepson, and Z. Kunda 1983 "The Use of Statistical Heuristics in Everyday Inductive Reasoning." *Psychological Review* 90:339–363.

Payne, J. W., J. R. Bettman, and E. J. Johnson 1992 "Behavioral Decision Research: A Constructive Processing Perspective." *Annual Review of Psychology* 49:447–477.

Pelham, B. W., T. T. Sumarta, and L. Myaskovsky 1994 "The Easy Path from Many to Much: The Numerosity Heuristic." *Cognitive Psychology* 26:103–133.

Pruitt, D. G., and P. J. Carnevale 1993 *Negotiation in Social Conflict*. Pacific Grove, Calif.: Brooks/Cole.

Rapoport, A., and A. M. Chammah 1965 *Prisoner's Dilemma: A Study in Conflict and Cooperation*. Ann Arbor, Mich.: University of Michigan Press.

Samuelson, W., and R. Zeckhauser 1988 "Status-Quo Bias in Decision Making." *Journal of Risk and Uncertainty* 1:7–59.

Schwarz, N., and G. L. Clore 1983 "Mood, Misattribution, and Judgments of Well-Being: Informative and Directive Functions of Affective States." *Journal of Personality and Social Psychology* 45:513–523.

Shapira, Z. 1995 *Risk Taking: A Managerial Perspective.* New York: Russell Sage Foundation.

Sherif, M., D. Taub, and C. I. Hovland 1958 "Assimilation and Contrast Effects of Anchoring Stimuli on Judgments." *Journal of Experimental Psychology* 55:150–155.

Slovic, P., and S. Lichtenstein 1983 "Preference Reversals: A Broader Perspective." *American Economic Review* 73:596–605.

Slugoski, B. R., and A. E. Wilson 1998 "Contribution of Conversation Skills to the Production of Judgmental Errors." *European Journal of Social Psychology* 28:575–601.

Stanovich, K. E., and R. F. West 1998 "Individual Differences in Rational Thought." *Journal of Experimental Psychology: General* 127:161–188.

Stevenson, M. K., J. R. Busemeyer, and J. C. Naylor 1990 "Judgment and Decision-Making Theory." In M. D. Dunette and L. M. Hough, eds., *Handbook of Industrial and Organizational Psychology*, 2d ed., vol. 1, 283–374. Palo Alto, Calif.: Consulting Psychologists Press.

Tversky, A., and D. Kahneman 1981 "The Framing of Decisions and the Psychology of Choice." *Science* 211:453–458.

—— 1982 "Evidential Impact of Base Rates." In D. Kahneman, P. Slovic, and A. Tversky, eds., *Heuristics and Biases: Judgments Under Uncertainty.* Cambridge, U.K.: Cambridge University Press.

—— 1983 "Extensional Versus Intuitive Reasoning: The Conjunction Fallacy in Probability Judgment." *Psychological Review* 90:293–315.

—— 1992 "Advances in Prospect Theory: Cumulative Representations of Uncertainty." *Journal of Risk and Uncertainty* 5:297–323.

Tversky, A., S. Sattath, and P. Slovic 1988 "Contingent Weighting in Judgment and Choice." *Psychological Review* 95:371–384.

von Neumann, J., and O. Morganstern 1947 *Theory of Games and Economic Behavior*, 2d ed. Princeton, N.J.: Princeton University Press.

Wever, E. G., and K. E. Zener 1928 "The Method of Absolute Judgment in Psychophysics." *Psychological Review* 35:466–493.

EVAN THACKERAY PRITCHARD

DEDUCTION/INDUCTION

See Experiments; Quasi-Experimental Research Designs; Scientific Explanation; Statistical Inference.

DEMOCRACY

Democracy is one of the most important subjects in the social sciences. From the work of de Tocqueville in the early nineteenth century through the work of the best contemporary scholars, democracy has been studied closely and debated widely (Tocqueville 1969). Democracy has drawn this attention primarily because, in spite of the fact that it is quite rare historically, it has come to have enormous legitimacy in the eyes of many individuals worldwide. This has not always been the case. Democracy has been severely criticized by those on both the political right and left. But few scholars today question whether democracy is a social good.

Democracy is also important because many historically undemocratic countries have adopted it as a system of government. Many such changes have occurred only in the years since the Cold War (Huntington 1991). By 1994, over half the countries in the world had some form of democratic governance, a doubling of the number of nation-states so organized within 25 years (Lipset 1994).

At the core of most discussions of democracy is a common understanding that democracy is a method of governance or decision making for organizations or societies in which the members of that organization or society participate, directly or indirectly, in the decision making of that group. Further, members affect decision making to such an extent that they can be thought of as actually governing that organization or society. In short, democracy is a system of governance in which members control group decision making.

Not all considerations on democracy have shared this understanding. For example, those working in the Marxist tradition saw any state, democratic or not, as the expression of a class struggle. As such, any state was inherently undemocratic, absent the creation of a classless, communist, and hence truly democratic, society (Held

1995). Subsequent to the collapse of the Soviet Union and its affiliated states, and the full exposure of the failures of those regimes, such an extreme view has been almost entirely rejected.

The common understanding of democracy as participation by members or citizens in the decision making of an organization or society still leaves considerable room for dispute. Two issues are central: First, who are, or should be, considered members of the society? Second, what does, or should, constitute a minimum level of control over decision making by members for a system to be thought of as democratic? In short, how much participation is necessary for a system to be democratic? These questions are not simply matters of empirical observation of the world, but also matters for moral and political philosophy.

Three additional factors add to the difficulty of approaching democracy as a field of sociological research. First, analysts of democracy all too often use different definitions of democracy, or fail to define democracy clearly. Democratic systems of governance can be characterized by many attributes—frequency of member participation, the form of member participation, and so forth. Establishing whether a particular system of governance is democratic, involves making decisions about which attributes are essential to a democratic system. Where there is no specific definition of democracy or where definitions conflict, evaluating research on democracy can be tasking (Macpherson 1972).

A second factor increasing the difficulty of this subject matter is that democracy is a system of governance found in many different kinds of collectivities, including states, formal organizations, and informal groups. It is thus necessary to be cautious in applying models, findings, and relationships across different types of collectivities. When general propositions about democracy are advanced, it is important to evaluate those propositions at multiple levels of analysis.

A third difficulty is that social scientists are interested in democracy not just for its own sake, but also because it is thought to be associated with other critical issues. Many important questions involve considerations of democracy: What is the effect of democracy on the success of organizations and nation-states? Does democracy promote individual liberty? What is the effect of democracy on income inequality and social stratification? What is the relationship between democracy and civil society? Can market economies prosper in the absence of democracy? All these and more force sociologists to consider the consequences, as well as the causes, of democracy.

While the difficulties of studying democracy are daunting, much significant work has been done in this field. Democracy has been studied as an outcome and as a cause, and has been studied at both the level of the nation-state, and at the level of the organization.

To begin with, there is work in the sociology of democracy on the question of who is or should be members or citizens of a democratic polity. Most systems commonly thought to be democratic have throughout history excluded some portion of those subject to the will of the democracy from participation in the decision-making process. Such exclusion has occurred on the basis of race, sex, income, relationship to property, criminal status, mental health, religion, age, and other characteristics. While use of many of these categories as a justification for excluding individuals from participation has declined in recent times, others remain, and there is continuing disagreement about the moral and political bases for excluding or including specific groups or categories of individuals. Migrant workers in Western Europe, for example, are subject to the action of the state on a long-term basis and yet remain excluded from full political participation in those states (Brubaker 1989). At the level of the organization, there are individuals affected by the decisions of the organization who may have little or no say in the decisions that affect them. These can include individuals both outside the organization ("stakeholders") and inside the organization. Regarding affected individuals outside the organization, there are occasional movements to increase the power of stakeholders over the decisions of the organization (Nader, Green, and Seligman 1976). While unsuccessful at a general level, there has been a shift toward permitting stakeholders increased access to legal redress, for example, in class action lawsuits and in environmental litigation. And regarding those within the organization, one way to understand the management trends toward "total quality management," participatory management, and economic democracy is that they are attempts to increase democratic participation of workers in decisions that affect them (Jarley, Fiorito, and Delaney 1997).

Sociologists have often focused on the forms of influence and participation that individuals have in decision making. *Representative democracy* is that form of governance in which members of the organization or polity exercise their control over the organization through the regular election of members of a decision-making body. It is traditional to view representative democracies as democratic because they provide for the expression of interests through the election of representatives. For example, in the United States, citizens directly elect senators and representatives to the U.S. Congress, which in turn makes political decisions about the actions of the federal government. Theorists since the Enlightenment have argued that representative democracy is an appropriate means for conveying participation in decision making in large-size organizations, where individuals are thought not to be able to participate in all decisions (Hobbes 1968; Locke 1980; Mill 1962; Rousseau 1977).

But this view has been attacked by numerous critics, many of them sociologists. One of the most scathing criticisms, building on work by Mosca, is the analysis of democracy by Michels (Mosca 1939). Michels's argument is that in any large organization (and, by extension, in any nation-state), a democratic system of governance inevitably leads to the rise of an oligarchy, and worse, to an oligarchy whose leaders have interests that differ from those of the ordinary members or citizens (Michels 1949). Why is this inevitable? In every instance of large democratic organization, Michels argues, oligarchy arises as a result of the organization's requirement for experienced, skilled leaders. Experience in leadership, however, tends to give leaders access to key organizational resources, such as mailing lists, publicity, and greater experience, that are significant resources that the leadership

can use to return themselves to office year after year. And as leaders remain in office over an extended time, their interests and attitudes are likely to diverge from those of members. The divergence of interests is a result of the changed work and social experiences that accrue to leaders. Hence Michels, while arguing that formal organization is necessary for social life, and especially for politics, also believes that democracy in such organizations is essentially impossible.

Michels's analysis has been taken very seriously in the social sciences, and there is some supporting evidence for his propositions. Weber described, and Heclo and Wilson separately concede, that there is a tendency for the civil service and bureaucracy to become unresponsive to the wishes of the people, as their experiences and needs differ from the people (Heclo 1977; Weber 1978; Wilson 1989). Lincoln and Zeitz have shown that as unions tend to get more professional, there is less member participation in decision making (Lincoln and Zeitz 1980). And for both unions and social movement organizations, Michels's critique is taken so seriously as to generate sometimes drastic proposals for counteracting the oligarchical tendencies in these organizations (Kochan 1980). Piven and Cloward argue that reform movements of the poor should waste few resources on creating long-lasting organizations, but should instead create massive and disruptive protests (Piven and Cloward 1977).

However, Michels is not without his critics. Nyden argues that democratic unions are possible (Nyden 1985). Weber himself, who was Michels's teacher, was critical of his conclusions. Michels overstated the case, Weber argued, because he insisted on relying upon too pure or strict a definition of democracy. Having started with such an idealistic vision of democracy, Michels was bound to find that reality comes up short (Scaff 1981).

That too pure a definition of democracy can lead to a misplaced understanding of how democracy works, and a failure to appreciate its achievements, is the key assumption behind the most significant defense of democracy in the 1950s and 1960s—the *pluralist* account of democracy. Dahl's account defends democracy by admitting its weakness: voting in elections is not a terribly effective system for ensuring that the will of the people will be carried out. Instead, Dahl focuses attention on whether non-electoral forms of influence can yield democratic decision making in keeping with the wishes and interests of the public. Interest groups thus become not the bane, but the hope of democracy. Through lobbying in all its forms, interest groups are able to exert power and influence over decision making beyond elections; if they do this, then the system, with all its flaws, can be considered democratic (Dahl 1961).

A problem with the pluralist view is that not all groups in society may be able effectively to form interest groups to pursue their goals. Olson, in an early effort in what is now known as *rational choice theory*, argued that individuals must be assumed to be rational, and that rational individuals will not contribute to the formation of interest groups when they will obtain the benefits achieved by the interest group anyway. This is the *free rider* or *collective action* problem: if an interest group lobbies for clean air, and a person cannot be denied clean air because he or she does not belong to the interest group, why should that person contribute to the group? Only those interest groups with a particularly small constituency or those interest groups who are able to use "special" incentives—those available only to members of the group—to attract contributors will be able to form to lobby to advance their interests. Groups representing weak and powerless individuals may be unable to supply such special incentives (Olson 1971).

Olson's pessimism about the chances for the disadvantaged to gain a voice in decision making has been the focus of much attention. Oliver and Marwell suggest that social movements are more likely to be formed as interest groups grow in size (Oliver and Marwell 1988). Knoke argues that the use of selective incentives may attract apathetic members, whereas a focus on the goal of lobbying may attract highly active members, thereby creating more effective organizations (Knoke 1988). Clemens points out that as interest groups come into existence, they are themselves models or templates for others to imitate. Those templates will

then increase the likelihood of the formation of more interest groups (Clemens 1997). These criticisms of Olson's analysis of the collective action problem may actually serve to strengthen the pluralist account of democracy.

Yet many sociologists remain deeply critical of the pluralist account. Domhoff argues that pluralism is flawed not because the collective action problem retards the capacity of the disadvantaged to organize. Rather, pluralism is flawed because in the United States, and in other industrialized democracies, there is a governing class (Domhoff 1998). This governing class is composed of elites from business, the social upper class, and those in charge of organizations, both within and outside government, that are powerfully involved in the formation of public policy. While Domhoff admits that there is some conflict within these groups, he views them as cohesive in their opposition to the interests of the poor and the working class. Through their control of important organizations, through the strength of their social ties, and through the use of agenda-setting, the governing class achieves enormous power. And, Domhoff argues, the governing class is able to use that power consistently to defeat the interests of the majority.

Other critics of the pluralist account have drawn attention to the relationship between social class and voting. For some years, it appeared that class-based voting in the United States appeared to be declining (Clark, Lipset, and Rempel 1993; Manza, Hout, and Brooks 1995). Yet some scholars believe that class remained a significant factor in voting behavior (Burnham 1981). Piven and Cloward argued that the pluralist account failed because there was a systematic pattern to who voted and who did not. Because the poor and the working classes disproportionately failed to vote in elections, they were inadequately represented in the competition between interests; hence the poor were excluded from the pluralist democracy (Piven and Cloward 1988). It has been shown that class remains a powerful determinant of how people vote, even if the working class no longer votes for the Democratic party in the United States with as great a frequency as it did in the years immediately after WWII (Hout, Brooks, and Manza 1995).

Researchers in the 1970s and 1980s criticized pluralism for adopting a definition of democracy that was too satisfied with the status quo of only limited participation in decision making. These participatory democratic theories emphasized that as members participate in decision making, they learn more about the criteria that need to be used in effective decision making and become better at making decisions. But members also, it was argued, become better at evaluating the choice of candidates where representatives must be elected. Accordingly, empirical researchers began to investigate the causes and consequences of increased participation in decision making (Finley 1973; Pateman 1970).

In keeping with this view, researchers increasingly moved to consider cases of participation throughout society (Alford and Friedland 1975). Participation in decision making in unions, community organizations, municipalities, and protest groups has been analyzed and touted (Gans 1989; Cole 1975). In organization theory, research on different forms of worker participation in organizational decision making has gained increasing prominence. Total quality management, participatory management, and worker control all have been studied closely, not just for improvement in productivity and quality, but also for democracy. Much of this research emphasizes how democracy is consistent with both effectiveness and the improvement of the condition of workers (Jarley, Fiorito, and Delaney 1997). Some have even come to see the spread of democratic management as inevitable, although this is almost certainly exaggerated (Collins 1997). Yet many have worked to show that democratic systems of management are more broadly possible than has been thought, although the conditions under which such systems of decision making can be created and maintained remain under debate (Burawoy 1982; Kanter 1983).

Renewed definitions of democracy beg a central question in democratic research: Where do democracies come from? The question has been most closely studied for nation-states. Lipset identifies a set of central conditions that are associated with the rise of democracy in nation-states. The presence of a market economy appears to be a necessary, although not a sufficient, condition for democracy. A minimum level of economic development is associated with democracy, although a key debate is the extent to which development leads to democracy (Bollen and Jackman 1995; Muller 1995). Also associated with democracy is a political culture in which the tolerance for the rights of others is recognized. Finally, countries with Protestant religious traditions have been more likely to be democratic, though the significance of that effect may be fading in the recent transition to democracy (Lipset 1994).

One of the most significant contributions to the account of the origins of democracy is that by Moore (Moore 1966). His analysis, standing in contrast to a Marxist emphasis on the role of the working class as a force in history, identified the relationship between peasant and lord prior to capitalism as the critical factor in determining whether a society became democratic or autocratic. In countries such as China, France, Japan, or Germany, repressive control over peasants by a dominant class led either to revolution or to continued autocracy. In China, revolution led to Communist autocracy; in France, because of the existence of a commercial class, revolution led, through fits and starts, to democracy. In Japan and Germany, the failure or absence of revolution led to continued dominance of repressive classes, leading to the rise of fascist regimes. Moore argued that in a country such as England, however, the greater status of labor, coupled with the nobility's increasing dependence on market-based agriculture, led to an eventual democratic solution to social conflict.

Moore's work has provoked considerable criticism and extension (Ross et al. 1998). Downing has shown conclusively that the nature of military conflicts affects the success of democracy in a country. How a nation fights its wars, and how often it must fight, is critically determinative of the need for repression in the mobilization of men and weapons to fight. England's peculiar move toward democracy is thus critically dependent on its position as an island nation, free from the necessity to fight long-term, massive land wars on the continent of Europe, and the necessity to maintain a state and military administrative structure capable of that task (Downing 1992). Friedman has shown that former British colonies tend to be democratic, whereas countries ruled by Leninist parties tend to remain autocratic (Friedman 1998).

Students of social movements have tended to argue that social movements are significant sources of democracy (Giugni, McAdam, and Tilly 1998). There is evidence that social movements can push the transition to democracy faster (Hipsher 1998; Sandoval 1998). Certainly this is consistent with Tilly's theoretical model of democratization, in which he argues that social conflict, as embodied in social movements, and where mediated by third parties, can lead to the creation of rights essential for democracy (Tilly 1998). But surely the effects of social movements on democracy are contingent on many factors, and sociologists must be careful not to assume that the outcome of social protest will be democratization (Melucci and Lyyra 1998). Clearly this has not always been the case.

The sources of democracy in organizations is an understudied area. Two findings are worth noting. Knoke has argued that in the present-day United States, a minimum level of democratic procedure is just a part of the institutional building blocks from which organizations are constructed; in short, organizations such as unions may have democratic procedures simply because everybody expects them to have those procedures (Knoke 1990). And, returning to the tension between democracy and effectiveness identified by Michels, Jarley has found that the causes of democratic procedures in unions are independent of those which drive bureaucratization (Jarley, Fiorito, and Delaney 1997). Yet much more systematic work needs to be done in this area.

The other side of the coin in the study of democracy is the question of the relationship between democracy and other core subjects of sociological interest. The relationship between democracy and equality is a central issue and has been a focus of research since de Tocqueville (Tocqueville 1969). In recent years, research has centered around this specific question: Does democracy promote or retard income inequality in nation-states? There is some evidence that democracy does not increase inequality, at least directly, and it might lead to increased equality (Bollen and Jackman 1985; Muller 1988).

Another question is whether democracies can be effective. The central issue, echoing Michels, is whether or not organizations, such as unions or parties or, for that matter, businesses, can be successful in competitive environments against organizations that are autocratically run. The evidence is conflicting. Some argue that democracy and effectiveness are in conflict in the context of unions (Lipset, Trow, and Coleman 1959; Piven and Cloward 1977). Others argue that democracy leads to effectiveness in achieving goals (Stepan-Norris and Zeitlin 1994). As yet, there seems to be no definitive answer, and the issue certainly merits more research.

Finally, the subject of democracy has been intimately tied in the 1990s to two related subjects.

The first is the subject of globalization. As the world has become more closely connected, as communications technologies radically change again, and as the world economy has grown larger, some have raised questions about the implications of this trend for democracy. Held, for example, has argued that decisions that affect citizens are increasingly being made at a level beyond that of the nation-state; in supra-national organizations and in the international economy. As a consequence of this globalization, the extent of democratic control over decisions is seen to have weakened (Held 1995). Others have criticized this argument, and the subject is still very much subject to research and debate (Hirst and Thompson 1996).

The second related subject is civil society. A focus of scholarly attention in part because of the demands for it from those who have emerged from socialist rule, civil society is commonly conceived as space for associational activity between the state and the individual (Gellner 1994). Many now see organizations and associations, independent of the state, as crucial to democracy, constituting a critical element of democratic society (Streeck and Schmitter 1985). Certainly, they are not the same: as Hall puts it, "Democracy can be decidedly uncivil" (Hall 1995). But democracy depends on civil society (Somers 1993). This view echoes Tocqueville's assertion that the knowledge of how to combine is fundamental to democracy (Tocqueville 1969). Already attracting significant attention, much room remains to answer questions about the relationship between civil society and democracy.

In conclusion, it is well to remember that there are many forms of democracy: those with weaker or stronger civil liberties; those with weaker or stronger civil societies; those with weaker or stronger tolerance for diversity. Nor can it be assumed that these different forms are internally consistent: the rights of the community to choose what it wishes to be, and the rights of the individual to live as he or she wishes, are not easily reconciled.

It is also well to remember that democracy is not inevitable (Berger 1992). Neither, we should also recall, is democracy a simple outcome that, once achieved, is a permanent condition (Friedman 1998). Democracy can be strengthened; democracy can be weakened. And it can, as it has in the past, disappear. While democracy is today in the ascendant, the lessons of the French Revolution and of Weimar Germany should not be forgotten; although in both instances democracy was regained, it was not regained quickly or without cost. And in Germany, as in Japan, democracy was not regained from within, but imposed from without. History should teach us that we still have much to learn about democracy.

(SEE ALSO: *Capitalism, Development, Inequality, Civil Society, Individualism in Less Developed Countries, Political Sociology, Rational Choice Theory.*)

REFERENCES

Alford, Robert R., and Roger Friedland 1975 "Political Participation and Public Policy." *Annual Review of Sociology* 1:429–479.

Berger, Peter 1992 "The Uncertain Triumph of Democratic Capitalism." *Journal of Democracy* 3:7–17.

Bollen, Kenneth A., and Robert W. Jackman 1985 "Political Democracy." *American Sociological Review* 50:438–457.

—— 1995 "Income Inequality and Democratization Revisited: Comment on Muller." *American Sociological Review* 60:983–989.

Brubaker, William Rogers 1989 *Immigration and the Politics of Citizenship in Europe and North America.* Lanham, Md.: University Press of American; German Marshall Fund of the United States.

Burawoy, Michael 1982 *Manufacturing Consent.* Chicago: University of Chicago Press.

—— 1997 "Review Essay: The Soviet Descent into Capitalism." *American Journal of Sociology* 102:1430–1444.

Burke, Edmund 1955 *Reflections on the Revolution in France.* Indianapolis: Bobbs-Merrill.

Burnham, Walter Dean 1981 *The Current Crisis in American Politics.* New York: Oxford University Press.

Clark, Terry Nichols, Seymour Martin Lipset, and Michael Rempel 1993 "The Declining Political Significance of Class." *International Sociology* 8:323–333.

Clemens, Elisabeth S. 1997 *The People's Lobby: Organizational Innovation and the Rise of Interest Group Politics in the United States, 1890–1925.* Chicago: University of Chicago Press.

Cole, Richard L. 1975 "Citizen Participation in Municipal Politics." *American Journal of Political Science* 19:761–782.

Collins, Denis 1997 "The Ethical Superiority and Inevitability of Participatory Management as an Organizational System." *Organization Science.*

Dahl, Robert A. 1961 *Who Governs?* New Haven: Yale University Press.

Domhoff, G. William 1998 *Who Rules America? Power and Politics in the Year 2000.* Mountain View, Calif.: Mayfield Publishing Company.

Downing, Brian M. 1992 *The Military Revolution and Political Change: Origins of Democracy and Autocracy in Early Modern Europe.* Princeton, N.J.: Princeton University Press.

Finley, M. I. 1985 *Democracy: Ancient and Modern.* London: Hogarth Press.

Friedman, Edward 1998 "Development, Revolution, Democracy, and Dictatorship: China versus India?" In Theda Skocpol, ed., *Democracy, Revolution, and History,* 102–123. Ithaca, N.Y. and London: Cornell University Press.

Gans, Herbert J. 1989 "Comment on Vareene's Review of Middle American Individualism: The Future of

Liberal Democracy." *American Journal of Sociology* 95:188–190.

Gellner, Ernest 1994 *Conditions of Liberty: Civil Society and its Rivals*. London: Penguin Books.

Giugni, Marco G., Doug McAdam, and Charles Tilly 1998 "From Contention to Democracy." Lanham, Md.: Rowman and Littlefield.

Hall, John A. 1995 "In Search of Civil Society." In John A. Hall, ed., *Civil Society: Theory, History, Comparison* 1–27. Cambridge, England: Polity Press.

Hartz, Louis 1948 *Economic Policy and Democratic Thought: Pennsylvania 1776–1860*. Cambridge, Mass.: Harvard University Press.

Heclo, Hugh 1977 *A Government of Strangers*. Washington, D.C.: Brookings Institution.

Held, David 1995 *Democracy and the Global Order: From the Modern State to Cosmopolitan Governance*. Stanford, Calif.: Stanford University Press.

Hipsher, Patricia L. 1998 "Democratic Transitions and Social Movement Outcomes: The Chilean Shantytown Dwellers' Movement in Comparative Perspective." In Marco G. Giugni, Doug McAdam, and Charles Tilly, eds., *From Contention to Democracy* 149–168. Lanham, Md.: Rowman and Littlefield.

Hirst, Paul, and Grahame Thompson 1996 *Globalization in Question: The International Economy and the Politics of Governance*. Cambridge, England: Polity Press.

Hobbes, Thomas 1968 *Leviathan*. New York: Penguin Books.

Hout, Michael, Clem Brooks, and Jeff Manza 1995 "The Democratic Class Struggle in the United States, 1948–1992." *American Sociological Review* 60:805–828.

Huntington, Samuel P. 1991 *The Third Wave: Democratization in the Late Twentieth Century*. Norman, Okla.: University of Oklahoma.

Jarley, Paul, Jack Fiorito, and John Thomas Delaney 1997. "A Structural Contingency Approach to Bureaucracy and Democracy in U.S. National Unions." *Academy of Management Journal* 40:831–861.

Kanter, Rosabeth Moss 1983 *The Change Masters*. New York: Touchstone.

Knoke, David 1988 "Organizational Incentives." *American Sociological Review* 53:311–329.

—— 1990 *Organizing for Collective Action: The Political Economies of Associations*. New York: de Gruyter.

Kochan, T. H. 1980 *Collective Bargaining and Industrial Relations: From Theory to Policy and Practice*. Homewood, Ill.: Irwin.

Lincoln, J. R., and G. Zeitz 1980 "Organizational Properties from Aggregate Data: Separating Individual and Structural Effects." *American Sociological Review* 45:391–408.

Lipset, Seymour Martin 1994 "The Social Requisites of Democracy Revisited: 1993 Presidential Address." *American Sociological Review* 59:1–22.

——, Martin A. Trow, and James S. Coleman 1959 *Union Democracy*. Glencoe, Ill.: Free Press.

Locke, John 1980 *The Second Treatise of Government*. Indianapolis, Ind.: Hackett Publishers.

Macpherson, C. B. 1972 *The Real World of Democracy*. New York: Oxford University Press.

Manza, Jeff, Michael Hout, and Clem Brooks 1995 "Class Voting in Capitalist Democracies since WWII." *Annual Review of Sociology* 21:137–163.

Melucci, Alberto, and Timo Lyyra 1998 "Collective Action, Change, and Democracy." In Marco G. Giugni, Doug McAdam, and Charles Tilly, eds., *From Contention to Democracy* 203–228. Lanham, Md.: Rowman and Littlefield.

Michels, Robert 1949 *Political Parties: A Sociological Study of the Oligarchical Tendencies of Modern Democracy*. New York: Free Press.

Mill, John Stuart 1962 *Considerations on Representative Government*. South Bend, Ind.: Gateway Editions.

Moore, Barrington 1966 *Social Origins of Dictatorship and Democracy: Lord and Peasant in the Making of the Modern World*. Boston: Beacon Press.

Mosca, Gaetano 1939 *The Ruling Class*. New York: McGraw-Hill.

Muller, Edward N. 1988 "Democracy, Economic Development, and Income Inequality." *American Sociological Review* 53:50–68.

—— 1995 "Economic Determinants of Democracy." *American Sociological Review* 60:966–982.

Nader, Ralph, Mark Green, and E. J. Seligman 1976 *Constitutionalizing the Corporation: The Case for the Federal Chartering of Giant Corporations*. Washington, D.C.: Corporate Accountability Research Group.

Nyden, Philip W. 1985 "Democratizing Organizations: A Case Study of a Union Reform Movement." *American Journal of Sociology* 90:1179–1203.

Oliver, Pamela E., and Gerald Marwell 1988 "The Paradox of Group Size in Collective Action." *American Sociological Review* 53:1–8.

Olson, Mancur 1971 *The Logic of Collective Action*. Cambridge, Mass.: Harvard University Press.

Pateman, Carole 1970 *Participation and Democratic Theory*. Cambridge: Cambridge University Press.

Piven, Frances Fox, and Richard Cloward 1977 *Poor People's Movements*. New York: Pantheon.

—— 1988 *Why Americans Don't Vote*. New York: Pantheon.

Ross, George, Theda Skocpol, Tony Smith, and Judith Eisenberg Vichniac 1998 "Barrington Moore's Social Origins and Beyond: Historical Social Analysis since the 1960s." In Theda Skocpol, ed., *Democracy, Revolution, and History* 1–21. Ithaca, N.Y. and London: Cornell University Press.

Rousseau, Jean-Jacques 1977 *The Social Contract and Discourse on the Origin of Inequality*. New York: Washington Square Press.

Sandoval, Salvador A. M. 1998 "Social Movements and Democratization: The Case of Brazil and the Latin Countries." In Marco G. Giugni, Doug McAdam, and Charles Tilly, eds., *From Contention to Democracy* 169–202. Lanham, Md.: Rowman and Littlefield.

Scaff, Lawrence A. 1981 "Max Weber and Robert Michels." *American Journal of Sociology* 86:1269–1286.

Schumpeter, Joseph A. 1976 *Capitalism, Socialism, and Democracy*. New York: Harper and Row.

Somers, Margaret A. 1993 "Citizenship and the Place of the Public Sphere: Law, Community, and Political Culture in the Transition to Democracy." *American Sociological Review* 58:587–620.

Stepan-Norris, Judith, and Maurice Zeitlin 1994 "Union Democracy, Radical Leadership, and the Hegemony of Capital." *American Sociological Review* 1995:829–850.

Streeck, Wolfgang, and Philippe C. Schmitter 1985 "Community, Market, State—and Associations? The Prospective Contribution of Interest Governance to Social Order." In Wolfgang Streeck and Philippe C. Schmitter, eds., *Private Interest Government* 1–29. London: Sage Publications.

Tilly, Charles 1998 "Where Do Rights Come From?" In Theda Skocpol, ed., *Democracy, Revolution, and History* 55–72. Ithaca, N.Y. and London: Cornell University Press.

Tocqueville, Alexis de 1969 *Democracy in America*. Garden City, N.J.: Harper Perennial.

Weber, Max 1978 "Parliament and Government in a Reconstructed Germany: A Contribution to the Political Critique of Officialdom and Party Politics." In Guenther Roth and Claus Wittich, eds., *Economy and Society: An Outline of Interpretive Sociology* 1381–1469. Berkeley: University of California Press.

Wilson, James Q. 1989 *Bureaucracy: What Government Agencies Do and Why They Do It*. New York: Basic Books.

ANDREW L. CREIGHTON

DEMOGRAPHIC METHODS

Demographic methods are used to provide researchers and policymakers with useful information about the size and structure of human populations and the processes that govern population changes. A population, of course, may range in size from a small number of individuals surveyed locally to a large national population enumerated in periodic censuses to even larger aggregated entities.

We use demographic methods not only in purely demographic applications, but also in a variety of other fields, among them sociology, economics, anthropology, public health, and business. Demographers, like all researchers, must pay careful attention to the quality of data that enter into their analyses. Some circumstances under which we use these methods are more trying than others. In cases in which the data are viewed to be accurate and complete, the methods we use to analyze them are more straightforward than those that are applied to data of imperfect quality.

DESCRIPTION OF DATA

First we must develop ways to describe our data in a fashion that allows the most important facts to leap out at us. As one example, let us examine a population's age structure or distribution. Simple descriptive statistics are doubtless helpful in summarizing aspects of population age structure, but demographers often use age "pyramids" to convey to an audience the youthfulness of a population, for example, or even to convey a rough sense of a nation's history.

We might note, for example, that 20 percent of Norway's population in 1997 was under the age of fifteen. In contrast, 39 percent of Mexico's population seven years earlier fell into this category. But it is perhaps more dramatic to create a visual display of these figures in the form of age pyramids.

An age pyramid is typically constructed as a bar graph, with horizontal bars—one representing each sex—emanating in both directions from a central vertical age axis. Age increases as one proceeds up the axis and the unit of the horizontal axis is either the proportion of the total population in each age group or the population size itself.

We see in panel A of figure 1 that Mexico's population is described by a very broad-based pyramid—actually, in two-dimensional space, a triangle, but by convention we refer to it as a pyramid—which reveals a remarkably large proportion of the population not yet having reached adulthood. The median age of this population is about twenty years. Such a distributional shape is common particularly among high fertility populations. In stark contrast we have the pyramid shown in panel B, representing the population of Norway. Rather than triangular, its age distribution is somewhat more rectangular in shape, which is typically seen among countries that have experienced an extended period of low fertility rates. It is easy to see that Norway's median age (about thirty-six years) is considerably higher than that of Mexico.

As mentioned above, not only can we examine the age structure of populations through the use of pyramids, but we can also gain much insight into a nation's history insofar as that history has either directly or indirectly influenced the size of successive birth cohorts. Note, for example, the age pyramid reflecting the population age structure of France on 1 January 1962 (figure 2).

In this figure, several notable events in France's history are apparent. We see (1) the military losses experienced in World War I by male birth cohorts of the mid to late 1890s, (2) the remarkable birth dearth brought about by that war (the cohort aged in their mid-forties or so in 1962), followed by (3) the return of prewar childbearing activity once the

war ended (the cohort who in 1962 were in their early forties), and a similar pattern revolving around World War II, during which (4) a substantial decline in births took place (the cohort around age twenty in 1962), succeeded by (5) a dramatic baby boom in the years immediately following (those around age fifteen in 1962).

COMPARISON OF CRUDE RATES

Much of the work in which social scientists are engaged is comparative in nature. For example, we might seek to contrast the mortality levels of the populations of two countries. Surely, if the two countries in question have accurate vital registration and census data, this task would appear to be trivial. For each country, we would simply divide the total number of deaths (D) in a given year by the total population (P) at the midpoint of that year. Thus we would define the crude death rate (CDR) for country A as:

$$\text{CDR}^A = \frac{D^A[t,t+1]}{P^A[t+.5]} = \frac{\sum_{x=0,n}^{\omega-n} \left[{}_nM_x^A \cdot {}_nP_x^A \right]}{\sum_{x=0,n}^{\omega-n} {}_nP_x^A} \quad (1)$$

where t denotes the beginning of the calendar year, ω is the oldest age attained in the population, ${}_nM_x^A$ is the death rate of individuals aged x to $x + n$, and ${}_nP_x^A$ is the number of individuals in that same age group. ${}_nM_x^A$ and ${}_nP_x^A$ are centered on the midpoint of the calendar year. The rightmost segment of this equation reminds us that the crude death rate is but the sum of the age-specific death rates weighted by the proportion of the population at each age.

Unfortunately, comparisons of crude death rates across populations can lead to misleading conclusions. This problem is in fact general to any sort of comparison based on crude rates that do not account for the confounding effects of factors that differentiate the two populations.

Let us examine the death rates of two very different countries, Mexico and Norway. The crude death rate (for both sexes combined) in Mexico in 1990, 5.2 per 1000, was approximately half that for

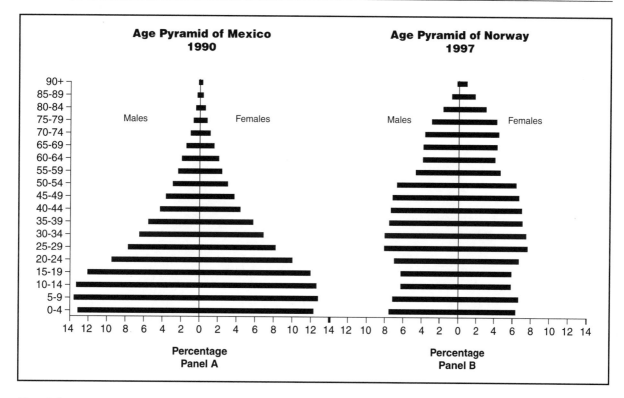

Figure 1

NOTE: Age pyramids for Mexico and Norway

Norway, 10.1, seven years later, in 1997. Knowing nothing else about these two countries, we might infer that the health of the Mexican population was considerably superior to that of the Norwegian population. However, once we standardize the crude death rates of the two countries on a common population age structure, we find just the reverse is true.

To accomplish this standardization, instead of applying the above equation to our data, we use the following:

$$\text{ASCDR}^A = \frac{\sum\limits_{x=0,n}^{\omega\text{-}n} \left[{}_nM_x^A \cdot {}_nP_x^s \right]}{\sum\limits_{x=0,n}^{\omega\text{-}n} {}_nP_x^s} \qquad (2)$$

where ASCDR^A is the age-standardized crude death rate of country A, and ${}_nP_x^s$ is the number of individuals in the standardized population of that same age group. Any age distribution may be chosen as the standard, however, it is common simply to use the average of the two proportionate age distributions (i.e., each normalized to one in order to account for unequal population sizes).

Table 1 gives the death rates and number of persons for each country by five-year age groups (zero through four, five through nine, and so on through eighty and above). The first fact we glean from the table is that the mortality rates of the Norwegian population are substantially lower than those of their Mexican counterparts at virtually all ages. We see that nearly 40 percent of the Mexican population is concentrated in the three age groups having the lowest death rates (ages five through nineteen). Only half that proportion of the Norwegian population is found in the same age range. In contrast, only 6 percent of the Mexican population is above sixty years of age, an age range with which its highest level of mortality is associated. At the same time, about 20 percent of the Norwegian population is sixty or older. Compared with the Mexican crude death rate, then, the Norwegian rate is disproportionately weighted toward the relatively high age-specific death rates that exist in the older ages.

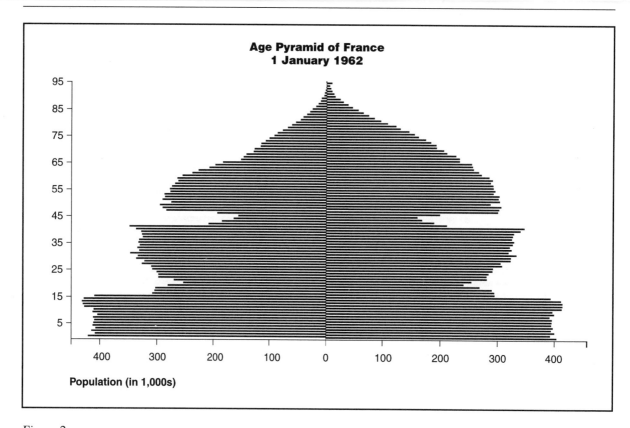

Figure 2

NOTE: Age pyramid France

Applying the standardization method described by the above equation to the average of Norway's and Mexico's proportionate age distributions, we find that the resulting crude death rates are consistent with what we would infer from the two series of age-specific mortality rates. Mexico's age-standardized crude death rate, 8.7 per 1000 population, is one-third greater than that of Norway, 6.6 per 1000.

LIFE TABLES

The *life table* is a methodological device used by demographers and others to examine the life—either literal or figurative—of a particular duration-dependent phenomenon. The original application of the life table was to the mortality patterns of human populations. Today, the life table technique is applied to such diverse areas as contraceptive efficacy, marital formation and dissolution, and organizational failure. Thus it is a remarkably

general tool for examining the time-dependent survivorship in a given state.

To illustrate the use of the life table method, suppose we use as an example the mortality experience of the United States population in 1996. We might wish to derive the average number of years that an individual would live, subject to the series of age-specific death rates attributed to that population. To find the answer, we could construct a *complete life table*, as in table 2. It is complete in the sense that it is highly age-detailed, focusing on single years of age. This is in contrast to the *abridged life table*, which is usually constructed using five-year age groups. The abridged life table shown in table 3 refers also to the total population of the United States in 1996.

Most life tables that we see are called *period* or *current life tables*. They refer to a particular snapshot in time. Although they describe the mortality experience of an actual population, they do not

**Standardization using Death Rates and Population Distributions
from Mexico (1990) and Norway (1997)**

Age Group	Mexico		STANDARD DISTRIBUTION (%)	Norway	
	Population in 1000s (% distribution)	Death Rate (per 1000)		Population in 1000s (% distribution)	Death Rate (per 1000)
0-4	10,257 (12.62)	8.40	9.75	303 (6.88)	1.06
5-9	10,627 (13.08)	0.61	9.96	301 (6.83)	0.19
10-14	10,452 (12.86)	0.52	9.43	264 (6.00)	0.14
15-19	9,723 (11.97)	0.99	9.00	265 (6.02)	0.48
20-24	7,877 (9.69)	1.50	8.24	299 (6.78)	0.54
25-29	6,444 (7.93)	1.88	7.86	343 (7.78)	0.68
30-34	5,420 (6.67)	2.21	7.17	338 (7.68)	0.77
35-39	4,607 (5.67)	2.88	6.46	319 (7.25)	0.94
40-44	3,519 (4.33)	3.80	5.72	313 (7.11)	1.55
45-49	2,990 (3.68)	5.30	5.28	303 (6.89)	2.45
50-54	2,408 (2.96)	7.30	4.73	286 (6.50)	3.88
55-59	1,906 (2.35)	11.32	3.48	203 (4.61)	6.19
60-64	1,621 (2.00)	15.17	2.97	174 (3.94)	10.31
65-69	1,191 (1.47)	23.57	2.74	177 (4.02)	16.55
70-74	832 (1.02)	33.27	2.53	177 (4.03)	28.66
75-79	594 (0.73)	54.53	2.13	156 (3.53)	57.11
80+	780 (0.96)	108.52	2.55	182 (4.14)	122.48

Table 1

SOURCE: http://www.ssb.no/www-open/english/yearbook/ and http://www.census.gov/ipc/www/idbprint.html

Complete Life Table* for the United States, 1996

Exact Age x	$_{1}q_{x}$	ℓ_{x}	$_{1}d_{x}$	$_{1}L_{x}$	T_{x}	e_{x}
0	.00732	100,000	732	99,370	7,611,825	76.1
1	.00054	99,268	53	99,240	7,512,455	75.7
2	.00040	99,215	40	99,193	7,413,215	74.7
3	.00031	99,175	31	99,158	7,314,022	73.7
4	.00026	99,144	26	99,130	7,214,864	72.8
5	.00023	99,118	23	99,106	7,115,734	71.8
6	.00021	99,095	21	99,084	7,016,628	70.8
7	.00020	99,074	19	99,064	6,917,544	69.8
8	.00018	99,055	18	99,046	6,818,480	68.8
9	.00016	99,037	15	99,029	6,719,434	67.8
10	.00014	99,022	14	99,014	6,620,405	66.9
⋮	⋮	⋮	⋮	⋮	⋮	⋮
80	.05967	49,276	2,940	47,668	411,547	8.4
81	.06566	46,336	3,043	44,676	363,879	7.9
82	.07250	43,293	3,139	41,586	319,203	7.4
83	.08033	40,154	3,225	38,403	277,617	6.9
84	.08936	36,929	3,300	35,141	239,214	6.5
85	(1.00000)	33,629	33,629	204,073	204,073	6.1

Table 2

NOTE: *This is technically an "interpolated life table" and not a complete life table based on single-year data.
SOURCE: This life table is available on the web at http://www.cdc.gov/nchswww/datawh/statab/unpubd/mortabs/lewk2.htm

describe the experience of an actual birth cohort—that is, a group of individuals who are born within a (narrowly) specified interval of time. If we wished to portray the mortality history of the birth cohort of 2000, for example, we would have to wait until the last individual of that cohort has died, or beyond the year 2110, before we would be able to calculate all of the values that comprise the life table. In such a life table, called a *generation* or *cohort life table*, we can explicitly obtain the probability of individuals surviving to a given age. As is intuitively clear, however, a generation life table is suitable primarily for historical analyses of cohorts now extinct. Any generation life table that we could calculate would be very much out of date and would in no way approximate the present mortality experience of a population. Thus, we realize the need for the period life table, which

treats a population at a given point in time as a *synthetic* or *hypothetical cohort*. The major drawback of the period life table is that it refers to no particular cohort of individuals. In an era of mortality rates declining at all ages, such a life table will underestimate true life expectancy for any cohort.

The most fundamental data that underlie the formation of a period life table are the number of deaths attributed to each age group in the population for a particular calendar year ($_{n}D_{x}$), where x refers to the exact age at the beginning of the age interval and n is the width of that interval, and the number of individuals living at the midpoint of that year for each of those same age groups ($_{n}P_{x}$).

To begin the life table's construction, we take the ratio of these two sets of input data—$_{n}D_{x}$ and $_{n}P_{x}$—to form a series of age-specific death rates, or $_{n}M_{x}$:

Abridged Life Table for the United States, 1996

Exact Age x	$_nD_x$	$_nP_x$ (in 1,000s)	$_nq_x$	ℓ_x	$_nd_x$	$_nL_x$	T_x	e_x
0	28,487	3,769	.00732	100,000	732	99,370	7,611,825	76.1
1	5,948	16,516	.00151	99,268	150	396,721	7,512,455	75.7
5	3,780	19,441	.00097	99,118	96	495,329	7,115,734	71.8
10	4,550	18,981	.00118	99,022	117	494,883	6,620,405	66.9
15	14,663	18,662	.00390	98,905	386	493,650	6,125,522	61.9
20	17,780	17,560	.00506	98,519	499	491,372	5,631,872	57.2
25	20,730	19,007	.00544	98,020	533	488,766	5,140,500	52.4
30	30,417	21,361	.00710	97,487	692	485,746	4,651,734	47.7
35	42,499	22,577	.00944	96,795	914	481,820	4,165,988	43.0
40	53,534	20,816	.01283	95,881	1,230	476,549	3,684,168	38.4
45	67,032	18,436	.01801	94,651	1,705	469,305	3,207,619	33.9
50	77,297	13,934	.02733	92,946	2,540	458,779	2,738,314	29.5
55	96,726	11,362	.04177	90,406	3,776	443,132	2,279,535	25.2
60	136,999	9,999	.06649	86,630	5,760	419,530	1,836,403	21.2
65	200,045	9,892	.09663	80,870	7,814	385,659	1,416,873	17.5
70	273,849	8,778	.14556	73,056	10,634	339,620	1,031,214	14.1
75	321,223	6,873	.21060	62,422	13,146	280,047	691,594	11.1
80	342,067	4,557	.31754	49,276	15,647	207,474	411,547	8.4
85	576,541	3,762	1.00000	33,629	33,629	204,073	204,073	6.1

Table 3

SOURCE: $_nD_x$ and $_nP_x$ values are obtained from Peters, Kochanek, and Murphy 1998, and from the web site, http://www.cdc.gov/nchswww/datawh/statab/unpubd/mortabs/pop6096.htm, respectively.

$$_nM_x = \frac{_nD_x}{_nP_x} \qquad (3)$$

For each death rate, we compute the corresponding probability of dying within that age interval, given that one has survived to the beginning of the interval. This value, denoted by $_nq_x$, is computed using the following equation:

$$_nq_x = \frac{n \cdot {}_nM_x}{1 + (n - {}_na_x) \cdot {}_nM_x} \qquad (4)$$

where $_na_x$ is the average number of years lived by those who die within the age interval x to $x+n$. (Except for the first year of life, it is typically assumed that deaths are uniformly distributed within an age interval, implying that $_na_x = n/2$.) Given the values of q and a, we are able to generate the entire life table.

The life table may be thought of as a tracking device, by which a cohort of individuals is followed from the moment of their birth until the last surviving individual dies. Under this interpretation, the various remaining columns are defined in the following manner: l_x equals the number of individuals in the life table surviving to exact age x. We arbitrarily set the number "born into" the life table, l_o, which is otherwise known as the *radix*, to some value—most often, 100,000. We generate all subsequent l_x values by the following equation:

$$\ell_{x+n} = \ell_x \cdot [1 - {}_nq_x] \qquad (5)$$

$_nd_x$ equals the number of deaths experienced by the life table cohort within the age interval x to $x+n$. It is the product of the number of individuals alive at exact age x and the conditional probability of dying within the age interval:

$$_nd_x = \ell_x \cdot {}_nq_x \qquad (6)$$

The concept of "person-years" is critical to understanding life table construction. Each individual who survives from one birthday to the next contributes one additional person-year to those tallied by the cohort to which that person belongs. In the year in which the individual dies, the decedent contributes some fraction of a person-year to the overall number for that cohort.

$_nL_x$ equals the total number of person-years experienced by a cohort in the age interval, x to $x+n$. It is the sum of person-years contributed by those who have survived to the end of the interval and those contributed by individuals who die within that interval:

$$_nL_x = [n\ell_{x+n}] + [_na_x \cdot _nd_x] \qquad (7)$$

T_x equals the number of person-years lived beyond exact age x:

$$T_x = \sum_{a=x,n}^{\infty} {}_nL_a = T_{x+n} + {}_nL_x \qquad (8)$$

e_x equals the expected number of years of life remaining for an individual who has already survived to exact age x. It is the total number of person-years experienced by the cohort above that age divided by the number of individuals starting out at that age:

$$e_x = \frac{T_x}{\ell_x} \qquad (9)$$

The $_nL_x$ and T_x columns are generated from the oldest age to the youngest. If the last age category is, for example, eighty-five and above (it is typically "open-ended" in this way), we must have an initial value for T_{85} in order to begin the process. This value is derived in the following fashion: Since for this oldest age group, $l_{85} = {}_{\infty}d_{85}$ (due to the fact that the number of individuals in a cohort who will die at age eighty-five or beyond is simply the number surviving to age eighty-five) and $T_{85} = {}_{\infty}L_{85}$, we have:

$$e_{85} = \frac{T_{85}}{\ell_{85}} = \frac{1}{\ell_{85} / T_{85}} =$$

$$\frac{1}{{}_{\infty}d_{85} / {}_{\infty}L_{85}} \approx \frac{1}{{}_{\infty}M_{85}} \qquad (10)$$

From the life table, we can obtain mortality information in a variety of ways. In table 2, we see, for example, that the expectation of life at birth, e_0, is 76.1 years. If an individual in this population survives to age eighty, then he or she might expect to live 8.4 years longer. We might also note that the probability of surviving from birth to one's tenth birthday is l_{10}/l_0, or 0.99022. Given that one has already lived eighty years, the probability that one survives five additional years is l_{85}/l_{80}, or 33,629/49,276=0.68246.

POPULATION PROJECTION

The life table, in addition, is often used to project either total population size or the size of specific age groups. In so doing, we must invoke a different interpretation of the $_nL_x$'s and the T_x's in the life table. We treat them as representing the age distribution of a *stationary population*—that is, a population having long been subject to zero growth. Thus, $_5L_{20}$, for example, represents the number of twenty- to twenty-four-year-olds in the life table "population," into which l_0, or 100,000, individuals are born each year. (One will note by summing the $_nd_x$ column that 100,000 die every year, thus giving rise to stationarity of the life table population.)

If we were to assume that the United States is a *closed population*—that is, a population whose net migration is zero—and, furthermore, that the mortality levels obtaining in 1996 were to remain constant for the following ten years, then we would be able to project the size of any U.S. cohort up to ten years into the future. Thus, if we wished to know the number of fifty- to fifty-four-year-olds in 2006, we would take advantage of the following relation that is assumed to hold approximately:

$$\frac{_nP_{x+t}^{\tau+t}}{_nP_x^{\tau}} \approx \frac{_nL_{x+t}^{\tau+t}}{_nL_x^{\tau}} \qquad (11)$$

where τ is the base year of the projection (e.g., 1996) and t is the number of years one is projecting the population forward. This equation implies that the fifty- to fifty-four-year-olds in 2006, $_5P_{50}^{2006}$, is simply the number of forty- to forty-four-year-olds ten years earlier, $_5P_{40}^{1996}$, multiplied by the proportion of forty- to forty-four-year-olds in the life table surviving ten years, $_5L_{50}/_5L_{40}$.

In practice, it is appropriate to use the above relation in population projection only if the width of the age interval under consideration, n, is sufficiently narrow. If the age interval is very broad—for example, in the extreme case in which we are attempting to project the number of people aged ten and above in 2006 from the number zero and above (i.e, the entire population) in 1996—we cannot be assured that the life table age distribution within that interval resembles closely enough the age distribution of the actual population. In other words, if the actual population's age distribution within a broad age interval is significantly different from that within the corresponding interval of the life table population, then implicitly by using this projection device we are improperly weighing the component parts of the broad interval with respect to survival probabilities.

Parenthetically, if we desired to determine the size of any component of the population under t years old—in this particular example, ten years old—we would have to draw upon fertility as well as mortality information, because at time τ these individuals had not yet been born.

HAZARDS MODELS

Suppose we were to examine the correlates of marital dissolution. In a life table analysis, the break-up of the marriage (as measured, e.g., by separation or divorce) would serve as the analogue to death, which is the means of exit in the standard life table analysis.

In the study of many duration-dependent phenomena, it is clear that several factors may affect whether an individual exits from a life table. Certainly, it is well-established that a large number of socioeconomic variables simultaneously impinge on the marital dissolution process. In many populations, whether one has given birth premaritally, cohabited premaritally, married at a young age, or had little in the way of formal education, among a whole host of other factors, have been found to be strongly associated with marital instability. In such studies, in which one attempts to disentangle the intricately related influences of several variables on survivorship in a given state, we invoke a hazards model approach. Such an approach may be thought of as a multivariate statistical extension of the simple life table analysis presented above (for theoretical underpinnings, see, e.g., Cox and Oakes 1984 and Allison 1984; for applications to marital stability, see, e.g., Menken, Trussell, Stempel, and Babakol 1981 and Bennett, Blanc, and Bloom 1988).

In the marital dissolution example, we would assume that there is a hazard, or risk, of dissolution at each marital duration, d, and we allow this duration-specific risk to depend on individual characteristics (such as age at marriage, education, etc.). In the *proportional hazards model*, a set of individual characteristics represented by a vector

of covariates shifts the hazard by the same proportional amount at all durations. Thus, for an individual i at duration d, with an observed set of characteristics represented by a vector of covariates, Z_i, the hazard function, $\mu_i(d)$, is given by:

$$\mu_i(d) = \exp[\lambda(d)] \exp[Z_i \beta] \qquad (12)$$

where β is a vector of parameters and $\lambda(d)$ is the underlying duration pattern of risk. In this model, then, the underlying risk of dissolution for an individual i with characteristics Z_i is multiplied by a factor equal to $\exp[Z_i\beta]$.

We may also implement a more general set of models to test for departures from some of the restrictive assumptions built into the proportional hazards framework. More specifically, we allow for time-varying covariates (for instance, in this example, the occurrence of a first marital birth) as well as allow for the effects of individual characteristics to vary with duration of first marriage. This model may be written as:

$$\mu_i(d) = \exp[\lambda(d)] \exp[Z_i(d)\beta(d)] \qquad (13)$$

where $\lambda(d)$ is defined as in the proportional hazards model, $Z_i(d)$ is the vector of covariates, some of which may be time-varying, and $\beta(d)$ represents a vector of parameters, some of which may give rise to nonproportional effects. The model parameters can be estimated using the method of maximum likelihood. The estimation procedure assumes that the hazard, $\mu_i(d)$, is constant within duration intervals. The interval width chosen by the analyst, of course, should be supported on both substantive and statistical grounds.

INDIRECT DEMOGRAPHIC ESTIMATION

Unfortunately, many countries around the world have poor or nonexistent data pertaining to a wide array of demographic variables. In the industrialized nations, we typically have access to data from rigorous registration systems that collect data on mortality, marriage, fertility, and other demographic processes. However, when analyzing the demographic situation of less developed nations, we are often confronted with a paucity of available data on these fundamental processes. When such data are in fact collected, they are often sufficiently inadequate to be significantly misleading. For example, in some countries we have learned that as few as half of all actual deaths are recorded. If we mistakenly assume the value of the actual number to be the registered number, then we will substantially overestimate life expectancy in these populations. In essence, we will incorrectly infer that people are dying at a slower rate than is truly the case.

The Stable Population Model. Much demographic estimation has relied on the notion of stability. A *stable population* is defined as one that is established by a long history of unchanging fertility and mortality patterns. This criterion gives rise to a fixed proportionate age distribution, constant birth and death rates, and a constant rate of population growth (see, e.g., Coale 1972). The basic stable population equation is:

$$c(a) = be^{-ra}p(a) \qquad (14)$$

where $c(a)$ is the proportion of the population exact age a, b is the crude birth rate, r is the rate of population growth, and $p(a)$ is the proportion of the population surviving to exact age a. Various mathematical relationships have been shown to obtain among the demographic variables in a stable population. This becomes clear when we multiply both sides of the equation by the total population size. Thus, we have:

$$N(a) = Be^{-ra}p(a) \qquad (15)$$

where $N(a)$ is the number of individuals in the population exact age a and B is the current annual number of births. We can see that the number of people aged a this year is simply the product of the number of births entering the population a years ago—namely, the current number of births times a growth rate factor, which discounts the births according to the constant population growth rate, r (which also applies to the growth of the number of births over time)—and the proportion of a birth cohort that survives to aged a today. Note that the constancy over time of the mortality schedule, $p(a)$, and the growth rate, r, are crucial to the validity of this interpretation.

When we assume a population is stable, we are imposing structure upon the demographic relationships existing therein. In a country where data

are inadequate, indirect methods allow us—by drawing upon the known structure implied by stability—to piece together sometimes inaccurate information and ultimately derive sensible estimates of the population parameters. The essential strategy in indirect demographic estimation is to infer a value or set of values for a variable whose elements are either unobserved or inaccurate from the relationship among the remaining variables in the above equation (or an equation deriving from the one above). We find that these techniques are robust with respect to moderate departures from stability, as in the case of quasi-stable populations, in which only fertility has been constant and mortality has been gradually changing.

The Nonstable Population Model. Throughout much of the time span during which indirect estimation has evolved, there have been many countries where populations approximated stability. In recent decades, however, many countries have experienced rapidly declining mortality or declining or fluctuating fertility and, thus, have undergone a radical departure from stability. Consequently, previously successful indirect methods, grounded in stable population theory, are, with greater frequency, ill-suited to the task for which they were devised. As is often the case, necessity is the mother of invention and so demographers have sought to adapt their methodology to the changing world.

In the early 1980s, a methodology was developed that can be applied to populations that are far from stable (see, e.g., Bennett and Horiuchi 1981; and Preston and Coale 1982). Indeed, it is no longer necessary to invoke the assumption of stability, if we rely upon the following equation:

$$c(a) = b \cdot \exp \left[-\int_0^a r(x)\, dx \right] \cdot p(a) \qquad (16)$$

where $r(x)$ is the growth rate of the population at exact age x. This equation holds true for any closed population, and, indeed, can be modified to accommodate populations open to migration.

The implied relationships among the age distribution of living persons and deaths, and rates of growth of different age groups, provide the basis for a wide range of indirect demographic methods that allow us to infer accurate estimates of basic demographic parameters that ultimately can be used to better inform policy on a variety of issues. Two examples are as follows.

First, suppose we have the age distribution for a country at each of two points in time, in addition to the age distribution of deaths occurring during the intervening years. We may then estimate the completeness of death registration in that population using the following equation (Bennett and Horiuchi 1981):

$$\tilde{N}(a) = \int_a^\infty D(x) \, \exp \, [\int_a^x r(u) \, du] \, dx \qquad (17)$$

where $\hat{N}(a)$ is the estimated number of people at exact age a, $D(x)$ is the number of deaths at exact age x and $r(u)$ is the rate of the growth of the number of persons at exact age u between the two time points. By taking the ratio of the estimated number of persons with the enumerated population, we have an estimate of the completeness of death registration in the population relative to the completeness of the enumerated population. This relative completeness (in contrast to an "absolute" estimate of completeness) is all that is needed to determine the true, unobserved age-specific death rates, which in turn allows one to construct an unbiased life table.

A second example of the utility of the nonstable population framework is shown by the use of the following equation:

$$\frac{N(x)}{N(a)} = {}_{x-a}p_a \exp \, [\int_a^x r(u) \, du] \qquad (18)$$

where $N(x)$ and $N(a)$ are the number of people exact ages x and a, respectively, and ${}_{x-a}p_a$ is the probability of surviving from age a to age x according to period mortality rates. By using variants of this equation, we can generate reliable population age distributions (e.g., in situations in which censuses are of poor quality) from a trustworthy life table (Bennett and Garson 1983).

MORTALITY MODELING

The field of demography has a long tradition of developing models that are based upon empirical regularities. Typically in demographic modeling, as in all kinds of modeling, we try to adhere to the principle of parsimony—that is, we want to be as efficient as possible with regard to the detail, and therefore the number of parameters, in a model.

Mortality schedules from around the world reveal that death rates follow a common pattern of relatively high rates of infant mortality, rates that decline through early childhood until they bottom out in the age range of five to fifteen or so, then rates that increase slowly through the young and middle adult years, and finally rising more rapidly during the older adult ages beyond the forties or fifties. Various mortality models exploit this regular pattern in the data. Countries differ with respect to the overall level of mortality, as reflected in the expectation of life at birth, and the precise relationship that exists among the different age components of the mortality curve.

Coale and Demeny (1983) examined 192 mortality schedules from different times and regions of the world and found that they could be categorized into four "families" of life tables. Although overall mortality levels might differ, within each family the relationships among the various age components of mortality were shown to be similar. For each family, Coale and Demeny constructed a "model life table" for females that was associated with each of twenty-five expectations of life at birth from twenty through eighty. A comparable set of tables was developed for males. In essence, a researcher can match bits of information that are known to be accurate in a population with the corresponding values in the model life tables, and ultimately derive a detailed life table for the population under study. In less developed countries, model life tables are often used to estimate basic mortality parameters, such as e_0 or the crude death rate, from other mortality indicators that may be more easily observable.

Other mortality models have been developed, the most notable being that by Brass (1971). Brass noted that one mortality schedule could be related to another by means of a linear transformation of the logits of their respective survivorship probabilities (i.e., the vector of l_x values, given a radix of one). Thus, one may generate a life table by applying the logit system to a "standard" or "reference" life table, given an appropriate pair of parameters that reflect (1) the overall level of mortality in the population under study, and (2) the relationship between child and adult mortality.

MARRIAGE, FERTILITY, AND MIGRATION MODELS

Coale (1971) observed that age distributions of first marriages are structurally similar in different populations. These distributions tend to be smooth, unimodal, and skewed to the right, and to have a density close to zero below age fifteen and above age fifty. He also noted that the differences in age-at-marriage distributions across female populations are largely accounted for by differences in their means, standard deviations, and cumulative values at the older ages, for example, at age fifty. As a basis for the application of these observations, Coale constructed a standard schedule of age at first marriage using data from Sweden, covering the period 1865 through 1869. The model that is applied to marriage data is represented by the following equation:

$$g(a) = \frac{E}{\sigma} 1.2813 \exp\left\{-1.145\left(\frac{a-\mu}{\sigma} + 0.805\right) - \exp\left[-1.896\left(\frac{a-\mu}{\sigma} + 0.805\right)\right]\right\}$$ (20)

where $g(a)$ is the proportion marrying at age a in the observed population and μ, σ, and E are, respectively, the mean and the standard deviation of age at first marriage (for those who ever marry), and the proportion ever marrying.

The model can be extended to allow for covariate effects by stipulating a functional relationship between the parameters of the model distribution and a set of covariates. This may be specified as follows:

$$\mu_i = \mathbf{X}_i' \alpha \ ,$$
$$\sigma_i = \mathbf{Y}_i' \beta \ ,$$ (20)
$$E_i = \mathbf{Z}_i' Y \ ,$$

where X_i, Y_i, and Z_i are the vector values of characteristics of an individual that determine, respectively, μ_i, σ_i, and E_i, and α, β, and Y are the associated parameter vectors to be estimated.

Because the model is parametric, it can be applied to data referring to cohorts who have yet to complete their marriage experience. In this fashion, the model can be used for purposes of projection (see, e.g., Bloom and Bennett 1990). The model has also been found to replicate well the first birth experience of cohorts (see, e.g., Bloom 1982).

Coale and Trussell (1974), recognizing the empirical regularities that exist among age profiles of fertility across time and space and extending the work of Louis Henry, developed a set of model fertility schedules. Their model is based in part on a reference distribution of age-specific marital fertility rates that describes the pattern of fertility in a *natural fertility population*—that is, one that exhibits no sign of controlling the extent of child-bearing activity. When fitted to an observed age pattern of fertility, the model's two parameters describe the overall level of fertility in the population and the degree to which their fertility within marriage is controlled by some means of contraception. Perhaps the greatest use of this model has been devoted to comparative analyses, which is facilitated by the two-parameter summary of any age pattern of fertility in question.

Although the application of indirect demographic estimation methods to migration analysis is not as mature as that to other demographic processes, strategies similar to those invoked by fertility and mortality researchers have been applied to the development of model migration schedules. Rogers and Castro (1981) found that similar age patterns of migration obtained among many different populations. They have summarized these regularities in a basic eleven-parameter model, and, using Brass and Coale logic, explore ways in which their model can be applied satisfactorily to data of imperfect quality.

The methods described above comprise only a small component of the methodological tools available to demographers and to social scientists, in general. Some of these methods are more readily applicable than others to fields outside of demography. It is clear, for example, how we may take advantage of the concept of standardization in a variety of disciplines. So, too, may we apply life table analysis and nonstable population analysis to problems outside the demographic domain. Any analogue to birth and death processes can be investigated productively using these central methods. Even the fundamental concept underlying the above mortality, fertility, marriage, and migration models—that is, exploiting the power to be found in empirical regularities—can be applied fruitfully to other research endeavors.

REFERENCES

Allison, Paul D. 1984 *Event History Analysis*. Beverly Hills, Calif.: Sage Publications.

Bennett, Neil G., Ann K. Blanc, and David E. Bloom 1988 "Commitment and the Modern Union: Assessing the Link between Premarital Cohabitation and Subsequent Marital Stability." *American Sociological Review* 53:127–138.

Bennett, Neil G., and Lea Keil Garson 1983 "The Centenarian Question and Old-Age Mortality in the Soviet Union, 1959–1970." *Demography* 20:587–606.

Bennett, Neil G., and Shiro Horiuchi 1981 "Estimating the Completeness of Death Registration in a Closed Population." *Population Index* 47:207–221.

Bloom, David E. 1982 "What's Happening to the Age at First Birth in the United States? A Study of Recent Cohorts." *Demography* 19:351–370.

——, and Neil G. Bennett 1990 "Modeling American Marriage Patterns." *Journal of the American Statistical Association* 85 (December):1009–1017.

Coale, Ansley J. 1972 *The Growth and Structure of Human Populations*. Princeton, N.J.: Princeton University Press.

—— 1971 "Age Patterns of Marriage." *Population Studies* 25:193–214.

——, and Paul Demeny 1983 *Regional Model Life Tables and Stable Populations*, 2nd ed. New York: Academic Press.

Coale, Ansley J., and James Trussell 1974 "Model Fertility Schedules: Variations in the Age Structure of Childbearing in Human Populations." *Population Index* 40:185–206.

Cox, D. R., and D. Oakes 1984 *Analysis of Survival Data*. London: Chapman and Hall.

Menken, Jane, James Trussell, Debra Stempel, and Ozer Babakol 1981 "Proportional Hazards Life Table Models: An Illustrative Analysis of Sociodemographic Influences on Marriage Dissolution in the United States." *Demography* 18:181–200.

Peters, Kimberley D., Kenneth D. Kochanek, and Sherry L. Murphy 1998 "Deaths: Final Data for 1996." *National Vital Statistics Reports*, vol. 47, no. 9. Hyattsville, Md.: National Center for Health Statistics.

Preston, Samuel H., and Ansley J. Coale 1982 "Age Structure, Growth, Attrition, and Accession: A New Synthesis." *Population Index* 48:217–259.

Rogers, Andrei, and Luis J. Castro 1981 "Model Migration Schedules." (Research Report 81–30) Laxenburg, Austria: International Institute for Applied Systems Analysis.

NEIL G. BENNETT

DEMOGRAPHIC TRANSITION

The human population has maintained relatively gradual growth throughout most of history by high, and nearly equal, rates of deaths and births. Since about 1800, however, this situation has changed dramatically, as most societies have undergone major declines in mortality, setting off high growth rates due to the imbalance between deaths and births. Some societies have eventually had fertility declines and emerged with a very gradual rate of growth as low levels of births matched low levels of mortality.

There are many versions of demographic transition theory (Mason 1997), but there is some consensus that each society has the potential to proceed sequentially through four general stages of variation in death and birth rates and population growth. Most societies in the world have passed through the first two stages, at different dates and speeds, and the contemporary world is primarily characterized by societies in the last two stages, although a few are still in the second stage.

Stage 1, presumably characterizing most of human history, involves high and relatively equal birth and death rates and little resulting population growth.

Stage 2 is characterized by a declining death rate, especially concentrated in the years of infancy and childhood. The fertility rate remains high, leading to at least moderate population growth.

Stage 3 involves further declines in mortality, usually to low levels, and initial sustained declines in fertility. Population growth may become quite high, as levels of fertility and mortality increasingly diverge.

Stage 4 is characterized by the achievement of low mortality and the rapid emergence of low fertility levels, usually near those of mortality. Population growth again becomes quite low or negligible.

While demographers argue about the details of demographic change in the past 200 years, clearcut declines in birth and death rates appeared on the European continent and in areas of overseas European settlement in the nineteenth century, especially in the last three decades. By 1900, life expectancies in "developed" societies such as the United States were probably in the mid-forties, having increased by a few years in the century (Preston and Haines 1991). By the end of the twentieth century, even more dramatic gains in mortality were evident, with life expectancies reaching into the mid- and high-seventies.

The European fertility transition of the late 1800s to the twentieth century involved a relatively continuous movement from average fertility levels of five or six children per couple to bare levels of replacement by the end of the 1930s. Fertility levels rose again after World War II, but then began another decline about 1960. Some countries now have levels of fertility that are well below long-term replacement levels.

With a few exceptions such as Japan, most other parts of the developing world did not experience striking declines in mortality and fertility until the midpoint of the twentieth century. Gains in life expectancy became quite common and very rapid in the post-World War II period throughout the developing world (often taking less than twenty years), although the amount of change was quite variable. Suddenly in the 1960s, fertility transitions emerged in a small number of societies, especially in the Caribbean and Southeast Asia, to be followed in the last part of the twentieth century by many other countries.

Clear variations in mortality characterize many parts of the world at the end of the twentieth century. Nevertheless, life expectancies in countries throughout the world are generally greater than those found in the most developed societies in 1900. A much greater range in fertility than mortality characterizes much of the world, but fertility declines seem to be spreading, including in "laggard" regions such as sub-Saharan Africa.

The speed with which the mortality transition was achieved among contemporary lesser-developed countries has had a profound effect on the magnitude of the population growth that has occurred during the past few decades. Sweden, a model example of the nineteenth century European demographic transition, peaked at an annual rate of natural increase of 1.2 percent. In contrast, many developing countries have attained growth rates of over 3.0 percent. The world population grew at a rate of about 2 percent in the early 1970s but has now declined to about 1.4 percent, as fertility rates have become equal to the generally low mortality rates.

CAUSES OF MORTALITY TRANSITIONS

The European mortality transition was gradual, associated with modernization and raised standards of living. While some dispute exists among demographers, historians, and others concerning the relative contribution of various causes (McKeown 1976; Razzell 1974), the key factors probably included increased agricultural productivity and improvements in transportation infrastructure which enabled more efficient food distribution and, therefore, greater nutrition to ward off disease. The European mortality transition was also probably influenced by improvements in medical knowledge, especially in the twentieth century, and by improvements in sanitation and personal hygiene. Infectious and environmental diseases especially have declined in importance relative to cancers and cardiovascular problems. Children and infants, most susceptible to infectious and environmental diseases, have showed the greatest gains in life expectancy.

The more recent and rapid mortality transitions in the rest of the world have mirrored the European change with a movement from infectious/environmental causes to cancers and cardiovascular problems. In addition, the greatest beneficiaries have been children and infants. These transitions result from many of the same factors as the European case, generally associated with economic development, but as Preston (1975) outlines, they have also been influenced by recent advances in medical technology and public health measures that have been imported from the highly-developed societies. For instance, relatively inexpensive vaccines are now available throughout the world for immunization against many infectious diseases. In addition, airborne sprays have been distributed at low cost to combat widespread diseases such as malaria. Even relatively weak national governments have instituted major improvements in health conditions, although often only with the help of international agencies.

Nevertheless, mortality levels are still higher than those in many rich societies due to such factors as inadequate diets and living conditions, and inadequate development of health facilities such as hospitals and clinics. Preston (1976) observes that among non-Western lesser-developed countries, mortality from diarrheal diseases (e.g., cholera) has persisted despite control over other forms of infectious disease due to the close relationship between diarrheal diseases, poverty, and ignorance—and therefore a nation's level of socioeconomic development.

Scholars (Caldwell 1986; Palloni 1981) have warned that prospects for future success against high mortality may be tightly tied to aspects of social organization that are independent of simple measures of economic well-being: Governments may be more or less responsive to popular need for improved health; school system development may be important for educating citizens on how to care for themselves and their families; the equitable treatment of women may enhance life expectancy for the total population.

Recent worldwide mortality trends may be charted with the help of data on life expectancy at age zero that have been gathered, sometimes on the basis of estimates, by the Population Reference Bureau (PRB), a highly respected chronicler of world vital rates. For 165 countries with relatively stable borders over time, it is possible to relate estimated life expectancy in 1986 with the same figure for 1998. Of these countries, only 13.3 percent showed a decline in life expectancy during the time period. Some 80.0 percent had overall increasing life expectancy, but the gains were highly variable. Of all the countries, 29.7 percent actually had gains of at least five years or more, a sizable change given historical patterns of mortality.

An indication of the nature of change may be discerned by looking at Figure 1, which shows a graph of the life expectancy values for the 165 countries with stable borders. Each point represents a country and shows the level of life expectancy in 1986 and in 1998. Note the relatively high levels of life expectancy by historical standards for most countries in both years. Not surprisingly, there is a strong tendency for life expectancy values to be correlated over time. A regression straight line, indicating average life expectancy in 1998 as a function of life expectancy in 1986 describes this relationship. As suggested above, the levels of life expectancy in 1998 tend to be slightly higher than the life expectancy in 1986. Since geography is highly associated with economic development, the points on the graph generally form a continuum from low to high life expectancy. African countries tend to have the lowest life expectancies, followed by Asia, Oceania, and the Americas. Europe has the highest life expectancies.

The African countries comprise virtually all the countries with declining life expectancies, probably a consequence of their struggles with acquired immune deficiency syndrome (AIDS), malnutrition, and civil disorder. Many of them have lost several years of life expectancy in a very short period of time. However, a number of the African countries also have sizeable increases in life expectancies.

Asian and American countries dominate the mid-levels of life expectancy, with the Asian countries showing a strong tendency to increase their life expectancies, consistent with high rates of economic development.

Unfortunately, Figure 1 does not include the republics of the former Soviet Union, since exactly comparable data are not available for both time points. Nevertheless, there is some consensus among experts that life expectancy has deteriorated in countries such as Russia that have made the transition from communism to economically-unstable capitalism.

WHAT DRIVES FERTILITY RATES?

The analysis of fertility decline is somewhat more complicated analytically than mortality decline. One may presume that societies will try, if given resources and a choice, to minimize mortality levels, but it seems less necessarily so that societies have an inherent orientation toward low fertility, or, for that matter, any specific fertility level. In addition, fertility rates may vary quite widely across

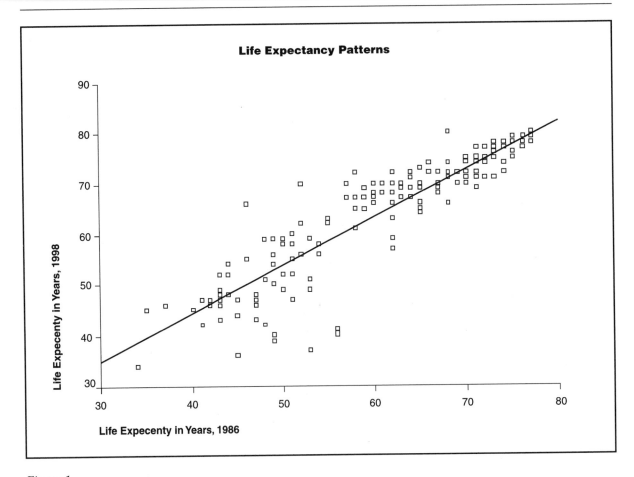

Figure 1

societies due to factors (Bongaarts 1975) that have little relationship to conscious desires such as prolonged breastfeeding which supresses reproductive ovulation in women, the effectiveness of birth control methods, and the amount of involuntary foetal abortion. As a result of these analytic ambiguities, scholars seem to have less consensus on the social factors that might produce fertility than mortality decline (Hirschman 1994; Mason 1997).

Coale (1973), in an attempt to reconcile the diversity of circumstances under which fertility declines have been observed to occur, identified three major conditions for a major fall in fertility:

1. Fertility must be within the calculus of conscious choice. Parents must consider it an acceptable mode of thought and form of behavior to balance the advantages and disadvantages of having another child.

2. Reduced fertility must be viewed as socially or economically advantageous to couples.

3. Effective techniques of birth control must be available. Sexual partners must know these techniques and have a sustained will to use the them.

Beyond Coale's conditions, little consensus has emerged on the causes of fertility decline. There are, however, a number of major ideas about what causes fertility transitions that may be summarized in a few major hypotheses.

A major factor in causing fertility change may be the mortality transition itself. High-mortality societies depend on high fertility to ensure their survival. In such circumstances, individual couples will maximize their fertility to guarantee that at least a few of their children survive to adulthood, to perpetuate the family lineage and to care for them in old age. The decline in mortality may also have other consequences for fertility rates. As mortality declines, couples may perceive that they can control the survival of family members by changing health and living practices such as cleanliness and diet. This sense of control may extend itself to the realm of fertility decisions, so that couples decide to calculate consciously the number of children they would prefer and then take steps to achieve that goal.

Another major factor may be the costs and benefits of children. High-mortality societies are often characterized by low technology in producing goods; in such a situation (as exemplified by many agricultural and mining societies), children may be economically useful to perform low-skilled work tasks. Parents have an incentive to bear children, or, at the minimum, they have little incentive not to bear children. However, high-technology societies place a greater premium on highly-skilled labor and often require extended periods of education. Children will have few economic benefits and may become quite costly as they are educated and fed for long periods of time.

Another major factor that may foster fertility decline is the transfer of functions from the family unit to the state. In low-technology societies, the family or kin group is often the fundamental unit, providing support for its members in times of economic distress and unemployment and for older members who can no longer contribute to the group through work activities. Children may be viewed as potential contributors to the unit, either in their youth or adulthood. In high-technology societies, some of the family functions are transferred to the state through unemployment insurance, welfare programs, and old age retirement systems. The family functions much more as a social or emotional unit where the economic benefits of membership are less tangible, thus decreasing the incentive to bear children.

Other major factors (Hirschman 1994; Mason 1997) in fertility declines may include urbanization and gender roles. Housing space is usually costly in cities, and the large family becomes untenable. In many high-technology societies, women develop alternatives to childbearing through employment outside their homes, and increasingly assert their social and political rights to participate equally with men in the larger society. Because of socialization, men are generally unwilling to assume substantial child-raising responsibilities, leaving partners with little incentive to participate in sustained childbearing through their young adult lives.

No consensus exists on how to order these theories in relative importance. Indeed, each theory may have more explanatory power in some circumstances than others, and their relative importance may vary over time. For instance, declines in mortality may be crucial in starting fertility transitions, but significant alterations in the roles of children may be key for completing them. Even though it is difficult to pick the "best" theory, every country that has had a sustained mortality decline of at least thirty years has also had some evidence of a fertility decline. Many countries seem to have the fertility decline precondition of high life expectancy, but fewer have achieved the possible preconditions of high proportions of the population achieving a secondary education.

EUROPEAN FERTILITY TRANSITION

Much of what is known about the process of fertility transition is based upon research at Princeton University (known as the European Fertility Project) on the European fertility transition that took place primarily during the seventy-year period between 1870 and 1940. Researchers used aggregate government-collected data for the numerous "provinces" or districts of countries, typically comparing birth rates across time and provinces.

In that almost all births in nineteenth-century Europe occurred within marriage, the European model of fertility transition was defined to take place at the point marital fertility was observed to fall by more than 10 percent (Coale and Treadway 1986). Just as important, the Project scholars identified the existence of varying levels of natural fertility (birth rates when no deliberate fertility control is practiced) across Europe and throughout European history (Knodel 1977). Comparative use of natural fertility models and measures derived from these models have been of enormous use to demographers in identifying the initiation and progress of fertility transitions in more contemporary contexts.

Most scholars have concluded that European countries seemed to start fertility transitions from very different levels of natural fertility but moved at quite similar speeds to similar levels of controlled fertility on the eve of World War II (Coale and Treadway 1986). As the transition progressed, areal differences in fertility within and across countries declined, while the remaining differences were heavily between countries (Watkins 1991).

Although some consensus has emerged on descriptive aspects of the fertility transition, much less agreement exists on the social and economic factors that caused the long-term declines. Early theorists of fertility transitions (Notestein 1953) had posited a simple model driven by urban-industrial social structure, but this perspective clearly proved inadequate. For instance, the earliest declines did not occur in England, the most urban-industrial country of the time, but were in France, which maintained a strong rural culture. The similarity of the decline across provinces and countries of quite different social structures also seemed puzzling within the context of previous theorizing. Certainly, no one has demonstrated that variations in the fertility decline across countries, either in the timing or the speed, were related clearly to variations in crude levels of infant mortality, literacy rates, urbanization, and industrialization. Other findings from recent analysis of the European experience include the observation that in some instances, reductions in fertility preceded reductions in mortality (Cleland and Wilson 1987), a finding that is inconsistent with the four-stage theory of demographic transition.

The findings of the European Fertility Project have led some demographers (Knodel and van de Walle 1979) to reformulate ideas about why fertility declined. They suggest that European couples were interested in a small family well before the actual transition occurred. The transition itself was especially facilitated by the development of effective and cheap birth control devices such as the condom and diaphragm. Information about birth control rapidly and widely diffused through European society, producing transitions that seemed to occur independently of social structural factors such as mortality, urbanization, and educational attainment. In addition, these scholars argue that "cultural" factors were also important in the decline. This is based on the finding that provinces of some countries such as Belgium differed in their fertility declines on the basis of areal religious composition (Lesthaeghe 1977) and that, in other countries such as Italy, areal variations in the nature of fertility decline were related to political factors such as the Socialist vote, probably reflecting anticlericalism (Livi-Bacci 1977). Others (Lesthaeghe 1983) have also argued for "cultural" causes of fertility transitions.

While the social causes of the European fertility transition may be more complex than originally thought, it may still be possible to rescue some of the traditional ideas. For instance, mortality data in Europe at the time of the fertility transition were often quite incomplete or unreliable, and most of the studies focused on infant (first year of life) mortality as possible causes of fertility decline. Matthiessen and McCann (1978) show that mortality data problems make some of the conclusions suspect and that infant mortality may sometimes be a weak indicator of child survivorship to adulthood. They argue that European countries with the earliest fertility declines may have been characterized by more impressive declines in post-infant (but childhood) mortality than infant mortality.

Conclusions about the effects of children's roles on fertility decline have often been based on rates of simple literacy as an indicator of educational system development. However, basic literacy was achieved in many European societies well before the major fertility transitions, and the major costs of children would occur when secondary education was implemented on a large scale basis, which did not happen until near the end of the nineteenth century (Van de Walle 1980). In a time-series analysis of the United States fertility decline from 1870 to the early 1900s, Guest and Tolnay (1983) find a nearly perfect tendency for the fertility rate to fall as the educational system expanded in terms of student enrollments and length of the school year. Related research also shows that educational system development often occurred somewhat independently of urbanization and industrialization in parts of the United States (Guest 1981).

An important methodological issue in the study of the European transition (as in other transitions) is how one models the relationship between social structure and fertility. Many of the research reports from the European Fertility Project seem to assume that social structure and fertility had to be closely related at all time points to support various theories about the causal importance of such factors as mortality and children's roles, but certain lags and superficial inconsistencies do not seem to prove fundamentally that fertility failed to respond as some of the above theories would suggest. The more basic question may be whether fertility eventually responded to changes in social structure such as mortality.

Even after admitting some problems with previous traditional interpretations of the European fertility transition, one cannot ignore the fact that the great decline in fertility occurred at almost the same time as the great decline in mortality and was associated (even if loosely) with a massive process of urbanization, industrialization, and the expansion of educational systems.

FERTILITY TRANSITIONS IN THE DEVELOPING WORLD

The great majority of countries in the developing world have undergone some fertility declines in the second half of the twentieth century. While the spectacularly rapid declines (Taiwan, South Korea) receive the most attention, a number are also very gradual (e.g. Guatemala, Haiti, Iraq, Cambodia), and a number are so incipient (especially in Africa) that their nature is difficult to discern.

The late twentieth century round of fertility transitions has occurred in a very different social context than the historical European pattern. In the past few decades, mortality has declined very rapidly. National governments have become very attuned to checking their unprecedented national growth rates through fertility control. Birth control technology has changed greatly through the development of inexpensive methods such as the intrauterine device (IUD). The world has become more economically and socially integrated through the expansion of transportation and developments in electronic communications, and "Western" products and cultural ideas have rapidly diffused throughout the world. Clearly, societies are not autonomous units that respond demographically as isolated social structures.

Leaders among developing countries in the process of demographic transition were found in East Asia and Latin America, and the Carribbean

(Coale 1983). The clear leaders among Asian nations, such as South Korea and Taiwan, generally had experienced substantial economic growth, rapid mortality decline, rising educational levels, and exposure to Western cultural influences (Freedman 1998). By 1998, South Korea and Taiwan had fertility rates that were below long-term replacement levels. China also experienced rapidly declining fertility, which cannot be said to have causes in either Westernization or more than moderate economic development, with a life expectancy estimated at seventy-one years and a rate of natural increase of 1.0 percent (PRB 1998).

Major Latin American nations that achieved substantial drops in fertility (exceeding 20 percent) in recent decades with life expectancies surpassing sixty years include Argentina, Brazil, Chile, Columbia, the Dominican Republic, Jamaica, Mexico, and Venezuela. All of these have also experienced substantial changes in mortality, education, or both, and economic development.

Unlike the European historical experience, fertility declines in the post-1960 period have not always sustained themselves until they reached near replacement levels. A number of countries have started declines but then leveled off with three or four children per reproductive age woman. For instance, Malaysia was considered a "miracle" case of fertility decline, along with South Korea and Taiwan, but in recent years its fertility level has stabilized somewhat above the replacement level.

Using the PRB data for 1986 and 1998, we can trace recent changes for 166 countries in estimated fertility as measured by the Total Fertility Rate (TFR), an indicator of the number of children typically born to a woman during her lifetime. Some 80.1 percent of the countries showed declines in fertility. Of all the countries, 37.3 percent had a decline of at least one child per woman, and 9.0 percent had a decline of at least two children per woman.

The region that encompasses countries having the highest rates of population growth is sub-Saharan Africa. Growth rates generally exceed 2 percent, with several countries having rates that clearly exceed 3 percent. This part of the world has been one of the latest to initiate fertility declines, but in the 1986–1998 period, Botswana, Kenya, and Zimbabwe all sustained fertility declines of at least two children per woman, and some neighboring societies were also engaged in fertility transition. At the same time, many sub-Saharan countries are pre-transitional or only in the very early stages of a transition. Of the twenty-five countries that showed fertility increases in the PRB data, thirteen of them were sub-Saharan nations with TFRs of at least 5.0.

In general, countries of the Middle East and regions of Northern Africa populated by Moslems have also been slow to embark on the process of fertility transition. Some (Caldwell 1976) found this surprising since a number had experienced substantial economic advances and invited the benefits of Western medical technology in terms of mortality reduction. Their resistance to fertility transitions had been attributed partly to an alleged Moslem emphasis on the subordinate role of women to men, leading them to have limited alternatives to a homemaker role. However, the PRB data for 1986–1998 indicate that some of these countries (Algeria, Bangladesh, Jordan, Kuwait, Morocco, Syria, Turkey) are among the small number that achieved reduction of at least two children per woman.

The importance of the mortality transition in influencing the fertility transition is suggested by Figure 2. Each dot is a country, positioned in terms of graphical relationship in the PRB data between life expectancy in 1986 and the TFR in 1998. The relationship is quite striking. No country with a life expectancy less than fifty has a TFR below 3.0. Remember that before the twentieth century, virtually all countries had life expectancies below fifty years. In addition, the figure shows a very strong tendency for countries with life expectancies above seventy to have TFRs below 2.0.

For a number of years, experts on population policy were divided on the potential role of contraceptive programs in facilitating fertility declines (Davis 1967). Since contraceptive technology has become increasingly cheap and effective, some (Enke 1967) argue that modest international expenditures on these programs in high-fertility countries could have significant rapid impacts on reproduction rates. Others (Davis 1967) point out, however, that family planning programs would only permit couples to achieve their desires, which may not be compatible with societal replacement

level fertility. The primary implication was that family planning programs would not be effective without social structures that encouraged the small family. A recent consensus on the value of family planning programs relative to social structural change seems to have emerged. Namely, family planning programs may be quite useful for achieving low fertility where the social structure is consistent with a small family ideal (Mauldin and Berelson 1978).

While the outlook for further fertility declines in the world is good, it is difficult to say whether and when replacement-level fertility will be achieved. Many, many major social changes have occurred in societies throughout the world in the past half-century. These changes have generally been unprecented in world history, and thus we have little historical experience from which to judge their impact on fertility, both levels and speed of change (Mason 1997).

Some caution should be excercised about future fertility declines in some of the societies that have been viewed as leaders in the developing world. For instance, in a number of Asian societies, a strong preference toward sons still exists, and couples are concerned as much about having an adequate number of sons survive to adulthood as they are about total sons and daughters. Since pre-birth gender control is still difficult, many couples have a number of girl babies before they are successful in bearing a son. If effective gender control is achieved, some of these societies will almost certainly attain replacement-level fertility.

In other parts of the world such as sub-Saharan Africa, the future of still-fragile fertility transitions may well depend on unknown changes in the organization of families. Caldwell (1976), in a widely respected theory of demographic transition that incorporates elements of both cultural innovation and recognition of the role of children in traditional societies in maintaining net flows of wealth to parents, has speculated that the traditional extended kinship family model now predominant in the region facilitates high fertility. Families often form economic units where children are important work resources. The extended structure of the household makes the cost of any additional member low relative to a nuclear family structure. Further declines in fertility will depend on the

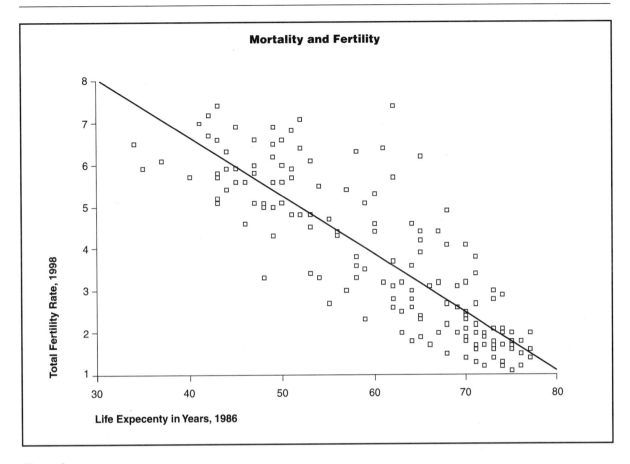

Figure 2

degree to which populations adopt the "Western" nuclear family, either through cultural diffusion or through autonomous changes in local social structure.

Taking the long view, the outlook for a completed state of demographic transition for the world population as a whole generally appears positive if not inevitable, although demographers are deeply divided on estimates of the size of world population at equilibrium, the timing of completed transition, the principal mechanisms at work, and the long-term ecological consequences. Certainly, the world population will continue to grow for some period of time, if only as a consequence of the previous momentum of high fertility relative to mortality. Most if not all demographers, however, subscribe to the view expressed by Coale (1974, p. 51) that the entire process of global demographic transition and the phase of phenomenal population growth that has accompanied

it will be a transitory (albeit spectacular) episode in human population history.

REFERENCES

Bongaarts, John 1975 "Why High Birth Rates are So Low." *Population and Development Review* 1:289–296.

Caldwell, John 1976 "Toward a Restatement of Demographic Transition Theory."*Population and Development Review* 2:321–366.

—— 1986 "Routes to Low Mortality in Poor Countries." *Population and Development Review* 12:171–220.

Cleland, John, and Christopher Wilson 1987 "Demand Theories of the Fertility Transition: An Iconoclastic View." *Population Studies* 41:5–30.

Coale, Ansley 1973 "The Demographic Transition." *International Population Conference, IUSSP.* Liege, Belgium.

—— 1974 "The History of Human Population." *Scientific American* 23:41–51.

—— 1983 "Recent Trends in Fertility in Less Developed Countries." *Science* 221:828–832.

——, and Roy Treadway 1986 "A Summary of the Changing Distribution of Overall Fertility, Marital Fertility, and the Proportion Married in the Provinces of Europe." In Ansley Coale and Susan Watkins, eds., *The Decline of Fertility in Europe*. Princeton: Princeton University Press.

Davis, Kingsley 1967 "Population Policy: Will Current Programs Succeed?" *Science* 158:730–739.

Enke, Stephen 1967 "The Economic Case for Birth Control." *Challenge/Magazine of Economic Affairs* 15:30–31.

Freedman, Ronald 1998 "Observing Taiwan's Demographic Transition: A Memoir." Research Report 98–426. Ann Arbor: Population Studies Center, University of Michigan.

Guest, Avery 1981 "Social Structure and U.S. Inter-State Fertility Differentials in 1900." *Demography* 18:453–486.

—— and Stewart Tolnay 1983 "Children's Roles and Fertility: Late Nineteenth Century United States," *Social Science History* 7:355–380.

Hirschman, Charles 1994 "Why Fertility Changes." *Annual Review of Sociology* 20:203–233.

Knodel, John 1977 "Family Limitation and the Fertility Transition: Evidence from the Age Patterns of Fertility in Europe and Asia." *Population Studies* 32:481–510.

——, and Etienne van de Walle 1979 "Lessons from the Past: Policy Implications of Historical Fertility Studies." *Population and Development Review* 5:217–245.

Lesthaeghe, Ron 1983 "A Century of Demographic Change in Western Europe: An Exploration of Underlying Dimensions." *Population and Development Review* 9:411–436.

Mason, Karen Oppenheim 1997 "Explaining Fertility Transitions." *Demography* 34:443–454.

Matthiessen, Paul C., and James C. McCann 1978 "The Role of Mortality in the European Fertility Transition: Aggregate-level Relations." In Samuel H. Preston, ed., *The Effects of Infant and Child Mortality on Fertility*. New York: Academic Press.

Mauldin, W. Parker, and Bernard Berelson 1978 "Conditions of Fertility Decline in Developing Countries." *Studies in Family Planning* 9:89–148.

McKeown, Thomas 1976 *The Modern Rise of Population*. New York: Academic Press.

Notestein, Frank 1953 "Economic Problems of Population Change." *Proceedings of the Eighth International Conference of Agricultural Economics*, 13–31. London: Oxford University Press.

Palloni, Alberto 1981 "Mortality in Latin America: Emerging Patterns." *Population and Development Review* 7:623–649.

Population Reference Bureau 1986 *World Population Data Sheet*. Washington, D.C.

—— 1998 *World Population Data Sheet*. Washington, D.C.

Preston, Samuel 1975 "The Changing Relationship Between Mortality and Level of Economic Development." *Population Studies* 29:231–248.

—— 1976 *Mortality Patterns in National Populations*. New York: Academic Press.

——, and Michael Haines 1991 *Fatal Years: Child Mortality in Late Nineteenth-Century America*. Princeton: Princeton University Press.

Razzell, P.E. 1974 "An Interpretation of the Modern Rise of Population in Europe - a Critique." *Population Studies* 28:5–17.

van de Walle, Francine 1980 "Education and the Demographic Transition in Switzerland." *Population and Development Review* 6:463–472.

Watkins, Susan 1991 *From Provinces into Nations: Demographic Integration in Western Europe, 1870–1960*. Princeton: Princeton University Press.

Avery M. Guest
Gunnar Almgren

DEMOGRAPHY

Demography is the study of human populations. It is an important part of sociology and the other social sciences because all persisting social aggregates—societies, states, communities, racial or ethnic groups, professions, formal organizations, kinship groups, and so on—are also populations. The size of the population, its growth or decline, the location and spatial movement of its people, and their changing characteristics are important features of an aggregate whether one sees it as a culture, an economy, a polity, or a society. As a result some anthropologists, economists, historians, political scientists, and sociologists are also demographers, and most demographers are members of one of the traditional social science disciplines.

A central question for each of the social sciences is: How does the community, society, or whatever, seen as a culture, an economy, a polity, or whatever, produce and renew itself over the years? Formal demography answers this question for aggregates seen as populations. This formal part of demography is fairly independent of the traditional social sciences and has a lengthy history in mathematics and statistics (Smith and Keyfitz 1977; Stone 1997; Desrosières 1998). It depends on a definition of age and on the relationship of age to fertility and mortality. Those relationships certainly are socially conditioned, but their major outlines are constrained by biology.

Beyond pursuing formal demography, the task of most social scientist-demographers is detailing the relationships between demographic change and other aspects of social change. Working with concepts, methods, and questions arising from the traditions of each of the social science disciplines as well as those of demography per se, scholars have investigated the relationship between demographic changes and such social changes as those in the nature of families (Davis 1985; Sweet and Bumpass 1987; Bumpass 1990; Waite 1995), levels of economic growth (Johnson and Lee 1987; Nerlove and Raut 1997), the development of colonialism (McNeill 1990), changes in kinship structures (Dyke and Morrill 1980), nationalism and interethnic strife (Tietelbaum and Winter 1998), and the development of the nation-state (Watkins 1991).

FORMAL DEMOGRAPHY

At the heart of demography is a body of strong and useful mathematical theory about how populations renew themselves (Keyfitz 1968, 1985; Coale 1972; Bourgeois-Pichat 1994). The theory envisions a succession of female birth cohorts living out their lives subject to a schedule of age-specific mortality chances and age-specific chances of having a female baby. In the simplest form of the model the age-specific rates are presumed constant from year to year.

Each new annual birth cohort is created because the age-specific fertility rates affect women in earlier birth cohorts who have come to a specific age in the year in question. Thus, the mothers of a new cohort of babies are spread among previous cohorts. The size of the new cohort is a weighted average of the age-specific fertility rates. The sizes of preceding cohorts, survived to the year in question, are the weights.

As a cohort of women age through their fertile period, they die and have children in successive years according to the age-specific rates appropriate to those years. Thus, the children of a single birth cohort of women are spread over a sequence of succeeding birth cohorts.

The number of girls ever born to a birth cohort, taken as a ratio to the initial size of the cohort, is implicit in the age-specific fertility and mortality rates. This ratio, called the net reproduction rate, describes the growth rate over a generation that is implicit in the age-specific rates. The length of this generation is also implicit in the age-specific rates as the average age of mothers at the birth of the second-generation daughters. With a rate of increase over a generation and a length of the generation, it is clear that an annual rate of increase is intrinsic to the age-specific rates.

The distribution of the children of a birth cohort over a series of succeeding cohorts has an important effect. If an unusually small or large birth cohort is created, the effects of its largeness or smallness will be distributed among a number of succeeding cohorts. In each of those succeeding cohorts, the effect of the unusual cohort is averaged with that of other birth cohorts to create the new cohort's size. Those new cohorts' "inherited" smallness or largeness, now diminished by averaging, will also be spread over succeeding cohorts. In a few generations the smallness or largeness will have averaged out and no reflection of the initial disturbance will be apparent.

Thus, without regard to peculiarities in the initial age distribution, the eventual age distribution of a population experiencing fixed age-specific fertility and mortality will become proportionately constant. As this happens, the population will take on a fixed aggregate birth and death rate and, consequently, a fixed rate of increase. The population so created is called a stable population and its rates, called intrinsic rates, are those implicit in the net reproduction rate and the length of a generation. Such rates, as well as the net reproduction rates, are frequently calculated for the age-specific fertility and mortality rates occurring for a single year as a kind of descriptive, "what if" summary.

This theory is elaborated in a number of ways. In one variant, age-specific rates are not constant but change in a fixed way (Lopez 1961). In another elaboration the population is divided into a number of states with fixed age-specific migration or mobility among the states (Land and Rogers 1982; Schoen 1988). States may be geographic regions, marital circumstances, educational levels, or whatever.

In part, the value of this theory is in the light it sheds on how populations work. For example, it explains how a population can outlive all of its contemporary members and yet retain its median age, percent in each race, and its regional distribution.

The fruit of the theory lies in its utility for estimation and forecasting. Using aspects of the theory, demographers are able to elaborate rather modest bits and pieces of information about a population to a fairly full description of its trajectory (Coale and Demeny 1983). Combined with this mathematical theory is a body of practical forecasting techniques, statistical estimation procedures, and data-collection wisdom that makes up a core area in demography that is sometimes called formal demography (United Nations 1983; Shryock and Siegel 1976; Pollard, Yusuf, and Pollard 1990; Namboodiri 1991; Hinde 1998).

DEMOGRAPHIC DATA

Generating the various rates and probabilities used in formal demography requires two different kinds of data. On the one hand are data that count the number of events occurring in the population in a given period of time. How many births, deaths, marriages, divorces, and so on have occurred in the past year? These kinds of data are usually collected through a vital registration system (National Research Council 1981; United Nations 1985, 1991). On the other hand are data that count the number of persons in a given circumstance at a given time. How many never-married women age twenty to twenty-four were there on July 1? These kinds of data are usually collected through a population census or large-scale demographic survey (United Nations 1992; Anderson 1988; Anderson and Fienberg 1999). From a vital registration system one gets, for example, the number of births to black women age twenty. From a census one collects the number of black women at age twenty. The division of the number of events by the population exposed to the risk of having the event occur to them yields the demographic rate, that is, the fertility rate for black women age twenty. These

two data collection systems—vital statistics and census—are remarkably different in their character. To be effective, a vital statistics system must be ever alert to see that an event is recorded promptly and accurately. A census is more of an emergency. Most countries conduct a census every ten years, trying to enumerate all of the population in a brief time.

If a vital registration system had existed for a long time, were very accurate, and there were no uncounted migrations, one could use past births and deaths to tally up the current population by age. To the degree that such a tallying up does not match a census, one or more of the data collections systems is faulty.

SOCIAL DEMOGRAPHY

One of the standard definitions of demography is that given by Hauser and Duncan: "Demography is the study of the size, territorial distribution and composition of populations, changes therein, and the components of such change, which may be identified as natality, mortality, territorial movement (migration) and social mobility (change of status)" (1959, p. 2). Each of these parts—size, territorial distribution, and composition—is a major arena in which the relationships between demographic change and social change are investigated by social scientist-demographers. Each part has a somewhat separate literature, tradition, method, and body of substantive theory.

Population Size. The issue of population size and change in size is dominated by the shadow of Malthus (Malthus 1959), who held that while food production can grow only arithmetically because of diminishing returns to investment in land and other resources, population can grow geometrically and will do so, given the chance. Writing in a time of limited information about birth control and considerable disapproval of its use, and holding little hope that many people would abstain from sexual relations, Malthus believed that populations would naturally grow to the point at which starvation and other deprivations would curtail future expansion. At that point, the average level of living would be barely above the starvation level. Transitory improvements in the supply of food would only lead to increased births and subsequent deaths as the population returned to its equilibrium size. Any permanent improvement in food supplies due to technological advances would, in Malthus's theory, simply lead to a larger population surviving at the previous level of misery.

Although there is good evidence that Malthus understood his contemporary world quite well (Lee 1980; Wrigley 1983), he missed the beginnings of the birth control movement, which were contemporaneous (McLaren 1978). The ability to limit births, albeit at some cost, without limiting sexual activity requires important modifications to the Malthusian model.

Questions of the relationship among population growth, economic growth, and resources persist into the contemporary period. The bulk of the literature is in economics. A good summary of that literature can be found in T. P. Schultz (1981), in Rosensweig and Stark (1997), and in a National Research Council report on population policy (1985). A more polemical treatment, but one that may be more accessible to the noneconomist, is offered by the World Bank (1985).

Sharing the study of population size and its change with Malthusian issues is a body of substantive and empirical work on the *demographic revolution* or *transition* (Notestein 1945). The model for this transition is the course of fertility and mortality in Europe during the Industrial Revolution. The transition is thought to occur concurrently with "modernization" in many countries (Coale and Watkins 1986) and to be still in process in many less developed parts of the world (United Nations 1990). This transition is a change from (1) a condition of high and stable birthrates combined with high and fluctuating death rates, through (2) a period of initially lowering death rates and subsequently lowering birthrates, to (3) a period of low and fairly constant death rates combined with low and fluctuating birthrates. In the course of part (2) of this transition, the population grows very considerably because the rate of increase, absent migration, is the difference between the birthrate and the death rate.

In large measure because of anxiety that fertility might not fall rapidly enough in developing countries, a good deal of research has focused on the fertility part of the transition. One branch of this research has been a detailed historical investigation of what actually happened in Europe, since that is the base for the analogy about what is

thought likely to happen elsewhere (Coale and Watkins 1986). A second branch was the World Fertility Survey, perhaps the largest international social science research project ever undertaken. This project conducted carefully designed, comparable surveys with 341,300 women in seventy-one countries to investigate the circumstances of contemporary fertility decline (Cleland and Hobcraft 1985). In 1983, a continuation of this project was undertaken under the name Demographic and Health Surveys. To date, this project has provided technical assistance for more than 100 surveys in Africa, Asia, the Near East, Latin America, and the Caribbean. For more complete information about current activities see their web site at http://www.macroint.com/dhs/.

Scholars analyzing these projects come to a fairly similar assessment of the roots of historical and contemporary fertility decline as centering in an increased secular rationality and growing norms of individual responsibility.

Detailed investigation of the mortality side of the European demographic transition has primarily been conducted by historians. A particularly useful collection of papers is available in Schofield, Reher, and Bideau (1991). For the United States, a particularly useful book on child and infant mortality at the turn of the twentieth century is by Haines and Preston (1991).

The utility of the idea of a demographic transition to understand population change in the developing world has, of course, been a matter of considerable debate. A good summary of this literature is found in Jones et al. (1997).

Territorial Distribution. Research on the territorial distribution of populations is conducted in sociology, geography, and economics. The history of population distribution appears to be one of population dispersion at the macroscopic level of continents, nations, or regions, and one of population concentration at the more microscopic level of larger towns and cities.

The diffusion of the human population over the globe, begun perhaps as the ice shields retreated in the late Pleistocene, continues to the present (Barraclough 1978; Bairoch 1988). More newly inhabited continents fill up and less habitable land becomes occupied as technological and social change makes it possible to live in previously remote areas. Transportation lines, whether caravan, rail, or superhighway, extend across remote areas to connect distant population centers. Stops along the way become villages and towns specializing in servicing the travelers and the goods in transit. These places are no longer "remote." Exploitation of resources proximate to these places may now become viable because of the access to transportation as well as services newly available in the stopover towns.

As the increasing efficiency of agriculture has released larger and larger fractions of the population from the need to till the soil, it has become possible to sustain increasing numbers of urban people. There is a kind of urban transition more or less concomitant with the demographic transition during which a population's distribution by city size shifts to larger and larger sizes (Kelley and Williamson 1984; Wrigley 1987). Of course, the continuing urban transition presents continuing problems for the developing world (United Nations 1998).

Population Composition. The characteristics included as compositional ones in demographic work are not predefined theoretically, with the exception, perhaps, of age and sex. In general, compositional characteristics are those characteristics inquired about on censuses, demographic surveys, and vital registration forms. Such items vary over time as social, economic, and political concerns change. Nonetheless, it is possible to classify most compositional items into one of three classes. First are those items that are close to the reproductive core of a society. They include age, sex, family relationships, and household living arrangements. The second group of items are those characteristics that identify the major, usually fairly endogamous, social groups in the population. They include race, ethnicity, religion, and language. Finally there is a set of socioeconomic characteristics such as education, occupation, industry, earnings, and labor force participation.

Within the first category of characteristics, contemporary research interest has focused on families and households because the period since 1970 has seen such dramatic changes in developed countries (Van de Kaa 1987; Davis 1985; Farley 1996, ch. 2). Divorce, previously uncommon, has become a common event. Many couples now live together without record of a civil or religious ceremony having occurred. Generally these unions are not initially for the purposes of procreation, although children are sometimes born into them. Sometimes they appear to be trial marriages and are succeeded by legal marriages. A small but increasing fraction of women in the more developed countries seem to feel that a husband is not a necessary ornament to motherhood. Because of these changes, older models of how marriage comes about and how marriage relates to fertility (Coale and McNeil 1972; Coale and Trussell 1974) are in need of review as demographers work toward a new demography of the family (Bongaarts 1983; Keyfitz 1987).

Those characteristics that indicate membership in one or another of the major social groupings within a population vary from place to place. Since such social groupings are the basis of inequality, political division, or cultural separation, their demography becomes of interest to social scientists and to policy makers (Harrison and Bennett 1995). To the degree that endogamy holds, it is often useful to analyze a social group as a separate population, as is done for the black population in the United States (Farley 1970). Fertility and mortality rates, as well as marital and family arrangements, for blacks in the United States are different from those of the majority population. The relationship between these facts, their implications, and the socioeconomic discrimination and residential segregation experienced by this population is a matter of historic and continuing scholarly work (Farley and Allen 1987; Lieberson 1980; Farley 1996, ch. 6).

For other groups, such as religious or ethnic groups in the United States, the issue of endogamy becomes central in determining the continuing importance of the characteristic for the social life of the larger population (Johnson 1980; Kalmijn 1991). Unlike the black population, ethnic and religious groups seem to be of decreasing appropriateness to analyze as separate populations within the United States, since membership may be a matter of changeable opinion.

The socioeconomic characteristics of a population are analyzed widely by sociologists, economists, and policy-oriented researchers. Other than being involved in the data production for much of this research, the uniquely demographic contributions come in two ways. First is the consideration of the relationship between demographic change and change in these characteristics. The relationship between female labor force participation and changing fertility patterns has been a main topic of the "new home economics" within economic demography (Becker 1960; T. W. Schultz 1974; T. P. Schultz 1981; Bergstrom 1997). The relationship between cohort size and earnings is a topic treated by both economists and sociologists (Winsborough 1975; Welch 1979). A system of relationships between cohort size, economic well-being, and fertility has been proposed by Easterlin (1980) in an effort to explain both fertility cycles and long swings in the business cycle.

A second uniquely demographic contribution to the study of socioeconomic characteristics appears to be the notion of a cohort moving through its socioeconomic life course (Duncan and Hodge 1963; Hauser and Featherman 1977; Mare 1980). The process of leaving school, getting a first job, then subsequent jobs, each of which yields income, was initially modeled as a sequence of recursive equations and subsequently in more detailed ways. Early in the history of this project it was pointed out that the process could be modeled as a multistate population (Matras 1967), but early data collected in the project did not lend itself to such modeling and the idea was not pursued.

POPULATION POLICY

The consideration and analysis of various population policies is often seen as a part of demography. Population policy has two important parts. First is policy related to the population of one's own nation. The United Nations routinely conducts inquiries about the population policies of member nations (United Nations 1995). Most responding governments claim to have official positions about a number of demographic issues, and many have policies to deal with them. It is interesting to note that the odds a developed country that states its fertility is too low has a policy to raise the rate is about seven to one, while the odds that a less developed country that states that its fertility is too high has a policy to lower the rate is about 4.6 to one. The prospect of declining population in the United States has already begun to generate policy proposals (Teitelbaum and Winter 1985).

The second part of population policy is the policy a nation has about the population of other countries. For example, should a country insist on family-planning efforts in a developing country prior to providing economic aid? A selection of opinions and some recommendations for policy in the United States are provided in Menken (1986) and in the National Research Council (1985).

IMPORTANT CURRENT RESEARCH AREAS

Three areas of demographic research are of especially current interest. Each is, in a sense, a sequela of the demographic transition. They are:

1. Institutional arrangements for the production of children,

2. Immigration, emigration, ethnicity, and nationalism,

3. Population aging, morbidity, and mortality.

Institutional arrangements for the production of children. The posttransition developed world has seen dramatic changes in the institutional arrangements for the production of children. Tracking these changes has become a major preoccupation of contemporary demography. Modern contraception has broken the biological link between sexual intercourse and pregnancy. Decisions about sexual relations can be made with less concern about pregnancy. The decision to have a child is less colored by the need for sexual gratification. People no longer must choose between the celibate single life or the succession of pregnancies and children of a married one. Women are employed before, during, and after marriage. Their earning power makes marriage more an option and a context for child raising than an alternative employment. Women marry later, are older when they have children, and are having fewer children than in the past. Divorce has moved from an uncommon event to a common one. Cohabitation is a new, and somewhat inchoate, lifestyle that influences the circumstances for childbearing and child rearing. Although only a modest number of children are currently born to cohabiting couples, most children will spend some time living with a parent in such a relationship before they are adults (Bumpass and Lu 1999). Changes such as these have occurred in most of Europe and North America and appear to be increasing in those parts of Asia where the demographic transitions occurred first. The changes have, of course, been met with considerable resistance in many places. Will they continue to occur in other countries as the demographic transitions proceed around the world? How serious will the resistance be in countries more patriarchal than those of Europe? These issues await future demographic research.

Immigration, emigration, ethnicity, and nationalism. The difference between immigration and emigration is, of course, net migration as a component of population growth. In general, the direct impact of net migration on growth has been modest. Certainly emigration provided some outlet for population growth in Europe during the transition (Curtin 1989) and played a role in the population of the Americas, Australia, and New Zealand. Most of the effect of immigration to the New World was indirect, however. It was the children of immigrants who peopled the continents rather than the immigrants themselves. Contemporary interest in international migration has three sources. First is an abiding concern for refugees and displaced persons. Second is interest in a highly mobile international labor force in the construction industry. Third, and perhaps most important, is the migration of workers from less developed countries to developed ones in order to satisfy the demand for labor in a population in real or incipient decline (Teitelbaum and Winter 1998). In France, Germany, and England immigrants who come and stay change the ethnic mix of the population. In the United States, legal and illegal immigration from Mexico has received considerable attention (Chiswick and Sullivan 1995). The immigration of skilled Asians raises issues of another kind. In all of these countries, the permanent settlement of new immigrants arouses powerful nationalistic concerns. The situation provides ample opportunity for the investigation of the development of ethnicity and the place of endogamy in its maintenance. As with changes for child rearing, these changes seem consequences of the demographic transition. Below-replacement fertility seems to generate the need for imported workers and their consequent inclusion in the society. If this speculation is true, how will countries more recently passing through the transition react to this opportunity and challenge? This is another arena for future demographic investigation.

Population aging, morbidity, and mortality. Accompanying the reduction of fertility and of population growth is the aging of the population (Treas and Torrecilha 1995). Much of the developed world is experiencing this aging and its concomitants. Countries that made a rapid demographic transition have especially dramatic imbalances in their age distribution. Concerns about retirement, health, and other programs for the elderly generate interest in demographic research in these areas. Will increasing life expectancy add years to the working life so that retirement can begin later? Or will the added years all be spent in nursing homes? These questions are currently of great policy interest and pose interesting and difficult problems for demographic research (Manton and Singer 1994). Traditional demographic modeling has assumed that frailty, the likelihood of death, varies according to measurable traits such as age, sex, race, education, wealth, and so on, but are constant within joint values of these variables. But what happens if frailty is a random variable? In survival models, randomness in frailty is not helpful, or at least benign, as it is in so many other statistical circumstances. Rather, it can have quite dramatic effects (Vaupel and Yashin 1985). How one models frailty appears to make a considerable amount of difference in the answers one gets to important policy questions surrounding population aging.

DEMOGRAPHY AS A PROFESSION

Most demographers in the United States are trained in sociology. Many others have their highest degree in economics, history, or public health. A few are anthropologists, statisticians, or political scientists. Graduate training of demographers in the United States and in much of the rest of the world now occurs primarily in centers. Demography centers are often quasi-departmental organizations that serve the research and training needs of scholars in several departments. In the United States there are about twenty such centers, twelve of which have National Institutes of Health grants. The Ford Foundation has supported similar demography centers at universities in the less developed parts of the world.

Today, then, most new demographers, without regard for their disciplinary leanings, are trained at a relatively few universities. Most will work as faculty or researchers within universities or at demography centers. Another main source of employment for demographers is government agencies. Census bureaus and vital statistics agencies both provide much of the raw material for demographic work and employ many demographers around the world. There is a small but rapidly growing demand for demographers in the private sector in marketing and strategic planning.

Support for research and training in demography began in the United States in the 1920s with the interest of the Rockefeller Foundation in issues related to population problems. Its support led to the first demography center, the Office of Population Research at Princeton University. The Population Council in New York was established as a separate foundation by the Rockefeller brothers in the 1930s. Substantial additional foundation support for the field has come from the Ford Foundation, the Scripps Foundation, and, more recently, the Hewlett Foundation. Demography was the first of the social sciences to be supported by the newly founded National Science Foundation in the immediate post-World War II era. In the mid-1960s the National Institute of Child Health and Human Development undertook support of demographic research.

(SEE ALSO: *Birth and Death Rates*; *Census*; *Demographic Methods*; *Demographic Transition*; *Life Expectancy*; *Population*)

REFERENCES

Anderson, Margo 1988 *The American Census: A Social History*. New Haven: Yale University Press.

——, and Stephen Fienberg 1999 *Who Counts: The Politics of Census-Taking in Contemporary America*. New York: Russell Sage Foundation.

Barraclough, Geoffrey (ed.) 1978 *The Times Atlas of World History*. London: Times Books.

Becker, G. S. 1960 "An Economic Analysis of Fertility." In Becker, ed., *Demographic and Economic Change in Developed Countries*. Princeton, N.J.: National Bureau of Economic Research.

Bergstrom, Theodore 1997 "A Survey of Theories of the Family." In Mark Rosenzweig and Oded Stark, eds., *Handbook of Family and Population Economics*. Amsterdam: North-Holland.

Bongaarts, John 1983 "The Formal Demography of Families and Households: An Overview." *IUSSP Newsletter* 17:27–42.

Bourgeois-Pichat, Jean 1994 *La Dynamique Des Populations: Populations Stables, Semi-stable, Quasi-stables*. Paris: Presses Universitaires de France.

Bumpass, Larry L. 1990 "What's Happening to the Family? Interactions Between Demographic and Institutional Change." *Demography* 27:483–498.

——, and H-H Lu 1999 "Trends in Cohabitation and Implications for Children's Family Contexts in the U.S." Forthcoming in *Population Studies*.

Chiswick, Barry, and Teresa Sullivan 1995 "The New Immigrants." In Reynolds Farley, ed., *State of the Union: America in the 1990s, V2, Social Trends*. New York: Russell Sage Foundation.

Cleland, John, and John Hobcraft 1985 *Reproductive Change in Developing Countries: Insights from the World Fertility Survey*. London: Oxford University Press.

Coale, Ansley 1972 *The Growth and Structure of Human Populations: A Mathematical Investigation*. Princeton, N.J.: Princeton University Press.

——, and Paul Demeny 1983 *Regional Model Life Tables and Stable Populations*. New York: Academic Press.

Coale, Ansley, and D. R. McNeil 1972 "Distribution by Age of Frequency of First Marriage in a Female Cohort." *Journal of the American Statistical Association* 67:743–749.

——, and James Trussell 1974 "Model Fertility Schedules: Measurement and Use in Fertility Models." *Population Index* 40:182–258.

Coale, Ansley, and Susan C. Watkins (eds.) 1986 *The Decline of Fertility in Europe*. Princeton, N.J.: Princeton University Press.

Curtin, Philip 1989 *Death by Migration: Europe's Encounter with the Tropical World in the Nineteenth Century*. Cambridge, Mass.: Cambridge University Press.

Davis, Kingsley (ed.) 1985 *Contemporary Marriage*. New York: Russell Sage Foundation.

Desrosières, Alain 1998 *The Politics of Large Numbers: A History of Statistical Reasoning*. Translated by Camille Naish. Cambridge, Mass.: Harvard University Press.

Duncan, O. D., and William Hodge 1963 "Education and Occupational Mobility." *American Journal of Sociology* 68:629–644.

Dyke, Bennett, and Warren Morrill (eds.) 1980 *Genealogical Demography*. New York: Academic Press.

Easterlin, Richard 1980 *Birth and Fortune: The Impact of Numbers on Personal Welfare*. New York: Basic Books.

Farley, Reynolds 1970 *Growth of the Black Population: A Study of Demographic Trends*. Chicago: Markham.

—— (ed.) 1995 *State of the Union: America in the 1990's.* Vol. 1, *Economic Trends.* Vol. 2, *Social Trends.* New York: Russell Sage Foundation.

—— 1996 *The New American Reality: Who We Are, How We Got There, Where We Are Going.* New York: Russell Sage Foundation.

——, and Walter R. Allen 1987 *The Color Line and the Quality of Life in America.* New York: Russell Sage Foundation.

Haines, M., and S. Preston 1991 *The Fatal Years: Child Mortality in Late Nineteenth-Century America.* Princeton, N.J.: Princeton University Press.

Harrison, Roderick, and Claudette Bennett 1995 "Racial and Ethnic Diversity." In Farley, ed., *State of the Union: America in the 1990s, V2, Social Trends* New York: Russell Sage Foundation.

Hauser, Philip M., and Otis Dudley Duncan 1959 *The Study of Population: An Inventory and Appraisal.* Chicago: University of Chicago Press.

Hauser, Robert M., and David L. Featherman 1977 *The Process of Stratification: Trends and Analyses.* New York: Academic Press.

Hinde, Andrew 1998 *Demographic Methods.* London: Arnold.

Johnson, D. Gale, and Ronald D. Lee (eds.) 1987 *Population Growth and Economic Development: Issues and Evidence.* Madison: University of Wisconsin Press.

Johnson, Robert A. 1980 *Religious Assortative Marriage in the United States.* New York: Academic Press.

Jones, Gavin et al. (eds.) 1997 *The Continuing Demographic Transition.* Oxford: Clarendon Press.

Kalmijn, Matthijs 1991 "Shifting Boundaries: Trends in Religious and Educational Homogamy." *American Sociological Review* 56:786–800.

Kelley, Allen, and Jeffrey Williamson 1984 "Modeling the Urban Transition." *Population and Development Review* 10:419–442.

Keyfitz, Nathan 1968 *Introduction to the Mathematics of Populations.* Reading, Mass.: Addison-Wesley.

—— 1985 *Applied Mathematical Demography.* New York: Springer-Verlag.

—— 1987 "Form and Substance in Family Demography." In J. Bongaarts, T. Burch, and K. Wachter, eds., *Family Demography.* New York: Oxford University Press.

Land, Kenneth C., and Andrei Rogers (eds.) 1982 *Multidimensional Mathematical Demography.* New York: Academic Press.

Lee, Ronald 1980 "An Historical Perspective on Economic Aspects of the Population Explosion: The Case of Preindustrial England." In Richard Easterlin, ed., *Population and Economic Change in Developing Countries.* Chicago: University of Chicago Press.

Lieberson, Stanley 1980 *A Piece of the Pie: Black and White Immigrants Since 1880.* Berkeley: University of California Press.

Lopez, A. 1961 *Some Problems in Stable Population Theory.* Princeton, N.J.: Office of Population Research.

Malthus, Thomas R. 1959 *Population: The First Essay.* Ann Arbor: University of Michigan Press.

Mare, Robert D. 1985 "Social Background and School Continuation Decisions." *Journal of the American Statistical Association* 75:295–305.

Matras, Judah 1967 "Social Mobility and Social Structure: Some Insights from the Linear Model." *American Sociological Review* 33:608–614.

McLaren, Angus 1978 *Birth Control in Nineteenth-Century England.* New York: Holmes & Meier.

McNeill, William H. 1990 *Population and Politics Since 1750.* Charlottesville: University of Virginia Press.

Menken, Jane (ed.) 1986 *World Population and U.S. Policy: The Choices Ahead.* New York: W. W. Norton.

Namboodiri, Krishnan 1991 *Demographic Analysis: A Stochastic Approach.* San Diego: Academic Press.

National Research Council 1981 *Collecting Data for Estimation of Fertility and Mortality.* Report no. 6, Committee on Population and Demography, Assembly of Behavioral and Social Sciences, National Research Council. Washington, D.C.: National Academy Press.

—— Working Group on Population Growth and Economic Development, Committee on Population, Commission on Behavioral and Social Sciences and Education 1985 *Population Growth and Economic Development: Policy Questions.* Washington, D.C.: National Academy Press.

Nerlove, Marc, and Lakshmi Raut 1997 "Growth Models with Endogenous Population: A General Framework." In Mark Rosenzweig and Oded Stark, eds., *Handbook of Family and Population Economics* Amsterdam: North-Holland.

Notestein, Frank W. 1945 "Population—The Long View." In Theodore W. Schultz, ed., *Food for the World.* Chicago: University of Chicago Press.

Pollard, A. H., Farhat Yusuf, and G. N. Pollard 1990 *Demographic Techniques.* Sydney: Pergamon Press.

Rosenzweig, Mark, and Oded Stark (eds.) 1997 *Handbook of Population and Family Economics.* Amsterdam: Elsevier.

Schoen, Robert 1988 *Modeling Multigroup Populations.* New York: Plenum Press.

Schofield, R., D. Reher, and A. Bideau (eds.) *The Decline of Mortality in Europe*. Oxford: Clarendon Press.

Schultz, T. Paul 1981 *Economics of Population*. Reading, Mass.: Addison-Wesley.

Schultz, T. W. (ed.) 1974 *Economics of the Family*. Chicago: University of Chicago Press.

Shryock, Henry S., and Jacob S. Siegel 1976 *The Methods and Materials of Demography*. New York: Academic Press.

Singer, B., and K. Manton 1994 "What's the Fuss About the Compression Morbidity?" *Chance*. Fall 1994.

Smith, David P., and Nathan Keyfitz (eds.) 1977 *Mathematical Demography: Selected Essays*. Berlin and New York: Springer-Verlag.

Stone, Richard 1997 *Some British Empiricists in the Social Sciences: 1650–1900*. Cambridge, Mass.: Cambridge University Press.

Sweet, James A., and Larry L. Bumpass 1987 *American Families and Households*. New York: Russell Sage Foundation.

Teitelbaum M., and J. Winter 1985 *The Fear of Population Decline*. Orlando, Fla.: Academic Press.

—— 1998 *A Question of Numbers: High Migration, Low Fertility, and the Politics of National Identity*. New York: Wang and Hill.

Treas, Judith, and Ramon Torrecilha 1995 "The Older Population." In Reynolds Farley, ed., *State of the Union: The 1990 Census Research Project*. New York: Russell Sage Foundation.

United Nations, Department of International Economic and Social Affairs 1983 *Manual X: Indirect Techniques for Demographic Estimation*. Population Studies, no. 81, ST/ESA/SER.A/81.

—— 1985 *Handbook of Vital Statistics Systems and Methods, Volume II: Review of National Practices*. ST/STAT/SER.F/35 V2.

—— 1991 *Handbook of Vital Statistics Systems and Methods, Volume I: Legal, Organizational and Technical Aspects*. ST/STAT/SER.F/35V.1.

—— 1992 *Handbook of Population and Housing Censuses*. ST/STAT/SER.F/54 V.1,2.

—— 1995 *Results of the Seventh United Nations Population Inquiry Among Governments*. ST/ESA/SER.R/140.

—— 1998 *World Urbanization Prospects: The 1996 Revision*. ST/ESA/SER.A/170.

Van de Kaa, Dirk 1987 "Europe's Second Demographic Transition." *Population Bulletin* 42:1.

Vaupel, James W., and Anatoli I.Yashin. 1985 "Heterogeneity's Ruses: Some Surprising Effects of Selection on Population Dynamics." *American Statistician* 39:176–185.

Waite, Linda 1995 "Does Marriage Matter?" *Demography* 32:483–507.

Watkins, Susan C. 1991 *From Provinces into Nations: Demographic Integration in Western Europe, 1870–1960*. Princeton, N.J.: Princeton University Press.

Welch, F. 1979 "Effect of Cohort Size on Earnings: The Baby Boom Babies' Financial Bust." *Journal of Political Economy* 2:565–598.

Winsborough, H. 1975 "Age, Period, Cohort, and Education Effects of Earnings by Race—An Experiment with a Sequence of Cross-Sectional Surveys." In Kenneth Land and Seymour Spilerman, eds., *Social Indicator Models*. New York: Russell Sage Foundation.

World Bank 1985 *Population Change and Economic Development*. New York: Oxford University Press.

Wrigley, E. A. 1987 *People, Cities and Wealth: The Transformation of Traditional Society*. Oxford: Basil Blackwell.

HALLIMAN H. WINSBOROUGH

DEPENDENCY THEORY

Conceived in the 1960s by analysts native to developing countries, dependency theory is an alternative to Eurocentric accounts of modernization as universalistic, unilinear evolution (Addo 1996). Instead, contemporary underdevelopment is seen as an outgrowth of asymmetrical contacts with capitalism. The thesis is straightforward: Following the first wave of modernization, less-developed countries are transformed by their interconnectedness with other nations, and the nature of their contacts, economies, and ideologies (Keith 1997). Interaction between social orders is never merely a benign manifestation of economic or cultural diffusion. Rather, both the direction and pace of change leads to internal restructuring designed to bolster the interests of the more powerful exchange partner without altering the worldwide distribution of affluence.

Widely utilized as both a heuristic and empirical template, dependency theory emerged from neo-Marxist critiques of the failure of significant capital infusion, through the United Nations Economic Commission for Latin America, to improve overall quality of life or provide significant returns to countries in the region. Dependency theory quickly became an instrument for political commentary as well as an explanatory framework as it couched its arguments in terms of the consequences of substituting cash crops for subsistence farming and replacing local consumer goods with export commodities destined for developed markets. Frank (1967, 1969), an early proponent, established the premise for dependency theory; contemporary underdevelopment is a result of an international division of labor exploited by capitalist interests.

Frank's innovation was to incorporate the vantagepoint of underdeveloped countries experiencing capital infusion into the discussion of the dynamics of economic, social, and political change. In so doing he discounted Western and European models of modernization as self-serving, ethnocentric, and apolitical. He asserted that explanations of modernization have been disassociated from the colonialism that fueled industrial and economic developments characteristic of the modern era. However, much of the first wave of modernization might have been driven by intrinsic, internal factors; more recent development has taken place in light of change external to individual countries. Central to Frank's contention was a differentiation of undeveloped from underdeveloped countries. In the latter, a state of dependency exists as an outgrowth of a locality's colonial relationship with "advanced" areas. Frank referred to the "development of underdevelopment" and the domination of development efforts by advanced countries, using a "metropolis–satellite" analogy to denote the powerful center out of which innovations emerge and a dependent hinterland is held in its sway. He spoke of a chain of exploitation—or the flow and appropriation of capital through successive metropolis–satellite relationships, each participating in a perpetuation of relative inequalities even while experiencing some enrichment. Galtung (1972) characterized this same relationship in terms of "core and periphery," each with something to offer the other, thereby fostering a symbiotic but lopsided relationship. The effect is a sharp intersocietal precedence wherein the dominant core grows and becomes more complex, while the satellite is subordinated through the transfer of economic surpluses to the core in spite of any absolute economic changes that may occur (Hechter 1975).

Dos Santos (1971) extended Frank's attention to metropolis–satellite relationships. He maintained that whatever economic or social change that does take place occurs primarily for the benefit of the dominant core. This is not to say that the outlying areas are merely plundered or picked clean; to ensure their long-run usefulness, peripheral regions are allowed, indeed encouraged, to develop. Urbanization, industrialization, commercialization of agriculture, and more expedient social, legal, and political structures are induced. In this way the core not only guarantees a stable supply of raw materials, but a market for finished goods. With the bulk of economic surplus exported to the core, the less-developed region is powerless to disseminate change or innovation across multiple realms. Dos Santos distinguished colonial, financial-industrial, and technological-industrial forms of dependencies. Under colonialism there is outright control and expropriation of valued resources by absentee decision makers. The financial-industrial dimension is marked by a locally productive economic sector characterized by widespread specialization and focus ministering primarily to the export sector that coexists alongside an essential subsistence sector. The latter furnishes labor and resources but accrues little from economic gains made in the export sector. In effect, two separate economies exist side by side.

In the third form of dependency, technological-industrial change takes place in developing regions but is customarily channeled and mandated by external interests. As the core extends its catchment area, it maximizes its ascendancy by promoting a dispersed, regionalized division of labor to maximize its returns. International market considerations affect the types of activities local export sectors are permitted to engage in by restricting the infusion of capital for specified purposes only. So, for example, the World Bank makes loans for certain forms of productive activity while eschewing others, and, as a result, highly segmented labor markets occur as internal inequities proliferate. The international division of labor is reflected in local implementation of capital-intensive technology, improvements in the infrastructure—transportation, public facilities, communications—and, ultimately, even social programming occurring principally in central enclaves or along supply corridors that service export trade (Hoogvelt 1977; Jaffee 1985; So 1990). Dos Santos maintained that the balance of payments is manipulated, ex parte, not only to bring about desired forms of change, but to ensure the outflow of capital accumulation to such a degree that decapitalization of the periphery is inescapable. Or, at the very least, that capitalist-based economic development leaves local economies entirely dependent on the vagaries of markets well beyond their control. International interests establish the price of local export products and also set purchase prices of those technological-industrial products essential to maintaining the infrastructure of development. There may be a partial diffusion of technology, since growth in the periphery also enhances profits for the core, but it also creates unequal pockets of surplus labor in secondary labor markets, thereby impeding growth of internal markets as well as deteriorating the quality of life for the general populace (Portes 1976; Jaffee 1985).

Because international capital is able to stipulate the terms of the exchange, external forces shape local political processes if only through disincentives for capitalization of activities not contributing to export trade (Cardoso and Faletto 1979). As Amin (1976) pointed out, nearly all development efforts are geared to enhancing productivity and value in the export sector, even as relative disadvantages accrue in other sectors and result in domestic policies aimed at ensuring stability in the export sector above all else. Internal inequalities are thereby exacerbated as those facets of the economy in contact with international concerns become more capital intensive and increasingly affluent while other sectors languish as they shoulder the transaction costs for the entire process. One consequence of the social relations of the new production arrangements standing side by side with traditional forms is a highly visible appearance of obsolescence as status in conferred by and derived from a "narrow primary production structure" (Hoogvelt 1977, p.96). DeJanvry (1981) spoke of the social disarticulation that results as legitimization and primacy are granted to those deemed necessary to maintain externally valued economic activities. Although overall economic growth may occur as measured by the value of exports relative to Gross Domestic Product (GDP), debt loads remain high and internal disparities bleak as few opportunities for redistribution occur even if local decision makers were so inclined in the face of crushing debt-service. As Ake

(1988) put it, even per capita income figures may be insufficient as they represent averages while GDP may be suspect in light of differences between economic growth and distributive development. Finally, although local economies may manifest substantial growth, profits are exported along with products so that capital accumulation is not at the point of production in the periphery but at the core. In its various guises, and despite substantial criticisms, dependency theory provides global-orienting principles for analyses of international capitalism, interlocking monetary policies, and their role in domestic policy in developing countries.

Baran's (1957) analysis of the relationship between India and Great Britain is frequently cited as an early effort to examine the aftermath of colonialism. The imperialism of Great Britain was said to exploit India, fostering a one-sided extraction of raw materials and the imposition of impediments to industrialization, except insofar as they were beneficial to Great Britain. Precolonial India was thought to be a locus of other-worldly philosophies and self-sustaining subsistence production. Postcolonial India came to be little more than a production satellite in which local elites relished their relative advantages as facilitators of British capitalism. In Baran's view, Indian politics, education, finance, and other institutional arrangements were restructured to secure maximal gain to British enterprise. With independence, sweeping changes were undertaken, including many exclusionary practices, as countermeasures to the yoke of colonial rule.

Latin American concerns gave rise to the dependency model, and many of the *dependistas*, as they were originally known, have concentrated on regional case studies to outline the nature of contact with international capitalism. For the most part they focused less on colonialism per se and more on Dos Santos's (1971) second and third types of dependency. Despite substantial resources, countries in the region found themselves burdened with inordinate trade deficits and international debt loads which had the potential to inundate them (Sweezy and Magdoff 1984). As a consequence, one debt restructuring followed another to ensure the preservation of gains already made, to maintain some modicum of political stability, and to ensure that interest payments continued or, in worst-case scenarios, bad debts could be written down and tax obligations reduced. In many instances the World Bank and the International Monetary Fund (IMF) exercised control and supervision, one consequence of this action being promotion of political regimes unlikely to challenge the principle of the loans (So 1990). Chile proved an exception, but one with disastrous and disruptive consequences. In all cases, to default would be to undermine those emoluments and privileges accorded local elites likely to seek further rather than fewer contacts with external capital.

Dos Santos's third form of dependency has also been widely explored. Landsberg (1979) looked to Asia to find empirical support. Through an analysis of manufacturing relationships in Hong Kong, Singapore, Taiwan, and South Korea with the industrial West, he concluded that despite improvement in local circumstances, relative conditions remained little affected due to the domination of manufacturing and industrial production by multinational corporations. These corporations moved production "off-shore," to Asia or other less-developed regions, in order to limit capitalization and labor costs while selling "on-shore," thereby maximizing profits. Landsberg asserted that because external capital shapes the industrialization of developing nations, the latter becomes so specialized as to have little recourse when international monopolistic practices become unbearable.

Few more eloquent defenders of the broad dependency perspective have emerged than Brazil's Cardoso (1973, 1977). He labeled his rendering a *historical-structural model* to connote the manner in which local traditions, preexisting social patterns, and the time frame of contact serve to color the way in which generalized patterns of dependency play out. He also coined the phrase *associated-dependent development* to describe the nurturing of circumscribed internal prosperity in order to enhance profit realization on investments (Cardoso 1973). He recognized that outright exploitation may generate immediate profit but can only lead to stagnation over the long run. Indeed, the fact that many former colonies remain economic losers seems to suggest that global development has not been ubiquitous (Bertocchi and Conova 1996). Instead, foreign capital functions as a means to development, underwriting dynamic progress in those sectors likely to further exports

but able, as well, to absorb incoming consumer goods. In the process, internal inequalities are heightened in the face of wide-ranging economic dualities as the physical quality of life for those segments of the population not immediately necessary to export and production suffer as a consequence.

In his analysis of Brazil, Cardoso also broadened the discussion to political consequences of dependency spurred by capital penetration. His intent was not to imply that only a finite range of consequences may occur, but to suggest that local patterns of interaction, entitlements, domination, conflict, and so on have a reciprocal impact on the conditions of dependency. By looking at changes occurring under military rule in Brazil, Cardoso succeeded in demonstrating that foreign capital predominated in essential manufacturing and commercial arenas (foreign ownership of industries in Brazil's state of Rio Grande do Sul were so extensive that Brazilian ownership was notable for being an exception). At the same time, internal disparities were amplified as interests supportive of foreign capital gained advantage at the expense of any opposition. In the process, wages and other labor-related expenses tended not to keep pace with an expanding economy, thereby resulting in ever-larger profit margins. As the military and the bourgeoisie served at the behest of multinational corporations, they defined the interests of Brazil to be consonant with their own.

By the early 1980s the Brazilian economy had stagnated, and as the country entered the new millennium it appeared headed for recursive hard times. Evans (1983) examined how what he termed the "triple alliance"—the state, private, and international capital interests—combined to alter the Brazilian economic picture pretty drastically while managing to preserve their own interests. In an effort to continue an uninterrupted export of profits, international capitalists permitted some accumulation among a carefully circumscribed local elite, so that each shared in the largess of favorable political decisions and state-sponsored ventures. Still, incongruities abounded; per capita wages fell as GDP increased and consumer goods flourished as necessities became unattainable. At the same time, infant and female mortality remained high and few overall gains in life expectancy were experienced. An exacerbation of local inequalities may have contributed to the downswing but so too did international financial shifts which eventually dictated that the majority of new loans were earmarked for servicing old debts.

In the face of these shifts, foreign capital gained concessions, subsidies, and favored-nation accommodations. The contradictions proliferated. Unable to follow through on promises to local capital, the Brazilian government had little choice but to rescind previous agreements, at the same time incurring the unintended consequence of reducing regional market-absorption capabilities. Without new orders and in the face of loan payments, local capital grew disillusioned and moderated its support for state initiatives despite a coercive bureaucracy that sent Brazil to the verge of economic failure. The value of Evans's work is that it highlights the entanglements imposed on local politics, policies, and capitalists by a dependent-development agenda lacking significant national autonomy. What became apparent was that governments legitimate themselves more in terms of multinational interests than in terms of local capital—and certainly more than in terms of local less-privileged groups seeking to influence government expenditures. In an examination of forty-five less-developed countries, Semyonov and Lewin-Epstein (1996) discovered that though external influences shape the growth of productive services, internal processes frequently remain capable of moderating the effect these changes have on other sectors.

In an analysis of Peru, Becker (1983) contended that internal alignments created close allegiances based on mutual interests and that hegemonic control of alliances in local decision making leads to the devaluing and disenfranchising of those who challenge business as usual or represent old arrangements. Bornschier (1981) asserted that internal inequalities increase and the rate of economic growth decreases in inverse proportion to the degree of dependency and in light of narrow sectoral targeting of foreign capital's development dollars. A recurrent theme running through their findings and those of other researchers is that internal economic disparities grow unchecked as tertiary-sector employment eventually becomes the predominant form (Bornschier 1981; Semyonov and Lewin-Epstein 1986; Delacroix and Ragin 1978; Chase-Dunn 1981; Boyce 1992).

Nearly all advocates of dependency models contend that many facets of less-developed countries, from structure of the labor force to mortality, public health, forms and types of services provided, and the role of the state in public welfare programs, are products of the penetration of external capital and the particulars of activities in the export sector. As capital-intensive production expands, surplus labor is relegated back to agrarian pursuits or to other tertiary and informal labor. It also fosters a personal-services industry in which marginal employees provide service to local elites but whose own well-being is dependent on the economic well-being of the elites. Distributional distortions, as embodied in state-sponsored social policies, are also thought to reflect the presence of external capitalism (Kohli et al. 1984; Clark and Phillipson 1991). Evans is unmistakable: the relationship of dependency and internal inequality ". . . is one of the most robust, quantitative, aggregate findings available" (1979, p.532).

Not everyone is convinced. As investigations of dependency theory proliferated, many investigators failed to find significant effects that could be predicted by the model (Dolan and Tomlin 1980). In fact, Gereffi's (1979) review of quantitative studies of "third world" development led him to maintain that there was little to support the belief that investment of foreign capital had any discernable effect on long-term economic gain. In fact, it is commonly claimed that most investigations rely on gross measures of the value of exports relative to GDP, thus treating all exports as contributing equally to economic growth (Talbot 1998). But when a surplus of primary commodities, "raw" extraction or agricultural products, is exported, prices become unstable, with the consequences being felt most explicitly in producing regions. When manufactured goods are exported, prices remain more stable, and local economies are less affected. Relying on covariant analysis of vertical trade (export of raw materials, import of manufactured goods), commodity concentration, and export processing, Jaffee (1985) maintained that when exports grow so too does overall economic viability. Yet he did note that consideration of economic vulnerabilities and export enclaves does yield "conditional effects" whereby economic growth is significantly reduced or even takes a negative turn.

In their research on what is sometimes termed the "resource curse" in resource-rich countries,

Auty (1993) and Khalil and Mansour (1993) suggest that competition between export sectors such as minerals, oil, and agriculture often impedes prosperity of the other two or one another. In countries where that occurs, governments tend to adopt lax economic policies that, for example, increase agricultural dependencies in favor of oil exports. Internal conflicts then become self-perpetuating and play out in the physical and economic well-being of the populace. Some investigators also point out that the internal dynamics of different types of export commodities will have differential impacts on the economy as a whole and on state bureaucracies as differing degrees of infrastructure are implicated (Talbot 1998).

A number of critics have asserted that dependency theory is flawed, fuzzy, and unable to withstand empirical scrutiny (Peckenham 1992; Ake 1988; Becker 1983). Even Marxist theorists find fault with dependency theory for overemphasizing external, exploitative factors at the expense of attention to the role of local elite (Shannon 1996). Other critics have focused on the evidence mustered and suggested that only about one-third of the variance in inequality among nations is accounted for by penetration of multinational corporations or other forms of foreign investment (Kohli et al. 1984; Bornschier, Chase-Dunn, and Rubinson 1978). Interestingly, still others have concluded that economic development of the type being discussed here is a significant facilitator for political democracy (Bollen 1983).

Defenders react by challenging measures of operationalization, the way variables are defined, and whether the complex of concepts embraced by the multidimensionality of the notion of dependency can be assessed in customary ways or in the absence of a comparative framework juxtaposing developing nations with their industrial counterparts (Ragin 1983; Robinson and Holtzman 1982; Boyce 1993). Efforts to isolate commodity concentration and multinational corporate investments have not proven to be reliable indicators and, as noted, even per capita GDP has its detractors. While important questions on heterogeneity, dispersion, or heteroskedasticity can be addressed by slope differences and recognized estimation techniques (Delacroix and Ragin 1978), proponents of the model are adamant that contextualized historical analysis is not only appropriate but mandated by the logic of dependency itself (Bach

1977; Bertocchi and Canova 1996). In their investigation of former colonies in Africa, Bertocchi and Canova (1996) concluded that colonial status is central to explaining relatively poor economic performance in ensuing years.

Proponents have also turned to sophisticated statistical procedures to elucidate their claims. For example, Bertocchi and Canova (1996) ran regression models on forty-six former colonies and dependencies in Africa to test their contention that colonialization makes a difference in subsequent societal and economic well-being. In a separate examination of state size and debt size among African nations, Bradshaw and Tshandu (1990) concluded that international capital penetration in the face of a mounting debt crisis may precipitate antagonism and austerity measures as the IMF and foreign capital debt claims are pitted against local claimants such as governmental subsidies and wages. In discussing capital penetration and the debt crises facing many developing nations, Bradshaw and Huang (1991) attributed incidences of political turmoil to austerity measures imposed on domestic welfare programs by IMF conditions and transnational financial institutions. They went on to assert that dependency theorists must take into consideration international recessions and global monetary crises if they are to understand structural accommodations and shifts in the quality of life in developing nations. In light of interlocking monetary policies, a single country teetering on the brink of economic adversity portends consequences for not only its trading partners but many other countries as well.

Several dependency analysts have utilized advanced analytic techniques to examine whether income inequality within countries is related to status in the world economy (Rubinson 1976; London and Robinson 1989; Boyce 1993). Both Rubinson (1976) and London and Robinson (1989) looked at interlocking world economies and their affect on governmental bureaucracies and internal structural differentiation. London and Robinson (1989) noted that the extent of multinational corporate penetration, and indirectly, its affect on income inequality, is associated with political malaise. Walton and Ragin (1990) concurred, maintaining that the involvement of international economic interests in domestic political-economic policy combine with "overurbanization" and associated dependency to help pave the way to political protest.

Boswell and Dixon (1990) carried the analysis a step further. Using regression and path analysis, they examined both economic and military dependency, concluding that both forms contribute to political instability through their effects on domestic class and state structures. They asserted that corporate penetration impedes real growth while exacerbating inequalities and the type of class polarization that leads to political violence. In his analysis of the economic shambles created in the Philippines under Ferdinand Marcos, Boyce (1993) concluded that the development strategies adopted during the Marcos era were economically disastrous for the bulk of the populace as "imperfections" in world markets precluded even modest capital accumulation for all but a privileged few. Though not speaking strictly in terms of dependency theory, Milner and Keohane (1996) point out that domestic policies are inevitably affected by global economic currents insofar as new policy preferences and coalitions are created as a result, by triggering domestic political and economic crises or by the undermining of governmental autonomy and thereby control over local economic policy. Dependency theorists customarily incorporate attention to all three in addressing the role international markets play in local economic policy.

Alternative interpretations of underdevelopment began to gain strength in the early 1970s. The next step was a world systems perspective, which saw global unity accompanied by an international division of labor with corresponding political alignments. Wallerstein (1974), Chirot and Hall (1982), and others shifted the focus from spatial definitions of nation-states as the unit of analysis to corporate actors as the most significant players able to shape activities—including the export of capital—according to their own interests. Wallerstein suggested that the most powerful countries of the world constitute a de facto collective core that disperses productive activities so that dependent industrialization is an extension of what had previously been geographically localized divisions of labor. World systems analysts see multinational corporations rather than nation-states as the means by which articulation of global economic arrangements is maintained. So powerful have multinationals become that even the costs of corporate organization are borne by those countries in which the corporations do business, with costs calculated according to terms dictated by the multinational

corporations themselves. Yet state participation is undoubtedly necessary as a kind of subsidization of multinational corporate interests and as a means for providing local management that, in addition to facilitating political compliance and other functions, promotes capital concentration for more efficient marketing and the maintenance of demand for existing goods and services. Thus production, consumption, and political ideologies are transplanted globally, legitimated, and yield a thoroughgoing stratification that, while it cuts across national boundaries, always creates precedence at the local level.

Dependency theory and collateral notions have become dispositional concepts utilized by numerous investigations of the effect of dependent development on diverse dimensions of inequality. Using a liberal interpretation of the model, many investigators have sought to understand how political economy affects values, types of rationality, definitions of efficiency and so on, as well as evaluations of those who do not share those values, views, or competencies. The social organization of the marketplace is thus thought to exert suzerainty over many types of social relationships and will continue to drive analysis of internal disparities in underdeveloped regions (Zeitlin 1972; Hechter 1975; Ward 1990; Shen and Williamson 1997). It remains to be seen how the absence of Soviet influence, often underemphasized during the formative period of dependency theory, will play out in analyses of international economic development in the twenty-first century (Pai 1991).

Substituting a figurative, symbolic relationship for spatial criteria, a generalized dependency model alloyed ideas of internal colonialism and has been widely employed as an explanatory framework wherein social and psychological distance from the center of power is seen as a factor in shaping well-being and other aspects of quality of life such as school enrollment, labor force participation, social insurance programs, longevity and so on. Likely as not, the political economics of development will continue to inform analysis of ancillary spheres for some time to come.

Gamson's (1968) concept of "stable unrepresentation" helped emphasize how the politics of inequality are perpetuated by real or emblematic core complexes. Internal colonialism and political economic variants have been widely adopted in examinations of many types of social problems. Blauner's (1970) analysis of American racial problems is illustrative of one such application. So too is Marshall's (1985) investigation of patterns of industrialization, investment debt, and export dependency on the status of women in sixty less-developed countries. While she was unable to draw firm conclusions relative to dependency per se, Marshall did assert that with thoughtful specification, gender patterns in employment and education may be found to be associated with dependency-based economic change. In a manner similar to Blauner, Townsend (1981) spoke of "the structured dependency of the elderly" as a consequence of economic utility in advanced industrial societies. Many analysts have advocated the use of dependency-driven approaches to examine various consequences of dependency and development such as fertility, mortality, differential life expectancy, health patterns, and education (Hendricks 1982, 1995; Neysmith and Edwardth 1984; London 1988; Ward 1990; Lena and London 1993; Shen and Williamson 1997). Such a perspective casts the situation of the elderly as a consequence of shifts in economic relationships and state policies designed to provide for their needs. For example, Neysmith (1991) maintained that as debts are refinanced to retain foreign capital, domestic policies are rewritten in such a way as to disenfranchise vulnerable populations within those countries in favor of debt service. To support her point, Neysmith cites a United Nations finding that human development programs tend to benefit males, households in urban areas, and middle- or higher-income people, while relatively fewer are targeted at women, rural residents, or low-income persons (United Nations Department of International Economic and Social Affairs 1988). Interestingly, according to a United Nations report issued two decades ago, women account for approximately half the world's adult population, one-third of the formal labor force, and two-thirds of all the recorded work hours, yet receive one-tenth of the earned income (cited in Tiano 1988; Ward 1990). In an examination of capital penetration in eighty-six countries, Shen and Williamson (1997) suggest that as penetration increases and sectorial inequalities are exacerbated between tertiary and informal labor markets vis-à-vis other sectors, there is a degradation of women's status in all economic activities. At the same time, fertility rates remain high partly because child labor provides an integral component of household income.

Variation in the life experiences of subpopulations is one of the enduring themes of sociology. Despite wide disparities, a central focus has been the interconnections of societal arrangements and political, economic, and individual circumstances. It is through them that norms of reciprocity and distributive justice are fostered and shared. As contexts change, so too will norms of what is appropriate. The linkage between political and moral economies is nowhere more apparent than in dependency theory as it facilitates our understanding of the dynamic relationship between individuals and structural arrangements.

REFERENCES

Addo, Herb 1996 "Developmentalism: A Eurocentric Hoax, Delusion, and Chicanery." In Sing C. Chew and Robert A. Denemark, eds., The *Underdevelopment of Development*. Thousand Oaks, Calif.: Sage.

Ake, Claude 1988 "The Political Economy of Development: Does it Have a Future?" *International Social Science Journal* 40:485–497.

Amin, Samir 1976 *Unequal Development: An Essay on the Social Formation of Peripheral Capitalism*. New York: Monthly Review Press.

Auty, Richard M. 1993 "Sustainable Development in Mineral Exporting Economies." *Resources-Policy* 19:14–29 (cited in Talbot).

Bach, Robert 1977 "Methods of Analysis in the Study of the World Economy: A Comment on Rubinson." *American Sociological Review* 42:811–814.

Baran, Paul 1957 *The Political Economy of Growth*. New York: Monthly Review Press.

Becker, David G. 1983 *The New Bourgeoisie and the Limits of Dependency: Mining, Class, and Power in "Revolutionary" Peru*. Princeton: Princeton University Press.

Bertocchi, Graziella, and Fabio Canova 1996 "Did Colonization Matter for Growth? An Empirical Exploration into the Historical Causes of Africa's Underdevelopment." Discussion Paper No. 1444, Center for Economic Policy Research, London.

Blauner, Robert 1970 "Internal Colonialism and Ghetto Revolt." In J. H. Skolnick and E. Curries, eds., *Crisis in American Institutions*. Boston: Little, Brown.

Bollen, Kenneth 1983 "World System Position, Dependency, and Democracy: The Cross-National Evidence." *American Sociological Review* 48:468–479.

Bornschier, Volker 1981 "Dependent Industrialization in the World Economy." *Journal of Conflict Resolution* 25:371–400.

———, C. Chase-Dunn, and R. Rubinson 1978 "Cross-National Evidence of the Effects of Foreign Investment: A Study of Findings and Analysis." *American Journal of Sociology* 84:651–683.

Boswell, Terry, and William J. Dixon 1990 "Dependency and Rebellion: A Cross-National Analysis." *American Sociological Review* 55:540–559.

Boyce, James K. 1993 *The Philippines: The Political Economy of Growth and Impoverishment in the Marcos Era.* Honolulu: University Of Hawaii Press.

Bradshaw, York W., and Zwelakhe Tshandu 1990 "Foreign Capital Penetration, State Intervention, and Development in Sub-Saharan Africa." *International Studies Quarterly* 34:229–251.

———, and Jie Huang 1991 "Intensifying Global Dependency: Foreign Debt, Structural Adjustment, and Third World Underdevelopment." *Sociological Quarterly* 32:321–342.

Cardoso, Fernando H. 1973 "Associated-Dependent Development: Theoretical and Practical Implications." In Alfred Stephen, ed., *Authoritarian Brazil.* New Haven: Yale University Press.

——— 1977 "The Consumption of Dependency Theory in the United States." *Latin American Research Review* 12:7–24.

———, and Enzo Faletto 1979 *Dependency and Development In Latin America.* Berkeley, Calif.: University of California Press.

Chase-Dunn, Christopher 1981 "Instate System and Capitalist World-Economy: One Logic or Two?" *International Studies Quarterly* 25:19–42.

Chirot, Daniel, and Thomas D. Hall 1982 "World System Theory." *Annual Review of Sociology* 8:81–106.

Clark, Roger, and Rachel Filinson 1991 "Multinational Corporate Penetration, Industrialism, Region, and Social Security Expenditures: A Cross-National Analysis." *International Journal of Aging and Human Development* 32:143–159.

DeJanvry, Alain 1981 *The Agrarian Question and Reformism in Latin America.* Baltimore, Md.: Johns Hopkins University Press.

Delacroix, Jacques, and Charles Ragin 1978 "Modernizing Institutions, Mobilization, and Third World Development." *American Journal of Sociology* 84:123–149.

Dolan, M., and B. W. Tomlin 1980 "First World–Third World Linkages: The Effects of External Relations upon Economic Growth, Imbalance, and Inequality in Developing Countries." *International Organization* 34:41–63.

Dos Santos, Theotonio 1971 "The Structure of Dependence." In K. T. Kan and Donald C. Hodges, eds., *Readings in U.S. Imperialism.* Boston: Expanding Horizons.

Evans, Peter 1979 *Dependent Development: The Alliance of Multinational State and Local Capital in Brazil.* Princeton: Princeton University Press.

Frank, Andre Gunder 1967 *Capitalism and Underdevelopment in Latin America.* New York: Monthly Review Press.

——— 1969 *Latin America: Underdevelopment or Revolution.* New York: Monthly Review Press.

Galtung, Johan 1972 "A Structural Theory of Imperialism." *African Review* 1:93–138.

Gamson, William A. 1968 "Stable Unrepresentation in American Society." *American Behavioral Scientist* 12:15–21.

Gereffi, Gary 1979 "A Critical Evaluation of Quantitative, Cross-National Studies of Dependency." Paper presented to International Studies Association Annual Meeting. Toronto, March 1979.

Hechter, Michael 1975 *Internal Colonialism: The Celtic Fringe in British National Development, 1536–1966.* Berkeley: University of California Press.

Hendricks, Jon 1982 "The Elderly in Society: Beyond Modernization." *Social Science History* 6:321–345.

——— 1995 "The Contributions of Older Women to Social and Economic Development." *Ageing International* (July): 4–9.

Hoogvelt, A. M. M. 1977 *The Sociology of Developing Societies.* Atlantic Heights, N.J.: Humanities Press.

Jaffee, David 1985 "Export Dependence and Economic Growth: A Reformulation and Respecification." *Social Forces* 64:102–118.

Keith, Nelson W. 1997 *Reframing International Development: Globalism, Postmodernity and Difference.* Thousand Oaks, Calif.: Sage.

Khalil, Mohammad, and Ali H. Mansour 1993 "Development Patterns of Oil Exporting Countries." *Journal of Economics and Finance* 17:43–49.

Kohli, Atul, M. F. Altfeld, S. Lotfian, and R. Mardon 1984 "Inequality in The Third World." *Comparative Political Studies* 17:283–318.

Landsberg, Martin 1979 "Export-Led Industrialization in the Third World: Manufacturing Imperialism." *Review of Radical Political Economics* 11:50–63.

Lena, Hugh F., and Bruce London 1993 "The Political and Economic Determinants of Health Outcomes: A

Cross-National Analysis." *International Journal of Health Services* 23:585–602.

London, Bruce 1988 "Dependence, Distorted Development, and Fertility Trends in Noncore Nations: A Structural Analysis of Cross-National Data." *American Sociological Review* 53:606–618.

——, and Thomas D. Robinson 1989 "The Effects of International Dependence on Income Inequality and Political Violence." *American Sociological Review* 54:305–308.

Marshall, Susan E. 1985 "Development, Dependence, and Gender Inequality in the Third World." *International Studies Quarterly* 29:217–240.

Milner, Helen V., and Robert O. Keohane 1996 "Internationalization and Domestic Policies: A Conclusion." In Robert O. Keohand and Helen V. Milner, eds., *Internationalization and Domestic Politics*. Cambridge, Eng.: Cambridge University Press.

Neysmith, Sheila M. 1991 "Dependency Among Third World Elderly: A Need for New Direction in the Nineties." In M. Minkler and C. L. Estes, eds., *Critical Perspectives on Aging: The Political and Moral Economy of Growing Old*. Amityville, N.Y.: Baywood Publishing.

——, and Joey Edwardth 1984 "Economic Dependency in the 1980s: Its Impact on Third World Elderly." *Ageing and Society* 5:21–44.

O'Donnell, Guillermo 1988 *Bureaucratic Authoritarianism: Argentina, 1966–1973, in Comparative Perspective*. Berkeley: University of California Press.

Packenham, Robert A. *The Dependency Movement: Scholarship and Politics in Development Studies*. Cambridge, Mass.: Harvard University Press.

Pai, Sudha 1991 "Problems in the Comparative Analysis of Third World Societies." *Indian Journal of Social Science* 4:591–603.

Portes, Alejandro 1976 "On the Sociology of National Development: Theories and Issues." *American Journal of Sociology* 29:339–357.

Ragin, Charles 1983 "Theory and Method in the Study of Dependency and International Inequality." *International Journal of Comparative Sociology* 24:121–136.

Rubinson, Richard 1976 "The World-Economy and the Distribution of Income within States: A Cross-National Study." *American Sociological Review* 41:638–659.

——, and Deborah Holtzman 1982 "Comparative Dependence and Economic Development." *International Journal of Comparative Sociology* 22:86–101.

Semyonov, Moshe, and Noah Lewin-Epstein 1986 "Economic Development, Investment Dependence, and the Rise of Services in Less Developed Nations." *Social Forces* 64:582–598.

Shannon, Thomas R. 1996 *An Introduction to the World-System Perspective*. Boulder, Colo.: Westview.

Shen, Ce, and John B. Williamson 1997 "Child Mortality, Women's Status, Economic Dependency, and State Strength: A Cross-National Study of Less Developed Countries." *Social Forces* 76:667–687.

So, Alvin Y. 1990 *Social Change and Development: Modernization, Dependency, and World-System Theories*. Newbury Park, Calif.: Sage.

Sweezy, Paul, and Harry Magdoff 1984 "The Two Faces of Third World Debt: A Fragile Financial Environment and Debt Enslavement." *Monthly Review* 35:1–10.

Talbot, John M. 1998 "Export Sectors and Economic Development: Do Sectors Shape the Development Prospects of States?" Paper presented to the annual meeting of the American Sociological Association. San Francisco, August 21–25, 1998.

Tiano, Susan 1988 "Women's Work in the Public and Private Spheres: A Critique and Reformulation." In M. Francis Abraham and P. Subhadra Abraham, eds., *Women, Development and Change: The Third World Experience*. Bristol, Ind.: Wyndham Hall Press.

Townsend, Peter 1981 "The Structured Dependency of the Elderly." *Ageing and Society* 1:5–28.

United Nations Department of International Economic and Social Affairs 1988 *Human Resources Development: A Neglected Dimension of Development Strategy*. New York: United Nations.

Wallerstein, Immanuel 1974 "The Rise and Future Demise of the World Capitalist System: Concepts for Comparative Analysis." *Comparative Studies in Society and History* 16:387–415.

Walton, John, and Charles Ragin 1990 "Global and National Sources of Political Protest: Third World Responses to the Debt Crisis." *American Sociological Review* 55:876–890.

Ward, Kathryn B. (ed.) 1990 *Women Workers and Global Restructuring*. Cornell, N.Y.: ILR Press.

Zeitlin, I. M. 1972 *Capitalism and Imperialism*. Chicago: Markham.

JON HENDRICKS

DEPRESSION

INTRODUCTION

The term "depression" covers a wide range of thoughts, behaviors, and feelings. It is also one of the most commonly used terms to describe a wide range of negative moods. In fact there are many types of depression, each of which vary in the number of symptoms, their severity, and persistence. The prevalence of depression is surprisingly high. Between 5 and 12 percent of men and 10 to 20 percent of women in the United States will suffer from a major depressive episode at some time in their lives. Approximately half of these individuals will become depressed more than once, and up to 10 percent will experience manic phases where they are elated and excited, in addition to depressive ones; an illness known as "manic-depressive" or bipolar disorder. Depression can involve the body, mood, thoughts, and many aspects of life. It affects the way people eat and sleep, the way they feel about themselves, and the way they think about things. Without treatment, symptoms can last for weeks, months, or years. Appropriate treatment, however, can help most people who suffer from depression.

TYPES OF DEPRESSION

Depression can be experienced for either a short period of time or can extend for years. It can range from causing only minor discomfort, to completely mentally and physically crippling the individual. The former case of short-term, mild depression is what is most commonly referred to as "the blues" or when people report "feeling low." It is technically referred to as *dysphoric mood*. Feelings of depression tend to occur in almost all individuals at some point in their lives, and dsyphoric mood has been associated with many key life events varying from minor to major life transitions (e.g., graduation, pregnancy, the death of a loved one). The feelings of separation and loss associated with leaving a town one has grown up in, moving to a new city for a job or school, or even leaving a work environment that one has grown accustomed to, can cause bouts of depression signaled by a loss of motivation and energy, and sadness. Other common features of dysphoric mood, include sighing, an empty feeling in the stomach, and muscular weakness, are also associated with changes such as the breakup of a dating relationship, divorce, or separation. In the case of bereavement, most survivors experience a dysphoric mood that is usually called grief (although some studies have shown that these feelings may be distinct from depression).

Many of these feelings are seen as representing the body's short-term response to stress. Other

kinds of stressful events like losing a job; being rejected by a lover; being unable to pay the rent or having high debts; or losing everything in a fire, earthquake, or flood; may also bring on feelings of depression. Most of these feelings based on temporary situations are perfectly normal and tend to fade away.

A more severe type of depression than dysphoric mood, *dysthymia* (from the Greek word for defective or diseased mood), involves long-term, chronic symptoms that do not disable, but keep those individuals from functioning at their best or from feeling good. People with dysthymia tend to be depressed most of the day, more days than not, based on their own description or the description of others. Dysthymics have a least two of the following symptoms: eating problems, sleeping problems, tiredness and concentration problems, low opinions of themselves, and feelings of hopelessness. Unlike major depression, dysthymics can be of any age. Often people with dysthymia also experience major depressive episodes.

If "the blues" persist, it is more indicative of major depression, also referred to as *clinical depression* or a *depressive disorder*. Major depression is manifested by a combination of symptoms that interfere with the ability to work, sleep, eat, and enjoy once-pleasurable activities. These disabling episodes of depression can occur once, twice, or several times in a lifetime. Clinical practitioners (both clinical psychologists and psychiatrists) make use of a multiple-component classification system designed to summarize the diverse information relevant to an individual case rather than to just provide a single label. Using a specified set of criteria in the *Diagnostic and Statistical Manual of Mental Disorders* (referred to as *DSM-IV*, American Psychiatric Association 1994), a diagnosis of depressive disorder includes symptoms such as dissatisfaction and anxiety; changes in appetite, sleep, and psychological and motor functions; loss of interest and energy; feelings of guilt; thoughts of death; and diminished concentration. It is important to keep in mind that many of these symptoms are also reported by individuals who are not diagnosed with clinical depression. Only having many of these symptoms at any one time qualifies as depression. An individual is said to be experiencing a "major depressive episode" if he or she experiences a depressed mood or a loss of interest or pleasure in almost all activities and exhibits at least four other symptoms from the following list: marked weight loss or gain when not dieting, constant sleeping problems, agitated or greatly slowed-down behavior, fatigue, inability to think clearly, feelings of worthlessness, and frequent thoughts about death or suicide. Anyone experiencing these symptoms for a prolonged period of time should see a doctor or psychiatrist immediately.

Another type of depression is *bipolar disorder*, formerly called manic-depressive illness. Not nearly as prevalent as other forms of depressive disorders, bipolar disorder involves interspersed periods of depression and elation or mania. Sometimes the mood switches are dramatic and rapid, but most often they are gradual. When in the depressed cycle, individuals have any or all of the symptoms of a depressive disorder. When in the manic cycle, individuals tend to show inappropriate elation, social behavior, and irritability; have disconnected and racing thoughts; experience severe insomnia and increased sexual appetite; talk uncontrollably; have grandiose notions; and demonstrate a marked increase in energy. Mania often affects thinking, judgment, and social behavior in ways that cause serious problems and embarrassment. For example, unwise business or financial decisions may be made when an individual is in a manic phase. Bipolar disorder is often a chronic condition. For more details on types of depression, including symptoms, see either a good textbook on abnormal psychology (e.g., Sarason and Sarason 1999), DSM-IV (American Psychiatric Association 1994) or use the search term "depression" on the web site for the National Institute of Health (http://search.info.nih.gov/).

THEORIES OF DEPRESSION

Most theorists agree that depression can be best studied using what health psychologists refer to as a *biopsychosocial approach*. This holds that depression has a biological component (including genetic links and biochemical imbalances), a psychological component (including how people think, feel, and behave), and a social component (including family and societal pressures and cultural factors). Individual theories have tended to emphasize one or the other of these components. The main theories of depression are biological and cognitive in nature, although there are also psychodynamic and behavioral explanations which are discussed below.

Psychodynamic Theories of Depression. The psychological study of depression was essentially begun by Sigmund Freud and Karl Abraham, a German physician. Both described depression as a complex reaction to the loss of a loved person or thing. This loss could be real or imagined, through death, separation, or rejection. For Abraham (1911/1968), individuals who are vulnerable to depression experience a marked ambivalence toward people, with positive and negative feelings alternating and blocking the expression of the other. These feelings were seen to be the result of early and repeated disappointments. Depression, or melancholy, as Freud called it, was grief out of control (Freud 1917/1957). Unlike those in mourning, however, depressed persons appeared to be more self-denigrating and lacking self-esteem. Freud theorized that the anger and disappointment that had previously been directed toward the lost person or thing was internalized, leading to a loss of self-esteem and a tendency to engage in self-criticism. Theorists who used a similar approach and modified Freud's theories for depression were Sandot Rado and Melanie Klein, and most recently John Bowlby (1988).

Behavioral Theories of Depression. In contrast to a focus on early-childhood experiences and internal psychological processes, behavioral theories attempt to explain depression in terms of responses to stimuli and the overgeneralization of these responses. For example, loss of interest to a wide range of activities (food, sex, etc.) in response to a specific situation (e.g., loss of a job). The basic idea is that if a behavior is followed or accompanied by something good (a reward), the behavior will increase and persist. If the reward is taken away, lessened, or worse still, if the behavior is punished, the behavior will lessen or disappear. B. F. Skinner, a key figure in the behaviorist movement, postulated that depression was the result of a weakening of behavior due to the interruption of an established sequence of behavior that had been positively reinforced by the social environment. For example, the loss of a job would stop a lot of the activities that having a salary provides (e.g., dining out often, entertainment). Most behavioral theories extended this idea, focusing on specific others as the sources of reinforcement (e.g., spouses, friends).

Cognitive Theories of Depression. Although it is probably indisputable that the final common pathways to clinical depression and even dysphoric mood involve biological changes in the brain, the most influential theories of depression today focus on the thoughts of the depressed individual. This cognitive perspective also recognizes that behavior and biochemistry are important components of depression, but it is more concerned with the quality, nature, and patterns of thought processes. Cognitive therapists believe that when depressive cognitions are changed, behavior and underlying biological responses change as well. Cognitive theories of depression differ from behavioral theories in two major ways (see Gotlieb and Hammen 1992 for a more detailed description). First, whereas behavioral theories focus on observable behaviors, cognitive theories emphasize the importance of intangible factors such as attitudes, self-statements, images, memories, and beliefs. Second, cognitive approaches to depression consider maladaptive, irrational, and in some cases, distorted thoughts to be the cause of the disorder and of its exacerbation and maintenance. Depressive behaviors, negative moods, lack of motivation, and physical symptoms that are seen to accompany depression are all seen as stemming from faulty thought patterns. There are three main cognitive theories of depression: *Beck's cognitive-distortion model, Seligman's learned helplessness model,* and the *hopelessness theory of depression.*

Beck's cognitive-distortion model. The most influential of these theories is Aaron Beck's cognitive-distortion model of depression (1967). Beck believes that depression is composed of three factors: negative thoughts about oneself, the situation, and the future. A depressed person misinterprets facts in a negative way, focuses on negative aspects of a situation, and has no hope for the future. Thus any problem or misfortune experienced, like the loss of a job, is completely assumed to be one's own fault. The depressed individual blames these events on his or her own personal defects. Awareness of these presumed defects becomes so intense that it overwhelms any positive aspects of the self and even ambiguous information is interpreted as evidence of the defect in lieu of positive explanations. A depressed person might focus on a minor negative exchange within an entire conversation and interpret this as a sign of complete rejection. These types of thought patterns, also referred to as "automatic thoughts" when responses based on insufficient information are made, are persistent and act as negative filters for all of life's experiences. Excellent descriptions of the way these thoughts operate can be found in books by the psychologist Norman Endler (*Holiday of Darkness*, 1990) and the writer William Styron (*Darkness Visible: A Memoir of Madness*, 1982).

Together with the idea that depressed individuals mentally distort reality and engage in faulty processing of information, the most important part of Beck's cognitive model of depression is the notion of a "negative self-schema." A schema is a stored body of knowledge that affects how information is collected, processed, and used, and serves the function of efficiency and speed. In the context of depression, schemas are mental processes that represent a stable characteristic of the person, influencing him or her to evaluate and select information from the environment in a negative and pessimistic direction. Similar to psychoanalytical theories, negative self-schemas are theorized to develop from negative experiences in childhood. These schemas remain with the individual throughout life, functioning as a vulnerability factor for depression. Cognitive treatments of depression necessarily work to change these negative schemas and associated negative-automatic thought patterns.

Seligman's learned helplessness model. Based on work on animals (later replicated in humans), Martin Seligman's (1975) theory of learned helplessness and his model of depression holds that when individuals are exposed to uncontrollable stress they fail to respond to stimulation and show marked decrements in the ability to learn new behaviors. Because this theory did not sufficiently account for the self-esteem problems faced by depressed individuals, it was reformulated by Abramson who hypothesized that together with uncontrollable stress, people must also expect that future outcomes are uncontrollable. When they believe that these negative uncontrollable outcomes are their own doing (internal versus external), will be stable across time and will apply to everything they do (global), they feel helpless and depressed.

Hopelessness theory of depression. The most recent reformulation of the learned helplessness theory, referred to as the "hopelessness theory" of depression (Abramson, Seligman, and Alloy 1989) holds that depression is a result of expectations that highly undesired outcomes will occur and that one is powerless to change these outcomes. The hopelessness theory of depression is receiving a large amount of attention as it has been found to be particularly useful in predicting the likelihood of suicide among depressed people.

Biological Theories of Depression. The most compelling of the recent theories of depression rely heavily on the biological bases of behavior. Biological theories assume the cause of depression lies in some physiological problem, either in the genes themselves or in the way neurotransmitters (the chemicals that carry signals between nerve cells in our brains and around our bodies) are produced, released, transported, or recognized (see Honig and van Praag 1997 for a detailed review of biological theories of depression). Most of the work focuses on neurotransmitters, especially a category of chemicals in our bodies called the monoamines, the main examples of which are norepinephrine (also called noradrenalin), dopamine, and serotonin. These chemicals first attracted attention in the 1950s when physicians discovered that severe depression arose in a subset of people who were treated for hypertension with a drug (reserpine) that depleted monoamines. Simultaneously, researchers found that a drug that increased the monoamines, this time given to medicate tuberculosis, elevated mood in users who were depressed. Together these results suggested that low levels of monoamines in the brain cause depression. The most important monoamine seems to be norepinephrine although it is now acknowledged that changes in levels of this neurochemical do not influence moods in everyone. Nevertheless, this biochemical theory has received much experimental support.

Apart from the neurochemicals, there are also other physiological differences between depressed and nondepressed individuals. Hormones are chemical substances that circulate in the blood and enable communication between different systems of the body. Some hormones control the release of other hormones which then stimulate growth and help prepare the body to deal with,

and respond to, stress (e.g., adrenocorticotropic hormone or ACTH). Depressed patients have repeatedly been demonstrated to show abnormal functioning of these hormones (see Nemerof 1998 for a detailed review). Another difference is seen in one of the major systems of the body that affects how we respond to stress; the hypothalamic-pituitary-adrenal (HPA) axis. From the late 1960s and early 1970s, researchers have found increased activity in the HPA axis in unmedicated depressed patients as evidenced by increased levels of stress markers in bodily fluids. Now a large volume of studies confirm that substantial numbers of depressed patients display overactivity of the HPA axis. According to Charles Nemeroff (1998) and his colleagues, and based on studies on animals, all these biological factors including genetic inheritance of depression, neurotransmitter and hormonal levels, and HPA axis and related activity, could relate to early childhood abuse or neglect, although this theory has yet to be fully substantiated. The antecedents and consequences notwithstanding, it is well accepted that one of the major causes of depression is based in our biology.

RISK FACTORS

Depression can have many different causes as indicated by the different theories that have been formulated to explain it. Accordingly, there are different factors that indicate a risk for depression. Some of the main risk factors for long-term depression include heredity, age, gender, and lack of social support.

Studies of twins and of families clearly suggest a strong genetic component to clinical depression, which increases with genetic closeness. There is a much greater risk of developing a major depression if one's identical twin has had it than if one's parent, brother, or sister developed it. Chances are even less if no close relatives have ever had it. Furthermore, the younger people are when they experience depression, the higher the chances that one of their relatives will also get severely depressed. Relatives of people who were over forty when they first had a major depression have little more than the normal risk for depression.

One of the most clear risk factors is gender. Women are at least twice as likely to experience all types of depressed states than are men and this seems to occur from an early age. There are no gender differences in depression rates in prepubescent children, but after the age of fifteen, girls and women are about twice as likely to be depressed as boys and men. Many models have been advanced for how gender differences in depression might develop in early adolescence. For example, one model suggests that the causes of depression can be assumed to be the same for girls and boys, but these causes become more prevalent in girls than in boys in early adolescence. According to another model, there are different causes of depression in girls and boys, and the causes of girls' depression become more prevalent than the causes of boys' depression in early adolescence. The model that has received the most support suggests that girls are more likely than boys to carry risk factors for depression even before early adolescence, but these risk factors lead to depression only in the face of challenges that increase in early adolescence (Nolen-Hoeksema and Girgus 1994). For a review of the epidemiology of gender differences in depression including prominent theories for why women are more vulnerable to depression, cross-cultural studies of gender differences in depression, biological explanations for the gender difference in depression (including postpartum depression, premenstrual depression, pubescent depression), personality theories (relationship with others, assertiveness), and social factors for the gender difference (increases in sexual abuse in adolescent females) see Susan Nolen-Hoeksema (1995).

Age by itself is a major risk factor for depression, although as described this varies for each gender. For women, the risk for a first episode of depression is highest between the ages of twenty and twenty-nine. For men, the risk for a first episode is highest for those aged forty to forty-nine. A related risk concerns when a person was born. People born in recent decades have been found to have an increased risk for depression as compared to those born in earlier cohorts.

Another significant risk factor for depression is the availability and perception of social support. People who lack close supportive relationships are at added risk for depression. Additionally, the presence of supportive others may prevent depression in the face of severe life stressors. Support is especially important in the context of short-term depression that can result from events like conflictual work or personal interactions, unemployment, the loss of a job, a relationship break-up, or the loss of a loved one.

MEASUREMENT OF DEPRESSION

Most of the commonly used techniques to assess for depression come from clinical psychology and are heavily influenced by the cognitive theories of depression. For example, the work of Beck and other cognitive theorists has led to the development of many ways to measure the thoughts that depressed individuals may have. Most of these measures are completed by the individuals themselves, while some are administered in an interview format where the therapist asks a series of questions. Some interviews are delivered by trained clinical administrators (e.g., the Structured Clinical Interview for DSM-IV), while others are highly structured, can be computer scored to achieve diagnoses based on the DSM-IV, and can be administered by lay interviewers with minimal training (e.g., the Diagnostic Interview Schedule). Separate measures have also been designed for adults and children to compensate for differences in level of comprehension and sophistication, although measures of symptoms and diagnoses in children and adolescents are less-extensively studied. The methods used work well for children provided that information from both parent and child sources are included in the final decisions.

There are different types of self-report measures for depression. It can be assessed by having the patient fill out a questionnaire. Because our thought processes may operate at varying levels of consciousness, we may not always be able to access what they are to report on them. For this reason different cognitive measures of depression were designed to operate at various levels of consciousness. For example, the most direct measures ask about the frequency with which negative automatic thoughts have "popped" into a person's head in the past week (e.g., "no one understands me"). Another type of measure attempts to get at the cognitive and social cognitive mechanisms by which people formulate their beliefs and expectations. Because many negative thoughts take the form of comparing the self with others, these types of scales try to understand the negative comparisons. An example of this type of measure is one where individuals are asked about the circumstances (interactions with people, idle thoughts, etc.), the dimensions (social skills, intelligence), the gender, and the type of relationship with the comparison target, and the individual's mood before and after the interaction. To get at the least-accessible level of thoughts, those that are believed to store, organize, and direct the processing of personally relevant information, researchers have used measures like the Stroop color-word task. Individuals are asked to name the color of the ink in which a word is printed but to ignore the meaning of the word itself. Slower response rates are thought to indicate greater effort to suppress words that are highly descriptive of the self. For example, depressed individuals take longer to name the color in which words like "sad" and "useless" are printed compared to the color for positive words.

In health, clinical, and counseling research and evaluation settings, the two most common measures of depression are the Beck Depression Inventory (BDI) and the Center for Epidemiological Studies Depression Scale (CESD). The BDI was designed to measure "symptom-attitude categories" associated with depression (Beck 1967). These include, among others, mood, pessimism, and sense of failure as well as somatic preoccupation. Many of the items reflect Beck's belief in the relevance of negative cognitions or self-evaluations in depression. Each item includes a group of statements that reflect increasing levels of one of these symptom-attitude categories. The test taker is asked to choose the statement within each item that reflects the way he or she has been feeling in the past week. The items are scored on a scale from 0–3, and reflect increasing levels of negativity. A sample item includes 0 = "I do not feel like a failure," to 3 = "I feel I am a complete failure as a person." The CESD is a twenty-item scale, is a widely used measure of depressive symptomatology, and has been shown to be valid and reliable in many samples. Participants are asked to best describe how often they felt or behaved during the previous week, in a variety of ways reflective of symptoms of depression, using a scale ranging from 0 (*Rarely or none of the time[less than 1 day]*) to 3 (*Most or all of the time [5–7 days]*). For example, participants are asked how often their sleep was restless or they felt that everything they did was an effort. Other self-report measures include the Minnesota Multiphasic Personality Inventory Depression Scale (MMPI-D), the Zung Self-Rating Depression Scale (SDS), and the Depression Adjective Check List (DACL). Complete descriptions of these scales can be found in Constance Hammen (1997).

TREATMENT

As can be expected, the type of treatment depends on the type of depression and to some extent the favored theory of the health-care provider (physician, psychologist, or therapist) one goes to for treatment.

Biologically based treatments. The most common treatment for depression that is thought to have a physiological basis is antidepressant medication. Based on biological theories suggesting that depression results from low levels of the monoamines serotonin, norepinephrine, and dopamine, antidepressant medications act to increase the levels of these chemicals in the bloodstream. These drugs work by either preventing the monoamines from being broken down and destroyed (referred to as monoamine oxidase (MOA) inhibitors and tricyclics) or by preventing them from being removed from where they work (referred to as selective serotonin inhibitors [SSRIs]). Elavil, Norpramin, and Tofranil are the trade names of some MAO inhibitors. Prozac, Paxil, Zoloft, and Luvox are examples of SSRIs.

Although these medications have been proven to be effective in reducing depression, they also have a variety of side effects and need to be taken only under medical supervision. For example, tricyclics also cause dry mouth, constipation, dizziness, irregular heartbeat, blurred vision, ringing in the ears, retention of urine, and excessive sweating. Some of the SSRIs were developed with an eye toward reducing side effects and are correspondingly more often prescribed. Unfortunately, they are most commonly associated with prescription drug overdoses resulting in many thousands of deaths a year.

Several medicinal herbs have antidepressant effects. The most powerful is St. John's wort, a natural MAO inhibitor. In addition, ginkgo and caffeine may also help. Although much more research remains to be done, studies to date support the effectiveness of such alternative medicine. For example, a group of researchers in Texas, in collaboration with German scientists, surveyed studies including a total of 1,757 outpatients with mainly mild or moderately severe depressive disorders, and found that extracts of St. John's wort were more effective than placebos (i.e., inactive pills) and as effective as standard antidepressant medication in the treatment of depression. They also had fewer side effects than standard antidepressant drugs (Linde et al. 1996).

In extreme cases of depression when drugs have been tried and found to not have an effect, and when the patient does not have the time to wait for drugs to take an effect (sometimes up to two or three weeks), electroconvulsive therapy (ECT) is recommended. ECT involves passing a current of between 70 and 130 volts through the patient's head after the administration of an anesthetic and muscle relaxant (to prevent injury from the convulsion caused by the charge). ECT is effective in treating severe depression although the exact mechanisms by which it works have not been determined.

Cognitive treatments. Cognitive therapists focus on the thoughts of the depressed person and attempt to break the cycle of negative automatic thoughts and negative self-views. Therapy sessions are well structured and begin with a discussion of an agenda for the session, where a list of items is drawn up and then discussed one by one. The therapist then tries to identify, understand, and clarify the misinterpretations and unrealistic expectations held by the client. Therapists use several techniques to identify these thoughts including asking direct questions, asking the client to use imagery to evoke the thoughts, or role-playing. Identifying these thoughts is a critical part of cognitive therapy and clients are also asked to keep daily diaries to list automatic thoughts when they occur as they are often unnoticed by depressed individuals. The client is then asked to provide a written summary of the major conclusions from the session to solidify what has been achieved and finally, the therapist prescribes a "homework assignment" designed to help the client practice skills and behaviors worked on during the session. Behavioral therapy is closely related to cognitive therapy and involves training the client to have better social skills and behaviors that enable them to develop better relationships with others.

Which are more effective treatments: cognitive or biological? A large National Institute of Mental Health study suggests that there is little difference in the effectiveness of the two therapies although the two treatments seem to produce different effects over time. Patients who received cognitive therapy were less likely to have a return of depression over time as compared to patients with biological therapy, although the small sample size used in this study precludes a definite answer to this question. Both therapies have been found to be effective, and it is likely that one is better with some forms of depression than the other, depending on how long the person has been depressed and the exact nature of his or her symptoms. In general both treatments, whether cognitive or biological, are recommended to be continued for a short time after the depressed episode has ended in order to prevent relapse.

CONCOMITANTS

A wide body of research has documented the links between depression and a wide variety of other factors. It is both a component of many other psychological disorders as well as something that follows many other disorders. In fact, some studies have shown that out of all the people at a given time with depression, only 44 percent of them display what can be called "pure" depression, whereas the others have depression and at least one other disorder or problem. The most common of these associated problems are anxiety, substance abuse, alcoholism, and eating disorders (see Hammen 1997 for more details). Given the symptoms of depression, individuals with the disorder also experience associated social problems including strained relationships with spouses, family, and friends, and in the workplace. Most alarming perhaps is that the children of depressed parents (especially mothers) are especially at risk for developing problems of their own.

Depression has also been linked to positive factors although not always with good results. For example, there is some evidence that depression is linked to creativity. Artists tend to suffer more than their share of depression according to psychiatrists at Harvard medical school, who charted the psychological histories of fifteen mid-twentieth-century artists. They found that at least half of them, including artists like Jackson Pollock and Mark Rothko, suffered from varying degrees of depression (Schildkraut and Aurora 1996). Many of these artists eventually committed suicide, which is perhaps one of the most significant and dangerous results of depression. At least 15 percent of people with depression complete the act of suicide, but an even higher proportion will attempt it. Consequently, individuals with severe cases of depression may experience many suicide-related thoughts and sometimes need constant surveillance.

Depression is often seen in patients with chronic or terminal illnesses and in patients who are close to dying. For example, depression is a common experience of AIDS patients, and is related to a range of factors such as physical symptomatology, number of days spent in bed, and in the perceived sufficiency of social support. Depression has also been linked to factors that influence mortality and morbidity. Higher depressed mood has been significantly associated with immune parameters pertinent to HIV activity and progression: lower levels of CD4 T cells, immune activation, and a lower proliferative response to PHA (a natural biological reaction that is essential to good health). Depression is also a critical variable with respect to compliance with treatment, especially in HIV-positive women of low-socioeconomic status.

Depression is strongly related to the number and duration of stressors experienced, or chronic burden. Chronic burden, defined by Leonard Pearlin and Carmi Schooler (1978) as ongoing difficulties in major social roles, including difficulties in employment, marriage, finances, parenting, ethnic relations, and being single/separated/divorced contributes to depression and increases vulnerability to health problems by reducing the ability of the body to respond to a physiological challenge, such as mounting an immune response to a virus. Related to chronic burden, many aspects of depression are concomitants of low-socioeconomic status, traditionally measured by education, income, and occupation. Research showing clear social-class differences in depression also suggest the contribution of the stress of poverty, exposure to crime, and other chronic stressors that vary with social class. Jay Turner, Blair Wheaton, and David Lloyd (1995) found that individuals of low-socioeconomic status were exposed to more chronic strain in the form of life difficulties in

seven domains (e.g., parenting, relationships, and financial matters) than individuals of high-socioeconomic status, which could account for higher levels of depression.

The influence of culture is one factor that has not been sufficiently studied in the context of depression. To date, most clinical-disorder classification systems do not sufficiently acknowledge the role played by cultural factors in mental disorders. The experience of depression has very different meanings and forms of expression in different societies. Most cases of depression worldwide are experienced and expressed in bodily terms of aching backs, headaches, fatigue, and a wide assortment of symptoms that lead patients to regard this condition as a physical problem (Sarason and Sarason 1999). Only in contemporary Western societies is depression seen principally as an internal psychological experience. For example, many cultures tend to view their mental health problems in terms of physical bodily problems. That is, they tend to manifest their worries, guilt feelings, and strong negative emotions (such as depression) as physical complaints. This could be because bodily complaints do not carry the stigma or negative social consequences that psychological problems do, and are correspondingly easier to talk about.

Although not an essential part of aging, many people over age sixty-five develop clinical depression. Surveys suggest that only about 5 percent of healthy elderly people living independently suffer depression at any given moment, but more than 15 percent experience depression at some point during their elderly years, and the condition tends to be more chronic than in younger people. In addition, some 25 percent of elderly individuals experience periods of persistent sadness that last two weeks or longer, and more than 20 percent report persistent thoughts of death and dying. The likelihood of depression varies with the situation the person is in, and is more likely when the elderly person is away from his or her family in a novel setting. For example, some 20 percent of nursing home residents are depressed. Depression is also antagonized by serious medical conditions that elderly men and women may have. Correspondingly, depression is commonly associated with illnesses like cancer, heart attack, and stroke. Depression often goes undiagnosed and untreated in the elderly and is something that caregivers (spouse, children, family, and friends) should be especially watchful for given the relationship between depression and suicide.

CONCLUSIONS

Many people still carry the misperception that depression is either a character flaw, a problem that happens because of personal weaknesses, or is completely "in the head." As described above, there are psychological, physiological, and societal components to depression. Most importantly, it is something that can and should be treated. There are too few people who see a doctor when they recognize symptoms of depression or think of getting medical treatment for it. Depression is so prevalent that it is often seen as a natural component of life events like pregnancy and old age, and depressed mothers and elderly men and women often do not get the attention they need. Today, much more is known about the causes and treatment of this mental-health problem, with the best form of treatment being a combination of medication and psychotherapy. Depression need not be "the end."

REFERENCES

Abraham, Karl 1968 "Notes on the Psychoanalytic Investigation and Treatment of Manic-Depressive Insanity and Allied Conditions" (1911). In K. Abraham, ed., *Selected Papers of Karl Abraham*. New York: Basic Books.

Abramson, Lauren, Y., G. I. Metalsky, and L. B. Alloy 1989 "Hopelessness Depression: A Theory-Based Subtype of Depression." *Psychological Review* 96:358–372.

American Psychiatric Association 1994 *Diagnostic and Statistical Manual of Mental Disorders: DSM-IV*, 4th ed. Washington, D.C. : American Psychiatric Association.

Beck, Aaron T. 1967 *Depression: Clinical, Experimental and Theoretical Aspects*. New York: Harper and Row.

Beckham, E. E., and W. R. Leber (eds.) 1995 *Handbook of Depression: An Updated Review and Integration*, 2nd ed. New York: Guilford.

Bowlby, John 1988 *A Secure Base: Parent-Child Attachment and Healthy Human Development*. New York: Basic Books.

Brown, G. W., and T. O. Harris 1978 *Social Origins of Depression*. London: Free Press.

Endler, Norman S. 1990 *Holiday of Darkness: A Psychologist's Personal Journey Out of His Depression*. New York: John Wiley and Sons.

Freud, S. 1957 "Mourning and Melancholia" (1917). In J. Strachey, ed., *The Standard Edition of the Complete Psychological Works of Sigmund Freud*, vol 14. London: Hogarth.

Gotlib, Ian H., and Constance L. Hammen 1992 *Psychological Aspects of Depression: Toward a Cognitive-Interpersonal Integration*. New York: John Wiley and Sons.

Hammen, Constance 1997 *Depression*. Hove, East Sussex, Eng.: Psychology Press.

Honig, A., and H. M. van Praag (eds.) 1997 *Depression: Neurobiological, Psychopathological, and Therapeutic Advances*. New York: John Wiley and Sons.

Linde K., G. Ramirez, C. D. Mulrow, A. Pauls, W. Weidenhammer, and D. Melchart 1996 "St. John's Wort for Depression: A Meta-Analysis of Randomized Clinical Trials." *British Medical Journal*, 313, 253.

Nemeroff, Charles B. 1998 "The Neurobiology of Depression." *Scientific American* 278:42–49.

Nolen-Hoeksema, Susan 1995 "Epidemiology and Theories of Gender Differences in Unipolar Depression." In M. V. Seeman, ed., *Gender and Psychopathology*, 63–87. Washington, D.C.: American Psychiatric Press.

——, and J. S. Girgus 1994 "The Emergence of Gender Differences in Depression During Adolescence." *Psychological Bulletin* 115:424–443.

Pearlin, L. I., and C. Schooler 1978 "The Structure of Coping." *Journal of Health and Social Behavior* 19:2–21.

Sarason, Irwin G., and Barbara R. Sarason 1999 *Abnormal Psychology: The Problem of Maladaptive Behavior*, 9th ed. Upper Saddle River, N.J.: Prentice-Hall.

Schildkraut, J. J., and A. Otero (eds.) 1996 *Depression and the Spiritual in Modern Art: Homage to Miro*, 112–130. New York: John Wiley and Sons.

Seligman, Martin E. P. 1975 *Helplessness: On Depression, Development and Death*. San Francisco: Freeman.

Styron, William 1990 *Darkness Visible: A Memoir of Madness*. New York: Random House.

Turner, R. J., B. Wheaton, and D. A. Lloyd 1995 "The Epidemiology of Social Stress." *American Sociological Review* 60:104–125.

REGAN A. R. GURUNG, PH. D.

DESCRIPTIVE STATISTICS

Descriptive statistics include data distribution and the summary information of the data. Researchers use descriptive statistics to organize and describe the data of a sample or population. The characteristics of the sample are statistics while those of the population are parameters. Descriptive statistics are usually used to describe the characteristics of a sample. The procedure and methods to infer the statistics to parameters are the statistical inference. Descriptive statistics do not include statistical inference.

Though descriptive statistics are usually used to examine the distribution of single variables, they may also be used to measure the relationship of two or more variables. That is, descriptive statistics may refer to either univariate or bivariate relationship. Also, the level of the measurement of a variable, that is, nominal, ordinal, interval, and ratio level, can influence the method chosen.

DATA DISTRIBUTION

To describe a set of data effectively, one should order the data and examine the distribution. An eyeball examination of the array of small data is often sufficient. For a set of large data, the aids of tables and graphs are necessary.

Tabulation. The table is expressed in counts or rates. The *frequency table* can display the distribution of one variable. It lists attributes, categories, or intervals with the number of observations reported. Data expressed in the frequency distribution are *grouped data*. To examine the central tendency and dispersion of large data, using grouped data is easier than using ungrouped data. Data usually are categorized into intervals that are mutually exclusive. One case or data point falls into one category only. Displaying frequency distribution of quantitative or continuous variables by intervals is especially efficient. For example, the frequency distribution of age in an imaginary sample can be seen in Table 1.

Here, age has been categorized into five intervals, i.e., 15 and below, 16–20, 21–25, 26–30, and 31–35, and they are mutually exclusive. Any age falls into one category only. This display is very efficient for understanding the age distribution in our imaginary sample. The distribution shows that twenty cases are aged fifteen or younger, twenty-five cases are sixteen to twenty years old, thirty-six cases are twenty-one to twenty-five years old, twenty cases are twenty-six to thirty years old, and nineteen cases are thirty-one to thirty-five years old. To compare categories or intervals and to

compare various samples or populations, the reporting percent or relative frequency of each category is important. The third column shows the percent of sample in each interval or category. For example, 30 percent of the sample falls into the range of twenty-one to twenty-five years old. The fourth column shows the proportion of observation for each interval or category. The proportion was called *relative frequency*. The cumulative frequency, the cumulative percent, and the cumulative relative frequency are other common elements in frequency tabulation. They are the sum of counts, percents, or proportions below or equal to the corresponding category or interval. For instance, the cumulative frequency of age thirty shows 101 persons or 84.2 percent of the sample age thirty or younger.

The frequency distribution displays one variable at a time. To study the *joint distribution* of two or more variables, we cross-tabulate them first. For example, the joint distribution of age and sex in the imaginary sample can be expressed in Table 2.

This table is a two-dimensional table: age is the column variable and sex is the row variable. We call this table a "two-by-five" table: two categories for sex and five categories for age. The marginal frequency can be seen as the frequency distribution of the corresponding variables. For example, there are fifty seven men in this sample. The marginal frequency for age is called *column frequency* and the marginal frequency for sex is called *row frequency*. The joint frequency of age and sex is *cell frequency*. For example, there are seventeen women twenty-one to twenty-five years old in this sample. The second number in each cell is *column percentage*; that is, the cell frequency divided by the column frequency and times 100 percent. For example, 47 percent in the group of twenty-one to twenty-five year olds are women. The third number in each cell is *row percentage*; that is, the cell frequency divided by the row frequency. For example, 27 percent of women are twenty-one to twenty-five years old. The *marginal frequency* can be seen as the frequency distribution of the corresponding variables. The row and column percentages are useful in examining the distribution of on variable conditioning on the other variable.

Charts and Graphs. Charts and graphs are efficient ways to show data distribution. Popular

Age Distribution of an Imaginary Sample

Codes	Frequency	Percent	Relative Frequency	Cumulative Frequency	Cumulative Percent
15 and below	20	16.7	.17	20	16.7
16–20	25	20.8	.21	45	37.5
21–25	36	30.0	.30	81	67.5
26–30	20	16.7	.17	101	84.2
31–35	19	15.8	.16	120	100
Total	**120**	**100**	**1.0**		

Table 1

graphs for single variables are *bar graphs, histograms,* and *stem-and-leaf plots.* The bar graph shows the relative frequency distribution of discrete variables. A bar is drawn over each category with height of the bar representing the relative frequency of observations in that category. The histogram can be seen as a bar graph for the continuous variable. By connecting the midpoints of tops of all bars, a histogram becomes the *frequency polygon.* Histograms effectively show the shape of the distribution.

Stem-and-leaf plots represent each observation by its higher digit(s) and its lowest digit. The value of higher digits is the stem while the value of the final digit of each observation is the leaf. The stem-and-leaf plot conveys the same information as the bar graph or histogram. Additionally, it tells the exact value of each observation. Despite providing more information than bar graphs and histograms, stem-and-leaf plots are used mostly for small data.

Other frequently used graphs include *line graphs, ogives,* and *scatter plots.* Line graphs and ogives show the relationship between time and the variable. The line graph usually shows trends. The ogive is a form of a line graph for cumulative relative frequency or percentage. It is commonly used for survival data. The scatter plot shows the relationship between variables. In a two-dimensional scatter plot, *x* and *y* axises label values of the data. Conventionally, we use the horizontal axis (*x*-axis) for the explanatory variable and use the vertical axis (*y*-axis) for the outcome variable. The plain is naturally divided into four areas by two axises. For continuous variables, the value at the joint point of two axises is zero. When the *x*-axis

goes to the right or *y*-axis goes up, the value ascends; when the *x*-axis goes to the left or *y*-axis goes down, the value descends. The data points, determined by the joint attributes of the variables, are scattered in four areas or along the axises.

SUMMARY STATISTICS

We may use measures of central tendency and dispersion to summarize the data. To measure the central tendency of a distribution is to measure its center or typicality. To measure the dispersion of a distribution is to measure its variation, heterogeneity, or deviation.

Central Tendency. Three popular measures of the central tendency are *mean, median,* and *mode.* The arithmetic mean or average is computed by taking the sum of the values and dividing by the number of the values. It is the balanced point of the sample or population weighted by values. Mean is an appropriate measure for continuous (ratio or interval) variables. However, the information might be misleading because the arithmetic mean is sensitive to the extreme value or outliers in a distribution. For example, the ages of five students are 21, 19, 20, 18, and 20. The ages of another five students are 53, 9, 12, 13, and 11. Though their distributions are very different, the mean age for both groups is 19.6.

Median is the value or attribute of the central case in an ordered distribution. If the number of cases is even, the median is the arithmetic average of the central two cases. In an ordered age distribution of thirty-five persons, the median is the age of the eighteenth person, while, in a distribution of thirty-six persons, the median is the average age of

Age

Sex	15 and below	16–20	21-25	26–30	31-25	Total
Male	9	12	19	9	8	57
	45.0%	48.0%	52.8%	45.0%	42.1%	47.5%
	15.8%	21.1%	33.3%	15.8%	14.0%	
Female	11	13	17	11	11	63
	55.0%	52.0%	47.2%	55.0%	57.9%	52.5%
	17.5%	20.6%	27.0%	17.5%	17.5%	
	20	25	36	20	19	120
Total	16.7%	20.8%	30.0%	16.7%	15.8%	100%

Table 2

the seventeenth and eighteenth persons. The median, like mean, can only tell the value of the physical center in an array of numbers, but cannot tell the dispersion. For example, the median of 21, 30, 45, and 100 is 27.5 and the median of 0, 27, 28, and 29 is also 27.5, but the two distributions are different. The mode is the most common value, category, or attribute in a distribution. Like the median, the mode has its limitations. For a set of values of 0, 2, 2, 4, 4, 4, 4, 5, and 10, the mode is four. For a set of values of 0, 0, 1, 4, 4, 4, 5, and 6, the mode is also four. One cannot tell one distribution from the other simply by examining the mode or median alone. The mode and median can be used to describe the central tendency of both continuous and discrete variables, and values of mode and median are less affected by the extreme value or the outlier than the mean.

One may also use upper and lower quartiles and percentiles to measure the central tendency. The n percentile is a number such that n percent of the distribution falls below it and $(100-n)$ percent falls above it. The lower quartile is the twenty-fifth percentile, the upper quartile is the seventy-fifth percentile, and the median is the fiftieth percentile. For example, the lower quartile or the twenty-fifth percentile is two and the upper quartile or the seventy-fifth percentile is seven for a set of values of 1, 2, 3, 4, 5, 6, 7, and 8. Apparently, the upper and lower quartiles and the percentiles can provide more information about a distribution than the other measures of the central tendency.

Dispersion. The central tendency per se does not provide much information on the distribution. Yet the combination of measures of central tendency and dispersion becomes useful to study a distribution. The most popular measures of dispersion are *range, standard deviation*, and *variance*. Range is the crude measure of a distribution from the highest value to the lowest value or the difference between the highest and the lowest values. For example, the range for a set of values of 1, 2, 3, 4, and 5 is one to five. The range is sensitive to the extreme value and may not provide sufficient information about the distribution. Alternatively, the dispersion can be measured by the distance between the mean and each value. The standard deviation is defined as the square root of the arithmetic mean of the squared deviation from the mean. For example, the standard deviation for a set of values of 1, 2, 3, 4, and 5 is 1.44. We take the square root of the squared deviation from the mean because the sum of the deviation from the mean is always zero. The variance is the square of the standard deviation. The variance is two in the previous array of numbers. The standard deviation is used as a standardized unit in statistical inference. Comparing with standard deviation, the unit of the variance is not substantively meaningful. It is, however, valuable to explain the relationship between variables. Mathematically, the variance defines the area of the normal curve while the standard deviation defines the average distance between the mean and each data point. Since they are derived from the distance from the mean, standard deviation and variance are sensitive to the extreme values.

The *interquartile range* (IQR) and *mean absolute deviation* (MAD) are also commonly used to measure the dispersion. The IQR is defined as the difference between the first and third quartiles. It is more stable than the range. MAD is the average absolute values of the deviation of the observations from the mean. As standard deviation, MAD can avoid the problem that the sum of the deviation from the mean is zero, but it is not as useful in statistical inference as variance and standard deviation.

Bivariate Relationship. One may use the *covariance* and *correlation coefficients* to measure the direction and size of a relationship between two variables. The covariance is defined as the average product of the deviation from the mean between two variables. It also reports the extent to which the variables may vary together. On average, while one variable deviates one unit from the mean, the covariance tells the extent to which the corresponding value of the other variable may deviate from its own mean. A positive covariance suggests that, while the value of one variable increases, that of the other variable tends to increase. A negative covariance suggests that, while the value of one variable increases, that of the other variable tends to decrease. The correlation coefficient is defined as the ratio of the covariance to the product of the standard deviations of two variables. It can also be seen as a covariance rescaled by the standard deviation of both variables. The value of the correlation coefficient ranges from −1 to 1, where zero means no correlation, −1 means perfectly negatively related, and 1 means perfectly positively related. The covariance and correlation are measures of the bivariate relationship between continuous variables. Many measures of association between categorical variables are calculated using cell frequencies or percentages in the cross-tabulation, for example, Yule's Q, phi, Goodman's tau, Goodman's gamma, and Somer's d. Though measures of association alone show the direction and size of a bivariate relationship, it is statistical inference to test the existence of such a relationship.

RELATIONSHIPS BETWEEN GRAPHS AND SUMMARY STATISTICS

The *box plot* is a useful tool to summarize the statistics and distribution. The box plot is consisted of a rectangular divided box and two extended lines attached to the ends of the box. The ends of the box define the upper and lower quartiles. The range of the distribution on each side is shown by an extended line attached to each quartile. A line

dividing the box shows the median. The plot can be placed vertically or horizontally. The box plot became popular because it can express the center and spread of the data simultaneously. Several boxes may be placed next to one another for comparison.

The order of mode, median, and mean is related to the shape of the distribution of a continuous variable. If mean, median, and mode are equal to each other, the shape of the histogram approximates a bell curve. However, a uniform distribution, in which all cases are equally distributed among all values and three measures of the central tendency are equal to each other, has a square shape with the width as the range and the height as the counts or relative frequency. In a bimodal distribution, two modes are placed in two ends of the distribution equally distanced from the center where the median and the mean are placed. We seldom see the true bell-curved, uniform, and bimodal distributions. Most of the distributions are more or less skewed to the left or to the right. If the mean is greater than median and the median is greater than mode, the shape is skewed to the right. If the mean is smaller than the median, and the median is smaller than the mode, the shape is skewed to the left. The outliers mainly lead the direction.

The shape and direction of the scatter plot can diagnose the relationship of two variables. When the distribution directs from the upper-right side to the lower-left side, the correlation coefficient is positive; when it directs from the upper-left side to the lower-right side, the correlation coefficient is negative. The correlation of a loosely scattered plot is weaker than that of a tightly scattered plot. A three-dimensional scatter plot can be used to show a bivariate relationship and its frequency distribution or a relationship of three variables. The former is commonly seen as a graph to examine a joint distribution.

Descriptive statistics is the first step in studying the data distribution. In omitting this step, one might misuse the advanced methods and thus be led to wrong estimates and conclusions. Some summary statistics such as standard deviation, variance, mean, correlation, and covariance, are also essential elements in statistical inference and advanced statistical methods.

REFERENCES

Agresti, Alan, and Barbara Finlay 1997 *Statistical Methods for the Social Sciences*, 3rd ed. New York: Simon & Schuster.

Blalock, Jr., Hubert M. 1979 *Social Statistics*, rev. 2nd ed. New York: McGraw-Hill.

Johnson, Allan G. 1988 *Statistics*. New York: Harcourt Brace Jovanovich.

Wonnacott, Thomas H., and Ronald J. Wonnacott 1990 *Introductory Statistics*. 5th ed. New York: John Wiley & Sons, Inc.

DAPHNE KUO

DEVIANCE

See Alienation; Anomie; Criminalization of Deviance; Deviance Theories; Legislation of Morality.

DEVIANCE THEORIES

Since its inception as a discipline, sociology has studied the causes of deviant behavior, examining why some persons conform to social rules and expectations and why others do not. Typically, sociological theories of deviance reason that aspects of individuals' social relationships and the social areas in which they live and work assist in explaining the commission of deviant acts. This emphasis on social experiences, and how they contribute to deviant behavior, contrasts with the focus on the internal states of individuals taken by disciplines such as psychology and psychiatry.

Sociological theories are important in understanding the roots of social problems such as crime, violence, and mental illness and in explaining how these problems may be remedied. By specifying the causes of deviance, the theories reveal how aspects of the social environment influence the behavior of individuals and groups. Further, the theories suggest how changes in these influences may yield changes in levels of deviant behaviors. If a theory specifies that a particular set of factors cause deviant behavior, then it also implies that eliminating or altering those factors in the environment will change levels of deviance. By developing policies or measures that are informed by sociological theories, government agencies or programs focused on problems like crime or violence are more likely to yield meaningful reductions in criminal or violent behavior.

Despite their importance, deviance theories disagree about the precise causes of deviant acts. Some look to the structure of society and groups or geographic areas within society, explaining deviance in terms of broad social conditions in which deviance is most likely to flourish. Others explain deviant behavior using the characteristics of individuals, focusing on those characteristics that are most highly associated with learning deviant acts. Other theories view deviance as a social status conferred by one group or person on others, a status that is imposed by persons or groups in power in order to protect their positions of power. These theories explain deviance in terms of differentials in power between individuals or groups.

This chapter reviews the major sociological theories of deviance. It offers an overview of each major theory, summarizing its explanation of deviant behavior. Before reviewing the theories, however, it may prove useful to describe two different dimensions of theory that will structure our discussion. The first of these, the *level of explanation*, refers to the scope of the theory and whether it focuses on the behavior and characteristics of individuals or on the characteristics of social aggregates such as neighborhoods, cities, or other social areas. *Micro-level* theories stress the individual, typically explaining deviant acts in terms of personal characteristics of individuals or the immediate social context in which deviant acts occur. In contrast, *macro-level* theories focus on social aggregates or groups, looking to the structural characteristics of areas in explaining the origins of deviance, particularly rates of deviance among those groups.

Theories of deviance also vary in relation to a second dimension, *causal focus*. This dimension divides theories into two groups, those that explain the social origins of norm violations and those explaining societal reactions to deviance. *Social origin* theories focus on the causes of norm violations. Typically, these theories identify aspects of the social environment that trigger norm violations; social conditions in which the violations are most likely to occur. In contrast, *social reaction* theories argue that deviance is often a matter of social construction, a status imposed by one person or group on others and a status that ultimately may influence the subsequent behavior of the designated deviant. Social reaction theories argue that some individuals and groups may be designated or labeled as deviant and that the process of labeling may trap or engulf those individuals or groups in a deviant social role.

These two dimensions offer a four-fold scheme for classifying types of deviance theories. The first, *macro-level origin theories*, focus on the causes of norm violations associated with broad structural conditions in the society. These theories typically examine the influences of such structural characteristics of populations or communities like the concentration of poverty, levels of community integration, or the density and age distribution of the population on areal rates of deviance. The theories have clear implications for public policies to reduce levels of deviance. Most often, the theories highlight the need for altering structural characteristics of society, such as levels of poverty, that foster deviant behavior.

The second, *micro-level origin theories* focus on the characteristics of the deviant and his or her immediate social environment. These theories typically examine the relationship between a person's involvement in deviance and such characteristics as the influence of peers and significant others, persons' emotional stakes in conformity, their beliefs about the propriety of deviance and conformity, and their perceptions of the threat of punishments for deviant acts. In terms of their implications for public policy, micro-level origin theories emphasize the importance of assisting individuals in resisting negative peer influences while also increasing their attachment to conforming lifestyles and activities.

A third type of theories may be termed *micro-level reaction theories*. These accord importance to those aspects of interpersonal reactions that may seriously stigmatize or label the deviant and thereby reinforce her or his deviant social status. According to these theories, reactions to deviance may have the unintended effect of increasing the likelihood of subsequent deviant behavior. Because labeling may increase levels of deviance, micro-level reaction theories argue that agencies of social control (e.g. police, courts, correctional systems) should adopt policies of "nonintervention."

Finally, *macro-level reaction theories* emphasize broad structural conditions in society that are associated with the designation of entire groups or segments of the society as deviant. These theories tend to stress the importance of structural characteristics of populations, groups, or geographic areas, such as degrees of economic inequality or concentration of political power within communities or the larger society. According to macro-level reaction theories, powerful groups impose the status of deviant as a mechanism for controlling those groups that represent the greatest political, economic, or social threat to their position of power. The theories also imply that society can only achieve reduced levels of deviance by reducing the levels of economic and political inequality in society.

The rest of this article is divided into sections corresponding to each of these four "types" of deviance theory. The article concludes with a discussion of new directions for theory—the development of explanations that cut across and integrate different theory types and the elaboration of existing theories through greater specification of the conditions under which those theories apply.

MACRO-LEVEL ORIGINS OF DEVIANCE

Theories of the macro-level origins of deviance look to the broad, structural characteristics of society, and groups within society, to explain deviant behavior. Typically, these theories examine one of three aspects of social structure. The *first* is the pervasiveness and consequences of poverty in modern American society. Robert Merton's (1938) writing on American social structure and Richard Cloward and Lloyd Ohlin's (1960) subsequent work on urban gangs laid the theoretical foundation for this perspective. Reasoning that pervasive materialism in American culture creates unattainable aspirations for many segments of the population, Merton (1964) and others argue that there exists an environmental state of "strain" among the poor. The limited availability of legitimate opportunities for attaining material wealth forces the poor to adapt through deviance, either by achieving wealth through illegitimate means or by rejecting materialistic aspirations and withdrawing from society altogether.

According to this reasoning, deviance is a byproduct of poverty and a mechanism through which the poor may attain wealth, albeit illegitimately. Thus, "strain" theories of deviance interpret behaviors such as illegal drug selling, prostitution, and armed robbery as innovative adaptations to blocked opportunities for legitimate economic or occupational success. Similarly, the theories interpret violent crimes in terms of the frustrations of poverty, as acts of aggression triggered by those frustrations (Blau and Blau 1982). Much of the current research in this tradition is examining the exact mechanisms by which poverty and economic inequality influence rates of deviant behavior.

Although once considered a leading theory of deviance, strain theory has come under criticism for its narrow focus on poverty as the primary cause of deviant behavior. Recent efforts have sought to revise and extend the basic principles of the theory by expanding and reformulating ideas about strain. Robert Agnew (1992) has made the most notable revisions to the theory. His reformulation emphasizes social psychological, rather than structural, sources of strain. Agnew also broadens the concept of strain, arguing that poverty may be a source of strain, but it is not the *only* source. Three sources of strain are important: failure to achieve positively valued goals, removal of positively valued stimuli, and confrontation with negative stimuli. The first type of strain, failure to achieve positively valued goals, may be the result of a failure to live up to one's expectations or aspirations. Strain may also result if an individual feels that he or she is not being treated in a fair or just manner. The removal of a positively valued stimulus, such as the death of a family member or the loss of a boyfriend or girlfriend, can also result in strain. Finally, strain can also be produced by the presentation of negative stimuli, such as unpleasant school experiences. Thus, although this reformulation of strain theory retains the notion that deviance is often the result of strain, the concept of strain is broadened to include multiple sources of strain.

The second set of macro-level origin theories examine the role of culture in deviant behavior. Although not ignoring structural forces such as poverty in shaping deviance, this class of theories reasons that there may exist cultures within the larger culture that endorse or reinforce deviant values; deviant subcultures that produce higher rates of deviance among those segments of the population sharing subcultural values.

Subcultural explanations have their origin in two distinct sociological traditions. The first is writing on the properties of delinquent gangs that identifies a distinct lower-class culture of gang members that encourages aggression, thrill seeking, and antisocial behavior (e.g., Miller 1958). The second is writing on cultural conflict that recognizes that within complex societies there will occur contradictions between the conduct norms of different groups. Thorsten Sellin (1938) suggests that in heterogeneous societies several different subcultures may emerge, each with its own set of conduct norms. According to Sellin, the laws and norms applied to the entire society do not necessarily reflect cultural consensus but rather the values and beliefs of the dominant social groups.

Subcultural theories emerging from these two traditions argue that deviance is the product of a cohesive set of values and norms that favors deviant behavior and is endorsed by a segment of the general population. Perhaps most prominent among the theories is Marvin Wolfgang and Franco Ferracuti's (1967) writing on subcultures of criminal violence. Wolfgang and Ferracuti reason that there may exist a distinct set of beliefs and expectations within the society; a subculture that promotes and encourages violent interactions. According to Wolfgang and Ferracuti, this violent subculture is pervasive among blacks in the United States and may explain extremely high rates of criminal homicide among young black males.

Although Wolfgang and Ferracuti offer little material specifying the subculture's precise causes, or empirical evidence demonstrating the pervasiveness of subcultural beliefs, other writers have extended the theory by exploring the relationship between beliefs favoring violence and such factors as the structure of poverty in the United States (Curtis 1975; Messner 1983), the history of racial oppression of blacks (Silberman 1980), and ties to the rural South and a southern subculture of violence (Gastil 1971; Erlanger 1974). Even these writers, however, offer little empirical evidence of violent subcultures within U.S. society.

A third class of theories about the macro-level origins of deviance began with the work of sociologists at the University of Chicago in the 1920s. Unlike strain and subcultural theories, these stress the importance of the social integration of neighborhoods and communities—the degree to which neighborhoods are stable and are characterized by a homogenous set of beliefs and values—as a force influencing rates of deviant behavior. As levels of integration increase, rates of deviance decrease. Based in the early work of sociologists such as Clifford Shaw and Henry McKay, the theories point to the structure of social controls in neighborhoods, arguing that neighborhoods lacking in social controls are "disorganized," that is, areas in which there is a virtual vacuum of social norms. It is in this normative vacuum that deviance flourishes. Therefore, these theories view deviance as a property of areas or locations rather than specific groups of people.

Early writers in the "disorganization" tradition identified industrialization and urbanization as the causes of disorganized communities and neighborhoods. Witnessing immense growth in eastern cities such as Chicago, these writers argued that industrial and urban expansion create zones of disorganization within cities. Property owners move from the residential pockets on the edge of business and industrial areas and allow buildings to deteriorate in anticipation of the expansion of business and industry. This process of natural succession and change in cities disrupts traditional mechanisms of social control in neighborhoods. As property owners leave transitional areas, more mobile and diverse groups enter. But the added mobility and diversity of these groups translate into fewer primary relationships—families and extended kinship and friendship networks. And as the number of primary relationships decline, so will informal social controls in neighborhoods. Hence, rates of deviance will rise.

Recent writing from this perspective focuses on the mechanisms by which specific places in urban areas become the spawning grounds for deviant acts (Bursik and Webb 1982; Bursik 1984; and others). For example, Rodney Stark (1987) argues that high levels of population density are associated with particularly low levels of supervision of children. With little supervision, children perform poorly in school and are much less likely to develop "stakes in conformity"—that is, emotional and psychological investments in academic achievement and other conforming behaviors. Without such stakes, children and adolescents are much more likely to turn to deviant alternatives. Thus, according to Stark, rates of deviance will be high in densely populated areas because social controls in the form of parental supervision are either weak or entirely absent.

Similarly, Robert Crutchfield (1989) argues that the structure of work opportunities in areas may have the same effect. Areas characterized primarily by secondary-sector work opportunities—low pay, few career opportunities, and high employee turnover—may tend to attract and retain persons with few stakes in conventional behavior—a "situation of company" in which deviance is likely to flourish.

Recent writing from the disorganization perspective has also taken the form of ethnographies; qualitative studies of urban areas and the deviance producing dynamics of communities. As Sullivan (1989, p. 9) states, ethnographies describe the community "as a locus of interaction, intermediate between the individual and the larger society, where the many constraints and opportunities of the total society are narrowed to a subset within which local individuals choose." At the heart of Sullivan's argument is the idea that social networks in neighborhoods are important in understanding whether individuals are capable of finding meaningful opportunities for work. For example, youth were less likely to turn to crime in those neighborhoods where they could take advantage of family and neighborhood connections to blue collar jobs. Because of the greater employment opportunities in these neighborhoods, even youth who become involved in crime were less likely to persist in high-risk criminal behaviors.

Similarly, Jay MacLeod (1995) attempts to explain how the aspirations of youth living in urban areas have been "leveled," or reduced to the point where the youths have little hope for a better future. In an analysis of two urban gangs, MacLeod argues that the youths' family and work experiences, along with their relationships with their peers, help explain why a predominantly white gang had lower aspirations and engaged in more delinquent and antisocial behavior than the other gang, predominantly comprised of African Americans. According to MacLeod, the parents of white youth were much less likely to discipline their children or to encourage them to achieve and do well in school. Also, white youth had more experience on the job market than the African American youth. This contributed to a more pessimistic outlook and a lowering of their future aspirations.

Finally, MacLeod argues that the white youths' immersion in a subculture, which emphasized rejecting the authority of the school, reinforced their negative attitudes to a much greater extent than the African American peer group.

In sum, theories of the macro-level origins of deviance argue that many of the causes of deviance may be found in the characteristics of groups within society, or in the characteristics of geographic areas and communities. They offer explanations of group and areal differences in deviance—for example, why some cities have relatively higher rates of crime than other cities or why blacks have higher rates of serious interpersonal violence than other ethnic groups. These theories make no attempt to explain the behavior of individuals or the occurrence of individual deviant acts. Indeed, they reason that deviance is best understood as a property of an area, community, or group, regardless of the individuals living in the area or community, or the individuals comprising the group.

The theories' implications for public policy focus on the characteristics of geographic areas and communities that lead to deviance. The impact of change on neighborhoods, for example, can be reduced if the boundaries of residential areas are preserved. By preserving such boundaries, communities are less likely to become transitional neighborhoods that foster deviance and crime. Also, by maintaining residential properties people become invested in their own community, which helps foster the mechanisms of informal social control that make deviance less likely. Strengthening schools and other stabilizing institutions in neighborhoods, such as churches and community centers, can also contribute to a reduction in deviance. Finally, establishing networks for jobs and job placement in disadvantaged areas may increase the opportunities of employment among youth. If they succeed in increasing employment, the networks should decrease the chances that youth will turn to careers in crime.

MICRO-LEVEL ORIGINS OF DEVIANCE

Many explanations of deviance argue that its causes are rooted in the background or personal circumstances of the individual. Micro-level origin theories have developed over the past fifty years, identifying mechanisms by which ordinarily conforming individuals may become deviant. These theories assume the existence of a homogeneous, pervasive set of norms in society and proceed to explain why persons or entire groups of persons violate the norms. There exist two important traditions within this category of theories. The first tradition involves "social learning theories"—explanations that focus on the mechanisms through which people learn the techniques and attitudes favorable to committing deviant acts. The second tradition involves "social control theories"—explanations that emphasize factors in the social environment that regulate the behavior of individuals, thereby preventing the occurrence of deviant acts.

Edwin Sutherland's (1947) theory of differential association laid the foundation for learning theories. At the heart of this theory is the assumption that deviant behavior, like all other behaviors, is learned. Further, this learning occurs within intimate personal groups—networks of family members and close friends. Thus, according to these theories individuals learn deviance from persons closest to them. Sutherland specified a process of differential association, reasoning that persons become deviant in association with deviant others. Persons learn from others the techniques of committing deviant acts and attitudes favorable to the commission of those acts. Further, Sutherland reasoned that persons vary in their degree of association with deviant others; persons regularly exposed to close friends and family members who held beliefs favoring deviance and who committed deviant acts would be much more likely than others to develop those same beliefs and commit deviant acts.

Sutherland's ideas about learning processes have played a lasting role in micro-level deviance theories. Central to his perspective is the view that beliefs and values favoring deviance are a primary cause of deviant behavior. Robert Burgess and Ronald Akers (1966) and subsequently Akers (1985) extended Sutherland's ideas, integrating them with principles of operant conditioning. Reasoning that learning processes may best be understood in terms of the concrete rewards and punishments given for behavior, Burgess and Akers argue that deviance is learned through associations with others and through a system of rewards and punishments, imposed by close friends and relatives, for participation in deviant acts. Subsequent empirical studies offer compelling support for elements of learning theory (Matsueda 1982; Akers et al. 1979; Matsueda and Heimer 1987).

Some examples may be useful at this point. According to the theory of differential association, juveniles develop beliefs favorable to the commission of delinquent acts and knowledge about the techniques of committing deviant acts from their closest friends, typically their peers. Thus, sufficient exposure to peers endorsing beliefs favoring deviance who also have knowledge about the commission of deviant acts will cause the otherwise conforming juvenile to commit deviant acts. Thus, if adolescent peer influences encourage smoking, drinking alcohol, and other forms of drug abuse—and exposure to these influences occurs frequently, over a long period of time, and involves relationships that are important to the conforming adolescent—then he or she is likely to develop beliefs and values favorable to committing these acts. Once those beliefs and values develop, he or she is likely to commit the acts.

The second class of micro-level origin theories, control theories, explores the causes of deviance from an altogether different perspective. Control theories take for granted the existence of a cohesive set of norms shared by most persons in the society and reason that most persons want to and will typically conform to these prevailing social norms. The emphasis in these theories, unlike learning theories, is on the factors that bond individuals to conforming lifestyles. The bonds act as social and psychological constraints on the individual, binding persons to normative conformity (Toby 1957; Hirschi 1969). People deviate from norms when these bonds to conventional lifestyles are weak, and hence, when they have little restraining influence over the individual. Among control theorists, Travis Hirschi (1969) has made the greatest contributions to our knowledge about bonding processes and deviant behavior. Writing on the causes of delinquency, he argued that four aspects of bonding are especially relevant to control theory: emotional attachments to conforming others, psychological commitments to conformity, involvements in conventional activities, and beliefs consistent with conformity to prevailing norms.

Among the most important of the bonding elements are emotional attachments individuals may have to conforming others and commitments to conformity—psychological investments or stakes people hold in a conforming lifestyle. Those having weak attachments—that is, people who are insensitive to the opinions of conforming others—and who have few stakes in conformity, in the form of commitments to occupation or career and education, are more likely than others to deviate (see, e.g., Paternoster et al. 1983; Thornberry and Christenson 1984; Liska and Reed 1985). In effect, these individuals are "free" from the constraints that ordinarily bond people to normative conformity. Conversely, individuals concerned about the opinions of conforming others and who have heavy psychological investments in work or school will see the potential consequences of deviant acts—rejection by friends or loss of a job—as threatening or costly, and consequently will refrain from those acts.

A related concern is the role of sanctions in preventing deviant acts. Control theorists like Hirschi reason that most people are utilitarian in their judgments about deviant acts, and thus evaluate carefully the risks associated with each act. Control theories typically maintain that the threat of sanctions actually prevents deviant acts when the risks outweigh the gains. Much of the most recent writing on sanctions and their effects has stressed the importance of perceptual processes in decisions to commit deviant acts (Gibbs 1975, 1977; Tittle 1980; Paternoster et al. 1982, 1987; Piliavin et al. 1986; Matsueda, Piliavin, and Gartner 1988). At the heart of this perspective is the reasoning that individuals perceiving the threat of sanctions as high are much more likely to refrain from deviance than those perceiving the threat as low, regardless of the actual level of sanction threat.

Writing from the social control perspective attempts to build on and extend the basic assumptions and propositions of control theory. Michael Gottfredson, in conjunction with Hirschi, has developed a general theory of crime that identifies "low self-control," as opposed to diminished social control, as the primary cause of deviant behavior (Hirschi and Gottfredson 1987; Gottfredson and Hirschi 1990). Arguing that all people are inherently self-interested, pursuing enhancement of personal pleasure and avoiding pain, Gottfredson and Hirschi suggest that most crimes, and for that matter most deviant acts, are the result of choices to maximize pleasure, minimize pain, or both.

Crimes occur when opportunities to maximize personal pleasure are high and when the certainty of painful consequences is low. Further, people who pursue short-term gratification with little consideration for the long-term consequences of their actions are most prone to criminal behavior. In terms of classical control theory, these are individuals who have weak bonds to conformity or who disregard or ignore the potentially painful consequences of their actions. They are "relatively unable or unwilling to delay gratification; they are indifferent to punishment and the interests of others" (Hirschi and Gottfredson 1987, pp. 959–960).

Building on traditional control theory, Charles Tittle (1995) reasons that it helps explain why individuals conform, but it also helps to explain why they engage in deviant behavior. Tittle (1995, p. 135) argues that "the amount of control to which an individual is subject, relative to the amount of control he or she can exercise, determines the probability of deviance occurring as well as the type of deviance likely to occur." Conformity results when individuals are subjected to and exert roughly equal amounts of control—there is "control balance." According to Tittle, however, individuals who are subjected to more control than they exert will be motivated to engage in deviance in order to escape being controlled by others.

Robert Sampson and John Laub (1993) have also expanded on the basic propositions of control theory. In their research, Sampson and Laub focus on stability and change in the antisocial behavior of individuals as they grow from juveniles to adults. Sampson and Laub argue that family, school, and peer relationships influence the likelihood of deviant behavior among juveniles. In particular, Sampson and Laub argue that the structure of the family (e.g., residential mobility, family size) affects family context or process (e.g., parental supervision, discipline), which, in turn, makes deviance among children more or less likely. Many adolescent delinquents grow up to become adult criminals because their juvenile delinquency makes the formation of adult social bonds to work and family less likely. Despite this continuity in antisocial behavior from adolescence to adulthood, however, Sampson and Laub argue that many juvenile delinquents do not commit deviant acts as adults because they develop adult social bonds, such as attachment to a spouse or commitment to a job.

In sum, micro-level origin theories look to those aspects of the individual's social environment that influence her or his likelihood of deviance. Learning theories stress the importance of deviant peers and other significant individuals, and their impact on attitudes and behaviors favorable to the commission of deviant acts. These theories assume that the social environment acts as an agent of change, transforming otherwise conforming individuals into deviants through peer influences. People exposed to deviant others frequently and sufficiently, like persons exposed to a contagious disease who become ill, will become deviant themselves. Control theories avoid this "contagion" model, viewing the social environment as a composite of controls and restraints cementing the individual to a conforming lifestyle. Deviance occurs when elements of the bond—aspects of social control—are weak or broken, thereby freeing the individual to violate social norms. Sanctions and the threat of sanctions are particularly important to control theories, a central part of the calculus that rational actors use in choosing to commit or refrain from committing deviant acts.

The policy implications of micro-level origin theories are obvious. If, as learning theories argue, deviance is learned through association with deviant peers, then the way to eliminate deviance is to assist youths in resisting deviant peer influences and helping them to develop attitudes that disapprove of deviant behavior. Control theories, on the other hand, suggest that deviance can be reduced with programs that help families develop stronger bonds between parents and children. Control theory also implies that programs that help youths develop stronger commitments to conventional lines of activity and to evaluate the costs and benefits of deviant acts will also result in a reduction of problematic behavior.

MICRO-LEVEL REACTIONS TO DEVIANCE

Unlike micro-level origin theories, micro-level reaction theories make no assumptions about the existence of a homogeneous, pervasive set of norms in society. These theories take an altogether different approach to explaining deviant behavior, viewing deviance as a matter of definition; a social status imposed by individuals or groups on others. Most argue that there exists no single pervasive set of norms in society and that deviant behavior may best be understood in terms of norms and their enforcement. These theories typically stress the importance of labeling processes—the mechanisms by which acts become defined or labeled as "deviant—and the consequences of labeling for the person so labeled. Many of these theories are concerned with the development of deviant lifestyles or careers; long-term commitments to deviant action.

One of the most important writers in this tradition is Howard Becker (1963). Becker argues that deviance is not a property inherent in any particular form of behavior but rather a property conferred on those behaviors by audiences witnessing them. Becker (1963, p. 9) notes that ". . . deviance is *not* a quality of the act the person commits, but rather a consequence of the application by others of rules and sanctions to an 'offender.' The deviant is one to whom that label has been successfully applied; deviant behavior is behavior that people so label." Thus, Becker and others in this tradition orient the study of deviance on rules and sanctions, and the application of labels. Their primary concern is the social construction of deviance—that is, how some behaviors and classes of people come to be defined as "deviant" by others observing and judging the behavior.

Building on the idea that deviance is a property conferred on behavior that is witnessed by a social audience, Becker (1963) also developed a simple typology of deviant behavior. The dimensions upon which the typology is based are whether or not the individual is perceived as deviant and whether or not the behavior violates any rule. *Conforming* behavior is behavior that does not violate any rules and is not perceived as deviant. Individuals in the opposite scenario, in which the person both violates rules and is perceived by others as deviant, Becker labeled *pure deviants*. Some individuals, according to Becker, may be perceived as deviant, even though they have not violated any rules. Becker identified these individuals as the *falsely accused*. Finally, the *secret deviant* is one who has violated the rules, but, nonetheless, is not perceived by others as being deviant.

Equally important is the work of Edwin Lemert (1951). Stressing the importance of labeling to subsequent deviant behavior, he argues that repetitive deviance may arise from social reactions to initial deviant acts. According to Lemert (1951, p. 287), deviance may often involve instances where "a person begins to employ his deviant behavior. . . as a means of defense, attack or adjustment to the. . . problems created by the consequent social reactions to him." Therefore, a cause of deviant careers is negative social labeling; instances where reactions to initial deviant acts are harsh and reinforce a "deviant" self-definition. Such labeling forces the individual into a deviant social role, organizing his or her identity around a pattern of deviance that structures a way of life and perpetuates deviant behavior (Becker 1963; Schur 1971, 1985).

Perhaps the most significant developments in this tradition have contributed to knowledge about the causes of mental illness. Proponents of micro-level reaction theories argue that the label "mental illness" can be so stigmatizing to those labeled, especially when mental-health professionals impose the label, that they experience difficulty returning to nondeviant social roles. As a result, the labeling process may actually exacerbate mental disorders. Former mental patients may find themselves victims of discrimination at work, in personal relationships, or in other social spheres (Scheff 1966). This discrimination, and the widespread belief that others devalue and discriminate against mental patients, may lead to self-devaluation and fear of social rejection by others (Link 1982, 1987). In some instances, this devaluation and fear may be associated with demoralization of the patient, loss of employment and personal income, and the persistence of mental disorders following treatment (Link 1987).

Hence, micro-level reaction theories reason that deviant behavior is rooted in the process by which persons define and label the behavior of others as deviant. The theories offer explanations of individual differences in deviance, stressing the importance of audience reactions to initial deviant acts. However, these theories make no attempt to explain the origins of the initial acts (Scheff 1966). Rather, they are concerned primarily with the development and persistence of deviant careers.

Micro-level reaction theories have very different implications for public policy than macro- and micro-level origins theories. Micro-level reaction theories argue that unwarranted labeling can lead to deviant careers. In effect, the reaction to deviance can cause deviant behavior to escalate. Thus, in order to reduce deviance, agencies of social control must adopt policies of nonintervention. Rather than being formally sanctioned and labeled as deviant, nonintervention policies must encourage diversion and deinstitutionalization. Formal sanctioning must be highly selective, focusing only on the most serious and threatening deviant acts.

MACRO-LEVEL REACTIONS TO DEVIANCE

The final class of theories looks to the structure of economic and political power in society as a cause of deviant behavior. Macro-level reaction theories—either Marxist or other conflict theories—view deviance as a status imposed by dominant social classes to control and regulate populations that threaten political and economic hegemony. Like micro-level reaction theories, these theories view deviance as a social construction and accord greatest importance to the mechanisms by which society defines and controls entire classes of behavior and people as deviant in order to mediate the threat. However, these theories reason that the institutional control of deviants has integral ties to economic and political order in society.

Marxist theories stress the importance of the economic structure of society and begin with the assumption that the dominant norms in capitalist societies reflect the interests of the powerful economic class; the owners of business. But contemporary Marxist writers (Quinney 1970, 1974, 1980; Spitzer 1975; Young 1983) also argue that modern capitalist societies are characterized by large "problem populations"—people who have become displaced from the workforce and alienated from the society. Generally, the problem populations include racial and ethnic minorities, the chronically unemployed, and the extremely impoverished. They are a burden to the society and particularly to the capitalist class because they create a form of social expense that must be carefully controlled if the economic order is to be preserved.

Marxist theories reason that economic elites use institutions such as the legal, mental-health, and welfare systems to control and manage society's problem populations. In effect, these institutions define and process society's problem populations as deviant in order to ensure effective management and control. In societies or communities characterized by rigid economic stratification, elites are likely to impose formal social control in order to preserve the prevailing economic order.

Conflict theories stress the importance of the political structure of society and focus on the degree of threat to the hegemony of political elites, arguing that elites employ formal social controls to regulate threats to political and social order (Turk 1976; Chambliss 1978; Chambliss and Mankoff 1976). According to these theories, threat varies in relation to the size of the problem population, with large problem populations substantially more threatening to political elites than small populations. Thus, elites in societies and communities in which those problem populations are large and perceived as especially threatening are more likely to process members of the problem populations as deviants than in areas where such problems are small.

Much of the writing in this tradition has addressed the differential processing of people defined as deviant. Typically, this writing has taken two forms. The first involves revisionist histories linking the development of prisons, mental asylums, and other institutions of social control to structural changes in U.S. and European societies. These histories demonstrate that those institutions often target the poor and chronically unemployed independent of their involvement in crime and other deviant acts, and thereby protect and serve the interests of dominant economic and political groups (Scull 1978; Rafter 1985).

A second and more extensive literature includes empirical studies of racial and ethnic disparities in criminal punishments. Among the most important of these studies is Martha Myers and Suzette Talarico's (1987) analysis of the social and structural contexts that foster racial and ethnic disparities in the sentencing of criminal offenders. Myers and Talarico's research, and other studies examining the linkages between community social structure and differential processing (Myers 1987, 1990; Peterson and Hagan 1984; Bridges, Crutchfield, and Simpson 1987; Bridges and Crutchfield 1988), demonstrate the vulnerability of minorities to differential processing during historical periods and in areas in which they are perceived by whites as serious threats to political and social order. In effect, minorities accused of crimes during these periods and in these geographic areas are perceived as threats to white hegemony, and therefore become legitimate targets for social control.

In addition to studying the connections between community social structure and the differential processing of racial and ethnic minorities, researchers have also begun to examine how court officials' perceptions of offenders can influence disparities in punishments. Bridges and Steen (1998), for example, show how court officials' perceptions of white and minority youths differ, and how these different perceptions contribute to different recommendations for sentencing. Probation officers often attribute the offenses of minority youths to internal characteristics of the youths (i.e., aspects of their personality), while attributing the offenses of white youths to external characteristics (i.e., aspects of their environments). As a result of these differential attributions, minority youths are perceived as more threatening, more at risk for re-offending than whites and more likely to receive severe recommendations for sentences.

Thus, macro-level reaction theories view deviance as a by-product of inequality in modern society, a social status imposed by powerful groups on those who are less powerful. Unlike micro-level reaction theories, these theories focus on the forms of inequality in society and how entire groups within the society are managed and controlled as deviants by apparatuses of the state. Like those theories, however, macro-level reaction theories make little or no attempt to explain the origins of deviant acts, claiming instead that the status of "deviant" is, in large part, a social construction designed primarily to protect the interests of the most powerful social groups. The primary concern of these theories is explicating the linkages between inequality in society and inequality in the labeling and processing of deviants.

Since macro-level reaction theories view deviance as a status imposed by powerful groups on those with less power, the most immediate policy implication of these theories is that imbalances in power and inequality must be reduced in order to reduce levels of deviance and levels of inequality in the sanctioning of deviance. More effective monitoring of government agencies that are used to control problem populations, such as the criminal justice system, can also help to reduce the disproportionate processing of less powerful groups, such as racial minorities, as deviant.

NEW THEORETICAL DIRECTIONS

A recurring issue in the study of deviance is the contradictory nature of many deviance theories. The theories often begin with significantly different assumptions about the nature of human behavior and end with significantly different conclusions about the causes of deviant acts. Some scholars maintain that the oppositional nature of these theories—the theories are developed and based on systematic rejection of other theories (Hirschi 1989)—tends toward clarity and internal consistency in reasoning about the causes of deviance. However, other scholars argue that this oppositional nature is intellectually divisive—acceptance of one theory precludes acceptance of another—and "has made the field seem fragmented, if not in disarray" (Liska, Krohn, and Messner 1989, p. 1).

A related and equally troublesome problem is the contradictory nature of much of the scientific evidence supporting deviance theories. For each theory, there exists a literature of studies that supports and a literature that refutes major arguments of the theory. And although nearly every theory of deviance may receive empirical confirmation at some level, virtually no theory of deviance is sufficiently comprehensive to withstand empirical falsification at some other level. The difficult task for sociologists is discerning whether and under what circumstances negative findings should be treated as negating a particular theory (Walker and Cohen 1985).

In recent years, these two problems have renewed sociologists' interest in deviance theory and, at the same time, suggested new directions for the development of theory. The oppositonal nature of theories has spawned interest in theoretical integration. Many scholars are dissatisfied with classical theories, arguing that their predictive power is exceedingly low (see Elliott 1985; Liska, Krohn, and Messner 1989). Limited to a few key explanatory variables, any one theory can explain only a limited range and amount of deviant behavior. And because most scholars reason that the causes of deviance are multiple and quite complex, most also contend that it may be "necessary to combine different theories to capture the entire range of causal variables" (Liska, Krohn, and Messner 1989, p. 4).

Because it combines the elements of different theories, the new theory will have greater explanatory power than theories from which it was derived. However, meaningful integration of deviance theories will require much more than the simple combination of variables. Scholars must first reconcile the oppositional aspects of theories, including many of their underlying assumptions about society, the motivations of human behavior, and the causes of deviant acts. For example, learning theories focus heavily on the motivations for deviance, stressing the importance of beliefs and values that "turn" the individual to deviant acts. In contrast, control theories accord little importance to such motivations, examining instead those aspects of the social environment that constrain people from committing deviant acts. Reconciling such differences is never an easy task, and in some instances may be impossible (Hirschi 1979).

The problem of contradictory evidence suggests a related but different direction for deviance theory. Theories may vary significantly in the conditions—termed *scope conditions*—under which they apply (Walker and Cohen 1985; Tittle 1975; Tittle and Curran 1988). Under some scope conditions, theories may find extensive empirical support, and under others virtually none. For instance, macro-level origin theories concerned with the frustrating effects of poverty on deviance may have greater applicability to people living in densely populated urban areas than those living in rural areas. The frustration of urban poverty may be much more extreme than in rural areas, even though the actual levels of poverty may be the same. As a result, the frustrations of urban poverty may be more likely to cause deviant adaptations in the form of violent crime, drug abuse, and vice than those of rural poverty. In this instance, "urbanness" may constitute a condition that activates strain theories linking poverty to deviance. Obviously, the same theories simply may not apply in rural areas or under other conditions.

Effective development of deviance theory will require much greater attention to the specification of such scope conditions. Rather than combining causal variables from different theories as integrationists would recommend, this approach

to theory development encourages scholars to explore more fully the strengths and limitations of their own theories. This approach will require more complete elaboration of extant theory, explicitly specifying those circumstances under which each theory may be meaningfully tested and thus falsified. The result will be a greater specification of each theory's contribution to explanations of deviant behavior.

These two directions have clear and very different implications for the development of deviance theory. Theoretical integration offers overarching models of deviant behavior that cut across classical theories, combining different levels of explanation and causal focuses. If fundamental differences between theories can be reconciled, integration is promising. The specification of scope conditions offers greater clarification of existing theories, identifying those conditions under which each theory most effectively applies. Although this direction promises no general theories of deviance, it offers the hope of more meaningful and useful explanations of deviant behavior.

REFERENCES

Agnew, Robert 1992 "Foundation for a General Strain Theory of Crime and Delinquency." *Criminology* 30:47–88.

Akers, Ronald L. 1985 *Deviant Behavior: A Social Learning Approach.* Belmont, Calif.: Wadsworth.

——, Marvin D. Krohn, Lonn Lanza-Kaduce, and Marcia Radosevich 1979 "Social Learning and Deviant Behavior: A Specific Test of a General Theory." *American Sociological Review* 44:636–655.

Becker, Howard 1963 *The Outsiders.* Chicago: University of Chicago Press.

Blau, Judith, and Peter Blau 1982 "Metropolitan Structure and Violent Crime." *American Sociological Review* 47:114–128.

Bridges, George S., and Robert D. Crutchfield 1988 "Law, Social Standing and Racial Disparities in Imprisonment." *Social Forces* 66:699–724.

——, and Edith Simpson 1987 "Crime, Social Structure and Criminal Punishment." *Social Problems* 34:344–361.

——, and Sara Steen 1998 "Racial Disparities in Official Assessments of Juvenile Offenders: Attributional Stereotypes as Mediating Mechanisms." *American Sociological Review* 63:554–570.

Burgess, Robert L., and Ronald Akers 1966 "A Differential Association-Reinforcement Theory of Criminal Behavior." *Social Problems* 14:128–147.

Bursik, Robert J. 1984 "Urban Dynamics and Ecological Studies of Delinquency." *Social Forces* 63:393–413.

——, and J. Webb 1982 "Community Change and Ecological Studies of Delinquency." *American Journal of Sociology* 88:24–42.

Chambliss, William 1978 *On the Take*. Bloomington: Indiana University Press.

——, and Milton Mankoff 1976 *Whose Law, What Order?* New York: Wiley.

Cloward, Richard 1959 "Illegitimate Means, Anomie and Deviant Behavior." *American Sociological Review* 24:164–176.

——, and Lloyd E. Ohlin 1960 *Delinquency and Opportunity*. New York: Free Press.

Crutchfield, Robert D. 1989 "Labor Stratification and Violent Crime." *Social Forces* 68:489–513.

Curtis, Lynn 1975 *Violence, Race and Culture*. Lexington, Mass.: Heath.

Elliott, Delbert 1985 "The Assumption That Theories can be Combined with Increased Explanatory Power: Theoretical Integrations." In Robert F. Meier, ed., *Theoretical Methods in Criminology*. Beverly Hills, Calif.: Sage.

Erlanger, Howard 1974 "The Empirical Status of the Subculture of Violence Thesis." *Social Problems* 22:280–292.

Gastil, Raymond 1971 "Homicide and a Regional Culture of Violence." *American Sociological Review* 36:412–427.

Gibbs, Jack P. 1975 *Crime, Punishment and Deterrence*. New York: Elsevier.

—— 1977 "Social Control, Deterrence, and Perspectives on Social Order." *Social Forces* 62:359–374.

Gottfredson, Michael R., and Travis Hirschi 1990 *A General Theory of Crime*. Palo Alto, Calif.: Stanford University Press.

Hirschi, Travis 1969 *Causes of Delinquency*. Berkeley: University of California Press.

—— 1979 "Separate and Unequal is Better." *Journal of Research in Crime and Delinquency* 16:34–37.

—— 1989 "Exploring Alternatives to Integrated Theory." In Steven F. Messner, Marvin D. Krohn, and Allen E. Liska, eds., *Theoretical Integration in the Study of Deviance and Crime: Problems and Prospects*. Albany, N.Y.: SUNY Press.

——, and Michael R. Gottfredson 1987 "Causes of White Collar Crime." *Criminology* 25:949–974.

Lemert, Edwin 1951 *Social Pathology*. New York: McGraw-Hill.

Link, Bruce 1982 "Mental Patient Status, Work and Income: An Examination of the Effects of a Psychiatric Label." *American Sociological Review* 47:202–215.

—— 1987 "Understanding Labeling Effects in the Area of Mental Disorders: An Assessment of the Effects of Expectations of Rejection." *American Sociological Review* 52:96–112.

Liska, Allen E., Marvin D. Kroh, and Steven S. Messner 1989 "Strategies and Requisites for Theoretical Integration in the Study of Deviance and Crime." In Steven S. Messner, Marvin D. Krohn, and Allen E. Liska, eds., *Theoretical Integration in the Study of Deviance and Crime: Problems and Prospects*. Albany, N.Y.: SUNY Press.

MacLeod, Jay 1995 *Ain't No Makin' It*. Boulder, Colo.: Westview.

Matsueda, Ross L. 1982 "Testing Control Theory and Differential Association: A Causal Modeling Approach." *American Sociological Review* 47:36–58.

——, and Karen Heimer 1987 "Race, Family Structure and Delinquency: A Test of Differential Association and Social Control Theories." *American Sociological Review* 52:826–840.

——, Irving Piliavin, and Rosemary Gartner 1988 "Ethical Assumptions Versus Empirical Research." *American Sociological Review* 53:305–307.

Merton, Robert K. 1938 "Social Structure and Anomie." *American Sociological Review* 3:672–682.

—— 1964 *Social Theory and Social Structure*. New York: Free Press.

Messner, Steven F. 1983 "Regional and Racial Effects on the Urban Homicide Rate: The Subculture of Violence Revisited." *American Journal of Sociology* 88:997–1,007.

Miller, Walter B. 1958 "Lower Class Culture as a Generating Milieu of Gang Delinquency." *Journal of Social Issues* 14:5–19.

Myers, Martha 1987 "Economic Inequality and Discrimination in Sentencing." *Social Forces* 65:746–766.

—— 1990 "Economic Threat and Racial Disparities in Incarceration: The Case of Postbellum Georgia." *Criminology* 28:627–656.

——, and Suzette Talarico 1987 *Social Contexts of Criminal Sentencing*. New York: Springer-Verlag.

Paternoster, Raymond L., Linda Saltzman, Gordon P. Waldo, and Theodore Chiricos 1982 "Perceived Risk and Deterrence: Methodological Artifacts in Deterrence Research." *Journal of Criminal Law and Criminology* 73:1,243–1,255.

—— 1983 "Perceived Risk and Social Control." *Journal of Criminal Law and Criminology* 74:457–480.

Peterson, Ruth D., and John Hagan 1984 "Changing Conceptions of Race: Toward an Account of Anomalous Findings of Sentencing Research." *American Sociological Review* 49:56–70.

Piliavin, Irving, Rosemary Gartner, Craig Thornton, and Ross L. Matsueda 1986 "Crime, Deterrence and Rational Choice." *American Sociological Review* 51:101–120.

Quinney, Richard 1970 *The Social Reality of Crime.* Boston: Little, Brown.

—— 1974 *Critique of Legal Order.* Boston: Little, Brown.

—— 1980 *Class, State and Crime.* New York: Longman.

Rafter, Nicole Hahn 1985 *Partial Justice: Women in State Prisons, 1800–1935.* Boston: Northeastern University Press.

Sampson, Robert J., and John H. Laub 1993 *Crime in the Making: Pathways and Turning Points Through Life.* Cambridge, Mass.: Harvard University Press.

Scheff, Thomas 1966 *Being Mentally Ill.* Chicago: Aldine.

Schur, Edwin 1971 *Labeling Deviant Behavior.* New York: Harper and Row.

—— 1985 *Labeling Women Deviant: Gender, Stigma and Social Control.* New York: Harper and Row.

Scull, Andrew T. 1978 *Museums of Madness.* London: Heinemann.

Sellin, Thorsten 1938 *Culture, Conflict and Crime.* New York: Social Science Research Council.

Shaw, Clifford 1930 *The Jack-Roller.* Chicago: University of Chicago Press.

——, and Henry McKay 1942 *Juvenile Delinquency and Urban Areas.* Chicago: University of Chicago Press.

Silberman, Charles 1980 *Criminal Justice, Criminal Violence.* New York: Vintage.

Spitzer, Steven 1975 "Toward a Marxian Theory of Deviance." *Social Problems* 22:638–651.

Stark, Rodney 1987 "Deviant Places: A Theory of the Ecology of Crime." *Criminology* 25:893–910.

Sullivan, Mercer L. 1989 *Getting Paid: Youth Crime and Work in the Inner City.* Ithaca, N.Y.: Cornell University Press.

Sutherland, Edwin H. 1947 *Principles of Criminology*, 4th ed. Philadelphia: Lippincott.

Thornberry, Terence P, and R. L. Christenson 1984 "Unemployment and Criminal Involvement: An Investigation of Reciprocal Causal Structures." *American Sociological Review* 49:398–411.

Tittle, Charles R. 1975 "Deterrents or Labeling?" *Social Forces* 53:399–410.

—— 1980 *Sanctions and Social Deviance.* New York: Praeger.

—— 1995 *Control Balance: Toward a General Theory of Deviance.* Boulder, Colo.: Westview Press.

——, and Barbara A. Curran 1988 "Contingencies for Dispositional Disparities in Juvenile Justice." *Social Forces* 67:23–58.

Toby, Jackson 1957 "Social Disorganization and Stakes in Conformity: Complimentary Factors in the Predatory Behavior of Hoodlums." *Journal of Criminal Law and Criminology and Police Science* 48:12–17.

Turk, Austin T. 1976 "Law as a Weapon in Social Conflict." *Social Problems* 23:276–291.

Walker, Howard, and Bernard P. Cohen 1985 "Scope Statements." *American Sociological Review* 50:288–301.

Wolfgang, Marvin E., and Franco Ferracuti 1967 *The Subculture of Violence: Towards an Integrated Theory in Criminology.* London: Tavistock.

Young, Peter 1983 "Sociology, the State and Penal Relations." In David Garland and Peter Young, eds., *The Power to Punish.* London: Heinemann.

George S. Bridges
Scott A. Desmond

DIFFERENTIAL ASSOCIATION

See Crime, Theories of; Deviance Theories.

DIFFUSION THEORIES

The concept of *diffusion* inherently focuses upon *process.* Diffusion refers to the dissemination of any physical element, idea, value, social practice, or attitude through and between populations. Diffusion is among the rare concepts used across the physical, natural, and social sciences, as well as in the arts. Diffusion is most closely associated with the social sciences, particularly rural sociology, anthropology, and communication. Diffusion thinking offers a logic through which to describe and perhaps explain myriad types of change that involve equally diverse foci, ranging from the adoption of internet technology (Adams 1997), to the spread of belief systems (Dean 1997).

Work connected to the concept of diffusion is arguably structured as theory. Certainly there is no single, unified, deductively structured collection of propositions, widely regarded by social scientists as identifying the principal mechanisms of diffusion that could be employed across all substantive areas. There are however, many distinct collections of propositions, a few well-tested over decades, that describe different diffusion phenomena in different content areas. Indeed, in the area of innovation diffusion, Everett Rogers (1983) produced a formal theory that is broadly recognized, often tested, and that has been adapted to other content areas including disaster research and technology transfer. Part of the problem in formalizing diffusion theories is that the concept does not inherently specify content (rather a framework or process to structure thinking). However, it cannot be examined empirically without tying it to some substance. That is, studies of diffusion focus on *something* (a technology, idea, practice, attitude, etc.) that is being diffused. Consequently, the research on diffusion that would drive theory building has remained scattered in the literatures of different sciences, and as such it is not readily pulled together. These conditions do not facilitate ready assembly of information that would encourage creation of a general theory of diffusion. Thus, one must look to the growth of formal theory in sub-areas, although Rogers (in press) has begun to cross content spheres.

There are at least three traditions or theory families that can be historically discerned in the study of diffusion. Rogers (1983, p. 39) has pointed out that for many years these traditions remained largely distinct, with little overlap and cross-fertilization. Since the late 1970s the level of research and theoretical isolation has decreased, leading to an enhanced awareness among the perspectives and some integration of empirical findings into more general theoretical statements. The three theory families are: (1) cultural diffusion; (2) diffusion of innovations; and (3) collective behavior.

CULTURAL DIFFUSION

The earliest social scientific use of the term *diffusion* is found in Edward Tylor's (1865) treatment of culture change. Anthropologists have long attempted to explain similarities and differences among cultures, especially those that were geographically adjacent. Tylor's work on culture change first proposed the notion of diffusion as a means of explaining the appearance of similar culture elements in different groups and of understanding the progressive alteration of elements within the same group. As the twentieth century began, diffusion arose as an alternative to evolution as a basis for understanding cultural differences and change. Evolutionists argued that cultural similarities probably arose through independent invention. Those who embraced diffusion presented it as a more parsimonious explanation, emphasizing that traits and institutions could pass between groups by means of contact and interaction.

Historical Development. The English anthropologists W. J. Perry and Elliot Smith devised the most extreme position on cultural diffusion. These scholars held that human culture originated in Egypt and progressively diffused from that center over the remainder of the earth. In Germany, Fritz Graebner (1911) argued that critical aspects of cultures—toolmaking, for example—originated in a small number of geographically isolated societies. This hypothesis formed the basis for *culture circles* ("kulturkreise"), collections of societies sharing similar cultures. Unlike British diffusionists who emphasized tracking the movement of single culture elements, Graebner and others in his tradition focused on the dissemination of collections of elements or cultural complexes.

American anthropologists are credited with developing a social scientifically workable concept of diffusion. Franz Boas (1896) conceived of diffusion as a viable mechanism for culture exchanges among geographically adjacent areas. His view figured prominently in the intellectual move away from the deterministic view of diffusion proposed by early British anthropologists. Alfred Kroeber (1923, p. 126) and Robert Lowie (1937, p. 58)—students of Boas—subsequently developed a position called *moderate diffusionism*, which is currently widely accepted in anthropology. This position allowed for the coexistence of a variety of mechanisms of change and transfer—independent invention, acculturation, etc.—in addition to diffusion in accounting for culture change and differentiation. Clark Wissler (1929), a Kroeber contemporary, established an empirical basis for culture diffusion by identifying ten culture areas (regions with similar cultural inventories) in North and South America and the Caribbean.

Theory in Cultural Diffusion. In terms of theory development, *cultural diffusion* is the actual movement of a given social institution or physical implement, while *stimulus diffusion* is the exchange or movement of the *principle* upon which an institution or implement is based. In the cultural diffusion literature, scholars have enumerated assumptions, stated principles, and reviewed empirical work with the objective of identifying propositions tested repeatedly and not found to be false. Indeed, beginning with the work of early twentieth century anthropologists, one can identify at least five broadly accepted and empirically supported claims that form the core of what is called cultural diffusion theory. First, borrowed elements usually undergo some type of alteration or adaptation in the new host culture. Second, the act of borrowing depends on the extent to which the element can be integrated into the belief system of the new culture. Third, elements that are incompatible with the new culture's prevailing normative structure or religious belief system are likely to be rejected. Fourth, acceptance of an element depends upon its utility for the borrower. Finally, cultures with a history of past borrowing are more likely to borrow in the future. These claims constitute the "core propositions" of culture diffusion theory; over the years, each has been qualified and elaborated upon, and corollaries have been created (Stahl 1994).

Currently, diffusion is seen as a mechanism for culture change that typically accounts for a large proportion of any particular culture inventory. The deterministic, linear view of diffusion has been discredited by the empirical record. The concept of culture diffusion as a means of understanding cultural inventories is entrenched in the field of cultural anthropology. As the twenty-first century dawns, a principal controversy among cultural anthropologists centers on the definition of culture, rather than upon the acceptability of culture diffusion. Diffusion theory remains prominent in the archaeology literature, particularly as a means of tracing culture inventories for groups over time (Posnansky and DeCorse 1986).

Sociologists were initially involved in the use of cultural diffusion theory as a means of looking at cultural change (largely in terms of nonmaterial culture) in the United States. Initially theory drawn from anthropology was used (Chapin 1928), but over time the sociological focus became identifying social psychological motivations and mechanisms supporting the diffusion process (Park and Burgess 1921, p. 20). Recently, sociological work directly on culture is bifurcated, with one group of scientists still emphasizing the social psychological issues in culture meaning (Wuthnow and Witten 1988), and another more concerned with structural (mathematical or statistical) models of culture processes themselves (Griswold 1987). Neither group has especially focused on diffusion theory as a mechanism to track or identify the content-outcomes of culture change.

DIFFUSION OF INNOVATIONS

The diffusion of innovations has historically focused on the spread of an idea, procedure, or implement within a single social group or between multiple groups. For the most part, scholars of this tradition define diffusion as the process through which some innovation is communicated within a social system. Also important is the notion of a time dimension reflecting the *rate* of diffusion, and the importance of the individual adopter (or non-adopter) reflecting the role of social influence.

The study of innovation diffusion began rather narrowly, grew to dominate the field of rural sociology for a time, contracted in popularity for many years, and then spawned wide interest across several disciplines. Innovation diffusion study contains several groups: those who focus on content or the specific innovation being diffused; those who emphasize theoretical elaborations of generic principles of innovation diffusion; and those concerned with creating structural models to track diffusion. Particularly in the past decade, the literature has seen much cross-fertilization, although mathematical modelers tend to appear less often in the work of other diffusion scholars. Although the roots of innovation diffusion theory are seen to be largely in rural sociology, more recently the field has become distinctly interdisciplinary with major advancements made especially in the discipline of communication.

Historical Development. The definitive history of the diffusion of innovations as a paradigm was published by Thomas Valente and Everett Rogers (1995). The roots of innovation diffusion are usually traced to Gabriel Tarde (1890) who didn't use the term *diffusion*, but was the first to address the notions of *adopters* and the role of social influence in adoption, as well as to identify the S-shaped curve associated with the rate of an innovation's adoption. The formative empirical work on innovation diffusion can be traced to Bryce Ryan's Iowa State University-based study of hybrid corn seeds (published with Gross in 1943), and Raymond Bowers's (1937) study of the acceptance and use of ham radio sets. For more than two decades following this pioneering work, the study of innovation diffusion and particularly theory development took place within the context of rural sociology. This circumstance was a function of a variety of forces, principal among which were the location of rural sociologists in land grant institutions charged with the dissemination of agricultural innovations to farmers (Hightower 1972) and the communication and stimulation accorded by the North Central Rural Sociology Committee's (a regional professional society) formation of a special subcommittee to deal with the issue of diffusion of agricultural innovations (Valente and Rogers 1995, p. 254).

Most scholars agree that contemporary views of innovation diffusion grew from hybrid corn seeds; specifically the research on adoption done by Bryce Ryan and Neal Gross (1943). These studies ultimately defined most of the issues that occupied diffusion researchers and builders of innovation diffusion theory for decades to come: the role of social influence, the timing of adoptions, the adoption process itself, and interactions among adopter characteristics and perceived characteristics of the innovation. From the middle 1940s through the 1950s, rural sociologists vigorously developed a body of empirical information on the diffusion of innovations. Most of these studies remained tied to agriculture and farming, and focused on the diffusion of new crop management systems, hybridizations, weed sprays, insect management strategies, chemical fertilizers, and machinery. A common criticism of the studies of this era is that many of the studies seem to be almost replications of the Ryan and Gross work, the main difference among them being the specific innovation studied. While it is true that these studies tend to share a common methodology and linear conception of diffusion, it is also true that they provide a strong foundation of empirical case studies.

Indeed, the replications that these studies represent substantially facilitated the later sophisticated theoretical work initiated in the early 1960s (Rogers 1962), and continued in the 1980s (Rogers 1983, 1988).

The 1960s marked the beginning of the decline of the central role of rural sociologists in innovation diffusion research. In large part this was due to changes in the field of rural sociology, but it also reflected the increasing involvement of researchers from other disciplines, changing the sheer proportion of rural sociologists working on innovation diffusion. After more than two decades of extensive research on the diffusion of agricultural innovations, rural sociologists—like other social scientists of the time—began to devote more time to the study of social problems and the consequences of technology. Indeed, Crane (1972) argued that around 1960 rural sociologists began to believe that the critical questions about innovation diffusion had already been answered. Although the late 1960s saw rural sociologists launch a series of diffusion studies on agricultural change in the international arena (particularly Latin America, Asia and Africa), by 1965 research on diffusion of innovations was no longer dominated by members of that field. Of course, innovation diffusion research by rural sociologists has continued, including studies of the impacts of technological innovation diffusion, and diffusion of conservation practices and other ecologically-based innovations (Fliegel 1993).

The infusion of researchers from many disciplines studying a variety of specific innovations initiated the process of expanding the empirical testing of innovation diffusion tenets. This began with studies in education addressing the diffusion of kindergartens and driver education classes in the 1950s, as well as Richard Carlson's (1965) study of the diffusion of modern math. Another major contribution came from the area of public health. Elihu Katz, Herbert Menzel, and James Coleman launched extensive studies of the diffusion of a new drug (the antibiotic tetracycline); first in a pilot study (Menzel and Katz 1955) and then in studies of four Illinois cities (Coleman, Menzel, and Katz 1957; Coleman, Katz, and Menzel 1966). This research greatly expanded knowledge of interpersonal diffusion networks, and in particular its influence in adoption. Interestingly, as Elihu Katz, M. L. Levine, and Harry Hamilton

(1963) indicated, the drug studies truly represented an independent replication of the principles of innovation diffusion developed by rural sociologists because the public health researchers were unaware of the agricultural diffusion research. Other studies in the public health arena focused on dissemination of new vaccines, family planning, and new medical technology.

Beginning in the late 1960s, there was a substantial increase in the amount of diffusion research in three disciplines: business marketing, communication, and transportation-technology transfer. Marketing research principally addressed the characteristics of adopters of new products and the role of opinion leaders in the adoption process (Howes 1996). This literature is based almost exclusively on commercial products, ranging from coffee brands and soap to touch-tone telephones, the personal computer, and internet services. The studies tend to be largely atheoretical, methodologically similar, and aimed simply at using knowledge of diffusion either to improve marketing and sales of the product or to describe product dissemination.

In sharp contrast, work done on innovation diffusion by scholars trained in communication has been considerably more theoretically oriented. Throughout the 1960s, universities in America began to establish separate departments of communication (Rogers 1994). Since diffusion of innovations was widely seen as one type of communication process, scholars in these new departments adopted this type of research as one staple of their work. Beginning with studies of the diffusion of news events (Deutschmann and Danielson 1960), this research tradition has branched out to study the dissemination of a wide variety of specific innovations (McQuail 1983, p. 194). Scholars working in this tradition have been principally responsible for the progressive refinements of formalized theory of innovation diffusion. Everett Rogers has consistently remained the leader in theory development in communication, revising and extending his 1962 book *Diffusion of Innovations* with help from co-author Floyd Shoemaker to produce *Communication of Innovations* in 1971. Subsequently, Rogers (1983, in press) restored the original title *Diffusion of Innovations*, broadened the theoretical base and incorporated diffusion studies and thinking from other disciplines. Generally, Rogers and other communication scholars

have studied the diffusion of many target material elements, phenomena, and other intangibles, but they have continued to produce theoretical statements dealing with communication channels, diffusion networks, interpersonal influence and the innovation-decision process. Finally, the technology dissemination and transfer issues have involved work by geographers, engineers, and others beginning in the 1970s. The primary focus of such studies has been the spread or dissemination of technology (Sahal 1981) and the development of network models of innovation diffusion (Valente 1995).

Theory in Innovation Diffusion. The theoretical work of Everett Rogers initially resulted in the collection of knowledge gained from the rural sociology tradition, then facilitated the transition to communication perspectives, and now has served as the mainstay of what is developing as a more cross-disciplinary focus on innovation diffusion. His contribution is twofold. First, he created inventories of findings from many disciplines and from many types of innovation. These inventories provided impetus for the development of a definition of innovation diffusion that was not bound by discipline. Second, Rogers assembled and refined theoretical structures aimed at explaining the principal features of innovation diffusion. The theoretical work has cemented a core of knowledge and principles that are widely identified (and used empirically) as the bases of the diffusion of innovations. Rogers's (1983) theory includes eighty-one generalizations (propositions) that have undergone empirical testing.

The theory of innovation diffusion may be understood as capturing the innovation-decision process, innovation characteristics, adopter characteristics, and opinion leadership. The innovation-decision process represents the framework on which diffusion research is built. It delineates the process through which a decision maker (representing any unit of analysis) chooses to adopt, reinvent (modify), or reject an innovation. This process consists of five stages. *Knowledge* is the initial stage when the decision maker detects the existence of the innovation and learns of its function. In the *persuasion* stage, the decision maker forms a positive or negative attitude toward the innovation. The third stage, *decision*, deals with the decision-maker's choice to accept or reject the innovation. *Implementation*, the fourth stage, follows a decision to accept and involves putting the innovation into some use (in either its accepted form or some modified form). During the final stage of *confirmation*, decision makers assess an adopted innovation, gather information from significant others, and choose to continue to use the innovation as is, modify it (reinvention), or reject it. While some have criticized the stage model as too linear, Rogers (1983) has convincingly argued that existing formulations afford a degree of interpretative and predictive flexibility that averts historical problems with stage models in social science.

Different innovations have different probabilities of adoption and hence, different adoption rates. That is, they travel through the innovation-decision process at varying speeds. The literature demonstrates that five characteristics of innovations influence the adoption decision. *Compatibility* refers to the congruence between an innovation and the prevailing norms, values, and perceived needs of the potential adopter. Higher levels of compatibility are associated with greater likelihood of adoption. Innovation *complexity*, on the other hand, is negatively associated with adoption. The extent to which use of an innovation is visible to the social group—called *observability*—is positively related to adoption. *Relative advantage* refers to the extent to which an innovation is perceived to be "better" than the idea, practice, or element that it replaces. Higher relative advantage increases the probability of adoption. Finally, *trialability*—the extent to which an innovation may be experimented with—also increases the probability of adoption.

The third component of diffusion of innovation theory addresses adopter characteristics. Adopter categories are classifications of individuals by how readily they adopt an innovation. Rogers (1983, p. 260) identifies nine socioeconomic variables, twelve personality variables, and ten personal communication characteristics that have been demonstrated to bear upon adoption choices. In general, the literature holds that early adopters are more likely to be characterized by high socioeconomic status, high tolerance of uncertainty and change, low levels of fatalism and dogmatism, high integration into the social system, high exposure to mass media and interpersonal communication channels, and frequent engagement in information seeking.

Identifying the characteristics of people who adopt innovations raises the question of interpersonal influence. Three issues are addressed in the development of propositions about the role of interpersonal influence in the innovation decision process: information flow, opinion leadership, and diffusion networks. Over time, information flow has been seen as a "hypodermic needle" model, a two-step flow (to opinion leaders, then other adopters), and a multi-step flow. Currently, information flows are seen as multi-step in nature and are described in terms of *homophily* and *heterophily*—the degree to which pairs of interacting potential adopters are similar or dissimilar. Opinion leadership denotes the degree to which one member of a social system can influence the attitude and behavior of others. This concept is presently discussed relative to spheres of influence, wherein a given person may be a leader or follower depending upon the part of the diffusion network being referenced. The diffusion or communication network is the structural stage upon which social influence takes place. Considerable attention has been devoted to developing analysis strategies and tactics for such networks (Wigand 1988).

COLLECTIVE BEHAVIOR

While diffusion is not a commonly used term in collective behavior, processes of diffusion are important in connection with understanding crowds, fashion, and some aspects of disaster behavior. In all cases, analytic concern centers on the dissemination of emotions, social practices, or physical elements through a collectivity. The study of human behavior in disasters is recent and multidisciplinary. In this field there has been a concern with diffusion in the classic sense of tracking ideas and practices through networks. The principle foci of research have been the adoption of protective measures and the dissemination of warning messages (Lindell and Perry 1992), with the aim of research being both the development of general theories of protective behaviors and more effective protection of endangered populations.

All three diffusion theory traditions converge in the study of crowd behavior. In proposing *imitation* as an explanatory mechanism for crowd actions, Gabriel Tarde (1890, p. 45) drew upon Edward Tylor's concept of cultural diffusion. Subsequently, Gustave LeBon (1895) and Gabriel Tarde

(1901) approached crowd behavior in terms of *social contagion*: rapid dissemination of emotions among interacting people. Although Floyd Allport (1924) and Herbert Blumer (1939) extended and formalized the concept of contagion, it has been largely displaced as a theory of crowd behavior by convergence theory (Turner and Killian 1987, p.19).

Changes in dress have been conceptualized as diffusion processes. Alfred Kroeber (1919) studied *fashion cycles* which he believed diffused systematically through civilizations. Katz and Lazarsfeld (1955, p. 241) moved away from the initial concern with movement of fashion through networks to focus more on social influence. Herbert Blumer (1969) firmly established social psychological motivations as the basis for fashion behavior. Current theoretical work on fashion continues to emphasize social psychological approaches wherein fashion diffusion issues are peripheral (Davis 1985; Nagasawa, Hutton, and Kaiser 1991).

REFERENCES

Adams, Tyronne 1997 "Using Diffusion of Innovations Theory to Enrich Virtual Organizations in Cyberspace." *Southern Communication Journal* 62:133–141.

Allport, Floyd 1924 *Social Psychology*. Boston: Houghton-Mifflin.

Blumer, Herbert 1939 "Collective Behavior." In Robert Park, ed., *Outline of the Principles of Sociology*. New York: Barnes and Noble.

—— 1969 "Fashion." *Sociological Quarterly* 10:275–291.

Boas, Franz 1896 *The Limitations of the Comparative Method of Anthropology*. New York: Alfred Knopf.

Bowers, Raymond 1937 "The Direction of Intra-Societal Diffusion." *American Sociological Review* 2:826–836.

Carlson, Richard 1965 *Adoption of Educational Innovations*. Eugene: University of Oregon Center for the Advanced Study of Educational Administration.

Chapin, F. Stuart 1928 *Cultural Change*. New York: Century.

Coleman, James, Herbert Menzel, and Elihu Katz 1957 "The Diffusion of an Innovation among Physicians." *Sociometry* 20:253–270.

—— 1966 *Medical Innovation: A Diffusion Study*. New York: Bobbs-Merrill.

Crane, Diana 1972 *Invisible Colleges*. Chicago: University of Chicago Press.

Davis, Fred 1985 "Clothing and Fashion as Communication." *Symbolic Interaction* 5:111–126.

Dean, John 1997 "The Diffusion of American Culture in Western Europe since World War Two." *Journal of American Culture* 20:11–32.

Deutschmann, P. J., and W. A. Danielson 1960 "Diffusion of Knowledge of the Major News Story." *Journalism Quarterly* 37:345–355.

Fliegel, Frederick 1993 *Diffusion Research in Rural Sociology*. Westport, Conn.: Greenwood.

Graebner, Fritz 1911 *Methode der Ethnologie*. Heidelberg, Germany: Carl Winter.

Griswold, William 1987 "A Methodological Framework for the Sociology of Culture." *Sociological Methodology* 14:1–35.

Hightower, James 1972 *Hard Tomatoes, Hard Times*. Cambridge, Mass.: Shenkman.

Howes, David 1996 *Cross-Cultural Consumption*. New York: Routledge.

Katz, Elihu, and Paul Lazarsfeld 1955 *Personal Influence*. New York: Free Press.

Katz, Elihu, M. L. Levine, and H. Hamilton 1963 "Traditions of Research on Diffusion of Innovation." *American Sociological Review* 28:237–253.

Kroeber, Alfred 1919 "On the Principle of Order in Civilization as Exemplified by Changes of Fashion." *American Anthropologist* 21:235–263.

—— 1923 *Anthropology*. New York: Harcourt.

LeBon, Gustave 1895 *Psychologie des foules*. Paris: Alcan.

Lindell, Michael, and Ronald Perry 1992 *Behavioral Foundations of Community Emergency Planning*. Washington, D.C.: Hemisphere Publishers.

Lowie, Robert 1937 *The History of Ethnological Theory*. New York: Rinehart and Company.

McQuail, Denis 1983 *Mass Communication Theory*. Beverly Hills, Calif.: Sage.

Menzel, Herbert, and Elihu Katz 1955 "Social Relations and Innovation in the Medical Profession." *Public Opinion Quarterly* 19:337–352.

Nagasawa, Richard, Sandra Hutton, and Susan Kaiser 1991 "A Paradigm for the Study of the Social Meaning of Clothes." *Clothing and Textiles Research Journal* 10:53–62.

Park, Robert, and Ernest Burgess 1921 *Introduction to the Science of Sociology*. Chicago: University of Chicago Press.

Posnansky, M., and C. R. DeCorse 1986 "Historical Archaeology in Sub-Saharan Africa." *Historical Archaeology* 20:1–14.

Rogers, Everett 1962, 1995 *Diffusion of Innovations*. New York: Free Press.

—— 1988 "The Intellectual Foundation and History of the Agricultural Extension Model." *Knowledge* 9:492–510.

—— 1994 *A History of Communication Study.* New York: Free Press.

——, and Floyd Shoemaker 1971 *Communication of Innovations.* New York: Free Press.

Ryan, Bryce, and Neal Gross 1943 "The Diffusion of Hybrid Seed Corn in Two Iowa Communities." *Rural Sociology* 8:15–24.

Sahal, Devendra 1981 *Patterns of Technological Innovation.* Reading, Mass.: Addison-Wesley.

Stahl, Ann 1994 "Innovation, Diffusion and Culture Contact." *Journal of World Prehistory* 8:51–112.

Tarde, Gabriel 1890 *Les Lois de l'imitation.* Paris: Alcan.

—— 1901 *L'opinion et la foule.* Paris: Alcan.

Turner, Ralph, and Lewis Killian 1987 *Collective Behavior.* Englewood Cliffs, N.J.: Prentice-Hall.

Tylor, Edward 1865 *Early History of Mankind and the Development of Civilisation.* London: John Murray.

Valente, Thomas 1995 *Network Models of the Diffusion of Innovations.* Cresskill, N.J.: Hampton.

——, and Everett Rogers 1995 "The Origins and Development of the Diffusion of Innovations Paradigm." *Science Communication* 16:242–273.

Wigand, Rolf 1988 "Communication Network Analysis." In G. Goldhaber and G. Barnett, eds., *Handbook of Organizational Communication.* Norwood, N.J.: Ablex Publishing.

Wissler, Clark 1929 *An Introduction to Social Anthropology.* New York: Henry Holt.

Wuthnow, Robert, and Marsha Witten 1988 "New Directions in the Study of Culture." *Annual Review of Sociology* 14:49–67.

RONALD W. PERRY

DISASTER RESEARCH

SOCIOHISTORY OF THE FIELD

Descriptions of calamities exist as far back as the earliest human writings, but systematic empirical studies and theoretical treatises on social features of disasters appeared only in the twentieth century. The first major publications in both instances were produced by sociologists. Samuel Prince (1920) wrote a doctoral dissertation in sociology at Columbia University that examined the social change consequences of a munitions ship explosion in the harbor of Halifax, Canada. Pitirim Sorokin (1942) two decades later wrote *Man and Society in Calamity* that mostly speculated on how war, revolution, famine, and pestilence might affect the mental processes and behaviors, as well as the social organizations and the cultural aspects of impacted populations. However, there was no building on these pioneering efforts.

It was not until the early 1950s that disaster studies started to show any continuity and the accumulation of a knowledge base. Military interest in possible American civilian reactions to post-World War II threats from nuclear and biological warfare led to support of academic research on peacetime disasters. The National Opinion Research Center (NORC) undertook the key project at the University of Chicago between 1950 and 1954. This work, intended to be multidisciplinary, became dominated by sociologists as were other concurrent studies at the University of Oklahoma, Michigan State, and the University of Texas (Quarantelli 1987, 1994). The NORC study not only promoted field research as the major way for gathering data, but also brought sociological ideas from the literature on collective behavior and notions of organizational structure and functions into the thinking of disaster researchers (Dynes 1988; Dynes and Tierney 1994).

While the military interest quickly waned, research in the area obtained a strategic point of salience and support when the U.S. National Academy of Sciences in the late 1950s created the Disaster Research Group (DRG). Operationally run by sociologists using the NORC work as a prototype, the DRG supported field research of others as well as conducted its own studies (Fritz 1961). When the DRG was phased out in 1963, the Disaster Research Center (DRC) was established at the Ohio State University. DRC helped the field of study to become institutionalized by its continuous existence to the present day (having moved to the University of Delaware in 1985). In its thirty-six years of existence DRC has trained dozens of graduate students, built the largest specialized library in the world on social aspects of disasters, produced over six hundred publications and about three dozen Ph. D. dissertations (see http://www.udel.edu/DRC/homepage.htm), continually and consciously applied a sociological perspective to new disaster research topics, initiated an interactive computer net of researchers in the area, and intentionally helped to create international networks and critical masses of disaster researchers.

DRC was joined in time in the United States by two other major social science research centers (both currently headed by sociologists). The Natural Hazards Center at the University of Colorado has as part of its prime mission the linking of disaster researchers and research-users in policy and operational areas. The Hazards Reduction and Recovery Center at Texas A & M University has a strong multidisciplinary orientation. The organization of these groups and others studying disasters partly reflects the fact that the sociological work in the area was joined in the late 1960s by geographers with interest in natural hazards (Cutter 1994), in the 1980s by risk analysts (including sociologists such as Perrow 1984; Short 1984) especially concerned with technological threats, and later by political scientists who initially were interested in political crises (Rosenthal and Kouzmin 1993). More important, in the 1980s disaster research spread around the world, which led to the development of a critical mass of researchers. This culminated in 1986 in the establishment within the International Sociological Association of the Research Committee on Disasters (# 39) (http:// sociweb.tamu.edu/ircd/), with membership in over thirty countries; its own professional journal, *The International Journal of Mass Emergencies and Disasters* (www.usc.edu/dept/sppd/ijmed); and a newsletter, *Unscheduled Events*. At the 1998 World Congress of Sociology, this committee organized fourteen separate sessions with more than seventy-five papers from several dozen countries. The range of papers reflected that the initial focus on emergency time behavior has broadened to include studies on mitigation and prevention, as well as recovery and reconstruction.

CONCEPTUALIZATION OF "DISASTER"

Conceptualizations of "disaster" have slowly evolved from employing everyday usages of the term, through a focus on social aspects, to attempts to set forth more sociological characterizations. The earliest definitions equated disasters with features of physical agents and made distinctions between "acts of God" and "technological" agents. This view was followed by notions of disasters as phenomena that resulted in significant disruptions of social life, which, however, might not involve a physical agent of any kind (e.g., a false rumor might evoke the same kind of evacuation behavior that an actual threat would). Later, disasters came to be seen as crises resulting either from certain social constructions of reality, or from the application of politically driven definitions, rather than necessarily from one initial and actual social disruption of a social system. Other researchers equated disasters with occasions where the demand for emergency actions by community organizations exceeds their capabilities for response. By the late 1980s, disasters were being seen as overt manifestations of latent societal vulnerabilities, basically of weaknesses in social structures or systems (Schorr 1987; Kreps 1989).

Given these variants about the concept, it is not surprising that currently no one formulation is totally accepted within the disaster research community (see Quarantelli 1998 where it is noted that postmodernistic ideas are now also being applied). However, there would be considerable agreement that the following is what is involved in using the term "disaster" as a sensitizing concept: Disasters are relatively sudden occasions when, because of perceived threats, the routines of collective social units are seriously disrupted and when unplanned courses of action have to be undertaken to cope with the crisis.

The notion of "relatively sudden occasions" indicates that disasters have unexpected life histories that can be designated in social space and time. Disasters involve the perceptions of dangers and risks to valued social objects, especially people and property. The idea of disruption of routines indicates that everyday adjustive social mechanisms cannot cope with the perceived new threats. Disasters necessitate the emergence of new behaviors not available in the standard repertoire of the endangered collectivity, a community, which is usually the lowest social-level entity accepted by researchers as able to have a disaster. In the process of the refinement of the concept, sociologists have almost totally abandoned the distinction between "natural" and "technological" disasters, derived from earlier notions of "acts of God" and "man-made" happenings. Any disaster is seen as inherently social in nature in origin, manifestation, or consequences. However, there is lack of consensus on whether social happenings involving intentional, deliberate human actions to produce social disruptions such as occur in riots, civil disturbances, terrorist attacks, product tampering or sabotage, or wars, should be conceptualized as disasters. The majority who oppose their inclusion argue that conflict situations are inherently different in their origins, careers, manifestations, and consequences. They note that in disaster occasions there are no conscious attempts to bring about negative effects as there are in conflict situations (Quarantelli 1993). Nevertheless, there is general agreement that both conflict- and consensus-type crises are part of a more general category of collective stress situations, as first suggested by Allan Barton (1969).

MAJOR RESEARCH FINDINGS

While the research efforts have been uneven, much has been learned about the behavior of individuals and households, organizations, communities, and societies in the pre-, trans-, and postimpact time periods (Quarantelli and Dynes 1977; Kreps 1984; Drabek 1986). A separation of the disaster-planning cycle into mitigation, preparedness, response, and recovery phases has won partial acceptance at some policy and operational levels in the United States. However, international usage of the terms is far from total and there also is disagreement regarding what should be considered under mitigation. Therefore we will continue to discuss findings under the older "time" breakdown.

Preimpact behavior. *Individuals and households.* Most residents show little concern about disasters before they happen, even in risk-prone areas and where threats are recognized. Citizens tend to see disaster planning as primarily a moral even more than a legal responsibility of the government. Very few households ever plan in any concrete way for possible disasters. Exceptions to these passive attitudes are where there are many recurrent experiences of disasters as occur in some localities, where disaster subcultures (institutionalized expectations) have developed, and where potential disaster settings (such as at chemical complexes or nuclear plants) are the focus of activist citizen groups.

Organizations. Except for some disaster-oriented groups such as police and fire departments, there usually is little organizational planning for disasters. Even agencies that plan tend to think of disasters as extensions of everyday emergencies and fail, according to researchers, to recognize the qualitative as well as quantitative differences between routine crises and disaster occasions. In disasters the responding organizations have to quickly relate to more and different groups than normal, adjust to losing part of their autonomy to overall coordinating groups, apply different performance standards and criteria, operate within a closer-than-usual public and private interface, and cannot function well when their own facilities and operations may be directly impacted by the disaster agent.

Communities. Low priority usually is given to preparing localities for disasters, and when there is some effort it is usually independent of general community development and planning. This reflects the reactive rather than proactive orientation of most politicians and bureaucrats and the fact that the issue of planning very seldom becomes a matter of broad community interest as would be indicated by mass media focus, discussions in the political arena, or the existence of advocacy groups. Efforts to initiate overall disaster preparedness often are hindered by prior organizational and community conflicts, cleavages, and disputes. Starting in the 1990s, major systematic efforts from the top down have been made in a few countries to push for the implementation of local mitigation measures. For programs to be implemented, however, people must accept the realistic criticism that while a disaster may be a high-impact, it is a very low-probability event.

Societies. Generally, disaster planning does not rank very high on the agenda of most societies. However, increasingly there are exceptions in developing countries when major recurrent disasters have had major impact on the gross national product and developmental programs. Also, in developed societies certain even distant catastrophes such as a Bhopal or Chernobyl can become symbolic occasions that lend impetus to instituting preparedness measures for specific disaster agents. Increasingly too, attention to national-level disaster planning has increased as citizens have come to expect their governments to provide more security in general for the population. Also, mitigation or prevention of disasters is being given higher priority than in the past.

Transemergency Period Behavior. *Individuals and households.* When disasters occur, individuals generally react very well. They are not paralyzed by a threat but actively seek relevant information and attempt to do what they can in the emergency. Victims while usually very frightened, not only act positively but also show little deviant behavior; they extremely seldom break in panic flight; they do not act irrationally especially from their perspective; and they very rarely engage in antisocial activities, although stories of such contrary behavior as looting may circulate very widely. Prosocial behavior especially comes to the fore, with the initial search and rescue being undertaken quickly and mostly by survivors in the immediate area. Most sudden needs, such as emergency housing, are met by kin and friends rather than official relief agencies. Family and household relationships are very important in affecting immediate reactions to disasters such as whether evacuation will occur or if warnings will be taken seriously, because mass media reports are filtered through primary ties.

Organizations. As a whole, organizations do not react as well to disasters as do individuals and households. But while there are many organizational problems in coping with the emergency time demands of a disaster, these difficulties are often not the expected ones. Often it is assumed that if there has been organizational disaster planning, there will be successful crisis or emergency management. But apart from the possibility of planning being poor in the first place, planning is not management and the former does not always translate well into the latter in community disasters. There typically are problems in intra- and interorganizational information flow, and in communication between and to organizations and the general public. Groups initially often have to struggle with major gaps in knowledge about the impacts of a disaster. There can be organizational problems in the exercise of authority and decision making. These can stem from losses of higher-echelon personnel because of overwork, conflict regarding authority over new disaster tasks, and clashes over organizational jurisdictional differences. Generally, there is much decentralization of organizational response which in most cases is highly functional. Organizations operating with a command and control model of response do not do well at emergency times. There often too are problems associated with strained organizational relationships created by new disaster tasks and by the magnitude of a disaster impact.

Communities. Since disasters almost always cut across formal governmental boundaries, problems of coordination among different impacted political entities are all but inevitable. The greater the impact of a disaster, the more there will be the emergence of new and adaptive community structures and functions, especially emergent groups (that is, those without any preimpact existence). The greater the disaster also, the more organized improvisations of all kinds appear accompanied by pluralistic decision making. In addition, the mass convergence of outside but nonimpacted personnel and resources on impacted communities, while functional in some ways, creates major coordination problems.

Societies. Few societies ignore major disasters, but this sometimes occurs especially in the case of slow and diffuse occasions such as droughts and famines, especially if they primarily affect subgroups not in the mainstream of a developing country. In responding to domestic disasters, typically massive help is provided to impacted areas. Increasingly, most societies, including governmental officials at all levels, obtain their view of what is happening in their disasters from mass media accounts (what has been called the "CNN syndrome"); this also affects what is often remembered about the occasions. There is also a spreading belief, so far unsupported by research, that new technologies—especially computer-related ones—will allow major improvements in disaster planning and management.

Postimpact Behavior. *Individuals and households.* Overall, there is little personal learning as a result of undergoing a single disaster. While the experience of a major disaster is a memorable one from a social-psychological point of view, there are seldom lasting and widespread negative behavioral consequences. Disasters very seldom produce new psychoses or severe mental illnesses. They often, but not always, generate subclinical, short-lived and self-remitting surface reactions, such as loss of appetite, sleeplessness, and anxiety. More common are many problems in living that stem more from inefficient and ineffective relief and recovery efforts of helping organizations rather than from the direct physical impacts of disasters. However, not all postimpact effects are negative; sometimes, the experience of undergoing a disaster results in positive self-images and closer social ties among victims.

Organizations. Organizational changes, whether for planning for disasters or for other purposes in the postimpact period, is not common and selective at best. Most modifications are simply accelerations of noncrisis-related changes already planned or underway. Postimpact discussion of how to improve disaster planning seldom gets translated into concrete actions (unlike civil disturbances which in American society in the 1960s led to many changes in organizations). However, overall, both in the United States and elsewhere, there have been in recent decades the growth of small, locally based, formal social groups primarily concerned with emergency time disaster planning and management. Partly because of seemingly constantly escalating economic losses, certain businesses in such sectors as banking and insurance have increasingly become interested in disaster preparedness and recovery.

Communities. There are selective longer-run outcomes and changes in communities that have been impacted by disasters. There can be acceleration of some ongoing and functional community trends (e.g., in local governmental arrangements and power structures), and generation of some limited new patterns (e.g., in providing local mental-health services or some mitigation measures such as floodproofing regulations). On the other hand, particularly as the result of rehousing and rebuilding, there can be magnifications of preimpact community conflicts as well as the generation of new ones; some of the latter is manifested in blame assignation, which, however, tends to deflect attention away from social structural flaws to mass-media–influenced search for individual scapegoats. It is also being recognized after disasters that changes in technology that create diffuse networks and systems, such as among lifeline organizations, are increasingly creating the need for regional rather than just community-based disaster planning.

Societies. In developed societies, there are few long-run negative consequences of disaster losses whether of people or property, since such effects are absorbed by the larger system. In developing

societies and very small countries, this is not necessarily true; a catastrophic disaster may reduce the gross national product five to ten percent as well as producing tens of thousands of casualties. Nevertheless, changes or improvement in national disaster planning often does not occur except in certain cases such as after the Mexico City earthquake where an unusual set of circumstances existed, including a "political will" to do something. But increasingly, in the aftermath of major disasters, to the extent that planning is instituted or improved, it is being linked to developmental planning, a move strongly supported by international agencies such as the World Bank.

UNIVERSALITY OF GENERALIZATIONS FROM AN UNEVEN RESEARCH BASE

Cross-societal and comparative research increased markedly in the 1990s. Studies have ranged from cooperative work on local mass-media reporting of community disasters in Japan and the United States (Mikami, Hiroi, Quarantelli, and Wenger 1992) and flood responses and crisis management in four Western European countries (Rosenthal and Hart 1998), to comparisons of perceptions of recurrent floods in Bangladesh by European engineers and local residents (Schmuck-Widmann 1996), and cross-national analyses of post-disaster political unrest in a dozen countries (Olson and Drury 1997), as well as methodological issues involved in cross-societal research in Italy, Mexico, Turkey, Peru, the United States, and Yugoslavia (Bates and Peacock 1993). However, this kind of comparative empirical research so far has been limited. Furthermore, although the bulk of disasters occur in developing countries, the majority of studies from which the generalizations advanced have been derived, have been done in developed societies. Thus, the question of the universality of disaster behaviors in different social systems has increasingly been raised. Some universals appear to have been found: Prosocial rather than antisocial behavior clearly predominates in responses everywhere; household members and significant others are crucial in validating warning messages, and the larger kin system is vital in providing emergency assistance; emergent groups always appear at the height of the crisis period; organizations have relatively more difficulty in adjusting to and coping with disasters than do individuals and small groups; the disaster recovery period is fraught with problems at the household, organization, and community levels; mitigation measures are given little priority even in disaster-prone localities; and social change is seldom an outcome of most disasters.

Generalizations of a more limited nature also seem to exist. There are social-system–structure-specific behaviors. For example, there often is a major delay in the response to catastrophic disasters from centralized, compared to decentralized, governmental systems. There also may be culturally specific differences. For example, reflecting cultural values, individual volunteers in disasters very rarely appear in some societies such as Japan whereas they are typical in almost all American disasters.

THE FUTURE

There is a dialectical process at work: There will be more and worse disasters at the same time that there will be more and better planning. Why more and worse disasters? Risks and threats to human beings and their societies are increasing. Traditional natural-disaster agents, such as earthquakes and floods, will simply have more to impact as the result of normal population growth and higher, denser concentration of inhabitants in risk-prone localities, such as floodplains or hurricane-vulnerable shorelines that otherwise are attractive for human occupancy. There is an escalating increase in certain kinds of technological accidents and mishaps in the chemical, nuclear, and hazardous-waste areas that were almost unknown before World War II. There are technological advances that create risks and complexities to old threats such as when fires are prevented in high-rise buildings by constructing them with highly toxic materials, or when the removal of hazardous substances from solid sewage waste generates products that contain dangerous viruses and gases. New versions of old threats are also appearing, such as the increasing probability of urban rather than rural droughts, or the potential large-scale collapse of the infrastructure of older metropolitan area lifeline systems. Finally, there is the continual development of newer kinds of risks ranging from the biological threats that are inherent in genetic engineering, to the crises that will be generated as the

world increasingly becomes dependent on computers that are bound to fail somewhere at some key point, with drastic consequences for social systems. In addition, the newer threats are frequently dangerous at places and times distant from their initial source or origin as dramatized by the Chernobyl nuclear radiation fallout in European countries and smog pollution episodes such as forest fires in Indonesia which had negative effects in many Southeast Asian countries.

On the other hand, there is increasing concern and attention being paid to disaster planning of all kind. The future augers well for more and better planning. Citizens almost everywhere are coming to expect that their governments will take steps to protect them against disasters; this is often actualized in planning for emergency preparedness and response. Whereas two decades ago a number of societies had no preimpact disaster planning of any kind, this is no longer the case. A symbolic manifestation of this trend was the proclamation by the United Nations of the 1990s as The Decade for Natural-Disaster Reduction. This international attention accelerated efforts to prevent, prepare for, respond to, and recover from disasters. The effect was especially notable in the increased disaster planning in developed countries.

In developed societies, a focus on disaster planning and crisis management had started earlier, partly as a result of sociological and related research. By the 1980s, social scientists were increasingly influencing policies, political agenda settings, and operational matters regarding disasters. This can be seen in a variety of ways. Social scientists were represented on almost all national committees set up for the U. N. Decade, and contributed significantly to the reports prepared to mark the midpoint of the decade. The Board on Natural Disasters, established in 1992 in the U.S. National Academy of Sciences, always has had members from sociology and related disciplines. Sociologists have had major roles in national-disaster legislation in Greece and Italy. American social science disaster researchers typically testify before state and congressional committees considering disaster-related laws and policies. Many sociological disaster researchers provide both paid and unpaid consultant services to international, national, and local public and private groups involved in disaster-related activities. In places such as the United States, Australia, New Zealand, and some European countries, the emergency-management and disaster-planning community has become more open to recognizing the practical implications of social science research.

However, a caveat is in order for the generally correct view that studies by sociologists and others have increasingly influenced policy decisions and operational activities in the disaster area. Research results and questions are sometimes more than counterbalanced by other factors: These include the vested interests of powerful professional and bureaucratic elites to maintain traditional stances, resistance to seriously questioning the viabilities and competencies of specific organizations, and an unwillingness to face up to false assumptions of some cultural beliefs and values. Research to the contrary, for example, has had little effect on the fad-like spread of the "Incident Command System" as a model for the emergency time operations of organizations, or an ever-spreading acceptance that victims are likely to suffer posttraumatic stress disorders, or the current common belief that mitigation measures are necessarily a better strategy for disaster planning than giving priority to improving resilience and response to crises.

RELATIONSHIP TO SOCIOLOGY

Although not true everywhere, sociologists have been increasingly accepted as having an important contribution to make to disaster planning and management. In part this stems from the fact that in many countries such as Germany, Italy, Russia, and the United States, they have played the lead role among social scientists in undertaking disaster studies. While many reasons account for this, probably the crucial factor has been that much in general sociology can be used in doing research in the area.

There has been a close relationship between disaster studies and sociology from the earliest days of work in the area. In part this is because sociologists, being among the leading pioneers and researchers in the area, have tended to use what they could from their discipline. Thus, sociology has contributed to the research techniques used (e.g., field studies and open-ended interviewing), the research methodology utilized (e.g., the

"grounded theory" approach and the employment of inductive analytical models), the theoretical ideas used (e.g., the notion of emergence from collective-behavior thinking and the idea of informal and formal structures of organizations), and the general perspectives employed (e.g., that there can be latent as well as dysfunctional aspects of any behavior and that societies and communities have a social history that is not easily set aside). In the volume entitled *Sociology of Disasters: Contributions of Sociology to Disaster Research* (Dynes, De Marchi, and Pelanda 1987), these and other contributions to disaster theory, disaster research methods, disaster models, and disaster concepts are set forth in considerable detail.

The relationship has not been one-sided, since disaster research has also contributed to sociology. The field of collective behavior has been most influenced and this has been explicitly noted (Wenger 1987). Other significant contributions include the study of formal organizations, social roles, social problems, organizational and social change, mass communications, medical sociology, and the urban community (see Drabek 1986; Dynes, De Marchi, and Pelanda 1987; Dynes and Tierney 1994). A symposium on social structure and disaster, coattended by disaster researchers and prominent sociological theorists, examined how disaster studies not only are informed by but could also inform sociological theory; the proceedings were published in *Social Structure and Disaster* (Kreps 1989). It is also perhaps of interest that for several decades now, many introductory sociology textbooks have a section on disaster behavior, usually in the collective behavior chapter.

REFERENCES

Barton, Allan 1969 *Communities in Disaster: A Sociological Analysis*. Garden City, N.Y.: Anchor.

Bates, F., and W. Peacock 1993 *Living Conditions, Disasters and Development: An Approach to Cross-Cultural Comparisons*. Athens, Ga.: University of Georgia Press.

Cutter, Susan, ed. 1994 *Environmental Risks and Hazards*. Englewood Cliffs, N.J.: Prentice-Hall.

Drabek, Thomas 1986 *Human System Responses to Disasters: An Inventory of Sociological Findings*. New York: Springer Verlag.

Dynes, R. R., ed. 1988 "Disaster Classics Special Issue." *International Journal of Mass Emergencies and Disasters* 6:209–395.

——, and K. Tierney, eds. 1994 *Disasters, Collective Behavior, and Social Organization.* Newark, Del.: University of Delaware Press.

Dynes, R. R., B. De Marchi, and C. Pelanda (eds.) 1987 *Sociology of Disasters: Contributions of Sociology to Disaster Research.* Milan: Franco Angeli.

Fritz, C. 1961 "Disasters." In R. K. Merton and R. A. Nisbet, eds., *Contemporary Social Problems.* New York: Harcourt.

Kreps, G. 1984 "Sociological Inquiry and Disaster Research." *Annual Review of Sociology* 10:309–330.

—— 1989 *Social Structure and Disaster.* Newark, Del.: University of Delaware Press.

Mikami, S., O. Hiroi, E. L. Quarantelli, and D. Wenger 1992 "A Cross-Cultural Comparative Study of Mass Communication in Disasters." *Bulletin of Faculty of Sociology. Toyo University* 29:59–202.

Olson, Richard, and A. Cooper Druy 1997 "Un-Therapeutic Communities: A Cross-National Analysis of Post-Disaster Political Unrest." *International Journal of Mass Emergencies and Disasters* 15:221–238.

Perrow, C. 1984 *Normal Accidents: Living With High-Risk Technologies.* New York: Basic Books.

Prince, S. 1920 *Catastrophe and Social Change.* New York: Columbia University Press.

Quarantelli, E. L. 1987 "Disaster Studies: An Analysis of the Social Historical Factors Affecting the Development of Research in the Area." *International Journal of Mass Emergencies and Disasters* 5:285–310.

—— 1993 "Community Crises: An Exploratory Comparison of the Characteristics and Consequences of Disasters and Riots." *Journal of Contingencies and Crisis Management* 1:67–78.

—— 1994 "Disaster Studies: The Consequences of the Historical Use of a Sociological Approach in the Development of Research." *International Journal of Mass Emergencies and Disasters* 12:25–49.

——,ed. 1998 *What is a Disaster? Perspectives on the Question.* London: Routledge.

——, and R. R. Dynes 1977 "Response to Social Crisis and Disaster." *Annual Review of Sociology* 3:23–49.

Rosenthal, U., and P. Hart, eds. 1998 *Flood Response and Crisis Management in Western Europe: A Comparative Analysis.* New York: Springer Verlag.

Rosenthal, U., and A. Kouzmin 1993 "Globalizing an Agenda for Contingencies and Crisis Management." *Journal of Contingencies and Crisis Management* 1:1–12.

Schmuck-Widmann, Hanna 1996 *Living with the Floods: Survival Strategies of Char-Dwellers in Bangladesh.* Berlin: FDCL.

Schorr, J. 1987 "Some Contributions of German Katastrophensoziologie to the Sociology of Disaster." *International Journal of Mass Emergencies and Disasters* 5:115–135.

Short, James F. 1984 "The Social Fabric at Risk: Toward the Social Transformation of Risk Analysis." *American Sociological Review* 49:711–725.

Sorokin, Pitirim 1942 *Man and Society in Calamity.* New York: Dutton.

Wenger, Dennis 1987 "Collective Behavior and Disaster Research." In R. R. Dynes, B. De Marchi, and C. Pelanda, eds., *Sociology of Disasters: Contribution of Sociology to Disaster Research*, 213–238. Milan: Franco Angeli.

E. L. Quarantelli

DISCRIMINATION

Discrimination, in its sociological meaning, involves highly complex social processes. The term derives from the Latin *discriminatio*, which means to perceive distinctions among phenomena or to be selective in one's judgment. Cognitive psychology retains the first of these meanings, popular usage the second. Individual behavior that limits the opportunities of a particular group is encompassed in many sociological considerations of discrimination. But exclusively individualistic approaches are too narrow for robust sociological treatment. Instead, sociologists understand discrimination not as isolated individual acts, but as a complex system of social relations that produces intergroup inequities in social outcomes.

This definitional expansion transforms "discrimination" into a truly sociological concept. But in its breadth, the sociological definition leaves room for ambiguity and controversy. Obstacles to consensus on what constitutes discrimination stem from two sources—one empirical, the other ideological and political. First, deficiencies in analysis and evidence limit our ability to trace thoroughly the dynamic web of effects produced by discrimination. Second, because social discrimination is contrary to professed national values and law, a judgment that unequal outcomes reflect discrimination is a call for costly remedies. Variable willingness to bear those social costs contributes to dissension about the extent of discrimination.

The broadest sociological definitions of discrimination assume that racial minorities, women, and other historical target groups have no inherent characteristics that warrant inferior social outcomes. Thus, all inequality is seen as a legacy of discrimination and a social injustice to be remedied. By contrast, political conservatives favor a far narrower definition that limits the concept's scope by including only actions *intended* to restrict a group's chances. For solid conceptual reasons, sociologists seldom follow suit (but see Burkey 1978, p. 79). First, an intentionality criterion returns the concept to the realm of psychology and deflects attention from restraining social structure. Second, the invisibility of intentions creates insuperable obstacles to documenting discrimination.

DIRECT AND INDIRECT DISCRIMINATION

Sociologists' understanding of intricate societal patterns sensitizes them to the fact that disadvantage accruing from intentional discrimination typically cumulates, extends far beyond the original injury, and long outlives the deliberate perpetration. Many sociologists distinguish between *direct* and *indirect* discrimination (Pettigrew 1985). Direct discrimination occurs at points where inequality is generated, often intentionally. When decisions are based explicitly on race, discrimination is direct. Indirect discrimination is the perpetuation or magnification of the original injury. It occurs when the inequitable results of direct discrimination are used as a basis for later decisions ("past-in-present discrimination"), or decisions in linked institutions ("side-effect discrimination") (Feagin and Feagin 1986). Hence, discrimination is indirect when an ostensibly nonracial criterion serves as a *proxy* for race in determining social outcomes.

To illustrate with wages, direct discrimination exists when equally qualified blacks and whites or men and women are paid at different rates for the same work. Indirect discrimination exists when the two groups are paid unequally because *prior* discrimination in employment, education, or housing created apparent differences in qualifications or channeled the groups into better- and worse-paying jobs. This direct/indirect distinction resembles the legal distinction between disparate treatment and disparate impact. While intentional direct discrimination may have triggered the

causal chain, the original injury is often perpetuated and magnified by unwitting accomplices. Intentionality criteria deny that the continuing disadvantage is a legacy of discrimination.

Years ago, Williams outlined the concept differently: "Discrimination may be said to exist to the degree that individuals of a given group who are otherwise *formally qualified* are not treated in conformity with these nominally *universal institutionalized codes*." (Williams 1947, p. 39, italics added). For Antonovsky (1960, p. 81), discrimination involves ". . . injurious treatment of persons on grounds *rationally irrelevant* to the situation" (italics added). Economists use starker terms. Becker (1968, p. 81) held that economic discrimination occurs ". . . against members of a group whenever their earnings fall short of the amount *'warranted'* by their abilities" (italics added).

Two problems arise with these definitions. First, the assessment of "abilities" and of what treatment is "rationally" relevant or "warranted" is no easy task. Critical examination of common practice uncovers many instances where formal qualifications and "nominally universal institutionalized codes" prove *not* to provide a logical basis for distinctions. Employment testing litigation demonstrates that when hiring criteria once legitimized by tradition or "logic" are put to scientific test, they often fail to predict job performance in the assumed fashion. Analogous fallacies have been identified in the conventional wisdom guiding admission to advanced education. Hence, nominally universalistic standards may provide an altogether illogical basis for decision making. If such misguided selection procedures also work to the disadvantage of historical victims of discrimination, these practices are not exempted from the charge of discrimination by their universalistic facade.

The second problem with these definitions is that they ignore another, prevalent form of indirect discrimination. Even where nominally universalistic standards do serve some legitimate social function, such as selecting competent workers, adverse impact of these standards on those who bear the cumulated disadvantage of historical discrimination cannot be disregarded.

The complexity of discrimination and unresolved issues about its definition impede easy application of social science methods to inform institutional policy. Apparently rigorous quantitative analyses often only camouflage the crucial issues, as critical examination of wage differential decompositions reveals.

THE DECOMPOSITION APPROACH

Assessments of discrimination produced by decomposing gross race or gender differences in wages or other social outcomes are common in sociology (e.g., Corcoran and Duncan 1978; Farley 1984, Rosenfeld and Kalleberg 1990) as well as in economics (e.g., Gill 1989). One segment of the gross intergroup differential is defined by its empirical linkage to "qualifications" and other factors deemed legitimate determinants of social rewards. The second, residual segment not demonstrably linked to "legitimate" determinants of the outcomes often is presented as the estimate of discrimination. However, in the absence of better information than usually available and greater agreement on what constitutes discrimination, no *unique* estimate is possible. Through their choice of control variables to index "legitimate" determinants of social outcomes and their interpretation of findings, researchers wittingly or unwittingly shape their answers. Any appearance of scientific certitude is an illusion. For example, estimated proportions of the gender earnings gap caused by discrimination in the United States range from Sanborn's (1969) 10 percent or less to Blinder's (1973) 100 percent. Predictably, each has been challenged (Bergman and Adelman 1973; Rosensweig and Morgan 1976).

An Illustrative Decomposition Study. An analysis of gender differentials in faculty salaries at a large university illustrates the difficulty of separating "legitimate" wage differentials from inequity (Taylor 1988). About 90 percent of a $10,000 gender difference in faculty salaries was empirically linked to three factors widely considered legitimate determinants of faculty pay: academic rank, age, and discipline. Women tend to hold lower academic rank, to be younger, and more often to be affiliated with poorly-paid disciplines than men. Insofar as women's lower salaries are linked to rank, age, and discipline, is the salary differential untainted by gender discrimination? Conventional wage differentials imply an unequivocal yes. If a simple answer is given, it should be no. But in truth, when policy makers ask for dollar estimates

of inequity that the institution is obliged to remedy, the answers are neither unequivocal nor simple.

If the university's promotion system has operated fairly, a gender gap reflecting differences in rank may be warranted. If gender bias has existed in the university's promotion system, depressing the average academic rank of women faculty, the resulting deficit in women's salaries reflects indirect discrimination. Attention should then be directed to the offending promotion processes. However, direct salary adjustments may also be in order, because gender bias in promotions weakens the link between rank and merit. Inequitable depression of women's ranks would not necessarily lessen their actual contributions to the faculty, just their status. Using rank as a universalistic determinate of salary would then undermine the goal this practice is claimed to promote—the matching of rewards to contributions.

Salary differences tied to the age differential of female and male faculty also raise troublesome questions. If the relative youth of women faculty reflects lower retention and higher turnover as a result of discriminatory review processes or generally inhospitable conditions, salary differentials tied to age differences are again examples of indirect discrimination. The evidence would signal a need for institutional efforts to improve the retention of women faculty. But here it is not clear that salary adjustments are warranted. Because faculty contributions may be a function of experience, application of the universalistic age criterion is arguably reasonable. Any gender gap in salary tied to age differentials could, then, be both a legacy of discrimination and a reasonable conditioning of rewards on contributions. Complicating the issue further is the fact that affirmative action efforts often meet with greatest success in recruiting junior candidates. Thus, without supplementary data, it is not even clear whether an age-linked gender gap in salary reflects continuing institutional discrimination or affirmative hiring.

Gender differences in salary associated with discipline present even more complicated interpretational problems. Women and men are distributed across academic disciplines in a fashion that mirrors the gender distribution across occupations. Disciplinary differences in average salary likewise mirror wage differentials across occupations. But are the differing occupational distributions simply a matter of gender differences in preferences or abilities with no implication of discrimination? Or are women steered away from lucrative fields, so that gender differentials in salary linked to disciplinary affiliation represent indirect discrimination in training, recruitment, and hiring? Or does the pattern of occupational wage differentials mirrored in disciplinary differences represent direct discrimination, an influence of gender composition per se on occupational wage structures (England et al. 1988)? In the latter case, assignment of responsibility for remedy presents particular problems. The university, like any other single employer, is simultaneously vulnerable to competitive forces of the wider labor market and a constituent element of that market. Defiance of the market by a single organization is costly to that organization; adherence by all organizations to the broader occupational wage structure perpetuates gender inequity and carries broader costs.

This faculty salary study did not examine the role of scientific "productivity." But the inclusion of productivity measures among the control variables raises further difficulties. On standard "productivity" measures, women faculty average lower scores than men (Fox 1990). Thus, an institutional study of salary differentials might find some segment of the male/female salary gap linked to productivity differences. Fox's research demonstrates, however, that gender differences in scientific productivity reflect contrasting levels of resources that institutions provide to male and female faculty. Like age and rank, the gender difference in productivity may itself be a product of institutional discrimination. Thus, salary differentials based on male/female productivity differences also may represent indirect discrimination. The new ingredient here is that institutional shaping of productivity is subtle. Scientific productivity is ordinarily seen as an outgrowth of talent and effort, not potentially gender-biased institutional resource allocation. Solid documentation of this indirect discrimination process offers another challenge for researchers.

COMPLEXITIES OF DISCRIMINATION AND REMEDY

Critical reflection on this decomposition study highlights a set of interrelated points about the complex nature of discrimination and unresolved issues of remedy.

1. In American society today, the injuries of indirect discrimination are often far more extensive than those of direct discrimination. This conclusion does not imply that direct discrimination no longer exists (Reskin 1998). The continued operation of direct forms of discrimination is indicated by employment complaint records. American women and minorities have filed almost 1.5 million job discrimination complaints since 1965 (Blumrosen 1996, p. 4). In 1994 alone, over 150,000 such complaints were filed; 91,000 to local and state agencies and 64,000 to the U.S. Equal Employment Opportunity Commission (Leonard 1994, p. 24). Of course, not all complaints reflect genuine discrimination; on the other hand, not all discrimination prompts formal complaints. Many major corporations were found guilty of direct race or gender discrimination in the 1990s. And employment audits using paired, equally qualified applicants reveal widespread direct discrimination (Reskin 1998, pp. 25–29).

2. Apparently reasonable universalistic principles may on closer examination be unnecessary or even disfunctional. Scrutiny of employment criteria prompted by the Supreme Court's 1971 *Griggs v. Duke Power Co.* decision has provided useful models for challenging nominally universalistic standards. Where it is possible to substitute standards that do as well or better at screening or evaluation without adversely affecting historical targets of discrimination, there are gains for all involved.

3. When gaps in actual qualifications are a legacy of discrimination, more extensive remedies are needed. Where training deficits impair employability, or inadequate preparation impedes admission to higher education, attention should be given to the earlier schooling processes that generated these deficiencies. This form of remedy aids future generations. In the meantime, compensatory training can

reduce the liabilities of those who have already fallen victim to inferior schools.

4. Microcosms cannot escape the discriminatory impact of the societal macrocosm. Just as salary differences across academic disciplines reflect general occupational wage structures, institutions are often both prey to and participant in broader social forces. Narrow, legalistic approaches to remedy are inadequate for addressing this dynamic of discrimination.

5. Empirical research on group discrimination must mirror the phenomenon in its variety and complexity. The regression decomposition approach has proven useful but has its limitations (see also Dempster 1988, and the ensuing commentary). Regression analyses could provide more pertinent information if based on more homogeneous job groups (Conway and Roberts 1994) and on structural equation models that test reciprocal causation. Most important, if the aim is to guide policy, a framework far more complex than the dichotomous discrimination-or-not approach is required. The sociological arsenal of methods offers other promising approaches. Research that traces the actual processes of institutional discrimination is essential (e.g., Braddock and McPartland 1987, 1989). Also needed is attention to victims' perceptions of discrimination (e.g., Feagin and Sikes 1994) and investigation of the changes generated by anti-discrimination efforts. Another approach involves cross-national comparative research, which we consider below.

EFFECTIVE REMEDIAL INTERVENTIONS

Direct racial and gender discrimination in the United States has declined in recent decades—more slowly in the 1980s and 1990s than in the 1960s and 1970s. But what caused this decline? Many factors were involved, but governmental intervention was an important impetus. For example, blacks in South Carolina made dramatic economic gains in manufacturing during the late 1960s. Heckman and Payner (1989) demonstrated that human capital, supply shifts, and tight labor

markets could not explain the sudden improvements. It was federal anti-discrimination programs, they concluded, that made a decisive contribution to the gains.

More general assessments also show that anti-discrimination legislation did reduce direct job discrimination nationally (Burstein 1985). It did not, however, eliminate the problem. Nor did such laws effectively attack indirect discrimination. For this more difficult problem, affirmative action programs were needed and have had some success (Reskin 1998). The resistance to such programs, however, underscores the difficulty of establishing effective remedies for the more subtle forms of discrimination.

DISCRIMINATION IN WESTERN EUROPE

Beyond racial and gender discrimination in the United States, the same basic concerns and principles arise for other nations and targets. Discrimination against Western Europe's new immigrant minorities is pervasive (Castles 1984; MacEwen 1995; Pettigrew 1998). Both direct and indirect discrimination are involved, though the indirect forms are largely unrecognized in Europe.

Investigators have repeatedly uncovered direct discrimination in England (Amin et al. 1988; Daniel 1968; Gordon and Klug 1984; Smith 1976). Controlled tests reveal the full litany of discriminatory forms involving employment, public accommodations, housing, the courts, insurance, banks, even car rentals. Employment discrimination poses the most serious problem. In every European Union nation, minorities have far higher unemployment rates than the majority group. In 1990 in the Netherlands, Moroccans and Turks had unemployment rates above 40 percent compared with the native Dutch rate of 13 percent (Pettigrew and Meertens 1996). During the 1974–1977 recession, West German manufacturing reduced its labor force by 765,000—42 percent of whom were foreign workers (Castles 1984, p. 148).

As in the United States, there are many reasons for minority unemployment disparities. The "last-in, first-out" principle selectively affects the younger minority workers. Typically less skilled, they are more affected by job upgrading. Minorities also are more likely to be in older, declining industries. But these patterns are not accidental. Planners put minorities into these industries for cheaper labor precisely because of their decline. In addition, these multiple factors offer insufficient explanations for the greater unemployment of minorities. Veenman and Roelandt (1990) found that education, age, sex, region, and employment level explained only a small portion of the differential unemployment rates in the Netherlands.

Indirect discrimination arises when the inability to obtain citizenship restricts the opportunities of non-European Union minorities. It limits their ability to get suitable housing, employment, and schooling. A visa is necessary in order to travel to other European Union countries. In short, the lives of Europe's non-citizens are severely circumscribed (Wilpert 1993). Castles (1984) contends that the guest-worker system that brought many of the immigrants to Europe was itself a state-controlled system of institutional discrimination. It established the newcomers as a stigmatized "out-group" suitable for low-status jobs but not citizenship. Widespread indirect discrimination was inevitable for these victims of direct discrimination.

Anti-discrimination remediation has been largely ineffective in Europe. Basic rights in Germany are guaranteed only to citizens. So, the disadvantages of non-citizenship include limited means to combat discrimination. There is extensive German legislation to combat anti-Semitism and Nazi ideology, but these laws have proved difficult to apply to non-citizens. The German constitution explicitly forbids discrimination on the basis of origin, race, language, beliefs, or religion—but not citizenship. Indeed, the Federal Constitutional Court has ruled that differential treatment based on citizenship is constitutional if there is a reasonable basis for it and if it is not wholly arbitrary. Hence, a German court upheld higher taxes for foreign bar owners than German bar owners. And restaurants can refuse service to Turks and others on the grounds that their entry might lead to intergroup disturbances (Layton-Henry and Wilpert 1994).

Few means of combatting discrimination are available in France either. Commentators often view discrimination as "natural," as something universally triggered when a "threshold of tolerance" (seuil de tolerance) is surpassed (MacMaster

1991). Without supporting evidence, this rationalization supports quotas and dispersal policies that limit minority access to suitable housing.

The Netherlands, United Kingdom, and Sweden have enacted anti-discrimination legislation that specifically applies to the new immigrant minorities. And the Dutch have instituted modest affirmative action programs for women and minorities (De Vries and Pettigrew 1994). Not coincidentally, these countries make citizenship easier to obtain than Germany. Yet this legislation has been largely ineffective for two interrelated reasons. First, European legal systems do not allow class action suits—a forceful North American weapon to combat discrimination. Second, European efforts rely heavily on individual complaints rather than systemic remediation. Britain's 1976 Act gave the Commission for Racial Equality the power to cast a broad net, but individual complaints remain the chief tool (MacEwen 1995).

It is a sociological truism that individual efforts are unlikely to alter such systemic phenomena as discrimination. Mayhew (1968) showed how individual suits and complaints are largely nonstrategic. Minorities bring few charges against the worst discriminators, because they avoid applying for jobs with them in the first place. Complaints about job promotion are common, but they are made against employers who hire minorities. Thus, effective anti-discrimination laws must provide broad powers to an enforcement agency to initiate strategic, institutionwide actions that uproot the structural foundations of discrimination. Mayhew's American analysis proves to be just as accurate in Western Europe.

CONCLUSIONS

A comprehensive understanding of societal discrimination in both North America and Western Europe must encompass two propositions.

1. The long-lasting character of discrimination means that the effects typically outlive the initiators of discriminatory practices. Apart from its importance to the law, this feature of modern discrimination has critical implications for sociological theory. Discrimination is fundamentally normative; its structural web operates in large part independent of the dominant group's

present "tastes," attitudes, or awareness. Hence, models based primarily on individual prejudice or "rationality," whether psychological or economic, will uniformly understate and oversimplify the phenomenon.

2. Discrimination is typically cumulative and self-perpetuating. For example, an array of research on black Americans has demonstrated that neighborhood racial segregation leads to educational disadvantages, then to occupational disadvantage, and thus to income deficits (Pettigrew 1979, 1985). To be effective, structural remedies must reverse this "vicious circle" of discrimination. Affirmative action programs are one such remedy.

Seen in sociological perspective, then, discrimination is considerably more intricate and entrenched than commonly thought. The complexity of discrimination presents major challenges to social-scientific attempts to trace its impact. This complexity also precludes any one-to-one correspondence between perpetration and responsibility for remedy. Broad social programs will be necessary if the full legacy of direct and indirect discrimination is finally to be erased.

REFERENCES

Amin, K., M. Fernandes, and P. Gordon 1988 *Racism and Discrimination in Britain: A Select Bibliography, 1984–87.* London: Runnymede Trust.

Antonovsky, A. 1960 "The Social Meaning of Discrimination." *Phylon* 11:81–95.

Becker, G. 1968 "Economic Discrimination." In D. L. Sills, ed., *International Encyclopedia of the Social Sciences*, vol. IV. New York: Macmillan.

Bergman, B. R., and I. Adelman 1973 "The 1973 Report of the President's Council of Economic Advisors: The Economic Role of Women." *American Economic Review* 63:509–514.

Blinder, A. S. 1973 "Wage Discrimination: Reduced Form and Structural Estimates." *Journal of Human Resources* 8:436–455.

Blumrosen, A. W. 1996 *Declaration.* Statement submitted to the Supreme Court of California in response to Proposition 209 (Sept. 26, 1996).

Braddock, J. H. II, and J. M. McPartland 1987 "How Minorities Continue to be Excluded from Equal Employment Opportunities: Research on Labor Market and Institutional Barriers." *Journal of Social Issues* 43:5–39.

—— 1989 "Social Psychological Processes that Perpetuate Racial Segregation: The Relationship Between School and Employment Desegregation." *Journal of Black Studies* 19:267–289.

Burkey, R. 1978 *Ethnic and Racial Groups: The Dynamics of Dominance.* Menlo Park, Calif.: Cummings.

Burstein, P. 1985 *Discrimination, Jobs, and Politics.* Chicago: University of Chicago Press.

Castles, S. 1984 *Here for Good: Western Europe's New Ethnic Minorities.* London: Pluto Press.

Conway, D. A., H.V. and Roberts 1994 "Analysis of Employment Discrimination through Homogeneous Job Groups." *Journal of Econometrics* 61:103–131.

Corcoran M., and G. J. Duncan 1978 "Work History, Labor Force Attachment, and Earning Differences Between Races and Sexes." *Journal of Human Resources* 14:3–20.

Daniel, W. W. 1968 *Racial Discrimination In England.* Harmondsworth, UK: Penguin.

Dempster, A. P. 1988 "Employment Discrimination and Statistical Science." *Statistical Science* 3:149–195.

De Vries, S., and T. F. Pettigrew 1994 "A Comparative Perspective on Affirmative Action: *Positieve aktie* in the Netherlands." *Basic and Applied Social Psychology* 15:179–199.

England, P., G. Farkas, B. Kilbourne, and T. Dou 1988 "Explaining Occupational Sex Segregation and Wages: Findings from a Model with Fixed Effects." *American Sociological Review* 53:544–558.

Farley, R. 1984 *Blacks and Whites: Narrowing the Gap?* Cambridge, Mass.: Harvard University Press.

Feagin, J. R., and C. B. Feagin 1986 *Discrimination American Style: Institutional Racism and Sexism*, 2d ed. Malabar, Fla.: Krieger.

Feagin, J. R., and M. P. Sikes 1994 *Living with Racism: The Black Middle-Class Experience.* Boston, Mass.: Beacon Press.

Fox, M. F. 1991 "Gender, Environmental Milieux, and Productivity in Science." In J.Cole, H. Zuckerman, and J. Bruer, eds., *The Outer Circle: Women in the Scientific Community.* New York: Norton.

Gill, A. M. 1989 "The Role of Discrimination in Determining Occupational Structure." *Industrial and Labor Relations Review* 42:610–623.

Gordon, P., and F. Klug 1984 *Racism and Discrimination in Britain: A Select Bibliography, 1970–83.* London: Runnymede Trust.

Heckman, J. J., and B. S. Payner 1989 "Determining the Impact of Federal Antidiscrimination Policy on the Economic Status of Blacks: A Study of South Carolina." *American Economic Review* 79:138–177.

Layton-Henry, Z., and C. Wilpert 1994 *Discrimination, Racism and Citizenship: Inclusion and Exclusion in Britain and Germany*. London: Anglo-German Foundation for the Study of Industrial Society.

Leonard, J. S. 1994 "Use of Enforcement Techniques in Eliminating Glass Ceiling Barriers." Report to the Glass Ceiling Commission. U. S. Dept. of Labor, Washington, D.C.

MacEwen M. 1995 *Tackling Racism in Europe: An Examination of Anti-Discrimination Law in Practice*. Washington, D.C.: Berg.

MacMaster N. 1991 "The 'Seuil de Tolerance': The Uses of a 'Scientific' Racist Concept." In M. Silverman, ed., *Race, Discourse and Power in France*. Aldershot, UK: Avebury.

Mayhew, L. H. 1968 *Law and Equal Opportunity: A Study of the Massachusetts Commission Against Discrimination*. Cambridge, Mass.: Harvard University Press.

Pettigrew, T. F. 1979 "Racial Change and Social Policy." *Annals of the American Association of Political and Social Science* 441:114–131.

—— 1985 "New Black-White Patterns: How Best to Conceptualize Them?" *Annual Review of Sociology* 11:329–346.

—— 1998 "Responses to the New Minorities of Western Europe." *Annual Review of Sociology* 24:77–103.

——, and R. W. Meertens 1996 "The Verzuiling Puzzle: Understanding Dutch Intergroup Relations." *Current Psychology* 15:3–13.

Reskin, B. F. 1998 *The Realities of Affirmative Action in Employment*. Washington, D.C.: American Sociological Association.

Rosenfeld, R. A., and A. L. Kalleberg 1990 "A Cross-national Comparison of the Gender Gap in Income." *American Journal of Sociology* 96:69–105.

Rosensweig, M. R., and J. Morgan 1976 "Wage Discrimination: A Comment." *Journal of Human Resources* 11:3–7.

Sanborn, H. 1969 "Pay Differences Between Men and Women." *Industrial and Labor Relations Review* 17:534–550.

Smith, D. J. 1976 *The Facts of Racial Disadvantage: A National Survey*. London: PEP.

Taylor, M. C. 1988 "Estimating Race and Sex Inequity in Wages: Substantive Implications of Methodological Choices." Paper presented at the 1989 Research Conference of the Association for Public Policy Analysis and Management. Seattle, Wash.

Veenman, J., and T. Roelandt 1990 "Allochtonen: Achterstand en Achterstelling." In J. J. Schippers, ed., *Arbeidsmarkt en Maatschappelijke Ongelijkheid*. Groningen, The Netherlands: Wolters-Noordhoff.

Williams, R. M., Jr. 1947 *The Reduction of Intergroup Tensions*. New York: Social Science Research Council.

Wilpert, C. 1993 "Ideological and Institutional Foundations of Racism in the Federal Republic of Germany." In J. Solomos and J. Wrench, eds., *Racism and Migration in Western Europe*. Oxford, UK: Berg.

THOMAS F. PETTIGREW
MARYLEE C. TAYLOR

DISENGAGEMENT THEORY

See Aging and the Life Course; Retirement.

DISTRIBUTION-FREE STATISTICS

See Nonparametric Statistics.

DISTRIBUTIVE JUSTICE

See Human Rights/Children's Rights; Social Justice.

DIVISION OF LABOR

The division of labor is a multifaceted concept that applies to several levels of analysis: small groups, families, households, formal organizations, societies, and even the entire "world system" (Wallerstein 1979). Each level of analysis requires a slightly different focus; the division of labor may refer to the emergence of certain roles in groups, to the relative preponderance of industrial sectors (primary, secondary, tertiary) in an economy, to the distribution of societal roles by sex and age, or to variability among occupational groupings. Sociologists at the micro-level are concerned with "who does what," while macrosociologists focus on the larger structural issues of societal functions.

All of the major sociological theorists considered the division of labor to be a fundamental concept in understanding the development of modern society. The division of labor in society has been a focus of theoretical debate for more than a century, with some writers most concerned about hierarchical divisions, or the vertical dimension, and others emphasizing the heterogeneity or the horizontal dimension, of a social system. The analysis here is primarily theoretical, and so does not deal with debates about the technical problems of measurement (but see Baker 1981; Clemente 1972; Gibbs and Poston 1975; Land 1970; Rushing and Davies 1970).

THE DIVISION OF LABOR IN SMALL GROUPS

Most small groups exhibit "role differentiation," as first described by Simmel (1890), Whyte (1943), and Bales and Slater (1955). The research on informal work groups stresses a hierarchical form of the division of labor, or the emergence of leadership; in particular, the emergence of both a "task leader" and a "social leader." It appears that defining group goals and enforcing norms is a type of activity incompatible with maintaining group cohesion, and therefore most groups have a shared leadership structure. Even in same-sex groups, this structure of coleadership is apparent; also, the degree of role differentiation appears be greater in larger groups. The functional need for a social leader depends in part on the degree to which group members are task oriented, and on the degree to which the task leader is perceived as a legitimate authority (with the power to reward and punish other group members). Burke (1969) has also noted that a "scapegoat" role may emerge within task groups, reducing the need for a social leader to maintain harmony among the rest of the group members.

HOUSEHOLD AND FAMILY DIVISION OF LABOR

When the family or household is the unit of analysis, issues concerning the division of tasks between spouses are of primary interest to sociologists. One major finding has been the persistence of disproportionately high levels of traditional housework by the wife, even when she is employed outside the home. This reflects the "provider" vs. "homemaker" role distinction that formerly characterized most nuclear families in industrialized societies. Another major family role, occupied almost exclusively by the wife, is that of "kinkeeper." The maintenance of family traditions, the recording of important family anniversaries, and the coordination of visits between households are all vital elements of this role. The classic works by Bott (1957) and Blood and Wolfe (1960) documented the spousal division of labor as it was influenced by wider social networks and the relative power of the husband and wife. Kamo (1988) has noted that cultural ideology is a strong factor in the determination of spousal roles, although it is not entirely independent of the resources available to husband and wife.

Within a household, both age and sex structure the division of labor. Young children have few responsibilities, while parents have many, and males and females tend to do very different tasks. For example, White and Brinkerhoff (1981) studied the reported allocation of a variety of household tasks among a sample of Nebraska households, and found that the youngest cohort of children (aged two to five) performed relatively few household tasks and showed little differentiation by sex. Older children, however, diverged considerably in their roles (males doing more outdoor work, females more responsible for cooking or childcare). At the other end of the lifespan, the roles of the grandparent generation were strongly influenced by geographical proximity, the ages of the grandparents, and the ages of the children. Divorce among the parental generation can also substantially impact the roles adopted by grandparents (see Bengston and Robertson 1985).

FORMAL ORGANIZATIONS AND OCCUPATIONAL SPECIALIZATION

Formal organizations are always structured by an explicit division of labor (an organization chart contains the names of functions, positions, or subunits). The horizontal differentiation in an organization, or task specialization, is normally based on functional units that are of roughly equivalent levels in the hierarchy of authority. The division of labor may also be constructed on a geographical basis, with the extreme examples being transnational corporations that draw raw resources and labor from the developing nations, and management from the developed nations.

Labor is also organized hierarchically, into levels of authority. Max Weber was one of the first sociologists to analyze the emergence of modern bureaucracies, where the division of labor is fundamental. Weber's approach suggests a maximum possible level of specialization, so that each position can be filled by individuals who are experts in a narrow area of activity. An extreme form of the bureaucratic division of labor was advocated by Frederick Taylor's theory of "Scientific Management" (1911). By studying in minute detail the physical motions required to most efficiently operate any given piece of machinery, Taylor pioneered "time and motion studies." Along with Henry Ford, he also made the assembly line a standard industrial mode of production in modern society. However, this form of the division of labor can lead to isolation and alienation among workers, and so more recent organizational strategies, in some industrial sectors, emphasize the "craft" approach, in which a team of workers participate more or less equally in many aspects of the production process (see Blauner 1964; Hedley 1992).

SOCIETAL DIVISION OF LABOR

Macrosociologists measure the societal division of labor in a number of ways, most commonly by considering the number of different occupational categories that appear in census statistics or other official documents (see Moore 1968). These lists are often implicitly or explicitly ranked, and so both horizontal and vertical division of labor can be analyzed. This occupational heterogeneity is dependent in part on the official definitions, but researchers on occupational prestige (the vertical dimension) have shown comparable levels in industrialized societies such as the United States, Canada, England, Japan, Sweden, Germany, and France (see Treiman 1977). The "world system" as described by Wallerstein (1979) is the upper limit of the analysis of the division of labor. Entire societies are characterized as "core" or "periphery" in Wallerstein's analysis of the global implications of postindustrialism.

THEORETICAL APPROACHES

Adam Smith, in *The Wealth of Nations* (1776), produced the classic statement of the economic efficiencies of a complex division of labor. He observed that the manufacture of steel pins could be more than two hundred times more productive if each separate operation (and there were more than a dozen) were performed by a separate worker. The emergence of the systematic and intentional division of labor probably goes back to prehistoric societies, and is certainly in evidence in the ancient civilizations of China, Egypt, Greece, and Rome. The accumulation of an agricultural surplus and the establishment of markets both created and stimulated the differentiation of producers and consumers. Another phase in the transformation in Europe was the decline of the "craft guilds" that dominated from the twelfth to the sixteenth centuries. When labor became free from the constraints of the journeyman/apprentice system and when factories began to attract large numbers of laborers, the mechanization of modern work flourished. (For economic and political perspectives on the division of labor see Krause 1982; Putterman 1990).

Early sociologists such as Herbert Spencer considered the growth of societies as the primary determinant of the increased specialization and routinization of work; they also emphasized the positive impacts of this process. Spencer, like other functionalists, viewed human society as an organic system that became increasingly differentiated as it grew in size, much as a fertilized egg develops complex structures as it develops into a full-fledged embryo. In his *Principles of Sociology* (1884), Spencer considered the evolution of human society as a process of increasing differentiation of structure and function.

Karl Marx(1867) argued that the increasing division of labor in capitalist societies is a primary cause of alienation and class conflict, and therefore is a force in the eventual transformation to a socialist/communist society. In fact, a specific question asking for details of the division of labor appeared on one of the earliest questionnaire surveys in sociology done by Marx in 1880. Marx and his followers called for a new form of the division of labor, supported by an equalitarian ethos, in which individuals would be free to choose their productive roles; labor would not be alienating because of the common ideology and sense of community.

Weber (1947) painted a darker picture when he documented the increasing "rationalization" of society, especially the ascendence of the bureaucratic division of labor with its coordinated system of roles, each highly specialized, with duties specified in writing and incumbents hired on the basis of their documented competence at specific tasks. The ideal-type bureaucracy was in actuality subject to the negative consequences of excessive specialization, however. Weber pointed out that the "iron cage" placed stifling limits on human freedom within the organization, and that decisions by bureaucrats often became so rule bound and inflexible that the clients were ill served.

Georg Simmel's "differentiation and the principle of saving energy" (1976 [1890]) is a little-known essay that similarly describes the inevitable problems that offset the efficiencies gained by the division of labor; he called these "friction, indirectness, and superfluous coordination." He also echoed Marx and Engels when he described the effects of high levels of differentiation upon the individual:

> ... *differentiation of the social group is evidently directly opposed to that of the individual. The former requires that the individual must be as specialized as possible, that some single task must absorb all his energies and that all his impulses, abilities and interests must be made compatible with this one task, because this specialization of the individual makes it both possible and necessary to the highest degree for him to be different from all other specialized individuals. Thus the economic setup of society forces the individual for life into the most monotonous work, the most extreme specialization, because in this way he will acquire the skill which makes possible the desired quality and cheapness of the product.* (Simmel 1976, p. 130)

While the foregoing theorists contributed substantially to the understanding of the division of labor, Emile Durkheim's *The Division of Labor in Society* (1893) stands as the classic sociological statement of the causes and consequences of the historical shift from "mechanical solidarity" to "organic solidarity." The former is found in smaller, less-advanced societies where families and villages are mostly self-sufficient, independent, and united by similarities. The latter is found in larger, urbanized societies where specialization creates interdependence among social units.

Following Spencer's lead, Durkheim noted that the specialization of functions always accompanies the growth of a society; he also observed that increasing population density—the urbanization of society that accompanies modernization—greatly increases the opportunities for further increases in the division of labor.

It should be noted that the shift to a modern division of labor could not have occurred without a preexisting solidarity; in his chapter on "organic and contractual solidarity" he departed from Spencer's utilitarian explanation of social cohesion, and noted that the advanced division of labor can occur only among members of an existing society, where individuals and groups are united by preexisting similarities (of language, religion, etc.).

A sense of trust, obligation, and interdependence is essential for any large group in which there are many diverse roles; indirect exchanges occur; and individuals form smaller subgroupings based on occupational specialization. All of these changes create high levels of interdependence, but with increasing specialization, and different world views develop, along with different interests, values, and belief systems. This is the problem Durkheim saw in the shift from mechanical to organic solidarity; he feared the "anomie" or lack of cohesion that might result from a multiplicity of views, languages, and religions within a society (as in the France of his times, and even more so today). The problems of inequality in modern industrial society were not lost on Durkheim, either; he noted how the "pathological form of the division of labor" posed a threat to the full development of social solidarity (see Giddens 1971). Although many simplistic analyses of Durkheim's approach suggest otherwise, he dealt at length with the problems of "the class war" and the need for justice and fraternity.

The division of labor is treated as a key element in Peter Blau's book, *Inequality and Heterogeneity* (1977). This important work emphasizes the primacy of differentiation (division of labor) as an influence on mobility, prejudice, conflict, affiliation, intermarriage, and inequality. In Blau's scheme, a society may be undifferentiated (all persons or positions are independent, self-sufficient, etc.) or strongly differentiated (a high degree of specialization and interdependence). This differentiation may be a matter of degree, on dimensions such as authority, power, prestige, etc.; this constitutes inequality. Or the differentiation may be a matter of kind, such as occupational differentiation—the division of labor.

Blau, like Durkheim, distinguished two major types of division of labor: *routinization* and *expert specialization*.

> *The two major forms of division of labor are the subdivision of work into repetitive routines and its subdivision into expert specialties. . . when jobs are divided into repetitive routines, the training and skills needed to perform them are reduced, whereas when they are divided into fields of specialists, the narrower range of tasks permits greater expertness to be acquired and applied to the work, increasing the training and skills required to perform it.* (Blau 1977, p. 188)

Blau has shown that the division of labor always increases inequality in the organization. The managerial and technical experts coordinate the increasing number and diversity of routinized positions. As organizations and societies increase in size and population density, the division of labor increases. At the same time, the forces of industrialization and urbanization require and encourage further specialization, and in most cases, increase inequality, and indirectly, social integration. Some of the confounding boundaries include the degree of linguistic, ethnic, or cultural heterogeneity (all of which can inhibit integration), and social or geographic mobility (which can increase integration).

In a rare display of explicitly stated definitions and propositions, Blau created a landmark theory of social organization. Here are the most important of Blau's assumptions and theorems relating to the division of labor:

- The division of labor depends on opportunities for communication.

- Population density and urbanization increase the division of labor.

- Rising levels of education and qualifications promote an advanced division of labor.

- Large work organizations promote the division of labor in society.

- Linguistic heterogeneity impedes the division of labor.

- The more the division of labor is in the form of specialization rather than routinization, the higher are rates of associations among different occupations, which produces higher integration.

- The more the division of labor intersects with other nominal parameters (including kinship, language, religion, ethnicity, etc.) the greater is the probability that intergroup relations strengthen society's integration.

- The smaller an organization, the more its internal division of labor increases the probabilities of intergroup and interstratum associations, and therefore the higher the degree of integration. (Summarized from Blau 1977, pp. 214–215)

Blau concludes by noting that "Advances in the division of labor tend to be accompanied by decreases in various forms of inequality but by increases in inequality in power. Although the advancing division of labor does not generate the growing concentration of power, the two are likely to occur together, because the expansion of work organizations promotes both." (p. 214).

CONCLUSION

Ford's moving assembly lines began to produce the frames for Model T automobiles in 1913, at a rate of about one every two working days, but within months, refinements on the assembly process reduced this to four units per day. This eightfold increase in efficiency was accompanied by a decrease in the price of the cars and indirectly stimulated a very large industry. Now, automated factories, using robotics and highly specialized computer systems, have dramatically increased the efficiency of the automobile industry. The effects on morale and the environment, however, appear to be less salutary.

(SEE ALSO: *Bureaucracy, Complex Organizations, Convergence Theories, Family and Household Structure, Family Roles, Industrial Sociology, Industrialization, Parental Roles, Social Change, Social Structure, Technology and Society,* and *Work and Occupations.*)

REFERENCES

Baker, P.M. 1981 "The Division of Labor: Interdependence, Isolation, and Cohesion in Small Groups." *Small Group Behavior* 12(1):93–106.

Bales, R.F,. and P.E. Slater 1955 "Role Differentiation in Small Decision-Making Groups." In T. Parsons et al., eds., *Family, Socialization, and Interaction Process.* Glencoe, Ill.: Free Press.

Bengston, V.L., and J.F. Robertson 1985 *Grandparenthood.* Beverly Hills, Calif.: Sage.

Blau, P.M. 1977 *Inequality and Heterogeneity.* New York: Free Press.

Blauner, R. 1964 *Alienation and Freedom.* Chicago: University of Chicago Press.

Blood, R., and D. Wolfe 1960 *Husbands and Wives: The Dynamics of Married Living.* New York: Free Press.

Bott, E. 1957 *Family and Social Network.* London: Tavistock Publications.

Burke, P.J. 1969 "Scapegoating: An Alternative to Role Differentiation." *Sociometry* 32(June):159–168.

Clemente, R. 1972 "The Measurement Problem in the Analysis of an Ecological Concept: The Division of Labor." *Pacific Sociological Review* 15:30–40.

Durkheim, E. (1893) 1933 *The Division of Labor in Society.* New York: Free Press.

Gibbs, J.P., and D.L. Poston 1975 "The Division of Labor: Conceptualization and Related Issues." *Social Forces* 53 (March) 468–476.

Giddens, A. 1971 *Capitalism and Modern Social Theory: Analysis of the Writings of Marx, Durkheim, and Max Weber.* Cambridge: Cambridge University Press.

Hedley, R.A. 1992 *Making a Living: Technology and Change.* New York: Harper Collins.

Kamo, Y. 1988 "Determinants of Household Labor: Resources, Power, and Ideology." *Journal of Family Issues* 9:177–200.

Krause, E.A. 1982 *The Division of Labor: A Political Perspective.* Westport, Conn.: Greenwood Press.

Land, K.C. 1970 "Mathematical Formalization of Durkheim's Theory of Division of Labor." E.F. Borgatta, ed., *Sociological Methodology 1970,* 257–282. San Francisco: Jossey-Bass.

Marx, K. (1867) 1977 *Capital: A Critique of Political Economy.* New York: Vintage Books.

Moore, W.E. 1968 *Economy and Society.* New York: Random House.

Putterman, L. 1990 *Division of Labor and Welfare: An Introduction to Economic Systems.* New York: Oxford University Press.

Rushing, W.A., and V. Davies 1970 "Note on the Mathematical Formalization of a Measure." *Social Forces* 48(March):394–396.

Simmel, G. (1890) 1976 "On Social Differentiation." In P. Lawrence, ed., *Georg Simmel, Sociologist and European.* New York: Nelson.

Smith, Adam (1776) 1985 *An Inquiry into the Nature and Causes of the Wealth of Nations.* New York: Modern Library.

Smith, D., and R. Snow 1976 "The Division of Labor: Conceptual and Methodological Issues." *Social Forces* 55:520–528.

Spencer, H. 1884 *Principles of Sociology.* New York: Appleton-Century-Crofts.

Taylor, F. 1911 *Scientific Management.* New York: Harper.

Treiman, D. 1977 *Occupational Prestige in Comparative Perspective.* New York: Academic Press.

Wallerstein, I. 1979 *The Capitalist World-Economy.* New York: Cambridge University Press.

Weber, M. (1908) 1947 *The Theory of Social and Economic Organization.* New York: Free Press.

Whyte, W.F. 1943 *Street Corner Society.* Chicago: Chicago University Press.

PAUL MORGAN BAKER

DIVORCE

Divorce is of sociological significance for several reasons. To begin, divorce rates are often seen as indicators of the health of the institution of marriage. When divorce rates rise or fall, many sociologists view these changes as indicating something about the overall quality of marriages or, alternatively, the stability of social arrangements more generally. Viewed from another perspective, divorce interests sociologists as one of several important transitions in the life course of individuals. The adults and children who experience divorce have been studied to understand both the causes and consequences. From this perspective, a divorce is as much an event in the biography of family members, as other life-course transitions (remarriage, childbirth, and retirement). The sociological interest in divorce also focuses on the social trends it is part of, figuring prominently in any sociological analysis of industrialization, poverty rates, educational attainment, strategies of conflict resolution, or law.

For sociologists, divorce may characterize an individual, a family, a region, a subgroup, a historical period, or an entire society. It may be studied as either the cause or consequence of other phenomena. Still, the overriding concern of almost all research on this topic has been the increase in divorce over time. Divorce is now almost as common as its absence in the lives of recently married couples. The National Center for Health Statistics estimates that 43 percent of marriages begun in the early 1990s will end in divorce (NCHS 1998), a significant decline from the estimates of 50 percent to 65 percent in the late 1980s (Martin and Bumpass 1989). The decline in divorce rates in the recent past is probably a result of the aging of the post-World War II Baby Boom generation who are no longer at high risk of divorce because of their age. It is also possible that American marriages are becoming somewhat more stable than they were a decade ago. Still, the fluctuations in divorce rates one decade to the next do not mask the more general trend for the past two centuries. Understanding the increase in divorce has been the larger sociological endeavor regardless of the particular perspective employed. A historical account of trends is necessary before considering contemporary issues associated with divorce.

A BRIEF HISTORICAL RECORD OF DIVORCE IN AMERICA

The Colonial Period. Divorce was not legal in any but the New England settlements. The Church of England allowed for legal separations (*a mensa et thoro*), but not for divorce. The New England Puritans who first landed at Plymouth in 1621, however, were disenchanted with this, as well as many other Anglican doctrines. Divorce was permitted on the grounds of adultery or seven-year desertion as early as 1639 in Plymouth. Other New England colonies followed similar guidelines. Divorce governed by rudimentary codified law was granted by legislative decree. Individual petitions for divorce were debated in colonial legislatures

and were effected by bills to dissolve a particular marriage. Still, though legal, divorce was very rare. During the seventeenth century, there were fifty-four petitions for divorce in Massachusetts, of which forty-four were successful (Phillips 1988, p. 138). The middle colonies provided annulments or divorces for serious matrimonial offenses such as prolonged absence or bigamy. The southern colonies afforded no provisions for divorce whatsoever.

Post-Revolutionary War. Immediately after the Revolutionary War, without British legal impediments to divorce, the states began discussion of laws to govern divorce. In New England and the middle states, divorce became the province of state courts while in the more restrictive southern states it was more often a legislative matter. By the turn of the nineteenth century, almost all states had enacted some form of divorce law. And by the middle of the century, even southern states were operating within a judicial divorce system.

The shift to judicial divorce is significant. By removing divorce deliberations from legislatures, states were forced to establish grounds that justified a divorce. Such clauses reflected the prevailing sentiments governing normative marriage—they indicated what was expected of marriage at the time. And by investing judges with the authority to interpret and adjudicate, such changes significantly liberalized the availability of divorce. Northern and southern states permitted divorces for specific offenses such as adultery, desertion, bigamy, and increasingly with time, cruelty. In the newer frontier western states, grounds resembled those of the East plus "any other cause for which the court shall deem it proper that the divorce shall be granted" (Phillips 1988, p. 453).

Throughout the nineteenth century, there was a gradual liberalization of divorce laws in the United States and a corresponding increase in divorce as well. Where divorces totaled a few hundred at the beginning of the nineteenth century, the numbers grew exponentially as the century wore on; 7,380 divorces in 1860, 10,962 in 1870, 19,663 in 1880, 33,461 in 1890, and 55,751 in 1900 (U.S. Bureau of the Census 1975). These figures assume greater significance when growth in population is removed from them. Whereas the divorce rate (number of divorces per 1,000 marriages) was but 1.2 in 1869, it had climbed to 4.0 by 1900. In short, the increase in divorce outstripped the increase in population several times.

A number of factors have been identified as causes of such dramatic increases. In part, these can be described as social changes, which made marriage less essential. The growth of wage labor in the nineteenth century afforded women an alternative to economic dependence on a husband. In an economy dominated by individuals rather than families, marriage was simply less essential. Life as a single individual gradually lost its legal or social stigma (New England settlements had forbidden solitary dwelling while southern communities had taxed it heavily).

More important, however, were fundamental shifts in the meaning of marriage. Divorce codes reflected the growing belief that marriages should be imbued with heavy doses of affection and equality. Divorce grounds of cruelty or lack of support indicate that marriage was increasingly viewed as a partnership. Where a century earlier men had been granted greater discretion in their personal lives, latter nineteenth-century morality attacked such double standards. Men were not necessarily less culpable than women for their vices. Victorian morality stressed the highest standards of sexual behavior for both husbands and wives. Changing divorce codes coincided with the passage of laws restricting husbands' unilateral control over their wifes' property. The passage of married women's property acts throughout the nation in the latter nineteenth century acknowledged married women's claims to property brought to or acquired in marriage. By 1887, thirty-three states and the District of Columbia gave married women control over their property and earnings (Degler 1980, p. 332).

Divorce codes including omnibus grounds such as "cruelty" (which could justify a divorce from a drunkard husband, for example) may be viewed as reflecting a Victorian American belief that women were morally sensitive and fragile, and in need of protection (Phillips 1988, p. 500). More particularly, the growing use of offenses against the intimate and emotional aspects of marriage reflected a growing belief that such things constituted matrimonial essentials. If a failure of intimacy could justify the dissolution of a marriage, then intimacy may be viewed as a core expectation of marriage.

The Twentieth Century. The first half of the twentieth century was a continuation of trends established in the latter nineteenth century. Two world wars and the Great Depression interrupted gradually increasing divorce rates, however. During each war and during the Depression, divorce rates dropped. After each, rates soared before falling to levels somewhat higher than that which preceded these events. Sociological explanations for these trends focus on women's employment opportunities. Women's labor force participation permits the termination of intolerable unions. The separations, hastily timed marriages, and sexual misalliances characteristic of wartime were also undoubtedly factors in the post-war divorces rates. Further, the increases in divorce following these difficult times may be seen, in part, as a delayed reaction. Once the Depression or war was over, the reservoir of impending divorces broke. And finally, postwar optimism and affluence may have contributed to an unwillingness to sustain an unhappy marriage.

The second half of the century witnessed even more dramatic increases in divorce. With the exception of the peculiar 1950s (for an explanation of this anomaly, see Cherlin 1992), the trend for the second half of the 1900s was a regular and exponential growth in divorce until around 1980, at which point the increase stopped.

Though specific explanations for the increase in divorces during the twentieth century vary, several themes may be noted. First, marriage has lost much of its central economic and social significance—especially for women. For example, divorce was undoubtedly inhibited by the fact that prior to the twentieth century, custody of children was uniformly awarded to fathers (since they were legally responsible for financial support). With the acceptance of Freudian ideas of psychosexual development and similar ideas about intellectual and cognitive growth, the so-called Tender Years Doctrine became accepted practice in courts during the early 1900s which then awarded custody to mothers as regularly as they had once done to fathers. And as it became more commonplace, remarriage began to lose some of its stigma. All these changes made it possible for women to divorce their husbands if they wished. But why did so many wish to obtain divorces?

The simplest explanation is that more divorce is a consequence of higher expectations of marriage. More and more grounds for divorce are developed as there are higher and higher expectations for what a marriage should be. In the nineteenth century, drunkenness, cruelty, and failure to provide were added to more traditional grounds of adultery and desertion. In the early twentieth century, cruelty was continually redefined to include not only physical, but mental cruelty as well.

The post-war surges in divorce created sufficient numbers of divorced persons so that the practice lost much of its stigma. The increase in divorce becomes more understandable when the loss of stigma is considered alongside the increase in women's employment since the mid 1960s. When women are employed, there is less constraint on them to remain in a marriage. But there is also less constraint on their husbands who will not be required to support their employed ex-wives after a divorce.

Since 1970, divorce has been fundamentally redefined. No-fault divorce laws passed since the early 1970s have defined as unacceptable those marriages in which couples are "incompatible," have "irreconcilable differences" or in which the marriage is "irretrievably broken." Prior to the no-fault regime, divorces required proof of a fault (crime) on the part of one spouse. The court decided whether to grant the divorce. Divorce proceedings were intentionally adversarial. Today, the non-adversarial grounds for divorce are almost entirely based on the failures of emotional essentials. Emotional marital breakdown may have been a feature of large numbers of marriages in earlier historical periods. Only now, however, is such a situation viewed as solely sufficient grounds for terminating the marriage.

DIVORCE IN THE WEST

Any theory of divorce must be able to account for the broad similarities in historical (twentieth century) trends throughout the entire Western world. These similarities exist despite notable differences in national economies, forms of government, and the role of the church. The trends are well known. There was very little divorce until the end of the nineteenth century, a slow but constant growth in divorce rates through the first half of the twentieth century (interrupted by two world wars and an international economic depression), and significant increases in divorce rates since the 1960s. The

twentieth century, in short, is when most significant changes in divorce rates occurred. And the changes noted in America were seen in most other Western nations.

Between World Wars I and II, there were widespread changes in divorce laws that reflected changing beliefs about matrimony and its essentials. The strains of war and the associated problems that produced more divorces made the practice more conspicuous and consequently more acceptable. There is no doubt one cause of divorce is divorce. When obscure, the practice was stigmatized and there was little to counter stereotypes associated with its practice. When divorce became more commonplace, it lost some of its stigma.

Social changes pertaining to women's roles are a large part of the story of divorce during the postwar era. One sign of these changes was the growth, throughout the West, of women's labor force participation. But the most conspicuous symbol of the changing role of women was the passage of suffrage legislation throughout the Western world. Before 1914, women were permitted to vote only in New Zealand, Australia, Finland, Norway, and eleven western U.S. states. In the United States, women were enfranchised in 1920. In Britain, Sweden, Germany, and many other European countries, suffrage passed soon after World War I.

Divorce laws, similarly, were altered between the wars in accordance with changing views of marriage and the role of women. The British Parliament enacted divorce reform in 1937 by significantly extending the grounds for divorce (including cruelty) and granting women new options for filing for divorce. Scotland reformed its divorce laws in 1938 by extending grounds for divorce to include failures of emotional essentials—cruelty and habitual drunkenness, for example. In 1930, the Canadian Parliament for the first time empowered judicial magistrates to grant divorce rather than requiring legislative decrees. And the Spanish divorce law of 1932 was the most liberal in contemporary Europe—providing divorce by mutual consent (Phillips 1988, p. 539). Even Nazi Germany permitted no-fault divorce by 1938 (though divorce law was aimed at increasing the number of Aryan children born).

Following World War II, divorce rates throughout the Western world stabilized after an initial increase. The low divorce rates, high fertility, and

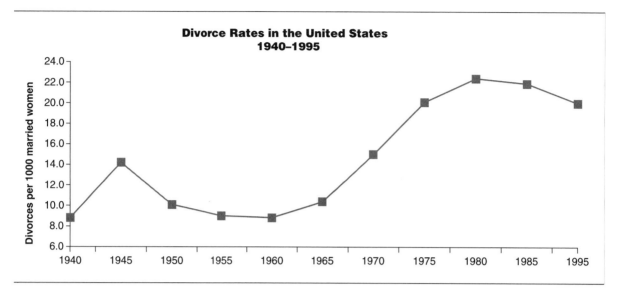

**Divorce Rates in the United States
1940–1995**

Figure 1

SOURCE: Vital Statistics of the United States

lower age at marriage that characterized all Western nations after World War II are trends that have not been adequately explained. Whether these trends reflected the consequences of war, the effects of having grown up during the worldwide depression, or a short-term rise in social conservatism is now debated. Regardless of the cause, the decade of the 1950s is universally regarded as a temporary aberration in otherwise long-term and continuous twentieth century trends. Not until the 1960s were there additional significant changes in divorce laws or divorce rates.

The 1960s were years of significant social change in almost all Western nations. The demographic consequences of high fertility during the 1950s became most apparent in the large and vocal youth movements challenging conventional sexual and marital norms, censorship, the war in Vietnam, and educational policies. Challenges to institutional authority were commonplace. Divorce laws were not immune to the general liberalization. "Between 1960 and 1986 divorce policy in almost all the countries of the West was either completely revised or substantially reformed" (Phillips 1988, p. 562). Most such reforms occurred in the late 1960s to the late 1970s. Unlike earlier divorce law reforms, those during the post-World War II era did not extend the grounds for divorce so much as they redefined the jurisdiction over it. The passage

of no-fault divorce laws signaled a profound shift in the way divorce was to be handled.

Most significantly, divorce became the prerogative of the married couple with little involvement of the state. No-fault divorce laws do not require either spouse to be guilty of an offense. Instead, they focus on the breakdown of the emotional relationship between the spouses. These statutes typically require a period of time during which the spouses do not live together. Beyond that, evidence must be adduced to substantiate one or both spouses' claim that the marriage is irretrievably broken. The significance of no-fault divorce lies entirely in the fact that decisions about divorce are no longer the prerogative of the state or church but rather of the married couple.

The passage of no-fault divorce laws in the West is properly viewed as a response to changing behaviors and attitudes. Indeed, social science research has shown that divorce rates began to increase significantly prior to passage of such laws and did not change any more dramatically afterward (Stetson and Wright 1975).

The changes in divorce law and actual divorce behaviors in the West are a reflection of the redefinition of marriage. More vulnerable and fragile emotional bonds have replaced the economic constraints that once held spouses together. The availability of gainful employment for women makes marriage less essential and divorce more possible. Indeed, the significant changes in women's social positions and the corresponding changes in normative expectations (i.e., gender) have been the subject of significant sociological research. These changes are recognized as fundamentally altering almost all social institutions. Marriage is no exception.

The redefinition of marriage in the latter twentieth century throughout the West reflects the profound changes in relationships between men and women that have occurred. No longer an economic institution, marriage is now defined by its emotional significance. Love and companionship are not incidents of the institution. Rather, they are essentials. Meeting these high expectations may be difficult, but sustaining them is certainly more so.

Taken together, the changes in the second half of the twentieth century may be summarized as redefining the meaning of marriage. Children are not economic assets. Spouses are not economic necessities. Marriage is a conjugal arrangement where the primary emphasis is on the relationship between husband and wife. The reasons for divorce are direct consequences of the reasons for marriage. As one changes so does the other. Since it is more difficult to accomplish and sustain matrimonial essentials, it is easier to terminate the legal framework surrounding them. Divorce has become less costly (financially, legally, and reputationally) as marriage has become more so (in terms of the investments required to accomplish what is expected of it).

CORRELATES OF DIVORCE

Sociologists have documented a number of demographic and personal characteristics that correlate with the probability of divorce. These include early age at marriage, premarital births, premarital cohabitation, divorce from a previous marriage, and low educational attainments. Social class is inversely related to divorce, yet wives' employment significantly increases divorce probabilities (see Huber and Spitze 1988 for a review).

Half of all recent marriages began with cohabitation (unmarried couples living together) (Bumpass and Sweet 1989). Repeated national studies have found that married couples who cohabited (either with each other, or with others) before marrying

have higher divorce rates than those who never cohabited (Nock 1995). The reason is still unclear. Research shows that cohabiting individuals are less committed to the idea of marriage or marital permanence. They are also less religious and tend to be drawn from lower social classes (both of which are associated with higher divorce rates) (Nock 1995). Cohabitation appears to foster (or reflect) a belief that problems in intimate relationships are solvable by ending the relationship. When such beliefs are carried into marriage, the result is higher divorce rates.

Race correlates with divorce—even after controls are imposed for socioeconomic correlates of race—with black individuals having divorce rates approximately twice those of whites. However, such large differences associated with race are recent in origin. Not until the late 1950s did significant differences in divorce, separation, and other marital statuses emerge between blacks and whites, even though a pattern of marginally higher marital disruption has been found among blacks for at least a century. Such findings suggest that the differences stem more from contemporary than historical circumstances. As Cherlin suggests, the recent changes in black Americans' family situations resemble those of other racial and ethnic groups, though they are more pronounced. The restructuring of the American economy, the decline in semi-skilled jobs, and the rise in service occupations has resulted in higher rates of black male unemployment or low wages, and better opportunities for black women. "Faced with difficult times economically, many blacks responded by drawing upon a model of social support that was in their cultural repertoire, a way of making it from day to day passed down by African Americans who came before them. This response relied heavily on extended kinship networks and deemphasized marriage" (Cherlin 1992, p. 113).

CONSEQUENCES OF DIVORCE

For Children. A central concern of much of the recent research on divorce is how children fare. Developmental psychologists describe five ways in which marital disruption may affect children's adjustment. First, some adults and some children are more vulnerable to the stress and strain of divorce. Personality characteristics, ethnicity, or

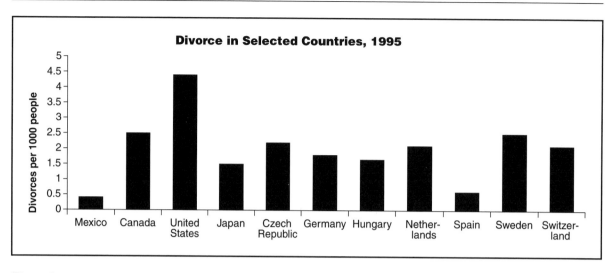

Figure 2

SOURCE: United Nations 1996 Demographic Yearbook

age for example, may make some individuals more susceptible to negative outcomes. Second, the absence of one parent, per se, may affect children's adjustment to divorce. Boys, in particular, appear to benefit from the presence of a male adult. Third, the loss of income creates many indirect problems for children, including changes in residence, school, neighborhood, and peer networks. Fourth, divorce often diminishes the custodial parent's ability to provide supportive and appropriate parenting, especially if depression follows marital disruption. And finally, negative, conflictual, and dysfunctional family relationships between parents, parents and children, and siblings are probably the most damaging consequence of divorce for children. (Hetherington, Bridges, and Insabella 1998).

Longitudinal research has shown that children who experience divorce differ from others before the disruption occurs. Cherlin showed that children whose parents were still married, but who would later divorce, showed more behavior problems and did less well in school than children whose parents would remain married (Cherlin et al. 1991).

Even after such predisruption differences are considered, divorce takes a toll in the lives of children who experience it. Divorce significantly increases the chances that young people will leave their homes due to friction with a parent, increases

the chances of premarital cohabitation, and increases the odds of premarital pregnancies or fatherhood (Cherlin, Kiernan, and Chase-Lansdale 1995). The effects of divorce in young adulthood include higher rates of unemployment and lower educational attainments. Divorce weakens young people's connections to their friends and neighbors due to higher rates of residential mobility (McLanahan and Sandefur 1994). Following divorce, many children are subjected to changes in residence, often to disadvantaged neighborhoods where peers have lower educational prospects. The lack of connections to others affects parents' ability to monitor their children. It also limits young people's knowledge about local employment opportunities.

The changed economic circumstances caused by divorce affects children in many indirect ways. The loss of available income may affect the quality of schools children attend if custodial parents move to poorer neighborhoods. The lack of income may limit children's opportunities for extracurricular activities (e.g., travel, or music lessons). The need for income often compels custodial parents to work more hours, reducing their ability to monitor children's after-school activities.

In their socioeconomic attainments, children who experienced their parents' divorce average one to two fewer years of educational attainment than children from intact homes (Krein and Beller

1988; Hetherington, Camara, and Featherman 1983). Such effects are found even after rigorous controls are imposed for such things as race, sex, years since the divorces, age at time of divorce, parental income, parental education, number of siblings, region of residence, educational materials in the home, or the number of years spent in the single-parent family. There are comparable effects of divorce on occupational prestige, income and earnings, and unemployment (Nock 1988).

White women who spent some childhood time in a single-parent family as a result of divorce are 53 percent more likely to have teenage marriages, 111 percent more likely to have teenage births, 164 percent more likely to have premarital births, and 92 percent more likely to experience marital disruptions than are daughters who grew up in two-parent families. The effects for black women are similar, though smaller. Controls for a wide range of background factors have little effect on the negative consequences of divorce. Further, remarriage does not remove these effects of divorce. And there is no difference between those who lived with their fathers and those who lived with their mothers after divorce. Experiencing parents' divorce has the same (statistical) consequences as being born to a never-married mother (McLanahan and Bumpass 1988; McLanahan and Sandefur 1994).

Such large and consistent negative effects have eluded simple explanation. Undoubtedly much of the divorce experience is associated with the altered family structure produced—in almost 90 percent of all cases a single-mother family—and the corresponding changes in family functioning. Such a structure is lacking in adult role models, in parental supervision, and in hierarchy. On this last dimension, research has shown that divorced women and their children are closer (less distinguished by generational distinctions) to one another than is true in intact families. Parent and child are drawn together more as peers, both struggling to keep the family going. The excessive demands on single parents force them to depend on their children in ways that parents in intact families do not, leading to a more reciprocal dependency relationship (Weiss 1975, 1976). Single mothers are "... likely to rely on their children for emotional support and assistance with the practical problems of daily life" (Hetherington, Camara,

and Featherman 1983, p. 218). In matters of discipline, single mothers have been found to rely on restrictive (authoritarian as opposed to authoritative) disciplinary methods—restricting children's freedom and relying on negative sanctions—a pattern psychologists believe reflects a lack of authority on the part of the parent (Hetherington 1972). Whatever else it implies, the lack of generational boundaries means a less hierarchical family and less authoritative generational distinctions.

The institutional contexts within which achievement occurs, however, are decidedly hierarchical in nature. Education, the economy, and occupations are typically bureaucratic structures in which an individual is categorically subordinate to a superior—an arrangement Goffman described as an "eschelon authority structure" (1961, p. 42). The nuclear family has been described as producing in children the skills and attitudes necessary for competition within such eschelon authority relationships in capitalist production and family childrearing. "The hierarchical division of labor (in the economy) is merely reflected in family life" (Bowles and Gintis 1976, p. 144–147). The relative absence of clear subordinate-superordinate relationships in single-parent families has been argued to inadequately socialize children, or place them in a disadvantageous position when and if they find themselves in hierarchical organizations (Nock 1988).

For Adults. A wide range of psychological problems has been noted among divorcing and recently divorced adults. A divorce occasions changes in most every aspect of adult life; residence, friendship networks, economic situation, and parental roles. Marriage in America makes significant contributions to individual well-being. Thus, regardless of the quality of the marriage that ends, emotional distress is a near-universal experience for those who divorce (Weiss 1979). Anxiety, anger, and fear are dominant psychological themes immediately before and after divorce. At least for a year or two after divorce, men and women report psychosomatic symptoms of headaches, loss of appetite, overeating, drinking too much, trembling, smoking more, sleeping problems, and nervousness (Group for the Advancement of Psychiatry 1980).

The emotional problems occasioned by divorce are accompanied by major changes in economic situations, as well—especially for women.

The vast majority of those involved in divorce experience a significant decline in their immediate standard of living. This problem is especially acute for women who—in almost 90 percent of cases—assume custody of children. Immediately after a divorce, women suffer an average 30 percent to 40 percent decline in their overall standards of living (Hoffman and Duncan 1988; Peterson 1989). Either in anticipation of or as a consequence of divorce, there is typically an increase in divorced women's labor force participation. Analyzing national longitudinal data, Peterson estimates that one year before the divorce decree (when most divorcing individuals are separated), women's average standard of living (total family income divided by the poverty threshold for a family of a particular size) is 70 percent of its level in the previous year. As a consequence of increased hours worked, the standard of living increases one year after divorce and by five or six years after divorce, "the standard of living of divorced women is about 85 percent of what it had been before separation" (1989, p. 48). Women who have not been employed during their marriages, however, are particularly hard-hit; the majority ending up in poverty.

Child support payments are not a solution to the economic problems created by divorce for two reasons. First, about one-quarter (24 percent) of women due child support receive none (39 percent of men awarded child support receive none). Another one-quarter receive less than the court-ordered amount. In 1991, the average amount of child support received by divorced mothers was $3,011 per year ($2,292 for men) (U.S. Bureau of the Census 1995). About 16.7 million, or 85 percent of the 19.8 million children in single-parent families in 1997 were living with the mother; 60 percent of whom were divorced (U.S. Bureau of the Census 1998a). Their median family income was $22,999 compared with $34,802 for those in single-father situations, and $51,681 for children in households where both parents were present (U.S. Bureau of the Census 1998a). Families headed by single mothers are the most likely to be in poverty, and represent 55 percent of all poor families. In 1997, a third (31.6 percent) of all single-mother families were in poverty compared to 5.2 percent of two-parent families (U.S. Bureau of the Census 1998b). Analyzing national longitudinal data, Duncan concluded that changes in

family status—especially divorce and remarriage—are the most important cause of change in family economic well-being and poverty among women and children (1984).

Single-parent families in America have grown dramatically as a result of increasing divorce rates. And even though most divorced persons remarry, Bumpass has shown that the average duration of marital separation experienced by children under age 18 was 6.3 years and 7.5 years for whites and blacks respectively. In fact 38 percent of white and 73 percent of black children are still in a single-parent family 10 years after the marital disruption—a reflection of blacks' lower propensity to remarry and their longer intervals between divorce and remarriage (1984). The role of divorce in the formation of single-parent families differs by race. Among all single-parent white families, 25 percent are maintained by never-married mothers, 47 percent by divorced (or separated) mothers, 7 percent by never-married men, and 13 percent by divorced or separated men. Among black single-parent families, 59 percent are maintained by never-married women, 28 percent by divorced or separated women, 4 percent by never-married men, and only 3 percent by divorced or separated men. Divorce is the primary route to single-parenthood for white mothers, whereas out-of-wedlock childbearing is for black mothers (U.S. Bureau of the Census 1998c, Table 11; 1998d).

Families headed by single women with children are the poorest of all major demographic groups regardless of how poverty is measured. Combined with frequent changes in residence and in employment following divorce, children and mothers in such households experience significant instabilities—a fact reflected in the higher rates of mental health problems among such women (Garfinkel and McLanahan 1986, pp. 11–17).

CONCLUSION

High rates of remarriage following divorce clearly indicate that marital disruption does not signify a rejection of marriage. There is no evidence of widespread abandonment of conjugal life by Americans. Admittedly, marriage rates have dropped in recent years. However, such changes are best seen to be the result of higher educational attainments, occupational commitments, and lower fertility expectations; not a rejection of marriage per se. Rather, increasing divorce rates reflect the fact that marriage is increasingly evaluated as an entirely emotional relationship between two persons. Marital breakdown, or the failure of marriage to fulfill emotional expectations, has come increasingly to be a cause for divorce. Since the 1970s, our laws have explicitly recognized this as justification for terminating a marriage—the best evidence we have that love and emotional closeness are the *sine qua non* of modern American marriage. Contemporary divorce rates thus signal a growing unwillingness to tolerate an unsatisfying emotional conjugal relationship.

The consequences of divorce for children are difficult to disentangle from the predictable changes in household structure. Whether the long-term consequences are produced by the single-parent situation typically experienced for five to ten years, or from the other circumstances surrounding divorce is not clear. It is quite apparent, however, that divorce occasions significant instabilities in children's and mothers' lives.

Our knowledge about the consequences of divorce for individuals is limited at this time by the absence of controlled studies that compare the divorced to the nondivorced. Virtually all research done to date follows the lives of divorced individuals without comparing them to a comparable group of individuals who have not divorced. A related concern is whether the consequences of divorce reflect the experience itself, or whether they reflect various selection effects. That is, are people who divorce different from others to begin with? Are their experiences the results of their divorce, or of antecedent factors?

When almost half of all marriages are predicted to end in divorce, it is clear that marital disruption is a conspicuous feature of our family and kinship system. Divorce creates new varieties of kin not traditionally incorporated in our dominant institutions. The rights and obligations attached to such kinship positions as spouse of the noncustodial father are ambiguous—itself a source of problems. The social institution of the family is redefined as a consequence of divorce. Entering marriage, for example, is less commonly the beginning of adult responsibilities. Ending marriage is less commonly the consequence of death. Parents are not necessarily co-residents with their children. And new categories of "quasi" kin are invented to accommodate the complex connections among previously married spouses and their new spouses and children. In many ways, divorce itself has become a dominant institution in American society. It is, however, significantly less structured by consensual normative beliefs than the family institutions to which it is allied.

REFERENCES

Bennett, Neil G., David E. Bloom, and Patricia H. Craig 1989 "The Divergence of Black and White Marriage Patterns." *American Journal of Sociology* 95 (3):692–772.

Bowles, Samuel, and Herbert Gintis 1976 *Schooling in Capitalist America*. New York: Basic Books.

Bumpass, Larry L. 1984 "Children and Marital Disruption: A Replication and Update." *Demography* 21:71–82.

——, and James A. Sweet 1989 "National Estimates of Cohabitation." *Demography* 26:615–625.

Cherlin, Andrew J. 1981 *Marriage, Divorce, and Remarriage*. Cambridge, Mass.: Harvard University Press.

——, F.F. Furstenberg, Jr., P.L. Chase-Lansdale, K.E. Kiernam, P.K. Robins, D.R. Morrison, and J.O. Teitler 1991 "Longitudinal Studies of Effects of Divorce on Children in Great Britain and the United States." *Science* 252 (June 7):1386–1389.

Cherlin, Andrew J., Kathleen E. Kiernam, and P. Lindsay Chase-Lansdale 1995 "Parental Divorce in Childhood and Demographic Outcomes in Young Adulthood." *Demography* 32 (No. 3):299–318.

Degler, Carl N. 1980 *At Odds: Women and the Family in America from the Revolution to the Present*. New York: Oxford University Press.

Duncan, Greg J. 1984 *Years of Poverty, Years of Plenty*. Ann Arbor, Mich.: University of Michigan, Institute for Social Research.

Garfinkel, Irwin, and Sara S. McLanahan 1986 *Single Mothers and their Children*. Washington, D.C.: The Urban Institute Press.

Goffman, Irving 1961 *Asylums*. New York: Anchor.

Group for the Advancement of Psychiatry 1980 *Divorce, Child Custody, and the Family*. San Francisco: Jossey-Bass.

Hetherington, E. Mavis 1972 "Effects of Paternal Absence on Personality Development in Adolescent Daughters." *Developmental Psychology* 7:313–326.

——, Margaret Bridges, and Glendessa M. Insabella 1998 "What Matters? What Does Not? Five Perspectives on the Association Between Marital Transitions and Children's Adjustment." *American Psychologist* 53 (No.2):167–184.

Hetherington, E.M., K.A. Camara, and D.L. Featherman 1983 "Achievement and Intellectual Functioning of Children in One Parent Households." In J. T. Spence, ed., *Achievement and Achievement Motives*, 205–284 San Francisco: W. H. Freeman.

Hoffman, Saul D., and Greg J. Duncan 1988 "What are the Economic Costs of Divorce?" *Demography* 25:641–645.

Huber, Joan, and Glenna Spitze 1988 "Trends in Family Sociology." In N. J. Smelser, ed., *Handbook of Sociology*. Beverly Hills, Calif.: Sage.

Krein, Sheila F., and Andrea H. Beller 1988 "Educational Attainment of Children from Single-Parent Families: Differences by Exposure, Gender, and Race." *Demography* 25:221–234.

Martin, Teresa C., and Larry L. Bumpass 1989 "Recent Trends in Marital Disruption." *Demography* 26 (1):37–51.

McLanahan, Sara S., and Larry Bumpass 1988 "Intergenerational Consequences of Family Disruption." *American Journal of Sociology* 94 (1):130–152.

National Center for Health Statistics 1998 FASTATS: "Divorce." www.cdc.gov/nchswww/fastats/divorce.htm

Nock, Steven L. 1988 "The Family and Hierarchy." *Journal of Marriage and the Family* 50 (Nov):957–966.

—— 1995 "A Comparison of Marriages and Cohabiting Relationships." *Journal of Family Issues* 16:53–76.

Peterson, Richard R. 1989 *Women, Work, and Divorce*. Albany: State University of New York Press.

Phillips, Roderick 1988 *Putting Asunder: A History of Divorce in Western Society*. New York: Cambridge University Press.

Stetson, Dorothy M., and Gerald C. Wright, Jr. 1975 "The Effects of Law on Divorce in American States." *Journal of Marriage and the Family* (August):537–547.

U.S. Bureau of the Census 1975 *Historical Statistics of the United States: Colonial Times to 1970. Part I*. Washington, D.C.: U.S. Government Printing Office.

—— 1989 "Child Support and Alimony: 1985." *Current Population Reports*. P-23, No. 154.

—— 1989 "Studies in Marriage and the Family." *Current Population Reports*. P-23, No. 162.

—— 1995 "Who Receives Child Support?" *Statistical Brief*. www.census.gov/socdemo/www/chldsupp.html

—— 1998a "Money Income in the United States: 1997." *Current Population Reports*. P-60, No. 200.

—— 1998b "Poverty in the United States: 1997." *Current Population Reports*. P-60, No. 201.

—— 1998c "Household and Family Characteristics: 1997." *Current Population Reports*. P-20, No. 515.

—— 1998d "Marital Status and Living Arrangements: 1997." *Current Population Reports*. P-20, No. 506.

Weiss, Robert 1975 *Marital Separation*. New York: Basic Books.

—— 1976 "The Emotional Impact of Marital Separation." *Journal of Social Issues* 32:135–145.

—— 1979 *Going it Alone: The Family Life and Social Situation of the Single Parent*. New York: Basic Books.

STEVEN L. NOCK
ALISON BURKE

DRAMATURGY

See Symbolic Interaction Theory.

DRUG ABUSE

Drug abuse has been a major social problem in the United States for almost a century and we are now in the second decade of a continuing war on drugs. Drug abuse is a health and criminal justice problem that also has implications for nearly every facet of social life. It is a major element in the high cost of health care, a central reason for the United States's extraordinarily high rate of incarceration, and a focus of intensive education and treatment efforts. Substance abuse is an equal-opportunity problem that affects both high- and low-income persons, although its consequences are most often felt by those persons and communities that have the lowest social capital.

Substance abuse, with its connotations of disapproval or wrong or harmful or dysfunctional usage of mood-modifying substances, is a term that was developed in the United States. The more neutral term, *dependence*, is often used in other countries. *Addiction*, which formerly communicated the development of tolerance after use and a physical withdrawal reaction after a drug became unavailable, has assumed less explicit meanings. Whatever terminology is employed, there is intense societal concern about the use of psychoactive mood-altering substances that involve loss of control. This concern is manifest particularly for young people in the age group most likely to use such substances. Society is concerned that adolescents

710

and young adults, who should be preparing themselves for crucial educational, vocational, and other significant life choices, are instead diverted by the use of controlled substances.

The United States has the highest rate of drug abuse of any industrialized country and, not surprisingly, spends more public money than any other country to enforce laws that regulate the use of psychoactive drugs. Its efforts to control drug abuse reach out across its borders. The United States also plays a critical role in developing knowledge about substance abuse; more than 85 percent of the world's drug abuse research is supported by the National Institute on Drug Abuse.

EPIDEMIOLOGY

Information on incidence and prevalence of drug use and abuse derives from a range of sources: surveys of samples of households and schools; hospital emergency room and coroners' reports; urine testing of samples of arrestees; treatment programs; and ethnographic studies. Such epidemiological information enables us to assess drug abuse programs and decide on allocation of resources (Winick 1997).

Since World War II, the peak years for illicit drug use were in the late 1970s, when approximately 25 million persons used a proscribed substance in any thirty-day period. Overall illicit drug use has been declining since 1985. The yearly National Household Survey on Drug Abuse, which is the most influential source of epidemiology data, reported that in 1997 marijuana was used by 11.1 million persons or 80 percent of illicit drug users (Office of Applied Studies 1999). Sixty percent only used marijuana but 20 percent used it along with another illicit substance. During the 1990s, the rate of marijuana initiation among youths aged twelve to seventeen reached a new high, of approximately 2.5 million per year. The level of current use of this age group (9.4 percent) is substantially less than the rate in 1979 (14.2 percent).

Twenty percent of illicit drug users in 1997, ingested a substance other than marijuana in the month preceding the interviews. Some 1.5 million Americans, down from 5.7 million in 1985, used cocaine in the same period; the number of crack users, approximately 600,000, has remained nearly constant for the last ten years. At least 408,000

individuals used heroin in 1997, with the estimated number of new users at the highest level in thirty years.

Data on incidence and prevalence of use must be interpreted in terms of social structure. Thus, one out of five of the American troops in Vietnam were addicted to heroin, but follow-up studies one year after veterans had returned to the United States found that only 1 percent were addicted (Robins, Helzer, Hesselbrook et al. 1980). In Vietnam, heroin use was typically found among enlisted men and not among officers. Knowing such aspects of social setting and role can help in understanding the trends and can contribute to understanding the use of other substances in other situations. In any setting, the frequency of substance use, the length of time over which it was taken, the manner of ingestion, whether it was used by itself or with other substances, its relationship to criminal activity and other user characteristics (e.g., mental illness), the degree to which its use was out of control, the setting, and whether it was part of a group activity are also important.

Rates of use by subgroup can vary greatly. Thus, for example, prevalence rates of drug use are higher among males than females and highest among males in their late teens through their twenties. Over half the users of illicit drugs work full time. About one-third of homeless persons and more than one-fourth of the mentally ill are physically or psychologically dependent on illicit drugs. The first survey of mothers delivering liveborns, in 1993, found that 5.5 percent had used illicit drugs at some time during their pregnancy. A survey of college students reported that in the previous year, 26.4 percent had used marijuana and 5.2 percent had used cocaine. National Household Survey data indicate that use of illicit drugs by persons over thirty-five, which was 10.3 percent in 1979, jumped to 29.4 percent by 1991 and was 33.5 percent in 1997.

Rates of cigarette smoking are of interest because of their possible relationship to the use of other psychoactive substances. Approximately one-eighth of cigarette smokers also use illicit drugs. In a typical month in 1997, 30 percent of Americans, or 64 million, had smoked cigarettes and one-fifth of youths between the ages of twelve and seventeen, were current smokers. Almost half of all American adults who ever smoked have stopped smoking. Drug abusers may also be involved with alcohol.

POLICY

A central contributor to current American policy toward mood-modifying drugs was the Harrison Act of 1914, which prevented physicians from dispensing narcotics to addicts (Musto 1987). The Marijuana Tax Act of 1937 and strict penalties for sale and possession of narcotics that were imposed by federal legislation in 1951 and 1966 expanded punitive strategies. An important change took place in 1971, when President Nixon—who had campaigned vigorously against drug use—established a national treatment network. Nixon was the only president to devote most of the federal drug budget to treatment; his successors have spent most of the budget on law enforcement.

In 1972, the Commission on Marijuana and Drug Abuse recommended a dual-focused policy that is both liberal and hard-line. The policy, which continues to the present, is liberal in that users who need help are encouraged to obtain treatment. But it is hard-line because it includes harsh criminal penalties for drug possession and sales. As a result, nearly two-thirds of the federal resources devoted to drug use are now spent by the criminal justice system to deter drug use and implement a zero-tolerance philosophy.

President Carter's 1977 unsuccessful attempt to decriminalize marijuana was the only effort by a national political leader to lessen harsh penalties for drug possession. Between 1981 and 1986, President Reagan doubled enforcement budgets to fight the "war on drugs." Politicians generally have felt that the traditional hard-line policy served their own and the country's best interests and there has been limited national support for legalization or decriminalization (Evans and Berent 1992).

Originating in several European countries, the policy of *harm reduction* has, during the last decade, generated growing interest in the United States as a politically viable alternative to legalization (Heather, Wodak, Nadelmann et al. 1998). It attempts to understand drug use nonevaluatively in the context of people's lives and to urge that the policies that regulate drug use should not lead to more harm than the use of the substance itself causes. A representative harm-reduction initiative

is the establishment of needle exchanges, for injecting users of heroin and other drugs, in order to minimize the possibility of HIV transmission resulting from the sharing of infected needles. The use of needles to inject illegal substances has been linked to one-third of the cumulative number of AIDS cases in the United States. In the United States, the use of federal government money for needle exchanges is prohibited, although there are approximately 1.3 million injecting drug users. Critics of these programs believe that such exchanges increase heroin use and send a latent message that it is acceptable to use drugs like heroin. Harm reductionists disagree and argue that needle exchanges lead to a decline in rates of HIV infection without encouraging use.

Another policy disagreement between America and other countries involves marijuana. In the United States many federal benefits, including student loans, are not available to those convicted of marijuana crimes. In contrast, marijuana has been decriminalized in a number of Western European countries, including Italy, Spain, and Holland. It is openly available in coffee houses in Holland, where officials believe that its use is relatively harmless and can deter young people from using heroin or cocaine. In America, marijuana is viewed by federal authorities as possibly hazardous and a potential "stepping stone" to heroin or cocaine use, and approximately 695,000 persons were arrested for its possession in 1997.

Other countries have experimented with ways to make drugs such as heroin legally available, albeit under control. Thus, in Switzerland, heroin addicts have been legally maintained. In England, methadone (a heroin substitute) can be obtained by prescription from a physician. In the United States, by contrast, an addict must enroll in a program to be able to receive methadone.

In the United States prevention of drug abuse has never been as important a policy dimension as treatment or law enforcement, in part because it requires legislators to commit resources in the present to solve a future problem. Prevention has, thus, accounted for less than one-seventh of the drug abuse budget. Because of the variety of prevention approaches and because of the American local approach to education, there are many viewpoints on how to conduct programs that will prevent young people from becoming drug users and abusers. An information-didactic approach, often with the assistance of law enforcement personnel, has been traditional. A role-training, peer-oriented, values-clarification, alternatives, affective-education approach emerged in the 1970s, along with psychological inoculation. Addressing the social structure and family in which young people live, and targeted community action, attracted substantial support in the 1980s and 1990s.

National policy toward drug use is systematically promulgated by the Office of National Drug Control Policy (1999). The office has established the goal of reducing drug use and availability by 50 percent and reducing the rate of related crime and violence by 30 percent by 2007. It is proposed that these goals will be achieved by expanding current approaches.

Although drug abuse has been called "the American disease," physicians have had little impact on policy. Between 1912 and 1925, clinics in various states dispensed opiates to users. More recently, however, the federal government has opposed making marijuana available for medicinal purposes, even to treat persons with terminal or debilitating illnesses. Nevertheless, eleven states decriminalized marijuana possession in the 1970s and others, by referendum vote in the 1990s, have permitted physicians to recommend and patients to use marijuana medically.

CONTROL

In the United States, programs to control the supply of mood-modifying substances are intended to interdict the importation of illicit materials, enforce the laws, and cooperate with other countries that are interested in minimizing the availability of controlled substances. In addition to illicit substances (such as heroin, that has no established medical use), prescription products can be abused. These include substances such as barbiturates, that are used without medical supervision in an inappropriate manner. The problem also includes over-the-counter drug products that are not used for the purpose for which they were manufactured. Some nondrug substances like airplane model glue and other inhalants that can provide a "high" and are difficult to regulate, are also considered part of the country's substance abuse burden.

Preventing illicit drugs from entering the United States is difficult because of heavily trafficked, long, porous borders. Large tax-free profits provide incentives for drug entrepreneurs to develop new ways to evade customs barriers, process the drug for the market, and sell it (Johnson, Goldstein, Preble et al. 1985). For example, approximately seven-eighths of the retail price represents profit after all costs of growing, smuggling, and processing cocaine for illegal sale in the United States. The increasing globalization of the world economy further facilitates the international trade in illicit substances.

A key component in efforts to reduce the supply of stimulants, depressants, and hallucinogens is the Comprehensive Drug Abuse and Control Act of 1970, which established a national system of schedules that differentiated the public health threat of various drugs of abuse. This law, which has been modified over the years, classifies controlled substances into five categories, based on their potential for abuse and dependency and their accepted medical use. Schedule I products, such as peyote, have no acceptable safe level of medical use. Schedule II products, such as morphine, have both medicinal value and high abuse potential. Schedule III substances, such as amphetamines, have medical uses but less abuse potential than categories I or II. Also acceptable medicinally, Schedule IV substances, such as phenobarbital have low abuse potential, although the potential is higher than Schedule V products, such as narcotics that are combined with non-narcotic active ingredients. Conviction for violation of federal law against possession or distribution of scheduled products can lead to imprisonment, fines, and asset forfeiture.

Ever since it assumed a major role in promoting the Hague Opium Convention of 1912, the United States has been a leader in the international regulation of drugs of abuse. The United States convened the 1961 Single Convention on Narcotic Drugs and the 1971 Convention on Psychotropic Substances. Some countries, like England and Holland, subscribe to the treaties but interpret them more liberally than does the United States. The United States has also provided technical assistance, financing, and encouragement to other countries to minimize the growth of drugs such as cocaine and marijuana. Programs have been conducted in Mexico and Turkey to eradicate these crops and related programs have been encouraged in Peru and Columbia.

Since 1930, the U.S. Treasury Department has had responsibility for drug regulation in the United States. In 1973, the Drug Enforcement Administration of the Justice Department assumed the police and control function under federal law. Each state has laws that generally parallel the federal laws on possession and distribution of controlled substances and all states have a single state agency that coordinates other programs related to drug abuse.

Regular or frequent drug users, without outside income, are likely to engage in a range of criminal activities in order to buy controlled substances. They typically engage in six times more criminal activity when using than when they are not using drugs. Urine testing of arrestees, under the federal Arrestees Drug Abuse Monitoring program, indicates that some two-thirds of those arrested in urban communities had used an illicit substance prior to arrest. It is, thus, not surprising that the rates of street crimes tend to be positively correlated with the number of illegal drug users in a community.

During the last fifteen years, both state and federal prison populations have experienced a massive increase due to the number of people convicted and jailed for selling or using drugs. Other developments contributing to the surge in the prison population include aggressive enforcement, longer sentences, the decline of parole, and mandatory sentencing procedures that provide less latitude for judges. Thus, for example, federal penalties for possession of crack, a rock-like form of cocaine that became popular in the 1980s and sells for a low price on the street, are 100 times greater than for powdered cocaine. Sellers targeting crack to urban minorities represent one of several factors that have led to a disproportionate number of young blacks in federal and state prisons, for violation of possession laws. Ninety percent of prisoners in federal prisons for crack violations are black, although twice as many whites as blacks use it.

Survey and other data consistently report that the use of mood-modifying drugs is distributed among all the socioeconomic and ethnic groups in the United States; nevertheless, arrests, convictions, deaths, and other negative outcomes of drug use are disproportionately concentrated in specific geographic areas and population subgroups. In state prisons, blacks make up some 60 percent of the drug-law violators although they represent 12 percent of the country's population and 15 percent of regular drug users. Selective enforcement of the laws might reasonably be considered a possible contributor to such statistics.

American attitudes toward drug use have historically reflected ethnic and class-related prejudices. Thus, earlier in the twentieth century, negative attitudes toward cocaine were associated with the hostility that Southern blacks, among whom cocaine use was thought to be widespread, were believed to harbor toward whites. The public's suspicion of Chinese immigrants was a reflection of their use of opium. A number of stereotypes about marijuana reflected beliefs about its use by Mexican immigrants and some occupations that had low status at the time, such as jazz musicians.

For members of both majority and minority groups sentenced to prison, recidivism rates are high and represent one reason that the United States has higher rates of incarceration (approaching two million) than any industrialized nation. Although treatment of former drug users in prison settings has produced some promising results, treatment opportunities in prison are scarce and have not kept pace with the growth in the population of incarcerated former users. Approximately one in eight state inmates and one in ten federal inmates have taken part in treatment since their admission to prison. On a limited basis, treatment is being offered in an effort to keep offenders from returning to prison.

TREATMENT

The treatment of substance abuse has consistently been a lower priority than efforts to control drug abuse through interdiction and criminal sanctions, although cost-benefit studies have demonstrated that every dollar invested in treatment saves seven dollars in other costs. The federal government has usually spent more than two-thirds of its substance abuse budget (which now totals nearly $20 billion) on such supply-reduction and criminal justice system strategies. Only a small minority of drug abusers have access to treatment, since health insurers tend to discriminate against persons with substance abuse problems and there are inadequate treatment resources.

Current treatment for drug abuse, in addition to withdrawal, ranges from psychotherapeutic interventions (provided in both inpatient and outpatient settings), pharmacology agents, and various forms of milieu therapy. It frequently includes information on relapse prevention. Psychotherapy is often used in combination with other forms of treatment, and is provided both on an individual and group basis by therapists trained in medicine, psychology, social work, nursing and education. Pharmacological treatments include approaches, that substitute or block the effect of an abused substance, such as methadone maintenance for heroin (Ball and Ross 1991). Milieu therapies include a variety of residential programs where drug abusers can learn or relearn how to live substance free. Although some relatively short-term hospital-based programs exist (particularly for those with independent resources to pay for such services), the most common milieu consists of longer-term therapeutic communities such as Phoenix House, where drug users live in a setting in which they are closely monitored. The residents' progress through the several levels of the program's hierarchical social structure depends on their ability to implement the program's rules for "right living" (De Leon 1997).

Although often not considered a treatment, various fellowship groups deriving from the Alcoholics Anonymous model are widely used by drug abusers. Thus, for example, groups such as Narcotics Anonymous, Cocaine Anonymous, and parallel groups for spouses and parents of drug users exist in almost every community. Such groups, which have no professional staff and rely on the reinforcement of abstinence, support drug abusers in maintaining drug-free lives and help family members aid their drug-abusing relatives. Many treatment programs encourage their patients or clients to participate in such a twelve-step fellowship simultaneously with the treatment period or after treatment is completed.

Although substantial resources have been devoted to treatment outcome research, our knowledge of who does best in what treatment is limited. Particularly for cocaine, the use of which can lead to dependence in a short period of time, effective

pharmacological treatments are not available. A combination of strategies is often most effective especially if it recognizes that drug abuse is a chronic relapsing disorder that is likely to include multiple treatment failures on the way to an ultimately favorable outcome. Of the treatment approaches to drug abuse, milieu treatments have been among the most intensely studied. For those able to participate in such programs, they can have extremely high rates of relatively enduring positive outcomes. Whatever the treatment modality, it must include job readiness, habilation and vocational rehabilitation, and other dimensions that will enable the former user to function effectively in the modern information-oriented community and economy.

PREVENTION

In the late 1980s, the social problems associated with drug abuse, particularly in terms of the possession and sale of cocaine in urban areas, were perceived to have reached crisis dimensions and there was a marked increase in criminal justice efforts to control substance use. Another positive response was a renewed emphasis on the prevention of drug abuse and the collateral development of broad-based community strategies designed to reduce demand for illicit drugs. Currently, such demand-reduction efforts are undergoing systematic study in several long-term longitudinal public and private programs.

There has been a transformation in views of substance abuse as we have moved from a focus on individual pathology to programs that engage community institutions. Such efforts aim to change norms about substance use through the involvement of community members and the integration of the substance-abuse programs pursued by public and private agencies. The 1990s saw the expansion of community-based programs to include a broad range of institutions, including the police and courts, the voluntary sector, as well as the media (Falco 1994). Fostered by the government's Center for Substance Abuse Prevention (part of the Substance Abuse and Mental Health Administration) and efforts of the Robert Wood Johnson Foundation, the country's largest health foundation, hundreds of communities are engaged in broad-based efforts to change the culture within which substance abuse takes place (Saxe, Reber, HalFors, et al. 1997).

The belief that substance abuse is sustained by community norms represents an ecological approach. Environmental conditions, whether they reflect physical conditions in the community, poverty, or available health care, are thus seen as risk factors for drug use and abuse. Supporters of this view believe that what is needed are coordinated, community-wide efforts to address drug abuse at multiple levels of social organization and the collaboration of many groups. The idea that multicomponent community-action efforts can prevent drug abuse derives from earlier studies of programs designed to cope with cardiovascular disease. It is consistent with efforts to promote a variety of other health issues, but substance abuse is now a primary focus of these efforts.

The largest of these comprehensive efforts is the federal government's Community Partnership Program, which has supported over 250 partnerships. The Community Partnership Program was initiated in 1990 after the Robert Wood Johnson Foundation had begun to develop a model and sponsor broad-based community efforts. Called "Fighting Back" programs, they now provide long-term support to more than a dozen communities to develop comprehensive demand-reduction interventions. The foundation has also provided support and technical assistance to hundreds of additional communities through groups such as Join Together.

A significant element of many such prevention programs is the presence of a strong media component. The Partnership for a Drug-Free America, for example, develops and places hundreds of millions of dollars of advertising each year, and communities are encouraged to leverage local media to present anti-drug messages directed at youth. Although there is limited direct evidence of the effectiveness of media campaigns, it is likely that they reinforce education and prevention messages being delivered to youth through other means.

Schools play a central role in prevention programs, under the assumption that drug abuse will be more easily prevented if programs are started early. The goal of these programs is to provide youth with the skills to become successful adults and to teach them the community's norms and values. There is substantial evidence that positive school experiences are linked to lower levels of drug use and conversely, that drug use is related to delinquency and problems in school.

The role of school environments in affecting adolescent substance use has been validated by specific school-based trials. In both the Midwestern Prevention Project and Project Northland, significant reductions in the prevalence of substance use by adolescents were reported (Pentz, Dwyer, MacKinnon, et al. 1989; Perry, William, Veblen-Martenson 1996). Designed for students in grades six through eight, the programs include academic curricula, along with parental and community involvement. Often, a significant mass media component is part of the effort, with a focus on correcting misperceptions about the consequences of drug use and providing alternative positive behavior. The D.A.R.E. program (Drug Abuse Resistance Education) also has been a widely used school-based prevention strategy.

Schools are not the only public institution that affect youths' likelihood to abuse drugs. The police and justice agencies, as well as the network of health and social service agencies that serve a community, have a crucial influence and prevention activities typically involve such agencies. The ability of health and social service professionals to attend to drug use is clearly important, but their role is often reactive, providing treatment rather than prevention.

One of the most important programs that has contributed to attempts by law enforcement agencies to deal with drug abuse is community policing. It represents a shift from reactive policing where the goal is to arrest offenders, to an active strategy designed to identify crime problems and work with citizens—including offenders—to avoid further difficulties. The heart of the approach is that officers get to know citizens and help them deal with minor transgressions and, in so doing, avoid serious crime. A collateral approach, widely used in the 1990s ("fixing broken windows") is designed to improve morale and confidence and stem the physical and social deterioration of communities by prompt attention to small visible manifestations of community dysfunction or decay. There is evidence that such approaches are, at least partly, responsible for declines in violent crime, which is closely related to substance-abuse problems.

A community's resources and social institutions have a critical impact on drug use, but the attitudes and behavior of peers and family may have an even more direct influence. The affluence of a community and the quality of its schools have a substantial effect on the initiation of drug use, but their impact is mediated by adolescents' peer relationships and their interactions with significant adults in their lives. Thus, peers and parents are perhaps the most vital elements of the community context—directing or guiding youngsters' needs and desires through the obstacles in their environment. Some of the most important programs designed to address community substance abuse focus on changing peer culture and addressing family attitudes and behavior.

Parents (or other adult "guides") arguably have the greatest potential effect on how the youngster learns to negotiate the environment as it exists (good or bad), and they can also affect the influence that the youngsters' peers exert. The use of drugs by parents significantly increases the likelihood that their youngsters will also use drugs. Although this might seem to be a clear example of youngsters modeling the behavior of their parents, the influence of parents' own use of drugs is probably more complicated. Some research suggests that it is not merely that youngsters mimic parents' behavior, but instead such modeling interacts with what they see in their peers. If both peers and parents engage in substance use, there is far greater likelihood that young people will become regular users.

The influences of peers and parents may interact in complex ways and each community is different—its resources and institutions function differently. Communities can be directed to the key levers, but there is no simple formula available to determine which activities will be most important for a particular community. What is clear, however, is that to understand and develop strategies that reduce adolescent substance abuse, it is necessary to consider the social context in which a child lives. Only by identifying the resources available within a community, the roles played by the social institutions within that community, and the behaviors and values of the individuals (parents and children) who live in that community, can the interactions among the multiple forms and levels of influence begin to be understood.

RESEARCH

Social science research has played a critical role in the identification of the substance-abuse problem, it social consequences, and strategies to arrest the use of illicit drugs. There is now a long-standing tradition of surveys to identify drug use and attitudes toward the use of mood-modifying substances and their consequences. Surveys, such as the National Household Survey on Drug Abuse (which assesses the drug use of a random sample of U.S. residents over twelve years old) and Monitoring the Future (a school-based survey of junior and senior high school students), have each been conducted for more than two decades. Although there is considerable discussion about the validity of these surveys and how to ensure veridical data (Beveridge, Kadushin, Saxe, et al. forthcoming), there is no question that they have influenced social policy.

More recently, much of the focus of social research has shifted to assessing strategies to prevent drug use and to evaluate treatment programs. Under the auspices of the National Institute on Drug Abuse (a component of the National Institutes of Health), a variegated research program includes both biological and sociopsychological components. An emphasis of research is on assessment of programs such as D.A.R.E., the Community Partnership Program, and Fighting Back. Determining whether these programs achieve their goals of preventing substance abuse is a particularly difficult challenge. The programs are implemented differently across communities and the research design needs to separate the effects of race, socioeconomic status, and other factors from program implementation (Rindskopf and Saxe 1998).

It is also the case that antidrug programs develop loyal followings and their proponents develop a stake in showing that their efforts are successful. Thus, for example, there has been a major debate about the D.A.R.E. program and whether it is successful, with researchers claiming that the evidence suggests it is not effective. In other cases, such as the Community Partnership Program and Fighting Back, the issue has been the availability of data that can show the effects of the program over time.

One development that will likely allow much better utilization of social research is the availability of sophisticated methodologies. Thus, for example, meta-analytic techniques are now available that permit the synthesis of data across multiple studies, allowing us to amalgamate multiple small-scale tests of programs. In addition, new analytic strategies are being developed to allow construction of multilevel statistical models. Such hierarchical linear modeling permits one to take account of the fact that programs are conducted in particular settings and facilitates the segregation of community effects from overall program effects. Qualitative ethnographic techniques have been used to track the life cycle of substance abuse and the structure of the illegal markets.

FUTURE

The war on drugs is far from being "won," but drug abuse appears to have stabilized, with use remaining nearly constant. Two trends, that could be counterreactions, have emerged and may help to shape future use of illicit drugs. The first is the call for legalization or decriminalization of the possession of drugs such as marijuana. Several national organizations have emerged to promote this goal and to urge a harm reduction approach. The second trend is the increased licit use of mood-altering prescription substances, such as Prozac and Ritalin. Such powerful psychotropic agents are being prescribed by physicians for depression, difficulties in concentration, and similar problems. As the medical options increase, misuse of prescription drugs will likely increase and it may be more difficult to control the sale of less powerful nonprescription drugs.

(SEE ALSO: *Alcohol*)

REFERENCES

Ball, J. C. , and A. Ross 1991 *The Effectiveness of Methadone Maintenance Treatment*. New York: Springer-Verlag.

Beveridge, A., C. Kadushin, L. Saxe, D. Rindskopf, and D. Livert forthcoming "Survey Estimates of Drug Use Trends in Urban Communities: General Principles and Cautionary Examples." *Substance Use and Misuse*.

De Leon, G. (ed.) 1997 *Community As Method: Therapeutic Communities for Special Populations and Special Settings*. Westport, Conn.: Praeger.

Evans, R., and I. Berent 1992 *Drug Legalization: For and Against*. La Salle, Ill.: Open Court Press.

Falco, M. 1994 *The Making of A Drug Free America: Programs That Work*. New York: Times Books.

Gerstein, D. R., and H. J. Harwood (eds.) 1990 *Treating Drug Problems*. Washington, D.C.: National Academy Press.

Heather, N., A. Wodak, E. Nadelmann, et al. 1998 *Psychoactive Drugs and Harm Reduction*. London, U.K.: Whurr Publishers.

Johnson, B. D., P. Goldstein, E. Preble, et al. 1985 *Taking Care of Business: The Economics of Crime by Heroin Abusers*. Lexington, Mass.: Lexington Books.

Kleiman, M. A. R. 1992 *Against Excess: Drug Policy for Results*. New York: Basic Books.

Musto, D. F. 1987 *The American Disease: Origins of Narcotic Control*. New York: Oxford University Press.

Office of Applied Studies 1999 *National Household Survey on Drug Abuse Main Findings 1997*. Rockville, Md.: Substance Abuse and Mental Health Services Administration.

Office of National Drug Control Policy 1999 *The National Drug Control Strategy 1999*. Washington D.C.: The White House.

Pentz, M. A., J. H. Dwyer, D. P. MacKinnon, et al. 1989 "A Multi-Community Trial for Primary Prevention of Adolescent Drug Use: Effects on Drug Use Prevalence." *Journal of the American Medical Association* 261:3259–3266.

Perry, C. L., C. L. Williams, S. Veblen-Martenson, et al. 1996 "Project Northland: Outcome of A Community Wide Alcohol Use Prevention Program for Early Adolescence." *American Journal of Public Health* 86:956–965.

Rindskopf, D., and L. Saxe 1998 "Zero Effects in Substance Abuse Programs: Avoiding False Positives and False Negatives in the Evaluation of Community-based Programs." *Evaluation Review* 22:78–94.

Robins, L. N., J. E. Helzer, M. Hesselbrook, et al. 1980 "Vietnam Veterans Three Years After Vietnam." In L. Brill and C. Winick, eds., *Yearbook of Substance Use and Abuse*, vol. 2, 213–232.New York: Human Sciences Press.

Saxe, L., E. Reber, D. Halfors, C. Kadushin, D. Jones, D. Rindskopf, and A. Beveridge 1997 "Think locally, act globally: Assessing the impact of community-based substance abuse prevention." *Evaluation and Program Planning* 20:357–366.

Winick, C. 1983 "Addicts and Alcoholics as Victimizers." In D.E.J. Mac Namara and A. Karmen, eds., *Deviants: Victims or Victimizers?* Beverly Hills, Calif.: Sage Publications.

—— "Epidemiology." In J.H. Lowinson, P. Ruiz, R.B. Millman, et al. eds., *Substance Abuse: A Comprehensive Textbook* 3rd ed. 10–16. Baltimore, Md.: Williams and Wilkins.

——(ed.) 1974 *Sociological Aspects of Drug Dependence.* Cleveland, Oh: CRC Press.

LEONARD SAXE
CHARLES WINICK

ISBN 0-02-864849-8

90000